Webster's

Dictionary
& Thesaurus

® Landoll, Inc.
© 1997 Landoll, Inc.
Ashland, Ohio 44805

A, a The first letter of the English alphabet; the highest grade, meaning excellent or best

aah *v.* to exclaim in joy

aard-vark *n.* a burrowing African animal which resembles the anteater and feeds on ants and termites

aard-wolf *n.* hyena-like mammal feeding chiefly on carrion and insects

ab-a-ca *n.* a plant from the Philippines whose leafstalks are the source of Manila hemp.

a-back *adv.* unexpectedly; by surprise; startled; confused

abac-te-ri-al *adj.* not being caused by bacteria

ab-a-cus *n.* a frame holding parallel rods with beads used for manual computation abacuses n., abaci n.

a-baft *adv.* toward the stern of a ship

ab-a-lo-ne *n.* a member of the genus of gastropod mollusks that will cling to rocks and have a shell which is flat and lined with mother of pearl.

a-ban-don *v.* to yield utterly; to desert; to forsake; to withdraw protection, support, or help
abandonment n., abandoner n.

a-ban-don-ed *adj.* to be deserted; to be foresaken

a-base *v.* to lower in rank, position, prestige, or estimation; to cast down, to humble abasement *n*

a-bash *v.* embarrass abashment n.

a-bate *v.* reduce in quantity, or value, to deduct; to make less
abatement n., abater n.

ab-ba-cy *n.* a jurisdiction or an office of an abbot

ab-ba-tial *adj.* to be pertaining or related to an abbey or abbot.

ab-be *n.* a French title given to a priest.

ab-bess *n.* the femal superior of an abbey of nuns and possessing the same authority as an abbot

ab-bey *n.* monastery abbeys pl.

ab-bot *n.* the superior of the monastery

ab-bre-vi-ate *v.* make briefer; to shorten to reduce to a briefer form, as a word or phrase abbreviated, abbreviating *v.*

ab-bre-vi-a-tion *n.* shortened form of a word or phrase

ABC soil *n.* a type of soil where there are three well-defined layers.

ab-do-men *n.* the part of the human body that lies between the thorax and the pelvis and contains the stomach, spleen, liver, kidneys, bladder, pancreas, and intestines
abdominal adj.

ab-duct *v.* carry away wrongfully by force or fraud; to kidnap; to draw aside, or away; to move apart abductor n.

a-beam *adv. or adj.* right angles to the keel of a ship

ab-er-rant *adj.* straying from the right course; wandering; varying from aberrance n., aberrantly adv.

a-bet *v.* incite abetment n., abettor n.

ab-hor *v.* dislike intensely abhorrer n.

a-bide *v.* to tolerate; to remain; to last; to conform to abider n., abided v.

a-bil-i-ty *n.* state of being able; competence; -ties *n., pl.*

ab-ject *adj.* sunk to a low condition abjection *n.*, abjectly adv., -ness n.

ab-jure *v.* renounce solemnly abjured v.

a-blaze *adv.* on fire, glowing

a-ble *adj.* having sufficient ability

a-ble--bodied *adj.* having a strong body ablebodies adj.

ab-lu-tion *n.* washing of the body as a part of religious rites ablutionary adj.

ab-ne-gate *v.* deny; to refuse or renounce abnegator n., abnegation n.

ab-nor-mal *adj.* not normal -ity *n.*

a-board *adv.* on board a ship, onto

a-bode *n.* temporary dwelling place

a-bol-ish *v.* put an end to, destroy

a-bom-i-na-ble *adj.* detestable; loathsome abominably adv.

a-bort *v.* to terminate or cause to terminate an operation or procedure before completion aborter n.

a-bor-tion *n.* induced termination of pregnancy before the fetus can survive abortionist n.

a-bound *v.* to have plenty

a-bout *adv.* approximately, all sides

a-bove *adv.* higher or greater than

ab-ra-ca-dab-ra *n.* a word believed to have magical powers, used in casting spells; nonsense, foolish talk

a-brade *v.* to wear or rub off abrading *v.*

a-breast *adv. or adj.* side by side

a-bridge *v.* to make smaller, fewer or shorter while maintaining essential contents abridger *n*

a-broad *adv.* widely, beyond

ab-ro-gate *v.* put an end to -ed v.

ab-rupt *adj.* happening suddenly

ab-scess *n.* infected sore containing pus abscessed adj.

ab-scind *v.* to sever; to separate

ab-scond *v.* to flee from justice

ab-sent *adj.* not present absently adv.

ab-sent--mind-ed *adj.* always forgetting things; not paying attention

ab-so-lute *adj.* unconditional

ab-solve *v.* to set free from guilt

ab-sorb v. to take in **absorbable adj.**

ab-stain v. refrain from doing something **abstainer** n.

ab-ste-mi-ous adj. showing moderation **abstemiously** adv.

ab-stract v. summarize **abstractable adj.**

ab-struse adj. difficult to understand **abstruseness** n., **abstrusely** adv.

ab-surd adj. clearly unreasonable **absurdness** n., **absurdly** adv.

a-bun-dance n. ample supply; plenty

a-buse v. use in an improper or wrong way **abusable adj., abuser** n.

a-but v. to border **abutted, abutting** v.

a-but-ment n. bridge support

a-bys-mal adj. extension downward, inward, or inward **abysmally** adv.

a-byss n. deep crack or gap in the earth, great space, bottomless

a-ca-cia n. thorny tree or shrub

a-cad-e-my n. private school

acap-pel-la adj. singing without instrumental accompaniment

ac-cede v. to consent **-ed v., -ing v.**

ac-cel-er-ate v. work faster; to increase, gain **acceleratingly** adv.

ac-cent v. emphasize **accentless adj.**

ac-cept v. take what is given

ac-cept-able adj. satisfactory; proper, capable of being accepted

ac-cep-tance n. approval, being accepted or acceptable

ac-cess n. admission, entrance

ac-ces-si-ble adj. easy access or approach **accessibleness** n., **accessibly** adv.

ac-ces-sory n. -ies contributing

ac-ci-dent n. unexpected happening **accidental** adj., **accidentally** adv.

ac-claim v. greet with strong approval, praise **acclaimer** n.

ac-cli-mate v. become accustomed

ac-co-lade n. award; praise

ac-com-mo-date v. to give room or lodging; to adjust **accommodating adj.**

ac-com-pa-ni-ment n. something that goes well with another, unit

ac-com-pa-nist n. someone who plays a musical accompaniment

ac-com-pa-ny v. go along with

ac-com-plice n. companion in crime

ac-com-plish v. to do **accomplishment** n.

ac-cord n. harmony **accordance** n.

ac-cord-ing-ly adv. in a proper way

ac-cor-di-on n. musical instrument

ac-cost v. approach in an unfriendly manner, speak in a challenging or aggressive manner

ac-count n. description; record **accountable** adj.

ac-count-ing n. system of keeping business records or accounts

ac-cred-it v. give official power

ac-crete v. grow together

ac-crue v. to increase at certain times **accruable adj., accrued** v.

ac-cu-mu-late v. collect or gather

ac-cu-rate adj. without mistakes; careful and exact **accurately** adv.

ac-curs-ed adj. unpleasant **-ness** n.

ac-cu-sa-tion n. charge of guilty

ac-cuse v. find fault with; charge someone with breaking the law

ac-custom v. familiarize by habit **accustomed** adj., **accustomation** n.

ace n. playing card marked with one spot; score in tennis

ac-e-tate n. salt, acetic acid

a-ce-tic acid n. main ingredient for production of vinegar

a-cet-y-lene n. inflammable gas

ache v. have a dull, steady pain

a-chieve v. to succeed **achievement** n.

ac-id n. a chemical compound **acidity** n., **acidness** n., **acidly** adv.

acid rock n. song lyrics suggesting drug related experiences

a-cid-u-late v. to become or make acid **acidulated** v., **acidulating** v.

ack-ack n. anti-aircraft fire or gun

ac-know-ledge v. to admit the truth **acknowledgement** n., **-able adj.**

ac-me n. the highest point

ac-ne n. skin disease; pimples

ac-o-lyte n. altar boy, assistant

ac-o-nite n. a poisonous plant

a-corn n. nut of the oak tree

a-cous-tic adj. having to do with sound **acoustical** adj., **acoustically** adv.

a-cous-tics n. study of sound

ac-quaint v. to make familiar **acquaintance** n., **acquaintanceship**

ac-qui-esce v. agree without arguing **acquiesced** v., **acquiescing** v.

ac-quire v. become the owner **acquirement** n., **acquired,** v.

acquired immunity n. immunity against disease

ac-qui-si-tion n. something acquired

ac-quit v. rule not guilty **acquital** n.

a-cre n. a measurement of land, great quantity **acreage** n.

ac-rid adj. a sharp, bitter taste **acridity** n., **acridness** n., **-ly adv.**

ac-ri-mo-ni-ous adj. bitter in speech or manner **acrimoniousness** n.

ac-ro-bat n. one skilled in gymnastic feats **acrobatic** adj., **-lly adv.**

ac-ro-pho-bi-a n. unusual fear of being at great heights

a-cross prep. side to side, opposites

acrylic fiber *n.* synthetic textile fiber

act *n.* a thing done; a deed -ing *adj.*

ac-tion *n.* process of doing or acting, act of will, bringing about

ac-ti-vate *v.* put into action
activation *n.*, activated *v.*, -ing *v.*

ac-tive *adj.* full of action; busy, quick
actively *adv.*, activeness n.

ac-tiv-ism *n.* action to affect changes in government activistic adj.

act of God *n.* uncontrollable happening caused by nature

ac-tor *n.* performer actorish adj.

ac-tress *n.* female actor -es n.

ac-tu-al *adj.* existing in fact; real

ac-tu-ate *v.* put into mechanical motion or action actuation *n.*

a-cute *adj.* sharp and quick
acutely *adv.*, acuteness n., -er adj.

ad-age *n.* proverb, metaphorical

ad-a-mant *adj.* standing firm

a-dapt *v.* to adjust to new conditions
adaption, adaptness *n.*

add *v.* join together addable adj.

ad-der *n.* poisonous snake

ad-dict *n.* a person with a strong habit with a drug addiction *n.*

ad-di-tion *n.* adding of numbers to find the total additional *adj.*

ad-dle *v.* become or make confused

ad-dress *v.* to speak to; place where mail or goods can be delivered

ad-duce *v.* offer as proof or give as a reason adducer n., -ed v., -ing v.

ad-e-noids *n.* lymphoid tissue growths which obstructs breathing, relating to the adenoids

a-dept *adj.* highly skilled adeptly *adv.*, adeptness *n.*

ad-e-quate *adj.* sufficient -ly adv.

ad-here *v.* to stick and not come loose
adhered v., adhering v.

ad-her-ent *n.* one who follows a leader
adherently adv.

ad-he-sive *adj.* having a sticky surface
adhesively adv., adhesiveness n.

a-dieu *n.* good-by adieus, adieux pl.

ad-in-ter-im *adj.* in the meantime

ad-ja-cent *adj.* close to or nearby

ad-jec-tive *n.* word used to describe a noun or pronoun adjectively adv.

ad-join *v.* be next to, attach or add

ad-journ *v.* close a meeting or session, to relocate adjournment *n.*

ad-judge *v.* decide by judicial procedure
adjudged v., adjudging v.

ad-jure *v.* ask urgently adjuration *n.*

adjust *v.* to arrange or change
adjustability *n.*, adjustable adj.

ad-just-er *n.* person who estimates

damages for settlement adjustor n.

ad-lib *v.* to improvise adlibbed v.

ad-man *n.* person working in the business of advertising

ad-min-is-ter *v.* direct or manage

ad-min-is-tra-tion *n.* people who manage a school, or company
administrator *n.*, -al adj., -ist n.

ad-mi-ra-ble *adj.* worthy of being admired admirableness adv.

ad-mi-ral *n.* highest ranking naval officer, is above a vice-admiral

ad-mire *v.* regard with wonder

ad-mis-si-ble *adj.* capable of being admitted admissibility n.

ad-mit *v.* to confess; give the right to enter or access admittance *n.*

ad-mix-ture *n.* blend; mingling

ad-mon-ish *v.* to give a person advice
admonishtion *n.* admonishingly adv.

a-do *n.* fuss, excitement

a-do-be *n.* building material made from clay and straw

ad-o-les-cence *n.* between childhood and adulthood, growing up

a-dopt *v.* legally take into one's family
adoption *n.*, -ability n.

a-dor-a-ble *adj.* very likable -ness n.

a-dore *v.* to love greatly; to worship

a-dorn *v.* to add splendor or beauty, to decorate adornment *n.*

a-drift *adv.* floating freely; having no purpose, without guidance

a-droit *adj.* skillful and clever, with the hands adroitly *adv.*

ad-u-late *v.* give greater praise
adulation *n.*, adulator n., -ed v.

a-dult *n.* person who is fully grown
adulthood *n.*, adultness n., -ly adv.

a-dul-ter-ate *v.* to make impure

a-dul-tery *n.* voluntary sexual intercourse with someone other than a spouse

ad-vance *v.* to move ahead -ment *n.*

ad-vanced *adj.* ahead in time

ad-van-tage *n.* better chance
advantageous *adj.*

ad-vent *n.* the four Sundays before Christmas as a season of prayer

ad-ven-ture *n.* an exciting experience
adventured v., adventuring v.

ad-verb *n.* word used to describe a verb or adjective adverbial *adj.*

ad-verse *adj.* opposed; against someone or something, opposite

ad-ver-si-ty *n.* bad luck or misfortune, a condition of suffering

ad-ver-tise *v.* draw public attention to a product advertiser *n.*

ad-vice *n.* opinion on a course of action, recommendation

ad-vis-ed-ly *adv.* deliberately

ad-vise-ment *n.* careful thought

ad-viser *n.* person who gives an opinion, one who gives advice

advocate *v.* write or speak in favor of advocated v., advocating n.

aer-ate *v.* to purify, to supply

aer-i-al *adj.* antenna for television or radio aerially adv.

aer-i-al-ist *n.* aerial acrobat

aer-o-bics *n.* strenuous exercise for the heart aerobically adv.

aer-o-nau-tics *pl., n.* science of designing aircraft aeronautical adj.

aer-o-sol *n.* liquid substance under pressurized conditions

aes-thet-ic *adj.* having a love for or judgements concerning beauty

a-far *adv.* far away, great distance

af-fa-ble *adj.* good natured; friendly

af-fair *n.* an event or happening

af-fect *v.* to move emotionally affecting adj., affectability n.

af-fec-tion *n.* fond feeling for another affectionless adj.

af-fec-tion-ate *adj.* loving and gentle affectionately adv.

af-fi-da-vit *n.* sworn written statement, has made an oath

af-fil-i-ate *v.* join or associate with common ownership affiliation n.

af-fin-i-ty *n.* natural attraction or liking, relationship by marriage

af-firm *v.* to declare positively affirmative n., affirmable adj.

af-fix *n.* to attach; to add at the end

af-flict *v.* a persistent cause of suffering or pain affliction n.

af-flu-ence *n.* wealth; abundance

af-ford *v.* be able to provide

af-fray *n.* noisy fight

af-front *v.* to confront

af-ghan *n.* a knitted or crocheted blanket of colored wool

a-fire *adv.* burning, on fire

a-float *adv.* floating on water

a-flut-ter *adj.* nervously excited

a-foot *adj.* walking, on foot

a-fore-men-tioned *adj.* mentioned before, previously

a-foul *adv.* tangled, in conflict with

a-fraid *adj.* filled with fear; reluctant, unwanting of a situation

a-fresh *adj.* to something again

aft *adv.* toward the rear of a ship

af-ter *adv. prep.* following

af-ter-math *n.* consequence

af-ter-thought *n.* idea occurring later, not thought of originally

a-gain *adv.* once more

a-gainst *prep.* in exchange for

a-gape *adv.* open-mouthed, wide

ag-ate *n.* type of quartz

age *n.* length of time a person has lived aged v., aging v.

aged *adj.* grown or become old

age-less *adj.* existing forever

a-gen-cy *n.* business that acts for others agencies n.

a-gen-da *n.* list of things to be done

a-gent *n.* one who acts as the representative of another

ag-glom-er-ate *v.* to collect

ag-gran-dize *n.* to extend, to make greater aggrandizement n.

ag-gra-vate *v.* to annoy, bothersome

ag-gre-gate *adj.* to gather together

ag-gres-sion *n.* hostile action

ag-gres-sive *adj.* pushy; offensive

a-ghast *adj.* appalled, amazement

ag-ile *adj.* ability to move easily

ag-i-tate *v.* to stir or move with violence agitation, agitator n.

a-gleam *adj.* gleaming, reflecting

ag-nos-tic *n.* disbeliever in God

a-go *adj. & adv.* in the past

a-gog *adj.* excited, interest

ag-o-nize *v.* afflict with great anguish agonized, agonizing adj.

ag-o-ny *n., pl.* -nies mental distress

a-gree *v.* to give consent agreed n. agreeable adj., agreeness n.

a-gree-ment *n.* harmony

ag-ri-cul-ture *n.* raising of livestock and crops, cultivation of soil

a-ground *adv. & adj.* stranded; beached, on or onto a shore

a-head *adv.* in advance

a-hoy *interj.* nautical greeting

aid *v.* to give help

AIDS *n.* Acquired Immune Deficiency Syndrome

ail *v.* to feel sick, pain

aim *v.* to direct a weapon; to direct purpose aimless adj., aimlessness n.

air *n.* nitrogen and oxygen mixture; a breeze airlessness n.

air conditioner *n.* equipment to control temperature indoors

air-craft *n.* a machine that flies

air-field *n.* paved runways at an airport airfields n.

air-mail & air mail *n.* mail sent via air

air-port *n.* airplane terminal

air raid *n.* bombing attack

air-ship *n.* dirigible; lighter-than-air aircraft having propulsion

aisle *n.* passageway between rows of seats

a-jar *adv. & adj.* partially opened

a-kin *adj.* related, as in a family

al-a-bas-ter *n.* white, fine-grained gypsum **alabastrine** *adj.*

a-lac-ri-ty *n.* readiness; eagerness

a la mode *n.* pie served with ice cream, fashionable

a-larm *n.* a warning of danger; bell or buzzer of a clock **alarming** *adv.*

a-las *interj.* expressive of anxiety

a-late *or* **alated** *adj.* having wings

alb *n.* white robe worn by the clergy

al-ba-core *n.* large marine fish

al-ba-tross *n.* large sea bird

al-bi-no *n.* person with abnormal whiteness of the skin and hair

al-bum *n.* a book for photographs, etc, for making a collection

al-bu-men *n.* white of an egg

al-caz-ar *n.* a spanish fortress or palace

al-co-hol *n.* intoxicating liquor

al-co-hol-ism *n.* a habit or addiction, continuous use of a drug

al-cove *n.* partly enclosed extension of a room, an arched opening

ale *n.* beverage similar to beer

a-lert *adj.* vigilant; watchful **alertly** *adv.*, **alertness** *n.*

al-fal-fa *n.* plant grown for forage

al-fres-co *adv. & adj.* outside

al-ge-bra *n.* form of math

a-li-as *n.*, *pl.* **aliases** assumed name

al-i-bi *n.* form of defense

a-li-en *adj.* owing allegiance to a country, differing in nature

a-light *v.* to dismount; to come down **alightment** *n.*, **alighting** *v.*

a-lign *v.* to arrange in a line

a-like *adj.* similar; having close resemblance **alikeness** *n.*

al-i-mo-ny *n.* court ordered allowance for support

a-live *adj.* having life

al-ka-loid *n.* nitrogen containing organic bases obtained from plants

all *adj.* being a whole amount

al-lay *v.* to calm; to pacify **-er** *n.*

al-lege *v.* to assert; to be true

al-le-giance *n.* loyalty to one's nation, obligation, devotion

al-le-lu-ia *interj.* expressing praise to God

al-ler-gist *n.* doctor specializing in allergies

al-ler-gy *n.* **-gies** abnormal reaction to environmental substances

al-le-vi-ate *v.* make more bearable **alleviation** *n.*, **alleviator** *n.*

al-ley *n.* passageway behind buildings, narrow street **alley's** *n.*

al-li-ga-tor *n.* large amphibious reptiles

having broad heads

al-lo-cate *v.* to assign **allocation** *n.*

allot *v.* to distribute or set aside. **alloted** *v.*, **allotting** *v.*, **allotter** *n.*

al-low *v.* to make a provision for; to permit **allowable** *adj.*

al-low-ance *n.* a regular amount of money, food, etc **allowanced** *v.*

all right *adj.* meets satisfaction; dependable, agreeable, dependable

all-round *adj.* versatile

all-star *adj.* composed entirely of star performers or participants

al-lude *n.* refer to something indirectly, to play with

al-lure *v.* to entice; to tempt **allurement** *n.*, **allured** *v.*, **alluring** *v.*

al-lu-sion *n.* a hint **allusive** *adj.*

al-ly *v.* unite in a close relationship or bond **allied** *v.*, **allying** *v.*

al-ma ma-ter *n.* the school or university attended by a person

al-ma-nac *n.* an annual calender publication containing data

al-might-y *adj.* having absolute power, having control

al-mond *n.* oval nut

al-most *adv.* not quite

alms *pl.*, *n.* money given to the poor

a-loft *adv.* toward the upper rigging of a ship, a great height, in air

a-lo-ha *interj.* hawaiian greeting

a-lone *adj.* away from other people

a-long *adv.* following the length or path through woods, grass, etc.

a-loof *adj.* distant; indifferent, at a distance **aloofness** *n.*

a-loud *adv.* audibly, loud mannered

alp *n.* high mountain, large

al-pac-a *n.* a mammal related to the llama, having fine woolly hair

al-pen-stock *n.* long staff used by mountain climbers for support

al-pha *n.* first letter of the Greek alphabet, something that is first

al-pha-bet *n.* letters arranged in order, used in writing

al-pha-bet-ize *v.* to arrange in alphabetical order

al-read-y *adv.* by this or a specified time in the past

al-so *adv.* likewise; in addition

al-tar *n.* elevated holy table

al-ter *v.* to change or make different

al-ter-ca-tion *n.* noisy quarrel

al-ter-na-tive *n.* choice between two or more possibilities

al-ter-na-tor *n.* electric generator producing alternating current

al-though *conj.* even though

al-tim-e-ter *n.* instrument for measuring altitude

al-ti-tude *n.* height above sea level

al-to *n.* low female singing voice

al-to-geth-er *adv.* entirely

al-tru-ism *n.* selfless concern for others, unconcerned

a-lu-mi-num *n.* silvery metallic element, used in science

a-lum-na *n.* a female graduate of a school or university

a-lum-nus *n.* a male graduate of a school or university

al-ways *adv.* forever; at all times

am *n.* first person, singular

a-mal-ga-mate *v.* to mix; to blend amalgation, *n.*

a-man-dine *adj.* garnished with almonds, to decorate with almonds

am-a-teur *n.* one who lacks expertise amateurish *adj.*

a-maze *v.* to astound amazement *n.*

am-bass-a-dor *n.* official representative of a country

am-ber *n.* brownish-yellow resin

am-bi-ance *n.* environment

am-bi-dex-trous *adj.* using both hands with equal facility

am-bi-ent *adj.* surrounding, circling

am-big-u-ous *adj.* uncertain; doubtful ambiguousness n.

am-bi-tion *n.* strong desire to succeed ambitionless adj.

am-bi-tious *adj.* challenging

am-ble *v.* move at a leisurely pace, to make comfortable ambler *n.*

am-bu-lance *n.* vehicle to transport the injured or sick to a hospital

am-bush *n.* surprise attack

a-me-lio-rate *v.* to make better

a-men *interj.* ending of a prayer

a-me-na-ble *adj.* responsible -ility *n.*

a-mend *v.* to correct; to improve, make better amendment *n.*

a-mends *pl., n.* compensation for injury or sickness

a-men-i-ty *n.* agreeableness

a-merce *v.* to punish, correct

America *n.* United States of America, a free country

A-mer-ica-n *n.* a native U.S. citizen

am-e-thyst *n.* purple gemstone

a-mi-a-ble *adj.* friendly and pleasant

am-i-ca-ble *adj.* harmonious amicability *n.*

a-mid *prep.* to be in the middle of something, to be occupied

a-mi-go *n.* friend

a-miss *adj.* out of order or place

am-mo-nia *n.* colorless, pungent gas

am-mu-ni-tion *n.* projectiles fired from guns or other weapons

am-ne-sia *n.* the loss of memory

am-nes-ty *n.* pardon for political offenders

a-mor-al *adj.* neither moral nor immoral

a-mor-phous *adj.* something which is lacking definite form

am-or-tize *v.* liquidate a loan

a-mount *n.* sum or total quantity

am-per-age *n.* strength of an electric current, hot wires

am-pere *n.* unit of electric current

am-per-sand *n.* sign that represents and (&), used as an abbreviation

am-phet-a-mine *n.* a drug

am-phib-i-an *n.* an animal able to live on land and in water

am-ple *adj.* sufficient; abundant

am-pul *n.* small, sealed vial

am-pu-tate *v.* to remove a limb from the body, get rid of amputation *n.*

a-muck *adv.* in an uncontrolled manner, uncontrollable

am-u-let *n.* charm worn to protect against evil, protection

a-muse *v.* entertain amusement *n.*

an *adj.* one sort of, others

a-nad-ro-mous *adj.* migrating up river to breed in fresh water

an-a-gram *n.* formation of a new word from another

a-nal *adj.* relating to the anus

an-al-ge-sia *n.* inability to feel pain analgesic *adj.*

a-nal-o-gous *adj.* similar, alikeness

a-nal-y-sis *v.* examining parts

an-a-lyze *v.* to make an analysis of

an-ar-chy *n.* state of policial disorder, absence of government

a-nat-o-mize *v.* examine in great detail, to look over carefully

a-nat-o-my *n.* structure of an organ anatomical *adj.*

an-ces-tor *n.* forefather

an-ces-try *n.* line of descent

an-chor *n.* device to keep a ship from drifting, to keep in place

an-chor-age *n.* place for anchoring a ship

an-cho-vy *n.* small fish

an-cient *adj.* very old ancientness *n.*

and *conj.* along with; as well as; added to, to put with

an-dan-te *adv.* slow in tempo

and-i-ron *n.* heavy metal support for logs in a fireplace

an-dro-gen *n.* hormone that maintains masculine characteristics

an-ec-dote *n.* short account of a story, a long story short

a-ne-mi-a *n.* condition in which blood does not have enough red corpuscles, in hemoglobin

a-nent *prep.* regarding; concerning

an-es-thet-ic *n.* drug used during an operation to take away pain

a-new *adv.* again, to do over

an-gel *n.* an immortal being **angelic** *adj.*

an-ger *n.* feeling of extreme hostility

an-gi-na *n.* disease marked by painful choking spasms

an-gle *v.* shape that makes a corner

An-glo *n.* root word meaning "English", Anglo-American

an-go-ra *n.* silky hair of the Angora rabbit; used in sweater making

an-gry *adj.* feeling of anger, hostility toward someone **angrily** *adv.*

an-guish *n.* great suffering or grief

an-gu-lar *adj.* gaunt; bony; lean

an-hy-drous *adj.* does not contain any water, without

an-i-mal *n.* any four-footed creature; beast; having four feet

an-i-mate *v.* give life or spirit to something that is still **animation**

an-i-mos-i-ty *n.* hostility

an-ise *n.* licorice-flavored herb

an-kle *n.* joint that connects the foot with the leg, support

an-klet *n.* short sock

an-nals *n.* descriptive record

an-neal *v.* treatment to make glass less brittle, not fragile

an-nex *v.* join a smaller thing to a larger one **annexation** *n.*

an-ni-hi-late *v.* destroy completely

an-ni-ver-sa-ry *n., pl.* -ries date on which something happened at an earlier time in history

an-nounce *v.* to give notice, to make public **announcement** *n.*

an-nounc-er *n.* performer on radio or television who entertains

an-noy *v.* to bother **annoyance** *n.*

an-nu-al *adj.* recurring the same time each year; again

an-nu-i-ty *n.* annual payment of an income; once a year

an-nul *v.* to cancel a marriage or a law **annulment** *n.*

an-nun-ci-ate *v.* to proclaim

a-noint *v.* apply oil in a religious ceremony; to bless someone

a-non *adv.* in a short period of time

a-non-y-mous *adj.* an unknown or withheld name, agency

an-oth-er *adj.* additional

an-swer *n.* written or spoken reply

ant *n.* small insect

an-tag-o-nize *v.* arouse hostility

ant-eat-er *n.* animal with a long snout which feeds on ants

an-te-ce-dent *adj.* event that precedes another; afterwards

an-te-lope *n.* swift-running mammal; quick-running

an-te me-rid-i-em *n.* time before noon; before 12 o'clock

an-ten-na *n.* feelers of an insect; aerial; helps in movement

an-te-ri-or *adj.* toward or at the front; a head of

an-te-room *n.* waiting room

an-them *n.* hymn of praise

an-ther *n.* part of the flower

an-thol-o-gy *n.* collection of stories

an-thra-cite *n.* hard coal

an-thrax *n.* infectious disease found in cattle and sheep

an-thro-poid *n.* gorillas

an-thro-pol-o-gy *n.* study on the origin, and development of man

an-ti *n.* one who opposes policy or proposal; against; not for

an-ti-bi-ot-ic *n.* substance used as a germ killer; a medicine

an-ti-bod-y *n.* proteins that counteract diseases; help heal

an-tic *n.* mischievous caper or act

an-tic-i-pate *v.* to look forward; excitement anticipation *n.*

an-ti-cli-max *n.* letdown or decline

an-ti-dote *n.* substance to counteract poison -al *adj.*

an-ti-freeze *n.* substance, mixed with water to lower the freezing point

an-ti-his-ta-mine *n.* a drug to relieve symptoms of allergies

an-ti-knock *n.* substance to reduce engine knock in a vehicle

an-ti-mo-ny *n.* silver-white metallic element used in medicines

an-ti-pasto *n.* appetizer

an-ti-per-spi-rant *n.* sustance to reduce perspiration and odor

an-ti-pode *n.* a direct opposite

an-tique *n.* an object that is over 100 years old

an-tiquity *n., pl.* **antiquities** quality of being old

an-ti--Sem-ite *n.* person hostile toward Jews; against

an-tith-e-sis *n.* direct opposition

ant-ler *n.* horns of a deer

an-to-nym *n.* word opposite in meaning antonymous *adj.*, antonymy *n.*

a-nus *n.* lower opening of the alimentary canal; anal

an-vil *n.* block for forming metal

anx-i-e-ty *n.* state of uncertainty
anx-ious *adj.* worried; upset
any *adj.* no matter which
any-body *pron.* anyone; any person
any-how *adv.* in any way; whatever
any-thing *pron.* any occurrence
any-time *adv.* at any time
any-way *adv.* in any manner
any-where *adv.* to any place
a-or-ta *n.* main artery from the heart; branching out from heart
a-pace *adv.* rapid in pace; faster
a-part *adv.* separate or at a distance
a-part-heid *n.* non-white racial discrimination in South Africa
a-part-ment *n.* suite in a building
ap-a-thy *n.* lack of emotions or feelings; lack of concern
ape *n.* large mammal
ap-er-ture *n.* an opening
a-pex *n.* the highest point
a-pha-sia *n.* loss of the ability to express ideas; loss of expression
aphid *n.* small insects which move
aph-o-rism *n.* brief statement of truth; giving the truth
aph-ro-dis-i-ac *adj.* arousing the sexual desire
a-pi-ary *n.* place where bees are kept; collection of hives
a-piece *adv.* for or to each one
a-plomb *n.* poise; confident
ap-o-gee *n.* point most distant from earth; toward the outer layer
a-pol-o-get-ic *adj.* expression of apology; giving sympathy
ap-o-plex-y *n.* loss of muscular control; non-movement
a-pos-tle *n.* person sent on a mission; to accomplish something
a-pos-tro-phe *n.* mark (') of punctuation used in writing
ap-pall *v.* overcome by shock or dismay appalled *v.*, appalling *v.*
ap-pa-ra-tus *n.* instrument for a specific operation or useage
ap-par-el *v.* to adorn; clothes
ap-par-ent *adj.* open to the mind; visible; open minded
ap-pa-ri-tion *n.* unusual appearance
ap-peal *n.* an earnest plea appealable *adj.* appealingly *adv.*
ap-pear *v.* to come into public view, in sight appearance *n.*
ap-pease *v.* to pacify; to quiet
ap-pel-late *adj.* review the decisions of the lower courts
ap-pend *v.* add an appendix
ap-pen-dec-to-my *n.* a surgical removal of the appendix

ap-petite *n.* craving or desire for food appetitive *adj.*
ap-pe-tiz-er *n.* food served before a meal for enjoyment
ap-plaud *v.* express approval by clapping; agreeable
ap-ple *n.* edible fruit having sweatness; with seeds
ap-ple-jack *n.* brandy
ap-pli-ance *n.* equipment designed for a particular use
ap-pli-ca-ble *adj.* appropriate; suitable applicability *n.*
ap-pli-cant *n.* person applying for a job with an organization
ap-pli-ca-tion *n.* request or petition
ap-ply *v.* to put into use; useage
ap-point *v.* to fix or set officially appointment *n.*
ap-por-tion *v.* divide and share; divided into portions apportment *n.*
ap-po-site *adj.* pertinent
ap-prais-al *n.* evaluation of property
ap-praise *v.* estimate the value of; to set a value appraiser *n.*
ap-pre-ci-ate *v.* recognize the worth
ap-pre-hend *v.* anticipate with anxiety; arrest; seize; take away
ap-pre-hen-sive *adj.* view the future with anxiety or alarm
ap-pren-tice *n.* person learning a trade through on-hands training
ap-prise *v.* to inform; make aware
ap-proach *v.* to come near; in contact approachable *adj.*
ap-prove *v.* express a favorable opinion; to agree with
ap-prox-i-mate *adj.* almost exact approximately *adv.*
apri-cot *n.* oval, orange-colored fruit having sweatness
apron *n.* garment used to protect clothing; protection against
ap-ro-pos *adv.* by the way
apse *n.* polygonal projection of a church, semicircular
apt *adj.* appropriate aptly *adv.*
ap-ti-tude *n.* natural talent or ability
aqua *n.* water, greenish-blue color
aqua-naut *n.* scuba diver
aquar-i-um *n.* an artificial pond
aq-ue-ous *adj.* resembling water
ar-a-ble *adj.* land suitable for plowing; fit for cultivation
ar-bi-tra-tor *n.* a person chosen to decide a dispute; settlement
ar-bor *n.* garden shelter
ar-bor-vi-tae *n.* ever-green tree
arc *n.* Something that is curved or arched.

arch *n.* the structure that spans over an open area; usually curved

ar-chae-ol-o-gy *n.* scientific study of ancient times archaeologist *n.*

arch-bishop *n.* a bishop of the highest rank; the highest

arch-di-o-cese *n.* district of an archbishop archdiocesan *adj.*

ar-cher-y *n.* art of shooting with a bow and arrow archer *n.*

ar-chi-tect *n.* person who designs and supervises construction

arch-way *n.* an arch over a passage

arc-tic *adj.* extremely cold or frigid

ar-dor *n.* extreme warmth or passion; to have feelings for

ar-e-a *n.* flat piece of ground

a-re-na *n.* area for public entertainment; usually a spherical shape

ar-go-sy *n.* fleet of ships

ar-gue *v.* to dispute, quarrel; to disagree on something arguement *n.*

ar-gyle *n.* knitted diamond-shaped designs in solid or outline

ar-id *adj.* dry; insufficient rain

a-right *adv.* correctly

a-rith-me-tic *adj.* branch of math

ark *n.* ship Noah built

arm *n.* upper limb of the human body extended outward armer *n.*

ar-ma-da *n.* fleet of warships

ar-ma-dil-lo *n.* burrowing nocturnal animal

ar-ma-ment *n.* military supplies and weapons needed for strength

ar-ma-ture *n.* main moving part of an electric device

arm-chair *n.* chair with armrests

arm-ful *n.* as much as the arm can hold; what can be carried

arm-hole *n.* an opening in a garment for the arm to go through

ar-mi-stice *n.* mutual agreement; truce; trusting agreement; bond

arm-let *n.* band worn on the upper arm made of cloth or metal

ar-moire *n.* large wardrobe

ar-mor *n.* covering to protect the body made of metal

ar-mory *n.* place where military equipment is stored

arm-pit *n.* hollow area under connection of the arm and shoulder

arm-rest *n.* support for the arm on a chair

arm-twist-ing *n.* direct pressure to achieve a desired effect

ar-my *n.* the land forces of a country; to defend a country

a-ro-ma *n.* distinctive fragrance or odor, long lasting aromatic *adj.*

a-round *adv.* to or on all sides

around-the-clock *adj.* lasting for a period of 24 hours; one day

arouse *v.* wake up from a sleep

ar-peg-gi-o *n.* chord produced in succession

ar-rack *n.* alcoholic beverage

ar-raign *v.* called before a court arraignment *n.*

ar-range *v.* put in correct order or sequence arrangement *n.*

ar-rant *adj.* extreme; without moderation; notoriously

ar-ras *n.* wall hanging of tapestry

ar-ray *v.* place or set in order; arrange arrayer *n.*

ar-rears *n., pl.* state of being behind, as an obligation, etc.

ar-rest *n.* to capture; to seize

arrest-ee *n.* person under arrest

ar-rest-ing *adj.* very impressive or striking; catching the attention of

ar-rhyth-mia *n.* alteration in rhythm of the heartbeat; irregular

ar-rhyth-mic *adj.* lacking regularity or rhythm; irregularity

ar-ri-ve *v.* reach or get to a destination; to make an appearance

ar-ro-gance *n.* overbearing manner arrogant *adj.,* arrogantly *adv.*

ar-row *n.* weapon shot from a bow; sign to show direction

ar-row-head *n.* striking end of an arrow; part which does damage

ar-row-root *n.* starch-yielding plant

ar-rowy *adj.* to move swiftly

ar-se-nal *n.* collection of weapons; place where military equipment is stored; manufacturing of weapon

ar-se-nic *n.* element used to make insecticide or weed killer

ar-son *n.* fraudulent burning of property; destroying arsonist *n.*

art *n.* human expression of objects by painting, etc.

ar-ter-y *n.* blood vessel that carries blood from the heart to the body

ar-te-sian well *n.* well that produces water without a pump; natural

art form *n.* form of an artistic expression

art glass *n.* glass designed for decorative purposes

ar-thral-gia *n.* pain in one or more joints arthralgic *adj.*

ar-thritic *n.* person who has arthritis; pain in joints

ar-thri-tis *n.* inflammation of joints

ar-thro-pod *n.* animal with jointed limbs

and segmented body, as a spider and other insects

ar-ti-choke *n.* plant with an edible thistle-like head; produces fruit

ar-ti-cle *n.* term or clause in a contract; a paragraph or section

ar-tic-u-late *adj.* able to express oneself clearly; feelings

ar-ti-fact *n.* something made by man showing human modification artifactual adj.

ar-ti-fice *n.* artful or clever skill

ar-ti-fi-cial *adj.* not genuine; made by man artificialy *adv.*

ar-til-lery *n.* weapons, especially cannons used in wars

ar-ti-san *n.* a craftsman

art-ist *n.* a person who practices the fine arts of painting, etc.

ar-tiste *n.* an expert in the theatrical profession; actor or actress

ar-tis-tic *adj.* characteristic of an artist; unique in design

art-ist-ry *n.* ability, or quality of workmanship; artistic ability

art-less *adj.* crude; simple; lacking art and skill artlessly *adv.*

art-mobile *n.* trailer that carries an art collection for exhibition on road tours; transportation of art

art-work *n.* the artistic work of an artist; expression of an artist

as *adv.* in the manner like; similar to; the same as

as-bes-tos *n.* mineral form of magnesium silicate used in fire-proofing; for putting out fires

as-cend *v.* to rise up from a lower level; to climb; to mount

as-cen-dant *adj.* rising; moving up

as-cent *n.* a way up; a slope

as-cer-tain *v.* to find out for certain; to make sure; to be correct

as-cet-icism *n.* practice of strict self-denial; measure of discipline

as-cot *n.* scarf or broad tie

as-cribe *v.* assign or attribute to something ascribable, *v.*

a-sex-u-al *adj.* lacking sexual reproductive organs asexuality *n.*

ash *n.* tree with a hard, elastic wood

a-shamed *adj.* feeling guilt, or shame; feeling unworthy; embarrassed ashamedly *adv.*

a-shore *adv.* on or to the shore

ash-tray *n.* container or receptacle for discarding tobacco ashes

aside *adv.* out of the way; to one side; off to the side

ask *v.* to request; to seek information;

to find out about

askance *adv.* with suspicion or distrust

askew *adv. or adj.* out of line, not straight; in a different direction

a-slant *adv.* in a slanting direction

a-sleep *adv.* in a state of sleep

a-slope *adv.* in a slanting or sloping position or direction

a-so-cial *adj.* selfish, not social

as-par-a-gus *n.* a vegetable with tender shoots; edible

as-pect *n.* the situation, position, view, or appearance of something

as-pen *n.* a tree known as the trembling poplar, having leaves that flutter in the lightest wind

as-per-i-ty *n., pl.* -ties roughness in manner or sound

as-per-sion *v.* false charges or slander; defamation; maligning

as-phalt *n.* a sticky, thick, blackish-brown mixture of petroleum tar

as-phyx-i-ate *v.* to suffocate, to prevent from breathing asphyxiation *n.*, asphyxiator *n.*

as-pic *n.* a savory jelly made from fish, meat; used to garnish meat

as-pi-rate *v.* to give pronunciation with a full breathing sound

as-pire *v.* to desire with ambition; to strive towards something that is higher aspiringly *adv.*

as-pi-rin *n.* medication used for the relief of pain and fever

ass *n.* a hoofed animal; a donkey

as-sail *v.* to attack violently with words or blows assailant *n.*

as-sas-sin *n.* murderer especially one that murders a politically important person either for fanatical motives or for hire

as-sas-si-nate *v.* to murder a prominent person by secret or sudden attack -tion, -or *n.*

as-sault *n.* a very violent physical or verbal attack on a person assaulter *n.*, assaultive adj.

as-say *n.* to evaluate or to assess; to try; to attempt assayer *n.*

as-sem-blage *n.* a collection of things or people; a gathering

as-sem-ble *v.* to put together the parts of something; to come together as a group assembly *n.*

as-sem-bly-man *n.* a member of an assembly line; a part of

as-sent *v.* to agree on something

as-sert *v.* to declare or state positively, to maintain; to defend

as-sess *v.* to fix or assign a value to

something **assessor** n.

as-sess-ment n. the official determination of value for tax purposes; the amount assessed

as-set n. a value placed on goods owned by a person

as-sev-er-ate v. to state positively, firmly, and seriously

as-sign v. to designate as to duty; to give or allot; to attribute

assignable adj., assignor n.

as-sign-ee n. the person appointed to act for another

as-sign-ment n. a given amount of work or task to undertake; a post, position, or office to which one is assigned; to be completed

as-sim-i-late v. to take in, to understand; to make similar assimilation n.

as-sist v. to give support, to aid, to give help assistance, assistant n.

as-size n. a fixed or customary standard;

as-so-ci-ate v. to connect or join together n. a partner, colleague, or companion

as-so-ci-a-tion n. an organized body of people having a common interest; a society; as one

as-so-nance n. the repetition of sound in words or syllables

as-sort v. to distribute into groups of a classification; divide

as-sort-ed adj. made up of different or various kinds

as-sort-ment n. the act or state of being assorted; a collection of different things or persons

as-suage v. to quiet, pacify; to put an end to by satisfying to soothe; to lessen intensity assuagement n.

as-sua-sive adj. having a smooth, pleasant effect or quality

as-sume v. to take upon oneself to complete a job or duty; to take responsibility for; complete

assumeable adj., assumeably adv.

as-sump-tion n. an idea or statement believed to be true without proof; taken for granted

as-sur-ance n. a statement made to inspire confidence of mind or manner; to give word

as-sure v. to give the feeling of confidence; to make sure

as-sured adj. satisfied as to the truth or certainty assuredly adv.

as-sur-er n. a person who gives assurance to someone or something

as-ter n. a plant having white, bluish, purple, or pink daisy-like flowers

as-ter-isk n. the character (*) used to in-

dicate letters omitted or as a reference to a footnote

a-stern adv. & adj. toward the rear or back of an aircraft or ship

as-ter-oid n. one of thousands of small moving planets between Jupiter and Mars

asth-ma n. a respiratory disease marked by labored breathing, accompanied by wheezing asthmatic adj., cally adv.

as though conj. as if

astig-ma-tism n. a defect of the lens of an eye resulting in blurred or imperfect images

a-stir adj. to be out of bed, awake; in motion; to be up and around

as to prep. with reference to or regard to; concerning

as-ton-ish v. to strike with sudden fear, wonder, or surprise

as-ton-ish-ing adj. causing surprise or astonishment astonishingly adv.

as-ton-ish-ment n. the state of being amazed or astonished

as-tound v. to fill with wonder and bewilderment astoundingly adv.

as-tra-khan n. the curly fur from a young lamb of the southeast U.S.S.R.

as-tral adj. resembling, or related to the stars; in resemblence

a-stray adv. away from a desirable or proper path; different path

a-stride prep. one leg on either side of something; placed or lying on both sides of; extending across or over astride adv.

as-trin-gent adj. able to draw together or to constricting tissue astringency n., astringently adv.

as-tro-dome n. a large stadium covered by a dome for protection

as-tro-labe n. instrument formerly used to determine the altitude of a celestial body

as-trol-o-gy n. the study of the supposed influences of the planets and stars and their movements and positions on human affairs -ical adj., astrologer n.

as-tro-naut n. person who travels in a spacecraft beyond the earth's atmosphere; explores space

as-tro-nau-tics n. the technology and science of the construction and operation of a spacecraft -cal adj.

as-tro-nom-i-cal adj. relating to astronomy; something enormously large astronomically adv.

as-tron-o-my n. the science of the celestial bodies and their motion, magnitudes, and constitution

astronomer n.

as-tro-phys-ics n. branch of astronomy dealing with the chemical and physical constitution of the celestial bodies **astrophysicist** n., **astrophysical adj.**

as-tute adj. sharp in discernment; very shrewd **astutely** adv., **astuteness** n.

a-sun-der adv. separate into parts or positions apart from each other

asy-lum n. a refuge or institution for the care of the needy or sick

at prep. to indicate presence, occurrence, or condition

at-a-vism n. a hereditary characteristic that skips several generations **atavistic** adj.

at-el-ier n. an artist's workshop

a-the-ism n. the disbelief that God exists; **athe-ist** n. a person who does not believe in the existence of God

a-thirst adj. having a strong, eager desire for something

ath-lete n. person who participates in the playing of sports

ath-lete's foot n. a contagious skin infection of the feet (a fungus)

ath-let-ic adj. relating to athletes

a-thwart adv. opposition to the expected or right

a-tilt adj. & adv. inclined upward or tilted in some way

Atlantic Ocean n. the second largest ocean in the world

at-las n. a collection or book of maps for states and countries

at-mos-phere n. a gaseous mass that surrounds a celestial body

at-oll n. an island of coral that encircles a lagoon

at-om n. the smallest unit of an element

atom bomb or **atomic bomb** n. a bomb that explodes violently

a-ton-al adj. marked by the deliberate avoidance of a traditional key or tonal center **atonally** adv.

a-tone v. to make amends

a-tone-ment n. amends for a wrongdoing; reconciliation

atop adj. on the top of something

atri-um n. one of the four chambers of the heart

a-tro-cious adj. cruel or evil

a-troc-i-ty n., pl. -ties the condition of being atrocious

a-tro-phy v. decrease in size or wasting away; progressive decline

at-tach v. to fasten or become fastened **attachable** adj.

at-ta-che n. an expert on the diplomatic staff of an embassy

attache case n. a briefcase or a small suitcase used for carrying important materials

at-tach-ment n. the state of being attached; a tie of affection or loyalty; together

at-tack v. to threaten with force or violence, to assault

at-tain v. to arrive at or reach a goal **attainability** n., **attainable adj.**

at-tain-der n. the loss of civil rights that occurs following a criminal conviction or sentencing

at-tain-ment n. accomplishment; achievement; reached a goal

at-taint v. to disgrace or stain; to achieve or obtain by effort

at-tar n. the fragrant oil from flowers; fragrance

at-tempt v. to make an effort to do something

at-tend v. to be present; to take charge of or to look after

at-ten-dance n. the number of times a person attends something

at-ten-dant n. one who provides a service for another; caregiver

at-ten-tion n. observation, or mental concentration **attentiveness** n.

at-ten-u-ate v. to lessen the force, amount or value; to become thin **attenuation** n., **attenuated** v.

at-test v. ive testimony or sign one's name as a witness **attestation** n.

at-tic n. the space directly below the roof of a building; for storage

at-tire n. a person's dress or clothing worn on a daily basis

at-ti-tude n. a mental position; the feeling one has for oneself

at-tor-ney n., pl. **attorneys** person with legal training who is appointed by another to transact business for him

attorney general n. the chief law officer of a state or nation

at-tract v. to draw by appeal

at-trib-ute v. explain by showing a cause **attributable** adj.

at-tune v. bring something into harmony **attunement** n.

atwit-ter adj. excited; nervously concerned about something

au-burn adj. a reddish brown color; moderately brown

au cou-rant adj. fully familiar or informed; aware of surroundings

auc-tion n. a public sale of merchandise to the highest bidder **auctioneer** n.,**auctioned** v., **-ing** v.

auc-to-ri-al adj. having to do with an

author; writer

au-da-cious *adj.* bold, daring, or fearless; insolent **audaciously** *adv.*

au-di-ble *adj.* capable of being heard and understandable

au-di-ence *n.* a group of spectators or listeners

au-di-o *adj.* relating to sound or its high-fidelity reproduction

au-dit *n.* verification or examination of financial accounts

au-di-tion *n.* trial performance given by an entertainer as to demonstrate ability

au-di-tor *n.* a person who listens or hears; one who audits accounts

au-di-to-ri-um *n.* a large room in a public building or a school that holds many people

au-di-to-ry *adj.* related to the organs or sense of hearing

aught *n.* zero (0)

aug-ment *v.* to add to or increase; to enlarge **augmentable** adj., **augmentor** n.

au jus *adj.* served in the juices obtained from roasting

auk *n.* sea bird living in the arctic regions and cold regions

aunt *n.* sister of a person's father or mother

au-ra *n., pl.* **auras, aurae** an emanation said to come from a person's or an animal's body

au-ral *adj.* relating to the ear or the sense of hearing

au-re-ate *adj.* of a brilliant golden color or radiance

au re-voir *interj.* used in expressing farewell to someone

au-ri-cle *n.* the two of the four upper chambers of the heart

au-ro-ra *n.* the brilliant display of moving and flashing lights in the night sky **auroral** *adj.*

aus-tere *adj.* stern in manner and appearance **austereness** n.

aus-tral *adj.* southern

au-then-tic *adj.* real; genuine; worthy of acceptance; original

au-then-ti-cate *v.* to prove that something is true or genuine **authenticity** n., **authentication** n.

author *n.* a person who writes an original literary work **author** v.

au-thor-i-tar-i-an *adj.* blind submission and absolute, unquestioned obedience to authority

au-thor-i-ty *n., pl.* **-ties** group or person with power; an expert

au-thor-ize *v.* give authority; to approve;

to justify **authorzation** n.

au-tism *n.* absorption in a self-centered mental state, such as fantasies, daydreams or hallucinations **autistic** *adj.*

au-to-bahn *n.* highway in Germany

au-to-bi-og-ra-phy *n., pl.* **-phies** the life story of a person, written by that person **autobiographer** n.

au-toch-tho-nous *adj.* native to an area or region of land

au-toc-ra-cy *n.* government by one person who has unlimited power

au-to-di-dact *n.* a person who has taught himself to do something

au-to-graph *n.* a handwritten signature **autography** n.

au-to-mate *v.* to operate by automation **automatable adj**

au-to-mat-ic *adj.* operating with very little control **automatically** *adv.*

automatic pilot *n.* the device for automatically steering aircraft and ships in one direction

au-to-ma-tion *n.* the equipment used to acquire automation

au-to-mo-bile *n.* a four-wheeled passenger vehicle commonly propelled by an internalcombustion engine **automobilist n.**

au-to-mo-tive *adj.* relating to self-propelled vehicles

au-top-sy *n., pl.* **-sies** the examination of a body after death to determine the cause of death

au-to-stra-da *n.* an expressway in Italy

au-tumn *n.* the season between summer and winter **-al n.**

aux-il-ia-ry *adj.* providing help or assistance to someone

auxin *n.* hormone in a plant that stimulates growth

a-vail *v.* to be of advantage or use; to use; to result in

a-vail-able *adj.* present and ready for immediate use; attainable

av-a-lanche *n.* a large mass of rock or snow that slides or falls down a mountainside or hill

a-vant--garde *n.* people who invent new ideas and styles in a certain field of study

a-venge *v.* to take revenge for something **avenger** n.

av-e-nue *n.* a street lined with trees

a-ver *v.* to state positively

av-er-age *n.* typical or usual, not being exceptional; regularly

a-verse *adj.* having a feeling of repugnance

a-ver-sion *n.* a feeling of strong dislike; the act of turning away

a-vert *v.* prevent or keep from happening; to ward off

a-vi-ary *n.* a place where birds are kept and confined

a-vi-a-tion *n.* the operation of planes and other aircraft

a-vi-a-tor *n.* pilot of an aircraft

av-id *adj.* greedy **avidly** *adv.*

av-o-ca-do *n.* pear-shaped edible fruit from the avocado tree

av-o-ca-tion *n.* activity in addition to the regular work; a hobby

a-void *v.* to stay away from; to shun

a-vouch *v.* to guarantee

a-vow *v.* state openly on a subject

a-wake *v.* to be alert or watchful

a-ward *v.* confer as being deserved or merited

a-ware *adj.* being conscious of something; knowing of all things

a-wash *adj.* flooded; to be washed by water; to ruin by water

a-way *adv.* at a distance; apart from

awe *n.* a feeling of wonder **awe** *v.*

a-wea-ry *adj.* tired

a-weigh *adj.* hang just clear of a ship's anchor

awe-some *adj.* expressive of awe

aw-ful *adj.* very unpleasant; disagreeable **awfully** *adv.*

a-while *adv.* for a short time

a-whirl *adj.* to spin around

awk-ward *adj.* not graceful; clumsy **awkwardly** *adv.*

awl *n.* tool used to make holes in leather or in wood

awn-ing *n.* structure that serves as a shelter over a window

a-wry *adv.* in a twisted or turned position; other than upright

ax *or* **axe** *n.* tool used to split wood

ax-i-om *n.* something assumed to be true without proof

ax-is *n.* the line around an object or body that rotates

ax-le *n.* shaft around which a wheel or pair of wheels revolve

a-yah *n.* nursemaid or maid in India

a-zal-ea *n.* a shrub grown for their many colored flowers

AZT *abbr.* azidothymidine; a drug that improves the symptoms of Acquired Imune Difficiency Syndrome

Az-tec *n.* Indian people of Mexico

az-ure *n.* blue color of the sky; the unclouded sky

azurite *n.* a mineral consisting of blue basic carbonate of copper

B, b The second letter of the English alphabet.

babble *v.* to chatter senselessly

babe *n.* a very young child or infant

ba-boon *n.* a species of the monkey family **baboonish** *adj.*

ba-by *n., pl. babies* infant, very young child **babish** *adj.*

baby grand *n.* a type of piano

bac-ca-lau-re-ate *n.* a college degree

bach-e-lor *n.* an unmarried male

ba-cil-lus *n., pl.* **bacilli** rod-like microscopic organism

back *n.* the rear part of the human body **back-less** *adj.*

back-bite *v.* gossip or speak in a nasty way **back-biter** *n.*

back-board *n.* a board that gives support

back-bone *n.* spinal column

back-er *n.* someone who gives support

back-field *n.* football players behind the line of scrimmage

back-fire *n.* explosion of ignited fuel in an engine **backfire** *v.*

back-gam-mon *n.* a board game

back-ground *n.* area behind which objects are represented

back-hand *n.* a stroke in the game of tennis

back-ing *n.* support; endorsment

back-lash *n.* violent backward movement **back-lash-er** *n.*

back-log *n.* accumulation of unfinished work

back-pack *n.* equipment to carry items on the back

back-pedal *v.* to move backward or retreat

back room *n.* a room in the rear of a building

back-side *n.* the buttocks

back-slide *v.* to lapse back into a less desirable condition

back-stage *n.* area behind the performing area in a theatre

back-stop *n.* screen to stop a ball

back-stretch *n.* side opposite the homestretch on a racecourse

back-stroke *n.* a swimming stroke

back-talk *n.* a smart or insolent reply

back-track *v.* to retrace one's previous steps or course

back-up *n.* alternative or substitute

back-ward *adv.* in a reverse order **backwardness** *n.*

back-woods *n., pl.* heavily wooded area **back-woods-man** *n.*

ba-con *n.* salted and smoked pork

bac-te-ri-cide *n.* substance that kills bacteria

bad *adj.* naughty or disobedient; inferior in quality or performance

badger *n.* burrowing mammal *v.* harass

bad-min-ton *n.* a court game

baf-fle *v.* to perplex

bag *n.* flexible container for storing, or carrying something

ba-gel *n.* round roll with a chewy texture

bag-gage *n.* personal belongings of a traveler

bag-gy *adj.* loose baggily *adv.*

bag-pipe *n.* a wind instrument bagpiper *n.*

ba-guette *n.* a long, narrow rectangle gem

bag-worm *n.* type of moth larva

bail *n.* money given to guarantee appearance of prisoners

bail-iff *n.* officer who guards prisoners

bail-i-wick *n.* office of a bailiff

bails-man *n.* person who puts up bail for another

bait *v.* to lure

bake *v.* to cook in an oven baker *n.*

baker's dozen *n.* thirteen pieces

baking powder *n.* leavening agent

baking soda *n.* sodium bicarbonate

bal-a-lai-ka *n.* musical instrument

bal-ance *n.* scale for weighing of something

bal-co-ny *n.* platform projecting from the wall of a building

bald *adj.* lacking hair on the head

bal-der-dash *n.* nonsense

bale *n.* large, bound package or bundle

ba-leen *n.* a whalebone

balk *v.* to refuse to go on balky *adj.*

ball *n.* round object

bal-lad *n.* folk song

bal-last *n.* heavy material for stability

ball bearing *n.* bearing to reduce friction

bal-le-ri-na *n.* a female ballet dancer

bal-let *n.* artistic expression of dance bal-let-ic *adj.*

bal-loon *n.* a bag inflated with gas

bal-lot *n.* slip of paper used in voting

ball-point *n.* self-inking writing pen

bal-ly-hoo *n.* exaggerated advertising

balm *n.* a fragrant soothing ointment

ba-lo-ney *n., Slang* nonsense

bal-sa *n.* wood very light in weight

bal-us-ter *n.* upright post supporting a handrail

bam-boo *n.* tall grass with hollow stems

bam-boo-zle *v.* to trick

ban *v.* to prohibit

ba-nal *adj.* trite

ba-nan-a *n.* crescent-shaped yellow fruit

band *n.* a group of musicians

band-age *n.* strip of cloth to protect an injury bandage *v.*

ban-dan-na *n.* brightly colored hankerchief

ban-deau *n.* narrow band worn in the hair

ban-dit *n.* a gangster or robber banditry *n.*

ban-do-leer *n.* a belt

ban-dy *adv.* crooked

bane *n.* cause of destruction or ruin

ban-gle *n.* a bracelet

ban-ish *v.* to drive away banishment *n.*

ban-jo *n.* a stringed instrument

bank *n.* land at rivers edge; establishment for saving and lending money

bank-rupt *n.* person legally insolvent

ban-ner *n.* flag

ban-nock *n.* unleavened or flat cake

ban-quet *n.* elaborate dinner or feast

ban-yan *n.* a tree

bap-tism *n.* Christian sacrament

bap-tize *v.* sprinkle with water during baptism

barb *n.* fishhook point

bar-bar-i-an *n.* uncivilized culture

bar-be-cue *n.* outdoor pit for roasting meat

bar-bell *n.* exercise bar with weights

bar-ber *n.* person who cuts and dresses hair

bard *n.* a poet

bare *adj.* exposed to view bareness *n.*

bare-back *adv. & adj.* ride without a saddle

bare-ly *adv.* sparsely

barf *v. Slang* to vomit

bar-gain *n.* agreement on the sale of an item

barge *n.* a flat-bottomed boat

bar-i-tone *n.* male voice between tenor and bass

bark *n.* outer covering of a tree

bar-ley *n.* type of grain for making whiskey and beer

barn *n.* a farm building

bar-na-cle *n.* fish attached to an underwater surface

ba-rom-et-er *n.* device recording atmospheric changes

ba-roque *adj.* ornate artistic style

bar-rack *n.* building for housing soldiers

bar-ra-cu-da *n.* fish with a narrow body

bar-rage *n.* discharge of missiles

bar-rel *n.* round wooden container

bar-ren *adj.* sterile

bar-rette *n.* bar used to hold hair in place

bar-ri-cade *n.* barrier

bar-ri-er *n.* structure to restrict entrance

bar-room *n.* place to purchase alcoholic

beverages

bar-tend-er *n.* one who serves drinks at a bar

bar-ter *v.* to trade

ba-salt *n.* volcanic rock

base *n.* fundamental part; headquarters

base-ball *n.* game using a ball and bat

base-ment *n.* foundation of a home

bash *v.* hit with a heavy blow

bash-ful *adj.* shy

ba-sic *adj.* forming the basis

BASIC *n.* computer programming language

bas-il *n.* an herb

bas-o-lisk *n.* tropical American lizard

ba-sin *n.* a washbowl

ba-sis *n., pl.* **bases** the main part

bask *v.* relax in the warmth of the sun

bas-ket *n.* woven straw, container basketry *n.*

bas-ket-ball *n.* game played on a court

bass *n.* fresh water fish

bas-si-net *n.* infant's crib

bas-soon *n.* a woodwind instrument

bas-tard *n.* an illegitimate child

baste *v.* loose stitch; moisten meat

bat *n.* wooden stick; nocturnal flying mammal

bath *n.* the act of washing the body

bat-tal-ion *n.* a military unit

bat-ten *v.* to secure

bat-ter *v.* beat or strike continuously

bat-tery *n.* device for storing electricity

bat-tle *n.* combat between opposing forces

bawd *n.* a prostitute

bawl *v.* cry loudly

bay *n.* inlet of a body of water

bay-o-net *n.* spear-like weapon

ba-zaar *n.* a fair

be *v.* to exist; a verb to show action

beach *n.* sandy shore of a lake or river

bea-con *n.* signaling device

bead *n.* ball with a hole for threading

beak *n.* bill of a bird

beak-er *n.* widemouthed cup for drinking

beam *n.* wood or metal used in construction

bean *n.* edible seed pod

bear *n.* bears large mammal *v.* to endure

beard *n.* hair growing on the chin beardless *adj.*

beast *n.* four-legged animal beastly *adj.*

beat *v.* to strike repeatedly

be-a-tif-ic *adj.* showing extreme bliss

beau *n.* sweetheart

beau-ty *n.* quality pleasing to the eye beautifully, *adv.*

be-cause *conj.* for a reason; since

beck *n.* a summons

be-come *v.* come to be

bed *n.* furniture for sleeping

be-dazzle *v.* confuse with bright lights

bed-bug *n.* wingless insect

bed-lam *n.* state of confusion

be-drag-gled *adj.* limp and wet; soiled

bee *n.* a stinging insect

beef *n.* cow, steer, or bull meat beefy *adj.*

beer *n.* an alcoholic beverage

beet *n.* red root vegetable

bee-tle *n.* an insect

be-fit *v.* be suitable

be-fore *adv.* earlier

be-friend *v.* be a friend to someone

beg *v.* ask for charity beggar *n.*

be-gan *v.* past tense of begin

be-get *v.* to produce

be-gin *v.* to start

be-go-nia *n.* a tropical plant

be-grudge *v.* envy someone's possessions

be-guile *v.* to delight

be-half *n.* support or interest of another

be-have *v.* function in a certain manner

be-head *v.* remove the head from the body

be-hind *adv.* at the back; slow in arriving

be-hold *v.* to look at

beige *n. or adj.* light brownish, grey color

being *n.* existence

be-lat-ed *adj.* tardy belatedly *adv.*

belch *v.* to expel stomach gas

bel-fry *n.* bell tower

be-lief *n.* something trusted or believed

be-lieve *v.* to accept as true or real

be-lit-tle *v.* speak in a slighting manner

bell *n.* hollow instrument that sounds when struck

bell--bot-toms *pl., n.* pants with flared legs

bel-lig-er-ent *adj.* hostile belligerence *n.*

bel-low *v.* make a deep, powerful roar

bel-lows *n.* instrument that produces air

bel-ly *n.* the abdomen

be-long *n.* to be a part of

be-loved *adj.* to be dearly loved

be-low *adv.* at a lower level or place

belt *n.* band worn around the waist

belt-way *n.* a highway

be-muse *v.* to bewilder

bench *n.* long seat

bend *v.* arch; curve

beneath *adv.* below; underneath

ben-e-dict *n.* newly married bachelor

ben-e-dic-tion *n.* a blessing

ben-e-fac-tion *n.* a gift

ben-e-fice *n.* fixed capital assets

be-nef-i-cence *n.* quality of being kind

ben-e-fi-cial *adj.* helpful
beneficially *adv.*

ben-e-fit *n.* aid; help

be-nev-o-lence *n.* act of kindness
benevolent *adj.*

be-nign *adj.* having a kind disposition

ben-i-son *n.* blessing

bent *adj.* curved

be-numb *v.* to dull

be-queath *v.* leave by a will; to hand down

be-rate *v.* scold severely

be-reave *v.* to suffer the loss of a loved one bereavement *n.*

be-ret *n.* a round, woolen cap

berg *n.* a large mass of ice; iceberg

ber-i-ber-i *n.* nervous disorder

berry *n., pl.* berries an edible fruit

ber-serk *adj.* destructively violent

berth *n.* space for a ship or boat to dock

be-seech *v.* to ask

be-side *prep.* at the side of; next to

be-siege *v.* to harass with requests

be-smear *v.* to soil

be-som *n.* broom made of twigs

be-spat-ter *v.* to soil

be-speak *v.* to indicate; foretell

best *adj.* exceeding all others in quality

bes-tial *adj.* animal-like
bestially *adv.*

be-stir *v.* to rouse into action

best man *n.* attendant at a wedding

be-stow *v.* to give honor

be-stride *v.* to straddle

bet *n.* amount risked on a stake or wager

be-take *v.* move or to go

be-tide *v.* to happen to; to take place

be-to-ken *v.* show by a visible sign

be-tray *v.* to be disloyal or unfaithful

be-troth *v.* promise to take or give in marriage betrothal *n.*

be-trothed *n.* person engaged to be married

bet-ter *adj.* more suitable, useful

be-tween *prep.* in the middle; shared by two

be-twixt *prep.* between

bev-el *n.* angle at which one surface meets another

bev-er-age *n.* refreshing liquid to drink

bev-y *n.* a flock of birds

be-wail *v.* express regret or sorrow

be-ware *v.* cautious

be-wilder *v.* to perplex or puzzle
bewilderment *n.*

be-witch *v.* fascinate completely

be-yond *prep.* outside the reach or scope of

bez-el *n.* flange or groove

be-zique *n.* card game

bi-a-ly *n.* baked roll with onions on top

bi-an-nu-al *adj.* twice a year; semiannual

bi-as *n.* diagonal line; prejudice

bib *n.* protective cloth for small children

Bi-ble *n.* book of Old and New Testaments

bib-u-lous *adj.* inclined to drink

bi-cen-ten-ni-al *adj.* every 200 years

bi-ceps *n.* large muscle of the upper arm

bick-er *v.* to argue

bi-con-cave *adj.* bowing in on two sides

bi-cus-pid *n.* tooth with two roots

bi-cy-cle *n.* two-wheeled vehicle

bid *v.* to offer to pay a certain price

bid-dy *n.* hen

bide *v.* to wait

bi-det *n.* a basin for bathing genital and anal areas

bi-en-ni-al *adj.* every two years
biennially *adv.*

bier *n.* stand on which a coffin is placed

bi-fo-cal *adj.* having two focal lengths

bi-fur-cate *v.* divide into two parts

big *adj.* very large in intensity; grownup

big-a-my *n.* married to two people at the same time bigamist *n.*

big head *adj.* conceited person

big--hearted *adj.* generous and kind

big-ot *n.* person devoted to one group

big-wig *n.* person of authority

bi-ki-ni *n.* scanty, two-piece bathing suit

bi-lat-er-al *adj.* having two sides

bile *n.* liquid that is secreted by the liver

bilge *n.* inside hull of a ship

bi-lin-gual *adj.* fluent in two languages

bil-ious *adj.* gastric distress

bilk *v.* to swindle

bill *n.* itemized fees for services rendered

bill-board *n.* sign for advertisements

bill-fold *n.* wallet

bil-liards *n.* game played on a table

bil-lion *n.* one thousand million

bil-lion-aire *n.* wealthy person

bill of lading *n.* list of merchandise shipped

bil-low *n.* large swell of water; wave
billowy *adj.*

bil-ly club *n.* wooden club for protection

billy goat *n.* male goat

bi-month-ly *adj., pl.* bimonthlies every two months

bin *n.* storage place

bi-na-ry *adj.* having two different parts

bind *v.* to bandage

bind-er n. a notebook

bind-er-y n. place where books are bound

binge n. a spree

bin-go n. a game of chance

bin-oc-u-lar n. device to bring objects far away into focus

bi-o-chem-is-try n. chemistry of biological processes

bi-o-de-grad-a-ble adj. decomposable by natural processes

bi-ol-o-gy n. science of living organisms **biological** adj.

bi-o-phys-ics n. the physics of living organisms

bi-op-sy n. examination for the detection of a disease

bi-par-ti-san adj. support by two parties **bipartisanship** n.

bi-plane n. glider or airplane

birch n. tree with close-grained wood **birch-en** adj.

bird n. warm-blooded, egg-laying animal **bird-like** adj.

bird-brain n., Slang a person who acts silly

bird-ie n. stroke under par; a shuttlecock

bi-ret-ta n. priests cap

birth n. beginning of existence

birth control n. a technique to control or prevent the number of children born; lessening

birth-day n. the day a person is born; day of origin

birth-mark n. an unusual mark on the skin at birth

birth-rate n. ratio of births to a population

bis adv. again; encore

bis-cuit n. type of bread or cracker

bi-sect v. to divide

bi-sex-u-al adj. relating to or having characteristics of both sexes

bish-op n. Christian clergyman

bi-son n. large buffalo

bisque n. creamy soup made from fish or of the flesh of birds

bis-sex-tile adj. the extra day occurring in a leap year

bis-tro n. bar or small nightclub

bit n. tiny piece

bitch n. a female dog; spiteful woman

bite v. crush with the teeth **bitingly** adv.

bit-ter adj. a sharp, unpleasant taste; disagreeable taste

bit-ter-sweet n. root, with a bitter, then a sweet taste

bi-valve n. a mollusk

biv-ou-ac n. temporary military camp under little shelter

bi-week-ly n. every two weeks

bi-year-ly n. every two years

bi-zarre adj. extremely strange and odd; out of the ordinary

blab v. reveal a secret indiscreetly

black adj. very dark in color; depressing

black--and--blue adj. discolored skin caused by bruising

black-ball n. vote to prevent admission; vote against

black belt n. expert in karate

black-berry n. plant with black berries; edible fruit

black-board n. slate-like board written on with chalk

black box n. container that protects the tape recordings of airline

black eye n. bruise around the eye

black-head n. dirt that clogs the pores and creates blemishes

black-jack n. card game

blacklight n. invisible infrared light

black-mail n. threat of exposing a past discreditable act

black market n. selling illegal merchandise

black-out n. temporary loss of electrical power

black-smith n. person who shapes iron **blacksmithing** n.

black-top n. asphalt

black widow n. a poisonous spider

blad-der n. sac that holds urine

blade n. cutting part of a knife

blame v. to find fault **blameless** n.

blanch v. remove color; scald vegetables

bland adj. tasteless

blan-dish v. coax; flatter

blank adj. empty; confused **blankly** adv.

blan-ket n. covering used on a bed

blare v. loud sound

blar-ney n. talk that is deceptive

blast n. strong gust of air; sound of a horn

blast-off n. launching of a space ship

bla-tant adj. offensively loud; shameless; obvious, conspicuous

blaze n. a sudden burst of fire

bla-zon v. to make known; to announce; armorial bearings

bleach v. remove the color from a fabric; to make white or lighter

bleach-ers pl., n. tiered planks used for seating of spectators

bleak adj. depressing; barren; cold; harsh

bleat *n.* the cry of a sheep or goat

bleed *v.* to lose blood, as from an injury; to feel anguish or pain

bleep *n.* a signal with a quick, loud sound

blem-ish *n.* a flaw or defect

blend *v.* to mix together smoothly

bless *v.* to confer prosperity or well-being

bless-ed *adj.* Holy; enjoying happiness; bringing pleasure

bless-ing *n.* a short prayer before a meal; the act of one that blesses

blight *n.* disease of plants

blimp *n.* a large aircraft

blind *adj.* not having eyesight; unable to see; unable to discern

blind-ers *pl., n.* flaps restricting side vision

blind-fold *v.* cover the eyes with a cloth; unable to see

blink *v.* open and close the eyes quickly

blink-er *n.* a light to indicate turns

blintz *n.* hin pancake stuffed with fillings

blip *v.* erase sounds from a recording; a short crisp sound

bliss *n.* great happiness or joy

blissful *adj.*

blis-ter *n.* swelling of skin containing a watery liquid

blithe *adj.* carefree or casual

blitheness *n.*

blitz *n.* a sudden attack

bliz-zard *n.* a severe winter storm

bloat *v.* to swell or puff out

blob *n.* a small shapeless mass

bloc *n.* group formed for a common purpose

block *n.* solid piece of matter

blockage *n.*

block-ade *n.* the closure of an area

blond *adj.* a golden or flaxen color

blondish *adj.*

blonde *adj.* a person with blond hair; having light hair

blood *n.* the red fluid circulated by the heart, arteries, and capilaries

blood count *n.* the number of white and red corpuscles in a specific amount of blood

blood-hound *n.* breed of hunting dogs remarkable for senses

blood-shot *adj.* red irritation of the eyes; inflammation

blood vessel *n.* canal in which blood flows and circulates

bloom *v.* bear flowers; to flourish

blooming *adj.*

bloom-ers *n., pl.* loose pants gathered at the knee or just below the knee

bloop-er *n.* embarrassing mistake made in public

blot *n.* a spot

blotch *n.* area of skin that is discolored; difference in shade

blouse *n.* loosely fitting shirt or top

blow *v.* move or be in motion because of a current of air

blow--by--blow *adj.* very descriptive

blow dry *v.* dry one's hair with a hair dryer; to dry completely

blow-out *n.* the sudden deflation of a tire; a bursting by pressure

blow-torch *n.* handheld tool to melt soft metals

blow-up *n.* photo enlargement

blubber *n.* fat removed from whales

blue *n.* the color of a clear sky

blue baby *n.* infant with inadequate oxygen in the blood

blue-berry *n., pl.* **blueberries** small, seedless berry

blue-collar *adj.* wage earners who do manual labor

blue-fish *n.* game fish of the tropical waters; various dark fishes

blue-grass *n.* folk music

blue jay *n.* a bird

blue-nose *n.* a snob

blue-print *n.* reproduction of technical drawings or plans

blue ribbon *n.* award for first place in a contest or competition

blues *pl., n.* style of jazz music

blue spruce *n.* an evergreen tree

bluff *v.* mislead

blun-der *n.* an error or mistake

blun-der-buss *n.* gun with a flared muzzle; a blundering person

blunt *adj.* abrupt; dull

blur *v.* to smudge or smear; to become hazy

blush *v.* to turn red in the face; to feel ashamed **blushingly** *adv.*

blus-ter *n.* violent noisy wind in a storm

bo-a *n.* large nonvenomous snake

boar *n.* wild pig

board *n.* piece of sawed lumber; area where games are played

board-walk *n.* wooden walkway along a beach

boast *v.* to brag

boat *n.* a small open craft or ship

boat-swain *n.* petty officer in charge of the rigging

bob *v.* move up and down in a quick, jerky movement

bob-bin *n.* spool that holds thread

bobby socks *pl., n.* ankle sock

bob-cat *n.* wildcat

bob-sled *n.* sled with steering controls **bobsledder** n.

bod-ice *n.* upper piece of a dress

bod-y *n.* main part; physical part of a person **bodily** *adv.*

body-guard *n.* person hired to protect another from harm

body-surf *v.* surf on without a surfboard **bodysurfer** n.

bog-gle *v.* pull away from with astonishment

bo-gus *adj.* counterfeit; worthless

bo-he-mi-an *n.* unconventional lifestyle

boil *v.* heat liquid till it bubbles

boil-er *n.* vessel used to heat water for power

bois-ter-ous *adj.* violent; undisciplined **boisterously** *adv.*

bold *adj.* courageous **boldly** *adv.*

bold-face *n.* style of printing type

bo-le-ro *n.* a short jacket

bo-lo-gna *n.* smoked sausage

bol-ster *n.* round pillow

bolt *n.* threaded metal pin

bomb *n.* weapon detonated upon impact; to attack with bombs

bom-bard *v.* attack with missiles or bombs **bombardment** *n.*

bom-bast *n.* very ornate speech

bomber *n.* military aircraft

bo-na fide *adj.* genuine; authentic

bo-nan-za *n.* great prosperity

bon-bon *n.* candy

bond *n.* something that fastens or binds; together

bond-age *n.* slavery

bone *n.* calcified tissue of the skeleton

bone-dry *adj.* without water

bon-er *n., Slang* mistake or blunder

bon-fire *n.* an open outdoor fire

bo-ni-to *n.* game fish related to the tuna; medium sized

bon-kers *adj., Slang* acting crazy

bon-net *n.* a woman's hat

bon-sai *n.* a small ornamental shrub

bo-nus *n.* over and above what is expected; extra

bon voyage *n.* a farewell wish

boo *n.* expression of disapproval

boog-ie *v., Slang* dance to rock and roll music

book *n.* bound, printed literary work

book-case *n.* shelving for storing books

book-end *n.* support for holding books

book-ie *n., Slang* a bookmaker

book-ing *n.* engagement

book-keep-ing *n.* recording transactions of a business **bookeeper** *n.*

book-worm *n.* one who reads a lot

boo-mer-ang *n.* curved, missile that returns to the thrower

boon *n.* something beneficial

boon-docks *pl., n. Slang* an out-of-the-way place; country with brush

boor *n.* person with little refinement; peasant

boost *v.* lift by pushing up from below; an increase in amount

boost-er *n.* promoter

boot *n.* a protective covering for the foot usually with high tops

boot camp *n.* a military camp used for basic training

booth *n.* small compartment or area **booths** pl.

boot-leg *v., Slang.* sell, or transport liquor illegally

bo-rax *n.* cleaning compound

bor-der *n.* margin or edge

bore *v.* make a hole using a drill

born *adj.* brought into life or being

bor-ough *n.* self-governing town

bor-row *v.* receive money with the intentions of returning it

bos-om *n.* the female's breasts

boss *n.* supervisor **bossiness** *n.*

bot-a-ny *n.* science of plants **otanical** *adj.,* **botanist** *n.*

botch *v.* ruin something by clumsiness; accidental

both *adj.* two in conjunction with one; together as one

both-er *v.* to pester **bothersome** *adj.*

bot-tle *n.* receptacle made of glass

bot-tle-neck *n.* narrow passage

bot-tom *n.* lowest or deepest part **bottomless** *adj.*

bot-u-lism *n.* food poisoning

bough *n.* large branch of a tree

bouil-lon *n.* a clear seasoned broth made from lean meat

boul-der *n.* large round rock

boul-e-vard *n.* broad city street

bounce *v.* rebound or cause to rebound **bounced** v., **bouncing** v.

bounc-er *n.* person who removes disorderly people

bounc-ing *adj.* lively and spirited

bound-a-ry *n.* a limit or border

bound-en *adj.* under an obligation

bound-less *adj.* without limits **boundlessly** *adv.*

boun-te-ous *adj.* plentiful or generous; excess

boun-ti-ful *adj.* abundant; plentiful

bounty *n.* reward for the return of something

bou-quet *n.* cut flowers

bour-bon *n.* whiskey

bour-geois *pl., n.* member of the middle class society

bout *n.* a contest

bou-tique *n.* small retail shop

bou-ton-niere *n.* flower worn in the buttonhole of a man's jacket

bo-vine *adj.* relating to an ox or cow

bow *n.* front section of a boat

bow-el *n.* digestive tract

bow-ie knife *n.* thick-bladed hunting knife which is curved cconcavely

bowl *n.* container for food or liquids

bow-leg *n.* outward curvature of the leg **bowlegged adj.**

bowling alley *n.* building used for bowling

bowl over *v.* astound

box *n.* small container or chest

box-car *n.* enclosed railway car

box-er *n.* person who boxes professionally

box office *n.* where tickets are purchased for an upcoming event

boy *n.* male youth or child **boyhood** *n.*

boy-cott *v.* a means of protest

bra *n.* brassiere

brace *n.* device that supports something; something with connects

brace-let *n.* ornamental band for the wrist; for show

brack-en *n.* large species of fern

brack-et *n.* support to hold a shelf

brack-ish *adj.* distasteful

brad *n.* small nail

brag *v.* assert or talk boastfully

brag-ga-do-ci-o *n., pl.* cockiness or arrogant manner

brag-gart *n.* person who brags

braid *v.* interweave three or more strands;; to make by braiding

braille *n.* system of printing for the blind; reading with fingers

brain *n.* ·large mass of nerve tissue enclosed in the cranium **brainless** *adj.*

brain-storm *n.* sudden idea or inspiration; a harebrained idea

brain-wash-ing *n.* intensive indoctrination

brain wave *n.* rhythmic fluctuation between parts of the brain

braise *v.* brown meat, then simmer

brake *n.* device to stop or slow a vehicle; to decrease in speed

brake fluid *n.* liquid contained in hydraulic brake cylinders

bran *n.* husk of cereal grains

branch *n.* extension from the trunk of a tree; extension outward

brand *n.* trademark or label; mark of

shame **brander** *n.*

bran-dish *v.* to wave or flourish a weapon; an aggressive manner

brand name *n.* a company's trademark

brand-new *adj.* unused

bran-dy *n.* an alcoholic liquor **brandied** *adj.*

brash *adj.* unthinking; insolent; impudent

brass *n.* alloy of zinc, copper and other metals

bras-siere *n.* woman's undergarment with bust support

brat *n.* an ill-mannered child

brat-wurst *n.* fresh pork sausage

brave *adj.* having courage

bra-vo *Interj.* expressing approval

brawl *n.* noisy fight

brawn *n.* well-developed muscles

bray *v.* make a loud cry like a donkey; loudness

braze *v.* to solder

bra-zen *adj.* shameless or impudent

bra-zier *n.* person who works with brass; a utensil for holding coals

breach *n.* a break in friendly relations; ruptered or torn condition

bread *n.* leavened food made from flour and yeast *Slang* Money

breadth *n.* distance from side to side; a comprehensive quality

breadwinner *n.* one who supports a household; a means of livelihood

break *v.* to collapse or give way

breakdown *n.* failure to function

breaker *n.* a wave

breakfast *n.* the first meal of the day

breakthrough *n.* sudden advance in technique; breaking through an obstruction

breast *n.* milk-producing glandular organs; used in breast-feeding

breast-bone *n.* the sternum

breast-stroke *n.* a swimming stroke

breathe *v.* draw air into and expel from the lungs **breathless** *adj.*

breath-tak-ing *adj.* awesome **breathtakingly** *adv.*

breech *n., pl.* breeches the buttocks

breed *v.* genetic strain of domestic animals; to produce

breeze *n.* slight gentle wind

breeze-way *n.* roofed area between two buildings

bre-vi-ar-y *n.* book of prayers and psalms for the canonical hours

brev-i-ty *n , pl.* -ties brief duration

brew *v.* to make beer

brew-er-y *n.* plant where beer is brewed and produced

bribe *v.* induce by giving a token of value

bric--a--brac *n.* collection of objects usually having a value

brick *n.* molded block of baked clay used in building

brick-lay-er *n.* person who lays bricks side by side

bride *n.* women just married

bride-groom *n.* man just married

brides-maid *n.* woman who attends a bride

bridge *n.* structure over water

bri-dle *n.* harness to guide a horse

brief *n.* concise, formal statement of a case **briefly** *adv.*

brief-case *n.* a small bag for carrying papers and books

bri-er *n.* prickly plant

brig *n.* prison on a ship; sailing ship

bri-gade *n.* military unit

bright *adj.* brilliant in color; vivid **brightness** *n.*

bril-liant *adj.* radiant; intelligent

brim *n.* edge or rim of a cup

brim-stone *n.* sulfur

brin-dle *adj.* having dark streaks or flecks; a brindled animal

brine *n.* water contained in the oceans

bring *v.* to carry to a certain place

brink *n.* upper edge of a very steep slope

bri-quette *n.* brick-shaped piece of charcoal

brisk *adj.* moving or acting quickly

bris-ket *n.* meat from the breast of an animal

bris-tle *n.* short, stiff, coarse hair

britch-es *pl.* *n.* trousers

brit-tle *adj.* fragile

broach *n.* tapered tool for enlarging a hole

broad *adj.* covering a wide area -ly *adv.*

broad-cast *v.* to make widely known

broad-cloth *n.* cloth with a lustrous finish

broad-mind-ed *adj.* fair

broad-side *n.* side of a ship above the water; used on one side

bro-cade *n.* silk fabric

broc-co-li *n.* green vegetable

bro-chure *n.* pamphlet

brogue *n.* strong regional accent

broil *v.* cook by direct radiant heat **broiler** *n.*

broke *adj.* completely without money; without something

bro-ken *adj.* separated violently into parts; damaged or altered

bro-ken-hearted *adj.* overcome by grief or despair

bro-mide *n.* a sedative

bron-chi-al *adj.* pertaining to the bronchi **bronchially** *adv.*

bron-co *n.* wild horse

bron-to-saur *n.* very large dinosaur

bronze *n.* alloy of tin, copper, and zinc **bronzed** *v.*, **bronzing** *v.*

brooch *n.* decorative pin

brood *n.* the young of an animal

brood-er *n.* enclosed heated area for raising young chickens

brook *n.* small fresh-water stream

broom *n.* long-handled implement for sweeping

broth *n.* liquid from cooking meats

broth-er *n.* male who shares the same parents as another

brow *n.* ridge above the eye

brow-beat *v.* bully

brown *n.* color between yellow and red in hue; medium lightness

brown bag-ging *n.* practice of bringing one's lunch to work

brown-ie *n.* chewy chocolate cake

browse *v.* look over something casually; glance at

bruise *n.* discoloration of the skin

brunch *n.* late breakfast and an early lunch combined together

bru-net *adj.* person with dark brown hair

brush *n.* device for painting or grooming the hair

bru-tal *adj.* very harsh or cruel **brutally** *adv.*

bub-ble *n.* round hollow object

bu-bon-ic plague *n.* contagious fatal disease

buck *n.* male deer

buck-et *n.* vessel used to carry liquids; pail

buckle *v.* to warp

bud *n.* something not developed completely; not yet mature

bud-dy *n.* companion

budge *v.* move slightly

bud-get *n.* money for a certain purpose; financial position

buff *v.* shine

buf-fa-lo *n.* wild ox

buff-er *n.* a special tool used to polish or shine something

buf-fet *n.* a side table for serving food; counter for refreshments

buf-foon *n.* clown

bug *n.* small insect; listening device

bu-gle *n.* brass instrument without keys

build *v.* erect by uniting materials

build-ing *n.* roofed and walled structure built for permanent use

bulb *n.* light for electric lamps

bulge *n.* swelling of the surface

bulk *n.* large mass

bulk-head *n.* retaining wall on the waterfront; an upright partition

bull *n.* adult male in cattle

bull-doze *v.* dig up land

bull-dozer *n.* machine for moving earth; one that buldozes

bul-let *n.* projectile fired from a gun bulletproof adj.

bul-le-tin *n.* a public notice

bull-head-ed *adj.* stubborn

bul-lion *n.* refined gold or silver

bull-pen *n.* area where pitchers warm up; a cell where prisoners are held until brought to court

bull's eye *n.* center of a target

bul-ly *n.* mean or cruel person

bul-rush *n.* tall grass

bul-wark *n.* strong support

bum *n.* one who begs from others

bum-ble-bee *n.* large bee

bump *v.* collide with

bump-er *n.* device that absorbs shock and prevents damage

bumper--to--bumper *adj.* long line of vehicles moving very slowly

bump-kin *n.* awkward country person bumpkinly adj., -ish adj.

bump-tious *adj.* forward; pushy

bun *n.* plain or sweet small breads; tightly rolled hair

bunch *n.* group of items

bun-co *n.* swindling scheme

bun-dle *n.* anything wrapped or held together

bundle up *v.* dress warmly

bun-ga-low *n.* one-story cottage

bun-gle *v.* act awkwardly **bungling adj., bungler** *n.,* **bunglingly adv.**

bun-ion *n.* painful swelling of the big toe

bunk *n.* narrow bed

bunk-er *n.* tank for storing fuel on a ship **bunkered** *v.,* **bunkering** *v.*

bun-ny *n.* small rabbit

bunt *v.* tap a pitched ball with a half swing; middle part of square sail

bunt-ing *n.* hooded blanket for a baby; various stout-billed birds

buoy *n.* floating channel marker

buoy-an-cy *n.* tendency to remain afloat; ability to recover quickly

bur-den *n.* something hard to bear; a duty; something that is carried

bu-reau *n.* low chest; body of non-elected officials in government

bur-geon *v.* put forth new life

bur-glar *n.* person who steals -ize *v.*

bur-i-al *n.* act of burying

burl *n.* growth on a tree

bur-lap *n.* coarse cloth woven from hemp; lightweight material

bur-lesque *n.* theatrical entertainment **burlesqued** *v.,* **burlesquely adv.**

burn *v.* be destroyed by fire; consume fuel and give off heat

bur-nish *v.* to polish; make shiny

burp *n.* a belch

bur-ro *n.* a small donkey

bur-row *n.* tunnel dug in the ground by an animal for burrying

bur-si-tis *n.* inflammation of the joints

burst *adj.* explode and experience a sudden outbreak

bus *n.* large passenger vehicle

bus boy *n.* waiter's assistant; person who cleans the tables

bus-by *n.* a fur hat

bush *n.* a low plant with branches near the ground; a dense tuft or growth; land that is covered intensely with undergrowth

bushed *adj.,* Slang extremely exhausted; tired

bush-el *n.* a unit of dry measurement which equals four pecks; a container that holds a bushel

bush-ing *n.* metal lining that reduces friction; electrical

bush-mas-ter *n.* the largest New World venomous snake

bush-whack *v.* to travel through thick woods by cutting bushes and small trees; to ambush **bushwhacker** *n.*

busi-ness *n.* person's professional dealings or occupation; an industrial or commercial establishment; role; function

bust *n.* a sculpture that resembles the upper part of a human body; the breasts of a women *v.* to break or burst; to become short of money Slang to place a person under arrest

bus-tle *n.* a padding that gives extra bulk to the back of a woman's skirt **bustled** *v.,* **bustling v.**

bus-y *adj.* full of activity; engaged in some form of work **busily adv., business** *n.*

busy-body *n.* an inquisitive person who interferes with someone else's business

but *conj.* on the contrary to; other than; if not; except for the fact

bu-tane *n.* a gas produced from petroleum, used as a fuel refrigerant and aerosol propellant

butch-er *n.* one who slaughters animals and dresses them for food butchered v., butchering v.

butt n. the object of ridicule; the thick large or blunt end of something. v. To hit with horns or the head; to place end to end

but-ter n. a yellow substance churned from milk

but-ter-cup n. a colorful plant with glossy yellow flowers

but-ter-fat n. the natural fat from milk that floats to the top of unpasteurized milk

but-ter-fin-gers n. an awkward or clumsy person

but-ter-fly n. a narrow-bodied insect with four broad, colorful wings; resembles a butterfly

but-ter-milk n. the liquid that remains after butter has been churned from milk

but-ter-scotch n. a candy made from brown sugar and melted butter

but-tocks pl., n. the two round fleshy parts of the rump

but-ton n. a small disk that interlocks with a buttonhole

but-ton-hole n. the slit through which a button is inserted

but-tress n. a support made of either brick or stone

bux-om adj. lively; full of life; happy; pleasantly plump

buy v. to purchase in exchange for money. n. Anything that is bought

buy-er v. a person who buys from a store or an individual

buzz v. to make a low vibrating sound, as a bee; to signal

buz-zard n. a broad-winged vulture from the same family as the hawk

buzz-er n. an electrical signaling device that makes a buzzing sound; the sound of a buzzer

by prep. up to and beyond; to go past; not later than

bye n. a position in which a contestant has no opponent after pairs are drawn for a tournament, and, therefore, advances to the next round

bye-bye Slang farewell

by-gone adj. gone by; past

by-law n. a rule or law governing internal affairs of a group or organization

by--product n. material that is left over when something is manufactured but also has a market value of its own

byte n. in computer science, a sequence of adjacent binary digits operated on as a unit

by-word n. well-known proverb

C, c The third letter of the English alphabet

cab n. a taxicab; the compartment where a person sits to drive a large truck or machinery

ca-bal n. a group that conspires against a government or other public intstitution

ca-ban-a n. a small shelter on the beach with living facilities

cab-a-ret n. a restaurant that provides dancing and live entertainment

cab-bage n. a plant with large, edible green leaves, eaten as a vegetable

cab-in n. a small house; a private room on a ship

cab-i-net n. a storage unit

cab-i-net-maker n. a person who specialized in the construction of furniture

cu-ble n. a very heavy rope having great strength

cable stitch n. a knitting stitch that produces the look of a cable

cable television n. a private television system which picks up signals from television stations and transmits them by cable

ca-boo-dle n. Slang the entire unit, amount, or colletion

ca-boose n. the last car of a train

ca-ca-o n. any tree of the chocolate family; the dried seed of the cacao tree from which chocolate and cocoa are made

cache n. a safe place

ca-dav-er n. a dead body

ca-det n. a military student

caf-e-te-ri-a n. a restaurant with self-service

caf-feine n. a stimuiant **caffeinic** adj.

cake n. a sweet dessert

cal-a-mine n. a lotion for skin irritations

ca-lam-i-ty n. a misfortune calamitously adv.

cal-ci-fy v. to become stony calcification n.

cal-ci-um n. an element found in teeth and bones

cal-cu-late v. to estimate something calculable, calculated adj.

cal-dron n. a cooking kettle

calf n. the offspring of a domestic cow

cal-i-co n. a cotton fabric used in clothing

call v. to call out; to telephone

cal-lus n. thickening of the skin

calm adj. an absence of motion

cal-o-rie n. a measurement of food energy

cam-el *n.* a desert animal living in Africa and Asia

cam-e-o *n.* a precious gem

cam-er-a *n.* an apparatus for taking pictures

cam-i-sole *n.* a short sleeveless undergarment for women

cam-ou-flage *v.* to disguise or conseal something from view

camp *n.* a temporary lodging

cam-pus *n.* the grounds of a college

can *v.* to be physically or mentally able

ca-nal *n.* a man-made water channel

ca-nar-y *n.* a small, colorful songbird

ca-nas-ta *n.* a card game

can-cel *v.* to invalidate or annul cancelation *n.*

can-cer *n.* a malignant tumor -ous *adj.*

can-di-date *n., pl.* a person seeking an office candidacy *n.*

can-dle *n.* a wax tallow burned to produce light

cane *n.* a walking stick

ca-nine *adj.* of the dog family

can-is-ter *n.* a container to store food in

can-ker *n.* an erosive sore in the mouth which causes great discomfort

can-ni-bal *n.* a person who eats human flesh

can-non *n.* a heavy war weapon

can-ny *adj.* cautious

ca-noe *n.* a light-weight, slender boat canoeist *n.*

can-on *n.* the laws of a church

can-o-py *n.* a cloth covering over a bed

can-tan-ker-ous *adj.* bad-tempered; illnatured cantankerously *adv.*

can-teen *n.* a container for carrying water

can-ter *n.* movement that is slower than a gallop

can-vas *n.* a fabric used in making tents

can-vass *v.* to solicit opinions or votes; to examine very carefully

can-yon *n.* a deep, narrow gorge

cap *n.* a covering for the head

ca-pa-ble *adj.* having the ability to perform

ca-pac-i-ty *n.* the volume of something; the ability to hold

cape *n.* a covering for the shoulders

cap-il-lary *n.* small vessels that connect

cap-i-tal *n.* the seat of government

ca-pit-u-late *v.* to surrender -tor *n.*

ca-pon *n.* a young rooster

cap-size *v.* to overturn in a boat

cap-sule *n.* a gelatinous case for oral medicine

cap-tain *n.* the chief leader of a group

cap-tion *n.* a subtitle

cap-ti-vate *v.* to hold the attention of someone or thing

cap-tive *n.* a prisoner

cap-ture *v.* to take by force captuer *n.*

ca-rafe *n.* a wine bottle

car-a-mel *n.* a chewy candy

car-at *n.* a unit of weight for gems

car-a-van *n.* a group of people traveling together

car-bo-hy-drate *n.* organic compounds

car-bon *n.* a nonmetallic element carbonize *v.*, carbonic *adj*

carbon monoxide *n.* a poisonous gas

car-bun-cle *n.* an infection of the skin

car-bu-re-tor *n.* a device to mix vapor, fuel, and air

car-ci-no-ma *n.* a malignant tumor

car-di-ac *adj.* of the heart

car-di-gan *n.* a sweater with buttons down the front

car-di-ol-o-gy *n.* the study of the heart cardiologist *n.*, cardiological *adj*

card-sharp *n.* a person who cheates when playing cards

care *n.* a feeling of concern

ca-reer *n.* an occupation

care-free *adj.* free from all worries

care-ful *adj.* exercising care

ca-ress *v.* to touch gently

car-go *n.* freight

car-il-lon *n.* a set of tuned bells in a tower

car-nage *n.* a massacre

car-ni-val *n.* an amusement show

car-ol *n.* a song

car-pen-ter *n.* one who works with lumber

car-pet *n.* a floor covering

car-rot *n.* an orange root vegetable

car-ry *v.* to transport from one place to another

car-tel *n.* a group of companies organized to control prices, etc.

car-ti-lage *n.* connective tissue

car-toon *n.* a funny caricature -ist *n.*

cart-wheel *n.* a sideways handspring

cas-cade *n.* a waterfall

case *n.* a particular occurrence

cash *n.* money

cash-ew *n.* an edible nut

cash-ier *n.* an employee who handles cash

ca-si-no *n.* a public place for gambling

cask *n.* a barrel

cas-ket *n.* a coffin

cas-se-role *n.* a dish used for baking

cas-sette *n.* tape used in tape recorders

cast *v.* hurl or throw with force castway *adj.*

cast-er *n.* a small set of swiveling rollers

cas-ti-gate *v.* to punish or criticize severely

cas-tle *n.* a fort

cast-off *adj.* to discarded or throw away

cas-trate *v.* to spay

ca-su-al *adj.* informal

ca-su-al-ty *n.* one injured or killed

cat-a-combs *n.* underground passage

cat-a-log *n.* publication listing of names and addresses

cat-a-ma-ran *n.* a pleasure boat

ca-tas-tro-phe *n.* a terrible disaster

catch *v.* to capture or seize

cat-e-go-ry *n.* a grouping of something

ca-ter *v.* to provide food

cat-er-pil-lar *n.* the larva of a moth or butterfly

cat-fish *n.* a freshwater fish

ca-the-dral *n.* a large church

cat-nap *n.* a short nap

CAT scan *n.* x-ray; using computerized axial tomography

cat-tle *n., pl.* farm animals

cau-cus *n.* the meeting of a political party

cau-li-flow-er *n.* a vegetable

caulk *v.* to seal seams against leakage

cause *v.* to produce a result

cause-way *n.* a highway through a marsh tract

cau-ter-ize *v.* to burn with a hot instrument

cau-tion *n.* a warning

cav-al-cade *n.* horse-drawn carriages

cav-al-ry *n.* army troops on horseback

cave *n.* an underground tomb or chamber

cav-i-ar *or* cav-i-are *n.* eggs of a large fish

cav-i-ty *n.* a decayed place in a tooth

cease *v.* to stop

cease-fire *v.* to stop fighting

cease-less *adj.* endless ceaselY *adv.*

ce-dar *n.* an evergreen tree

ceil-ing *n.* an overhead covering of a room

cel-e-brate *v.* to observe with ceremonies celebration *n.*

cel-leb-ri-ty *n., pl.* -ies a famous person

cel-er-y *n.* a vegetable with an edible stalk

ce-les-tial *adj.* heavenly

cell *n.* a small room in a prison

cel-lar *n.* an underground area of a house

cel-lu-lite *n.* a fatty deposit

cel-lu-lose *n.* a carbohydrate

ce-ment *n.* a hard construction material

cem-e-ter-y *n.* a place for burying the dead

cen-sor *n.* a person who examines films censorship *n.*

cen-sure *n.* an expression of criticism

cen-sus *n.* the count of the population

cen-ter *n.* the equal distance from all sides

cen-tral *adj.* the center or main part centralize *v.*

cen-tu-ry *n.* a period of 100 years

ce-ram-ic *adj.* material made by firing clay

ce-re-al *n.* an edible grain; breakfast food

cer-a-bel-lum *n.* the lower part of the brain

cer-e-brum *n.* the upper part of the brain

cer-e-mo-ny *n.* a ritual

cer-tain *adj.* to be very sure -ly *adv.*

cer-tif-i-cate *n.* a document stating the truth

cer-ti-fy *v.* to declare in writing to be true

ces-sa-tion *n.* the act of stopping or ceasing

ces-sion *n.* the act of giving up rights

chafe *v.* to become sore by rubbing

chafing dish *n.* a dish for cooking food

cha-grin *n.* the feeling of disappointment

chain *n.* connecting links

chair *n.* a seat with four legs and a back

chair-man *n.* a person presiding at a meeting

cha-let *n.* a cottage

chal-ice *n.* a drinking goblet

chalk *n.* a soft mineral used for writing

chal-lah *n.* a loaf of braided bread

chal-lis *n.* a lightweight printed cloth

cham-ber *n.* a judge's office

chamber-maid *n.* maid at a hotel

champ *n.* a champion

cham-pagne *n.* a white sparkling wine

chance *n.* accidental

chan-cel *n.* an area of a church

chan-cel-lor *n.* a chief director -ship *n.*

chan-croid *n.* a lesion in the genital area

chan-de-lier *n.* a large light fixture

change *v.* to become or make different; alter

chan-nel *n.* the deepest part of a harbor, lake or river

chant *n.* a melody sung on the same note

cha-os *n.* total disorder

chap *n., Slang* a fellow

chap-el *n.* a place to worship

chap-er-on *n.* a woman who supervises younger women

chap-lain *n.* clergyman

chaps *pl., n.* leather overpants

chap-ter *n.* one division or part of a book

char-ac-ter *n.* a persons quality or trait

char-coal *n.* a material used for fuel

chard *n.* an edible white beet

charge *v.* to give full responsibility to; price

charg-er *n.* an apparatus to recharge a battery

char-i-ot *n.* a horse-drawn vehicle

char-i-ty *n.* money given to the needy

cha-ri-va-ri *n.* a playful serenade to newlyweds

charm *n.* an ability to please; ornament

chart *n.* a map

char-ter *n.* an official document

chase *v.* to run after

chasm *n.* a deep crack in the earth's surface

chas-sis *n.* the framework for automobiles

chaste *adj.* pure

chas-tise *v.* to reprimand

chat *v.* to converse in a friendly manner

chat-tel *n.* movable personal property

chauf-feur *n.* a person who drives someone

cheap *adj.* inexpensive; low in cost

cheapen *v.* to lessen the value

cheap-skate *n.* one who tries to avoid spending money

cheat *v.* to break the rules cheater *n.*

check *v.* to restrain; examine for correctness

check-book *n.* a book with blank checks

check-ers *n.* a board game

check-mate *n.* a winning chess move

ched-dar *n.* a firm, smooth cheese

cheek *n.* the fleshy part of the face

cheek-bone *n.* the facial bone below the e y e s

cheerful *adj.* having good spirits

cheer-leader *n.* person who cheers at a sporting event

cheese *n.* food made from the curd of milk

cheese burg-er *n.* a hamburger with cheese

cheese-cake *n.* dessert cake

chee-tah *n.* a swift-running wildcat

chef *n.* a male cook

che-mise *n.* woman's loose undergarment

chem-ist *n.* a person versed in chemistry

che-mo-ther-a-py *n.* a treatment for cancer

che-nille *n.* a soft cord used to make rugs, etc.

cher-ish *v.* to hold dear

cher-ry *n.* fruit tree bearing red fruit

cher-ub *n.* an angel resembling a child

chess *n.* game for two played on a chessboard chessman *n.*

chest *n.* the part of the upper body

chest-nut *n.* a tree with edible nuts

chev-ron *n.* an insignia or emblem

chew *v.* to crush or grind with the teeth

chic *adj.* fashionable

chick *n.* a young chicken

chick-a-dee *n.* a bird

chick-en *n.* a domestic fowl

chicken pox *n.* a contagious childhood disease

chick-pea *n.* a plant with edible pea-like seeds

chic-le *n.* the juice of a tropical tree

chic-o-ry *n.* a herb used in salads

chide *v.* to scold or find fault

chief *n.* a person of highest rank; a boss

chief-tain *n.* a head of a group, or tribe

chif-fon *n.* a sheer fabric

chif-fo-nier *n.* a tall chest of drawers

chig-ger *n.* an insect

chi-gnon *n.* hair worn on the back of the neck

child *n.* a young person of either sex childish *adj.*

child abuse *n.* the sexual or physical maltreatment of a child

child-birth *n.* the act of giving birth

chil-i *n.* a hot pepper

chill *v.* to reduce to a lower temperature

chill-y *adj.* very cold condition

chime *n.* a set of bells tuned to a scale

chi-me-ra *n.* an absurd fantasy

chim-ney *n.* a flue for smoke to escape

chim-pan-zee *n.* an ape

chin *n.* the lower part of the face

chi-na *n.* fine porcelain from China

chin-chil-la *n.* a rodent from South America

chintz *n.* printed, glazed cotton fabric

chintz-y *adj.* cheap

chip *n.* a small broken off piece; disk used in the game of poker

chip-munk *n.* striped rodent

chi-ro-prac-tic *n.* a method of therapy chiropractor *n.*

chirp *n.* the high-pitched sound of a bird

chis-el *n.* tool with a sharp edge to shape

chit *n.* voucher for food or drink

chit-chat *n.* casual conversation

chiv-al-ry *n.* brave qualities of a knight

chive *n.* herb used as flavoring in cooking

chlo-rine *n.* compound used to purify water

chock *n.* wedge placed under a wheel

choc-o-late *n.* ground cacao nuts chocolaty *adj.*

choice *n.* select or choose

choir *n.* an organized group of singers

chok-er *n.* short necklace

cho-les-ter-ol *n.* fatty substance present in blood cells

choose *v.* select or pick out

chop *v.* cut by making downward stroke

choppy *adj.* rough

chop-sticks *pl.*, *n.* sticks of wood for eating

cho-ral *adj.* sung by a choir or chorus

cho-rale *n.* hymn with a simple melody

chore *n.* a daily task

cho-re-a *n.* acute nervous disease

cho-re-og-ra-phy *n.* creation of a dance routine in ballets

chor-is-ter *n.* a member of a choir

cho-rus *n.* a group of people singing together

cho-sen *adj.* preferred above all others

chow *n.*, *Slang* food

chow-der *n.* soup made with fish or clams

Christ *n.* Jesus; The Messiah

chris-ten *v.* to baptize; give a Christian name

Christ-mas *n.* December 25th; believed to be the birthday of Jesus Christ by Christians

chrome *n.* anything plated with chromium

chron-ic *adj.* frequently recurring

chron-i-cle *n.* record of events in order

chry-san-the-mum *n.* cultivated plants

chub-by *adj.* plumb

chuck-hole *n.* hole in the street

chuck-le *v.* laugh quietly -er *n.*

chum *n.* a close friend or pal

chunk *n.* a thick piece; a lump

churl *n.* a rude person

churn *n.* container for making butter

chut-ney *n.* condiment made with fruit

ci-der *n.* juice from apples

ci-gar *n.* rolled tobacco leaves

cig-a-rette *n.* amount of tobacco rolled in thin paper

cinch *n.* strap for holding a saddle

cin-der *n.* piece of burned wood

cin-e-ma *n.* a motion picture

cin-e-mat-o-garaph *n.* movie pro-jector

cin-e-ma-tog-ra-phy *n.* art of photographing a motion picture

cin-na-mon *n.* bark of a tree used for spice

ci-pher *n.* zero

cir-ca *prep.* approximate

cir-cle *n.* process that ends at its starting point

cir-cuit *n.* path where electric current flows

cir-cu-lar *adj.* moving in a circle

cir-cu-late *v.* pass from place to place

cir-cum-cise *v.* remove skin on the male penis

cir-cum-fer-ence *n.* perimeter of a circle

cir-cum-scribe *v.* confine within boundaries

cir-cum-stance *n.* fact to consider when making a decision

cir-cum-stan-tial *adj.* not essential

cir-cum-stan-ti-ate *adj.* provide circumstantial evidence

cir-cum-vent *v.* gain advantage

cir-cus *n.* show featuring clowns, and trained animals

cir-rho-sis *n.* liver disease

cir-rus *n.* white, wispy cloud

cis-tern *n.* man-made tank for holding rain water

cit-a-del *n.* fortress

ci-ta-tion *n.* official summons from a court

cit-i-zen *n.* native or naturalized person

cit-ron *n.* fruit

cit-y *n.* place larger than a town

civ-et *n.* cat-like mammal

civ-ic *adj.* relating to or of a city

ci-vil-ian *n.* person not in active duty in the military or police force

civ-i-li-za-tion *n.* high level development

civ-i-lize *v.* tame

claim *v.* to hold something to be true claimable *adj.*

clair-voy-ance *n.* visualize objects hidden from the senses

clam *n.* freshwater bivalve mollusks

clam-ber *v.* climb using both hands and feet clamberer *n.*

clam-my *adj.* damp, cold, and sticky

clam-or *n.* loud noise or outcry

clamp *n.* device for holding things

clan *n.* group of people who are related

clan-des-tine *adj.* done in secrecy

clang *v.* make a loud, ringing sound

clap *v.* applaud

clap-board *n.* board covering for a house

clap-per *n.* part of a bell

clar-i-fy *v.* become or make clearer

clar-i-net *n.* woodwind instrument

clash *v.* to collide; conflict

clasp *n.* hook to hold objects together

class *n.* group with common interest

clas-sic *adj.* belonging in a certain category

clas-si-fy *v.* arrange into the same category

clause *n.* group of words part of a complex sentence

claus-tro-pho-bia *n.* fear of enclosed places

clav-i-chord *n.* key-board instrument

clav-i-cle *n.* bone that connecting breastbone and shoulder blade

claw *n.* sharp, curved nail on the foot of an animal

clay *n.* pliable earth that hardens when fired

clean *adj.* free from impurities

cleanse *v.* make pure or clean -er *n.*

clear *adj.* not cloudy; able to see easily

clearance *n.* distance between two objects

cleat *n.* metal projection to prevent slipping

cleav-er *n.* knife used by butchers

clef *n.* musical staff symbol

cler-gy *n.* women and men religious leaders

cler-gy-man *n.* member of the clergy

cler-i-cal *adj.* trained for office duties

clerk *n.* clerical worker in an office

clev-er *adj.* mentally quick cleverness *n.*

cli-ent *n.* a patron; a customer

cli-en-tele *n.* collection of customers

cliff *n.* steep edge or face of a rock

cli-mate *n.* weather conditions -tic *adj.*

cli-max *n.* point of greatest intensity

climb *v.* move to a higher location

clinch *v.* to settle definitively

cling *v.* hold fast to; to grasp or stick

clin-ic *n.* medical establishment

clink *v.* cause a light ringing sound

clip *v.* cut off

clip-per *n.* fast sailing vessel

clique *n.* exclusive group of people

clob-ber *v.*, *Slang* hit repeatedly

cloche *n.* woman's close-fitting hat

clock *n.* instrument that measures time

clog *v.* to choke up

clone *n.* identical reproduction

close *adj.* near, as in time; nearly even

clos-et *n.* compartment or room for storage

clot *n.* thick or solid mass, as of blood

cloth *n.* fabric, used to cover a table

clothe *v.* provide clothes

cloud *n.* something that obscures

clout *n.* a heavy blow with the hand; influence

clove *n.* a spice

clo-ver *n.* herb with trifoliolate leaves

clover-leaf *n.* junction of highway

clown *n.* professional comedian -ish *adj.*

cloy *v.* make sick with too much sweetness

club *n.* heavy wooden stick

clump *n.* thick cluster

clum-sy *adj.* lacking coordination

clus-ter *n.* a group of something

clutch *v.* to seize and hold tightly

clut-ter *n.* confused mass of disorder

coach *n.* director of athletics, drama, etc.

co-ad-ju-tor *n.* assistant

coal *n.* mineral widely used for fuel; ember

co-a-lesce *v.* come together

co-ali-tion *n.* temporary alliance

coarse *adj.* lacking refinement -ness *v.*

coast *n.* land bordering the sea

coat *n.* outer garment

coax *v.* persuade by gentleness coaxingly *adv.*

cob *n.* male swan; a corncob

co-balt *n.* metallic element resembling iron and nickel

cob-ble *v.* make or repair shoes

co-bra *n.* venomous snake

cob-web *n.* fine thread spun into a web

co-caine *n.* narcotic used as a local anesthetic

coch-le-a *n.* spiral tube of the inner ear

cock *n.* adult male in the domestic fowl; the rooster

cock-a-too *n.* crested parrot

cock-le *n.* edible bivalve mollusk

cock-ney *n.* dialect of East End Londoners

cock-pit *n.* compartment where the pilot and the crew sit

cock-roach *n.* fast running nocturnal insect

co-co *n.* fruit of the coconut palm

co-coa *n.* powder from kernels of the cacao

co-coon *n.* silky, protective case spun by insect larvae

cod *n.* large fish of the North Atlantic

cod-dle *v.* to cook just below boiling point

code *n.* set of rules; set of secret words

co-ed-u-ca-tion *n.* educational system for both men and women

co-erce *v.* dominate with force

co-ex-ist *v.* exist together

cof-fee *n.* beverage prepared from ground beans

cof-fin *n.* box for burying a corpse

cog *n.* series of a teeth on the rim of a wheel

co-gent *adj.* forceful cogently *adv.*

cog-i-tate *v.* think carefully about

co-gnac *n.* fine brandy made in France

co-hab-it *v.* live as husband and wife

co-here *v.* stick or hold together

co-hort *n.* group of people united in

one effort

coif *n.* hat worn under a nun's veil

coil *n.* series of connecting rings

coin *n.* piece of metal used as money

co-in-cide *v.* happen at the same time

co-in-ci-dence *n.* two events happening at the same time

coke *n.* arbonaceous fuel; cocaine

cold *adj.* having a low temperature **coldness** *n.*

cold—blooded *adj.* without feeling

col-ic *n.* sharp pain in the abdomen caused by muscular cramps

col-i-se-um *n.* large amphitheater

col-lab-o-rate *v.* work with another person

col-lapse *v.* fall; to give way

col-lar *n.* part of a garment around the neck

col-lar-bone *n., Anat.* the clavicle

col-late *v.* assemble in correct sequence

col-lat-er-al *adj.* security for a loan

col-league *n.* one who works in the same profession

col-lect *v.* gather or assemble

col-lege *n.* institution of higher education

col-lide *v.* come together with impact

col-lo-quy *n.* formal conference

col-lusion *n.* secret agreement

co-lon *n.* punctuation mark (:); section of the large intestine

colo-nel *n.* an officer in the armed forces **colonelcy** *n.*

col-o-ny *n.* group of emigrants living in a new land

col-or *n.* a hue or tint **colorful** *adj.*

col-or-a-tion *n.* arrangement of different colors or shades

col-or—blind *adj.* not able to distinguish colors

col-or-fast *adj.* color that will not fade

col-os-sal *adj.* large or gigantic in size

colt *n.* very young male horse **-ish** *adj.*

col-umn *n.* decorative, supporting pillar

col-um-nist *n.* person who writes a newspaper column

co-ma *n.* deep unciousness sleep

comb *n.* instrument for aranging the hair

com-bat *v.* oppose; to struggle

com-bi-na-tion *n.* series of numbers or letters to open locks

com-bine *v.* unite; to merge

com-bus-ti-ble *adj.* capability of burning

come *v.* arrive; to approach

com-e-dy *n.* humorous, entertaining performance

com-et *n.* celestial body orbiting the sun **cometic** *adj.*

com-fort *v.* console in time of grief or fear

com-fort-er *n.* heavy quilt; one who comforts

com-ic *adj.* characteristic of comedy

com-i-cal *adj.* funny

com-ma *n.* punctuation mark (,) indicating a break or series

com-mand *v.* to give orders; to dominate

com-mem-o-rate *v.* honor the memory of **commemorative** *adj.*

com-mence *v.* begin; start

com-mence-ment *n.* graduation ceremony

com-mend *v.* give praise **-able** *adj.*

com-men-su-rate *adj.* equal in duration **commensurately** *adv.*

com-ment *n.* statement of observation

com-merce *n.* exchanging of products

com-mer-cial *adj.* relating to a product

com-mis-er-ate *v.* feel sympathy for someone

com-mis-sary *n.* store on a military base

com-mis-sion *n.* moneys paid sales

com-mit-tee *n.* people appointed perform a task or function

com-mode *n.* movable wash-stand

com-mo-dore *n.* naval officer

com-mon *adj.* general, ordinary

common denominatior *n.* number that can be evenly divided

com-mu-ni-ca-ble *adj.* capable of being transmitted, as with a disease **communicably** *adv.*

com-mu-ni-cate *v.* make known

com-mu-ni-ca-tion *n.* act of transmitting ideas

com-mun-ion *n.* mutual sharing of feelings and thoughts

com-mu-nism *n.* system of government

com-mu-ni-ty *n.* group of people living in the same area

com-mute *v.* travel to one's job each day

com-pact *adj.* packed together

com-pan-ion *n.* an associate

com-pan-ion-a-ble *adj.* friendly **companionably** *adv.*

com-pa-ny *n.* gathering of persons for a social purpose

com-pa-ra-ble *adj.* capable of comparison

com-pare *v.* note the likenesses of

com-part-ment *n.* enclosed area

com-pass *n.* instrument to determine geographic direction

com-pas-sion *n.* sympathy for someone

com-pat-i-ble *adj.* live together harmoniously

com-pa-tri-ot *n.* person of the same country **compatriotic** *adj.*

com-pel v. urge or force action

com-pen-dium n. short summary

com-pen-sate v. make up for; to pay

com-pete v. to engage in a contest

com-pe-tent adj. having sufficient ability

com-pe-ti-tion n. a trial of skill or ability competitive adj.

com-pet-i-tor n. one who competes against another

com-pile v. to put together information from other documents

com-plain-ant n. person filing a formal charge

com-plaint n. expression of dissatisfaction, or resentment

com-plai-sance n. willingness to please

com-ple-ment n. something that adds to

com-plete adj. having all the necessary parts; whole

com-plex adj. consisting of intricate parts

com-plex-ion n. natural color and texture of the skin

com-pli-ance n. agreement

com-pli-cate v. make or become complex

com-pli-ment n. expression of praise

com-pli-men-ta-ry adj. giving a compliment

com-ply v. to consent

com-po-nent n. a constituent part

com-port v. conduct oneself in a certain way

com-pose v. make up from elements or parts composer n.

com-pos-ite adj. made from separate elements

com-po-si-tion n. artistic literary work

com-post n. fertilizing mixture of vegetable matter

com-po-sure n. tranquillity

com-pote n. fruit preserved or stewed in syrup

com-pound n. combination of two or more parts compounable adj.

com-pre-hend v. to perceive -sion n.

com-pre-hen-sive adj. large in scope

com-pres-sor n. a machine that for compressing air

com-prise v. to be made up of

com-pro-mise n. settling of differences

comp-trol-ler n. person who examines accounts

com-pute v. determine by the use of math; to make calculations

com-puter n. electronic machine which performs logical calculations

computerize v. process or store information on a computer

com-rade n. associate who shares one's interest or occupation

con v. Slang to swindle or trick

con-cat-e-nate v. join, or link together

con-cave adj. hollowed and curved inward concavly adv.

con-ceal v. keep from sight; to hide concealment n.

con-cede v. yield to a privilege; acknowledge as true conceded adj.

con-ceive v. become pregnant; to create a mental image

con-cen-trate v. give intense thought to something

con-cen-tra-tion n. state of being concentrated

con-cept n. generalized idea conceptual adj.

con-cep-tion n. union of sperm and egg

con-cern n. sincere interest -ed adj.

con-cert n. musical performance

con-cer-to n. one or more solo instruments in a composition

con-ces-sion n. act of conceding

con-ces-sion-aire n. operator or holder of a concession

conch n. a tropical marine mollusk

con-cil-i-ate v. win over or to gain a friendship conciliation n.

con-cise adj. short and to the point

con-clave n. private or secret meeting to elect a new pope

con-clude v. bring to an end conclusion n.

con-com-i-tant adj. accompanying

con-cord n. accord; harmony

con-course n. open space for passage of crowds

con-crete n. construction material

con-cu-pis-cence n. a strong sexual desire

con-cur v. to agree or express approval

con-cur-rent adj. acting together

con-cus-sion n. sudden and violent jolt

con-demn v. to find to be wrong condemnable adj.

con-dense v. to make more compact condenser n.

con-di-ment n. relish, or sauce used to season food

con-di-tion n. state or existence of something

con-di-tion-al adj. tentative conditionally adv.

con-di-tioned adj. prepared for a certain process or action

con-di-tion-er n. application that improves a substance

con-dom n. thin rubber sheath to cover the penis during sexual intercourse

con-do-min-i-um n. building in which all units are owned separately

con-done n. to forgive

con-duct v. lead and direct a band; lead the way

con-duc-tor n. person who conducts a musical ensemble

con-duit n. pipe to pass electric wires through

cone n. solid body tapered evenly to a point

con-fab-u-late v. chat informally

con-fec-tion-er-y n. candy and sweets

con-fed-er-a-cy n. union of southern states

con-fed-er-ate n. ally or friend

con-fer v. consult with another conferment n.

con-fer-ence n. meeting for discussion

con-fess v. to make known or tell something

con-fet-ti pl., n. small pieces of paper thrown during a happy occasion

con-fide v. entrust a secret to another confiding adj.

con-fi-dence n. a feeling of self-assurance

con-fi-den-tial adj. hold as a secret confidentiality n.

con-fig-u-ra-tion n. arrangement of parts or things

con-fine v. keep within a certain boundary or limit confinement n.

con-firm v. establish or support the truth of something

con-fir-ma-tion n. act of confirming to show proof

con-fis-cate v. seize for public use; to officially seize confiscation n.

con-flict n. a battle; a clash -tive adj.

con-form v. similar in form or character conformably adv.

con-for-ma-tion n. the manner in which something is shaped

con-found v. to amaze, to confuse

con-front v. stand face to face with defiance confrontation n.

con-fuse v. mislead or bewilder

con-fu-sion n. state of being confused; disorder

con-fute v. prove to be invalid or false confutable adj.

con-geal v. jell; to solidify

con-gen-ial adj. having agreeable characteristics

con-gen-i-tal adj. existing from the time of birth, but not from heredity

con-gest v. enlarge with an excessive accumulation of blood; to clog, as with traffic congestion n.

con-glom-er-ate n. business consisting of many different companies

con-grat-u-late v. acknowledge an achievement with praise

con-grat-u-la-tions pl., n. expression of or the act of congratulating

con-gre-gate v. assemble together in a crowd congregator n.

con-gre-ga-tion n. group of people meeting for worship

Con-gress n. united States legislative body congressional adj.

con-gru-ent adj. agreeing to conform

con-jec-ture n. guess or conclusion based on incomplete evidence conjectural adj.

con-join v. to unite

con-ju-gate adj. change the form of a verb; to join in pairs -ly adv.

con-junct adj. combined

con-junc-tion n. act of joining; the state of being joined

con-junc-ti-va n. the membrane lining of the eyelids

con-junc-tive adj. connective

con-junc-ti-vi-tis n. Pathol. inflammation of the membrane that lines the eyelids

con-jure v. bring into the mind; to appeal or call on solemnly

con-nect v. join; to unite

con-nec-tion n. association of one person or thing to another

con-nec-tive adj. capable of connecting; tending to connect connectivity n.

con-nive v. ignore a known wrong, therefore implying sanction connivance n.

con-nois-seur n. a person whose expertise in an area of art or taste allows him to be a judge; an expert

con-no-ta-tion n. the associative meaning of a word in addition to the literal meaning

con-note v. imply along with the literal meaning

con-nu-bi-al adj. having to do with marriage or the state of marriage

con-quer v. subdue; to win

con-science n. ability to recognize right and wrong

con-sci-en-tious adj. honest

con-scious adj. aware of one's own existence and environment

con-script n. one who is drafted for a service or a job

con-se-crate v. declare something to be holy consecration n.

con-sec-u-tive adj. following in uninterrupted succession consecutively adv.

con-sen-sus n. a collective opinion

con-sent v. to agree; give permission

con-se-quent adj. following as a natural result or effect consequentially adv.

con-serv-a-tive *adj.* opposed to change consequentively *adv.*

con-ser-va-to-ry *n.* a school of dramatic art or music

con-serve *v.* save something from decay, loss, or depletion conservable *adj.*

con-sid-er *v.* seriously think about; to examine mentally

con-sid-er-a-ble *adj.* large in amount or extent; important considerably *adv.*

con-sid-er-a-tion *n.* taking into account of circumstance before forming an opinion

con-sign *v.* commit to the care of another; to deliver merchandise consignable *adj.* consignment *n.*

con-sist *v.* be made up of

con-sis-ten-cy *n.* degree of texture, viscosity, or density consistent *adj.*

con-sole *v.* give comfort to someone consolable *adj.*

con-sol-i-date *v.* combine in one or to form a union of; to form a compact mass consolidation *n.*

con-so-nant *n.* sound in speech other than a vowel consonantly *adv.*

con-sort *n.* spouse; companion or partner; agreement

con-spic-u-ous *adj.* noticeable -ly *adv.*

con-spir-a-cy *n.* plan or act of two or more persons to do an evil act

con-spire *v.* plan a wrongful act in secret conspirator *n.*

con-sta-ble *n.* peace officer

con-stant *adj.* unchanging; steady in action, purpose, and affection constancy *n.*, constantly *adv.*

con-ster-na-tion *n.* sudden confusion or amazement

con-sti-pa-tion *n.* condition of the bowels characterized by inability to empty the bowels

con-stit-u-ent *adj.* having the power to elect a representative

con-sti-tu-tion *n.* fundamental laws that govern a nation; structure or composition

con-strain *v.* restrain by physical or moral means constrained *adj.*

con-straint *n.* the threat or use of force; confinement

con-struct *v.* to create, make, or build constructor *n.*

con-struc-tion *n.* the act of constructing or building something -al *adj.*

con-struc-tive *adj.* useful; helpful; advancing, or improving constructively *adv.*, -ness *n.*

con-strue *v.* interpret; to translate

con-sul *n.* an official that resides in a for-

eign country

con-sult *v.* seek advice or information from; to compare views consulter *n.*

con-sume *v.* to ingest; to eat or drink; to absorb consumable *adj.*

consumer *n.* person who buys services or goods

con-sump-tion *n.* fulfillment; the act of consuming

con-sump-tive *adj.* tending to destroy or waste away

con-tact *n.* place, or junction where two or more surfaces or objects touch

con-ta-gion *n.* transmitting of a disease by contact

con-tain *v.* include or enclose

con-tain-er *n.* something that holds or carries

con-tam-i-nate *v.* pollute or make inferior

con-temn *v.* scorn or despise

con-tem-plate *v.* to ponder -ation *n.*

con-tempt *n.* viewing something as mean, vile, or worthless

con-temp-tu-ous *adj.* feeling or showing contempt

con-tend *v.* dispute; to fight; to debate; to argue

con-tent *n.* something contained within; subject matter of a book -ment *n.*

con-ten-tion *n.* competition

con-test *n.* a competition; strife; conflict contestant *n.*

con-text *n.* a sentence, or phrase

con-ti-nent *n.* one of the seven large masses of the earth

con-tin-ue *v.* maintain without interruption; to resume continuance *n.*

con-ti-nu-i-ty *n.* quality of being continuous

con-tin-u-ous *adj.* uninterrupted or unbroken

con-tort *v.* severely twist out of shape contortive *adj.*

con-tor-tion-ist *n.* an acrobat who exhibits unnatural body positions

con-tour *n.* the outline of a body, figure, or mass

con-tra-band *n.* illegal or prohibited traffic; smuggled goods

con-tra-cep-tion *n.* voluntary prevention of impregnation -tive *adj. or n.*

con-tract *n.* formal agreement between two or more parties

con-trac-tion *n.* a shortening of a word by using an apostrophe (')

con-trac-tile *adj.* having the power to contract

con-tra-dict *v.* express the opposite side or idea contradiction *n.*

con-tral-to n., pl. -tos lowest female singing voice

con-tra-puntal adj. relating to counterpoint

con-trast v. note the differences between two or more people, things, etc.

con-tra-vene v. be contrary; to violate

con-trib-ute v. give something to someone contribution n.

con-trol v. have the authority to regulate, direct, or dominate a situation controlable adj.

con-trol-ler n. the chief accounting officer of a business

con-tro-ver-sy n. a dispute; a debate; a quarrel controversial adj.

co-nun-drum n. a riddle with an answer that involves a pun

con-va-lesce v. grow strong after a long illness convalescent adj.

con-vene v. meet or assemble formally

con-ven-ience n. quality of being suitable

con-vent n. local house of a religious order, especially for nuns

con-ven-tion n. formal meeting; a regulatory meeting between people, or nations

con-ven-tion-al adj. commonplace

con-verge v. come to a common point

con-ver-sa-tion n. an informal talk

converse v. involve oneself in conversation with another

con-ver-sion n. state of changing to adopt new opinions or beliefs conversional adj.

con-vex adj. curved outward

con-vey v. transport; pass information on to someone else

con-vict v. prove someone guilty

con-vince v. persuade to believe without doubt

con-voy n. group of vehicles traveling together

con-vulse v. move or shake violently

con-vul-sion n. an involuntary muscular contraction

cook v. apply heat to food; to prepare food

cook-ie n. sweet, flat cake

cool adj. without warmth

coop n. enclosed area to contain chickens

co-op-er-ate v. work together -tion n.

co-op-er-a-tive adj. willing to cooperate with others

coot n. bird

cop n., Informal police officer

cope v. to struggle or contend with something

cop-ier n. machine that makes copies

co-pi-lot n. assistant pilot on an aircraft

co-pi-ous n. large in quantity; abundant

cop-per n. metallic element; conductor of electricity

cop-per-head n. venomous snake

cop-ra n. dried coconut meat

cop-u-late v. have sexual intercourse

copy v. reproduce an original

copy-right n. satutory right to distribute literary work

copy writer n. person who writes copy

co-quette n. woman who flirts

cor-al n. small sea creature

coral snake n. venomous snake

cord n. string or twine; an insulated wire

cor-dial adj. warm-hearted and sincere

cor-don n. circle of ships to guard an area

cor-du-roy n. durable ribbed cotton fabric

core n. innermost part of something

cork n. elastic bark of the oak tree

cork-screw n. device for removing corks from bottles

corn n. vegetable

corn bread n. bread made from crushed cornmeal

corn cob n. cone where kernels grow

corncrib n. building for storing corn

cor-ne-a n. membrane of the eyeball

cor-ner n. angle where surfaces meet

corner back n. the defensive halfback

corner-stone n. stone that forms part of a building

cor-net n. brass musical instrument

corn-row v. braid the hair in rows

corn-starch n. starch made from corn used to thicken food

corn syrup n. sweet syrup

cor-nu-co-pi-a n. a curved goat's horn

co-rol-la n. petals of a flower

cor-ol-lary n. something that naturally follows or accompanies

cor-o-nar-y adj. relating to the arteries of the heart muscles

coronary thrombosis n. blockage of the coronary artery

cor-po-ral n. noncommissioned officer

cor-po-rate adj. combined into one joint body

cor-po-ra-tion n. group of merchants

corps n. branch of the armed forces

corpse n. dead body

cor-pu-lence n. excessive body fat; obesity

cor-pus-cle n. living cell in the blood

cor-pus delicti n. evidence pertaining to a crime

cor-ral n. enclosure for containing animals

cor-rect v. make free from fault or mistakes correctable adj.

cor-rel-a-tive adj. having a mutual relation

cor-re-spond v. communicate by written words correspondence n.

cor-ri-dor n. long hall

cor-ri-gen-dum n. an error accompanied by its correction

cor-ri-gi-ble adj. able to correct

cor-rob-o-rate v. support with evidence corroboration n.

cor-rode v. eat away corrosion n.

cor-rupt adj. dishonest; evil

cor-sage n. small bouquet of flowers

cor-sair n. pirate; a fast moving vessel

cor-set n. woman's undergarment for support

cor-tege n. a funeral procession

cor-tex n. external layer of an organ

cor-ti-sone n. hormone from the adrenal cortex

cor-us-cate v. to sparkle

cor-vette n. armed warship

co-ry-za n. acute inflammation of the respiratory system

co-sign v. sign a document jointly

co-sig-na-to-ry n. one who cosigns a document

cos-met-ic n. preparation to beautify the face

cos-me-tol-o-gy n. study of cosmetics cosmetologist n.

cos-mog-o-ny n. creation of the universe

cos-mo-naut n. a Soviet astronaut

cos-mo-pol-i-tan adj. being at home anywhere in the world

cos-mos n. orderly systematic universe

cos-set v. to pamper; pet

cost n. amount paid or charged for a purchase

cos-tive adj. causing constipation

cos-tume n. clothes worn for playing a part or dressing up in a disguise

cot n. small, often collapsible bed

cot-tage n. small house

cotter pin n. metal pin with flared ends

cot-ton n. fabric created by the weaving cotton fibers

cotton candy n. spun sugar

cot-ton-mouth n. water moccasin snake

couch n. piece of furniture

cou-gar n. mountain lion, panther, and puma

cough v. suddenly expel air from the lungs

could v. past tense of can

could-n't contr. could not

cou-lomb n. unit to measure electricity

coun-cil n. group of people assembled for consultation; advisory body councilman n.

coun-sel n. advice through consultation

coun-sel-or n. a lawyer

count v. find the total number of units; to name numbers in order

count-down n. counting in descending order

coun-te-nance n. expression of the face

coun-ter-act v. oppose; make ineffective

coun-ter-at-tack n. attack made in response to an enemy attack

coun-ter-bal-ance n. a weight that balances another; counterpoise

coun-ter-claim n. contrary claim made to offset another

coun-ter-clock-wise adj. & adv. opposite direction

coun-ter-es-pi-o-nage n. espionage aimed at thwarting enemy espionage

coun-ter-feit v. closely imitate or copy

coun-ter-foil n. stub of a check or ticket

coun-ter-man n. one who works at a counter

coun-ter-mand v. reverse a command by issuing a contrary order

coun-ter-of-fen-sive n. a military offensive

coun-ter-pane n. a covering

coun-ter-part n. one who complements another

coun-ter-plea n. plea in answer to a previous plea

coun-ter-point n., Mus. combined melodies

coun-ter-pro-duc-tive adj. hinder rather than aid

coun-ter-vail v. counteract

coun-ter-weight n. an equivalent weight

count-ess n. wife of an earl or count

count-ing house n. room used for keeping books

count-less adj. too numerous to be counted

coun-tri-fied adj. rural; unsophisticated

coun-try n. the land of one's birth

coun-try-man n. a compatriot

coun-try-side n. rural area

coun-ty n. territorial division

cou-pe n. car with two doors

cou-ple n. a pair; a few

cou-plet n. rhyming lines of poetry

cou-pon n. form to obtain a discount

cour-age n. strength to face danger without fear courageous adj.

cou-ri-er n. a messenger

course n. a series or sequence; a series of studies

court n. a place where trials are conducted; area marked off for game playing

cour-te-ous *adj.* respect for others

cour-te-san *n.* prostitute

cour-te-sy *n.* courteous behavior

court-house *n.* building holding courts of law

court-yard *n.* open space enclosed by walls

cous-in *n.* child of one's uncle or aunt

cove *n.* small inlet or bay

cov-e-nant *n.* formal, binding agreement

cov-er *v.* place something on or over

cov-et *v.* to crave possessions of someone else

cov-ey *n.* small drain that runs under a road

cum-ber-some *adj.* unwieldy

cum-mer-bund *n.* group of birds

cow *n.* mature female of cattle

cow-ard *n.* one showing great fear or timidity **cowardice** *n.*

cowl *n.* hood or long hooded cloak

cox-comb *n.* conceited foolish person

cox-swain *n.* one who steers a boat

coy *adj.* quieting or shy

coy-o-te *n.* small wolf-life animal

coz-en *v.* swindle, cheat, or deceive; win over by coaxing

co-zy *adj.* comfortable and warm; snug

crab *n.* one of numerous crustaceans

crab-by *adj.* ill-tempered and cross

crack *v.* to break without completely separating *n.* addictive form of cocaine

cra-dle *n.* small bed for infants

craft *n.* special skill or ability

crag *n.* steep, jagged rock or cliff

cram *v.* pack tightly; prepare hastily for an exam

cramp *n.* painful contraction of a muscle; abdominal pain

cran-ber-ry *n.* tree with tart red berries

crane *n.* large bird; machine for lifting heavy objects

cra-ni-um *n.* the skull

crank *n.* device to turn a shaft

crank-y *adj.* grouchy **crankiness** *n.*

cran-ny *n.* small crevice

craps *v.* gambling game with two dice

crash *v.* break noisily; collapse

crate *n.* container for shipping or storage

cra-ter *n.* depression in a volcano

cra-vat *n.* a necktie

crave *v.* desire intensely

cra-ven *adj.* lacking courage

crav-ing *n.* intense longing or desire

craw *n.* the stomach of a lower animal

crawl *v.* move on hands and knees; progress slowly

cray-on *n.* stick of wax used for coloring

craze *v.* to become insane

cra-zy *adj.* insane **craziness** *n.*

creak *v.* squeaking or grating noise

cream *n.* fatty part of milk; pale yellow-white color

crease *n.* line made by folding and pressing

cre-ate *v.* bring something into existence

cre-a-tion *n.* something created

cre-a-tive *adj.* inventive; imaginative **creativeness** *n.*

cre-a-tor *n.* God

crea-ture *n.* a living being

cre-den-za *n.* a buffet or sideboard

cred-i-ble *adj.* reasonable grounds for belief

cred-it *n.* money available in a bank; acknowledgment; college unit

cred-u-lous *adj.* gullible

creed *n.* religious belief

creek *n.* narrow stream

creel *n.* wicker basket for holding fish

creep *v.* advance at a slow pace

cre-mate *v.* reduce to ashes by burning

cre-o-sote *n.* oily liquid mixture

cre-pus-cu-lar *adj.* relating to twilight

cre-scen-do *adv.* gradually increasing in loudness

cres-cent *n.* quarter shape of the moon

cress *n.* plant with edible leaves

crest *n.* top line of a mountain or hill; ridge of a wave or roof

cre-tin-ism *n.* condition of physical stunting and mental deficiency

cre-tonne *n.* cotton or linen cloth

cre-vasse *n.* deep crack in a glacier

crev-ice *n.* narrow crack

crew *n.* group of people that work together

crew-el *n.* yarn used in embroidery

crib *n.* small baby's bed with high sides

crick-et *n.* leaping insect; a game

crime *n.* an act forbidden by law

crimp *v.* to pinch in or together

crimson *n.* deep purplish color

cringe *v.* shrink or recoil in fear

crin-kle *v.* wrinkle

crin-o-line *n.* fabric used for stiffening garments

crip-ple *n.* one who is partially disabled

cri-sis *n.* an uncertain time; turning point of a disease

crisp *adj.* brittle; brisk or cold

crisp-er *n.* compartment to keep fruits and vegetables fresh

criss-cross *v.* mark with intersecting lines

cri-te-ri-on *n., pl.* **criteria** rule by which something can be judged

crit-ic *n.* one who expresses an opinion

crit-i-cal *adj.* tending to criticize harshly
critically *adv.*

crit-i-cize *v.* to find fault with

croak *n.* hoarse, raspy cry of a frog

cro-chet *n.* needlework with a hooked
needle

crock *n.* earthenware pot or jar

croc-o-dile *n.* large, tropical reptiles

cro-cus *n.* first spring plant.

crone *n.* old woman

cro-ny *n.* close friend

crook *n.* bend or curve; dishonest person

croon *v.* sing in a gentle, low voice

crop *n.* plants harvested for use or for
sale

cro-quet *n.* outdoor game

cro-quette *n.* small patty of minced food

cross *n.* an upright post with a crossbar

cross-breed *v.* breeding different species

crotch *n.* angle formed by the junction of
two parts

crouch *v.* bend at the knees

croup *n.* spasmodic loud, harsh cough

crou-pi-er *n.* one who collects and pays
bets at a gambling table

crou-ton *n.* piece of toasted bread

crow *n.* large, black bird

crowd *n.* large group of people together

crown *n.* head covering made of precious metal and jewels

CRT *abbr.* Cathode Ray Tube

cru-cial *adj.* extremely important

cru-ci-fy *v.* put to death on a cross

crude *adj.* lacking refinement

cruel *adj.* inflicting suffering cruelty *n.*

cru-et *n.* container for oil or vinegar

cruise *v.* drive or sail about for pleasure

crumb *n.* fragment of bread

crum-ble *v.* break into small pieces

crunch *v.* chew with a crackling noise

cru-sade *n.* religious journey

crush *v.* squeeze or force to damage

crust *n.* hardened exterior of bread; shell
of a pie

crus-ta-cean *n.* crabs, lobsters, etc.

crutch *n.* support to or an aid for walking

crux *n.* a main or central feature

cry *v.* shed tears

crypt *n.* underground chamber or vault

cryp-tic *adj.* intended to be obscure

cryp-tog-ra-phy *n.* deciphering of messages in secret code

crys-tal *n.* glassware

crystal ball *n.* globe for seeing the future

crys-tal-lize *v.* to form crystals; coat with
crystals

cub *n.* young of the lion, wolf, or bear

cub-by-hole *n.* small enclosed area

cube *n.* solid with six equal squares

cubic *adj.* having three dimensions

cu-bi-cle *n.* small partitioned area

cu-bit *n.* ancient unit of measurement

cu-cum-ber *n.* fruit with a green rind of
the gourd family

cud *n.* food rechewed by cattle

cud-dle *v.* caress fondly and hold close

cue *n.* signal to an actor

cuff *n.* lower part of a sleeve or pants

cui-sine *n.* style of preparing food

cull *v.* select the best

cul-mi-nate *v.* reach the highest point

cul-prit *n.* person guilty of a crime

cult *n.* system of religious worship

cul-ti-vate *v.* improve land by fertilizing
and plowing

cul-ture *n.* form of civilization, beliefs,
arts, and customs

cul-vert *n.* drain that runs under a road

cum-ber-some *adj.* unwieldy.

cum-mer-bund *n.* wide sash worn by
men

cu-mu-lus *n.* white, fluffy cloud

cun-ning *adj.* crafty

cup *n.* container with handle for drinking

cu-po-la *n.* rounded roof

cu-ra-tor *n.* person in charge of a
museum

curb *n.* control; edge of a street

curd *n.* portion of milk for making
cheese

cure *n.* recovery from a sickness

cur-few *n.* an order to be home at a certain hour

cu-ri-o *n.* unusual or rare object

cu-ri-ous *adj.* inquisitive curiousity *n.*

curl *v.* twist into curves

cur-rant *n.* small seedless raisin

cur-ren-cy *n.* money in circulation

cur-rent *adj.* occur in the present time

cur-ric-u-lum *n.* courses offered in a
school

cur-ry *n.* spice

cur-ry-comb *n.* special comb to curry a
horse

curse *n.* a wish for harm to come to
someone or something

cursor *n.* computer screen indicator

cur-sive *n.* flowing writing

curt *adj.* abrupt; rude

cur-tail *v.* shorten

cur-tain *n.* material that covers a window

curt-sy *n.* a bow

cush-ion *n.* pillow with a soft filling

cus-pid *n.* pointed tooth

cus-pi-dor *n.* spittoon

cuss *v.* use profane language

cus-tard *n.* baked dessert milk, eggs, sugar, and flavoring

cus-to-di-an *n.* one who has the custody or care of something

cus-to-dy *n.* the act of guarding; the care and protection of a minor

cus-tom *n.* accepted practice of a community or people; the usual manner of doing something **customary** *adj.*

customs *n.* tax one must pay on imported goods

custom--built *adj.* built to one's special order

cus-tomer *n.* person with whom a merchant or business person must deal

cus-tom house *n.* office of business where customs are paid

cut *v.* penetrate with a sharp edge, as with a knife

cut-and-dried *adj.* without changes

cut back *v.* to reduce

cute *adj.* attractive in a delightful way

cut glass *n.* glass shaped and decorated by using a cutting instrument

cut-lass *n.* thick, short, curved sword formerly was used by sailors aboard warships

cut-lery *n.* cutting instruments used to prepare food for cooking

cut-let *n.* a thin piece of meat **cut-off** *n.* a short cut; the act of cutting something off

cut-out *n.* something intended to be cut or already cut out

cut--rate *adj.* offering merchandise at a lower than normal price

cut-ter *n., Naut.* a fast-sailing vessel with a single mast

cut-throat *n.* a murderer

cut up *v.* act foolishly

cy-a-nide *n., Chem.* a poison

cyc-la-men *n.* a plant with red, white, or pink flowers

cy-cle *n.* time in which an event occurs repeatedly; a bicycle or motorcycle

cy-clist *n.* a person who rides a cycle

cyn-ic *n.* one who believes that all people have selfish motives

cy-no-sure *n.* person or object that attracts admiration

cy-press *n.* evergreen tree

cys-tic fi-bro-sis *n.* disease of the lungs and pancreas

cys-ti-tis *n.* inflammation of the bladder

cy-tol-ogy *n.* scientific study of cell formation

czar *n.* former emperors of Russia

cza-ri-na *n.* the woman married to the czar of Russia

D, d The fourth letter of the English alphabet.

dab *v.* touch with light, short strokes

dab-ble *v.* play in a liquid with the hands

da ca-po *adv.* from the beginning

dachs-hund *n.* small long bodied dog with long drooping ears

dac-tyl *n.* the fact that the three syllables have the fist one longest like the joints of the finger

dac-ty-lol-o-gy *n.* the art of communicating ideas by signs made with the fingers; sign language

dac-ty-lous *adj.* having fingers or toes

dad *n., Informal* father

dad-dy--long-legs *n.* an insect with very long legs

daf-fo-dil *n.* a bulbous plant with yellow flowers

daft *adj.* crazy; foolish; insane **daftly** *adv.* **daftness** *n.*

dag-ger *n.* pointed, short-edged weapon

dahl-ia *n.* perennial plant having tuberous roots

dai-ly *adj.* to occur or happen every day of the week

dain-ty *adj.* delicately beautiful; having or showing refined taste **daintiness** *n.*

dai-qui-ri *n.* cocktail made with rum and lime juice

dair-y *n.* business that processes milk for resale **dairymaid** *n.* **dairyman** *n.*

dai-sy *n.* plant with yellow and white flowers

dal-ly *v.* waste time; to dawdle; to flirt **dallier** *n.*, **dalliance** *n.*

dam *n.* barrier to control water level

dam-age *n.* injury to person or property **damageable** *adj.*, **damagingly** *adv.*

dam-ask *n.* reversible fabric

dame *n.* mature woman

damn *v.* to swear or curse at; to pronounce as bad, worthless, or a failure **damnation** *n.*, **damnableness** *n.*

damp *adj.* between dry and wet

dam-sel *n.* a maiden; a young unmarried woman

dam-son *n.* tree with an oval purple plum of the same name

dance *v.* move rhythmically to music

dan-de-lion *n.* a weed of North America; an herb; having yellow flowers

dan-dle *v.* to move a child or infant up and down on the knees or in the arms with a gentle movement

dan-druff *n.* scaly material which forms on the scalp and is shed

dan-dy *n.* elegantly dressed man; fine appearance **dandyish** *adj.*

dan-ger *n.* exposure to injury, evil, or

loss; a case of danger

dan-ger-ous *adj.* unsafe dangerously *adv.* dangerousness *n.*

dan-gle *v.* hang loosely and swing to and fro danglingly *adv.*, dangler *n.*

dank *adj.* damp; wet and cold dankness *n.*, dankly *adv.*

dan-seuse *n.* female ballet dancer

dap-per *adj.* stylishly dressed

dap-ple *v.* to make variegated in color

dare *v.* have courage to take a risk or undertan an adventure; to challenge a person as to show proof of courage; **dare-devil** *n.* reckless or bold person daredevilry n, daredeviltry n.

dark *adj.* dim; to have little or no light

dark-en *v.* make dark or become dark darkish *adj.*, darkly *adv.*

dar-ling *n.* someone who is very dear; favorite person; a person tenderly loved darlingly *adv.*

darn *v.* mend a hole darner *n.*

dart *n.* pointed missile

dash *v.* to move quickly; to rush; to finish or perform a duty in haste; with sudden speed dasher *n.*

da-ta *pl.*, *n.* facts or firures from which conclusions may be drawn

data bank *n.* location in a computer where information is stored

date *n.* a particular point in time; the exact time at which something happens; an edible fruit date *v.*

date-line *n.* the date of newspaper publication; imaginary line

da-tum *n.* single piece of information datums pl., data *n.*

daub *v.* coat or smear with grease, plaster or an adhesive substance

daugh-ter *n.* female offspring of a man or woman; realtion to parent

daughter--in--law *n.* one's son's wife daughters-in-law pl.

daunt *v.* intimidate or discourage

dav-it *n.* small crane on the side of a ship used for boats or anchors

daw-dle *v.* waste time dawdler n.

dawn *n.* the beginning of a new day; to begin to understand, perceive or develop; first light appearance

day *n.* period of time between dawn and night-fall; one rotation of the earth

day-care *n.* supervision and training for children of working parents

daze *v.* stun or bewilder with a heavy blow or shock dazedly *adv.*

D--Day *n.*, *Milit.* June 6, 1944

dea-con *n.* clergyman who ranks immediately below a priest

dead *adj.* without life; dormant

dead-end *n.* cannot progress

deadline *n.* time when something must be finished; the final day

dead-ly *adj.* very dangerous; likely to cause death

deaf *adj.* totally or partially unable to hear; refusing or unwilling to listen

deal *v.* pass out playing cards; to be concerned with a certain matter

deal-er-ship *n.* franchise to sell a certain item in a specified area, as a car dealer

deal-ing *n.*, *Slang* involved in the buying and selling of illegal drugs

dean *n.* head administrator of a college, or university deanship *n.*

dear *adj.* greatly cherished; loved dearly *adv.*, dearness n.

death *n.* termination; permanent cessation of all vital functions

deathly *adj.* fatal; causing death

death-trap *n.* unsafe structure

death-watch *n.* vigil kept on a person who is dying

deb *n.* debutante

de-ba-cle *n.* sudden downfall or failure

de-base *v.* lower in character or value debasement n., debaser *n.*

de-bate *v.* discuss or argue opposing points debatable *adj.*

de-bauch *v.* to corrupt debauchment *n.*

de-ben-ture *n.* voucher given as an acknowledgment of debt

de-bil-i-tate *v.* make feeble or weak

deb-it *n.* item recorded in an account; a sum of items entered

de-brief *v.* question or interrogate to obtain information

de-bris *n.* discarded or scattered remains or waste

debt *n.* that which someone owes as money or goods or services

debt-or *n.* person owing a debt to another, usually money, etc.

de-bug *v.* find and remove a concealed listening device; to remove errors

de-bunk *v.* expose false pretensions

de-but *n.* first public appearance; beginning of a new career; introduction

deb-u-tante *n.* young woman making her debut in society

dec-ade *n.* period of ten years; a set of ten; division of the rosary

de-ca-dence *n.* process of deterioration or decay; a period of decline

de-caf-fein-at-ed *adj.* having the caffeine removed; without

dec-a-gon *n.*, *Geom.* a polygon with ten sides and ten angles

dec-a-gram *n.* in the metric system, weight equal to 10 grams

de-cal *n.* design or picture that is transferred by decalsomania

de-cal-co-ma-ni-a *n.* process of transferring pictures or designs to somehting

dec-a-li-ter *n.* in the metric system, measure equal to 10 liters

dec-a-logue *n.* the Ten Commandments; a basic set of rules

dec-a-me-ter *n.* in the metric system, measure equal to 10 feet

de-camp *v.* break camp; to leave or depart suddenly **decampment** n.

de-cant-er *n.* decorative stoppered bottle for serving wine or other liquids

de-cap-i-tate *v.* cut off the head; to behead **decapitation** n.

de-cath-lon *n.* an athletic event with ten different track and field events

de-cay *v.* decline; to rot

de-cease *v.* die **decedent** *n.*

de-ceit *n.* falseness; deception

de-ceive *v.* mislead by falsehood; to lead into error; to delude

de-cel-er-ate *v.* decrease in velocity

de-cen-ni-al *adj.* happening once every 10 years; for a period of ten

de-cent *adj.* satisfactory; generous; adequate **decently** adv.

de-cen-tral-ize *v.* divide the administrative functions among local authorities

de-cep-tion *n.* act of deceiving

de-cep-tive *adj.* having the power to deceive **deceptively** adv.

de-ci-bel *n.* measurement of sound

de-cide *v.* to make up one's mind; to settle **decided** v., **deciding** v.

de-cid-ed *adj.* definite or unquestionabie; determination **decidedly** adv.

de-cid-u-ous *adj.* shedding or falling off at maturity

dec-i-gram *n.* in the metric sysstem, the tenth part of a gram

dec-i-li-ter *n.* in the metric system, the tenth part of a liter

dec-i-mal *n.* proper fraction based on the number 10

decimal point *n.* period to the left of a decimal fraction

dec-i-mate *v.* destroy or kill a large proportion of something

dec-i-meter *n.* in the metric system, the tenth part of a meter

de-ci-pher *v.* to decode; to translate from code to text **decipherable** adj.

de-ci-sion *n.* a judgmeut or conclusion; act of deciding

de-ci-sive *adj.* ending uncertainty

deck *n.* set of playing cards; platform; resembling a ship's deck

deck hand *n.* member of a ship's crew

who performs manual duties

de-claim *v.* speak loudly and rhetorically; to give speech **declamation** n.

de-clare *v.* to state formally or officially **declaration** *n.*, **declarative** adj.

de-clas-si-fy *v.* make public

de-clen-sion *n.* sloping downward; a decline; falling off or away

de-cline *v.* reject or refuse something **declinable adj.**, **declinational** adj.

de-cliv-i-ty *n.* steep down-ward slope or surface **declivitous**, **declivous** adj.

de-coct *v.* extract by boiling; condense; to make concentrate **decoction** n.

de-code *v.* convert from coded message into plain language **decoder** n.

de-com-pose *v.* decay **decomposition** *n.*

de-com-press *v.* relieve of pressure

de-con-ges-tant *n.* agent that relieves congestion

de-con-tam-i-nate *v.* make free of contamination **decontamination** n.

de-con-trol *v.* remove all controls

de-cor *n.* style of decorating

dec-o-rate *v.* adorn with fashionable or beautiful things; dress up

dec-o-ra-tion *n.* art, process, or act of decorating; a thing or group of things which decorate; an emblem

dec-o-ra-tive *adj.* ornamental; suit-abe for decoration **decoratively** adv.

de-co-rum *n.* proper behavior

de-coy *n.* artificial animal to lure game

de-crease *v.* grow less or smaller

de-cree *n.* formal order

de-crep-it *adj.* worn out by old age

de-cry *v.* denounce

ded-i-cate *v.* commit oneself to a certain cause **deducated** v.

de-duce *v.* derive a conclusion by reasoning

de-duct *v.* subtract or take away from

deed *n.* notable achievement or feat

deem *v.* judge or consider

deep *adj.* extending far below a surface **deepness** *n.*

deep-en *v.* become or make deep or deeper **deepened** v., **deepening** v.

deep-freeze *v.* quick-freeze food

deep-root-ed *adj.* firmly implanted

deep-six *v.*, *Slang* to throw overboard; toss out

deer *n.*, *pl.* deer hoofed ruminant mammal

deer fly *n.* bloodsucking flies

deer-skin *n.* deer's hide or leather made from it

de-es-ca-late *v.* decreased gradually

de-face *v.* spoil or mar the surface of something

de fac-to *adj.* actually exercising authority

de-fal-cate *v.* to misuse funds; to embezzle

de-fame *v.* to slander

de-fault *v.* neglect to fulfill an obligation

de-feat *v.* to win a victory

de-feat-ism *n.* accepting defeat as inevitable

def-e-cate *v.* discharge feces from the bowels

de-fect *n.* lack of perfection; a fault

de-fec-tive *adj.* imperfect; less than normal intelligence

de-fend *v.* protect

de-fend-ant *n.* person charged in a lawsuit; being on the devensive

de-fense *n.* action of defending

de-fer *v.* delay or postpone

de-fi-ance *n.* strong opposition

de-fi-cient *adj.* lacking a necessary element **deficiently** *adv.*

def-i-cit *n.* deficiency in amount

de-flate *v.* remove air; collapse

de-flect *v.* turn aside; swerve from a course **deflector** *n.*

de-flower *v.* rob one's virginity; to violate **deflowerer** *n.*

de-fog *v.* remove fog from

de-for-est *v.* to clear of trees

de-form *v.* distort the form of; to spoil the natural form of

de-fraud *v.* cheat; to swindle

de-fray *v.* make payment on something **defrayable** *adj.*

de-frost *v.* cause to thaw out; to remove the ice or frost from

deft *adj.* skillful and neat in one's actions **deftness** *n.*

de-funct *adj.* deceased

de-fuse *v.* remove the detonator or fuse from; to make less dangerous or harmful

de-fy *v.* confront or resist boldly; to dare **defier** *n.*, **defying** *n.*

de-gauss *v.* neutralize a magnetic field **degausser** *n.*

de-gen-er-ate *v.* decline in quality or value; to become worse

de-grade *v.* reduce in rank; demote

de-gree *n.* succession of stages or steps; academic title; amount

de-horn *v.* remove the horns from an animal **dehorner** *n.*

de-hu-man-ize *v.* deprive of human qualities or personality

de-hu-mid-i-fy *v.* remove moisture from **dehumidifier** *n.*, **dehumidification** *n.*

de-hy-drate *v.* lose moisture or water; to deprive **dehydrator** *n.*

de-ice *v.* keep free of ice **deicer** *n.*

de-i-fy *v.* glorify or idealize; raise in high regard **deified** *n.*, **deifying** *n.*

deign *v.* to grant

de-ism *n.* belief in the existence of God; but not that he has control

de-ject *v.* lower the spirits; to dishearten; to make gloomy

de-ject-ed *adj.* sad; low in spirit

de ju-re *adv.*, *L.* legally or rightfully

de-lay *v.* put off until a later time; to defer **delayer** *n.*, **delaying** *adj.*

de-le *n.*, *Print* mark in typesetting to delete **deled** *v.*, **deleing** *v.*

de-lec-ta-ble *adj.* giving great pleasure **delectability** *n.*, **delectableness** *n.*

de-lec-ta-tion *n.* enjoyment or pleasure; delight

del-e-gate *n.* representative for another; a deputy or agent

del-e-ga-tion *n.* state of being delegated **deleted** *v.*, **deleting** *v.*

de-lete *v.* cancel; to take out by cutting or erasing **deletion** *n.*, **deleting** *n.*

del-e-te-ri-ous *adj.* causing physical injury; harmful **deleteriously** *adv.*

delft *n.* glazed earthenware

del-i *n.*, *Slang* delicatessen

de-lib-er-ate *v.* say or do something intentionally **deliberateness** *n.*

del-i-ca-cy *n.* select or choice food

del-i-cate *adj.* exquisite and fine in quality **delicately** *adv.*

del-i-ca-tes-sen *n.* specialty store

de-li-cious *adj.* enjoyable and pleasant to the taste **deliciously** *adv.*

de-li-cious *n.* variety of red, sweet apples **deliciously** *adv.*

de-light *n.* a giving of great joy or pleasure **delighted** *adj.*

de-light-ful *adj.* extremely pleasing

de-lim-it *v.* set or prescribe the limits

de-lir-i-um *n.* temporary mental disturbance characterized by confusion, disorder speech, and hallucinations

delirium tremens *n.* acute delirium resulting from use of alcohol

de-liv-er *v.* to hand over; assist at a birth of an offspring **delivered** *v.*, **-ing** *v.*

de-liv-er-y *n.* act of conveying; process or act of giving birth **deliveries** *pl.*

del-phin-ium *n.* perennial plant

delta ray *n.* electron ejected from ionizing radiation

de-lude *v.* mislead the mind; to deceive

del-uge *v.* flood with water; to overwhelm **deluging** *v.*, **deluged** *v.*

de-lu-sion *n.* false belief in spite of contrary evidence **delusionary** *adj.*

de-luxe *adj.* elegance or luxury

delve *v.* search carefully for information

de-mag-net-ize *v.* remove the magnetic properties demagnetization *n.*

dem-a-gogue *n.* person who appeals to the emotions to gain power or fame

de-mand *v.* ask for in a firm tone; claim as due demander *n.*, demandable *adj.*

de-mar-cate *v.* set boundaries or limits

de-mean *v.* behave or conduct oneself in a particular manner

de-mean-or *n.* person's conduct to others

de-men-tia *n.* irreversible deterioration of the mind demential *adj.*

de-mer-it *n.* a defect

de-mesne *n.* manor house; a domain

dem-i-god *n.* mythological, semidivine being demigoddess *n.*

dem-i-john *n.* narrow-necked bottle

de-mil-i-ta-rize *v.* remove the military characteristics from

dem-i-monde *n.* class of women supported by wealthy lovers

de-mise *n.* death; a transfer of an estate by lease or will demised *v.*, -ing *v.*

dem-i-tasse *n.* small cup of very strong black coffee; the cup used to serve

dem-o *n.* demonstration to show product

de-mo-bi-lize *v.* disband; release from the military service -ation *n.*

de-moc-ra-cy *n., pl.* democracies form of government by and for the people

dem-o-crat *n.* one who believes in social and political equality

de-mog-ra-phy *n.* study of the characteristics of human population

de-mol-ish *v.* tear down; to raze

dem-o-li-tion *n.* a process of demolishing something demolitionist *n.*

de-mon.*n.* evil spirit; a devil

de-mon-e-tize *v.* deprive the currency of its standard value demonization *n.*

de-mo-ni-ac *adj.* like or befitting a demon demonically *adv.*

de-mon-ol-o-gy *n.* belief or study in demons

de-mon-stra-ble *adj.* obvious or apparent

dem-on-strate *v.* show or prove by evidence demonstration *n.*

de-mon-stra-tive *adj.* able to prove beyond any doubt; conclusive

de-mor-al-ize *v.* undermine the morales

de-mote *v.* reduce in rank, or grade demotion *n.*

de-mul-cent *n.* a soothing substance

de-mur *v.* take issue; to object

de-mure *adj.* reserved and modest

de-murrer *n.* plea to dismiss a lawsuit

den *n.* shelter for animals; small room

de-na-ture *v.* change the nature of

den-drol-ogy *n.* botanical study of trees

den-gue *n., Pathol.* infectious tropical disease transmitted by mosquitoes

de-ni-al *n.* refusal to comply with a request or truth

den-i-grate *v.* to slander

den-im *n.* strong cotton used for jeans

de-nom-i-nate *v.* give a name to

de-nom-i-na-tion *n.* name of a group or classification

de-nom-i-na-tor *n.* the bottom half of a fraction

de-no-ta-tion *n.* meaning of or object designated by a word

de-note *v.* make known

de-noue-ment *n.* final solution of a novel

de-nounce *v.* condemn openly; accuse formally

dense *adj.* thick; slow to understand; stupid

den-si-ty *n.* state or quality of being dense

dent *n.* small surface depression

den-tal *adj.* pertaining to the teeth

dental floss *n.* a strong thread to clean between the teeth

dental hygienist *n.* dental professional who provides preventive dental care

den-ti-frice *n.* preparation for cleaning the teeth

den-tine *n.* calcified part of the tooth

den-tist *n.* licensed dental doctor

den-ti-tion *n.* number, and arrangement of teeth

den-ture *n.* set of artificial teeth

de-nude *v.* remove all covering; cause to be naked

de-nun-ci-a-tion *n.* disapproval of a person or action; an accusation

de-ny *v.* declare untrue; refuse to acknowledge

de-o-dor-ant *n.* product to prevent unpleasant odors

de-o-dor-ize *v.* destroy the odor of

de-ox-i-dize *v.* remove oxygen from

de-part *v.* leave; to go away; to deviate

de-part-ment *n.* the distinct division of something

de-part-men-tal-ize *v.* divide into organized departments

department store *n.* large retail store usually in many places

de-par-ture *n.* act of taking leave; deviation

de-pend *v.* rely on

de-pend-a-ble *adj.* trust-worthy dependability *n.*

de-pend-ence *n.* trust or reliance

de-pend-ent *adj.* needing the help of another for support

de-pict *v.* represent in a picture

de-pil-a-to-ry *n.* chemical which removes hair

de-plane *v.* disembark or leave an aircraft

de-plete *v.* exhaust, empty, or use up

de-plor-a-ble *adj.* very bad; grievous; wretched **deplorably** *adv.*

de-plore *v.* show great disapproval of something

de-ploy *v.* spread out; place or position according to plans **deployment** *n.*

de-po-lit-i-cize *v.* remove the political status or aspect from

de-po-nent *n.* a person testifing under an oath

de-pop-u-late *v.* lower the population by massacre or disease

de-port *v.* banish from a country

de-port-ment *n.* one's conduct

de-pose *v.* remove position or office

de-pos-it *v.* set something down; put money in a bank

dep-o-si-tion *n.* in law, written testimony given under oath

de-pos-i-to-ry *n.* place for safekeeping

de-pot *n.* railroad station

de-prave *v.* render bad or worse **depravity** *n.*

dep-re-cate *v.* express regret or disapproval; belittle

de-pre-ci-ate *v.* lessen in value or price

de-pre-ci-a-tion *n.* loss in value from usage

de-press *v.* make gloomy; lower the spirits

de-pres-sant *adj.* act to lower the nervous activities

de-press-ed *adj.* sad; low in spirits

de-press-ed area *n.* area with severe unemployment

de-pres-sion *n.* severe decline in business; condition of deep dejection

de-pres-sive *adj.* related to psychological depression

de-prive *v.* take something away from; to keep from using

depth *n.* distance downward; intensity of of sound; comprehension

depth charge *n.* underwater bomb

dep-u-ta-tion *n.* person acting for another or others

de-pute *v.* appoint as a deputy, an agent; delegate; to transfer

dep-u-tize *v.* to appoint as a deputy

dep-u-ty *n.* person designated act for or assist a sheriff

de-rail *v.* cause a train to run off the rails **derailment** *n.*

de-range *v.* to disturb the normal order of

der-by *n.* horse race for 3-year-olds; stiff hat with narrow brim

de-reg-u-late *v.* remove from regulation or control

der-e-lict *adj.* neglectful; remiss

der-e-lic-tion *n.* voluntary neglect

de-ride *v.* ridicule

de ri-gueur *adj.* required by manners, custom, or fashion

der-i-va-tion *n.* process of deriving

de-riv-a-tive *adj.* made from derived elements

de-rive *v.* receive or obtain from a source

der-mal *adj.* relating to or of the skin

der-ma-ti-tis *n., Pathol.* inflammation of the skin

der-ma-tol-o-gy *n.* the medical study of the skin and the diseases **dermatologist** *n.*

der-o-gate *v.* to take away from; to distract

de-rog-a-tory *adj.* effect of belittling; lessening

der-rick *n.* machine to lift heavy loads; framework of an oil well

der-ri-ere *n.* the buttocks

der-ring--do *n.* daring action or spirit

de-salt *v.* remove the salt from sea water

des-cant *v.* play or sing a varied melody

de-scend *v.* move from a higher to a lower level

de-scen-dent *n.* offspring from another individual

de-scen-dant *adj.* proceeding downward

de-scent *n.* a slope; lowering in level or status

de-scribe *v.* explain in written or spoken words **describable** *adj.*

de-scrip-tion *n.* discourse to give a mental image of something

de-scry *v.* catch sight of

des-e-crate *v.* violate something sacred **desecration** *n.*

de-seg-re-gate *v.* eliminate racial segregation in

de-sen-si-tize *v.* make less sensitive

des-ert *v.* abandon or forsake

des-ert *n.* dry, barren region

de-ser-tion *n.* act of deserting or leaving

de-serve *v.* be worthy of or entitled to

de-served *adj.* merited; earned **deservingly** *adv.*

des-ic-cant *n.* silica gel to absorb moisture

des-ic-cate *v.* preserve food by drying; dehydrate

de-sid-er-a-tum *n.* desired and necessary thing

de-sign *v.* sketch preliminary outlines; create in the mind

des-ig-nate v. assign a name or title to; specify

de-sign-ing adj. relating to the art making designs

de-sir-a-ble adj. attractive, or valuable desirableness n.

de-sire v. long for; to wish

de-sir-ous adj. have a craving or strong desire

de-sist v. stop doing something

desk n. school and office furniture for writing

des-o-late adj. forlorn; forsaken desolately adv.

des-o-la-tion n. wasteland; de-serted; loneliness

de-spair v. lose or give up hope

des-per-a-do n. a dangerous, or violent criminal

des-per-ate adj. rash, without care; intense

des-per-a-tion n. state of being desperate

des-pi-ca-ble adj. hateful; contemptable

de-spise v. regard with contempt

de-spite prep. notwithstanding.

de-spoil v. rob; strip of possessions by force

de-spond v. lose hope, courage, or spirit

de-spon-den-cy n. dejection of spirits from loss hope

des-pot n. an absolute ruler; a tyrant

des-sert n. sweet food, as pastry, etc.

des-ti-na-tion n. goal; end of journey

des-tine v. determined in advance

des-ti-ny n. fate; predetermined course of events

des-ti-tute adj. impoverished; poor destitution n.

de-stroy v. ruin; to to demolish; to kill

de-stroy-er n. one that destroys; small maneuverable warship

de-struct n., Aeros. deliberate destruction of a defective missile

de-struc-ti-ble adj. capable of being destroyed

des-ue-tude n. condition or state of disuse

de-sul-fur-ize v. remove sulfur from

des-ul-to-ry adj. something occuring by chance

de-tach v. unfasten, or separate

de-tached adj. apart; separate

de-tach-ment n. process of separating

de-tail n. part considered sep-arately; task

de-tain v. keep from proceeding

de-tect v. find out; to expose or uncover, as a crime detectable adj.

de-tec-tive n. person that investigates crimes

de-tent n. a pawl

de-ten-tion n. hold in custody

de-ter v. prevent someone from acting by intimidation determent n.

de-ter-gent n. cleansing agent

de-te-ri-o-rate v. to worsen; to depreciate deterioration n.

de-ter-mi-nate adj. definitely fixed or limited; conclusive

de-ter-mine v. settle or decide conclusively determination n.

de-ter-mined adj. having a fixed purpose

de-ter-rent n. something which deters deterrently adv.

de-test v. dislike strongly detestable adj.

de-throne v. remove from the throne

det-o-nate v. explode suddenly violently detonation n.

det-o-na-tor n. fuse used to detonate an explosive

de-tour n. deviation from a direct route

de-tox-i-fy v. free oneself from dependence on drugs or alcohol detoxification n.

de-tract v. take away from; to divert detraction n.

de-train v. leave a railroad train detrainment n.

det-ri-ment n. damage; injury; loss detrimental adj.

de-tri-tus n. loose fragments from disintegration

deuce n. two

deut-sche mark n. standard monetary unit of Germany

de-val-u-ate v. reduce or lessen the value of devaluation n.

dev-as-tate v. destroy; to ruin devastation n.

de-vel-op v. expand the potentialities; to enlarge; process film

de-vel-op-er n. person who builds and sells homes; chemical to process film

de-vel-op-ment n. group of homes; improvement

de-vi-ant adj. stray from the norm deviantance n.

de-vi-ate v. turn away from prescribed behavior or course

de-vice n. something built and used for a specific purpose

dev-il n. spirit of evil, the ruler of Hell; Satan; wicked person

dev-il-ish adj. resemble or have the characteristics of a devil

dev-il—may—care adj. reckless

dev-il-ment n. reckless mischief

devil's advocate n. one who argues for the sake of arguing

dev-il-try n. malicious mischief; cruelty

or wickedness

de-vi-ous *adj.* leading away from the direct course **deviously** *adv.*

de-vise *v.* form in the mind; contrive; give real estate by will

de-vi-see *n.* person to whom a devise is made

de-vi-sor *n.* person who devises property

de-vi-tal-ize *v.* make weak

de-void *adj.* empty; lacking

de-voir *n.* act or expression of courtesy or respect

de-volve *v.* pass duty or authority on to a successor

de-vote *v.* apply oneself completely to some activity

de-vot-ed *adj.* feeling or showing loyalty devotedly *adv.*

dev-o-tee *n.* enthusiastic supporter

de-vo-tion *n.* strong attachment or affection **devotionly** *adv.*

de-vout *adj.* extreemely and earnestly religions; showing sincerity devoutly *adv.*

dew *n.* moisture condensed from the atmosphere in small drops onto cool surfaces

dew-claw *n.* rudimentary toe in some dogs and other mammals

dew-lap *n.* the loosee skin under the throat and neck of cattle and certain dogs

dex-ter-i-ty *n.* proficiency or skill in using the hands or body; cleverness; skillful

deex-ter-ous *adj.* skillful or adroit in the use of the hands

di-a-gram *n.* a sketch, plan or outline designed to demonstrate the similarity among partsof a whole

di-al *n.* graduated circular plate or face where a measurement is indicated by means of a pointer

di-a-logue *n.* conversation involving two or more persons

di-am-e-ter *n.* a straight line which passes through the center of a circle

di-a-met-ri-cal *adj.* along or relating to a diameter

dia-mond *n.* a very hard highly refractive colorless or white crystalline of carbon used as a gem

di-a-pa-son *n.* full range of a voice or an instrument

di-a-per *n.* baby's pants of absorbent material

di-aph-a-nous *adj.* transparent or translucent

di-a-phragm *n., Anat.* muscular wall between chest and abdomen; contraceptive device

di-ar-rhe-a *n.,Pathol.* disorder of the intestines

di-a-ry *n.* a daily record

di-as-tro-phism *n., Geol.* processes through which the earth's crust are formed

di-a-ther-my *n., pl.* **diathermies** *Med.* generation of heat in the body tissues

di-as-to-le *n.* rhythmnical expansion of the heart

di-a-tom *n.* various tiny planktonic algae

di-a-tom-ic *adj.* having two atoms in a molecule

di-a-ton-ic *adj., Mus.* relating to a musical scale having eight tones to an octave

di-a-tribe *n.* malicious criticism

dib-ble *n.* gardener's pointed tool for planting bulbs

dice *pl., n.* small cubes used in a game of chance

di-chot-o-my *n., pl.* dichotomies division into two mutually exclusive subclasses

dick-er *v.* haggle or work towards a deal or bargain

dick-ey *n.* a woman's blouse front worn under a jacket

di-cot-y-le-don *n.* plant having two seed leaves

dic-tate *v.* speak aloud for another to record or transcribe **dictation** *n.*

dic-ta-ting ma-chine *n.* phonographic machine which records speech

dic-ta-tor *n.* person having absolute authority and supreme governmental powers **dictatorship** *n.*

dic-ta-to-ri-al *adj.* tending to dictate

dic-tion *n.* arrangement of words in speaking and writing

dic-tion-ar-y *n.* book containing words, definitions and usages

dic-tum *n.* authoritative utterance

did *v.* past tense of do

di-dac-tic *adj.* inclined to teach excessively

did-dle *v.* cheat; to swindle

did-n't *contr.* did not

die *v.* expire; to stop living

die casting *n.* process of giving an alloy or metal a desired shape

die-hard *n.* stubborn person

diel-drin *n.* highly toxic chemical used as an insecticide

di-e-lec-tric *n., Elect.* nonconductor of electricity

die-sel *n.* vehicle driven by a diesel engine

diesel engine *n.* internalcombustion engine run by an air-fuel mixture

die-sink-er *n.* person who engraves

metal dies

di-et n. regulated selection of food and drink

di-e-tet-ics pl., n. study of diet and regulations of a diet

di-eth-yl-bes-trol n. a synthetic estrogen to treat menstrual disorders

di-e-ti-tian n. diet planner

dif-fer v. have different opinions

dif-fer-ence n. state, or degree of being different or unlike

dif-fer-ent adj. not the same

dif-fer-en-tia n. a specific difference

dif-fer-en-tial adj. showing a difference or differences

dif-fer-en-ti-ate v. show, or distinguish the difference

dif-fi-cult adj. hard to do, or accomplish; hard to please

dif-fi-cul-ty n., pl. difficulties quality or state of being difficult

dif-fi-dent adj. lacking confidence in oneself; timid diffidently adv.

dif-frac-tion n., Phys. modification of light rays

dif-fuse v. spread freely in all directions; to scatter

dig v. break up the earth

di-gest v. summarize; change ingested food into usable form

di-gest-ion n. dissolving food in the stomach

dig-it n. toe or finger

dig-i-tal adj. expressed in digits, as for computer use

digital computer n. computer using data resented as digits to perform operations

dig-i-tal-is n. drug prepared from dried leaves of foxglove

dig-ni-fied adj. stately; poised

dig-ni-fy v. to give distinction to something

dig-ni-tary n., pl. dignitaries person of high rank

dig-ni-ty n., pl. dignities quality being excellent

di-graph n. pair of letters that represents a single sound

di-gress v. to wander

dik-dik n. small African antelope

dike n. embankment made of earth, control flood waters

di-lap-i-dat-ed adj. state of decay or disrepair

di-late v. become larger dilateable adj.

dil-a-to-ry adj. delaying; slow; tardy

di-lem-ma n. perplexing situation

dil-et-tante n. superficial interest in something

dil-i-gent adj. industrious

dill n. aromatic herb

di-lute v. reduce concentration

dim adj. dull

dime n. U. S. coin worth ten cents

di-men-sion n. measurable extent

di-min-ish v. make smaller

di-min-u-en-do adv. gradually lessening in volume

di-min-u-tive adj. very small

dim-ple n. depression in the skin

din n. loud noise

dine v. to eat dinner

di-nette n. small dining room

din-ghy n., pl. dinghies a small rowboat

din-ky adj., Informal insignificant or small; tiny dinkier adv.

din-ner n. last meal of the day

di-no-saur n., Paleon. extinct reptiles dinosauric adj.

dip v. put into a liquid momentarily

diph-the-ri-a n., Pathol. acute infectious disease

di-plo-ma n. document from school

dip-lo-mat n. government representative

dip-per n. long-handled cup

dip-so-ma-ni-a n. insatiable craving for alcohol

dire adj. dreadful or terrible

di-rect v. give orders

di-rec-tion n. act of directing; instruction

di-rect-ly adv. immediately; at once

di-rec-tor n. person who manages

di-rec-to-ry n., pl. directories book listing data

dirge n. slow mournful song

dir-i-gi-ble n. lighter-than-air plane

dirn-dl n. dress with a full skirt

dirt n. soil or earth

dirt-y adj. not clean dirtiness n.

dis-a-ble v. to incapacitate

dis-ad-van-tage n. unfavorable inferior condition

dis-a-gree v. vary in opinion disagreeable adj.

dis-al-low v. refuse to allow

dis-ap-pear v. vanish disappearance n.

dis-ap-point v. fail to satisfy

dis-ap-pro-ba-tion n. disapproval

dis-ap-prove v. refuse to approve

dis-arm v. make harmless

dis-ar-range v. disturb the order disarramgement n.

dis-ar-ray n. state of confusion or disorder

dis-as-sem-ble v. to take apart

dis-as-so-ci-ate v. break away or detach from an association

dis-as-ter n. event that causes distress; a

suden misfortune

dis-a-vow v. disclaim or deny

dis-band v. disperse

dis-bar v. expelled from the legal profession **disbarment** n.

dis-be-lieve v. refuse to believe

dis-burse v. pay out money

disc or **disk** n., *Informal* phonograph record that holds information

dis-card v. to throw out

dis-cern v. understand

dis-charge v. to release

dis-ci-ple n. follower

dis-ci-pline n. train; punishment to correct poor behavior

dis-claim v. to deny interest in or assocation with

dis-close v. make known **discloseure** n.

dis-co n., pl. **discos** discotheque

dis-color v. alter or change the color of

dis-com-fit v. defeat in battle

dis-com-fort n. uneasiness; pain

dis-com-mode v. inconvenience

dis-com-pose v. disrupt composure of something

dis-con-cert v. upset

dis-con-nect v. break the connection of something

dis-con-so-late adj. unhappy

dis-con-tent n. dissatisfaction

dis-con-tin-ue v. bring to an end

dis-cord n. lacking harmony

dis-co-theque n. nightclub with

dis-count v. sell for lower price than usual or regular price

dis-coun-te-nance v. look upon with disfavor; weary

dis-cour-age v. deprived of enthusiasm or courage

dis-course n. conversation; lengthy discussion

dis-cour-te-ous adj. lacking courteous manners

dis-cov-er v. make known or visible **discoverable** adj.

dis-cred-it v. cast disbelief on

dis-creet adj. tactful; careful of appearances; modest

dis-crep-an-cy n., pl. **discrepancies** difference in facts

dis-crete adj. separate; made up of distinct parts

dis-cre-tion n. act of being discreet

dis-crim-i-nate v. distinguish between

dis-cur-sive adj. covering a wide field of subjects in a quick manner

dis-cuss v. to talk

dis-dain v. ignore; scorn

dis-ease n. sickness; illness **diseased** adj.

dis-em-bark v. unload

dis-em-body v. to free from the body

dis-en-chant v. free from false beliefs; disbeliefs

dis-en-gage v. to set free

dis-en-tan-gle v. free from involvement; know nothing of

dis-fig-ure v. deform appearance

dis-fran-chise v. deprive the legal right

dis-gorge v. to regurgitate; to pour out

dis-grace n. loss of honor

dis-guise v. alter appearance

dis-gust v. version

dish n. eating utensil

dis-har-mo-ny n. discord

dis-heart-en v. lose spirit

di-shev-el v. disarrange

dis-hon-est adj. lacking honesty

dis-hon-or n. disgrace

dis-il-lu-sion v. to disenchant

dis-in-fect v. free from infection

dis-in-gen-u-ous adj. lacking frankness

dis-in-her-it v. deprive of inheritance

dis-in-te-grate v. break into small particles; decompose

dis-in-ter-est-ed adj. unselfish, or not interested

dis-join v. to become detached

dis-like v. regard with disapproval

dis-lo-cate v. put out of place

dis-lodge v. remove from

dis-loy-al adj. untrue to obligations or duty **disloyalty** adj.

dis-mal adj. depressing

dis-man-tle v. to take apart

dis-may v. disheartened

dis-mem-ber v. cut into pieces

dis-miss v. to discharge

dis-mount v. get down from

dis-o-bey v. refuse or fail to obey

dis-o-blige v. act contrary to wishes

dis-or-der n. confussion

dis-or-gan-ize v. destroy or break up the unity; unorganizational

dis-own v. refuse to claim as one's own **disownment** n.

dis-patch v. send off on a particular destination

dis-pel v. drive or away

dis-pense v. give out

dis-perse v. scatter in various directions; to give out or distribute

dis-place v. change the position of

dis-play v. put in view

dis-please v. cause disapproval or annoyance of; to be offensive to

dis-pose v. put in place; arrange

dis-prove v. prove to be false

dis-pute v. to debate or argue

dis-qual-i-fy v. deprive of the required conditions

dis-qui-si-tion *n.* formal inquiry

dis-re-gard *v.* to neglect

dis-re-pute *n.* state of low esteem

dis-re-spect *n.* lack of respect

dis-robe *v.* undress

dis-rupt *v.* throw into disorder

dis-sat-is-fy *v.* fail to satisfy

dis-sect *v.* cut into pieces

dis-sem-ble *v.* conceal; disguise

dis-sem-i-nate *v.* spread; distribute

dis-sen-sion *n.* difference of opinion

dis-sent *v.* differ in opinion

dis-ser-ta-tion *n.* written essay

dis-serv-ice *n.* ill turn

dis-sim-i-lar *adj.* different

dis-sim-u-late *v.* dissemble

dis-si-pate *v.* disperse or drive

dis-so-ci-ate *v.* break association

dis-solve *v.* cause to fade away

dis-so-nance *n., Mus.* lack of agreement; unagreeable

dis-suade *v.* alter the course of action; to change direction

dis-tance *n.* separation in time or space distanced *v.,* distancing *v.*

dis-tant *adj.* separate by a specified amount of time or space

dis-taste *v.* feeling aversion to

dis-tem-per *n.* contagious viral disease of dogs

dis-tend *v.* expand

dis-till *v.* extract by distillation

dis-til-late *n.* the condensed substance sep-arated by distillation

dis-tinct *adj.* clearly seen

dis-tinc-tion *n.* act of distinguishing

dis-tinc-tive *adj.* serving to give style or distinction to

dis-tin-guish *v.* to recognize as beeing different

dis-tort *v.* to twist or bend out of shape distortion *n.*

dis-tract *v.* to draw or divert one's attention distractingly *adv.*

dis-trait *adj.* absentminded

dis-traught *adj.* deeply agitated with doubt or anxiety

dis-trict *n.* an administrative or political section of a territory; a division of space district *v.*

dis-turb *v.* to destroy the tranquillity of; to unsettle mentally disturber

ditch *n.* trench in the earth

dive *v.* to plunge into water headfirst; to submerge

di-verge *v.* to move or extend in different directions from a common point diverged *v.,* diverging *v.*

di-veerse *adj.* unlike in characteristics; different; not similar

di-ver-si-fy *v.* to give variety to something; to engage in varied operations

di-ver-sion *n.* the act of diverting from a course or activity

di-vert *v.* to undress or strip, especially of clothing or dispossess of property

di-vide *v.* to separate into parts; to cause to be apart

di-vi-sion *n.* separation; something which divides or marks off

div-ot *n.* a square of turf or sod

diz-zy *adj.* having a whirling sensation in the head

do-cent *n.* a teacher at a college or university; conducts groups

doc-ile *adj.* easily led, taught, or managed docility *n.*

dock *n.* a landing slip or pier for ships or boats; a loading area for trucks or trains

dock-et *n.* a brief written summary of a document

doc-tor *n.* a person trained and licensed to practive medicine

doc-tor-ate *n.* the degreee, status, or title of a doctor

doc-trine *n.* something taught as a body of principles

doc-u-ment *n.* official paper documentation *n.*

doc-u-men-ta-ry *adj.* relating to or based on documents

dodge *v.* avoid by moving suddenly

doe *n.* mature female deer

does-n't *contr.* does not

dog *n.* domesticated carnivorous mammal

dog-ged *adj.* stubbornly determined

dog-ma *n.* rigidly held doctrine

dog-mat-ic *adj.* marked by an authoritative assertion

dol-drums *pl., n.* a period of listlessness

dole *n.* distribution of food or money to the needy

dole-ful *adj.* filled with sadness

doll *n.* child's toy

dol-lar *n.* standard monetary unit of the U.S.

dol-men *n.* prehistoric monument

do-lor-ous *adj.* marked by grief; mournful

dol-phin *n.* aquatic mammal

dolt *n.* stupid person

do-main *n.* territory under one government

dome *n.* round shaped roof

do-mes-tic *adj.* relating to house-hold

dom-i-cile *n.* dwelling place

dom-i-nant *adj.* prevailing

dom-i-nate *v.* rule or control

dom-i-no *n.* a small rectangular block with dots on the face

don *v.* to put on

don-key *n., pl.* **donkeys** domesticated ass

do-nor *n.* one who donates or contributes

don't *contr.* do not

doo-dle *v.* to scribble or draw aimlessly

doom *n.* an unhappy destiny

door *n.* means of entrance or exit

dope *n.* drug or narcotic

dor-mant *adj.* asleep; state of rest

dor-sal *adj., Anat.* of or relating to back

do-ry *n., pl.* **dories** small flatbottomed boat

dose *n.* measured amount of medicine take at one time

dos-si-er *n.* complete data on a person

dot *n.* small round mark

dote *v.* show excessive affection

dou-ble *adj.* twice as much

double—cross *v., Slang* to betray

double--deck-er *n.* vehicle with two decks for passengers

doubt *v.* **doubter** *n.* uncertain of something

dough *n.* soft pastry mixture of flour and other ingredients

dough-nut *or* **donut** *n.* small cake made of rich, light dough

douse *v.* plunge into liquid or throw water on

dove *n.* any of numerous pigeons

dow-dy *adj.* not neat or tidy; old-fashioned **dowdiest** *adj.*

dow-el *n.* round wooden object that fastens two joined pieces

down *adv.* from higher to lower

down-er *n., Slang* depressant drug; a barbiturate

doz-en *n.* twelve of a kind

drab *adj.* unexciting; yellow-brown **drabness** *n.*

draft *n.* current of air; sketch or plan *Milit.* mandatory selection for service **draftee** *n.*

drag *v.* pull along by force

drag-on *n.* mythical, serpent-like monster

drain *v.* to draw off liquid gradually

drake *n.* male duck

dram *n.* small drink; a small portion

dra-ma *n.* a play recounting a serious story

drape *v.* to cover or adorn with something

dras-tic *adj.* extreme or severe

draw *v.* cause to move toward a position to sketch

draw-back *n.* undesirable feature

draw-bridge *n.* bridge that is raised or lowered

drawer *n.* one that draws pictures; a sliding receptacle in furniture

draw-ing *n.* picture; process of choosing lots

drawl *v.* to speak slowly

dray *n.* heavy cart used for hauling

dread *v.* fear greatly

dread-ful *adj.* inspiring dread; awful

dream *n.* series of thoughts or images which occur during sleep or the REM state of sleep

drea-ry *adj.* bleak and gloomy; dull **dreariness** *n.*

dredge *v.* remove sand or mud from under water **dredger** *n.*

dregs *pl., n.* sediment of a liquid

drench *v.* wet thoroughly

dress *n.* an outer garment for women and girls to put clothes on

drib-ble *v.* to slobber or drool; to bounce a ball repeatedly

drift *v.* to be carried along by a current to move about aimlessly

drill *n.* tool used in boring holes; the act of training soldiers by repeated exercise

drink *v.* to take liquid into the mouth and swallow

drip *v.* to fall in drops *n.* the sound made by falling drops

drive *v.* to propel, push, or press onward

driv-el *v.* to slobber

driz-zle *n.* fine, quiet, gentle rain

droll *adj.* whimsically comical

drom-e-dar-y *n.* one-humped camel

drone *n.* a male bee; unmanned boat or aircraft

drool *v.* to let saliva dribble from the mouth

droop *v.* to hang or bend downward

drop *n.* tiny, rounded mass of liquid; smallest unit of liquid measure

drop *v.* fall in drops; let fall

drop-sy *n., Med.* diseased condition with excessive water in the body

dross *n.* impurity forming molten metal

drought *n.* prolonged period of dryness; being without water

drove *n.* herd of cattle

drown *v.* die by suffocating in a liquid of any kind

drowse *v.* to doze

drub *v.* hit with a stick

drudge *n.* person who does menial tasks **drudgery** *n.*

drug *n.* substance for treatment of disease or illness

drum *n.* musical percussion instrument

drunk *adj.* intoxicated with alcohol

drunk-ard *adj.* person habitually drunk

drupe *n.* one seeded fruit, as the peach

dry *adj.* free from moisture; having no rain; thirsty

dry--clean *v.* clean fabrics with chemical solvents

dry goods *n.* textile fabrics

du-al *adj.* made up or composed of two parts

dub *v.* confer knighthood upon; nickname

du-bi-ous *adj.* causing doubt; unsettled in judgment

duch-ess *n.* wife or widow of a duke

duck *n.* swimming birds with short necks and legs

duct *n.* bodily tube or canal

duc-tile *adj.* capable of being shaped

dud *n., Informal* bomb or explosive round which fails to detonate; a failure

dude *n., Informal* a city person vacationing on a ranch

dudg-eon *n.* displeased, or indignant mood

due *adj.* owed; payable

dues *n., pl.* fee or charge for membership

du-el *n.* premeditated combat between two people

du-et *n.* musical composition for two performers duetted *v.*

duf-fel bag *n.* large cloth bag for personal belongings

duke *n.* noble ranking below a prince; a nobleman of the highest hereditary rank dukedom n.

dul-cet *adj.* melodious

dul-ci-mer *n.* musical stringed instrument of trapezoidal shape played with light hammers held in hands dulcimore n.

dull *adj.* stupid; with a blunt edge or point; not exciting dullness *n.*

du-ly *adv.* in a proper or due manner

dumb *adj.* unable to speak; uneducated dumbness *n.*

dumb-bell *n.* short bar with weights

dumb-waiter *n.* small elevator used to convey food or dishes, from one floor to another

dum-dum bullet *n.* small-arms bullet designed to expand on contact

dum-found *v.* to confound with amazement

dum-my *n.* one who is stupid; hand in bridge

dump *v.* throw down or discard; dispose of garbage

dump-ling *n.* mass of dough cooked in soup or stew

dun *v.* press a debtor for payment dun *adj.*

dunce *n.* slow-witted person

dune *n.* hill of sand drifted by the wind

dung *n.* excrement of animals; manure

dun-ga-ree *n.* sturdy, cotton fabric, especially blue denim; pants or overalls made from this material

dun-geon *n.* dark, underground prison chamber

dunk *v.* dip a piece of food into liquid before eating

du-o-de-num *n., pl.* -denums first portion of the small intestine

dupe *n.* person who is easily deceived

du-pli-cate *n.* identical; exact copy of an original duplication *n.*

du-ra-ble *adj.* able to continue for a long period of time without deterioration durability *n.*

du-ra-tion *n.* period of time during which something lasts or exists

du-ress *n.* constraint by fear or force; forced restraint

dur-ing *prep.* throughout the time of; within the time of

dusk *n.* earliest part of the evening, just before darkness

dust *n.* fine, dry particles of dirt

duty *n.* something a person must do; a moral obligation

dwarf *n.* a human being, or animal of a much smaller than normal size dwarfish *adj.*

dwell *v.* to live, as an inhabitant -er *n.*

dwell-ing *n.* house or building in which one lives

dwin-dle *v.* to waste away

dye *v.* fix a color in or stain materials; color with a dye

dying *adj.* coming to the end of life; about to die

dy-nam-ic *adj.* forceful; energic; productive activity or change; of or relating to energy, motion, or force -al adj.

dy-nam-ics *n., Phys.* part of physics dealing with force, energy, and motion and the relationship between them

dy-na-mo *n.* machine producing electric current

dys-en-ter-y *n.* infection of the lower intestinal tract

dys-lex-i-a *n.* an impairment in one's ability to read dyslexic *adj.*

dys-pep-sia *n.* indigestion

dys-pro-si-um *n.* metallic element

dys-tro-phy *n.* various neuromuscular disorders, especially muscular dystrophy

E, e The fifth letter of the English alphabet.

each *adj.* everyone

each other *pron.* each of two or more in reciprocal action or relation

ea-ger *adj.* marked by enthusiastic interest **eagerness** *n.*

eager beaver *n.* one who is extremely zealous in performing his assigned duties and in volunteering for more

ea-gle *n.* large, powerful bird

eagle eye *n.* the ability to see or observe with exceptional keeness; one that observes

eagle ray *n.* any of several widely distributed large active stingrays with broad pectoral fins like wings

ea-glet *n.* young eagle

ear *n., Anat.* hearing organ in vertebrates

earl *n.* British nobleman **earldom** *n.*

ear-ly *adj.* occurring before the usual time

earn *v.* payment for work done or services rendered **earner** *n.*

ear-nest *n.* serious intent **earnestly, earnestness** *n.*

earn-ings *pl., n.* something earned, such as a salary

earth *n.* the outer layer of the world; ground; soil; dirt

ease *n.* state of being comfortable

ea-sel *n.* frame used to support a canvas or picture

east *n.* the direction in which the sun rises **eastly** *adj. & adv.,* **eastward** *adj. & adv.*

Easter *n.* Christian festival that celebrates the resurrection of Christ

easy *adj.* little difficulty **easily** *adv.,* **easiness** *n.*

eat *v.* chew and swallow food; to erode **eater** *n.*

ebb *n.* recede of a tide towards the sea; leassening; to weaken

eb-o-ny *n., pl.* **ebonies** dark, hard, colored wood; black or very deep brown

ec-cen-tric *adj.* different or peculiar

ec-cle-si-as-ti-cal *n.* a clergyman; a person officially serving a church

ech-e-lon *n.* formation of military troops

ech-o *n., pl.* echoes repetition of a sound

ec-lec-tic *adj.* having components from diverse sources **eclectic** *n.*

e-clipse *n.* total or partial blocking of one celestial body by another

e-clip-tic *n., Astron.* the suns apparent path

ec-logue *n.* short pastoral poem in dialogue form

e-col-o-gy *n.* scientific study of the environment **ecologist** *n.*

ec-o-nom-ic *adj.* science relating to the necessities of life

ec-o-nom-i-cal *adj.* not wasteful **economically** *adv.*

ec-o-nom-ics *pl., n.* science which studies wealth

e-con-o-mize *v.* to manage thriftily **economizer** *n.*

e-con-o-my *n., pl.* economies system for the management of resources and production of goods

ec-ru *n.* light yellowish brown

ec-sta-sy *n., pl.* **ecstasies** state of intense joy or delight

ec-u-men-i-cal *adj.* worldwide; un-iversal

ec-ze-ma *n.* noncontagious skin disease marked by itching and scaly patches

ed-dy *n., pl.* eddies wind or water running against the main current

edge *n.* cutting side of a blade; sharpness

ed-i-ble *adj.* safe or fit for consumption

e-dict *n.* public decree

ed-i-fy *v.* improve or educate

ed-it *v.* correct for publication; to compile for an edition **editor** *n.*

e-di-tion *n.* form in which a book is published

ed-i-to-ri-al *n.* article in a newspaper or magazine **editorially** *adv.*

ed-u-cate *v.* supply with training or schooling **educator** *n.*

e-duce *v.* to call forth or bring out

eel *n., pl.* eel *or* eels snake-like fish

ee-rie *or* **ee-ry** *adj.* weird; scary; spooky **eerily** *adv.,* **eeriness** *n.*

ef-face *v.* remove or rub out

ef-fect *n.* power to produce a desired result

ef-fec-tive *adj.* producing an expected effect or result **effectiveness** *n.*

ef-fem-i-nate *adj.* having a more woman-like quality or trait

ef-fer-ent *adj., Physiol.* carrying away or outward from an organ or part **efferently** *adv.*

ef-fete *adj.* exhausted of effectiveness or force

ef-fi-ca-cious *adj.* producing an intended effect **efficaciously** *adv.*

ef-fi-cient *adj.* adequate in performance with minimum effort

ef-fi-gy *n., pl.* effigies image of a hated person

ef-flo-res-cence *n.* slow process of development

ef-flu-vi-um *n.*, *pl.* effluvivia *or* ef-fluviums unpleasant vapor of something

ef-fort *n.* earnest attempt or achievement effortless *adj.*

ef-fron-ter-y *n.*, *pl.* effronteries shameless; boldness; impudence

ef-ful-gent *adj.* shining brilliantly

ef-fu-sion *n.* unrestrained outpouring of feeling

egg *n.* reproductive cell of female animals

egg-beat-er *n.* tool with rotating blades used to mix food

egg-nog *n.* drink of beaten eggs, sugar, and milk or cream

egg-plant *n.* a purple, egg-shaped, edible fruit

e-go *n.* self thinking

e-go-cen-tric *adj.* thinking of oneself as the object of all experiences

e-go-ma-ni-a *n.* self obsession

e-gre-gious *adj.* remarkably bad

e-gress *n.* act of coming out; means of departing

e-gret *n.* white wading birds

ei-der *n.* large sea duck found in northern regions

eight *n.* cardinal number which follows seven.

ei-ther *pron.* one or the other; *adv.* likewise; also

e-jac-u-late *v.* eject abruptly; to exclaim

e-ject *v.* to throw out; to expel ejection, ejector *n.*

eke out *v.* obtain with great effort

e-lab-o-rate *adj.* planned or carried out with great detail

e-lapse *v.* slip or glide away

e-las-tic *adj.* capable of easy adjustment

e-late *v.* make proud of elation *n.*

el-bow *n.*, *Anat.* outer joint of the arm between the upper arm and forearm

elbow-room *n.* ample room to move about

eld-er *adj.* older; senior

e-lect *v.* choose or select by vote

e-lec-tric *or* e-lec-tri-cal *adj.* relating or pertaining to electricity

e-lec-tric-i-ty *n.*, *Phys.*, *Chem.* force that causes bodies to attract or repel each other; form of energy

e-lec-tro-cute *v.* kill by the use of electric current electrocution *n.*

e-lec-trode *n.* a conductor of electricity into or out of a battery

e-lec-tro-mag-net *n.* magnet that operates through an electric source

e-lec-tron *n.*, *Elect.* subatomic particle with a negative electric charge

e-lec-tro-type *n.* duplicate metal plate used in printing

el-e-gance *n.* refinement in appearance

el-e-gy *n.*, *pl.* elegies poem expressing sorrow for one who is dead elegist *n.*

el-e-ment *n.* constituent part

el-e-men-ta-ry *adj.* fundamental; essential

el-e-phant *n.* large mammal having a long, flexible trunk

el-e-vate *v.* lift up or raise

e-lev-en *n.* cardinal number equal to ten plus one eleventh *n.*

elf *n.*, *pl.* elves imaginary being with magical powers

e-lic-it *v.* bring or draw out

e-lide *v.* to omit; to slur over in pronunciation

e-lim-i-nate *v.* get rid of or remove

e-lite *n.* most skilled members of a group

e-lix-ir *n.*, *Phar.* sweetened aromatic liquid of alcohol and water

elk *n.* large deer

el-lipse *n.*, *Geom.* closed curve oval in shape

elm *n.* various valuable timber and shade trees

el-o-cu-tion *n.* art of effective public speaking

e-lope *v.* run away, especially in order to marry

el-o-quent *adj.* having the power to speak fluently

else *adj.* different; other; more

else-where *adv.* to or in another place

e-lu-ci-date *v.* make clear, clarify; to explain

e-lude *v.* to evade or avoid

e-ma-ci-ate *v.* to become extremely thin emaciation *n.*

em-a-nate *v.* to come or give forth

e-man-ci-pate *v.* liberate; to set free emancipation *n.*

e-mas-cu-late *v.* to castrate

em-balm *v.* treat a corpse with preservatives to protect from decay

em-bank *v.* support, protect or defend enbankment *n.*

em-bar-go *n.*, *pl.* embargoes a restraint on trade

em-bark *v.* to set out on a venture

em-bar-rass *v.* feel selfconscious; to confuse embarrassment *n.*

em-bas-sy *n.*, *pl.* embassies headquarters of an ambassador

em-bat-tle *v.* to prepare for battle

em-bed *v.* to enclose tightly in a surrounding mass

em-bel-lish *v.* to adorn; to decorate embellishment *n.*

em-ber *n.* small piece of glowing coal

em-bez-zle *v.* take money or other items fraudulently

em-bit-ter *v.* to create feelings of hostility embitterment *n.*

em-bla-zon *v.* decorate in bright colors

em-blem *n.* symbol of something; a distinctive design

em-bod-y *v.* give a bodily form to

em-bold-en *v.* to encourage; to make bold

em-bo-lism *n., Med.* blockage of a blood vessel

em-bon-point *n.* plumpness; stoutness

em-boss *v.* shape or decorate with raised designs

em-brace *v.* to clasp or hold in the arms

em-bro-cate *v.* moisten and rub liquid medicine

em-broi-der *v.* to decorate with ornamental needlework

em-broil *v.* to throw into confusion embroilment *n.*

em-bry-o *n., pl.* embryos organism in the early development stage embryonic *adj.*

em-cee *n., Informal* master of ceremonies emcee *v.*

e-mend *v.* correct or remove faults emendation *n.*

em-er-ald *n.* bright-green gemstone

e-merge *v.* to rise into view

e-mer-gen-cy *n., pl.* emergencies sudden and unexpected situation

e-mer-i-tus *adj.* retired from active duty with honor

e-met-ic *adj.* medicine used to induce vomiting

em-i-grate *v.* to move from one country or region emigration *n.*

e-mi-gre *n.* refugee

em-i-nent *adj.* high in esteem or rank eminently *adv.*

em-is-sar-y *n., pl.* emissaries person sent out on a mission

e-mit *v.* to send forth; to throw or give out

e-mol-lient *n.* substance for softening of the skin emollient *adj.*

e-mol-u-ment *n.* profit; compensation

e-mote *v.* to show emotion

e-mo-tion *n.* strong feeling of sorrow, hate and love

em-pa-thy *n., Physiol.* understanding the feelings of another person

em-pen-nage *n.* rear section of an aircraft

em-per-or *n.* ruler of an empire

em-pha-sis *n., pl.* emphases importance attached to anything

em-pire *n.* nations governed by a single supreme authority

em-pir-i-cal *or* em-pir-ic *adj.* gained from observation or experience empirically *adv.*

em-place-ment *n.* platform for guns or military equipment

em-ploy *v.* engage the service or use of -able *adj.*, emoloyer, employment *n.*

em-ploy-ee *or* em-ploy-e *n.* person who works for another in return for pay

em-po-ri-um *n., pl.* emporiums *or* emporia large store which carries general merchandise

em-pow-er *v.* to authorize; to delegate

em-press *n.* woman who rules an empire

emp-ty *adj.* containing nothing; lacking substance

em-u-late *v.* strive to equal, by imitating

e-mul-sion *n., Chem.* mixture of small droplets, one within the other

en-a-ble *v.* to make able

en-act *v.* to make into law; to decree enactment *n.*

e-nam-el *n.* protective coating

en-am-or *v.* to inflame with love; to charm

en-camp *v.* to form or stay in a camp encampment *n.*

en-cap-su-late *v.* enclose or encase in a capsule

en-ceph-a-li-tis *n., Pathol.* inflammation of the brain

en-chain *v.* put in chains

en-chant *v.* to put under a spell enchantment *n.*

en-cir-cle *v.* to form a circle around encirclement *n.*

en-close *v.* to surround on all sides

en-co-mi-um *n., pl.* encomiums *or* encomia high praise

en-com-pass *v.* to surround

en-core *n.* audience's demand for a repeat performance

en-coun-ter *n.* unexpected meeting or conflict

en-cour-age *v.* inspire with courage or hope encouragement *n.*

en-croach *v.* intrude upon the rights of another encroacher, encroachment *n.*

en-crust *v.* cover with a crust; to crust

en-cum-ber *v.* hinder or burden with difficulties

en-cy-clo-pe-di-a *n.* a book of references covering a broad range of subjects

en-cyst *v.* to become enclosed in a sac encystment *n.*

end *n.* terminal point where something is concluded

en-dan-ger *v.* to expose to danger

endangerment n.

en-dear v. to make beloved or dear
endearingly adv.

endearment n. state of being endeared

en-deav-or n. attempt to attain or do
something

en-dem-ic adj. peculiar to a particular
area

en-dog-e-nous adj., Biol. originating or
growing from within

en-dor-phin n. painkilling hormones
secreted by the brain

en-dorse v. to write one's signature on
the back of a check endorsement n.

en-dow v. to bestow upon endowment n.

en-dure v. to undergo

end-wise adv. on end; lengthwise

en-e-ma n. injection of a liquid into the
rectum for cleansing

en-e-my n. a hostile force

en-er-gy n., pl. energies vigor; growth
Phys. electric power

en-er-vate v. to weaken

en-fee-ble v. to weaken enfeeblement n.

en-fold v. enclose; wrap in layers

en-force v. impose by force or firmness
enforceable adj., enforcement n.

en-fran-chise v. to grant to give a
franchise to

en-gage v. to secure or bind; pledge to
marry

en-gen-der v. to exist

en-gine n. mechanical machine

en-gorge v. to swallow greedily
engorgement n.

en-graft v., Bot. join or fasten

en-grave v. to etch into a surface

en-gross v. occupy attention

en-gulf v. enclose completely

en-hance v. make greater -ment n.

e-nig-ma n. anything puzzling

en-join v. to prohibit

en-joy v. feel joy or find pleasure

en-large v. make larger in size

en-list v. enroll or sign up for

en-mesh v. to entangle

en-mi-ty n., pl. enmities deep hatred;
hostility

en-no-ble v. to confer the rank of
nobility

en-nui n. boredom; weariness

e-nor-mity n., pl. enormities wickedness

e-nor-mous adj. very great in size
enormously adv.

e-nough adj. adequate to satisfy demands

en-rage v. put into a rage

en-rap-ture v. to delight

en-rich v. make rich or richer

en-roll or en-rol v. to enter one's name
on a register or record

en-sconce v. to settle securely

en-sem-ble n. group of complementary
parts that are in harmony

en-shrine v. to hold saced

en-shroud v. cover with a shroud

en-sign n. identifying flag; commissioned
Navy officer

en-slave v. to put in bondage
enslavement n.

en-snare v. to catch; to trap

en-sue v. to follow as a consequence

en-sure v. to make certain of

en-tail v. necessary accompaniment or
result entailment n.

en-tan-gle v. to complicate; to confuse
entanglement n.

en-ter v. go into; to penetrate; to begin

en-ter-prise n. large or risky undertaking; project with risks

en-ter-tain v. to amuse; consider
entertainment n.

en-thrall v. to fascinate; captivate
enthrallment n.

en-thu-si-asm n. intense feeling

en-tice v. to attract by arousing desire

en-tire adj. whole; complete

en-ti-tle v. furnish with a right

en-ti-ty n., pl. entities something that exists alone

en-tomb v. to place in a tomb
entombment n.

en-to-mol-o-gy n. study of insects

en-trails pl., n. internal organs of man

en-trance n. the means or place of entry

en-trance v. to fascinate

en-trap v. catch in a trap entrapment n.

en-treat v. to make an earnest request of

en-trench v. to fix or sit firmly
entrenchment n.

en-tre-pre-neur n., Fr. person who un-
dertakes business ventures

en-trust v. transfer to another for care

en-try n., pl. entries opening or place for
entering

en-twine v. twine about or together

e-nu-mer-ate v. count off one by one

e-nun-ci-ate v. to pronounce with clarity;
to announce

en-ve-lope n. paper covering for a letter

en-ven-om v. to make poisonous; to embitter

en-vi-a-ble adj. highly desirable

en-vi-ron-ment n. surroundings

en-vi-ron-men-tal-ist n. person who tries
to preserve the natural environment

en-vi-rons pl., n. surrounding region; a
place

en-vis-age v. form a mental image of; to
visualize

en-voy n. messenger or agent; a

diplomatic representative

en-vy *n., pl.* **envies** resentment for someone else's possessions

e-o-li-an *adj., Geol.* caused by or transmitted by the wind

e-on *n.* indefinite period of time

ep-au-let *or* **ep-au-lette** *n.* shoulder ornament on a military uniform

e-pergne *n.* centerpiece for holding flowers

e-phed-rine *n., Chem.* alkaloid used to relieve nasal congestion

e-phem-er-al *adj.* lasting a very short time

ep-ic *n.* long narrative poem

ep-i-cure *n.* a person having refined tastes

ep-i-dem-ic *adj.* something that effects many individuals

ep-i-der-mis *n., Anat.* outer nonvascular layer of the skin

ep-i-gram *n.* clever, witty observation

ep-i-lep-sy *n., Pathol.* nervous disorder with attacks of unconsciousness

ep-i-logue *or* **ep-i-log** *n.* short speech given by an actor to the audience at the end of a play; an appended chapter placed at the end of a novel or book, etc.

ep-i-neph-rine *or* **ep-i-neph-rin** *n., Biochem.* a hormone secreted by the adrenal medulla of the adrenal glands

e-piph-a-ny *n.* Christian festival held on January 6th.

e-pis-co-pa-cy *n., pl.* **episcopacies** government of a church by bishops

e-pis-co-pal *adj.* pertaining to or governed by bishops

e-pis-co-pate *n.* term, rank, or position of a bishop

ep-i-sode *n.* a section of a poem, novel, etc., that is complete in itself **episodic** *adj.*

e-pis-tle *n.* a formal letter **Epistle** one of the letters in the New Testament

ep-i-taph *n.* inscription, as on a tomb or gravestone

ep-i-the-li-um *n.* thin membranous tissue covering the outer bodily surface

ep-i-thet *n.* word used to characterize something

e-pit-o-me *n.* concise summary; typical example

e-pit-o-mize *v.* be a perfect example

ep-och *n.* point in time marking a new era

ep-ox-y *n., pl.* **epoxies** *Chem.* corrosion-resistant resin used glues and coatings

eq-ua-ble *adj.* not changing; evenly proportioned

e-qual *adj.* same quantity, or value; having the same privileges or rights

e-qual-ize *v.* become or make equal **equalization** *n.*

e-qua-nim-i-ty *n.* composure

e-quate *v.* consider or make equal

e-qua-tion *n.* act of being equal; mathematical statement of equality, usually shown as $(=)$

e-qua-tor *n.* imaginary circle around the earth

eq-uer-ry *n.* the officer in charge of the horses of royalty

e-ques-tri-an *n.* person who rides or performs on a horse

e-qui-an-gu-lar *adj., Geom.* having all angles equal

e-qui-dis-tant *adj.* having equal distances

e-qui-lat-er-al *adj.* having all sides equal

e-qui-lib-ri-um *n.* balance between two opposing forces; state of adjustment, or balance

e-quine *adj.* pertaining to or like a horse

e-qui-nox *n.* twice a year the sun crosses the equator and days and nights are equal in time

e-quip *v.* furnish with what is needed for any undertaking

eq-ui-page *n.* carriage that is equipped with horses and attendants

e-quip-ment *n.* material provided for a special purpose

e-qui-poise *n.* a state of balance

eq-ui-ta-ble *adj.* being impartial in treatment or judgment **equitableness** *n.*

eq-ui-ta-tion *n.* art or act of horse riding

eq-ui-ty *n.* fairness or impartiality; value of property beyond a mortgage or liability

e-quiv-a-lent *adj.* being equal **equivalence** *n.*

e-quiv-o-cal *adj.* ambiguous; questionable **equivocally** *adv.*

e-quiv-o-cate *v.* use intentionally evasive or vague language **equivocation** *n.*

-er *n., suff.* person concerned with a trade; one from a certain area, as a northerner

e-ra *n.* historical period in history

e-rad-i-cate *v.* to destroy utterl

e-rase *v.* remove something written **erasable** *adj.*

er-bi-um *n., Chem.* metallic, silvery, rare-earth element

ere *prep., Poet.* prior to; before

e-rect *adj.* in a vertical position; standing up straight; upright

ere-long *adv., Archaic* before long

er-e-mite *n.* a hermit

er-go *conj. & adv.* consequently; therefore

er-got *n.* disease of cereal plants; drug used to contract involuntary muscles

er-mine *n.* weasel with white fur

e-rode *v.* wear away gradually; to corrode

e-rog-e-nous *adj.* responsive to sexual stimulation

e-ro-sion *n.* state of being eroded

e-ro-sive *adj.* tending to erode erosiveness *n.*

e-rot-ic *adj.* pertaining to or promoting sexual desire

err *v.* make a mistake; to sin

er-rand *n.* trip to carry a message or perform a task

er-rant *adj.* wandering in search of adventure; straying from what is proper

er-rat-ic *adj.* lacking a fixed course; inconsistent erratically *adv.*

er-ra-tum *n., pl.* errata an error in writing or printing

er-ro-ne-ous *adj.* having or contain an error erroneously *adv.*

er-ror *n.* something done incorrectly; a mistake

er-satz *adj.* substitute usually inferior; artificial

erst-while *adj., Archaic* former

e-ruct *v.* to belch eructation *n.*

er-u-dite *adj.* scholarly

er-u-di-tion *n.* informed; great learning

e-rupt *v.* burst forth violently; explode with steam, lava, etc

er-y-sip-e-las *n.* an acute, inflammatory, skin disease resulting from streptococcus

es-ca-late *v.* intensify, increase, or enlarge

es-ca-la-tor *n.* a moving stairway

es-cal-lop *n. & v.* variation of scallop

es-ca-pade *n.* reckless behavior; a prankish trick

es-cape *v.* break free from confinement, restraint, etc.

es-cape-ment *n., Mech.* device in timepieces to control the movement of the wheel

es-cap-ism *n.* escape from unpleasant realities through day-dreams escapist *n. & adj.*

es-ca-role *n.* endive leaves used for salads

es-carp-ment *n.* a steep slope or drop

-escense *n., suff.* give off light in a certain way, as florescence

es-chew *v.* shun or avoid

es-cort *n.* person accompanying another to give protection

es-cri-toire *n.* a writing desk

es-crow *n.* money placed in the custody of a third party until specified conditions are met

es-cutch-eon *n.* surface with an emblem bearing a coat of arms

-ese *n. & adj., suff.* anative of; in the language or style of

e-soph-a-gus *n., pl.* esophagi *Anat.* membranous tube through which food passes to the stomach

es-o-ter-ic *adj.* confidential; kept secret

es-pa-drille *n.* canvas shoe

es-pal-ier *n.* framework used to train shrubs to grow a particular way

es-pe-cial *adj.* having a very special place; exceptional especially *adv.*

es-pi-o-nage *n.* act of spying to obtain secret intelligence

es-pla-nade *n.* flat, open stretch of land along a shoreline

es-pou-sal *n.* support or adoption of a cause

es-pouse *v.* to make something one's own; to take as a spouse

es-pres-so *n.* strong coffee brewed by steam pressure

es-prit *n.* spirit; wit; mental liveliness

es-prit de corps *n., Fr.* a group's spirit of enthusiasm to the common goals of the group

es-py *v.* catch a quick view

-esque *adj., suff.* resembling

es-quire *n.* title of courtesy or respect

-ess *n., suff.* female

es-say *n.* short composition dealing with a single topic

es-sence *n.* the most important element; being

es-sen-tial *adj.* indispensable necessary essentially *adv.*

-est *adj. & adv., suff.* used to form the superlative degree of adverbs and adjectives

es-tab-lish *v.* make permanent, or secure; to create or find

es-tab-lish-ment *n.* a place of residence; those of influence and status in a society

es-tate *n.* large piece of land containing a large house

es-teem *v.* regard with respect

es-ter *n., Chem.* organic compounds formed by the reaction of an acid with an alcohol

es-ti-ma-ble *adj.* worthy of respect or admiration

es-ti-mate *v.* give an approximate opinion or calculation estimation *n.*

es-ti-val *adj.* pertaining to or of summer

es-ti-vate *v.* pass the summer in a state of

dormancy

es-trange v. arouse hated; disassociate or remove oneself

es-tro-gen n., Biochem. steroid hormones that regulate female reproductive functions

es-tu-ar-y n., pl. -ies wide mouth of a river where the current meets the sea

etch v. engrave or cut into the surface by the action of acid etcher n.

etch-ing n. process of engraving using a sharp instrument and acid

e-ter-nal adj. existing without beginning or end; unending

e-ter-ni-ty n., pl. externities forever; the immeasurable extent of time

eth-ane n., Chem. gasous hydrocarbon contained in crude petroleum

eth-a-nol n., Chem. the intoxicant in liquors, wines, and beers; alcohol

e-ther n., Chem. an anesthetic

e-the-re-al adj. highly refined; delicate

eth-ic n. the system of moral values

eth-i-cal adj. conforming to right principles of conduct

eth-nic adj. relating to or of a cultural, or racial group

eth-nog-ra-phy n., pl. ethnographies branch of anthropology dealing with primitive human cultures

eth-nol-o-gy n., pl. -gies the study of racial groups, their cultures, and origins

eth-yl-ene n., Chem. flammable gas used as a fuel

e-ti-ol-o-gy n. science and study of causes or origins

et-i-quette n. prescribed rules of behavior in society

-ette n., suff. small; female

et-y-mol-o-gy n., pl. -gies branch of linguistics that deals with etymologies

eu-ca-lyp-tus n. large, native Australian tree with aromatic leaves

Eu-cha-rist n. the Christian sacrament of Communion

eu-chre n. card game for two to four players

eu-gen-ics n. science of improving the physical and mental qualities of human beings

eu-lo-gize v. deliver a eulogy for eulogist n.

eu-lo-gy n., pl. eulogies a speech that honors a person or thing

eu-nuch n. a castrated man

eu-phe-mism n. substitution for a word thought to be too strong

eu-pho-ny n., pl. -nies agreeable sound of spoken words

eu-pho-ri-a n. very strong feeling of ela-

tion or well-being euphoric adj.

eu-re-ka interj. an expression of triumph

eu-sta-chian tube n., Anat. passage between the middle ear and the pharynx

eu-tha-na-sia n. act of putting to death painlessly a person suffering from an incurable disease

eu-then-ics n. study of improving the physical and mental qualities of human beings

e-vac-u-ate v. to leave a threatened area evacuation n.

e-vac-u-ee n. a person evacuated from a hazardous place

e-vade v. to elude; to get away from by using tricks

e-val-u-ate v. to determine the value of; to appraise evaluation n.

ev-a-nesce v. to fade away

ev-a-nes-cent adj. vanishing or passing quickly; fleeting

e-van-gel-i-cal adj. relating to the Christian gospel

e-van-gel-ism n. preaching and spreading of the gospel

e-van-gel-ist n. Protestant preacher or missionary

e-van-gel-ize v. to preach the gospel

e-vap-o-rate v. convert into vapor; remove the liquid or moisture from milk

e-va-sive adj. being intentionally vague evasively adv.

eve n. the evening before a special holiday; evening

e-ven adj. having a level surface; equally matched

e-ven-hand-ed adj. fair; impartial evenhandedly adv.

eve-ning n. the time between sunset and bedtime

e-ven-song n. an evening prayer

e-vent n. a significant occurrence; something that takes place eventful adj.

e-ven-tide n. evening

e-ven-tu-al adj. expected to happen in due course of time eventually adv.

e-ven-tu-al-i-ty n. the conceivable outcome

e-ven-tu-ate v. to come out eventually

ev-er adv. at any time; throughout the entire course of time

ev-er-glade n. tract of low, swampy land

ev-er-green adj. tree with green foliage throughout the year

ev-er-last-ing adj. existing or lasting forever everlastingly adv.

ev-er-more adv., Poet. for and at all time to come; always

e-vert v. to turn inside out or outward

eve-ry *adj.* without exceptions

eve-ry-body *pron.* every person

eve-ry-day *adj.* happening every day; daily

eve-ry-one *pron.* every person

eve-ry-place *adv.* everywhere

eve-ry-thing *pron.* all things; the essential thing

eve-ry-where *adv.* in, at, or to everyplace

e-vict *v.* to put out a tenant by legal process eviction *n.*

ev-i-dence *n.* facts on which a conclusion can be based

ev-i-dent *adj.* easily seen; obvious evidently *adv.*

e-vil *adj.* morally bad or wrong; low in public esteem

e-vil-do-er *n.* person who does evil to another

e-vil--mind-ed *adj.* obsessed with evil thoughts or intentions

e-vince *v.* demonstrate or indicate clearly

e-vis-cer-ate *v.* remove the vital part of something

e-voke *v.* call or summon forth to produce a reaction

ev-o-lu-tion *n.* gradual process of development or change -ary *adj.*

e-volve *v.* develop or change gradually; developed by evolutionary processes

ewe *n.* female sheep

ew-er *n.* wide-mouthed pitcher or jug

ex- *pref.* former

ex-ac-er-bate *v.* make more severe or worse

ex-act *adj.* accurate in every detail

ex-act-ing *adj.* making severe demands; rigorous exactingly *adv.*

ex-act-i-tude *n.* the quality of being exact

ex-ag-ger-ate *v.* represent something as being greater than it really is exaggeration *n.*

ex-alt *v.* raise in honor, rank, etc.; to praise or glorify exalted *adj.*

ex-am *n., Slang* an examination

ex-am-i-na-tion *n.* a test of skill or knowledge

ex-am-ine *v.* observe or inspect; to test by questions

ex-ample *n.* representative as a sample; one worthy of imitation

ex-as-per-ate *v.* make frustrated or angry

ex-ca-vate *v.* dig a hole or cavity excavation *n.*

ex-ceed *v.* surpass in quantity; to go beyond the limit

ex-ceed-ing-ly *adv.* greater than

ex-cel *v.* surpass or to do better than others

ex-cel-lence *n.* quality of being superior; superior quality

ex-cel-lent *adj.* the best quality

ex-cel-si-or *n.* wood shavings to protect delicate materials

ex-cept *prep.* with the omission or exclusion of; aside from

ex-cep-tion *n.* something that is excluded or does not conform

ex-cep-tion-a-ble *adj.* open to objection exceptionably *adv.*

ex-cep-tion-al *adj.* unusual; well above average exceptionally *adv.*

ex-cerpt *n.* passage from a book, etc.

ex-cess *n.* amount beyond what is necessary

ex-ces-sive *adj.* exceeding what is necessary; extreme

ex-change *v.* return for something else; trade

ex-cheq-uer *n.* treasury of a nation

ex-cise *n.* internal tax on the sale of a commodity

ex-cise *v.* remove surgically

ex-cit-a-ble *adj.* be easily excited excitableness *n.*

ex-cite *v.* stir up strong emotion; simulate the emotions of excitant *n.*

ex-claim *v.* cry out abruptly

ex-cla-ma-tion *n.* a sudden forceful utterance

ex-clude *v.* keep out; to omit from consideration

ex-clu-sive *adj.* intended for a single source; having no duplicate -ly *adv.*

ex-com-mu-ni-cate *v.* deprive the right of church membership -ation *n.*

ex-co-ri-ate *v.* to censure harshly

ex-cre-ment *n.* bodily waste

ex-cre-ta *pl., n.* excretions from the body such as sweat

ex-crete *v.* eliminate waste matter from the body

ex-cru-ci-at-ing *adj.* intensely painful excruciatingly *adv.*

ex-cul-pate *v.* free from wrong doing exculpation *n.*

ex-cur-sion *n.* short trip for pleasure

ex-cur-sive *adj.* go in one direction and then another; digressive

ex-cuse *v.* ask forgiveness or pardon for oneself; apologize for excuseable *adj.*

ex-e-cra-ble *adj.* extremely bad -ness *n.*

ex-e-crate *v.* to detest; abhor

ex-e-cute *v.* to carry out; put to death by the legal authority

ex-e-cu-tion *n.* act of executing a task; the death penalty

ex-e-cu-tion-er *n.* a person who carries out a legal execution

ex-ec-u-tive *n.* administrator in an organization; branch of government responsible for activating the laws of a country

ex-ec-u-tor *n.* person appointed to carry out the execution of a will

ex-em-plar *n.* something serving as a worthy model; a typical example

ex-em-pla-ry *adj.* worthy of imitation; commendable

ex-em-pli-fy *v.* show by giving examples

ex-empt *v.* free or excuse from an obligation or duty exemption *n.*

ex-er-cise *n.* the act of training or developing oneself

ex-ert *v.* put oneself through a strenuous effort exertion *n.*

ex-hale *v.* breathe out

ex-haust *v.* make extremely tired; drain oneself of strength

ex-haust *n.* discharge of waste gases; device through which waste gases are released

ex-hib-it *v.* display for public view

ex-hi-bi-tion-ism *n.* practice of drawing undue attention to oneself

ex-hil-a-rate *v.* to elate or refresh

ex-hort *v.* to urge by earnest appeal

ex-hume *v.* ig up and remove from a grave exhumation *n.*

ex-i-gen-cy *n.* urgency

ex-ig-u-ous *adj.* extremely small; scanty

ex-ile *n.* banishment; one who has been driven from his or her country

ex-ist *v.* have actual being or reality

ex-is-tence *n.* state of existing, or occurring

ex-is-ten-tial *adj.* based on experience existentially *adv.*

ex-is-ten-tial-ism *n.* a philosophy that stresses the active role of the will rather than of reason

ex-it *n.* a way or passage out

ex-o-bi-ol-o-gy *n.* the study of extraterrestrial life

ex-o-dus *n.* a departure of large numbers of people

ex-on-er-ate *v.* free one from accusation or blame; free from responsibility

ex-or-bi-tant *adj.* beyond usual and proper limits

ex-or-cise *v.* cast out or expel an evil spirit by prayers exorcism *n.*

ex-o-ther-mic *adj.* releasing rather than absorbing heat

ex-ot-ic *adj.* strangely different and fascinating

ex-pand *v.* increase the scope, or size; develop more fully expandable *adj.*

ex-panse *n.* a wide, open stretch

ex-pan-sion *n.* amount of increase in volume

ex-pan-sive *adj.* broad and extensive

ex-pa-ti-ate *v.* to talk or write at length

ex-pa-tri-ate *v.* to leave one's country and reside in another

ex-pect *v.* look forward to something as probable or certain

ex-pec-tan-cy *n.* state of expecting; expectation

ex-pec-tant *adj.* pregnant

ex-pec-ta-tion *n.* something that is expected and looked forward to

ex-pec-to-rant *n.* medicine used to promote expectoration

ex-pec-to-rate *v.* to spit

ex-pe-di-en-cy *n.* quality of being expedient

ex-pe-di-ent *adj.* determined by selfish interests only

ex-pe-dite *v.* speed up the progress of something

ex-pe-di-tion *n.* a journey for a definite purpose

ex-pe-di-tion-ar-y *adj.* sent on military service abroad

ex-pe-di-tious *adj.* quick; speedy

ex-pel *v.* drive or force out

ex-pend *v.* to pay out or use up

ex-pend-a-ble *adj.* available for spending expendability *n.*

ex-pen-di-ture *n.* an amount spent

ex-pense *n.* outlay or consumption of money; funds allotted to cover incidental costs

ex-pen-sive *adj.* high-priced

ex-pe-ri-ence *n.* the knowledge or skill acquired from actual participation or training in an activity

ex-pe-ri-enced *adj.* be knowledgeable through actual practices, etc

ex-per-i-ment *n.* test performed to demonstrate a truth experimental *adj.*

ex-pert *n.* a person having great knowledge, or skill

ex-per-tise *n.* specialized skill in a particular area

ex-pi-ate *v.* to make amends for

ex-pire *v.* to come to an end; to exhale

ex-plain *v.* make understandable; to account for

ex-ple-tive *n.* an exclamation, often profane

ex-pli-cate *v.* to clear up the meaning of

ex-plic-it *adj.* plainly expressed; straightforward

ex-plode *v.* burst or blow up violently with a loud noise

ex-ploit *n.* a deed or act that is notable

ex-plore *v.* examine in a systematic way

ex-plo-sion *n.* sudden, violent release of

energy

ex-plo-sive *n.* a chemical preparation that explodes

ex-po-nent *n.* person who speaks for a cause or group

ex-port *v.* send merchandise to other countries for resale

ex-pose *v.* lay open, as to ridicule; to lay bare; to reveal the identity of someone

ex-po-si-tion *n.* a statement of intent; a public exhibition

ex post facto *adj., L.* after the fact

ex-pos-tu-late *v.* try to dissuade against an action

ex-po-sure *n.* an indication of which way something faces

ex-pound *v.* give a detailed statement of something

ex-press *v.* to formulate in words; to comunicate

ex-pres-sion *n.* communication of feeling; a facial ok that conveys a feeling

ex-pres-sive *adj.* serving to indicate or express; full of expression

ex-press-way *n.* a multilane highway

ex-pro-pri-ate *v.* take property from the owner for public use

ex-pul-sion *n.* act of expelling

ex-punge *v.* to delete or remove; to erase

ex-pur-gate *v.* remove objectionable material from a play, etc.

ex-qui-site *adj.* intricately beautiful in craftsmanship

ex-tant *adj.* still in existence; not destroyed; surviving

ex-tem-po-ra-ne-ous *adj.* performing with little or no advance preparation; not memorized -ously *adv.*

ex-tem-po-rize *v.* do, with little or no advance preparation

ex-tend *v.* open to full length; to prolong; offer the hand

ex-ten-sion *n.* additional time to pay a debt

ex-ten-sive *adj.* wide-spread; far-reaching

ex-tent *n.* degree to which anything is extended; the size

ex-ten-u-ate *v.* minimize the seriousness of something

ex-te-ri-or *adj.* the outside; the external layer

ex-ter-mi-nate *v.* to destroy completely exterminator *n.*

ex-ter-nal *adj.* outside; exterior

ex-tinct *adj.* no longer existing

ex-tin-guish *v.* put an end to; to make extinct extinguishable *adj.*

ex-tir-pate *v.* pull up by the roots

ex-tol *v.* to praise highly

ex-tort *v.* obtain money by threat, or

abuse of authority extortist *n.*

ex-tra *adj.* over and above what is normal

ex-tract *v.* pull or draw out by force

ex-trac-tion *n.* act of extracting; one's origin or ancestry

ex-tra-cur-ric-u-lar *adj.* outside the usual duties

ex-tra-dite *v.* surrender by extradition

ex-tra-di-tion *n.* legal surrender of a criminal for trial

ex-tra-dos *n.* the upper curve of an arch

ex-tra-ga-lac-tic *adj.* coming from beyond the galaxy

ex-tra-mar-i-tal *adj.* adulterous

ex-tra-mu-ral *adj.* involving teams from different schools

ex-tra-ne-ous *adj.* coming from without extraneously *adv.*

ex-tra-or-di-nar-y *adj.* beyond what is usual; remarkable

ex-tra-sen-so-ry *adj.* beyond the range of normal perception

ex-tra-ter-res-tri-al *adj.* orginating outside the earth

ex-trav-a-gant *adj.* overly lavish; wasteful; unrestrained extravagantly *adv.*

ex-trav-a-gan-za *n.* a lavish, showy entertainment

ex-treme *adj.* going far beyond the bounds of moderation; of the highest or utmost degree extremely *adv.*

ex-trem-ist *n.* person who resorts to extreme measures

ex-trem-i-ty *n.* utmost or farthest point; appendage or limb of the body

ex-tri-cate *v.* free from entanglement; to disengage

ex-trin-sic *adj.* outside the nature of something; external

ex-tro-vert *n.* out going person

ex-trude *v.* 'sh or thrust out; to protrude

ex-u-ber-ant *adj.* full of high spirits exuberance *n.*

ex-ude *v.* to ooze or trickle forth, as sweat

ex-ult *v.* jubilant; to rejoice greatly exultation *n.*

ex-ur-bi-a *n.* well-to-do residential area

eye *n.* an organ of sight; central area of a hurricane

eye-ful *n.* a satisfying or complete view

eye opener *n.* a startling revelation

eye-sight *n.* power of sight; the range of vision

eye-sore *n.* something ugly that offends the sight

eye-wit-ness *n.* person who testifies to something he has seen

F, f The sixth letter of the English alphabet

fa-ba-ceous *adj.* or or relating to the legume family

Fa-bi-an *adj.* of, relating to, or in the manner of the Roman general Quintus Fabius Maximus known for his defeat of Hannibal in the Secon Punic War by the avoidance of decisive contests

fa-ble *n.* a fictitious story having a moral **fabler** *n.*

fab-ric *n.* cloth produced by knitting or spinning fibers

fab-ri-cant *n.* manufacturer

fab-ri-cate *v.* make or manufacture; build **fabrication** *n.*

fab-u-lar *adj.* of, relating to, or having the form of a fable

fab-u-list *adj.* a creator or writer of fables; liar

fab-u-lous *adj.* incredible

fa-cade *n., Arch.* face or front of a building

face *n.* front surface of the head

face angle *n.* an angle formed by two edges of polyhedral angle

face card *n.* a king, queen, or jack in a deck of cards

face--cloth *n.* washcloth

face--down *adv.* with the face down

face fly *n.* European fly that is similar to the house fly, is widely established in North America, and causes great distress in livestock by clustering about the face

face--harden *v.* to harden the suface of

face--lift-ing *n.* plastic surgery for improving the facial appearance

face--off *n.* putting a puck into play by dropping it between two players

fac-er *n.* a stunning check or defeat

face--saver *n.* something that saves space

face--saving *n.* the act of preserving one's dignity

fac-et *n.* polished surface on a gemstone; aspect of a person

fa-ce-tious *adj.* humorous -ly *adv.*

fact--to--face *adj.* being within each other's sight or presence

face-up *v.* to meet without shrinking

face value *n.* apparent value of something

fa-cial *adj.* near, of, or for the face

facial index *n.* the ratio of the breadth of the face to its length times 100

facial nerve *n.* cranial nerves that supply mnnotor fibers to the muyscles of the face and jaw

fac-ile *adj.* requiring little effort

fa-cil-i-tate *v.* make easier

fa-cil-i-ty *n.* ease in performance, or doing something

fac-ing *n.* lining sewn to a garment

fac-sim-i-le *n.* an exact copy

fact *n.* something that actually occurred; piece of information

fact finder *n.* one that tries to determine the realities of a case

fac-tion *n.* self-seeking group in a government

fac-tious *adj.* creating friction; divisive

fac-ti-tious *adj.* produced by man rather than nature

fac-ti-tive *adj.* relating to a transitive verb that in some constructions requires an objective complement as well as an object

fac-tor *n.* one transacting business for another for commission

fac-tor-age *n.* the charges made by a factor for certain services

factor analysis *n.* the transformation of statistical data into linear combinations of variables that are not correlated

fac-to-ry *n.* plant where goods are manufactured

fac-to-tum *n.* employee having many duties and responsibilites

fac-tu-al *adj.* consisting of or based on facts

fac-ul-ty *n.* natural ability or power; branch of learnig or teaching

fad *n.* temporary fashion -ish *adj.*

fade *v.* lose brightness gradually

fag *v.* exhaust by hard work

fag end *n.* frayed end of a rope or cloth

fag-ot *n.* bundle of sticks, etc. used for fuel

Fahr-en-heit *adj.* temperature scale in which the freezing point of water is 32 degrees and the boiling point is 212 degrees

fa-ience *n.* earthenware decorated with a colorful opaque glaze

fail *v.* be totally ineffective; receive a grade below standard

faille *n.* ribbed material

fail--safe *adj.* a system designed to prevent equipment failure

fail-ure *n.* a breaking down in strength, or efficiency

faint *adj.* having little vigor; lacking brightness; dizzy

faint-hearted *adj.* lacking courage

fair *adj.* visually light in coloring; not stormy; exhibit of livestock, etc.

fair ball *n.* batted ball with in the foul lines

fair-way n. part of a golf course between the tee and the green

fair-y n. a tiny imaginary being

fair-y-land n. delightful, enchanting place

fair-y tale n. fictitious tale of fanciful creatures

fait ac-com-pli n. irreversible accomplished fact or deed

faith n. belief in the value, or trustworthiness of someone or something

faith-ful adj. true and trustworthy in obligations, etc. faithfully adv.

fake adj. having a misleading appearance; not genuine

fal-con n. bird of prey

fall v. drop down from a higher place; collapse

fal-la-cious adj. deceptive; misleading

fal-li-ble adj. capable of making an mistake fallibility n.

fall-ing-out n. fight, or quarrel

fall-ing star n. a meteor

fall-off n. a decrease in something

fal-lo-pi-an tube n. ducts serving as a passage for the ovum

fall-out n. descent of minute particles of radioactive material

fal-low n. unplanted plowed ground; light brown color

false adj. incorrect; deliberately untrue falsely adv.

false face n. mask used as a disguise on Halloween

false-hood n. act of lying; untrue statement

fal-set-to n. high male singing voice

fal-si-fy v. give an untruthful account; misrepresent

fal-ter v. be uncertain in action or voice falteringly adv.

fame n. public esteem

fa-mil-iar adj. being well-acquainted with

fa-mil-i-ar-i-ty n. the knowledge of something

fa-mil-iar-ize v. make oneself familiar with something familarization n.

fam-i-ly n. a group of people connected by blood or marriage

fam-ine n. widespread scarcity of food

fam-ish v. to starve

fa-mous adj. well-known; renowned

fan n. device for putting air into motion

fa-nat-ic n. one moved by enthusiasm

fan-ci-er n. person having a special interest in something

fan-cy n. imagination whimsical nature

fan-cy-free adj. unattached

fan-fare n. short, loud trumpet flourish

fang n. long, pointed tooth

fan-jet n. aircraft with turbojet engines

fan-ny n. Slang the buttocks

fan-ta-sia n. composition according to the composer's fancy

fan-ta-size v. create mental pictures

fan-tas-tic adj. unreal; wildly exaggerated fantastically adv.

fan-ta-sy n. creative imagination

far adv. at a considerable distance

farce n. theatre comedy with ludicrous situations

fare n. fee paid for hired transportation

fare-well n. goodby

far-fetched adj. highly improbable

far-flung adj. widely distributed

far-i-na-ceous adj. rich in, or composed of starch

farm n. land used for agriculture raising animals

far-off adj. remote

far-out adj. very unconventional

far-ra-go n. a confused mixture

far-row n. litter of pigs

far-sighted adj. seeing distance objects more clearly than nearby things

far-ther adv. at a more distant point

far-ther-most adj. most distant

far-thest adj. at the greatest distance

far-thing n. something of little worth

fas-ci-nate v. attract irresistibly; captivate -nation n.

fas-cism n. one-party system of government

fashion n. mode or manner of dress

fast adj. swift; rapid

fast v. abstain from food

fast-back n. car with a downward slope roof

fast-en v. connect; securely fix something fastener n.

fast-food n. restaurant specializes in foods prepared and served quickly

fas-tid-i-ous adj. delicate or refined

fat adj. obese; plump

fat-al adj. causing death; inevitable fatally adv.

fa-tal-ism n. belief that things are predetermined by fate

fa-tal-i-ty n. death caused by a disaster or accident

fat cat n., Slang powerful and wealthy person

fate n. predetermine events

fate-ful adj. governed by fate

fa-ther n. male parent Father a priest

fath-om n. length equal to six feet

fath-om-less adj. too deep to measure

fa-tigue n. condition of extreme tiredness

fatigues n. military clothes
fat-ty adj. greasy
fat-u-ous adj. silly and foolish
fau-cet n. valve to draw liquids from a pipe
faugh interj. exclamation of contempt
fault n. impairment or defect
fault-find-er n. a petty critic
fau-vism n. art movement noted for flamboyant colors
faux pas n. a false step; a social blunder
fa-vor n. a helpful or considerate act
fa-vor-a-ble adj. expressing approval favorableness n.
fa-vor-ite n. preferred above all others favoritism n.
fawn n. a young deer; yellowish brown color
fay n. fairy or elf
faze v. to disconcert
fe-al-ty n. loyalty owed to a feudal lord
fear n. anticipation of danger
fear-less adj. without fear; brave
fea-si-ble adj. capable of being accomplished
feast n. a delicious meal
feat n. notable achievement
feath-er n. protective covering of birds feathery adj.
feather bed n. feather stuffed mattress
feather-stitch n. an embroidery stitch
feather-weight n. light weight boxer
fea-ture n. appearance or shape of the face
feb-ri-fuge n. medicine used to reduce fever
feb-rile adj. relating to a fever
fe-ces pl. n. bodily waste; excrement
feck-less adj. weak; worthless
fe-cund adj. fruitful; productive
fe-cun-date v. make fertile
fed-er-al adj. agreement between two or more states
fed-er-ate v. unite in a federal union
fed-er-a-tion n. two or more states joining a confederacy
fe-do-ra n. soft hat
fed up adj. extremely annoyed
fee n. fixed charge; charge for a professional service
fee-ble adj. very weak
feeble minded adj. mentally deficient
feed v. supply with food
feel v. perceive through the sense of touch
feel-ing n. sensation by touch
feign v. make a false show of; to fabricate feigned adj.
feint n. deceptive or misleading movement

fe-lic-i-tate v. to wish happiness felicitation n.
fe-lic-i-tous adj. most appropriate
fe-lic-i-ty n. great hapiness; bliss
fe-line adj. relating to cats
fel-low n. boy or man
fel-low-ship n. group with common interests
fel-ly n. rim of a wooden wheel
fel-on n. one who has committed a felony
fel-o-ny n. serious crime
felt n. unwoven fabric
fe-male n. sex that produces ova
fem-i-nine adj. pertaining to the female sex femininity n.
femme fa-tale n. seductive, charming woman
fe-mur n. leg bone
fen n. low marshy land
fence n. boundary or barrier
fenc-ing n. sport of using a foil or saber
fend v. ward off
fend-er n. covering for the wheel of a car
fen-nel n. herb of the carrot family
fe-ral adj. not tame or domesticated
fer--de--lance n. snake
fer-men-ta-tion n. decomposition of complex organic compounds
fern n. flowerless, seedless plants
fe-ro-cious adj. extremely savage
fer-ret n. small, red-eyed polecat
fer-rous adj. containing iron
fer-rule n. cap at the end of a cane
fer-ry n. boat to transport people and vehicles
fer-tile adj., Biol. ability to reproduce
fer-til-ize v. make fertile
fer-til-iz-er n. manure which enriches soil
fer-ule n. stick to punish children
fer-vent adj. passionate; very hot
fer-vor n. great intensity
fes-cue n. tough perennial grass
fes-ter v. develop pus
fes-ti-val n. holiday or celebration
fes-toon n. garland of flowers, etc.
fet-a n. Greek cheese white in color
fetch v. go after and return with
fetch-ing adj. very attractive or pleasing
fete n. large elaborate party
fet-id adj. having a foul odor; stinking fetidly adv.
fet-ish n. object having magical powers
fet-lock n. tuft of hair on the back of the leg of a horse
fet-ter n. chain to prevent escape
fe-tuc-ci-ne n. pasta
fe-tus n. unborn organism carried within

the womb

feud *n.* bitter family quarrel

fe-ver *n.* abnormally high body temperature

fever blister *n.* cold sore

few *adj.* small in number

fey *adj.* acting as if under a spell

fez *n.* red felt, black-tasseled hat

fi-an-ce *n.* man engaged to be married

fi-an-cee *n.* woman engaged to be married

fi-as-co *n.* complete or total failure

fi-at *n.* positive order or decree

fib *n.* trivial lie

fi-ber *n.* piece of synthetic material

fiber-board *n.* tough building material

fiber-glass *n.* non-flammable material of spun glass

fiber optics *pl., n.* light transmitted through flexible glass rods

fib-ril-la-tion *n., Pathol.* uncoordinated contraction of the muscle of the heart

-fic *adj., suffix* causing; rendering

-fication *n., suffix* production

fi-chu *n.* scarf

fick-le *adj.* inconstant; changeable

fic-tion *n.* something created or imaginary **fictional** *adj.*

fic-ti-tious *adj.* nonexistent; imaginary **fictitiously** *adv.*

fid-dle *v.* play a violin; spend time on a fruitless activity

fiddler crab *n.* small burrowing crab

fid-dle-sticks *interj.* to express mild disgust

fi-del-i-ty *n.* faithfulness or loyalty

fidg-et *v.* move nervously or restlessly

fidgets *pl, n.* condition of being nervous **fidgetity** *adj.*

fief *n.* feudal estate

field *n.* piece of cultivated land

field marshal *n.* army official in Europe

fiend *n.* evil spirit or demon

fierce *adj.* savage and violent

fier-y *adj.* composed of fire

fi-es-ta *n.* religious holiday or festival

fife *n.* small, shrilltoned instrument

fig *n.* tree bearing an edible fruit

fight *v.* argue or quarrel **fighting** *n.*

fight-er *n.* person who fights; airplane

fig-ment *n.* invention or fabrication

fig-u-ra-tive *adj.* containing a figure of speech **figuratively** *adv.*

fig-ure *n.* symbol that represents a number; human form or body

figure eight *n.* ice skating maneuver

figure-head *n.* person with nominal leadership

fig-u-rine *n.* molded figure; a statuette

fil-a-ment *n.* finely spun thread, or wire

fil-bert *n.* edible nut; **filch** *v.* to steal

file *n.* device for storing papers; grinding tool

fi-let *n.* filet of meat or fish

filet mi-gnon *n.* small, tender cut of beef

fil-i-al *adj.* relating to a son or daughter

fil-i-buster *n.* attempt to hinder legislative action

fil-i-gree *n.* lace-like ornamental work

fill *v.* supply fully; satisfy a need; put into **filling** *n.*

fill-er *n.* something added to increase weight or bulk

fil-lip *n.* snap of the finger

fil-ly *n.* female horse

film *n.* photosensitive paper used in photography

film-strip *n.* strip of film for projection on a screen

fil-ter *n.* device used to purify

filth *n.* dirty or foul

filth-y *adj.* covered with filth; dirty **filthiness** *n.*

fin *n.* extension of the body for swimming

fi-na-gle *v., Slang* get something by trickery

fi-nal *adj.* pertaining to the end; last **finally** *adv.*

fi-na-le *n.* last part; final scene in a play

fi-nal-ist *n.* person in the final round of a contest

fi-nal-ize *v.* put into final form **finalization** *n.*

fi-nance *n.* science of monetary affairs **financial** *adj.*

fin-an-cier *n.* expert in large-scale financial affairs

finch *n.* small bird

find *v.* come upon unexpectedly

find-ing *n.* something discovered

fine *adj.* superior in skill or quality; healthy **finely** *adv.*

fin-er-y *n.* elaborate jewels and clothes

fin-esse *n.* highly refined skill

fin-ger *n.* digits of the hand

finger-board *n.* wood on the neck of a stringed instrument

finger bowl *n.* bowl of water for cleansing the fingers

finger-nail *n.* transparent covering of the dorsal surface of each finger

fin-i-al *n.* ornamental projection on a lamp shade

fin-ick-y *adj.* hard to please; choosy

fi-nis *n.* the end

fin-ish *v.* bring to an end; to conclude **finished** *adj.*

fi-nite *adj.* having bounds or limits

fink *n.* person who breaks a strike; unsavory person

fir *n.* evergreen tree

fire *n.* chemical reaction of burning

fire alarm *n.* device to alert an outbreak of fire

fire-arm *n.* small weapon

fire-ball *n.* very bright meteor

fire-break *n.* strip of land cleared to prevent a fire from spreading

fire-bug *n.* one who enjoys setting fire

fire-cracker *n.* small explosive set off to make noise

fire engine *n.* vehicle to carry firemen and their equipment

fire escape *n.* emergency exit from a building

fire extinguisher *n.* apparatus containing fire-extinguishing chemicals

fire fighter *n.* person who fights fires as an occupation

fire-fly *n.* insect that glows at night

fire-proof *adj.* resistant to fires

fire-trap *n.* unsafe building

fire-works *pl. n.* explosives for entertainment

firm *adj.* solid or unyielding to pressure

fir-ma-ment *n.* the sky

first *adj.* preceding all others

first aid *n.* temporary medical care

first-born *n.* child who is born first

first class *n.* highest group in a classifaction

first-hand *adj.* directly from the original source

firth *n.* narrow inlet or arm of the sea

fis-cal *adj.* relating to the finances or treasury of a nation

fish *n., pl.* cold-blooded, aquatic animal **fishing** *n.*

fish-y *adj.* creating doubt of suspicion

fis-sile *adv.* capable of being separated

fis-sion *n.* process of splitting into parts

fis-sure *n.* narrow crack in a rock

fist *n.* the hand closed tightly

fit *v.* be the proper size and shape; be in good physical condition

fitch *n.* hide of a polecat

fit-ful *adj.* capricious; restless

fit-ing *adj.* suitable or proper

five *n.* number equal to 4 + 1

fix *v.* make firm; mend; repair

fix-a-tion *n.* state of being fixed

fix-ture *n.* part or appendage of a house

fizz *n.* hissing or bubbling sound

flab *n.* excessive, loose body tissue

flabbergast *v.* overwhelm with shock; astound

flac-cid *adj.* lacking resilience or firmness

flac-on *n.* small, decorative bottle

flag *n.* banner of a country or nation

flag-el-lant *n.* whipping for sexual excitement

fla-grant *adj.* disgraceful; notorious

flair *n.* aptitude or talent for something

flak *n.* antiaircraft fire

flake *n.* thin piece peeled off a surface

flam-boy-ant *adj.* ornate; showy; florid

flame *n.* mass of burning vapor from a fire

fla-men-co *n.* a fiery percussive dance

flame-out *n.* failure of a jet aircraft engine while in flight

fla-min-go *n.* large, tropical wading bird

flam-ma-ble *adj.* capable of catching fire

flange *n.* collar used to strengthen or guide a wheel

flank *n.* fleshy part of the hip

flan-nel *n.* woven wool fabric

flap-per *n.* woman of the 1920's

flare *v.* blaze up with a bright light

flash *v.* burst into a brilliant fire or light

flash-back *n.* interruption of a story, for something that happened earlier

flash card *n.* card with numbers, letters, etc. used as a learning tool

flash-y *adj.* tastelessly showy; gaudy

flask *n.* glass container used in laboratories

flat *adj.* extending horizontally; prostrate or prone

flat-bed *n.* truck without sides

flat-car *n.* railroad car with no roof or sides

flat-ten *v.* to knock down; make flat

flat-ter *v.* praise extravagantly

flat-ter-y *n.* insincere compliments

flat-top *n.* aircraft carrier; short haircut

flat-u-lent *adj.* having gas in the intestine

flat-ware *n.* eating utensils

flaunt *v.* display showily

flau-tist *n.* a flutist

fla-vor *n.* distinctive taste of something **flavorful** *adj.*

fla-vor-ing *n.* substance used to increase the flavor

flaw *n.* defect or blemish

flaw-less *adj.* without defects; perfect

flax *n.* plant that yields linseed oil

flay *v.* remove the skin of; to scold harshly

flea *n.* blood-sucking, parasitic

flea market *n.* place to sell secondhand items

fleck *n.* tiny spot

fledg-ling *n.* a young bird; immature or inexperienced person

flee *v.* run away; to move swiftly away

fleece *n.* soft wool covering a sheep

fleet *n.* number of warships

flesh n. soft tissue of the human body

flesh-ly adj. pertaining to the body; sensual; worldly

fleur-de-lis n., pl. fleurs-de-lis heraldic emblem

flex v. to contract a muscle

flex-i-ble adj. capable of being bent; capable of adjusting to new situations; pliable

flex time n. system allowing employees to set their own work schedules

flick n. light, quick snapping movement

flick-er v. burn or shine unsteadily

fli-er n. aviator; printed advertisement of handbill

flight n. a scheduled airline trip

flight-y adj. inclined to act in a fickle fashion flightiness n.

flim-flam n. Slang swindle; trick; hoax

flim-sy adj. lacking substance; of inferior workmanship

flinch v. wince or pull back in pain

fling v. throw or toss violently; period devoted to self-indulgence

flip v. throw suddenly with a jerk

flip-flop n. sound of something flapping loosely; sudden reverse of direction

flip-pant adj. showing disrespect

flip-per n. flat limb of a seal for swimming

flip side n. reverse or opposite side

flirt v. make teasing romantic overtures flirtation n.

flit v. move rapidly or abruptly

flit-ter v. to flutter

float n. suspend on water; cork on a fishing line

flock n. group of animals

floe n. large, flat mass of floating ice

flog v. beat hard with a whip or stick flogger n.

flood n. an overflow of water onto land

flood-gate n. valve to control flow or depth of water

flood-light n. intensely bright beam of light

floor n. level base of a room

floor exercise n. competitive gymnastics event with tumbling maneuvers

floor show n. entertainment at a night club

flop v. fall down clumsily

flop house n. cheap, rundown hotel

floppy disk n. flexible plastic disk used to record and store computer data

flo-ra n. plants grown in a specific region

flo-ral adj. pertaining to flowers

flor-id adj. rosy color or redness; ornate; covered with flowers

flo-rist n. one who grows or sells flowers

floristry n.

floss n. embroidery thread; dental floss

flo-til-la n. fleet of small vessels

flot-sam n. debris from sunken ships

floun-der v. struggle clumsily for footing; flat fish

flour n. ground meal of wheat

flour-ish v. thrive; prosper and succeed

flout v. show open contempt for floutingly adv.

flow v. move freely, as a fluid

flow-er n. cluster of colored petals

flub v. botch; to make a mess of

fluc-tu-ate v. shift irregularly; to change fluctuation n.

flue n. pipe for escaping smoke

flu-ent adj. capable of flowing; facile in speech fluently adv.

flu-id n. substance, as water cap-able of flowing

fluke n. flat fish; stroke of good luck

flunk v., Slang fail an examination or course

flun-ky n. person who does menial work; servant

flu-o-res-cence n., Chem., Phys. electromagnetic radiation

fluorescent lamp n. tubular electric lamp

fluor-i-date v. sodium compound to prevent tooth decay

flu-o-rine n. pale yellow, gasous element

flu-o-ro-scope n. instrument used for observing the human body by means of x-rays

flur-ry n. sudden gust of wind; brief, light fall of snow

flush v. flow or rush out suddenly; become red in the face

flus-ter v. make nervous or confused

flute n. highpitched, woodwind instrument

flut-ist n. a flute player

flut-ter v. flap or wave irregularly

flux n. a constant flow or movement

flux-ion n. constant change

fly v. move through the air on wings or wing-like parts; travel by air flyable adj.

flying saucer n. unidentified moving objects in the sky described as being saucershaped

fly-wheel n. rotating wheel to regulate the speed of a machine shaft

foal n. young horse, especially one under a year old

foam n. mass of bubbles on liquid; roth foamy adj.

fob n. chain attached to a pocket watch

fo-cus v. produce a sharp clear image of; adjust a lens

fod-der *n.* coarse feed for livestock

foe *n.* enemy in war; adversary

fog *n.* vapor mass of condensed water lying close to the ground

fog-horn *n.* horn sounded to give warning in a fog

fo-gy *n.* a person with old-fashioned attitudes and ideas

foi-ble *n.* minor flaw; weakness

foil *v.* prevent from being successful; to thwart

foist *v.* pass off as valuable or genuine; force to accept by deceit

fold *v.* double or lay one part over another

fol-de-rol *n.* pretty but useless ornament

fo-li-age *n.* leaves on plants and trees

fo-li-o *n.* folder for loose papers

folk *n., pl.* **folk** *or* **folks** ethnic group of people forming a nation or tribe; a person's parents

fol-li-cle *n.* small anatomical cavity

fol-low *v.* proceed or come after; to pursue

fol-ly *n., pl.* **fillies** an instance of foolishness; costly or unprofitable undertaking

fo-ment *v.* to rouse; to incite; treat with moist heat

fond *adj.* affectionate; cherished with great affection **fondness** *n.*

fon-dant *n.* sweet soft preparation of sugar used in candies

fon-dle *v.* stroke or caress tenderly

fond-ly *adv.* in a willingly credulous manner

fon-due *n.* preparation of melted cheese and wine for dipping food into

font *n.* receptacle that holds baptismal or holy water; assortment of printing type

food *n.* substance consisting of carbohydrates and protein to sustain life

fool *n.* one lacking good sense or judgment

foot *n., pl.* **feet** lower extremity of the leg upon which one stands; unit of measurement equal to 12 inches

foot-ball *n.* game played with an inflated ball

foot-bridge *n.* bridge for pedestrians

foot-hill *n.* hill at the foot of a mountain

foot-hold *n.* place to support the foot

foot-ing *n.* stable position for placement of the feet; a foundation

foot-locker *n.* trunk for personal belongings

foot-loose *adj.* having no ties; free to move about

foot-note *n.* note of reference below the text; a commentary

foot-path *n.* narrow path for people on foot

foot-print *n.* outline of the foot on a surface

foot-stool *n.* low stool for resting the feet

foot-work *n.* use of the feet, as in boxing

fop *n.* man concerned with his appearance **foppish** *adj.*

for *prep.* used to indicate the extent of something; behalf of someone; to be in favor of

for-age *n.* food for domestic animals; search for supplies or food **forager** *n.*

for-ay *n.* a raid to plunder

for-bear *v.* refrain from; to cease from **forbearance** *n.*

for-bid *v.* command not to do something; to prohibit by law

forbidding *adj.* very difficult; disagreeable

force *n.* energy or power; strength; intellectual influence **forceful** *adj.*

force-meat *n.* ground meat, fish, etc., used in stuffing

for-ceps *n.* forceps *pl.* instrument resembling a pair of tongs used in surgery

forc-i-ble *adj.* achieved or accomplished by force

ford *n.* shallow place in a body of water for crossing

fore *adj. & adv.* situated in, at, or toward the front; golfer's warning

fore--and--aft *adj.* from stem to stern

fore-arm *n.* part of the arm between the elbow and the wrist

fore-bear *or* **for-bear** *n.* an ancestor

fore-bode *v.* give a warning in advance; have a premonition of something evil

fore-cast *v.* estimate in advance; predict the weather

fore-cas-tle *n.* living quarters for the crew of a merchant ship

fore-close *v.* recall a mortgage in default; to exclude; to shut out

fore-fa-ther *n.* ancestor

fore-fin-ger *n.* finger next to the thumb

fore-foot *n.* front foot of an animal

fore-front *n.* very front of something; the vanguard

fore-go *v.* to precede in time, place, etc.

for-eign *adj.* outside one's native country

for-eign-er *n.* person from a different place or country; an alien

fore-knowl-edge *n.* prior knowledge of something

fore-lock *n.* lock of hair growing over the forehead

fore-man *n.* person who oversees a group

of people; spokesperson for a jury

fore-most *adj. & adv.* first in rank or order

fo-ren-sic *adj.* relating to a formal debate

fore-or-dain *v.* appoint advance; predestine

fore-see *v.* know or see beforehand **foreseeable** *adj.*

fore-sight *n.* capacity of foreseeing; concern for the future **forsighted** *adj.*

for-est *n.* tract of land covered with trees

forest ranger *n.* man in charge of protecting a public forest

fore-tell *v.* tell in advance; to predict

for-ev-er *adv.* for eternity; without end

fore-warn *v.* warn in advance

for-feit *n.* something taken away as punishment; a penalty **forfeitable** *adj.*

for-gath-er *v.* come together; to assemble

forge *n.* furnace to heat metals; a smithy *v.* give shape to; defraud

for-get *v.* lose the memory of -ful *adj.*

for-give *v.* pardon; to cease to feel resentment against

for-go *or* **fore-go** *v.* to give up or refrain from **forgoer** *n.*

fork *n.* eating utensil with prongs; division in a river or road

for-lorn *adj.* left in distress; hopeless; forsaken **forlornly** *adv.*

form *n.* contour of something; human body; manner determined by etiquette; fitness training; document

form *suff.* having the form or shape of; cuneiform

for-mal *adj.* adhering to convention; explicit; correct manners

for-mal-de-hyde *n.* colorless, gaseous chemical used as a disinfectant

for-mat *n.* style of a publication; basic design

for-ma-tion *n.* a given arrangement

for-ma-tive *adj.* having the power to form; pertaining to growth, or development

for-mer *adj.* previous; being the first of two persons mentioned or referred to

for-mer-ly *adv.* previously

for-mi-da-ble *adj.* extremely difficult; causing fear by size or strength **formidably** *adv.*

for-mu-la *n.* prescribed rules to be used; milk substitute for infants

for-mu-late *v.* state or express as a formula **formulation** *n.*

for-ni-ca-tion *n.* illicit sexual intercourse

for-sake *v.* abandon or renounce; to give up

for-sooth *adv.* in truth; certainly

for-swear *v.* renounce emphatically or upon oath; swear falsely; to perjure oneself

for-syth-i-a *n.* shrub with earlyblooming, bright, yellow flowers

fort *n.* fortified enclosure for defense against an enemy

forte *n.* activity one does with excellence; person's strong point

forth *adv.* out from seclusion; forward in order, place, or time

forth-with *adv.* at once; promptly

for-ti-fy *v.* provide physical strength; give courage to; enrich food with vitamins, etc.

for-ti-tude *n.* strength of mind; courage

fort-night *n.* period of two weeks **fortnightly** *adj. & adv.*

for-tress *n.* a fort

for-tu-i-tous *adj.* occurring by chance; lucky; fortunate

for-tu-nate *adj.* having good fortune

for-tune *n.* force that determines events; large amount of money

for-tune--tell-er *n.* person who predicts the future

for-ty *n.* number equal to four times ten

forty winks *n., Slang* short nap

fo-rum *n.* public market-place in ancient Rome where business is transacted; a judicial assembly

for-ward *adj.* toward a place or time in advance **forwardly** *adv.*

fos-sil *n.* remains of a past geologic age

fos-ter *v.* give parental care to; nurture

foul *adj.* spoiled or rotten; vulgar or obscene; dirty

found *v.* establish; to set up; melt metal and pour into a mold

foun-da-tion *n.* base of a building; make-up base

foun-dry *n.* place where metal is cast

fount *n.* a fountain; abundant source

foun-tain *n.* natural spring of water from the earth; artifically created spray of water

four-score *adj.* four times twenty; eighty

fourth *n.* gear in a motor vehicle

Fourth of July *n.* American Independence Day

fowl *n.* bird used as food or hunted as game

fox *n.* wild mammal; sly or crafty person

fox-hole *n.* shallow pit dug by a soldier to protect him from enemy fire

fox--trot *n.* ballroom dance

fox-y *adj.* sly or crafty; sharp

foy-er *n.* lobby of a hotel, theatre, etc.; entrance hall

fra-cas *n.* noisy quarrel or disturbance

frac-tion *n.* small part of; quantity less

than a whole number **fractional** *adj.*

frac-ture *n.* act of breaking; broken bone

frag-ile *adj.* easily broken; frail

frag-ment *n.* broken or detached part

fra-grant *adj.* having an agreeable sweet odor **frangrance** *n.*

frail *adj.* physically weak; fragile

frame *v.* enclosed border for a picture

frame-up *Slang* make someone appear guilty

fran-chise *n.* license to market a company's goods **franchiser** *n.*

fran-gi-ble *adj.* breakable; delicate **frangibility** *n.*

frank-furt-er *n.* smoked sausage made of beef or beef and pork

frank-in-cense *n.* aromatic gum resin used as incense

fran-tic *adj.* emotionally out of control with worry or fear **frantically** *adv.*

fra-ter-nal *adj.* pertaining to brothers **fraterrnalism** *n.*

frat-er-nize *v.* associate with others in a friendly way; mingle

frat-ri-cide *n.* killer of one's brother or sister **fratricidal** *adj.*

fraud *n.* deception for unlawful gain; imposter

fraud-u-lent *adj.* practicing fraud **fraudulently** *adv.*

fraught *adj.* accompanied by something specified

fray *n.* heated argument or dispute

fraz-zle *v., Slang* wear out; completely fatigue

freak *n.* seemingly capricious event; person with abnormalities; **freak out** experience hallucinations from drug use **freakish** *adj.*

freck-le *n.* brownish, suninduced spots on the skin

free *adj.* not imprisoned; costing nothing; under no obligation

free-bie *n.* something given or received with out charge

free-dom *n.* state of being free; independence

freeze *v.* become ice through loss of heat; set prices at a certain level

freight *n.* mode of shipping cargo; charge for shipping freight

freight-er *n.* ship for transporting cargo

fren-zy *n.* state of excitement or violent agitation

fre-quent *adj.* happening often or time after time

fres-co *n.* art of painting on moist plaster

fresh *adj.* newlymade, or obtained; not stale **freshness** *n.*

fresh-man *n.* first year student in college

fret *v.* anxious or irritated; ripple water **fretfully** *adv.*

fri-a-ble *adj.* easily crumbled; brittle **friableness** *n.*

fri-ar *n.* member of a Roman Catholic order

fric-as-see *n.* dish of meat or poultry in gravy

fric-tion *n.* rubbing one surface against another; a conflict or clash -al *adj.*

friend *n.* close personal companion **friendship** *n.*

frieze *n.* decorative band along a wall

frig-ate *n.* square-rigged warship

fright *n.* sudden alarm or fear

fright-en *v.* fill with fear; arousing fear **frighteningly** *adv.*

frig-id *adj.* very cold; sexually unresponsive **frigidity** *n.*

frill *n.* decorative ruffle; gathered border

fringe *n.* edging that consists of hanging threads, or loops

frisk *v.* skip or leap about playfully; to search someone for a concealed weapon by running the hands over the clothing quickly

frit-ter *v.* squander or waste little by little

friv-o-lous *adj.* trivial; insignificant; not serious; silly

frizz *v.* form into small, tight curls **frizziness** *n.*

fro *adv.* away from; back, as running to and fro

frock *n.* loosefitting robe; a robe worn by monks

frol-ic *n.* merriness; a playful, carefree occasion; playful

from *prep.* starting at a particular time or place; used to indicate a source; used to indicate differentiation, as knowing right from left

frond *n.* large leaf of a tropical fern, usually divided into smaller leaflets

front *n.* forward surface of an object or body; area or position located ahead

fron-tier *n.* part of an international border or the area adjacent to it; an unexplored area of knowledge or thought **frontiersman** *n.*

fron-tis-piece *n.* an illustration that usually precedes the title page of a book

frost *n.* feathery covering of minute ice crystals on a cold surface; icing on a cake **frostiness** *n.*

froth *n.* mass of bubbles on or in a liquid, resulting from agitation or fermentation; a salivary foam, as of an animal, resulting from disease

froth-i-ness n.

frou-frou n. rustling sound, as of silk; a frilly dress or decoration

frown v. contract the brow as in displeasure or concentration; to look on with distaste or disapproval

frow-zy adj. appearing unkempt

fro-zen adj. changed into, or made into ice; extremely cold, as a climate; immobilized or made rigid, as by fear; kept at a fixed level

fruc-tose n. sugar

fru-gal adj. economical; thrifty

fruit n., pl. **fruit** or **fruits** ripened, mature, seed-bearing part of a flowering plant, as a pod or berry; edible, fleshy plant part an apple or plum -**ful** adj.

fru-i-tion n. accomplishment of something worked for or desired; the state of bearing fruit

frump-y adj. unfashionable; dowdy **frumpiness** n.

frus-trate v. keep from attaining a goal or fulfilling a desire; to thwart

fry v. cook in hot fat or oil, especially over direct heat; n. dish of any fried food

fud-dy-dud-dy n., pl. **fuddy-duddies** an old-fashioned person

fuel n. combustible matter consumed to generate energy, such as wood, coal, or oil burned to generate heat; v. take in or supply with fuel; to stimulate, as an argument **fueler** n.

fu-gi-tive adj. fleeing or having fled, as from arrest, pursuit, etc. n. One who flees or tries to escape

ful-crum n., pl. **fulcrums** or **fulcra** point on which a lever turns

ful-fill v. convert into actuality; to effect; to carry out; to satisfy **fulfillment** n.

ful-mi-nate v. condemn severely; to explode

ful-some adj. offensively insincere **fulsomeness** n.

fum-ble v. to blunder; to mishandle a baseball or football; n. a fumbled ball

fume n., often **fumes** irritating smoke, gas, or vapor; v. to show or feel anger or distress

fu-mi-gate v. subject to fumes in order to exterminate vermin or insects -**gator** n.

fun n. enjoyment; amusement

func-tion n. characteristics or proper activity of a person or thing; specific occupation, duty, or role; an official ceremony

fund n. a sum of money reserved for a specific purpose; v. to furnish or accumulate a fund for

fun-da-men-tal adj. basic or essential; of major significance

fu-ner-al n. service performed in conjunction with the burial or cremation of a dead person

fun-gus n. **funguses** numerous sporebearing plants including mushrooms **fungal** adj.

fu-nic-u-lar n. a cable railway along which cable cars are drawn up a mountain counterbalancing one another

funk n. cowardly fright or panic; fear; a state of depression

funk-y adj., Slang an earthy quality that is characteristic of the blues -**iness** n.

fun-nel n. coneshaped utensil for pouring liquid

fur-be-low n. decorative ruffle on clothing

fur-bish v. make bright by rubbing; renovate

fu-ri-ous adj. extremely angry; fit of rage **furiously** adv.

furl v. roll up and secure something

fur-lough n. permission to be absent from duty

fur-nace n. device to produce intense heat

fur-nish v. outfit or equip with furniture **furnisher** n.

fur-ni-ture n. beds, lamps, chairs and tables, etc.

fu-ror n. violent anger; an uproar

fur-rier n. dealer in furs

fur-row n. long, narrow trench; deep wrinkle in the skin

fur-tive adj. done in secret; obtained underhandedly

fu-ry n. uncontrolled anger; turbulence

fuse n. electrical safety device; device to detonate explosives

fu-see n. friction match; signal flare

fus-se-lage n. central section of an airplane

fu-sil-lade n. discharge of a number of firearms

fu-sion n. act of melting together by heat

fuss v. argue; bother

fussy adj. giving close attention to details

fu-tile adj. ineffectual; serving no useful purpose; hopeless

fu-til-i-ty n. the state or quality of being futile

fu-ture n. time yet to come **future** adj.

fu-tur-is-tic adj. relating to the future

fuzz n. small particles of fibers that may sometime collect as a ball **fuzzy** adj.

fyke n. a long net bag that is kept open with hoops

G, g The seventh letter of the English alphabet.

gab v., Slang talk or chat idly

gab-ar-dine n. a firm cotton, wool, or rayon material, having a diagonal raised weave, used for suits or coats

gab-ble v. to speak rapidly or incoherently gabble n.

Gabriel n. a special messenger of God mentioned in the Bible

gad v. to wander about restlessly

gad-a-bout n., Slang person who seeks excitement

gad--fly n. a fly that bites or annoys cattle and horses; an irritating, critical, but often constructively provocative person.

gadg-et n., Slang small or tool for various jobs

gad-o-lin-i-um n. a metallic element, silvery-white in color, of the lanthanide series, symbolized by Gd

Gae-a n. in Greek mythology, the mother and wife of Uranus, the goddess of earth.

Geal n. one of the Celts of Scotland, Ireland, or the Isle of Man

gaff n. sharp iron hook used for landing fish

gaf-fer n. an old man

gag n. wadded cloth, forced into the mouth to prevent speach Slang practical joke

ga-ga adj. Slang crazy; silly

gage n. something, as a wadded cloth, forced into or over the mouth to prevent someone from speaking or crying out; an obstacle to or any restraint of free speech, such as by censorship; Slang a practical joke

gag-gle n. flock of geese

gai-e-ty n., pl. gaieties state of being happy; cheerfulness

gain v. to earn or acquire possession

gain-ful adj. producing profits

gain-say v. to deny; to contradict

gait n. a way or manner of moving on foot; one of the foot movements in which a horse steps or runs

gai-ter n. a covering, as of leather or canvas, that covers the leg and extends from the knee to the instep; an old-fashioned shoe with a high top and elastic sides

gal n., Slang a girl

ga-la n. festive celebration

ga-lac-tose n. the sugar typically occurring in lactose

gal-ax-y n., pl. galaxies Astron. very large cluster of stars

gale n., Meteor. very powerful wind

ga-le-na n. a metallic, dull gray mineral that is the principal or of lead

gall n., Physiol. bitter fluid secreted by the liver; bile

gal-lant adj. polite and attentive to women

gal-lant-ry n. nobility and bravery

gall-blad-der or gall bladder n. small sac under the right liver that stores bile

gal-le-on n. large sailing ship

gal-ler-y n., pl. -ries group of spectators; building that displays works of art

gal-ley n., pl. galleys a long medieval ship ;that was propelled by sails and oars; the long tray used bvy printers to hold set type; a printer's proof made from composed type, used to detect and correct errors

gal-li-nule n. a wading bird with dark iridescent plumage

gal-li-um n. a slivery metallic element used in semiconductor technology and as a component or various low-melting alloys, symbolized by Ga

gal-li-vant v. roam about in search of pleasure

gal-lon n. liquid measurement equal to 4 quarts

gal-lop n. horse's gait

gal-lows n. framework used for execution by hanging

gall-stone n., Pathol. small, stony mass that forms in the gall bladder

ga-lore adj. in great numbers

gal-va-nism n. electricity produced by chemical action

gal-va-nize v. to protect iron or steel with rust resistant zinc

gal-va-nom-e-ter n., Electr. apparatus that detects electric and its strength and direction

gam-bit n. an opening in chess where a piece is sacrificed

gam-ble v. to take a chance

gam-bol v. frolic, skip, or leap about in play

game n. contest having rules; animals or birds hunted for sport or food

gam-ete n., Biol. mature reproductive cells

gam-in n. homeless child

gam-mer n. elderly woman

gam-ut n. whole range or extent of anything

gan-der n. male goose Slang quick glance

gang n. group of persons who work together or socialize regularly gan-gling *adj.* tall and thin

gan-grene *n., Pathol.* the death and decay of tissue in the body

gang-ster *n.* member of a criminal gang

gap *n.* opening or wide crack

gape *v.* open the mouth wide

gar *n.* fish having a spearlike snout and elongated body

garb *n.* clothing

gar-bage *n.* food wastes; trash

gar-ble *v.* mix up or confuse

gar-den *n.* place for growing plants

gar-de-nia *n.* tropical shrub with fragrant white flowers

gar-gan-tu-an *adj.* of enormous size

gar-gle *v.* to cleanse or medicate the back of the mouth and throat

gar-ish *adj.* too showy and bright; gaudy

gar-land *n.* wreath of flowers or leaves

gar-lic *n.* plant having a strong odor, resembling an onion

gar-ment *n.* article of clothing

gar-ner *v.* gather and store

gar-net *n.* dark-red gemstone

gar-nish *v.* to add decoration

gar-ret *n.* room in an attic

gar-ri-son *n.* military post

gar-ter *n.* band worn to hold a stocking in place

gas *n., pl.* gases combustible mixture used as fuel; gasoline

gash *n.* long, deep cut

gas-ket *n., Mech.* seal to prevent the escape of fluid or gas

gas-o-hol *n.* fuel blended from unleaded gasoline and ethanol

gasp *v.* labored attempts to breathe

gas-tric *adj.* pertaining to the stomach

gas-tri-tis *n., Pathol.* inflammation of the stomach lining

gas-tron-o-my *n.* art of good eating

gate *n.* movable opening in a wall or fence

gath-er *v.* bring or come together into one place

gaud-y *adj.* too highly decorated for good taste

gauge *or* gage *n.* standard measurement

gaunt *adj.* thin in appearance

gaunt-let *or* gant-let *n.* challenge to fight

gauze *n.* loosely-woven material used for bandages

gav-el *n.* mallet used to call for order

ga-vi-al *n.* large crocodile

gawk *v.* to gape; to stare stupidly

gawk-y *adj.* Clumsy or awkward

gay *adj.* merry; happy

gaze *v.* to look steadily at something to stare

ga-zette *n.* newspaper

gear *n., Mech.* toothed wheel

gee-zer *n., Slang* an old man

geld *v.* to castrate

gem-ol-o-gy *or* gem-mol-o-gy *n.* study of gems

gen-der *n.* quality of being either male or female

gene *n., Biol.* means by which hereditary characteristics are given

ge-ne-al-o-gy *n., pl.* -ies record or study of ones ancestory

gen-er-al-ize *v.* draw a general conclusion from facts or observations

gen-er-al-i-za-tion *n.* something arrived at by generalizing

gen-er-ate *v.* cause to be; to produce

gen-er-a-tion *n.* group of individuals born about the same time

ge-ner-ic *adj.* relating to an entire class or group; general

gen-er-ous *adj.* sharing freely; abundant

gen-e-sis *n., pl.* -ses act or state of originating

ge-net-ic *adj.* pertaining to the development of something

gen-ial *adj.* cheerful, pleasant and good-humored

gen-i-tal *adj.* pertaining to the reproductive organs

genitals *pl.,n.* the external sexual organs

gen-i-tive *adj., Gram.* indicating origin, source, or possession

gen-ius *n., pl.* -ses exceptional intellectual ability a strong, natural talent

gen-o-cide *n.* systematic extermination of a race or cultural group

gen-teel *adj.* refined or well-bred

gen-tian *n.* annual or perennial plant

Gen-tile *n.* a Christian; non-Jew

gen-tle *adj.* not harsh, mild in manner

gen-tle-man *n.* man of noble birth and social position

gen-tle-wom-an *n.* woman of noble birth and social position

gen-try *n.* people of high social standing

gen-u-flect *v.* to bend down on one knee

gen-u-ine *adj.* real; not counterfeit

ge-o-cen-tric *adj.* relating to the earth's center

ge-og-ra-phy *n., pl.* -hies the scientific study of the earth's features and population

ge-om-e-try *n., pl.* ies mathematics dealing with lines, planes, and solids

ge-o-ther-mal *adj.* relating to the internal heat of the earth

ger-i-at-rics *pl., n.* medical study that deals with diseases and hygiene of old age

germ *n.* small cell from which a new organism may develop

ger-mane *adj.* relevant to what is being considered or discussed

germ cell *n.* egg or sperm cell

ger-mi-cide *n.* agent used to destroy or disease germs

ger-mi-nate *v.* to grow, develop, or sprout

gest *n.* notable deed or feat

ges-tic-u-late *v.* make expressive gestures

ges-ture *n.* bodily motion, especially with the hands in speaking

get *v.* to receive or come into the possession of

get-up *n.* an outfit; a costume

gey-ser *n.* natural spring that ejects hot water and steam

ghast-ly *adj.* horrible; terrifying

gher-kin *n.* very small pickle

ghet-to *n.* section of a city in which members of an ethnic group lives

ghost *n.* the spirit of a dead person which is believed to appear to or haunt living persons; a spirit

gib-ber *v.* to talk or chatter incoherently or unintelligibly

gib-ber-ish *n.* meaningless speech

gib-bet *n.* a gallows *v.* To execute by hanging on a gibbet

gib-bon *n.* a slender, long-armed Asian ape

gibe *v.* to ridicule or make taunting remarks giber *n.*

gib-let *n.*, *or* giblets the heart, liver, and gizzard of a fowl

gid-dy *adj.* affected by a reeling or whirling sensation; dizzy giddily *adv.*, giddiness *n.*

gift *n.* something that is given from one person to another

gifted *adj.* having a special ability; talented

gig *n.* a light, two-wheeled carriage drawn by one horse. *Naut.* A speedy, light rowboat

gi-gan-tic *adj.* of tremendous size; huge gigantically *adv.*

gig-gle *v.* to laugh in highpitched, repeated, short sounds giggler *n.*, giggly *adj.*

gig-o-lo *n.*, a man who is supported by a woman not his wife

gild *v.* to coat with a thin layer of gold; to brighten or adorn gilded *adj.*, gilding, gilder *n.*

gill *n.*, *Zool.* the organ, as of fishes and various other aquatic invertebrates, used for taking oxygen from water

gilt *adj.* covered with or of the color of gold

gim-crack *n.* a cheap and useless object of little or no value

gim-let *n.* a small, sharp tool with a bar handle and a pointed, spiral tip used for boring holes

gimp *n.*, *Slang* a person who walks with a limp; a cripple

gin *n.* an aromatic, clear, alcoholic liquor distilled from grain and flavored with juniper berries

gin-ger *n.* a tropical Asian plant with a pungent aromatic root, used in medicine and cooking

ginger ale *n.* an effervescent soft drink flavored with ginger

gin-ger-ly *adv.* doing something very cautiously

ging-ham *n.* a cotton fabric woven in solid colors and checks

gin-gi-vi-tis *n.*, *Pathol.* inflammation of the gums

gin rummy *n.* a variety of the card game rummy

gird *v.* to surround, encircle, or attach with or as if with a belt

gird-er *n.* a strong, horizontal beam, as of steel or wood

gir-dle *n.* a cord or belt worn around the waist; a supporting undergarment worn by women

girl *n.* a female child or infant; a young, unmarried woman

girth *n.* the circumference or distance around something

gis-mo *n.*, *Slang* a part or device whose name is unknown or forgotten

gist *n.* the central or main substance

give *v.* to make a present of; to bestow; donate or contribute; to apply

giv-en *adj.* bestowed; presented

giz-zard *n.* the second stomach in birds

gla-brous *adj.*, *Biol.* having no hair or down glabrousness *n.*

glacial epoch *Geol.* a portion of geological time when ice sheets covered much of the earth's surface

glad *adj.* displaying, experiencing, or affording joy and pleasure; being happy

glad-den *v.* to make glad

glade *n.* a clearing in a forest

glad-some *adj.* giving cheer

glam-or-ize *or* glam-our-ize *v.* to make glamorous

glam-our *or* glam-or *n.* alluring fascination or charm

glance *v.* to take a brief or quick look at something

gland *n.*, *Anat.* any of various body organs which excrete or secrete substances

glare v. to stare fiercely or angrily

glau-co-ma n., *Pathol.* a disease of the eye

glau-cous adj. yellowish green

gleam n. a momentary ray or beam of light

glean v. to collect or gather facts by patient effort -er n., -ings pl., n.

glee n. joy; merriment

glen n. a small, secluded valley

glib adj. spoken easily and fluently; superficial **glibly** adv., **glibness** n.

glide v. to pass or move smoothly with little or no effort **glidingly** adv.

glid-er n. one that glides; *Aeron.* an aircraft without an engine

glim-mer n. a faint suggestion; an indication; a dim unsteady light

glimpse n. a momentary look

glis-san-do n., pl. -di a rapid passing from one tone to another by a continuous change of pitch

glis-ten v. to shine softly as reflected by light

glitch n. a minor mishap or malfunction

glit-ter n. a brilliant sparkle

gloam-ing n. twilight

gloat v. to express, feel, or observe with great malicious pleasure or selfsatisfaction **gloater** n.

glob n. a drop of something

glob-al adj. spherical; involving the whole world **globalize** v.

globe n. a spherical object; anything that is perfectly rounded

glob-u-lin n., *Biochem.* any of a class of simple proteins found widely in blood, milk, tissue, muscle and plant seeds

gloom n. partial or total darkness **gloomily** adv., **gloominess** n.

glop n., *Slang* a messy mixture of food; something that is considered worthless

glo-ri-fy v. to worship and give glory to **glorification** n.

glo-ri-ous adj. magnificent -ly adv.

glory n., pl. -ies distinguished praise or honor

gloss n. the sheen or luster of a polished surface

glos-sa-ry n., pl. -ries a list of words and their meanings

glot-tis n., pl. -ises or -ides *Anat.* the opening or cleft between the vocal cords

glow v. to have a bright, warm, ruddy color

glow-er v. to look sullenly or angrily at; to glare

glox-in-i-a n. a tropical South American

plant

glu-cose n., *Chem.* a substance less sweet than cane sugar, found as dextrose in plants and animals and obtained by hydrolysis

glut v. to feed or supply beyond capacity. n. An overabundance

glu-ten n. a mixture of plant proteins that is used as an adhesive **glutenous** adj.

glut-ton n. someone who eats immoderately

glyc-er-ol n., *Chem.* a sweet, oily, syrupy liquid derived from fats and oils

gly-co-side n., *Chem.* any of a group of carbohydrates which, when decomposed, produce glucose or other sugar

gnarl n. a hard, protruding knot on a tree **gnarled** adj.

gnash v. to grind or strike the teeth together

gnat n. a small, winged insect, specially one that bites or stings

gnaw v. to bite or eat away with persistence **gnawer** n.

gnome n. in folklore, a dwarf-like creature

go v. to proceed or pass along; to leave; pass, as of time n. an attempt; a try

go--ahead n. permission; a signal to move ahead or proceed

goal n. a purpose

goat-ee n. a short, pointed beard on a man's chin

goat-skin n. the skin of a goat

gob n. a piece or lump of something

gob-ble v. to eat and swallow food greedily

gob-bler n. a male turkey

go--be-tween n. a person who acts as an agent between two parties

gob-let n. a drinking glass

gob-lin n. in folklore, an ugly, grotesque creature said to be mischievous and evil

god n. someone considered to be extremely important or valuable

God n. the Supreme Being

god-less adj. not recognizing a god **godlessness** n.

god-ly adj. filled with love for God.

god-send n. something received unexpectedly that is needed or wanted

go--get-ter n. an enterprising, aggressive person

gog-gle n., pl. -gles spectacles or eyeglasses to protect the eyes

go-ing n. the act of moving, leaving, or departing

goi-ter n., *Pathol.* any abnormal enlargement of the thyroid gland

goitrous *adj.*

gold *n.* a soft, yellow, metallic element that is highly ductile and resistant to oxidation

gold-en *adj.* made of or containing gold; bright yellow in color

gold-fish *n.* a reddish or brass-colored freshwater fish

Gol-go-tha *n.* the place near Jerusalem where Jesus was crucified; also known as Calvary

Go-li-ath *n.* in the Bible, a giant Philistine killed by David with a stone from a sling shot

gon-ad *n., Anat.* the male or female sex gland where the reproductive cells develop; an ovary or testis

gon-do-la *n.* a long, narrow, flat-bottomed boat

gong *n.* a heavy metal disk with a deep resonant tone

gon-o-coc-cus *n., pl.* -cocci the bacterium which causes gonorrhea **gonococcic** *adj.*

gon-or-rhe-a *n., Pathol.* a contagious venereal infection transmitted chiefly by sexual intercourse

goo *n.* any sticky substance

goo-ber *n., Regional* a peanut

good *adj.* having desirable or favorable qualities or characteristics; morally excellent **better, best** *adj.*

Good Book *n.* the Bible

good--by *or* **good--bye** *interj.* used to express farewell *n.* a farewell; a parting word

good--look-ing *adj.* handsome

good--na-tured *adj.* having an easygoing and pleasant disposition

good-ness *n.* the state or quality of being good

good-y *n., pl.* -ies something that is good to eat; a prissy person

goof *n., Slang* a mistake *v.* to blunder; to make a mistake

goof--off *n.* a person who shuns responsibility or work

goof-y *adj.* ridiculous; silly

gook *n., Slang* a slimy, sludgy, or dirty substance

goon *n., Slang* a thug or hoodlum hired to intimidate or injure someone

goose *n., pl.* **geese** a large water bird related to swans and ducks

go-pher *n.* a burrowing rodent with large cheek pouches

gore *v.* to stab or pierce *n.* blood that has been shed

gorge *n.* a deep, narrow ravine; deep or

violent disgust **gorger** *n.*

gor-geous *adj.* beautiful; dazzling

go-ril-la *n.* a large African jungle ape

gorse *n.* a spiny plant bearing fragrant yellow flowers

go-ry *adj.* covered or stained with blood; resembling gore

gos-hawk *n.* a large, shortwinged hawk formerly used in falconry

gos-ling *n.* a young goose

gos-pel *or* **Gos-pel** *n.* the teachings of Christ and the apostles

gos-sa-mer *n.* the fine film or strands of a spider's web floating in the air **gossamer** *adj.*

gos-sip *n.* idle, often malicious talk *v.* to spread or engage in gossip

got *v.* past tense of get

gour-mand *n.* a person who takes excessive pleasure in eating

gour-met *n.* someone who appreciates and understands fine food and drink

gout *n., Pathol.* a disease caused by a defect in metabolism and characterized by painful inflammation of the joints **gouty** *adj.*

gov-ern *v.* to guide, rule, or control by right or authority **governable** *adj.*

gov-ern-ment *n.* the authoritative administration of public policy and affairs of a nation, state or city -al *adj.*

gov-er-nor *n.* one who governs, as the elected chief executive of any state in the United States **governorship** *n.*

grab *v.* to snatch or take suddenly **grabber** *n.*, **grabby** *adj.*

gra-ben *n., Geol.* an elongated depression in the earth, caused by the downward faulting of a portion of the earth's crust

grace *n.* seemingly effortless beauty, ease, and charm of movement or form

gra-da-tion *n.* a gradual and orderly arrangement or progression according to quality, size, rank, or other value **gradational** *adj.*

grade *n.* a step or degree

gra-di-ent *n.* a slope or degree of inclination *Phys.* a rate of change in variable factors, as temperature or pressure

grad-u-al *adj.* moving or changing slowly by degrees -ly *adv.*, -ness *n.*

grad-u-ate *v.* to receive or be granted an academic diploma or degree upon completion of a course of study

grad-u-a-tion *n.* the state of graduating; a commencement ceremony

graf-fi-to *n., pl.* **graffiti** an inscription or drawing made on a public wall

gra-ham n. whole wheat flour

grail n. the legendary cup used by Christ at the Last Supper

grain n. a small, hard seed or kernel of cereal, wheat, or oats; the seeds or fruits of such plants as a group; texture; basic nature

grain alcohol n. ethanol

grain-y adj. having a granular texture **graininess** n.

gram n. a metric unit of mass and weight equal to 1/1000 kilogram and nearly equal to one cubic centimeter of water at its maximum density

gram-mar n. the study and description of the classes of words, their relations to each other, and their arrangement into sentences

gram molecule n., Chem. the quantity of a compound, expressed in grams, that is equal to the molecular weight of that compound

gran-a-ry n., pl. **ries** a building for storing threshed grain

grand adj. large in size, extent, or scope; magnificent

gran-deur n. the quality or condition of being grand

gran-dil-o-quent adj. speaking in or characterized by a pompous or bombastic style **grandiloquence** n.

gran-di-ose adj. impressive and grand; pretentiously pompous -ly adv.,

grand mal n., Pathol. a form of epilepsy characterized by severe convulsions and loss of consciousness

gran-ite n. a hard, coarsegrained igneous rock composed chiefly of quartz, mica, and orthoclase

gran-ite-ware n. ironware utensils coated with hard enamel

gran-ny or **gran-nie** n. a grandmother; an old woman

gra-no-la n. rolled oats mixed with dried fruit and seeds

grant v. to allow; to consent to **granter, grantor** n.

gran-u-lar adj. composed or seeming to be composed or containing grains or granules **granularity** n.

gran-u-late v. to make or form into granules or crystals -tion n.

gran-ule n. a very small grain or particle

graph n. a diagram representing the relationship between sets of things

graph-ic or **graph-i-cal** adj. describing in full detail

graph-ite n. a soft black form of carbon having a metallic luster and slippery texture, used in lead pencils, lubricants, paints, and coatings **graphitic** adj.

graph-ol-o-gy n. the study of handwriting for the purpose of analyzing **graphologist** n.

grap-nel n. a small anchor with several flukes at the end

grap-ple n. an instrument with iron claws used to fasten an enemy ship alongside for boarding -er n.

grasp v. to seize and grip firmly n. the power to seize and hold

grasp-ing adj. urgently desiring material possessions; greedy **graspingly** adv., **graspingness** n.

grass n. any of numerous plants having narrow leaves and jointed stems Slang Marijuana -iness n., -y adj.

grate v. to reduce, shred or pulverize by rubbing against a rough or sharp surface n. a rasping noise -er n., -ing adj.

grate n. a framework or bars placed over a window or other opening

grate-ful adj. thankful or appreciative for benefits or kindnesses **gratefully** adv.

grat-i-fy v. to give pleasure or satisfaction to **gratification** n.

grat-ing n. a grate

grat-is adv. & adj. free

grat-i-tude n. the state of appreciation and gratefulness

gra-tu-i-tous adj. given or obtained without payment; unjustified **gratuitously** adv.,

gra-tu-i-ty n., pl. -ies a gift given in return for a service rendered

gra-va-men n., pl. -mens or -mina in law, the part of an accusation or charge weighing most heavily against the accused

grave n. a burial place for a dead body adj. very serious or important in nature

grav-el n. loose rock fragments often with sand Pathol. the deposit of sandlike crystals that form in the kidneys

gra-vim-e-ter n. an implement for determining specific gravity **gravimetry** n.

grav-i-tate v. to be drawn as if by an irresistible force

grav-i-ta-tion n., Physics the force or attraction any two bodies exert towards each other -ive adj., -ally adv.

grav-i-ty n., pl. -ies the gravitational force mani-fested by the tendency of material bodies to fall toward the center of the earth

gray-ling n., pl. -ling or -lings any of several freshwater food and game fish with a small mouth and a large dorsal fin

gray matter *n.* the grayish-brown nerve tissue of the spinal cord and brain

graze *v.* to feed upon growing grasses or herbage

grease *n.* melted or soft animal fat *v.* to lubricate or coat with grease

great *adj.* very large in size or volume; very good or firstrate **greatly** *adv.*,

great-heart-ed *adj.* noble in spirit

greed *n.* selfish desire to acquire more than one needs or deserves

greed-y *adj.* excessively eager to acquire or gain something

green-er-y *n., pl.* -ies green foliage or plants

green-eyed *adj.* jealous

green thumb *n.* a special skill for making plants thrive

greet *v.* to address someone in a friendly way; to welcome **greeter** *n.*

greet-ing *n.* a word of salutation.

gre-gar-i-ous *adj.* habitually associating with others as in groups, flocks, or herds; sociable

grem-lin *n.* a mischievous elf

gre-nade *n.* a small explosive device detonated by a fuse and thrown by hand or projected from a rifle

grew *v.* past tense of grow

grid *n.* an arrangement of regularly spaced bars

grid-dle *n.* a flat pan used for cooking

grid-i-ron *n.* a metal framework used for broiling meat, fish, and other foods; a football field

grief *n.* deep sadness or mental distress caused by a loss

griev-ance *n.* a real or imagined wrong which is regarded as cause for complaint or resentment

grieve *v.* to cause, or feel sorrow

grille *or* **grill** *n.* a grating with open metalwork

grim *adj.* stern or forbidding in appearance or character; gloomy; dismal **grimly** *adv.*, **grimness** *n.*

grim-ace *n.* a facial expression of pain, disgust

grime *n.* dirt, especially soot clinging to or coating a surface **griminess** *n.*, **grimy** *adj.*

grin *v.* to smile broadly

grind *v.* to reduce to fine particles; to sharpen; *n.* a person who works hard

grip *n.* a firm hold; a grasp; the ability to seize or maintain a hold

gripe *v.* to cause sharp pain or cramps in the bowels; to anger

grippe *n.* influenza **grippy** *adj.*

gris-ly *adj.* ghastly; gruesome

gris-tle *n.* cartilage of meat

grit *n.* small, rough granules; having great courage and fortitude **gritty** *adj.*

grits *pl., n.* coarsely ground hominy; coarse meal

griz-zle *v.* to become gray

gro-cer *n.* a storekeeper who deals in various household supplies

grog-gy *adj.* dazed, weak, or not fully conscious, as from a blow **groggily** *adv.*

groom *n.* a person hired to tend horses; a stableman; a bridegroom

gro-tesque *adj.* incongruous or ludicrous in appearance; bizarre; outlandish

grot-to *n., pl.* -toes *or* -tos a cave or cave-like structure

grouch *n.* an habitually irritable or complaining person **grouchily** *adv.*,

ground *n.* the surface of the earth

ground *v.* past tense of grind

ground hog *n.* a woodchuck

ground-less *adj.* without foundation or basis

group *n.* a collection or assemblage of people, or things

grov-el *v.* to lie or crawl face downward, as in fear; to act with abject humility

grow *v.* to increase in size, develop, and reach maturity; to expand; to increase **grower** *n.*

grub *v.* to dig up by the roots; to lead a dreary existence

grub-by *adj.* sloppy, unkempt

grudge *n.* a feeling of ill will, rancor, or deep resentment

gru-el *n.* a thin liquid made by boiling meal in water or milk

gru-el-ing *or* **gru-el-ling** *adj.* extremely tiring **gruelingly** *adv.*

grue-some *adj.* causing horror or fright **gruesomely** *adv.*,

gruff *adj.* brusque and rough in manner; harsh in sound; hoarse **gruffly** *adv.*, **gruffness** *n.*

grum-ble *v.* to complain in low, throaty sounds; to growl **grumbler** *n.*

grump-y *adj.* irritable and moody; ill tempered

grun-gy *adj., Slang* dirty, run-down, or inferior in condition

grunt *n.* the deep, guttural sound of a hog

guar-an-tee *n.* the promise or assurance of the durability or quality of a product; something held or given as a pledge or security

guar-an-ty *n., pl.* -ies a pledge or promise

to be responsible for the debt, duty, or contract of another person

guard v. to watch over or shield from danger or harm; to keep watch

guard-i-an n. one who is legally assigned responsibility for the care of the person unable to be do for himself **guardianship** n.

gub-ba v., *Slang* to tickle the neck area

guess v. to make a judgment or form an opinion on uncertain or incomplete knowledge

guest n. one who is the recipient of hospitality from another

guf-faw n. a loud burst of laughter **guffaw** v.

guid-ance n. the act, process, or result of guiding

guide n. one who leads or directs another **guider** n.

guilt n. the condition of having committed a crime or wrongdoing; the feeling of responsibility for having done something wrong

gul-let n., *Pathol.* the passage from the mouth to the stomach; esophagus; the throat

gul-li-ble adj. easily cheated

gul-ly n., pl. -ies a ditch cut in the earth by running water

gump-tion n., *Slang* boldness; initiative; enterprise

gust n. a sudden, violent rush of wind or air; a sudden outburst **gustily** adv., **gusty** adj.

gus-ta-to-ry adj. of or pertaining to the sense of taste

gus-to n. hearty enjoyment

gut n. the alimentary canal or part of it v. to disembowel guts bowels; entrails

guts-y n., *Slang* courageous

guy n., *Slang* a man; a fellow

gym-na-si-um n., pl. -ums or -sia a building equipped for indoor sports

gy-ne-col-o-gy n. the branch of medicine dealing with the female reproductive organs **gynecological**,

gyp v., *Informal* to swindle, cheat, or defraud n. a fraud **gypper** n.

gy-rate v. to rotate or revolve around a fixed point or axis adj. coiled or winding about **gyratory** adj.

gy-ro n. a gyroscope or gyrocompass

gy-ro-scope n. a spinning wheel or disk whose spin axis maintains its angular orientation when not subjected to external torques

gy-ro-sta-bi-liz-er n. a gyroscopic instrument designed to reduce the rolling motion of ships

H, h The eighth letter of the English alphabet.

ha-be-as cor-pus n. in law, a writ commanding a person to appear before a judge or court for the purpose of releasing that person from unlawful detention or restraint

hab-er-dash-er n. a person who deals in men's clothing and men's furnishings

ha-bil-i-ment n. clothing characteristic of an office, rank, or occasion

hab-it n. involuntary pattern of behavior acquired by frequent repetition

hab-it-a-ble adj. suitable for habitation **habitably** adv.

hab-i-tat n. the region in which an animal or plant lives or grows

hab-i-ta-tion n. a place of residence

hab-it--form-ing adj. producing physiological addiction

ha-bit-u-al adj. practicing by or acting according to havit; resorted to on a regular basis; regular

ha-ci-en-da n. a large estate or ranch in Spanish speaking countries

hack v. to cut with repeated irregular blows; to manage ;successfully; n. a tool used for hacking; taxi driver

hack-ney n. a horse of medium size for ordinary driving or riding

hack-neyed adj. trite

hack-saw n. a saw in a narrow frame for cutting metal

had-dock n. a food fish

had-n't cont. had not

haft n. a handle of a weapon or tool

hag n. a malicious, ugly old woman; a witch **haggish** adj.

hag-gard wornout, exhausted, and gaunt look, as from hunger or fatigue

hag-gle v. to argue or bargain on price or terms **haggler** n.

hag-i-og-ra-phy n., pl. **hagiographies** biography of the lives of saints or revered persons

hai-ku n. an unrhymed Japanese verse form with three short lines

hail n. precipitation of small, hard lumps of ice and snow; a hailstone; an exclamation, greeting, acclamation

hake n. a marine food fish related to the cod

hal-berd n. a medieval weapon used in the 15th and 16th centuries

hal-cy-on adj. calm and tranquil; peaceful; prosperous

hale adj. healthy and robust; free from defect v. to compel to go **haleness** n.

half n., pl. **halves** one of two equal parts

into which a thing is divisible

half-wit *n.* a mentally disturbed person

hal-ite *n.* large crystal or masses of salt; salt rock

hal-i-to-sis *n.* a condition of having bad breath

hal-le-lu-jah *interj.* used to express joy, praise, or jubilation **hallelujah** *n.*

hal-low *v.* to sanctify; to make holy; to honor

hal-lu-ci-na-tion *n.* an illusion of seeing something that is nonexistent **hallucinate** *v.*

hal-lu-ci-no-gen *n.* a drug or other agent which causes hallucination **hallucinogenic** *adj.*

ha-lo *n.* a ring of colored light surrounding the head; an aura of glory

hal-o-gen *n.* any of the group of nonmentallic elements including flourine, chlorine, bromine, iodine, and astatine **halogenous** *adj.*

hal-ter *n.* a rope or strap for leading or tying an animal

halve *v.* to divide into two equal parts

hal-yard *n.* a rope for hoisting or lowering a sail, flag, or yard

ham *n.* the meat of a hog's thigh

ham-let *n.* a small rural village or town

ham-mer *n.* a hand tool with a heavy head used to drive or strike forcefully

ham-mock *n.* a hanging bed or couch of fabric or heavy netting

ham-per *v.* to interfere with movement or progress of

ham-ster *n.* any of various rodents with large cheek pouches and a short tail

ham-string *n.* either of two tendons located at the back of the human knee

hand *n.* the part of the arm below the wrist, consisting of the palm, four fingers and a thumb

hand-gun *n.* a gun that can be held and fired with one hand

hand-i-craft *or* **hand-craft** *n.* skill and expertise in working with the hands

han-dle *v.* to touch, pick up, or hold with the hands

hand-made *adj.* made by hand or by a hand process

hand-maid *or* **hand-maid-en** *n.* a female maid or personal servant

hand-y *adj.* easy to use or reach; helpful or useful

hang *v.* to be attached to from above and unsupported from below

han-gar *n.* a building for housing aircraft

han-ger *n.* a device from which something may be hung or on which something hangs

hang-up *n.,* *Slang* a psychological or emotional problem; an obstacle

hank *n.* a loop, coil, or piece of hair, thread, or yarn

han-ker *v.* to have a yearning or craving for something

Ha-nuk-kah *or* **Ha-nu-kah** *n.* an eight-day Jewish holiday remembering the rededication of the Temple in Jerusalem

hao-le *n.* a person who is not of the Hawaiian race, especially a Caucasian

hap-haz-ard *adj.* occurring by accident; happening by chance or at random

hap-less *adj.* unfortunate; unlucky **haplessly** *adv.*

hap-pen *v.* to occur or come to pass; to take place; to discover by chance

hap-pen-ing *n.* a spontaneous event or performance

happen-stance *n.* an event occurring by chance

hap-py *adj.* enjoying contentment and well-being; glad, joyous, satisfied or pleased **happiness** *n.*

ha-rass *v.* to disturb or annoy constantly; to torment persistently **harassment** *n.*

har-bin-ger *n.* a person that initiates or pioneers a major change

har-bor *n.* a place of refuge or shelter; a bay or cove; an anchorage for ships

hard *adj.* difficult to perform, endure, or comprehend; solid in texture or substance **hardness** *n.*

hard copy *n.* in computer science, the printed information or data from a computer

hard disk *n.* in computer science, magnetic storage consisting of a rigid disk of aluminum coated with a magnetic recording substance; contained within a removable cartridge or mounted in the hard disk of a microcomputer

hard-en *v.* to make or become hard or harder

har-di-hood *n.* resolute courage; audacious boldness; vitality; vigor

hard-ly *adj.,* *Slang* very little; almost certainly not. *adv.* forcefully; painfully

hard-ship *n.* a painful, difficult condition

hard-tack *n.* a hard, crackerlike biscuit made with flour and water

hard-ware *n.* manufactured machine parts, such as tools and utensils; the mechanical components of a computer installation

har-dy *adj.* bold and robust

hark *v.* to listen closely

har-le-quin *n.* a jester; a clown

har-lot *n.* a prostitute

harm *n.* emotional or physical damage or injury. *v.* to cause harm to **harmful** *adj.*

harm-less *adj.* without harm

har-mon-ic *adj.* relating to musical harmony

har-mo-ni-ous *adj.* pleasing to the ear **harmoniously** *adv.*

har-mo-ny *n., pl.* -**ies** complete agreement, as of feeling or opinion; pleasing sounds

har-ness *n.* the working gear, other than a yoke, of a horse or other draft animal **harnesser** *n.*

harp *n.* a musical instrument having a triangular upright frame with strings plucked with the fingers

har-poon *n.* a barbed spear used in hunting whales and large fish **harpoon** *v.*

harp-si-chord *n.* a piano-like instrument whose strings are plucked by using quills or leather points **harpsichordist** *n.*

har-py *n., pl.* **harpies** a vicious woman; a predatory person

har-ri-dan *n.* a mean, hateful old woman

har-ri-er *n.* a slender, narrow-winged hawk that preys on small animals

har-row *n.* a tool with sharp teeth for breaking up and smoothing soil

har-ry *v.* to harass

harsh *adj.* disagreeable; extremely severe **harshly** *adv.*

hart *n.* a fully grown male deer after it has passed its fifth year

har-um-scar-um *adj.* reckless

har-vest *n.* the process or act of gathering a crop

hash-ish *n.* the leaves and flowering tops of the hemp plant

has-sle *n., Slang* a quarrel or argument

has-sock *n.* a firm upholstered cushion used as a footstool

haste *n.* speed; swiftness of motion or action **hasten** *v.*

hasty *adj.* rapid; swift; made or done with excessive speed **hastily** *adv.*

hat *n.* a covering for the head with a crown and brim

hatch *n.* a small opening or door, as in a ship's deck

hatch-et *n.* a small ax with a short handle

hate *v.* to feel hostility or animosity toward; to dislike intensely

haugh-ty *adj.* arrogantly proud; disdainful

haul *v.* to pull or draw with force; to move or transport

haunch *n.* the hip; the buttock and upper thigh of a human or animal

haunt *v.* to appear to or visit as a ghost or spirit; to linger in the mind **haunting** *adj.*

haut-bois *or* **haut-boy** *n.* an oboe

hau-teur *n.* a disdainful arrogance

have *v.* to hold or own, as a possession or as property **have** to need to; must **have had** it suffered or endured all that one can tolerate

hav-oc *n.* mass confusion; wide-spread destruction

haw *n.* a hesitating sound made by a speaker who is groping for words

haw-ser *n.* a heavy cable or rope for towing or securing a ship

hay *n.* alfalfa or grass that has been cut and dried for animal food

hay-wire *adj., Slang* broken; emotionally out of control

haz-ard *n.* a risk; chance; an accident or source of danger **hazardous** *adj.*

ha-zel-nut *n.* the edible nut of the hazel

haz-y *adj.* lacking clarity; vague **hazily** *adv.*, **haziness** *n.*

head *n.* the upper part of a human or animal body, containing the brain

head-ing *n.* a title or caption that acts as a front, beginning, or upper part of anything

head-set *n.* a pair of headphones

head-strong *adj.* not easily restrained; obstinate

heal *v.* to restore to good health; to mend **healable** *adj.*, **healer** *n.*

health *n.* the overall sound condition or function of a living organism at a particular time **healthful** *adj.*

heap *n.* a haphazard assortment of things

hear *v.* to perceive by the ear; to listen with careful attention

hear-ing *n.* one of the five senses; the range by which sound can be heard

heark-en *v.* to listen carefully

hear-say *n.* information heard from another; common talk; rumor

heart *n.* the hollow, primary muscular organ of vertebrates which circulates blood throughout the body; the emotional center, such as in love, hate, consideration, or compassion

heart-ache *n.* emotional grief; sorrow; mental anguish

heart attack *n.* an acute malfunction or interrupted heart function

hearth *n.* the floor of a fireplace, furnace

heart-y *adj.* marked by exuberant warmth; full of vigor; nourishing

heat *n.* a quality of being hot or warm; a degree of warmth; depth of feeling

hea-then *n.* a person or nation that does

not recognize the God of Christianity, Judaism, or Islam; in the Old Testament

heave v. to raise or lift, especially forcibly

heav-en n. the sky; the region above and around the earth; the abode of God, the angels, and the blessed souls of the dead **heavenly** adj.

heav-y adj. of great weight; very thick or dense

heck-le v. to badger or annoy, as with questions, comments, or gibes **heckler** n.

hec-tic adj. intensely active, rushed, or excited

he'd conj. he had; he would

he-don-ism n. the doctrine devoted to the pursuit of pleasure

heed v. to pay attention; to take notice of something

heft n., Slang weight; bulk. v. to gauge or estimate the weight of by lifting

heft-y adj. bulky; heavy; sizable

he-gem-o-ny n. dominance or leadership, as of one country over another

he-gi-ra n. a journey or departure to flee an undesirable situation

heif-er n. a young cow, particularly one that has not produced a calf

height n. the quality of being high; the highest or most advanced point

Heim-lich maneuver n. an emergency maneuver used to dislodge food from a choking person's throat; the closed fist is placed below the rib cage and pressed inward to force air from the lungs upward

hei-nous adj. extremely wicked; hateful or shockingly wicked

heir n. a person who inherits another's property or title

heist v., Slang to take from; to steal n. a robbery

hel-i-cal adj. of or pertaining to the shape of a helix

hel-i-con n. a large, circular tuba that encircles the player's shoulder

hel-i-cop-ter n. an aircraft propelled by rotors which can take off vertically

he-li-um n. an extremely light, nonflammable, odorless, gaseous element, symbolized by He

hell or **Hell** n. the abode of the dead souls condemned to eternal punishment

he'll contr. he will

helm n. a wheel or steering apparatus for a ship

hel-met n. a protective covering for the head made of metal, leather, or plastic

helms-man n. one who guides a ship

help v. to assist or aid. n. Assistance; relief; one hired to help **helper** n., **helpful** adj.

hel-ter--skel-ter adv. in a confused or hurried manner; in an aimless way adj. rushed and confused

helve n. a handle on a tool such as an axe or hatchet

he--man n. Slang a man marked by strength; a muscular man

he-ma-tol-o-gy n. the branch of biological science that deals with blood and blood-generating organs **hematologist** n.

hem-i-sphere n. a half sphere that is divided by a plane passing through its center

he-mo-glo-bin n. the respiratory pigment in the red blood cells of vertebrates containing iron and carrying oxygen to body tissues

he-mo-phil-i-a n., Pathol. an inherited blood disease characterized by severe, protracted, sometimes spontaneous bleeding

hem-or-rhage n. bleeding, especially excessive bleeding **hemorrhage** v.

hem-or-rhoid n., Pathol. a painful mass of dilated veins in swollen anal tissue

he-mo-stat n. an agent that stops bleeding; a clamp-like instrument for preventing or reducing bleeding

hen n. a mature female bird

hence-forth, hence-for-ward adv. from this time on

hep-a-rin n., Biochem a substance found especially in liver tissue having the power to slow or prevent blood clotting

her-ald n. a person who announces important news

her-ald-ry n., pl. -ries the art or science of tracing genealogies

herb-age n. grass or vegetation used especially for grazing

her-bar-i-um n., pl. herbariums or herbaria a collection of dried plant specimens that are scientifically arranged for study

her-bi-cide n. a chemical agent used to kill weeds

her-bi-vore n. a herbivorous animal

her-biv-o-rous adj. feeding chiefly on plant life or vegetables -ly adv.

her-cu-le-an adj. of unusual size, force, or difficulty

here-af-ter adv. from now on; at some future time

here-by adv. by means or by virtue of

this

he-red-i-tar-y *adj.* passing or transmitted from an ancestor to a legal heir

he-red-i-ty *n.* the genetic transmission of physical traits from parents to offspring

here-in *adv.* in or into this place

here-of *adv.* relating to or in regard to this

her-e-sy *n., pl.* heresies a belief in conflict with orthodox religious beliefs

here-to *adv.* to this matter, proposition, or thing

here-with *adv.* together or along with this; hereby

her-maph-ro-dite *n.* a person having both male and female reproductive organs

her-met-ic *or* her-met-i-cal *adj.* tightly sealed against air and liquids
hermeticly *adv.*

her-mit *n.* a person who lives in seclusion, often for religious reasons

her-ni-a *n.* the protrusion of a bodily organ, as the intestine, through an abnormally weakened wall that usually surrounds it; a rupture hernial *adj.*

he-ro *n., pl.* heroes a figure in mythology and legend renowned for exceptional courage and fortitude

heroic couplet *n.* a verse consisting of two rhyming lines of iambic pentameter

her-o-in *n.* a highly addictive narcotic derivative of morphine

her-o-ine *n.* a woman of heroic character

her-o-ism *n.* heroic behavior

her-pes *n., Pathol.* a viral infection, characterized by small blisters on the skin or mucous membranes

her-pe-tol-o-gy *n.* the scientific study and treatment of reptiles and amphibians

her-ring *n.* a valuable food fish of the North Atlantic

hertz *n.* a unit of frequency equalling one cycle per second

he's *contr.* he has; he is

hes-i-tant *adj.* given to hesitating hesitancy *n.*

hes-i-tate *v.* to pause or to be slow before acting, speaking, or deciding hesitation *n.*

het-er-o-sex-u-al *adj.* of or having sexual desire to the opposite sex heterosexuality *n.*

hew *v.* to make or shape with or as if with an axe

hex *n.* one held to bring bad luck; a jinx. *v.* to put under an evil spell; to bewitch

hex-a-gon *n.* a polygon having six sides and six angles

hex-am-e-ter *n.* a line of verse containing six metrical feet

hi-a-tus *n.* a slight gap, break, or lapse in time from which something is missing

hi-ba-chi *n., pl.* hibachis a deep, portable charcoal grill used for cooking food

hi-ber-nate *v.* to pass the winter in an inactive, dormant, sleep-like state

hi-bis-cus *n.* a chiefly tropical shrub or tree

hick *n., Slang* a clumsy, unsophisticated country person

hide *v.* to put, or keep out of sight; to keep secret; to obscure from sight; *n.* the skin of an animal

hid-e-ous *adj.* physically repulsive; extremely ugly

hi-er-ar-chy *n., pl.* hierarchies an authoritative body or group of things or persons arranged in successive order

hi-er-o-glyph-ic *n.* a pictorial symbol representing an idea, object, or sound hieroglyphically *adv.*

high *adj.* extending upward; located at a distance above the ground

high-fa-lu-tin *adj.* pretentious or extravagant in manner or speech

high-ness *n.* the state of being high

high--pres-sure *adj., Informal* using insistent persuasive methods or tactics

high--spirit-ed *adj.* unbroken in spirit; proud

high--strung *adj.* very nervous and excitable

hi-lar-i-ous *adj.* boisterously happy or cheerful

hill *n.* a rounded, elevation of the earth's surface, smaller than a mountain
hilly *adj.*

hilt *n.* the handle of a dagger or sword to the hilt fully; completely; thoroughly

him *pron.* the objective case of the pronoun he

him-self *pron.* that identical male one; a form of the third person, singular masculine pronoun

hind *adj.* located at or toward the rear part; posterior

hin-der *v.* to interfere with the progress or action of

hind-most *adj.* farthest to the rear or back

hin-drance *n.* the act of hindering or state of being hindered

hind-sight *n.* comprehension or understanding of an event after it has happened

hip *n.* the part of the human body that projects outward below the waist and thigh; the hip joint

hip *n.* the bright, red seed case of a rose

hip *adj., Slang* said to be aware of or informed about current goings on

hip-pie *or* **hip-py** *n., pl.* **hippies** a young person who adopts unconventional dress and behavior

hip-po-pot-a-mus *n.* a large, aquatic mammal, native to Africa

hire *v.* to obtain the service of another for pay

his *adj.* the possessive case of the pronoun he

hir-sute *adj.* covered with hair

hiss *n.* a sound resembling a prolonged, sibilant sound, as that of

his-tol-o-gy *n., pl.* **-ies** the study of the minute structures of animal and plant tissues as seen through a microscope **histological** *adj.*

his-to-ri-an *n.* a person who specializes in the writing or study of history

his-tor-ic *adj.* significant or famous in history

his-to-ry *n., pl.* **-ries** past events, especially those involving human affairs

his-tri-on-ics *pl., n.* theatrical arts; feigned emotional display

hitch *v.* to fasten or tie temporarily, with a hook or knot *Slang* to unite in marriage

hith-er *adv.* to this place *adj.* situated toward this side

hith-er-to *adv.* up to now

hive *n.* a natural or man-made structure serving as a habitation for honeybees

hives *pl., n.* any of various allergic conditions marked by itching welts

hoarse *adj.* having a husky, gruff, or croaking voice

hoars-en *v.* to become or make hoarse

hoar-y *adj.* ancient; aged; gray or white with age

hoax *n.* a trick or deception

hob-by *n., pl.* **hobbies** an activity or interest undertaken for pleasure during one's leisure time

hob-gob-lin *n.* an imaginary cause of terror or dread

hob-nob *n.* to associate in a friendly manner

ho-bo *n., pl.* **hoboes** *or* **hobos** a vagrant who travels aimlessly about; a tramp

hod *n.* a V-shaped trough held over the shoulder to carry loads, as bricks or mortar

hodge-podge *n.* a jumbled mixture or collection

Hodg-kin's disease *n., Pathol.* a disease characterized by progressive enlargement of the lymph nodes, lymphoid tissue, and spleen, generally fatal

hoe *n.* a tool with a long handle and flat blade used for weeding

hoist *v.* to haul or raise up *n.* a machine used for raising large objects

hold *v.* to take and keep as in one's hand; to grasp

hold-ing *n.* property, as land, money, or stocks

hole *n.* a cavity or opening in a solid mass or body

ho-li-ness *n.* the state of being holy

hol-ler *v.* to shout loudly; to yell **holler** *n.*

hol-low *adj.* having a cavity or space within; concaved or sunken

hol-mi-um *n.* a metallic element of the rare-earth group, symbolized by Ho

hol-o-grah *n.* a handwritten document, as a lethoistered

ho-ly *adj.* regarded with or characterized by divine power

Holy Communion *n.* the Eucharist

Holy Ghost *n.* the third person of the Trinity

Holy Land *n.* palestine

Holy Spirit *n.* the Holy Ghost

hom-age *n.* great respect or honor

home *n.* the place where one resides; a place of origin

ho-me-op-a-thy *n.* a system of treating a disease with minute doses of medicines that produce the symptoms of the disease being treated

ho-me-o-sta-sis *n., Biol.* a state of equilibrium that occurs between different but related functions or elements **homeostatic** *adj.*

home-spun *adj.* something made, woven, or spun at home; anything that is simple and plain

home-y *or* **hom-y** *adj.* suggesting the coziness, intimacy, and comforts of home

hom-i-cide *n.* the killing of one person by another

hom-i-let-ic *n.* pertaining to the nature of a sermon

hom-i-ly *n., pl.* **homilies** a sermon, particularly one based on a Biblical text

ho-mo-ge-ne-ous *adj.* of the same or similar nature or kind

hom-o-graph *n.* a word that is identical to another in spelling, but different from it in origin and meaning

hom-o-nym *n.* a word that has the same sound and often the same spelling as another but a different meaning and origin

hom-o-phone *n.* one of two or more words that have the same sound but different spelling, origin, and meaning

Ho-mo sa-pi-ens *n.* the scientific name for the human race

ho-mo-sex-u-al *adj.* having sexual attraction or desire for persons of the same sex **homosexuality** *n.*

hon-cho *n., pl.* **honchos** the main person in charge; the boss; the manager

hon-est *adj.* not lying, cheating, or stealing; having or giving full worth or value

honey-suck-le *n.* a shrub or vine bearing a tubular, highly fragrant flower

hon-ky--tonk *n., Slang* a cheap bar or nightclub

hon-or *n.* high regard or respect; personal integrity; reputation; privilege

hon-or-ar-y *adj.* relating to an office or title bestowed as an honor, without the customary powers, duties, or salaries

hood *n.* a covering for the head and neck; cover of an automobile engine **hooded** *adj.*

hood *suff.* the quality or state of; sharing a given quality or state

hood-lum *n.* a young, tough, wild, or destructive fellow

hoo-doo *n.* voodoo *Slang* one who is thought to bring bad luck

hoo-ey *n., & interj., Slang* nonsense

hoof *n., pl.* **hooves** the horny covering of the foot in various mammals; *Slang* to dance; to walk; **on the hoof** alive; not butchered

hook *n.* a curved or bent piece of metal used to catch, drag, suspend, or fasten something

hook-er *n., Slang* a prostitute

hook-worm *n.* a parasitic intestinal worm with hooked mouth parts

hook-y *n., Slang* truant **to play hooky** to be out of school without permission

hoop-la *n., Slang* noise and excitement

hoose-gow *n., Slang* a jail

hoot *n.* the loud sound or cry of an owl **hooter** *n.,* **hoot** *v.*

hoot *n., Slang* a very insignificant amount **not give a hoot** not caring

hope *v.* to want or wish for something with a feeling of confident expectation **to hope against hope** to continue hoping for something even when it may be in vain **hopeful** *adj. & n.*

hop-per *n.* one that hops; a jumping insect; a receptacle in which coal, sand, grain, or other materials are held ready for discharge

horde *adj.* a large crowd

ho-ri-zon *n.* the line along which the earth and sky seem to meet

hor-mone *n., Physiol.* an internal secretion carried by the bloodstream to other parts of the body where it has a specific effect

hor-net *n.* any of various wasps which are capable inflicting a severe sting

horn-swog-gle *v.* to deceive

hor-o-scope *n.* a chart or diagram of the relative positions of the planets and signs of the zodiac at a certain time, as that of a person's birth; used to predict the future

hor-ri-ble *adj.* shocking; inducing or producing horror *Informal* excessive; inordinate **horribly** *adv.*

hor-rid *adj.* horrible

hor-ri-fy *v.* to cause a feeling of horror; to dismay or shock

hor-ror *n.* the painful, strong emotion caused by extreme dread, fear, or repugnance

horse sense *n., Slang* common sense

hor-ti-cul-ture *n.* the art or science of raising and tending fruits, vegetables, flowers, or ornamental plants **horticultural** *adj.*

ho-san-na *interj.* used to praise or glorify God

ho-sier-y *n.* stockings and socks

hos-pice *n.* a lodging for travelers or the needy

hos-pi-ta-ble *adj.* treating guests with warmth and generosity; receptive

hos-pi-tal *n.* an institution where the injured or sick receive medical, surgical, and emergency care

hos-pi-tal-i-ty *n.* hospitable treatment, disposition, or reception

host *n.* one who receives or entertains guests

hos-tage *n.* a person held as security that promises will be kept or terms met by a third party

host-ess *n.* a woman who entertains socially; a woman who greets patrons at a restaurant and escorts them to their tables

hos-tile *adj.* of or relating to an enemy; antagonistic

hos-til-i-ty *n., pl.* **-ies** a very deepseated opposition or hatred; war

hot *adj.* having heat that exceeds normal body temperature; electrically charged, as a hot wire *Slang* recently and or illegally obtained

hot air n., Slang idle talk

hot-el n. a business that provides lodging, meals, entertainment, and other services for the public

hot-foot v. to hasten

house n. a building that serves as living quarters for one or more families; home

how adv. in what manner or way; to what effect; in what condition or state; for what reason; with what meaning

how-dy interj. a word used to express a greeting

how-ev-er adv. in whatever manner or way conj. never-the-less

howl v. to utter a loud, sustained, plaintive sound, as the wolf howl-er n.

how-so-ev-er adv. to whatever degree or extent

hub n. the center of a wheel; the center of activity

hud-dle n. a crowd together

huff n. a fit of resentment or of ill temper

hug v. to embrace; to hold fast; to keep, cling, or stay close to

huge adj. of great quantity, size, or extent

hulk n. a heavy, bulky ship; the body of an old ship no longer fit for service

hulk-ing adj. unwieldy or awkward

hull n. the outer cover of a fruit or seed; the framework of a boat

hul-la-ba-loo n. a confused noise; a great uproar

hum v. to make a continuous low-pitched sound; to be busily active; to sing with the lips closed hummer n.

hu-man adj. of, relating to, or typical of man

hu-mane adj. to be marked by compassion, sympathy, or consideration for others

hum-ble adj. marked by meekness or modesty; unpretentious; lowly

hum-drum n., Slang bōring; dull

hu-mid adj. containing or characterized by a large amount of moisture; damp

hu-mid-i-ty n. a moderate amount of wetness in the air; dampness

hu-mil-i-ate v. to reduce one's dignity or pride to a lower position -tion n.

hu-mor n. something that is or has the ability to be comical or amusing

hunch n. a strong, intuitive feeling about a future event or result

hun-ger n. a strong need or desire for food

hurl v. to throw something with great force

hur-rah interj. used to express approval, pleasure, or exultation

hur-ri-cane n. a tropical cyclone with winds exceeding 74 miles per hour

hur-ry v. to move or cause to move with haste n. the act of hurrying

hurriedly adv.

hurt v. to experience or inflict with physical pain; to cause physical or emotional harm to; to damage -ful adj.

hus-band n. a man who is married

hush v. to make or become quiet; to calm; to keep secret n. a silence

hus-sy n., pl -ies a saucy or mischievous girl; a woman with doubtful morals

hus-tle v. to urge or move hurriedly along; to work busily and quickly Slang to make energetic efforts to solicit business or make money

hustle, hustler n.

hy-brid n. an offspring of two dissimilar plants or of two animals of different races, breeds, varieties, or species

hy-dro-gen n. a colorless, normally odorless, highly flammable gas that is the simplest and lightest of he elements, symbolized by H

hy-dro-pho-bi-a n. a fear of water hydrophobic adj.

hy-giene n. the science of the establishment and maintenance of good health and the prevention of disease

hy-men n. the thin membrane that partly closes the external vaginal orifice

hymn n. a song of praise giving thanks to God; a song of joy hymn v.

hype v., Slang to put on; to stimulate; to promote or publicize extravagantly

hy-per-ac-tive adj. abnormally active hyperactivity n.

hy-per-ten-sion n. the condition of abnormally high blood pressure

hy-phen n. a punctuation mark (-) used to show connection between two or more words hyphen v.

hyp-no-sis n., pl. hypnoses a state that resembles sleep but is brought on or induced by another person whose suggestions are accepted by the subject

hy-po-chon-dri-a n. a mental depression accompanied by imaginary physical ailments

hys-ter-ec-to-my n., pl. -ies surgery on a female which partially or completely removes the uterus

hys-ter-ia n. a psychological condition characterized by emotional excess and or unreasonable fear

hys-ter-i-cal adj. emotionally out of control hysterically adv.

I, i the ninth letter of the English alphabet; the Roman numeral for one

I *pron.* the person speaking or writing *n.* the self; the ego

I *or* **i** *abbr.* island; isle

IAAF *abbr.* International Amateur Athletic Federation

i-amb *or* **i-am-bus** *n.* a metrical foot consisting of a short or unstressed syllable followed by an accented syllable

i-at-ro-gen-ic *adj.* induced inadvertently by a physician or his treatment **iatrogenically** *adv.*

ib *or* **ibid** *abbr., L.* ibidem, in the same place

I band *n.* a type of isotropic band that is of the striated muscle fiber

Ibe-ri-an *n.* a person who is a member of the group of people who inhabited the Caucasus in Asia

i-bex *n.* an Old World mountain goat with long curved horns

i-bis *n.* a long-billed wading bird related to the heron and stork

ice *n.* solidly frozen water; a dessert of crushed ice which is flavored and sweetened *Informal* extreme coldness of manner *v.* to change into ice; to cool or chill; to cover with icing **icily** *adv.*, **iciness** *n.*, **icy** *adj.*

ice age *n.*, *Geol.* a time of widespread glaciation

ice bag *n.* a small, flexible, waterproof bag designed to hold ice, used on parts of the body

ice-berg *n.* a thick mass of floating ice separated from a glacier

ice-boat *n.* a vehicle with runners and usually a sail, used for sailing over ice; an icebreaker

ice-bound *adj.* obstructed or covered by ice

ice-box *n.* a structure designed for holding ice in which food and other perishables are stored

ice-break-er *n.* a sturdy vessel for breaking a path through icebound waters; a pier or dock apron for deflecting floating ice from the base of a pier or bridge

ice cap *n.* an extensive perennial covering of ice and snow that covers a large area of land

ice cream *n.* a smooth mixture of milk, cream, flavoring, sweeteners, and other ingredients, beaten and frozen

ice hock-ey *n.* a version of hockey played on ice

ice-house *n.* a building where ice is stored

ice-land *n.* an island country in the North Atlantic near the Arctic Circle **Icelander** *n.*, **Icelandic** *adj.*

ice milk *n.* a food similar to ice cream but made with skim milk

ice pack *n.* a large mass of floating, compacted ice; a folded bag filled with ice and applied to sore parts of the body

ice pick *n.* a pointed tool used for breaking ice into small pieces

ice skate *n.* shoe or boot with a runner fixed to it for skating on ice **ice-skate** *v.*

ich-thy-ol-o-gy *n.* the zoological study of fishes **ichthyologic, ichthyological** *adj.*, **ichthyologist** *n.*

i-ci-cle *n.* hanging spike of ice formed by dripping water that freezes

ic-ing *n.* sweet preparation for coating cakes and cookies

i-con *or* **i-kon** *n.* a sacred Christian pictorial representation of Jesus Christ, the Virgin Mary, or other sacred figures

i-con-o-clast *n.* one who opposes the use of sacred images; one who attacks traditional or cherished beliefs **iconoclasm** *n.*, **iconoclastic** *adj.*

id *n.*, *Psychol.* the unconscious part of the psyche associated with instinctual needs and drives

I'd *contr.* I had; I should; I would

i-de-a *n.* something existing in the mind; conception or thought; an opinion; a plan of action

i-de-al *n.* concept or imagined state of perfection; highly desirable; perfect; an ultimate objective; an honorable principle or motive *adj.* conforming to absolute excellence **ideally** *adv.*

i-de-al-ism *n.* the practice or tendency of seeing things in ideal form; pursuit of an ideal; a philosophical system believing that reality consists of ideas or perceptions **idealist** *n.*, **idealistic** *adj.*

i-de-al-ize *v.* to regard or represent as ideal **idealization** *n.*

i-dem *pron. & adj., L.* the same; used to indicate a previously mentioned reference

i-den-ti-cal *adj.* being the same; exactly equal or much alike; designating a twin or twins developed from the same ovum **identically** *adv.*

i-den-ti-fi-ca-tion *n.* the act of identifying; the state of being identified; a means of identity

i-den-ti-fy v. to recognize the identity of; to establish as the same or similar; to equate; to associate oneself closely with an individual or group **identifiable** adj.

i-den-ti-ty n., pl. **identities** the condition or state of being a specific person or thing and recognizable as such; the condition or fact of being the same as something else

id-e-o-gram or id-e-o-graph n. pictorial symbol used in a writing system to represent an idea or thing, as Chinese characters; a graphic symbol, as $ or %

i-de-ol-o-gy n., pl. **ideologies** body of ideas that influence a person, group, culture, or political party **ideological** adj.

ides pl., n. in the ancient Roman calendar, the fifteenth day of March, May, July, and October or the thirteenth day of the other months

id-i-o-cy n., pl. -cies a condition of an idiot

id-i-om n. form of expression having a meaning that is not readily understood from the meaning of its component words; the dialect of people or a region; a kind of language or vocabulary **idiomatic** adj., **idiomatically** adv.

id-i-o-syn-cra-sy n., pl. -sies peculiarity, as of behavior **idiosyncratic** adj., **idiosyncratically** adv.

id-i-ot n. a mentally deficient person; an extremely foolish or stupid person **idiotic** adj., **idiotically** adv.

i-dle adj. doing nothing; inactive; moving lazily; slowly; running at a slow speed or out of gear; unemployed or inactive **idleness, idler** n., **idly** adv.

i-dol n. a symbol or representation of a god or deity that is worshiped; a person or thing adored

i-dol-a-try n. the worship of idols; blind adoration; devotion; to admire **idolater** n., **idolatrous** adj.

i-dol-ize v. to admire with excessive admiration or devotion; to worship as an idol **idolization, idolizer** n.

i-dyll or i-dyl n. a poem or prose piece about country life; a scene, event, or condition of rural simplicity; a romantic interlude **idyllic** adj., **idyllically** adv.

-ie suff. little; dear

if-fy adj., Slang marked by unknown qualities or conditions

ig-loo n. dome-shaped Eskimo dwelling often made of blocks of snow

ig-ne-ous adj., Geol. relating to fire; formed by solidification from a molten magma

ig-nite v. to start or set a fire; to render luminous by heat

ig-ni-tion n. an act or action of igniting; a process or means for igniting the fuel mixture in an engine

ig-no-ble adj. dishonorable in character or purpose; not of noble rank **ignobly** adv.

ig-no-min-i-ous adj. marked by or characterized by shame or disgrace; dishonorable **ignominy** n.

ig-no-ra-mus n. totally ignorant person

ig-no-rant adj. lacking education or knowledge; not aware; lacking comprehension **ignorance** n.

ig-nore v. to pay no attention to; to reject **ignorable** adj.

i-gua-na n. large, dark-colored tropical American lizard

il-e-i-tis n. inflammation of the ileum

il-e-um n., pl. **ilea** the lower part of the small intestine between the jejunum and the large intestine

ilk n. sort; kind

ill adj. not healthy; sick; destructive in effect; harmful; hostile; unfriendly; not favorable; not up to standards adv. in an ill manner; with difficulty; scarcely n. evil; injury or harm; something causing suffering

I'll contr. I will; I shall

ill--ad-vised adj. done without careful thought or sufficient advice

ill--bred adj. ill-mannered; impolite; rude

il-le-gal adj. contrary to law or official rules **illegality** n., **illegally** adv.

il-leg-i-ble adj. not readable; not legible **illegibly** adv., **illegibility** n.

il-le-git-i-mate adj. against the law; unlawful; born out of wedlock **illegitimacy** n., **illegitimately** adv.

ill--fat-ed adj. destined for misfortune; doomed; unlucky

ill--fa-vored adj. unattractive; objectionable; offensive; unpleasant

ill--got-ten adj. obtained in an illegal or dishonest way

ill--hu-mored adj. irritable; cross **ill-humoredly** adv.

il-lic-it adj. not permitted by custom or law; unlawful **illicitly** adv.

il-lit-er-ate adj. unable to read and write; uneducated **illiteracy, illiterate** n.

ill--man-nered adj. lacking or showing a lack of good manners; rude

ill--na-tured *adj.* disagreeable or unpleasant disposition

ill-ness *n.* sickness; a state of being in poor health

il-log-i-cal *adj.* contrary to the principles of logic; not logical
illogicality *n.*, illogically *adv.*

ill--tem-pered *adj.* having or showing a cross temper or disposition

il-lu-mi-nate *v.* to give light; to make clear; to provide with understanding; to decorate with pictures or designs
illumination, illuminator *n.*

ill--use *v.* to treat cruelly or unjustly *n.* unjust treatment

il-lu-sion *n.* a misleading perception of reality; an overly optimistic idea or belief; misconception
illusive, illusory *adj.*

il-lus-trate *v.* to explain or clarify, especially by the use of examples; to clarify by serving as an example; to provide a publication with explanatory features
illustrator *n.*

il-lus-tra-tion *n.* the act of illustrating; an example or comparison used to illustrate

il-lus-tra-tive *adj.* serving to illustrate

il-lus-tri-ous *adj.* greatly celebrated; renowned illustriousness *n.*

ill will *n.* unfriendly or hostile feelings; malice

I'm *contr.* I am

im-age *n.* a representation of the form and features of someone or something; an optically formed representation of an object made by a mirror or lens; a mental picture of something imaginary *v.* to make a likeness of; to reflect; to depict vividly

im-age-ry *n.*, *pl.* -ies mental pictures; existing only in the imagination

im-ag-in-a-ble *adj.* capable of being imagined imaginably *adv.*

im-ag-i-nar-y *adj.* existing only in the imagination

im-ag-i-na-tion *n.* the power of forming mental images of unreal or absent objects; such power used creatively; resourcefulness
imaginative *adj.*, imaginatively *adv.*

im-ag-ine *v.* to form a mental picture or idea of; to suppose; to guess

i-ma-go *n.*, *pl.* -goes *or* -gines an insect in its sexually mature adult stage

i-mam *n.* a prayer leader of Islam; rulers that claim descent from Muhammad

im-bal-ance *n.* a lack of functional balance; defective coordination

im-be-cile *n.* a mentally deficient person

imbecile, imbecilic *adj.*, imbecility *n.*

im-bibe *v.* to drink; to take in imbiber *n.*

im-bri-cate *adj.* with edges over-lapping in a regular arrangement, as roof tiles or fish scales

im-bro-glio *n.*, *pl.* -glios a complicated situation or disagreement; a confused heap; a tangle

im-bue *v.* to saturate, as with a stain or dye

im-i-ta-ble *adj.* capable or worthy of imitation

im-i-tate *v.* to copy the actions or appearance of another; to adopt the style of; to duplicate; to appear like imitator *n.*

im-i-ta-tion *n.* an act of imitating; something copied from an original

im-mac-u-late *adj.* free from sin, stain, or fault; impeccably clean
immaculately *adv.*

im-ma-nent *adj.* existing within; restricted to the mind; subjective
immanence, immanency *n.*, -ly *adv.*

im-ma-te-ri-al *adj.* lacking material body or form; of no importance or relevance immaterially *adv.*,
immaterialness *n.*

im-ma-ture *adj.* not fully grown; undeveloped; suggesting a lack of maturity immaturely *adv.*, -ity *n.*

im-meas-ur-a-ble *adj.* not capable of being measured immeasurably *adv.*

im-me-di-a-cy *n.*, *pl.* -ies the quality of being immediate; directness; something of urgent importance

im-me-di-ate *adj.* acting or happening without an intervening object, agent, or cause; directly perceived; occurring at once; close in time, location, or relation immediately *adv.*

im-me-mo-ri-al *adj.* beyond the limits of memory, tradition, or records

im-mense *adj.* exceptionally large
immensely *adv.*, immensity *n.*

im-merse *v.* to put into a liquid; to baptize by submerging in water; to engross; to absorb
immersible *adj.*, immersion *n.*

im-mi-grant *n.* one who leaves his country to settle in another

im-mi-grate *v.* to leave one country and settle in another immigration *n.*

im-mi-nent *adj.* about to happen imminence *n.*

im-mo-bile *adj.* not moving or incapable of motion immobility *n.*

im-mo-bi-lize *v.* to render motionless immobilization *n.*

im-mod-er-ate *adj.* exceeding normal bounds **immoderately** *adv.*

im-mod-est *adj.* lacking modesty; indecent; boastful **immodestly** *adv.*, **immodesty** *n.*

im-mo-late *v.* to kill, as a sacrifice; to destroy completely **immolator** *n.*

im-mor-al *adj.* not moral **immorally** *adv.*

im-mo-ral-i-ty *n.*, *pl.* **-ies** lack of morality; an immoral act or practice

im-mor-tal *adj.* exempt from death; lasting forever, as in fame *n.* a person of lasting fame **immortality** *n.*, **immortally** *adv.*

im-mov-a-ble *adj.* not capable of moving or being moved **immovably** *adv.*

im-mune *adj.* not affected or responsive; resistant, as to a disease **immunity** *n.*

im-mu-nize *v.* to make immune **immunization** *n.*

im-mu-nol-o-gy *n.* the study of immunity to diseases **immunologic, immunological** *adj.*, **-ally** *adv.*

im-mu-no-sup-pres-sive *adj.* acting to suppress a natural immune response to an antigen

im-mure *v.* to confine by or as if by walls; to build into a wall

im-mu-ta-ble *adj.* unchanging or unchangeable **immutability** *n.*, **-bly** *adv.*

imp *n.* a mischievous child

im-pact *n.* a collision; the impetus or force produced by a collision; an initial, usually strong effect *v.* to pack firmly together; to strike or affect forcefully

im-pac-ted *adj.* wedged together at the broken ends, as an impacted bone; wedged inside the gum in such a way that normal eruption is prevented, as an impacted tooth

im-pac-tion *n.* something wedged in a part of the body

im-pair *v.* to diminish in strength, value, quantity, or quality **impairment** *n.*

im-pa-la *n.* large African antelope, the male of which has slender curved horns

im-pale *v.* to pierce with a sharp stake or point; to kill by piercing in this fashion **impalement** *n.*

im-pal-pa-ble *adj.* not perceptible to touch; not easily distinguished **impalpability** *n.*, **impalpably** *adv.*

im-part *v.* to grant; to bestow; to make known; to communicate

im-par-tial *adj.* not partial; unbiased **impartiality** *n.*, **impartially** *adv.*

im-pass-a-ble *adj.* impossible to travel over or across

im-passe *n.* a road or passage having no exit; a difficult situation with no apparent way out; a deadlock

im-pas-sioned *adj.* filled with passion

im-pas-sive *adj.* unemotional; showing no emotion; expressionless **impassively** *adv.*

im-pa-tient *adj.* unwilling to wait or tolerate delay; expressing or caused by irritation at having to wait; restlessly eager; intolerant **impatience** *n.*, **impatiently** *adv.*

im-peach *v.* to charge with misconduct in public office before a proper court of justice; to make an accusation against **impeachable** *adj.*, **impeachment** *n.*

im-pec-ca-ble *adj.* having no flaws; perfect; not capable of sin **impeccably** *adv.*

im-pe-cu-ni-ous *adj.* having no money **impecuniousness** *n.*

im-ped-ance *n.* a measure of the total opposition to the flow of an electric current, especially in an alternating current circuit

im-pede *v.* to obstruct or slow down the progress of

im-ped-i-ment *n.* one that stands in the way; something that impedes, especially an organic speech defect

im-ped-i-men-ta *pl.*, *n.* things that impede or encumber, such as baggage

im-pel *v.* to spur to action; to provoke; to drive forward; to propel **impeller** *n.*

im-pend *v.* to hover threateningly; to be about to happen

im-pen-e-tra-ble *adj.* not capable of being penetrated; not capable of being seen through or understood; unfathomable **impenetrability** *n.*, **-bly** *adv.*

im-pen-i-tent *adj.* not sorry; unrepentant **impenitence** *n.*

im-per-a-tive *adj.* expressing a command or request; empowered to command or control; compulsory **imperative** *n.*, **imperatively** *adv.*

im-per-cep-ti-ble *adj.* not perceptible by the mind or senses; extremely small or slight **imperceptibly** *adv.*

im-per-fect *adj.* not perfect; of or being a verb tense which shows an uncompleted or continuous action or condition *n.* the imperfect tense **imperfectly** *adv.*

im-per-fec-tion *n.* the quality or condition of being imperfect; a defect

im-pe-ri-al *adj.* of or relating to an empire or emperor; designating a nation or government having dependent

colonies; majestic; regal n. a pointed beard on the lower lip or chin
imperially adv.

im-pe-ri-al-ism n. the national policy or practice of acquiring foreign territories or establishing dominance over other nations
imperialist n., imperialistic adj.

imperial moth n. a large New World moth with yellow wings and brownish or purplish markings

im-per-il v. to put in peril; endanger

im-pe-ri-ous adj. commanding; domineering; urgent
imperiousness n., imperiously adv.

im-per-ish-a-ble adj. not perishable
imperishably adv.

im-per-ma-nent adj. not permanent; temporary impermanence n., -ly adv.

im-per-me-a-ble adj. not permeable
impermeability n., impermeably adv.

im-per-mis-si-ble adj. not permissible; not allowed

im-per-son-al adj. having no personal reference or connection; showing no emotion or personality -ly adv.

im-per-son-ate v. to assume the character or manner of impersonation, impersonator n.

im-per-ti-nent adj. overly bold or disrespectful; not pertinent; irrelevant
impertinence n., impertinently adv.

im-per-turb-a-ble adj. unshakably calm
imperturbability n., imperturbably adv.

im-per-vi-ous adj. incapable of being penetrated or affected
imperviously adv., imperviousness n.

im-pe-ti-go n. a contagious skin disease marked by pustules

im-pet-u-ous adj. marked by sudden action or emotion; impulsive
impetuosity n., impetuously adv.

im-pe-tus n. a driving force; an incitement; a stimulus; momentum

im-pi-e-ty n., pl. -ies the quality of being impious; irreverence

im-pinge v. to strike or collide; to impact; to encroach impingement n.

im-pi-ous adj. not pious; irreverent; disrespectful impiously adv.

imp-ish adj. mischievous
impishly adv., impishness n.

im-pla-ca-ble adj. not capable of being placated or appeased
implacability n., implacably adv.

im-plant v. to set in firmly; to fix in the mind; to insert surgically
implant, implantation n.

im-plau-si-ble adj. difficult to believe; unlikely -bility n., implausibly adv.

im-ple-ment n. a utensil or tool v. to put into effect; to carry out; to furnish with implements implementation n.

im-pli-cate v. to involve, especially in illegal activity; to imply

im-pli-ca-tion n. the act of implicating or state of being implicated; the act of implying; an indirect expression; something implied

im-plic-it adj. contained in the nature of someone or something but not readily apparent; understood but not directly expressed; complete; absolute

im-plode v. to collapse or burst violently inward implosion n.

im-plore v. to appeal urgently to
implorer n., imploringly adv.

im-ply v. to involve by logical necessity; to express indirectly; to suggest

im-po-lite adj. rude

im-pol-i-tic adj. not expedient; tactless

im-pon-der-a-ble adj. incapable of being weighed or evaluated precisely
imponderable n.

im-port v. to bring in goods from a foreign country for trade or sale; to mean; to signify; to be significant n. something imported; meaning; significance; importance importer n.

im-por-tance n. the quality of being important; significance

im-por-tant adj. likely to determine or influence events; significant; having fame or authority importantly adv.

im-por-ta-tion n. the act or business of importing goods; something imported

im-por-tu-nate adj. persistent in pressing demands or requests -ly adv.

im-por-tune v. to press with repeated requests importunity, importuner n.

im-pose v. to enact or apply as compulsory; to obtrude or force oneself or a burden on another; to take unfair advantage; to palm off imposition n.

im-pos-ing adj. awesome; impressive
imposingly adv.

im-pos-si-ble adj. not capable of existing or happening; unlikely to take place or be done; unacceptable; difficult to tolerate or deal with
impossibility n., impossibly adv.

im-post n. a tax or duty

im-pos-tor or im-pos-ter n. one who assumes a false identity or title for the purpose of deception

im-pos-ture n. deception by the assumption of a false identity

im-po-tent adj. without strength or vigor; having no power; ineffectual; incapable of sexual intercourse impotence,impotency n.,impotently adv.

im-pound v. to confine in or as if in a pound; to seize and keep in legal custody; to hold water, as in a reservoir impoundment n.

im-pov-er-ish v. to make poor; to deprive or be deprived of natural richness or fertility impoverishment n.

im-prac-ti-ca-ble adj. incapable of being done or put into practice impracticableness, impracticability n., impracticably adv.

im-prac-ti-cal adj. unwise to put into effect; unable to deal with practical or financial matters efficiently impracticality n.

im-pre-cise adj. not precise

im-preg-nate v. to make pregnant; to fertilize, as an ovum; to fill throughout; to saturate impregnation, -tor n.

im-pre-sa-ri-o n., pl. -os a theatrical manager or producer, especially the director of an opera company

im-press v. to apply or produce with pressure; to stamp or mark with or as if with pressure; to fix firmly in the mind; to affect strongly and usually favorably n. the act of impressing; a mark made by impressing; a stamp or seal for impressing impressible adj., impresser n.

im-pres-sion n. a mark or design made on a surface by pressure; an effect or feeling retained in the mind as a result of experience; an indistinct notion or recollection; a satiric or humorous imitation; the copies of a publication printed at one time

im-pres-sion-a-ble adj. easily influenced

im-pres-sion-ism n. a style of late nineteenth century painting in which the immediate appearance of scenes is depicted with unmixed primary colors applied in small strokes to simulate reflected light impressionist n., impressionistic adj.

im-pres-sive adj. making a strong impression; striking impressively adv., impressiveness n.

im-pri-ma-tur n. official permission to print or publish; authorization

im-print v. to make or impress a mark or design on a surface; to make or stamp a mark on; to fix firmly in the mind n. a mark or design made by imprinting; a lasting influence or effect; a publisher's name, often with the date and place of publication, printed at the bottom of a title page

im-pris-on v. to put in prison

imprisonment n.

im-prob-a-ble adj. not likely to occur or be true improbability n., -bly adv.

im-promp-tu adj. devised or performed without prior planning or preparation impromptu adv.

im-prop-er adj. unsuitable; indecorous; incorrect improperly adv.

improper fraction n. a fraction having a numerator larger than or the same as the denominator

im-pro-pri-e-ty n., pl. -ies the quality or state of being improper; an improper act or remark

im-prove v. to make or become better; to increase something's productivity or value improvable adj.

im-prove-ment n. the act or process of improving or the condition of being improved; a change that improves

im-prov-i-dent adj. not providing for the future improvidence n., improvidently adv.

im-pro-vise v. to make up, compose, or perform without preparation; to make from available materials improvisation, improviser, improvisator n., improvisatory, improvisatorial adj., -torially adv.

im-pru-dent adj. not prudent; unwise imprudence n., imprudently adv.

im-pu-dent adj. marked by rude boldness or disrespect impudence n., impudently adv.

im-pugn v. to attack as false; to cast doubt on

im-pulse n. a driving force or the motion produced by it; a sudden spontaneous urge; a motivating force; a general tendency Physiol. a transfer of energy from one neuron to another

im-pul-sive adj. acting on impulse rather than thought; resulting from impulse; uncalculated impulsively adv., impulsiveness n.

im-pu-ni-ty n. exemption from punishment

im-pure adj. not pure; unclean; unchaste or obscene; mixed with another substance; adulterated; deriving from more than one source or style impurely adv., impurity n.

im-pute v. to attribute something as a mistake, to another; to charge imputation n.

in abbr. inch

in ab-sen-tia adv. in the absence of

in-ac-ces-si-ble adj. not accessible inaccessibility n., inaccessibly adv.

in-ac-tive adj. not active or inclined to

be active; out of current use or service
inactively *adv.*, **inactivity, -ness** *n.*

in-ad-e-quate *adj.* not adequate
inadequacy *n.*, **inadequately** *adv.*

in-ad-ver-tent *adj.* unintentional; accidental; inattentive
inadvertently *adv.*

in-al-ien-a-ble *adj.* not capable of being given up or transferred
inalienably *adv.*, **inalienability** *n.*

in-ane *adj.* without sense or substance
inanely *adv.*, **inanity** *n.*

in-an-i-mate *adj.* not having the qualities of life; not animated
inanimately *adv.*, **inanimateness** *n.*

in-a-ni-tion *n.* exhaustion, especially from malnourishment

in-ap-pre-cia-ble *adj.* too slight to be significant **inappreciably** *adv.*

in-ar-tic-u-late *adj.* not uttering or forming intelligible words or syllables; unable to speak; speechless; unable to speak clearly or effectively; unexpressed **inarticulately** *adv.*, **inarticulateness** *n.*

in-as-much as *conj.* because of the fact that; since

in-au-gu-ral *adj.* of or for an inauguration

in-au-gu-rate *v.* to put into office with a formal ceremony; to begin officially **inauguration, inaugurator** *n.*

in--be-tween *adj.* intermediate *n.* an intermediate or intermediary
in between *adv. & prep.* between

in-board *adj.* within a ship's hull; close to or near the fuselage of an aircraft **inboard** *adv.*

in-born *adj.* possessed at birth; natural; hereditary

in-bound *adj.* incoming

in-breed *v.* to produce by repeatedly breeding closely related individuals

inc *or* **Inc** *abbr.* income; increase; incorporated

In-ca *n.*, *pl.* **-ca** *or* **-cas** an Indian people who ruled Peru before the Spanish conquest in the sixteenth century **Incan** *adj.*

in-cal-cu-la-ble *adj.* not calculable; indeterminate; unpredictable; very large **incalculably** *adv.*

in-can-des-cent *adj.* giving off visible light when heated; shining brightly; ardently emotional or intense **incandescence** *n.*

incandescent lamp *n.* a lamp in which a filament is heated to incandescence by an electric current

in-can-ta-tion *n.* a recitation of magic charms or spells; a magic formula for chanting or reciting

in-ca-pac-i-tate *v.* to render incapable; to disable; in law, to disqualify **incapacitation** *n.*

in-ca-pac-i-ty *n.*, *pl.* **-ies** inadequate ability or strength; a defect; in law, a disqualification

in-car-cer-ate *v.* to place in jail **incarceration** *n.*

in-car-na-tion *n.* the act of incarnating or state of being incarnated; the embodiment of God in the human form of Jesus; one regarded as personifying a given abstract quality or idea

in-cen-di-ar-y *adj.* causing or capable of causing fires; of or relating to arson; tending to inflame; inflammatory **incendiary** *n.*

in-cense *v.* to make angry *n.* a substance, as a gum or wood, burned to produce a pleasant smell; the smoke or odor produced

in-cen-tive *n.* something inciting one to action or effort; a stimulus

in-cep-tion *n.* a beginning; an origin **inceptive** *adj.*

in-cer-ti-tude *n.* uncertainty; lack of confidence; instability

in-ces-sant *adj.* occurring without interruption; continuous **incessantly** *adv.*

in-cest *n.* sexual intercourse between persons so closely related that they are forbidden by law to marry
incestuous *adj.*, **incestuously** *adv.*

inch *n.* a unit of measurement equal to 1/12th of a foot *v.* to move slowly

in-cho-ate *adj.* in an early stage; incipient **-ly** *adv.*, **inchoateness** *n.*

in-ci-dence *n.* the extent or rate of occurrence

in-ci-dent *n.* an event; an event that disrupts normal procedure or causes a crisis

in-ci-den-tal *adj.* occurring or likely to occur at the same time or as a result; minor; subordinate *n.* a minor attendant occurrence or condition **incidentally** *adv.*

in-cin-er-ate *v.* to burn up **incineration** *n.*

in-cin-er-a-tor *n.* one that incinerates; a furnace for burning waste

in-cip-i-ent *adj.* just beginning to appear or occur **incipience** *n.*, **incipiently** *adv.*

in-cise *v.* to make or cut into with a sharp tool; to carve into a surface; to engrave

in-ci-sion *n.* the act of incising; a cut or notch, especially a surgical cut

in-ci-sive *adj.* having or suggesting sharp intellect; penetrating; cogent and effective; telling
incisively *adv.*, incisiveness *n.*

in-ci-sor *n.* a cutting tooth at the front of the mouth

in-cite *v.* to provoke to action
incitement, inciter *n.*

in-clem-ent *adj.* stormy or rainy; unmerciful inclemency *n.*

in-cli-na-tion *n.* an attitude; a disposition; a tendency to act or think in a certain way; a preference; a bow or tilt; a slope

in-cline *v.* to deviate or cause to deviate from the horizontal or vertical; to slant; to dispose or be disposed; to bow or nod *n.* an inclined surface

in-clude *v.* to have as a part or member; to contain; to put into a group or total inclusion *n.*, inclusive *adj.*, -ly *adv.*

in-cog-ni-to *adv. & adj.* with one's identity hidden

in-co-her-ent *adj.* lacking order, connection, or harmony; unable to think or speak clearly or consecutively
incoherence *n.*, incoherently *adv.*

in-com-bus-ti-ble *adj.* incapable of burning incombustible *n.*

in-come *n.* money or its equivalent received in return for work or as profit from investments

income tax *n.* a tax on income earned by an individual or business

in-com-ing *adj.* coming in or soon to come in

in-com-men-su-rate *adj.* not commensurate; disproportionate; inadequate incommensurately *adv.*

in-com-mode *v.* to inconvenience; to disturb

in-com-mu-ni-ca-do *adv. & adj.* without being able to communicate with others

in-com-pa-ra-ble *adj.* incapable of being compared; without rival
incomparably *adv.*

in-com-pat-i-ble *adj.* not suited for combination or association; inconsistent
incompatibility *n.*, incompatibly *adv.*

in-com-pe-tent *adj.* not competent
incompetence, incompetency, *n.*

in-com-plete *adj.* not complete
incompletely *adv.*, incompleteness *n.*

in-con-gru-ous *adj.* not corresponding; disagreeing; made up of diverse or discordant elements; unsuited to the surrounding or setting
incongruity *n.*, incongruously *adv.*

in-con-se-quen-tial *adj.* without impor-

tance; petty inconsequentially *adv.*

in-con-sid-er-a-ble *adj.* unimportant; trivial inconsiderably *adv.*

in-con-sid-er-ate *adj.* not considerate; thoughtless inconsiderately *adv.*, inconsiderateness *n.*

in-con-sol-a-ble *adj.* not capable of being consoled inconsolably *adv.*

in-con-spic-u-ous *adj.* not readily seen or noticed inconspicuously *adv.*, inconspicuousness *n.*

in-con-stant *adj.* likely to change; unpredictable; faithless; fickle
inconstancy *n.*, inconstantly *adv.*

in-con-ti-nent *adj.* not restrained; uncontrolled; unable to contain or restrain something specified; incapable of controlling the excretory functions
incontinence *n.*, incontinently *adv.*

in-con-tro-vert-i-ble *adj.* unquestionable; indisputable incontrovertibly *adv.*

in-con-ven-ience *n.* the quality or state of being inconvenient; something inconvenient *v.* to cause inconvenience to; to bother

in-con-ven-ient *adj.* not convenient
inconveniently *adv.*

in-cor-po-rate *v.* to combine into a unified whole; to unite; to form or cause to form a legal corporation; to give a physical form to; to embody
incorporation, incorporator *n.*

in-cor-po-re-al *adj.* without material form or substance incorporeally *adv.*

in-cor-ri-gi-ble *adj.* incapable of being reformed or corrected incorrigibility, incorrigible *n.*, incorrigibly *adv.*

in-cor-rupt-i-ble *adj.* not capable of being corrupted morally; not subject to decay
incorruptibility *n.*, incorruptibly *adv.*

in-crease *v.* to make or become greater or larger; to have offspring; to reproduce *n.* the act of increasing; the amount or rate of increasing
increasingly *adv.*

in-cred-i-ble *adj.* too unlikely to be believed; unbelievable; extraordinary; astonishing incredibility *n.*, incredibly *adv.*

in-cred-u-lous *adj.* skeptical; disbelieving; expressive of disbelief
incredulity *n.*, incredulously *adv.*

in-cre-ment *n.* an increase; something gained or added, especially one of a series of regular additions
incremental *adj.*

in-crim-i-nate *v.* to involve in or charge with a wrongful act, as a crime
incrimination *n.*, incriminatory *adj.*

in-cu-bate v. to warm and hatch eggs, as by bodily heat or artificial means; to maintain a bacterial culture in favorable conditions for growth incubation n.

in-cu-ba-tor n. a cabinet in which a desired temperature can be maintained, used for bacterial culture; an enclosure for maintaining a premature infant in a controlled environment; a temperature controlled enclosure for hatching eggs

in-cu-bus n., pl. -buses or -bi an evil spirit believed to seize or harm sleeping persons; a nightmare; a nightmarish burden

in-cul-cate v. to impress on the mind by frequent repetition or instruction inculcation, inculcator n.

in-cul-pate v. to incriminate

in-cum-bent adj. lying or resting on something else; imposed as an obligation; obligatory; currently in office n. a person who is currently in office incumbency n., incumbently adv.

in-cu-nab-u-lum n., pl. -la a book printed before 1501

in-cur v. to become liable or subject to, especially because of one's own actions incurrence n.

in-cu-ri-ous adj. lacking interest; detached

in-cur-sion n. a sudden hostile intrusion into another's territory

in-cus n., pl. incudes an anvil-shaped bone in the middle ear of mammals

in-debt-ed adj. obligated to another, as for money or a favor; beholden indebtedness n.

in-de-cent adj. morally offensive or contrary to good taste indecency n., indecently adv.

in-de-ci-pher-a-ble adj. not capable of being deciphered or interpreted

in-de-ci-sion n. inability to make up one's mind; irresolution

in-de-ci-sive adj. without a clear-cut result; marked by indecision indecisively adv., indecisiveness n.

in-dec-o-rous adj. lacking good taste or propriety indecorously adv., indecorousness n.

in-deed adv. most certainly; without doubt; in reality; in fact interj. used to express surprise, irony, or disbelief

in-de-fat-i-ga-ble adj. tireless indefatigably adv.

in-de-fin-a-ble adj. not capable of being defined indefinableness n., indefinably adv.

in-def-i-nite adj. not decided or specified; vague; unclear; lacking fixed limits indefinitely adv., -ness n.

in-del-i-ble adj. not able to be erased or washed away;permanent indelibly adv.

in-del-i-cate adj. lacking sensitivity; tactless indelicacy n., indelicately adv.

in-dem-ni-fy v. to secure against hurt, loss, or damage; to make compensation for hurt, loss, or damage indemnification, indemnifier n.

in-dem-ni-ty n., pl. -ties security against hurt, loss, or damage; a legal exemption from liability for damages; compensation for hurt, loss, or damage

in-dent v. to set in from the margin, as the first line of a paragraph; to notch the edge of; to serrate; to make a dent or depression in; to impress; to stamp n. an indentation

in-den-ta-tion n. the act of indenting or the state of being indented; an angular cut in an edge; a recess in a surface

in-den-ture n. a legal deed or contract; a contract obligating one party to work for another for a specified period of time v. to bind into the service of another

in-de-pend-ence n. the quality or state of being independent

In-de-pend-ence Day n. July 4, a legal holiday in the United States, commemorating the adoption of the Declaration of Independence in 1776

in-de-pend-ent adj. politically self-governing; free from the control of others; not committed to a political party or faction; not relying on others, especially for financial support; providing or having enough income to enable one to live without working n. one who is independent, especially a candidate or voter not committed to a political party independently adv.

in-depth adj. thorough; detailed

in-de-scrib-a-ble adj. surpassing description; incapable of being described indescribably adv.

in-de-ter-mi-nate adj. not determined; not able to be determined; unclear or vague indeterminacy n., indeterminately adv.

in-dex n., pl. -dexes or -dices a list for aiding reference, especially an alphabetized listing in a printed work which gives the pages on which various names, places, and subjects are mentioned; something serving to guide or point out, especially a printed character calling attention to a paragraph or section; something that measures or indicates; a pointer, as in an instrument; in mathematics, a small number just above and to the left of a radical sign indicating what root is to be extracted; any number or symbol indicating an operation to be performed on a expression; a number or scale indicating change in magnitude, as of prices, relative to the magnitude at some specified point usually taken as one hundred (100) *v.* to provide with or enter in an index; to indicate; to adjust through

in-dex-a-tion *n.* the linkage of economic factors, as wages or prices, to a cost-of-living index so they rise and fall within the rate of inflation

in-dex fin-ger *n.* the finger next to the thumb

in-dex of re-frac-tion *n.* the quotient of the speed of light in a vacuum divided by the speed of light in a medium under consideration

In-di-an *n.* a native or inhabitant of India; a member of any of various aboriginal peoples of the Americas

Indian Ocean *n.* an ocean that extends from southern Asia to Antarctica and from eastern Africa to southeastern Australia

In-di-an sum-mer *n.* a period of mild weather in late autumn

in-di-cate *v.* to point out; to show; to serve as a sign or symptom; to signify; to suggest the advisability of; to call for indication, indicator *n.*

in-dic-a-tive *adj.* serving to indicate; of or being a verb mood used to express actions and conditions that are objective facts *n.* the indicative mood; a verb in the indicative mood

in-dict *v.* to accuse of an offense; to charge; to make a formal accusation against by the findings of a grand jury indictable *adj.*, indictor, indictment *n.*

in-dif-fer-ent *adj.* having no marked feeling or preference; impartial; neither good nor bad indifference *n.*, indifferently *adv.*

in-dig-e-nous *adj.* living or occurring naturally in an area; native

in-di-gent *adj.* impoverished; needy indigence *n.*

in-di-ges-tion *n.* difficulty or discomfort in digesting food

in-dig-nant *adj.* marked by or filled with indignation indignantly *adv.*

in-dig-na-tion *n.* anger aroused by injustice, unworthiness, or unfairness

in-dig-ni-ty *n., pl.* -ies humiliating treatment; something that offends one's pride

in-di-go *n., pl.* -gos *or* -goes a blue dye obtained from a plant or produced synthetically; a dark blue

in-di-go bunt-ing *n.* a small North American bird, the male of which has deep-blue plumage

in-di-go snake *n.* a non-venomous bluish-black snake found in the southern United States and northern Mexico

in-di-rect *adj.* not taking a direct course; not straight to the point indirection *n.*, indirectly *adv.*

in-dis-creet *adj.* lacking discretion indiscreetly *adv.*, indiscretion *n.*

in-dis-pen-sa-ble *adj* necessary; essential indispensability, indispensable *n.*, indispensably *adv.*

in-dite *v.* to write; to compose; to put down in writing inditer *n.*

in-di-um *n.* a soft, silver-white, metallic element used for mirrors and transistor compounds, symbolized by In.

in-di-vid-u-al *adj.* of, for, or relating to a single human being individually *adv.*

in-di-vis-i-ble *adj.* not able to be divided

in-doc-tri-nate *v.* to instruct in a doctrine or belief; to train to accept a system of thought uncritically indoctrination *n.*

In-do--Eu-ro-pe-an *n.* a family of languages comprising most of the languages of Europe and parts of southern Asia Indo-European *adj.*

in-do-lent *adj.* disinclined to exert oneself; lazy indolence *n.*

in-dom-i-ta-ble *adj.* incapable of being subdued or defeated -ably *adv.*

in-du-bi-ta-ble *adj.* too evident to be doubted indubitably *adv.*

in-duce *v.* to move by persuasion or influence; to cause to occur; to infer by inductive reasoning inducer *n.*

in-duce-ment *n.* the act of inducing; something that induces

in-duct *v.* to place formally in office; to admit as a new member; to summon into military service inductee *n.*

in-duc-tance *n.* a circuit element, usually a conducting coil, in which electromagnetic induction generates electromotive force

in-duc-tion *n.* the act of inducting or of being inducted; reasoning in which conclusions are drawn from particular instances or facts; the generation of electromotive force in a closed circuit by a magnetic field that changes with time; the production of an electric charge in an uncharged body by bringing a charged body close to it

in-dulge v. to give in to the desires of, especially to excess; to yield to; to allow oneself a special pleasure -ger n.

in-dus-tri-al adj. of, relating to, or used in industry industrially adv.

in-dus-tri-ous adj. working steadily and hard; diligent industriously adv., industriousness n.

in-dus-try n., pl. -tries the commercial production and sale of goods and services; a branch of manufacture and trade; industrial management as distinguished from labor; diligence

in-e-bri-ate v. to make drunk; to intoxicate inebriated, inebriant adj. & n., inebriation n.

in-ef-fa-ble adj. beyond expression; indescribable ineffably adv.

in-ef-fi-cient adj. wasteful of time, energy, or materials inefficiency n., inefficiently adv.

in-e-luc-ta-ble adj. not capable of being avoided or overcome ineluctably adv.

in-ept adj. awkward or incompetent; not suitable ineptitude, ineptness n., ineptly adv.

in-e-qual-i-ty n., pl. -ies the condition or an instance of being unequal; social or economic disparity; lack of regularity; in mathematics, an algebraic statement that a quantity is greater than or less than another quantity

in-eq-ui-ty n., pl. -ies injustice; unfairness

in-ert adj. not able to move or act; slow to move or act; sluggish; displaying no chemical activity inertly adv., inertness n.

in-er-tia n. the tendency of a body to remain at rest or to stay in motion unless acted upon by an external force; resistance to motion or change inertial adj., inertially adv.

in-ev-i-ta-ble adj. not able to be avoided or prevented inevitability n., inevitably adv.

in-ex-o-ra-ble adj. not capable of being moved by entreaty; unyielding inexorably adv.

in-ex-pe-ri-ence n. lack of experience

in-ex-pli-ca-ble adj. not capable of being explained inexplicably adv.

in ex-tre-mis adv. at the point of death

in-ex-tri-ca-ble adj. not capable of being untied or untangled; too complex to resolve inextricably adv.

in-fal-li-ble adj. not capable of making mistakes; not capable of failing; never

wrong infallibility n., infallibly adv.

in-fa-mous adj. having a very bad reputation; shocking or disgraceful infamously adv.

in-fa-my n., pl. -ies evil notoriety or reputation; the state of being infamous; a disgraceful, publicly known act

in-fan-cy n., pl. -ies the condition or time of being an infant; an early stage of existence; in law, minority

in-fant n. a child in the first period of life; a very young child; in law, a minor

in-fan-ti-cide n. the killing of an infant

in-fan-tile adj. of or relating to infants or infancy; immature; childish

in-fan-tile pa-ra-ly-sis n. poliomyelitis

in-fan-try n., pl. -ries the branch of an army made up of soldiers who are trained to fight on foot infantryman n.

in-farct n. an area of dead tissue caused by an insufficient supply of blood infarcted adj., infarction n.

in-fat-u-ate v. to arouse an extravagant or foolish love in infatuated adj., infatuation n.

in-fect v. to contaminate with disease-causing microorganisms; to transmit a disease to; to affect as if by contagion infective adj.

in-fec-tion n. invasion of a bodily part by disease-causing microorganisms; the condition resulting from such an invasion; an infectious disease

in-fe-lic-i-tous adj. not happy; unfortunate; not apt, as in expression infelicity n., infelicitously adv.

in-fer v. to conclude by reasoning; to deduce; to have as a logical consequence; to lead to as a result or conclusion inferable adj.

in-fer-ence n. a conclusion based on facts and premises

in-fe-ri-or adj. located under or below; low or lower in order, rank, or quality inferior, inferiority n.

in-fer-nal adj. of, like, or relating to hell; damnable; abominable infernally adv.

in-fer-no n. a place or condition suggestive of hell

in-fest v. to spread in or over so as to be harmful or offensive infestation n.

in-fi-del n. one who has no religion; an unbeliever in a religion, especially Christianity

in-field n. in baseball, the part of a playing field within the base lines infielder n.

in-fil-trate v. to pass or cause to pass

into something through pores or small openings; to pass through or enter gradually or stealthily **infiltration** *n.*

in-fi-nite *adj.* without boundaries; limitless; immeasurably great or large; in mathematics, greater in value than any specified number, however large; having measure that is infinite **infinite** *n.*, **infinitely** *adv.*

in-fin-i-tes-i-mal *adj.* immeasurably small **infinitesimally** *adv.*

in-fin-i-ty *n.*, *pl.* -ies the quality or state of being infinite; unbounded space, time, or amount; an indefinitely large number

in-firm *adj.* physically weak, especially from age; feeble; not sound or valid

in-fir-ma-ry *n.*, *pl.* -ries an institution for the care of the sick or disabled

in-flame *v.* to set on fire; to arouse to strong or excessive feeling; to intensify; to produce, affect or be affected by inflammation

in-flam-ma-ble *adj.* tending to catch fire easily; easily excited

in-flam-ma-tion *n.* localized redness, swelling, heat, and pain in response to an injury or infection

in-flate *v.* to fill and expand with a gas; to increase unsoundly; to puff up; to raise prices abnormally **inflatable** *adj.*

in-fla-tion *n.* the act or process of inflating; a period during which there is an increase in the monetary supply, causing a continuous rise in the price of goods

in-flect *v.* to turn; to veer; to vary the tone or pitch of the voice, especially in speaking; to change the form of a word to indicate number, tense, or person **inflective** *adj.*, **inflection** *n.*

in-flex-i-ble *adj.* not flexible; rigid; not subject to change; unalterable **inflexibility** *n.*, **inflexibly** *adv.*

in-flict *v.* to cause to be suffered; to impose **inflicter, inflictor,** -tion *n.*

in-flo-res-cence *n.* a characteristic arrangement of flowers on a stalk **inflorescent** *adj.*

in-flu-ence *n.* the power to produce effects, especially indirectly or through an intermediary; the condition of being affected; one exercising indirect power to sway or affect *v.* to exert influence over; to modify **influential** *adj.*

in-flu-en-za *n.* an acute, infectious viral disease marked by respiratory inflammation, fever, muscular pain, and often intestinal discomfort; the flu

in-flux *n.* a stream of people or things coming in

in-form-ant *n.* one who discloses or furnishes information which should remain secret

in-for-ma-tive *adj.* providing information; instructive

in-frac-tion *n.* a violation of a rule

in-fra-red *adj.* of, being, or using electromagnetic radiation with wave lengths longer than those of visible light and shorter than those of microwaves

in-fra-son-ic *adj.* producing or using waves or vibrations with frequencies below that of audible sound

in-fra-struc-ture *n.* an underlying base or foundation; the basic facilities needed for the functioning of a system

in-fringe *v.* to break a law; to violate; to encroach; to trespass **infringement** *n.*

in-fu-ri-ate *v.* to make very angry or furious; to enrage **infuriatingly** *adv.*, **infuriation** *n.*

in-fuse *v.* to introduce, instill or inculcate, as principles; to obtain a liquid extract by soaking a substance in water **infusion** *n.*

-ing *suff* used in forming the present participle of verbs and adjectives resembling participles; activity or action; the result or a product of an action

in-gen-ious *adj.* showing great ingenuity; to have inventive ability; clever **ingeniously** *adv.*, **ingeniousness** *n.*

in-ge-nu-i-ty *n.*, *pl.* -ies cleverness; inventive skill

in-gen-u-ous *adj.* frank and straightforward; lacking sophistication

in-gest *v.* to take or put food into the body by swallowing **ingestion** *n.*, **ingestive** *adj.*

in-gle-nook *n.* a recessed area or corner near or beside a fireplace

in-glo-ri-ous *adj.* not showing courage or honor; dishonorable **ingloriously** *adv.*

in-got *n.* a mass of cast metal shaped in a bar or block

in-grain *v.* to impress firmly on the mind or nature *n.* fiber or yarn that is dyed before being spun or woven

in-grained *adj.* to be worked into the inmost texture; deep-seated

in-grate *n.* a person who is ungrateful

in-gra-ti-ate *v.* to gain favor or confidence of others by deliberate effort or manipulation **ingratiatingly** *adv.*, **ingratiation** *n.*, **ingratiatory** *adj.*

in-grat-i-tude *n.* lack of gratitude

in-gre-di-ent *n.* an element that enters into the composition of a mixture; a part of anything

in-gress n. a going in or entering of a building **ingression** n., **ingressive** adj.

in-grown adj. growing into the flesh; growing abnormally within or into **ingrowing** adj.

in-gui-nal adj., Anat. of, pertaining to, or located in the groin

in-hab-it v. to reside in; to occupy as a home **inhabitability, inhabiter, inhabitation** n., **inhabitable** adj.

in-hab-i-tant n. a person who resides permanently, as distinguished from a visitor

in-ha-la-tion n. the act of inhaling

in-ha-la-tor n. a device that enables a person to inhale air, anesthetics, medicated vapors, or other matter

in-hale v. to breathe or draw into the lungs, as air or tobacco smoke; the opposite of exhale **inhalation** n.

in-hal-er n. one that inhales; a respirator

in-here v. To be an essential or permanent feature; to belong

in-her-ent adj. forming an essential element or quality of something **inherently** adv.

in-her-it v. to receive something, as property, money, or other valuables, by legal succession or will Biol. to receive traits or qualities from one's ancestors or parents **inheritable** adj., **inheritor** n.

in-her-i-tance n. the act of inheriting; that which is inherited or to be inherited by legal transmission to a heir

in-her-i-tance tax n. a tax imposed on an inherited estate

in-hib-it v. to restrain or hold back; to prevent full expression **inhibitable** adj., **inhibitor, inhibiter** n., **inhibitive, inhibitory** adj.

in-hi-bi-tion n. the act of restraining, especially a self-imposed restriction on one's behavior; a mental or psychological restraint

in--house adj. of, relating to, or carried on within an organization

in-hu-man adj. lacking pity, emotional warmth, or kindness; monstrous; not being of the ordinary human type **inhumanly** adv.

in-hu-mane adj. lacking compassion or pity; cruel **inhumanely** adv.

in-hu-man-i-ty n., pl. -ties the lack of compassion or pity; an inhumane or cruel act

in-im-i-cal adj. harmful opposition; hostile; malign **inimically** adv.

in-im-i-ta-ble adj. incapable of being matched; unique **inimitably** adv.

in-iq-ui-ty n., pl. -ies the grievous violation of justice; wickedness; sinfulness **iniquitous** adj.

in-i-tial adj. of or pertaining to the beginning n. the first letter of a name or word v. to mark or sign with initials **initially** adv.

in-i-ti-ate v. to begin or start; to admit someone to membership in an organization, fraternity, or group; to instruct in fundamentals adj. **initiated initiator** n., **initiatory** adj.

in-i-ti-a-tive n. the ability to originate or follow through with a plan of action; the action of taking the first or leading step Govt. the power or right to propose legislative measures

in-ject v. to force a drug or fluid into the body through a blood vessel or the skin with a hypodermic syringe; to throw in or introduce a comment abruptly **injection** n.

in-junc-tion n. an authoritative command or order; in law, a court order requiring the party to do or to refrain from some specified action **-tive** adj.

in-jure v. to cause physical harm, damage, or pain

in-ju-ri-ous adj. causing injury, damage or hurt; slanderous; abusive **injuriously** adv., **injuriousness** n.

in-ju-ry n., pl. -ies damage or harm inflicted or suffered

in-jus-tice n. the violation of another person's rights; an unjust act; a wrong

ink n. any of variously colored liquids or paste, used for writing, drawing, and printing **inker** n.

ink-horn n. a small container to hold ink

ink-ling n. a slight suggestion or hint; a vague idea or notion

ink-stand n. a stand or device for holding writing tools and ink

ink-well n. a small container or reservoir for holding ink

ink-y adj. resembling ink in color; dark; black; containing or pertaining to ink

in-laid adj. ornamented with wood, ivory, or other materials embedded flush with the surface

in-land adj. pertaining to or located in the interior of a country **inlander** n.

in--law n. a relative by marriage

in-lay v. to set or embed something, as gold or ivory, into the surface of a decorative design

in-let n. a bay or stream that leads into land; a passage between nearby islands

in-mate *n.* a person who dwells in a building with another; one confined in a prison, asylum, or hospital

inn *n.* a place of lodging where a traveler may obtain meals and/or lodging

in-nards *pl. n., Slang* the internal organs or parts of the body; the inner parts of a machine

in-nate *adj.* inborn and not acquired; having as an essential part; inherent **innately** *adv.*

in-ner *adj.* situated or occurring farther inside; relating to or of the mind or spirit

in-ner ear *n.* the part of the ear which includes the semicircular canals, vestibule, and cochlea

in-ner-most *adj.* most intimate; farthest within

in-ner tube *n.* a flexible, inflatable rubber tube placed inside a tire

in-ning *n.* in baseball, one of nine divisions of a regulation baseball game, in which each team has a turn at bat

innings *pl.* in the game of cricket, the time or period during which one side bats

inn-keep-er *n.* the proprietor or manager of an inn

in-no-cent *adj.* free from sin, evil, or moral wrong; pure; legally free from blame or guilt; not maliciously intended; lacking in experience or knowledge; naive **innocence**, **innocent** *n.*, **innocently** *adv.*

in-noc-u-ous *adj.* having no harmful qualities or ill effect; harmless

in-nom-i-nate bone *n., Anat.* one of the two large, irregular bones which form the sides of the pelvis

in-no-vate *v.* to introduce or begin something new **innovative** *adj.*, **innovator** *n.*

in-nu-en-do *n., pl.* -dos or -does an indirect or oblique comment, suggestion or hint

in-nu-mer-a-ble *adj.* too numerous or too much to be counted; countless

in-oc-u-late *v.* to introduce a mild form of a disease or virus to a person or animal in order to produce immunity **inoculation** *n.*

in-op-er-a-ble *adj.* unworkable; incapable of being treated or improved by surgery

in-op-er-a-tive *adj.* not working; not functioning

in-op-por-tune *adj.* inappropriate; untimely; unsuitable **inopportunely** *adv.*, **inopportuneness** *n.*

in-or-di-nate *adj.* exceeding proper or normal limits; not regulated; unrestrained **inordinately** *adv.*

in-or-gan-ic *adj.* not having or involving living organisms, their remains, or products

in-pa-tient *n.* a patient admitted to a hospital for medical treatment

in-put *n.* the amount of energy delivered to a machine; in computer science, information that is put into a data-processing system *Elect.* the voltage, current, or power that is delivered to a circuit

in-quest *n.* a legal investigation into the cause of death

in-quire *v.* to ask a question; to make an investigation **inquirer** *n.*, **inquiringly** *adv.*

in-quir-y *n., pl.* -ies the act of seeking or inquiring; a request or question for information; a very close examination; an investigation or examination of facts or evidence

in-qui-si-tion *n.* a former Roman Catholic tribunal established to seek out and punish heretics; an interrogation that violates individual rights; an investigation **inquisitor** *n.*, **inquisitorial** *adj.*

in-quis-i-tive *adj.* curious; probing; questioning **inquisitively** *adv.*, **inquisitiveness** *n.*

in-sane *adj.* afflicted with a serious mental disorder impairing a person's ability to function; the characteristic of a person who is not sane **insanely** *adv.*, **insanity** *n.*

in-san-i-tar-y *adj.* not sanitary; not hygienic and dangerous to one's health

in-scribe *v.* to write, mark, or engrave on a surface; to enter a name in a register or on a formal list; to write a short note on a card *Geom.* to enclose one figure in another so that the latter encloses the former **inscriber** *n.*

in-scru-ta-ble *adj.* difficult to interpret or understand; incomprehensible -bility, **inscrutableness** *n.*, **inscrutably** *adv.*

in-sect *n., Zool.* any of a numerous cosmopolitan class of small to minute winged invertebrate animals with 3 pairs of legs, a segmented body, and usually 2 pairs of wings

in-sec-ti-cide *n.* a substance for killing insects

in-sec-tiv-o-rous *adj.* feeding on insects

in-se-cure *adj.* troubled by anxiety and apprehension; threatened; not securely guarded; unsafe; liable to

break, fail, or collapse
insecurely adv., **insecurity** n.

in-sem-i-nate v. to introduce semen into the uterus of; to make pregnant; to sow seed **insemination, inseminator** n.

in-sen-sate adj. showing a lack of humane feeling; unconscious

in-sen-si-ble adj. deprived of consciousness; unconscious; incapable of perceiving or feeling; unmindful; unaware **insensibility** n., **insensibly** adv.

in-sen-ti-ent adj. without sensation or consciousness **insentience** n.

in-sep-a-ra-ble adj. incapable of being separated or parted
inseparability n., **inseparably** adv.

in-sert v. to put in place; to set n. in printing, something inserted or to be inserted **insertion** n.

in-set v. to set in; to implant; to insert

in-shore adj. near or moving toward the shore **inshore** adv.

in-side n. the part, surface, or space that lies within

insides n. The internal parts or organs **inside** adj.

in-sid-er n. one having special knowledge or access to confidential information

in-sid-i-ous adj. cunning or deceitful; treacherous; seductive; attractive but harmful **insidiously** adv., **invidiousness** n.

in-sight n. perception into the true or hidden nature of things
insightful adj., **insightfully** adv.

in-sig-ni-a n., pl. **-nia** or **-nias** a badge or emblem used to mark membership, honor, or office

in-sin-cere adj. not sincere; hypocritical **insincerely** adv., **insincerity** n.

in-sin-u-ate v. to suggest something by giving a hint; to introduce by using ingenious and sly means
insinuating adv., **insinuation** n.

in-sip-id adj. lacking of flavor; tasteless; flat; dull; lacking interest
insipidly adv., **insipidness** n.

in-sist v. to demand or assert in a firm way; to dwell on something repeatedly, as to emphasize **insistence** n., **insistent** adj., **insistently** adv.

in-so-far adv. to such an extent

in-sole n. the fixed inside sole of a shoe or boot; a removable strip of material put inside a shoe for protection or comfort

in-sol-u-ble adj. incapable of being dissolved; not soluble; not capable of being solved **insolubility,**

insolubleness n., **insolubly** adv.

in-sol-vent adj. in law, unable to meet debts; bankrupt

in-som-ni-a n. the chronic inability to sleep **insomniac** n.

in-sou-ci-ant adj. lighthearted and cheerful; unconcerned; not bothered **insouciance** n.

in-spect v. to examine or look at very carefully for flaws; to examine or review officially **-ion, inspector** n.

in-spi-ra-tion n. the stimulation within the mind of some idea, feeling, or impulse which leads to creative action; a divine or holy presence which inspires; the act of inhaling air
inspirational adj., **inspirationally** adv.

in-spire v. to exert or guide by a divine influence; to arouse and create high emotion; to exalt; to inhale; breathe in **inspirer** n., **inspiringly** adv.

inst abbr. instant; institute; institution

in-sta-bil-i-ty n., pl. **-ties** lacking stability

in-stall or **in-stal** v. to put in position for service; to place into an office or position; to settle **installation, installer** n.

in-stall-ment or **in-stal-ment** n. one of several payments due in specified amounts at specified intervals

in-stance n. an illustrative case or example; a step in proceedings v. to illustrate

in-stant n. a very short time; a moment; a certain or specific point in time adj. instantaneously; immediate; urgent

in-stan-ta-ne-ous adj. happening with no delay; instantly; completed in a moment **instantaneously** adv.

in-stant-ly adv. immediately; at once

in-stead adv. in lieu of that just mentioned

in-step n., Anat. the arched upper part of the human foot

in-sti-gate v. to urge forward; to stir up; to foment; to provoke
instigation, instigator n.

in-still or **in-stil** v. to introduce by gradual instruction or effort; to pour in slowly by drops **instillation, instiller** n.

in-stinct n. the complex and normal tendency or response of a given species to act in ways essential to its existence, development, and survival **-tive,** **instinctual** adj., **instinctively** adv.

in-sti-tute v. to establish or set up; to find; to initiate; to set in operation; to start n. an organization set up to promote or further a cause; an institution for educating

in-sti-tu-tion *n.* the principle custom that forms part of a society or civilization; an organization which performs a particular job or function, such as research, charity, or education; a place of confinement such as a prison or mental hospital institutionalize *v.*, institutional *adj.*, institutionally *adv.*

in-struct *v.* to impart skill or knowledge; to teach; to give orders or direction instructive *adj.*

in-struc-tion *n.* The act of teaching or instructing; important knowledge; a lesson; an order or direction

in-struc-tor *n.* one who instructs; a teacher; a low-rank college teacher, not having tenure instructorship, instructress *n.*

in-stru-ment *n.* a mechanical tool or implement; a device used to produce music; a person who is controlled by another; a dupe; in law, a formal legal document, deed, or contract

in-stru-men-tal *adj.* acting or serving as a means; pertaining to, composed for, or performed on a musical instrument instrumentally *adv.*

in-stru-men-tal-ist *n.* a person who plays or performs with a musical instrument

in-stru-men-tal-i-ty *n., pl.* -ies anything that serves to accomplish a purpose; means or agency

in-stru-men-ta-tion *n.* the use of instruments or work performed with instruments *Mus.* the arrangement of music for instruments

in-sub-or-di-nate *adj.* not obedient; not obeying orders insubordinately *adv.*, insubordination *n.*

in-sub-stan-tial *adj.* unreal; imaginary; not solid or firm; flimsy insubstantiality *n.*

in-suf-fi-cient *adj.* inadequate; not enough insufficiently *adv.*, insufficiency *n.*

in-su-lar *adj.* of or related to an island; typical or suggestive of life on an island; narrow-minded; limited in customs, opinions, and ideas insularity *n.*

in-su-late *v.* to isolate; to wrap or surround with nonconducting material in order to prevent the passage of heat, electricity, or sound into or out of; to protect with wrapping or insulation insulation, insulator *n.*

in-su-lin *n., Biochem.* the hormone released by the pancreas, essential in regulating the metabolism of sugar; a preparation of this hormone removed from the pancreas of a pig or an ox, used in the treatment of diabetes

in-sult *v.* to speak or to treat with insolence or contempt; to abuse verbally *n.* an act or remark that offends someone insulter *n.*, insulting *adj.*, insultingly *adv.*

in-su-per-a-ble *adj.* insurmountable; not able to be overcome insuperability *n.*, insuperably *adv.*

in-sur-ance *n.* protection against risk, loss, or ruin; the coverage an insurer guarantees to pay in the event of death, loss, or medical bills; a contract guaranteeing such protection on future specified losses in return for annual payments; any safeguard against risk or harm insurability *n.*, -able *adj.*

in-sure *v.* to guarantee against loss of life, property, or other types of losses; to make certain; to ensure; to buy or issue insurance insurability *n.*, insurable *adj.*

in-sured *n.* a person protected by an insurance policy

in-sur-er *n.* the person or company which insures someone against loss or damage

in-sur-mount-a-ble *adj.* incapable of being overcome insurmountably *adv.*

in-sur-rec-tion *n.* an open revolt against an established government insurrectional *adj.*, insurrectionist *n* insurrectionary *adj. & n.*,

in-sus-cep-ti-ble *adj.* immune; incapable of being infected insusceptibility *n.*

in-tact *adj.* remaining whole and not damaged in any way intactness *n.*

in-take *n.* the act of taking in or absorbing; the amount or quantity taken in or absorbed

in-tan-gi-ble *adj.* incapable of being touched; vague or indefinite to the mind intangibility, intangibleness *n.*, intangibly *adv.*

in-te-ger *n.* any of the numbers 1, 2, 3, etc., including all the positive whole numbers and all the negative numbers and zero; a whole entity

in-te-gral *adj.* being an essential and indispensable part of a whole; made up, from, or formed of parts that constitute a unity

in-te-grate *v.* to make into a whole by joining parts together; to únify; to be open to people of all races or ethnic groups integration *n.*, integrative *adj.*

in-teg-ri-ty *n.* uprightness of character; honesty; the condition, quality, or state of being complete or undivided

in-tel-lect *n.* the power of the mind to

understand and to accept knowledge; the state of having a strong or brilliant mind; a person of notable intellect

in-tel-lec-tu-al *adj.* pertaining to, possessing, or showing intellect; inclined to rational or creative thought *n.* a person who pursues and enjoys matters of the intellect and of refined taste **intellectuality** *n.*, **intellectually** *adv.*

in-tel-lec-tu-al-ize *v.* to examine objectively so as not to become emotionally involved

intellectualization, intellectualizer *n.*

in-tel-li-gence *n.* the capacity to perceive and comprehend meaning; information; news; the gathering of secret information, as by military or police authorities; information so collected

in-tel-li-gent *adj.* having or showing intelligence **intelligently** *adv.*

in-tel-li-gi-ble *adj.* having the capabilities of being understood; understanding

in-tend *v.* to have a plan or purpose in mind; to design for a particular use **intended** *adj.*

in-tense *adj.* extreme in strength, effect, or degree; expressing strong emotion, concentration, or strain; profound **intensely** *adv.*, **intenseness** *n.*

in-ten-si-fy *v.* to become or make more intense or acute **intensification** *n.*

in-ten-si-ty *n.*, *pl.* -ies the quality of being intense or acute; a great effect, concentration, or force

in-ten-sive *adj.* forceful and concentrated; marked by a full and complete application of all resources **intensively** *adv.*

intensive care *n.* the hospital care provided for a gravely ill patient in specially designed rooms with monitoring devices and life-support systems

in-tent *n.* a purpose, goal, aim, or design **intently** *adv.*, **intentness** *n.*

in-ten-tion *n.* a plan of action; purpose, either immediate or ultimate

in-ten-tion-al *adj.* deliberately intended or done -lity *n.*, **intentionally** *adv.*

in-ter *v.* to place in a grave; bury **interment** *n.*

inter- *pref.* mutually; with each other; together; among or between

in-ter-act *v.* to act on each other or with each other

interaction *n.*, **interactive** *adj.*

in-ter-breed *v.* to crossbreed; to breed together two different species

in-ter-cede *v.* to argue or plead on another's behalf **interceder** *n.*

in-ter-cept *v.* to interrupt the path or

course of; to seize or stop **intercept, interception** *n.*

in-ter-cep-tor *or* **in-ter-cept-er** *n.* one who or that which intercepts; a fighter plane designed for the pursuit and interception of enemy aircraft

in-ter-ces-sion *n.* an entreaty or prayer on behalf of others **intercessor** *n.*, **intercessional, intercessory** *adj.*

in-ter-change *v.* to put each in the place of another; to give and receive in return *n.* the intersection of a highway which allows traffic to enter or turn off without obstructing other traffic **interchangeable** *adj.*, **interchanger** *n.*

in-ter-col-le-gi-ate *adj.* involving or pertaining to two or more colleges

in-ter-com *n.*, *Informal* a two-way communication system, as used in different areas of a home or business

in-ter-com-mu-ni-cate *v.* to communicate with each other -tion *n.*, **intercommunicate** *adj.*

in-ter-con-ti-nen-tal *adj.* pertaining to or involving two or more continents

in-ter-course *n.* mutual exchange between persons or groups; communication; sexual intercourse

in-ter-dict *v.* to forbid or prohibit by official decree interdiction, **interdictor** *n.*, **interdictory** *adj.*

in-ter-est *n.* curiosity or concern about something; that which is to one's benefit; legal or financial right, claim, or share, as in a business; a charge for a loan of money, usually a percent of the amount borrowed

in-ter-est-ed *adj.* having or displaying curiosity; having a right to share in something **interestedly** *adv.*

in-ter-est-ing *adj.* stimulating interest, attention, or curiosity **interesting** *adv.* **interestingness** *n.*

in-ter-face *n.* a surface forming a common boundary between adjacent areas; in computer science, the software or hardware connecting one device or system to another **interface** *v.*, **interfacial** *adj.*

in-ter-fere *v.* to come between; to get in the way; to be an obstacle or obstruction **interference** *n.*

in-ter-ga-lac-tic *adj.* between galaxies

in-ter-im *n.* a time between events or periods *adj.* temporary.

in-te-ri-or *adj.* of, or contained in the inside; inner; away from the coast or border; inland; private; not exposed to view

in-ter-ject *v.* to go between other parts

or elements; to add something between other things **interjector** *n.*, **interjectory** *adj.*

in-ter-jec-tion *n.* a word used as an exclamation to express emotion, as *Oh! Heavens! Super!* **interjectional** *adj.*

in-ter-lace *v.* to join by weaving together; to intertwine; to blend

in-ter-lin-e-ar *adj.* situated or inserted between lines of a text

in-ter-lock *v.* to join closely

in-ter-loc-u-tor *n.* one who takes part in a conversation

in-ter-loc-u-to-ry *adj.* having the nature of a dialogue; in law, pronounced while a suit is pending and temporarily in effect

in-ter-lope *v.* to intrude or interfere in the rights of others

in-ter-lude *n.* a period of time that occurs in and divides some longer process; light entertainment between the acts of a show, play, or other more serious entertainment

in-ter-mar-ry *v.* to marry someone who is not a member of one's own religion, class, race, or ethnic group **intermarriage** *n.*

in-ter-me-di-ar-y *n., pl.* **-ies** a mediator *adj.* coming between; intermediate

in-ter-me-di-ate *adj.* situated or occurring in the middle or between **intermediately** *adv.*, **intermediateness** *n.*

in-ter-min-gle *v.* to blend or become mixed together

in-ter-mis-sion *n.* a temporary interval of time between events or activities; the pause in the middle of a performance

in-ter-mit-tent *adj.* ceasing from time to time; coming at intervals

in-tern *or* **in-terne** *n.* a medical school graduate undergoing supervised practical training in a hospital *v.* to confine, as in wartime **internment**, **internship** *n.*

in-ter-nal *adj.* of or pertaining to the inside; pertaining to the domestic affairs of a country; intended to be consumed by the body from the inside

in-ter-nal--com-bus-tion en-gine *n.* an engine in which fuel is burned inside the engine

in-ter-nal med-i-cine *n.* the branch of medicine that studies and treats the nonsurgical diseases

in-ter-na-tion-al *adj.* pertaining to or involving two or more nations **internationally** *adv.*

in-ter-na-tion-al-ism *n.* the policy of cooperation among nations where politics and economics are concerned **internationalist** *n.*

in-ter-nec-ine *adj.* mutually destructive to both sides; involving struggle within a group

in-tern-ee *n.* a person who is confined or interned

in-ter-nist *n.* a physician who is a specialist in internal medicine

in-ter-play *n.* action, movement, or influence between or among people **interplay** *v.*

in-ter-po-late *v.* to insert between other things or elements; to change something by introducing additions or insertions **interpolation**, **interpolator** *n.*

in-ter-pose *v.* to put between parts; to put in or inject a comment into a conversation or speech; to intervene **interposer**, **interposition** *n.*

in-ter-pret *v.* to convey the meaning of something by explaining or restating; to present the meaning of something, as in a picture; to take words spoken or written in one language and put them into another language **-able** *adj.*, **interpretation**, **interpreter** *n.*

in-ter-pre-ta-tive *or* **in-ter-pre-tive** *adj.* of or based on interpreting; to provide an interpretation **interpretatively** *adv.*

in-ter-ra-cial *adj.* between, among, or affecting different races

in-ter-reg-num *n., pl.* **-nums** *or* **-na** an interval between two successive reigns; a break in continuity

in-ter-re-late *v.* to have or to put into a mutual relationship **interrelation**, **interrelationship** *n.*

in-ter-ro-gate *v.* to question formally **interrogation**, **interrogator** *n.*

in-ter-rog-a-tive *adj.* asking or having the nature of a question *n.* a word used to ask a question **interrogatively** *adv.*

in-ter-rupt *v.* to break the continuity of something; to intervene abruptly while someone else is speaking or performing **interrupter**, **interruption** *n.*, **interruptive** *adj.*

in-ter-scho-las-tic *adj.* conducted between or among schools

in-ter-sect *v.* to divide by cutting through or across; to form an intersection; to cross

in-ter-sec-tion *n.* a place of crossing; a place where streets or roads cross; in mathematics, the point common to two or more geometric elements

in-ter-sperse *v.* to scatter among other things **interspersion** *n.*

in-ter-state *adj.* between, involving, or among two or more states

in-ter-stel-lar *adj.* among or between the stars

in-ter-stice *n.* the small space between things interstitial *adj.*

in-ter-twine *v.* to unite by twisting together intertwinement *n.*

in-ter-ur-ban *adj.* between or among connecting urban areas

in-ter-val *n.* the time coming between two points or objects; a period of time between events or moments *Mus.* the difference in pitch between two tones

in-ter-vene *v.* to interfere or take a decisive role so as to modify or settle something; to interfere with force in a conflict intervention *n.*

in-ter-view *n.* a conversation conducted by a reporter to elicit information from someone; a conversation led by an employer who is trying to decide whether to hire someone interview *v.*, interviewer *n.*

in-ter-weave *v.* to weave together; to intertwine

in-tes-tate *adj.* having made no valid will; not disposed of by a will intestacy *n.*

in-tes-tine or in-tes-tines *n. Anat.* the section of the alimentary canal from the stomach to the anus intestinal *adj.*, intestinally *adv.*

in-ti-mate *adj.* characterized by close friendship or association intimately *adv.*, intimacy, -ness *n.*

in-tim-i-date *v.* to make timid or fearful; to frighten; to discourage or suppress by threats or by violence intimidation, intimidator *n.*

in-to *prep.* to the inside of; to a form or condition of; to a time in the midst of

in-tol-er-a-ble *adj.* not tolerable; unbearable intolerability, intolerableness *n.*, intolerably *adv.*

in-tol-er-ant *adj.* not able to endure; not tolerant of the rights or beliefs of others intolerance *n.*, intolerantly *adv.*

in-to-na-tion *n.* the manner of speaking, especially the meaning and melody given to speech by changing levels of pitch

in-tone *v.* to utter or recite in a monotone; to chant intoner *n.*

in to-to *adv.*, *L.* totally

in-tox-i-cate *v.* to make drunk; to elate or excite intoxicant, intoxication *n.*

intra- *prefix* within

in-tra-cel-lu-lar *adj.* within a cell or cells

in-tra-cra-ni-al *adj.* within the skull

in-trac-ta-ble *adj.* hard to manage; difficult to cure or treat

in-tra-dos *n.*, *pl.* -dos *or* -doses the interior curve of an arch or vault

in-tra-mu-ral *adj.* taking place within a school, college, or institution; competition limited to a school community

in-tra-mus-cu-lar *adj.* within a muscle

in-tran-si-gent *adj.* refusing to moderate a position; uncompromising intransigence, intransigency, intransigent *n.*

in-tra-oc-u-lar *adj.* within the eyeball

in-tra-state *adj.* within a state

in-tra-u-ter-ine *adj.* within the uterus

in-tra-u-ter-ine de-vice *n.* a metal or plastic loop, ring, or spiral inserted into the uterus as a means of contraception

in-tra-ve-nous *adj.* within a vein intravenously *adv.*

in-trep-id *adj.* courageous; unshaken by fear; bold intrepidly *adv.*, intrepidness *n.*

in-tri-cate *adj.* having many perplexingly entangled parts or elements; complex; difficult to solve or understand intricacy *n.*, intricately *adv.*

in-trigue *v.* to arouse the curiosity or interest; to fascinate; to plot; to conspire; to engage in intrigues *n.* a secret or illicit love affair; a secret plot or plan intriguer *n.*

in-trin-sic *adj.* belonging to the true or fundamental nature of a thing; inherent intrinsically *adv.*

in-tro-duce *v.* to present a person face to face to another; to make acquainted; to bring into use or practice for the first time; to bring to the attention of introducer, introduction *n.*, introductory *adj.*

in-tro-it or In-tro-it *n.* a hymn or psalm sung at the beginning of a Roman Catholic Mass

in-tro-vert *n.*, *Psychol.* a person who directs his interest to himself and not to friends or social activities introversion *n.*, introversive, introverted *adj.*

in-trude *v.* to thrust or push oneself in; to come in without being asked or wanted

in-tu-it *v.* to understand through intuition

in-tu-i-tion *n.* the direct knowledge or awareness of something without conscious attention or reasoning; knowledge that is acquired in this way intuitive *adj.*, intuitively *adv.*

in-un-date *v.* to overwhelm with abundance or excess, as with work inundation *n.*

in-ure *v.* to become used to accepting something which is undesirable inurement *n.*

in-vade *v.* to enter by force with the intent to conquer or pillage; to penetrate and overrun harmfully; to violate; to encroach upon invader *n.*

in-va-lid *n.* a chronically sick, bedridden, or disabled person invalid *adj. & v.*

in-val-id *adj.* disabled by injury or disease; not valid; unsound invalidity *n.*, invalidly *adv.*

in-val-i-date *v.* to nullify; to make invalid invalidation, invalidator *n.*

in-val-u-able *adj.* priceless; of great value; to be of great help or use invaluably *adv.*, invaluableness *n.*

in-var-i-a-ble *adj.* constant and not changing invariably *adv.*

in-va-sion *n.* the act of invading; an entrance made with the intent of overrunning or occupying invasive *adj.*

in-veigh *v.* to angrily protest inveigher *n.*

in-vei-gle *v.* to win over by flattery inveiglement, inveigler *n.*

in-vent *v.* to devise or create by original effort or design inventor *n.*

in-ven-tion *n.* the act or process of inventing; a new process, method, or device conceived from study and testing

in-ven-tive *adj.* skillful at invention or contrivance; ingenious inventively *adv.*, inventiveness *n.*

in-ven-to-ry *n.*, *pl.* -ies a list of items with descriptions and quantities of each; the process of making such a list inventory *v.*

in-verse *adj.* reversed in order or sequence; inverted *n.* something opposite inversely *adv.*

in-ver-sion *n.* the act of inverting or the state of being inverted; that which is inverted

in-vert *v.* to turn upside down; to reverse the position, condition, or order of something inverter *n.*, invertible *adj.*

in-ver-te-brate *adj.* lacking a backbone or spinal column invertebrate *n.*

in-vest *v.* to use money for the purchase of stocks or property in order to obtain profit or interest; to place in office formally; to install; to make an investment investor *n.*

in-ves-ti-gate *v.* to search or inquire into; to examine carefully -tive *adj.*, investigation, investigator *n.*

in-ves-ti-ture *n.* the ceremony or act of investing or installing someone in a high office

in-vest-ment *n.* the act of investing money or capital to gain interest or income; property acquired and kept for future benefit

in-vig-o-rate *v.* to give strength or vitality to invigoratingly *adv.*, -tion *n.*

in-vin-ci-ble *adj.* incapable of being defeated invincibility *n.*, invincibly *adv.*

in-vi-o-la-ble *adj.* secure from profanation; safe from assault inviolability *n.*, inviolably *adv.*

in-vi-o-late *adj.* not violated inviolately *adv.*, inviolateness *n.*

in-vis-i-ble *adj.* not capable of being seen; not visible; not open to view; hidden invisibility *n.*, invisibly *adv.*

in-vi-ta-tion *n.* the act of inviting; the means or words that request someone's presence or participation

in-vite *v.* to request the presence or participation of; to make a formal or polite request for; to provoke; to entice; to issue an invitation

in-vit-ing *adj.* tempting; attractive invitingly *adv.*

in-vo-ca-tion *n.* an appeal to a deity or other agent for inspiration, witness, or help; a prayer used at the opening of a ceremony or service

in-voice *n.* an itemized list of merchandise shipped or services rendered, including prices, shipping instructions, and other costs; a bill invoice *v.*

in-voke *v.* to call upon for aid, support, or inspiration; to conjure invoker *n.*

in-vol-un-tar-y *adj.* not done by choice or willingly *n. Physiol.* muscles which function without an individual's control involuntariness *n.*

in-volve *v.* to include as a part; to make a participant of; to absorb; to engross involvement *n.*

in-vul-ner-a-ble *adj.* to be immune to attack; impregnable; not able to be physically injured or wounded invulnerability *n.*, invulnerably *adv.*

in-ward *adj.* situated toward the inside, center, or interior; of or existing in the mind or thoughts inwardness *n.*, inwardly *adv.*

i-o-dine *n.* a grayish-black, corrosive, poisonous element, symbolized by I; a solution made up of iodine, alcohol, and sodium iodide or potassium iodide which is used as an antiseptic

i-on *n.*, *Physics.* an atom or group of atoms which carries a positive or negative electric charge as a result of having lost or gained one or more electrons

i-on-ize *v.* to convert completely or partially into ions **ionization** *n.*

IOU *abbr.* I owe you

ip-so fac-to *adv.*, *L.* by that very fact or act

IQ *abbr.* intelligence quotient

i-ras-ci-ble *adj.* easily provoked to anger; quick-tempered **irascibly** *adv.*, **irascibility, irascibleness** *n.*

i-rate *adj.* raging; angry **irately** *adv.*

ir-i-des-cent *adj.* displaying the colors of the rainbow in shifting hues and patterns **iridescence** *n.*

i-ris *n.*, *pl.* **irises** *or* **irides** the pigmented part of the eye which regulates the size of the pupil by contracting and expanding around it *Bot.* a plant with narrow sword-shaped leaves and large, handsome flowers, as the gladiolus and crocus

I-rish *adj.* pertaining to Ireland and its people or their language

irk *v.* to annoy or to weary

Iron Age *n.* the most recent of three early stages of human progress, following the Stone Age and the Bronze Age

i-ron-bound *adj.* bound with iron; unyielding

i-ron-clad *adj.* covered with protective iron plates; strict; unbreakable

iron curtain *n.* an impenetrable political and ideological barrier between the Soviet bloc and the rest of the world

i-ron-ic *adj.* marked by or characterized by irony **ironical** *adj.*, **ironically** *adv.*

iron lung *n.* a tank which encloses the entire body with the exception of the head and regulates the respiration of a patient by alternately increasing and decreasing air pressure

i-ron-stone *n.* a heavy, white, glazed pottery

i-ro-ny *n.*, *pl.* **-ies** a literary device for conveying meaning by saying the direct opposite of what is really meant

ir-ra-di-ate *v.* to subject to ultraviolet light, radiation, or similar rays **irradiation, irradiator** *n.*

ir-ra-tion-al *adj.* unable to reason; contrary to reason; absurd; in mathematics, a number which is not expressible as an integer or a quotient of integers **irrationality** *n.*, **irrationally** *adv.*

ir-rec-on-cil-a-ble *adj.* not able or willing to be reconciled **irreconcilability** *n.*, **irreconcilably** *adv.*

ir-re-deem-a-ble *adj.* not capable of being recovered, bought back, or paid off; not convertible into coin

ir-re-duc-i-ble *adj.* not having the capabilities of reduction, as to a smaller amount **irreducibility** *n.*, **irreducibly** *adv.*

ir-ref-ra-ga-ble *adj.* cannot be refuted or disproved **irrefragably** *adv.*

ir-re-fut-able *adj.* cannot be disproved **irrefutability** *n.*, **irrefutably** *adv.*

ir-reg-u-lar *adj.* not according to the general rule or practice; not straight, uniform, or orderly; uneven *n.* one who is irregular **irregularity** *n.*, **irregularly** *adv.*

ir-rel-e-vant *adj.* not pertinent or related to the subject matter **-ly** *adv.*, **irrelevance, irrelevancy** *n.*

ir-re-lig-ious *adj.* lacking in religion; opposed to religion **irreligiously** *adv.*, **irreligiousness, irreligion** *n.*

ir-re-mis-si-ble *adj.* unpardonable, as for sin **irremissibility** *n.*

ir-re-mov-a-ble *adj.* not removable **irremovably** *adv.*

ir-rep-a-ra-ble *adj.* unable to be set right or repaired **irreparability** *n.*, **irreparably** *adv.*

ir-re-place-a-ble *adj.* unable to be replaced

ir-re-press-i-ble *adj.* impossible to hold back or restrain **irrepressibility** *n.*, **irrepressibly** *adv.*

ir-re-proach-a-ble *adj.* blameless; not meriting reproach **-ness** *n.*, **irreproachably** *adv.*

ir-re-sist-i-ble *adj.* completely fascinating; impossible to resist **irresistibility** *n.*, **irresistibly** *adv.*

ir-res-o-lute *adj.* lacking resolution; indecisive; lacking firmness of purpose **irresolutely** *adv.*, **irresoluteness** *n.*

ir-re-spec-tive *adj.* regardless of

ir-re-spon-si-ble *adj.* lacking in responsibility; not accountable **irresponsibility** *n.*, **irresponsibly** *adv.*

ir-re-triev-a-ble *adj.* unable to be retrieved or recovered

ir-rev-er-ence *n.* a lack of reverence; a disrespectful action **irreverent** *adj.*, **irreverently** *adv.*

ir-re-vers-i-ble *adj.* impossible to reverse **irreversibility** *n.*, **irreversibly** *adv.*

ir-rev-o-ca-ble *adj.* unable or incapable of being turned in the other direction; incapable of being repealed, annulled or undone **irrevocability** n., **irrevocably** adv.

ir-ri-gate v. to water the land or crops artificially, as by means of ditches or sprinklers; to refresh with water *Med.* to wash out with a medicated fluid or water **irrigation, irrigator** n., **irrigational** adj.

ir-ri-ta-ble adj. easily annoyed; ill-tempered *Pathol.* to respond abnormally to stimuli **irritability, irritableness** n., **irritably** adv.

ir-ri-tate v. to annoy or bother; to provoke; to be sore, chafed, or inflamed **irritator, irritation** n., **irritant** adj. & n., **irritatingly** adv.

ir-rupt v. to burst or rush in; to invade **irruption** n., **-ive** adj., **irruptively** adv.

IRS abbr. Internal Revenue Service.

is v. third person, singular, present tense of the verb to be

-ish suffix of or belonging to a nationality or ethnic group; characteristic of; the approximate age of; the approximate time of; somewhat

is-land n. a piece of land smaller than a continent, completely surrounded by water **islander** n.

isle n. a small island

ism n., *Slang* a distinctive cause, doctrine, or theory

-ism suffix practice; process; a manner of behavior characteristic of person or thing; a system of principles

is-n't contr. is not

i-so-late v. to set apart from the others; to put by itself; to place or be placed in quarantine **isolation, isolator** n.

i-so-la-tion-ism n. a national policy of avoiding political or economic alliances or relations with other countries **isolationist** n.

i-so-mer n. a compound having the same kinds and numbers of atoms as another compound but differing in chemical or physical properties due to the linkage or arrangement of the atoms **isomeric** adj.

i-sos-ce-les tri-an-gle n. a triangle which has two equal sides

i-so-therm n. a line on a map linking points that have the same temperature **isothermal** adj.

i-so-tope n. any of two or more species of atoms of a chemical element which contain in their nuclei the same number of protons but different numbers of neutrons **isotopic** adj., **isotopically** adv.

i-so-trop-ic adj. having the same value in all directions **isotropy** n.

Is-rae-li adj. of or pertaining to the country of Israel or its inhabitants **Israeli, Israel** n.

is-sue n. the act of giving out; something that is given out or published; a matter of importance to solve *Med.* a discharge as of pus or blood v. to come forth; to flow out; to emerge; to distribute or give out, as supplies **issuable** adj., **issuer** n.

isth-mus n. a narrow strip of land which connects two larger pieces of land **isthmian** adj.

it pron. used as a substitute for a specific noun or name when referring to places, things, or animals of unspecified sex

i-tal-ic adj. a style of printing type in which the letters slant to the right

i-tal-i-cize v. to print in italics **italicization** n.

itch n. a skin irritation which causes a desire to scratch; a contagious skin disease accompanied by a desire to scratch; a restless desire or craving **itch** v., **itchiness** n., **itchy** adj.

-ite suffix a native or inhabitant of; an adherent of; a sympathizer or follower

i-tem n. a separately-noted unit or article included in a category or series; a short article, as in a magazine or newspaper

i-tem-ize v. to specify by item; to list **itemizer, itemization** n.

it-er-ate v. to state or do again; to repeat **iteration** n.

i-tin-er-ant adj. traveling from place to place; wandering

i-tin-er-ar-y n., pl. -ies a scheduled route of a trip

it'll contr. it will; it shall

its adj. the possessive case of the pronoun it

it's contr. it is; it has

I've contr. I have

i-vo-ry n., pl. -ies a hard, smooth, yellowish-white material which forms the tusks of elephants, walruses, and other animals; any substance similar to ivory **ivory** adj.

ivory tower n. a condition or attitude of withdrawal from the world and reality

i-vy n., pl. -ies a climbing plant having glossy evergreen leaves

-ization n. suffix the process, action, or result of doing a specified thing

-ize suffix to cause to become or resemble

iz-zard n. the letter z

J, j The tenth letter of the English alphabet.

Ja *abbr.* joint account; judge advocate

jab *v.* to poke or thrust sharply with short blows; a rapid punch **jabbingly** *adv.*

jab-ber *v.* to speak quickly or without making sense

jab-i-ru *n.* a large white bird resembling the stork

jab-ot *n.* ruffle or decoration on the front of a blouse, dress, or shirt

ja-bot-i-ca-ba *n.* a shrubby tree of the tropics

ja-cal *n.* a small hut

jack *n.* the playing card that ranks just below a queen and bears a representation of a knave; any of various tools or devices used for raising heavy objects; the male of certain animals; a man or boy; fellow; a small flag on a ship that indicates nationality

jacks *n.* game played with a set of six-pronged metal pieces and a small ball

jack-al *n.* an African or Asian dog-like, carnivorous mammal

jack-a-napes *n.* an impudent person

jack-ass *n.* a male donkey or ass; a stupid person or one who acts in a stupid fashion

jack-boot *n.* a heavy military boot which reaches above the knee

jack-daw *n.* a glossy, black, crow-like bird

jack-et *n.* a short coat worn by men and women; an outer protective cover for a book; the skin of a cooked potato

Jack Frost *n.* a name given to frost or winter weather

jack-hammer *n.* a tool operated by air pressure, used to break pavement and to drill rock

jack--in--the--box *n.* a toy consisting of a small box from which a puppet springs up when the lid is unfastened

jack--in--the--pul-pit *n.* a common herb which grows from a turnip-shaped bulb

jack-knife *n.* a large pocketknife

jack-leg *adj.* deficient in skill; an amateur

jack--of--all--trades *n.* a person who is able to do many types of work

jack--o--lan-tern *n.* a lantern made from a hollowed out pumpkin which has been carved to resemble a face

jack pine *n.* large pine tree

jack-pot *n.* any post, prize, or pool in which the amount won is cumulative

jack rabbit *n.* a large American hare with long back legs and long ears

jade *n.* hard, translucent, green gemstone

jad-ed *adj.* fatigued; dulled; worn-out

jag *n.* a very sharp projection or point *Slang* a binge or spree

jag-ged *adj.* having jags or sharp notches; serrated **jaggedly** *adv.*, **jaggedness** *n.*

jag-uar *n.* large, spotted, feline mammal of tropical America with a tawny coat and black spots

jai alai *n.* game similar to handball in which players catch and throw a ball with long, curved, wicker baskets strapped to their arms

jail *n.* a place of confinement for incarceration

jail-bird *n.*, *Slang* a prisoner or ex-prisoner

jail-break *n.* prison escape using force

jail-er *n.* the officer in charge of a jail and its prisoners

ja-lop-y *n.*, *pl.* **-ies** *Slang* an old, rundown automobile

ja-lou-sie *n.* a window, blind, or door having adjustable horizontal slats

jam *v.* to force or wedge into a tight position *Mus.* to be a participant in a jazz session *Slang* to be in a jam *n.* a preserve of whole fruit boiled with sugar

jamb *n.* the vertical sidepiece of a door

jam-ba-lay-a *n.* a food dish made of rice, vegetables and various kinds of meats

jam-bo-ree *n.* a large, festive gathering

jam session *n.* an informal gathering of a group of jazz musicians

jan-gle *v.* to make a harsh unmusical sound *n.* a discordant sound **jangler** *n.*

jan-i-tor *n.* person who cleans and cares for a building **janitorial** *adj.*

ja-pan *n.* black varnish used for coating objects

jape *v.* to joke; to make fun of or mock by words or actions **japer**, **japery** *n.*

jar *n.* deep, cylindrical vessel with a wide mouth; a harsh sound *v.* to strike against or bump into; to affect one's feelings unpleasantly

jar-di-niere *n.* decorative pot or stand for flowers or plants

jar-gon *n.* technical or specialized vocabulary used among members of a particular profession **jargonistic** *adj.*

jas-mine *or* **jes-sa-mine** *n.* a shrub with fragrant yellow or white flowers

jas-per *n.* an opaque red, brown, or yellow variety of quartz

ja-to *n.* takeoff of an airplane which is assisted by an auxiliary rocket engine

jaun-dice *n.*, *Pathol.* a diseased condition

of the liver due to the presence of bile pigments in the blood

jaunt *n.* short journey for pleasure

jaun-ty *adj.* having a buoyantly carefree and self-confident air or matter about oneself -ily *adv.* -iness *n.*

Ja-va *n.*, *Slang* coffee

jave-lin *n.* a light spear thrown as a weapon

jaw *n.*, *Anat.* either of the two bony structures forming the framework of the mouth and holding the teeth

jaw-bone *n.* one of the bones of the jaw, especially the lower jaw

jaw-break-er *n.* very hard piece of candy. *Slang* A word which is hard to pronounce

jay *n.* any of various corvine birds of brilliant coloring

jay-walk *v.*, *Slang* to cross a street carelessly, violating traffic regulations and or signals **jaywalker** *n.*

jazz *n.* kind of music which has a strong rhythmic structure with frequent syncopation and often involving ensemble and solo improvisation -er *n.*, -y *adj.*

jeal-ous *adj.* suspicious or fearful of being replaced by a rival; resentful or bitter -ly *adv.*, -ness, *n.*

jean *n.* strong, twilled cotton cloth **jeans** Pants made of denim

jeep *n.* small, military, and civilian vehicle with four-wheel drive

jeer *v.* speak or shout derisively **jeer** *n.*, **jerringly** *adv.*

Je-ho-vah *n.* God, in the Christian translations of the Old Testament

je-june *adj.* lacking in substance or nourishment; immature

je-ju-num *n.*, *pl.* -na *Anat.* part of the small intestine which extends from the duodenum to the ileum

jel-ly *n.* *pl.* -ies food preparation made with pectin or gelatin and having a somewhat elastic consistency; a food made of boiled and sweetened fruit juice and used as a filler or spread; *v.* to make into jelly; to become or take the form of jelly; to become gelatinous; to assume or cause to assume definite form

jel-lybean *n.* small candy having a hard, colored coating over a gelatinous center

jel-ly-fish *n.*, *pl.* **fishes** any of a number of freeswimming marine animals of jelly-like substance

jeop-ard-ize *v.* to put in jeopardy; to expose to loss or danger

jeop-ard-y *n.* exposure to loss or danger

jer-bo-a *n.* any of a type of small, nocturnal rodent of Asia and Africa with long hind legs

jer-e-mi-ad *n.* lament or prolonged complaint

Jer-emi-ah *n.* Hebrew prophet of the seventh century B.C.

jerk *v.* give a sharp twist or pull to *n.* sudden movement, as a tug or twist *Physiol.* involuntary contraction of a muscle resulting from a reflex action **jerky**, **jerkily** *adv.*, **jerkiness** *n.*

jer-kin *n.* close-fitting jacket, usually sleeveless

jerk-wa-ter *adj.* of little importance

jer-ry—build *v.* build flimsily and cheaply

jer-sey *n.*, *pl.* -seys a soft ribbed fabric of wool, cotton, or other material; a knitted sweater, jacket, or shirt; fawn-colored, small dairy cattle which yield milk rich in butter fat

jest *n.* action or remark intended to provoke laughter; a joke; a playful mood **jester** *n.*

Jes-u-it *n.* member of the Society of Jesus, a religious order founded in 1534

Jesus *n.* founder of Christianity, son of Mary and regarded in the Christian faith as Christ the son of God, the Messiah; also referred to as Jesus Christ or Jesus of Nazareth

jet *n.* sudden spurt or gush of liquid or gas emitted through a narrow opening; a jet airplane **jet** *adj.*

jet lag *n.* mental and physical fatigue resulting from rapid travel through several time zones

jet set *n.* international social group of wealthy individuals who travel from one fashionable place to another for pleasure **jet setter** *n.*

jet stream *n.* high-velocity wind near the troposphere, generally moving from west to east often at speeds exceeding 250 mph.; a high-speed stream of gas or other fluid expelled from a jet engine or rocket

jet-ti-son *v.* throw cargo overboard; to discard a useless or hampering item

jet-ty *n.*, *pl.* -ies wall made of piling rocks, or other material which extends into a body of water to protect a harbor or influence the current; a pier

Jew *n.* descendant of the ancient Hebrew people; a person believing in Judaism

jew-el *n.* precious stone used for personal adornment; a person or thing of very rare excellence or value *v.* furnish with jewels **jewelry** *n.*

jew-eler or **jew-el-ler** n. person who makes or deals in jewelry

Jew's harp n. small musical instrument held between the teeth when played, consisting of a U-shaped frame with a flexible metal piece attached which is plucked with the finger to produce twanging sounds

jib n., Naut. triangular sail set on a stay extending from the head of the foremast to the bowsprit

jif-fy or **jiff** n. short time

jig n. any of a variety of fast, lively dances; the music for such a dance Mech. device used to hold and guide a tool **jig** v.

jig-ger n. small measure holding 1 1/2 oz. used for measuring liquor Naut. small sail in the stern of a sailing craft

jig-gle v. move or jerk lightly up and down n. jerky, unsteady movement

jig-saw n. saw having a slim blade set vertically, used for cutting curved or irregular lines

jigsaw puzzle n. puzzle consisting of many irregularly shaped pieces which fit together and form a picture

jilt v. discard a lover n. woman or girl who discards a lover

jim-my n., pl. -ies short crowbar, often used by a burglar v. to force open or break into with a jimmy

jim-son-weed n. tall, coarse, foul-smelling, poisonous annual weed with large, trumpet-shaped purplish or white flowers

jin-gle v. make a light clinking or ringing sound n. short, catchy song or poem, as one used for advertising

jin-go-ism n. extreme nationalism which is marked by a belligerent foreign policy **jingoist** n., **jingoistic** adj.

jinn n., pl. **jin-ni** in the Moslem legend, a spirit with supernatural powers

jinx n., Slang person or thing thought to bring bad luck

jit-ney n. vehicle carrying passengers for a small fee

jit-ter v., Slang to be intensely nervous **jittery** adj.

jit-ter-bug n., Slang lively dance or one who performs this dance **jitterbug** v.

jit-ters n. nervousness

jive n., Slang jazz or swing music and musicians

job n. anything that is done; work that is done for a set fee; the project worked on; a position of employment **jobless** adj., **joblessness** n.

job-ber n. one who buys goods in bulk from the manufacturer and sells them to retailers; a person who works by the job; a pieceworker

job-name n. Computer Science. code that is assigned to a specific job instruction in a computer program, for the operator's use

jock n., Slang male athlete in college; a person who participates in athletics

jock-ey n. person who rides a horse as a professional in a race

joc-u-lar adj. marked by joking; playful **jocularity** n., **jocularly** adv.

joc-und adj. cheerful; merry; suggestive of high spirits and lively mirthfulness **jocundity** n., **jocundly** adv.

jog n. slight movement or a slight shake; the slow steady trot of a horse; to exercise by running at a slow but steady pace **jogger** n.

jog-gle v. move or shake slightly

john n., Slang toilet; a prostitute's client

John n. one of the twelve Apostles

John Doe n., Law person in a legal proceeding whose true name is unknown

john-ny-cake n. thin bread made with cornmeal

John the Baptist n. baptizer of Jesus Christ

join v. bring or put together so as to form a unit

join-er n. person whose occupation is to build articles by joining pieces of wood

joint n. place where two or more things or parts are joined; a point where bones are connected adj. marked by cooperation, as a joint effort

join-ture n., Law settlement of property arranged by a husband which is to be used for the support of his wife after his death

joist n. any of a number of small parallel beams set from wall to wall to support a floor

joke n. something said or done to cause laughter, such as a brief story with a punch line; something not taken seriously v. to tell or play jokes **jokingly** adv.

jok-er n. person who jokes; a playing card

jol-li-fi-ca-tion n. merrymaking.

jol-ly adj. full of good humor; merry **jollity** n., **jolly** v.

jolt v. knock or shake about n. sudden bump or jar, as from a blow **jolty** adj.

jon-quil n. widely grown species of narcissus related to the daffodil

josh *v., Slang* make good-humored fun of someone

joss *n.* Chinese idol or image

jos-tle *v.* make one's way through a crowd by pushing, elbowing, or shoving

jot *v.* make a brief note of something *n.* tiny bit

jounce *v.* bounce; to bump; to shake **jouncey** *adj.*

jour-nal *n.* diary or personal daily record of observations and experiences; in bookkeeping, a book in which daily financial transactions are recorded

jour-nal-ese *n.* vocabulary and style of writing supposedly characteristic of most newspapers

jour-nal-ism *n.* occupation, collection, writing, editing, and publishing of newspapers and other periodicals -ist *n.*, -istic *adj.*, **journalistically** *adv.*

jour-ney *n.* trip from one place to another over a long distance

jour-ney-man *n., pl.* -men worker who has served an apprenticeship in a skilled trade

joust *n.* formal combat between two knights on horseback as a part of a medieval tournament

Jove *Interj.* mild expression of surprise or emphasis

jo-vi-al *adj.* good-natured; good-humored; jolly **joviality** *n.*

jowl *n.* fleshy part of the lower jaw; the cheek **jowly** *adj.*

joy *n.* strong feeling of great happiness; delight **joyfully** *adv.*, -fulness *n.*, -less *adj.*, -lessly *adv.*

joy-ous *adj.* joyful; causing or feeling joy **joyously** *adv.*

joy ride *Slang* ride taken for pleasure only

joy stick *Slang* control stick of an airplane or video game

ju-bi-lant *adj.* exultantly joyful or triumphant; expressing joy **jubilance** *n.*, **jubilantly** *adv.*

ju-bi-la-tion *n.* rejoicing; exultation

ju-bi-lee *n.* special anniversary of an event; any time of rejoicing

Ju-da-ism *n.* religious practices or beliefs of the Jews; a religion based on the belief in one God

judge *v., Law* public officer who passes judgment in a court *v.* decide authoritatively after deliberation

judg-ment or **judge-ment** *n.* ability to make a wise decision or to form an opinion; the act of judging *Law* sen-

tence or determination of a court **judgmental** *adj.*

ju-di-ca-ture *n.* function or action of administration of justice; law, courts, or judges as a whole

ju-di-cial *adj.* pertaining to the administering of justice, to courts of law, or to judges **judicially** *adv.*

ju-di-ci-ar-y *adj.* of, or pertaining to judges, courts, or judgments *n.* department of the government which administers the law

ju-di-cious *adj.* having, showing, or exercising good sound judgement **judiciously** *adv.*, **judiciousness** *n.*

ju-do *n.* system or form of self-defense, developed from jujitsu in Japan

jug *n.* small pitcher or similar vessel for holding liquids

jug-ger-naut *n.* destructive force or object

jug-gle *v.* keep several objects continuously moving from the hand into the air; to practice fraud or deception **juggler** *n.*

jug-u-lar *adj., Anat.* of or pertaining to the region of the throat or the jugular vein

jugular vein *n., Anat.* one of the large veins on either side of the neck

juice *n.* liquid part of a vegetable, fruit, or animal *Slang* electric current

juic-er *n.* device for extracting juice from fruit

juic-y *adj.* full of; abounding with juice; full of interest; richly rewarding, especially financially

ju-jit-su or **ju-jut-su** *n.* Japanese system of using holds, throws, and stunning blows to subdue an opponent

juke box *n.* large, automatic, coin-operated record player equipped with push buttons for the selection of records

ju-lep *n.* mint julep

ju-li-enne *adj.* cut into thin strips *n.* clear meat soup containing vegetables chopped or cut into thin strips

jum-ble *v.* to mix in a confused mass; to throw together without order

jum-bo *n.* very large person, animal, or thing *adj.* extremely large

jump *v.* spring from the ground, floor, or other surface into the air by using a muscular effort of the legs and feet; to move in astonishment

jump-er *n.* one who or that which jumps; a sleeveless dress, usually worn over a blouse

jump-y *adj.* nervous; jittery **jumpiness** n.

jump suit *n.* one piece clothing worn by parachutes

jun-co *n.* any of various small birds of North America

junc-tion *n.* place where lines or routes meet, as roads or railways; the process of joining or the act of joining

junc-ture *n.* point where two things join; a crisis; an emergency; a point in time

June beetle *or* **June bug** *n.* large, brightly colored beetle which flies in June and has larvae that live in the soil and often destroy crops

jun-gle *n.* densely covered land with tropical vegetation, usually inhabited by wild animals

jun-gle fe-ver *n.* disease of tropical regions where fever accompanies sickness

jun-gle-gym *n.* a structure with bars upon children can climb

jun-gle rot *n.* skin disease, such as a fungus

jun-ior *adj.* younger in years or rank, used to distinguish the son from the father of the same first name; the younger of two *n.* third year of high school or college

junior college *n.* college offering a two year course which is equivalent to the first two years of a four year college

junior high school *n.* school which includes the 7th, 8th, and 9th grades

ju-ni-per *n.* evergreen shrub or tree of Europe and America with dark blue berries, prickly foliage, and fragrant wood

jun-ket *n.* party, banquet, or trip -teer *n.*

junk-ie *or* **junk-y** *n.*, *Slang* drug addict that uses heroin

ju-ry *n.*, *pl.* -ies group of legally qualified persons summoned to serve on a judicial tribunal

just *adj.* fair and impartial in acting or judging; morally right justly *adv.*, justness *n.*

jus-tice *n.* principle of moral or ideal rightness; conformity to the law

jus-ti-fy *v.* to be just, right, or valid; to declare guiltless; to adjust or space lines to the proper length

jut *v.* extend beyond the main portion; to project

ju-ve-nile *adj.* young; youthful; not yet an adult *n.* a young person; an actor who plays youthful roles; a child's book

jux-ta-pose *v.* put side by side; to place together

K, k The eleventh letter of the English alphabet

kaa-ba *n.* building in the Great Mosque at Mecca that contains the sacred stone said to have been turned black in color, by the tears of the repentant pilgrims or by the sins of people ;who have rubbed or touched it

ka-bob *n.* small cubes of meat cooked with vegetables

ka-bu-ki *n.* traditional Japanese drama in which dances and songs are performed in a stylized fashion

Kad-dish *n.* a Jewish prayer recited by mourners after the death of a relative and during other daily prayers in the synagogue

kaf-fee-klatsch *n.* informal conversation over coffee

kaf-ir *n.* a grain sorghum that is cultivated in dry areas, having a tough leafy stalk and is used for fodder

kai-nite *n.* a mineral that is used as a fertilizer and a source of magnesium and potassium

kai-ser *n.* an Austrian ruler from 1804-1918; an emperor; the title given to German rulers between the years of 1871 and 1918

ka-ka *n.* a New Zealand parrot, having an olivebrown color

ka-ka-po *n.* a large parrot

kale *n.* a green cabbage having crinkled leaves which do not form a tight head

ka-lie-do-scope *n.* a tubular instrument rotated to make successive symmetrical designs by using mirrors reflecting the changing patterns made by pieces of loose colored glass ath the end of a tube

kal-yard school *n.* a school of writers form the 19th century who wrote about Scottish life in a very sentimental manner, using heavy dialect

kal-mi-a *n.* an evergreen shrub of North America, having pink, ;white, or purple flowers

kame *n.* short ridge of gravel and sand that remains after glacial ice melts

kam-ik *n.* boot made of sealskin, knee-high in length and worn in the eastern arctic regions

ka-mi-ka-ze *n.* a Japanese pilot in World War II trained to make a suicidal crash; an aircraft loaded with explosives used in a suicide attack

kan-ga-roo *n.*, *pl.* -roo, roos various herbivorous marsupials, of Australia, with short forelegs, large hind limbs, capable of jumping, and a large tail

kangaroo court *n.* self-appointed, illegal court, usually marked by incompetence or dishonesty

ka-o-lin *or* **ka-o-line** *n.* fine clay used in ceramics

ka-pok *n.* silky fiber manufactured from the fruit of the silk-cotton tree and used for stuffing cushions and life preservers

ka-put *adj., Slang* destroyed or out of order

kar-a-kul *n.* any of a breed of fat-tailed sheep of central Asia having a narrow body and coarse wiry, brown fur

kar-at *n.* unit of measure for the fineness of gold

ka-ra-te *n.* Japanese art of self-defense

kar-ma *n.* over-all effect of one's behavior, held in Hinduism and Buddhism to determine one's destiny in a future existence **kar-mic** *adj.*

ka-ty-did *n.* various green insects related to grasshoppers and crickets, having specialized organs on the wings of the male that make a shrill sound when rubbed together

kay-ak *n.* watertight Eskimo boat with a light frame and covered with sealskin **kayaker** *n.*

ka-zoo *n.* toy musical instrument with a paper membrane which vibrates symathelically when a player hums into the tube

kedge *n.* small anchor *v.* pull a ship by the rope of an anchor

keel *n.* central main stem on a ship or aircraft which runs lengthwise along the center line from bow to stern, to which a frame is built upwards *v.* to capsize. *keel over.* fall over suddenly; turn upside down -ed *adj.* -less *adj.*

keel-haul *v.* drag a person under the keel of a ship as a form of punishment

keel-son *n., Naut.* structural member fastened above and parallel to the keel to give additional strength

keen *adj.* having a sharp edge or point; acutely painful or harsh; intellectually acute; strong; intense *Slang* great *n.* wailing lament especially for the dead **keenly** *adv.*, **keenness** *n.*

keep *v.* to have and hold; to not let go; to maintain, as business records; to know a secret and not divulge it; to protect and defend

keep-sake *n.* memento or souvenir

keg *n.* small barrel

keg-ler *n.* bowler

kelp *n.* any of a large brown seaweeds

kel-pie *n.* sheep dog originally bred in Australia

ken-nel *n.* shelter for or a place where dogs or cats are bred, boarded, or trained **kennel** *v.*

ke-no *n.* game of chance resembling bingo; a lottery game

kep-i *n.* French military cap having a flat, round top and a visor

ker-a-tin *n.* fibrous protein which forms the basic substance of nails, hair, horns, and hoofs **keratinous** *adj.*

ker-a-ti-tis *n.* inflammation of the cornea

ker-chief *n.* piece of cloth usually worn around the neck or on the head; scarf; a handkerchief

ker-nel *n.* grain or seed, as of corn, enclosed in a hard husk; the inner substance of a nut; the central, most important part

ker-o-sene *or* **ker-o-sine** *n.* oil distilled from petroleum or coal and used for illumination

kes-trel *n.* small falcon, with gray and brown plumage

ketch *n.* small sailing vessel with two masts

ketch-up *n.* thick, smooth sauce made from tomatoes

ket-tle *n.* pot used for cooking

ket-tle-drum *n.* musical instrument with a parchment head which can be tuned by adjusting the tension

key *n.* an instrument by which the bolt of a lock is turned *adj.* of general importance

key-board *n.* bank of keys, as on a piano, typewriter, or computer terminal *v.* to set by means of a keyed typesetting machine; to generate letters by means of a word processor **keyboarder** *n.*

key club *n.* private club that offers entertainment amd serves liquor

key-note *n., Mus.* first and harmonically fundamental tone of a scale; main principle or theme

keynote address *n.* opening speech that outlines issues for discussion

key-punch *n.* machine operated from a keyboard that uses punched holes in tapes or cards for data processing systems **keypunch** *n.*, **keypuncher** *v.*

key-stone *n.* wedge-shaped stone at the center of an arch that locks its parts together; an essential part

key-stroke *n.* stroke of a key, as of a typewriter

key-way *n.* groove for a key

kg *abbr.* kilogram

khak-i *n.* yellowish brown or olive-drab color; a sturdy cloth being khaki in color **khakis** uniform of khaki cloth

khan *n.* Asiatic title of respect; a medieval Turkish, Mongolian or Tartar ruler **khanate** *n.*

khe-dive *n.* ruler of Egypt from 1867 to 1914 governing as a viceroy of the sultan of Turkey

kibble *n.* coarsely ground grain

kib-itz *v.* Slang look on and offer meddlesome advice to others **kibitzer** *n.*

kick *n.* sudden forceful thrust with the foot

kick-stand *n.* metal rod for holding up a two-wheeled bike

kick up *n.* provoke; to stir up

kid *n.* young goat; leather made from the skin of a young goat *Slang* child; youngster *v.* mock or tease playfully to deceive for fun; to fool **kidder** *n.*

kid leather *n.* soft pliable leather made from goatskin or lambskin

kid-nap *v.* seize and hold a person; unlawfully, often for ransom **kidnapper** *n.*

kid-ney *n.*, *pl.* **-neys** either of two organs situated in the abdominal cavity of vertebrates whose function is to keep proper water balance in the body and to excrete wastes in the form of urine

kidney bean *n.* bean grown for its edible seeds

kidvid *n.*, *Slang* television programming for children

kiel-ba-sa *n.* smoked Polish sausage

kill *n.* put to death; nullify; cancel; to slaughter for food

kill-deer *n.*, *pl.* **-deer**, **-deers** bird characterized by a plaintive, penetrating cry

killer whale *n.* black and white carnivorous whale, found in the colder waters of the seas

kil-lick *n.* small anchor usually made from a stone

kill-joy *n.* one who spoils the enjoyment of others

kiln *n.* oven or furnace for hardening or drying a substance, especially one for firing ceramics, pottery, etc.

ki-lo *n.* kilogram

kil-o-bit *n.* in computer science, one thousand binary digits

ki-lo-cy-cle *n.* unit equal to one thousand cycles, one thousand cycles per second

kil-o-gram *n.* measurement of weight in the meteric system equal to slightly more than one third of a pound

kil-o-ton *n.* one thousand tons; an explosive power equal to that of one thousand tons of TNT

kil-o-watt *n.* unit of power equal to one thousand watts

kil-o-watt-hour *n.* unit of electric power consumption of one thousand watts throughout one hour

kilt *n.* knee-length wool skirt with deep pleats, usually of tartan, worn especially by men in the Scottish Highlands

kil-ter *n.* good condition; proper or working order

ki-mo-no *n.* loose, Japanese robe with a wide sash; a loose robe worn chiefly by women

kin *n.* one's relatives by blood

kin-der-gar-ten *n.* school or class for young children from the ages of four to six

kin-der-gart-ner *n.* child who attends kindergarten

kind-heart-ed *adj.* a sympathetic nature **-ly** *adv.* **kindheartedness** *n.*

kin-dle *v.* ignite; to catch fire; to stir up; to arouse; to excite, as the feelings **kindler** *n.*

kin-dling *n.* easily ignited material such as, sticks, wood chips, etc. used to start a fire

kin-dred *n.* a person's relatives by blood *adj.* having a like nature; similar **kindredness** *n.*

kin-e-mat-ics *n.* the branch of dynamics that deals with motion considered apart from force and mass **kinematical** *adj.*, **-ally** *adv.*

kin-e-scope *n.* cathoderay tube in a television set which translates received electrical into a visable picture on a screen; a film of a television on broadcast

ki-net-ic *adj.* of, or pertaining to, or produced by motion

king-bolt *n.* verticle central vehicle to the front axle

king crab *n.* large crablike crustacean common in the coastal waters of Japan, Alaska, and Siberia

king-pin *n.* foremost pin of a set arranged in order for playing bowling or tenpins; the most important or essential person

kink *n.* tight twist or knotlike curl; a sharp painful muscle cramp; a mental quirk *v.* to form or cause to form a kink.

kink-a-jou *n.* tropical American mammal having large eyes, brown fur and a long prehensile tail

kink-y *adj.* tightly curled; sexually un-inhibited kinkily *adv.,* kinkiness *n.*

ki-osk *n.* small building used as a refreshment booth or newsstand

kip *n.* untanned skin of a calf, a lamb and or an adult of any small breed

kip-per *n.* salted and smoked herring or salmon *v.* to cure by salting, smoking, or drying

kir-tle *n.* woman's long skirt

kis-met *n.* fate; appointed lot

kitch-en *n.* room in a house or building used to prepare and cook food

kite *n.* light-weight framework of wood and paper designed to fly in a steady breeze at the end of a string; any of various predatory birds of the hawk family having a long, usually forked tail

kith *or* **kin** *n.* acquaintances or family

kitsch *n.* anything that is pretentious and in poor taste

kit-ten *n.* young cat

kit-ty--cor-nered *adj.* diagonally; cater-cornered

klep-to-ma-ni-a *n.* obsessive desire to steal or impulse to steal, especially without economic motive

klutz *n., Slang* stupid or clumsy person klutziness *n.,* klutzy *adj.*

km *abbr.* kilometer

knack *n.* natural talent; aptitude

knap-sack *n.* supply or equipment bag, as of canvas or nylon, worn strapped across the shoulders

knave *n.* tricky; or dishonest person knavish *adj.,* -ishness *n.*

knead *v.* work dough into a uniform mass; to shape by or as if by kneading

knee *n.* joint in the human body which connects the calf with the thigh

knell *v.* sound a bell, especially when rung for a funeral; to toll *n.* act or in-stance of knelling; a signal of disaster

knick-ers *pl. n.* short loose-fitting pants gathered at the knee

knick-knack *n.* trinket; trifling article

knight *n.* medieval soldier serving a monarch; a chess piece bearing the shape of a horse's head knighthood *n.,* knightly *adj.*

knish *n.* baked or fried dough stuffed with meat, cheese, or potatoes

knit *v.* to form by intertwining thread or yarn, by interlocking loops of a single yarn by means of needles; to fasten securely; to draw together knit *n.*

knitting needle *n.* long, slender, pointed rod for knitting

knob *n.* rounded protuber-ance; a lump; a rounded mountain; a rounded handle knobed *adj.*

knock *v.* hit or strike with a hard blow; to criticize; to collide

knock-down *adj.* designed to be easily assembled for storage or shipment

knockdown--drag--out *adj.* extremely violent or bitter

knock-er *n.* one who or that which knocks; as a metal ring for knocking on a door

knock-knee *n.* condition in which one or both knees turn inward and knock or rub together while walking knock-kneed *adj.*

knoll *n.* small round hill; a mound

knot *n.* interwinding as of string or rope; a fastening made by tying together lengths of material, as string; a unify-ing bond, especially of marriage; a hard node on a tree from which a branch grows *Naut.* unit of speed

knot-hole *n.* hole in lumber left by the falling out of a knot

knout *n.* whip or scourge for flogging criminals knout *v.*

know *v.* perceive directly as fact or truth; to believe to be true; to be certain of knowable *adj.,* knowledge *n.*

ko-a-la *n.* Australian marsupial which has large hairy ears, gray fur, and feeds on eucalyptus leaves

kohl-ra-bi *n.* a variety of cabbage having a thick stem and eaten as a vegetable

kook *n., Slang* crazy or eccentric person

ko-sher *adj.* conformant to eat accord-ing to Jewish dietary laws *Slang* ap-propriate; proper.

kow-tow *v.* show servile deference

kraal *n.* a village of southern African na-tives; an enclosure for animals in southern Africa.

krem-lin *n.* the citadel of Moscow which houses the major Soviet government offices; the Soviet government

kryp-ton *n.* a white, inert gaseous chemical used mainly in fluorescent lamps, symbolized by Kr

ku-dos *n.* acclaim or prestige resulting from notable achievement or high position

kum-quat *n.* small, round orange fruit having a sour pulp and edible rind

ky-ack *n.* a packsack for either side of a packsaddle

ky-pho-sis *n.* the abnormal backward curve of the spine

ky-rie *n.* a short prayer that consists of the words "Lord, have mercy"

L,l The twelfth letter of the English alphabet; the Roman numeral for fifty.

lab *n.* laboratory

la-bel *n.* something that identifies or describes **label** *v.*

la-bi-al *adj.* pertaining to or of the labia or lips

la-bi-um *n., pl.* **labia** any of the four folds of the vulva

la-bor *n.* physical or manual work done for hire

lab-o-ra-to-ry *n., pl.* **-ies** a place equipped for conducting scientific experiments, research, or testing

labor camp *n.* a group of prisoners who have been forced into labor; a place for migrant farm workers

Labor Day *n.* a legal holiday, the first Monday in September, which recognizes the contributions of working people

la-bored *adj.* bearing the marks of constraint and effort; produced with a great amount of labor; heavy

la-bo-ri-ous *adj.* toilsome; not easy; requiring much labor; diligent in service or work; industrious

la-bor-ite *n.* a person who promotes the theories, interests, and practices of a labor organization; one that belongs to a political party that is devoted mainly to labor interests

la-bret *n.* a decorative ornament worn by primitive tribes or people, usually made from a piece of wood, bone, ets. and placed through a pierced lip

la-brum *n.* the upper part of the mouth or an crustacean or insect

lab-y-rinth *n.* a system of winding, intricate passages; a maze **-thine** *adj.*

lac *n.* the resinous secretion left on certain trees by the lac insect and used in making paints and varnishes and the production of red color matter

lac-er-ate *v.* to open with a jagged tear **laceration** *n.*

lach-ry-mal or **lac-ri-mal** *adj.* relating to or producing tears

lack *n.* the deficiency or complete absence of something

lack-a-dai-si-cal *adj.* lacking life, interest, or spirit; melancholy

lack-ey *n.* a male servant of very low status

lack-lus-ter *adj.* lacking sheen

lac-tate *v.* to secrete or to milk **lactation** *n.*

lac-te-al *adj.* of, resembling, or like milk

lac-tic acid *n.* a limpid, syrupy acid that is present in sour milk, molasses, some fruits, and wines

lac-tose *n., Biochem.* a white, odorless, crystalline sugar

la-cu-na *n., pl.* **-nas, -nae** a space from which something is missing

lad *n.* a boy or young man

lad-der *n.* an implement used for climbing up or down

lad-en *adj.* heavily burdened; oppressed; loaded **laden** *v.*

lad-ing *n.* cargo; freight

la-dle *n.* a cup-shaped vessel with a deep bowl and a long handle **ladle** *v.*

la-dy *n., pl.* **ladies** a woman showing refinement, cultivation, and often high social position

lag *v.* to stray or fall behind; to move slowly

la-gniappe *n.* a small gift which is given to a purchaser by a storekeeper

la-goon *n.* a body of shallow water separated from the ocean by a coral reef or sandbars **lagoonal** *adj.*

lain *v.* past tense of lie

lais-sez--faire *n.* a policy stating that a government should exercise very little control in trade and industrial affairs

la-i-ty *n.* laymen, as distinguished from clergy

lake *n.* a large inland body of either salt or fresh water

La-maze method *n.* a method of childbirth in which the mother is prepared psychologically and physically to give birth

lamb *n.* a young sheep; the meat of a lamb used as food

lam-baste or **lambast** *v., Slang* to thrash or beat

lam-bent *adj.* lightly and playfully brilliant **lambency** *n.*

lame *adj.* disabled or crippled **lamely** *adv.*, **lameness** *n.*

la-me *n.* a brocaded fabric woven with gold or silver thread

lame duck *n.* an officeholder who has been defeated but continues in office until the inauguration of his or her successor

la-ment *v.* to express sorrow

lam-i-na *n., pl.* **-nae, -nas** a thin scale or layer *Bot.* the blade or flat part of a leaf

lam-i-nate *v.* to form or press into thin sheets **laminated** *adj.*

lamp *n.* a device for generating heat or light

lam-poon *n.* a satirical, but often humorous, attack in verse or prose

lam-prey *n.* ,*pl.* **preys** an eel-like fish

lance *n.* a spear-like implement used as a weapon by mounted knights or soldiers

lance corporal *n., Mil.* in the U.S. Marine Corps, an enlisted man who ranks above a private first class and below a corporal

land *n.* the solid, exposed surface of the earth as distinguished from the waters

lan-dau *n.* a four-wheeled vehicle with a closed carriage and a back seat with a collapsible top

land-er *n.* a space vehicle for landing on a celestial body

land--fill *n.* a system of trash and garbage disposal in which the waste is burned in low-lying land so as to build up the ground surface; a section built up by landfill

land grant *n.* a grant of land made by a government, especially for railroads, roads, or agricultural colleges

land-ing *n.* the act of coming, going, or placing ashore from any kind of vessel or craft; the act of descending and settling on the ground in an airpland

land-scape *n.* a view or vista of natural scenery as seen from a single point

lane *n.* a small or narrow path between walls, fences, or hedges

lan-guage *n.* the words, sounds, pronunciation and method of combining words

lan-guid *adj.* lacking in energy languidly *adv.,* languidness *n.*

lan-guish *v.* to become weak

lank *adj.* slender; lean

lan-o-lin *n.* wool grease obtained from sheep's wool and refined for use in ointments and cosmetics

lan-yard *n.* a piece of rope or line used to secure objects on ships

lap-in *n.* rabbit fur that is sheared and dyed

lap-is laz-u-li *n.* a semiprecious stone that is azure blue in color

lap-pet *n.* a flap or fold on a headdress or on a garment

lapse *n.* a temporary deviation or fall to a less desirable state

lar-ce-ny *n., pl.* -ies the unlawful taking of another person's property

lar-der *n.* a place, such as a pantry or room, where food is stored

large *adj.* greater than usual or average in amount or size

lar-gess *or* **lar-gesse** *n.* liberal or excessive giving to an inferior; generosity

lar-go *adv., Mus.* in a very slow, broad, and solemn manner largo *adj. & n.*

lar-i-at *n.* a long, light rope with a running noose at one end to catch livestock

lark *n.* a bird having a melodious ability to sing

lar-va *n., pl.* larvae the immature, wingless, often worm-like form of a newly hatched insect

lar-yn-gi-tis *n.* inflammation of the larynx

lar-ynx *n., pl.* larynges *or* larynxes the upper portion of the trachea which contains the vocal cords

lash *v.* to strike or move violently or suddenly

lass *n.* a young girl or woman

las-si-tude *n.* a condition of weariness; fatigue

last *adj.* following all the rest; of or relating to the final death

Last Supper *n.* the last meal eaten by Jesus Christ and his disciples, before his crucifixion

latch *n.* a device used to secure a gate or door, consisting of a bar that usually fits into a notch latch onto to grab onto

latch-et *n.* a narrow leather strap or thong used to fasten a shoe

latch-key *n.* a key for opening an outside door

late *adj.* coming, staying, happening after the proper or usual time; having recently died -ness *n.,* -ly *adv.*

lat-er-al *adj.* relating to or of the side laterally *adv.*

la-tex *n.* the milky, white fluid that is produced by certain plants, such as the rubber tree

lath *n.* a thin, narrow strip of wood nailed to joists, rafters, or studding

lathe *n.* a machine for holding material while it is spun and shaped by a tool

lat-i-tude *n.* the angular distance of the earth's surface north or south of the equator

la-trine *n.* a public toilet

lat-ter *adj.* being the second of two persons or two things

laud *v.* to praise; to extol laudable *adj.,* laudably *adv.*

laugh *v.* to express amusement, satisfaction laughable *adj.*

laun-dry *n., pl.* -ies an establishment where laundering is done professionally

lau-re-ate a person honored for his accomplishment

la-va *n.* molten rock which erupts or flows from an active volcano

lav-a-to-ry *n., pl.* **-ies** a room with permanently installed washing and toilet facilities

lav-en-der *n.* an aromatic plant having spikes of pale violet flowers

lav-ish *adj.* generous and extravagant in giving or spending
lavisher *n.,* **lavishly** *adv.*

law *n.* a rule of conduct or action, recognized by custom or decreed by formal enactment, considered binding on the members of a nation, community, or group

law-ren-ci-um *n.* a short-lived radioactive element

law-suit *n.* a case or proceeding brought before a court of law for settlement

law-yer *n.* a person trained in the legal profession who acts for and advises clients or pleads in court

lax *adj.* lacking disciplinary control
laxity, laxness *n.*

lax-a-tive *n.* a medicine taken to stimulate evacuation of the bowels

lay *v.* to cause to lie; to place on a surface; past tense of lie

lay-er *n.* a single thickness, coating, or covering that lies over or under another **layered** *adj.,* **layer** *v.*

lay-ette *n.* the clothing, bedding, and equipment for a newborn child

lay-off *n.* a temporary dismissal of employees

la-zy *adj.* unwilling to work; sluggish
lazily *adv.,* **laziness** *n.*

la-zy-bones *n. Slang* a lazy person

L-do-pa *n.* a drug used in treating Parkinson's disease

lea *n., Poetic.* a grassy field or meadow

leach *v.* to cause a liquid to pass through a filter

lead *v.* to go ahead so as to show the way; to control the affairs or action of

lead poisoning *n.* poisoning of a person's system by the absorption of lead or any of its salts

leaf *n., pl.* **leaves** a flat out-growth from a plant structure or tree

leaf-let *n.* a part or a segment of a compound leaf; a small printed handbill or circular

league *n.* an association of persons, organizations, or states for common action or interest

leak *n.* an opening, as a flaw or small crack, permitting an escape or entrance of light or fluid
leakage, leakiness *n.*

lean *v.* to rest or incline the weight of the body for support **leanly** *adv.,* **-ness** *n.*

lean-ing *n.* an inclination

learn *n.* the process of acquiring knowledge **learner** *n.*

lease *n.* a contract for the temporary use or occupation of property or premises in exchange for payment of rent

leash *n.* a strong cord or rope for restraining a dog or other animal

least-wise *adv., Slang* at least

leath-er *n.* an animal skin or hide with the hair removed

leave *v.* to go or depart from

leav-en *n.* an agent of fermentation, as yeast, used to cause batters and doughs to rise **leaven** *v.*

lech-er-y *n.* unrestrained indulgence in sexual activity **-er** *n.,* **-ous** *adj.*

lec-i-thin *n.* any of a group of phosphorus containing compounds found in plant and animal tissues

lec-tern *n.* a stand or tall desk, usually with a slanted top

lec-ture *n.* a speech on a specific subject

led *v., p.t. & p.p.* past tense of lead

ledg-er *n.* a book in which sums of money received and paid out are recorded

lee *n.* the side of a ship sheltered from the wind

leech *n.* any of various carnivorous or bloodsucking worms

leek *n.* a culinary herb of the lily family, related to the onion

leer *n.* a sly look or sideways glance expressing desire

lee-way *n., Naut.* the lateral drift of a plane or ship away from the correct course

left *adj.* pertaining to or being on the side of the body that faces north when the subject is facing east

leg-a-cy *n., pl.* **-ies** personal property, money, and other valuables that are bequeathed by will

le-gal *adj.* of, pertaining to, or concerned with the law or lawyers **-ity,** **-ization** *v.,* **legalize** *v.,* **legally** *adv.*

le-gal-ism *n.* a strict conformity to the law, especially when stressing the letter and forms of the law rather than the spirit of justice

le-ga-tion *n.* the official diplomatic mission in a foreign country, headed by a minister

le-ga-to *adv., Music* smooth and flowing with successive notes connected
legato *adj. & n.*

leg-end *n.* an unverifiable story handed down from the past **legendary** *adj.*

leg-horn *n.* a hat made from finely

plaited wheat straw

leg-i-ble *adj.* capable of being read **legibility** *n.,* **legibly** *adv.*

le-gion *n.* any various honorary or military organizations

leg-is-late *v.* to pass or make laws

leg-is-la-tion *n.* the act or procedures of passing laws

leg-is-la-ture *n.* a body of persons officially constituted and empowered to make and change laws

leg-ume *n.* a plant of the pea or bean family

lei *n., pl.* **leis** a wreath of flowers worn around the neck; the customary greeting of welcome in the state of Hawaii

lei-sure *n.* the time of freedom from work or duty **leisurely** *adj. & adv.*

lem-on *n.* an oval citrus fruit grown on a tree

lem-on-ade *n.* a drink made from water, lemon juice, and sugar

lend *v.* to allow the temporary use or possession of something **lender** *n.*

length *n.* the linear extent of something from end to end

length-wise *adv. & adj.* of or in the direction or dimension of length

le-ni-ent *adj.* gentle, forgiving, and mild **leniently** *adv.*

len-i-tive *adj.* having the ability to ease pain

lent *v.* past tense of lend

len-til *n.* a leguminous plant, having broad pods and containing edible seeds

leop-ard *n.* a large member of the cat family of Africa and Asia

le-o-tard *n.* a close-fitting garment worn by dancers and acrobats

lep-er *n.* one who suffers from leprosy

lep-re-chaun *n.* a mischief elf of Irish folklore

lep-ro-sy *n., Pathol.* a chronic communicable disease characterized by nodular skin lesions and the progressive destruction of tissue **leprotic** *adj.*

les-bi-an *n.* a homosexual woman

lese maj-es-ty *or n.* an offense against a ruler or supreme power of state

le-sion *n., Pathol.* an injury; a wound

less *adj.* smaller; of smaller or lower importance or degree

-less *suffix.* without; lacking

les-see *n.* one who leases a property

les-son *n.* an instance from which something is to be or has been learned

let *v.* to give permission; to allow

le-thal *adj.* pertaining to or being able to cause death

leth-ar-gy *n., Pathol.* a state of excessive drowsiness or abnormally deep sleep; laziness **lethargic** *adj.*

let's *contr.* let us

let-ter *n.* a standard character or sign used in writing or printing to represent an alphabetical unit or speech

leu-ke-mi-a *n., Pathol.* a generally fatal disease of the blood **leukemic** *adj.*

le-vee *n.* an embankment along the shore of a body of water, built to prevent over-flowing

lev-el *n.* a relative position, rank, or height on a scale. *v.* To make or become flat or level **-er,** **-ness** *n.*

lever *n.* a handle that projects and is used to operate or adjust a mechanism

lev-i-tate *v.* to rise and float in the air in apparent defiance of gravity **levitation** *n.*

Le-vit-i-cus *n.* the third book of the Old Testament

lev-i-ty *n., pl.* **-ies** lack of seriousness; frivolity; lightness

lev-y *v.* to impose and collect by authority or force, as a fine or tax

lewd *adj.* preoccupied with sex; lustful **lewdness** *n.*

lex-i-cog-ra-phy *n.* the practice or profession of compiling dictionaries

lex-i-con *n.* a dictionary; a vocabulary or list of words that relate to a certain subject, occupation, or activity

li-a-bil-i-ty *n., pl.* **-ies** the condition or state of being liable

li-a-ble *adj.* legally or rightly responsible

li-ai-son *n.* a communication, as between different parts of an armed force or departments of a government

li-ar *n.* a person who tells falsehoods

li-bel *n., Law* a written statement in published form that damages a person's character or reputation

lib-er-al *adj.* characterized by generosity or lavishness in giving; abundant; ample; inclining toward opinions or policies that favor progress or reform, such as religion or politics

liberal arts *pl. n.* academic courses that include literature, philosophy, history, languages, etc.

lib-er-ate *v.* to set free, as from bondage, oppression

lib-er-ty *n., pl.* **-ies** the state of being free from oppression

li-bi-do *n.* one's sexual desire or impulse; the psychic energy drive that is behind all human activities

li-brar-i-an *n.* a person in charge of a

library

li-brar-y n., pl. -ies a collection of books, pamphlets, magazines, and reference books kept for reading, reference, or borrowing

lice n. plural of louse

li-cense n. an official document that gives permission to engage in a specified activity or to perform a specified act

li-cen-ti-ate n. a person licensed to practice a specified profession

li-cen-tious adj. lacking in moral restraint; immoral

li-chen n. any of various flowerless plants consisting of fungi, commonly growing in flat patches on trees and rocks lichened, lichenous adj.

lic-it adj. lawful licitly adv.

lick v. to pass the tongue over or along the surface of something

lick-e-ty--split adv. full speed

lic-o-rice n. a perennial herb of Europe, the dried root of which is used to flavor medicines and candy

lid n. a hinged or removable cover for a container; an eyelid lidded, lidless adj.

lie v. to be in or take a horizontal recumbent position; to recline n. a false or untrue statement

liege n. a feudal lord or sovereign

lien n. the legal right to claim, hold, or sell the property of another to satisfy a debt or obligation

lieu n. place; stead in lieu of In place of

lieu-ten-ant n. a commissioned officer

life n., pl. lives the form of existence that distinguishes living organisms from dead organisms or inanimate matter in the ability to carry on metabolism, respond to stimuli, reproduce, and grow

lifer n. Slang a person sentenced to life in prison

life-time n. the period between one's birth and death

life zone n. a biogeographic zone

lift v. to raise from a lower to a higher position; to elevate; to take from; to steal

liftoff n. the vertical takeoff or the instant of takeoff of an aircraft or spacecraft

lig-a-ment n. a tough band of tissue joining bones or holding a body organ in place ligamentous adj.

li-gate v. to tie with a ligature

lig-a-ture n. something, as a cord, that is used to bind

light n. electromagnetic radiation that can be seen by the naked eye; a source of fire, such as a match lightness n.

light-ning n. the flash of light produced by a high-tension natural electric discharge into the atmosphere

lig-ne-ous adj. of or resembling wood; woody

lig-nite n. a brownish-black soft coal

lig-ro-in n. a volatile, flammable fraction of petroleum used as a solvent

lik-en v. to describe as being like; to compare

like-ness n. resemblance; a copy

like-wise adv. in a similar way

lilt n. a light song; a rhythmical way of speaking

lil-y n., pl. -ies any of various plants bearing trumpet-shaped flowers

limb n. a large bough of a tree; an animal's appendage used for movement or grasping; an arm or leg

lim-ber adj. bending easily; pliable; moving easily; agile

lime n. a tropical citrus edible green fruit; calcium oxide

lime-light n. a focus of public attention; the center of attention

lim-er-ick n. a humorous verse of five lines

lim-it n. a boundary; a maximum or a minimum number or amount

limn v. to describe; to depict by drawing limner n.

li-mo-nite n. a natural iron oxide used as an ore of iron

lim-ou-sine n. a luxurious large vehicle; a small bus used to carry passengers to airports and hotels

limp v. to walk lamely. adj. Lacking or having lost rigidity; not firm or strong

lim-pet n. any of numerous marine gastropod mollusks having a conical shell and adhering to tidal rocks

lim-pid adj. transparently clear limpidity n., limpidly adv.

lin-den n. any of various shade trees having heart-shaped leaves

lin-e-age n. a direct line of descent from an ancestor

lin-e-a-ment n. a contour, shape, or feature of the body and especially of the face

lin-e-ar adj. of, pertaining to, or resembling a line; long and narrow

lin-en n. thread, yarn, or fabric made of flax; household articles, such as sheets and pillow cases

ling n. any of various marine food fishes

related to the cod

lin-ger v. to be slow in parting or reluctant to leave; to be slow in acting; to procrastinate **linger** n., **-ingly** adv.

lin-ge-rie n. women's undergarment

lingo n., pl. goes language that is unfamiliar; a specialized vocabulary

lin-guist n. one who is fluent in more than one language

lin-i-ment n. a liquid or semiliquid medicine applied to the skin

lin-ing n. a material which is used to cover an inside surface

lin-net n. a small Old World finch

li-no-le-um n. a floor covering

lin-seed n. the seed of flax, used in paints and varnishes

lin-tel n. a horizontal beam across the top of a door which supports the weight of the structure above

li-on n. a large carnivorous mammal of the cat family, found in Africa and India

li-on-ize v. to treat someone as a celebrity

liq-ue-fy or **liq-ui-fy** v. to make liquid **liquefaction** n.

li-queur n. a sweet alcoholic beverage; a cordial

liq-ui-date v. to settle a debt by payment or other settlement; to close a business by settling accounts and dividing up assets; to get rid of, to kill **liquidation, liquidator** n.

liq-uor n. a distilled alcoholic beverage

lisle n. a fine, tightly twisted cotton thread

lisp n. a speech defect or mannerism marked by lisping

list n. a series of numbers or words; a tilt to one side

list-less adj. lacking energy or enthusiasm **listlessly** adv.

lit-a-ny n., pl. -ies a prayer in which phrases recited by a leader are alternated with answers from a congregation

li-tchi or **li-chee** n. a Chinese tree, bearing edible fruit

lit-er-al adj. conforming to the exact meaning of a word **literally** adv., **literalistic** adj.

lit-er-al-ism n. adherence to the explicit sense of a given test; literal portrayal; realism **literalist** n.

lit-er-ar-y adj. pertaining to literature; appropriate to or used in literature

lit-er-ate adj. having the ability to read and write **literacy** n.

lithe adj. bending easily; supple

lithely adv., **litheness** n.

lith-i-um n. a silver-white, soft metallic element symbolized by Li

li-thog-ra-phy n. a printing process **lithograph** n. & v.

li-thol-o-gy n. the microscopic study and classification of rocks **lithologist** n.

lit-i-gate v. to conduct a legal contest by judicial process **litigant, litigation** n.

lit-ter-bug n. one who litters a public area

lit-to-ral adj. relating to or existing on a shore n. a shore

lit-ur-gy n., pl. -ies a prescribed rite or body of rites for public worship

live-li-hood n. a means of support or subsistence

live-ly adj. vigorous **liveableness** n.

liv-er n. the large, very vascular, glandular organ of vertebrates which secretes bile

live-stock n. farm animals raised for human use

live wire n., Slang an energetic person

liv-id adj. discolored from a bruise; very angry

liz-ard n. one of various reptiles, usually with an elongated scaly body

load n. a mass or weight that is lifted or supported; anything, as cargo

loaf n., pl. loaves a food, especially bread, that is shaped into a mass v. to spend time in idleness

loam n. soil that consists chiefly of sand, clay, and decayed plant matter

loan n. money lent with interest to be repaid; something borrowed for temporary use v. to lend

loath adj. averse

loathe v. to dislike intensely

loath-ing n. intense dislike

loath-some adj. arousing disgust **loathsomely** adv., **loathsomeness** n.

lob v. to hit or throw in a high arc

lob-by n., pl. -ies a foyer, as in a hotel or theatre; a group of private persons trying to influence legislators

lobe n. a curved or rounded projection or division, as the fleshy lower part of the ear **lobar, lobed** adj.

lob-lol-ly n., pl. -ies a mudhole; mire

lo-bo n. the gray wolf

lo-bot-o-my n., pl. -mies surgical severance of nerve fibers by incision into the brain

lob-ster n. any of several large, edible marine crustaceans

lob-ule n. a small lobe; a subdivision of a lobe

lo-cal *adj.* pertaining to, being in, or serving a particular area or place **locally** *adv.*

lo-cale *n.* a locality where a particular event takes place; the setting or scene, as of a novel

lo-cate *v.* to determine the place, position, or boundaries of; to look for and find **locator** *n.*

loch *n., Scot.* a lake

lock *n.* a device used, as on a door, to secure or fasten

lock-et *n.* a small, ornamental case for a keepsake, often a picture, worn as a pendant on a necklace

lock-jaw *n.* tetanus

lock-smith *n.* a person who makes or repairs locks

lo-co *adj., Slang* insane

lo-co-mo-tion *n.* the act of moving

lo-co-mo-tive *n.* a self-propelled vehicle that is generally electric or diesel-powered and is used for moving railroad cars

lo-cust *n.* any of numerous grasshoppers which often travel in swarms and damage vegetation

loft *n.* one of the upper, generally unpartitioned floors of an industrial buildings

loge *n.* a small compartment, especially a box in a theatre; a small partitioned area

log-gi-a *n.* a roofed but open arcade along the front of a building; an open balcony

log-ic *n.* the science dealing with the principles of reasoning, especially of the method and validity of deductive reasoning

log-i-cal *adj.* something marked by consistency of reasoning **logically** *adv.*

lo-gis-tics *pl., n.* the methods of procuring, maintaining, and replacing material and personnel **logistic** *adj.*

lo-go-type *n.* identifying symbol for a company or publication

lo-gy *adj.* something marked by sluggishness **-iness** *n.*

loins the thighs and groin; the reproductive organs

loi-ter *v.* to stay for no apparent reason; to dawdle or delay **loiterer** *n.*

loll *v.* to move or act in a lax, lazy or indolent manner

lol-ly-gag *v., Slang* to fool around

lone *adj.* single; isolated; sole

lone-ly *adj.* being without companions **loneliness** *n.*

lon-er *n.* a person who avoids the company of others

long-bow *n.* a wooden bow that is approximately five to six feet in length

lon-gev-i-ty *n.* long life; long duration; seniority

lon-gi-tude *n.* the angular distance that is east and west of the prime meridian at Greenwich, England

lon-gi-tu-di-nal *adj.* of or relating to the length; relating to longitude

look *v.* to examine with the eyes; to see; to glance, gaze, or stare at

look-out *n.* a person positioned to keep watch

loom *v.* to come into view as a image; to seem to be threatening

loo-ny *or* **loo-ney** *adj.* loony *n.* crazy

loose *adj.* not fastened; not confined or fitting; free

loot *n.* goods, usually of significant value, taken in time of war; goods that have been stolen *v.* to plunder

lope *v.* to run with a steady gait **lope, lopper** *n.*

lop-sid-ed *adj.* larger or heavier on one side than on the ·other; tilting to one side **lopsidedly** *adv.,* **-ness** *n.*

lo-qua-cious *adj.* overly talkative **loquaciously** *adv.,* **loquacity** *n.*

Lord *n.* God. a man having dominion and power over other people

lore *n.* traditional fact; knowledge that has been gained through education or experience

lorn *n.* forlorn

lose *v.* to mislay; to fail to keep **loser** *n.*

loss *n.* the suffering or damage used by losing; someone or something that is lost. **losses** *pl. n.* killed, wounded, or captured

lost *adj.* unable to find one's way

lot *n.* fate; fortune; a parcel of land having boundaries

lo-tion *n.* a liquid medicine for external use on the hands and body

lounge *v.* to move or act in a lazy, relaxed manner. *n.* A room, as in a hotel or theatre; a couch **-er** *n.*

louse *n., pl.* lice a small, wingless biting or sucking insect which lives as a parasites on various animals and also on human beings.

lous-y *adj.* lice infested *Slang* mean; poor; inferior

lout *n.* an awkward, stupid person **loutish** *adj.*

love *n.* intense affection for another arising out of kinship or personal ties; a strong feeling of attraction resulting from sexual desire

lov-er *n.* a person who loves another; a sexual partner

low *adj.* not high; being below or under normal height, rank, or level; depressed

low-brow *n.* an uncultured person

low-down *n.* the whole truth; all the facts *adj.* despicable; mean; depressed

low frequency *n.* a radiowave frequency between 30 and 300 kilohertz

low-key *or* **low-keyed** *adj.* restrained

low-ly *adj.* low in position or rank **lowliness** *n.*

low profile *n.* a deliberately inconspicuous life style or posture

lox *n.* smoked salmon; liquid oxygen.

loy-al *adj.* faithful in allegiance to one's country and government; faithful to a person, cause, ideal

loy-al-ist *n.* one who is or remains loyal to political cause, party, government, or sovereign

lu-au *n.* a traditional Hawaiian feast

lub-ber *n.* an awkward, clumsy or stupid person; an inexperienced sailor

lu-bri-cant *n.* a material, as grease or oil, applied to moving parts to reduce friction

lu-bri-cous *adj.* smooth, unstable; shifty **lubricity** *n.*

lu-cid *adj.* easily understood; mentally clear; rational; shining **lucidity** *n.*

Lucifer *n.* the devil; Satan

lu-cra-tive *adj.* producing profits or great wealth

lu-cre *n.* money; profit

lu-cu-brate *v.* to study or work laboriously

lu-di-crous *adj.* amusing or laughable through obvious absurdity; ridiculous

luge *n.* a small sled

lu-gu-bri-ous *adj.* mournful; dejected; especially exaggeratedly

lull *v.* to cause to rest or sleep; to cause to have a false sense of security

lul-la-by *n., pl.* -bies A song to lull a child to sleep

lum-ba-go *n.* painful rheumatic pain of the muscles and tendons of the lumbar region

lum-bar *adj.* part of the back and sides between the lowest ribs and the pelvis

lum-ber *n.* timber, sawed or split into boards

lu-mi-nar-y *n., pl.* -ies a celestial body, as the sun; a notable person

lu-mi-nes-cence *n.* an emission of light without heat, as in fluorescence

lu-mi-nous *adj.* emitting or reflecting light; bathed in steady light; illuminated

lum-mox *n.* a clumsy oaf

lump *n.* a projection; a protuber-ance; a swelling

lu-na-cy *n., pl.* -ies insanity

lu-nar *adj.* of, relating to, caused by the moon

lu-na-tic *n.* a crazy person

lunch-eon *n.* a lunch

lung *n.* one of the two spongy organs that constitute the basic respiratory organ of air-breathing vertebrates

lunge *n.* a sudden forward movement

lu-pus *n.* a bacterial disease of the skin

lure *n.* a decoy; something appealing; *v.* to attract or entice with the prospect of reward or pleasure

lurk *v.* to lie in concealment, as in an ambush

lus-cious *adj.* very pleasant to smell or taste; appealing to the senses

lush *adj.* producing luxuriant growth or vegetation *Slang* An alcoholic -ly *adv.*

lust *n.* intense sexual desire; an intense longing; a craving **lustful** *adj.*

lus-ter *or* **lus-tre** *n.* a glow of reflected light; sheen; brilliance or radiance

lust-y *adj.* vigorous; healthy; robust; lively **lustily** *adv.*

lute *n.* a medieval musical stringed instrument

lu-te-ti-um *or* **lu-te-ci-um** *n.* a silvery rare-earth metallic element symbolized by Lu

lux-u-ri-ant *adj.* growing or producing abundantly; lush; plentiful -tly *adv.*

lux-u-ri-ate *v.* to enjoy luxury or abundance

lymph node *n.* a roundish body of lymphoid tissue; lymph gland

lynch *v.* to execute without author-ity or the due process of law

lynx *n.* a wildcat *adj.* having acute eyesight

lyre *n.* an ancient Greek stringed instrument related to the harp

lyr-ic *adj.* concerned with thoughts and feelings; romantic; appro-priate for singing. *n.* a lyric poem **lyrically** *adv.*, **lyricism** *n.*

ly-ser-gic acid di-eth-yl-am-ide *n.* an organic compound which induces psychotic symptoms similar to those of schizophrenia; LSD

ly-so-some *n.* a cellular organelle containing various hydrolytic enzymes **lysosomal** *adj.*

ly-so-zyme *n.* a basic bateriolytic protein present in human tears and saliva

M, m The thirteenth letter of the English alphabet

ma-ca-bre *adj.* suggesting death and decay **macabrly** *adv.*

mac-ad-am *n.* pavement for roads consisting of layers of compacted, broken stone, usually cemented with asphalt and tar *v.* the laving down of layers of small stones, held together with asphalt or tar

mac-a-ro-ni *n.* dried pasta made into short tubes and prepared as food

mac-a-roon *n.* small cookie

ma-caw *n.* the largest type of tropical American parrots

mace *n.* an aromatic spice made by grinding the cover of the nutmeg

mac-e-doine *n.* a jellied salad, or mixture of diced vegetables or fruits

mac-er-ate *v.* to make a solid substance soft **maceration** *n.*

ma-chet-e *n.* a large, heavy type of knife used for cutting sugarcane

mach-i-nate *v.* to plot

ma-chine *n.* device built to use energy to do work **machinery** *n.*, **machinable** *adj.*, **machined** v.

ma-chine lan-guage *n.* in Computer Science, the system of numbers or instructions for coding input data which can be then directly processed by a computer

ma-chin-er-y *n.* a collection of machines as a whole; the mechanism or operating parts of a machine; literary devices

machine shop *n.* a work are where materials, especially metals, are cut and desigtned by machine tools

machine tool *n.* a machine that is power-driven and used for chaping or cutting metals, wood, etc.

ma-chin-ist *n.* the person who operates, assembles and repairs machines for others

ma-chis-mo *n.* an exaggerated sense of masculinity; a strong sense of

mach-me-ter *n.* an indicator that measures airspeed relative to the speed of sound, and then indicates the speed that an airplance using such an indiciator, can exceed without sustaining damage due to compressibility effects

ma-cho *adj.* exhibiting machismo in character; agressive

mack-er-el *n.* kind of fish that is found in the Atlantic Ocean

mack-in-tosh *n.* raincoat

mac-ra-me *n.* the craft of tying knots in a geometrical pattern

mac-ro-bi-ot-ic *adj.* being an extremely restricted diet to promote longevity; for the well-being of

ma-cron *n.* the (-) placed over a vowel to indicate a long sound

mac-ro-scop-ic *adj.* large enough to be seen by the naked eye

mad *adj.* being angry; insane **madder** **adj. madness** *n.*, **madly** *adv.*

mad-am *n.* title used to address a married woman; a polite address

made *v.* past tense of make

mad-e-moi-selle *n.* an unmarried French girl; used as a title

made--to--order *adj.* to be custom-made; designed a certain way

made--up *adj.* being fabricated; invented; falsely devised

mad-house *n.* a place of confusion uproar and disorder

mad-ri-gal *n.*, *Music* unaccompanied song **madrigalist** *n.*

mael-strom *n.* any irresistible or dangerous force; whirlpool

maes-tro *n.* a person mastering any art; a composer or conductor

mag-a-zine *n.* publication of reading marterial; explosives storehouse

ma-gen-ta *n.* a purplish red color or hue; known as fuchsine

mag-got *n.* the legless larva insects; an eccentric idea **maggoty** *adj.*

mag-ic *n.* art of illusions **magically** *adv.*, **magical** *adj.*

mag-is-trate *n.* civil officer of law **magistratically** *adv.*

mag-ma *n.* the molten rock beneath the earth's surface

mag-nan-i-mous *adj.* being forgiving; generous -ness *n.*, -ly *adv.*

mag-nate *n.* kind of business tycoon

mag-ne-sia *n.* a light, white powder used in medicine as an antacid

mag-ne-si-um *n.* a light, silvery metallic element which burns with a hot flame; the form of light

mag-net *n.* body attracting other magnetic material **magnetically** *adv.*, **magnetize** *v.*

mag-net-ic *adj.* pertaining to magnetism or a magnet **magnetically** **adv.**

magnetic field *n.* the area in the neighborhood of a magnet or of an electric current, marked by the existence of a detectable magnetic force

mag-net-ite *n.* a black iron oxide in mineral form of the spinel group

mag-net-ize *v.* to have magnetic properties **magnetizable** **adj.**

mag-ne-to *n.* small alternator that uses

magnets to operate

mag-nif-i-cent adj. beautiful
magnificence n., **magnificently** adv.

mag-ni-fy v. increase in size
magnification n., **magnifiable** adj.

mag-nil-o-quent adj. speaking in a lofty manner **magniloquently** adv.

mag-ni-tude n. the greatness in size

mag-no-lia n. flowering tree

mag-num n. wine bottle holding about two quarts

mag-pie n. large, noisy bird

ma-ha-ra-ja n. a king or prince who rules an Indian state

ma-ha-ra-ni n. the wife of the maharaja; a Hindu princess

ma-hat-ma n. a title of respect

ma-hog-a-ny n., pl. mahoganies trees with hard wood; brownish

maid n. a young unmarried woman or girl

maid-en n. young girl

maid-en-hair n. a delicate fern with dark stems and lightgreen, feathery fronds

maid-en name n. woman's family name before marriage

mail n. printed matter **mailable adj.**, **mailbox** n., **mailed** adj.

mail order n. goods which are ordered and sent by mail

maim v. to cripple or disfigure another **maimer** n.

main adj. being most important part **mainly** adv.

main-land n. the land part of a country as distinguished from an island

main-line v. to inject a drug directly into a vein; main highway

main-stream n. a main direction or line of thought or influence

main-tain v. keep in existence **maintainer** n., **maintainable** adj.

maize n. type of corn

maj-es-ty n. stateliness; one's exualted dignity **majesties** pl.

ma-jor adj. being greater in importance, rank, or dignity

ma-jor-ette n. a young woman who marches and twirls a baton in her hand usually in a parade

ma-jor-i-ty n. the state of having a greater number of something

ma-jor med-i-cal n. a type of insurance policy which one has

make v. create; cause to happen **maker** n., **makable** adj.

make--be-lieve n. something pretended; imagined; fantasy

make--up n. composition

mal-a-chite n. a green basic copper car-

bonate of copper

mal-a-droit adj. lacking skill **maladroitness** n., **maladroitly** adv.

mal-a-dy n., pl. maladies chronic disease or sickness

mal-aise n. the vague discomfort sometimes indicating the beginning of an illness

mal-a-prop-ism n. foolish misuse of a word; misapplication of a word

mal-ap-ro-pos adj. being not appropriate in style

ma-lar-i-a n., disease caused by the bite of sporozoan parasites in the red blood cells **malarious** adj.

ma-lar-key n. foolish or insincere talk

mal-con-tent adj. unhappy with surroundings; dissatisfied

mal-de-mer n. seasickness

male adj. being a man

mal-e-dic-tion n. a curse; execration; to speak evil of

mal-for-ma-tion n. a defective form of something; wrong-doing

mal-func-tion n. the failure to work

mal-ice n. the desire to harm others **maliciously** adv., **maliciousness** n.

ma-lign v. to speak evil of **malignly** adv., **maligner** n.

ma-lig-nant adj., Pathol. to be relating to tumors **malignantly** adv., -cy n.

ma-lin-ger v. pretend sickness to avoid work **malingerer** n.

mal-lard n. wild duck

mal-let n. hammer with a short handle; barrel-shaped head

mal-nour-ished adj. being underfed; lacking food; without food

mal-oc-clu-sion n. improper alignment of the teeth

mal-prac-tice n. the mistreatment by a doctor; negligent

malt n. grain **malty** adj.

mal-treat v. to treat another unkindly **maltreatment** n.

mam-mal n. the group of animals who suckle their young **mammalian** adj.

mam-mog-ra-phy n. x-ray of the breast for detection of cancer

mam-moth n. extinct form of an elephant with large, curved tusks

man n. the adult male; the human race; a human being; manhood

man-a-cle n. handcuffs

man-age v. direct or control **manageable** adj., -ability n.

man-ag-er n. one in charge of a situation **managership** n.

man-a-tee n. type of aquatic mammal with a broad round tail

man-date *n.* an order or command

man-da-to-ry *adj.* required

man-do-lin *n.* a musical instrument mandolinist *n.*

mane *n.* long and heavy hair growing on animals necks maned *adj.*

mange *n.* the skin disease of the dogs marked by the loss of hair

man-ger *n.* the box for animal feed

man-gle *v.* to disfigure or to mutilate mangled, mangling v.

man-grove *n.* tropical tree

man-han-dle *v.* to handle roughly manhandled *adj.*

man-hole *n.* sewer drain

ma-ni-a *n.* the desire for something

man-i-cot-ti *n.* pasta

man-i-cure *n.* the taking care of the fingernails manicurist *n.*

man-i-fest *n.* the list of cargo a vehicle carries manifestation *n.*

man-i-fold *adj.* to be having many parts, or types; having a variety

ma-nip-u-late *v.* to manage shrewdly manipulation *n.*

man-kind *n.* human race

man-made *adj.* not developed naturally; made by mankind

man-ner *n.* way in which things are done mannerless *adj.*

man-ner-ly *adj.* being well-behaved; good manners mannerliness *n.*

ma-nom-e-ter *n.* instrument to measure pressure

man-or *n.* estate manorial *adj.*

man-slaugh-ter *n., Law* the unlawful killing of another without malice

man-tel *n.* shelf over a fireplace mantelpiece *n.*

man-til-la *n.* light scarf

man-u-al *adj.* operated by the hand manually *adv.*

man-u-fac-ture *v.* make a product manufacturer *n.,* -able *adj.*

ma-nure *n.* animal dung used for fertilizer on crops and grass

man-u-script *n.* a typed copy of an article, or book

man-y *adj.* indefinite number

map *n.* plane surface of a region mapper *n.,* mapped v.,mapping v.

ma-ple syr-up *n.* concentrating the sap of the sugar maple

mar *v.* deface marer *n.*

mar-a-thon *n.* the foot race of 26 miles

mar-ble *n.* the limestone marblize v., marbling *n.*

march *v.* to walk with measured steps marching *n.*

mare *n.* female of the horse

mar-ga-rine *n.* kind of butter substitute

mar-gin *n.* edge of printed text marginal *adj.,* marginally *adv.*

mar-i-jua-na *n.* kind of hallucinogenic drug; a wild tobacco

ma-ri-na *n.* harbor for boats

mar-i-nade *n.* brine for soaking meat, fish, or vegetables

ma-rine *adj.* to be pertaining to the sea mariner *n.*

mar-i-o-nette *n.* puppet operated by strings

mark *n.* visible impression

mar-ket *n.* public place to purchase or sell goods

marks-man *n.* the skill in the firing of a gun at a marked target

mar-lin *n.* large marine game fish

ma-roon *v.* to abandon one on the shore; a dark red color

mar-riage *n.* the legal union of two people in wedlock marriageability *n.,* -able *adj.*

mar-row *n.* the tissue in bone cavities marrowy *adj.*

marsh *n.* low, wet land; swamp marshy *adj.* marshiness *n.*

mar-shal *n.* military officer

marsh-mal-low *n.* kind of soft confection which is edible

mar-su-pi-al *n.* animals with external pouches such as a kangaroo

mar-tial arts *pl., n.* self-defense, such as karate

mar-ti-ni *n.* cocktail of gin and dry vermouth; vodka may be used

mar-tyr *n.* person who would die for a cause martyrdom *n.*

mar-zi-pan *n.* paste of almonds, sugar and egg whites made into candy shaped into various forms

mar-vel *n.* be in awe

mas-car-a *n.* the cosmetic used for coloring the eyelashes

mas-cot *n.* object to bring good luck

mas-cu-line *adj.* male sex

mash *n.* the mixture to distill alcohol; to gain the affection of

mask *n.* covering to conceal the face

mas-o-chism *n.* the sexual pleasure from pain masochistic *adj.,* masochist *n.*

ma-son *n.* brick layer

mas-quer-ade *n.* a costume party or gathering for entertainment

mass *n.* body of matter with no form; a Eucharistic celebration

mas-sa-cre *n.* savage killing of human beings massacrer *n.*

mas-sage *n.* rub down of one's body to relieve tension massager *n.*

mas-sive *adj.* of great intensity

mast *n.* pole which supports the sails of boats

mas-ter *n.* person with the control

mas-ter-piece *n.* work of art

mas-ti-cate *v.* to chew -able *adj.*

mas-to-don *n.* kind of extinct mammal which differ from mammoths

mas-tur-ba-tion *n.* ones sexual stimulation without intercourse

mat-a-dor *n.* bullfighter

match *n.* identical; piece of wood that ignites matcher *n.*

ma-te-ri-al-ize *v.* to take form or shape; to make material

ma-te-ri-el *n.* the equipment or the supplies used by an organization

ma-ter-nal *adj.* relating to mother maternally *adv.*, maternalistic *adj.*

math-e-mat-ics *n.* the study of form, quantity and magnitude of numbers mathematically *adv.*, -cal *adj.*

mat-i-nee *n.* afternoon movie

mat-ri-cide *n.* one who kills his mother matricidal *adj.*

ma-tric-u-late *v.* enroll into a college matriculation *n.*

mat-ri-mo-ny *n.* ceremony of marriage matrimonial *adj.*

ma-tron *n.* married woman

mat-ter *n.* the substance of anything

ma-ture *adj.* completely developed maturity *n.*, maturer *adj.*, -est *adj.*

mat-zo *n.* flat piece of unleavened bread eaten at the Passover

maud-lin *adj.* sentimental

maul *n.* heavy hammer

maun-der *v.* talk incoherent

mau-so-le-um *n.* large tomb

mav-er-ick *n.* an unbranded calf

max-i-mum *n.* greatest possible quantity or value

may *v.* permitted or allowed

may-be *adv.* perhaps

may-on-naise *n.* the dressing used for salads and sandwiches

may-or *n.* chief magistrate of a city or town mayoralty *n.*

maze *n.* a complicated network of passages mazy *adj.*

mead *n.* alcoholic beverage

mead-ow *n.* a tract of grassland

mea-ger *adj.* thin; lean in quantity meagerness *n.*, meagerly *adv.*

mean *v.* purpose or intent; bad tempered meanness *n.*

me-an-der *v.* wander about meanderingly *adv.*, -drous *adj.*

mea-sles *n.* kind of contagious disease marked by red circular spots

mea-sly *adj.* very small

meas-ure *n.* the dimension of anything measurer *n.*

meat *n.* tissue of an animal used as food; the core of something

me-chan-ic *n.* person skilled with tools mechanical *adj.*

mech-a-nism *n.* the parts of a machine which help it run

med-al *n.* an award medalist *n.*

med-dle *v.* to interfere in other's affairs or business meddlesome *adj.*, -er *n.*

me-di-al *adj.* being situated in the middle; between two

me-di-ate *v.* to help settle or decide a dispute mediative *adj.*

med-ic *n.* intern; corpsman

med-i-cal *adj.* the study of medicine medically *adv.*

med-i-cine *n.* the treatment of diseases or illness

me-di-o-cre *adj.* being common; plain mediocrity *n.*

med-i-tate *v.* in contemplative thought meditator *n.*, meditative *adj.*

me-di-um *n.* the middle; intermediary professing to give messages from the dead

med-ley *n.* a jumble; musical composition made up of songs

meek *adj.* to be lacking in spirit meekness *n.*

meet *v.* to come upon

meg-a-ton *n.* weight equal to one million tons

mel-an-chol-y *adj.* gloomy or sad -lness *n.* melancholically *adv.*

mel-a-no-ma *n.*, *pl.* melanomas *or* melanomata malignant mole

mel-io-rate *v.* to improve meliotor *n.*, meliorateable *adj.*

mel-lif-er-ous *adj.* to be producing or yielding honey

mel-o-dra-ma *n.* type of dramatic presentation -tic *adj.*, -tics *n.*

mel-on *n.* the fruit of the gourd family eaten raw as fruits

melt *v.* change from solid to liquid melter *n.*, meltable *adj.*

melt-down *n.* melting of a nuclear-reactor core

mem-ber *n.* a person belonging to a club membership *n.*, -less *adj.*

mem-brane *n.* thin layer of skin membranous *adj.*

me-men-to *n.* keepsake

mem-oir *n.* an autobiography of a person; a remembrance

mem-o-ra-ble *adj.* worth remembering memorably *adv.*

mem-o-rize v. to commit to one's memory -zation n., -zable adj.

men-ace n. a threatening person menacly adv.

me-nar-che n. beginning of the menstruation cycle

me-ni-al adj. requiring little skill menially adv.

men-o-pause n., Physiol. time of final menstruation menopausal adj.

men-tal adj. of the mind

men-tal re-tar-da-tion n. a mental deficiency

men-tion v. refer to briefly mentioner n., mentionable adj.

men-u n. the list of the food at a restaurant

mer-can-tile adj. to be relating to commerce

mer-ce-nar-y n. a greedy person mercenarily adv.

mer-cer-ize v. to treat cotton yarn

mer-chan-dise n. goods bought and sold merchandiser n.

mer-chant n. person who operates a retail business

mer-cu-ry n. the silvery liquid found in thermometers

mer-cy n., pl. mercies kind treatment -iless adj., mercifully adv.

mere adj. no more than is stated merely adv., merest adj.

merge v. to unite as one mergence n.

mer-it n. act worthy of praise meritedly adv., meritless adj.

mer-maid n. an imaginary sea creature half woman half fish

mer-ry-go-round n. kind of carrousel; seats in animal form

me-sa n. flat-topped hill

mesh n. open spaces in wire

mess n., pl. messes disorderly confused heap

mes-sage n. the information which is sent from one person to another by word of mouth

mes-sen-ger n. one who does errands for another person

mess-y adj. untidy; dirty

me-tab-o-lism n. chemical changes in living cells

met-a-gal-ax-y n. the universe

met-a-mor-pho-sis n. change in the structure and formation of living animals metamorphoses pl.

me-te-or n. moving particle in the solar system resembling light

me-te-or-ol-o-gy n. the science of weather forecasting -al adj.

meth-a-done n. man-made narcotic used

to treat heroin addiction

meth-od n. the process of carrying out something

me-tic-u-lous adj. very precise meticulously adv.

met-ro n. subway system

met-ro-nome n. instrument designed to mark musical time -nomic adj.

me-trop-o-lis n. the large capital city of a state, country or region

mew n. hideaway

mez-za-nine n. the lowest balcony

mi-crobe n. minute living organism microbial adj.

mi-cro-com-put-er n. type of computer using a microprocessor

mi-cro-film n. film used to record reduced size printed material

mi-cro-phone n. instrument which amplifies sound

mi-cro-proc-es-sor n. semiconductor processing unit

mi-cro-scope n. device to magnify small objects

mi-cro-scop-ic adj. very small; minute microscopically adv.

mi-cro-wave n. a rather short electromagnetic wave

mi-cro-wave o-ven n. the oven using microwaves to heat food quickly

mid-day n. noon

mid-dle adj. the center

midg-et n. very small person

mid-night n. 12 o'clock p.m.

mid-point n. near the middle

mid-riff n. midsection of the human torso; a section of garment

mid-ship-man n. person who is in training at the U.S. Naval Academy; a student

mid-term n. the middle of academic an term

miff n. a displeasure

might n. a force mighty adj., -ily adv.

mi-graine n. kind of severe headaches migrainous adj.

mi-grant n. a person constantly moving to find work

mi-grate v. move from place to place -tory adj., migration n.

mild adj. gentle in manner mildness n., mildly adv.

mile n. 5,280 feet

mil-i-ta-rize v. train for war

mi-li-tia n. armed forces used only in an emergency

Milk-y Way n. luminous galaxy in the solar system

mil-li-ner n. one who designs, makes, or sells women's hats mil-lion *n.* number equal to 1,000 x 1,000; a very large number

mim-e-o-graph *n.* kind of duplicating machine which uses stencils

mim-ic *v.* imitate another person mimical *adj.*

mince *v.* to chop something into small pieces mincing *adj.*, mincer *n.*

mind *n.* organ for thought mindful *adj.*, mindfulness *n.*

mine *n.* underground excavation; personal belongings

min-er-al *n.* an inorganic crystalline

min-e-stro-ne *n.* kind of thick veg-etable soup

min-gle *v.* to mix together

min-i-a-ture *n.* copy greatly reduced in size; smaller than usual

mini-disk *n.* 5.25 inch floppy disk used for storing important data

min-i-mum *n.* least amount

min-is-ter *n.* pastor of a church ministerial *adj.*

mink *n.* an animal with valuable fur

min-now *n.* small, fresh water fish

mi-nor *adj.* not of legal age

mi-nor-i-ty *n., pl.* minorities smaller in number of two groups

min-u-et *n.* kind of slow, stately dance; graceful

mi-nus *prep., Math.* reduced, by subtraction of numbers

min-ute *n.* 60 seconds in time; small in size; short space of time

mir-a-cle *n.* kind of supernatural event; extremely unusual

mi-rage *n.* optical illusion

mir-ror *n.* a glass which reflects images as they are seen

mirth *n.* a merriment or a joyousness mirthfulness *n.*, mirthful *adj.*

mis-an-thrope *n.* the hatred or distrusts of mankind

mis-ap-pro-pri-ate *v.* to embezzle money misappropriation *n.*

mis-car-riage *n.* the premature birth of a fetus before it is viable

mis-cel-la-ne-ous *adj.* mixed variety of parts, etc.; many different

mis-chief *n.* a behavior causing harm or damage something

mis-con-ceive *v.* to misunderstand the meaning of something

mis-de-mean-or *n., Law* a crime less serious than a felony

mis-er *n.* person who hoards money miserly *adj.*, miserliness *n.*

mis-er-a-ble *adj.* very unhappy

mis-er-ly *n.* the state of great unhappiness; depression

mis-fire *v.* fail to explode

mis-fit *n.* one not adjusted to his environment; a poor fit

mis-for-tune *n.* bad luck

mis-giv-ing *n.* the feeling of doubt

mis-han-dle *v.* to manage inefficiently, wrong, or ignorantly

mis-hap *n.* an unfortunate accident

mish-mash *n.* jumble or hodgepodge

mis-in-ter-pret *v.* understand incorrectly misinterpreter *n.*

mis-judge *v.* make a mistake in judgment misjudgment *n.*

mis-lay *v.* lose something

mis-lead *v.* to deceive misleader *n.*, misleading *adj.*

mis-no-mer *n.* an inappropriate name misnomered *adj.*

mi-sog-a-my *n.* the hatred of the marriage

mis-pro-nounce *v.* to pronounce incorrectly or in an incorrect way

mi-sog-y-ny *n.* the hatred of women

Miss *n.* the title for unmarried girl

mis-sile *n.* object that shot at a target

mis-sion *n.* kind of task to be carried out to obtain a result

mis-take *n.* wrong decision

mis-tle-toe *n.* parasitic plant

mis-tress *n.* a woman in authority

mis-trust *v.* have doubt

mite *n.* very small insect

mit-i-gate *v.* to make less painful mitigator *n.*, mitigative *adj.*

mitt *n.* the women's hand warmer; baseball glove

mix *v.* blend; combine; unite mixable *adj.*, mixability *n.*

mix-up *n.* state of confusion

moan *n.* dull sound of pain

moat *n.* kind of trench around a castle moatlike *adj.*

mob *n.* an unruly crowd or group of people mobbish *adj.*

mock-up *n.* a model used for demonstration

mode *n.* a method of doing something

mod-el *n.* clothing displayer

mod-er-ate *adj.* not excessive moderateness *n.*, moderately *adv.*

mod-ern *adj.* up-to-date

mod-ern-ize *v.* to improve on something modernzation *n.*

mod-est *adj.* shy; reserved modesty *n.*, modestly *adv.*

mod-i-fy *v.* make different in form modifier *n.*, modifiable *adj.*

mod-ule *n.* a series of standardized components modular *adj.*

mod-us op-er-an-di *n.* the method of

operating; procedure

moist *adj.* sightly wet; damp
moisten *v.*, moistly *adv.*

mois-ture *n.* dampness
moisturize *v.*, moisturizer *n.*

mo-lar *n.* the grinding tooth

mo-las-ses *n.* the light brown syrup produced from sugar

mold *n.* growth produced on damp organic matter; pattern
moldy *adj.*, moldeer *n.*

mole *n.* spot on the human skin

mol-e-cule *n.* smallest part retaining its identity

mo-lest *v.* to accost someone sexually molestation *n.*

mol-li-fy *v.* make less angry
molifier *n.*, molifiable *adj.*

molt *v.* to cast off or shed feathers
molter *n.*

mol-ten *adj.* transform to liquid form by heat moltenly *adv.*

mo-men-tous *adj.* being of a great importance

mo-men-tum *n.*, *pl.* -ta *or* -tums increasing force; body in motion

mon-arch *n.* one who reigns an empire or kingdom; ruler

mon-as-ter-y *n.*, *pl.* monasteries the place where monks work and live

mon-e-tar-y *adj.* to be relating to money
monetarily *adv.*

mon-ey *n.* the medium of exchange

mon-grel *n.* the mixed breed animal

mo-ni-tion *n.* the caution or warning about something

monk *n.* a member of a religious order
monkishness *n.*, monkishly *adv.*

mon-key *n.*, *pl.* monkeys member of the primates, excluding man

mon-o-cle *n.* the eyeglass used for one eye

mo-nog-a-my *n.* sexual relationship with only one person

mon-o-logue *n.* speech by one person
monologuist *n.*

mon-o-ma-ni-a *n.* mental disorder
monomaniacal *adj.*

mon-o-nu-cle-o-sis *n.* kind of infectious disease

mo-nop-o-ly *n.*, *pl.* monopolies the exclusive ownership

mon-o-rail *n.* train traveling on a single rail to a specific destination

mon-o-the-ism *n.* the belief there is just one God; the one and only

mon-o-tone *n.* the sounds uttered in a single unvarying tone -ic *adj.*

mo-not-o-nous *adj.* lacking variety
monotoness *n.*, monotonously *adv.*

mon-ox-ide *n.* oxide containing one oxygen atom per molecule

mon-soon *n.* periodic wind

mon-ster *n.* animal having abnormal form

mon-tage *n.* a composite picture

month-ly *adj.* being payable each month; twelve times a year

mon-u-ment *n.* the object in memory of a person monumental *adj.*, -ally *adv.*

mooch *v. Slang* acquire by begging
moocher *n.*

mood *n.* the temporary state of one's mind

mood-y *adj.* being gloomy
moodiness *n.*, moodily *adv.*

moon *n.* earth's only satellite
moony *adj.*, mooniness *n.*

moon-lit *adj.* lit by the moon

moor *v.* fasten with anchors

moose *n.* very large deer

moot *v.* debate; argue

mope *v.* to be dejected

mo-ped *n.* motorbike

mor-al *adj.* referring to conduct of right or wrong

mo-rale *n.* an individual's state of mind

mor-a-to-ri-um *n.* temporary pause

mor-bid *adj.* gruesome; gloomy
morbidness *n.*, morbidly *adv.*

more *adj.* being of greater number or degree

more-o-ver *adv.* furthermore

mo-res *n.*, *pl.* moral customs of a social group

morgue *n.* place to keep dead bodies until they are claimed

morn-ing *n.* the early part of the day; before noon

mo-roc-co *n.* soft leather made of goatskin tanned with sumac

mo-ron *n.* an adult with a low intelligence level moronism *n.*, moronic *adj.*, moronity *n.*

mor-ose *adj.* marked by gloom
morosity *n.*, morosely *adv.*

mor-phine *n.* a highly addictive narcotic, derived from opium

mor-sel *n.* a small quantity of food

mor-tal *adj.* to having caused death; about to cause death

mort-gage *n.* conveyance as security for the repayment of a debt

mor-ti-cian *n.* undertaker

mo-sa-ic *n.* decorative inlaid design of tile

moss *n.* small green plants

most *adj.* majority of; greatest in quantity

mo-tel *n.* establishment which provides

lodging for travelers

moth *n.* nocturnal insect

moth-er *n.* female parent

mo-tif *n.* the main element or theme of something

mo-tile *adj.* being capable of moving alone

mo-tion *n.* the act of changing position; a proposal for action

mo-tive *n.* the need or the desire to act motivator *n.*

mo-tor *n.* the device which develops energy for motion

mot-tle *v.* marked with spots or streaks of colors

mot-to *n.* phrase, or word expressing purpose

mound *n.* small hill of earth

mourn *v.* to express one's grief or sorrow over something

mov-ie *n.* motion picture

mow *v.* to cut down

much *adj.* being of great amount or quantity; many in number

muck *n.* moist, sticky soil

mu-cus *n.* the liquid secreted by glands in the body

mud *n.* the mixture of water and solid material such as earth

muf-fle *v.* to suppress; to deaden sound; to conceal or protect

mug *n.* large drinking cup

mug-gy *adj.* being humid and being sultry muggily *adv.*, -ness *n.*

mul-ber-ry *n.* trees having an edible fruit

mulch *n.* protective covering of compost or wood chips

mull *v.* ponder; think over

multi- *prefix* multiple; two or more

mul-ti-far-i-ous *adj.* having great variety multifariousness *n.*

mul-ti-ple *adj.* to be consisting of more than one individual or part

mul-ti-ply *v.* increase in amount or number

mul-ti-tude *n.* large amount or number of something

mum *adj.* not speaking

mum-ble *v.* to speak in a confused indistinct manner

mum-my *n.*, *pl.* mummies body embalmed for burial mummify *v.*

munch *v.* chew noisily

mun-dane *adj.* relating to the world mundanely *adv.*

mu-nic-i-pal *adj.* relating to local affairs; local self-government

mu-ral *n.* kind of painting created on a wall

mur-der *n.* the crime of killing a person by will

mur-mur *n.* a low sound

mus-cle *n.* bodily tissue which produces strength

mus-cu-lar *adj.* brawny

mu-sic *n.* the organized tones in sequences; melodious

mu-si-cian *n.* a performer of music

mus-lin *n.* a sheer, or coarse fabric

muss *v.* to mess up

mus-sel *n.* a type of freshwater bivalve mollusk

must *v.* to be forced to

mus-tache *n.* hair growing on the human upper lip

mus-tang *n.* wild horse

mus-tard *n.* from the seeds of the mustard plant

mus-ter *v.* to come or bring things together

mustn't *contr.* must not

mute *adj.* unable to speak

mu-ti-late *v.* maim or cripple

mu-ti-ny *n.*, *pl.* mutinies revolt against lawful authority

mutt *n.*, *Slang* a dog that is of a mixed breed

mut-ter *v.* to speak or utter in a low voice with the lips partialy closed

mut-ton *n.* the flesh of a fully grown sheep used for food

mu-tu-al *adj.* having the same relationship mutuality *n.*

my *adj.* of myself *interj.* to express surprise, dismay, or pleasure

my-ce-li-um *n.*, *pl.* mycelia the mass of filaments which form the main structure of a fungus

my-col-o-gy *n.* scientific study of fungi mycologist *n.*

my-e-li-tis *n.* the inflammation of the spinal cord or the bone marrow

my-elo-ma *n.* the tumor of the bone marrow

myo-car-dio-graph *n.* recording tool which traces the action of the heart muscles

myo-car-di-um *n.* muscular layer of the heart; along the heart wall

my-o-pia *n.* a visual defect

myr-i-ad *adj.* having large, indefinite aspects

myr-mi-don *n.* loyal follower

myr-tle *n.* evergreen shrub

my-self *pron.* one identical with me

mys-ter-y *n.*, *pl.* mysteries something that is not understood

mys-tic *n.* person practicing or believing in mysticism mystical *adj.*, -cally *adv.*

mys-ti-fy *v.* to perplex

N, n. The fourteenth letter of the English alphabet.

nab v., *Slang* to seize

na-cho n. a tortilla, often small and triangular in shape, topped with cheese or chili sauce and baked

nag v. to bother by scolding or constant complaining n. a worthless horse **nagger** n.

nai-ad n. *Gr. Mythol.* a nymph presiding over and living in springs, brooks, and fountains

nail n. a thin pointed piece of metal for hammering into wood and other material to hold pieces together

na-ked adj. without clothes on the body; nude; exposed; uncovered **nakedly** adv., **nakedness** n.

nam-by--pam-by adj. weak; indecisive; lacking in substance

name n. a title or word by which something or someone is known v. to give a name **nameable** adj.

nape n. the back of the neck

nap-kin n. a cloth or soft paper, used at the dinner table for wiping the lips and fingers

nar-cis-sus n. a widely grown type of bulbous plant

nar-co-sis n. a deep drug induced state of stupor or unconsciousness

nar-cot-ic n. a drug which dulls the senses, relieves pain, and induces a deep sleep; if abused, it can become habit-forming and cause convulsions or comas

nar-rate v. to tell a story or give a description in detail **narration** n., **narrator** v.

nar-row adj. slender or small in width **narrowly** adj.

narrow--mind-ed adj. lacking sympathy or tolerance

nar-whal n. an aquatic mammal of the Arctic regions, closely related to the white whale

na-sal adj. of or pertaining to the nose

na-stur-tium n. a five-petaled garden plant usually having red, yellow, or orange flowers

nas-ty adj. dirty, filthy, or indecent **nastily** adv., **nastiness** n.

na-tal adj. pertaining to or associated with birth

na-tion n. a group of people made up of one or more nationalities under one government -al adj., **nationally** adv.

na-tion-al-ism n. devotion to or concern for one's nation

na-tion-al-i-ty n. the fact or condition of belonging to a nation

na-tion-al-ize v. to place a nation's resources and industries under the control of the state

na-tive n. a person born in a country or place adj. belonging to one by nature or birth

na-tiv-i-ty n. birth, circumstances, or con-ditions; the birth of Christ

nat-u-ral adj. produced or existing by nature; not artificial *Mus.* a note that is not sharp or flat **naturalness** n., **naturally** adv.

natural child-birth n. childbirth with little stress or pain; childbirth requiring training for the mother and father and medical supervision, but without the use of drugs, anesthesia, or surgery

nat-u-ral-ize v. to confer the privileges and rights of full citizenship **naturalization** n.

na-ture n. the universe and its phenomena; kind, sort, or type **natured** adj.

naught n. nothing; the number 0

naugh-ty adj. unruly; not proper **naughtily** adv., **naughtiness** n.

nau-se-a n. an upset stomach with a feeling that one needs to vomit -ous adj.

nau-ti-cal adj. pertaining to ships or seamanship nautically adv.

na-val adj. of or relating to ships

na-vel n. a small mark or scar on the abdomen where the umbilical cord was attached

nav-i-ga-ble adj. sufficiently deep and wide enough to allow ships to pass

nav-i-gate v. to plan the course of a ship or aircraft; to steer a course **navigation**, **navigator** n.

na-vy n. one of a nation's organizations for defense; a nation's fleet of ships; a very dark blue

Ne-an-der-thal adj. suggesting a caveman in behavior or appearance; primitive or crude **Neanderthal** n.

neap tide n. a tide in the minimum range which occurs twice a month

near adv. at, to, or within a short time or distance adj. closely or intimately related **nearness** n.

near-by adj. & adv. adjacent

near-sight-ed adj. able to see clearly at short distances only

neat adj. tidy and clean; free from disorder and dirt **neatly** adv., **neatness** n.

neb-u-lous adj. confused or vague

nec-es-sar-y adj. unavoidable **necessarily** adv.

ne-ces-si-tate v. to make necessary; to

oblige; to require

ne-ces-si-ty n., pl. -ies the condition of being necessary

neck n. the part of the body which connects the head and trunk; a narrow part or projection, as of land, a stringed instrument, or bottle. v. to caress and kiss

neck-tie n. a narrow strip of material worn around the neck

nec-tar n. a good-tasting beverage; a sweet fluid in various flowers, gathered by bees to help make honey nectarous adj.

nee n. born; the surname a woman was born with

need n. the lack of something desirable, useful, or necessary

nee-dle n. a slender, pointed steel implement which contains an eye through which thread is passed

needle-point n. decorative stitching done on canvas

need-n't contr. need not

ne-far-i-ous adj. extremely wicked

ne-gate v. to nullify; to deny; to rule out negation n.

neg-a-tive adj. expressing denial or disapproval; not positive negatively adj., negativeness n.

neglect v. to ignore; to pay no attention to neglectful adj.

neg-li-gee n. a woman's loose-fitting dressing gown

neg-li-gent adj. to neglect what needs to be done; neglectful

ne-go-ti-ate v. to confer with another person to reach an agreement negotiation, negotiator n.

Ne-gro n. a member of the Black race; a black person

ne-groid adj. of or relating to the Black race negroid n.

neigh-bor n. one who lives near another; fellowman

neighbor-hood n. a section or small region that possesses a specific quality

nei-ther adj. not one or the other pron. Not the one or the other conj. Not either; also not

neo prefix recent; new

neo-dym-i-um n. a metallic element of the rare-earth group, symbolized by Nd.

ne-on n. an inert gaseous element used in lighting fixtures, symbolized by Ne

ne-o-nate n. a newborn child less than a month old

ne-o-na-tol-o-gy n. the medical study of the first 60 days of a baby's life

neo-phyte n. a novice; a beginner.

ne-o-plasm n. a tumor tissue serving no physiologic function neoplastic adj.

neph-ew n. the son of one's sister, brother, sister-in-law, or brother-in-law

ne-phrit-ic adj. relating to the kidneys

nep-o-tism n. the act of showing favoritism to relatives or friends in the work force nepotist n.

nep-tu-ni-um n. a radioactive metallic element, symbolized by Np

nerve n. the bundles of fibers which convey sensation and originate motion through the body

nerv-ous adj. affecting the nerves or the nervous system -ly adv., -ness n.

nervous system n., Physiol. the body system that coordinates, regulates, and controls the various internal functions and responses to stimuli

nest n. a shelter, or home built by a bird to hold its eggs and young

nest egg n. a supply of money accumulated or saved for future use

nes-tle v. to settle snugly; to lie close to nestler n.

net n. a meshed fabric made of cords, ropes, threads, or other material knotted or woven together; the profit, weight, or price which remains after all additions, subtractions, or adjustments have been made

neth-er adj. situated below or beneath

net-tle n. a plant having toothed leaves covered with stinging hairs

net-work n. a system of interlacing tracks, channels, or lines

neu-ral adj. relating to a nerve or the nervous system

neu-ral-gia n. pain that occurs along the course of a nerve

neu-ri-tis n. an inflammation of a nerve which causes pain, the loss of reflexes, and muscular decline neurotic adj.

neu-rol-o-gy n. the medical and scientific study of the nervous system and its disorders neurological adj., neurologist n.

neu-ron or neu-rone n., Anat. a granular cell nerve which is the main functional unit of the nervous system

neu-ro-sis n. any one of various functional disorders of the mind or emotions having no physical cause neurotic adj., n., neurotically adv.

neu-ter adj. neither feminine nor masculine n. a castrated animal

neu-tral adj. not supporting either side of a debate, quarrel, or party; a color which does not contain a decided hue *Chem.* neither alkaline nor acid

neu-tral-i-ty *n.*, neutrally *adv.*

neu-tral-ize *v.* to make or declare neutral

neu-tron *n.* an uncharged particle in the nucleus of an atom

nev-er *adv.* not ever

nev-er-the-less *adv.* nonetheless

new *adj.* not used before; unaccustomed; unfamiliar

news *n.*, *pl.* current information and happenings

news-cast *n.* a television or radio news broadcast

news-pa-per *n.* a weekly or daily publication which contains recent news and information

news-print *n.* an inexpensive machinefinished paper made from wood pulp and used chiefly for newspapers and some paperback books

New Testament *n.* the second part of the Christian Bible containing the Gospels, Acts, Epistles, and the Book of Revelation

next *adj.* immediately following or proceeding

nib-ble *v.* to bite a little at a time nibble, nibbler *n.*

nice *adj.* pleasing; enjoyable nicely *adv.*, niceness *n.*

niche *n.* a recess or alcove in a wall, usually used for displays

nick *n.* a small chip or cut on a surface; the final critical moment

nick-el *n.* a hard, silver, metallic element used in alloys and symbolized by Ni; a United States coin worth five cents

nick-el-o-de-on *n.* a movie theatre which charged five cents for admission; a coin-operated juke box

nick-name *n.* the familiar form of a proper name, expressed in a shortened form nickname *v.*

nic-o-tine *or* nicotin *n.* a poisonous alkaloid found in tobacco and used in insecticides and medicine

niece *n.* a daughter of one's sister or brother or one's sister-in-law or brother-in-law

nigh *adv.* near in relationship, time, or space

night *n.* the time between dusk and dawn or the hours of darkness

nightcap *n.* an alcoholic drink usually taken before retiring for the night

night-in-gale *n.* a songbird with brownish plumage, noted for the sweet, nocturnal song of the male

night-mare *n.* a frightening and horrible dream

nim-ble *adj.* marked by a quick, light movement; quick-witted nimbleness *n.*, nimbly *adv.*

nin-com-poop *n.* a silly or stupid person

nine *n.* the cardinal number that is equal to $8+1$ nine *adj.*, *pron.*

ni-o-bi-um *n.* a gray, metallic element used in alloys, symbolized by Nb

nip *v.* to pinch, bite, or grab something nipper *n.*

nip-ple *n.* the small projection of a mammary gland through which milk passes

ni-tro-gen *n.* a nonmetallic gaseous element which is essential to life, symbolized by N

ni-tro-glyc-er-in *n.* a highly flammable, explosive liquid, used to make dynamite and, in medicine, to dilate blood vessels

no *adv.* used to express rejection

no-bel-i-um *n.* a radioactive element, symbolized by No

Nobel prize *n.* an award given to people with achievements in literature, economics, medicine, and other fields, established by the last will and testament of Alfred Nobel

no-bil-i-ty *n.*, *pl.* -ies the state or quality of being noble

no-ble *adj.* morally good; superior in character or nature -ness *n.*, -y *adv.*

no-bod-y *pron.* not anybody

noc-tur-nal *adj.* pertaining to or occurring during the night; active at night and quiet during the daylight hours nocturnally *adv.*

nod *n.* a quick downward motion of the head as one falls off to sleep; a downward motion of the head indicating acceptance or approval

node *n.* a swollen or thickened enlargement

no-el *n.* a Christmas carol

noise *n.* a sound which is disagreeable or loud; in computer science, unwanted data in an electronic signal noisy *adj.*, noisily *adv.*

no-mad *n.* a member of a group of people who wander from place to place nomadic *adj.*, nomadism *n.*

no-men-cla-ture *n.* the set of names used to describe the elements of art, science, and other fields

nom-i-nal *adj.* of or relating to something that is in name or form only nominally *adv.*

nom-i-nate *v.* to select a candidate for an elective office; to appoint or designate to a position nomination, -tor n.

nom-i-nee n. a person nominated for a position or office

non- prefix not

non-a-ge-nar-i-an adj. a person between the ages of 90 and 100 years

non-cha-lant adj. giving an effect of casual unconcern -ance n., -ly adv.

non com-pos men-tis adj. mentally unbalanced; not of sound mind

non-con-form-ist n. a person who does not feel compelled to follow or accept his community's customs or traditions

none pron. not any; not one

non-sec-tar-i-an adj. not associated with or restricted to one religion, faction, or sect

non-sense n. something that seems senseless or foolish; something which is very unimportant nonsensical adj.

non seq-ui-tur n. an inference that does not follow as the logical result of what has preceded it

non-sex-ist adj. not discriminating on the basis of gender

noo-dle n. a flat strip of dried dough made with eggs and flour Slang the head

nook n. a corner, recess, or secluded place

noon n. the middle of the day; 12:00 o'clock

noose n. a loop of rope secured by a slipknot, allowing it to decrease in size as the rope is pulled

nor conj. not either; or not

norm n. a rule, model, or pattern typical for a particular group

nor-mal adj. ordinary, average, usual; having average intelligence; standard normalcy, normality n., normally adv.

north n. the direction to a person's left while facing east

nose n. the facial feature containing the nostrils; the sense of smell

nose-dive n. a sudden plunge as made by an aircraft

nos-tal-gia n. a yearning to return to the past nostalgic adj.

nos-tril n. the external openings of the nose

nos-y or **nos-ey** adj. snoopy; inquisitive; prying

not adv. in no manner; used to express refusal or denial

no-ta-ble adj. remarkable; distinguished n. a person or thing which is notable notably adv.

no-ta-rize v. to acknowledge and certify as a notary public

notary public n. a person who is legally authorized as a public officer to witness and certify documents

no-ta-tion n. a process or system of figures or symbols used in specialized fields to represent quantities, numbers, or values notational adj.

notch n. a v-shaped indentation or cut

note n. a record or message in short form Mus. a tone or written character

not-ed adj. famous; well-known

noth-ing n. not any thing; no part or portion adv. in no way; not at all

no-tice n. an announcement; a notification v. to give notice; to become aware of noticeable adj., -ably adv.

no-ti-fy v. to give notice of; to announce notifier, notification n.

no-tion n. an opinion; a general concept; an idea notions pl., n. small useful articles, as thread or buttons

no-to-ri-ous adj. having a widely known and usually bad reputation

not-with-stand-ing prep. in spite of adv. nevertheless; anyway conj. although

noun n. a word which names a person, place, or thing

nour-ish v. to furnish with the nutriment and other substances needed for growth and life nourishing adj., nourishment n.

nou-veau riche n. a person who has recently become rich

no-va n., pl. -vae or -vas a star which flares up and fades away after a few years or months

nov-el n. an inventive narrative dealing with human experiences; a book

nov-el-ty n., pl. -ies something unusual or new

nov-ice n. a person who is new and unfamiliar with an activity or business

now adv. at the present time

no-where adv. not in or at any place

nox-ious adj. harmful; obnoxious

noz-zle n. a projecting spout or vent of something

nu-ance n. a slight variation

nub n. a knob; a small piece or lump

nu-bile adj. suitable or ready for marriage

nu-cle-ar adj. pertaining to and resembling a nucleus

nu-cle-us n., pl. -clei or -cleuses a central element around which other elements are grouped

nude adj. unclothed; naked nudity, nudist n.

nudge v. to poke or push gently nudge n.

nug-get *n.* a lump, as of precious metal

nui-sance *n.* a source of annoyance

null *adj.* invalid; having no value or consequence; having no legal value nullification *n.*

nul-li-fy *v.* to counteract

numb *adj.* lacking physical sensation; paralyzed or stunned numbness *n.*

num-ber *n.* a word or symbol which is used in counting or which indicates how many or which one in a series

number-less *adj.* too many to be counted

nu-meral *n.* a symbol, figure, letter, word, or a group of these which represents a number

nu-mer-a-tor *n.* the term in mathematics indicating how many parts are to be taken; the number in a fraction which appears above the line

nu-mer-ous *adj.* consisting or made up of many units

nun *n.* a woman who has joined a religious group and has taken vows to give up worldly goods and never to marry

nup-tial *adj.* of or pertaining to a wedding nuptials *pl.*, *n.* a wedding

nurse *n.* a person who is specially trained to care for disabled or sick persons *v.* To feed a baby from a mother's breast; to provide care to a sick or disabled person

nurs-er-y *n.*, *pl.* -ies a room reserved for the special use of infants or small children; a business or place where trees, shrubs, and flowers are raised and sold

nur-ture *n.* the upbringing, care, or training of a child nurture *v.*, nurturer *n.*

nut *n.* a hard-shelled fruit or seed which contains an inner, often edible kernal *Slang* a person who does crazy or silly things

nu-tri-ent *n.* a substance which nourishes or promotes growth and repairs natural wastage of organic life

nu-tri-tion *n.* the process by which a living being takes in food and uses it to live and grow nutritive, nutritional *adj.*, nutritionally *adv.*

nu-tri-tious *adj.* nourishing and healthy nutritiously *adv.*

nuts *adj.*, *Slang* foolish, crazy

nuz-zle *v.* to gently rub against something with the nose; to cuddle

ny-lon *n.* a strong, elastic material; yarn or fabric made from nylon nylons stockings made of nylon

nys-tag-mus *n.* · the rapid involuntary movement of the eyeballs -mic *adj.*

O, o The fifteenth letter of the English alphabet.

O *n.* a word used before a name when talking to that person; an interjection

oaf *n.* a stupid or clumsy person oafish *adj.*, oafishly *adv.*

oak *n.* a large tree of durable wood bearing acorns oaken *adj.*

oar *n.* a long pole, flat at one end, used in rowing a boat

oar-lock *n.* a u-shaped device, on a pivot used to hold an oar during rowing.

oars-man *n.* a person who is skilled in the use of oars

oasis *n.*, *pl.* oases a fertile section in the desert which contains water

oat *n.* a cultivated cereal grass whose grain or seed is used as food

oat-cake *n.* a thin, brittle cake made of oatmeal

oath *n.* a solemn promise in the name of God or on a Bible

oat-meal *n.* a cooked cereal food made from rolled oats

ob-bli-ga-to *adj.* necessary to; indispensable

ob-du-rate *adj.* stubborn obduracy *n.*

o-be-di-ence *n.* the havit of obeying; compliance; submission

o-be-di-ent *adj.* obeying or willing to do what one is told obedience *n.*

ob-e-lisk *n.* a tall, four-sided stone pillar which slopes from a pointed top

o-bese *adj.* very fat obesity *n.* ·

o-bey *v.* to carry out instructions obeyer *n.*

ob-fus-cate *v.* to obscure; to confuse, muddle, or bewilder

o-bi *n.* a sash that is tied over a kimono and worn by the Japanese female

o-bit *n. Slang* an obituary

o-bit-u-ar-y *n.*, *pl.* -ies a published announcement that a person has died

ob-ject *v.* to voice disapproval *Grammar* a word in a sentence which explains who or what is acted upon

object ball *n.* in billiards the first ball struck by the cue ball.

object glass *n.* the lens or combination of lenses in a microscope or telescope, that first receives the rays from an object and forms the image through the eyepiece

ob-jec-tion *n.* a feeling of opposition or disagreement, etc.; the reason for a disagreement

ob-jec-tion-a-ble *adj.* provoking diapproval or protest; offensive or reprehensible

ob-jec-tive *adj.* pertaining to or dealing

with material objects rather than mental concepts

ob-la-tion n. a religious offering or the act of sacrifice

ob-li-ga-tion n. a promise or feeling of duty; something one must do because one's conscience or law demands it

ob-lig-a-to-ry adj. binding legally or morally; imperative, compulsory; recording an

o-blige v. to constrain; to put in one's debt by a service or favor
obliger n., obligingly adv.

ob-li-gee n. the person to whom another is obligated or bound by a legal agreement

o-blig-ing adj. disposed to do favors or perform special services; willing; kind

ob-li-gor adj. a person who is legally bound to discharge an obligation

o-blique adj. inclined; not level or straight up and down
obliqueness, obliquity n.

ob-liq-ui-ty n. divergence from ones moral standards, an instance of mental deviation; a confusing statement

o-blit-er-ate v. to blot out or eliminate completely; to wipe out
obliteration, obliterator n., obliterative adj.

o-bliv-i-on n. the condition of being utterly forgotten

ob-liv-i-ous adj. not aware or conscious of what is happening; unmindful
obliviously adv., obliviousness n.

ob-long adj. rectangular; longer in one direction than the other oblong n.

ob-lo-quy n. abusive languange; a strongly condemnatory utterance

ob-nox-ious adj. very unpleasant; repugnant obnoxiousness n.

o-boe n. a double-reed, tube-shaped woodwind instrument
oboist, ob-scene adj. indecent

ob-scene adj. indecent; disgusting; objectionable; tending to 9incit lust

ob-scure adj. remote; not clear; faint v. to make dim; to conceal by covering
obscurely adv., obscurity n.

ob-serve v. to pay attention; to watch
observable, observant adj., observably adv., observer n.

ob-ser-vant adj. paying strict attention to something

ob-ser-va-tion n. the act of observing something; that which is observed; a judgment or opinion
observational adj. -ally adv.

ob-ser-va-to-ry n., pl. -ies a building or station furnished with instruments for

studying the natural phenomenon

ob-sess v. to preoccupy the mind with an idea or emotion obsession n.

ob-so-lete adj. no longer in use; out-of-date obsolescence n., obsolescent adj.

ob-sta-cle n. an obstruction; anything which opposes or stands in the way of

ob-ste-tri-cian n. a physician who specializes in the care of a woman during pregnancy and childbirth

ob-stet-rics pl., n. the branch of medicine which deals with pregnancy and childbirth

ob-sti-na-cy n. the instance, state, or quality of being obstinate

ob-sti-nate adj. stubbornly set to an opinion or course of action
obstinacy n., obstinately adv.

ob-strep-er-ous adj. noisy, unruly, or boisterous in resistance to advice or control

ob-struct v. to block, hinder or impede obstructor, obstruction n., -tive adj.

ob-struc-tion-ism n. the deliberate interference the progress or business

ob-tain v. to acquire or gain possession of obtainable adj., obtainer n.

ob-trude v. to thrust forward without request or warrant; to call attention to oneself

ob-tuse adj. lacking acuteness of feeling; insensitive; not distinct or clear to the senses, as pain or sound

ob-vert v. to turn in order to present a different view or surface

ob-vi-ate v. to counter or prevent by effective measures

ob-vi-ous adj. easily seen, discovered, or understood

oc-ca-sion n. the time an event occurs; the event itself; a celebration v. to bring about

oc-ca-sion-al adj. appearing or occurring irregularly or now and then

oc-ci-den-tal adj. western

oc-cip-i-tal bone n. Anat. the bone which forms the back of the skull

oc-cult adj. concealed n. the action or influence of supernatural agencies or secret knowledge of them
occultist, occultism n.

oc-cult-ism n. study or belief in the influence or action of supernatural powers

oc-cu-pan-cy n. the state or act of being occupied; the act of holding in possession

oc-cu-pant n. a person who acquired title by occupancy

oc-cu-pa-tion n. a job, profession, or vocation; a foreign military force which controls an area

occupational therapy *n. Med.* the treatment of mental, nervous, or physical disabilities by means of work designed to promote recovery or readjustment

oc-cu-py *v.* to take and retain possession of; to live in **occupier** *n.*

oc-cur *v.* to suggest; to have something come to mind; to happen
occurrence *n.,* **-rent** *adj. and n.*

o-cean *n.* an immense body of salt water which covers 3/4 of the earth's surface **oceanic** *adj.*

ocean-ar-i-um *n.* a large contained marine aquarium used for the display of fish

o-ce-an-ic *adj.* pertaining to , occurring in the ocean

ocean-front *n.* an area or building that faces the ocean

ocean-going *adj.* being capable or designed for ocean travel

o-ce-an-og-ra-phy *n.* the science of oceanic phenomena dealing with underwater research

o'clock *adv.* of, or according to the clock

oc-ta-gon *n.* a polygon with eight angles and eight sides
octagonal *adj.,* **octagonally** *adv.*

oc-tane *n.* any of several hydrocarbon compounds which occur in petroleum

oc-tave *n., Music* a tone on the eighth degree above or below another tone

Oc-to-ber *n.* the 10th month of the calendar year, having 31 days

oc-to-ge-nar-i-an *n.* a person between the ages of 80 and 90

oc-to-pus *n., pl.* **-es** *or* **-pi** a cephalopod with a sac-like body and eight tentacles containing double rows of suckers

oc-u-lar *adj.* of or relating to the eye

OD *n. Slang* an overdose of a drug; one who has taken an overdose *v.* to overdose; to die from an overdose

odd *adj.* unusual; strange; singular; left over; not even **oddly** *adv.,* **oddness** *n.*

odds *pl, n.* an equalizing advantage given to a weaker opponent

ode *n.* a lyric poem usually honoring a person or event

o-dom-e-ter *n.* a device in a vehicle used to measure distance traveled **-try** *n.*

o-dor *n.* a smell; a sensation which occurs when the sense of smell is stimulated

od-ys-sey *n.* a long voyage marked by many changes of fortune; a spiritual quest

of *prep.* proceeding; composed of; relating to

off *adv.* from a position or place; no longer connected or on *adj.* canceled *prep.* away from

of-fend *v.* to make angry; to arouse resentment; to break a law **offender** *n.*

of-fense *n.* a violation of a duty, rule, or a propriety; the act of causing displeasure; the act of assaulting or attacking

of-fen-sive *adj.* disagreeable or unpleasant; causing resentment; insulting

of-fer *v.* to present for acceptance or rejection; to present as an act of worship; to make available

of-fer-ing *n.* the act of one who offers; a contribution, as money, given to the support of a church

off-hand *adv. or adj.* without preparation or premeditation

of-fice *n.* a place where business or professional duties are conducted

of-fi-cer *n.* a person who holds a title, or position of authority

of-fi-cial *adj.* something derived from proper authority *n.* one who holds a position or office; a person who referees a game such as football, basketball, or soccer
officialism *n.,* **officially** *adv.*

of-fi-ci-ate *v.* to carry out the duties and functions of a position or office

of-fi-cious *adj.* offering one's services or advice in an unduly forward manner **officiously** *adv.,* **officiousness** *n.*

off-spring *n., pl.* **-springs** the descendants of a person, plant, or animal

of-ten *adv.* frequently

oh *interj.* used to express surprise, fear, or pain

oil *n.* any of various substances, usually thick, which can be burned or easily melted; a lubricant *v.* to lubricate

oil field *n.* an area rich in petroleum; an area which has been made ready for oil production

oint-ment *n.* an oily substance used on the skin as an aid to healing or to soften the skin

o-kra *n.* a tall tropical and semitropical plant with green pods that can be either fried or cooked in soups

old *adj.* having lived or existed for a long time; of a certain age *n.* former times

old-en *adj.* of or relating to times long past; ancient

old--fash-ioned *adj.* pertaining to or characteristic of former times or old customs; not modern or up-to-date

Old Glory *n.* the flag of the United States of America

Old Testament *n.* the first of two parts of the Christian Bible, containing the history of the Hebrews, the laws of Moses, the writings of the prophets, the Holy Scriptures of Judaism, and other material

Old World *n.* the eastern hemisphere, including Asia, Europe, and Africa

ol-fac-tory *adj.* pertaining to the sense of smell

oli-gar-chy *pl., n.* -ies a government controlled by a small group for corrupt and selfish purposes; the group exercising such control

ol-ive *n.* a small oval fruit from an evergreen tree with leathery leaves and yellow flowers, valuable as a source of oil

O-lym-pic Games *pl., n.* international athletic competition held every four years, based on an ancient Greek festival

om-buds-man *pl. n.* -men a government official appointed to report and receive grievances against the government

om-e-let *or* **om-e-lette** *n.* a dish made from eggs and other items, such as bacon, cheese, and ham, and cooked until set

o-men *n.* a phenomenon which is thought of as a sign of something to come, whether good or bad

om-i-nous *adj.* fore-shadowed by an omen or by a presentiment of evil; threatening

o-mis-sion *n.* the state or act of being omitted; anything neglected or left out

o-mit *v.* to neglect; to leave out

om-ni-bus *n.* a public vehicle designed to carry a large number of people; a bus *adj.* covering a complete collection of objects or cases

om-nip-o-tent *adj.* having unlimited or infinite power or authority

om-nis-cient *adj.* knowing all things; having universal or complete knowledge

om-niv-or-ous *adj.* feeding on both vegetable and animal substances; absorbing everything **omnivorously** *adv.*

on *prep.* positioned upon; indicating proximity; indicating direction toward; with respect to *adv.* in a position of covering; forward

once *adv.* a single time; at any one time *conj.* As soon as

once-over *n., Slang* a swift but comprehensive glance

on-col-o-gy *n.* the study of tumors **oncological,** -gic *adj.,* **oncologist** *n.*

one *adj.* single; undivided *n.* a single person; a unit; the first cardinal number (1). **oneself** *pron.* one's own self

one--sid-ed *adj.* partial to one side; unjust **one-sidedness** *n.*

on-ion *n.* an edible bulb plant having a pungent taste and odor

on--line *adj. Computer Science* controlled directly by a computer

on-ly *adj.* sole; for one purpose alone *adv.* without anyone or anything else *conj.* except; but

on-o-mat-o-poe-ia *n.* the use of a word, as buzz or hiss, which vocally imitates the sound it denotes **onomatopoeic, onomatopoetic** *adj.*

on-shore *adj.* moving or coming near or onto the shore **onshore** *adv.*

on-slaught *n.* a fierce attack

on-to *prep.* to a position or place; aware of

o-nus *n.* a burden; a responsibility or duty which is difficult or unpleasant; the blame

on-ward *adv.* moving forward in time or space **onwards** *adj.*

on-yx *n.* a gemstone; a chalcedony in layers of different colors

oo-dles *pl., n., Slang* a great or large quantity

ooze *n.* a soft deposit of slimy mud on the bottom of a body of water; muddy or marshy ground; a bog *v.* to flow or leak slowly; to disappear little by little

o-pal *n.* a translucent mineral composed of silicon, often marked with an iridescent play of colors **opaline** *adj.*

o-paque *adj.* not transparent; dull; obscure **opacity, opaqueness** *n.*

OPEC *abbr.* Organization of Petroleum Exporting Countries.

o-pen *adj.* having no barrier; not covered, sealed, locked, or fastened *n.* a contest for both amateurs and professionals *v.* to begin or start **openness** *n.,* **openly** *adv.*

open--and--shut *adj.* easily settled; simple to decide

op-era *n.* a drama having music as a dominant factor, an orchestral accompaniment, acting, and scenery

op-er-ate *v.* to function, act, or work effectively; to perform an operation, as surgery **operative** *adj.*

op-er-a-tion *n.* the process of operating; the system or method of operating; a series of acts to effect a certain purpose; a process; a procedure performed on the human body with surgical instruments to restore health; various mathematical or logical processes

op-er-a-tor n. a person who operates a machine; the owner or person in charge of a business *Slang* a shrewd person

oph-thal-mol-o-gy- n. a branch of medical science dealing with diseases of the eye, its structure, and functions

o-pin-ion n. a judgment held with confidence; a conclusion held without positive knowledge

o-pi-um n. a bitter, highly addictive drug; a narcotic

o-pos-sum n., pl. -sum or -sums a nocturnal animal which hangs by its tail and carries its young in a pouch

op-po-nent n. an adversary; one who opposes another

op-por-tune adj. occurring at the right or appropriate time
opportunist n., **opportunely** adv.

op-por-tu-ni-ty n., pl. -ies a favorable position; a chance for advancement

op-pose v. to be in direct contention with; to resist; to be against
opposable adj., **opposition** n.

op-po-site adj. situated or placed on opposing sides **oppositeness** n.

op-press v. to worry or trouble the mind; to weigh down; to burden as if to enslave **oppression, oppressor** n.

op-tic adj. pertaining or referring to sight or the eye

op-ti-cal adj. pertaining to sight; constructed or designed to assist vision **optically** adv.

op-ti-cian n. a person who makes eyeglasses and other optical articles

op-ti-mism n. a doctrine which emphasizes that everything is for the best

op-ti-mum n., pl. -ma the degree or condition producing the most favorable result adj. conducive to the best result

op-tion n. the act of choosing or the power of choice; a choice -ally adv.

op-tion-al adj. left to one's decision; elec-tive; not required

op-tom-e-try n. the occupation or profession of examining the eyes and prescribing corrective lenses

op-u-lence n. wealth in abundance; affluence

or conj. a word used to connect the second of two choices or possibilities, indicating uncertainty *suffix* indicating a person or thing which does something

or-a-cle n. a seat of worship where ancient Romans and Greeks consulted the gods for answers; a person of unquestioned wisdom **oracular** adj.

o-ral adj. spoken or uttered through the mouth; taken or administered through the mouth **orally** adv.

oral contraceptive n. a pill containing hormones, taken monthly to prevent pregnancy

or-ange n. a citrus fruit which is round and orange in color adj. Yellowish-red

o-rang-u-tan n., pl. -tans a large, anthropoid ape, having brownish-red hair and very long arms

o-rate v. to speak in an elevated manner

orb n. a globe or sphere

or-bit n. the path of a celestial body or a manmade object v. to revolve or move in an orbit; to circle **orbital** adj.

or-chard n. land that is devoted to the growing of fruit trees

or-ches-tra n. a group of musicians performing together on various instruments **orchestral** adj.

orchestra pit n. in theatres, the space reserved for musicians

or-chid n. a plant found the world over having three petals in various colors

or-dain v. to appoint as a minister, priest, or rabbi by a special ceremony; to decree

or-deal n. a painful or severe test of character or endurance

or-der n. a condition where there is a logical arrangement or disposition of things; sequence or suc-cession; method; an instruction for a person to follow; a request for certain objects v. to command; to demand

orderly adj. neat, tidy.

or-di-nance n. a command, rule, or order; a law issued by a municipal body

or-di-nar-y adj. normal; having no exceptional quality; common; average; plain

ore n. a natural underground substance, as a mineral or rock, from which valuable matter is extracted

o-reg-a-no n. a bushy perennial herb of the mint family, used as a seasoning for food

or-gan n. a musical instrument of pipes, reeds, and keyboards which produces sound by means of compressed air; a part of an animal, human, or plant that performs a definite function, as the heart, a kidney, or a stamen

or-gan-dy *or* or-gan-die *n., pl.* -ies a translucent, stiff fabric of cotton or silk

or-gan-ic *adj.* effecting or pertaining to the organs of an animal or plant; of or relating to the process of growing plants with natural fertilizers with no chemical additives organically *adv.*

or-gan-i-za-tion *n.* the state of being organized or the act of organizing; a group of people united for a particular purpose organizational *adj.*

or-gan-ize *v.* to assemble or arrange with an orderly manner; to arrange by planning organization *n.*

or-gasm *n.* Physiol. intensive emotional excitement; the culmination of a sexual act

o-ri-ent *v.* to determine the bearings or right direction with respect to another source

Orient *n.* the countries located east of Europe Oriental *adj.*

or-i-fice *n.* an opening through which something may pass; a mouth

or-i-gin *n.* the cause or beginning of something; the source; a beginning place

o-rig-i-nal *adj.* belonging to the first or beginning *n.* a new idea produced by one's own imagination; the first of a kind originality *n.,* originally *adv.*

or-i-ole *n.* a songbird having brightly colored yellow and black plumage in the males

or-na-ment *n.* a decoration. *v.* To adorn or beautify ornamental *adj.*, ornamentally *adv.*, ornamentation *n.*

or-nate *adj.* excessively ornamental; elaborate; showy, as a style of writing

or-phan *n.* a child whose parents are deceased orphan *v.*, orphanage *n.*

or-ris *n.* any of several species having a fragrant root and used in medicine, perfumes, and cosmetics

or-tho-don-tics *n.* the branch of dentistry dealing with the correction and prevention of irregularities of the teeth

or-tho-dox *adj.* following established traditions and beliefs, especially in religion

Orthodox Judaism *n.* the branch of Jewish faith which accepts the Mosaic Laws as interpreted in the Talmud

or-tho-pe-dics *n.* the branch of surgery or manipulative treatment concerned with the disorders of the bones, joints, and muscles orthopedist *n.*

os-cil-late *v.* to swing back and forth with regular motion, as a pendulum oscillation, oscillator *n.,* -tory *adj.*

os-mi-um *n.* a hard, but brittle metallic element symbolized as OS

os-mo-sis *n.* the tendency of fluids separated by a semipermeable membrane to pass through it and become mixed and equal in strength osmotic *adj.*

os-ten-ta-tion *n.* the act of displaying pretentiously in order to excite

osteo *n. comb. form* bone; pertaining to the bones

os-te-op-a-thy *n.* a medical practice based on the theory that diseases are due chiefly to abnormalities of the body, which can be restored by manipulation of the parts by therapeutic measures

os-teo-po-ro-sis *n.* a disorder causing gradual deterioration of bone tissue, usually occurring in older women

os-tra-cize *v.* to exile or exclude from a group; to shut out

oth-er *adj.* additional; alternate; different from what is implied or specified *pron.* a different person or thing

oth-er-wise *adv.* under different conditions of circumstances

ot-ter *n., pl.* -ter *or* -ters web-footed aquatic mammals, related to the weasel

ouch *n. interj.* an exclamation to express sudden pain

ought *v.* used to show or express a moral duty or obligation; to be advisable or correct

ounce *n.* a unit of weight which equals 1/16 of a pound

our *adj.* of or relating to us ourselves *pron.* the possessive case of the pronoun we ourselves our own selves

oust *v.* to eject; to remove with force

out *adv.* away from the center or inside *adj.* away *n.* a means of escape *prep.* through; forward from

out-age *n.* a loss of electricity

out-break *n.* a sudden outburst; an occurrence

out-cast *n.* a person who is excluded; a homeless person

out-come *n.* a consequence or result

out-dated *adj.* old-fashioned and obsolete

out-do *v.* to excel in achievement

out-fit *n.* the equipment or tools required for a specialized purpose; the clothes a person is dressed in *v.* to supply

out-land-ish *adj.* extremely ridiculous,

unusual, or strange

out-last v. to exceed; to outlive; to last longer that something else in comparison

out-law n. a person who habitually defies or breaks the law; a criminal v. to ban; prohibit; to deprive of legal protection

out-let n. an exit

out-line n. a rough draft showing the main features of something outline v.

out-look n. a person's point of view; an area offering a view of something

out-num-ber v. to go over or exceed in number

out-pa-tient n. a patient who visits a clinic or hospital for treatment but does not spend the night

out-post n. troops stationed at a distance away from the main group as a guard against attack; a frontier or outlying settlement

out-put n. production or yield during a given time

out-rage n. an extremely violent act of violence or cruelty; the violent emotion such an act engenders outrageous adj., outrage v.

out-right adj. free from reservations or complications; complete; entire

out-side n. the area beyond the boundary lines or surface; extreme adv. outdoors

out-spo-ken adj. spoken without reserve; candid outspokenly adv.

out-stand-ing adj. excellent; prominent; unsettled, as a bill owed; projecting

out-ward adj. pertaining to the outside or exterior; superficial outwards adv.

out-wit v. to trick, baffle, or outsmart with ingenuity

o-val adj. having the shape of an egg; an ellipse

o-va-ry n., pl. -ies one of the pair of female reproductive glands -rian adj.

o-va-tion n. an enthusiastic display of approval for a person or a performance; applause

ov-en n. an enclosed chamber used for baking, drying, or heating

o-ver-act v. to act in an exaggerated way

o-ver prep. above; across; upon adv. covering completely; thoroughly; again; repetition adj. higher; upper prefix excessive, as overstuffed or overcrowded

over-act v. to act in an exaggerated way

over-all adj. including or covering everything; from one side or end to another; generally n. pants with a bib and shoulder straps

over-arm adj. thrown or executed with the arms raised above the shoulders

over-bear v. to crush or bear down by superior force or weight overbearing adj.

over-board adv. over the side of a boat or ship into the water

over-cast adj. gloomy; obscured Meteor. clouds covering more than 9/10 of the sky

over-coat n. a coat worn over a suit for extra warmth

over-come v. to prevail; to conquer or defeat overcomer n.

over-con-fi-dence n. extreme or excessive confidence

over-do v. to do anything excessively; to overcook

over-dose n. to take an excessive dose of medication, especially narcotics

over-draw v. to withdraw money over the limits of one's credit

over-drive n. a gearing device in a vehicle that turns a drive shaft at a greater speed than that of the engine, therefore decreasing power output

over-due adj. past the time of return or payment

over-flow v. to flow beyond the limits of capacity; to overfill

over-hand v. to execute something with the hand above the level of the elbow or shoulder overhanded adv.

over-haul v. to make all needed repairs

over-head n. the operating expenses of a company, including utilities, rent, and upkeep adj. situated above the level of one's head

over-look v. to disregard or fail to notice something purposely; to ignore

over-night adj. lasting the whole night; from dusk to dawn overnight adv.

over-pass n. a raised section of highway which crosses other lines of traffic v. to cross, pass over, or go through something; to overlook

over-plus n. a surplus of something

over-ride v. to disregard; to take precedence over; to declare null and void

over-rule v. to put aside by virtue of higher authority

over-run v. to spread out; to extend or run beyond

over-seas adv. abroad, across the seas overseas adj.

over-see v. to supervise; to direct overseer n.

over-sexed adj. having an overactive interest in sex

over-shoe *n.* a galosh worn over a shoe for protection from snow or water

over-sight *n.* a mistake made inadvertently

over-size or oversized *adj.* larger than the average size of something

over-step *v.* to go beyond a limit or restriction

overt *adj.* open to view

over-the-counter *adj.* not traded on an organized security ex-change; of or relating to drugs or medicine which can be purchased without a prescription

over-throw *v.* to remove from power by force; to bring about destruction

over-time *n.* the time worked beyond or before the specified hours

over-whelm *v.* to overcome completely; to make helpless

o-void *adj.* having the shape of an egg

ovu-late *n.* to discharge or produce eggs from an ovary

o-vum *n., pl.* **ova** the female reproductive cell

owe *v.* to be in debt for a certain amount; to have a moral obligation

owl *n.* a predatory nocturnal bird, having large eyes, a short hooked bill, and long powerful claws **owlish** *adj.*

own *adj.* belonging to oneself *v.* to possess; to confess; to admit **owner** *n.*

ox *n., pl.* **oxen** a bovine animal used domestically in much the same way as a horse; an adult castrated bull

ox-ford *n.* a shoe which is laced and tied over the instep

ox-ide *n.* a compound of oxygen and another element

oxy-ac-id *n.* an acid containing oxygen

ox-y-gen *n.* a colorless, odorless, tasteless gaseous element essential to life, symbolized by O

ox-y-gen-ate *v.* to combine or treat with oxygen

oxygen mask *n.* a device worn over the mouth and nose through which a person can receive oxygen as an aid to breathing

ox-y-gen tent *n.* the protective cover that is placed over the upper body of a patient, and makes it possible for delivering and retaining pure oxygen to aid breathing

oys-ter *n.* an edible marine mollusk

o-zone *n.* a pale-blue gas formed of oxygen with an odor like chlorine, formed by an electrical discharge in the air *Slang* fresh air

P p The sixteenth letter of the English alphabet.

pab-u-lom *n.* type of food such as in absorable solution

pa-ca *n.* type of large and borwn rodent that is from Central and South America having white spots

pace *n.* a person's step in walking or the length of a person's step; stride **pace** *v.*, **pacer** *n.*

pace car *n.* the automobile that leads a field of competitors around the track, in order to warm up the engines then falls aout and does not continue in the race

pace lap *n.* the warm up lap before the start of a car race

pace-mak-er *n.* the person who sets the pace for another in a race; a type of surgically implanted electronic instrument used to stabilize or stimulate the heartbeat

pac-er *n.* one that sets

pa-chi-si *n.* another name for the game Parcheesi; ancient board game played with dice

pach-y-derm *n.* a group of animals which contains the elephant, the rhinoceros, and hippo; animals having thisk skins

pach-y-san-dra *n.* a type of species of the evergreen trailing herbs of the box family and is grown for the purpose of ground cover in areas that are shaded

pa-cif-i-ca-tion *n.* the state of something being pacified or calmed

pac-i-fi-er *n.* a person or something that will pacify another; nipple shaped device for babies to such on

pac-i-fism *n.* the policy dealing with the establishment of universal peace between all nations; opposition to violence or war as a means of settling problems or disputes

pac-i-fy *v.* to quiet or soothe anger or distress; to calm **pacification** *n.*

pack *n.* a bundle; a group or number of things tied or wrapped up

pack-age *n.* something tied up, wrapped or bound together

pack-age deal *n.* an agreement or offer that involves a number of related items, the items offered

pack-age store *n.* a retail establishment that sells alcoholic beverages only in sealed containers

pack animal *n.* an animal used to carry heavy packs

pack-board *n.* a metal fram that is usuallyt covered with canvas, used to carry goods and equipment over ones shoulder

pack-er n. a person who packs; one who works in an establishment that packs meat; a machine that automatically packs

pact n. an agreement between nations, groups, or people

pad-dy wag-on n., *Slang* a police vehicle

pa-dre n. a title used in Spain and Italy for a priest

pa-gan n. a person who does not acknowledge God in any religion; a heathen **pagan** *adj.*, **paganism** n.

page n. a person hired to deliver messages or run errands; one side of the leaf of a book or letter

pag-eant n. an elaborate exhibition or spectacular parade for public celebration **pageantry** n.

pa-go-da n. a sacred Buddhist tower built as a memorial or shrine

paid v. past tense of pay

pail n. a cylindrical container usually having a handle

pain n. the unpleasant feeling resulting from injury or disease **-ful, -less** *adj.*

paint n. a mixture of colors or pigments which are spread on a surface as protection or as a decorative coating **painter, painting** n.

pair n., *pl.* **pairs, pair** two things which are similar and used together

pa-ja-mas *pl.*, n. a loose fitting garment for sleeping, consisting of a jacket and pants

pal-ace n. the royal residence of a sovereign **palatial** *adj.*

pal-at-a-ble *adj.* pleasant to the taste

pale n. the pointed stake of a fence; a picket **palely** *adv.*

pal-ette n. a thin oval board with a hole for the thumb, on which an artist lays and mixes colors

pal-in-drome n. a word, number, or sentence which reads the same backward or forward

pal-i-sade n. a fence made of stakes for protection

pall n. a heavy cloth used to cover a bier or coffin

pal-la-di-um n. a silvery-white metallic element symbolized by Pd.

pall-bear-er n. a person who assists in carrying a coffin at a funeral

pal-lid *adj.* deficient in color

pal-lor n. lacking color; paleness

palm n. the inner area of the hand between the fingers and the wrist

pal-sy n., *pl.* **-ies** paralysis; the loss of ability to control one's movements

pam-per v. to treat with extreme care

pam-phlet n. a brief publication which is not permanently bound

pan-a-ce-a n. a remedy for all diseases, difficulties, or ills

pan-cake n. a thin, flat cake made from batter and fried on a griddle

pan-cre-as n., *Anat.* a large, irregularly shaped gland situated behind the stomach which releases digestive enzymes and produces insulin **-tic** *adj.*

pan-da n. a large bear-like animal of China and Tibet

pan-de-mo-ni-um n. a place marked with disorder and wild confusion

pan-der or panderer n. a go-between in sexual affairs; a pimp

pan-el n. a flat, rectangular piece of material, often wood, which for-ms a part of a surface **panelist** n.

pan-ic n. a sudden unreasonable fear which overpowers **panicky** *adj.*

pan-nier n. one of a pair of large baskets which are carried on either side of an animal

pan-o-ply n., *pl.* **-lies** the complete equipment of a warrior

pan-o-ram-a n. an unlimited or complete view in all directions

pan-sy n., *pl.* **-ies** a garden plant with flowers bearing blossoms

pant v. to breathe in rapid or short gasps; to yearn

pan-the-ism n. the belief that the laws and forces of nature are all manifestations of God

pantheist n., **pantheistic** *adj.*

pan-ther n. a black leopard in its unspotted form

pan-to-mime n. communication done solely by means of facial and body gestures

pan-try n., *pl.* **-ies** a closet or room for storage

pants *pl*, n. trousers; underpants

pap n. a soft food for invalids or babies

pa-pa-cy n., *pl.* **-ies** the dignity or jurisdiction of a pope

pa-per n. a substance made of pulp from wood and rags

pa-poose n. a North American Indian child or baby

pa-pri-ka n. a dark red seasoning powder made by grinding red peppers

Pap test n. a test in which a smear of bodily secretion from the uterus is examined for the early detection of cancer

par-a-ble n. a short, fictitious story which illustrates a moral lesson

par-a-chute *n.* a folding umbrella-shaped apparatus of light fabric used to make a safe landing after a free fall from an airplane

pa-rade *n.* an organized public procession parader *n.*

par-a-dise *n.* a state or place of beauty, bliss or delight; heaven paradisiac, paradisiacal *adj.*

par-a-dox *n.* a statement which seems opposed to common sense or contradicts itself paradoxical *adj.*, paradoxically *adv.*

par-a-gon *n.* a pattern or model of excellence or perfection

par-a-graph *n.* a section of a composition dealing with a single idea, containing one or more sentences

par-a-keet *n.* a small parrot with a long, wedge-shaped tail

par-al-lel *adj.* moving in the same direction but separated by a distance, as railroad tracks parallel *v.* parallelism *n.*

par-al-lel-o-gram *n.* a four-sided figure having parallel opposite sides which are equal

pa-ral-y-sis *n., pl.* -ses complete or partial loss of the ability to feel any sensation or to move -tic *adj. & n.*

par-a-lyze *v.* to cause to be inoperative or powerless

par-a-med-ic *n.* a person trained to give emergency medical treatment until a doctor is available

par-a-mount *adj.* superior to all others in rank, importance, and power

par-a-noi-a *n.* mental insanity marked by systematic delusions of persecution or grandeur

par-a-pher-na-lia *n.* personal effects or belongings

par-a-phrase *v.* to put something written or spoken into different words while retaining the same meaning

par-a-site *n., Biol.* an organism which lives, grows, feeds, and takes shelter in or on another organism

par-a-sol *n.* a small umbrella used as protection from the sun

par-boil *v.* to precook something in boiling water

par-cel *n.* a wrapped package; a portion of land parcel *v.*

parch *v.* to become very dry from intense heat

parch-ment *n.* goatskin or sheepskin prepared with a pumice stone and used as a material for writing or drawing

par-don *v.* to forgive someone for an offense pardonable *adj.*, pardonably *adv.*, pardon *n.*

pare *v.* to cut away or remove the outer surface gradually

par-e-go-ric *n.* a medication used to relieve stomach pains

par-ent *n.* a mother or father; a forefather; an ancestor parenthood *n.*, parental *adj.*

pa-ren-the-sis *n., pl.* -ses one of a pair of curved lines ( ) used to enclose a qualifying or explanatory remark

park *n.* a tract of land used for recreation

par-ka *n.* a cloth jacket with an attached hood

Par-kin-son's disease *n., Pathol.* a progressive disease marked by partial facial paralysis, muscular tremor, weakness, and impaired muscular control

par-lia-ment *n.* the assembly which constitutes the lawmaking body of various countries

par-lor *n.* a room for entertaining visitors or guests

pa-ro-chi-al *adj.* belonging to a local parish; having to do with a parish

par-o-dy *n., pl.* -ies a composition, song, or poem which mimics another in a ridiculous way

pa-role *n.* the conditional release of a prisoner before his sentence expires parole *v. & adj.*

par-ox-ysm *n.* a violent attack or outburst; a spasm

par-ri-cide *n.* the crime of murdering one's parents parricidal *adj.*

par-rot *n.* a brightly colored, semitropical bird

par-ry *v.* to avoid something; to turn aside parry *n.*

parse *v.* to identify the parts of speech in a sentence and to indicate their relationship to each other

par-si-mo-ny *n.* extreme reluctance to use one's resources or to spend money -ious *adj.*, parsimoniously *adv.*

pars-ley *n.* an herb with curly leaves which is used for seasoning and garnishing

pars-nip *n.* a plant from the carrot family cultivated for its long, edible root

par-son *n.* a pastor or clergyman

parsonage *n.* the home provided by a church for its parson

part *n.* a segment, portion, or division of a whole

par-take *v.* to have a share or part; to

take

par-tial *adj.* incomplete; inclined to favor one side more than the other partiality *n.*, partially *adv.*

par-tic-i-pate *v.* to join in or share; to take part

par-ti-cle *n.* a very small piece of solid matter

par-tic-u-lar *adj.* having to do with a specific person, group, thing, or category particularly *adv.*

part-ing *n.* a division; a separation; the place where a division or separation occurs *adj.* done, given, or said on departing

par-ti-tion *n.* a separation or division *v.* to divide

part-ner *n.* one who shares something with another

part-ner-ship *n.* two or more persons who run a business together and share in the profits and losses

par-tridge *n., pl.* partridges a plump or stout-bodied game bird

par-ty *n., pl.* -ies a group of persons who gather for pleasure or entertainment

pass *v.* to proceed; to move; to transfer; to go away or come to an end

pas-sage *n.* the act of going, proceeding, or passing

pas-sen-ger *n.* one who travels in a vehicle, car, plane, or boat

pas-sion *n.* a powerful feeling; lust; sexual desire; an outburst of strong feeling

pas-sive *adj.* not working, acting, or operating; inactive passivity *n.*

pass-port *n.* an official permission issued to a person allowing him to travel out of this country and to return

past *adj.* having to do with or existing at a former time *n.* Before the present time

pas-tel *n.* a crayon made of ground pigments; a drawing made with crayons of this kind

pas-teur-i-za-tion *n.* the process of killing disease-producing microorganisms by heating the liquid to a high temperature

pas-time *n.* spending spare time in a pleasant way; a diversion

pas-tor *n.* a Christian clergyman in charge of a church or congregation

pas-tor-al *adj.* referring to the duties of a pastor

past par-ti-ci-ple *n.* a participle used with reference to actions and conditions in the past

pas-try *n.* food made with dough or

having a crust made of dough

pas-ture *n.* an area for grazing of domestic animals

pat *v.* to tap lightly with something flat *n.* a soft, caressing stroke

patch *n.* a piece of fabric used to repair a weakened or torn area in a garment patchy, patchable *adj.*

pat-ent *n.* a governmental protection assuring an inventor the exclusive right of manufacturing, using, exploiting, and selling an invention *adj.* evident patentee, patency *n.*, patently *adv.*

pa-ter-nal *adj.* relating to or characteristic of a father; inherited from a father paternally *adv.*, paternalism *n.*

path *n.* a track or course; a route; a course of action

pa-thet-ic *adj.* rousing pity, tenderness, or sympathy pathetically *adv.*

pa-thol-o-gy *n.* the science that deals with facts about diseases, their nature and causes -ic, -ical *adj.*, -gist *n.*

pa-thos *n.* a quality in a person that evokes sadness or pity

pa-tience *n.* the quality, state, or fact of being patient; the ability to be patient

pa-tient *adj.* demonstrating uncomplaining endurance under distress

pa-ti-o *n.* an area attached to a house, used for enjoyment and entertainment

pa-tri-arch *n.* the leader of a tribe or family who rules by paternal right; a very old and revered man patriarchal *adj.*

pa-tri-ot *n.* a person who loves and defends his country patriotic *adj.*, patriotism *n.*

pa-trol *n.* walking around an area for the purpose of maintaining or observing security patrol *v.*

pa-tron *n.* a person who fosters, protects, or supports some person, enterprise, or thing; a regular customer patroness *n.*

pat-sy *n., pl.* -ies *Slang* a person who is taken advantage of

pat-tern *n.* anything designed or shaped to serve as a guide in making something else; a sample

pat-ty *n., pl.* -ies a small, flat piece of chopped meat

pau-per *n.* a very poor person who depends on charity pauperism *n.*, pauperize *v.*

pause *v.* to linger, hesitate, or stop for a time pause *n.*

pave *v.* to surface with gravel, concrete, asphalt, or other material

pavement *n.* a surface that has been

paved

pa-vil-ion *n.* a large, roofed structure used for shelter

paw *n.* the foot of an animal *v.* To handle clumsily or rudely

pay *v.* to give a person what is due for a debt, purchase, or work completed; to compensate

pay-ment *n.* the act of paying

pay-roll *n.* the amount of money to be paid to a list of employees

pea *n.* a round edible seed contained in a pod and grown on a vine

peace *n.* a state of physical or mental tranquillity; calm; serenity; the absence of war peaceable, -ful *adj.*

peach *n.* a round, sweet, juicy fruit

pea-cock *n.* a male bird with brilliant blue or green plumage and a long iridescent tail

peak *n.* a projecting edge or point; the top *v.* to bring to the maximum

pea-nut *n.* a nutlike seed which ripens underground; the plant bearing this nut

pear *n.* a juicy, edible fruit which grows on a tree

peas-ant *n.* a farmhand or rustic workman; an uneducated person of the lowest class

peat *n.* the black substance formed when plants begin to decay in wet ground, as bogs peaty *adj.*

peb-ble *n.* a small, smooth stone

pe-can *n.* a large tree of the central and southern United States with an edible oval, thin-shelled nut

peck *v.* to strike with the beak; to eat without any appetite, taking only small bites

pec-tin *n.* a complex carbohydrate found in ripe fruits and used in making jelly pectic *adj.*

pe-cu-liar *adj.* odd; strange peculiarity *n.*, peculiarly *adv.*

ped-al *n.* a lever usually operated by the foot

ped-dle *v.* to travel around in an attempt to sell merchandise

ped-es-tal *n.* a support or base for a statue to put on a pedestal to hold something in high respect

pe-des-tri-an *n.* a person traveling by foot

pe-di-at-rics *n.* the branch of medicine dealing with the care of children and infants pediatric *adj.*, pediatrician *n.*

ped-i-cure *n.* the cosmetic care of the toenails and feet

ped-i-gree *n.* a line of ancestors, especially of an animal of pure breed

ped-i-ment *n.* a broad, triangular architectural or decorative part above a door

pe-dom-e-ter *n.* an instrument which indicates the number of miles one has walked

pe-dun-cle *n.*, *Biol.* a stalk-like support in some plants and animals

peek *v.* to look shyly or quickly from a place of hiding; to glance

peel *n.* the natural rind or skin of a fruit *v.* to pull or strip the skin or bark off peeler *n.*

peen *n.* the ball-shaped end of a hammer opposite the flat, striking surface

peep *v.* to utter a very small and weak sound, as of a young bird

peer *v.* to look searchingly

pee-vish *adj.* irritable in mood peevishly *adv.*, peevishness *n.*

peg *n.* a small pin peg *v.*

pei-gnoir *n.* a woman's loose fitting dressing gown

pe-koe *n.* a superior black tea made from young or small leaves

pel-i-can *n.* a large, webfooted bird with a large pouch under the lower bill for the temporary storage of fish

pel-let *n.* a small round ball made from paper or wax; a small bullet

pelt *n.* the skin of an animal with the fur

pel-vis *n.*, *pl.* -vises *or* -ves the structure of the vertebrate skeleton which rests on the lower limbs, supporting the spinal column

pen *n.* an instrument used for writing pen *v.*

pe-nal *adj.* of or pertaining to punishment or penalties

pen-al-ty *n.*, *pl.* -ties. the legal punishment for an offense or crime

pen-ance *n.* a voluntary act to show sorrow or repentance for sin

pen-cil *n.* a writing or drawing implement made from graphite

pen-dant *or* pen-dent *n.* an ornament which hangs from a necklace

pend-ing *adj.* not yet decided; imminent *prep.* during; until

pen-du-lous *adj.* hanging downward so as to swing

pen-du-lum *n.* a suspended object free to swing back and forth

pen-e-trate *v.* to force a way through or into; to pierce -ing *adj.*, penetration *n.*

pen-guin *n.* a webfooted, flightless, marine bird

pen-i-cil-lin *n.* a powerful antibiotic derived from mold and used to treat certain types of bacterial infections

pen-in-su-la *n.* a piece of land projecting into water from a larger land mass

pe-nis *n., pl.* -nises *or* -nes the male sex organ

pen-i-tent *adj.* having a feeling of guilt or remorse for one's sins or misdeeds; sorry penitence *n.*

pen-ny *n., pl.* -ies a U. S. coin worth one cent ($.01)

pen-sion *n.* the amount of money a person receives regularly after retirement

pen-sive *adj.* involved in serious, quiet reflection

pen-ta-gon *n.* any object or building having five sides and five interior angles

pent-house *n.* an apartment built on the roof of a building

pe-on *n.* a servant; a person engaged in menial work

pe-o-ny *n., pl.* -nies a plant with a large, fragrant red, white, or pink flower

peo-ple *n., pl.* people human beings

pep-per *n.* a strong, aromatic condiment *v.* to pelt or sprinkle

pep-tic *adj.* pertaining to or aiding digestion

per an-num *adv.* for, by, or in each year; annually

per-cale *n.* a closely woven cotton fabric

per--cap-i-ta *adj. & adv., Latin* of each individual

per-ceive *v.* to become aware of by the senses; to understand; to feel or observe -able *adj.*, -ably *adv.*

per-cent-age *n.* the rate per hundred; a part or proportion in relation to a whole

per-cept *n.* a mental impression of something perceived

perch *n.* a place on which birds rest or alight; any place for standing or sitting

per-cip-i-ent *adj.* having the power of perception percipience, percipiency *n.*

per-co-late *v.* to pass or cause to pass through a porous substance; to filter percolation, percolator *n.*

per-en-ni-al *adj.* lasting from year to year; perpetual perennially *adv.*

per-fect *adj.* having no defect or fault perfectly *adv.*, perfectness *n.*

per-form *v.* to execute or carry out an action performance *n.*

per-fume *n.* a fragrant substance which emits a pleasant scent; one distilled from flowers

per-haps *adv.* possibly; maybe; not sure

per-i-gee *n.* the point of an orbit when a satellite of the earth is closest to the earth

per-il *n.* a source of danger; exposure to the chance of injury perilous *adj.*, perilously *adv.*

pe-ri-od *n.* an interval of time marked by certain conditions

pe-riph-er-y *n., pl.* -ies the outer part, boundary, or surface peripheral *adj.*

per-ish *v.* to ruin or spoil; to suffer an untimely or violent death

per-i-win-kle *n.* any of several edible marine snails

per-jure *v.* to give false testimony while under oath

per-ma-nent *adj.* continuing in the same state; lasting indefinitely; enduring

per-me-ate *v.* to spread through; to pervade

per-mis-sion *n.* the act of permitting something; consent

per-mit *v.* to consent to; to allow

per-ni-cious *adj.* very harmful; malicious perniciously *adv.*

per-ox-ide *n., Chem.* oxide containing the highest proportion of oxygen for a given series

per-pen-dic-u-lar *adj.* being at right angles to the plane of the horizon perpendicularity *n.*

per-pe-trate *v.* to perform; to commit; to be guilty

per-pet-u-al *adj.* lasting or continuing forever or an unlimited time perpetually *adv.*

per-plex *v.* to confuse or be confused; to make complicated perplexing *adj.*

per-se-cute *v.* to harass or annoy persistently; to oppress because of one's religion, beliefs, or race

per-se-vere *v.* to persist in any purpose or idea; to strive in spite of difficulties

per-sim-mon *n.* a tree having reddish orange, edible fruit

per-sist *v.* to continue firmly despite obstacles; to endure

per-son *n.* a human being; an individual

per-son-al *adj.* belonging to a person or persons

per-son-i-fy *v.* to think of or represent as having human qualities or life; to be a symbol of personifier, -fication *n.*

per-son-nel *n.* the body of people working for a business or service

per-spec-tive *n.* a painting or drawing technique in which objects seem to have depth and distance

per-spi-ra-tion *n.* the salty fluid excreted from the body by the sweat glands

per-spire *v.* to give off perspiration

per-suade *v.* to cause to convince or

believe by means of reasoning or argument

per-tain v. to relate to; to refer to; to belong as a function, adjunct or quality

per-ti-na-cious adj. adhering firmly to an opinion, belief, or purpose; stubbornly persistent **pertinacity** n.

per-ti-nent adj. relating to the matter being discussed

per-turb v. to disturb, make anxious, or make uneasy; to cause confusion

per-vade v. to spread through every part of something; to permeate
pervasive adj.

per-ver-sion n. the act of being led away from the accepted course; a deviant form of sexual behavior **perverted** adj.

pes-si-mism n. the tendency to take a gloomy view of affairs or situations and to anticipate the worst
pessimist n., **pessimistic** adj.

pest n. a person or thing which is a nuisance; an annoying person or thing; a destructive insect, plant, or animal

pes-ter v. to harass with persistent annoyance; to bother

pes-ti-cide n. a chemical substance used to destroy rodents, insects, and pests

pes-ti-lence n. a widespread and often fatal infectious disease

pet n. an animal, bird, or fish one keeps for companionship

pet-al n., Bot. one of the leaf-like parts of a flower

pe-tite adj. small in size; little

pe-ti-tion n. a solemn request or prayer; a formal written request addressed to a group or person in authority
petitioner n.

pet-ri-fy v. to convert into a stony mass; to make fixed or immobilize, as in the face of danger

pe-tro-le-um n. an oily, thick liquid which develops naturally below the ground surface, used in products such as gasoline, fuel oil, and kerosene

pet-ty adj. to have little importance or value; insignificant; trivial

pe-tu-nia n. a widely grown tropical plant

pew n. a row of bench-like seats for seating people in church

pew-ter n. an alloy of tin with copper

pfen-nig n., pl. -nigs or -nige a small coin of Germany

phal-lus n., pl. -li or -luses a representation of the penis, often as a symbol of generative power **phallic** adj.

phan-tasm n. the creation of an imaginary image; a fantasy; a phantom

phar-ma-cy n., pl. -cies a drugstore

phar-ynx n., pl. -ynges or -ynxes the part of the throat located between the palate and the esophagus

phase n. any decisive stage in development or growth

phe-nom-e-non n. something that can be observed or perceived; a rare occurrence

phi-lan-der v. to make love without feeling or serious intentions
philanderer n.

phi-lat-e-ly n. the collection and study of postage stamps and postmarked material **philatelist** n.

phil-har-mon-ic adj. pertaining to a symphony orchestra

phi-los-o-phy n., pl. -ies the logical study of the nature and source of human knowledge or human values; the set of values

pho-bi-a n. a compulsive fear of a specified situation or object

phone n., Slang a telephone v. to call or communicate by telephone

phon-ic adj. pertaining to sounds in speech; using the same symbol for each sound **phonically** adv.

pho-no-graph n. a machine which uses a needle to reproduce sound from a grooved disc or record

pho-ny adj. Informal counterfeit; fraudulent; not real or genuine

phos-phate n., Chem. a salt or phosphoric acid which contains mostly phosphorus and oxygen

phos-pho-rus n. a highly flammable, poisonous, nonmetallic element

pho-to n. Slang a photograph

pho-to-cop-y v. to reproduce printed material using a photographic process
photocopier, photocopy n.

pho-to-graph n. a picture or image recorded by a camera **photography** n.

pho-to-syn-the-sis n., Biochem. the chemical process by which plants use light to change carbon dioxide and water into carbohydrates, releasing oxygen as a byproduct
photosynthesize v., **photosynthetic** adj.

phrase n., Gram. a brief or concise expression which does not contain a predicate

phre-nol-o-gy n. the study of or the theory that the conformation of the human skull indicates the degree of intelligence and character

phys-i-cal adj. relating to the human

body apart from the mind or emotions

phy-si-cian *n.* a person licensed to practice medicine

phys-ics *n.* the scientific study which deals with energy, matter, motion, and related areas of science

phys-i-ol-o-gy *n., pl.* **-ies** the scientific study of living animals, plants, and their activities and functions

phys-i-o-ther-a-py *n.* the treatment of disease or physical defects by the use of heat and massage.

pi-ca *n.* a printer's type size of 12 points, equal to about 1/6 inch

pic-co-lo *n.* a small flute with a brilliant sound pitched an octave above the flute

pick *v.* to select or choose

pick-le *n.* a cucumber preserved in a solution of brine or vinegar

pic-nic *n.* an outdoor social gathering where food is provided **picnicker** *n.*

pic-ture *n.* a visual representation on a surface, which is printed, drawn or photographed

piece *n.* an element, unit, or part of a whole

piece-meal *adv.* gradually

pier *n.* a structure extending into the water, used to secure, protect, and provide access to vessels

pierce *v.* to penetrate or make a hole in something

pi-e-ty *n., pl.* **-ties** devoutness toward God

pig *n.* a cloven footed mammal with short legs, bristly hair, and a snout for rooting

pi-geon *n.* a bird with short legs, a sturdy body, and a small head

pig-gy-back *adv.* carried on the back and shoulders

pig-ment *n.* a material used as coloring matter, suitable for making paint

pike *n.* a long pole with a sharp, pointed steel head

pile *n.* a quantity of anything thrown in a heap

pil-fer *v.* to steal in little quantities **pilferage** *n.*

pil-grim *n.* a person who travels to a sacred place; a wanderer

pill *n.* a small tablet containing medicine which is taken by mouth **the pill** *Slang* an oral contraceptive drug taken by women

pil-lar *n.* a freestanding column which serves as a support

pil-low *n.* a cloth case filled with feathers or other soft material

pi-lot *n.* a person who is licensed to operate an aircraft

pi-men-to *n.* a sweet pepper used as a stuffing for olives or as a relish

pimp *n.* a person who arranges customers for prostitutes

pim-ple *n.* a small eruption of the skin, having an inflamed base **pimpled, pimply** *adj.*

pin *n.* a small, stiff piece of wire with a blunt head and a sharp point

pin-a-fore *n.* a sleeveless apron-like garment

pin-cer *n.* an implement having two handles and a pair of jaws working on a pivot

pinch *v.* to squeeze between a finger and thumb causing pain or discomfort

pine *n., Bot.* any of various cone-bearing evergreen trees

pine-ap-ple *n.* a tropical American plant with spiny, curved leaves bearing a large edible fruit *Slang* a hand grenade

pink-eye *n., Pathol.* an acute, contagious conjunctivitis of the eye

pin-na-cle *n.* the highest peak

pi-noch-le *or* **pi-noc-le** *n.* a card game for two, three, or four people, played with a double deck of 48 cards

pint *n.* a liquid or dry measurement equal to half of a quart or two cups

pin-to *n., pl.* **-tos** *or* **-toes** a horse with spots

pin-worm *n.* a nematode parasite which infests the human intestines and rectum

pi-o-neer *n.* one of the first settlers of a new region or country

pi-ous *adj.* reverently religious; devout **piously** *adv.,* **piousness** *n.*

pipe *n.* a hollow cylinder for conveying fluids

pique *n.* a feeling of resentment or irritation

pi-rate *n.* a robber of the high seas **piracy** *n.,* **piratical** *adj.*

pis-til *n.* the seed-producing female reproductive organ of a flower

pis-tol *n.* a small hand-held firearm

pis-ton *n., Mech.* a solid cylinder fitted into a larger cylinder, moving back and forth under liquid pressure

pit *n.* an artificial or manmade hole in the ground; a slight indentation in the skin

pitch *n.* a thick, sticky, dark substance which is the residue of the distillation of petroleum or coal tar

pith *n., Bot.* the sponge-like soft tissue at the center of the branch or stem of many plants

pit-i-ful *adj.* evoking or meriting pity
pitifully *adv.*

pit-y *n., pl.* -ies. a feeling of compassion
or sorrow

piv-ot *n.* a thing or person upon which
development, direction, or effect
depends *v.* to turn

piz-za *n.* an Italian food consisting of a
doughy crust covered with tomato
sauce, cheese, and other toppings and
then baked

place *n.* a region; an area; a building or
location used for a special purpose

place-ment *n.* the act of being placed

pla-cen-ta *n., pl.* -tas or -tae *Anat.* the
vascular, membranous structure which
supplies a fetus with nourishment
before its birth

plague *n.* anything that is troublesome
Pathol. a highly contagious and often
fatal epidemic disease

plaid *n.* a rectangular wool cloth or garment, usually worn by men and
women, having a crisscross or
checkered design

plain *adj.* level; flat; clear; open, as in
view; not rich or luxurious; not highly
gifted or cultivated
plainly *adv.,* plainness *n.*

plain-tiff *n.* a person who brings suit

plan *n.* a scheme or method for achiev-
ing something

plane *n.* a tool for smoothing or leveling
a wood surface

plan-et *n., Astron.* a celestial body which
is illuminated by light from the star
around which it revolves

plank *n.* a broad piece of wood

plant *n.* a living organism belonging to
the vegetable kingdom

plaque *n.* a flat piece, made from metal,
porcelain, ivory, or other materials,
engraved for mounting

plas-ma *n.* the clear fluid part of blood,
used for transfusions

plas-tic *n.* a synthetically made material
which is molded and then hardened
into objects plasticity *n.,* plasticize *v.*

plastic surgery *n.* surgery dealing with
the restoration or repair of deformed
or destroyed parts of the body or skin

plate *n.* a shallow, flat vessel made from
glass, crockery, plastic, or other
material from which food is served or
eaten

pla-teau *n.* an extensive level expanse of
elevated land

plat-form *n.* any elevated or raised surface used by speakers; a formal decla-

ration of principles or policy of a
political party

plat-i-num *n.* a silver-white, metallic element which is corrosiveresistant, used
in jewelry

pla-toon *n.* a military unit subdivision
commanded by a lieutenant

plat-ter *n.* a large, oblong, shallow dish
for serving food

plau-si-ble *adj.* seeming to be probable

play *v.* to amuse or entertain oneself, as
in recreation; to take part in a game *n.*
a dramatic presentaton

playful *adj.* lightly humorous

plea *n.* an urgent request; in law, an allegation made by either party in a law
suit

plead *v.* to ask earnestly

pleas-ant *adj.* giving or promoting the
feeling of pleasure -ly *adv.*

please *v.* to make happy; to give pleasure

pleas-ur-a-ble *adj.* pleasant

pleas-ure *n.* a feeling of satisfaction or
enjoyment

pleat *n.* a fold in a cloth made by dou-
bling the cloth back and fastening it
down

plebe *n.* a freshman or first year student
at the United States Naval Academy

pledge *n.* a solemn promise; a deposit of
something as security for a loan; a
promise to join a fraternity

plen-ti-ful *adj.* having great abundance

plen-ty *n.* an ample amount

pleu-ra *n., pl.* pleurae *Anat.* the
membranous sac which envelops the
lungs and provides a lining for the
thoracic cavity

pli-a-ble *adj.* flexible

pli-ers *pl. n.* a pincers-like implement
used for holding, bending, or cutting

plight *n.* a distressing circumstance,
situation, or condition

plod *n.* to walk in a heavy way

plow *n.* an implement for breaking up or
turning over the soil

pluck *v.* to remove by pulling out or off
plucker *n.*

plug *n.* anything used to stop or close a
hole or drain *Electr.* a two-pronged
device attached to a cord and used in
a jack or socket to make an electrical
connection plugger *n.*

plum *n.* a small tree bearing an edible
fruit with a smooth skin and a single
hard seed

plum-age *n.* the feathers of a bird

plumb *n.* a lead weight tied to the end of
a string, used to test the exact perpendicular line of something

plumb-er *n.* a person who repairs or installs plumbing in a home or business

plumb-ing *n.* the profession or trade of a plumber

plume *n.* a feather used as an ornament

plun-der *v.* to deprive of goods or property in a violent way **plunderer** *n.*

plunge *v.* to thrust or cast something, as into water

plunk *v.* to put down or place suddenly **plunker** *n.*

plu-ral *adj.* consisting of or containing more than one

plus *prep.* add the symbol (+) which indicates addition

plu-to-ni-um *n.* a radioactive metallic element symbolized by Pu.

ply *v.* to mold, bend, or shape *n.* a layer of thickness; the twisted strands of thread, yarn, or rope

pneu-mo-nia- *n.* an inflammation caused by bacteria, virus of the lungs, or irritation

pock-et *n.* a small pouch within a garment, having an open top and used for carrying items

pod *n., Bot.* aseed vessel, as of a bean or pea *Aeron* a separate and detachable compartment in a spacecraft

po-di-a-try *n.* professional care and treatment of the feet

po-di-um *n.,pl.* **-ia** *or* **-iums** a small raised platform for an orchestra conductor or a speaker

po-em *n.* a composition in verse with language selected for its beauty and sound

po-et *n.* a person who writes poetry

po-et-ry *n.* the art of writing stories, poems, and thoughts into verse

point *n.* the sharp or tapered end of something; a mark of punctuation, as a period (.); a geometric object which does not have property or dimensions other than locaton; a degree, condition, or stage

poise *v.* to bring into or hold one's balance *n.* equilibrium; selfconfidence; the ability to stay calm in all social situations

poi-son *n.* a substance which kills, injures **poisonous** *adj.*

poke *v.* to push or prod at something with a finger or other implement

po-lar *adj.* having to do with the poles of a magnet or sphere

po-lar-ize *v.* to cause something to vibrate in an exact pattern; to break up into opposite groups **-ation** *n.*

pol-i-o-my-e-li-tis *n.* inflammation of the spinal cord causing paralysis; also polio

po-lice *n.* a division or department organized to maintain order. *v.* to patrol; to enforce the law

po-liceman *n.* a member of the police force **policewoman** *n.*

pol-i-cy *n., pl.* **-ies** any plan or principle which guides decision making

pol-ish *v.* to make lustrous and smooth by rubbing; to become refined or elegant

po-lite *adj.* refined, mannerly, and courteous

po-lit-i-cal *adj.* concerned with or pertaining to government; involved in politics

pol-i-ti-cian *n.* a person active in governmental affairs or politics

pol-i-tics *n.* the activities and methods of a political party

poll *n.* the recording of votes in an election; a public survey on a given topic

pol-len *n.* the yellow dust-like powder which contains the male reproductive cells of a flowering plant

pol-lute *v.* to contaminate; to make unclear or impure; to dirty **pollution** *n.*

po-lo-ni-um *n.* a radioactive metallic element symbolized by PO.

pol-ter-geist *n.* a mischievous ghost or spirit which makes much noise

pol-y-es-ter *n.* a strong lightweight synthetic resin used in fibers

pol-y-graph *n.* a machine designed to record different signals given off by the body, as respiration, blood pressure, or heartbeats; may be used to detect a person who may be lying

pol-y-he-dron *n.* a solid bounded by polygons

pom-pa-dour *n.* a hairstyle which is puffed over the forehead

pomp-ous *adj.* a showing or appearance of dignity or importance

pond *n.* a body of still water, smaller in size than a lake

pon-der *v.* to weigh or think about very carefully; to meditate

pon-der-ous *adj.* massive; having great weight

pon-tiff *n.* a pope

po-ny *n., pl.* **-ies** a small horse

pool *n.* a small body of water

poor *adj.* lacking possessions and money; not satisfactory; broke; needy; destitute

pop-lar *n.* a rapid growing tree having a light, soft wood

pop-u-lar *adj.* approved of; widely liked;

suited to the means of the people

pop-u-la-tion *n.* the total number of people in a given area, country, or city

por-ce-lain *n.* a hard, translucent ceramic which has been fired and glazed

porch *n.* a covered structure forming the entrance to a house

por-cu-pine *n.* a clumsy rodent covered with long sharp quills

pore *v.* to ponder or meditate on something

pork *n.* the edible flesh of swine

por-no *n., Slang* pornography

por-nog-ra-phy *n.* pictures, films, or writing which deliberately arouse sexual excitement

por-poise *n.* an aquatic mammal with a blunt, rounded snout

port *n.* a city or town with a harbor for loading and unloading cargo from ships; the left side of a ship; a dark-red, sweet, fortified wine

port-a-ble *adj.* capable of being moved easily

por-ter *n.* a person hired to carry baggage

port-fo-li-o *n.* a carrying case for holding papers and other items

por-tion *n.* a section or part of a whole; a share

por-tray *v.* to represent by drawing, writing, or acting

pose *v.* to place or assume a position, as for a picture

po-si-tion *n.* the manner in which something is placed; an attitude; a viewpoint; a job; employment

pos-i-tive *adj.* containing, expressing, or characterized by affirmation; very confident; absolutely certain; not negative **positively** *adv.*

pos-se *n.* a deputized group or squad

pos-ses-sion *n.* the fact or act of possessing property; the state of being possessed

pos-ses-sive *adj.* having a strong desire to possess; not wanting to share *n.* the noun or pronoun case which indicates ownership

pos-si-ble *adj.* capable of being true, happening, or being accomplished **possibility** *n.*

post *n.* an upright piece of wood or metal support; a position or employment *v.* to put up information in a public place *prefix.* after; in order; or time; behind

post-age *n.* the charge or fee for mailing something

pos-te-ri-or *adj.* located in the back *n.*

the buttocks

post-mor-tem *adj.* the examination of a body after death; an autopsy

post-op-er-a-tive *adj.* following surgery

post-pone *v.* to put off; to defer to a later time

post-script *n.* a short message added at the end of a letter

pos-ture *n.* the carriag or position of the body

pot *n.* a rounded, deep container used for cooking and other domestic purposes *Slang* a large sum of money; marijuana **potful** *n.*

po-tas-si-um *n.* a silvery-white, highly reactive metallic element

po-ta-to *n., pl.* -toes a thick, edible, underground tuber plant native to America

po-tent *adj.* having great strength or physical powers; having a great influence on the mind or morals

po-ten-tial *adj.* possible, but not yet actual

pot-pour-ri *n.* a mixture of sweet-smelling dried flower petals and spices, kept in an airtight jar

pot-ter-y *n., pl.* -ies objects molded from clay and fired by intense heat

pouch *n.* a small bag or other container for holding or carrying money, tobacco, and other small articles *Zool.* the sac-like structure in which some animals carry their young

poul-try *n.* domestic fowl as ducks and hens, which are raised for eggs or meat

pound *n., pl.* **pounds** A measure of weight equal to sixteen ounces; a public enclosure where stray animals are fed and housed *v.* to strike repeatedly or with force

pov-er-ty *n.* the condition or state of being poor and needing money

pow-der *n.* a dry substance which has been finely ground or pulverized; dust; an explosive, such as gunpowder *v.* to dust or cover

pow-er-ful *adj.* possessing energy or great force; having authority

prac-ti-cal *adj.* serving an actual use or purpose

pract-ice *n.* a custom or habit of doing something

prai-rie *n.* a wide area of level or rolling land with grass and weeds but no trees

praise *v.* to express approval; to glorify

prank *n.* a mischievous, playful action or trick

pra-seo-dym-i-um *n.* a metallic element

of the rare-earth group

prawn *n.* an edible shrimp-like crustacean found in both salt and fresh water

pray *v.* to address prayers to God; to ask or request

prayer *n.* a devout request; the act of praying; a formal or set group of words used in praying

pre- *pref* earlier or prior to something; in front

preach *v.* to advocate; to proclaim; to deliver a sermon **-er,** **-ment** *n.,* **-y** *adj.*

pre-am-ble *n.* an introduction to something, as a law, which states the purpose and reasons for the matter which follows

pre-cau-tion *n.* a measure of caution or care taken in advance to guard against harm

pre-cede *v.* to be or go before in time, or position

prec-e-dent *n.* an instance which may serve as a rule or example in the future

pre-cept *n.* a rule, order, or commandment meant to guide one's conduct

pre-cinct *n.* an electoral district of a county, township, city, or town; an enclosure with definite boundaries

pre-cious *adj.* having great worth or value; beloved; cherished

pre-cip-i-ta-tion *n.* condensed water vapor which falls as snow, rain, sleet or hail

pre-cip-i-tous *adj.* very steep; marked with very steep cliffs

pre-cise *adj.* exact; definite; strictly following rules

pre-ci-sion *n.* exactness; the quality of being precise

pre-clude *v.* to shut out; to make impossible; to prevent

pre-co-cious *adj.* showing and developing skills and abilities very early in life

pre-con-ceive *v.* to form a notion or conception before knowing all the facts

pre-da-cious *adj.* living by preying on other animals

pred-a-tor *n.* a person who lives or gains by stealing from another person; an animal that survives by killing and eating other animals

pre-des-ti-na-tion *n.* destiny; fate; the act by which God has predestined all events

pred-i-ca-ble *adj.* capable of being predicated: to foretell

pred-i-cate *n.* *Gram.* the word or words which say something about the subject

of a clause or sentence; the part of a sentence which contains the verb *v.* to establish

pre-dict *v.* to tell beforehand; to foretell

pre-dom-i-nant *adj.* superior in strength, authority, or number

pree-mie *n.* *Slang* a baby born before the expected due date

pre-empt *v.* to take or get hold of before someone else; to take the place of; to do something before someone else has a chance to do it **-ion** *n.,* **-ive** *adj.*

pre-fab-ri-cate *v.* to construct in sections beforehand

pref-ace *n.* the introduction at the beginning of a book or speech

pre-fect *n.* a high administrative official **prefecture** *n.*

pre-fer *v.* to select as being the favorite; to promote

pref-er-ence *n.* a choice; a special liking for anything over another **-ential** *adj.*

pre-fix *v.* to put at the beginning; to put before

preg-nant *adj.* carrying an unborn fetus; significant

pre-his-tor-i-cal *adj.* of or related to the period before recorded history

pre-judge *v.* to judge before one knows all the facts

prej-u-dice *n.* a biased opinion based on emotion rather than reason; bias against a group, race, or creed

pre-lim-i-nar-y *adj.* leading up to the main action

prel-ude *n.* an introductory action *Music* the movement at the beginning of a piece of music

pre-ma-ture *adj.* occurring or born before the natural or proper time **prematurely** *adv.*

pre-med-i-tate *v.* to plan in advance or beforehand

pre-mi-er *adj.* first in rank or importance **premiership** *n.*

pre-na-tal *adj.* existing prior to birth

pre-oc-cu-py *v.* to engage the mind or attention completely

prep *Slang* preparatory school; preparation

prep-a-ra-tion *n.* the process of preparing for something

pre-par-a-to-ry *adj.* serving as preparation

pre-pare *v* to make ready or qualified; to equip

pre-pay *v.* to pay for in advance

pre-pon-der-ate *v.* to have superior importance, weight, force, influence, or other qualities **preponderance** *n.*

prep-o-si-tion *n.*, *Gram.* a word placed in front of a noun or pronoun to show a connection with or to something or someone

pre-pos-ter-ous *adj.* absurd; ridiculous; beyond all reason

prep-pie *n.* *Slang* a student attending a prep school; a young adult who behaves and dresses very traditionally

pre-rog-a-tive *n.* the unquestionable right belonging to a person

pres-age *n.* an omen or indication of something to come

pre-school *adj.* of or for children usually between the ages of two and five

pre-scribe *v.* to impose as a guide; to recommend

pre-scrip-tion *n.*, *Med.* a physician's written order for medicine

pres-ence *n.* the state of being present; the immediate area surrounding a person or thing

pres-ent *adj.* now going on; not past or future *Gram.* denoting a tense or verb form which expresses a current state or action

pres-en-ta-tion *n.* a formal introduction of one person to another; to present something as an exhibition, show, or product

pre-serv-a-tive *adj.* keeping something from decay or injury **preservation** *n.*

pre-serve *v.* to keep or save from destruction or injury

pre-side *v.* to have a position of authority or control; to run or control a meeting

pres-i-dent *n.* the chief executive officer of a government, corporation, or association

presidency *n.*, **presidential** *adj.*

press *v.* to act upon or exert steady pressure or force; to squeeze out or extract by pressure; to smooth by heat and pressure **presser** *n.*

pres-sure *n.* the act of or the state of being pressed; a constraining moral force; any burden, force, painful feeling, or influence; the depressing effect of something hard to bear

pres-tige *n.* importance based on past reputation and achievements

pres-to *adv.*, *Music* very fast and quick; at once

pre-sume *v.* to take for granted; to take upon oneself without permission

pre-sump-tion *n.* arrogant conductor speech; something that can be logically assumed true until disproved

pre-tend *v.* to make believe; to act in a false way **pretender** *n.*

pre-tense *n.* a deceptive and false action or appearance

pre-ten-tions *n.* having or making claims to worth, excellence, etc.

pre-text *n.* a motive assumed in order to conceal the true purpose

pret-ty *adj.* pleasant; attractive; characterized by gracefulness; pleasing to look at

pret-zel *v.* a hard, cooked dough usually twisted in a knot and sprinkled with salt

pre-vail *v.* to succeed; to win control over something

pre-vent *v.* to keep something from happening; to keep from doing something

pre-ven-tive *or* **preventative** *adj.* protecting or serving to ward off harm, disease, or other problems

pre-view *or* **prevue** *n.* an advance showing or viewing to invited guests

pre-vi-ous *adj.* existing or occurring earlier **-ly** *adv.*

price *n.* the set amount of money expected or given for the sale of something

prick *n.* a small hole made by a sharp point

pride *n.* a sense of personal dignity; a feeling of pleasure because of something achieved **pride** *v.*

priest *n.* a clergyman in the Catholic church who serves as mediator between God and His worshipers

pri-ma-ry *adj.* first in origin, time, series, or sequence; basic

prime *adj.* first in importance, time, or rank *n.* a period of full vigor, success, or beauty

prim-i-tive *adj.* of or pertaining to the beginning or earliest time; resembling the style or manners of an earlier time

primp *v.* to dress or arrange with superfluous attention to detail

prince *n.* the son of a king; a king

prin-cess *n.* the daughter of a king

prin-ci-pal *adj.* chief; most important; owner *n.* the headmaster or chief official of a school; a sum of money invested or owed which is separate from the interest

prin-ci-ple *n.* the fundamental law or truth upon which others are based; a moral standard

print *n.* an impression or mark made with ink; the design or picture which is transferred from an engraved plate or other impression

printer *n.* a person whose occupation is printing

print-out *n. Computer Science* the output of a computer, printed on paper

pri-or *adj.* previous in order or time

pri-or-i-ty *n.* something which takes precedence; something which must be done or taken care of first

prism *n.* a solid figure with triangular ends and rectangular sides, used to disperse light into a spectrum

pris-on *n.* a place of confinement where people are kept while waiting for a trial or while serving time for breaking the law; jail

pri-vate *adj.* secluded or removed from the public view; secret; intimate; owned or controlled by a group or person rather than by the public

priv-i-lege *n.* a special right or benefit granted to a person

priv-i-leged *adj.* to have or enjoy a given privilege

prize *n.* an award or something given to the winner of a contest

pro *n.* an argument in favor of or supporting something

prob-a-bil-i-ty *n., pl.* **-ies** the state or quality of being probable; a mathematical statement or prediction of the odds of something happening or not happening

prob-a-ble *adj.* likely to become a reality, but not certain or proved

pro-bate *n.* the act of legally proving that a will is genuine

pro-ba-tion *n.* a period used to test the qualifications and character of a new employee; the early release of lawbreakers

probe *n.* an instrument used for investigating an unknown environment; a careful investigation or examination

prob-lem *n.* a perplexing situation or question; a question presented for consideration, solution, or discussion **problematic** *adj.*

pro-ce-dure *n.* a certain pattern or way of doing something; the normal methods or forms to be followed

pro-ceed *v.* to carry on or continue an action or process

pro-ceeds *pl., n.* the profits received from a fundraising venture

proc-ess *n.* the course, steps, or methods toward a desired result *Law* any judicial request or order; in Computer Science, the sequence of operations which gives a desired result *v.* to compile, compute, or assemble; data

pro-ces-sion *n.* a group which moves along in a formal manner; a parade

pro-ces-sion-al *n.* a hymn sung during a procession *adj.* the opening of a church service

pro-ces-sor *n. Computer Science* the central unit of a computer which processes data

pro-claim *v.* to announce publicly

proc-la-ma-tion *n.* an official public declaration or announcement

pro-cras-ti-nate *v.* to put off, defer, or postpone to a later time **procrastination, procrastinator** *n.*

proc-tor *n.* a person in a university or college whose job it is to see that order is maintained during exams **proctorial** *adj.*

pro-cure *v.* to acquire; to accomplish

prod *v.* to arouse mentally; to poke with a pointed instrument *n.* a pointed implement used to prod or poke

prod-i-gal *adj.* wasteful expenditure of money, strength, or time; extravagance *n.* one who is a spendthrift or is wasteful

pro-duce *v.* to bear or bring forth by a natural process; to manufacture; to make; to present or bring into view **producer** *n.*

prod-uct *n.* something produced, manufactured, or obtained *Math.* the answer obtained by multiplying

pro-duc-tion *n.* the process or act of producing; something produced

pro-fane *adj.* manifesting disrespect toward sacred things; vulgar

pro-fess *v.* to admit or declare openly; to make an open vow

pro-fess-sion-al *adj.* having to do with a job or profession; referring to or engaging in an occupation

pro-fes-sor *n.* a faculty member of the highest rank in a college or university

pro-fi-cient *adj.* highly skilled in a field of knowledge

pro-file *n.* the outline of a person's face or figure as seen from the side; a short biographical sketch indicating the most striking characteristics

prof-it *n.* the financial return after all expenses have been accounted for *v.* to gain an advantage or a financial reward **profitable** *adj.*

pro-found *adj.* deeply held or felt

pro-fuse *adj.* extravagant; giving forth lavishly; over-flowing **profusely** *adv.*

prog-e-ny *n., pl.* **-ies** one's offspring, children, or descendants

prog-no-sis *n., pl.* **-noses** a prediction of the outcome and course a disease may take

pro-gram *n.* any prearranged plan or course; a show or performance, as one given at a scheduled time; in Computer Science, a sequence of commands which tell a computer how to perform a task or sequence of tasks

prog-ress *n.* forward motion or advancement to a higher goal; an advance; steady improvement

pro-hib-it *v.* to forbid legally; to prevent

pro-ject *n.* a plan or course of action; a proposal; a large job

pro-jec-tile *n.* anything hurled forward through the air

pro-jec-tion *n.* the act or state of being projected; the state or part that sticks out

pro-lif-er-ate *v.* to grow or produce with great speed, as cells in tissue formation

pro-logue *n.* an introductory statement at the beginning of a poem, song, or play

pro-long *v.* to extend or lengthen in time

prom-e-nade *n.* an unhurried walk for exercise or amusement; a public place for such a walk

prom-i-nent *adj.* jutting out; widely known; held in high esteem

pro-mis-cu-ous *adj.* lacking selectivity or discrimination

prom-ise *n.* an assurance given that one will or will not do something; a pledge

pro-mote *v.* to raise to a higher rank or position; to work on behalf of

prompt *adj.* arriving on time; punctual; immediate

prone *adj.* lying flat; face down pronely *adv.*, proneness *n.*

prong *n.* a pointed, projecting part, as the end of a sharp instrument or the end of an antler

pro-noun *n.*, *Gram.* a word which can be used in the place of a noun

pro-nounce *v.* to deliver officially; to articulate the sounds pronunciation *n.*

proof *n.* the establishment of a fact by evidence

prop *n.* a support to keep something upright

prop-a-gate *v.* to reproduce or multiply by natural causes; to pass on qualities or traits propagation *n.*

pro-pel *v.* to thrust or cause to move forward; to motivate

prop-er *adj.* appropriate; especially adapted or suited; conforming to social convention; correct

prop-er-ty *n.*, *pl.* -ies any object of value owned or lawfully acquired, as real estate; a piece of land

proph-e-cy *n.*, *pl.* -ies a prediction made under divine influence

proph-et *n.* one who delivers divine messages; one who foretells the future

pro-pi-ti-ate *v.* to win the goodwill of; to stop from being angry propitiation *n.*

pro-po-nent *n.* one who supports or advocates a cause

pro-por-tion *n.* the relation of one thing to another in size, degree, or amount proportional, proportionate *adj.*

pro-pose *v.* to present or put forward for consideration or action; to suggest someone for an office or position; to make an offer; to offer marriage

prop-o-si-tion *n.* a scheme or plan offered for consideration; a subject or idea to be proved or discussed

pro-pri-e-ty *n.*, *pl.* -ies the quality or state of being proper in accordance with recognized principles or usage

pro-pul-sion *n.* the act or process of propelling

pro-rate *v.* to distribute or divide proportionately

pro-scribe *v.* to banish; to outlaw

prose *n.* ordinary language, speech, or writing which is not poetry

pros-e-cute *v.* to carry on *Law* to bring suit against a person; to seek enforcement for legal process prosecution *n.*

pros-pect *n.* something that has the possibility of future success; a possible customer *v.* to explore

pros-per *v.* to be successful; to achieve success prosperous *adj.*

pros-tate *n.* a small gland at the base of the male bladder

pros-ti-tute *n.* one who sells the body for the purpose of sexual intercourse

pros-trate *adj.* lying with the face down to the ground *v.* to overcome

prot-ac-tin-i-um *n.* a radioactive metallic element symbolized by Pa.

pro-tect *v.* to guard or shield from attack of injury; to shield protective *adj.*

pro-tein *n.*, *Biochem.* any of a very large group of highly complex nitrogenous compounds occurring in living matter and composed of amino acids which are essential for tissue repair and growth

pro-test *v.* to make a strong formal objection; to object to protester *n.*

Prot-es-tant *n.* a member of any of the Christian churches who believes Jesus is the son of God and died for man's sins

pro-to-col *n.* the code and rules of diplomatic and state etiquette

pro-ton *n., Physics* a unit of positive charge equal in magnitude to an electron

pro-tract *v.* to extend in space

pro-trude *v.* to project; to thrust outward

proud *adj.* showing or having a feeling that one is better than the others; having a feeling of satisfaction; having proper self-respect or proper self-esteem

prove *v.* to show with valid evidence that something is true provable *adj.*

prov-erb *n.* an old saying which illustrates a truth

pro-vide *v.* to supply or furnish with what is needed

pro-vi-sion *n.* a supply of food or needed equipment

pro-voke *v.* to cause to be angry; to annoy

prox-i-mate *adj.* immediate; direct

prox-y *n., pl.* proxies the authority, usually written, to act for another

prude *n.* a person who is very modest, especially in matters related to sex

pru-dent *adj.* cautious; discreet; managing very carefully

psalm *n.* a sacred hymn, taken from the Book of Psalms in the Old Testament

pso-ri-a-sis *n., Pathol.* a noncontagious, chronic, inflammatory skin disease characterized by reddish patches and white scales

psych *v., Slang* to prepare oneself emotionally or mentally; to outwit or outguess

psy-chi-a-try *n.* the branch of medicine which deals with the diagnosis and treatment of mental disorders

psy-chic *adj.* cannot be explained by natural or physical laws *n.* a person who communicates with the spirit world

psy-chol-o-gy *n., pl.* psychologies the science of emotions, behavior, and the mind psychological *adj.*, psychologist *n.*

psy-cho-path *n.* a person suffering from a mental disorder characterized by aggressive antisocial behavior psychopathic *adj.*

pu-ber-ty *n.* the stage of development in which sexual reproduction can first occur pubertal, puberal *adj.*

pub-lic *adj.* pertaining to or affecting the people or community; for everyone's use

pub-li-ca-tion *n.* the business of publishing; any pamphlet, book, or magazine

pub-lic-i-ty *n.* the state of being known to the public

pub-lish *v.* to print and distribute a book, magazine, or any printed matter to the public publisher *n.*

puck *n.* a hard rubber disk used in playing ice hockey

pud-dle *n.* a small pool of water

puff *n.* a brief discharge of air or smoke *v.* to breathe in short heavy breaths

pull *v.* to apply force; to cause motion toward or in the same direction of

pulp *n.* the soft juicy part of a fruit; a soft moist mass

pul-pit *n.* the elevated platform lectern used in a church from which a service is conducted

pul-sate *v.* to beat rhythmically pulsation

pulse *n., Physiol.* the rhythmical beating of the arteries caused by the action of the heart pulse *v.*

pul-ver-ize *v.* to be reduced to dust or powder by crushing

pump *n.* a mechanical device for moving a gas or liquid *v.* to raise with a pump; to obtain information through persistent questioning

pump-kin *n.* a large, edible yellow-orange fruit having a thick rind and many seeds

punch *n.* a tool used for perforating or piercing; a blow with the fist; a drink made of an alcoholic beverage and a fruit juice or other nonalcoholic beverage

punc-tu-al *adj.* prompt; arriving on time

punc-tu-ate *v.* to mark words or written material with punctuation; to give or show emphasis

punc-ture *v.* to prick or pierce with a pointed instrument *n.* the act or effect of puncturing

pun-gent *adj.* sharp or acrid in smell or taste

pun-ish *v.* to subject a person to confinement or impose a penalty for a crime

pun-ish-ment *n.* a penalty which is imposed for breaking the law or a rule

punk *n., Slang* a young, inexperienced boy *adj.* of or relating to a bizarre style of clothing; relating to punk rock bands

pup *n.* a puppy, young dog, or the young of other animals

pupil *n.* a person who attends school and receives instruction by a teacher

pup-pet *n.* a small figure of an animal or person which is manipulated by hand or by strings puppeteer pur-chase v. to receive by paying money as an exchange purchaser n.

pure adj. free from anything that damages, weakens, or contaminates

purge v. to make clean; to free from guilt or sin; to rid of anything undesirable

pu-ri-fy v. to make clean or pure purification, purifier n.

pu-ri-ty n. the quality of being pure; freedom from guilt or sin

pur-ple n. a color between red and violet purplish adj.

pur-port v. to give the appearance of intending; to imply, usually with the intent to deceive

pur-pose n. a desired goal; an intention purposely adv.

purse n. a small pouch or bag for money; a handbag; a pocketbook; the sum of money offered as a prize

pur-sue v. to seek to achieve; to follow in an attempt to capture pursuer n.

pur-suit n. the act of pursuing an occupation

pur-vey v. to supply provisions as a service purveyor n.

pus n. a yellowish secretion formed in infected tissue which contains bacteria

push v. to move forward by exerting force; to force oneself through a crowd; to sell illegally Slang to sell illegal drugs

put v. to cause to be in a location; to bring forward for debate or consideration, as to put up for

pu-ta-tive adj. commonly supposed

pu-tre-fy v. to cause to decay

putt n. in golf, a light stroke made on a putting green to get the ball into the hole

puz-zle v. to bewilder; to confuse n. a toy, board game, or word game

pyg-my n., pl. pygmies a very small person or animal; a dwarf

py-lon n. a tower serving as a support for electrical power lines

py-or-rhe-a n., Pathol. inflammation of the gums and sockets of the teeth

pyr-a-mid n. a solid structure with a square base and triangular sides which meet at a point

pyre n. a pile of combustible material for burning a dead body

py-ro-ma-ni-a n. a compulsion to set fires

py-ro-met-al-lur-gy n. chemical metallurgy depending on heat action pyrometallurgical adj.

py-tho-ness n. a woman who practices divination pythonic adj.

Q, q the seventeenth letter of the English alphabet

qat n. a small plant found in Africa, the fresh leaf is chewed for a stimulating effect

Qa-tar n. country of located on the western coast of the Persian Gulf

qi-vi-ut n. yarn spun from the fine, soft hair of the musk ox

quack n. the harsh, croaking cry of a duck quack v., quackery n.

quad-ran-gle n., Math a plane figure with four sides and four angles

quad-rant n. a quarter section of a circle, subtending or enclosing a central angle of 90 degrees; an instrument which is used to measure altitudes

qua-draph-o-nyn. the recording of sound using four transmission channels

quad-rate adj. being square or almost square

qua-drat-ics n. a branch of algebra concerned with equations

quad-ra-ture n. an arrangement of two celestial bodies with a separation of 90 degrees

qua-dren-ni-um n. a period consisting of four years

quad-ri-cen-ten-ni-al n. an anniversary celebrating 400 years

quad-ri-ceps n. the muscle located in the front of the thigh

qua-dri-ga n. a chariot pulled by a team of four horses

qua-drille n. a square dance with five or six figures exected by four couples

quad-ril-lion n. a thousand trillions; one followed by fifteen zeros

quad-ri-par-tite adj. consisting of four persons or parts

quad-ri-ple-gic n. a person who is paralyzed in both arms and both legs

qua-dru-ma-na n. a group of primates distinguished by hand-shaped fgeet

quad-ru-ped n. any animal having four feet

quad-ru-ple adj. consisting of four parts; multiplied by four

qua-dru-plet n. one of four infants born t the same time

qua-dru-pli-cate n. consisting of four identical parts

quaff v. to drink with abundance

quag-ga n. a wild ass ofr Africa related to the zebras

quag-mire n. an area of soft muddy land that gives away underfoot; a marsh

quail n., pl. a small game bird

quaint adj. pleasing in an old-fashioned, unusual way

quake *v.* to shake or tremble voilently

Quak-er *n.* the religious sect called the Society of Friends

qual-i-fi-ca-tion *n.* an act of qualifying; the ability, skill, or quality which makes something suitable for a given position

qual-i-fy *v.* to prove something able; restrict; limit; modify

qual-i-ty *n., pl.* , **qualities** a distinguishing character which makes something such as it is

qualm *n.* a sudden feeling of sickness

quan-da-ry *n.* a state of perplexity

quan-ti-ty *n.* number; amount

quan-tum *n., pl.*, **quanta** an amount or quantity

quar-an-tine *n.* a period of enforced isolation for a specified period of time

quar-rel *n.* an unfriendly or angry disagreement

quar-ry *n., pl.* **quarries** an animal hunted for food; an open pit or excavation from which limestone or other material is being extracted

quart *n.* a unit of measurement equaling four cups

quar-ter *n.* one of four equal parts into which anything may be divided; a place of lodging

quar-ter-back *n., Football* the offensive player who directs the plays for his team

quar-ter-mas-ter *n.* the officer in charge of supplies for army troops

quar-tet *n.* a musical composition for four voices or instruments

quartz *n.* a hard, transparent crystallized mineral

qua-sar *n.* one of the most distant and brightest bodies in the universe

quea-sy *adj.* nauseated; sick
queasiness *n.*

queen *n.* the wife of a king; a woman sovereign or monarch; in chess, the most powerful piece on the board

queer *adj.* strange; unusual; different from the normal *Slang* homosexual

quell *v.* to put down with force

quench *v.* to extinguish or put out; to cool metal by thrusting into water

quer-u-lous *adj.* complaining or fretting; expressing complaints

que-ry *n.* an injury; a question

quest *n.* a search; pursuit; an expedition to find something

ques-tion *n.* an expression of inquiry which requires an answer

question mark *n.* a mark of punctuation, (?), used in writing to indicate a question

ques-tion-naire *n.* a written series of questions

quib-ble *v.* to raise trivial objection

quiche *n.* unsweetened custard baked in a pastry shell

quick *adj.* moving swiftly; occurring in a short time

quick-sand *n.* a bog of very fine, wet sand of considerable depth

quid *n.* a small portion of tobacco; a cow's cud

qui-et *adj.* silent; making very little sound; still; tranquil; calm

quill *n.* a strong bird feather; a spine from a porcupine

quilt *n.* a bed coverlet made of two layers of cloth with a soft substance between and held in place by lines of stitching

qui-nine *n., Chem.* a very bitter, colorless, crystalline powder used in the treatment of malaria

quin-sy *n., Pathol.* a severe inflammation of the tonsils

quin-tes-sence *n.* the most essential and purest form of anything

quin-tet *n.* a musical composition written for five people

quin-tu-ple *adj.* increased five times

quire *n.* twenty-five sheets of paper removed from a complete ream of paper

quirk *n.* a sudden, sharp bend or twist; a personal mannerism

quis-ling *n.* a person who is a traitor, working against his own country from within

quit *v.* to cease; to give up; to depart; to abandon

quite *adv.* to the fullest degree; really; actually

quix-ot-ic *adj.* extravagantly romantic; impractical

quiz *v.* to question, as with an informal oral or written examination

quoin *n.* the external corner or angle of a building

quo-ta *n.* an allotment or proportional share

quo-ta-tion *n.* the exact quoting of words as a passage

quo-ta-tion mark *n.* the marks of punctuation (" ") showing a direct quote

quote *v.* to repeat exactly what someone else has previously stated

quo-tient *n., Math* the amount or number which results when one number is divided by another

R, r The eighteenth letter of the English alphabet

rab-bet *n.* a recess or groove along the edge of a piece of wood cut to fit another piece to form a joint -ed *v.*

rab-bi *n.* an ordained leader of Jews; the leader and teacher of a Jewish congregation **rabbinic** *adj.*

rab-bin-i-cal *adj.* to be referring or pertaining to the rabbis

rab-bit *n.* a burrowing mammal related to but smaller than the hare

rab-ble *n.* a disorderly crowd **rabbling, rabbled** *v.*

rab-id *adj.* affected with rabies; mad; furious **rabidly** *adv.* **rabidness** *n.*

ra-bies *n.* an acute, infectious viral disease of the central nervous system, often fatal, which is transmitted by the bite of an infected animal

rac-coon *n., pl.* -coons, -coon a nocturnal mammal with a black, mask-like face and a black-and-white ringed, bushy tail

race *n.* the zoological division of the human population having common origin and other physical traits, such as hair form and pigmentation; a group of people having such common characteristics or appearances; people united by a common nationality

race *n.* a contest which is judged by speed; any contest, such as a race for an elective office **raced, racer** *n.*

ra-ceme *n.* a type of plant bearing flowers along its stalk

ra-chis *n.* a type of axial structure

ra-cial *adj.* a characteristic of a race of people

rac-ism *n.* a thought or belief that one race is better than another race **racist** *n.*

rack *n.* an open framework or stand for displaying or holding something; an instrument of torture used to stretch the body; a triangular frame used to arrange the balls on a pool table *Mech.* a metal bar with teeth designed to move a cogged bar and produce a rotary or linear motion *v.* to strain, as with great effort in thinking

rack-et or **racquet** *n.* a light-weight bat-like object with netting stretched over an oval frame, used in striking a tennis ball or a shuttlecock

rack-et-eer *n.* a person who engages in acts which are illegal

rac-on-teur *n.* one who is skilled in the act of telling stories

rac-y *adj.* having a spirited or strongly marked quality; slightly improper or immodest **racily** *adv.*, **raciness** *n.*

ra-dar *n.* a system which uses radio signals to detect the presence of an object or the speed the object is traveling

ra-dar as-tron-o-my *n.* astronomy that deals with investigations of the celestial bodies of the solar system by comparing characteristics of reflected radar wave with characteristics of ones transmitted from earth

ra-dar-scope *n.* a screen or oscilloscope that serves as a visual indicator in a radar receiver

rad-dled *adj.* to be in a state of confusion; broken down; worn; lacking composure

ra-di-al *adj.* pertaining to or resembling a ray or radius; developing from a center axis

ra-di-ance *n.* the quality of being shiny; the state of being radiant; relating or emitting to radiant heat

ra-di-ant *adj.* emitting rays of heat or light; beaming with kindness or love; projecting a strong quality **-ly** *adv.*

ra-di-ant heat *n.* heat that is transmitted by radiation

ra-di-ate *v.* to move out in rays, such as heat moving through the air **-ly** *adv.*

ra-di-a-tion *n.* an act of radiating; the process or action of radiating; the process of emitting radiant energy in the form of particles or waves **radiationless** *adj.*, **radiative** *adj.*

ra-di-a-tor *n.* something which radiates

rad-i-cal *adj.* proceeding from a foundation or root; drastic; making extreme changes in views, conditions, or habits; carrying convictions or theories to their fullest application **radically** *adv.*, **radicalness** *n.*

radii *pl. of* radius

ra-di-o *n.* the technique of communicating by radio waves; the business of broadcasting programmed material to the public via radio waves **radioing, radioed** *v.*

ra-dio-ac-tive *adj.* exhibiting radioactivity **radioactively** *adv.*

ra-di-o-ac-tiv-i-ty *n.*, *Physics* a spontaneous emission of electromagnetic radiation, as from a nuclear reaction

ra-di-o-fre-quen-cy *n.* a frequency which is above 15,000 cycles per second that is used in radio transmission

ra-di-o-gram *n.* a type of radiograph

ra-di-ol-o-gy *n.* a science which deals with rays for a radioactive substance

and use for medical diagnosis
radiologist *n.*

rad-ish *n.* the edible root of the radish plant

ra-di-um *n* a radioactive metallic element symbolized by Ra.

ra-di-us *n., pl.* **radii** or **raduses** a line from the center of a circle to its surface or circumference

ra-don *n.* a heavy, colorless, radioactive gaseous element symbolized by Rn

raf-fi-a *n.* a fiber from an African palm tree used for making baskets, hats, and other woven articles

raff-ish *adj.* something that is marked by crudeness or flashy vulgarity **raffishly** *adv.*, **raffishness** *n.*

raf-fle *n.* a game of chance; a lottery in which one buys chances to win something

raft *n.* a floating structure made from logs or planks and used for water trans-portation

raft-er *n.* a timber of a roof which slopes

rag *n.* a cloth which is useless and sometimes used for cleaning purposes

rag-a-muf-fin *n.* a child who is unkempt

rag-bag *n.* a miscellaneous grouping or collection; a bag for holding scrap pieces of material

rag doll *n.* a child's doll that is usually made from scrap material and has a hand painted face

rage *n.* violent anger **raging** *adj.*, **ragingly** *adv.*

rag-ged *adj.* to be torn or ripped **raggedness** *n.*, **raggedly** *adv.*

rag-weed *n.* a type of plant whose pollen can cause hay fever

raid *n.* a sudden invasion or seizure **raider** *n.*

rail *n.* a horizontal bar of metal, wood, or other strong material supported at both ends or at intervals; the steel bars used to support a track on a railroad

rail-bird *n.* a person who sits on or near a race track rail and watches a race or workout

rail-ing *n.* a barrier of wood

rain *n.* the condensed water from atmospheric vapor, which falls to earth in the form of drops

rain-bow *n.* an arc that contains bands of colors of the spectrum and is formed opposite the sun and reflects the sun's rays, usually visible after a light rain shower

rain-coat *n.* a water-resistant or waterproof coat

rain-fall *n.* the amount of measurable precipitation

rain gauge *n.* an instrument used to measure rain fall

rain-making *n.* the act or process of producing or attempting to produce rain by the use of artificial means

raise *v.* to cause to move upward; to build; to make greater in size, price, or amount; to increase the status; to grow; as plants; to rear as children; to stir ones emotions; to obtain or collect as funds or money

rai-sin *n.* a grape dried for eating

rake *n.* a tool with a long handle at the end and a set of teeth at the other end used to gather leaves and other matter; a slope or incline, as the rake of an auditorium **rake** *v.*

ral-ly *v.* to call together for a purpose *n.* a rapid recovery, as from depression, exhaustion, or any setback; in a meeting whose purpose is to rouse or create support

ram *n.* a male sheep; an implement used to drive or crush by impact; to cram or force into place

RAM *abbr.* random access memory

ram-ble *v.* to stroll or walk without a special destination in mind; to talk without sequence of ideas **ramble** *n.*, **ramblingly** *adv.*

ram-bunc-tious *adj.* rough or boisterous **rambunctiousness** *n.*

ramp *n.* an incline which connects two different levels; movable staircase allows passengers to enter or leave an aircraft

ram-page *n.* a course of destruction or violent behavior *v.* to storm about in a rampage **rampageous** *adj.*, **rampageously** *adv.*, **rampageousness** *n.*

ram-pan-cy *n.* the state or quality of being rampant

ram-pant *adj.* exceeding or growing without control; wild in actions; standing on the hind legs and elevating both forelegs **rampantly** *adv.*

ram-rod *n.* a metal rod used to drive or plunge the charge into a muzzle-loading gun or pistol; the rod used for cleaning the barrels of a rifle or other firearm

ram-shack-le *adj.* likely to fall apart from poor construction or maintenance

ranch *n.* a large establishment for raising cattle, sheep, or other livestock; a large farm that specializes in a certain crop or animals **rancher** *n.*

ran-cid *adj.* having a rank taste or smell

ran-dom *adj.* done or made in a way that

has no specific pattern or purpose; to select from a group whose members all had an even chance of being chosen

rang v. past tense of ring

range n. an area over which anything moves; an area of activity; a tract of land over which animals such as cattle and horses graze; an extended line or row especially of mountains; an open area for shooting at a target; large cooking stove with burners and oven. v. to arrange in a certain order; to extend or proceed in a particular direction

range finder n. instrument that is used in gunnery to determine the distance of a target

rank n. a degree of official position or status v. to place in order, class, or rank adj. a strong and disagreeable odor, smell, or taste

ran-sack v. to search or plunder through every part of something

ran-som n. the price demanded or paid for the release of a kidnaped person; the payment for the release of a person or property detained ransom v.

rant v. to talk in a wild, loud way

ra-pa-cious adj. living on prey seized alive; taking by force; plundering rapaciously adv., rapaciousness,

rape n. the crime of forcible sexual intercourse; abusive treatment rape v., rapist n.

rap-id adj. having great speed; completed quickly or in a short time rapidity, rapidness n.

ra-pi-er n. a long, slender, straight sword with two edges

rap-ine n. the forcible taking of another's property

rap-port n. a harmonious relationship

rapt adj. deeply absorbed or carried away with something and not to noticing any-thing else; engrossed raptness n., raptly adv.

rare adj. scarce; infrequent; often held in high esteem or admiration because of infrequency rareness n.

ras-cal n. a person full of mischief; a person who is not honest rascally adj.

rash adj. acting without consideration or caution n. a skin irritation or eruption caused by an allergic reaction

rasp n. a file with course raised and pointed projections v. to scrape or rub with a course file; to utter something in a rough, grating voice rasper n., raspy adj.

rasp-berry n. a small edible fruit, red or black in color and having many small seeds Slang contemptuous sound made by expelling air with the tongue between the lips in order to make a vibration

raspy adj. grating; irritable

rat n. a rodent similar to the mouse, but having a longer tail Slang a despicable person who betrays his friends or associates

rat-a-tat n. a sharp tapping, or repeated knocking

ratch-et n. a mechanism consisting of a pawl that allows a wheel or bar to move in one direction only

ratch-et wheel n. a wheel with teeth that is held place with a engaging handle

rate n. the measure of something to a fixed unit; the degree of price or value; a fixed ratio or amount v. to appraise

rath-er adv. preferably; with more reason or justice; more accurate or precise

rat-i-fy v. to approve something in an official way ratification n.

rat-ing n. a relative evaluation or estimate of something

ra-tio n., pl. ratios the relationship between two things in amount, size, degree, expressed as a proportion

ra-tion n. a fixed portion or share v. to provide or allot in rations rationing n.

ra-tion-al adj. having the faculty of reasoning; being of sound mind rationality n., -ally adv. rationalness n.

rat-tan n. an Asian palm whose strong stems are used to make wickerworks

rat-tle v. to make a series of rapid, sharp noises in quick succession; to talk rapidly; chatter n. a baby's toy made to rattle when shaken

rat-tler n., Slang a venomous snake which has a series of horny, modified joints which make a rattling sound when moved; a rattlesnake; one that rattle

rat-tle-trap n. something that is rickety or rattly

rau-cous adj. loud and rowdy; having a rough hoarse sound; disorderly raucously adv., raucousness n.

rav-age v. to bring on heavy destruction; devastate

rave v. to speak incoherently; to speak with enthusiasm n. the act of raving

rav-el v. to separate fibers or threads; to unravel ravelment n.

ra-ven n. a large bird, with shiny black

feathers *adj.* of or relating to the glossy sheen or color of the raven

ra-vine *n.* a deep gorge with steep sides in the earth's surface, usually created by flowing water

rav-ish *v.* to seize and carry off; to rape ravishment *n.*, ravisher *n.*

raw *adj.* uncooked; in natural condition; not processed inexperienced; damp, sharp, or chilly rawly *adv.*, rawness *n.*

ray *n.* a thin line of radiation or light; a small trace or amount; one of several lines coming from a point

ray-on *n.* a synthetic cellulose yarn; any fabric made from such yarn

ra-zor *n.* a sharp cutting instrument used especially for shaving

ra-zor-back *n.* a wild hog of the southeastern United States; the mascot of the University of Arkansas

razz *v.*, *Slang* to heckle; to tease

raz-zle--daz-zel *n.* a state of complete confusion

re- *prefix* again, anew or reverse action

reach *v.* to stretch out; to be able to grasp *n.* the act of stretching out

re-act *v.* to act in response to *Chem.* to undergo a chemical change; to experience a chemical reaction

re-ac-tor *n.* a person, object, device, or substance which reacts to something

read *v.* to visually go over something, as a book, and to understand its meaning; to learn or be informed; to perceive something in a meaning which may or may not actually be there

read-y *adj.* prepared for use or action; quick or prompt; willing

re-a-gent *n* any substance which causes a chemical reaction

re-al *adj.* something which is existing, genuine, true, or authentic *Law* property which is regarded as permanent or immovable

reel-to-reel *adj.* pertaining to magnetic tape which is threaded to a take-up reel, which moves from one reel to another

real estate *n.* land and whatever is attached such as natural resources or buildings

re-al-ism *n.* concern or interest with actual facts and things as they really are realist *n.*, -istic *adj.*, -stically *adv.*

re-al-i-ty *n.*, *pl.* the fact or state of being real or genuine; an actual situation or event

re-al-ize *v.* to understand correctly; to make real realizable *adj.*, realization *n.*, realizer *n.*

re-al-ly *adv.* actually; truly; indeed

realm *n.* a scope or field of any power or influence

ream *n.* a quantity of paper containing 500 sheets

reap *v.* to harvest a crop with a sickle or other implement

rear *n.* the back; *adj.* of or at the rear; *v.* to raise up on the hind legs; to raise as an animal or child

rea-son *n.* a statement given to confirm or justify a belief, promise, or excuse; the ability to decide things, to obtain ideas, to think clearly, and to make logical and rational choices and decisions; *v.* to discuss something logically reasoning *n.*

rea-son-a-ble *adj.* moderate; rational reasonableness *n.*, reasonably *adv.*

re-a-sur-ance *n.* the act of reassuring; reinsurance

re-bate *n.* a deduction allowed on items sold; a discount; money which is returned to the purchaser from the original payment; *v.* to return part of the payment rebater *n.*

re-bel *v.* to refuse allegiance; to resist any authority; to react with violence

re-bel-lion *n.* an organized uprising to change or overthrow an existing authority

re-bel-lious *adj.* engaged in rebellion; relating to a rebel or rebellion rebelliously *adv.*, rebelliousness *n.*

re-birth *n.* a revival or renaissance; reincarnation

re-bound *v.* to spring back; to recover from a setback or frustration; *n.* recoil

re-broad-cast *v.* to repeat or broadcast again rebroadcast *n.*

re-buff *v.* to refuse abruptly; to snub rebuff *n.*

re-build *v.* to make extensive repairs to something; to reconstruct; remodel

re-buke *v.* to criticize something sharply; to turn back rebuker *n.*

re-but *v.* to try and prove someone wrong by argument or evidence rebuttal *n.*, rebutable *adj.*

re-call *v.* to order or summon to return to ask for something to be returned; so that defects can be fixed or repaired; to remember; to recollect

re-cant *v.* to formally admit that a previously held belief was wrong by making public confession

re-cap *v.* to restore an old tire; to review or summarize something

re-cede *v.* to move back; as floodwater; to withdraw from an agreement re-ceipt *n.* the written acknowledgment of something received; *pl.*, receipts the amount of money received

re-ceive *v.* to take or get something; to greet customers or guests; to accept as true or correct receiver *n.*

re-cent *adj.* happening at a time just before the present recently *adv.*

re-cep-ta-cle *n.* anything which holds something; an electrical outlet designed to receive a plug

re-cep-tion *n.* the act or manner of receiving something; a formal entertainment of guests, as a wedding reception

re-cep-tion-ist *n.* an employee who greets callers and answers the telephone for a business

re-cep-tive *adj.* able to receive receptively *adv.*, -ness, receptivity *n.*

re-cess *n.* a break in the normal routine of something; a depression or niche in a smooth surface

re-ces-sion *n.* the act of receding; withdrawal; a period or time of reduced economic activity -ary *adj.*

rec-i-pe *n.* the directions and a list of ingredients for preparing food

re-cip-ro-cate *v.* to give and return mutually, one gift or favor for another

re-cite *v.* to repeat something from memory; give an account of something in detailt

reck-less *adj.* state of being careless and rash when doing something -ness *n.*

reck-on *v.* to calculate; to compute; to estimate; to consider; to assume

reck-on-ing *n.* the act of calculation or counting

re-claim *v.* to redeem; to reform; to recall; to change to a more desirable condition or state

rec-la-ma-tion *n.* the state of being eclaimed

re-cline *v.* to assume a prone position

rec-luse *n.* a person who chooses to live in seclusion

rec-og-ni-tion *n.* an acknowledgment which is formal

re-cog-ni-zance *n.* an amount of money which will be forfeited for a nonperformance of an obligation

rec-og-nize *v.* to experience or identify something or someone as having been known previously; to appreciative recognizable *adj.*, recognizably *adv.*

re-coil *v.* to fall back or to rebound recoilless *adj.*

rec-ol-lect *v.* to remember or recall to the mind recollection *n.*

rec-om-mend *v.* to suggest to another as desirable; advise recommendation *n.*, recommedable *adj.*

rec-om-pense *v.* to reward with something for a service

rec-on-cile *v.* to restore a friendship after an estrangement reconcilably *adv.*

rec-on-dite *adj.* being obscure

re-con-di-tion *v.* to return to a good condition

re-con-firm *v.* confirm something again

re-con-nais-sance *n.* an observation of territory such as that of the enemy

re-con-noi-ter *v.* to survey a region

re-con-sid-er *v.* to think about again with a view to changing a previous action or decision reconsideration *n.*

re-con-struct *v.* to build something again

re-con-struc-tion *n.* something which has been reconstructed or rebuilt

re-cord *v.* to write down for future use or permanent reference; to preserve sound on a tape or disk for replay; a phonograph record; *n.* information which is recorded and kept permanently

re-cord-er *n.* a person who records things such as official transactions

re-cord-ing *n.* the act of making a transcription of sounds

rec-ord play-er *n.* the machine which is used to play recordings

re-count *v.* to tell the facts; narrate or describe in detail; to count again; *n.* a second count to check the results of the first count

re-coup *v.* to be reimbursed; to recover

re-course *n.* a turning to or an appeal for help

re-cov-er *v.* to regain something which was lost; to be restored to good health; *Law* to obtain a judgment for damages

re-cov-er-y *n.* the power to regain something

rec-re-ant *adj.* cowardly; unfaithful

re-cre-ate *v.* to create again

rec-re-a-tion *n.* refreshment of body and mind; a pleasurable occupation or exercise recreational *adj.*

re-crim-i-nate *v.* the charging of another of the same account recriminatory, recriminative *adj.*, recrimination *n.*

re-cruit *v.* to enlist someone for military or naval purposes; to look for someone as for a service or employment recuiter *n.*

rec-tal *adj.* referring to the rectum of the body

rec-tan-gle *n.* a parallelogram with all

right angles rectangular *adj*.,
rectangularity *n*.

rec-ti-fi-er *n*. that which rectifies something

rec-ti-fy *v*. to make correct; *Chem*. to purify by repeated distillations; *Electr*. to make an alternating current a direct current

rec-ti-lin-e-ar *adj*. made up of or indicated by straight lines; bounded by straight lines

rec-ti-tude *n*. rightness in principles and conduct; correctness

rec-to *n*. the right-hand page of a book

rec-tor *n*. a member of the clergy in charge of a parish; a priest in charge of a congregation, church, or parish; the principal or head of a school or of a college

rec-tum *n*., *pl*. rectums, recta *Anat*. the lower terminal portion of the large intestine connecting the colon and anus

re-cum-bent *adj*. lying down or reclining

re-cu-per-ate *v*. to regain strength or to regain one's health; to recover from a financial loss recuperation *n*., recuperative *adj*.

re-cur *v*. to happen, to return, or to appear again recurrence, recurrent *adj*.

red *n*. having the color which resembles blood, as pigment or dye which colors red; *Slang* a communist; one who is in favor of the overthrow of an existing political of social order; a condition indicating a loss, as in the red

re-deem *v*. to buy back; to pay off; to turn something in, as coupons or rain checks and receive something in exchange

re-demp-tion *n*. the act of redeeming; rescue; ransom; that which redeems; salvation

re-doubt *n*. a small enclosed fortification

re-doubt-a-ble *adj*. to be dreaded redoubtably *adv*.

re-dound *v*. to have an effect on something

re-dress *v*. to put something right

red snap-per *n*. a saltwater fish which is red in color and can be found in the Gulf of Mexico and near Florida

red tape *n*. routines which are rigid and may cause a delay in a process

re-duce *v*. to decrease; lessen in number, degree, or amount; to put into order; to lower in rank; to lose weight by dieting

re-duc-tion *n*. the state of being reduced

re-dun-dant *adj*. exceeding what is necessary; repetitive

re-du-pli-cate *v*. to repeat something reduplication *n*.

red-wood *n*. a tree found in California which is very tall and wide

re-ech-o *v*. to reverberate again

reed *n*. tall grass with a slender stem, which grows in wet areas; a thin tongue of wood, metal, cane, or plastic; placed in the mouthpiece of an instrument to produce sounds by vibrating reediness *n*., reedy *adj*.

reef *n*. a chain of rocks, coral, or sand at or near the surface of the water

reef-er *n*. a jacket which is close-fitting

reek *v*. to emit vapor or smoke; to give off a strong offensive odor

reel *n*. a device which revolves on an axis and is used for winding up or letting out fishing line, rope, or other string-like material; a lively and fast dance

re-e-lect *v*. the act of electing someone again for an office

re-em-pha-size *v*. to stress something or an idea again

re-en-list *v*. to enlist or join a group or an armed force again reenlistment *n*.

re-enter *v*. to enter a room or area again

re-ex-am-ine *v*. examine something or someone another time or again reexamination *n*.

re-fec-to-ry *n*. the place in colleges where the students dine

re-fer *v*. to direct for treatment, information, or help

ref-e-ree *n*. a person who supervises a game, making sure all the rules are followed

ref-er-ence *n*. the act of referring some-one to someplace or to something

ref-er-en-dum *n*. a public vote on an item for final approval or for rejection

ref-er-ent *n*. what is referred to such as a person

re-fill *v*. to fill something with an item again

re-fine *v*. to purify by removing unwanted substances or material; to improve refined *adj*. refinement *n*.

re-fin-er-y *n*. a place or location which is used for the purpose of refining, such as sugar

re-fin-ish *v*. the act of putting a new surface onto something, such as wood

re-fit *v*. to repair something

re-flect *v*. to throw back rays of light from a surface; to give an image, as from a mirror; to ponder or think carefully about something reflection *n*. reflective *adj*.

re-flec-tor *n.* something which is able to reflect things, such as light

re-flex *adj.* turning, casting, or bending backward; *n.* an involuntary reaction of the nervous system to a stimulus

re-for-est *v.* the act of replanting a forest or wooded area with trees -ation *n.*

re-form *v.* to reconstruct, make over, or change something for the better; improve; to abandon or give up evil ways reformer *n.*, reformed *adj.*

re-for-ma-to-ry *n.* a jail-like institution for young criminals

re-fract *v.* the deflecting something, such as a ray of light refractive *adj.*

re-frac-tion *n.* the state of being refracted or deflected

re-frac-to-ry *adj.* unmanageable; obstinate; difficult to melt; resistant to heat; *n.* something which does not change significantly when exposed to high temperatures

re-frain *v.* to hold back

re-fresh *v.* to freshen something again

re-fresh-ment *n.* something which will refresh someone, such as a cold drink or snack

re-frig-er-ant *n.* an agent which cools something

re-frig-er-ate *v.* to chill or cool; to preserve food by chilling; to place in a refrigerator

re-frig-er-a-tor *n.* a box-like piece of equipment which chills food and other matter

re-fu-el *v.* to put fuel into something again

ref-uge *n.* shelter or protection from harm; any place one may turn for relief or help

ref-u-gee *n.* a person who flees to find safety

re-ful-gent *adj.* state of being radiant or putting off a bright light

re-fund *v.* to return or pay back; to reimburse refundable *adj.* refund *n.*

re-fur-bish *v.* to make clean; to renovate

re-fus-al *n.* the denial of something which is demanded

re-fuse *v.* to decline; to reject; to deny

ref-use *n.* rubbish; trash

re-fute *v.* to overthrow or to disprove with the use of evidence

re-gain *v.* to recover; to reach again

re-gal *adj.* of or appropriate for royalty regally *adv.*

re-gale *v.* to entertain or delight; to give pleasure

re-ga-li-a *n.* something which represents royalty such as a septer

re-gard *v.* to look upon closely; to consider; to have great affection for; *n.* careful attention or thought; esteem or affection; regards greetings of good wishes

re-gard-ful *adj.* state of being mindful

re-gard-less *adj.* state of being careless or showing no regard towards something or someone

re-gat-ta *n.* a boat race

re-gen-cy *n.*, *pl.* regenies the jurisdiction or office of a regent

re-gen-er-ate *v.* to reform spiritually or morally; to make or create anew; to refresh or restore

re-gent *n.* one who rules and acts as a ruler during the absence of a sovereign, or when the ruler is underage

re-gime *n.* an administration

reg-i-men *n.* government control; therapy

reg-i-ment *n.* a military unit of ground troops which is composed of several battalions regimental *adj.*

regimentation *n.*

re-gion *n.* an administrative, political, social, or geographical area

re-gion-al *adj.* typical or pertaining to a geographic region; limited to a particular region

reg-is-ter *n.* something which contains names or occurrences

reg-is-trar *n.* type of person who keeps a register

reg-is-tra-tion *n.* an act of recording things or names

re-gress *v.* to return to a previous state or condition regress, regression *n.*

re-gret *v.* to feel disappointed or distressed about; *n.* a sense of loss or expression of grief; a feeling of sorrow regretfully, regretably *adv.*, regretful, regretable *adj.*

reg-u-lar *adj.* usual; normal; customary; conforming to set principles, procedures, or discipline; well-ordered; not varying regularity *n.*, regularly *adv.*

reg-u-late *v.* to adjust to a specification or requirement regulative, regulatory *adj.*, regulator *n.*

reg-u-la-tion *n.* a rule that is set down in order to govern an area or people

re-gur-gi-tate *v.* to pour something forth

re-ha-bil-i-tate *v.* to restore; to a former state, by education and therapy rehabilitation *n.*, rehabilitative *adj.*

re-hash *v.* to rework or go over old material

re-hears-al *n.* the act of practicing for a performance rehearse *v.*

reign *n.* the period in time when the monarch rules over an area

re-im-burse *v.* to repay **reimbursement** *n.*

rein *n.* one of a pair of narrow, leather straps attached to the bit of a bridle and used to control a horse

rein-deer *n.* a large deer found in northern regions, both sexes having antlers

re-in-force *v.* to support; to strengthen with additional people or equipment **reinforcement** *n.*

re-in-state *v.* to restore something to its former position or condition **reinstatement** *n.*

re-it-er-ate *v.* to say or do something over and over again

re-ject *v.* to refuse; to discard as useless **reject, rejection** *n.*

re-joice *v.* to fill with joy; to be filled with joy

re-join *v.* to respond or to answer someone

re-join-der *n.* the answer to a reply made by someone to another

re-ju-ve-nate *v.* to restore to youthful appearance or vigor **rejuvenation** *n.*

re-kin-dle *v.* to inflame something again

re-lapse *v.* to fall back or revert to an earlier condition **relapse** *n.*

re-late *v.* to tell the events of; to narrate; to bring into natural association **relater** *n.*

re-lat-ed *adj.* to be in the same family; connected to each other by blood or by marriage

re-la-tion *n.* the relationship between people by marriage or blood lines **relational** *adj.*

re-la-tion-ship *n.* a connection by blood or family; kinship; friendship; a natural association

rel-a-tive *adj.* relevant; connected; considered in comparison or relation-ship to other; *n.* a member of one's family

rel-a-tiv-i-ty *n.* a condition or state of being relative

re-lax *v.* to make loose or lax; to relieve something from effort or strain; to become less formal or less reserved **relaxation** *n.*, **relaxedly** *adv.*

re-lay *n.* a race in which a fresh team replaces another; *v.* to pass from one group to another

re-lease *v.* to set free from confinement; to unfasten; to free; to relinquish a claim on something **releaser** *n.*

rel-e-gate *v.* to banish someone or something

re-lent *v.* to soften in temper, attitude, or determination; to slacken

relentless *adj.*

rel-e-vant *adj.* related to matters at hand

re-li-a-ble *adj.* dependable; capable of being relied upon

re-li-ance *n.* confidence and trust; something which is relied upon

re-li-ant *adj.* state of being confident or having reliance

re-lic *n.* something which is very old; a keepsake; an object whose cultural environment has disappeared

re-lief *n.* anything which decreases or lessens anxiety, pain, discomfort, or other unpleasant conditions or feelings

re-lief map *n.* a map which outlines the contours of the land

re-lieve *v.* to lessen or ease pain, anxiety, embarrassment, or other problems; to release or free from a duty by providing a replacement **reliever** *n.*, **relievable** *adj.*

re-lig-ion *n.* an organized system of beliefs, rites, and celebrations centered on a supernatural being power; belief pursued with devotion **religious** *adj.*

re-lin-quish *v.* to release something or someone

re-lish *n.* pleasure; a spicy condiment taken with food to lend it flavor

re-live *v.* to experience something again

re-lo-cate *v.* to move to another area **relocation** *n.*

re-luc-tance *n.* an unwillingness

re-luc-tant *adj.* unwilling; not yielding

re-ly *v.* to trust or depend

re-main *v.* to continue without change; to stay after the departure of others

remainder *n.* something left over; *Math* the difference which remains after division or subtraction

re-mains *pl., n.* what is left after all other parts have been taken away; corpse

re-mand *n.* state of being remanded

re-mark *n.* a brief expression or comment; to take notice; to observe; to comment

re-mark-a-ble *adj.* extraordinary **remarkably** *adv.*

re-me-di-a-ble *adj.* being able to be remedied

rem-e-dy *n., pl.* **remedies** a therapy or medicine which relieves pain; something which corrects an error or fault; *v.* to cure or relieve; to rectify

re-mem-ber *v.* to bring back or recall to the mind; to retain in the mind carefully; to keep a person in one's thought; to recall a person to another as a means of greetings

re-mem-brance *n.* something which is remembered by someone

re-mind *v.* to cause or help to remember

rem-i-nisce *v.* to recall the past things which have happened

rem-i-nis-cence *n.* the practice or process of recalling the past reminiscent *adj.*

re-miss *adj.* lax in performing one's duties; negligent remissness *n.*

re-mis-sion *n.* a forgiveness; act of remitting

re-mit *v.* to send money as payment for goods; to forgive, as a crime or sin; to slacken, make less violent, or less intense remittance *n.*

rem-nant *n.* a small piece or a scrap or something

re-mod-el *v.* to reconstruct something making it like new

re-mon-strance *n.* statement of reasons against an idea or something

re-mon-strate *v.* giving strong reasons against an act or an idea

re-morse *n.* deep moral regret for past misdeeds remorseful *adj.*

re-mote *adj.* distant in time; space or relation remotely *adv.*, remoteness *n.*

re-mount *v.* to mount something again

re-mov-a-ble *adj.* being able to be removed

re-mov-al *n.* the change of a site or place

re-move *v.* to get rid of; to extract; to dismiss from office; to change one's business or residence; *n.* an act of moving removable *adj.* removal *n.*

re-moved *adj.* state of being separate from others

re-mu-ner-ate *v.* pay an equivalent for a service

ren-ais-sance *n.* a revival or rebirth; the humanistic revival of classical art, literature, and learning in Europe which occurred during the 14th through the 16th centuries

re-nal *adj.* of or relating to the kidneys

re-nas-cence *n.* a revival or a rebirth

rend *v.* to remove from with violence; to split

ren-der *v.* to give or make something available; to submit or give; to represent artistically; to liquefy or melt fat by means of heat rendering *n.*

ren-dez-vous *n.* a meeting place that has been prearranged; *v.* to meet at a particular time and place

ren-di-tion *n.* an interpretation or a translation

ren-e-gade *n.* a person who rejects one allegiance for another; an outlaw; a traitor renegade *adj.*

re-nege *v.* to fail to keep one's word

re-new *v.* to make new or nearly new by restoring; to resume renewable *adj.*, renewal *n.*

ren-net *n.* an extract taken from a calf's stomach and used to curdle milk for making cheese

re-nounce *v.* to reject something or someone

ren-o-vate *v.* to return or to restore to a good condition

re-nown *n.* the quality of being widely honored renowned *adj.*

rent *n.* the payment made for the use of another's property; *v.* to obtain occupancy in exchange for payment rental *n.*

re-nun-ci-a-tion *n.* renouncing

re-or-gan-i-za-tion *n.* the process of reorganizing something

rep. *n., Slang* representative; *v.* represent

re-pair *v.* to restore to good or usable condition; to renew; refresh repairable *adj.*

re-pair-man *n.* the person who makes repairs of things that are broken

rep-a-ra-ble *adj.* being able to be corrected

rep-a-ra-tion *n.* the act of repairing something

rep-ar-tee *n.* a quick, witty response or reply

re-pa-tri-ate *v.* to go back to one's own country

re-pay *v.* to pay back money; to do something in return

re-peal *v.* to withdraw officially repeal *n.*, repealer *n.*

re-peat *v.* to utter something again; to do an action again

re-peat-er *n.* something or person which repeats

re-pel *v.* to discourage; to force away; to create aversion

re-pel-lent *adj.* able to repel

re-pent *v.* to feel regret for something which has occurred; to change one's sinful way repentance *n.*, repentant *adj.*

re-per-cus-sion *n.* an unforeseen effect produced by an action repercussive *adj.*

rep-er-toire *n.* the accomplishments or skills of a person

rep-er-to-ry *n.* a collection of things

rep-e-ti-tion *n.* the act of doing something over and over again; the act of repeating re-place v. to return something to its previous place replaceable adj., replacement n., replacer n.

re-plen-ish v. to add to something to replace what has gone or been used

re-plete adj. having plenty; abounding; full

rep-li-ca n. a reproduction or copy of something replicate v.

re-ply v. to give an answer to either verbally or in writing reply n.

re-port n. a detailed account; usually in a formal way; v. to tell about; to make oneself available; to give details of reportable adj., reporter n.

re-port card n. the report of the students progress

re-port-ed-ly adv. to be according to a report

re-pose n. the act of being at rest; v. to lie at rest reposeful adj.

re-pos-i-tor-y n. the location where things may be placed for preservation

re-pos-sess v. to restore ownership of something

rep-re-hend v. to show or express disapproval of reprehension n., reprehensible adj.

rep-re-sent v. to stand for something; to serve as the official representative for

rep-re-sen-ta-tion n. the act of representing

rep-re-sent-a-tive n. a person or thing serving as an example or type; adj. of or relating to government by representation; typical

re-press v. to restrain; hold back; to remove from the conscious mind repression n., repressive adj.

re-prieve v. to postpone punishment; to provide temporary relief reprievable adj., reprieve n., reprieve, reprieving v.

rep-ri-mand v. to censure severely; rebuke reprimand n.

re-print n. an additional printing of a book exactly as the previous one reprint v., reprinter n.

re-pri-sal n. retaliation with intent to inflict injury in return for injury received

re-proach v. to blame; to rebuke reproachful adj.

rep-ro-bate adj. the state of being morally depraved

re-pro-duce v. to produce an image or copy; Biol. to produce an offspring; to recreate or produce; again reproducer n., reproducible adj., reproduction n., reproductive adj.

re-proof n. a censure

re-prove v. to tell or express a disapproval of something

rep-tile n. a cold-blooded, egg-laying vertebrate, as a snake, lizard, or turtle reptilian n., adj.

re-pub-lic n. a political unit or state where representatives are elected to exercise the power

re-pub-li-can adj. having the character of a republic

re-pub-li-can-ism n. the Republican principles

Republican Party n. one of the two political parties in the United States

re-pu-di-ate v. to cast away; to refuse to pay something

re-pug-nance n. the state or condition of being opposed

re-pug-nant adj. distasteful; repulsive; offensive

re-pulse v. to repel or drive back; to repel or reject rudely; to disgust or be disgusted repulsion n.

re-pul-sive adj. state of causing aversion

rep-u-ta-ble adj. to be honorable reputability n.

re-put-a-tion n. the commonly held evaluation of a person's character

re-pute v. to account or to consider something

re-quest v. to ask for something request n.

re-qui-em n. the Roman Catholic mass for a deceased person

re-quire v. to demand or insist upon requirement n.

req-ui-site adj. absolutely needed; necessary

req-ui-si-tion n. a demand or a request

re-quit-al n. the act of requiting something

re-quite v. to reward; to repay someone

re-run n. a television show which is shown again

re-sale n. the act of selling something again

re-scind v. to repeal; to void rescindable adj., rescission n.

res-cue v. to free from danger; n. an act of deliverance rescuer n.

re-search n. a scientific or scholarly investigation; to carefully seek out researcher n.

re-sem-ble v. to have similarity to something resemblance n.

re-sent v. to feel angry about resentful adj., resentfully adv., resentment n.

res-er-va-tion n. the act of keeping something back

re-serve *v.* to save for a special reason; to set apart; to retain; to put off; *n.* something that is saved for a future point in time; the portion of a country's fighting force kept inactive until called upon

res-er-voir *n.* a body of water stored for the future; large reserve; a supply

re-side *v.* to dwell permanently; to exist as a quality or attribute **residence** *n.*

res-i-due *n.* matter remaining after treatment or removal of a part; something which remains

re-sign *v.* to give up; to submit to something as being unavoidable; to quit **resignation** *n.*

res-in *n.* a plant substance from certain plants and trees used in varnishes and lacquers **resinous** *adj.*

re-sist *v.* to work against or actively oppose; to withstand **resistible** *adj.*

res-o-lute *adj.* coming from or characterized by determination **resolutely** *adv.*, **resolution** *n.*

re-solve *v.* to make a firm decision on something; to find a solution **resolvable** *adj.*, **resolver** *n.*, **resolution** *n.*

re-sort *v.* to go frequently or customarily *n.* a place, or recreation, for rest, and for a vacation

re-sound *v.* to be filled with echoing sounds; to reverberate; to ring or sound loudly **resounding** *adj.*, **resoundingly** *adv.*

re-source *n.* a source of aid or support which can be drawn upon if needed; **resources** one's available capital or assets **resourceful** *adj.*

re-spect *v.* to show consideration or esteem for; to relate to; *n.* courtesy or considerate treatment **respectfully** *adv.* **respectful** *adj.*

res-pi-ra-tion *n.* the process or act of inhaling and exhaling; the act of breathing; the process in which an animal or person takes in oxygen from the air and releases carbon dioxide **respirator** *n.*

res-pite *n.* a temporary postponement

re-spond *v.* to answer or reply; to act when prompted by something or someone

re-sponse *n.* a reply; the act of replying **responsive** *adj.*

re-spon-si-ble *adj.* trustworthy; in charge; having authority; being answerable for one's actions or the actions of others **responsibility** *n.*

rest *n.* a cessation of all work, activity, or motion; *Mus.* an interval of silence equal in time to a note of same value; *v.* to stop work; to place or lay **restful** *adj.*, **restfully** *adv.*

res-tau-rant *n.* a place which serves meals to the public

res-ti-tu-tion *n.* the act of restoring something to its rightful owner; compensation for injury, loss, or damage

res-tive *adj.* nervous or impatient because of a delay **restively** *adv.*, **restiveness** *n.*

re-store *v.* to bring back to a former condition; to make restitution of **restoration** *n.*

re-strain *v.* to hold back or be held back; to control, limit, or restrict **restraint** *n.*

re-strict *v.* to confine within limits **restriction** *n.*, **restrictive** *adj.*, **restrictively** *adv.*

re-sult *v.* to happen or exist in a particular way; *n.* the consequence of an action, course, or operation

re-sume *v.* to start again after an interruption **resumption** *n.*

res-u-me *n.* a summary of one's personal history, background, work, and education

re-sus-ci-ate *v.* to return to life; to revive **resuscitation** *n.*, **resuscitator** *n.*

re-tail *v.* the sale of goods or commodities to the public; *v.* to sell to the consumer **retail** *adj.*, **retailer** *n.*

re-tain *v.* to hold in one's possession; to remember; to employ someone, as for his services

re-tain-er *n.* a person or thing that retains; a fee paid for one's services

re-tard *v.* to delay or slow the progress of. **retardant** *n. & adj.*

re-tar-da-tion *n.* a condition in which mental development is slow or delayed; a condition of mental slowness

re-ten-tion *n.* the act or condition of being retained

ret-i-na *n.*, *pl.* **retinas, retinae** the light sensitive membrane lining the inner eyeball connected by the optic nerve to the brain **retinal** *adj.*

re-tire *v.* to depart for rest; to remove oneself from the daily routine of working; *Baseball* to put a batter out **retirement** *n.*, **retired** *adj.*, **retiree** *n.*

re-trace *v.* to go back over

re-tract *v.* to draw back or to take back something that has been said **retractable** *adj.*, **retraction** *n.*

re-tread v. to replace the tread of a worn tire retread n.

re-treat n. the act of withdrawing from danger; a time of study; prayer; and meditation in a quiet; isolated location retreat v.

re-trieve v. to regain; to find something and carry it back retrievable adj., retrieval n.

ret-ro-ac-tive adj. taking effect on a date prior to enactment

ret-ro-spect n. a review of things in the past retrospectively adv., retrospective adj.

re-turn v. to come back to an earlier condition; to reciprocate; n. the act of sending, bringing, or coming back returns n. a yield or profit from investments; a report on the results of an election returnable adj., returnee n. returner n.

re-un-ion n. a reuniting; the coming together of a group which has been separated for a period of time

re-veal v. to disclose or make known; to expose or bring into view

rev-eil-le n. the sounding of a bugle used to awaken soldiers in the morning

rev-el v. to take great delight in reveler n.

rev-e-la-tion n. an act of or something revealed; a manifestation of divine truth; evelation the last book in the New Testament

re-venge v. to impose injury in return for injury received revengeful adj., revenger n.

re-verse adj. turned backward in position; n. the opposite of something; a change in fortune usually from better to worse; change or turn to the opposite direction; to transpose or exchange the positions of; Law to revoke a decision reverser n.

re-vert v. to return to a former practice or belief reversion n.

re-view v. to study or look over something again; to give a report on; n. a reexamination; a study which gives a critical estimate of something reviewer n.

re-vise v. to look over something again with the intention of improving or correcting it reviser n., revision n.

re-viv-al n. the act or condition or reviving; the return of a film or play which was formerly presented; a meeting whose purpose is religious reawakening

re-vive v. to restore, refresh, or recall; to return to consciousness or life

re-voke v. to nullify or make void by recalling revocation n.

re-volt n. to try to overthrow authority; to fill with disgust

rev-o-lu-tion n. the act or state of orbital motion around a point; the abrupt overthrow of a government; a sudden change in a system

re-volve v. to move around a central point; to spin; to rotate revolvable adj.

re-vue n. a musical show consisting of songs, dances, skits, and other similar entertainment

re-ward n. something given for a special service; v. to give a reward

R.F.D. abbr. rural free delivery

rhap-so-dy n., pl. rhapsodies an excessive display of enthusiasm

rhe-ni-um n. a metallic element symbolized by Re

rhet-o-ric n. effective expression in writing or speech; language which is not sincere

Rh fac-tor n. a substance found in the red blood cells of 85% of all humans; the presence of this factor is referred to as PH positive; the absence as PH negative

rhi-noc-er-os n. a very large mammal with one or two upright horns on the snout

Rhode Is-land n. a state located in the northeastern part of the United States

rho-di-um n. a metallic element symbolized by Rh

rhu-barb n. a garden plant with large leaves and edible stalks used for pies

rhyme or rime n. a word or verse whose terminal sound corresponds with another rhyme v. rhymer n.

rhy-thm n. Music, speech, or movements which are characterized by equal or regularly alternating beats rhythmical, rhythmic adj. rhythmically adv.

RI abbr. Rhode Island

rib n. one of a series of curved bones enclosed in the chest of man and animals; Slang to tease

rib-bon n. a narrow band or strip of fabric, such as satin, used for trimming

rice n. a cereal grass grown extensively in warm climates

rich adj. having great wealth; of great value; satisfying and pleasing in voice, color, tone, or other qualities; extremely productive; as soil or land

rick-rack n. a zigzag braid used in trimming

rick-ets *n., Pathol.* a disease occurring in early childhood resulting from a lack of vitamin D and insufficient sunlight, characterized by defective bone growth and deformity

rid *v.* to make free from anything objectionable

rid-dle *v.* to perforate with numerous holes; *n.* a puzzling problem or question which requires a clever solution

ride *v.* to travel in a vehicle or on an animal; to sit on and drive, as a motorcycle

rid-er *n.* one who rides as a passenger; a clause, usually having little relevance, which is added to a document

ridge *n.* a long, narrow crest; a horizontal line formed where two sloping surfaces meet **ridge** *v.*

ridge-pole *n.* timber located at the top of a roof which is horizontal

rid-i-cule *n.* actions or words intended to make a person or thing the object of mockery **ridicule** *v.*

ri-dic-u-lous *adj.* to be causing derision or ridicule

rife *adj.* state of being abundant or abounding

rif-fle *n.* ripply water which is caused by a ridge

riff-raff *n.* the rabble; low persons in society

ri-fle *n.* a firearm having a grooved bore designed to be fired from the shoulder

ri-fling *n.* the act of putting or cutting spiral grooves in the barrel of a gun.

rift *n.* a fault; disagreement; a lack of harmony

rig *v.* to outfit with necessary equipment; *n.* the arrangement of sails, masts, and other equipment on a ship; the apparatus used for drilling water or oil wells

right *adj.* in accordance with or conformable to law, justice, or morality; proper and fitting; properly adjusted, disposed, or placed; orderly; sound in body or mind; *n.* the right side, hand, or direction; the direction opposite left; *adv.* immediately; completely; according to justice, morality, or law **rightness** *n.*

right an-gle *n., Geom.* an angle of 90 degrees; an angle with two sides perpendicular to each other

rig-id *adj.* not bending; inflexible; severe; stern **rigidity, rigidness** *n.*

rig-or *n.* the condition of being rigid or stiff; stiffness of temper; harshness

rigorous *adj.*, **rigorously** *adv.*

rind *n.* a tough outer layer which may be taken off or pealed off

ring *n.* a circular mark, line, or object; a small circular band worn on a finger; a group of persons acting together; especially in an illegal way; *v.* to make a clear resonant sound, as a bell when struck; *n.* the sound made by a bell

ring-worm *n., Pathol.* a contagious skin disease caused by fungi and marked by discolored, ring-shaped, scaly patches on the skin

rink *n.* a smooth area covered with ice used for hockey or ice-skating; a smooth wooden surface for roller-skating

rinse *v.* to wash lightly with water; *n.* the act of rinsing; a hair coloring or conditioning solution

ri-ot *n.* a wild and turbulent public disturbance; *Slang* an irresistibly amusing person **riotous** *adj.*

rip *v.* to tear apart violently; to move violently or quickly; *n.* a torn place; **rip-off** *Slang* to steal

rip-cord *n.* a cord which, when pulled, releases a parachute from its pack

ripe *adj.* fully developed or aged; mature **ripeness** *n.*

rip-ple *v.* to cause to form small waves on the surface of water; to waver gently **ripple** *n.*

rise *v.* to move from a lower position to a higher one; to extend upward; to meet a challenge or demand; *n.* the act of going up or rising; an elevation in condition or rank

ris-er *n.* a person who rises

ris-i-ble *adj.* being inclined to or causing laughter

risk *n.* a chance of suffering or encountering harm or loss; danger **risky** *adj.*

rite *n.* a formal religious ceremony; any formal custom or practice

rit-u-al *n.* a prescribed method for performing a religious ceremony; *adj.* pertaining to or practiced as a rite **ritual** *adj.*, **ritualism** *n.*

ri-val *n.* one who strives to compete with another; one who equals or almost equals another

riv-er *n.* a relatively large natural stream of water, usually fed by another body of water

ri-vet *n.* a metal bolt used to secure two or more objects

RN *abbr.* Registered Nurse

roach *n.* a European freshwater fish; cockroach; *Slang* the butt of a marijuana cigarette

road *n.* a public highway used for vehicles, people, and animals; a path or course; a course toward the achievement of something; **road block** *n.* an obstruction in a road, which prevents passage

roam *v.* to travel aimlessly or without a purpose **roamer** *n.*

roar *v.* to utter a deep prolonged sound of excitement; to laugh loudly **roar, roarer** *n.*

roast *v.* to cook meat by using dry heat in an oven; *n.* a cut of meat.

rob *v.* to take property unlawfully from another person **robber** *n.*, **robbery** *n.*

robe *n.* a long loose garment usually worn over night clothes; a long flowing gar-ment worn on ceremonial occasions

rob-in *n.* a large North American bird with a black head and reddish breast

ro-bot *n.* a machine capable of performing human duties

ro-bust *adj.* full of strength and health; rich; vigorous **robustly** *adv.*, **robustness** *n.*

rock *n.* a hard naturally formed material; *Slang* one who is dependable

rock-er *n.* a curved piece, usually of wood, on which a cradle or chair rocks

rock-et *n.* a device propelled with the thrust from a gaseous combustion; *v.* to move rapidly

rode *v.* past tense of ride

ro-dent *n.* a mammal, such as a rat, mouse, or beaver having large incisors used for gnawing

ro-de-o *n.* a public show, contest, or demonstration of ranching skills, as riding and roping

roe *n.* the eggs of a female fish

rogue *n.* a scoundrel or dishonest person; an innocently or playful person

roll *v.* to move in any direction by turning over and over; to sway or rock from side to side, as a ship; to make a deep prolonged sound as thunder; *n.* a list of names; *Slang* a large amount of money

roll-er *n.* a cylinder for crushing, smoothing or rolling something; any of a number of various cylindrical devices

Roman Catholic Church *n.* the Christian church having priests and bishops and recognizing the Pope as its supreme head

ro-mance *n.* a love affair, usually of the young, characterized by ideals of devotion and purity; a fictitious story filled with extravagant adventures **romance** *v.* **romancer** *n.*

Ro-man nu-mer-al *n.* the letter or letters of the Roman system of numbering still used in formal contexts, as: $V = 5$, $X = 10$, $L = 50$, $C = 100$, $D = 500$, $M = 1000$

romp *v.* to run, play, or frolic in a carefree way

rood *n.* a measurement of land which equals 1/4 acre

rook-ie *n.* an untrained person; a novice or inexperienced person

room *n.* a section or area of a building set off by partitions or walls; *v.* to occupy or live in a room

roast *n.* a place or perch on which birds sleep or rest; a piece of meat which has been or is to be roasted

root *n.* the part of a plant which grows in the ground; *Math* a number which, when multiplied by itself, will produce a given quantity; *v.* to search or rummage for something; to turn up the earth with the snout, as a hog **rootless** *adj.*, **rootless** *adj.*

root beer *n.* a type of beverage which is made from herb and root extracts and this if fermented in sugar and yeast

root hair *n.* a type of filament which grows from the tip of a root

root-stock *n.* the source

rope *n.* a heavy cord of twisted fiber; **know the ropes** to be familiar with all of the conditions at hand **roping, roped** *v.*

rop-y *adj.* being stringy; being like a rope

ro-sa-ry *n.*, *pl.* **-ies** a string of beads for counting prayers; a series of prayers

rose *n.* a shrub or climbing vine having sharp prickly stems and variously colored fragrant flowers

ro-se-ate *adj.* being rosy; optimistic; being colored like a rose

rose-bud *n.* a bud of a rose

rose--col-ored *adj.* being pink or rosy; cheerful

rose-mar-y *n.* a type of a green shrub which is located in the Mediterranean region and its leaves are used for seasoning

ro-sette *n.* an ornament gathered to resemble a rose and made of silk or ribbon

rose wa-ter *n.* a fragrant product made from rose petals, steeped in water, and used in cosmetics

rose-wood *n.* a type of tropical South American tree

Rosh Ha-sha-nah *n.* the Jewish New Year

ros-in *n.* a resin which is formed as the oil of turpentine is distilled from crude turpentine

ros-ter *n.* a list of names

ros-trum *n.* the platform that a speaker gives his speach from

ros-y *adj.* being the of roses; cheerful rosiness *n.*

rot *v.* to decay

ro-ta-ry *adj.* turning or designed to turn; of or relating to axial rotation

ro-tate *v.* to turn on an axis; to alternate something in sequence rotatable *adj.*, rotation, rotator *n.*, rotatory *adj.*

ROTC *abbr.* Reserve Officer's Training Corps

ro-tis-ser-ie *n.* a rotation device with spits for roasting food

ro-tor *n.* a rotating part of a mechanical device

rot-ten *adj.* decomposed; morally corrupt; very bad

ro-tund *adj.* plump; rounded

rouge *n.* a cosmetic coloring for the cheeks

rough *adj.* having an uneven surface; violent or harsh; *n.* the part of a golf course with tall grass; *v.* to treat roughly; *adv.* in a very rude manner roughly *adv.*, roughness *n.*

rou-lette *n.* a gambling game in which players bet on which slot a small ball will land in

round *adj.* curved; circular; spherical; *v.* to become round; to surround; *adv.* throughout; prescribed duties, places, or actions roundness *n.*

rouse *v.* to awaken or stir up

route *n.* a course of travel; *v.* to send in a certain direction

rou-tine *n.* activities done regularly; *adj.* ordinary

rove *v.* to wander over a wide area rover *n.*, roving *adj.*

row *n.* a number of things positioned next to each other; a continuous line; *v.* to propel a boat with oars

roy-al *adj.* relating to a king or queen

roy-al-ty *n., pl.* royalties monarchs and or their families; a payment to someone for the use of his invention, copyright, or services

R.S.V.P. *abbr.* respondez s'il vous plait; please reply

rub *v.* to move over a surface with friction and pressure; to cause to become worn or frayed

rub-ber *n.* a resinous elastic material obtained from the coagulated and processed sap of tropical plants or produced synthetically rubbery *adj.*

rub-ber ce-ment *n.* a type of adhesive that is liquid and made of rubber

rub-ber-ize *v.* coat or cover something with rubber

rub-ber-neck *v.* to turn the head in order to see something

rub-ber plant *n.* type of plant that is found in East India and yields rubber

rub-ber stamp *n.* a type of rubber plate which is coated with ink and used for the purpose of leaving prints on paper or other objects

rub-bish *n.* worthless trash; nonsense rubbishy *adj.*

rub-ble *n.* the pieces of broken material or stones

ru-bel-la *n.* the German measles

ru-bi-cund *adj.* state of being of a red color or hue

ru-bid-i-um *n., Symbol* a silvery, highly reactive element symbolized by Rb

ru-bric *n.* a heading, title, or initial letter of a manuscript which appears in red

ru-by *n., pl.* rubies a deep-red precious stone

ruck-us *n., Slang* a noisy uproar, or commotion

rud-der *n., Naut.* a broad, flat, hinged device attached to the stern of a boat used for steering

rud-dy *adj.* being red in color or hue

rude *adj.* discourteous; offensively blunt

ru-di-ment *n.* a first step, element, skill, or principle; *Biol.* an undeveloped organ

rue *v.* to repent

rue-ful *adj.* to be causing sorrow or remorse

ruff *n.* a stiff collar which has pleats in it

ruf-fi-an *n.* a lawless, rowdy person

ruf-fle *n.* a pleated strip or frill; a decorative band; *v.* to disturb or destroy the smoothness

rug *n.* a heavy textile fabric used to cover a floor

rug-by *n.* a game similar to football in which the ball is propelled toward the opponents goal by carrying or kicking

rug-ged *adj.* strong; rough; having an uneven or rough surface ruggedness *n.*, ruggedly *adv.*

ru-in *n.* total destruction; *v.* to destroy ruination *n.*, ruinous *adj.*

rule *n.* controlling power; an authoritative direction or statement which regulates the method of doing something; a standard procedure; v. to have control over; to make a straight line using a ruler; to be in command

rul-er n. a straight edge used for measuring; a person who rules as a sovereign

rul-ing n. a type of decision which is handed down by a judge in a trial

rum n. a type of liquor made from molasses and is distilled

rum-ba n. a type of dance which has a complex rhythm

rum-ble v. to make a heavy, continuous sound; n. a long deep rolling sound

ru-mi-nant n. a cud-chewing animal; as a cow, deer, sheep, or giraffe; an animal which chews something which was swallowed

ru-mi-nate v. to chew a cud; to ponder at length rumination n., ruminative adj., ruminator n.

rum-mage v. to look or search thoroughly by digging or turning things over; to ransack

rum-mage sale n. a sale of second-hand objects, conducted to make money

rum-my n. a card game in which each player tries to get rid of his hand in sequences of three cards or more of the same suit

ru-mor n. an uncertain truth which is circulated from one person to another; gossip; v. to speed by rumor

ru-mor-mon-ger n. one who aids in the spreading of rumors

rump. the fleshy hind quarter of an animal; the human buttocks

rum-ple v. to form into creases or folds; to wrinkle

rum-pus room n. a type of room which is used for parties

run v. to hurry busily from place to place; to move quickly in such a way that both feet leave the ground for a portion of each step; to make a rapid journey; to be a candidate seeking an office; to drain or discharge; Law to be effective, concurrent with; n. a speed faster than a walk; a streak, as of luck; the continuous extent or length of something; an outdoor area used to exercise animals; in baseball, the method of scoring a point by running the bases and returning to home plate

run-a-bout n. a type of boat which is open

rund-let n. a type of barrel which is small in size

run-down adj. the state of being worn down

rung n. a bar or board which forms a step of a ladder

run-ner n. the person who runs in a race

run-ner--up n. a contestant who finishes second in a competition

run-ning adj. state of moving fast or rapidly

run-off n. that which runs off of something

run of the mill adj. ordinary; not special; average

runt n. the smallest animal in a litter

run-through n. the rehearsal of a play

run-way n. a path over which something runs; a platform which extends from a stage into the middle of an auditorium; a strip of paved ground for the landing and takeoff of airplanes

rup-ture n. a state of being broken; the act of bursting

ru-ral adj. pertaining to the country or country life

ru-ral-ize v. the act of moving to or living in the country or the rural area ruralization n.

ru-ral route n. a mail route which runs through the country

ruse n. a type of trick

rush v. to move quickly; to hurry; to be in a hurry

rus-set n. a reddish or yellowish brown color russet adj.

rust n. ferric oxide which forms a coating on iron material exposed to moisture and oxygen; deterioration through neglect; v. to form rust

rus-tic adj. characteristic of country life; n. a simple person rustically adv.

rus-ti-cate v. living and staying in the country or rural area -tor, -icity n.

rus-tle v. to move making soft sounds, such as those made by leaves of a tree

rus-tler n. a person who steals cattle

rust-proof adj. being unable to rust

rust-y adj. to be covered by rust rustiness n., rustily adv.

rut n. an indented track made by the wheels of vehicles

ru-ta-ba-ga n. type of vegetable which belongs to the mustard family that produces a tuber

ru-the-ni-um n. a metallic element symbolized by Ru

rut-ty adj. a state of having many ruts

rye n. a cultivated cereal grass whose seeds are used to make flour and whiskey

S, s The nineteenth letter of the English alphabet.

sab-a-dil-la *n.* a type of mexican plant such as of the lily family whose seeds can be used for insecticides

sab-bat *n.* the midnight assembly of the diabolists

Sab-ba-tar-i-an *n.* a person who observes the Sabbath on Saturday

Sab-bath *n.* seventh day of the week; set apart as the day of worship for Jews and some Christians; Sunday, the first day of the week, a day set apart as the day of worship by most Christians

sab-bat-i-cal *adj.* to be relating to the sabbath

Sa-bel-li-an *n.* the member of the early Italian people which includes the Sabines and Samnited

sa-ber *n.* lightweight sword

sa-ber saw *n.* a type of light and protable electric saw

sa-ber--toothed tiger *n.* a type of extinct cant which was charaterized by the great development of the upper canines

sa-bine *n.* the member of the people of the Appennines of the ancient times

sa-ble *n.* carnivorous mammal having soft, black or dark fur

sa-ble-fish *n.* a type of large spiny-finned fish which is grey or black and of the Pacific coast

sa-bot *n.* the kind of wooden shoe which is worn by the people in various European countries

sab-o-tage *n.* act of malicious destruction

sab-o-teur *n.* a person who commits sabotage

sac *n.*, *Biol.* membranous pouch in an animal or plant, containing a liquid

sa-ca-huis-te *n.* a kind of bear grass that has long linear leaves and is used for forage

sac-cade *n.* a type of small rapid jerky movement of the eye

sac-cate *adj.* to have the form of a pouch

sac-cha-rate *n.* a tyhpe of a compound of sugar usually with a bivalent metal

sac-char-i-fy *v.* to break some compound into a simple sugar

sac-cha-rim-e-ter *n.* a kind of device which is used for the purpose of measuring the amount of sugar in a solution

sac-cha-rin *n.* white, crystalline powder used as a noncaloric sugar substitute

sac-cha-rine *adj.* pertaining to or like sugar

sac-cha-roi-dal *adj.* being of fine granular texture

sac-cha-rom-e-ter *n.* a type of hydrometer that has a special scale

sac-cu-lar *adj.* to be resembling a sac

sac-cu-late *adj.* to be formed of a series of saccular expansions

sac-cule *n.* a chamber which is the smaller of the membranous labyrinth of the ear

sac-er-do-tal *adj.* pertaining to the priesthood or to priests

sa-chem *n.* a kind of North American Indian chief

sa-chet *n.* small bag of a sweet-smelling powder used to scent clothes

sack *n.* strong bag for holding articles *Slang* dismissal from a position or job

sack-ing *n.* the material that sacks are constructed from

sack out *v.* to go or to get into bed

sack race *n.* type of race where the contestants jump inside a sack to the finish line

sacque *n.* a type of infant jacket that is short and fastens at the neck

sa-cral *adj.* pertaining to the sacrum

sac-ra-ment *n.* a formal christian rite performed in a chruch, as a baptism

sac-ra-men-tal *adj.* pertaining to the character of the sacrament

sac-ra-men-tal-ism *n.* the use of the sacramental acts or rites

sa-crar-l-um *n.* a kind of ancient Roman shrine ;which holds sacred articles

sa-cred *adj.* dedicated to worship; holy sacredly *adv.*

sa-cred mush-room *n.* a type of New World hallucinogenic fungi

sac-ri-fice *n.* practice of offering something *v.* to give up something of value for something else sacrificial *adj.*

sad *adj.* marked by sorrow; unhappy; causing sorrow sadly *adv.*, sadness *n.*

sa-dism *n.*, *Psychol.* condition in which sexual gratification comes from inflicting pain on others; cruelty sadist *n.*, sadistic *adj.*, -tically *adv.*

sa-fa-ri *n.*, *pl.* safaris trip or journey; a hunting expedition in Africa

safe *adj.* secure from danger, harm, or evil; unharmed safely *adv.*, safeness *n.*

sag *v.* droop; to sink from pressure or weight sag *n.*

sa-ga *n.* long heroic story

sage *n.* person recognized for judgment and wisdom

said *v.* past tense of say

sake *n.* motive or reason for doing something

sa-la-ry *n., pl.* **salaries** set compensation paid on a regular basis for services rendered **salaried** *adj.*

sale *n.* exchange of goods for a price; disposal of items at reduced prices **salable** *adj.*

sa-li-ent *adj.* projecting beyond a line; conspicuous

sa-li-va *n.* tasteless fluid secreted in the mouth which aids in digestion

sal-i-vate *v.* to secrete saliva

sal-i-va-tion *n.* action or process of salivating

Salk vaccine *n.* vaccine used to immunize against polio

sal-low *n.* a European willow with broad leaves

sal-ly *n., pl.* **sallies.** sudden rush to launch an assault on something or someone

salm-on *n., pl.* **salmons** a large game fish with pinkish flesh

sal-mo-nel-la *n.* bacteria associated with food poison

sa-lon *n.* large drawing room; a business establishment pertaining to fashion

sa-loon *n.* place where alcoholic drinks are sold

salt *n.* white crystalline solid, mainly sodium chloride

sal-ta-tion *n.* sudden movement; dancing

salt-cel-lar *n.* a small personal dish used to hold salt

salt-ed *adj.* seasoned with salt; preserved

sal-tine *n.* a thin, salted cracker

salt mine *n.* a mine from which salt is dug

salt-y *adj.* tasting or containing salt **saltiness** *n.*

sal-u-tar-y *adj.* wholesome; healthful; beneficial

sal-u-ta-tion *n.* an expression; a greeting of good will **salutational** *adj.*

sa-lu-ta-to-ry *n.* message of welcome delivered at com-mencements

sa-lute *v.* to show honor *n.* act of respect or greeting by saluting **saluter** *n.*

sal-u-tif-er-ous *adj.* referring to something healthful or beneficial

salv-a-ble *adj.* something that may be salvaged **salvability** *n.*

salve *n.* medicated ointment used to soothe the pain of a burn or wound

sal-va-tion *n.* preservation from destruction or danger **-al** *adj.*, **-ism** *n.*

salve *v.* to salvage, as a ship

sa-mar-i-um *n.* a metallic element

same *adj.* identical; exactly alike; similar; not changing

sam-ple *n.* portion which represents the

whole *v.* to try a little; to examine

san-a-to-ri-um *n., pl.* **sanatoriums** an institution for treating chronic diseases

sanc-ti-fy *v.* to make holy **sanctification** *n.*

sanc-tion *n.* permission from a person of authority; a penalty to ensure compliance

sanc-tu-ar-y *n., pl.* **-ies.** sacred, holy place, as the part of a church, where services are held; a safe place; a refuge

sane *adj.* having a healthy, sound mind; showing good judgment **sanely** *adv.*, **sanity** *n.*

san-i-tar-y *adj.* free from bacteria or filth which endanger health

san-i-tize *v.* to make sanitary; to make clean or free of germs

sank *v.* past tense of sink

sa-pi-ent *adj.* wise

sap-phire *n.* a clear, deep-blue gem, used in jewelry

sar-casm *n.* insulting or mocking statement or remark **sarcastic** *adj.*, **sarcastically** *adj.*

sar-dine *n.* small edible fish of the herring family, often canned in oil

sar-don-ic *adj.* scornful; mockingly cynical

sass *n., Slang* rudeness; a disrespectful manner of speech

sas-sa-fras *n.* dried root of a North American tree, used as flavoring

sat-el-lite *n.* natural or man-made object which orbits a celestial body

sat-in *n.* smooth, shiny fabric made of silk, nylon, or rayon, having a glossy face and dull back

sat-ire *n.* use of mockery, sarcasm, or humor in a literary work to ridicule or attack human vice

sat-is-fac-tion *n.* anything which brings about a happy feeling; the fulfillment of a need, appetite, or desire

sat-is-fy *v.* fulfill; to give assurance to

sat-u-rate *v.* to make completely wet; to soak or load to capacity **saturation** *n.*

sau-cer *n.* small shallow dish for holding a cup

sav-age *adj.* wild; uncivilized; brutal *n.* vicious or crude person **-ly** *adv.*, **-ry** *n.*

save *v.* rescue from danger, loss, or harm; to prevent loss or waste; to keep for another time in the future

sav-ior *n.* one who saves Christ Savior

sa-voir-faire *n.* social skill

sa-vor *n.* the taste or smell of something to truly enjoy **savory** *adj.*

say *v.* speak aloud; to express oneself in words; to indicate; to show *n.* chance to speak

scab *n.* stiff, crusty covering which forms over a healing wound *Slang* person who continues to work while others are on strike

sca-bies *n.* contagious skin disease characterized by severe itching, caused by a mite under the skin

scald *v.* burn with steam or a hot liquid

scal-lop *n.* marine shellfish

scalp *n.* skin which covers the top of the human head

scal-pel *n.* small, straight knife with a narrow, pointed blade, used in surgery

scamp *n.* scheming or tricky person

scan *v.* examine all parts closely; to look at quickly **scan, scanner** *n.*

scan-dal *n.* something which brings disgrace when exposed to the public; gossip

scan-di-um *n.* metallic element symbolized by Sc.

scant *adj.* not plentiful or abundant; inadequate

scant-ling *n.* dimensions of material used in building

scap-u-la *n., pl.* **scapulae** one pair of large, flat, triangular bones which form the back of the shoulder **-ar** *adj.*

scar *n.* permanent mark which remains on the skin after a sore or injury has healed

scarce *adj.* not common or plentiful; rare **scarceness** *n.*

scar-la-ti-na *n.* mild form of scarlet fever

scar-let *n.* bright or vivid red

scat-ter *v.* spread around

scav-en-ger *n.* an animal, as a vulture, which feeds on decaying or dead animals or plant matter

sce-nar-i-o *n.* synopsis of a dramatic plot

scene *n.* view; the time and place where an event occurs; a public display of temper

scent *n.* smell; an odor *v.* to smell

sched-ule *n.* list or written chart which shows the times at which events will happen

scheme *n.* plan of action; an orderly combination of related parts; a secret plot

schol-ar *n.* student with a strong interest in learning

school *n.* place for teaching and learning

schoon-er *n.* sailing vessel with two or more masts

sci-ence *n.* study and theoretical explanation of natural phenomena in an orderly way; knowledge acquired through experience **scientific** *adj.*

scis-sors *pl., n.* a cutting tool

scle-ro-sis *n., pl.* **scleroses** a hardening of a part of the body, as an artery

scold *v.* accuse or reprimand harshly

sconce *n.* wall bracket for holding candles

scoop *n.* mall, shovel-like tool *v.* lift up or out

scoot *v.* go suddenly and quickly

scope *n.* range or extent of one's actions

scope *suff.* device for seeing or discovering

scorch *v.* burn slightly, changing the color and taste of something; to parch with heat

scorn *n.* contempt; disdain *v.* treat with scorn **scornful** *adj.*

scour *v.* clean by rubbing with an abrasive agent

scout *v.* observe activities in order to obtain information *n.* person whose job is to obtain information

scow *n.* a large barge with a flat bottom and square ends, used to transport freight, gravel, or other cargo

scowl *v.* make an angry look; to frown

scrab-ble *v.* scratch about frantically, as if searching for something **scrabbler** *n.*

scrag-gly *adj.* messy; irregular

scrap *n.* small section or piece

scrape *v.* rub a surface with a sharp object in order to clean *Slang* embarrassing situation

scratch *v.* mark or make a slight cut on; to mark with the fingernails

scrawl *n.* write or draw quickly and often illegibly

scraw-ny *adj.* very thin; skinny

scream *v.* utter a long, sharp cry, as of fear or pain *n.* long piercing cry

screech *v.* make a shrill, harsh noise **screech** *n.*

scrim-shaw *n.* art of carving designs on whale ivory or whalebone

scrip-ture *n.* sacred writing **Scriptures** the Bible

scroll *n.* roll of parchment or similar material used in place of paper

scro-tum *n., pl.* **scrota** external sac of skin which encloses the testes **scrotal** *adj.*

scrub *v.* clean something by rubbing; *Slang* cancel

scrump-tious *adj., Slang* delightful

scru-ple *n.* principle which governs one's actions **scrupulous** *adj.*

scu-ba *n.* apparatus used by divers for underwater breathing

scuff *v.* drag or scrape the feet while walking

sculp-tor *n.* person who creates statues from clay, marble, or other material

scum *n.* thin layer of waste matter floating on top of a liquid

scurf *n.* flaky dry skin; dandruff

scur-ry *v.* move quickly

scut-tle *n.* small opening with a movable lid in the hull of a ship

scythe *n.* tool with a long handle and curved, single-edged blade, used for cutting hay, grain and grass

sea *n.* body of salt water which covers most of the earth

seam *n.* line formed at the joint of two pieces of material

sear *v.* wither or dry up; to shrivel; to burn or scorch

search *v.* look over carefully search, searcher *n.*

sea-son *n.* one of the four parts of the year seasonal *adj.*,

seat *n.* place or spot, as a chair, stool, or bench, on which to sit

se-cede *v.* withdraw from an organization or group secessionist *n.*

se-clude *v.* isolate

sec-ond *n.* unit of time equal to 1/60 of a minute; a very short period of time; an object which does not meet first class standards

sec-on-dar-y *adj.* not being first in importance; inferior

se-cret *n.* knowledge kept from others; a mystery

sec-re-tary *n., pl.* secretaries person hired to write and keep records for an executive or an organization secretarial *adj.*

se-crete *v.* produce and give off; to release or discharge

sec-tion *n.* part or division of something; a separate part

sec-u-lar *adj.* relating to something worldly

se-cure *adj.* safe and free from doubt or fear; sturdy or strong; not likely to fail *v.* tie down, fasten, lock, or otherwise protect from risk or harm -ly *adv.*

se-cu-ri-ty *n., pl.* securities state of being safe and free from danger or risk; protection

se-date *adj.* serene and composed *v.* to keep or be kept calm through the use of drugs sedative *n.*

sed-i-ment *n.* material which floats in or settles to the bottom of a liquid sedimentary *adj.*, sedimentation *n.*

se-duce *v.* tempt and draw away from proper conduct seducer, seduction *n.*, sedative *adj.*

see *v.* have the power of sight; to understand

seed *n.* fertilized plant ovule with an embryo, capable of producing an offspring

seek *v.* search for; to try to reach; to attempt seeker *n.*

seem *v.* appear to be; to have the look of seeming *adj.*

seep *v.* leak or pass through slowly seepage *n.*

seer *n.* person who predicts the future

seg-ment *n.* any of the parts into which a thing is divided *v.* divide -al *adj.*

seg-re-gate *v.* separate or isolate from others

seg-re-ga-tion *n.* act of separating people based on the color of their skin

seine *n.* fishing net with weights on one edge and floats on the other

seize *v.* grasp or take possession forcibly

sel-dom *adv.* not often

se-lect *v.* to choose from a large group; to make a choice selection *adj.*, -or

se-le-ni-um *n.* element symbolized by Se.

self *n., pl.* selves complete and essential being of a person

self--de-fense *n.* act of defending oneself or one's belongings

sell *v.* exchange a product or service for money seller *n.*

se-man-tics *n.* study of word meanings and the relationships between symbols and signs

sem-a-phore *n.* system for signaling by using flags, lights or arms in various positions semaphore *v.*

se-men *n.* secretion of the male reproductive system, thick and whitish in color and containing sperm

se-mes-ter *n.* one of two periods of time in which a school year is divided

sem-i-an-nu-al *adj.* occurring twice a year

sem-i-co-lon *n.* punctuation mark (;) having a degree of separation stronger than a comma but less than a period

sem-i-nar *n.* course of study for students engaged in advanced study of a particular subject

sem-i-nar-y *n., pl.* seminaries school that prepares ministers, rabbis, or priests for their religious careers -ian *n.*

send *v.* cause something to be conveyed from one place to another; to dispatch

se-nile *adj.* having a mental deterioration often associated with old age senility *n.*

sen-ior *adj.* being the older of two; of higher office or rank; referring to the

last year of high school or college
seniority n.

sense n. sensation; feeling; the physical
ability which allows a person to be
aware of things around him; the five
senses: taste, smell, touch, sight, and
hearing

sen-si-bil-i-ty n., pl. **sensibilities** ability
to receive sensations

sen-si-ble adj. capable of being perceived through the senses; sensitive;
having good judgment **sensibly** adv.

sen-si-tive adj. capable of intense feelings **sensitivity** n.

sen-sor n. device which responds to a
signal

sen-su-al adj. preoccupied with the
gratification of the senses
sensuality n., **sensualous** adj.

sent v. past tense of send

sen-tence n. series of words arranged to
express a single complete thought; a
prison term for a convicted person

sen-ti-ment n. feelings of affection; an
idea, opinion, thought, or attitude
based on emotion rather than reason
sentimental adj.

sen-ti-nel n. who guards

se-pal n. one of the leaves which forms a
calyx in a flower

sep-a-rate v. divide or keep apart by
placing a barrier between; to go in different directions; to set apart from
others; adj. single; individual
separation n.

se-quence n. set arrangement; a number
of connected events; the regular order

ser-e-nade n. music performed as a
romantic expression of love

se-rene adj. calm; peaceful **serenity** n.

serf n. slave owned by a lord during the
Middle Ages

serge n. twilled, durable woolen cloth

se-ri-al adj. arranged in a series with one
part presented at a time

se-ries pl. n. number of related items
which follow one another

se-ri-ous adj. sober; grave; not trivial;
important **seriously** adv.,

ser-mon n. message or speech delivered
by a clergyman during a religious service

ser-pent n. snake

ser-rate adj. having sharp teeth; having a
notched edge **serration** n.

se-rum n., pl. **serums** or **sera** yellowish
fluid part of the blood which remains
after clotting

ser-vant n. one employed to care for
someone or his property

serve v. to take care of; to wait on; to
prepare and supply; to complete a
term of duty

serv-ice n. help given to others; a
religious gathering; the military

ses-a-me n. tropical plant and its edible
seeds

ses-sion n. meeting or series of meetings;
a meeting set for a specific purpose

set v. to put or place; to cause to do; to
regulate; to adjust; to arrange; to place
in a frame or mounting

set-tee n. small couch or bench with
arms and a back

set-tle v. arrange or put in order; to restore calm

sev-er v. cut off or separate **severance** n.

sev-er-al adj. being more than one or
two, but not many; being separate
severally adv.

se-vere adj. strict; stern; hard; not fancy;
extremely painful
severely adv., **severity** n.

sew v. fasten or fix; to make stitches with
thread and needle

sew-age n. solid waste material carried
away by a sewer

sew-er n. conduit or drain pipe used to
carry away waste

sex n. one of two divisions, male and
female, into which most living things
are grouped; sexual intercourse

sex-tet n. group of six people or things

shab-by adj. worn-out; ragged

shack n. small, poorly built building

shad n., pl. **shad** or **shads** edible fish
which swims upstream to spawn

shad-ow n. area from which light is
blocked; a shaded area **shadowy** adj.

shaft n. long, narrow part of something;
a beam or ray of light; a long, narrow
underground passage

shal-low adj. not deep; lacking intellectual depth

sham n. person who is not genuine but
pretends to be; a cover for pillows

sham-ble v. walk while dragging one's
feet

shame n. painful feeling of embarrassment or disgrace brought on by doing
something wrong; dishonor; disgrace

shank n. portion of the leg between the
ankle and the knee; a cut of meat
from the leg of an animal, such as a
lamb

shape n. outline or configuration of
something; the form of a human body

share n. part or portion given to or by
one person; one of equal parts, as the
capital stock in a corporation v. divide

or distribute portions **sharer** *n.*

shark *n.* large marine fish which eats other fish and is dangerous to man

sharp *adj.* having a thin edge or a fine point; capable of piercing or cutting; clever; quick-witted; painful

shat-ter *v.* burst suddenly into pieces

shave *v.* remove a thin layer; to cut body hair, as the beard, by using a razor; to come close to

she *pron.* female previously indicated by name

shear *v.* trim, cut, or remove the fleece or hair with a sharp instrument -er *n.*

sheath *n.* cover or case for a blade, as a sword

shed *v.* pour out or cause to pour; to throw off without penetrating; to cast off or leave behind, especially by a natural process

sheen *n.* luster

sheep *n.*, *pl.* **sheep** cud-chewing thick-fleeced mammal, widely domesticated for meat and wool

sheer *adj.* very thin; almost transparent; complete; absolute; very steep, almost perpendicular

sheet *n.* large piece of cloth for covering a bed; a single piece of paper

shelf *n.*, *pl.* **shelves** flat piece of wood, metal, plastic, or other rigid material attached to a wall or within another structure, used to hold or store things

shell *n.* hard outer covering of certain organisms

shel-ter *n.* something which gives protection or cover

shelve *v.* put aside; to place on a shelf

shep-herd *n.* person who takes care of a flock of sheep

sher-bet *n.* sweet frozen dessert made with fruit juices, milk or water, egg white, and gelatin

sher-iff *n.* high ranking lawenforcement officer

shield *n.* piece of protective metal or wood held in front of the body; anything which serves to conceal or protect; a badge or emblem **shield** *v.*, **shielder** *n.*

shift *n.* group of people who work together; a woman's loose-fitting dress; *v.* change direction or place

shim-mer *v.* shine with a faint sparkle **shimmerer** *n.*, **shimmery** *adj.*

shin *n.* front part of the leg from the knee to the ankle

shine *v.* give off light; to direct light; to polish shoes

shiner *n.* black eye

shin-gle *n.* thin piece of material, as asbestos, used to cover a roof or side of a house **shingler** *n.*

shin-gles *pl.*, *n.*, *Pathol.* acute, inflammatory viral infection, characterized by skin eruptions along a nerve path

ship *n.* large vessel for deep-water travel or transport; *v.* send or transport

ship-yard *n.* place where ships are built or repaired

shirt *n.* garment worn on the upper part of the body

shiv-er *v.* tremble or shake with excitement or chill **shiver** *n.*, **shivery** *adj.*

shoe *n.* outer cover for a foot

shone *v.* past tense of shine

shoot *v.* kill or wound with a missile, as a bullet, fired from a weapon; to discharge or throw rapidly

shore *n.* land bordering a body of water

short *adj.* having little height or length; less than normal in distance, time, or other qualities; less than the needed amount; **shorts** underpants or outerpants which end at the knee or above; **shortage** a lack in the amount needed; **short-change** give less than the correct amount, as change for money; **short circuit** an electrical malfunction

short-en-ing *n* a fat, such as butter, used to make pastry rich and light

shot *n.* discharging of a gun, rocket, or other device; an attempt; a try; an injection

should *v.* past tense of shall, used to express obligation, duty, or expectation

shoul-der *n.* part of the body located between the neck and upper arm

should-n't *contr.* should not

shout *v.* to yell; *n.* a loud cry

shov-el *n.* tool with a long handle and a scoop, used for picking up material or for digging

show *v.* put within sight; to point out; to explain; to put on display

shrank *v.* past tense of shrink

shrap-nel *n.*, *pl.* **shrapnel** large shell containing metal fragments

shred *n.* a narrow strip or torn fragment; a small amount

shrew *n.* a small mouse-like mammal, having a narrow, pointed snout

shriek *n.* loud, sharp scream or noise

shrill *adj.* high-pitched, sharp sound

shrimp *n.*, *pl.* **shrimp** or **shrimps** small, edible shellfish

shrine *n.* place for sacred relics; a place considered sacred because of an event or person associated with it

shrink *v.* make or become less or

smaller; to pull back from; to flinch; *Slang* psychiatrist

shroud *n.* a cloth in which a body is wrapped for burial; *v.* to cover

shrug *v.* to raise the shoulders briefly to indicate doubt or indifference **shrug** *n.*

shrunk *v.* past tense of shrink

shuck *n.* outer husk that covers an ear of corn

shud-der *v.* tremble uncontrollably, as from fear

shuf-fle *v.* drag or slide the feet; to mix together in a haphazard fashion; to rearrange or change

shun *v.* avoid deliberately

shut *v.* move a door, drawer, or other object to close an opening; to lock up; to cease or halt operations

shy *adj.* bashful; timid; easily frightened

sib-ling *n.* one of two or more children from the same parents

sick *adj.* in poor health; ill; nauseated; morbid **sickness** *n.*

sick-le *n.* tool with a curved blade attached to a handle, used for cutting grass or grain

side *n.* surface between the front and back or top and bottom of an object

SIDS *abbr., n.* Sudden Infant Death Syndrome; an unexpected death of a seemingly healthy baby

siege *n.* the action of surrounding a town or port in order to capture it; a prolonged sickness

si-er-ra *n.* rugged chain of mountains or hills

si-es-ta *n.* rest or short nap

sieve *n.* meshed or perforated device which allows small particles to pass through but which holds back larger particles; a device for separating liquids from solids **sieve** *v.*

sigh *v.* to exhale a long, deep breath, usually when tired, sad, or relieved **sigh** *n.*

sight *n.* the ability to see with the eyes; the range or distance one can see

sign *n.* a piece of paper, wood, metal, etc., with information written on it; a gesture that tells or means something

sig-nal *n.* a sign which gives a warning; the image or sound sent by television or radio

sig-na-ture *n.* the name of a person, written by that person; a distinctive mark which indicates identity

sig-nif-i-cance *n.* quality of being important

sig-ni-fy *v.* express or make known by a sign; to indicate

signification *n.*, **significant** *adj.*

si-lence *n.* state or quality of being silent; quiet

silent *adj.* making no sound; not speaking; mute

sil-i-con *n.* second most common chemical element, found only in combination with another substance

silk *n.* soft, thread-like fiber spun by silkworms; thread or fabric made from silk

sil-ly *adj.* foolish; lacking good sense, seriousness, or substance **silliness** *n.*

sil-ver *n.* soft, white metallic element used in tableware, jewelry, and coins

sim-i-lar *adj.* almost the same, but not identical

sim-mer *v.* to cook just below boiling; to be near the point of breaking, as with emotion

sim-ple *adj.* easy to do or understand; not complicated; ordinary

sim-plic-i-ty *n.* state of being easy to understand

sim-pli-fy *v.* to make easy or simple **simplification** *n.*

sim-u-late *v.* to have the appearance, effect, or form of **simulation**, **simulator** *n.*

si-mul-ta-ne-ous *adj.* occurring at exactly the same time **simultaneously** *adj.*

sin *n.* breaking of a religious law or a law of God

since *adv.* at a time before the present; *prep.* during the time later than

sin-cere *adj.* honest; not deceitful; genuine; true **sincerely** *adv.*, -**ity** *n.*

sing *v.* to use the voice to make musical tones; to make a humming or whistling sound **singer** *n.*

singe *v.* to slightly burn the surface of something

sin-gle *adj.* of or referring to only one, separate; individual; unmarried

sin-gu-lar *adj.* separate; one; extraordinary; denoting a single unit, thing or person

sink *v.* to submerge beneath a surface; to go down slowly

si-nus *n.*, *pl.* **sinuses** *Anat.* body cavity; one of eight air spaces in the bones of the face which drain into the nasal cavity

sip *v.* drink in small amounts

si-phon *also* syphon *n.* tube through which liquid from one container can be drawn into another by forced air pressure **siphon** *v.*

sir *n.* respectful term used when addressing a man

si-ren *n.* whistle which makes a loud wailing noise, as a warning or signal

sit *v.* rest the body with the weight on the buttocks; to cover eggs for hatching

siz-a-ble *adj.* large in size or dimensions

size *n.* measurement or dimensions of something

siz-zle *v.* make a hissing sound, as of fat frying

skate *n.* device with rollers or a blade which attaches to the shoe and allows one to glide over ice or roll over a wooden or cement surface

skate-board *n.* narrow piece of wood with wheels attached

skel-e-ton *n.* framework of bones that protects and supports the soft tissues and organs

skep-tic *n.* person who doubts or questions skepticism *n.*, skeptical *adj.*, skeptically *adv.*

sketch *n.* rough drawing or outline; a brief literary composition sketchy *adj.*

skew *v.* turn or slant; *n.* slant

skid *v.* slide to the side of the road; to slide along without rotating

skill *n.* ability gained through practice; expertise skilled *adj.*

skim *v.* remove the top layer; to remove floating matter

skimp *v.* economize; to hold back -y *adj.*

skin *n.* tough, outside covering of man and some animals; the outside layer of a vegetable or fruit

skirt *n.* piece of clothing that extends down from the waist

skull *n.* bony part of the skeleton which protects the brain

sky *n., pl.* skies upper atmosphere above the earth; the celestial regions

slab *n.* thick piece or slice

slack *adj.* not taut or tense; sluggish; lacking in strength

slain *v.* past tense of slay

slam *v.* shut with force; to strike with a loud impact

slam-mer *n., Slang* jail or prison

slan-der *n.* false statement that deliberately does harm to another's reputation slanderous *adj.*

slang *n.* informal language that contains made-up words or common words used in a different or uncommon way

slant *v.* lie in an oblique position; to slope; to report on something giving only one side or viewpoint

slap *n.* sharp blow with an open hand

slash *v.* cut with a fast sweeping stroke; to reduce or limit greatly *n.* long cut

slate *n.* fine grained rock that splits into thin layers, often used as a writing surface or roofing material slate *v.*

slaugh-ter *v.* kill livestock for food; to kill in great numbers; *Slang* to soundly defeat slaughterer *n.*

slave *n.* person held against his will and made to work for another

sled *n.* vehicle with runners, used to travel on snow or ice

sleek *adj.* smooth and shiny; neat and trim sleekly *adv.*

sleep *n.* natural state of rest for the mind and body; *v.* to rest in sleep

sleet *n.* rain that is partially frozen; a combination of snow and rain

sleeve *n.* part of a garment which covers the arm; a case for something

sleigh *n.* vehicle mounted on runners, usually pulled over ice and snow by horses

slen-der *adj.* slim; inadequate in amount slenderly *adv.*

slept *v.* past tense of sleep

slice *n.* thin cut; a portion or share

slick *adj.* smooth and slippery; quick; smart; clever

slick-er *n.* raincoat made of yellow oilcloth

slight *adj.* minor in degree; unimportant slightly *adv.*

slim *adj.* slender; meager; not much slimness *n.*

slime *n.* wet, slippery substance -y *adj.*

sling *n.* piece of material, as leather, or a strap which secures something; a piece of fabric worn around the neck used to support an injured hand or arm

slip *v.* move in a smooth, quiet way; to fall or lose one's balance; *Slang* to become less active, alert, or strong

slith-er *v.* slide or slip in an indirect manner; to move like a snake slithery *adj.*

sliv-er *n.* thin, narrow piece of something that has been broken off sliver *v.*

slob-ber *v.* dribble from the mouth slobber *n.*

slo-gan *n.* phrase used to express the aims of a cause

slope *v.* slant upward or downward

slosh *v.* to splash in a liquid, as water sloshy *adj.*

slot *n.* narrow, thin groove or opening; *Slang* place or scheduled time for an event

sloth *n.* laziness; a slow mammal found in South America

slouch *n.* drooping or sagging posture; a lazy person

slow *adj.* moving at a low rate of speed; requiring more time than usual; not lively; sluggish; not interestin; *adv.* at less speed; in a slow manner **slowly** *adv.*, **slowness** *n.*

slug *n.* slow animal related to the snail; a bullet or a lump of metal

sluice *n.* man-made ditch used to move water

slum *n.* crowded urban neighborhood marked by poverty

slum-ber *v.* to sleep; to doze; *n.* sleep **slumberer** *n.*

slump *v.* fall or sink suddenly

slur *v.* to slide over without careful consideration; to pronounce unclearly; *n.* an insult

slush *n.* melting snow **slushy** *adj.*

slut *n.* woman of bad character; a prostitute

sly *adj.* cunning; clever; sneaky **slyly** *adv.*, **slyness** *n.*

smack *v.* slap; press and open the lips with a sharp noise **small** *adj.* little in size, quantity, or extent; unimportant **smallness** *n.*

small-pox *n.* acute, contagious disease marked by high fever and sores on the skin

smart *adj.* intelligent; clever

smash *v.* break into small pieces; to ruin

smear *v.* spread or cover with a sticky, oily, or moist substance; *Slang* discredit one's reputation

smell *v.* notice an odor by means of the olfactory sense organs; *n.* odor

smelt *v.* heat metals or their ores to a high temperature in order to obtain pure metallic constituents

smile *n.* grin

smirk *v.* smile in a conceited way **smirk, smirker** *n.*

smite *v.* hit with great force using the hand

smock *n.* loose-fitting garment worn as a protection for one's clothes while working

smog *n.* mixture of smoke and fog **smoggy** *adj.*

smoke *n.* cloud of vapor released into the air when something is burning

smolder *v.* burn slowly without a flame and with little smoke **smolder** *n.*

smooth *adj.* not irregular; flat; without lumps; *adv.* evenly; *v.* to make less difficult

smor-gas-bord *n.* buffet meal with a variety of foods to choose from

smother *n.* failure to receive enough oxygen to survive; *v.* conceal

smothery *adj.*

smudge *v.* soil by smearing with dirt; *n.* dirty mark or smear

smug *adj.* complacent with oneself; self-satisfied

smug-gle *v.* import or export goods illegally without paying duty fees **smuggler** *n.*

snack *n.* small amount of food taken between meals

snag *n.* stump or part of a tree; a pull in a piece of fabric

snake *n.* any of a large variety of scaly reptiles, having a long tapering body; *Slang* an untrustworthy person

snap *v.* break suddenly with a sharp, quick sound; to fly off under tension

snare *n.* anything that entangles or entraps; a trap with a noose, used to catch small animals

snarl *v.* speak in an angry way; to cause confusion; to tangle or be tangled

snatch *v.* seize or grasp something suddenly

sneak *v.* act or move in a quiet, sly way; *n.* person who acts in a secret, underhanded way

sneer *v.* express scorn by the look on one's face

sneeze *v.* expel air from the nose suddenly and without control

sniff *v.* inhale through the nose in short breaths with a noise

snip *v.* cut off in small pieces and with quick strokes

snipe *n., pl.* **snipe** or **snipes** bird with a long bill which lives in marshy places; *v.* to shoot at people from a hidden position **sniper** *n.*

snob *n.* a person who considers himself better than anyone else

snoop *v., Slang* prowl or spy; *n.* one who snoops

snore *v.* to breath with a harsh noise while sleeping **snorer** *n.*

snor-kel *n.* tube that extends above the water, used for breathing while swimming face down

snort *n.* force air through the nostrils with a loud, harsh nois; *Slang* inhale a narcotic through the nose

snow *n.* vapor that forms crystals in cold air and falls to the ground in white flakes **snow** *v.*

snub *v.* treat with contempt or in an unfriendly way

snuff *v.* draw air in through the nostrils **snuff** *n.*

snug *adj.* warm, pleasant, comfortable and safe

so *adv.* to a degree or extent as a result; likewise; also; indeed; *conj.* in order that; therefore

soap *n.* cleansing agent made of an alkali and a fat, and used for washing

soar *v.* glide or fly high without any noticeable movement; to rise higher than usual

sob *v.* weep with short, quick gasps

so-ber *adj.* not drunk or intoxicated; serious; solemn **soberly** *adv.*, **soberness** *n.*

soc-cer *n.* game in which two teams of eleven men each try to kick a ball into the opposing team's goal

so-cia-ble *adj.* capable of friendly social relations; enjoying the company of others **sociableness** *n.*, **sociably** *adv.*

socialism *n.* system in which people as a whole, and not individuals, control and own all property

so-ci-e-ty *n.*, *pl.* **societies** people working together for a common purpose; companionship

so-ci-ol-o-gy *n.* study of society and the development of human society **sociologist** *n.*

sock *n.* short covering for the foot, ankle, and lower part of the leg; a hard blow

sock-et *n.* hollow opening into which something is fitted

so-da *n.* sodium carbonate; a flavored, carbonated drink

sod-den *adj.* completely saturate; very wet; lacking in expression

so-di-um *n.* metallic element symbolized by Na.

sod-om-y *n.* anal sexual intercourse

so-fa *n.* upholstered couch with arms and a back

soft *adj.* not stiff or hard; not glaring or harsh; mild or pleasant; gentle in sound

soft-ware *n.* in computer science, data, as routines, programs and languages, which is essential to the operation of computers

sog-gy *adj.* saturated with a liquid or moisture

sol-ace *n.* comfort in a time of trouble, grief, or misfortune **solacer** *n.*

so-lar *adj.* relating to or connected with the sun; utilizing the sun for power or light; measured by the earth's movement around the sun

so-lar-i-um *n.*, *pl.* **-ia** *or* **-ums** a glassed-in room exposed to the sun's rays

solar system *n.* the sun and the planets, asteroids, and comets that orbit it

sol-der *n.* alloy, as lead or tin, which is melted and used to mend or join other pieces of metal

soldier *n.* enlisted person who serves in the military

sole *n.* bottom of a foot or shoe; single, the only one

sol-emn *adj.* very serious; characterized by dignity; sacred **-ity**, **-ness** *n.*

so-lic-it *v.* try to obtain; to ask earnestly; to beg or entice a person persistently **solicition** *n.*

sol-id *adj.* having a definite firm shape and volume; having no crevices; not hollow; having height, weight and length; with-out interruption **-ify** *v.*

sol-i-taire *n.* single gemstone set by itself; a card game played by one person

sol-i-tude *n.* act of being alone or secluded; isolation

so-lo *n.* musical composition written for and performed by one person or played by one instrument

sol-u-ble *adj.* capable of being dissolved **solubility** *n.*

solve *v.* find the answer to **solvable** *adj.*

som-ber *adj.* dark; gloomy; melancholy

some *adj.* being an indefinite number or quantity; unspecified; *pron.* undetermined or indefinite quantity

some-day *adv.* an unspecified future time

somehow *adv.* in a way

som-nam-bu-lism *n.* act of walking during sleep

son *n.* male offspring

song *n.* piece of poetry put to music; the act or sound of singing

son-ic *adj.* pertaining to sound or the speed of sound

son-net *n.* poem made up of fourteen lines

soon *adv.* in a short time; in the near future; quickly

soot *n.* black powder generated by incomplete combustion of a fuel, such as coal or wood

soothe *v.* make comfortable; to calm

sop *v.* soak up a liquid; to absorb

so-pran-o *n.*, *pl.* **sopranos** *or* **soprani** highest female singing voice

sor-did *adj.* filthy, very dirty; morally corrupt

sore *adj.* tender or painful to the touch, as an injured part of the body; severe or extreme

so-ror-i-ty *n.*, *pl.* **sororities** social organization for women

sor-rel *n.* any of several herbs with sour-tasting leaves, used in salads

sor-row *n.* anguish; mental suffering; an expression of grief **-ful** *adj.*, **-fully** *adv.*

sor-ry *adj.* feeling or showing sympathy or regret; worthless

sort *n.* collection of things having common attributes or similar qualities

sought *v.* past tense of seek

soul *n.* spirit in man that is believed to be separate from the body and is the source of a person's emotional, spiritual, and moral nature

sound *n.* sensation received by the ears from air, water, noise, and other sources; *v.* make a sound; *adj.* free from flaw, disease, or damage **soundless** *adj.*, **soundly** *adv.*

soup *n.* liquid food made by boiling meat and/or vegetables, in water

sour *adj.* sharp to the taste; acid; unpleasant **sourly** *adv.*

source *n.* any point of origin or beginning

south *n.* direction opposite of north; *adv.* to or towards the south; *adj.* from the south **southerly** *adj.*, **southerner** *n.*

south-paw *n.* left-handed person

sou-ve-nir *n.* item kept as a remembrance of something or someplace

sov-er-eign *n.* ruler with supreme power; a monarch

soviet *adj.* having to do with the Soviet Union

sow *v.* scatter or throw seeds on the ground for growth; *n.* a female pig

space *n.* unlimited area in all directions in which events occur and have relative direction; an interval of time; the area beyond the earth's atmosphere

spade *n.* tool with a flat blade used for digging, heavier than a shovel **spade** *v.*

spa-ghet-ti *n.* pasta made in long, thin pieces

span *n.* the section between two limits or supports; *v.* to extend across

spank *v.* strike or slap the buttocks with an open hand as a means of punishment

spare *v.* to refrain from injuring, harming or destroying; to refrain from using

spark *n.* glowing or incandescent particle, as one released from a piece of burning wood or one produced by means of friction; *v.* to give off sparks

spar-kle *v.* emit or reflect light

spar-row *n.* small bird with grayish or brown plumage

sparse *adj.* scant; thinly distributed **sparsely** *adv.*

spasm *n.* involuntary muscle contraction

spat-ter *v.* scatter or splash a liquid

spat-u-la *n.* kitchen utensil with a flexible blade for mixing soft substances

spawn *n.* eggs of fish or other water animals, as oysters or frogs; *v.* to lay eggs

speak *v.* utter words; to express a thought in words

speak-er *n.* person who speaks, usually before an audience

spear *n.* weapon with a long shaft and a sharply pointed head; *v.* strike, pierce

spear-mint *n.* mint plant yielding an aromatic oil used as a flavoring

spe-cial-ist *n.* person, such as a doctor, who devotes his practice to one particular field

spe-cial-ize *v.* focus one's efforts or interests in one field of activity or study

spec-i-men *n.* sample; a representative of a particular thing

speck *n.* small particle, mark, or spot

spec-ta-cle *n.* public display of something unusual **spectacled** *adj.*

spec-trum *n.*, *Physics* band of colors produced when light is passed through a prism or other means, separating the light into different wave lengths

spec-u-late *v.* reflect and think deeply; to take a chance on a business venture in hopes of making a large profit

speech *n.* ability, manner, or act of speaking; a talk before the public

speed *n.* rate of action or movement; quickness; rapid motion; *Slang* a drug used strictly as a stimulant

spell *v.* say out loud or write in proper order the letters which make up a word; to relieve

spellbind *v.* fascinate or hold as if by magic

spend *v.* give out; to use up; to pay; to exhaust

sperm *n.* male cell of reproduction; semen

sphere *n.*, *Math* round object with all points the same distance from a given point; globe, ball, or other rounded object **spherical** *adj.*

sphinx *n.*, *pl.* **sphinxes** *or* **sphinges** ancient Egyptian figure having the head of a man, male sheep, or hawk and the body of a lion; a very mysterious person

spice *n.* pungently aromatic plant used as flavoring in food, as nutmeg, cinnamon, pepper, or curry **spicy** *adj.*

spi-der *n.* eight-legged insect

spike *n.* large, thick nail

spill *v.* allow or cause something to flow

or run out of something

spin v. draw out fibers and twist into thread; to run something around and around **spinner** n.

spin-ach n. widely cultivated plant with green leaves which are used in salads

spine n. spinal column; the backbone; the back of a bound book

spin-ster n. unmarried woman; an old maid

spir-it n. vital essence of man, considered divine in origin the mind; the Holy Ghost

spir-i-tual adj. of, like, or pertaining to the nature of spirit; relating to religion; sacred -ity n., -ize v.

spite n. hatred or malicious bitterness; a grudge; ill will -ful adj., -fully adv.

spit-toon n. a cuspidor or receptacle for spit

spitz n. small dog with a tail which curls over its back

splash v. spatter a liquid; to wet or soil with liquid; to make a splash **splashy** adj.

splash-down n. landing of a missile or spacecraft in the ocean

spleen n., Anat. highly vascular, flattened organ which filters and stores blood, located below the diaphragm

splen-did adj. illustrious; magnificent

splice v. join together by wearing, overlapping, and binding the ends **splice** n.

splint n. device used to hold a fractured or injured limb in the proper position for healing **splint** v.

splotch n. discolored and irregularly shaped spot

splutter v. make a slight, short spitting sound **splutter** n.

spoil v. destroy the value, quality, or usefulness

spoke n. one of the rods that serve to connect and support the rim of a wheel; v. past tense of speak

sponge n. any of a number of marine creatures with a soft, porous skeleton which soaks up liquid **spongy** adj.

spon-ta-ne-ous adj. done from one's own impulse without apparent external cause **spontaneousity** n., **spontaneously** adv.

spoof n. deception; nonsense

spook n., Slang a ghost; v. scare or frighten **spooky** adj.

spool n. small cylinder for holding thread, tape or wire

spoon n. eating or cooking utensil; a shiny metallic fishing lure Slang make love, as by kissing or caressing -ful n.

spo-rad-ic adj. occurring occasionally or at irregular intervals **sporadically** adv.

spore n., Bot. reproductive singlecelled structure produced by nonflowering plants; any cell capable of developing into a new organism, seed, or germ

sport n. interesting diversion; a particular game or physical activity with set rules

sport-ing adj. of or relating to risk taking or gambling; displaying sportsmanship

sports-man-ship n. fair play; the ability to win or lose graciously

spot n. a small area that differs in size, portion, or color; Slang a dangerous or difficult situation

spot-light n. powerful light thrown directly at one area

spouse n. one's husband or wife; a marriage partner

spout v. pour out forcibly, as under pressure; to cause to shoot forth **spouter** n.

sprain n. wrenching or twisting of a muscle or joint

sprawl v. sit or lie in an ungraceful manner; to develop haphazardly **sprawler** n.

spray n. liquid dispersed in a fine mist or droplets; v. disperse or send forth in a spray **sprayer** n.

spread v. unfold or open fully; to apply or distribute over an area; to force apart; to extend or expand **spread** v.

spree n. excessive indulgence in an activity; a binge

spright-ly adj. Vivacious, lively **sprightliness** n.

sprin-kle v. scatter in small particles or drops; to rain in small drops **sprinkle** n.

sprint n. short, fast race **sprinter** n.

sprock-et n., Mech. tooth-like projection from the rim of a wheel

sprung v. past tense of spring

spry adj. quick; brisk; energetic

spud n., Slang potato

spur n. sharp, projecting device worn on a rider's boot, used to nudge a horse

sput-nik n. unmanned Soviet earth satellite

sput-ter v. throw off small particles in short bursts; to speak in a confused or agitated manner

spu-tum n., pl. sputa saliva or mucus that is expectorated

spy n., pl. spies secret agent who obtains information; one who watches other people secretly

squab-ble v. engage in a petty argument

squad n. small group organized to perform a specific job

squan-der v. spend extravagantly or wastefully

square n. parallelogram with four equal sides; an implement having a T or L shape used to measure right angles; *Math.* to square root n. number which when multiplied by itself gives the given number

squash n. edible fruit of the gourd family; a sport played in a walled court with a hard rubber ball and racket

squat v. sit on the heels; to crouch; to settle on a piece of land in order to obtain legal title

squaw n. American Indian woman

squeak v. utter a sharp, penetrating sound

squea-mish adj. easily shocked or nauseated **squeamishly** adv.

squeeze v. press together; to extract by using pressure

squint v. view something through partly closed eyes

squirm n. twist the body in a wiggling motion **squirm** v.

squir-rel n. rodent with gray or brown fur, having a long bushy tail and dark eyes

squirt v. eject in a thin stream or jet; to wet with a squirt

sta-bi-lize v. make firm; to keep from changing **stabilization, stabilizer** n.

sta-ble n. building for lodging and feeding horses or other farm animals

stac-ca-to adj., *Music* Marked by sharp emphasis **staccato** n. & adv.

stack n. large pile of straw or hay; any systematic heap or pile; a chimney

sta-di-um n., pl. -dia large structure for holding athletic events or other large gatherings

staff n., pl. **staffs** or **staves** pole or rod used for a specific purpose; the people employed to assist in the day-to-day affairs of running a business.

stag n. adult male of various animals; a man who attends a social gathering without a woman companion

stag-ger v. walk unsteadily; to totter

stag-nant adj. not flowing; standing still; foul from not moving; inactive **stagnate** v.

stair n. step or a series of steps

staircase n. series or a flight of steps that connect one level to another

stake n. bet placed on a game of chance; a sharpened piece of wood for driving into the ground

stale adj. having lost freshness; deteriorated; lacking in interest; dull

stalk n. main axis of a plant v. approach in a stealthy manner

stall n. enclosure in a barn, used as a place to feed and confine animals; a sudden loss of power in an engine; a booth used to display and sell v. to delay

stal-lion n. uncastrated, fully grown male horse

sta-men n., pl. **stamens** *Bot.* pollen-producing organs of a flower

stam-i-na n. physical or moral endurance

stam-mer v. make involuntary halts or repetitions of a sound or syllable while speaking

stamp v. put the foot down with force; to imprint or impress with a die, mark, or design n. a postage stamp

stam-pede n. sudden rush of panic, as of a herd of horses or cattle

stance n. posture or position of a standing person or animal

stand v. to be placed in or maintain an erect or upright position; to take an upright position; to remain unchanged; to maintain a conviction; to resist n. a device on which something rests; a small booth for selling or displaying items

stand-ard n. model which stands for or is accepted as a basis for comparison

stand-ing n. status, reputation, or achievement; a measure of esteem adj. unchanging

sta-ple n. principle commodity grown in an area; a major element; a metal fastener designed to hold materials such as cloth or paper **staple** v., **stapler** n.

star n., *Astron.* self-luminous body that is a source of light; any of the celestial bodies that can be seen in the night sky; a symbol having five or six points and resembling a star

star-board n. right side of a ship or boat

starch n. nutrient carbohydrates that are found in foods such as rice and potatoes v. to stiffen clothing by using starch **starchiness** n., **starchy** adj.

stare v. look with an intent, direct gaze **stare, starer** n.

stark adj. bare; total; complete; forbidding in appearance **starkness** n., **starkly** adv.

star-ling n. common black or brown bird

star-tle v. cause a sudden surprise; to shock **startle** n.

starve v. suffer or die from not having food; to suffer from the need of food, love, or other necessities **starvation** n.

state n. situation, mode, or condition of something; a nation; the governing power or authority of; one of the subdivisions or areas of a federal government, as the United States v. make known verbally

stat-ic adj. not moving n. random noise heard on a radio -ally adv.

sta-tion n. place where someone or something is directed to stand; a scheduled stopping place; the place from which radio and television programs are broadcast

sta-tion-ar-y adj. not movable; unchanging

sta-tion-er-y n. writing paper and envelopes

sta-tis-tic n. estimate using an average or mean on the basis of a sample taken; numerical data

stat-ue n. form sculpted from wood, clay, metal, or stone

stave n narrow piece of wood used in forming part of a container, as a barrel

stay v. remain; to pause; to maintain a position; to halt or stop; to postpone or delay an execution n. short visit

stead n. position, place, or job of another

stead-y adj. firmly placed, fixed or set; not changing

steal v. take another person's property; to move in a sly way; to move secretly *Slang* real bargain

steam n. water in the form of vapor; the visible mist into which vapor is condensed by cooling

steam v., **steamy** adj.

steel n. various mixture of iron, carbon, and other elements; a strong material that can be shaped when heated **steely** adj.

stem n. main stalk of a plant; the main part of a word to which prefixes and suffixes may be added v. stop or retard the progress or flow of something

sten-cil n. form cut into a sheet of material, as cardboard or plastic, so that when ink or paint is applied, the pattern will reproduce on paper or another material

ste-nog-ra-phy n. skill of writing in shorthand **stenographer** n.

step n. single completed movement in walking, dancing, or running; the distance of such a step; the part of a ladder that one places the feet on in ascending or descending *Music* musical scale; a degree

ste-re-o n. record player with stereophonic sound

ster-e-o-type n. conventional opinion or belief; a metal printing plate

ster-ile adj. free from microorganisms; sanitary; unable to reproduce

ster-ling n. alloy of 92.5% silver and another metal, as copper

stern adj. inflexible; harsh n. rear of a boat or ship **sternly** adv., **sternness** n.

ster-num n., pl. -nums or -na long, flat bone located in the chest wall, connecting the collarbones and the cartilage of the first seven pairs of ribs **sternumal** adj.

steth-o-scope n. instrument used to listen to the internal sounds of the body

stew v. cook slowly; to simmer; to boil n. dish of stewed meat and potatoes *Slang* to worry

stew-ard n. manager of another's financial affairs; a person responsible for maintaining household affairs; a male attendant on an airplane or ship

stick n. slender piece of wood; a club, rod, or walking stick v. put a hole in something; to pierce; to cling; to become jammed

stiff adj. not flexible; not easily bent; awkward n., *Slang* dead body -ness n.

sti-fle v. suffocate; to cut off; to suppress; to keep back

stig-ma n., pl. -mata or -mas mark of disgrace **stigmata** part of a flower where pollen is deposited at pollination **stigmatic** adj.

still adj. silent; calm; peaceful; until now or another time adv. nevertheless **stillness** n.

stillbirth n. birth of a dead fetus

stilt n. one of a pair of long poles with foot supports, used for walking

stim-u-lant n. agent which arouses or accelerates physiological activity

stim-u-late v. excite to a heightened activity; to quicken **stimulation** n.

stim-u-lus n., pl. -li something that excites to action

sting v. prick with something sharp; to feel or cause to feel a smarting pain; to cause or feel sharp pain, either physical or mental n. act of stinging; the injury or pain caused by the stinger of a bee or wasp **stinger** n.

stin-gy adj. not giving freely; cheap

stink v. give off a foul odor that is highly offensive

stip-u-late v. settle something by agreement; to establish conditions of agreement stipulation *n.*

stir *v.* mix a substance by moving round and round; to agitate or provoke

stir-rup *n.* loop extending from a horse's saddle, used to support the rider's foot

stitch *n.* in sewing, a single loop formed by a needle and thread; the section of loop of thread

stock *n.* supply of goods kept on hand; animals living on a farm; a share in ownership, as in a company or corporation; the raw material or the base used to make something *v.* provide with stock *adj.* regular, common, or typical

stock-ade *n.* barrier placed around a fort for protection

stock-ing *n.* knitted covering for the foot

stock-y *adj.* sturdy and compact; built sturdily

stole *n.* long, narrow scarf that is usually worn around a woman's shoulders, as a mink stole *v.* past tense of steal

stom-ach *n., Anat.* organ into which food passes from the esophagus; one of the primary organs of digestion *v.* tolerate or stand; to put up with

stone *n.* rock; compacted earth or mineral matter; a gem or jewel; the seed or pit of certain fruits *Med.* hard rock that forms inside a body organ, as the kidney stoned to be overcome by an excessive amount of alcohol or drugs

stood *v.* past tense of stand

stool *n.* seat without a backrest and arms; a small version of this on which to rest the feet; a bowel movement

stoop *v.* bend the body forward and downward from the waist *n.* porch attached to a house

stop *v.* cease; to halt; to refrain from moving, operating, or acting; to block or obstruct

stor-age *n.* act of storing or keeping; in Computer Science, the part of a computer in which all information is held; the memory

store *n.* business offering merchandise for sale; a supply to be used in the future *v.* supply; to accumulate

stork *n.* large, wading bird

storm *n.* atmospheric condition marked by strong winds with rain, sleet, hail, or snow *v.* charge or attack with a powerful force

sto-ry *n., pl.* -ies. narration of a fictional tale or account; a lie; a level in a building or house

stout *adj.* strong; sturdy; substantial; courageous

stove *n.* apparatus in which oil, electricity, gas, or other fuels are consumed to provide the heat for cooking

stow *v.* pack or put away

strad-dle *v.* sit or stand with the legs on either side of something; to favor both sides of an issue -er *n.*

straight *adj.* being without bends, angles, or curves; upright; erect; honest; undiluted; unmodified; heterosexual straightly *adv.*

strain *v.* stretch beyond a proper limit; to injure by putting forth too much effort; to pass through a sieve to separate small particles from larger ones

strait *n.* narrow passageway which connects two bodies of water

strand *n.* land that borders a body of water; one of the threads that are twisted together to form a rope *v.* leave in a difficult situation

strange *adj.* not previously known or experienced;odd; peculiar; inexperienced; alien -ly *adv.*

stran-ger *n.* person unknown; a newcomer; an alien

stran-gle *v.* kill by choking strangler *n.*

strap *n.* long, narrow strip of leather or other material used to secure objects

strat-e-gy *n., pl.* -ies skillful planning and managing of an activity -gic *adj.*

stra-tum *n., pl.* -ta *or* -tums horizontal layer, as of the earth's crust

straw *n.* stalk of dried, threshed grain; a slender, plastic or paper straw used to suck up a liquid

straw-ber-ry *n.* low plant with white flowers and red fruit; the fruit of this plant

stray *v.* roam or wander *n.* lost or wandering animal or person *adj.* lost strayer *n.*

streak *n.* narrow line or stripe that is different from the surrounding area; a run of good or bad luck *v.* rush or move rapidly; to make a streak streaky *adj.*

stream *n.* small body of flowing water; a steady or continuous succession or procession. *v.* flow in or like a stream

street *n.* public thoroughfare in a town or city with buildings on either or both sides

strength *n.* quality of being strong; power in general; degree of concentration or potency

strengthen *v.* grow strong or stronger

stren-u-ous *adj.* necessitating or characterized by vigorous effort or exertion **strenuously** adv.

stress n. special significance; an emphasis given to a specific syllable, word, action, or plan; strain or pressure **stressful** adj.

stretch v. extend fully; to extend forcibly beyond proper limits; to prolong n. state or act of stretching **stretchable, stretchy** adj.

strew v. scatter about

strick-en adj. suffering, as from an emotion, illness, or trouble

strict adj. holding to or observing rules exactly; imposing absolute standards **strictly** adv., **-ness** n.

stride v. walk with a long, sweeping step

strike v. hit with the hand; to ignite, as with a match; to afflict suddenly with a disease; to discover; to conclude or make; to stop working as a protest against something or in favor of rules or demands presented to an employer

string n. strip of thin twine, wire, or catgut used on stringed musical instruments; a series of related acts, items, or events; in Computer Science, data arranged in an ascending or descending sequence according to a command within the data

strin-gent adj. of or relating to strict requirements; marked by obstructions or scarcity **stringently** adv.

strip v. take off the outer covering; to divest or pull rank; to remove one's clothes; to rob

stripe n. streak, band, or strip of a different color or texture; a piece of material or cloth worn on the sleeve of a uniform to indicate rank, award, or service

stroke n. movement of striking; a sudden action with a powerful effect; a single movement made by the hand or as if by a brush or pen Path. sudden interruption of the blood supply to the brain v. pass the hand over gently

stroll v. walk in a slow, leisurely way

strong adj. exerting or possessing physical power; durable; difficult to break **strongly** adv.

struc-ture n. construction made up of a combination of related parts **structure** v., **structural** adj.

strug-gle v. put forth effort against opposition

strych-nine n. extremely poisonous alkaloid derived from certain plants, used to kill rodents and as a neural stimulant

stub n. short, projecting part; the short end of something after the main part has been removed or used

stub-born adj. inflexible; difficult to control, handle, or manage

stuc-co n., pl. **-coes** or **-cos** fine plaster used to coat exterior walls and to decorate interior walls

stud n. upright post, as in a building frame, to which sheets of wallboard or paneling are fastened; a small removable button used as an ornament; a male horse used for breeding **stud** v.

stu-dent n. person who studies at a school or college

stu-di-o n. place of work for an artist, photographer, or other creative person; a place for filming movies

stud-y n., pl. **-ies** process of applying the mind to acquire knowledge

stum-ble v. trip and nearly fall over something; to come upon unexpectedly

stump n. part of a tree which remains after the top is cut down v. puzzle or be puzzled; to walk heavily; to campaign

stun v. render senseless by or as if by a blow

stu-pen-dous adj. astonishing or highly impressive **-ness** n., **stupendously** adv.

stu-pid adj. slow in apprehension or understanding **stupidity** n.

stur-dy adj. possessing robust strength and health **-ily** adv., **sturdiness** n.

stur-geon n. large freshwater fish highly valued as a source of caviar

stut-ter v. speak with involuntary repetitions of sound **stutter** n.

sty n., pl. **sties** inflammation of the edge of an eyelid

style n. method, manner, or way of performing, speaking, or clothing; elegance, grace, or excellence in performance or appearance **style** v., **stylish** adj.

suave adj. ingratiating; smoothly pleasant in manner

sub- prefix. beneath, under, or below

sub-con-scious adj. below the level of consciousness

sub-due v. bring under control by influence, training, persuasion or force

sub-ject n. word in a sentence that defines a person or thing; a person who is under the control of another's governing power **subjection** n.

sub-jec-tive adj. taking place within, relating to or preceding from an individual's emotions or mind **subjectively** adv., **subjectivity** n.

sub-ma-rine adj. operating or existing beneath the surface of the sea n. ship that travels underwater **submariner** n.

sub-merge v. plunge under the surface of the water

sub-mit v. give into or surrender to another's authority **submission,** -**tal** n., **submissive** adj.

sub-or-di-nate adj. being of lower class or rank; minor; inferior -**ation** n., **subordinative** adj.

sub-poe-na n. legal document requiring a person to appear in court for testimony

sub-se-quent adj. following in time, place, or order **subsequently** adv., **subsequentness** n.

sub-side v. move to a lower level or sink; to become less intense

sub-sid-i-ar-y adj., pl., n. -**ies**. providing assistance in a lesser capacity **subsidiaries** pl., n.

sub-si-dy n., pl. -**dies**. financial aid granted directly to a private commercial enterprise from the government

sub-sist v. have continued existence

sub-soil n. layer of earth that comes after the surface soil

sub-stance n. matter or material of which anything consists

sub-sti-tute n. something or someone that takes the place of another

sub-ten-ant n. a person who rents property from a tenant

sub-ter-ra-ne-an adj. located, situated, or operating underground

sub-ti-tle n. explanatory title, as in a document, book, etc.; a written translation that appears at the bottom of a foreign motion picture screen

sub-tract v. deduct or take away from

sub-trop-i-cal adj. pertaining to regions adjacent to the tropics

sub-urb n. residential community near a large city **suburban** adj.

sub-way n. underground electrical-lypowered train, usually used as a means of transportation

suc-ceed v. accomplish what is attempted; to come next or to follow

suc-cess n. achievement of something intended or desired; attaining wealth, fame, or prosperity

suc-ces-sion n. act or process of following in order; sequence; series; the order, sequence or act by which something changes hands

suc-ces-sive adj. following in order or

sequence -**ly** adv., -**ness** n.

suc-cu-lent adj. juicy; full of juice or sap -**ence** n., **succulently** adv.

such adj. of this or that kind or thing; a great degree or extent in quality pron. of a particular degree or kind; a person or thing of such

suck v. pull liquid in the mouth by means of a vacuum created by the lips and tongue n. action of sucking

su-crose n. sugar obtained from the sugar beet or sugar cane

suc-tion n. process or act of sucking

sud-den adj. happening very quickly without warning or notice; sharp; abrupt; marked by haste -**ly** adv.

suds pl., n. bubbles or soapy water **sudsy** adv.

suede n. leather with a soft, napped finish

su-et n. hard fat around the kidney and loins of sheep

suf-fer v. feel pain or distress; to sustain injury, loss, or damage **sufferer** n.

suf-fi-cient adj. as much that is needed or desired

suf-fix n. form affixed to the end of a word

suf-fo-cate v. kill by depriving something or someone of oxygen **suffocation** n.

sugar n. sweet, watersoluble, crystal-like carbohydrate Slang nickname for someone

sug-gest v. give an idea for action or consideration; to imply; hint or intimate

sug-ges-tion n. act of suggesting; a slight insinuation; hint

su-i-cide n. act of taking one's own life **suicidal** adj.

suit n. set of articles, as clothing, to be used or worn together; in cards, one of the four sets: spades, hearts, clubs, and diamonds that make up a deck v. meet the requirements of; to satisfy

sul-fur also **sulphur** n. light, yellow, nonmetallic element occurring naturally in both combined and free form, used in making matches, gunpowder and medicines

sulk v. to be sullenly silent

sul-len adj. ill-humored, melancholy; gloomy; depressing

sul-try adj. hot and humid; muggy

sum n. result obtained by adding; the whole amount, quantity, or number; summary

sum-ma-ry n., pl. -**ries**. giving the sum or substance adj. a statement covering the main points **summarily** adv.

sum-mer n. warmest of the four seasons,

following spring and coming before autumn

sum-mit *n.* top and highest point, degree, or level

sum-mons *n., pl.* -monses order or command to perform a duty; a notice to appear at a certain place

sun *n.* star around which other planets of the solar system orbit; the energy, visible light, and heat, that is emitted by the sun; sunshine **sunny** *adj.*

Sun-day *n.* Christian holy day; the first day of the week

sun-down *n.* time of day the sun sets

sunk-en *adj.* submerged or deeply depressed in

su-per *adj.* exceeding a norm; in excessive intensity or degree; surpassing most others; superior in rank, status or position; excellent *n. Slang* superintendent of a building

su-perb *adj.* of firstrate quality **superbly** *adv.*

su-per-fi-cial *adj.* pertaining to a surface; concerned only with what is not necessarily real

su-pe-ri-or *adj.* of higher rank, grade, or dignity *n.* person who surpasses another in rank or excellence **-ity** *n.*, **superiorly** *adv.*

su-per-la-tive *adj.* of the highest degree of excellence; pertaining to the degree of comparison of an adverb or adjective that shows extreme extent or level **superlatively** *adv.*

su-per-nat-u-ral *adj.* order of existence beyond the natural world; pertaining to a divine power **supernaturaly** *adv.*

su-per-sede *v.* take the place of; to set aside

su-per-son-ic *adj., Aero.* characterized by a speed greater than that of sound

su-per-sti-tion *n.* belief founded, despite evidence that it is irrational; a belief, resulting from faith in magic or chance

su-per-vise *v.* have charge in directing the work of other people **supervision, supervisor** *n.*, **supervisory** *adj.*

sup-per *n.* last or evening meal of the day

sup-ple-ment *n.* part that compensates for what is lacking -ary, -tal *adj.*

sup-ply *v., pl., n.* -plies. provide with what is needed; to make available **supplier** *n.*

sup-port *v.* bear or hold the weight of; to tolerate; to give assistance or approval *n.* act of supporting **supportable, -ive** *adj.*, **-er** *n.*

sup-pose *v.* think or assume as true; to consider probable **supposed** *adj.*, **supposedly** *adv.*

su-preme *adj.* of the highest authority, rank, or power

sur-charge *n.* extra fee added to the cost of something; to overcharge

sure *adj.* firm and sturdy; being impossible to doubt; inevitable; not liable to fail

sur-face *n.* exterior or outside boundary of something

surge *v.* increase suddenly *n.* large swell of water

sur-geon *n.* physician who practices surgery

sur-ger-y *n., pl.* -ies. branch of medicine in which physical deformity or disease is treated by an operative procedure

sur-mise *v.* guess; conjecture

sur-mount *v.* overcome; be at the top

sur-name *n.* person's family last name

sur-pass *v.* go beyond the limits of; to be greater than

sur-plus *n.* amount beyond what is needed

sur-prise *v.* come upon unexpectedly or suddenly; to cause to feel amazed or astonished **surpriser** *n.*, **surprisingly** *adv.*

sur-ren-der *v.* give up or yield possession or power *n.* act of surrendering

sur-ro-gate *n.* person who puts himself in the place of another **surrogate** *v.*

sur-round *v.* extend around all edges of something; to enclose or shut in

sur-veil-lance *n.* close observation kept over one, especially as a suspect

sur-vive *v.* continue to exist; to outlast; to outlive

su-shi *n.* Japanese dish of thin slices of fresh, raw fish

sus-pect *v.* have doubt or distrust; to have a suspicion or inkling of someone or something **suspect** *n.*

sus-pend *v.* bar from a privilege for a certain time, as a means of punishment; to hang so as to allow free movement

sus-pense *n.* feeling of being insecure or undecided, resulting from uncertainty

sus-pi-cion *n.* instance of suspecting something wrong without proof

sus-tain *v.* hold up and keep from falling; to suffer or undergo an injury

su-ture *n.* stitching together or joining the edges of an incision or cut

swad-dle *v.* wrap closely, using a long strip of flannel or linen

swag-ger *v.* walk with a proud or conceited air

swap v. trade something for something in return

swarm n. large number of insects, as bees; a large group of persons or things swarm v., **swarmer** n.

swat v. hit something with a sharp blow

sway v. move or swing from right to left or side by side; to exert influence or control n. dominating power

swear v. make an affirmation under oath **swearer** n.

sweat v. excrete a salty moisture from the pores of the skin *Informal* work hard; to cause to sweat *Slang* being impatient; having anxiety

sweat gland n., *Anat.* one of the tubular glands that secrete sweat externally through pores

sweep v. touch very lightly; to remove or clear away with a brush, broom, etc.; to move with an even action

sweet adj. having a sugary, agreeable flavor; arousing pleasant emotions; a beloved or dear person

swell v. increase in size or bulk; to grow in volume

swel-ter v. suffer from extreme heat

swerve v. turn aside from the regular course

swift adj. moving with great speed; accomplished or occurring quickly **swiftly** adv., **swiftness** n.

swim v. move oneself through water by moving parts of the body, as arms, head, and legs

swin-dle v. cheat out of property or money; to practice fraud **swindler** n.

swine n., pl. swine hoofed mammal with a snout, related to pigs and hogs; a low, despicable person

swirl v. move with a whirling, rotating motion swirl n.

swiv-el n. coupling device, ring, or pivot that allows attached parts to rotate or move freely **swivel** v.

sword n. weapon with a long, pointed cutting blade

syl-la-ble n., *Phonet.* word or part of one that consists of a single vocal impulse, usually consisting of one or more vowels or consonants

sym-bol n. something that stands for or represents something else symbolical adj.

sym-me-try n., pl. -tries. balance in form, size, and position of parts that are on two sides of an axis

sym-pa-thet-ic adj. having or showing kindness or sympathy for others

symathize v.

sym-pa-thy n., pl. -thies. mutual understanding or affection during a time of sadness or loss

sym-pho-ny n., pl. -nies. large orchestra with wind, percussion and string sections

symp-tom n. sign of change in a body's functions or appearance symptomatic adj.

syn-a-gogue n. place for Jewish worship and prayer

syn-chro-nize v. operate or take place at the same time

syn-di-cate n. organization set up to carry out business transactions

syn-drome n. set of concurrent symptoms that indicate or characterize a disorder or disease

syn-o-nym n. word that means the same or nearly the same as another synonymous adj.

syn-op-sis n., pl. -ses. shortened statement or narrative

syn-tax n. way in which words are put together or arranged to form sentences and phrases

syn-the-sis n. the combination of elements or parts to form a whole synthesist n.

syn-the-size v. to produce or combine by synthesis

syn-the-siz-er n. electronic equipment used to produce and control sound

syn-ton-ic adj. adaptive and normally responsive to the interpersonal or social environment syntonically adv.

syph-i-lis n. infectious venereal disease transmissible by direct contact and usually progressing in severity syphilitic adj.

syph-i-lol-o-gy n. a branch medicine dealing with syphilis

sy-ringe n. medical instrument used to inject or draw fluids

syr-up n. sticky, thick, sweet liquid, used as a topping for food

sys-tal-ic adj. to be marked by regular dilatation and contraction

sys-tem n. method or way of doing something **systemless** adj.

sys-to-le n., *Physiol.* regular rhythmic contraction of the heart that pumps blood through the aorta and pulmonary artery **systolic** adj.

sy-zy-gial adj. to be pertaining to syzygy

syz-y-gy n. a configuration of three celestial bodies in one gravitational system such as the moon, the sun, and earth when an eclipse is taking place

T, t The twentieth letter of the English alphabet.

tab *n.* strip, flap, or small loop that projects from something *slang* bill or total, as for a meal

tab-a-nid *n.* member of large bloodsucking insects such as the horse fly

tab-ard *n.* a type of domestic cat that has a coat which is mottled and striped

tab-er-na-cle *n.* portable shelter or structure used by the Jews during their journey out of Egypt

ta-bes *nl* the wasting that comes with or is accompanying a chronic disease

ta-bes for-sa-lis *n.* disease of the spinal cord

ta-bla *n.* a type of drum which is usually used in pairs of different sizes in the Hindu music

tab-la-ture *n.* a tabular surface or structure

ta-ble *n.* article of furniture
v. put off something until another time

tab-leau *n.* a striking picture representation

table-cloth *n.* a type of covering that is placed on the top of tables for protection or for decoration

ta-ble-ful *n.* the amount that a table is able to accomodate

ta-ble--hop *v.* to go from one table to another in order to talk with one's friends such as in a restaurant

ta-ble-land *n.* braod flat land; a plateau

table salt *n.* the salt that is suitable for use in cooking and at the table for the food

table-spoon *n.* a unit of measure; a large spoon for serving food

table sugar *n.* a type of white sugar which is granulated and used in foods

tab-let *n.* pad used for writing

ta-ble talk *n.* the conversation which is informal and takes place at the dinner table

ta-ble ten-nis *n.* a type of game that is like lawn tennis and is played on a table top with a plastic ball and wooden paddles

ta-ble-top *n.* a top of a table

ta-ble-ware *n.* the utensils such as forks, knives, and plates that are used on the table to eat with

ta-ble wine *n.* a type of wine that is wserved with the food and does not have more than 14 percent alcohol

tab-loid *n.* small newspaper

ta-boo *n.* custom or rule against doing, using, or mentioning something

tab-u-lar *adj.* pertaining to or arranged in a table or list

ta-chis-to-scope *n.* instrument for testing visual perception

ta-chom-e-ter *n.* instrument for measuring velocity and speed

tach-y-car-di-a *adj.* rapid heart movement or action

ta-chyg-ra-phy *n.* the art of shorthand; stenography

tac-it *adj.* understood; expressed or implied nonverbally; implicit

tac-i-turn *adj.* speaking infrequently taciturnity *n.*

tack-le *n.* equipment used for fishing or other sports or occupations tackled *v.*

tacky *adj.* slightly sticky; shabby; lacking style or good taste

ta-co *n., pl.* -cos type of Mexican or Spanish food made of a tortilla

tact *n.* having the ability to avoid what would disturb or offend someone

tac-tic *n.* way or method of working toward a goal

tad *n.* small boy; an insignificant degree or amount

tae-ni-a-sis *n.* a sickness due to the presence of tapeworms

taf-fe-ta *n.* stiff, smooth fabric of rayon, nylon, or silk taffetized *adj.*

taff-rail *n.* rail around the stern of a boat or ship

taf-fy *n.* candy made from sugar, butter and flavoring

taf-fy pull *n.* an informal party where guest make and pull taffy

tag *n.* piece of plastic, metal, paper, or other material that is attached to something in order to identify it; children's game tagger *n.*

tag-board *n.* very sturdy cardboard used to make posters, and signs

tail *n.* posterior extremity, extending from the end or back of an animal Tails opposite side of a coin from heads

tai-lor *n.* one whose profession is making, mending, and altering clothing *v.* adapt for a specific purpose

taint *v.* spoil, contaminate, or pollute *n.* blemish or stain

take *v.* seize or capture; to get possession of; to move to a different place; to choose

talc *n.* soft, fine-grained, smooth mineral used in making talcum powder

tale *n.* story or recital of relating events that may or may not be true

tal-ent *n.* aptitude, or ability of a person talented *adj.*

talk *v.* communicate by words or speech;

to engage in chatter or gossip

tall *adj.* greater than average height; of a designated or specified height; imaginary, as a tall tale **tallness** *n.*

tal-low *n.* hard fat rendered from sheep or cattle, used to make candles, lubricants, and soap **tallow** *adj.*

tal-ly *n., pl.* **-ies** record or counting of money, amounts, or scores

tal-on *n.* long, curved claw found on birds or animals

tam-bou-rine *n.* percussion instrument made of a small drum with jingling metal disks around the rim

tame *adj.* not wild or ferocious; domesticated or manageable *v.* make docile or calm **tamely** *adv.*, **tamer, tameness** *n.*

tam-per *v.* change, meddle, or alter something; to use corrupt measures; to scheme **tamperproof** *adj.*, **tamperer** *n.*

tan-dem *n.* any arrangement that involves two or more things, animals, or persons arranged one behind the other

tang *n.* sharp, distinct taste, smell, or quality

tan-gent *n.* line that touches a curved line but does not intersect or cross it; a sudden change from one course to another **tangency** *n.*, **tangential** *adj.*

tan-ger-ine *n.* small citrus fruit

tan-gi-ble *adj.* capable of being appreciated or felt by the sense of touch **tangibly** *adv.*

tan-gle *v.* mix, twist, or unite in a confused manner making separation difficult **tangle, tanglement** *n.*

tank *n.* large container for holding or storing a gas or liquid **tankful** *n.*

tan-ta-lize *v.* tease or tempt by holding or keeping something just out of one's reach **tantalizer** *n.*

tan-ta-lum *n.* metallic element symbolized by Ta

tan-trum *n.* fit; an outburst or a rage of bad temper

tap *v.* strike repeatedly, usually while making a small noise; to strike or touch gently

tape *n.* narrow strip of woven fabric

ta-per *n.* very slender candle *v.* become gradually smaller or thinner at one end

tap-es-try *n., pl.* **-ies** thick fabric woven with designs and figures

tap-i-o-ca *n.* bead-like substance used for thickening and for puddings

taps *n. pl. Mil.* bugle call that signals lights out, also sounded at memorial and funeral services

tar-dy *adj.* late; not on time **tardily** *adv.*, **tardiness** *n.*

tar-get *n.* object marked to shoot at; an aim or goal

tar-iff *n.* duty or tax on merchandise coming into or going out of a country

tar-nish *v.* become discolored or dull; to lose luster; to spoil **tarnishable** *adj.*

tar-ot *n.* set of 22 cards used for fortune-telling, each card showing a virtue, an elemental force, or a vice

tar-pau-lin *n.* sheet of waterproof canvas used as a protective covering

tar-ry *v.* linger, or delay

tart *adj.* sharp; sour; cutting, biting in tone or meaning **tartly** *adv.*, **tartness** *n.*

task *n.* bit of work, usually assigned by another; a job

tas-sel *n.* ornamental decoration made from a bunch of string or thread

taste *n.* ability to sense or determine flavor in the mouth; a personal liking or dislike **tasteful, tasteless** *adj.*, **taster** *n.*

tat-tle *v.* reveal the secrets of another by gossiping

tattle-tale *n.* one who betrays secrets concerning others; a person, usually a child, who informs on others

tat-too *n.* permanent design or mark made on the skin by pricking and inserting an indelible dye **tattooer** *n.*

taught *v.* past tense of teach

taut *adj.* tight; emotionally strained **tautly** *adv.*, **tautness** *n.*

tau-tol-o-gy *n., pl.* **-ies** redundancy; a statement which is an unnecessary repetition of the same idea

tav-ern *n.* inn; an establishment or business licensed to sell alcoholic beverages **taverner** *n.*

tax *n.* payment imposed and collected from individuals or businesses by the government *v.* strain

tax--ex-empt *adj.* exempted from tax

tax-i *v.* move along the ground or water surface on its own power before taking off

taxi-cab *n.* vehicle for carrying passengers for money

tax-i-der-my *n.* art or profession of preparing, stuffing, and mounting animal skins **taxidermist** *n.*

tea *n.* small tree or bush which grows where the climate is very hot and damp; a drink made by steeping the dried leaves of this shrub in boiling water

teach v. communicate skill or knowledge; to give instruction
teaching n., teachable adj.

teach-er n. person who teaches; one who instructs

team n. two or more players on one side in a game; a group of people trained to work together; two or more animals harnessed to the same implement

tear v. become divided into pieces; to separate; to rip into parts or pieces

tear n. fluid secreted by the eye to moisten and cleanse v. to cry teary adj.

tease v. make fun of; to bother; to annoy

tech-ne-tium n. metallic element symbolized by Tc.

tech-ni-cal adj. expert; derived or relating to technique; related to industry or mechanics technically adv.

tech-nique n. technical procedure or method of doing something

tech-nol-o-gy n., pl. -ies application of scientific knowledge to serve man in industry, commerce, medicine and other fields

te-di-ous adj. boring; taking a long time tediously adv.

teem v. swarm or crowd; to abound; to be full of

teens pl., n. ages between 13 and 19; the years of one's life between 13 and 19

teeth pl., n. plural of tooth

tel-e-cast n. television broadcast telecast v.

tel-e-gram n. message sent or received by telegraph

tel-e-graph n. system for communicating; a transmission sent by wire or radio

te-lep-a-thy n. communication by means of mental processes rather than ordinary means telepathic adj., telepathist n.

tel-e-phone n. system or device for transmitting conversations by wire

tel-e-pho-to adj. relating to a camera lens which produces a large image of a distant object telephotograph n.

tel-e-scope n. instrument which contains a lens system which makes distant objects appear larger and nearer telescopic adj.

tel-e-thon n. long telecast used to raise money for a worthy cause

tel-ex n. teletype communications by means of automatic exchanges

tell v. relate or describe; to command or order

tem-per n. state of one's feelings temperable adj.

tem-per-a-ment n. personality; a charac-

teristic way of thinking, reacting temperamental adj.

tem-per-ance n. moderation; restraint from drinking alcoholic beverages

tem-per-ate adj. avoiding extremes; moderate temperately adv.

tem-per-a-ture n. measure of heat or cold in relation to the body or environment; an elevation in body temperature above the normal 98.6

tem-pest n. severe storm, with snow, hail, rain, or sleet

tem-ple n. place of worship

tem-po n., pl. -pos or -pi Mus. rate of speed at which a musical composition is to be played

tem-po-rar-y adj. lasting for a limited amount of time

tempt n. encourage or draw into a foolish or wrong course of action

te-na-cious adj. persistent; stubborn tenaciously adv., tenaciousness n.

ten-ant n. person who pays rent to occupy another's property -able adj.

Ten Commandments n. ten rules of moral behavior which were given to Moses by God

tend v. to be inclined or disposed; to look after

ten-den-cy n., pl. -ies disposition to act or behave in a particular way

ten-der adj. fragile; soft; not hard or tough; painful or sore when touched

ten-don n. band of tough, fibrous tissues that connect a muscle and bone

ten-nis n. sport played with a ball and racket by 2 or 4 people

ten-or n. adult male singing voice, above a baritone

tense adj. taut or stretched tightly; nervous tense v.

ten-sion n. condition of stretching or the state of being stretched tensionless adj.

tent n. portable shelter made by stretchin material over a supporting framework

ten-ta-cle n. long, unjointed, flexible body part that projects from certain invertebrates, as the octopus

ten-ta-tive adj. experimental; not definite tentatively adv.

ten-ure n. the right, state, or period of holding something, as an office or property -ed, -ial adj.

tep-id adj. lukewarm

ter-cen-ten-a-ry n., pl. -ries. time span of 300 years

term n. phrase or word; a limited time or duration

ter-mi-nal adj. of, forming, or located at

the end; final

ter-mi-nate v. bring to a con-clusion or end **termination** n.

ter-mite n. winged or wingless insect which lives in large colonies feeding on wood

ter-race n. open balcony or porch

ter-ra cot-ta n. hard, baked clay used in ceramic pottery

ter-rain n. surface of an area, as land

ter-ra-pin n. edible turtle of North America

ter-res-tri-al adj. something earthly; not heavenly

ter-ri-ble adj. causing fear or terror; intense; extreme; horrid **terribly** adv., **terriblness** n.

ter-rif-ic adj. terrifying *Informal* excellent; causing amazement **terrifically** adv.

ter-ri-fy v. fill with fear or terror; to frighten; to menace **terrified, terrifying** adj.

ter-ri-to-ry n., pl. -ies area, usually of great size, which is controlled by a particular government **territorial** adj.

ter-ror n. extreme fear

ter-ror-ism n. the use of intimidation to attain one's goals or to advance one's cause

terse adj. brief; using as few words as possible without loss of force or clearness **tersely** adj., **terseness** n.

test n. examination to determine one's knowledge, skill, intelligence or other qualities **tester** n.

tes-ta-ment n. legal document which states how one's personal property is to be distributed upon his death **Testament** n. one of the two sections of the Bible **Testamentary** adj.

tes-tate adj. having left a valid will

tes-ti-fy v. give evidence while under oath **testifier** n.

tes-ti-mo-ni-al n. formal statement; a gift, dinner, reception, or other sign of appreciation given to a person as a token of esteem

tes-ti-mo-ny n., pl. -ies a solemn affirmation made under oath

tes-tis n., pl. **testes** sperm producing gland of the male

teth-er n. rope or chain which fastens an animal to something

text n. actual wording of an author's work; the main part of a book **textual** adj.

text-book n. book used by students to prepare their lessons

tex-tile n. cloth made by weaving; yarn or fiber for making cloth **textile** adj.

tex-ture n. look, surface, or feel of something

thal-li-um n. metallic element resembling lead, symbolized by Tl.

than conj. in comparison with or to something

thank v. express one's gratitude; to credit

thank-ful adj. feeling or showing gratitude

thanks pl., n. expression of one's gratitude

that adj., pl. those person or thing present or being mentioned

thaw v. change from a frozen state to a liquid or soft state; to melt **thaw** n.

the-a-tre or **the-a-ter** n. building adapted to present dramas, motion pictures, plays, or other performances

the-at-ri-cal adj. extravagant; designed for show, display, or effect **theatricals** n.

theft n. act or crime of stealing; larceny

their adj. & pron. possessive case of they

the-ism n. belief in the existence of God **theist** n., **theistic** adj.

them pron. objective case of they

theme n. topic or subject of something **thematic** adj.

them-selves pron. them or they; a form of the third person plural pronoun

then adv. at that time; soon or immediately adj. being or acting in or belonging to or at that time

thence adv. from that place

thenceforth, thence-for-ward adv. from that time on

the-oc-ra-cy n., pl. -ies government by God or by clergymen who think of themselves as representatives of God -tic adj., -tically adv.

the-ol-o-gy n., pl. -ies religious study of the nature of God, beliefs **theologian** n.

the-o-rize v. analyze theories

the-o-ry n., pl. -ies general principle or explanation which covers the known facts

ther-a-peu-tics n. medical treatment of disease **therapeutist** n.

ther-a-py n., pl. -ies treatment of certain diseases **therapist** n.

there adv. in, at, or about that place; toward, into, or to

thereabouts, thereafter, thereby, therefore, therefrom, adv.

ther-mal adj. having to do with or producing heat

ther-mo-plas-tic ad. pliable and soft when heated or warm but hard when cooled thermoplastic n.

ther-mo-stat n. device that automatically responds to temperature changes and activates equipment to adjust the temperature to correspond with the setting on the device -ic adj.

the-sau-rus n., pl. -ruses or -ri book which contains synonyms and antonyms

these pron. plural of this

the-sis n., pl. -ses formal argument or idea; a paper written by a student that develops an idea

they pron. two or more beings just mentioned

they'd contr. they had

they'll contr. they will

they're contr. they are

they've contr. they have

thick adj. having a heavy or dense consistency

thief n., pl. thieves person who steals

thieve v. take by theft thievery n.

thigh n. part of the leg between the hip and the knee of man

thin adj. having very little depth or extent from one side or surface to the other; not fat; slender thinly adv.

thing n. something not recognized or named; an idea, or conception

things one's belongings

think v. exercise thought; to use the mind thinkable adj.

third n. next to the second in time or place; the last in a series of three

thirst n. uncomfortably dry feeling in the throat and mouth; a desire for liquids

this pron., pl. these person or thing that is near, present, or just mentioned

this-tle n. prickly plant usually producing a purplish or yellowish flower

thith-er adv. to that place; there

thong n. narrow strip of leather used for binding

tho-rax n., pl. -raxes or -races section or part of the human body between the neck and abdomen

tho-ri-um n. radioactive metallic element symbolized by Th.

thorn n. sharp, pointed, woody projection on a plant stem thorny adj.

thor-ough adj. complete; intensive thoroughly adv.

thor-ough-bred adj. being of a pure breed of stock

thor-ough-fare n. public highway, road or street

those adj. & pron. plural of that

though adv. nevertheless; in spite of

thought n. process, act, or power of thinking; an idea
thoughtful, thoughtless adj.

thrash v. to beat or strike with a whip; to move violently about; to defeat
thrasher n.

threat n. expression or warning of intent to do harm

thresh v. to separate seed from a harvested plant mechanically

thresh-old n. horizontal piece of wood or other material which forms a doorsill

threw v. past tense of throw

thrice adv. three times

thrift n. careful use of money and other resources

thrill n. feeling of sudden intense excitement, fear, or joy
thrilling adj., thrillingly adv.

thrive v. to prosper; to be healthy; to do well in a position

throat n. front section or part of the neck containing passages for food and air

throb v. to beat, move, or vibrate in a pulsating way

throm-bo-sis n., pl. -ses development of a blood clot in a blood vessel or in the heart cavity

throng n. large group or crowd v. to crowd around or into

throt-tle n. valve which controls the flow of fuel to an engine

through prep. from the beginning to the end

through-out prep., adv. in every place; everywhere; at all times

throw v. to toss or fling through the air with a motion of the arm

thru prep., adv. & adj. through

thrush n. small songbird having a brownish upper body and spotted breast

thrust v. to push; to shove with sudden or vigorous force

thru-way or throughway n. major highway; an expressway

thud n. dull thumping sound

thug n. tough or violent gangster
thuggish adj.

thumb n. short first digit of the hand

thump n. blow with something blunt or heavy

thun-der n. loud explosive sound made as air is suddenly expanded by heat and then quickly contracted again

thus adv. in this or that way

thwack v. strike hard, using something flat

thwart *v.* prevent from happening

thy *adj.* pertaining to oneself

thyme *n.* an aromatic mint herb whose leaves are used in cooking

thy-roid *adj. Anat.* pertaining to the thyroid gland

thy-rox-ine *n.* hormone secreted by the thyroid gland

ti-ar-a *n.* bejeweled crown

tick *n.* one of a series of rhythmical tapping sounds made by a clock; a small bloodsucking parasite

tick-et *n.* printed slip of paper or cardboard allowing its holder to enter a specified event or to enjoy a privilege

tick-le *v.* to stroke lightly so as to cause laughter; to amuse or delight -ler *n.*

tid-bit *n.* choice bit of food, news, or gossip

tide *n.* rise and fall of the surface level of the ocean

tid-ings *pl., n.* news; information about events

ti-dy *adj.* well arranged; neat; orderly tidiness *n.*

tie *v.* to secure or bind with a rope or other similar material; to make a bow or knot in; to match an opponent's score

tier *n.* layer or row placed one above the other tiered *adj.*

ti-ger *n.* large carnivorous cat having tawny fur with black stripes

tiger-eye *n.* yellow-brown gemstone

tight *adj.* set closely together; bound or securely firm; not loose *adv.* firmly

tight-en *v.* to become or make tighter tightener *n.*

tights *pl., n.* skintight stretchable garment

till *prep. & conj.* until; unless or before *v.* to cultivate; to plow.

till-er *n.* machine or person that tills land

tilt *v.* to tip, as by raising one end

tim-ber *n.* wood prepared for building

timber line *n.* height on a mountain beyond which trees cannot grow

time *n.* continuous period measured by clocks, watches, and calendars *adj.* of or pertaining to time

tim-id *adj.* shy

tin *n.* white, soft, malleable me-tallic element, symbolized by Sn.

tinc-ture *n.* tinge of color; an alcohol solution of some medicinal substance

tin-der *n.* readily combustible substance or material

tine *n.* narrow pointed spike or prong,

as of a fork or antler

tinge *v.* to impart a faint trace of color *n.* trace of color

tin-gle *v.* to feel a stinging or prickling sensation

tin-kle *v.* to produce a slight, sharp series of metallic ringing sounds

tin-ny *adj.* pertaining to or composed of tin

tin-sel *n.* thin strips of glittering material used for decorations

tint *n.* slight amount or trace of color *v.* to color

ti-ny *adj.* minute; very small

tip-ple *v.* drink an alcoholic beverage to excess

tip-sy *adj.* partially intoxicated

ti-rade *n.* long, violent speech

tire *v.* become or make weary *n.* outer covering for a wheel, usually made of rubber, serving to absorb shock and to provide traction

tis-sue *n., Biol.* similar cells and their products developed by plants and animals

ti-ta-ni-um *n.* metallic element symbolized by Ti.

tithe *n.* income given voluntarily for the support of a church tithe *v.*, tither *n.*

tit-il-late *v.* excite or stimulate in a pleasurable way

ti-tle *n.* identifying name of a book, poem, play, or other creative work; a name or mark of distinction indicating a rank or an office

to *prep.* toward, opposite or near; in contact with; as far as; used as a function word indicating an action, movement, or condition suggestive of movement; indicating correspondence, dissimilarity, similarity, or proportion

toad *n.* tailless amphibian

toaster *n.* device for toasting bread

to-bac-co *n.* plant widely cultivated for its leaves

to-bog-gan *n.* long sled-like vehicle without runners

to-day *adv.* on or during the present day

tod-dle *v.* walk unsteadily

toddler *n.* small child

tod-dy *n., pl.* -ies drink made with hot water, sugar, spices, and liquor

toe *n.* one of the extensions from the front part of a foot; the part of a stocking, boot or shoe

tof-fee *n.* chewy candy made of butter and brown sugar

to-geth-er *adv.* in or into one group, mass, or body; regarded jointly

toil v. to labor very hard and continuously **toilsome** adj.

toi-let n. porcelain apparatus with a flushing device, used as a means of disposing body wastes

toi-lette n. act of washing, dressing, or grooming oneself

tol-er-ate v. to put up with; to endure; to suffer

toll n. fixed charge for travel across a bridge or along a road v. to sound a bell in repeated single, slow tones

tom n. male turkey or cat

tom-a-hawk n. ax used as a weapon or tool by North American Indians

to-ma-to n., pl. -toes garden plant cultivated for its edible fruit; the fruit of such a plant

tomb n. vault for burying the dead; a grave

tomb-stone n. stone used to mark a grave

to-mor-row n. day after the present day

ton n. measurement of weight equal to 2,000 pounds

tone n. vocal or musical sound that has a distinct pitch v. to change or soften the color

tongs pl., n. implement with two long arms joined at one end

tongue n. muscular organ attached to the floor of the mouth, used in tasting, chewing, and speaking

ton-ic n. medicine or other agent used to restore health

to-night n. this night; the night that is coming

ton-sil n. one of a pair of tissue similar to lymph nodes, found on either side of the throat

ton-sil-lec-to-my n. surgical re-moval of tonsils

too adv. also; as well; more than is needed

tool n. implement used to perform a task **tooling** n.

tooth n., pl. **teeth** one of the hard, white structures rooted in the jaw and used for chewing and biting; the small, notched, projecting part of any object, such as a gear, comb or saw
toothed, toothless adj.

top n. highest part or surface of anything; a covering or lid; the highest degree

to-paz n. gemstone

top-coat n. outer coat

top-ic n. subject discussed in an essay, thesis, speech or other discourse; the theme

top-most adj. uppermost

to-pog-ra-phy n., pl. -ies detailed description of a region or place

top-ple v. to fall; to overturn

To-rah n. body of law and wisdom contained in Jewish Scripture and oral tradition; a parchment scroll that contains the first five books of the Old Testament

torch n. stick of resinous wood which is burned to give light Slang to set fire to

tor-ment n. extreme mental anguish or physical pain v. to cause terrible pain; to pester, harass, or annoy
-ingly adv., tormentor n.

tor-na-do n., pl. -does or -dos whirling, violent windstorm accompanied by a funnel-shaped cloud that travels a narrow path over land

tor-pe-do n., pl. -oes large, selfpropelled, underwater missile launched from a ship, containing an explosive charge

tor-pid adj. having lost the power of motion or feeling; dormant
torpidity n., torpidly adv.

tor-rent n. swift, violent stream
torrential adj.

tor-rid adj. parched and dried by the heat torridly adv.

tor-sion n. act or result of twisting torsional adj.

tor-so n., pl. -sos or -si trunk of the human body

tort n., Law wrongful act requiring compensation for damages

tor-toise n. turtle that lives on the land

tor-tu-ous adj. marked by repeated bends, turns, or twists; devious tortuousness n.

tor-ture n. infliction of intense pain as punishment

toss v. fling or throw about continuously; to throw up in the air n. a throw

tot n. young child; a toddler

to-tal n. whole amount or sum; the entire quantity
adj. absolute; complete

to-tal-i-tar-i-an adj. characteristic of a government controlled completely by one party

tote v. carry something on one's arm or back

to-tem n. animal or plant regarded as having a close relationship to some family clan or group

tot-ter v. walk unsteadily

tou-can n. brightly colored tropical bird having a very large thin bill

touch *v.* allow a part of the body, as the hands, to feel or come into contact with; join; to come next to; to have an effect on; to move emotionally **touchable** *adj.*

tough *adj.* resilient and strong enough to withstand great strain without breaking or tearing; difficult to cut or chew *n.* unruly person; a thug **toughness** *n.*

tou-pee *n.* wig worn to cover a bald spot on one's head

tour *n.* trip with visits to points of interest; a journey **tourism, tourist** *n.*

tour-na-ment *n.* contest involving a number of competitors for a title or championship

tour-ni-quet *n.* device used to temporarily stop the flow of blood through an artery

tou-sle *v.* to mess up

tout *v.* to solicit customers

tow *v.* drag or pull, as by a chain or rope

to-ward or **towards** *prep.* in the direction of; just before; somewhat before; regarding

tow-el *n.* absorbent piece of cloth used for drying or wiping

tow-er *n.* very tall building or structure; a skyscraper **towering** *adj.*

town *n.* collection of houses and other buildings larger than a village and smaller than a city

tox-e-mi-a *n., Pathol.* blood poisoning; a condition in which the blood contains toxins

tox-ic *adj.* relating to a toxin; destructive, deadly, or harmful

tox-in *n.* poisonous substance produced by chemical changes in plant and animal tissue

toy *n.* object designed for the enjoyment of children; a small trinket; a bauble

trace *n.* visible mark or sign of a thing, person, or event; something left by some past agent or event

track *n.* mark, as a footprint, left by the passage of anything; a regular course; a set of rails on which a train runs; a circular or oval course for racing

tract *n.* extended area, as a stretch of land

trac-tor *n.* diesel or gasoline-powered vehicle used in farming

tractor trailer *n.* large truck having a cab and no body

trade *n.* business or occupation; skilled labor; a craft; an instance of selling or buying; a swap **trader** *n.*

trade-mark *n.* brand name which is legally the possession of one company and cannot be used by another

tra-di-tion *n.* customs passed down from one generation to another **-al** *adj.*

tra-duce *v.* to betray

traf-fic *n.* passage or movement of vehicles; trade, buying and selling

trag-e-dy *n., pl.* **-ies** extremely sad or fatal event or course of events

trail *v.* to draw, drag, or stream along behind; to follow in the tracks of

trail-er *n.* one who trails; a large vehicle that transports objects and is pulled by another vehicle

trait *n.* quality or distinguishing feature, such as one's character

trai-tor *n.* person who betrays his country

tra-jec-to-ry *n., pl.* **-ies** curved line or path of a moving object

tram-mel *n.* long, large net used to catch birds or fish

tramp *v.* to plod or walk with a heavy step

tram-ple *v.* to tread heavily; to stomp; to inflict injury, pain **trampler** *n.*

tram-po-line *n.* canvas device on which an athlete or acrobat may perform

trance *n.* stupor, daze, mental state, or condition, such as produced by drugs or hypnosis

tran-quil *adj.* very calm, quiet

trans-act *v.* to perform, carry out, conduct, or manage business in some way **transaction, transactor** *n.*

tran-scend *v.* to pass beyond; to exceed; to surpass

tran-scribe *v.* to make copies of something; to adopt or arrange

tran-script *n.* written copy

trans-cription *n.* process or act of transcribing

trans-fer *v.* remove, shift, or carry from one position to another **transferable** *adj.*

trans-fig-ure *v.* change the outward appearance or form **-ation** *n.*

trans-fix *v.* to pierce; to hold motionless, as with terror, awe or amazement **transfixion** *n.*

trans-form *v.* change or alter completely in nature, form or function **transformation**

trans-fuse *v.* transfer liquid by pouring from one place to another **transfusion**

trans-gress *v.* to go beyond the limit or boundaries

tran-sient *adj.* not staying or lasting very long; moving from one location to another **transiently** *adv.*

tran-sit *n.* passage or travel from one point to another

trans-late *v.* change from one language to another while retaining the original meaning translation, translator *n.*

trans-lu-cent *adj.* diffusing and admitting light but not allowing a clear view of the object

trans-mis-sion *n.* act or state of transmitting *Mech.* gears and associated parts of an engine which transmit power to the driving wheels of an automobile or other vehicle

trans-mit *v.* dispatch or convey from one thing, person, or place to another

trans-mute *v.* change in nature, kind, or substance

tran-som *n.* small, hinged window over a doorway

trans-par-ent *adj.* admitting light so that images and objects can be clearly viewed; obvious transparency *n.*

tran-spire *v.* to happen; to take place transpiration *n.*

trans-plant *v.* remove a living plant from where it is growing and plant it in another place; to remove a body organ from one person and implant it in the body of another, as a kidney transplant

trans-port *v.* carry or move from one place to another

trans-pose *v.* reverse the place or order of

trans-sex-u-al *n.* person whose sex has been changed surgically

trap *n.* device for holding or catching animals; anything which deliberately catches or stops people or things *v.* catch in a trap

tra-peze *n.* short horizontal bar suspended by two ropes, used for acrobatic exercise or stunts

trau-ma *n., pl.* -mas *or* -mata severe wound caused by a sudden physical injury; an emotional shock causing lasting and substantial damage to a person's psychological development

tra-vail *n.* strenuous mental or physical exertion

trav-el *v.* journey or move from one place to another

tra-verse *v.* pass over, across, or through

trawl *n.* strong fishing net which is dragged through water

tray *n.* flat container having a low rim, used for carrying, holding, or displaying something

treach-er-ous *adj.* disloyal; deceptive treachery *n.*

tread *v.* to walk along, on, or over; to trample

trea-son *n.* violation of one's allegiance to a sovereign or country, as giving or selling state secrets to another country or attempting to overthrow the government

treas-ure *n.* hidden riches; something regarded as valuable

treas-ur-y *n., pl.* -ies place where public or private funds are kept

treat *v.* behave or act toward; regard in a given manner; provide entertainment or food for another at one's own expense or cost

treat-ment *n.* manner or act of treating; medical care

tre-foil *n.* any of various plants having three leaflets with red, purple, yellow, or pink flowers

trek *v.* make a slow and arduous journey trekker *n.*

trel-lis *n.* latticework frame used for supporting vines

trem-ble *v.* shake involuntarily, as with fear or from cold

trembler *n.*, trembly *adj.*

tre-men-dous *adj.* extremely huge, large, or vast *Slang* wonderful

trem-or *n.* quick, shaking movement; any continued and involuntary trembling or quavering of the body

trench *n.* ditch; long, narrow excavation in the ground

trend *n.* general inclination, direction, or course; a fad

tres-pass *v.* infringe upon another's property

tres-tle *n.* bar or beam supported by four legs

tri-al *n.* in law, the examination and hearing of a case before a court of law

tri-an-gle *n., Geom.* plane figure bounded by three sides and having three angles triangular *adj.*

tribe *n.* group of people composed of several villages, districts, or other groups which share a common language, culture, and name

trib-u-la-tion *n.* great distress or suffering

trib-un-al *n.* decision making body

trib-ute *n.* action of respect or gratitude to someone

tri-ceps *n., Anat.* large muscle at the back of the upper arm

trick *n.* action meant to fool, as a scheme; a prank; a feat of magic tricky *adj.*

trick-er-y *n.* deception

trick-le v. flow in droplets or a small stream trickle n.

tri-col-or n. French color in the flag tricolored adj.

tri-cy-cle n. small vehicle having three wheels, propelled by pedals

tri-dent n. long spear with three prongs, used as a weapon

tried adj. tested and proven reliable or useful

tri-en-ni-al adj. happening every third year; lasting for a time period of three years

tri-fle n. something of little value or importance; a dessert made with cake, jelly, wine, and custard

trig-ger n. lever pulled to fire a gun; a device used to release or start an action v. to start

trim v. clip or cut off small amounts in order to make neater; to decorate adj. neat trim n.

tri-ni-tro-tol-u-ene n. very powerful explosive, abbreviated as TNT

trin-ket n. small piece of jewelry

tri-o n. set or group of three

trip n. travel from one place to another; a journey; a loss of balance

tripe n. stomach lining of oxen or similar animals, used as food

trip-le adj. having three parts

trip-let n. one of three born at the same time

tri-pod n. three-legged stand

trite adj. used too often; common

tri-umph v. be victorious n. victory triumphantly adv.

triv-i-al adj. insignificant; of little value or importance

trol-ley n. streetcar powered by electricity from overhead lines

tro-phy n., pl. -ies prize or object, such as a plaque, awarded to someone for his success, victory, or achievement

tro-po-sphere n. lowest atmosphere between the earth's surface and the stratosphere

troth n. good faith; the act of pledging one's fidelity

trou-ble n. danger; affliction; need; distress; an effort v. bother; to worry; to be bothered troubler n.

trough n. long, narrow, shallow container, especially one that holds food or water for animals

trounce v. whip or beat

troupe n. group, especially of the performing arts

trou-sers pl., n. outer garment that covers the body from the waist down

trous-seau n. wardrobe, linens, and other similar articles of a bride

tru-ant n. person who is absent from school without permission truancy n.

truce n. agreement to stop fighting; a cease fire

truck n. automotive vehicle used to carry heavy loads; any of various devices with wheels designed to move heavy loads trucker n.

trudge v. walk heavily and wearily; plod

true adj. in accordance with reality or fact; not false; real; loyal; faithful

trunk n. main part of a tree; the human body, excluding the head, arms and legs; a sturdy box for packing

truss v. fasten or tie securely Med. support or device worn to keep a hernia in place

trust n. confidence or faith in a person or thing

trust-y adj. reliable

truth n., pl. truths facts corresponding with actual events or happenings; sincerity or honesty

truthful adj., truthfully adv.

try v. make an attempt; to make an effort; to strain; to hear or conduct a trial; to place on trial trying adj.

tryst n. meeting between lovers; a prearranged meeting

tsu-na-mi n. extensive and destructive ocean wave caused by an underwater earthquake

tub n. round, low, flat-bottomed, vessel with handles on the side

tu-ba n. large, brass wind instrument having a low range

tu-ber-cu-lo-sis n. contagious lung disease of humans and animals caused by microorganisms

tuck n. flattened fold of material, usually stitched in place

tuft n. small cluster of feathers, threads, hair, or other material fastened or growing closely together

tug v. strain and pull vigorously n. hard pull

tu-i-tion n. payment for instruction, as at a private school or college

tu-lip n. bulb-bearing plant, having upright cup-like blossoms.

tum-ble v. fall or cause to fall; to perform acrobatic rolls, somersaults, and similar maneuvers

tum-ble-down adj. ramshackle; in need of repair

tum-brel n. cart which can discharge its load by tilting

tu-mor n., Pathol. swelling on or in any

part of the body; an abnormal growth which may be malignant or benign

tu-mult *n.* confusion and noise of a crowd; a riot

tu-na *n.*, *pl.* **-na** *or* **-nas** any of several large marine food fish

tun-dra *n.* treeless area in the arctic regions having a subsoil which is permanently frozen

tune *n.* melody which is simple and easy to remember; agreement

tung-sten *n.* element also known as wolfram, symbolized by W.

tu-nic *n.* loose garment extending to the knees, worn by ancient Romans and Greeks

tun-nel *n.* underground or underwater passageway

tur-ban *n.* Moslem headdress that consists of a long scarf wound around the head

tur-bine *n.* motor having one or more rotary units mounted on a shaft, which are turned by the force of gas or a liquid

tur-bu-lent *adj.* marked by a violent disturbance

tu-reen *n.* large dish used to serve soup or stew

turf *n.* layer of earth with its dense growth of grass and matted roots

tur-moil *n.* state of confusion or commotion

turn *v.* to move or cause to move around a center point; to revolve or rotate **turn to** seek comfort or advice from; to open a book to a certain page **turn down** refuse or deny **turn in** go to bed **turn off** be or cause to be disgusted with something **in turn** one after another **turn over** to ponder; to think about; to give up or transfer to another **turn on** *v.*, *Slang* cause a person to experience with intense stimulation, as by means of LSD or marijuana

turn-key *n.* person in charge of the keys at a prison

turn-over *n.* process or act of turning over; an upset; a change or reversal

tur-pen-tine *n.* thick sap of certain pine trees; a clear liquid manufactured from this sap

tusk *n.* long, curved tooth, as of an elephant or walrus

tus-sle *n.* hard fight or struggle with a problem or person **tussle** *v.*

tu-tor *n.* person who teaches another person privately

tu-tu *n.* very short ballet skirt

tux-e-do *n.* semiformal dress suit worn by men

tweak *v.* pinch and twist sharply

twice *adv.* double; two times

twid-dle *v.* to turn or twirl in an aimless way

twig *n.* small branch which grows from a larger branch on a tree

twi-light *n.* soft light of the sky between sunset and darkness

twilight sleep *n.* a state of feeling in which pain is dulled

twill *n.* weave that produces the parallel rib on the surface of a fabric

twin *n.* one of two persons born at the same time to the same mother; one of two similar persons or things

twine *v.* weave or twist together

twinge *n.* sudden, sharp pain

twin-kle *v.* gleam or shine with quick flashes; to sparkle

twirl *v.* to rotate or cause to turn around and around

twist-er *n.*, *Slang* tornado; a cyclone; one that twists

twit *v.* tease about a mistake

twitch *v.* move or cause to move with a jerky movement

twit-ter *v.* utter a series of chirping sounds; to chatter nervously

two-bits twenty-five cents

two-faced double-dealing

ty-coon *n.*, *Slang* business person of wealth and power

tyke *n.* small child

type *n.* class or group of persons or things

ty-phoid *n.*, *Path.* acute, infectious disease caused by germs in drink or food, resulting in high fever and intestional hemorrhaging

ty-phoon *n.* tropical hurricane

typ-i-cal *adj.* exhibiting the characteristics of a certain class or group **typically** *adv.*

typ-i-fy *v.* be characteristic or typical of **typification** *n.*

typ-ist *n.* operator of a type-writer

ty-po *n.*, *Slang* error in typewriting or in setting type; any printed error which was not the fault of the author

ty-ran-no-sau-rus *n.* large, flesh-eating dinosaur which walked on its hind legs

tyr-an-ny *n.* harsh, absolute, and unfair rule by a king or other ruler; complete control

tyr-an-nize *v.* rule or control completely

ty-rant *n.* absolute, unjust, or cruel ruler control unfairly

ty-ro *n.* a novice; a beginner

U, u The twenty-first letter of the English alphabet.

obi-qui-none *n.* the quinone which is able to function as an electron transfer agent in the Kreb's cycle

ubiq-ui-ty *n.* a presence in many places or locations at the same time

ud-der *n.* milk-producing organ pouch of some female animals, having two or more teats

ugh *interj.* used to express disgust or horror

ug-li-fy *v.* to make something ugly

ug-ly *adj.* offensive; unpleasant to look at

uh *interj.* to express hesitation.

u-ku-le-le *n.* small, four-stringed musical instrument

ul-cer *n.* festering, inflamed sore on a mucous membrane or on the skin that results in the destruction of the tissue

ul-na *n., Anat.* one of the two bones of the forearm

ul-ti-mate *adj.* final; ending; most extreme **ultimately** *adv.*

ul-ti-ma-tum *n., pl* **-tums, -ta** final demand, proposal, or choice

ultra- *prefix* beyond the scope, range, or limit of something

ul-tra-mod-ern *adj.* extremely advanced or modern in style

ul-tra-son-ic *adj.* relating to sound frequencies inaudible to humans

ul-tra-vi-o-let *adj.* producing radiation having wave-lengths just shorter than those of visible light and longer than those of X rays

um-bil-i-cal cord *n.* structure by which a fetus is attached to its mother, serving to supply food and dispose of waste

um-brel-la *n.* collapsible frame covered with plastic or cloth, held above the head as protection from sun or rain

um-pire *n.* in sports, the person who rules on plays in a game *v.* act as an umpire

ump-teen *adj., Slang* indefinitely large number

un- *prefix* reverse or opposite of an act; removal or release from

un-able *adj.* not having the mental capabilities

un-ac-com-pa-nied *adj.* alone; without a companion *Mus.* Solo

un-ac-count-a-ble *adj.* without an explanation; mysterious; not responsible

un-ac-cus-tomed *adj.* not used to or in the habit of; not ordinary

u-nan-i-mous *adj.* agreed to completely; based on the agreement of all

un-armed *adj.* lacking means for protection

un-as-sum-ing *adj.* modest and not showy

un-at-tach-ed *adj.* not engaged, going steady, or married

un-a-void-able *adj.* inevitable; unstoppable **-ly** *adv.*

un-a-ware *adj.* not realizing

un-bear-a-ble *adj.* not possible to endure; intolerable

un-be-com-ing *adj.* unattractive; not pleasing; not proper, polite or suitable for the situation

un-be-known *or* **unbeknownst** *adj.* not known; without one's knowledge

un-be-liev-able *adj.* incredible; hard to accept; not to be believed

un-called for *adj.* not necessary or needed; not requested

un-can-ny *adj.* strange, odd, or mysterious; exceptional

un-cer-tain *adj.* doubtful; not sure; not known; hard to predict

un-chang-ed *adj.* having nothing new or different

un-civ-i-lized *adj.* without culture or refinement; without an established cultural

un-cle *n.* brother of one's mother or father

un-clean *adj.* immoral; dirty; not decent

un-clothe *v.* uncover or undress

un-com-fort-a-ble *adj.* disturbed; not at ease physically or mentally

un-com-mon *adj.* rare; odd; unusual; extraordinary

un-com-pro-mis-ing *adj.* firm; unwilling to give in or to compromise

un-con-cern *n.* lack of interest; disinterest; indifference

un-con-di-tion-al *adj.* without conditions **unconditionally** *adv.*

un-con-scious *adj.* not mentally aware; done without thought; not on purpose

un-con-sti-tu-tion-al *adj.* contrary to the constitution or the basic laws of a state or country

un-couth *adj.* acting or speaking crudely, unrefined; clumsy or awkward

un-cov-er *v.* remove the cover from something; to disclose

un-de-cid-ed *adj.* unsettled; having made no firm decision; open to change

un-de-ni-able *adj.* not open to doubt or denial; not possible to contradict

un-der *prep.* below, in place or position; in a place lower than another; less in degree, number, or other quality; inferior in rank, quality, or character;

during the reign or period; in accordance with; less than the required amount; insufficient

under *prefix.* location beneath or below; lower in importance or rank

un-der-brush *n.* small bushes, vines, and plants that grow under tall trees

un-der-clothes *pl., n.* clothes worn next to the skin; underwear

un-der-de-vel-oped *adj.* not fully mature or grown; lacking modern communications and industry

un-der-foot *adj.* underneath or below the feet; being so close to one's feet as to be in the way

un-der-go *v.* to have the experience of; to be subjected to

un-der-grad-u-ate *n.* college or university student studying for a bachelor's degree

un-der-hand *adj.* done deceitfully and secretly underhandedly *adv.*

un-der-line *v.* to draw a line directly under something

un-der-mine *v.* to weaken; to make less strong

un-der-neath *adv.* beneath or below; on the under side; lower

un-der-pass *n.* road or walk that goes under another

un-der-priv-i-leged *adj.* deprived of economic and social advantages

un-der-rate *v.* rate or value below the true worth

un-der-score *v.* emphasize

un-der-sell *v.* sell for less than a competitor

un-der-side *n.* side or part on the bottom

un-der-stand *v.* comprehend; to realize

un-der-stand-a-ble *adj.* able to comprehend -ly *adv.*

un-der-state *v.* make too little of the actual situation -ment *n.*

un-der-stood *adj.* agreed upon by all

un-der-stud-y *v.* to learn another person's part or role in order to be able to replace him if necessary

un-der-take *v.* set about to do a task; to pledge oneself to a certain job; to attempt

un-der-tak-er *n.* person who prepares the dead for burial

un-der-tone *n.* low, quiet voice; a pale or subdued color visible through other colors

un-der-tow *n.* underwater current which runs in the opposite direction of the surface current

un-der-wa-ter *adj.* occurring, happening

or used beneath the surface of the water

un-der-write *v.* sign or write at the end of something; to finance; to assume a risk by means of insurance assume responsibility for; to undertake to pay a written pledge of money underwriter *n.*

un-de-sir-a-ble *adj.* offensive; not wanted undesirably *adv.*

un-do *v.* cancel; to reverse; to loosen or unfasten

un-done *adj.* not finished; unfastened; ruined

un-du-late *v.* to move from side to side with a flowing motion; to have a wavy shape undulation *n.*

un-dy-ing *adj.* without end

un-earth *v.* dig up from the earth; to find or discover

unearthly *adj.* strange; not from this world

un-eas-y *adj.* feeling or causing distress or discomfort; embarrassed

un-em-ployed *adj.* without a job; without work unemployment *n.*

un-e-qual *adj.* not even; not fair; not of the same size or time

un-e-ven *adj.* not equal; varying in consistency or form; not balanced

un-e-vent-ful *adj.* lacking in significance; calm

un-expect-ed *adj.* surprising; happening without warning -ly *adv.*

un-fail-ing *adj.* constant, unchanging

un-fair *adj.* not honest; marked by a lack of justice

un-faith-ful *adj.* breaking a promise or agreement; without loyalty

un-fa-mil-iar *adj.* not knowing; strange; foreign

unfavorable *adj.,* not desired; harmful; unpleasant

un-feel-ing *adj.* without sympathy; hardhearted; without sensation

un-fit *adj.* not suitable; not qualified; in poor body or mental health

un-fold *v.* open up the folds of and lay flat; to reveal gradually

un-fore-seen *adj.* not anticipated or expected

un-for-get-ta-ble *adj.* impossible or hard to forget; memorable

un-for-tu-nate *adj.* causing or having bad luck, damage, or harm

un-found-ed *adj.* not founded or based on fact; groundless; lacking a factual basis

un-friend-ly *adj.* showing a lack of kindness; not friendly

un-furl v. unroll or unfold; to open up or out

un-fur-nished adj. without furniture

un-god-ly adj. wicked; evil; lacking reverence for God **ungodliness** n.

un-grate-ful adj. not thankful; no appreciation

un-guent n. healing or soothing salve; ointment

un-happy adj. sad; without laughter or joy; not satisfied or pleased

un-heard adj. not heard; not listened to

un-heard--of adj. not known or done before; without precedent

un-hook v. release or undo from a hook

u-ni-corn n. mythical animal resembling a horse, with a horn in the center of its forehead

u-ni-cy-cle n. one wheeled vehicle with pedals

un-i-den-ti-fied flying object n. flying object that cannot be explained or identified

u-ni-form n. identical clothing worn by the members of a group to distinguish them from the general population **uniformly** adv.

u-ni-fy v. come together as one; to unite

un-in-hab-it-ed adj. not lived in; empty

un-in-ter-est-ed adj. having no interest or concern in; not interested

un-ion n. act of joining together of two or more groups or things; a group of countries or states joined under one government; a mar-riage; an organized body of employees who work together to upgrade their working conditions and wages **Union** The United States

u-nique adj. unlike any other; sole

u-ni-sex adj. adaptable and appropriate for both sexes

u-ni-son n. in music, the exact sameness of pitch, as of a tone

u-nit n. any one of several parts regarded as a whole; an exact quantity that is used as a standard of measurement; a special section

u-nite v. join or come together for a common purpose

United Nations n. international organization formed in 1945; comprised of nearly all the countries of the world whose purpose is to promote security, economic development, and peace

United States of America n. country bordering the Atlantic and Pacific Oceans, Mexico, and Canada

u-ni-ty n., pl. -ies fact or state of being one; accord; agreement; harmony

u-ni-valve n. mollusk having a one-piece shell, such as a snail

u-ni-ver-sal adj. having to do with the world or the universe in its entirety

u-ni-verse n. the world, stars, planets, space, and all that is contained

u-ni-ver-si-ty n., pl. -ies educational institution offering undergraduate and graduate degrees in a variety of academic areas

un-just adj. not fair; lacking justice or fairness

un-kempt adj. poorly groomed; messy

un-kind adj. harsh; lacking in sympathy, concern, or understanding

un-known adj. strange; unidentified; not known; not familiar

un-lead-ed adj. containing no lead

un-like prep. dissimilar; not alike; not equal in strength or quantity

un-lim-it-ed adj. having no boundaries or limitations

un-load v. take or remove the load; to unburden; to dispose or get rid of by selling in volume

un-lock v. open, release, or unfasten a lock; open with a key

un-loose v. loosen or undo; to release

un-luck-y adj. unfortunate; having bad luck; disappointing or unsuitable **unluckily** adv.

un-manned adj. designed to operate or be operated without a crew of people

un-men-tion-a-ble adj. improper or unsuitable

un-mis-tak-a-ble adj. very clear and evident; understood; obvious

un-mor-al adj. having no moral knowledge

un-nat-u-ral adj. abnormal or unusual; strange; artificial

un-nec-es-sar-y adj. not needed; not appropriate **unnecessarily** adv.

un-nerve v. frighten; to upset

un-num-bered adj. countless; not identified by number

un-oc-cu-pied adj. empty; not occupied

un-pack v. remove articles out of trunks, suitcases, or boxes

un-pleas-ant adj. not agreeable; not pleasant

un-pop-u-lar adj. not approved or liked

un-pre-dict-a-ble adj. not capable or being foretold; not reliable

un-pre-pared adj. not equipped or ready

un-pro-fes-sion-al adj. contrary to the standards of a profession; having no professional status

un-prof-it-a-ble adj. showing or giving no profit; serving no purpose

un-qual-i-fied *adj.* lacking the proper qualifications; unreserved

un-rav-el *v.* to separate threads; to solve; to clarify; to come apart

un-re-al *adj.* having no substance or reality

un-rea-son-a-ble *adj.* not according to reason; exceeding all reason-able limits

un-re-li-a-ble *adj.* unable to be trusted; not dependable

un-re-served *adj.* done or given without reserve; unlimited

un-re-strained *adj.* not held back, forced, or affected

un-ru-ly *adj.* disorderly; difficult to subdue or control

un-sat-is-fac-to-ry *adj.* unacceptable; not pleasing

un-screw *v.* to loosen or unfasten by removing screws from

un-scru-pu-lous *adj.* without morals, guiding principles, or rules

un-seat *v.* cause to lose one's seat; to force out of office

un-sel-fish *adj.* willing to share; thinking of another's well-being before one's own

un-set-tle *v.* cause to be upset or excited; to disturb

un-sheathe *v.* draw a sword from a sheath or other case

un-sight-ly *adj.* not pleasant to look at; ugly

un-skilled *adj.* having no skills or train-ing in a given kind of work

un-sound *adj.* having defects; not solidly made

un-speak-a-ble *adj.* of or relating to something which can not be expressed

un-sta-ble *adj.* not steady or firmly fixed; having the tendency to fluctuate or change

un-stead-y *adj.* not secure; unstable; variable

un-sub-stan-tial *adj.* lacking strength, weight, or solidity

un-suit-a-ble *adj.* unfitting; not suitable; not appropriate for a specific cir-cumstance

un-tan-gle *v.* free from snarls or en-tanglements

un-thank-ful *adj.* ungrateful

un-think-a-ble *adj.* unimaginable

un-ti-dy *adj.* messy; showing a lack of tidiness

un-tie *v.* unfasten or loosen; to free from a restraint or bond

un-til *prep.* up to the time of *conj.* to the time when; to the degree or place

un-time-ly *adj.* premature; before the expected time

un-told *adj.* not revealed; not told; inex-pressible; cannot be described

un-touch-a-ble *adj.* cannot be touched; incapable of being obtained or reached

un-true *adj.* not true; contrary to the truth; not faithful; disloyal

un-truth *n.* something which is not true **untruthful** *adj.*

un-used *adj.* not put to use; never having been used

un-u-su-al *adj.* not usual; uncommon **unusually** *adv.*

un-ut-ter-a-ble *adj.* incapable of being described or expressed; unpronounce-able

un-veil *v.* remove a veil from; to uncover; to reveal

un-war-y *adj.* not cautious or careful; careless

un-whole-some *adj.* unhealthy; morally corrupt or harmful

un-will-ing *adj.* reluctant; not willing

un-wind *v.* undo or reverse the winding of; to untangle

un-wise *adj.* lacking good judgment or common sense

un-wor-thy *adj.* not deserving; not be-coming or befitting; lacking merit or worth; shameful **-iness** *n.*

up *adv.* from a lower position to a higher one; on, in, or to a higher level, posi-tion, or place; to a greater degree or amount; in or into a specific action or an excited state, as they stirred up trouble; under consideration, as up for discussion; in a safe, protected place; totally, completely, as the building was burned up

up-beat *n., Mus.* relatively unaccented beat preceding the down beat *adj.* op-timistic; happy

up-bring-ing *n.* process of teaching and rearing a child

up-draft *n.* upward current of air

up-grade *v.* increase the grade, rank, or standard of

up-hill *adv.* up an incline *adj.* hard to accomplish; going up a hill or incline

up-hol-ster *v.* cover furniture with fabric covering

up-keep *n.* cost and work needed to keep something in good condition

up-on *prep.* on

up-per *adj.* higher in status, position or location *n.* the part of a shoe to which the sole is attached

up-per--class *adj.* economically or socially superior

up-right *adj.* having a vertical direction or position; honest *n.* something standing vertically

up-ris-ing *n.* revolt; a rebellion; an insurrection

up-roar *n.* confused, loud noise; a commotion

up-root *v.* detach completely by pulling up the roots

up-set *v.* capsize; to turn over; to throw into confusion or disorder; to overcome; to beat unexpectedly *adj.* capsized; overturned; distressed; troubled

up-stage *adj. & adv.* toward or at the back part of a stage

up-start *n.* one who has risen quickly to power or wealth

up-tight *adv.* nervous, or tense

up-ward *or* **upwards** *adv.* from a lower position to or toward a higher one

u-ra-ni-um *n.* hard, heavy, shiny metallic element that is radioactive

urge *v.* encourage, push, or drive; to recommend persistently and strongly

ur-gent *adj.* requiring immediate attention

urine *n.* in man and other mammals, the yellowish fluid waste produced by the kidneys

Us *pl., pron.* objective case of we; used as an indirect object, direct object

us-a-ble *or* **useable** *adj.* fit or capable of being used **usability** *n.,* **usably** *adv.*

us-age *n.* way or act of using something; the way words are used

use *v.* put into action; to employ for a special purpose; to employ on a regular basis; to exploit for one's own advantage

u-su-al *adj.* ordinary or common; regular; customary

usually *adv.,* **usualness** *n.*

u-surp *v.* take over by force without authority **usurpation,** **-er** *n.*

u-ten-sil *n.* tool, implement, or container

u-ter-us *n.* organ of female mammals33 within which young develop and grow before birth **uterine** *adj.*

u-til-i-ty *n., pl.* **-ies** state or quality of being useful; a company which offers a public service

u-til-ize *v.* make or put to use

ut-most *adj.* of the greatest amount or degree; most distant **utmost** *n.*

u-to-pi-a *n.* condition or place of perfection or complete harmony

u-vu-la *n.* fleshy projection which hangs above the back of the tongue

uvular *adj.*

V, v The twenty-second letter of the English alphabet.

va-cant *adj.* empty; not occupied

va-cate *v.* leave; to cease

va-ca-tion *n.* period of time away from work for pleasure, relaxation, or rest

vac-ci-nate *v.* inject with a vaccine so as to produce immunity to an infectious disease

vac-ci-na-tion *n.* inoculation with a vaccine

vac-cine *n.* solution of weakened or killed microorganisms, as bacteria or viruses, injected into the body to produce immunity to a disease

vac-u-um *n., pl.* **vacuums, -ua** space which is absolutely empty; a void

vag-a-bond *n.* homeless person who wanders from place to place

va-gar-y *n., pl.* **vagaries** eccentric or capricious action or idea

va-gi-na *n., pl.* **vaginas, -nae** *Anat.* canal or passage extending from the uterus to the external opening of the female reproductive system

va-gi-ni-tis *n.* inflammation of the vagina

va-grant *n.* roaming from one area to another without a job

vague *adj.* not clearly expressed; not sharp or definite **vaguely** *adv.*

vain *adj.* conceited; lacking worth or substance **vainly** *adv.*

val-ance *n.* decorative drapery across the top of a window

vale *n.* a valley

val-e-dic-to-ri-an *n.* student ranking highest in a graduating class

val-en-tine *n.* card or gift sent to one's sweetheart on Valentine's Day, February 14th

val-et *n.* man who takes care of another man's clothes and other personal needs; a hotel employee

val-iant *adj.* brave; exhibiting valor **valiance, valor** *n.*

val-id *adj.* founded on facts or truth *Law* binding; having legal force **validity**

val-ley *n., pl.* **valleys** low land between ranges of hills

val-or *n.* bravery **valorous** *adj.*

val-u-a-ble *adj.* of great value or importance **valuableless** *adj.*

val-ue *n.* quality or worth of something that makes it valuable; material worth

valve *n.* movable mechanism which opens and closes to control the flow of a substance through a pipe or other passageway

va-moose *v. Slang* leave in a hurry

vam-pire *n.* in folklore, a dead person

believed to rise from the grave at night to suck the blood of sleeping persons; a person who preys on others

vampire bat *n.* a tropical bat that feeds on the blood of living mammals.

van *n.* large closed wagon or truck

va-na-di-um *n.* metallic element symbolized by

van-dal-ism *n.* malicious defacement or destruction of private or public property

vane *n.* metal device that turns in the direction the wind is blowing

va-nil-la *n.* flavoring extract used in cooking and baking

van-ish *v.* disappear suddenly; to drop out of sight

van-i-ty *n., pl.,* vanities conceit; extreme pride in one's ability

van-tage *n.* superior position; an advantage

va-por *n.* moisture or smoke sus-pended in air, as mist or fog
vaporish, vaporous *adj.*

var-i-able *adj.* changeable; tending to vary; inconstant
variableness *n.,* variably *adv.*

var-i-ance *n.* state or act of varying; difference; conflict

var-i-a-tion *n.* result or process of varying; the degree or extent of varying

var-i-e-gat-ed *adj.* having marks of different colors variegate *v.*

va-ri-e-ty *n., pl.,* varieties state or character of being varied or various; a number of different kinds; an assortment

var-i-ous *adj.* of different kinds

var-mint *n., Slang* a troublesome animal; an obnoxious person

var-nish *n.* solution paint used to coat or cover a surface with a hard, transparent, shiny film

var-si-ty *n., pl.,* varsities best team representing a college, university, or school

var-y *v.* change; to make or become different; to be different

vas-cu-lar *adj., Biol.* having to do with vessels circulating fluids, as blood

va-sec-to-my *n., pl.* vasectomies method of male sterilization

vast *adj.* very large or great in size
vastly *adv.,* vastness *n.*

vault *n.* room for storage and safekeeping, as in a bank, usually made of steel; a burial chamber

veg-e-ta-ble *n.* plant, as the tomato, green beans, lettuce, raised for the edible part

veg-e-tar-i-an *n.* person whose diet is limited to vegetables

veg-e-ta-tion *n.* plants or plant life which grow from the soil

ve-hi-cle *n.* a motorized device for transporting goods, equipment, or passengers

veil *n.* a piece of transparent cloth worn on the head or face for concealment or protection

vein *n., Anat.* vessel which transports blood back to the heart after passing through the body vein *v.*

ve-lour *n.* soft velvet-like woven cloth

vel-vet *n.* fabric made of rayon, cotton, or silk

vend-er *or* vendor *n.* person who sells, as a peddler

ven-det-ta *n.* fight or feud between blood-related persons

ven-er-a-ble *adj.* meriting or worthy of respect by reason of dignity, position, or age

venereal disease *n.* contagious disease, as syphilis, or gonorrhea, which is typically acquired through sexual intercourse

ve-ne-tian blind *n.* window blind having thin, horizontal slats

ven-i-son *n.* edible flesh of a deer

ven-om *n.* poisonous substance secreted by some animals, as scorpions or snakes venomous *adj.*

ve-nous *adj.* of or relating to veins

vent *n.* means of escape or passage from a restricted area; an opening which allows the escape of vapor, heat, or gas

ven-ti-late *v.* expose to a flow of fresh air for refreshing, curing, or purifying purposes
ventilation, ventilator *n.*

ven-ture *n.* course of action involving risk, chance, or danger, especially a business investment

ven-ue *n.* place where a crime or other cause of legal action occurs; the locale of a gathering

verb *n.* part of speech which expresses action, existence, or occurrence

ver-bal *adj.* expressed in speech; expressed orally; not written; relating to or derived from a verb *n.* an adjective, noun or other word which is based on a verb and retains some characteristics of a verb verbally *adv.,* verbalize *v.*

ver-ba-tim *adv.* word for word

ver-be-na *n.* American garden plant

verge *n.* extreme edge or rim; margin; the point beyond which something begins

ver-min *n.* a destructive, annoying

animal which is harmful to one's health

ver-sa-tile *adj.* having the capabilities of doing many different things; having many functions or uses

verse *n.* writing that has a rhyme; poetry; a subdivision of a chapter of the Bible

ver-sion *n.* an account or description told from a particular point of view; a translation from another language, especially a translation of the Bible

ver-so *n., pl.* versos left-hand page

ver-sus *prep.* against; in contrast to; as an alternative of

ver-te-bra *n., pl.* vertebrae, vertebras one of the bony or cartilaginous segments making up the spinal column

ver-tex *n., pl.* vertexes, vertices highest or topmost point; the pointed top of a triangle

ver-ti-cal *adj.* in a straight up-and-down direction

ver-y *adv.* to a high or great degree; truly; absolutely; exactly

ves-per *n.* evening prayer service; a bell to call people to such a service

ves-sel *n.* hollow or concave utensil, as a bottle, kettle, container, or jar; a hollow craft designed for navigation on water

vest *n.* a sleeveless garment open or fastening in front, worn over a shirt

ves-tige *n.* trace or visible sign of something that no longer exists

vestigial *adj.*, **vestigially** *adj.*

ves-try *n., pl.* vestries room in a church used for meetings

vet *n., Slang* veterinarian; a veteran

vet-er-an *n.* person with a long record or experience in a certain field; one who has served in the military

vet-er-i-nar-i-an *n.* one who is trained and authorized to give medical treatment to animals

vet-er-i-nar-y *adj.* pertaining to the science and art of prevention and treatment of animals

ve-to- *n., pl.* vetoes power of a government executive, as the President or a governor, to reject a bill passed by the legislature

vex *v.* to bother or annoy

vi-a *prep.* by way of; by means of

vi-a-duct *n.* bridge, resting on a series of arches

vi-al *n.* small, closed container used especially for liquids

vi-brate *v.* move or make move back and forth or up and down

vi-car-i-ous *adj.* undergoind or serving in the place of someone or something else; experienced through sympathetic or imaginative participation in the experience of another

vice *n.* immoral habit or practice; evil conduct

vi-ce ver-sa *adv.* with the order or meaning of something reversed

vi-chy-ssoise *n.* a soup made from potatoes, chicken stock, and cream, flavored with leeks or onions and usually served cold

vi-cin-i-ty *n., pl.* -ies surrounding area or district; the state of being near in relationship or space

vi-cious *adj.* dangerously aggressive; having the quality of immorality

vic-tim *n.* person who is harmed or killed by another **victimize** *v.*

vic-tor *n.* person who conquers; the winner

vic-to-ri-ous *adj.* being the winner in a contest **victoriously** *adv.*

vic-to-ry *n., pl.* victories defeat of those on the opposite side

vid-e-o *adj.* being, related to, or used in the reception or transmission of television

vid-e-o disc *n.* disc containing recorded images and sounds

vid-e-o game *n.* computerized game displaying on a display screen

vid-e-o term-in-al *n. Computer Science* computer device having a cathoderay tube for displaying data on a screen

vie *v.* strive for superiority

view *n.* act of examining or seeing; a judgment or opinion

vig-il *n.* a watch with prayers kept on the night before a religious feast; a period of surveillance

vig-or *n.* energy or physical strength; intensity of effect or action

vile *adj.* morally disgusting, miserable, and unpleasant

vil-la *n.* a luxurious home in the country; a country estate

vil-lage *n.* incorporated settlement, usually smaller than a town

vil-lain *n.* evil or wicked person

vin-ai-grette *n.* a small ornamental bottle with a periorated top, used for holding an aromatic preparation such as smelling salts

vin-di-cate *v.* to clear of suspicion; to set free **vindication** *n.*

vin-dic-tive *adj.* showing or possessing a desire for revenge; spiteful

vine *n.* plant whose stem needs support as it climbs or clings to a surface

vin-e-gar *n.* a tart, sour liquid derived from cider or wine

vin-tage *n.* the grapes or wine produced from a particular district in one season

vi-nyl *n.* variety of shiny plastics, similar to leather, often used for clothing and for covering furniture

vi-o-la *n.* stringed instrument, slightly larger and deeper in tone than a violin

vi-o-late *v.* break the law or a rule; to disrupt or disturb a person's privacy violation *n.*

vi-o-lence *n.* physical force or activity used to cause harm, damage, or abuse

vi-o-let *n.* small, low-growing plant with blue, purple, or white flowers; a purplish-blue color

vi-o-lin *n.* a small stringed instrument, played with a bow

vi-per *n.* a poisonous snake; an evil or treacherous person

vir-gin *n.* person who has never had sexual intercourse *adj.* in an unchanged or natural state

Vir-go *n.* the sixth sign of the zodiac; a person born betweeb August 23rd and September 22nd

vir-ile *adj.* having the qualities and nature of a man; capable of sexual performance in the male

vir-tu *n.* the love or knowledge of fine objects of art

vir-tue *n.* morality, goodness or uprightness; a special type of goodness virtuous *adj.*

vi-rus *n.* any of a variety of microscopic organisms which cause diseases

vi-sa *n.* an offical authorization giving permission on a passport to enter a specific country

vis-cid *adj.* sticky; having an adhesive quality

vise or vice *n.* a tool in carpentry and metalwork having two jaws to hold things in position

vis-i-bil-i-ty *n., pl.* -ies degree or state of being visible; the distance that one is able to see clearly

vis-i-ble *adj.* apparent; exposed to view

vi-sion *n.* power of sight; the ability to see; an image created in the imagination; a supernatural appearance

vis-it *v.* journey to or come to see a person or place *n.* a professional or social call *Slang* to chat

vi-su-al *adj.* visible; relating to seeing or sight

vi-tal *adj.* essential to life; very important vitally *adv.*

vi-ta-min *n.* any of various substances which are found in foods and are essential to good health

vit-re-ous *adj.* related to or similar to glass

vi-va-cious *adj.* filled with vitality or animation; lively

viv-id *adj.* bright; brilliant; intense; having clear, lively, bright colors

viv-i-fy *v.* give life to

vo-cab-u-lar-y *n., pl.* vocabularies list or group of words and phrases, usually in alphabetical order; all the words that a person uses or understands

vo-cal *adj.* of or related to the voice; uttered by the voice; to speak freely and loudly *n.* vocal sound

vogue *n.* leading style or fashion; popularity

voice *n.* sounds produced by speaking; the ability or power to produce musical tones *v.* to express; to utter

void *adj.* containing nothing; empty; not inhabited

voile *n.* a fine, soft, sheer fabric used for making light clothing and curtains

volt-age *n.* amount of electrical power, given in terms of the number of volts

vol-ume *n.* capacity or amount of space or room; a book; a quantity; the loudness of a sound

vol-un-tar-y *adj.* done cooperatively or willingly; from one's own choice

vol-un-teer *n.* one who offers himself for a service of his own free will *adj.* consisting of volunteers

vo-lup-tuous *adj.* full of pleasure; delighting the senses; sensuous; luxury

vom-it *v.* eject contents of the stomach through the mouth

vo-ra-cious *adj.* having a large appetite; insatiable

vote *n.* expression of one's choice by voice, by raising one's hand, or by secret ballot voter *n.*

vouch *v.* verify or support as true; to guarantee

vow *n.* solemn pledge or promise, especially one made to God; a marriage vow

vow-el *n.* sound of speech made by voicing the flow of breath within the mouth; a letter representing a vowel

vul-gar *adj.* showing poor manners; crude; improper; immoral or indecent

vul-ner-a-ble *adj.* open to physical injury or attack vulnerability *n.*, vulnerably *adv.*

vul-ture *n.* large bird of the hawk family, living on dead animals; a greedy person

W, w The twenty-third letter of the English alphabet.

wacky *adj.* amusingly or absurdly irrational

wad *n.* small crumpled mass or bundle

wade *v.* walk through a substance as mud or water which hampers one's steps

wad-able *adj.* having the capability of being wadded

wad-ding *n.* materials for wadding or wads; a sheet of loose fibers that is used for stuffing

wad-dle *v.* to walk with short steps and swing from side to side

wa-fer *n.* small, thin, crisp cracker, cookie, or candy

waf-fle *n.* pancake batter cooked in a waffle iron

waft *v.* drift or move gently, as by the motion of water or air **waft** *n.*

wag *v.* move quickly from side to side or up and down *n.* playful, witty person **waggish** *adj.*

wage *n.* payment of money for labor or services *v.* to conduct

wa-ger *v.* make a bet

wag-on *n.* four-wheeled vehicle used to transport goods; a station wagon; a child's four-wheeled cart with a long handle

waif *n.* abandoned, homeless, or lost child

wail *n.* loud, mournful cry or weep

waist *n.* narrow part of the body between the thorax and hips **waisted** *adj.*

wait *v.* stay in one place in expectation of; to await; to put off until a later time or date

wait-er *n.* man who serves food at a restaurant

wait-ress *n.* woman who serves food at a restaurant

waive *v.* forfeit of one's own free will; to postpone or dispense with

wake *v.* come to consciousness, as from sleep *n.* vigil for a dead body.

walk *v.* move on foot over a surface; to pass over, go on

walk-out *n.* labor strike against a company

wall *n.* vertical structure to separate or enclose an area *v.* to provide or close up, as with a wall

wal-la-by *n.* small or medium-sized kangaroo

wal-let *n.* flat folding case for carrying paper money

wal-lop *n.* powerful blow; an impact *v.* to move with disorganized haste **walloper** *n.*

wall-pa-per *n.* decorative paper for walls, usually having a colorful pattern

wal-nut *n.* edible nut with a hard, light-brown shell; the tree on which this nut grows

wal-rus *n.* large marine mammal of the seal family, having flippers, tusks, and a tough hide

waltz *n.* ballroom dance

wam-pum *n.* polished shells, once used as currency by North American Indians *Slang* Money

wand *n.* slender rod used by a magician

wan-der *v.* travel about aimlessly; to roam; to stray **wanderer** *n.*

wane *v.* decrease in size or extent; to decrease gradually *n.* gradual deterioration

wan-gle *v.* resort to devious methods in order to obtain something wanted **wangler** *n.*

want *v.* wish for or desire; to need; to lack; to fail to possess a required amount

war *n.* armed conflict among states or nations

ward *n.* section in a hospital. *v.* to keep watch over someone or something

ware *n.* manufactured items of the same general kind; items or goods for sale

ware-house *n.* large building used to store merchandise

warm *adj.* moderate heat; neither hot or cold

warn *v.* give notice or inform beforehand; to call to one's attention; to alert

warp *v.* become bent out of shape; to deviate from a proper course

war-rant *n.* written authorization giving the holder legal power to search, seize, or arrest **warrantable** *adj.*

war-ri-or *n.* one who fights in a war or battle

war-y *adj.* marked by caution; alert to danger

wash *v.* cleanse by the use of water; to remove dirt

wash-and-wear *adj.* requiring little or no ironing after washing

wash-board *n.* corrugated board on which clothes are rubbed in the process of washing

washed-out *adj., Slang* tired

wash-er *n.* small disk usually made of rubber or metal having a hole in the center, used with nuts and bolts; a washing machine

wash-ing *n.* clothes and other articles that are washed or to be washed; cleaning

was-n't *contr.* was not

wasp *n.* any of various insects, having a slim body with a constricted abdomen, the female capable of inflicting a painful sting

waste *v.* to be thrown away; to be available but not used completely -ful *adj.*

watch *v.* view carefully; to guard; to keep informed

watch-dog *n.* dog trained to guard someone or his property

watch-ful *adj.* carefully observant or attentive watchfully *adv.*

watch-man *n.* person hired to keep watch; a guard

wa-ter *n.* clear liquid making up oceans, lakes, and streams; the body fluids as tears or urine

water moccasin *n.* venomous snake

water polo *n.* water game between two teams

water power *n.* power or energy produced by swift-moving water

wa-ter-proof *adj.* capable of preventing water from penetrating.

wa-ter-shed *n.* The raised area between two regions that divides two sections drained by different river sources

wa-ter-ski *v.* travel over water on a pair of short, broad skis while being pulled by a motorboat

wa-ter-spout *n.* tube or pipe through which water is discharged

water table *n.* upper limit of the portion of the ground completely saturated with water

wa-ter-tight *adj.* closed or sealed so tightly that no water can enter

wa-ter-way *n.* navigable body of water; a channel for water

wa-ter-y *adj.* containing water; diluted; lacking effectiveness wateriness *n.*

watt *n.* unit of electrical power represented by current of one ampere, produced by the electromotive force of one volt

wave *v.* move back and forth or up and down; to motion with the hand

wa-ver *v.* sway unsteadily; to move back and forth; to weaken in force waver *n.*, waveringly *adv.*

wax *n.* natural yellowish substance made by bees, solid when cold and easily melted or softened when heated

way *n.* manner of doing something; a tendency or characteristic

way-far-er *n.* person who travels on foot

way-lay *v.* attack by ambush

way-ward *adj.* unruly; unpredictable

we *pl., pron.* used to refer to the person speaking and one or more other people

weak *adj.* having little energy or strength; easily broken; having inadequate skills weakness *n.*, weakly *adv.*

wealth *n.* abundance of valuable possessions or property

wean *v.* accustom an infant or small child to food other than a mother's milk or bottle

weap-on *n.* device which can be used to harm another person

wear *v.* to have on or put something on the body; to display wearable *adj.*

wea-ri-some *adj.* tedious, boring or tiresome

wea-ry *adj.* exhausted; tired; feeling fatigued wearily *adv.*, -iness *n.*

wea-sel *n.* mammal with a long tail and short legs; a sly, sneaky person

weath-er *n.* condition of the air or atmosphere in terms of humidity, temperature, and similar features

weath-er-man *n.* man who reports or forecasts the weather

weather vane *n.* device that turns, indicating the direction of the wind

weave *v.* make a basket, cloth, or other item by interlacing threads or other strands of material weaver *n.*

web *n.* cobweb; piece of interlacing material which forms a woven structure

wed *v.* take as a spouse; to marry

we'd *contr.* we had; we should

wed-ding *n.* marriage ceremony; an act of joining together in close association

wedge *n.* tapered, triangular piece of wood or metal used to split logs, to add leverage, and to hold something open or ajar

weed *n.* unwanted plant which interferes with the growth of grass, vegetables, or flowers

week *n.* period of seven days, beginning with Sunday and ending with Saturday

week-day *n.* any day of the week except Saturday or Sunday

week-end *n.* end of the week from the period of Friday evening through Sunday evening

weep *v.* to shed tears; to express sorrow, joy, or emotion wee-vil *n.* small beetle having a downward-curving snout

weigh *v.* determine the heaviness of an object by using a scale; to consider carefully in one's mind

weight *n.* amount that something weighs; heaviness; a heavy object used to hold or pull something down

weight-less *adj.* lacking the pull of gravity; having little weight

weight-y *adj.* burdensome; important

weird *adj.* having an extraordinary or strange character weirdly *adv.*

weird-o *n., Slang* person who is very strange

wel-come *v.* extend warm hospitality; to accept gladly

weld *v.* unite metallic parts by applying heat and sometimes pressure, allowing the metals to bond together

wel-fare *n.* state of doing well; governmental aid to help the disabled or disadvantaged

well *n.* hole in the ground which contains a supply of water; a shaft in the ground through which gas and oil are obtained

we'll *contr.* we will; we shall

well--be-ing *n.* state of being healthy, happy, or prosperous

well--done *adj.* completely cooked; done properly

well--groomed *adj.* clean, neat, and properly cared for

well--known *adj.* widely known

well--man-nered *adj.* polite; having good manners

well--mean-ing *adj.* having good intentions

well--to--do *adj.* having more than enough wealth

welsh *v., Slang* cheat by avoiding a payment to someone; to neglect an obligation

welt *n.* strip between the sole and upper part of a shoe; a slight swelling on the body

wel-ter-weight *n.* boxer weighing between 136 and 147 pounds

went *v.* past tense of go

wept *v.* past tense of weep

were *v.* second person singular past plural of be

we're *contr.* we are

were-n't *contr.* were not

west *n.* direction of the setting sun western *adj.*

whack *v.* strike with a hard blow, to slap *n.* an attempt

whale *n.* very large mammal resembling a fish which lives in salt water

wharf *n.* pier or platform built at the edge of water so that ships can load and unload

what *pron.* which one; which things; which type or kind

what-ev-er *pron.* everything or anything *adj.* no matter what

what's *contr.* what is

wheat *n.* grain ground into flour, used to make breads and similar foods

wheel *n.* a circular disk which turns on an axle

wheel-bar-row *n.* vehicle having one wheel, used to transport small loads

wheel-chair *n.* a mobile chair for disabled persons

wheel-er *n.* anything that has wheels

wheeze *v.* breathe with a hoarse whistling sound *n.* high whistling sound

whelk *v.* any of various large water snails, sometimes edible

when *adv.* at what time; at which time *pron.* what or which time *conj.* while; at the time that

whence *adv.* from what source or place; from which

when-ev-er *adv.* at any time; when *conj.* at whatever time

where *adv.* at or in what direction or place; in what direction or place

where-a-bouts *adv.* near, at, or in a particular location *n.* approximate location

where-as *conj.* it being true or the fact; on the contrary

where-by *conj.* through or by which

wher-ev-er *adv.* in any situation or place

whet *v.* to make sharp; to stimulate

wheth-er *conj.* indicating a choice; alternative possibilities; either

whet-stone *n.* stone used to sharpen scissors, knives, and other implements

whew *n., interj.* used to express relief; or tiredness

whey *n.* clear, water-like part of milk that separates from the curd

which *pron.* what one or ones; the one previously; whatever one or ones; whichever

which-ev-er *pron.* any; no matter which or what

whiff *n.* slight puff; a light current of air; a slight breath or odor

while *n.* length or period of time *conj.* during the time that; even though; at the same time

whim *n.* sudden desire or impulse

whim-per *v.* make a weak, soft crying sound

whim-si-cal *adj.* impulsive; erratic; light and spontaneous whimsically *adv.*

whine *v.* make a squealing, plaintive sound; to complain in an irritating, childish fashion

whin-ny *v.* neigh in a soft gentle way

whip *v.* spank repeatedly with a rod or stick; to punish by whipping *n.* flexible stick or rod used to herd or beat animals whipper *n.*

whip-lash *n.* injury to the spine or neck caused by a sudden jerking motion of the head

whip-poor-will *n.* brownish nocturnal bird of North America

whir *v.* move with a low purring sound

whirl *v.* rotate or move in circles; to twirl; to move

whirl-pool *n.* circular current of water

whirl-wind *n.* violently whirling mass of air; a tornado

whirl-y-bird *n., Slang* helicopter

whisk *v.* move with a sweeping motion; move quickly or lightly

whisk-er *n.* hair that grows on a man's face; the long hair near the mouth of dogs, cats, and other animals whiskers man's beard

whis-key *n.* alcoholic beverage distilled from rye, barley, or corn

whis-per *v.* speak in a very low tone; to tell in secret

whis-tle *v.* make a clear shrill sound by blowing air through the teeth, through puckered lips, or through a special instrument

white *n.* color opposite of black; the part of something that is white or light in color, as an egg or the eyeball; a member of the Caucasian group of people

white-cap *n.* wave having a top of white foam

white--col-lar *adj.* relating to an employee whose job does not require manual labor

white-wash *n.* mixture made of lime and other ingredients and used for whitening fences and exterior walls

whith-er *adv.* what state, place, or circumstance; wherever

whit-tle *v.* cut or carve off small shavings from wood with a knife; to remove or reduce gradually whittler *n.*

who *pron.* which or what certain individual, person, or group

who'd *contr.* who would; who had

who-ev-er *pron.* whatever person; all or any persons

whole *adj.* complete; having nothing missing; not divided or in pieces

whole-heart-ed *adj.* sincere; totally committed

whole-sale *n.* sale of goods in large amounts to a retailer

whole-some *adj.* contributing to good mental or physical health wholesomely *adv.*, -ness *n.*

whole wheat *adj.* made from the wheat kernel with nothing removed

who'll *contr.* who shall; who will

whol-ly *adv.* totally; exclusively

whom *pron.* form of who used as the direct object of a verb or the object of the preposition

whom-ev-er *pron.* form of whoever used as the object of a preposition or the direct object of a verb

whooping cough *n.* infectious disease of the throat and breathing passages

whooping crane *n.* large bird of North America, nearly extinct

whoosh *v.* make a rushing or gushing sound, as a rush of air

whop-per *n.* something of extraordinary size *Slang* a lie

whore *n.* prostitute

who's *contr.* who is; who has

whose *pron.* belonging to or having to do with one's belongings

why *adj.* for what reason or purpose *conj.* cause, purpose, or reason for which *interj.* expressing surprise or disagreement

wick *n.* soft strand of fibers which extends from a candle or lamp

wick-er *n.* thin, pliable twig used to make furniture and baskets

wick-et *n.* wire hoop in the game of croquet

wide *adj.* broad; covering a large area; completely extended or open *adv.* over a large area; full extent

wide-spread *adj.* fully spread out; over a broad area

wid-ow *n.* woman whose husband is no longer living

wid-ow-er *n.* man whose wife is no longer living

width *n.* distance or extent of something from side to side

wield *v.* use or handle something skillfully; to employ power effectively

wie-ner *n.* frankfurter; a hot dog

wife *n.* married female

wig *n.* artificial or human hair woven together to cover baldness or a bald spot on the head

wig-gle *v.* squirm; to move with rapid

side-to-side motions -er *n.*

wig-wam *n.* Indian dwelling place

wild *adj.* living in a natural, untamed state; not occupied by man; not civilized; strange and unusual *adv.* out of control *n.* wilderness region not cultivated or settled by man

wild-cat *n.* medium-sized wild, feline animal; one with a quick temper

wil-der-ness *n.* unsettled area; a region left in its uncultivated or natural state

wild-life *n.* animals and plants living in their natural environments

will *n.* mental ability to decide or choose for oneself; strong desire or determination; a legal document stating how one's property is to be distributed after death

wil-low *n.* large tree, usually having narrow leaves and slender flexible twigs

wilt *v.* cause or to become limp; to lose force; to deprive of courage or energy

win *v.* defeat others; to gain victory in a contest; to receive *n.* victory; the act of winning winner *n.*

winch *n.* apparatus with one or more drums on which a cable or rope is wound, used to lift heavy loads

wind *n.* natural movement of air windy *adj.*

wind *v.* wrap around and around something; to turn, to crank *n.* turning or twisting

wind-bag *n., Slang* person who talks excessively without saying anything of importance

wind-fall *n.* sudden or unexpected stroke of good luck

wind instrument *n.* musical instrument which produces sound when a person forces his breath into it

wind-mill *n.* machine operated or powered by the wind

win-dow *n.* opening built into a wall for light and air; a pane of glass

win-dow--shop *v.* look at merchandise in store windows without going inside to buy

wind-pipe *n.* passage in the neck used for breathing; the trachea

wine *n.* drink containing 10-15% alcohol by volume, made by fermenting grapes

wing *n.* one of the movable appendages that allow a bird or insect to fly; one of the airfoils on either side of an aircraft

wing-spread *n.* extreme measurement from the tips or outer edges of the wings of an aircraft, bird, or other insect

wink *v.* shut one eye as a signal or message

win-ning *adj.* defeating others; captivating *n.* victory

win-some *adj.* very pleasant; charming

win-ter *n.* coldest season, coming between autumn and spring *adj.* relating to or typically of winter

win-ter-green *n.* small plant having aromatic evergreen leaves

wipe *v.* clean by rubbing; to take off by rubbing *n.* act or instance of wiping

wire *n.* small metal rod used to conduct electricity; thin strands of metal twisted together to form a cable; the telephone or telegraph system

wis-dom *n.* ability to understand what is right, true, or enduring; good judgment; knowledge

wise *adj.* having superior intelligence; having great learning; having a capacity for sound judgment marked by deep understanding wisely *adv.*

wise-crack *n., Slang* witty remark or joke usually showing a lack of respect

wish *v.* desire or long for something; to command or request *n.* longing or desire

wish-bone *n.* bone of a bird, which, according to the superstition, when broken brings good luck to the person who has the longer end

wish-ful *adj.* having or expressing a wish; hopeful wishfully *adv.*

wish-y--wash-y *adj., Slang* not purposeful; indecisive

wisp *n.* tuft or small bundle of hay, straw, or hair; a thin piece wispy *adj.*

wit *n.* ability to use words in a clever way; a sense of humor

witch *n.* person believed to have magical powers; a mean, ugly, old woman

with *prep.* in the company of; near or alongside; having, wearing or bearing

with-draw *v.* take away; to take back; to retreat

with-draw-al *n.* process of with-drawing; a retreat; the act of removing money from an account

whither *v.* dry up or wilt from a lack of moisture; to lose freshness or vigor

with-hold *n.* hold back or keep

withholding tax *n.* tax on income held back by an employer in payment of one's income tax

with-in *adv.* inside the inner part; inside the limits; inside the limits of time, distance, or degree

with-out *adv.* on the outside; not in possession of

prep. something or someone lacking

with-stand *v.* endure

wit-ness *n.* person who has seen, experienced, or heard something; something serving as proof or evidence

wit-ty *adj.* amusing or cleverly humorous

wiz-ard *n.* very clever person; a person thought to have magical powers *Slang* one with amazing skill

wob-ble *v.* move unsteadily from side to side, as a rocking motion

woe *n.* great sorrow or grief; misfortune

wok *n.* convex metal cooker for stir-frying food

woke *v.* past tense of wake

wolf *n.* carnivorous animal found in northern areas; a fierce person *v.* eat quickly and with greed

  wolfish *adj.*, **wolfishly** *adv.*

woman *n.* mature adult human female; a person who has feminine qualities

womanhood *n.* state of being a woman

womb *n.* uterus; place where development occurs

won *v.* past tense of win

won-der *n.* feeling of amazement or admiration *v.* feel admiration; feel uncertainty

won-der-ment *n.* feeling or state of amazement

won-drous *adj.* wonderful; marvelous

won't *contr.* will not

won-ton *n.* noodle dumpling filled with minced pork and served in soup

wood *n.* hard substance which makes up the main part of trees

wood-chuck *n.* rodent having short legs and a heavyset body, which lives in a burrow

wood-en *adj.* made of wood; resembling wood; stiff; lifeless; lacking flexibility

wood-peck-er *n.* bird which uses its bill for drilling holes in trees looking for insects to eat

wood-wind *n.* group of musical instruments which produce sounds when air is blown through the mouthpiece, as the clarinet

wool *n.* soft, thick hair of sheep and other such mammals; a fabric made from such hair

word *n.* meaningful sound which stands for an idea; a comment

word processing *n.* system which produces typewritten documents with automated type and editing equipment

work-er *n.* person who works for wages; an employee; a bee or other insect which performs special work in the colony in which it lives

work-ing *adj.* adequate to permit work to be done; assumed to permit further work

work-man-ship *n.* skill or art of a craftsman; quality given to something in the process of making it

world *n.* planet Earth; the universe; the human race

worn *adj.* made weak or thin from use; exhausted

wor-ry *v.* concerned or troubled; to tug at repeatedly; to annoy; to irritate

wor-ship *n.* reverence for a sacred object; high esteem or devotion for a person *v.* revere; attend a religious service **worshiper** *n.*

worst *adj.* bad; most inferior; most disagreeable

worth *n.* quality or value of something; personal merit

wor-thy *adj.* valuable or useful; deserving admiration or honor

would-n't *contr.* would not

wound *n.* laceration of the skin *v.* injure by tearing, cutting, or piercing the skin

wow *interj.* expression of amazement, surprise, or excitement

wran-gle *v.* quarrel noisily

wrap *v.* fold in order to protect something; encase or enclose

wrath *n.* violent anger or fury

wreak *v.* inflict punishment upon another person

wreath *n.* decorative ring-like form of intertwined flowers, bows, and other articles

wreck *v.* ruin or damage by accident or deliberately

wrest *v.* twist or pull away in a violent way

wretch *n.* extremely unhappy person; a miserable person

wrig-gle *v.* squirm; move by turning and twisting

wring *v.* squeeze and twist by hand or machine; press together

wrin-kle *n.* small crease on the skin or on fabric

writ *n., Law* written court document directed to a public official or individual ordering a specific action

writhe *v.* twist, as in pain; suffer greatly with pain

wrong *adj.* incorrect; against moral standards; not suitable **wrongly** *adv.*

wrote *v.* past tense of write

wrought *adj.* fashioned; formed; beatened or hammered into shape

wrung *v.* past tense of wring

X, x The twenty-fourth letter of the English alphabet.

xan-thate *n.* salt of xanthic acid

xan-thic *adj.* colors that tend to be yellow and yellows in flowers

xan-thip-pe *n.* wife; female which is like a shrew

xan-tho-chroid *adj.* light-haired, Caucasion peoples

x-axis *n.* in Cartesian coordinate system, the horizontal line of a two-dimensional plane

X chro-mo-some *n.* sex female chromosome, associated with female characteristics; occurs paired in the female and single in the male chromosome pair

xe-non *n.* colorless, odorless gaseous element found in small quantities in the air, symbolized by Xe.

xen-o-phobe *n.* person who dislikes, fears, and mistrusts foreigners or anything strange xenophobia *n.*

X--Ra-di-a-tion *n.* treatment with X-rays

X ray *n.* energy that is radiated with a short wavelength and high penetrating power; a black and white negative image or picture of the interior of the body

xy-lo-phone *n.* musical instrument consisting of mounted wooden bars which produce a ringing musical sound when struck with two small wooden hammers xylophonist *n.*

Y, y The twenty-fifth letter of the English alphabet.

yacht *n.* small sailing vessel powdered by wind or motor, for pleasure cruises

yak *n.* longhaired ox of Tibet and mountains of central Asia

yam *n.* edible root; a variety of the sweet potato

yap *v.* bark in a high pitched, sharp way *Slang* talk in a loud, or stupid manner

yard *n.* unit of measure that equals 36 inches or 3 feet; ground around a house

yarn *n.* twisted fibers, as of wool, used in knitting or weaving *Slang* involved tale or story

yawn *v.* inhale a deep breath with the mouth open wide

Y-Chro-mo-some *n.* sex chromosome associated with male characteristics

ye *pron.* you, used especially in religious contexts, as hymns

yea *adv.* yes; indeed; truly

yeah *adv., Slang* yes

year *n.* period of time starting on January 1st and continuing through December 31st

yearn *v.* feel a strong craving

yeast *n.* fungi or plant cells used to make baked goods rise or fruit juices ferment

yell *v.* cry out loudly *n.* loud cry; cheer to show support for an athletic team

yel-low *n.* bright color of a lemon; the yolk of an egg *v.* make or become yellow *adj.* of the color yellow *Slang* cowardly

yellow fever *n.* acute infectious disease of the tropics, spread by the bite of a mosquito

yeo-man *n.* owner of a small farm; a petty officer who acts as a clerk

yes *adv.* express agreement

yes-ter-day *n.* day before today; a former or recent time *adv.* on the day before the present day

yet *adv.* up to now; at this time *conj.* nevertheless; but

yew *n.* evergreen tree having poisonous flat, dark-green needles and poisonous red berries

yield *v.* bear or bring forward; give up possession

yo-del *v.* sing in a way so that the voice changes from normal to a high shrill sound and then back again

yo-ga *n.* system of exercises which helps the mind and the body in order to achieve tranquillity and spiritual insight

yo-gurt *n.* thick custard-like food made from curdled milk and often mixed with fruit

yoke *n.* wooden bar used to join together two animals working together, as oxen

yo-del *n.* very unsophisticated country person; a bumpkin

yolk *n.* yellow, nutritive part of an egg

Yom Kip-pur *n.* Jewish holiday observed with fasting and prayer for the forgiveness of sins

you *pron.* person or persons addressed

you all *pron., Slang* y'all southern variation used for two or more people in direct address

you'd *contr.* you had; you would

you'll *contr.* you will; you shall

young *adj.* of or relating to the early stage of life *n.* offspring of an animal youngster *n.*

your *adj.* belonging to you or yourself or the person spoken to

you're *contr.* you are

your-self *pron.* form of you for emphasis when the object of a verb and the subject is the same

you've *contr.* you have

yowl *v.* make a loud, long cry or howl yowl *n.*

yt-ter-bi-um *n.* metallic element symbolized by Yb.

yule *n.* Christmas

yule-tide *n.* Christmas season

Z, z The twenty-sixth letter of the English alphabet.

za-ny *n., pl* -nies clown; person who acts silly or foolish *adj.* typical of being clownish
zaniness *n.*, zannily *adv.*

zap *v., Slang* destroy; do away with

zeal *n.* great interest or eagerness

zeal-ot *n.* fanatical person; a fanatic

zeal-ous *adj.* full of interest; eager; passionate zealously *adv.*

ze-bra *n.* African mammal of the horse family having black or brown stripes on a white body

zeph-yr *n.* gentle breeze

ze-ro *n., pl.* -ros, -roes number or symbol "0"; nothing; point from which degrees or measurements on a scale begin; the lowest point *v.* aim, point at, or close in on *adj.* pertaining to zero; nonexisting

zest *n.* enthusiasm; a keen quality
zestful *adj.*, zestfully, zesty *adj.*

zig-zag *n.* pattern with sharp turns in alternating directions *adv.* move in a zigzag course or path

zilch *n., Slang* nothing; zero

zil-lion *n., Slang* extremely large number

zinc *n.* bluish-white crystalline metallic element, used as a protective coating for steel and iron, symbolized by Zn.

zip *n.* act or move with vigor or speed *v.* move with energy, speed, or facility; open or close with a zipper
Slang energy; zero; nothing

zip code *n.* system to speed the delivery of mail by assigning a five digit number, plus four to each postal delivery location in the United States

zip-per *n.* fastener consisting of two rows of plastic or metal teeth that are interlocked by means of sliding a tab

zir-co-ni-um *n.* metallic element symbolized by Zr.

zit *n., Slang* pimple

zo-di-ac *n.* unseen path followed through the heavens by the moon, sun, and most planets; area divided into twelve astrological signs, bearing the name of a constellation

zom-bie *n.* person who resembles the walking dead

zone *n.* area or region set apart from its surroundings by some characteristic

zonk *v., Slang* stun; render senseless with alcohol or drugs

zoo *n., pl.* zoos public display or collection of living animals

zo-ol-o-gy *n.* science that deals with animals, animal life, and the animal kingdom zoologist *n.*

zoom *v.* move with a continuous, loud sound; move upward sharply

zuc-chi-ni *n., pl.* -ni summer squash that has a dark-green, smooth rind

zwie-back *n.* sweetened bread which is baked to make it crisp

zy-mur-gy *n.* chemistry of fermentation processes

NEW WEBSTER
THESAURUS

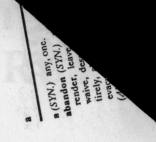

DICTIONARY FORMAT
OF
SYNONYMS AND ANTONYMS

**This book was not published by the original publisher of
the Webster's Dictionary, or by any of their successors.**

relinquish, resign, sur-
...give up, cease, forsake,
...ert, quit, vacate, abjure, en-
...bdicate, leave undone, discard,
...uate, withdraw.

(ANT.) support, keep, fulfill, uphold, depend, stay, maintain, embrace, cherish, favor, adopt, join, engage, unite, retain.

abandoned *(SYN.)* depraved, wicked, deserted, desolate, forsaken, rejected, cast off, profligate, degraded, loose, unrestrained, marooned, immoral, evil.

(ANT.) befriended, cherished, chaste, moral, respectable, virtuous, righteous.

abase *(SYN.)* make humble, reduce, bring down, degrade, demote, mock, scorn, belittle, shame, make lower, despise.

(ANT.) exalt, cherish, elevate, uplift, respect, dignify.

abash *(SYN.)* disconcert, bewilder, confuse, put off, discompose, nonplus.

(ANT.) comfort, relax, hearten, nerve.

abashed *(SYN.)* confused, ashamed, embarrassed, mortified, humiliated.

abate *(SYN.)* lessen, curtail, reduce, decrease, restrain, decline, stop, moderate, subside, slow, diminish, slacken.

(ANT.) grow, prolong, increase, extend, intensify, quicken, enhance, accelerate.

abbey *(SYN.)* nunnery, convent, cloisters.

abbot *(SYN.)* friar, monk.

abbreviate *(SYN.)* shorten, lessen, abridge, condense, curtail, reduce, cut, compress, trim, restrict, clip, contract.

(ANT.) lengthen, increase, expand, extend, prolong, enlarge, augment.

abbreviation *(SYN.)* abridgment, reduction, shortening, condensation.

(ANT.) expansion, extension, amplification, lengthening, dilation.

abdicate *(SYN.)* relinquish, renounce, vacate, waive, desert, forsake, abolish, quit, abandon, surrender, resign.

(ANT.) maintain, stay, retain, uphold.

abdomen *(SYN.)* paunch, belly, stomach.

abduct *(SYN.)* carry off, take, kidnap.

aberrant *(SYN.)* capricious, devious, irregular, unnatural, abnormal, unusual.

(ANT.) regular, usual, fixed, ordinary.

aberration *(SYN.)* oddity, abnormality, irregularity, deviation, quirk, monster, abortion, nonconformity, eccentricity.

(ANT.) norm, conformity, normality.

abet *(SYN.)* support, connive, encourage, conspire, help, incite, aid, assist.

(ANT.) deter, check, hinder, frustrate, oppose, discourage, resist.

abettor *SYN.)* accomplice, ally, confederate, associate, accessory.

(ANT.) opponent, rival, enemy.

abeyance *(SYN.)* inaction, cessation, pause, inactivity, rest, suspension, recess, dormancy, remission.

(ANT.) ceaselessness, continuation, continuity.

abhor *(SYN.)* dislike, hate, loathe, execrate, avoid, scorn, detest, despise.

abhorrent *(SYN.)* loathsome, horrible, detestable, nauseating, hateful, despicable, disgusting, foul, offensive, terrible, revolting.

abide *(SYN.)* obey, accept, tolerate, endure, dwell, stay, reside.

ability *(SYN.)* aptness, capability, skill, dexterity, faculty, power, talent.

(ANT.) incapacity, incompetency, weakness, ineptitude, inability, disability.

abject *(SYN.)* sordid, infamous, miserable, wretched, mean, base, contempt.

abjure *(SYN.)* relinquish, renounce, vacate, waive, desert, quit, leave, forsake, forewear, abdicate, resign, surrender.

(ANT.) cling to, maintain, uphold, stay.

able *(SYN.)* qualified, competent, fit, capable, skilled, having power, efficient, clever, talented, adequate, skillful.

(ANT.) inadequate, trained, efficient, incapable, weak, incompetent, unable.

abnegation *(SYN.)* rejection, renunciation, self-denial, abandonment, refusal, relinquishment, abjuration.

abnormal *(SYN.)* uncommon, unnatural, odd, irregular, monstrous, eccentric.

(ANT.) natural, usual, normal, average.

aboard *(SYN.)* on board.

abode *(SYN.)* dwelling, habitat, hearth, home, residence, address, quarters, lodging place, domicile.

abolish *(SYN.)* end, eradicate, annul, cancel, revoke, destroy, invalidate, overthrow, obliterate, abrogate, erase, exterminate, wipe out, eliminate.

(ANT.) promote, restore, continue, establish, sustain.

abominable *(SYN.)* foul, dreadful, hateful, revolting, vile, odious, loathsome, detestable, bad, horrible, terrible, aw-

ful, nasty, obnoxious, disgusting, unpleasant.
(ANT.) delightful, pleasant, agreeable, commendable, admirable, noble, fine.
abominate *(SYN.)* despise, detest, hate, dislike, abhor, loathe.
(ANT.) like, cherish, approve, admire.
abomination *(SYN.)* detestation, hatred, disgust, revulsion, antipathy, horror.
abort *(SYN.)* flop, fizzle, miscarry, abandon, cancel.
abortion *(SYN.)* fiasco, disaster, failure, defeat.
abortive *(SYN.)* unproductive, vain, unsuccessful, useless, failed, futile.
(ANT.) rewarding, effective, profitable, successful.
abound *(SYN.)* swarm, plentiful, filled, overflow, teem.
(ANT.) scarce, lack.
about *(SYN.)* relating to, involving, concerning, near, around, upon, almost, approximately, of, close to, nearby, ready to, nearly.
about-face *(SYN.)* reversal, backing out, shift, switch.
above *(SYN.)* higher than, overhead, on, upon, over, superior to.
(ANT.) under, beneath, below.
aboveboard *(SYN.)* forthright, open, frank, honest, overt, plain, straightforward, guileless, trustworthy.
(ANT.) underhand, ambiguous, sneaky, wily.
abracadabra *(SYN.)* voodoo, magic, charm, spell.
abrasion *(SYN.)* rubbing, roughness, scratching, scraping, friction, chap, chafe, chapping, scrape.
abrasive *(SYN.)* hurtful, sharp, galling, annoying, grating, cutting, irritating, caustic.
(ANT.) pleasant, soothing, comforting, agreeable.
abreast *(SYN.)* beside, side by side, alongside.
abridge *(SYN.)* condense, cut, abbreviate, make shorter, contract, shorten, reduce, summarize, curtail.
(ANT.) increase, lengthen, expand, extend.
abridgment *(SYN.)* digest, condensation, summary, abbreviation, shortening.
(ANT.) lengthening, expansion, enlarge-

ment.
abroad *(SYN.)* away, overseas, broadly, widely.
(ANT.) at home, privately, secretly.
abrogate *(SYN.)* rescind, withdraw, revoke, annul, cancel, abolish, repeal.
abrupt *(SYN.)* sudden, unexpected, blunt, curt, craggy, precipitous, sharp, hasty, unannounced, harsh, precipitate, brusque, rude, rough, short, steep.
(ANT.) foreseen, smooth, warm, courteous, gradual, smooth, expected, anticipated.
abscess *(SYN.)* pustule, sore, wound, inflammation.
absence *(SYN.)* nonexistence, deficiency, lack, need, shortcoming.
(ANT.) attendance, completeness, existence, presence.
absent *(SYN.)* away, truant, abroad, departed, inattentive, lacking, not present, out, off.
(ANT.) attending, attentive watchful, present.
absent-minded *(SYN.)* inattentive, daydreaming, preoccupied, absorbed, distrait, bemused, dreaming, forgetful.
(ANT.) observant, attentive, alert.
absolute *(SYN.)* unconditional, entire, actual, complete, thorough, total, perfect, essential, supreme, ultimate, unrestricted, positive, unqualified, whole.
(ANT.) partial, conditional, dependent accountable, restricted, qualified, limited, fragmentary, imperfect, incomplete.
absolutely *(SYN.)* positively, really, doubtlessly.
(ANT.) doubtfully, uncertainly.
absolution *(SYN.)* pardon, forgiveness, acquittal, mercy, dispensation, amnesty, remission.
absolutism *(SYN.)* autarchy, dictatorship, authoritarianism.
absolve *(SYN.)* exonerate, discharge, acquit, pardon, forgive, clear, excuse.
(ANT.) blame, convict, charge, accuse.
absorb *(SYN.)* consume, swallow up, engulf, assimilate, imbibe, engage, engross, take in, integrate, incorporate, occupy, suck up.
(ANT.) discharge, dispense, emit, exude, leak, eliminate, bore, tire, weary, drain.
absorbent *(SYN.)* permeable, spongy, pervious, porous.

(ANT.) moisture-proof, waterproof, impervious.

absorbing *(SYN.)* engaging, exciting, engaging, engrossing, entertaining, thrilling, intriguing, pleasing, fascinating.
(ANT.) dull, boring, tedious, tiresome.

abstain *(SYN.)* forbear, forego, decline, resist, hold back, withhold, refrain.
(ANT.) pursue.

abstemious *(SYN.)* abstinent, sparing, cautious, temperate, ascetic, self-disciplined, continent, sober.
(ANT.) uncontrolled, indulgent, abandoned, excessive.

abstinence *(SYN.)* fasting, self-denial, continence, forbearance, sobriety, refrain, do without, abstention.
(ANT.) gluttony, greed, excess, self-indulgence, pursue.

abstract *(SYN.)* part, appropriate, steal, remove, draw from, separate, purloin, unconcrete, abridge, summarize.
(ANT.) return, concrete, unite, add, replace, specific, clear, particular, restore.

abstracted *(SYN.)* parted, removed, stolen, abridged, taken away.
(ANT.) replaced, returned, alert, united, added.

abstraction *(SYN.)* idea, image, generalization, thought, opinion, impression, notion.
(ANT.) matter, object, thing, substance.

abstruse *(SYN.)* arcane, obscure, complicated, abstract, refined, mandarin, esoteric, metaphysical.
(ANT.) uncomplicated, direct, obvious, simple.

absurd *(SYN.)* ridiculous, silly, unreasonable, foolish, irrational, nonsensical, impossible, inconsistent, preposterous, self-contradictory, unbelievable.
(ANT.) rational, sensible, sound, meaningful, consistent, reasonable.

absurdity *(SYN.)* foolishness, nonsense, farce, drivel, joke, paradox, babble, drivel, senselessness, folly.

abundance *(SYN.)* ampleness, profusion, large amount, copiousness, plenty.
(ANT.) insufficiency, want, absence, dearth, scarcity.

abundant *(SYN.)* ample, overflowing, plentiful, rich, teeming, large amount, profuse, abounding.
(ANT.) insufficient, scant, not enough,

scarce, deficient, rare, uncommon, absent.

abuse *(SYN.)* maltreatment, misuse, reproach, defamation, dishonor, mistreat, damage, ill-use, reviling, aspersion, desecration, invective, insult, outrage, profanation, perversion, upbraiding, disparagement, misemploy, misapply, hurt, harm, injure, scold, berate.
(ANT.) plaudit, respect, appreciate, commendation. protect, praise, cherish.

abusive *(SYN.)* harmful, insulting, libelous, hurtful, slanderous, nasty, defamatory, injurious, scathing, derogatory.
(ANT.) supportive, helpful, laudatory, complimentary.

abut *(SYN.)* touch, border, meet, join, verge on, connect with.

abutment *(SYN.)* pier, buttress, bulwark, brace, support.

abysmal *(SYN.)* immeasurable, boundless, endless, stupendous, profound, un-believable, infinite, overwhelming, consummate.

abyss *(SYN.)* depth, chasm, void, infinitude, limbo, unknowable.

academic *(SYN.)* learned, scholarly, theoretical, erudite, bookish, formal, pedantic.
(ANT.) ignorant, practical, simple, uneducated.

academy *(SYN.)* college, school.

accede *(SYN.)* grant, agree, comply, consent, yield, endorse, accept, admit.
(ANT.) dissent, disagree, differ, oppose.

accelerate *(SYN.)* quicken, dispatch, facilitate, hurry, rush, speed up, forward, hasten, push, expedite.
(ANT.) hinder, retard, slow, delay, quicken.

accent *(SYN.)* tone, emphasis, inflection, stress, consent.

accept *(SYN.)* take, approve, receive, allow, consent to, believe, adopt, admit.
(ANT.) ignore, reject, refuse.

acceptable *(SYN.)* passable, satisfactory, fair, adequate, standard, par, tolerable, unobjectionable.
(ANT.) poor, substandard, inadmissible.

access *(SYN.)* entrance, approach, course, gateway, door, avenue.

accessible *(SYN.)* nearby, attainable, achievable, affable, democratic, accommodating.

(ANT.) remote, unobtainable, unachievable, standoffish, forbidding, unfriendly.

accessory *(SYN.)* extra, addition, assistant, supplement, contributory, accomplice.

accident *(SYN.)* casualty, disaster, misfortune, mishap, chance, calamity, contingency, fortuity, misadventure, mischance, injury, event, catastrophe.

(ANT.) purpose, intention, calculation.

accidental *(SYN.)* unintended, chance, casual, fortuitous, contingent, unplanned, unexpected, unforeseen.

(ANT.) calculated, planned, willed, intended, intentional, on purpose, deliberate.

acclaim *(SYN.)* eminence, fame, glory, honor, reputation, credit, applaud, distinction, approve, notoriety.

(ANT.) infamy, obscurity, disapprove, reject, disrepute.

acclimated *(SYN.)* adapted, habituated, acclimatized, accommodated, seasoned, inured, used to, weathered, reconciled.

accolade *(SYN.)* praise, honor, acclaim, recognition, applause, kudos, bouquet, crown, testimonial, acclamation, salute.

accommodate *(SYN.)* help, assist, aid, provide for, serve, oblige, hold, house.

(ANT.) inconvenience.

accommodating *(SYN.)* obliging, helpful, willing, kind, cooperative, gracious, cordial, sympathetic, unselfish.

(ANT.) unfriendly, selfish, hostile, uncooperative.

accommodation *(SYN.)* change, alteration, adaptation, convenience, adjustment, acclimatization, aid, help, boon, kindness, service, courtesy.

(ANT.) inflexibility, rigidity, disservice, stubbornness, disadvantage.

accommodations *(SYN.)* housing, lodgings, room, place, quarters, board.

accompany *(SYN.)* chaperon, consort with, escort, go with, associate with, attend, join.

(ANT.) abandon, quit, leave, desert, avoid, forsake.

accomplice *(SYN.* accessory, ally, associate, partner in crime, assistant, sidekick, confederate.

(ANT.) opponent, rival, enemy, adversary.

accomplish *(SYN.)* attain, consummate, achieve, do, execute, carry out, fulfill, complete, effect, perform, finish.

(ANT.) fail, frustrate, spoil, neglect, defeat.

accomplished *(SYN.)* proficient, skilled, finished, well-trained, gifted, masterly, polished, able.

(ANT.) unskilled, amateurish, crude.

accomplishment *(SYN.)* deed, feat, statute, operation, performance, action, achievement, transaction.

(ANT.) cessation, inhibition, intention, deliberation.

accord *(SYN.)* concur, agree, award, harmony, conformity, agreement, give, tale, sum, statement, record, grant.

(ANT.) difference, quarrel, disagreement.

accordingly *(SYN.)* consequently, therefore, whereupon, hence, so, thus.

accost *(SYN.)* approach, greet, speak to, address.

(ANT.) avoid, shun.

account *(SYN.)* description, chronicle, history, narration, reckoning, rate, computation, detail, narrative, relation, recital, consider, believe, deem, record, explanation, report, tale, story, anecdote, reason, statement, tale, ledger.

(ANT.) confusion, misrepresentation, distortion.

accountable *(SYN.)* chargeable, answerable, beholden, responsible, obliged, liable.

account for *(SYN.)* justify, explain, substantiate, illuminate, clarify, elucidate.

accredited *(SYN.)* qualified, licensed, deputized, certified, commissioned, vouched for, empowered.

(ANT.) illicit, unofficial, unauthorized.

accrue *(SYN.)* amass, collect, heap, increase, accumulate, gather, hoard.

(ANT.) disperse, dissipate, waste, diminish.

accrued *(SYN.)* accumulated, totaled, increased, added, enlarged, amassed, expanded.

accumulate *(SYN.)* gather, collect, heap, increase, accrue, assemble, compile, hoard, amass.

(ANT.) spend, give away, diminish, dissipate.

accumulation *(SYN.)* heap, collection, pile, store, hoard, stack, aggregation.

accurate *(SYN.)* perfect, just, truthful, unerring, meticulous, correct, all right.

(ANT.) incorrect, mistaken, false, wrong.

accursed *(SYN.)* ill-fated, cursed, condemned, doomed, bedeviled, ruined.
(ANT.) fortunate, hopeful.

accusation *(SYN.)* charge, incrimination, indictment, arraignment.
(ANT.) pardon, exoneration, absolve.

accuse *(SYN.)* incriminate, indict, censure, tattle, denounce, charge, arraign, impeach, blame.
(ANT.) release, vindicate, exonerate, acquit, absolve, clear.

accustom *(SYN.)* addict, familiarize, condition.

accustomed *(SYN.)* familiar with, used to, comfortable with.
(ANT.) strange, unusual, rare, unfamiliar.

ace *(SYN.)* champion, star, king, queen, winner, head.

acerbity *(SYN.)* bitterness, harshness, un-kindness, sourness, acidity, unfriendliness, acrimony, coldness, sharpness.
(ANT.) sweetness, gentleness, kindness, tenderness.

ache *(SYN.)* hurt, pain, throb.

achieve *(SYN.)* do, execute, gain, obtain, acquire, accomplish, realize, perform, complete, accomplish, finish, fulfill, reach, attain, secure, procure.
(ANT.) fail, lose, fall short.

achievement *(SYN.)* feat, accomplishment, attainment, exploit, realization, performance, completion, deed.
(ANT.) botch, dud, mess, omission, defeat, failure.

acid *(SYN.)* tart, sour, bitter, mordant, biting, biting.
(ANT.) pleasant, friendly, bland, mild, sweet.

acknowledge *(SYN.)* allow, admit, agree to, concede, recognize, answer, grant, accept, receive.
(ANT.) reject, refuse, disavow, refute, deny.

acme *(SYN.)* summit, top, zenith, peak, crown.
(ANT.) bottom.

acquaint *(SYN.)* inform, teach, enlighten, notify, tell.

acquaintance *(SYN.)* fellowship, friendship, cognizance, knowledge, intimacy, familiarity, companionship, associate,

colleague, companion.
(ANT.) inexperience, unfamiliarity, ignorance.

acquiesce *(SYN.)* submit, agree, concur, assent, comply, consent, succomb.
(ANT.) refuse, disagree, rebel, argue.

acquire *(SYN.)* attain, earn, get, procure, assimilate, obtain, secure, gain, appropriate.
(ANT.) miss, surrender, lose, forego, forfeit.

aquirement *(SYN.)* training, skill, learning, achievement, attainment, education, information.

aquisition *(SYN.)* procurement, gain, gift, purchase, proceeds, possession, grant.

aquisitive *(SYN.)* greedy, avid, hoarding, covetous.

acquit *(SYN.)* forgive, exonerate, absolve, cleanse, pardon, excuse, excuse, discharge, found not guilty.
(ANT.) doom, saddle, sentence, condemn.

acrid *(SYN.)* bitter, sharp, nasty, stinging, harsh.
(ANT.) pleasant, sweet.

acrimonious *(SYN.)* sharp, sarcastic, acerb, waspish, cutting, stinging, testy.
(ANT.) soft, kind, sweet, pleasant, soothing.

acrobat *(SYN.)* athlete, gymnast.

act *(SYN.)* deed, doing, feat, execution, accomplishment, performance, action, operation, transaction, law, decree, statute, edict, achievement, exploit, statute, judgment, routine, pretense.
(ANT.) inactivity, deliberation, intention, cessation.

acting *(SYN.)* officiating, substituting, surrogate, temporary, delegated.

action *(SYN.)* deed, achievement, feat, activity, exploit, movement, motion, play, behavior, battle, performance, exercise.
(ANT.) idleness, inertia, repose, inactivity, rest.

activate *(SYN.)* mobilize, energize, start, propel, nudge, push.
(ANT.) paralyze, immobilize, stop, deaden.

active *(SYN.)* working, operative, alert, agile, nimble, supple, sprightly, busy, brisk, lively, quick, industrious, energetic, vigorous, industrious, occupied, vivacious, dynamic, engaged.

(ANT.) passive, inactive, idle, dormant, lazy, lethargic.

activism *(SYN.)* engagement, confrontation, agitation, commitment, aggression, fervor, zeal.
(ANT.) detachment, lethargy, disengagement, fence-sitting.

activist *(SYN.)* militant, doer, enthusiast.

activity *(SYN.)* action, liveliness, motion, vigor, agility, exercise, energy, quickness, enterprise, movement, briskness.
(ANT.) idleness, inactivity, dullness, sloth.

actor *(SYN.)* performer, trouper, entertainer.

actual *(SYN.)* true, genuine, certain, factual, authentic, concrete, real.
(ANT.) unreal, fake, bogus, nonexistent, false.

actuality *(SYN.)* reality, truth, deed, occurrence, fact, certainty.
(ANT.) theory, fiction, falsehood, supposition.

acute *(SYN.)* piercing, severe, sudden, keen,sharp, perceptive, discerning, shrewd, astute, smart, intelligent.
(ANT.) bland, mild, dull, obtuse, insensitive.

adamant *(SYN.)* unyielding, firm, obstinate.
(ANT.) yielding.

adapt *(SYN.)* adjust, conform, accommodate, change, fit, alter, vary, modify.
(ANT.) misapply, disturb.

add *(SYN.)* attach, increase, total, append, sum, affix, augment, adjoin, put together, unite, supplement.
(ANT.) remove, reduce, deduct, subtract, detach, withdraw.

address *(SYN.)* greet, hail, accost, speak to, location, residence, home, abode, dwelling, speech, lecture, greeting, oration, presentation.
(ANT.) avoid, pass by.

adept *(SYN.)* expert, skillful, proficient.
(ANT.) unskillful.

adequate *(SYN.)* capable, commensurate, fitting, satisfactory, sufficient, enough, ample, suitable, plenty, fit.
(ANT.) lacking, scant, insufficient, inadequate.

adhere *(SYN.)* stick fast, grasp, hold, keep, retain, cling, stick to, keep, cleave.
(ANT.) surrender, abandon, release, separate, loosen.

adherent *(SYN.)* follower, supporter.
(ANT.) renegade, dropout, defector.

adjacent *(SYN.)* next to, near, bordering, adjoining, touching, neighboring.
(ANT.) separate, distant, apart.

adjoin *(SYN.)* connect, be close to, affix, attach.
(ANT.) detach, remove,

adjoining *(SYN.)* near to, next, next to, close to, touching, bordering.
(ANT.) distant, remote, separate.

adjourn *(SYN.)* postpone, defer, delay, suspend, discontinue, put off.
(ANT.) begin, convene, assemble.

adjust *(SYN.)* repair, fix, change, set, regulate, settle, arrange, adapt, suit, accommodate, modify, very, alter, fit.

administer *(SYN.)* supervise, oversee, direct, manage, rule, govern, control, conduct, provide, give, execute, preside, apply, contribute, help.

administration *(SYN.)* conduct, direction, management, supervision.

admirable *(SYN.)* worthy, fine, praisedeserving, commendable, excellent.

admiration *(SYN.)* pleasure, wonder, esteem, approval.
(ANT.) disdain, disrespect, contempt.

admire *(SYN.)* approve, venerate, appreciate, respect, revere. esteem, like.
(ANT.) abhor, dislike, despise, loathe, detest, hate.

admissible *(SYN.)* fair, justifiable, tolerable, allowable, permissible.
(ANT.) unsuitable, unfair, inadmissible.

admission *(SYN.)* access, admittance, entrance, pass, ticket.

admit *(SYN.)* allow, assent, permit, acknowledge, welcome, concede, agree, confess, accept, grant, own up to.
(ANT.) deny, reject, dismiss, shun, obstruct.

admittance *(SYN.)* access, entry, entrance.

admonish *(SYN.)* caution, advise against, warn, rebuke, reprove, censure.
(ANT.) glorify, praise.

admonition *(SYN.)* advice, warning, caution, reminder, tip.

ado *(SYN.)* trouble, other, fuss, bustle, activity, excitement, commotion, action, hubbub, upset, confusion, turmoil.
(ANT.) tranquillity, quietude.

adolescent *(SYN.)* young, youthful, immature, teenage.

(ANT.) grown, mature, adult.

adoration *(SYN.)* veneration, reverence, glorification, worship homage.

adore *(SYN.)* revere, venerate, idolize, respect, love, cherish, esteem, honor.

(ANT.) loathe, hate, despise.

adorn *(SYN.)* trim, bedeck, decorate, ornament, beautify, embellish, glamorize, enhance, garnish, embellish..

(ANT.) mar, spoil, deform, deface, strip, bare.

adrift *(SYN.)* floating, afloat, drifting, aimless, purposeless, unsettled.

(ANT.) purposeful, stable, secure, well-organized.

adroit *(SYN.)* adept, apt, dexterous, skillful, clever, ingenious, expert.

(ANT.) awkward, clumsy, graceless, un-skillful, oafish.

adult *(SYN.)* full-grown, mature.

(ANT.) infantile, immature.

advance *(SYN.)* further, promote, bring forward, propound, proceed, aggrandize, elevate, improve, adduce, allege, propose, progress, move, advancement, improvement, promotion, upgrade.

(ANT.) retard, retreat, oppose, hinder, revert, withdraw, flee, retardation.

advantage *(SYN.)* edge, profit, superiority, benefit, mastery, leverage, favor, vantage, gain.

(ANT.) handicap, impediment, obstruction, disadvantage, detriment, hindrance, loss.

adventure *(SYN.)* undertaking, occurrence, enterprise, happening, event, project, occurrence, incident, exploit.

adventurous *(SYN.)* daring, enterprising, rash, bold, chivalrous.

(ANT.) cautious, timid, hesitating.

adversary *(SYN.)* foe, enemy, contestant, opponent, antagonist.

(ANT.) ally, friend.

adverse *(SYN.)* hostile, counteractive, unfavorable, opposed, disastrous, contrary, antagonistic, opposite, unlucky, unfriendly, unfortunate.

(ANT.) favorable, propitious, fortunate, friendly, beneficial.

adversity *(SYN.)* misfortune, trouble, calamity, distress, hardship, disaster.

(ANT.) benefit, happiness.

advertise *(SYN.)* promote, publicize,

make known, announce, promulgate.

advertisement *(SYN.)* commercial, billboard, want ad, handbill, flyer, poster, brochure, blurb.

advice *(SYN.)* counsel, instruction, suggestion, warning, information, caution, exhortation, admonition, recommendation, plan, tip, guidance, opinion.

advisable *(SYN.)* wise, sensible, prudent, suitable, fit, proper, fitting.

(ANT.) ill-considered, imprudent, inadvisable.

advise *(SYN.)* recommend, suggest, counsel, caution, warn, admonish.

adviser *(SYN.)* coach, guide, mentor, counselor.

advocate *(SYN.)* defend, recommend, support.

(ANT.) opponent, adversary, oppose, opponent.

aesthetic *(SYN.)* literary, artistic, sensitive, tasteful, well-composed.

(ANT.) tasteless.

affable *(SYN.)* pleasant, courteous, sociable, friendly, amiable, gracious, approachable, communicative.

(ANT.) unfriendly, unsociable.

affair *(SYN.)* event, occasion, happening, party, occurrence, matter, festivity, business, concern.

affect *(SYN.)* alter, modify, concern, regard, move, touch, feign, pretend, influence, sway, transform, change, impress.

affected *(SYN.)* pretended, fake, sham, false.

affection *(SYN.)* fondness, kindness, emotion, love, feeling, tenderness, attachment, disposition, endearment, liking, friendly, friendliness, warmth.

(ANT.) aversion, indifference, repulsion, hatred, repugnance, dislike, antipathy.

affectionate *(SYN.)* warm, loving, tender, fond, attached.

(ANT.) distant, unfeeling, cold.

affirm *(SYN.)* aver, declare, swear, maintain, endorse, certify, state, assert, ratify, pronounce, say, confirm, establish.

(ANT.) deny, dispute, oppose, contradict, demur, disclaim.

afflict *(SYN.)* trouble, disturb, bother, agitate, perturb.

(ANT.) soothe.

affliction *(SYN.)* distress, grief, misfortune, trouble.
(ANT.) relief, benefit, easement.

affluent *(SYN.)* wealthy, prosperous, rich, abundant, ample, plentiful, well-off, bountiful, well-to-do.
(ANT.) poor.

afford *(SYN.)* supply, yield, furnish.

affront *(SYN.)* offense, slur, slight, provocation, insult.

afraid *(SYN.)* faint-hearted, frightened, scared, timid, fearful, apprehensive, cowardly, terrified.
(ANT.) assured, composed, courageous, bold, confident.

after *(SYN.)* following, subsequently, behind, despite, next.
(ANT.) before.

again *(SYN.)* anew, repeatedly, afresh.

against *(SYN.)* versus, hostile to, opposed to, in disagreement.
(ANT.) pro, with, for, in favor of.

age *(SYN.)* antiquity, date, period, generation, time, senility, grow old, senescence, mature, dotage, ripen, mature, era, epoch.
(ANT.) youth, childhood.

aged *(SYN.)* ancient, elderly, old.
(ANT.) youthful, young.

agency *(SYN.)* office, operation.

agent *(SYN.)* performer, doer, worker, actor, operator.

aggravate *(SYN.)* intensify, magnify, annoy, irritate, increase, heighten, nettle, make worse, irk, vex, provoke, embitter, worsen.
(ANT.) soften, soothe, appease, pacify, mitigate, ease, relieve.

aggregate *(SYN.)* collection, entirety, sum, accumulate, total, amount to, compile, conglomeration.
(ANT.) part, unit, ingredient, element.

aggression *(SYN.)* assault, attack, invasion, offense.
(ANT.) defense.

aggressive *(SYN.)* offensive, belligerent, hostile, attacking, militant, pugnacious.
(ANT.) timid, withdrawn, passive, peaceful, shy.

aghast *(SYN.)* surprised, astonished, astounded, awed, thunderstruck, flabbergasted, bewildered.

agile *(SYN.)* nimble, graceful, lively, active, alert, fast, quick, athletic, spry.

(ANT.) inept, awkward, clumsy.

agility *(ANT.)* quickness, vigor, liveliness, energy, activity, motion.
(ANT.) dullness, inertia, idleness, inactivity.

agitate *(SYN.)* disturb, excite, perturb, rouse, shake, arouse, disconcert, instigate, inflame, provoke, jar, incite, stir up, toss.
(ANT.) calm, placate, quiet, ease, soothe.

agitated *(SYN.)* jumpy, jittery, nervous, restless, restive, upset, disturbed, ruffled.

agony *(SYN.)* anguish, misery, pain, suffering, torture, ache, distress, throe, woe, torment, grief.
(ANT.) relief, ease, comfort.

agree *(SYN.)* comply, coincide, conform, concur, assent, accede, tally, settle, harmonize, unite, yield, consent.
(ANT.) differ, disagree, protest, contradict, argue, refuse.

agreeable *(SYN.)* amiable, charming, gratifying, pleasant, suitable, pleasurable, welcome, pleasing, acceptable, friendly, cooperative.
(ANT.) obnoxious, offensive, unpleasant, disagreeable, quarrelsome, contentious, touchy.

agreement *(SYN.)* harmony, understanding, unison, contract, pact, stipulation, alliance, deal, bargain, treaty, contract, arrangement, settlement, accord, concord.
(ANT.) variance, dissension, discord, disagreement, difference, misunderstanding.

agriculture *(SYN.)* farming, gardening, tillage, husbandry, cultivation, agronomy.

ahead *(SYN.)* before, leading, forward, winning, in advance.
(ANT.) behind.

aid *(SYN.)* remedy, assist, helper, service, support, assistant, relief, help.
(ANT.) obstruct, hinder, obstacle, impede, hindrance.

ail *(SYN.)* bother, trouble, perturb, disturb, suffer, feel sick.

ailing *(SYN.)* sick, ill.
(ANT.) hearty, hale, well.

ailment *(SYN.)* illness, disease, affliction, sickness.

aim *(SYN.)* direction, point, goal, object, target, direct, try, intend, intention, end, objective.

aimless *(SYN.)* directionless, adrift, purposeless.

air *(SYN.)* atmosphere, display, reveal, expose, publicize.

(ANT.) conceal, hide.

airy *(SYN.)* breezy, light, gay, lighthearted, graceful, fanciful.

aisle *(SYN.)* corridor, passageway, lane, alley, opening, artery.

ajar *(SYN.)* gaping, open.

akin *(SYN.)* alike, related, connected, similar, affiliated, allied.

alarm *(SYN.)* dismay, fright, signal, warning, terror, apprehension, affright, consternation, fear, siren, arouse, startle, bell.

(ANT.) tranquillity, composure, security, quiet, calm, soothe, comfort.

alarming *(SYN.)* appalling, daunting, shocking.

(ANT.) comforting, calming, soothing.

alcoholic *(SYN.)* sot, drunkard, tippler, inebriate.

alert *(SYN.)* attentive, keen, clear-witted, ready, nimble, vigilant, watchful, observant.

(ANT.) logy, sluggish, dulled, listless.

alias *(SYN.)* anonym, assumed name.

alibi *(SYN.)* story, excuse.

alien *(SYN.)* adverse, foreigner, strange, remote, stranger, different, extraneous.

(ANT.) germane, kindred, relevant, akin, familiar, accustomed.

alight *(SYN.)* debark, deplane, detrain, disembark.

(ANT.) embark, board.

alive *(SYN.)* existing, breathing, living, live, lively, vivacious, animated.

(ANT.) inactive, dead, moribund.

allay *(SYN.)* soothe, check, lessen, calm, lighten, relieve, soften, moderate, quite.

(ANT.) excite, intensify, worsen, arouse.

allege *(SYN.)* affirm, cite, claim, declare, maintain, state, assert.

(ANT.) deny, disprove, refute, contradict, gainsay.

allegiance *(SYN.)* faithfulness, duty, devotion, loyalty, fidelity, obligation.

(ANT.) treachery, disloyalty.

allegory *(SYN.)* fable, fiction, myth, saga, parable, legend.

(ANT.) history, fact.

alleviate *(SYN.)* diminish, soothe, solace, abate, assuage, allay, soften, mitigate,

extenuate, relieve, let up, ease, slacken, relax, weaken.

(ANT.) increase, aggravate, augment, irritate.

alley *(SYN.)* footway, byway, path, passageway, aisle, corridor, opening, lane.

alliance *(SYN.)* combination, partnership, union, treaty, coalition, association, confederacy, marriage, pact, agreement, relation, interrelation, understanding, relationship.

(ANT.) separation, divorce, schism.

allot *(SYN.)* divide, mete, assign, give, measure, distribute, allocate, share, grant, dispense, deal, apportion.

(ANT.) withhold, retain, keep, confiscate, refuse.

allow *(SYN.)* authorize, grant, acknowledge, admit, let, permit, sanction, consent, concede, mete, allocate.

(ANT.) protest, resist, refuse, forbid, object, prohibit.

allowance *(SYN.)* grant, fee, portion, ration, allotment.

allude *(SYN.)* intimate, refer, insinuate, hint, advert, suggest, imply, mention.

(ANT.) demonstrate, specify, state, declare.

allure *(SYN.)* attract, fascinate, tempt, charm, infatuate, captivate.

ally *(SYN.)* accomplice, associate, confederate, abettor, assistant, friend, partner.

(ANT.) rival, enemy, opponent, foe, adversary.

almighty *(SYN.)* omnipotent, powerful.

almost *(SYN.)* somewhat, nearly.

(ANT.) completely, absolutely.

alms *(SYN.)* dole, charity, donation, contribution.

aloft *(SYN.)* overhead.

alone *(SYN.)* desolate, unaided, only, isolated, unaided, lone, secluded, lonely, deserted, solitary, single, apart, solo, separate.

(ANT.) surrounded, attended, accompanied, together.

aloof *(SYN.)* uninterested, uninvolved, apart, away, remote, unsociable, standoffish, separate, disdainful, distant.

(ANT.) warm, outgoing, friendly, cordial.

also *(SYN.)* in addition, likewise, too, besides, furthermore, moreover, further.

alter *(SYN.)* adjust, vary, deviate, modify,

reserved, change.

(ANT.) maintain, preserve, keep.

alteration *(SYN.)* difference, adjustment, change, modification.

(ANT.) maintenance, preservation.

altercation *(SYN.)* controversy, dispute, argument, quarrel.

alternate *(SYN.)* rotate, switch, spell, interchange.

(ANT.) fix.

alternative *(SYN.)* substitute, selection, option, choice, replacement, possibility.

although *(SYN.)* though, even if, even though, despite, notwithstanding.

altitude *(SYN.)* elevation, height.

(ANT.) depth.

altogether *(SYN.)* totally, wholly, quite, entirely, thoroughly, completely.

(ANT.) partly.

altruism *(SYN.)* kindness, tenderness, generosity, charity, benevolence, liberality.

(ANT.) selfishness, unkindness, cruelty, inhumanity.

always *(SYN.)* evermore, forever, perpetually, ever, unceasingly, continually, constantly, eternally, everlastingly.

(ANT.) never, rarely, sometimes, occasionally.

amalgamate *(SYN.)* fuse, unify, unite, commingle, merge, blend, combine, consolidate.

(ANT.) decompose, disintegrate, separate.

amass *(SYN.)* collect, accumulate, heap up, gather, increase, compile, assemble, store up.

(ANT.) disperse, dissipate, spend.

amateur *(SYN.)* beginner, dilettante, learner, dabbler, neophyte, apprentice, novice, nonprofessional, tyro.

(ANT.) expert, master, adept, professional, authority.

amaze *(SYN.)* surprise, flabbergast, stun, dumb-found, astound, bewilder, aghast, thunderstruck, astonish.

(ANT.) bore, disinterest, tire.

ambiguous *(SYN.)* uncertain, vague, obscure, dubious, equivocal, unclear, deceptive.

(ANT.) plain, clear, explicit, obvious, unequivocal, unmistakable, certain.

ambition *(SYN.)* eagerness, goal, incentive, aspiration, yearning, longing, desire.

(ANT.) indifference, satisfaction, indolence, resignation.

ambitious *(SYN.)* aspiring, intent upon.

(ANT.) indifferent.

amble *(SYN.)* saunter, stroll.

ambush *(SYN.)* trap, hiding place.

amend *(SYN.)* change, mend, better, correct, improve.

(ANT.) worsen.

amends *(SYN.)* compensation, restitution, payment, reparation, remedy, redress.

amiable *(SYN.)* friendly, good-natured, gracious, pleasing, agreeable, outgoing, kindhearted, kind, pleasant.

(ANT.) surly, hateful, churlish, disagreeable, ill-natured, ill-tempered, cross, captious, touchy.

amid *(SYN.)* among, amidst, surrounded by.

amiss *(SYN.)* wrongly, improperly, astray, awry.

(ANT.) properly, rightly, right, correctly, correct.

ammunition *(SYN.)* shot, powder, shells, bullets.

among *(SYN.)* between, mingled, mixed amidst, amid, betwixt, surrounded by.

(ANT.) separate, apart.

amorous *(SYN.)* amatory, affectionate, loving.

amount *(SYN.)* sum, total, quantity, number, price, value, measure.

ample *(SYN.)* broad, large, profuse, spacious, copious, liberal, plentiful, full, bountiful, abundant, great, extensive, generous, wide, enough, sufficient, roomy.

(ANT.) limited, insufficient, meager, small, lacking, cramped, confined, inadequate.

amplification *(SYN.)* magnification, growth, waxing, accrual, enhancement, enlargement, heightening, increase.

(ANT.) decrease, diminishing, reduction, contraction.

amplify *(SYN.)* broaden, develop, expand, enlarge, extend.

(ANT.) confine, restrict, abridge, narrow.

amuse *(SYN.)* divert, please, delight, entertain, charm.

(ANT.) tire, bore.

amusement *(SYN.)* diversion, pastime, entertainment, pleasure, enjoyment, recreation.

(ANT.) tedium, boredom.

amusing *(SYN.)* pleasant, funny, pleasing, entertaining, comical.

(ANT.) tiring, tedious, boring.

analogous *(SYN.)* comparable, corresponding, like, similar, correspondent, alike, correlative, parallel, allied, akin.

(ANT.) different, opposed, incongruous, divergent.

analysis *(SYN.)* separation, investigation, examination.

analyze *(SYN.)* explain, investigate, examine, separate.

ancestral *(SYN.)* hereditary, inherited.

ancestry *(SYN.)* family, line, descent, lineage.

(ANT.) posterity.

anchor *(SYN.)* fix, attach, secure, fasten.

(ANT.) detach, free, loosen.

ancient *(SYN.)* aged, old-fashioned, archaic, elderly, antique, old, primitive.

(ANT.) new, recent, current, fresh.

anecdote *(SYN.)* account, narrative, story, tale.

anesthetic *(SYN.)* opiate, narcotic, sedative, painkiller, analgesic.

angel *(SYN.)* cherub, archangel, seraph.

(ANT.) demon, devil.

angelic *(SYN.)* pure, lovely, heavenly, good, virtuous, innocent, godly, saintly.

(ANT.) devilish.

anger *(SYN.)* exasperation, fury, ire, passion, rage, resentment, temper, indignation, animosity, irritation, wrath, displeasure, infuriate, arouse, nettle, annoyance, exasperate.

(ANT.) forbearance, patience, peace, self-control.

angry *(SYN.)* provoked, wrathful, furious, enraged, incensed, exasperated, maddened, indignant, irate, mad, inflamed.

(ANT.) happy, pleased, calm, satisfied, content, tranquil.

anguish *(SYN.)* suffering, torment, torture, distress, pain, heartache, grief, agony, misery.

(ANT.) solace, relief, joy, comfort, peace, ecstasy, pleasure.

animal *(SYN.)* beast, creature.

animate *(SYN.)* vitalize, invigorate, stimulate, enliven, alive, vital, vigorous.

(ANT.) dead, inanimate.

animated *(SYN.)* gay, lively, spry, viva-cious, active, vigorous, chipper, snappy.

(ANT.) inactive.

animosity *(SYN.)* grudge, hatred, rancor, spite, bitterness, enmity, opposition, dislike, hostility, antipathy.

(ANT.) good will, love, friendliness, kindliness.

annex *(SYN.)* join, attach, add, addition, wing, append.

annihilate *(SYN.)* destroy, demolish, end, wreck, abolish.

announce *(SYN.)* proclaim, give out, make known, notify, publish, report, herald, promulgate, advertise, broadcast, state, tell, declare, publicize.

(ANT.) conceal, withhold, suppress, bury, stifle.

announcement *(SYN.)* notification, report, declaration, bulletin, advertisement, broadcast, promulgation, notice, message.

(ANT.) silence, hush, muteness, speechlessness.

annoy *(SYN.)* bother, irk, pester, tease, trouble, vex, disturb, inconvenience, molest, irritate, harry, harass.

(ANT.) console, gratify, soothe, accommodate, please, calm, comfort.

annually *(SYN.)* once a year.

anoint *(SYN.)* grease, oil.

answer *(SYN.)* reply, rejoinder, response, retort, rebuttal, respond.

(ANT.) summoning, argument, questioning, inquiry, query, ask, inquire.

antagonism *(SYN.)* opposition, conflict, enmity, hostility, animosity.

(ANT.) geniality, cordiality, friendliness.

antagonist *(SYN.)* adversary, rival, enemy, foe, opponent.

(ANT.) ally, friend.

antagonize *(SYN.)* against, provoke, counter, oppose, embitter.

(ANT.) soothe.

anthology *(SYN.)* garland, treasury, collection.

anticipate *(SYN.)* await, foresee, forecast, hope for, expect.

anticipated *(SYN.)* expected, foresight, hoped, preconceived.

(ANT.) dreaded, reared, worried, doubted.

antics *(SYN.)* horseplay, fun, merrymaking, pranks, capers, tricks, clowning.

antipathy *(SYN.)* hatred.

antiquated *(SYN.)* old, out-of-date, outdated, old-fashion.

antique *(SYN.)* rarity, curio, old, ancient, old-fashioned, archaic, out-of-date.
(ANT.) new, recent, fresh.

anxiety *(SYN.)* care, disquiet, fear, concern, solicitude, trouble, worry, apprehension, uneasiness, distress, foreboding.
(ANT.) nonchalance, assurance, confidence, contentment, peacefulness, placidity, tranquillity.

anxious *(SYN.)* troubled, uneasy, perturbed, apprehensive, worried, concerned, desirous, bothered, agitated, eager, fearful.
(ANT.) tranquil, calm, peaceful.

anyway *(SYN.)* nevertheless, anyhow.

apartment *(SYN.)* suite, flat, dormitory.

apathy *(SYN.)* unconcern, indifference, lethargy.
(ANT.) interest, feeling.

aperture *(SYN.)* gap, pore, opening, cavity, chasm, abyss, hole, void.
(ANT.) connection, bridge, link.

apex *(SYN.)* acme, tip, summit, crown, top.

apologize *(SYN.)* ask forgiveness.

apology *(SYN.)* defense, excuse, confession, justification, alibi, explanation, plea.
(ANT.) denial, complaint, dissimulation, accusation.

apostate *(SYN.)* nonconformist, unbeliever, dissenter, heretic, schismatic.
(ANT.) saint, conformist, believer.

appall *(SYN.)* shock, stun, dismay, frighten, terrify, horrify.
(ANT.) edify, please.

appalling *(SYN.)* fearful, frightful, ghastly, horrid, repulsive, terrible, dire, awful.
(ANT.) fascinating, beautiful, enchanting, enjoyable.

apparatus *(SYN.)* rig, equipment, furnishings, gear, tackle.

apparel *(SYN.)* clothes, attire, garb, clothing, garments, dress, robes.

apparent *(SYN.)* obvious, plain, self-evident, clear, manifest, transparent, unmistakable, palpable, unambiguous, ostensible, illusory, visible, seeming, evident, understandable.
(ANT.) uncertain, indistinct, dubious, hidden, mysterious.

apparition *(SYN.)* illusion, ghost, phantom, vision, fantasy, dream.

appeal *(SYN.)* plea, petition, request, entreaty, request, plead, petition, beseech, beg, entreat, attract.
(ANT.) repulse, repel.

appear *(SYN.)* look, arrive, emanate, emerge, arise, seem, turn up.
(ANT.) vanish, withdraw, exist, disappear, evaporate.

appearance *(SYN.)* advent, arrival, aspect, demeanor, fashion, guise, apparition, manner, mien, look, presence.
(ANT.) disappearance, reality, departure, vanishing.

appease *(SYN.)* calm, compose, lull, quiet, relieve, assuage, pacify, satisfy, restraint, lesson, soothe, check, ease, alleviate, still, allay, tranquilize.
(ANT.) excite, arouse, incense, irritate, inflame.

append *(SYN.)* supplement, attach, add.

appendage *(SYN.)* addition, tail, supplement.

appetite *(SYN.)* zest, craving, desire, liking, longing, stomach, inclination, hunger, thirst, relish, passion.
(ANT.) satiety, disgust, distaste, repugnance.

appetizer *(SYN.)* hors d'oeuvre.

applaud *(SYN.)* cheer, clap, hail, approve, praise, acclaim.
(ANT.) disapprove, denounce, reject, criticize, condemn.

appliance *(SYN.)* machine, tool, instrument, device, utensil, implement.

applicable *(SYN.)* fitting, suitable, proper, fit, usable, appropriate, suited.
(ANT.) inappropriate, inapplicable.

apply *(SYN.)* affix, allot, appropriate, use, employ, petition, request, devote, avail, pertain, attach, ask, administer, petition, assign, relate, utilize.
(ANT.) give away, demand, detach, neglect, ignore.

appoint *(SYN.)* name, choose, nominate, designate, elect, establish, assign, place.
(ANT.) discharge, fire, dismiss.

appointment *(SYN.)* rendezvous, meeting, designation, position, engagement, assignment.
(ANT.) discharge, dismissal.

appraise *(SYN.)* value, evaluate, place a value on.

appreciate *(SYN.)* enjoy, regard, value, prize, cherish, admire, go up, improve, rise, respect, think highly of, esteem, appraise.
(ANT.) belittle, misunderstand, apprehend, degrade, scorn, depreciate, undervalue.

apprehend *(SYN.)* seize, capture, arrest, understand, dread, fear, grasp, perceive.
(ANT.) release, lose.

apprehension *(SYN.)* fear, misgiving, dread, uneasiness, worry, fearfulness, anticipation, capture, seizure.
(ANT.) confidence, composure, self-assuredness.

apprehensive *(SYN.)* worried, afraid, uneasy, bothered, anxious, concerned, perturbed, troubled, fearful.
(ANT.) relaxed.

apprentice *(SYN.)* amateur, recruit, novice, learner, beginner.
(ANT.) experienced, professional, master.

approach *(SYN.)* greet, inlet, come near, advance, access, passageway.
(ANT.) avoid, pass by, retreat.

appropriate *(SYN.)* apt, particular, proper, fitting, suitable, applicable, loot, pillage, purloin, rob, steal, embezzle, assign, becoming, apportion, authorize.
(ANT.) improper, contrary, inappropriate, buy, repay, restore, return, unfit, inapt.

approval *(SYN.)* commendation, consent, praise, approbation, sanction, assent, endorsement, support.
(ANT.) reproach, censure, reprimand, disapprove.

approve *(SYN.)* like, praise, authorize, confirm, endorse, appreciate, think well of, ratify, commend, sanction.
(ANT.) criticize, nullify, disparage, frown on, disapprove, deny.

approximate *(SYN.)* near, approach, roughly, close.
(ANT.) correct.

apt *(SYN.)* suitable, proper, appropriate, fit, suited, disposed, liable, inclined, prone, clever, bright, alert, intelligent, receptive.
(ANT.) ill-becoming, unsuitable, unlikely, slow, retarded, dense.

aptness *(SYN.)* capability, dexterity, power, qualification, skill, ability, aptitude.
(ANT.) incompetency, unreadiness, in-capacity.

aptitude *(SYN.)* knack, talent, gift, ability.

aqueduct *(SYN.)* gully, pipe, canal, waterway, channel.

arbitrary *(SYN.)* unrestricted, absolute, despotic, willful, unreasonable, unconditional, authoritative.
(ANT.) contingent, qualified, fair, reasonable, dependent, accountable.

arbitrate *(SYN.)* referee, settle, mediate, umpire, negotiate.

architecture *(SYN.)* structure, building, construction.

ardent *(SYN.)* fervent, fiery, glowing, intense, keen, impassioned, fervid, hot, passionate, earnest, eager, zealous, enthusiastic.
(ANT.) cool, indifferent, nonchalant, apathetic.

ardor *(SYN.)* enthusiasm, rapture, spirit, zeal, fervent, eager, glowing, eagerness.
(ANT.) unconcern, apathy, disinterest, indifference.

arduous *(SYN.)* laborious, hard, difficult, burdensome, strenuous, strained.
(ANT.) easy.

area *(SYN.)* space, extent, region, zone, section, expanse, district, neighborhood, size.

argue *(SYN.)* plead, reason, wrangle, indicate, prove, show, dispute, denote, imply, object, bicker, discuss, debate, disagree.
(ANT.) reject, spurn, ignore, overlook, agree, concur.

argument *(SYN.)* debate, dispute, discussion, controversy.
(ANT.) harmony, accord, agreement.

arid *(SYN.)* waterless, dry, flat, dull, unimaginative, stuffy.
(ANT.) fertile, wet, colorful.

arise *(SYN.)* enter, institute, originate, start, open, commence, emerge, appear.
(ANT.) terminate, end, finish, complete, close.

aristocrat *(SYN.)* noble, gentleman, peer, lord, nobleman.
(ANT.) peasant, commoner.

arm *(SYN.)* weapon, defend, equip, empower, fortify.

armistice *(SYN.)* truce, pact, deal, understanding, peace, treaty, contract, alliance, agreement.

army *(SYN.)* troops, legion, military,

forces, militia.

aroma *(SYN.)* smell, odor, fragrance, perfume, scent.

arouse *(SYN.)* stir, animate, move, pique, provoke, kindle, disturb, excite, foment, stimulate, awaken.
(ANT.) settle, soothe, calm.

arraign *(SYN.)* charge, censure, incriminate, indict, accuse.
(ANT.) acquit, release, vindicate, exonerate, absolve.

arraignment *(SYN.)* imputation, charge, accusation, incrimination.
(ANT.) pardon, exoneration, exculpation.

arrange *(SYN.)* classify, assort, organize, place, plan, prepare, devise, adjust, dispose, regulate, order, group, settle, adapt, catalog, systematize, distribute, prepare.
(ANT.) jumble, scatter, disorder, confuse, disturb, disarrange.

arrangement *(SYN.)* display, grouping, order, array.

array *(SYN.)* dress, adorn, attire, clothe, arrange, order, distribute, arrangement, display, exhibit.
(ANT.) disorder, disorganization, disarray.

arrest *(SYN.)* detain, hinder, restrain, seize, withhold, stop, check, obstruct, apprehend, interrupt, catch, capture.
(ANT.) free, release, discharge, liberate.

arrival *(SYN.)* advent, coming.
(ANT.) leaving, departure.

arrive *(SYN.)* come, emerge, reach, visit, land, appear.
(ANT.) exit, leave, depart, go.

arrogance *(SYN.)* pride, insolence.
(ANT.) humbleness, modesty, humility.

arrogant *(SYN.)* insolent, prideful, scornful, haughty, cavalier, proud.
(ANT.) modest, humble.

art *(SYN.)* cunning, tact, artifice, skill, aptitude, adroitness, painting, drawing, design, craft, dexterity, composition, ingenuity.
(ANT.) clumsiness, innocence, unskillfulness, honesty.

artery *(SYN.)* aqueduct, pipe, channel.

artful *(SYN.)* clever, sly, skillful, knowing, deceitful, tricky, crafty, cunning.
(ANT.) artless.

article *(SYN.)* story, composition, treatise, essay, thing, report, object.

artifice *(SYN.)* trick, clever, scheme, device.

artificial *(SYN.)* bogus, fake, affected, feigned, phony, sham, unreal, synthetic, assumed, counterfeit, unnatural, manmade, unreal, manufactured, false, feigned, pretended.
(ANT.) genuine, natural true, real, authentic.

artisan *(SYN.)* worker, craftsman, mechanic.

artist *(SYN.)* actor, actress, painter, sculptor, singer, designer.

artless *(SYN.)* innocent, open, frank, simple, honest, candid, natural, unskilled, ignorant, truthful, sincere.
(ANT.) artful.

ascend *(SYN.)* rise, scale, tower, mount, go up, climb.
(ANT.) fall, sink, descend, go down.

ascertain *(SYN.)* solve, learn, clear up, answer.

ascribe *(SYN.)* attribute, assign.

ashamed *(SYN.)* shamefaced, humiliated, abashed, mortified, embarrassed.
(ANT.) proud.

ask *(SYN.)* invite, request, inquire, query, question, beg, solicit, demand, entreat, claim, interrogate, charge, expect.
(ANT.) order, reply, insist, answer.

askance *(SYN.)* sideways.

askew *(SYN.)* disorderly, crooked, awry, twisted.
(ANT.) straight.

asleep *(SYN.)* inactive, sleeping, dormant.
(ANT.) alert, awake.

aspect *(SYN.)* appearance, look, view, outlook, attitude, viewpoint, phase, part, feature, side.

aspersion *(SYN.)* dishonor, insult, misuse, outrage, reproach, defamation, abuse, disparagement.
(ANT.) plaudit, respect, commendation, approval.

asphyxiate *(SYN.)* suffocate, stifle, smother, choke, strangle, throttle.

aspiration *(SYN.)* craving, desire, hope, longing, objective, passion, ambition.

aspire *(SYN.)* seek, aim, wish for, strive, desire, yearn for.

ass *(SYN.)* mule, donkey, burro, silly, dunce, stubborn, stupid, fool.

assail *(SYN.)* assault, attack.

assassinate *(SYN.)* purge, kill, murder.

assault *(SYN.)* invade, strike, attack, assail, charge, bombard, onslaught.
(ANT.) protect, defend.

assemble *(SYN.)* collect, gather, meet, congregate, connect, manufacture.
(ANT.) disperse, disassemble, scatter.

assembly *(SYN.)* legislature, congress, council, parliament.

assent *(SYN.)* consent to, concede, agree, approval, accept, comply, permission.
(ANT.) deny, dissent, refusal, denial, refuse.

assert *(SYN.)* declare, maintain, state, claim, express, defend, press, support, aver, uphold, consent, accept, comply, affirm, allege, emphasize.
(ANT.) deny, refute, contradict, decline.

assertion *(SYN.)* statement, affirmation, declaration.
(ANT.) contradiction, denial.

assess *(SYN.)* calculate, compute, estimate, levy, reckon, tax, appraise.

asset *(SYN.)* property, wealth, capitol, resources, goods.

assign *(SYN.)* apportion, ascribe, attribute, cast, allot, choose, appropriate, name, elect, appoint, distribute, designate, specify.
(ANT.) release, relieve, unburden, discharge.

assignment *(SYN.)* task, job, responsibility, duty.

assimilate *(SYN.)* digest, absorb, blot up.

assist *(SYN.)* help, promote, serve, support, sustain, abet, aid, back.
(ANT.) prevent, impede, hinder, hamper.

assistance *(SYN.)* backing, help, patronage, relief, succor, support.
(ANT.) hostility, resistance, antagonism, counteraction.

assistant *(SYN.)* accomplice, ally, associate, confederate, abettor.
(ANT.) rival, enemy, adversary.

associate *(SYN.)* affiliate, ally, join, connect, unite, combine, link, mingle, partner, mix.
(ANT.) separate, disconnect, divide, disrupt, estrange.

association *(SYN.)* organization, club, union, society, fraternity, sorority, companionship, fellowship.

assorted *(SYN.)* varied, miscellaneous, classified, different, several, grouped, various.

(ANT.) alike, same.

assortment *(SYN.)* collection, variety, mixture, conglomeration.

assuage *(SYN.)* calm, quiet, lessen, relieve, ease, allay, moderate, alleviate, restrain.

assume *(SYN.)* arrogate, affect, suspect, believe, appropriate, take, pretend, usurp, simulate, understand, postulate, presume, suppose.
(ANT.) doff, demonstrate, prove, grant, concede.

assumption *(SYN.)* presumption, guess, supposition, conjecture, postulate.

assure *(SYN.)* promise, convince, warrant, guarantee, pledge.
(ANT.) equivocate, deny.

astonish *(SYN.)* astound, amaze, surprise, shock.
(ANT.) tire, bore.

astound *(SYN.)* shock, amaze, astonish, stun, surprise, floor.

asunder *(SYN.)* divided, separate, apart.
(ANT.) together.

asylum *(SYN.)* shelter, refuge, home, madhouse, institution.

athletic *(SYN.)* strong, active, able-bodied, gymnastic, muscular, well-built.

atone *(SYN.)* repay, make up.

atrocious *(SYN.)* horrible, savage, brutal, ruthless, dreadful, awful, horrifying.
(ANT.) good, kind.

attach *(SYN.)* connect, adjoin, annex, join, append, stick, unite, adjoin, affix.
(ANT.) unfasten, separate, disengage.

attack *(SYN.)* raid, assault, besiege, abuse, censure, offense, seige, denunciation, aggression, push, criticism, invade.
(ANT.) surrender, defense, opposition, aid, defend, protect, repel.

attain *(SYN.)* achieve, acquire, accomplish, gain, get, reach, win.
(ANT.) discard, abandon, desert.

attainment *(SYN.)* exploit, feat, accomplishment, realization, performance.
(ANT.) omission, defeat, failure, neglect.

attempt *(SYN.)* essay, experiment, trial, try, undertaking, endeavor, effort.
(ANT.) laziness, neglect, inaction.

attend *(SYN.)* accompany, escort, watch, be serve, care for, follow, lackey, present, frequent, protect, guard.
(ANT.) desert, abandon, avoid.

attendant *(SYN.)* waiter, servant, valet.

attention *(SYN.)* consideration, heed, circumspection, notice, watchfulness, observance, application, reflection, study, care, alertness, mindfulness.
(ANT.) negligence, indifference, omission, oversight, disregard.

attentive *(SYN.)* careful, awake, alive, considerate, heedful, mindful, wary.
(ANT.) unaware, oblivious, apathetic.

attest *(SYN.)* testify, swear, vouch, certify.

attire *(SYN.)* apparel, dress, clothe.

attitude *(SYN.)* standpoint, viewpoint, stand, pose, aspect, position, posture.

attract *(SYN.)* enchant, interest, pull, fascinate, draw, tempt, infatuate, entice.
(ANT.) deter, repel, repulse, alienate.

attractive *(SYN.)* enchanting, winning, engaging, pleasant, pleasing, seductive.
(ANT.) unattractive, obnoxious, repellent, repulsive, forbidding.

attribute *(SYN.)* give, apply, place, trait, characteristic, feature, nature, credit.

audacious *(SYN.)* daring, bold, arrogant, foolhardy, cavalier, haughty, insolent.
(ANT.) humble, shy.

audacity *(SYN.)* effrontery, fearlessness, temerity, boldness.
(ANT.) humility, meekness, circumspection, fearfulness.

audible *(SYN.)* distinct, plain, clear.
(ANT.) inaudible.

augment *(SYN.)* enlarge, increase, raise, expand, broaden, extend.

auspicious *(SYN.)* lucky, timely, favorable, promising, fortunate.
(ANT.) untimely, unfortunate.

austere *(SYN.)* stern, severe, harsh, strict.
(ANT.) lenient, soft.

authentic *(SYN.)* real, true, genuine, pure, accurate, reliable, legitimate, factual.
(ANT.) false, spurious, artificial, counterfeit, erroneous.

authenticate *(SYN.)* validate, warrant, guarantee, verify, certify.

author *(SYN.)* father, inventor, maker, originator, writer, composer.

authoritative *(SYN.)* certain, secure, commanding, sure, tried, trustworthy, safe, influential, dependable.
(ANT.) uncertain, unreliable, dubious, fallible, questionable.

authority *(SYN.)* dominion, justification, power, permission, authorization, importance, domination, supremacy.

(ANT.) incapacity, denial, prohibition, weakness, impotence.

autocrat *(SYN.)* monarch, ruler, tyrant.

autograph *(SYN.)* endorse, sign, approve.

automatic *(SYN.)* self-acting, mechanical, spontaneous, uncontrolled, involuntary.
(ANT.) hand-operated, intentional, deliberate, manual.

automobile *(SYN.)* auto, car.

auxiliary *(SYN.)* assisting, helping, aiding.

avail *(SYN.)* help, profit, use, value, benefit, serve, advantage.

available *(SYN.)* obtainable, convenient, ready, handy, accessible, prepared.
(ANT.) unavailable, out of reach, inaccessible, unobtainable.

avarice *(SYN.)* lust, greed.

average *(SYN.* moderate, ordinary, usual, passable, fair, intermediate, medium.
(ANT.) outstanding, exceptional, extraordinary, unusual.

averse *(SYN.)* unwilling, opposed, forced, against, involuntary.
(ANT.) willing.

avert *(SYN.)* avoid, prevent, prohibit.
(ANT.) invite.

avid *(SYN.)* greedy, eager.

avoid *(SYN.)* elude, forestall, evade, escape, dodge, avert, forbear, eschew.
(ANT.) oppose, meet, confront, encounter, seek.

award *(SYN.)* reward, prize, medal, gift, trophy.

aware *(SYN.)* mindful, perceptive, informed, apprised, realizing, conscious.
(ANT.) unaware, ignorant, oblivious.

away *(SYN.)* absent, departed, distracted, gone, not at home.
(ANT.) present, attentive, attending.

awe *(SYN.)* surprise, respect, dread, astonishment, alarm.

awful *(SYN.)* frightful, horrible, awe-inspiring, dire, terrible, unpleasant.
(ANT.) humble, pleasant, commonplace.

awkward *(SYN.)* inept, unpolished, clumsy, gauche, rough, ungraceful.
(ANT.) adroit, graceful, polished, skillful.

awry *(SYN.)* askew, wrong, twisted, crooked, disorderly.
(ANT.) straight, right.

axiom *(SYN.)* fundamental, maxim, principle, theorem, adage, apothegm, byword, aphorism.

babble *(SYN.)* twaddle, nonsense, gibberish, prattle, balderdash, rubbish, chatter, baby talk, poppycock, jabber, maunder, piffle.

baby *(SYN.)* newborn, infant, neonate, babe, teeny, small, wee, little, undersized, midget, papoose, protect, cosset, pamper.

babyish *(SYN.)* infantile, childish, baby, whiny, unreasonable, immature, puerile, foolish, dependent.
(ANT.) mature, adult, sensible, reasonable, grown-up.

back *(SYN.)* help, assist, endorse, support, second, ratify, approve, stand by, approve, posterior, rear.
(ANT.) anterior, front, face, undercut, veto, undermine, progress, flow, leading, close, accessible, near.

backbiting *(SYN.)* gossip, slander, abuse, malice, cattiness, aspersion, derogation, belittling, badmouthing.
(ANT.) compliments, praise, loyalty, friendliness, approval.

backbone *(SYN.)* vertebrae, spine, pillar, support, staff, mainstay, basis, courage, determination, toughness, character.
(ANT.) timidity, weakness, cowardice, spinelessness.

backbreaking *(SYN.)* exhausting, fatiguing, tough, tiring, demanding, wearying, wearing, difficult.
(ANT.) light, relaxing, undemanding, slight.

back down *(SYN.)* accede, concede, acquiesce, yield, withdraw, renege.
(ANT.) persevere, insist.

backer *(SYN.)* underwriter, benefactor, investor, patron, sponsor, supporter.

backfire *(SYN.)* flop, boomerang, fail, founder, disappoint.
(ANT.) succeed.

background *(SYN.)* training, training, practice, knowledge, experience.

backing *(SYN.)* help, support, funds, money, assistance, grant, advocacy, subsidy, sympathy, endorsement.
(ANT.) criticism, detraction, faultfinding.

backlog *(SYN.)* inventory, reserve, hoard, amassment, accumulation.

backslide *(SYN.)* relapse, revert, return, weaken, regress, renege.

backward *(SYN.)* dull, sluggish, stupid,

loath, regressive, rearward, underdeveloped, slow, retarded.
(ANT.) progressive, precocious, civilized, advanced, forward.

bad *(SYN.)* unfavorable, wrong, evil, immoral, sinful, faulty, improper, unwholesome, wicked, corrupt, tainted.
(ANT.) good, honorable, reputable, moral, excellent.

badger *(SYN.)* tease, question, annoy, pester, bother, taunt, bait, provoke, torment, harass, hector.

baffle *(SYN.)* confound bewilder, perplex, puzzle, mystify, confuse, frustrate.
(ANT.) inform, enlighten.

bag *(SYN.)* catch, snare, poke, sack.

bait *(SYN.)* enticement, captivate, ensnare, tease, torment, pester, worry, entrap, question, entice, lure, trap, harass, tempt, badger.

balance *(SYN.)* poise, stability, composure, remains, residue, equilibrium, compare, weigh, equalize.
(ANT.) unsteadiness, instability.

bald *(SYN.)* bare, hairless, nude, open, uncovered, simple.
(ANT.) covered, hairy.

balk *(SYN.)* unwilling, obstinate, stubborn, hesitate, check, stop.
(ANT.) willing.

ball *(SYN.)* cotillion, dance, globe, sphere, spheroid.

ballad *(SYN.)* poem, song, ditty.

balloon *(SYN.)* puff up, enlarge, swell.
(ANT.) shrivel, shrink.

ballot *(SYN.)* choice, vote, poll.

balmy *(SYN.)* soft, gentle, soothing, fragrant, mild.
(ANT.) tempestuous, stormy.

ban *(SYN.)* prohibit, outlaw, disallow, block, bar, exclude, obstruct, prohibition, taboo, forbid.
(ANT.) allow, permit.

banal *(SYN.)* hackneyed, corny, vapid, trite, overused, humdrum.
(ANT.) striking, original, fresh, stimulating, novel.

band *(SYN.)* company, association, crew, group, society, belt, strip, unite, gang.

bandit *(SYN.)* thief, robber, highwayman, outlaw, marauder.

bang *(SYN.)* hit, strike, slam.

banish *(SYN.)* drive away, eject, exile, oust, deport, dismiss, expel.

(ANT.) receive, accept, shelter, admit, harbor, embrace, welcome.

bank *(SYN.)* barrier, slope, storage, treasury, row, series, string, shore.

banner *(SYN.)* colors, standard, pennant, flag.

banquet *(SYN.)* feast, celebration, festival, dinner, regalement, affair.

banter *(SYN.)* joke, tease, jest.

bar *(SYN.)* counter, impediment, saloon, exclude, obstacle, barricade, obstruct, shut out, hindrance, forbid, block, barrier, obstruction.
(ANT.) allow, permit, aid, encouragement.

barbarian *(SYN.)* brute, savage, boor, ruffian, rude, uncivilized, primitive, uncultured, coarse, cruel, barbaric, crude.
(ANT.) permit, allow, encouragement.

barbarous *(SYN.)* savage, remorseless, cruel, uncivilized, rude, unrelenting, merciless, crude, ruthless, inhuman.
(ANT.) kind, civilized, polite, humane, refined, tasteful, cultivated.

barber *(SYN.)* coiffeur, hairdresser.

bare *(SYN.)* naked, nude, uncovered, undressed, unclothed, unfurnished, plain, barren, empty, disclose, reveal, publicize, bald, expose, scarce, mere.
(ANT.) dressed, garbed, conceal, covered, hide, disguise, clothed.

barefaced *(SYN.)* impudent, bold, insolent, brazen, shameless, audacious, impertinent, rude.

barely *(SYN.)* hardly, scarcely, just.

bargain *(SYN.)* agreement, arrangement, deal, contract, arrange, sale.

baroque *(SYN.)* ornamented, elaborate, embellished, ornate.

barren *(SYN.)* unproductive, bare, unfruitful, infertile, sterile, childless.
(ANT.) productive, fruitful, fertile.

barricade *(SYN.)* fence, obstruction, shut in, fortification, barrier.
(ANT.) free, open, release.

barrier *(SYN.)* fence, wall, bar, railing, obstacle, hindrance, fortification, restraint, impediment, limit, barricade.
(ANT.) assistance, aid, encouragement.

barter *(SYN.)* exchange, deal, trade.

base *(SYN.)* bottom, rest, foundation, establish, found, immoral, evil, bad, wicked, depraved, selfish, worthless, cheap, debased, poor, support, stand, low, abject, menial.
(ANT.) exalted, righteous, lofty, esteemed, noble, honored, refined, valuable.

bashful *(SYN.)* timorous, abashed, shy, coy, timid, diffident, modest, sheepish, embarrassed, shame-faced, humble, recoiling, uneasy, awkward, ashamed.
(ANT.) fearless, outgoing, adventurous, gregarious, aggressive, daring.

basic *(SYN.)* underlying, chief, essential, main, fundamental.
(ANT.) subsidiary, subordinate.

basis *(SYN.)* presumption, support, base, principle, groundwork, presupposition, foundation, postulate, ground, assumption, premise, essential.
(ANT.) implication, trimming, derivative, superstructure.

basket *(SYN.)* hamper, creel, dossier, bassinet.

bastion *(SYN.)* mainstay, support, staff, tower, stronghold.

bat *(SYN.)* strike, hit, clout, stick, club, knock, crack.

batch *(SYN.)* group, set, collection, lot, cluster, bunch, mass, combination.

bath *(SYN.)* washing, shower, tub, wash, dip, soaping.

bathe *(SYN.)* launder, drench, swim, cover, medicate, immerse, wet, dip, soak, suffuse, rinse, saturate.

bathing suit *(SYN.)* maillot, swimsuit, trunks.

bathos *(SYN.)* mawkishness, soppiness, slush, sentimentality.

bathroom *(SYN.)* powder room, toilet, bath, lavatory.

baton *(SYN.)* mace, rod, staff, billy, crook, stick, fasces.

battalion *(SYN.)* mass, army, swarm, mob, drove, horde, gang, legion, regiment.

batten *(SYN.)* thrive, flourish, fatten, wax, expand, bloom, boom, grow.
(ANT.) decrease, weaken, fail.

batter *(SYN.)* pound, beat, hit, pommel, wallop, bash, smash, mixture, strike.

battery *(SYN.)* series, troop, force, rally, muster, set.

battle *(SYN.)* strife, fray, combat, struggle, contest, skirmish, conflict, fight, war, flight, warfare, action, campaign, strive against.
(ANT.) truce, concord, agreement, settle-

ment, harmony, accept, concur, peace.

battlement (SYN.) parapet, crenellation, rampart, fort, bastion, stronghold, escarpment.

bauble (SYN.) plaything, toy, trinket.

bawd (SYN.) procuress, prostitute.

bawdy (SYN.) vulgar, smutty, filthy, dirty, obscene, pornographic.

bawl (SYN.) sob, shout, wail, cry loudly, bellow, weep, cry.

bawl out (SYN.) scold, upbraid, censure, berate, reprove, reprimand.

bay (SYN.) inlet, bayou, harbor, lagoon, cove, sound, gulf.

bazaar (SYN.) fair, market, marketplace.

beach (SYN.) sands, seashore, waterfront, seaside, strand, coast, shore.

beacon (SYN.) light, signal, watchtower, guide, flare, warning, alarm.

bead (SYN.) globule, drop, pill, blob.

beak (SYN.) nose, bill, proboscis.

beam (SYN.) gleam, ray, girder, crossmember, pencil, shine, glisten, smile, glitter, gleam.

beaming (SYN.) joyful, bright, happy, radiant, grinning.
(ANT.) sullen, gloomy, threatening, scowling.

bear (SYN.) carry, support, take, uphold, suffer, convey, allow, stand, yield, endure, tolerate, produce, sustain, brook, transport, undergo, permit, suffer, abide, tolerate.
(ANT.) evade, shun, avoid, refuse, dodge.

bearable (SYN.) sufferable, supportable, manageable, tolerable.
(ANT.) terrible, painful, unbearable, awful, intolerable.

bearing (SYN.) course, direction, position, posture, behavior, manner, carriage, relation, reference, connection, application, deportment, air, way, conduct.

bearings (SYN.) orientation, whereabouts, location, direction, position, reading, course.

bear on (SYN.) affect, relate to.

bear out (SYN.) confirm, substantiate, justify, verify, prove.

bear up (SYN.) carry on, endure.

bear with (SYN.) tolerate, forbear.

beast (SYN.) monster, savage, brute, creature, animal.

beastly (SYN.) detestable, mean, low,

hateful, loathsome, nasty, unpleasant, despicable, obnoxious, brutal, brutish, offensive.
(ANT.) considerate, sympathetic, refined, humane, fine, pleasant.

beat (SYN.) pulse, buffet, pound, defeat, palpitate, hit, thump, belabor, knock, overthrow, thrash, pummel, rout, smite, throb, punch, subdue, pulsate, dash, strike, overpower, vanquish, conquer, batter, conquer, overcome, blow.
(ANT.) stroke, fail, defend, surrender, shield.

beaten (SYN.) disheartened, dejected, licked, discouraged, hopeless, downcast, down, depressed.
(ANT.) eager, hopeful, cheerful.

beatific (SYN.) uplifted, blissful, elated, happy, wonderful, joyful, divine.
(ANT.) awful, hellish, ill-fated, accursed.

beating (SYN.) whipping, drubbing, flogging, lashing, scourging, walloping.

beau (SYN.) lover, suitor, swain, admirer.

beautiful (SYN.) pretty, fair, lovely, charming, comely, handsome, elegant, attractive.
(ANT.) repulsive, hideous, unsightly, foul, homely, plainness, unattractive, ugly, ugliness.

beauty (SYN.) handsomeness, fairness, charm, pulchritude, attractiveness, loveliness, comeliness, grace, allegiance.
(ANT.) ugliness, disfigurement, homeliness, plainness, deformity, eyesore.

becalm (SYN.) calm, quiet, smooth, still, hush, repose, settle.

because (SYN.) inasmuch as, as, since, for.

because of (SYN.) as a result of, as a consequence of.

beckon (SYN.) call, signal, summon, motion, gesture, wave.

becloud (SYN.) obfuscate, confuse, befog, confound, obscure, muddle. (ANT.) illuminate, clarify, solve.

become (SYN.) change, grow, suit, be appropriate, befit.

becoming (SYN.) suitable, meet, befitting, appropriate, fitting, seemly, enhancing, attractive, pleasing, flattering, tasteful, smart, adorning, ornamental.
(ANT.) unsuitable, inappropriate, incongruent, ugly, unattractive, improper.

bed *(SYN.)* layer, cot, vein, berth, stratum, couch, accumulation, bunk, deposit, cradle.

bedazzle *(SYN.)* glare, blind, dumbfound, flabbergast, bewilder, furbish, festoon.

bedeck *(SYN.)* deck, adorn, beautify, smarten, festoon, garnish.

bedevil *(SYN.)* worry, fret, irk, torment, harass, pester, nettle, tease, vex, plague.
(ANT.) soothe, calm, delight, please.

bedlam *(SYN.)* tumult, uproar, madhouse, commotion, confusion, racket, rumpus, pandemonium.
(ANT.) calm, peace.

bedraggled *(SYN.)* shabby, muddy, sodden, messy, sloppy.
(ANT.) dry, neat, clean, well-groomed.

bedrock *(SYN.)* basis, foundation, roots, basics, essentials, fundamentals, bottom, bed, substratum, core.
(ANT.) top, dome, apex, nonessentials.

bedroom *(SYN.)* chamber, bedchamber.

beef *(SYN.)* brawn, strength, heft, gripe, sinew, fitness, huskiness, might.

beef up *(SYN.)* reinforce, vitalize, nerve, buttress, strengthen.
(ANT.) sap, weaken, enervate, drain.

beefy *(SYN.)* solid, strong, muscular, heavy, stocky.

befall *(SYN.)* occur, come about, happen.

before *(SYN.)* prior, earlier, in advance, formerly.
(ANT.) behind, following, afterward, latterly, after.

befriend *(SYN.)* welcome, encourage, aid, stand by.
(ANT.) dislike, shun, desert, avoid.

befuddle *(SYN.)* stupefy, addle, confuse, rattle, disorient.

beg *(SYN.)* solicit, ask, implore, supplicate, entreat, adjure, petition, beseech, request, importune, entreat, implore.
(ANT.) grant, cede, give, bestow, favor.

beget *(SYN.)* sire, engender, produce, create, propagate, originate, breed, generate, procreate, father.
(ANT.) murder, destroy, kill, abort, prevent, extinguish.

beggar *(SYN.)* scrub, tatterdemalion, pauper, wretch, ragamuffin, vagabond, starveling.

begin *(SYN.)* open, enter, arise, initiate, commence, start, inaugurate, originate, institute, create.

(ANT.) terminate, complete, finish, close, end, stop.

beginner *(SYN.)* nonprofessional, amateur, apprentice.
(ANT.) veteran, professional.

beginning *(SYN.)* outset, inception, origin, source, commencement, start, opening, initiation, inauguration.
(ANT.) termination, completion, end, close, consummation, closing, ending, finish.

begrime *(SYN.)* soil, dirty, smear, muddy, splotch, tarnish.
(ANT.) wash, clean, freshen, launder.

begrudge *(SYN.)* resent, envy, stint, withhold, grudge.

begrudging *(SYN.)* hesitant, reluctant, resentful, unwilling, forced.
(ANT.) willing, eager, quick, spontaneous.

beguiling *(SYN.)* enchanting, interesting, delightful, intriguing, engaging, bewitching, attractive, enthralling, captivating.
(ANT.) boring, dull, unattractive, tedious.

behalf *(SYN.)* benefit, welfare, support, aid, part, interest.

behave *(SYN.)* deport, comport, manage, act, demean, bear, interact, carry, operate, conduct.
(ANT.) rebel, misbehave.

behavior *(SYN.)* manners, carriage, disposition, action, deed, bearing, deportment, conduct, demeanor.
(ANT.) rebelliousness, misbehavior.

behead *(SYN.)* decapitate, guillotine, decollate.

behest *(SYN.)* order, command, decree, mandate, bidding.

behind *(SYN.)* after, backward, at the back, in back of.
(ANT.) frontward, ahead, before.

behold *(SYN.)* look, see, view, notice, observe, perceive, sight.
(ANT.) overlook, ignore.

being *(SYN.)* life, existing, existence, living, actuality, organism, individual.
(ANT.) death, nonexistence, expiration.

belabor *(SYN.)* repeat, reiterate, pound, explain, expatiate, din.

belated *(SYN.)* late, delayed, overdue, tardy.
(ANT.) well-timed, early.

belch *(SYN.)* emit, erupt, gush, disgorge, bubble, eructation, burp.

beleaguered *(SYN.)* bothered, beset, annoyed, beset, harassed, badgered, vexed, plagued, victimized.

belie *(SYN.)* distort, misrepresent, twist, disappoint.

belief *(SYN.)* trust, feeling, certitude, opinion, conviction, persuasion, credence, confidence, reliance, faith, view, creed, assurance.
(ANT.) heresy, denial, incredulity, distrust, skepticism, doubt.

believe *(SYN.)* hold, apprehend, fancy, support, accept, conceive, suppose, imagine, trust, credit.
(ANT.) doubt, reject, distrust, disbelieve, question.

believer *(SYN.)* adherent, follower, devotee, convert, zealot.
(ANT.) doubter, critic, scoffer, skeptic.

belittle *(SYN.)* underrate, depreciate, minimize, decry, disparage, diminish, demean, slight, discredit, militant, depreciate, humiliate.
(ANT.) esteem, admire, flatter, overrate, commend.

bell *(SYN.)* pealing, ringing, signal, tolling, buzzer, chime.

belligerent *(SYN.)* aggressive, warlike, hostile, offensive, combative, militant.
(ANT.) easygoing, compromising, peaceful.

bellow *(SYN.)* thunder, roar, scream, shout, yell, howl.

bellwether *(SYN.)* leader, pilot, guide, ringleader, boss, shepherd.

belly *(SYN.)* stomach, abdomen, paunch.

belonging *(SYN.)* loyalty, relationship, kinship, acceptance, rapport.

belongings *(SYN.)* property, effects, possessions.

beloved *(SYN.)* adored, sweet, loved, cherished, prized, esteemed, valued, darling.

below *(SYN.)* under, less, beneath, underneath, lower.
(ANT.) aloft, overhead, above, over.

belt *(SYN.)* girdle, sash, strap, cummerbund, band, waistband, whack, hit, wallop, punch.

bemoan *(SYN.)* mourn, lament, grieve, sorrow, regret, deplore.

bend *(SYN.)* turn, curve, incline, submit, bow, lean, crook, twist, yield, stoop, crouch, agree, suppress, oppress, mold,

kneel, deflect, subdue, influence.
(ANT.) resist, straighten, break, stiffen.

beneath *(SYN.)* under, below.
(ANT.) above, over.

benediction *(SYN.)* thanks, blessing, prayer.

beneficial *(SYN.)* salutary, good, wholesome, advantageous, useful, helpful, serviceable, profitable.
(ANT.) harmful, destructive, injurious, disadvantageous, unwholesome, deleterious, detrimental.

benefit *(SYN.)* support, help, gain, avail, profit, account, favor, aid, good, advantage, serve, interest, behalf, service.
(ANT.) handicap, calamity, trouble, disadvantage, distress.

benevolence *(SYN.)* magnanimity, charity, tenderness, altruism, humanity, philanthropy, generosity, liberality, beneficence, good will.
(ANT.) malevolence, unkindness, cruelty, selfishness, inhumanity.

benevolent *(SYN.)* kindhearted, tender, merciful, generous, altruistic, obliging, kind, good, well-wishing, philanthropy, liberal, unselfish, kindly, disposed, openhearted, humane, benign, friendly.
(ANT.) malevolent, greedy, wicked, harsh.

bent *(SYN.)* curved, crooked, resolved, determined, set, inclined, firm, decided.
(ANT.) straight.

berate *(SYN.)* scold.

beseech *(SYN.)* appeal, entreat, plead, ask, beg, implore.

beset *(SYN.)* surround, attack.

besides *(SYN.)* moreover, further, except for, also, as well, furthermore.

besiege *(SYN.)* assault, attack, siege, bombard, raid, charge.

bespeak *(SYN.)* engage, reserve, indicate, show, signify, express.

best *(SYN.)* choice, prime, select.
(ANT.) worst.

bestial *(SYN.)* brutal, beastly, savage, cruel.

bestow *(SYN.)* confer, place, put, award, give, present.
(ANT.) withdraw, withhold.

bet *(SYN.)* gamble, give, stake, wager, pledge, ante.

betray *(SYN.)* reveal, deliver, expose, mislead, trick, deceive, exhibit, show.

(ANT.) shelter, protect, safeguard.

betrothal *(SYN.)* marriage, engagement, contract.

better *(SYN.)* superior, preferable, improve.
(ANT.) worsen.

between *(SYN.)* among, betwixt.

beware *(SYN.)* take care, watch out, look sharp, be careful.

bewilder *(SYN.)* perplex, confuse, mystify, baffle, puzzle, overwhelm.
(ANT.) clarify, enlighten.

bewitch *(SYN.)* captivate, charm, delight, enchant.

beyond *(SYN.)* past, farther, exceeding.

bias *(SYN.)* slant, inclination, proneness, turn, bent, penchant, tendency, disposition, propensity, partiality, predisposition, leaning, proclivity, prejudice, influence, warp, slanting, predilection.
(ANT.) fairness, justice, evenhandedness, equity, detachment, impartiality.

bible *(SYN.)* guide, handbook, gospel, manual, sourcebook, guidebook.

bibulous *(SYN.)* guzzling, intemperate, winebibbing, sottish, alcoholic.
(ANT.) sober, moderate.

bicker *(SYN.)* dispute, argue, wrangle, quarrel.
(ANT.) go along with, agree.

bid *(SYN.)* order, command, direct, wish, greet, say, offer, instruct, invite, purpose, tender, proposal.

bidding *(SYN.)* behest, request, decree, call, charge, beck, summons, solicitation, invitation, instruction, mandate.

bide *(SYN.)* stay, tarry, delay, wait, remain.

big *(SYN.)* large, huge, bulky, immense, colossal, majestic, august, monstrous, hulking, gigantic, massive, great, enormous, tremendous, outgoing, important, kind, big-hearted, considerable, generous, grand.
(ANT.) small, little, tiny, immature, petite.

big-hearted *(SYN.)* good-natured, liberal, generous, unselfish, open-handed, unstinting, charitable, magnanimous.
(ANT.) cold, selfish, mean, uncharitable.

bigoted *(SYN.)* intolerant, partial, prejudiced, biased, unfair, chauvinist.

bigotry *(SYN.)* bias, blindness, intolerance, unfairness, prejudice, ignorance, passion, sectarianism.
(ANT.) acceptance, open-mindedness.

big-shot *(SYN.)* somebody, brass hat, big gun.
(ANT.) underling, nobody, nebbish, cipher.

bijou *(SYN.)* gem, bauble, jewel, ornament.

bile *(SYN.)* spleen, rancor, anger, bitterness, peevishness, ill-humor, nastiness, resentment, discontent, irascibility.
(ANT.) cheerfulness, affability, pleasantness.

bilge *(SYN.)* hogwash, drivel, gibberish, rubbish, bosh, foolishness, twaddle.

bilious *(SYN.)* petulant, crabby, ill-natured, cross, peevish, crotchety, cranky.
(ANT.) happy, agreeable, pleasant, good-natured.

bilk *(SYN.)* defraud, trick, cheat, hoodwink, deceive, fleece, rook, bamboozle.

bill *(SYN.)* charge, invoice, account, statement.

billet *(SYN.)* housing, quarters, berth, shelter, barrack, installation.

billingsgate *(SYN.)* swearing, scurrility, cursing, abuse, vulgarity, gutter, profanity.

billow *(SYN.)* surge, swell, rise, rush, peaking, magnification, amplification, augmentation, increase, intensification.
(ANT.) lowering, decrease.

bin *(SYN.)* cubbyhole. box, container, chest, cubicle, crib, receptacle, can.

bind *(SYN.)* connect, restrain, band, fasten, oblige, obligate, engage, wrap, connect, weld, attach, tie, require, restrict.
(ANT.) unlace, loose, unfasten, untie, free.

binding *(SYN.)* compulsory, obligatory, mandatory, compelling, unalterable, imperative, indissoluble, unconditional, unchangeable, hard-and-fast.
(ANT.) adjustable, flexible, elastic, changeable.

binge *(SYN.)* fling, spree, carousal, toot.

birth *(SYN.)* origin, beginning, infancy, inception.
(ANT.) finish, decline, death, disappearance, end.

biscuit *(SYN.)* bun, roll, cake, muffin, bread, rusk.

bit *(SYN.)* fraction, portion, scrap, fragment, particle, drop, speck, harness, small amount, restraint, morsel, sum.

bite *(SYN.)* gnaw, chew, nip, sting, pierce, mouthful, snack, morsel.

biting *(SYN.)* cutting, sharp, acid, sneering, sarcastic.

(ANT.) soothing, kind, gentle, agreeable.

bitter *(SYN.)* distasteful, sour, acrid, pungent, piercing, vicious, severe, biting, distressful, stinging, distressing, ruthless, hated, hostile, grievous, harsh, painful, tart.

(ANT.) sweet, mellow, pleasant, delicious.

bizarre *(SYN.)* peculiar, strange, odd, uncommon, queer, unusual.

(ANT.) usual, everyday, ordinary, inconspicuous.

black *(SYN.)* sooty, dark, ebony, inky, swarthy, soiled, filthy, dirty, stained, somber, depressing, sad, dismal, gloomy.

(ANT.) white, clean, pristine, glowing, pure, cheerful, light-skinned, sunny, bright.

blackball *(SYN.)* turn down, ban, blacklist, exclude, snub, reject, debar.

(ANT.) accept, include, invite, ask, bid.

blacken *(SYN.)* tar, ink, black, darken, besoot, smudge, begrime, discredit, defile, dull, dim, tarnish, ebonize, denounce, sully, libel, blemish, defame.

(ANT.) exalt, honor, whiten, brighten, shine, bleach.

blackmail *(SYN.)* bribe, payment, bribery, extortion, shakedown, coercion.

blackout *(SYN.)* faint, coma, unconsciousness, oblivion, amnesia, stupor, swoon.

bladder *(SYN.)* saccule, sac, vesicle, pouch, pod, cell, blister, container, cyst.

blade *(SYN.)* cutter, lancet, knife, sword.

blah *(SYN.)* lifeless, flat, jejune, lukewarm, stale, insipid, tasteless, pedestrian, tedious, dreary, uninteresting.

(ANT.) spirited, fascinating, vibrant, vigorous.

blame *(SYN.)* upbraid, criticize, fault, guilt, accuse, rebuke, charge, implicate, impeach, tattle, condemn, indict, responsibility, censure, denounce, reproach.

(ANT.) exonerate, credit, honor, absolve.

blameless *(SYN.)* moral, innocent, worthy, faultless.

(ANT.) blameworthy, culpable, guilty.

blanch *(SYN.)* whiten, bleach, decolorize, peroxide, fade, wash out, dim, dull.

bland *(SYN.)* soft, smooth, gentle, agreeable, vapid, insipid, mild, polite.

(ANT.) harsh, outspoken, disagreeable.

blandish *(SYN.)* praise, compliment, overpraise, cajole, puff, adulate, salve, fawn, court, toady, butter up, please, jolly.

(ANT.) insult, deride, criticize, belittle.

blandisher *(SYN.)* adulator, booster, sycophant, eulogist, apple polisher, flunkey.

(ANT.) knocker, faultfinder, belittler.

blandishment *(SYN.)* applause, cajolery, honey, adulation, plaudits, acclaim, fawning, compliments.

(ANT.) carping, belittling, criticism, deprecation.

blank *(SYN.)* unmarked, expressionless, uninterested, form, area, void, vacant, empty.

(ANT.) marked, filled, alert, animated.

blanket *(SYN.)* quilt, coverlet, cover, comforter, robe, padding, carpet, wrapper, mantle, envelope, housing, coat, comprehensive, universal, across-the-board, panoramic, omnibus.

(ANT.) limited, detailed, restricted, precise.

blare *(SYN.)* roar, blast, resound, jar, scream, swell, clang, peal, trumpet, toot, hoot.

blasphemous *(SYN.)* profane, irreverent, impious, godless, ungodly, sacrilegious, irreligious.

(ANT.) reverent, reverential, religious, pious.

blasphemy *(SYN.)* profanation, impiousness, cursing, irreverence, sacrilege, abuse, ecration, swearing, contempt.

(ANT.) respect, piety, reverence, devotion.

blast *(SYN.)* burst, explosion, discharge, blow-out.

blasted *(SYN.)* blighted, withered, ravaged, decomposed, spoiled, destroyed.

blastoff *(SYN.)* launching, expulsion, launch, shot, projection.

blatant *(SYN.)* shameless, notorious,

brazen, flagrant, glaring, bold, obvious.
(ANT.) deft, subtle, insidious, devious.
blaze *(SYN.)* inferno, shine, flare, marking, fire, outburst, holocaust, notch, flame.
(ANT.) die, dwindle.
bleach *(SYN.)* pale, whiten, blanch, whitener.
(ANT.) darken, blacken.
bleak *(SYN.)* dreary, barren, cheerless, depressing, gloomy, windswept, bare, cold, dismal, desolate, raw, chilly.
(ANT.) lush, hopeful, promising, cheerful.
bleary *(SYN.)* hazy, groggy, blurry, fuzzy, misty, clouded, overcast, dim, blear.
(ANT.) clear, vivid, precise, clear-cut.
bleed *(syn.)* pity, lose blood, grieve, sorrow.
blemish *(SYN.)* injury, speck, flaw, scar, disgrace, imperfection, stain, fault, blot.
(ANT.) purity, embellishment, adornment, perfection.
blend *(SYN.)* beat, intermingle, combine, fuse, unify, consolidate, unite, amalgamate, conjoin, mix, coalesce, intermix, join, merge, compound, combination, stir, mixture, commingle, mingle.
(ANT.) separate, decompose, analyze, disintegrate.
bless *(SYN.)* thank, celebrate, extol, glorify, adore, delight, praise, gladden, exalt.
(ANT.) denounce, blaspheme, slander, curse.
blessed *(SYN.)* sacred, holy, consecrated, dedicated, hallowed, sacrosanct, beatified, joyful, delighted, joyous, sainted, canonized, blissful.
(ANT.) miserable, sad, dispirited, cheerless.
blessing *(SYN.)* benison, sanction, favor, grace, benediction, invocation, approbation, approval, compliment, bounty, windfall, gift, benefit, advantage, kindness, felicitation, invocation.
(ANT.) disapproval, execration, curse, denunciation, malediction, rebuke, displeasure, condemnation, adversity, misfortune, mishap, calamity.
blight *(SYN.)* decay, disease, spoil, sickness, wither, ruin, damage, harm, decaying, epidemic, affliction, destroy.
blind *(SYN.)* sightless, unmindful,

rash, visionless, ignorant, unsighted, unconscious, discerning, heedless, oblivious, purblind, unknowing, screen, unaware, thoughtless, shade, unthinking, cover, curtain, without thought, headlong.
(ANT.) discerning, sensible, calculated, perceiving, perceptive, aware.
blink *(SYN.)* bat, glance, flicker, wink, twinkle.
bliss *(SYN.)* ecstasy, rapture, glee, elation, joy, blessedness, gladness, happiness, delight, felicity, blissfulness.
(ANT.) woe, sadness, sorrow, grief, unhappiness, torment, wretchedness, misery.
blissful *(SYN.)* happy, elated, rapturous, ecstatic, paradisiacal, joyous, enraptured.
blister *(SYN.)* bleb, swelling, welt, sore, blob, bubble, inflammation, boil, canker.
blithe *(SYN.)* breezy, merry, airy, lighthearted, light, gay, fanciful, graceful.
(ANT.) morose, grouchy, low-spirited, gloomy.
blitz *(SYN.)* strike, onslaught, thrust, raid, lunge, drive, incursion, assault, sally.
blizzard *(SYN.)* storm, snowstorm, snowfall, gale, tempest, blast, blow, swirl.
bloat *(SYN.)* distend, puff up, inflate, swell.
(ANT.) deflate.
blob *(SYN.)* bubble, blister, pellet, globule.
block *(SYN.)* clog, hinder, bar, impede, close, obstruct, barricade, blockade, obstruction, hindrance, obstacle, impediment, retard, check, stop.
(ANT.) forward, promote, aid, clear, advance, advantage, assist, further, open.
blockade *(SYN.)* barrier, fortification, obstruction, barricade.
blockhead *(SYN.)* dunce, dolt, fool, sap, idiot, simpleton, chump, booby, bonehead, woodenhead.
blood *(SYN.)* murder, gore, slaughter, bloodshed, ancestry, lineage, heritage.
bloodcurdling *(SYN.)* hair-raising, terrifying, alarming, chilling, stunning, scary.
bloodless *(SYN.)* dead, torpid, dull, drab,

cold, colorless, passionless, lackluster.
(*ANT.*) *passionate, vital, ebullient, animated, vivacious.*

bloodshed (*SYN.*) murder, killing, slaying, blood bath, massacre, carnage.

bloodthirsty (*SYN.*) murderous, cruel.

bloody (*SYN.*) cruel, pitiless, bloodthirsty, inhuman, ruthless, ferocious, murderous.
(*ANT.*) *kind, gentle.*

bloom (*SYN.*) thrive, glow, flourish, blossom, flower.
(*ANT.*) *wane, decay, dwindle, shrivel, wither.*

blooming (*SYN.*) flush, green, vigorous, thriving, vital, abloom, healthy, fresh, booming.
(*ANT.*) *flagging, declining, whithering.*

blooper (*SYN.*) muff, fluff, error, bungle, botch, blunder, fumble, howler, indiscretion.

blossom (*SYN.*) bloom, flower, flourish.
(*ANT.*) *shrink, wither, dwindle, fade.*

blot (*SYN.*) stain, inkblot, spot, inkstain, blemish, dishonor, disgrace, spatter, obliterate, soil, dry.

blot out (*SYN.*) wipe out, destroy, obliterate, abolish, annihilate, cancel, expunge, strike out, shade, darken, shadow, overshadow, obfuscate, cloud, eclipse.

blow (*SYN.*) hit, thump, slap, cuff, box, shock, move, drive, spread, breeze, puff, whistle, inflate, enlarge.

blowout (*SYN.*) blast, explosion, burst.

blue (*SYN.*) sapphire, azure, gloomy, sad, unhappy, depressed, dejected, melancholy.
(*ANT.*) *cheerful, optimistic, happy.*

blueprint (*SYN.*) design, plan, scheme, chart, draft, prospectus, outline, proposal, conception, project, layout.

blues (*SYN.*) dumps, melancholy, depression, doldrums, moodiness, dejection, despondency, gloominess, moroseness.

bluff (*SYN.*) steep, perpendicular, vertical, abrupt, precipitous, rough, open, frank, hearty, blunt, fool, mislead, pretend, deceive, fraud, lie, fake, deceit.

blunder (*SYN.*) error, flounder, mistake, stumble.

blunt (*SYN.*) solid, abrupt, rough, dull, pointless, plain, bluff, edgeless, unceremonious, obtuse, rude, outspoken,

unsharpened, rounded, worn, crude, direct, impolite, short, curt, gruff.
(*ANT.*) *tactful, polite, subtle, polished, suave, sharp, keen, pointed, diplomatic.*

blur (*SYN.*) sully, dim, obscure, stain, dull, confuse, cloud, smear, stain, smudge.
(*ANT.*) *clear, clarify.*

blush (*SYN.*) redden.

board (*SYN.*) embark, committee, wood, mount, cabinet, food, get on, lumber.

boast (*SYN.*) vaunt, flaunt, brag, glory, crow, exaggerate, bragging.
(*ANT.*) *humble, apologize, minimize, deprecate.*

body (*SYN.*) remains, bulk, mass, carcass, form, company, corpus, society, firmness, group, torso, substance, collection, cadaver, trunk, group, throng, company, crowd, band.
(*ANT.*) *spirit, intellect, soul.*

bogus (*SYN.*) counterfeit, false, pretend, fake, phony.
(*ANT.*) *genuine.*

boil (*SYN.*) seethe, bubble, pimple, fume, pimple, cook, swelling, rage, foam, simmer, stew.

boisterous (*SYN.*) rough, violent, rowdy, noisy, tumultuous.
(*ANT.*) *serene.*

bold (*SYN.*) daring, forward, pushy, striking, brave, dauntless, rude, prominent, adventurous, fearless, insolent, conspicuous, defiant, arrogant, cavalier, brazen, unafraid, intrepid, courageous, valiant, heroic, gallant, disrespectful, impudent, shameless.
(*ANT.*) *modest, bashful, cowardly, timid, retiring, flinching, fearful, timorous, polite, courteous, deferential.*

bolt (*SYN.*) break away, fastener, flee, take flight, lock.

bombard (*SYN.*) shell, open fire, bomb, rake, assail, attack.

bond (*SYN.*) fastener, rope, tie, cord, connection, attachment, link, tie, promise.
(*ANT.*) *sever, separate, untie, disconnect.*

bondage (*SYN.*) slavery, thralldom, captivity, imprisonment, servitude, confinement, vassalage, enslavement.
(*ANT.*) *liberation, emancipation, free, independence, freedom.*

bonds *(SYN.)* chains, cuffs, fetters, shackles, irons, bracelets.

bone up *(SYN.)* learn, master, study, relearn.

bonus *(SYN.)* more, extra, premium, gift, reward, bounty.

bony *(SYN.)* lean, lank, thin, lanky, rawboned, fleshless, skinny, gangling, weight.

(ANT.) plump, fleshy, stout.

book *(SYN.)* manual, textbook, work, booklet, monograph, brochure, tract, volume, pamphlet, treatise, publication, hardcover, paperback, novel, workbook, text.

bookish *(SYN.)* formal, scholarly, theoretical, academic, learned, scholastic, erudite.

(ANT.) simple, ignorant.

boom *(SYN.)* advance, grow, flourish, progress, gain, increase, roar, beam, rumble, reverberate, thunder, prosper, swell, thrive, pole, rush.

(ANT.) decline, fail, recession.

booming *(SYN.)* flourishing, blooming, thriving, vigorous, prospering, exuberant.

(ANT.) waning, dying, failing, declining.

boon *(SYN.)* gift, jolly, blessing, pleasant, godsend, windfall.

boondocks *(SYN.)* sticks, backwoods.

boor *(SYN.)* lout, clown, oaf, yokel, rustic, vulgarian, ruffian.

boorish *(SYN.)* coarse, churlish, uncivil, ill-mannered, ill-bred, uncivilized, crude, uncouth.

(ANT.) polite, cultivated, cultivated, well-mannered.

boost *(SYN.)* push, lift, help, hoist, shove.

(ANT.) depress, lower, belittle, submerge, disparage, decrease, decline, reduction, downturn.

booster *(SYN.)* supporter, fan, rooter, plugger, follower.

boot *(SYN.)* shoe, kick.

booth *(SYN.)* enclosure, cubicle, stand, compartment, box.

bootless *(SYN.)* purposeless, ineffective, profitless, useless.

(ANT.) favorable, successful, useful.

bootlicker *(SYN.)* flunky, fawner, toady, sycophant.

booty *(SYN.)* prize, plunder, loot.

booze *(SYN.)* spirits, drink, liquor, al-cohol.

border *(SYN.)* fringe, rim, verge, boundary, edge, termination, brink, limit, brim, outskirts, frontier, margin.

(ANT.) interior, center, mainland, core, middle.

borderline *(SYN.)* unclassifiable, indeterminate, halfway, obscure, inexact, indefinite, unclear.

(ANT.) precise, absolute, definite.

border on *(SYN.)* approximate, approach, resemble, echo, parallel, connect.

bore *(SYN.)* tire, weary, hole, perforate, pierce, drill.

(ANT.) arouse, captivate, excite, interest.

boredom *(SYN.)* ennui, doldrums, weariness, dullness, tedium.

(ANT.) stimulation, motive, activity, stimulus, excitement.

boring *(SYN.)* monotonous, dull, dead, flat, tedious, wearisome, trite, prosaic, humdrum, long-winded.

born *(SYN.)* hatched, produced.

borrow *(SYN.)* copy, adopt, simulate, mirror, assume, usurp, plagiarize, take.

(ANT.) allow, advance, invent, originate, credit, lend.

bosom *(SYN.)* chest, breast, feelings, thoughts, mind, interior, marrow, heart.

boss *(SYN.)* director, employer, oversee, direct, foreman, supervisor, manager.

(ANT.) worker, employee, underling.

bossy *(SYN.)* overbearing, arrogant, domineering, lordly, tyrannical, highhanded, arbitrary, oppress.

(ANT.) flexible, easygoing, cooperative.

botch *(SYN.)* blunder, bungle, fumble, goof, muff, mishandle, mismanage.

(ANT.) perform, realize.

bother *(SYN.)* haunt, molest, trouble, annoy, upset, fleeting, transient, harass, inconvenience, momentary, disturb, passing, pester, tease, irritate, worry, vex.

(ANT.) prolonged, extended, long, protracted, lengthy, comfort, solace.

bothersome *(SYN.)* irritating, vexatious, worrisome, annoying, distressing, troublesome, disturbing.

bottle *(SYN.)* container, flask, vessel, decanter, vial, ewer, jar.

bottleneck *(SYN.)* obstacle, obstruction, barrier, block, blockage, detour.

bottom *(SYN.)* basis, fundament, base,

groundwork, foot, depths, lowest part, underside, foundation, seat, buttocks, rear, behind.

(ANT.) top, peak, apex, summit, topside.

bough *(SYN.)* branch, arm, limb.

bounce *(SYN.)* recoil, ricochet, rebound.

bound *(SYN.)* spring, vault, hop, leap, start, surrounded, jump, limit, jerk, boundary, bounce, skip, tied, shackled, trussed, fettered, certain, sure, destined, compelled, required.

(ANT.) unfettered, free.

boundary *(SYN.)* bound, limit, border, margin, outline, circumference, perimeter, division, frontier, edge.

boundless *(SYN.)* limitless, endless, inexhaustible, unlimited, eternal, infinite.

(ANT.) restricted, narrow, limited.

bounteous *(SYN.)* plentiful, generous, liberal, abundant.

(ANT.) scarce.

bountiful *(SYN.)* bounteous, fertile, plentiful, generous, abundant.

(ANT.) sparing, infertile, scarce.

bounty *(SYN.)* generosity, gift, award, bonus, reward, prize, premium.

bourgeois *(SYN.)* common, ordinary, commonplace, middle-class, conventional.

(ANT.) upper-class, unconventional, loose, aristocratic.

bout *(SYN.)* round, contest, conflict, test, struggle, match, spell, fight.

bow *(SYN.)* bend, yield, kneel, submit, stoop.

bowels *(SYN.)* entrails, intestines, innards, guts, stomach.

bowl *(SYN.)* container, dish, pot, pottery, crock, jug, vase.

bowl over *(SYN.)* fell, floor, overturn, astound, nonplus, stagger, jar.

bow out *(SYN.)* give up, withdraw, retire, resign, abandon.

box *(SYN.)* hit, fight, crate, case, container.

boxer *(SYN.)* prizefighter, fighter.

boy *(SYN.)* male, youngster, lad, kid, fellow, buddy, youth.

(ANT.) girl, man.

boycott *(SYN.)* picket, strike, ban, revolt, blackball.

boy friend *(SYN.)* date, young man, sweetheart, courtier, beau.

brace *(SYN.)* strengthen, tie, prop, support, tighten, stay, strut, bind, truss, crutch.

bracelet *(SYN.)* armband, bangle, circlet.

bracing *(SYN.)* stimulating, refreshing, restorative, fortifying, invigorating.

bracket *(SYN.)* join, couple, enclose, relate, brace, support.

brag *(SYN.)* boast, flaunt, vaunt, bluster, swagger.

(ANT.) demean, debase, denigrate, degrade, depreciate, deprecate.

braid *(SYN.)* weave, twine, wreath, plait.

brain *(SYN.)* sense, intelligence, intellect, common sense, understanding, reason.

(ANT.) stupid, stupidity.

brake *(SYN.)* decelerate, stop, curb.

(ANT.) accelerate.

branch *(SYN.)* shoot, limb, bough, tributary, offshoot, part, division, expand, department, divide, spread, subdivision.

brand *(SYN.)* make, trademark, label, kind, burn, trade name, mark, stamp, blaze.

brave *(SYN.)* bold, daring, gallant, valorous, adventurous, heroic, magnanimous, chivalrous, audacious, valiant, courageous, fearless, intrepid, unafraid.

(ANT.) weak, cringing, timid, cowardly, fearful, craven.

brawl *(SYN.)* racket, quarrel, fracas, riot, fight, melee, fray, disturbance, dispute, disagreement.

brawn *(SYN.)* strength, muscle.

(ANT.) weakness.

brazen *(SYN.)* immodest, forward, shameless, bold, brassy, impudent, insolent, rude.

(ANT.) retiring, self-effacing, modest, shy.

breach *(SYN.)* rupture, fracture, rift, break, crack, gap, opening, breaking, quarrel, violation.

(ANT.) observation.

break *(SYN.)* demolish, pound, rack, smash, burst, rupture, disobey, violate, crack, infringe, crush, squeeze, transgress, fracture, shatter, wreck, crash, atomize, disintegrate, collapse, splinter, crack, gap, breach, opening, rupture.

(ANT.) restore, heal, join, renovate, mend, repair.

breed *(SYN.)* engender, bear, propagate,

father, beget, rear, conceive, train, generate, raise, procreate, nurture, create, mother, produce, originate, generate, raise, train, nurture.

(ANT.) murder, abort, kill.

breeze *(SYN.)* air, wind, zephyr, breath.

(ANT.) calm.

breezy *(SYN.)* jolly, spry, active, brisk, energetic, lively, carefree, spirited.

brevity *(SYN.)* briefness, conciseness.

(ANT.) length.

brew *(SYN.)* plot, plan, cook, ferment, prepare, scheme.

bribe *(SYN.)* buy off.

bridle *(SYN.)* control, hold, restrain, check, harness, curb, restraint, halter.

(ANT.) release, free, loose.

brief *(SYN.)* curt, short, fleeting, passing, compendious, terse, laconic, succinct, momentary, transient, temporary, concise, compact, condensed.

(ANT.) long, extended, prolonged, lengthy, protracted, comprehensive, extensive, exhaustive.

brigand *(SYN.)* bandit, robber, thief.

bright *(SYN.)* luminous, gleaming, clever, witty, brilliant, lucid, vivid, clear, smart, intelligent, lustrous, clever, shining, shiny, sparkling, shimmering, radiant, cheerful, lively, gay, happy, lighthearted, keen, promising, favorable, encouraging.

(ANT.) sullen, dull, murky, dark, gloomy, dim, lusterless, boring, colorless, stupid, backward, slow.

brilliant *(SYN.)* bright, clear, smart, intelligent, sparkling, shining, alert, vivid, splendid, radiant, glittering, talented, ingenious, gifted.

(ANT.) mediocre, dull, lusterless, second-rate.

brim *(SYN.)* border, margin, lip, rim, edge.

(ANT.) middle, center.

bring *(SYN.)* fetch, take, carry, raise, introduce, propose.

(ANT.) remove, withdraw.

brink *(SYN.)* limit, verge, rim, margin, edge.

brisk *(SYN.)* fresh, breezy, cool, lively, spry, refreshing, spirited, jolly, energetic, quick, active, animated, nimble, spry, agile, sharp, keen, stimulating, invigorating.

(ANT.) musty, faded, stagnant, decayed, hackneyed, slow, lethargic, sluggish, still, dull, oppressive.

briskness *(SYN.)* energy, exercise, motion, rapidity, agility, action, quickness, activity, vigor, liveliness, movement.

(ANT.) inertia, idleness, sloth, dullness, inactivity.

bristle *(SYN.)* flare up, anger, rage, seethe, get mad.

brittle *(SYN.)* crumbling, frail, breakable, delicate, splintery, crisp, fragile, weak.

(ANT.) tough, enduring, unbreakable, thick, strong, sturdy, flexible, elastic, supple.

broach *(SYN.)* set afoot, introduce, inaugurate, start, mention, launch, advance.

broad *(SYN.)* large, wide, tolerant, expanded, vast, liberal, sweeping, roomy, expansive, extended, general, extensive, full.

(ANT.) restricted, confined, narrow, constricted, slim, tight, limited, negligible.

broadcast *(SYN.)* distribute, announce, publish, scatter, circulate, spread, send, transmit, relay.

broaden *(SYN.)* spread, widen, amplify, enlarge, extend, increase, add to, expand, stretch, deepen, magnify.

(ANT.) tighted, narrow, constrict, straiten.

broad-minded *(SYN.)* unprejudiced, tolerant, liberal, unbigoted.

(ANT.) prejudiced, petty, narrow-minded.

brochure *(SYN.)* booklet, pamphlet, leaflet, mailing, circular, tract, flier.

broil *(SYN.)* cook, burn, heat, roast, bake, scorch, fire, grill, singe, sear, toast.

broken *(SYN.)* flattened, rent, shattered, wrecked, destroyed, reduced, smashed, crushed, fractured, ruptured, interrupted, burst, separated.

(ANT.) whole, integral, united, repaired.

brokenhearted *(SYN.)* disconsolate, forlorn, heartbroken, sad, grieving.

bromide *(SYN.)* banality, platitude, stereotype, commonplace, slogan, proverb.

brooch *(SYN.)* clasp, pin, breastpin, broach.

brood *(SYN.)* study, consider, ponder, reflect, contemplate, meditate, young, litter, offspring, think, muse, deliberate.

brook *(SYN.)* rivulet, run, branch, stream, creek.

brother *(SYN.)* comrade, man, kinsman, sibling.
(ANT.) sister.

brotherhood *(SYN.)* kinship, kindness, fraternity, fellowship, clan, society, brotherliness, bond, association, relationship, solidarity.
(ANT.) strife, discord, acrimony, opposition.

brotherly *(SYN.)* affectionate, fraternal, cordial, sympathetic, benevolent, philanthropic, humane, kindred, communal, altruistic.

brow *(SYN.)* forehead, eyebrow.

browbeat *(SYN.)* bully, domineer, bulldoze, intimidate, henpeck, oppress, grind.

brown study *(SYN.)* contemplation, reflection, reverie, musing, thoughtfulness, deliberation, rumination, self-communion.

browse *(SYN.)* scan, graze, read, feed.

bruise *(SYN.)* hurt, injure, wound, damage, abrasion, injury, contusion, mark, damage, harm, wound.

brunt *(SYN.)* force, impact, shock, strain, oppression, severity.

brush *(SYN.)* rub, wipe, clean, bushes, remove, shrubs, broom, whisk, paintbrush, hairbrush, underbrush, thicket.

brush-off *(SYN.)* dismissal, snub, slight, rebuff, turndown.

brusque *(SYN.)* sudden, curt, hasty, blunt, rough, steep, precipitate, rugged, craggy, gruff, surly, abrupt, short, bluff.
(ANT.) smooth, anticipated, courteous, expected, gradual, personable.

brutal *(SYN.)* brute, cruel, inhuman, rude, barbarous, gross, sensual, ferocious, brutish, coarse, bestial, carnal, remorseless, ruthless, savage, mean, savage, pitiless, barbaric.
(ANT.) kind, courteous, humane, civilized, gentle, kindhearted, mild.

brute *(SYN.)* monster, barbarian, beast, animal, wild, savage.

bubble *(SYN.)* boil, foam, seethe, froth.

buccaneer *(SYN.)* sea robber, privateer, pirate.

buck *(SYN.)* spring, jump, vault, leap.

bucket *(SYN.)* pot, pail, canister, can.

buckle *(SYN.)* hook, fastening, fastener, bend, wrinkle, clip, clasp, distort, catch, strap, fasten, collapse, yield, warp.

bud *(SYN.)* develop, sprout.

buddy *(SYN.)* companion, comrade, friend, partner, pal.

budge *(SYN.)* stir, move.

budget *(SYN.)* schedule, ration.

buff *(SYN.)* shine, polish, burnish, rub, wax.

buffet *(SYN.)* bat, strike, clout, blow, knock, beat, crack, hit, slap, cabinet, counter, server.

buffoon *(SYN.)* jester, fool, clown, jokester, zany, comedian, chump, boor, dolt.

bug *(SYN.)* fault, hitch, defect, catch, snag, failing, rub, flaw, snarl, weakness, annoy, pester, hector, vex, nag, nettle.

bugbear *(SYN.)* bogy, specter, demon, devil, fiend.

build *(SYN.)* found, rear, establish, constructed, raise, set up, erect, assemble.
(ANT.) raze, destroy, overthrow, demolish, undermine.

building *(SYN.)* residence, structure, house, edifice.

buildup *(SYN.)* gain, enlargement, increase, praise, commendation, promotion, jump, expansion, uptrend, testimonial, plug, puff, blurb, endorsement, compliment.
(ANT.) reduction, decrease, decline.

bulge *(SYN.)* lump, protuberance, bump, swelling, protrusion, extend, protrude.
(ANT.) hollow, shrink, contract, depression.

bulk *(SYN.)* lump, magnitude, volume, size, mass, most, majority.

bulky *(SYN.)* great, big, huge, large, enormous, massive, immense, monstrous, clumsy, cumbersome, unwieldy.
(ANT.) tiny, little, small, petite, handy, delicate.

bull *(SYN.)* push, force, press, drive, thrust, bump.

bulldoze *(SYN.)* cow, bully, coerce, thrust, push.

bulletin *(SYN.)* news, flash, message, statement, newsletter, circular.

bullheaded *(SYN.)* dogged, stiff-necked, stubborn, mulish, rigid, pigheaded, willful, tenacious, unyielding.

(*ANT.*) *flexible, submissive, compliant.*

bully *(SYN.)* pester, tease, intimidate, harass, domineer.

bulwark *(SYN.)* wall, bastion, abutment, bank, dam, rampart, shoulder, parapet, backing, maintainer, embankment, safeguard, reinforcement, sustainer.

bum *(SYN.)* idler, loafer, drifter, hobo, wretch, dwadler, beggar, vagrant.

bumbling *(SYN.)* bungling, inept, blundering, clumsy, incompetent, awkward, maladroit, lumbering, ungainly.

(*ANT.*) *facile, handy, dexterous, proficient.*

bump *(SYN.)* shake, push, hit, shove, prod, collide, knock, bang, strike.

bumpkin *(SYN.)* hick, yokel, rustic, yahoo.

bumptious *(SYN.)* arrogant, self-assertive, conceited, forward, overbearing, pushy, boastful, obtrusive.

(*ANT.*) *sheepish, self-effacing, retiring, shrinking, unobtrusive, diffident.*

bumpy *(SYN.)* uneven, jolting, rough, jarring, rocky, coarse, craggy, irregular.

(*ANT.*) *flat, smooth, flush, polished, level.*

bunch *(SYN.)* batch, bundle, cluster, company, collection, flock, group.

bundle *(SYN.)* package, mass, collection, batch, parcel, packet, box, carton, bunch.

bungalow *(SYN.)* ranch house, cabana, cabin, cottage, lodge, summer house, villa.

bungle *(SYN.)* tumble, botch, foul up, boggle, mess up, louse up, blunder.

bunk *(SYN.)* berth, rubbish, nonsense, couch, bed, cot.

buoyant *(SYN.)* light, jolly, spirited, effervescent, blithe, sprightly, lively, resilient.

(*ANT.*) *hopeless, dejected, sullen, depressed, heavy, despondent, sinking, low, pessimistic, downcast, glum.*

burden *(SYN.)* oppress, afflict, trouble, encumber, tax, weight, load, worry, contents, trial, lade, overload.

(*ANT.*) *lighten, alleviate, ease, mitigate, console, disburden.*

bureau *(SYN.)* office, division, department, unit, commission, chest, dresser.

bureaucrat *(SYN.)* clerk, official, functionary, servant, politician.

burglar *(SYN.)* thief, robber.

burial *(SYN.)* interment, funeral.

burn *(SYN.)* scorch, blaze, scald, sear, char, incinerate, fire, flare, combust.

(*ANT.*) *quench, extinguish.*

burrow *(SYN.)* tunnel, search, seek, dig, excavate, hunt, den, hole.

burst *(SYN.)* exploded, broken, erupt.

bury *(SYN.)* hide, inhume, conceal, immure, cover, inter, entomb, secrete.

(*ANT.*) *reveal, display, open, raise, disinter.*

business *(SYN.)* employment, profession, trade, work, art, engagement, vocation, occupation, company, concern, firm.

(*ANT.*) *hobby, avocation, pastime.*

bustle *(SYN.)* noise, flurry, action, fuss, ado, stir, excitement, commotion.

(*ANT.*) *calmness, composure, serenity, peacefulness.*

busy *(SYN.)* careful, industrious, active, patient, assiduous, diligent, perseverant.

(*ANT.*) *unconcerned, indifferent, careless, inactive, unemployed, lazy, indolent.*

busybody *(SYN.)* gossip, tattletale, pry, meddler, snoop.

but *(SYN.)* nevertheless, yet, however, though, although, still.

butcher *(SYN.)* kill, murder, slaughter, assassinate, slay, massacre.

(*ANT.*) *save, protect, vivify, animate, resuscitate.*

butt *(SYN.)* bump, ram, bunt, shove, jam, drive, blow, push, thrust, propulsion.

buttocks *(SYN.)* hind end, rump, posterior, behind, bottom, rear, butt.

button *(SYN.)* clasp, close, fasten, hook.

buttress *(SYN.)* support, brace, stay, frame, prop, reinforcement, bulwark.

buy *(SYN.)* procure, get, purchase, acquire, obtain.

(*ANT.*) *vend, sell.*

buzz *(SYN.)* whir, hum, drone, burr.

by *(SYN.)* near, through, beside, with, from, at, close to.

bygone *(SYN.)* bypast, former, earlier, past, onetime, forgotten.

(*ANT.*) *present, current, modern.*

bypass *(SYN.)* deviate from, go around, detour around.

bystander *(SYN.)* onlooker, watcher, viewer, observer, witness, kibitzer.

byway *(SYN.)* passage, detour, path.

byword *(SYN.)* adage, proverb, axiom, shibboleth, apothegm, motto, slogan.

cab *(SYN.)* coach, taxi, car, hack, taxicab, carriage.

cabin *(SYN.)* cottage, shack, shanty, hut, dwelling, house.

cabinet *(SYN.)* ministry, council, committee, case, cupboard.

cable *(SYN.)* wire, cord, rope, telegraph.

cache *(SYN.)* bury, hide, cover, store.

cad *(SYN.)* knave, rascal, scoundrel, rogue.

cafe *(SYN.)* coffeehouse.

cafeteria *(SYN.)* cafe, diner, restaurant.

cagey *(SYN.)* cunning, wary, clever, tricky, cautious, shrewd, evasive. *(ANT.) innocent, straightfoward, guileless, naive.*

calamity *(SYN.)* ruin, disaster, casualty, distress, hardship, trouble, misfortune, bad luck, catastrophe. *(ANT.) blessing, fortune, welfare.*

calculate *(SYN.)* count, compute, figure, estimate, consider, tally, determine, measure, subtract, add, divide, multiply, judge, reckon. *(ANT.) guess, miscalculate, assume, conjecture.*

calculating *(SYN.)* crafty, shrewd, scheming, cunning. *(ANT.) simple, guileless, direct, ingenuous.*

calculation *(SYN.)* figuring, reckoning, computation, estimation. *(ANT.) guess, assumption.*

calendar *(SYN.)* timetable, schedule, diary.

call *(SYN.)* designate, name, yell, cry, ask, shout, speak, cry out, call out, exclaim, command, term, label, phone, ring up, collect, waken, awaken, ring, wake, arouse, rouse, outcry, need, demand, claim, assemble, telephone, occasion, invite.

calling *(SYN.)* occupation, profession, trade.

callous *(SYN.)* insensitive, impenitent, obdurate, unfeeling, indurate, hard, insensible, heartless. *(ANT.) soft, compassionate, tender.*

calm *(SYN.)* appease, lull, quiet, soothe, composed, tranquilize, dispassionate, still, imperturbable, peaceful, pacify, alloy, assuage, unruffled, mild, tranquil, smooth, serene, cool, level-headed, unexcited, aloof, detached, stillness, calm-

ness, serenity, composure. *(ANT.) tempestuous, disturbed, emotional, turmoil, incite, inflame, roiled, incense, upheaval, excite, upset, disturb, arouse.*

campaign *(SYN.)* movement, cause, crusade.

can *(SYN.)* tin, container.

canal *(SYN.)* gully, tube, duct, waterway.

cancel *(SYN.)* eliminate, obliterate, erase, delete, nullify, repeal, revoke, cross out, expunge, void, recall, set aside, abolish, rescind. *(ANT.) perpetuate, confirm, ratify, enforce, enact.*

candid *(SYN.)* free, blunt, frank, plain, open, sincere, honest, straightforward, direct, outspoken. *(ANT.) sly, contrived, wily, scheming.*

candidate *(SYN.)* applicant, aspirant, nominee.

canine *(SYN.)* pooch, dog, puppy.

canny *(SYN.)* artful, skillful, shrewd, clever, cautious, cunning, careful.

canopy *(SYN.)* awning, screen, shelter, cover.

cant *(SYN.)* dissimulation, patois, jargon, shoptalk, deceit, argot, pretense. *(ANT.) honesty, condor, frankness, truth.*

cantankerous *(SYN.)* crabby, grouchy, irritable, surly, ill-natured, grumpy, irascible.

canyon *(SYN.)* gulch, gully, arroyo, ravine, gorge.

cap *(SYN.)* top, cover, crown, beat, lid, excel.

capability *(SYN.)* aptness, ability, capacity, aptitude, dexterity, power, efficiency, qualification. *(ANT.) incapacity, disability, incompetency.*

capable *(SYN.)* clever, qualified, able, efficient, competent, skilled, fit, skillful, accomplished, fitted. *(ANT.) unfitted, incapable, incompetent, unskilled, inept, inadequate.*

capacity *(SYN.)* capability, power, ability, talent, content, skill, volume, size. *(ANT.) inability, stupidity, incapacity, impotence.*

cape *(SYN.)* pelisse, cloak, mantle, neck, point, headland, peninsula.

caper *(SYN.)* romp, frisk, cavort, frolic, gambol.

capital *(SYN.)* leading, chief, important, property, wealth, money, city, cash, assets, principal, resources, major, primary, first, funds.
(ANT.) unimportant, trivial, secondary.

capricious *(SYN.)* undependable, erratic, inconstant, fickle, changeable, irregular, inconsistent, unstable.

captain *(SYN.)* commander, authority, supervisor, leader, skipper, commander, master, officer.

caption *(SYN.)* heading, title, headline.

captivate *(SYN.)* fascinate, charm, delight.

captive *(SYN.)* convict, prisoner, hostage.

captivity *(SYN.)* detention, imprisonment, custody, confinement, bondage, slavery.
(ANT.) liberty, freedom.

capture *(SYN.)* catch, grip, apprehend, clutch, arrest, snare, seize, nab, seizure, catching, grasp, take prisoner, grab, recovery, trap.
(ANT.) set free, lose, liberate, throw, free, release.

car *(SYN.)* auto, automobile, motorcar, vehicle.

carcass *(SYN.)* remains, frame, corpse, form, bulk, mass, corpus, association, body, cadaver.
(ANT.) mind, spirit, intellect, soul.

cardinal *(SYN.)* chief, primary, important, prime, leading, major, essential.
(ANT.) subordinate, secondary, auxiliary.

care *(SYN.)* concern, anxiety, worry, caution, solicitude, charge, ward, attention, regard, supervision, consider, consideration, keeping, protection, attend, watch, supervise, keep, guardianship, custody.
(ANT.) neglect, disregard, indifference, unconcern, negligence.

career *(SYN.)* occupation, profession, job, calling, vocation, trade.

carefree *(SYN.)* lighthearted, happy, unconcerned, breezy, jolly, uneasy, nonchalant, happy-go-lucky, lively.

careful *(SYN.)* prudent, thoughtful, attentive, cautious, painstaking, scrupulous, heedful, circumspect, vigilant, guarded, discreet, watchful, wary, concerned, meticulous, thorough, lax, negligent.
(ANT.) nice, careful, heedless, messy, careless, accurate, incautious, sloppy, meticulous.

careless *(SYN.)* imprudent, heedless, un-concerned, inattentive, lax, indiscreet, desultory, reckless, negligent.
(ANT.) careful, nice, cautious, painstaking, prudent, accurate.

caress *(SYN.)* hug, fondle, embrace, pet, pat, stroke, kiss, cuddle.
(ANT.) spurn, vex, buffet, annoy, tease.

cargo *(SYN.)* freight, load, freightload, shipment.

caricature *(SYN.)* exaggeration, parody, spoof, takeoff, lampoon, satire, burlesque.

carnage *(SYN.)* massacre, liquidation, slaughter, genocide, butchery, extermination, annihilation.

carnal *(SYN.)* base, corporeal, animal, lustful, worldly, sensual, bodily, gross, fleshy, voluptuous.
(ANT.) intellectual, spiritual, exalted, temperate.

carnival *(SYN.)* fete, fair, jamboree, festival.

carol *(SYN.)* hymn, song, ballad.

carp *(SYN.)* pick, praise, complain.

carpet *(SYN.)* mat, rug.

carping *(SYN.)* discerning, exact, captions, accurate, fastidious, important, hazardous.
(ANT.) superficial, cursory, approving, encouraging, unimportant, insignificant.

carriage *(SYN.)* bearing, conduct, action, deed, behavior, demeanor, disposition, deportment.

carry *(SYN.)* convey, transport, support, bring, sustain, bear, hold, move, transfer, take.
(ANT.) drop, abandon.

carry off *(SYN.)* seize, abduct, capture, kidnap.
(ANT.) set free, let go. liberate.

carry on *(SYN.)* go on, continue, proceed, misbehave.
(ANT.) stop.

carry out *(SYN.)* succeed, complete, fulfill, win, accomplish, effect.

carve *(SYN.)* hew, shape, cut, whittle, chisel, sculpt.

case *(SYN.)* state, covering, receptacle, condition, instance, example, occurrence, happening, illustration, sample, suit, action, claim, lawsuit, crate, container, carton, box.

cash *(SYN.)* currency, money.

casket *(SYN.)* coffin, box, crate.

cast *(SYN.)* fling, toss, throw, pitch, form, company, shape, sort, mold, hurl, sling, shed, direct, impart, turn, actors, players, type, variety.

caste *(SYN.)* class, grade, order, category, status, elegance, set, rank, station, social standing, denomination, excellence, genre.

castle *(SYN.)* mansion, palace, chateau.

casual *(SYN.)* chance, unexpected, informal, accidental, incidental, offhand, unplanned, relaxed, fortuitous, unintentional, spontaneous.
(ANT.) planned, expected, calculated, formal, deliberate, dressy, premeditated, pretentious.

casualty *(SYN.)* calamity, fortuity, mishap, loss, injured, dead, wounded, accident, contingency, victim, sufferer, misfortune.
(ANT.) design, purpose, intention, calculation.

catalog *(SYN.)* classify, roll, group, list, inventory, directory, index, record, file.

catastrophe *(SYN.)* mishap, calamity, disaster, adversity, accident, ruin.
(ANT.) fortune, boon, triumph, blessing, advantage, welfare.

catch *(SYN.)* hook, snare, entrap, ensnare, capture, grip, apprehend, grasp, take, grab, nab, arrest, contract, snare, seize, apprehension, latch, bolt, pin, clasp, trap.
(ANT.) lose, free, liberate, throw, release.

catching *(SYN.)* contagious, pestilential, communicable, infectious, virulent.
(ANT.) noncommunicable, healthful.

catchy *(SYN.)* tricky, misleading, attractive.

category *(SYN.)* class, caste, kind, order, genre, rank, classification, sort, elegance, type, set, excellence.

cater *(SYN.)* coddle, oblige, serve, humor, baby, mollycoddle, pamper, spoil, indulge, provide.

cause *(SYN.)* effect, incite, create, induce, inducement, occasion, incentive, prompt, principle, determinant, reason, origin, motive.

caustic *(SYN.)* bitter, disagreeable, distasteful, acrid, sour, spiteful, pungent, tart, painful, cruel, insulting, peevish, mean, ruthless, malicious, hateful, harsh.

(ANT.) mellow, sweet, delicious, pleasant.

caution *(SYN.)* heed, vigilance, care, prudence, counsel, warning, wariness, advice, warn, injunction, admonish, watchfulness.
(ANT.) carelessness, heedlessness, incaution, abandon, recklessness.

cautious *(SYN.)* heedful, scrupulous, attentive, prudent, thoughtful, discreet, guarded, circumspect, vigilant, watchful, wary, careful.
(ANT.) improvident, headstrong, heedless, foolish, forgetful, indifferent.

cavalcade *(SYN.)* column, procession, parade.

cavalier *(SYN.)* contemptuous, insolent, haughty, arrogant.

cave *(SYN.)* grotto, hole, shelter, lair, den, cavern.

cave in *(SYN.)* fall in, collapse.

cavity *(SYN.)* pit, hole, crater.

cavort *(SYN.)* caper, leap, frolic, hop, prance.

cease *(SYN.)* desist, stop, abandon, discontinue, relinquish, end, terminate, leave, surrender, resign.
(ANT.) occupy, continue, persist, begin, endure, stay.

cede *(SYN.)* surrender, relinquish, yield.

celebrate *(SYN.)* honor, glorify, commemorate, keep, solemnize, extol, observe, commend, praise.
(ANT.) decry, overlook, profane, disregard, disgrace.

celebrated *(SYN.)* eminent, glorious, distinguished, noted, illustrious, famed, well-known, popular, renowned, famous.
(ANT.) obscure, hidden, anonymous, infamous, unknown.

celebrity *(SYN.)* somebody, personage, heroine, hero, dignitary, notable.

celestial *(SYN.)* godlike, holy, supernatural, divine, paradisiacal, utopian, transcendent, superhuman.
(ANT.) diabolical, profane, mundane, wicked.

cement *(SYN.)* solidify, weld, fasten, secure.

cemetery *(SYN.)* graveyard.

censure *(SYN.)* denounce, reproach, upbraid, blame, disapproval, reprehend, condemn, criticism, disapprove, crit-

icize, reprove.
(ANT.) *commend, approval, forgive, approve, praise, applaud, condone.*
center *(SYN.)* heart, core, midpoint, middle, nucleus, inside, hub, focus.
(ANT.) *rim, boundary, edge, border, periphery, outskirts.*
central *(SYN.)* chief, necessary, main, halfway, dominant, mid, middle, inner, focal, leading, fundamental, principal.
(ANT.) *side, secondary, incidental, auxiliary.*
ceremonious *(SYN.)* correct, exact, precise, stiff, outward, external, solemn, formal.
(ANT.) *material, unconventional, easy, heartfelt.*
ceremony *(SYN.)* observance, rite, parade, formality, pomp, ritual, protocol, solemnity.
(ANT.) *informality, casualness.*
certain *(SYN.)* definite, assured, fixed, inevitable, sure, undeniable, positive, confident, particular, special, indubitable, secure, unquestionable.
(ANT.) *probable, uncertain, doubtful, questionable.*
certainly *(SYN.)* absolutely, surely, definitely.
(ANT.) *dubiously, doubtfully, questionably.*
certainty *(SYN.)* confidence, courage, security, assuredness, firmness, assertion, statement.
(ANT.) *humility, bashfulness, modest, shyness.*
certificate *(SYN.)* affidavit, document.
certify *(SYN.)* validate, affirm, verify, confirm, authenticate, substantiate.
certitude *(SYN.)* confidence, belief, conviction, feeling, faith, persuasion, trust.
(ANT.) *doubt, incredulity, denial, heresy.*
cessation *(SYN.)* ending, finish, stoppage, termination, conclusion, end.
chafe *(SYN.)* heat, rub, warm, annoy, disturb.
chagrin *(SYN.)* irritation, mortification, embarrassment, annoyance, vexation, worry, bother, shame, annoy, irk, humiliation, irritate, vex, frustrate, humiliate, embarrass, mortify, exasperate, disappoint, disappointment.
chain *(SYN.)* fasten, bind, shackle, restrain.

chairman *(SYN.)* speaker.
challenge *(SYN.)* question, dare, call, summon, threat, invite, threaten, demand.
chamber *(SYN.)* cell, salon, room.
champion *(SYN.)* victor, winner, choice, best, conqueror, hero, support, select.
chance *(SYN.)* befall, accident, betide, disaster, opportunity, calamity, occur, possibility, prospect, happen, luck, fate, take place.
(ANT.) *design, purpose, inevitability, calculation, certainty, intention.*
change *(SYN.)* modification, alternation, alteration, mutation, variety, exchange, shift, alter, transfigure, veer, vary, variation, substitution, substitute, vicissitude.
(ANT.) *uniformity, monotony, settle, remain, endure, retain, preserve, steadfastness, endurance, immutability, stability.*
changeable *(SYN.)* fitful, fickle, inconstant, unstable, shifting, wavering.
(ANT.) *stable, uniform, constant, unchanging.*
channel *(SYN.)* strait, corridor, waterway, artery, duct, canal, way, trough, groove, passageway.
chant *(SYN.)* singing, incantation, hymn, intone, sing, carol, psalm, song, ballad.
chaos *(SYN.)* confusion, jumble, turmoil, anarchy, disorder, muddle.
(ANT.) *organization, order, tranquillity, tidiness, system.*
chaotic *(SYN.)* confused, disorganized, disordered, messy.
(ANT.) *neat, ordered, systematic, organized.*
chap *(SYN.)* break, fellow, person, crack, split, man, rough, individual, boy.
chaperon *(SYN.)* associate with, escort, convoy, accompany, consort with.
(ANT.) *avoid, desert, leave, abandon, quit.*
chapter *(SYN.)* part, section, division.
char *(SYN.)* scorch, singe, burn, sear.
character *(SYN.)* description, class, kind, repute, mark, individuality, disposition, traits, personality, reputation, symbol, features, quality, eccentric, nature.
characteristic *(SYN.)* exclusive, distinctive, special, mark, feature, property, typical, unique, attribute, distinguishing, trait, quality.

charge *(SYN.)* arraignment, indictment, accusation, sell for, attack, assail, assault, indict, blame, allegation, care, custody, imputation.
(ANT.) pardon, flee, exculpation, excuse, absolve, retreat, exoneration.

charitable *(SYN.)* benevolent, generous, liberal, altruistic, kind, obliging, considerate, unselfish.
(ANT.) petty, mean, harsh, wicked, greedy, narrow-minded, stingy, malevolent.

charity *(SYN.)* benevolence, kindness, magnanimity, altruism, generosity.
(ANT.) malevolence, cruelty, selfishness.

charm *(SYN.)* allure, spell, enchantment, attractiveness, magic, witchery, amulet, talisman, lure, enchant, bewitch, fascinate, captivate.

charmer *(SYN.)* siren, temptress, enchantress, vamp, seductress, seducer, enchanter.

charming *(SYN.)* attractive, enchanting, fascinating, alluring, appealing, winsome, agreeable, bewitching, winning.
(ANT.) revolting, repugnant, repulsive.

chart *(SYN.)* design, plan, cabal, plot, sketch, stratagem, map, diagram, conspiracy, graph, intrigue.

charter *(SYN.)* lease, hire, rent, alliance.

chase *(SYN.)* hunt, run after, pursue, trail, follow, persist, scheme.
(ANT.) escape, flee, abandon, elude, evade.

chasm *(SYN.)* ravine, abyss, canyon, gorge.

chaste *(SYN.)* clear, immaculate, innocent, sincere, bare, clean, modest, pure, decent, virtuous, virginal, sheer, absolute, spotless.
(ANT.) polluted, tainted, foul, impure, sinful, worldly, sullied, defiled.

chasten *(SYN.)* chastise, restrain, punish, discipline.

chastise *(SYN.)* punish, castigate, correct.
(ANT.) release, acquit, free, exonerate.

chat *(SYN.)* argue, jabber, blab, plead, consult, converse, lecture, discuss, talk, conversation, tattle.

chatter *(SYN.)* dialogue, lecture, speech, conference, talk, discourse.
(ANT.) silence, correspondence, writing.

cheap *(SYN.)* poor, common, inexpensive, shabby, low-priced, beggary, low-cost, shoddy, mean, inferior.
(ANT.) honorable, dear, noble, expensive, costly, well-made, elegant, dignified.

cheat *(SYN.)* deceive, fool, bilk, outwit, victimize, dupe, gull, hoodwink, circumvent, swindler, cheater, trickster, phony, fraud, defraud, charlatan, crook, chiseler, con artist, hoax, swindle.

check *(SYN.)* dissect, interrogate, analyze, contemplate, inquire, question, scrutinize, arrest, stop, halt, block, curb, control, investigate, review, examine, test, counterfoil, stub, barrier, watch.
(ANT.) overlook, disregard, advance, foster, continue, promote, omit, neglect.

checkup *(SYN.)* medical examination, physical.

cheek *(SYN.)* nerve, effrontery, impudence, gall, impertinence.

cheer *(SYN.)* console, gladden, comfort, encourage, applause, encouragement, joy, glee, gaiety, mirth, soothe, sympathize, approval, solace.
(ANT.) depress, sadden, discourage, derision, dishearten, discouragement, antagonize.

cheerful *(SYN.)* glad, jolly, joyful, gay, happy, cherry, merry, joyous, lighthearted.
(ANT.) mournful, sad, glum, depressed, gloomy, sullen.

cherish *(SYN.)* prize, treasure, appreciate, nurse, value, comfort, hold dear, foster, nurture, sustain.
(ANT.) disregard, neglect, deprecate, scorn, reject, undervalue, abandon.

chest *(SYN.)* bosom, breast, coffer, box, case, trunk, casket, dresser, commode, cabinet, chifforobe.

chew *(SYN.)* gnaw, munch, bite, nibble.

chic *(SYN.)* fashionable, modish, smart, stylish, trendy.

chide *(SYN.)* admonish, rebuke, scold, reprimand, criticize, reprove.
(ANT.) extol, praise, commend.

chief *(SYN.)* chieftain, head, commander, captain, leader, principal, master, boss, leading, ruler.
(ANT.) servant, subordinate, secondary, follower, incidental, accidental, auxiliary, attendant.

chiefly *(SYN.)* mainly, especially, mostly.

childish *(SYN.)* immature, childlike, infantile, babyish.

grownup.

chill *(SYN.)* coolness, cold, cool, coldness, brisk, frosty.
(ANT.) hot, warm, heat, heated, warmth.

chilly *(SYN.)* cold, frigid, freezing, arctic, cool, icy, passionless, wintry, unfeeling.
(ANT.) fiery, heated, passionate, ardent.

chirp *(SYN.)* peep, cheep, twitter, tweet, chirrup.

chivalrous *(SYN.)* noble, brave, polite, valorous, gallant, gentlemanly, courteous.
(ANT.) crude, rude, impolite, uncivil.

chivalry *(SYN.)* courtesy, nobility, gallantry, knighthood.

choice *(SYN.)* delicate, elegant, fine, dainty, exquisite, pure, refined, subtle, splendid, handsome, option, selection, beautiful, minute, pretty, pick, select, uncommon, rare, precious, valuable, thin, small.
(ANT.) coarse, rough, thick, blunt, large.

choke *(SYN.)* throttle, gag, strange.

choose *(SYN.)* elect, decide between, pick, select, cull, opt.
(ANT.) reject, refuse.

chop *(SYN.)* hew, cut, fell, mince.

chore *(SYN.)* routine, task, job, duty, work.

chronic *(SYN.)* persistent, constant, lingering, continuing, perennial, unending, sustained, permanent.
(ANT.) fleeting, acute, temporary.

chronicle *(SYN.)* detail, history, narrative, account, description, narration, recital.
(ANT.) misrepresentation, confusion, distortion.

chuckle *(SYN.)* titter, laugh, giggle.

chum *(SYN.)* friend, pal, buddy, companion.

cinema *(SYN.)* effigy, film, etching, appearance, drawing, engraving, illustration, likeness, image, panorama, painting, picture, photograph.

circle *(SYN.)* disk, ring, set, group. class, club, surround, encircle, enclose, round.

circuit *(SYN.)* circle, course, journey, orbit, revolution, tour.

circuitous *(SYN.)* distorted, devious, indirect, roundabout swerving, crooked, tortuous.
(ANT.) straightforward, straight, direct, honest.

honest.

circular *(SYN.)* chubby, complete, curved, bulbous, cylindrical, round, ringlike, globular, entire, rotund.
(ANT.) straight.

circumference *(SYN.)* border, perimeter, periphery, edge.

circumspection *(SYN.)* care, worry, solicitude, anxiety, concern, caution, attention, vigilance.
(ANT.) neglect, negligence, indifference.

circumstance *(SYN.)* fact, event, incident, condition, happening, position, occurrence, situation.

circumstances *(SYN.)* facts, conditions, factors, situation, background, grounds, means, capital, assets, rank, class.

cite *(SYN.)* affirm, assign, allege, advance, quote, mention, declare, claim, maintain.
(ANT.) refute, gainsay, deny, contradict.

citizen *(SYN.)* native, inhabitant, national, denizen, subject, dweller, resident.

city *(SYN.)* metropolis, municipality, town.

civil *(SYN.)* courteous, cultivated, accomplished, public, municipal, respectful, genteel, polite, considerate, gracious, urban.
(ANT.) uncouth, uncivil, impertinent, impolite, boorish.

civilization *(SYN.)* cultivation, culture, education, breeding, enlightenment, society, refinement.
(ANT.) ignorance, vulgarity.

civilize *(SYN.)* refine, tame, polish, cultivate, instruct, teach.

claim *(SYN.)* aver, declare, allege, assert, affirm, express, state, demand, maintain, defend, uphold.
(ANT.) refute, deny, contradict.

clamor *(SYN.)* cry, din, babel, noise, racket, outcry, row, sound tumult, shouting, shout, uproar.
(ANT.) hush, serenity, silence, tranquility, stillness, quiet.

clan *(SYN.)* fellowship, kindness, solidarity, family, brotherliness, association, fraternity.
(ANT.) discord, strife, opposition, acrimony.

clandestine *(SYN.)* covert, hidden, latent, private, concealed, secret, unknown.

(ANT.) exposed, known, conspicuous, obvious.

clarify *(SYN.)* educate, explain, expound, decipher, illustrate, clear, resolve, define, interpret, unfold.

(ANT.) darken, obscure, baffle, confuse.

clash *(SYN.)* clank, crash, clang, conflict, disagreement, opposition, collision, struggle, mismatch, contrast, disagree, collide, interfere.

(ANT.) accord, agreement, harmony, blend, harmonize, match, agree.

clasp *(SYN.)* grip, hold, grasp, adhere, clutch, keep, have, maintain, possess, occupy, retain, support, confine, embrace, fastening, check, detain, curb, receive.

(ANT.) relinquish, vacate, surrender, abandon.

class *(SYN.)* category, denomination, caste, kind, genre, grade, rank, order, elegance, classification, division, sort, family, species, set, excellence.

classic *(SYN.)* masterpiece.

classification *(SYN.)* order, category, class, arrangement, ordering, grouping, organization.

classify *(SYN.)* arrange, class, order, sort, grade, group, index.

clause *(SYN.)* condition, paragraph, limitation, article.

claw *(SYN.)* hook, talon, nail, scratch.

clean *(SYN.)* mop, tidy, neat, dustless, clear, unsoiled, immaculate, unstained, untainted, pure, dust, vacuum, scour, decontaminate, wipe, sterilize, cleanse, scrub, purify, wash, sweep.

(ANT.) stain, soil, pollute, soiled, impure, dirty, stain.

cleanse *(SYN.)* mop, purify, wash, sweep.

(ANT.) stain, soil, dirty, pollute.

clear *(SYN.)* fair, sunny, cloudless, transparent, apparent, limpid, distinct, intelligible, evident, unmistakable, understandable, unclouded, uncloudy, light, bright, certain, manifest, lucid, plain, obvious, unobstructed.

(ANT.) obscure, unclear, muddled, confused, dark, cloudy, blocked, obstructed, questionable, dubious, blockaded, foul, overcast.

clearly *(SYN.)* plainly, obviously, evidently, definitely, surely, certainly.

(ANT.) questionably, dubiously.

clemency *(SYN.)* forgiveness, charity, compassion, grace, mercy, leniency, pity, mildness.

(ANT.) punishment, vengeance, retribution.

clerical *(SYN.)* ministerial, pastoral, priestly, celestial, holy, sacred, secretarial.

clerk *(SYN.)* typist, office worker, office girl, saleslady, salesperson, salesclerk.

clever *(SYN.)* apt, dexterous, quick, adroit, quick-witted, talented, bright, skillful, witty, ingenious, smart, intelligent, shrewd, gifted, expert, sharp.

(ANT.) unskilled, slow, stupid, backward, maladroit, bungling, dull, clumsy.

cleverness *(SYN.)* intellect, intelligence, comprehension, mind, perspicacity, sagacity, fun.

(ANT.) sobriety, stupidity, solemnity, commonplace, platitude.

client *(SYN.)* patron, customer.

cliff *(SYN.)* scar, tor, bluff, crag, precipice, escarpment.

climate *(SYN.)* aura, atmosphere, air, ambience.

climax *(SYN.)* apex, culmination, peak, summit, consummation, height, acme, zenith.

(ANT.) depth, base, anticlimax, floor.

climb *(SYN.)* mount, scale, ascend.

(ANT.) descend.

clip *(SYN.)* snip, crop, cut, mow, clasp.

cloak *(SYN.)* conceal, cover, disguise, clothe, cape, guard, envelop, hide, mask, protect, shield.

(ANT.) divulge, expose, reveal, bare, unveil.

clod *(SYN.)* wad, hunk, gobbet, lump, chunk, clot, gob, dunce, dolt, oaf, fool.

clog *(SYN.)* crowd, congest, cram, overfill, stuff.

cloister *(SYN.)* monastery, priory, hermitage, abbey, convent.

close *(SYN.)* adjacent, adjoining, immediate, unventilated, stuffy, abutting, neighboring, dear, oppressive, mean, impending, nearby, near, devoted.

(ANT.) afar, faraway, removed, distant.

close *(SYN.)* seal, shut, clog, stop, obstruct, cease, conclude, complete, end, terminate, occlude, finish.

(ANT.) unlock, begin, open, unbar, inaugurate, commence, start.

closet *(SYN.)* cabinet, locker, wardrobe, cupboard.

cloth *(SYN.)* fabric, goods, material, textile.

clothe *(SYN.)* garb, dress, apparel.

(ANT.) strip, undress.

clothes *(SYN.)* array, attire, apparel, clothing, dress, garb, dress, garments, raiment, drapery, vestments.

(ANT.) nudity, nakedness.

clothing *(SYN.)* attire, clothes, apparel, array, dress, drapery, garments, garb, vestments.

(ANT.) nudity, nakedness.

cloud *(SYN.)* fog, mist, haze, mass, collection, obscure, dim, shadow.

cloudy *(SYN.)* dim, dark, indistinct, murky, mysterious, indefinite, vague, sunless, clouded, obscure, overcast, shadowy.

(ANT.) sunny, clear, distinct, limpid, lucid, clarified, cloudless, clearheaded, brilliant, bright.

club *(SYN.)* society, association, set, circle, organization, bat, cudgel, stick, blackjack.

clue *(SYN.)* sign, trace, hint, suggestion.

clumsy *(SYN.)* bungling, inept, rough, unpolished, bumbling, awkward, ungraceful, gauche, ungainly, unskillful, untoward.

(ANT.) polished, skillful, neat, graceful, dexterous, adroit.

cluster *(SYN.)* batch, clutch, group, bunch, gather, pack, assemble, crowd.

clutch *(SYN.)* grip, grab, seize, hold.

coalition *(SYN.)* combination, association, alliance, confederacy, entente, league, treaty.

(ANT.) schism, separation, divorce.

coarse *(SYN.)* unpolished, vulgar, refined, rough, smooth, impure, rude, crude, gruff, gross, cultivated, delicate, cultured.

(ANT.) delicate, smooth, refined, polished, genteel, cultivated, suave, fine, cultured.

coast *(SYN.)* seaboard, seashore, beach, shore, drift, glide, ride.

coax *(SYN.)* urge, persuade, wheedle, cajole.

(ANT.) force, bully, coerce.

coddle *(SYN.)* pamper, baby, spoil, indulge.

coerce *(SYN.)* constrain, compel, enforce, force, drive, oblige, impel.

(ANT.) prevent, persuade, convince, induce.

coercion *(SYN.)* emphasis, intensity, energy, dint, might potency, power, vigor, strength, compulsion, force, constraint, violence.

(ANT.) impotence, frailty, feebleness, weakness, persuasion.

cognizance *(SYN.)* apprehension, erudition, acquaintance, information, learning, knowledge, lore, science, scholarship, understanding.

(ANT.) illiteracy, misunderstanding, ignorance.

cognizant *(SYN.)* conscious, aware, apprised informed, mindful, observant, perceptive.

(ANT.) unaware, ignorant, oblivious, insensible.

coherent *(SYN.)* logical, intelligible, sensible, rational, commonsensical, reasonable.

coiffeur *(SYN.)* hairdresser.

coiffure *(SYN.)* haircut, hairdo.

coincide *(SYN.)* acquiesce, agree, accede, assent, consent, comply, correspond, concur, match, tally, harmonize, conform.

(ANT.) differ, disagree, protest, contradict.

coincidence *(SYN.)* accident, chance.

(ANT.) plot, plan, prearrangement, scheme.

coincident *(SYN.)* identical, equal, equivalent, distinguishable, same, like.

(ANT.) distinct, contrary, disparate, opposed.

coincidental *(SYN.)* unpredicted, unexpected, chance, unforeseen, accidental, fortuitous.

cold *(SYN.)* cool, freezing, chilly, frigid, icy, frozen, wintry, arctic, unfriendly, indifferent, phlegmatic, stoical, passionless, chill, unemotional, heartless, unfeeling.

(ANT.) hot, torrid, fiery, burning, ardent, friendly, temperate, warm, passionate.

collapse *(SYN.)* descend, decrease, diminish, fail, downfall, failure, decline, fall, drop, sink, subside, topple.

(ANT.) soar, steady, limb, mount, arise.

colleague *(SYN.)* companion, attendant,

comrade, associate, crony, mate, friend, partner.

(ANT.) enemy, stranger, adversary.

collect *(SYN.)* assemble, amass, concentrate, pile, accumulate, congregate, obtain, heap, gather, solicit, secure, procure, raise, get, mass, hoard, consolidate.

(ANT.) divide, dole, assort, dispel, distribute, disperse.

collected *(SYN.)* cool, calm, composed, peaceful, imperturbable, placid, sedate, quiet.

(ANT.) excited, violent, aroused, agitated.

collection *(SYN.)* amount, conglomeration, sum, entirety, aggregation, hoard, accumulation, pile, store, aggregate, total, whole.

(ANT.) part, unit, particular, element, ingredient.

collide *(SYN.)* hit, smash, crash, strike.

collision *(SYN.)* conflict, combat, duel, battle, encounter, crash, smash, fight, contention, struggle, discord.

(ANT.) concord, amity, harmony, consonance.

collusion *(SYN.)* combination, cabal, intrigue, conspiracy, plot, treason, treachery.

color *(SYN.)* hue, paint, pigment, complexion, dye, shade, tone, tincture, stain, tint, tinge.

(ANT.) paleness, transparency, achromatism.

colorful *(SYN.)* impressive, vivid, striking, full-color, multicolored, offbeat, weird, unusual.

(ANT.) flat, dull, uninteresting.

colossal *(SYN.)* enormous, elephantine, gargantuan, huge, immense, gigantic, prodigious.

(ANT.) little, minute, small, miniature, diminutive, microscopic, tiny.

combat *(SYN.)* conflict, duel, battle, collision, encounter, fight, contest, oppose, war, contention, struggle, discord.

(ANT.) consonance, harmony, concord, yield, surrender, succumb, amity.

combination *(SYN.)* association, confederacy, alliance, entente, league, compounding, mixture, blend, composite, federation, mixing, compound, blending, union.

(ANT.) separation, division, schism, divorce.

combine *(SYN.)* adjoin, associate, accompany, conjoin, connect, link, mix, blend, couple, unite, join.

(ANT.) detach, disjoin, divide, separate, disconnect.

come *(SYN.)* near, approach, reach, arrive, advance.

(ANT.) depart, leave, go.

comedian *(SYN.)* comic, wit, humorist, gagman, wag.

comely *(SYN.)* charming, elegant, beauteous, beautiful, fine, lovely, pretty, handsome lovely.

(ANT.) hideous, repulsive, foul, unsightly.

come-on *(SYN.)* lure, inducement, enticement, temptation, premium.

comfort *(SYN.)* contentment, ease, enjoyment, relieve, consolation, relief, cheer, console, calm, satisfaction, soothe, encourage, succor, luxury, solace.

(ANT.) depress, torture, discomfort, upset, misery, disturb, agitate, affliction, discompose, uncertainty, suffering.

comfortable *(SYN.)* pleasing, agreeable, convenient, cozy, welcome, acceptable, relaxed, restful, cozy, gratifying, easy, contented, rested, satisfying, pleasurable.

(ANT.) miserable, distressing, tense, strained, troubling, edgy, uncomfortable.

comical *(SYN.)* droll, funny, humorous, amusing, ludicrous, witty, ridiculous, odd, queer.

(ANT.) sober, solemn, sad, serious, melancholy.

command *(SYN.)* class, method, plan regularity, rank, arrangement, series, sequence, point, aim, conduct, manage, guide, bid, system, succession, bidding, direct, order, demand, direction, rule, dictate, decree.

(ANT.) consent, obey, misdirect, distract, deceive, misguide, license, confusion.

commandeer *(SYN.)* take, possession, seize, confiscate, appropriate.

commanding *(SYN.)* imposing, masterful, assertive, authoritative, positive.

commence *(SYN.)* open, start.

(ANT.) stop, end, terminate, finish.

commend *(SYN.)* laud, praise, applaud, recommend.

(ANT.) censure, blame, criticize.

commendable *(SYN.)* deserving, praise-

worthy.
(ANT.) bad, deplorable, lamentable.

commendation *(SYN.)* approval, applause, praise, recommendation, honor, medal.
(ANT.) criticism, condemnation, censure.

commensurate *(SYN.)* keep, celebrate, observe, honor, commend, extol, glorify, laud, praise, honor.
(ANT.) decry, disgrace, disregard, overlook, profane, dishonor.

comment *(SYN.)* assertion, declaration, annotation, explanation, review, commentary, report, remark, observation, utterance, criticism, statement.

commerce *(SYN.)* business, engagement, employment, art, trade, marketing, enterprise, occupation.
(ANT.) hobby, pastime, avocation.

commission *(SYN.)* board, committee, command, permit, order, permission, delegate, authorize, deputize, entrust.

commit *(SYN.)* perpetrate, perform, obligate, do, commend, consign, relegate, bind, delegate, empower, pledge, entrust, authorize, trust.
(ANT.) neglect, mistrust, release, free, miscarry, fail, loose.

commitment *(SYN.)* duty, promise, responsibility, pledge.

committee *(SYN.)* commission, bureau, board, delegate, council.

commodious *(SYN.)* appropriate, accessible, adapted, favorable, handy, fitting, timely.
(ANT.) inconvenient, troublesome, awkward.

commodity *(SYN.)* article, merchandise, wares, goods.

common *(SYN.)* ordinary, popular, familiar, mean, low, general, vulgar, communal, mutual, shared, natural, frequent, prevalent, joint, conventional, plain, usual, universal.
(ANT.) odd, exceptional, scarce, noble, extraordinary, different, separate, outstanding, rare, unusual, distinctive, refined.

commonplace *(SYN.)* common, usual, frequent, ordinary, everyday.
(ANT.) distinctive, unusual, original.

commonsense *(SYN.)* perceptible, alive, apprehensible, aware, awake, cognizant, conscious, comprehending, perceptible.

(ANT.) unaware, impalpable, imperceptible.

commotion *(SYN.)* confusion, chaos, disarray, ferment, disorder, stir, tumult, agitation.
(ANT.) tranquillity, peace, certainty, order.

communicable *(SYN.)* infectious, virulent, catching, transferable, contagious.
(ANT.) hygienic, noncommunicable, healthful.

communicate *(SYN.)* convey, impart, inform, confer, disclose, reveal, relate, tell, advertise, publish, transmit, publicize, divulge.
(ANT.) withhold, hide, conceal.

communication *(SYN.)* disclosure, transmission, declaration, announcement, notification, publication, message, report, news, information.

communicative *(SYN.)* unreserved, open, frank, free, straightforward, unrestrained.
(ANT.) close-mouthed, secretive.

communion *(SYN.)* intercourse, fellowship, participation, association, sacrament, union.
(ANT.) nonparticipation, alienation.

community *(SYN.)* public, society, city, town, village, township.

compact *(SYN.)* contracted, firm, narrow, snug, close, constricted, packed, vanity, treaty, agreement, tense, taught, tight, niggardly, close-fisted, parsimonious, compressed, stingy.
(ANT.) slack, open, loose, relaxed, unconfined, unfretted, sprawling, lax.

companion *(SYN.)* attendant, comrade, consort, friend, colleague, partner, crony, mate, associate.
(ANT.) stranger, enemy, adversary.

companionship *(SYN.)* familiarity, cognizance, acquaintance, fellowship, knowledge, intimacy.
(ANT.) unfamiliarity, inexperience, ignorance.

company *(SYN.)* crew, group, band, party, throng, house, assemblage, troop, fellowship, association, business, concern, partnership, corporation, companionship, firm.
(ANT.) seclusion, individual, solitude, dispersion.

comparable *(SYN.)* allied, analogous,

alike, akin, like, correspondent, correlative, parallel.

(ANT.) opposed, incongruous, dissimilar, unalike, different, divergent.

compare *(SYN.)* discriminate, match, differentiate, contrast, oppose.

comparison *(SYN.)* likening, contrasting, judgment.

compartment *(SYN.)* division, section.

compassion *(SYN.)* mercy, sympathy, pity, commiseration, condolence.

(ANT.) ruthlessness, hardness, brutality, inhumanity, cruelty.

compassionate *(SYN.)* sympathizing, benign, forbearing, good, tender, affable, humane, indulgent, kind, sympathetic, kindly.

(ANT.) inhuman, merciless, unkind, cold-hearted, unsympathetic, cruel.

compatible *(SYN.)* consistent, agreeing, conforming, accordant, congruous, harmonious, cooperative, agreeable, constant, consonant, correspondent.

(ANT.) discrepant, paradoxical, disagreeable, contradictory.

compel *(SYN.)* drive, enforce, coerce, constrain, force, oblige, impel.

(ANT.) induce, coax, prevent, wheedle, persuade, cajole, convince.

compensate *(SYN.)* remunerate, repay, reimburse, recompense, balance.

compensation *(SYN.)* fee, earnings, pay, payment, recompense, allowance, remuneration, remittance, settlement, stipend, repayment, salary, wages.

(ANT.) present, gratuity, gift.

compete *(SYN.)* rival, contest, oppose, vie.

(ANT.) reconcile, accord.

competence *(SYN.)* skill, ability, capability.

competent *(SYN.)* efficient, clever, capable, able, apt, proficient, skillful, fitted, qualified.

(ANT.) inept, incapable, unfitted, awkward, incompetent, inadequate.

competition *(SYN.)* contest, match, rivalry, tournament.

competitor *(SYN.)* rival, contestant, opponent.

(ANT.) ally, friend, colleague.

complain *(SYN.)* lament, murmur, protest, grouch, grumble, regret, moan, remonstrate, whine, repine.

remonstrate, whine, repine.

(ANT.) rejoice, praise, applaud, approve.

complaint *(SYN.)* protest, objection, grievance.

complement *(SYN.)* supplement, complete.

(ANT.) clash, conflict.

complete *(SYN.)* consummate, entire, ended, full, thorough, finished, full, whole, concluded, over, done, terminate, unbroken, total, undivided.

(ANT.) unfinished, imperfect, incomplete, start, partial, begin, commence, lacking.

completion *(SYN.)* achievement, attainment, end, conclusion, close, finish, wind-up, accomplishment, realization.

(ANT.) omission, neglect, failure, defeat.

complex *(SYN.)* sophisticated, compound, intricate, involved, perplexing, elaborate, complicated.

(ANT.) basic, simple, rudimentary, uncompounded, uncomplicated, plain.

complexion *(SYN.)* paint, pigment hue, color, dye, stain, tincture, tinge, tint, shade.

(ANT.) paleness, transparency, achromatism.

compliant *(SYN.)* meek, modest, lowly, plain, submissive, simple, unostentatious, unassuming, unpretentious.

(ANT.) proud, vain, arrogant, haughty, boastful.

complicated *(SYN.)* intricate, involved, complex, compound, perplexing.

(ANT.) simple, plain, uncompounded.

compliment *(SYN.)* eulogy, flattery, praise, admiration, honor, adulation, flatter, commendation, tribute.

(ANT.) taunt, affront, aspersion, insult, disparage, criticism.

complimentary *(SYN.)* gratis, free.

comply *(SYN.)* assent, consent, accede, acquiesce, coincide, conform, concur, tally.

(ANT.) differ, dissent, protest, disagree.

component *(SYN.)* division, fragment, allotment, moiety, apportionment, scrap, portion, section, share, segment, ingredient, organ.

(ANT.) whole, entirety.

comport *(SYN.)* carry, conduct, behave, act, deport, interact, operate, manage.

compose *(SYN.)* forge, fashion, mold,

make, construct, create, produce, shape, form, constitute, arrange, organize, make up, write, invent, devise, frame.
(ANT.) *misshape, dismantle, disfigure, destroy.*

composed *(SYN.)* calm, cool, imperturbable, placid, quiet, unmoved, sedate, peaceful, collected, tranquil.
(ANT.) *aroused, violent, nervous, agitated, perturbed, excited.*

composer *(SYN.)* author, inventor, creator, maker, originator.

composition *(SYN.)* paper, theme, work, essay, compound, mixture, mix.

composure *(SYN.)* calmness, poise, control, self-control, self-possession.
(ANT.) *anger, rage, turbulence, agitation.*

compound *(SYN.)* blend, confound, jumble, consort, aggregate, complicated, combination, combined, mixture, complex, join.
(ANT.) *segregate, separate, divide, simple, sort.*

comprehend *(SYN.)* apprehend, discern, learn, perceive, see, grasp, understand.
(ANT.) *mistake, misunderstand, ignore.*

comprehension *(SYN.)* insight, perception, understanding, awareness, discernment.
(ANT.) *misconception, insensibility.*

comprehensive *(SYN.)* wide, inclusive, complete, broad, full.
(ANT.) *fragmentary, partial, limited, incomplete.*

compress *(SYN.)* press, compact, squeeze, pack, crowd.
(ANT.) *spread, stretch, expand.*

comprise *(SYN.)* contain, hold, embrace.
(ANT.) *emit, encourage, yield, discharge.*

compulsion *(SYN.)* might, energy, potency, strength, vigor.
(ANT.) *persuasion, impotence, frailty.*

compulsory *(SYN.)* required, obligatory, necessary, unavoidable.
(ANT.) *elective, optional, free, unrestricted.*

computation *(SYN.)* reckoning, record.
(ANT.) *misrepresentation.*

compute *(SYN.)* count, calculate, determine, figure, reckon.
(ANT.) *conjecture, guess, miscalculate.*

comrade *(SYN.)* attendant, companion, colleague, associate, friend.
(ANT.) *stranger, enemy, adversary.*

swindle.

conceal *(SYN.)* disguise, cover, hide, mask, screen, secrete, veil, withhold.
(ANT.) *reveal, show, disclose, expose.*

concede *(SYN.)* permit, suffer, tolerate, grant, give, admit, acknowledge, allow, yield.
(ANT.) *forbid, contradict, protest, refuse, deny, negate, resist.*

conceit *(SYN.)* pride, vanity, complacency, conception, idea, egotism, self-esteem, caprice, fancy, whim.
(ANT.) *humility, meekness, humbleness, modesty.*

conceited *(SYN.)* proud, arrogant, vain, smug, egotistical.
(ANT.) *humble, modest, self-effacing.*

conceive *(SYN.)* design, create, imagine, understand, devise, concoct, perceive, frame, grasp, invent.
(ANT.) *imitate, reproduce, copy.*

concentrate *(SYN.)* localize, focus, condense, ponder, meditate, center, scrutinize.
(ANT.) *scatter, diffuse, dissipate, disperse.*

concentrated *(SYN.)* compressed, thick, dense.
(ANT.) *sparse, quick, dispersed.*

concept *(SYN.)* fancy, conception, image, notion, idea, sentiment, thought.
(ANT.) *thing, matter, substance, entity.*

conception *(SYN.)* consideration, deliberation, fancy, idea, notion, regard, thought, view.

concern *(SYN.)* matter, anxiety, affair, disturb, care, business, solicitude, interest, affect, involve, touch, trouble, interest, worry.
(ANT.) *unconcern, negligence, disinterest, tire, bore, calm, soothe, indifference.*

concerning *(SYN.)* regarding, about, respecting.

concerted *(SYN.)* united, joint, combined.
(ANT.) *individual, unorganized, separate.*

concession *(SYN.)* admission, yielding, granting.
(ANT.) *insistence, demand.*

concise *(SYN.)* pity, neat, brief, compact, succinct, terse.
(ANT.) *wordy, lengthy, verbose, prolix.*

conclude *(SYN.)* decide, achieve, close, complete, end, finish, terminate, ar-

complete, end, finish, terminate, arrange, determine, settle, perfect, perform.

(ANT.) start, begin, commence.

concluding *(SYN.)* extreme, final, last, terminal, utmost.

(ANT.) first, foremost, opening, initial.

conclusion *(SYN.)* end, finale, termination, deduction, close, settlement, decision, finish, resolution, determination, completion, issue, judgment.

(ANT.) commencement, inception, opening, start, beginning.

conclusive *(SYN.)* decisive, eventual, final, terminal, ultimate.

(ANT.) original, first, inaugural.

concord *(SYN.)* agreement, unison, understanding, accordance, stipulation.

(ANT.) disagreement, discord, dissension.

concrete *(SYN.)* solid, firm, precise, definite, specific.

(ANT.) undetermined, vague, general.

concur *(SYN.)* agree, assent, consent, accede.

(ANT.) dissent, protest, differ.

condemn *(SYN.)* denounce, reproach, blame, upbraid, convict, rebuke, doom, judge, censure, reprehend, punish, reprobate, sentence.

(ANT.) condone, forgive, absolve, praise, applaud, extol, approve, pardon, laud, excuse, commend.

condense *(SYN.)* shorten, reduce, abridge, abbreviate, concentrate, digest, compress, diminish.

(ANT.) enlarge, increase, swell, expand.

condition *(SYN.)* circumstance, state, situation, case, plight, requirement, position, necessity, stipulation, predicament, provision, term.

conditional *(SYN.)* dependent, relying.

(ANT.) casual, original, absolute.

condolence *(SYN.)* commiseration, concord, harmony, pity, sympathy, warmth.

(ANT.) harshness, indifference, unconcern.

conduct *(SYN.)* control, deportment, supervise, manage, behavior, deed, actions, act, behave, manners, deportment.

confederate *(SYN.)* ally, abettor, assistant.

(ANT.) enemy, rival, opponent, adversary.

confederation *(SYN.)* combination, league, union, marriage, treaty.

(ANT.) separation, divorce.

confer *(SYN.)* gossip, grant, speak, tattle, blab, chat, deliberate, consult, award, give, bestow, talk, mutter.

(ANT.) retrieve, withdraw.

confess *(SYN.)* avow, acknowledge, admit, concede, grant, divulge, reveal.

(ANT.) disown, renounce, deny, conceal.

confession *(SYN.)* defense, justification, excuse, apology.

(ANT.) dissimulation, denial, complaint.

confidence *(SYN.)* firmness, self-reliance, assurance, faith, trust, pledge, declaration, self-confidence, reliance, self-assurance, courage, statement.

(ANT.) distrust, shyness, mistrust, bashfulness, diffidence, doubt, modesty, suspicion.

confident *(SYN.)* certain, sure, dauntless, self-assured.

(ANT.) uncertain, timid, shy.

confine *(SYN.)* enclose, restrict, hinder, fence, limit, bound.

(ANT.) release, expose, free, expand, open.

confirm acknowledge, establish, settle, substantiate, approve, fix, verify, assure, validate, ratify, corroborate, strengthen.

(ANT.) disclaim, deny, disavow.

confirmation *(SYN.)* demonstration, experiment, test, trail, verification.

(ANT.) fallacy, invalidity.

confirmed *(SYN.)* regular, established, habitual, chronic.

(ANT.) occasional, infrequent.

conflict *(SYN.)* duel, combat, fight, collision, discord, encounter, interference, inconsistency, contention, struggle, opposition, clash, oppose, battle, controversy, contend, engagement, contest, variance.

(ANT.) consonance, harmony, amity.

confiscate *(SYN.)* capture, catch, gain, purloin, steal, take, clutch, grip, seize, get, obtain, bear.

conflagration *(SYN.)* flame, glow, heat, warmth, fervor, passion, vigor.

(ANT.) apathy, cold, quiescence.

conform *(SYN.)* adapt, comply, yield, submit, obey, adjust, agree, fit, suit.

(ANT.) misapply, misfit, rebel, vary, dis-

conformity *(SYN.)* congruence, accord, agreement, correspondence.

confound *(SYN.)* confuse, baffle, perplex, puzzle, bewilder.

confront *(SYN.)* confront, defy, hinder, resist, thwart, withstand, bar.

(ANT.) submit, agree, support, succumb.

confuse *(SYN.)* confound, perplex, mystify, dumbfound, baffle, puzzle, jumble, mislead, mix up, mistake, bewilder.

(ANT.) explain, instruct, edify, illumine, enlighten, illuminate, solve.

confused *(SYN.)* deranged, indistinct, disordered, muddled, bewildered, disconcerted, disorganized, perplexed.

(ANT.) organized, plain, clear, obvious.

confusion *(SYN.)* commotion, disarray, agitation, disorder, chaos, ferment, stir, perplexity, tumult, bewilderment, disarrangement, uncertainty, muss, mess, turmoil.

(ANT.) order, tranquillity, enlightenment, comprehension, understanding, tidiness, organization, peace.

congregate *(SYN.)* gather, foregather, meet, convene.

(ANT.) scatter, dispel, disperse, dissipate.

congress *(SYN.)* parliament, legislature, assembly.

congruous *(SYN.)* agreeing, conforming, constant, correspondent.

(ANT.) incongruous, inconsistent, discrepant.

conjecture *(SYN.)* law, supposition, theory.

(ANT.) proof, fact, certainty.

conjunction *(SYN.)* combination, junction, connection, link.

(ANT.) separation, disconnection, separation, diversion.

connect *(SYN.)* adjoin, link, combine, relate, join, attach, unite, associate, attribute, affix.

(ANT.) detach, separate, disjoin, untie, dissociation, disconnect, disassociation, unfasten.

connection *(SYN.)* conjunction, alliance, link, affinity, bond, tie, association, relationship, union.

(ANT.) isolation, dissociation, separation, disassociation, disunion.

conquer *(SYN.)* master, beat, humble, defeat, overcome, rout, win, succeed, achieve, gain, overpower, quell, subdue,

achieve, gain, overpower, quell, subdue, crush, vanquish.

(ANT.) cede, yield, retreat, surrender.

conquest *(SYN.)* triumph, victory, achievement.

(ANT.) surrender, failure, defeat.

conscientious *(SYN.)* upright, straight, honest, incorruptible, scrupulous.

(ANT.) careless, irresponsible, slovenly.

conscious *(SYN.)* cognizant, informed, perceptive, aware, intentional, sensible, awake, purposeful, deliberate, sensible.

(ANT.) unaware, insensible, asleep, comatose, ignorant.

consecrate *(SYN.)* exalt, extol, hallow, honor.

(ANT.) mock, degrade, debase, abuse.

consecrated *(SYN.)* holy, divine, devout, spiritual.

(ANT.) evil, worldly, secular.

consent *(SYN.)* permission, leave, agree, let, assent, agreement, license, permit.

(ANT.) refusal, opposition, denial, dissent, prohibition.

consequence *(SYN.)* outcome, issue, result, effect, significance, importance.

(ANT.) impetus, cause.

consequential *(SYN.)* significant, important, weighty.

(ANT.) trivial, unimportant, minor, insignificant.

consequently *(SYN.)* hence, thence, therefore.

conservative *(SYN.)* conventional, reactionary, cautious, moderate, careful.

(ANT.) radical, liberal, rash, foolhardy, reckless.

conserve *(SYN.)* save, retain, reserve, guard, keep, support, sustain.

(ANT.) dismiss, neglect, waste, reject, discard.

consider *(SYN.)* heed, ponder, contemplate, examine, study, weigh, reflect, think about, regard, deliberate, respect.

(ANT.) ignore, overlook, disdain, disregard, neglect.

considerable *(SYN.)* much, noteworthy, worthwhile, significant, important.

considerate *(SYN.)* careful, considerate, heedful, prudent, kind, thoughtful, polite, introspective, reflective.

(ANT.) thoughtless, heedless, inconsiderate, selfish, rash.

consideration *(SYN.)* kindness, care,

heed, politeness, empathy, notice, watchfulness, kindliness, thoughtfulness, courtesy, concern, sympathy, thought, attention, reflection, fee, pay, study.
(ANT.) omission, oversight, negligence.

consistent *(SYN.)* conforming, accordant, compatible, agreeing, faithful, constant, harmonious, expected, regular, congruous, correspondent.
(ANT.) paradoxical, discrepant, contrary, antagonistic, opposed, eccentric, inconsistent, incongruous.

consolation *(SYN.)* enjoyment, sympathy, relief, ease, contentment, comfort, solace.
(ANT.) discomfort, suffering, discouragement, torture, burden, misery.

console *(SYN.)* solace, comfort, sympathize with, assuage, soothe.
(ANT.) worry, annoy, upset, disturb, distress.

consolidate *(SYN.)* blend, combine, conjoin, fuse, mix, merge, unite.
(ANT.) decompose, separate, analyze, disintegrate.

consort *(SYN.)* companion, comrade, friend.
(ANT.) stranger, enemy, adversary.

conspicuous *(SYN.)* distinguished, clear, manifest, salient, noticeable, striking, obvious, prominent, visible.
(ANT.) hidden, obscure, neutral, common, inconspicuous.

conspiracy *(SYN.)* machination, combination, treason, intrigue, cabal, treachery, plot, collusion.

conspire *(SYN.)* plan, intrigue, plot, scheme.

constancy *(SYN.)* devotion, faithfulness, accuracy, precision, exactness.
(ANT.) faithlessness, treachery, perfidy.

constant *(SYN.)* continual, invariable, abiding, permanent, faithful, invariant, true, ceaseless, enduring, unchanging, steadfast, unchangeable, loyal, stable, immutable, staunch, steady, fixed.
(ANT.) fickle, irregular, wavering, off-and-on, infrequent, occasional, mutable.

constantly *(SYN.)* eternally, ever, evermore, forever, unceasingly.
(ANT.) rarely, sometimes, never, occasionally.

consternation *(SYN.)* apprehension, dismay, alarm, fear, fright, dread, horror, terror.
(ANT.) bravery, courage, boldness, assurance.

constitute *(SYN.)* compose, found, form, establish, organize, create, appoint, delegate, authorize, commission.

constitution *(SYN.)* law, code, physique, health, vitality.

constrain *(SYN.)* necessity, indigence, need, want, poverty.
(ANT.) luxury, freedom, uncertainty.

construct *(SYN.)* build, form, erect, make, fabricate, raise, frame.
(ANT.) raze, demolish, destroy.

construction *(SYN.)* raising, building, fabricating.

constructive *(SYN.)* useful, helpful, valuable.
(ANT.) ruinous, destructive.

construe *(SYN.)* explain, interpret, solve, render, translate.
(ANT.) distort, confuse, misconstrue.

consult *(SYN.)* discuss, chatter, discourse, gossip, confer, report, rumor, deliberate, speech, talk.
(ANT.) writing, correspondence, silence.

consume *(SYN.)* engulf, absorb, use up, use, expend, exhaust, devour, devastate, destroy, engross.
(ANT.) emit, expel, exude, discharge.

consumer *(SYN.)* user, buyer, purchaser.

consummate *(SYN.)* close, conclude, do finish, perfect, terminate.

consummation *(SYN.)* climax, apex, culmination, peak.
(ANT.) depth, base, floor.

contact *(SYN.)* meeting, touching.

contagious *(SYN.)* infectious, virulent, communicable, catching.
(ANT.) noncommunicable, healthful, hygienic.

contain *(SYN.)* embody, hold, embrace, include, accommodate, repress, restrain.
(ANT.) emit, encourage, yield, discharge.

contaminate *(SYN.)* corrupt, sully, taint, defile, soil, pollute, dirty, infect, poison.
(ANT.) purify.

contemplate *(SYN.)* imagine, recollect, consider, study, reflect upon, observe, deliberate, muse, ponder, plan, intend, view, regard, think about, reflect, think, mean.
(ANT.) forget, guess, conjecture.

contemplative *(SYN.)* simultaneous,

meditative, thoughtful, contemporaneous, pensive, studious.
(ANT.) inattentive, indifferent, thoughtless.

contemporary (SYN.) modern, present, simultaneous, fashionable, coexisting, contemporaneous, up-to-date.
(ANT.) old, antecedent, past, ancient, succeeding, bygone.

contempt (SYN.) detestation, malice, contumely, disdain, derision, scorn.
(ANT.) respect, reverence, admiration, esteem, awe.

contemptible (SYN.) base, mean, vile, vulgar, nasty, low, detestable, selfish, miserable, offensive.
(ANT.) generous, honorable, noble, exalted, admirable.

contemptuous (SYN.) disdainful, sneering, scornful, insolent.
(ANT.) modest, humble.

contend (SYN.) dispute, combat, contest, assert, claim, argue, maintain.

content (SYN.) pleased, happy, contented, satisfied.
(ANT.) restless, dissatisfied, discontented.

contented (SYN.) delighted, fortunate, gay, happy, joyous, lucky, merry.
(ANT.) gloomy, blue, depressed.

contention (SYN.) combat, duel, struggle, discord, battle, variance.
(ANT.) concord, harmony, amity, consonance.

contentment (SYN.) delight, happiness, gladness, pleasure, satisfaction.
(ANT.) misery, sorrow, grief, sadness, despair.

contest (SYN.) dispute, debate, competition, tournament, oppose, discuss, quarrel, squabble.
(ANT.) allow, concede, agree, assent.

continence (SYN.) forbearance, temperance.
(ANT.) self-indulgence, excess, intoxication.

contingency (SYN.) likelihood, possibility, occasion, circumstance.

contingent (SYN.) depending, subject.
(ANT.) independent, original, casual.

continual (SYN.) constant, unceasing, everlasting, unremitting, endless, continuous, uninterrupted, regular, connected, consecutive, ceaseless.
(ANT.) periodic, rare, irregular, oc-

continue (SYN.) proceed, extend, endure, persist, resume, renew, recommence, last, remain, last, prolong, pursue.
(ANT.) check, cease, discontinue, stop, suspend.

continuous (SYN.) continuing, uninterrupted, ceaseless, unceasing, incessant, constant.
(ANT.) intermittent, irregular, sporadic.

contract (SYN.) condense, diminish, reduce, bargain, restrict, agreement, compact, pact, shrink, get, treaty, shorten.
(ANT.) lengthen, extend, swell, expand, elongate.

contraction (SYN.) reduction, shortening.
(ANT.) enlargement, expansion, extension.

contradict (SYN.) gainsay, counter, oppose, confute, dispute.
(ANT.) verify, confirm, agree, support.

contradictory (SYN.) inconsistent, conflicting, incompatible, paradoxical, unsteady.
(ANT.) congruous, consistent, correspondent.

contrary (SYN.) disagreeable, perverse, hostile, stubborn, opposite, opposing, opposed, disagreeing, disastrous, conflicting, headstrong, unlucky.
(ANT.) lucky, agreeable, propitious, favorable, like, obliging, similar, complementary, tractable, fortunate.

contrast (SYN.) differentiate, compare, distinction, disagreement, distinguish, differ, discriminate, difference, oppose.
(ANT.) agreement, similarity, likeness.

contribute (SYN.) grant, give, donate, bestow, provide, offer.
(ANT.) deny, withhold.

contribution (SYN.) grant, gift, offering, donation.

contrition (SYN.) grief, regret, self-reproach.
(ANT.) self-satisfaction, complacency.

contrive (SYN.) devise, intend, plan, make, invent, plot, hatch, form, project, arrange, manage, maneuver, scheme, sketch.

control (SYN.) govern, regulate, rule, command, dominate, direct, manage, check, repress, curb, management, mastery, direction, restraint, superintend,
(ANT.) ignore, forsake, follow, submit,

tend, restrain.

(ANT.) ignore, forsake, follow, submit, abandon.

controversy *(SYN.)* disagreement, dispute, debate.

(ANT.) agreement, harmony, accord, concord, decision.

convenience *(SYN.)* accessibility, aid, benefit, help, service, availability.

(ANT.) inconvenience.

convenient *(SYN.)* adapted, appropriate, fitting, favorable, handy, suitable, accessible, nearby, ready, available, advantageous, timely.

(ANT.) inconvenient, troublesome, awkward.

convention *(SYN.)* meeting, conference, assembly, practice, custom, rule.

conventional *(SYN.)* common, regular, usual, everyday, habitual, routine, accustomed.

(ANT.) exotic, unusual, bizarre, extraordinary.

conversant *(SYN.)* aware, intimate, familiar, versed, close, friendly, sociable.

(ANT.) affected, distant, cold, reserved.

conversation *(SYN.)* colloquy, dialogue, chat, parley, discussion, talk.

converse *(SYN.)* jabber, talk, argue, comment, harangue, plead, rant, spout, discuss, chat, talk, speak, reason.

conversion *(SYN.)* alteration, change, mutation, modification, metamorphosis.

convert *(SYN.)* change, alter, alter, turn, transform, shift, modify, exchange, win over, vary, veer.

(ANT.) establish, stabilize, settle, retain.

convey *(SYN.)* carry, bear, communicate, transport, transmit, support, sustain.

(ANT.) drop, abandon.

conveyance *(SYN.)* van, car, train, truck, plane.

convict *(SYN.)* felon, offender, criminal.

conviction *(SYN.)* opinion, position, view, faith, belief, confidence, feeling, reliance, trust.

(ANT.) doubt, heresy, incredulity, denial.

convince *(SYN.)* persuade, assure, exhort, induce, influence.

(ANT.) deter, compel, restrain, dissuade.

convivial *(SYN.)* jolly, social, jovial, gregarious.

(ANT.) solemn, stern, unsociable.

convoy *(SYN.)* with, attend, chaperone.

(ANT.) avoid, desert, quit, leave.

cool *(SYN.)* frosty, chilly, icy, cold, wintry, quiet, composed, collected, distant, unfriendly, quiet, moderate.

(ANT.) hot, warm, heated, overwrought, excited, hysterical, friendly, outgoing.

cooperate *(SYN.)* unite, combine, help, contribute, support.

coordinate *(SYN.)* attune, harmonize, adapt, match, balance.

copious *(SYN.)* ample, abundant, bountiful, overflowing, plentiful, profuse, rich.

(ANT.) scant, scarce, insufficient, meager, deficient.

copy *(SYN.)* facsimile, exemplar, imitation, duplicate, reproduction, likeness, print, carbon, transcript.

(ANT.) prototype, original.

cordial *(SYN.)* polite, friendly, affable, genial, earnest, gracious, warm, ardent, warmhearted, hearty, sincere.

(ANT.) unfriendly, cool, aloof, hostile, ill-tempered, reserved.

core *(SYN.)* midpoint, heart, kernel, center, middle.

(ANT.) outskirts, border, surface, outside, boundary, rim.

corporation *(SYN.)* business, organization, crew, group, troop, society, company, conglomerate, firm.

(ANT.) individual, dispersion, seclusion.

corpse *(SYN.)* cadaver, carcass, remains, body, form.

(ANT.) spirit, soul, mind, intellect.

corpulent *(SYN.)* obese, portly, chubby, stout.

(ANT.) slim, thin, slender, lean, gaunt.

correct *(SYN.)* true, set right, faultless, impeccable, proper, accurate, precise, mend, right, rebuke, punish, amend, rectify, better, emend, caution, discipline, exact, strict.

(ANT.) condone, aggravate, false, inaccurate, wrong, untrue, faulty.

correction *(SYN.)* order, improvement, regulation, instruction, amendment, emendation, remedy, rectification, repair, training, punishment.

(ANT.) confusion, turbulence, chaos.

correlative *(SYN.)* allied, correspondent, like, similar, parallel.

(ANT.) different, opposed, divergent.

correspond *(SYN.)* compare, coincide, match, agree, suit, fit, write.

(ANT.) differ, diverge, vary.

correspondent *(SYN.)* allied, alike, comparable, like, parallel, similar.

(ANT.) different, opposed, divergent, dissimilar.

corridor *(SYN.)* hallway, hall, foyer, passage, lobby, passageway.

corrode *(SYN.)* erode.

corrupt *(SYN.)* crooked, untrustworthy, treacherous, debased, unscrupulous, wicked, evil, low, contaminated, perverted, bribe, depraved, corrupted, demoralize, degrade, venal, putrid, tainted, dishonest, impure.

(ANT.) upright, honest, pure, sanctify, edify, purify, sanctified, scrupulous.

corrupted *(SYN.)* crooked, dishonest, impure, spoiled, unsound.

cost *(SYN.)* price, value, damage, charge, loss, sacrifice, penalty, worth.

costly *(SYN.)* dear, expensive.

(ANT.) cheap, inexpensive.

costume *(SYN.)* dress, clothes, apparel, clothing, garb.

couch *(SYN.)* davenport, sofa, loveseat.

council *(SYN.)* caution, instruction, committee, cabinet, board, suggestion.

counsel *(SYN.)* guidance, attorney, lawyer, counselor, hint, imply, opinion, advice, offer, advise.

(ANT.) declare, dictate, insist.

count *(SYN.)* consider, number, enumerate, total, figure, compute, tally, estimate.

(ANT.) conjecture, guess, miscalculate.

countenance *(SYN.)* visage, face, aspect, support, appearance, approval, encouragement, favor.

(ANT.) forbid, prohibit.

counteract *(SYN.)* thwart, neutralize, offset, counterbalance, defeat.

counterfeit *(SYN.)* false, fraudulent, pretended, pretend, sham, imitate, forgery, artificial, bogus, fake, spurious, imitation, unreal.

(ANT.) authentic, natural, real, genuine, true.

country *(SYN.)* state, nation, forest, farmland.

(ANT.) city.

couple *(SYN.)* team, pair, accompany, associate, attach, combine, connect, brace, join, link, unite.

(ANT.) detach, separate, disjoin, discon- nect.

courage *(SYN.)* fearlessness, boldness, chivalry, fortitude, mettle, spirit, daring, bravery, prowess, intrepidity, valor, resolution.

(ANT.) fear, timidity, cowardice.

courageous *(SYN.)* bold, dauntless, brave, daring, intrepid, valorous, plucky, fearless, heroic, valiant.

(ANT.) fearful, weak, timid, cowardly.

course *(SYN.)* passage, advance, path, road, progress, way, direction, bearing, route, street, track, trail, way.

courteous *(SYN.)* civil, respectful, polite, genteel, well-mannered, gracious, refined.

(ANT.) discourteous, rude, uncivil, impolite, boorish.

courtesy *(SYN.)* graciousness, politeness, respect.

(ANT.) discourtesy, rudeness.

covenant *(SYN.)* agreement, concord, harmony, unison, compact, stipulation.

(ANT.) variance, discord, dissension, difference.

cover *(SYN.)* clothe, conceal, disguise, curtain, guard, envelop, mask, cloak, shield, hide, screen, protect, embrace, top, lid, covering, stopper, protection, refuge, spread, overlay, include, veil.

(ANT.) bare, expose, reveal.

covert *(SYN.)* potential, undeveloped, concealed, dormant.

(ANT.) explicit, visible, manifest.

covetous *(SYN.)* grasping, greedy, acquisitive, avaricious.

(ANT.) generous.

coward *(SYN.)* dastard, milquetoast, cad.

(ANT.) hero.

cowardice *(SYN.)* dread, dismay, fright, dismay, panic, terror, timidity.

(ANT.) fearlessness, courage, bravery.

cowardly *(SYN.)* fearful, timorous, afraid, faint-hearted, yellow, pusillanimous, spineless.

cower *(SYN.)* wince, flinch, cringe, quail, tremble.

coy *(SYN.)* embarrassed, sheepish, shy, timid.

(ANT.) fearless, outgoing, bold, adventurous, daring.

crack *(SYN.)* snap, break, split.

cracker *(SYN.)* wafer, biscuit, saltine.

craft *(SYN.)* talent, skill, expertness,

ability, cunning, guile, deceit, trade, profession, occupation.

crafty *(SYN.)* covert, clever, cunning, skillful, foxy, tricky, sly, underhand, shrewd.
(ANT.) frank, sincere, gullible, open, guileless, ingenuous.

craggy *(SYN.)* rough, rugged, irregular, uneven.
(ANT.) level, sleek, smooth, fine, polished.

crank *(SYN.)* cross, irritable, bad-tempered, testy.
(ANT.) cheerful, happy.

crash *(SYN.)* smash, shatter, dash.

crave *(SYN.)* want, desire, hunger for.
(ANT.) relinquish, renounce.

craving *(SYN.)* relish appetite, desire, liking, longing, passion.
(ANT.) renunciation, distaste, disgust.

crazy *(SYN.)* delirious, deranged, idiotic, mad, insane, imbecilic, demented, foolish, maniacal.
(ANT.) sane, sensible, sound, rational, reasonable.

creak *(SYN.)* squeak.

create *(SYN.)* fashion, form, generate, engender, formulate, make, originate, produce, cause, ordain, invent, beget, design, construct, constitute.
(ANT.) disband, abolish, terminate, destroy, demolish.

creative *(SYN.)* imaginative, ingenious, original, resourceful, clever, inventive, innovative, mystical.
(ANT.) unromantic, dull, literal.

credence *(SYN.)* confidence, faith, feeling, opinion, trust.
(ANT.) doubt, incredulity, denial.

credible *(SYN.)* conceivable, believable.
(ANT.) inconceivable, unbelievable.

credit *(SYN.)* believe, accept, belief, trust, faith, merit, honor, apprehend, fancy, hold, support.
(ANT.) doubt, reject, question, distrust.

creditable *(SYN.)* worthy, praiseworthy.
(ANT.) dishonorable, discreditable, shameful.

credulous *(SYN.)* trusting, naive, believing, gullible, unsuspicious.
(ANT.) suspicious.

creed *(SYN.)* belief, precept, credo, faith, teaching.
(ANT.) practice, deed, conduct, perfor-

mance.

creek *(SYN.)* brook, spring, stream, rivulet.

crime *(SYN.)* offense, insult, aggression, wrongdoing, wrong, misdeed.
(ANT.) right, gentleness, innocence, morality.

criminal *(SYN.)* unlawful, crook, gangster, outlaw, illegal, convict, delinquent, offender, malefactor, culprit, felonious, felon, transgressor.

cripple *(SYN.)* hurt, maim, damage, injure.

crippled *(SYN.)* deformed, disabled, maimed, hobbling, limping, unconvincing, unsatisfactory.
(ANT.) robust, sound, vigorous, athletic.

crisis *(SYN.)* conjuncture, emergency, pass, pinch, acme, climax, contingency, juncture, exigency, strait.
(ANT.) calm, normality, stability, equilibrium.

crisp *(SYN.)* crumbling, delicate, frail, brittle.
(ANT.) calm, normality, stability.

criterion *(SYN.)* measure, law, rule, principle, gauge, proof.
(ANT.) fancy guess, chance, supposition.

critic *(SYN.)* reviewer, judge, commentator, censor, defamer, slanderer, faultfinder.

critical *(SYN.)* exact, fastidious, caviling, faultfinding, accurate, condemning, reproachful, risky, dangerous, momentous, carping, acute, hazardous, hypercritical, perilous, decisive, important.
(ANT.) shallow, uncritical, approving, insignificant, trivial, unimportant.

criticize *(SYN.)* examine, analyze, inspect, blame, censure, appraise, evaluate, scrutinize, reprehend.
(ANT.) neglect, overlook, approve.

critique *(SYN.)* criticism, inspection, review.

crony *(SYN.)* colleague, companion, chum, buddy, comrade, friend, mate.
(ANT.) stranger, enemy, adversary.

crooked *(SYN.)* twisted, corrupt, hooked, curved, criminal, dishonest, degraded, bent, zigzag, impaired.
(ANT.) improved, raised, straight, honest, vitalized, upright, enhanced.

crop *(SYN.)* fruit, produce, harvest, cut, mow, reaping, result, yield.

cross *(SYN.)* mix, mingle, traverse, interbreed, annoyed, irritable, cranky, testy, angry, mean, ill-natured.
(ANT.) cheerful.
crouch *(SYN.)* duck, stoop.
crow *(SYN.)* boast, brag.
crowd *(SYN.)* masses, flock, host, squeeze, mob, multitude, populace, press, cramp, throng, swarm.
crown *(SYN.)* coronet, apex, crest, circlet, pinnacle, tiara, skull, head, top, zenith.
(ANT.) base, bottom, foundation, foot.
crude *(SYN.)* rude, graceless, unpolished, green, harsh, rough, coarse, illprepared, unfinished, raw, boorish, unrefined, uncouth.
(ANT.) finished, refined, polished, cultured, genteel, cultivated.
cruel *(SYN.)* ferocious, mean, heartless, unmerciful, malignant, savage, brutal, pitiless, inhuman, ruthless, merciless.
(ANT.) humane, forbearing, kind, compassionate, merciful, benevolent, kindhearted, gentle.
cruelty *(SYN.)* harshness, meanness, savagery, brutality.
(ANT.) compassion, kindness.
crumb *(SYN.)* jot, grain, mite, particle, shred.
(ANT.) mass, bulk, quantity.
crunch *(SYN.)* champ, gnaw, nibble, pierce.
crush *(SYN.)* smash, break, crash.
cry *(SYN.)* yowl, yell, roar, shout, bellow, scream, wail, weep, bawl, sob.
cryptic *(SYN.)* puzzling, mysterious, enigmatic, hidden, secret, vague, obscure, occult, unclear.
cull *(SYN.)* elect, choose, pick, select.
(ANT.) reject, refuse.
culpable *(SYN.)* guilty, blameworthy.
(ANT.) innocent.
cultivate *(SYN.)* plant, seed, farm, till, refine, educate, teach.
cultivation *(SYN.)* farming, horticulture, tillage, agriculture.
cultural *(SYN.)* civilizing, educational, elevating, instructive.
cumbersome *(SYN.)* bulky, clumsy, awkward, unmanageable.
(ANT.) handy.
cunning *(SYN.)* clever, wily, crafty, foxy, skillful, tricky, ingenious, foxiness, ability, skill, wiliness, devious.

(ANT.) gullible, honest, naive, openness, straightforward, simple, direct.
curb *(SYN.)* check, restraint, hinder, hold, limit, control, stop, suppress.
(ANT.) aid, loosen, incite, encourage.
cure *(SYN.)* help, treatment, heal, medicine, restorative, relief, remedy.
curiosity *(SYN.)* marvel, rarity, phenomenon, admiration, amazement.
(ANT.) apathy, indifference, expectation.
curious *(SYN.)* interrogative, interested, peculiar, queer, nosy, peeping, prying, inquisitive, snoopy, inquiring, unusual.
(ANT.) unconcerned, incurious, ordinary, indifferent, uninterested, common.
current *(SYN.)* up-to-date, contemporary, present, new, tide, stream, modern.
(ANT.) antiquated, old, bygone, ancient, past.
curse *(SYN.)* ban, oath, denounce, swear, condemn.
(ANT.) boon, blessing, advantage.
cursory *(SYN.)* frivolous, shallow, slight.
(ANT.) complete, deep, profound, thorough.
curt *(SYN.)* hasty, short, abrupt, brusque, brief, blunt, rude, harsh.
(ANT.) friendly, smooth, gradual, polite, courteous.
curtail *(SYN.)* condense, contract, diminish, reduce, limit, abbreviate.
(ANT.) lengthen, extend.
curtain *(SYN.)* blind, drapery, drape, shade.
curve *(SYN.)* crook, deflect, bend, bow, incline, turn, twist.
(ANT.) resist, stiffen, straighten.
cushion *(SYN.)* pillow, pad, absorb.
custodian *(SYN.)* guard, keeper, guardian, watchman.
custody *(SYN.)* guardianship, care.
(ANT.) neglect, disregard, indifference.
custom *(SYN.)* fashion, rule, routine.
customary *(SYN.)* common, usual, regular, everyday, general.
(ANT.) exceptional, irregular, rare, unusual, abnormal.
customer *(SYN.)* patron, client, buyer.
cut *(SYN.)* slash, gash, prick, slit, sever, cleave, mow, incision, chop, lop, slice.
cutting *(SYN.)* bitter, stern, caustic, scathing, harsh, acerbic.
cylindrical *(SYN.)* circular, curved, plump, rotund, spherical, round.

dab *(SYN.)* coat, pat, smear.

dabble *(SYN.)* splatter, toy, splash, fiddle, putter.

dabbler *(SYN.)* amateur, dilettante, tinkerer, trifler.

(ANT.) master, expert, scholar, specialist, authority.

daft *(SYN.)* crazy, foolish, insane. **dagger** *(SYN.)* knife, dirk, blade.

daily *(SYN.)* every day, diurnal, regularly.

dally *(SYN.)* dawdle, linger, lag, delay.

(ANT.) rush, hurry, dash, bustle.

dam *(SYN.)* dike, levee, barrier, slow, stop, check, obstruct, block.

(ANT.) free, release, loose, unleash.

damage *(SYN.)* spoil, deface, impair, mar, hurt, injury, impairment, destruction.

(ANT.) repair, benefit, mend, rebuild, improve, ameliorate.

dame *(SYN.)* woman, lady.

damn *(SYN.)* ˙ denounce, descry, doom, curse, reprove, blame.

(ANT.) bless, honor, glorify, praise, accept, applaud, commend, consecrate.

damp *(SYN.)* humid, dank, moisture, wetness, dampness, humidity.

(ANT.) arid, dry.

dampen *(SYN.)* wet, depressed, moisten, dull, suppress, sprinkle, discouraged, retard, slow, inhibit, deaden, muffle.

(ANT.) dehumidify, increase, encourage.

dance *(SYN.)* bounce, flit, skip, sway, prance, bob, glide, caper, cavort, frisk.

dandle *(SYN.)* jounce, joggle, bounce, jiggle, nestle, cuddle, caress.

dandy *(SYN.)* coxcomb, fop, swell, great, fine, wonderful, excellent.

(ANT.) rotten, terrible, awful, miserable, slob.

danger *(SYN.)* jeopardy, risk, threat, hazard, uncertainty, peril.

(ANT.) safety, immunity, security, defense.

dangerous *(SYN.)* risky, insecure, threatening, critical, perilous, unsafe, uncertain, hazardous.

(ANT.) secure, protected, safe.

dangle *(SYN.)* swing, flap, hang, sag.

dank *(SYN.)* moist, muggy, wet.

(ANT.) dry.

dapper *(SYN.)* spruce, trim, natty, smart, well-tailored, dashing, neat.

(ANT.) untidy, shabby, messy, unkempt.

dappled *(SYN.)* spotted, flecked, brindl-

ed, variegated, piebald, pied.

(ANT.) uniform, solid, unvaried.

dare *(SYN.)* brave, call, question, defy, risk, challenge, summon.

daredevil *(SYN.)* lunatic, thrill-seeker, madcap, adventurer.

daring *(SYN.)* foolhardy, chivalrous, rash, fearless, courageous, intrepid, valiant, courage, bravery, brave, precipitate, bold.

(ANT.) timid, cowardice, timidity, cautious.

dark *(SYN.)* somber, obscure, gloomy, black, unilluminated, dim, evil, hidden, secret, swarthy, murky, opaque, dismal, mournful, sable, sullen, shadowy, sinister, dusky, mystic, shadowy, unlit, sunless, shaded, wicked, occult.

(ANT.) lucid, light, happy, cheerful, illuminated, pleasant.

darling *(SYN.)* dear, adored, sweetheart, favorite, cherished.

(ANT.) uncherished, unlovable, disagreeable, rejected, forlorn.

darn *(SYN.)* repair, mend.

dart *(SYN.)* scurry, arrow, barb, hurry, dash, throw, missile, run, hasten, scamper, toss, rush, cast.

dash *(SYN.)* pound, thump, beat, smite, buffet, thrash, smash, break, scurry, run, dart, rush, scamper, hint, pinch, hit, strike.

(ANT.) stroke, hearten, encourage, defend.

dashing *(SYN.)* swashbuckling, dapper, flamboyant, handsome.

(ANT.) dull, colorless, shabby, lifeless.

dastardly *(SYN.)* mean-spirited, craven, cowardly, mean, rotten, villainous, dishonorable.

(ANT.) heroic, brave, high-minded, courageous.

data *(SYN.)* information, statistics, proof, facts, evidence.

date *(SYN.)* interview, appointment, commitment, engagement, meeting, rendezvous, regale, entertain.

dated *(SYN.)* out-of-date, old-fashioned, outmoded.

(ANT.) latest, now, current, fashionable, hot.

daub *(SYN.)* coat, grease, soil, scribble, cover, stain, smear, scrawl.

daunt *(SYN.)* discourage, dishearten, intimidate, frighten, deter.

(ANT.) enspirit, encourage.

dauntless *(SYN.)* fearless, brave, bold, courageous, intrepid, valiant.

(ANT.) fearful, timid, cowardly.

dawn *(SYN.)* sunrise, start, outset, daybreak, origin, commencement.

(ANT.) dusk, sunset, nightfall, end, conclusion, finish.

daydream *(SYN.)* woolgather, muse.

daze *(SYN.)* perplex, stun, puzzle, bewilder, upset, confuse, ruffle, confusion, stupor, bewilderment.

dazzle *(SYN.)* surprise, stun, astonish, impress, bewilder, stupefy.

dead *(SYN.)* departed, lifeless, deceased, insensible, inanimate, dull, defunct, gone, lifeless, unconscious, inoperative, inactive, inert, motionless, spiritless.

(ANT.) animate, functioning, active, living, alive, stirring.

deaden *(SYN.)* anesthetize, numb, paralyze.

deadlock *(SYN.)* standstill, impasse, stalemate.

deadly *(SYN.)* lethal, mortal, fatal, deathly, baleful.

deaf *(SYN.)* stone-deaf, unhearing, unheeding, unaware, unheedful, stubborn, oblivious, inattentive.

(ANT.) aware, conscious.

deafening *(SYN.)* vociferous, noisy, stentorian, resounding, loud.

(ANT.) soft, inaudible, subdued.

deal *(SYN.)* act, treat, attend, cope, barter, trade, bargain, apportion, give, distribute, deliver.

dear *(SYN.)* valued, esteemed, expensive, beloved, costly, darling, high-priced, loved, precious.

(ANT.) hateful, reasonable, inexpensive, cheap, unwanted.

dearth *(SYN.)* shortage, lack, scarcity.

death *(SYN.)* decease, extinction, demise, passing.

(ANT.) life.

debase *(SYN.)* lower, degrade, alloy, adulterate, defile, humiliate, depress, abase, pervert, corrupt.

(ANT.) restore, improve, vitalize, enhance.

debate *(SYN.)* wrangle, discuss, plead, argue, discussion, contend, argument, controversy, dispute.

(ANT.) agreement, reject, accord, ignore, spurn.

debonair *(SYN.)* urbane, sophisticated, refined, dapper, well-bred.

debris *(SYN.)* rubbish, litter, junk, wreckage, refuse, detritus, ruins, trash, residue.

debt *(SYN.)* amount due, liability, obligation.

decay *(SYN.)* decrease, spoil, ebb, decline, waste, disintegrate, wane, dwindle, molder, deteriorate, perish, wither, rot, collapse, rottenness, putrefy, die, decompose.

(ANT.) progress, rise, increase, grow, flourish.

deceased *(SYN.)* lifeless, departed, dead, insensible, defunct.

(ANT.) living, alive.

deceit *(SYN.)* duplicity, cheat, fraud, chicanery, trick, cunning, deception, guile, beguilement, deceitfulness, dishonesty, wiliness.

(ANT.) truthfulness, openness, forthrightness, honesty, candor.

deceitful *(SYN.)* false, fraudulent, insincere, dishonest, deceptive.

(ANT.) sincere, honest.

deceive *(SYN.)* cheat, defraud, hoodwink, mislead, swindle.

decency *(SYN.)* decorum, dignity, propriety, respectability.

decent *(SYN.)* befitting, fit, suitable, becoming, respectable, adequate, seemly, fitting, comely, appropriate, proper, tolerable, decorous.

(ANT.) vulgar, gross, improper, unsuitable, indecorous, reprehensible, indecent, coarse.

deception *(SYN.)* trick, cheat, sham, deceit, trickery, craftiness, treachery, beguilement, cunning.

(ANT.) openness, frankness, candor, probity, truthfulness, honesty.

deceptive *(SYN.)* specious, fallacious, deceitful, false, delusive, unreliable, illusive, tricky, dishonest, deceiving, misleading, delusory.

(ANT.) honest, real, genuine, true, truthful, authentic.

decide *(SYN.)* resolve, determine, terminate, conclude, close, settle, adjudicate, choose, end.

(ANT.) waver, hesitate, vacillate, doubt,

suspend.

decipher *(SYN.)* render, unravel, construe, solve, decode, translate, elucidate, determine.

(ANT.) misconstrue, distort, misinterpret, confuse.

decision *(SYN.)* resolution, determination, settlement.

decisive *(SYN.)* determined, firm, decided, unhesitating, resolute.

declaration *(SYN.)* pronouncement, notice, affirmation, statement, announcement, assertion.

declare *(SYN.)* assert, promulate, affirm, tell, broadcast, express, proclaim, aver, say, pronounce, profess, announce.

(ANT.) deny, withhold, conceal, suppress.

decline *(SYN.)* descend, decay, dwindle, refuse, incline, wane, sink, depreciate, deny, diminish, weaken.

(ANT.) accept, ascend, ameliorate, increase.

decompose *(SYN.)* rot, disintegrate, molder, decay, crumble.

decorate *(SYN.)* trim, paint, deck, enrich, color, beautify, enhance, furbish, furnish, adorn, ornament.

(ANT.) uncover, mar, deface, defame, debase.

decoration *(SYN.)* ornamentation, embellishment, adornment, furnishing, award, citation, medal.

decoy *(SYN.)* lure, bait.

decrease *(SYN.)* lessen, wane, deduct, diminish, curtail, deduct, remove, lessening, decline.

(ANT.) expansion, increase, enlarge, expand, grow.

decree *(SYN.)* order, edict, statute, declaration, announce, act.

decrepit *(SYN.)* feeble, puny, weakened, infirm, enfeebled, languid, rickety, weak, run-down, tumble-down, dilapidated, faint.

(ANT.) strong, forceful, vigorous, energetic, lusty.

decry *(SYN.)* lower, belittle, derogate, minimize, undervalue.

(ANT.) praise, commend, magnify, aggrandize.

dedicate *(SYN.)* sanctify, consecrate, hallow, devote, assign.

dedicated *(SYN.)* disposed, true, affectionate, fond, wedded.

(ANT.) indisposed, detached, untrammeled, disinclined.

deduct *(SYN.)* lessen, shorten, abate, remove, eliminate, curtail, subtract.

(ANT.) grow, enlarge, add, increase, amplify, expand.

deed *(SYN.)* feat, transaction, action, performance, act, operation, achievement, document, certificate, title, accomplishment.

(ANT.) intention, cessation, inactivity, deliberation.

deem *(SYN.)* hold, determine, believe, regard, reckon, judge, consider, account, expound, view.

deep *(SYN.)* bottomless, low, unplumbed, acute, obscure, involved, absorbed.

(ANT.) shallow.

deface *(SYN.)* spoil, impair, damage, mar, hurt, scratch, mutilate, disfigure, injure, harm.

(ANT.) mend, benefit, repair, enhance.

defamation *(SYN.)* invective, reproach, upbraiding, abuse, insult, outrage, reviling, desecration.

(ANT.) respect, approval, laudation, commendation.

default *(SYN.)* loss, omission, lack, failure, want, dereliction.

(ANT.) victory, achievement, sufficiency, success.

defeat *(SYN.)* quell, vanquish, beat, overcome, overthrow, subdue, frustrate, spoil, conquest.

(ANT.) submit, retreat, cede, yield, surrender, capitulate, lose.

defect *(SYN.)* shortcoming, fault, omission, blemish, imperfection, forsake, leave, weakness, failure.

(ANT.) perfection, flawlessness, support, join, completeness.

defective *(SYN.)* faulty, imperfect, inoperative, flawed, inoperable.

(ANT.) flawless, perfect, faultless.

defend *(SYN.)* screen, espouse, justify, protect, vindicate, fortify, assert, guard, safeguard, shield. *(ANT.) oppose, assault, submit, attack, deny.*

defense *(SYN.)* resistance, protection, bulwark, fort, barricade, trench, rampart, fortress.

defer *(SYN.)* postpone, delay.

(ANT.) speed, hurry, expedite.

deference *(SYN.)* fame, worship, adora-

tion, reverence, admiration, respect, fame, dignity, homage.
(ANT.) dishonor, derision, reproach, contempt.
defiant *(SYN.)* rebellious, antagonistic, obstinate.
(ANT.) yielding, submissive.
deficient *(SYN.)* lacking, short, incomplete, defective, scanty, insufficient, inadequate.
(ANT.) enough, ample, sufficient, adequate.
defile *(SYN.)* pollute, march, corrupt, dirty, file, debase, contaminate.
(ANT.) purify.
define *(SYN.)* describe, fix, establish, label, designate, set, name, explain.
definite *(SYN.)* fixed, prescribed, certain, specific, exact, determined, distinct, explicit, correct.
(ANT.) indefinite, confused, undetermined, equivocal.
definitely *(SYN.)* certainly, assuredly, absolutely, positively, surely.
definition *(SYN.)* sense, interpretation, meaning, explanation.
deft *(SYN.)* handy, adroit, clever, adept, dexterous, skillful, skilled.
(ANT.) inept, clumsy, maladroit, awkward.
defunct *(SYN.)* lifeless, dead, departed, expired, extinct, spiritless, inanimate.
(ANT.) living, alive, stirring.
defy *(SYN.)* hinder, oppose, withstand, attack, resist, confront, challenge, flout, dare, thwart.
(ANT.) yield, allow, relent, surrender, submit, accede.
degenerate *(SYN.)* dwindle, decline, weaken, deteriorate, decrease.
(ANT.) ascend, ameliorate, increase, appreciate.
degrade *(SYN.)* crush, reduce, subdue, abash, humble, lower, shame, demote, downgrade, abase, mortify.
(ANT.) praise, elevate, honor.
degree *(SYN.)* grade, amount, step, measure, rank, honor, extent.
deign *(SYN.)* condescend, stoop.
dejected *(SYN.)* depressed, downcast, sad, disheartened, blue, discouraged.
(ANT.) cheerful, happy, optimistic.
delectable *(SYN.)* tasty, delicious, savory, delightful, sweet, luscious.

(ANT.) unsavory, distasteful, unpalatable, acrid.
delegate *(SYN.)* emissary, envoy, ambassador, representative, commission, deputize, authorize.
delete *(SYN.)* erase, cancel, remove.
(ANT.) add.
deleterious *(SYN.)* evil, unwholesome, base, sinful, bad, wicked, immoral, destructive, injurious, hurtful, damaging, detrimental, unsound.
(ANT.) moral, excellent, reputable, healthful, healthy, helpful, constructive, good.
deliberate *(SYN.)* studied, willful, intended, contemplated, premeditated, planned, methodical, designed.
(ANT.) fortuitous, hasty, accidental.
delicate *(SYN.)* frail, critical, slender, dainty, pleasing, fastidious, exquisite, precarious, demanding, sensitive, savory, fragile, weak.
(ANT.) tough, strong, coarse, clumsy, hearty, hale, vulgar, rude.
delicious *(SYN.)* tasty, luscious, delectable, sweet, savory.
(ANT.) unsavory, distasteful, unpalatable, unpleasant, acrid.
delight *(SYN.)* joy, bliss, gladness, pleasure, ecstasy, happiness, rapture.
(ANT.) revolt, sorrow, annoyance, displeasure, disgust, displease, revulsion, misery.
delightful *(SYN.)* pleasing, pleasant, charming, refreshing, pleasurable.
(ANT.) nasty, disagreeable, unpleasant.
delirious *(SYN.)* raving, mad, giddy, frantic, hysterical, violent.
deliver *(SYN.)* impart, publish, rescue, commit, communicate, free, address, offer, save, give, liberate,
(ANT.) restrict, confine, capture, enslave, withhold, imprison.
deluge *(SYN.)* overflow, flood.
delusion *(SYN.)* mirage, fantasy, phantasm, vision, dream, illusion, phantom, hallucination.
(ANT.) substance, actuality.
delve *(SYN.)* dig, look, search, scoop, explore, hunt.
demand *(SYN.)* claim, inquire, ask, need, require, obligation, requirement, ask for, necessitate.
(ANT.) tender, give, present, waive, relin-

quish, offer.

demean *(SYN.)* comport, bear, operate, carry, act, manage, deport.

demeanor *(SYN.)* manner, way, conduct, actions, behavior.

demented *(SYN.)* insane, crazy, mad, mental, psychotic, lunatic.

demolish *(SYN.)* ruin, devastate, ravage, annihilate, wreck, destroy, raze, exterminate, obliterate.

(ANT.) erect, make, save, construct, preserve, build, establish.

demolition *(SYN.)* wrecking, destruction.

(ANT.) erection, construction.

demon *(SYN.)* fiend, monster, devil, ogre, spirit.

demonstrate *(SYN.)* evince, show, prove, display, illustrate, describe, explain, manifest, exhibit.

(ANT.) hide, conceal.

demonstration *(SYN.)* exhibit, show, presentation, exhibition, display, rally.

demur *(SYN.)* waver, falter, delay, stutter, doubt, vacillate, hesitate, scruple.

(ANT.) proceed, decide, resolve, continue.

demure *(SYN.)* meek, shy, modest, diffident, retiring, bashful, coy.

den *(SYN.)* cave, lair, cavern.

denial *(SYN.)* disallowance, proscription, refusal, prohibition.

denounce *(SYN.)* condemn, blame, reprove, reprehend, censure, reproach, upbraid, reprobate.

(ANT.) condone, approve, forgive, commend, praise.

dense *(SYN.)* crowded, slow, close, obtuse, compact, dull, stupid, compressed, thick, concentrated, packed, solid.

(ANT.) sparse, quick, dispersed, clever, dissipated, empty, smart, bright.

dent *(SYN.)* notch, impress, pit, nick.

deny *(SYN.)* refuse, withhold, dispute, disavow, forbid, refute, contradict, abjure, confute, gainsay.

(ANT.) confirm, affirm, admit, confess, permit, allow, concede, assert.

depart *(SYN.)* quit, forsake, withdraw, renounce, desert, relinquish, die, perish, decease.

(ANT.) tarry, remain, come, abide, stay, arrive.

departure *(SYN.)* valediction, farewell.

depend *(SYN.)* trust, rely, confide.

dependable *(SYN.)* secure, trustworthy, certain, safe, trusty, reliable, tried.

(ANT.) unreliable, fallible, dubious, uncertain.

dependent *(SYN.)* relying, contingent, subordinate, conditional.

(ANT.) original, casual, absolute, independent.

depict *(SYN.)* explain, recount, describe, portray, characterize, relate, narrate.

deplore *(SYN.)* repine, lament, bemoan, wail, bewail, weep, grieve, regret.

deport *(SYN.)* exile, eject, oust, banish, expel, dismiss, ostracize, dispel, exclude.

(ANT.) receive, admit, shelter, accept, harbor.

deportment *(SYN.)* deed, behavior, manner, action, carriage, disposition, bearing, demeanor.

deposit *(SYN.)* place, put, bank, save, store, sediment, dregs, addition, entry.

(ANT.) withdraw, withdrawal.

depreciate *(SYN.)* dwindle, decrease, decay, belittle, disparage, weaken, minimize, descend, deteriorate.

(ANT.) ascend, ameliorate, praise, increase, applaud, appreciate.

depress *(SYN.)* deject, dishearten, sadden, dampen, devaluate, devalue, lessen, lower, cheapen, reduce, dispirit, discourage, sink.

(ANT.) exalt, cheer, exhilarate.

depression *(SYN.)* hopelessness, despondency, pessimism, dip, cavity, pothole, hole, despair, gloom, melancholy, sadness, sorrow, recession, decline, desperation, discouragement.

(ANT.) eminence, elation, optimism, happiness, confidence, elevation, hope.

deprive *(SYN.)* bereave, deny, strip.

(ANT.) provision, supply, provide.

derelict *(SYN.)* decrepit, shabby, dilapidated, neglected, forsaken, deserted, remiss, abandoned, lax.

dereliction *(SYN.)* want, lack, failure, miscarriage, loss, default, deficiency, omission, fiasco.

(ANT.) sufficiency, success, achievement, victory.

derision *(SYN.)* irony, satire, banter, raillery, sneering, gibe, ridicule.

derivation *(SYN.)* source, birth, inception, start, beginning, spring, commencement, foundation, origin.

(ANT.) issue, end, outcome, harvest, product.

derive *(SYN.)* obtain, acquire, get, receive.

descend *(SYN.)* wane, lower, move, slope, incline, decline, slant, sink.

(ANT.) increase, appreciate, ameliorate, ascend.

descendant *(SYN.)* child, issue, progeny, offspring.

describe *(SYN.)* portray, picture, recount, depict, relate, characterize, represent, narrate.

description *(SYN.)* history, record, recital, account, computation, chronicle, reckoning, narration, detail, narrative.

(ANT.) misrepresentation, confusion, caricature.

desecration *(SYN.)* profanation, insult, defamation, reviling, abuse, maltreatment, aspersion, perversion, dishonor.

(ANT.) respect, commendation, approval, laudation.

desert *(SYN.)* forsake, wilderness, resign, abjure, abandon, wasteland, waste, leave, surrender, abdicate, quit, barren, uninhabited.

(ANT.) uphold, defend, stay, maintain, accompany, join, support.

deserter *(SYN.)* runaway, renegade, fugitive, defector.

deserts *(SYN.)* right, compensation, due, reward, requital, condign.

deserve *(SYN.)* earn, warrant, merit.

design *(SYN.)* drawing, purpose, outline, devise, intend, draw, contrive, draft, cunning, plan, artfulness, delineation, scheming, sketch, intent, invent, objective, mean, contrivance, plotting, intention, create.

(ANT.) candor, accident, result, chance.

designate *(SYN.)* manifest, indicate, show, specify, denote, reveal, name, appoint, select, assign, disclose, signify, imply, nominate, intimate.

(ANT.) divert, mislead, conceal, falsify, distract.

desirable *(SYN.)* coveted, wanted.

desire *(SYN.)* longing, craving, yearning, appetite, lust, long for, crave, covet, want, request, ask, need, wish, aspiration, urge.

(ANT.) hate, aversion, loathing, abomination, detest, loathe, abhor, dis-
taste.

desist *(SYN.)* cork, stop, cease, hinder, terminate, abstain, halt, interrupt, seal, arrest, plug, bar.

(ANT.) promote, begin, speed, proceed, start.

desolate *(SYN.)* forlorn, waste, bare, lonely, abandoned, wild, deserted, uninhabited, empty, sad, miserable, wretched, unhappy, bleak, forsaken.

(ANT.) crowded, teeming, populous, happy, cheerful, fertile, attended.

despair *(SYN.)* discouragement, pessimism, depression, hopelessnêss, despondency, gloom, desperation.

(ANT.) elation, optimism, hope, joy, confidence.

desperado *(SYN.)* criminal, crook, thug, gangster, hoodlum.

desperate *(SYN.)* reckless, determined, despairing, wild, daring, hopeless, despondent, audacious.

(ANT.) optimistic, composed, hopeful, collected, calm, assured.

despicable *(SYN.)* vulgar, offensive, base, vile, contemptible, selfish, low, mean, worthless, nasty.

(ANT.) noble, exalted, admirable, generous, worthy, dignified.

despise *(SYN.)* hate, scorn, detest, loathe, disdain, abhor, condemn, dislike, abominate.

(ANT.) honor, love, approve, like, admire.

despite *(SYN.)* notwithstanding.

despoil *(SYN.)* plunder, rob, loot.

despondent *(SYN.)* sad, dismal, depressed, somber, ejected, melancholy, doleful, sorrowful.

(ANT.) joyous, cheerful, merry, happy.

despot *(SYN.)* tyrant, ruler, oppressor, dictator.

despotic *(SYN.)* authoritative, unconditional, absolute, tyrannous, entire, unrestricted.

(ANT.) dependent, conditional, qualified, accountable.

destiny *(SYN.)* fate, portion, outcome, consequence, result, fortune, doom, lot.

destitute *(SYN.)* poor, penurious, needy, impecunious, poverty-stricken, impoverished, indigent.

(ANT.) opulent, wealthy, affluent, rich.

destroy *(SYN.)* raze, devastate, ruin, end,

demolish, wreck, extinguish, annihilate, exterminate, obliterate, waste, slay, kill, eradicate.

(ANT.) make, construct, start, create, save, establish.

destroyed *(SYN.)* rent, smashed, interrupted, flattened, wrecked, broken, ruptured, crushed.

(ANT.) whole, repaired, integral, united.

destruction *(SYN.)* ruin, devastation, extinction, demolition.

(ANT.) beginning, creation.

destructive *(SYN.)* deadly, baneful, noxious, deleterious, injurious, pernicious, fatal, detrimental.

(ANT.) salutary, beneficial, creative.

detach *(SYN.)* deduct, remove, subtract, curtail, divide, shorten, decrease, disengage, reduce, separate, diminish.

(ANT.) hitch, grow, enlarge, increase, connect, amplify, attack, expand.

detail *(SYN.)* elaborate, commission, part, itemize, portion, division, fragment, assign, circumstance, segment.

detain *(SYN.)* impede, delay, hold back, retard, arrest, restrain, stay.

(ANT.) quicken, hasten, expedite, forward, precipitate.

detect *(SYN.)* discover, reveal, find, ascertain, determine, learn, originate, devise.

(ANT.) hide, screen, lose, cover, mask.

determinant *(SYN.)* reason, incentive, source, agent, principle, inducement.

(ANT.) result, effect, consequence, end.

determine *(SYN.)* decide, settle, end, conclude, ascertain, induce, fix, verify, resolve, establish, necessitate.

detest *(SYN.)* loathe, hate, despise.

(ANT.) savor, appreciate, like, love.

detriment *(SYN.)* injury, harm, disadvantage, damage.

(ANT.) benefit.

detrimental *(SYN.)* hurtful, mischievous, damaging, harmful.

(ANT.) salutary, advantageous, profitable, beneficial.

develop *(SYN.)* evolve, unfold, enlarge, amplify, expand, create, grow, advance, reveal, unfold, mature, elaborate.

(ANT.) wither, contract, degenerate, stunt, deteriorate, compress.

development *(SYN.)* growth, expansion, progress, unraveling, elaboration, evolution, maturing, unfolding.

(ANT.) compression, abbreviation, curtailment.

deviate *(SYN.)* deflect, stray, divert, diverge, wander, sidetrack, digress.

(ANT.) preserve, follow, remain, continue, persist.

device *(SYN.)* tool, utensil, means, channel, machine, agent, vehicle, gadget, apparatus, tools, instrument, contrivance.

(ANT.) preventive, impediment, hindrance, obstruction.

devilish *(SYN.)* diabolical, fiendish, diabolic, satanic, demonic.

devious *(SYN.)* tortuous, winding, distorted, circuitous, tricky, crooked, roundabout, cunning, erratic, indirect.

(ANT.) straight, direct, straightforward, honest.

devise *(SYN.)* create, concoct, invent, originate.

devote *(SYN.)* assign, dedicate, give, apply.

(ANT.) withhold, relinquish, ignore, withdraw.

devoted *(SYN.)* attached, dedicated, prone, wedded, addicted, ardent, earnest, loyal, disposed, inclined, fond, affectionate, faithful.

(ANT.) untrammeled, disinclined, detached, indisposed.

devotion *(SYN.)* piety, zeal, ardor, loyalty, dedication, religiousness, consecration, affection, love, devoutness, fidelity, attachment.

(ANT.) unfaithfulness, aversion, alienation, indifference.

devour *(SYN.)* consume, gulp, gorge, waste, eat, ruin, swallow, destroy.

devout *(SYN.)* sacred, religious, spiritual, holy, theological, pietistic, pious, sanctimonious, reverent.

(ANT.) profane, skeptical, atheistic, secular, impious.

dexterity *(SYN.)* talent, capability, qualification, aptness, skill, ability.

(ANT.) unreadiness, incapacity, disability, incompetency.

dexterous *(SYN.)* clever, adroit, handy, deft, facile, skillful, skilled, proficient.

(ANT.) awkward, clumsy.

dialect *(SYN.)* slang, jargon, cant, speech, idiom, tongue, diction, vernacular.

(ANT.) nonsense, drivel, babble, gibberish.

dialogue *(SYN.)* interview, chat, discussion, conference, exchange, talk, conversation.

diary *(SYN.)* memo, account, journal, words.

dicker *(SYN.)* haggle, bargain, negotiate.

dictate *(SYN.)* deliver, speak, record, command, order, direct.

dictator *(SYN.)* oppressor, tyrant, despot, persecutor, overlord, autocrat.

die *(SYN.)* fade, wane, cease, depart, wither, decay, decline, sink, expire, perish, decease, go, diminish, fail, languish, decrease.
(ANT.) live, begin, grow, survive, flourish.

difference *(SYN.)* inequality, variety, disparity, discord, distinction, dissension, dissimilarity, disagreement, contrast, separation.
(ANT.) harmony, similarity, identity, agreement, likeness, compatibility, kinship, resemblance.

different *(SYN.)* unlike, various, distinct, miscellaneous, divergent, sundry, contrary, differing, diverse, variant, incongruous, divers, unalike, changed, dissimilar, opposite.
(ANT.) similar, congruous, same, alike, identical.

differentiate *(SYN.)* separate, discriminate, distinguish, perceive, detect, recognize, discern.
(ANT.) confuse, omit, mingle, confound, overlook.

difficult *(SYN.)* involved, demanding, arduous, trying, complicated, hard, laborious, perplexing, hard, intricate.
(ANT.) simple, easy, facile, effortless.

difficulty *(SYN.)* trouble, hardship, fix, predicament, trouble.
(ANT.) ease.

diffuse *(SYN.)* spread, sparse, scattered, scanty, dispersed, thin, rare.
(ANT.) concentrated.

dig *(SYN.)* burrow, excavate, appreciate, understand.

digest *(SYN.)* consume, eat, reflect on, study, shorten, consider, summarize, abridge, abstract, abridgment, synopsis.

dignified *(SYN.)* serious, solemn, noble, stately, elegant.

dignify *(SYN.)* honor, elevate.
(ANT.) shame, degrade, humiliate.

dignity *(SYN.)* stateliness, distinction, bearing.

digress *(SYN.)* divert, wander, bend, stray, deflect, sidetrack, crook.
(ANT.) preserve, continue, remain, follow, persist.

dilate *(SYN.)* increase, widen, amplify, enlarge, augment, expand.
(ANT.) shrink, contract, restrict, abridge.

dilemma *(SYN.)* fix, strait, condition, scrape, difficulty, plight.
(ANT.) ease, calmness, satisfaction, comfort.

diligent *(SYN.)* patient, busy,` hardworking, active, perseverant, assiduous, industrious, careful.
(ANT.) unconcerned, indifferent, apathetic, lethargic, careless.

dim *(SYN.)* pale, shadowy, faint, faded, unclear, vague, darken, dull, indistinct.
(ANT.) brighten, brilliant, bright, illuminate, glaring.

dimension *(SYN.)* size, importance, measure, extent.

diminish *(SYN.)* suppress, lower, decrease, shrink, wane, abate, reduce, lessen, assuage.
(ANT.) enlarge, revive, amplify, increase.

diminutive *(SYN.)* small, wee, tiny, little, minute.
(ANT.) large, big, great, gigantic, huge.

din *(SYN.)* tumult, clamor, sound, babble, outcry, row, noise, racket.
(ANT.) quiet, stillness, hush.

dine *(SYN.)* lunch, eat, sup, feed.

dingy *(SYN.)* dull, dark, dismal, dirty, drab, murky, gray.
(ANT.) cheerful, bright.

dip *(SYN.)* immerse, plunge, submerge, wet, swim.

diplomacy *(SYN.)* knack, dexterity, skill, address, poise, tact, finesse.
(ANT.) vulgarity, blunder, awkwardness, incompetence.

diplomatic *(SYN.)* politic, adroit, tactful, discreet, judicious, gracious, polite, discriminating.
(ANT.) rude, churlish, gruff, boorish, impolite, coarse.

dire *(SYN.)* horrible, terrible, appalling, fearful, harrowing, grievous, ghastly, awful, horrid, terrifying, dreadful, frightful, horrifying, monstrous, horrendous, repulsive.
(ANT.) lovely, enchanting, fascinating,

beautiful, enjoyable.

direct *(SYN.)* rule, manage, bid, order, level, command, conduct, regulate, point, indicate, show, aim, control, sight, guide, instruct, train, govern.
(ANT.) swerving, untruthful, misguide, distract, indirect, crooked, deceive.

direction *(SYN.)* way, order, course, instruction, tendency, management, route, trend, guidance, administration, supervision, inclination.

directly *(SYN.)* immediately, straight.

dirt *(SYN.)* pollution, soil, filthiness, filth.
(ANT.) cleanliness, cleanness.

dirty *(SYN.)* muddy, base, pitiful, filthy, shabby, foul, soiled, nasty, mean, grimy, low, obscene, untidy, indecent, unclean, messy, squalid, contemptible, sloppy.
(ANT.) pure, neat, wholesome, clean, presentable.

disability *(SYN.)* inability, weakness, handicap, incapacity, injury, unfitness, incompetence, impotence.
(ANT.) power, ability, strength, capability.

disable *(SYN.)* weaken, incapacitate, cripple.
(ANT.) strengthen.

disabled *(SYN.)* deformed, limping, weak, crippled, maimed, defective, unsatisfactory, halt, unconvincing, feeble.
(ANT.) vigorous, athletic, sound, agile, robust.

disadvantage *(SYN.)* drawback, hindrance, handicap, inconvenience, obstacle.
(ANT.) advantage, benefit, convenience.

disagree *(SYN.)* quarrel, dispute, differ, conflict.
(ANT.) agree.

disagreement *(SYN.)* nonconformity, variance, difference, objection, challenge, remonstrance, dissent.
(ANT.) assent, acceptance, compliance, agreement.

disappear *(SYN.)* end, fade out, vanish.
(ANT.) emerge, appear.

disappoint *(SYN.)* fail, displease, mislead, dissatisfy.
(ANT.) please, satisfy, gratify.

disappointment *(SYN.)* dissatisfaction, defeat, discouragement, failure.
(ANT.) pleasure, satisfaction, gratification.

disapprove *(SYN.)* object to, disfavor, oppose.
(ANT.) approve.

disarm *(SYN.)* paralyze, demilitarize.

disaster *(SYN.)* casualty, mishap, misfortune, catastrophe, accident, adversity, ruin, calamity.
(ANT.) fortune, advantage, welfare.

disavow *(SYN.)* reject, revoke, disclaim, retract, disown.
(ANT.) recognize, acknowledge.

disband *(SYN.)* scatter, split, dismiss, separate.

disbelief *(SYN.)* doubt, incredulity, skepticism.
(ANT.) certainty, credulity.

discard *(SYN.)* scrap, reject.

discern *(SYN.)* distinguish, see, descry, separate, differentiate, perceive, discriminate, detect, observe, recognize.
(ANT.) omit, confuse, overlook, mingle, confound.

discernment *(SYN.)* perception, sharpness, intelligence, perspicacity, acuity, keenness.
(ANT.) dullness, stupidity.

discharge *(SYN.)* remove, relieve, dismiss, banish, unburden, shoot, fire, explosion, eject, detonation, liberation, release, unload, discard, send.
(ANT.) retain, employ, enlist, hire, accept, recall, detain.

disciple *(SYN.)* learner, follower, student, adherent, supporter, scholar, pupil, votary, devotee.
(ANT.) guide, leader.

discipline *(SYN.)* training, order, instruction, drill, restraint, regulation, practice, correction, control, self-control, train, teach, exercise.
(ANT.) carelessness, sloppiness, confusion, negligence, messiness, chaos, turbulence.

disclaim *(SYN.)* retract, reject, deny, renounce, disavow, revoke.
(ANT.) recognize, acknowledge.

disclose *(SYN.)* show, divulge, betray, uncover, discover, reveal, expose.
(ANT.) hide, cloak, mask, cover, obscure, conceal.

discomfit *(SYN.)* malaise, concern, confuse, baffle, perplex, disconcert.

discomfort *(SYN.)* malaise, concern, anxiety, uneasiness.

disconcerted *(SYN.)* disturbed, agitated, upset.

disconnect *(SYN.)* divide, separate, unhook, disengage, detach.
(ANT.) connect, bind, attach, unify, engage.

disconsolate *(SYN.)* depressed, downcast, sorrowful, dejected, dismal, sad, unhappy, wretched, somber, cheerless, morose, lugubrious, miserable, mournful.
(ANT.) delightful, merry, glad, cheerful, happy.

discontent *(SYN.)* displeased, disgruntled, unhappy, dissatisfied, vexed.

discontinue *(SYN.)* postpone, delay, adjourn, stay, stop, defer, suspend, end, cease, interrupt.
(ANT.) prolong, persist, continue, start, begin, proceed, maintain.

discord *(SYN.)* disagreement, conflict.
(ANT.) concord, accord, agreement.

discourage *(SYN.)* hamper, obstruct, restrain, block, dishearten, retard, check, dispirit, thwart, depress, hinder, stop.
(ANT.) expedite, inspire, encourage, promote, inspirit, assist, further.

discourteous *(SYN.)* gruff, rude, vulgar, blunt, impolite, saucy, uncivil, boorish, rough.
(ANT.) stately, courtly, civil, dignified, genteel.

discover *(SYN.)* find out, invent, expose, ascertain, devise, reveal, learn, determine, detect.
(ANT.) hide, screen, cover, conceal, lose.

discredit *(SYN.)* disbelieve, dishonor, doubt, disgrace, shame.

discreet *(SYN.)* politic, discriminating, judicious, adroit, prudent, cautious, wise, tactful, careful, diplomatic.
(ANT.) incautious, rude, coarse, boorish, tactless, imprudent, indiscreet, careless, gruff.

discrepant *(SYN.)* incompatible, wavering, contrary, irreconcilable, unsteady, illogical, contradictory.
(ANT.) correspondent, compatible, consistent.

discriminating *(SYN.)* exact, particular, critical, accurate, discerning.
(ANT.) unimportant, shallow, insignificant, superficial.

discrimination *(SYN.)* perspicacity, discernment, racism, wisdom, bias, sagacity, intolerance, prejudice, intelligence, understanding.
(ANT.) thoughtlessness, senselessness, arbitrariness.

discuss *(SYN.)* gossip, plead, discourse, blab, lecture, talk, chat, spout, mutter, deliberate, consider, reason, comment.

discussion *(SYN.)* speech, chatter, lecture, conference, talk, dialogue, conversation, rumor.
(ANT.) silence, correspondence, writing.

disdain *(SYN.)* derision, hatred, contempt, scorn, contumely, reject, haughtiness, detestation.
(ANT.) respect, esteem, reverence, admire, prize, honor, admiration, awe, regard.

disdainful *(SYN.)* haughty, scornful, arrogant, contemptuous.
(ANT.) awed, admiring, regardful.

disease *(SYN.)* malady, disorder, ailment, illness, affliction, infirmity, complaint, sickness.
(ANT.) soundness, health, vigor.

disentangle *(SYN.)* unwind, untie, clear, unravel, unknot, unsnarl, untangle.

disfigured *(SYN.)* deformed, marred, defaced, scarred.

disgrace *(SYN.)* odium, chagrin, shame, mortification, embarrassment, humiliate, scandal, dishonor, mortification.
(ANT.) renown, glory, respect, praise, dignity, honor.

disgraceful *(SYN.)* ignominious, shameful, discreditable, disreputable, scandalous, dishonorable.
(ANT.) renowned, esteemed, respectable, honorable.

disguise *(SYN.)* excuse, simulation, pretension, hide, camouflage, make-up, cover-up, mask, conceal, screen, affectation, pretext.
(ANT.) show, reality, actuality, display, reveal, sincerity, fact.

disgust *(SYN.)* offend, repulse, nauseate, revolt, sicken.
(ANT.) admiration, liking.

disgusting *(SYN.)* repulsive, nauseating, revolting, nauseous, repugnant

dish *(SYN.)* serve, container, give, receptacle.

dishearten *(SYN.)* depress, sadden, discourage.

disheveled *(SYN.)* mussed, sloppy, rumpled, untidy.

dishonest *(SYN.)* crooked, impure, unsound, false, contaminated, venal, corrupt, putrid, thievish, vitiated, tainted. *(ANT.)* upright, honest, straightforward.

dishonor *(SYN.)* disrepute, scandal, indignity, chagrin, mortification, shame, obloquy, defamation, humiliation, disgrace, scandal. *(ANT.)* renown, glory, praise, honor, dignity.

disinclined *(SYN.)* unwilling, reluctant, loath.

disingenuous *(SYN.)* tricky, deceitful, scheming, dishonest, underhanded, cunning, artful, crafty, insidious.

disintegrate *(SYN.)* decompose, dwindle, spoil, decay, wane, ebb, decline, rot. *(ANT.)* increase, flourish, rise, grow.

disinterested *(SYN.)* unbiased, openminded, neutral, impartial, unprejudiced.

dislike *(SYN.)* aversion, dread, reluctance, abhorrence, disinclination, hatred, repugnance. *(ANT.)* devotion, affection, enthusiasm, attachment.

disloyal *(SYN.)* false, treasonable, apostate, unfaithful, recreant, treacherous, untrue, perfidious, traitorous, faithless. *(ANT.)* true, devoted, constant, loyal.

dismal *(SYN.)* dark, lonesome, somber, bleak, dull, sad, doleful, sorrowful, cheerless, depressing, dreary, funeral, gloomy, melancholy. *(ANT.)* lively, gay, happy, lighthearted, charming, cheerful.

dismantle *(SYN.)* take apart, wreck, disassemble.

dismay *(SYN.)* disturb, bother, dishearten, horror, alarm, bewilder, frighten, scare, discourage, confuse. *(ANT.)* encourage, hearten.

dismiss *(SYN.)* remove, discharge, discard, release, liberate, exile, banish, eject, oust. *(ANT.)* retain, detain, engage, hire, accept, recall.

disobedient *(SYN.)* refractory, forward, unruly, insubordinate, defiant, rebellious, undutiful. *(ANT.)* submissive, compliant, obedient.

disobey *(SYN.)* invade, break, violate, infringe, defile.

disorder *(SYN.)* tumult, chaos, jumble, confusion, muddle, turmoil, anarchy. *(ANT.)* organization, neatness, system, order.

disorganization *(SYN.)* jumble, confusion, muddle, anarchy. *(ANT.)* system, order.

disorganized *(SYN.)* muddled, confused, indistinct, bewildered, mixed. *(ANT.)* organized, lucid, clear, plain.

disown *(SYN.)* deny, renounce, reject, repudiate, forsake, disinherit.

disparaging *(SYN.)* belittling, deprecatory, discrediting, deprecating.

disparage *(SYN.)* undervalue, depreciate, lower, belittle, derogate, minimize, decry, discredit. *(ANT.)* exalting, praise, aggrandize, magnify, commend.

disparagement *(SYN.)* lowering, decrying, undervaluing, belittling, minimizing. *(ANT.)* praise, exalting, aggrandizement, magnification.

dispassionate *(SYN.)* calm, cool, composed, controlled, unemotional, imperturbable.

dispatch *(SYN.)* throw, impel, transmit, emit, cast, finish, report, message, send, speed, achieve, conclude, communication, promptness, discharge. *(ANT.)* reluctance, get, retain, bring, slowness, hold.

dispel *(SYN.)* disseminate, scatter, disperse, separate, diffuse. *(ANT.)* collect, accumulate, gather.

dispense *(SYN.)* deal, give, allot, assign, apportion, mete, distribute, grant, allocate, measure. *(ANT.)* refuse, withhold, confiscate, retain, keep.

disperse *(SYN.)* dissipate, scatter, disseminate, diffuse, separate, dispel. *(ANT.)* collect, amass, gather, assemble, accumulate.

dispirited *(SYN.)* downhearted, unhappy, dejected, disheartened, sad, depressed, melancholy. *(ANT.)* cheerful, happy, optimistic.

displace *(SYN.)* remove, transport, lodge, shift, move. *(ANT.)* retain, leave, stay, remain.

display *(SYN.)* parade, exhibit, show, excover, flaunt.

(ANT.) hide, cover, conceal.

displeasure *(SYN.)* dislike, disapproval, dissatisfaction, distaste, discontentment.

disposal *(SYN.)* elimination, adjustment, removal, release, arrangement, administration, settlement.

dispose *(SYN.)* settle, adjust, arrange.

disposition *(SYN.)* behavior, character, deed, deportment, action, manner, bearing, temperament, nature, demeanor, personality, carriage.

dispossess *(SYN.)* eject, expel, evict, oust, dislodge.

disprove *(SYN.)* refute, deny, invalidate, controvert.

dispute *(SYN.)* squabble, debate, argument, controversy, contention, disagreement, bicker, contest, argue, contend, quarrel, contradict, discuss, deny, oppose, altercate.

(ANT.) harmony, concord, agreement, allow, concur, agree, concede, decision.

disregard *(SYN.)* slight, omit, ignore, inattention, oversight, skip, neglect, overlook.

(ANT.) regard, include.

disrepair *(SYN.)* ruin, decay, dilapidation, destruction.

disreputable *(SYN.)* dishonored, notorious, dishonorable, disgraced.

disrespectful *(SYN.)* fresh, impertinent, rude, impolite, impudent.

(ANT.) polite, respectful, courteous.

dissect *(SYN.)* examine, cut, analyze.

disseminate *(SYN.)* publish, circulate, spread, publish, broadcast.

dissent *(SYN.)* objection, challenge, disagreement, protest, remonstrance, difference, nonconformity, variance, noncompliance.

(ANT.) assent, acceptance, compliance, agreement.

dissertation *(SYN.)* thesis, treatise, disquisition.

dissimilar *(SYN.)* diverse, unlike, various, distinct, contrary, sundry, different, miscellaneous.

(ANT.) same, alike, similar, congruous.

dissimulation *(SYN.)* pretense, deceit, sanctimony, hypocrisy, cant.

(ANT.) honesty, candor, openness, frankness, truth.

dissipate *(SYN.)* misuse, squander,

dwindle, consume, waste, lavish, diminish.

(ANT.) save, conserve, preserve, accumulate, economize.

dissolve *(SYN.)* liquefy, end, cease, melt, fade, disappear.

distant *(SYN.)* stiff, cold, removed, far, afar, unfriendly, remote, faraway, separated, aloof, reserved.

(ANT.) nigh, friendly, close, cordial, near.

distasteful *(SYN.)* disagreeable, unpleasant, objectionable.

distend *(SYN.)* swell, widen, magnify, expand, enlarge.

distinct *(SYN.)* plain, evident, lucid, visible, apparent, different, separate, individual, obvious, manifest, clear.

(ANT.) vague, indistinct, uncertain, obscure, ambiguous.

distinction *(SYN.)* importance, peculiarity, trait, honor, fame, characteristic, repute, quality, renown, prominence, attribute, property.

(ANT.) nature, substance, essence, being.

distinctive *(SYN.)* odd, exceptional, rare, individual, eccentric, special, strange.

(ANT.) ordinary, general, common, normal.

distinguish *(SYN.)* recognize, differentiate, divide, classify, descry, discern, separate, perceive, detect.

(ANT.) mingle, conjoin, blend, found, omit, confuse, overlook.

distinguished *(SYN.)* eminent, illustrious, renowned, celebrated, elevated, noted, important, famous, prominent.

(ANT.) ordinary, common, unknown, undistinguished, obscure, unimportant.

distort *(SYN.)* contort, falsify, twist, misrepresent.

distract *(SYN.)* occupy, bewilder, disturb, divert, confuse.

(ANT.) focus, concentrate.

distracted *(SYN.)* abstracted, preoccupied, absent.

(ANT.) attentive, attending, watchful, present.

distraction *(SYN.)* entertainment, confusion, amusement, diversion.

distress *(SYN.)* torment, misery, trouble, worry, pain, agony, torture, anguish, anxiety, disaster, wretchedness, peril, danger, suffering.

(ANT.) joy, solace, comfort, relief.

distribute (SYN.) deal, sort, allot, mete, classify, share, issue, dole, apportion, allocate, dispense, group.

district (SYN.) domain, place, territory, country, region, division, neighborhood, section, area, land.

distrust (SYN.) scruple, unbelief, suspect, mistrust, hesitation, suspense, uncertainty, doubt, suspicion, ambiguity.

(ANT.) faith, conviction, trust, belief, determination.

disturb (SYN.) perturb, vex, confuse, worry, agitate, derange, unsettle, perplex, rouse, bother, trouble, annoy, interrupt, discompose.

(ANT.) quiet, order, calm, settle, pacify, soothe.

disturbance (SYN.) disorder, commotion, confusion, riot, fight, brawl.

(ANT.) calm, tranquillity, serenity.

disturbed (SYN.) neurotic, psychopathic, psychoneurotic, psychotic.

(ANT.) normal.

diverge (SYN.) fork, separate.

(ANT.) converge, join, merge.

diverse (SYN.) unlike, various, different, several.

diversify (SYN.) change, modify, alter.

diversion (SYN.) entertainment, sport, distraction, amusement, recreation.

divert (SYN.) detract, amuse, confuse, distract, deflect, entertain, tickle.

(ANT.) tire, bore, weary.

divide (SYN.) share, split, detach, cleave, apportion, sunder, part, distribute, allocate, disunite, estrange, separate, allot, sever.

(ANT.) merge, unite, convene, join, gather, combine.

divine (SYN.) holy, supernatural, godlike, transcendent, celestial, heavenly.

(ANT.) mundane, wicked, blasphemous, profane, diabolical.

division (SYN.) partition, separation, sharing, section, segment, part, portion.

(ANT.) union, agreement.

divorce (SYN.) disjoin, disconnect, separate, divide.

divulge (SYN.) discover, release, expose, show, betray, reveal, admit, disclose, uncover.

(ANT.) hide, conceal, cloak, cover.

dizzy (SYN.) staggering, unsteady, giddy, light-headed, confused.

(ANT.) rational, clearheaded, unconfused.

do (SYN.) effect, conduct, perform, work, suffice, accomplish, finish, transact, serve, discharge, execute, complete, carry on, make, settle, conclude, fulfill, consummate, produce, terminate, observe, practice.

docile (SYN.) pliant, tame, complaint, teachable, obedient, submissive, yielding.

(ANT.) unruly, obstinate, ungovernable, mulish.

dock (SYN.) moor, clip, anchor, tie.

doctor (SYN.) heal, treat, medic, remedy, cure.

doctrine (SYN.) tenet, precept, belief, dogma, teaching, principle, creed.

(ANT.) deed, practice, conduct, perform.

doctrinaire (SYN.) formal, dogmatic, overbearing, authoritarian, formal, arrogant, magisterial.

(ANT.) skeptical, indecisive, fluctuating.

document (SYN.) report, minute, memorial, vestige, account, note, trace.

dodge (SYN.) equivocate, recoil, elude, evade, avoid, duck.

dogma (SYN.) tenet, doctrine, belief, teaching, creed.

(ANT.) deed, practice, conduct, performance.

dogmatic (SYN.) formal, domineering, authoritarian, doctrinaire, opinionated, dictatorial, positive, arrogant, authoritative, overbearing, doctrinal, magisterial.

(ANT.) skeptical, indecisive, fluctuating.

doing (SYN.) feat, performance, act, deed, action, accomplishment, transaction.

(ANT.) intention, inactivity, cessation, inhibition.

dole (SYN.) deal, spread, allot, relief, divide, apportion, alms, welfare, distribute, dispense.

doleful (SYN.) dark, depressed, sad, dismal, dejected, bleak, dull, blue, sorrowful, unhappy, morose, lonesome, mournful, somber.

(ANT.) gay, lively, cheerful, joyous.

dolt (SYN.) blockhead, dunce.

domain (SYN.) place, division, region, territory, empire, country, charge, kingdom, realm, quarter, dominion, bailiwick, jurisdiction, land.

dom, realm, quarter, dominion, bailiwick, jurisdiction, land.

domestic *(SYN.)* family, tame, native, servant, homemade, household, internal.
(ANT.) alien, foreign, outside.

domesticate *(SYN.)* train, tame, housebreak, teach.

domicile *(SYN.)* dwelling, residence, home, abode.

dominate *(SYN.)* control, manage, rule, influence, subjugate, command, govern, tyrannize, direct, regulate.
(ANT.) follow, ignore, abandon, submit, forsake.

domination *(SYN.)* mastery, sway, ascendancy, transcendence.

don *(SYN.)* wear, slip on.

donation *(SYN.)* gift, bequest, present, benefaction, grant, contribution, offering, largess, boon.
(ANT.) earnings, purchase, deprivation, loss.

done *(SYN.)* complete, concluded, finished, over, terminated.

doom *(SYN.)* fortune, issue, result, destruction, destiny, consequence, fate, outcome, destine, ruin, death, lot.

doomed *(SYN.)* fated, predestined, destined, foreordained.

dormant *(SYN.)* unemployed, inert, lazy, unoccupied, idle, indolent.
(ANT.) working, employed, occupied, active, industrious.

dose *(SYN.)* quantity, amount, portion.

dote *(SYN.)* indulge, treasure, coddle, pamper, spoil.
(ANT.) ignore.

double *(SYN.)* copy, fold, duplicate.

doubt *(SYN.)* distrust, incredulity, suspicion, hesitation, uncertainty, question, scruple, ambiguity, skepticism, suspect, mistrust, unbelief, suspense.
(ANT.) conviction, belief, determination, trust, certainty.

doubtful *(SYN.)* uncertain, unsettled, dubious, questionable, unsure, undetermined.

doubtless *(SYN.)* certainly, undoubtedly, assuredly, positively, unquestionably.

dour *(SYN.)* gloomy, sulky, crabbed, morose, fretful.
(ANT.) joyous, pleasant, amiable, merry.

douse *(SYN.)* immerse, quench, dip, dunk, extinguish.

dowdy *(SYN.)* messy, unkempt, untidy, sloppy, shabby, frowzy.

downcast *(SYN.)* sad, disheartened, unhappy, downhearted, dejected, dispirited, discourage, depressed, glum.

downfall *(SYN.)* destruction, comedown.

downgrade *(SYN.)* reduce, lower, diminish, decrease, depreciate.
(ANT.) improve, upgrade, appreciate.

downhearted *(SYN.)* glum, discouraged, depressed, gloomy, downcast, sad, dejected.
(ANT.) enthusiastic, cheerful, happy.

downpour *(SYN.)* cloudburst, deluge, flood.

downright *(SYN.)* totally, positively, completely, definitely.

dowry *(SYN.)* endowment, gift, settlement, talent, ability.

drab *(SYN.)* flat, dull, lifeless, unattractive.

draft *(SYN.)* air, induction, wind, enrollment, drawing, outline.

drag *(SYN.)* heave, pull, tug, crawl, draw, tarry, tow, haul, delay.

drain *(SYN.)* empty, deprive, dry, filter, spend, tap, exhaust, waste, sap, use.
(ANT.) fulfill, fill.

drama *(SYN.)* show, play, production, piece.

dramatist *(SYN.)* playwright.

drape *(SYN.)* flow, cover, hang.

drastic *(SYN.)* severe, rough, extreme, violent, tough, intense.

draw *(SYN.)* tug, obtain, trace, lure, drag, attract, persuade, induce, haul, write, remove, extend, stretch, take out, allure, pull, prolong, extract, tow, draft, delineate, unsheathe, lure, depict, entice, sketch, infer.
(ANT.) shorten, contract, propel, alienate, drive.

drawback *(SYN.)* snag, hitch, disadvantage, handicap, deficiency, difficulty, check, obstacle, hindrance, impediment.
(ANT.) gain, benefit, windfall, advantage.

drawing *(SYN.)* likeness, print, view, engraving, portrait, sketch, illustration, picture, resemblance, scene.

drawn *(SYN.)* tired, haggard, taut, strained, harrowed, weary, tense, sapped, spent.
(ANT.) rested, relaxed, energetic, fresh.

draw out *(SYN.)* protract, extend, persist, prolong, lengthen, sustain, continue.
(ANT.) reduce, curtail, shorten, abridge.

draw up *(SYN.)* draft, write out, prepare, compose, indite, formulate, wait, stay.

dread *(SYN.)* awe, horror, fear, terror, alarm, reverence, apprehension, foreboding.
(ANT.) courage, boldness, assurance, confidence.

dreadful *(SYN.)* dire, inspiring, ghastly, appalling, horrid, impressive, terrible, awful, frightful, horrible, bad, hideous, awesome, outrageous, repulsive.
(ANT.) fascinating, beautiful, enjoyable, enchanting, lovely.

dream *(SYN.)* fantasy, wish, hope, vision, daydream, reverie, imagine, fantasize, fancy, invent, muse.

dream up *(SYN.)* cook up, create, think up, concost, contrive, originate, imagine, devise.

dreary *(SYN.)* dull, sad, bleak, lonesome, gloomy, chilling, somber, depressing, dismal, cheerless, dark.
(ANT.) lively, hopeful, gay, cheerful, bright, joyous.

dregs *(SYN.)* riffraff, scum, outcasts, dross, leftovers, flotsam.

drench *(SYN.)* wet, bathe, flood, soak, saturate.

dress *(SYN.)* garb, frock, gown, clothing, costume, apparel, attire, wardrobe, garments, vesture, clothes, habit, wear, don, robe, raiment.
(ANT.) undress, strip, divest, disrobe.

dresser *(SYN.)* dude, clotherhorse, fop, dandy.

dressing *(SYN.)* bandage, seasoning, medicine, sauce.

dressy *(SYN.)* flashy, swank, showy, dapper.
(ANT.) dowdy, drab, frumpy, shabby, tacky.

dribble *(SYN.)* fall, drip, leak, slaver, slobber.

drift *(SYN.)* roam, tendency, meander, sail, float, direction, wander, intention, stray.

drifter *(SYN.)* hobo, tramp, vagabond.

drill *(SYN.)* employment, lesson, task, use, activity, operation, training.
(ANT.) relaxation, indolence, rest, idleness, repose.

drink *(SYN.)* gulp, swallow, imbibe, beverage, refreshment, potion.

drip *(SYN.)* dribble, drop, trickle.

drive *(SYN.)* impel, coerce, oblige, force, push, direct, constrain, journey, urge, enforce, trip, handle, ride, propel, control, run, compel.

drivel *(SYN.)* slaver, drool, spit, spittle, dribble, slobber, saliva, nonsense, twaddle, rubbish, babble, gibberish.

driver *(SYN.)* motorist, operator, teamster, trucker, motorman, pilot, coachman.

droll *(SYN.)* laughable, funny, amusing, witty, comical.
(ANT.) sober, sad, solemn, melancholy.

drone *(SYN.)* buzz, hum, loafer, idler, nonworker.

drool *(SYN.)* drivel, slaver, dribble, spit, gibber, jabber, twaddle, trickle, salivate.

droop *(SYN.)* dangle, weaken, hang, sink, fail, settle, sag, weary, languish, despond.
(ANT.) stand, tower, extend, rise, straighten.

drop *(SYN.)* droop, dribble, topple, collapse, downward, drip, trickle, tumble, gob, droplet, reduction, slump, slip, decrease, fall, dismiss, decline.
(ANT.) ascend, mount, steady, arise, soar.

drop out *(SYN.)* back out, withdraw, stop, forsake, abandon, give up, leave, quit.

droppings *(SYN.)* faces, dung, waste, manure, excrement, ordure, guano.

dross *(SYN.)* dregs, impurity, leftovers, residue, debris, leavings, remains.

drove *(SYN.)* flock, herd.

drown *(SYN.)* sink, inundate, submerge, immerse.

drowse *(SYN.)* nap, doze, catnap, snooze, sleep, slumber, rest, drop off, repose.

drowsy *(SYN.)* dozing, torpid, soothing, dreamy, sleepy, comatose, sluggish, lulling, dull, calming, restful, lethargic.
(ANT.) alert, awake, sharp, keen, acute.

drub *(SYN.)* wallop, thrash, beat, thump, cane, flog, rout, outclass, overcome, belabor, pummel, defeat, outplay.

drubbing *(SYN.)* walloping, flogging, beating, pounding, pommeling, thwacking, thrashing, rout, licking, clobbering.

drudge *(SYN.)* work, labor, hack, slave, toil, grub, grind, toiler, flunky, menial, servant.

drudgery (SYN.) toil, travail, effort, task, work, endeavor, labor.

(ANT.) recreation, indolence, leisure.

drug (SYN.) remedy, medicine, stupefy, anesthetize, numb, benumb.

drugged (SYN.) numb, doped, numbed, stupefied, dazed, groggy, benumbed.

druggist (SYN.) apothecary, chemist, pharmacologist.

drunk (SYN.) tight, intoxicated, soused, drunken, inebriated, alcoholic, sozzled, besotted, sot, toper, boozer, wino, rummy, dipsomaniac, lush, tipsy.

drunkard (SYN.) sot, drunk, alcoholic, lush.

dry (SYN.) thirsty, dehydrated, vapid, plain, arid, uninteresting, drained, parched, barren, waterless, dull, tedious, boring, desiccated, tiresome.

(ANT.) fresh, wet, soaked, fascinating, attractive, lively, moist, interesting.

dub (SYN.) nickname, name, christen, call, style, term, confer, bestow, denominate, entitle, characterize, tag, label.

dubious (SYN.) unsure, uncertain, undecided, hesitant, spurious, unreliable, puzzling, untrustworthy, questionable, ambiguous.

(ANT.) decided, fixed, irrefutable, definite, genuine, unquestionable, sound, authentic, trustworthy.

duct (SYN.) pipe, tube, passage, vein, funnel, gutter, main, trough, artery.

due (SYN.) payable, unpaid, owing, owed, imminent, expected.

duel (SYN.) competition, contest, engagement, rivalry, combat, strife, encounter.

dues (SYN.) assessment, fees, cost, levy, admission, fare, toll, contribution.

duffer (SYN.) bungler, slouch, blunderer, novice, incompetent, fumbler, lummox.

(ANT.) master, expert, pro.

dull (SYN.) commonplace, slow, sad, dreary, boring, stupid, uninteresting.

(ANT.) clear, animated, interesting, lively.

dullard (SYN.) dolt, dunce, moron, clod, blockhead, numskull.

dumb (SYN.) dull, witless, ignorant, mute, speechless, brainless, dense.

(ANT.) bright, alert, clever, intelligent.

dump (SYN.) heap, fling down, drop,

empty, unload, clear out, dispose of.

(ANT.) store, fill, load, hoard, pack.

dunce (SYN.) deadhead, nitwit, booby, idiot, ignoramus, numskull, noddy, fool.

dungeon (SYN.) jail, prison, keep, cell.

dunk (SYN.) plunge, submerge, dip.

(ANT.) uplift, elevate, recover.

dupe (SYN.) sucker, victim, gull, pushover, fool, cheat, deceive, defraud.

duplicate (SYN.) replica, replicate, facsimile, copy, reproduce, clone, double, twin, transcript.

(ANT.) prototype.

duplicity (SYN.) dissimulation, deception, hypocrisy, deceitfulness, insincerity, artifice, cant, guile.

(ANT.) openness, artlessness, candor, straightforwardness, genuineness.

durability (SYN.) might, strength, force, sturdiness, intensity, potency, vigor.

(ANT.) weakness, frailty, feebleness.

durable (SYN.) constant, firm, fixed, unchangeable, enduring, abiding, lasting.

(ANT.) unstable, temporary, perishable, transitory.

duration (SYN.) time, term, period, while, stage, era, epoch, interim.

duress (SYN.) force, demand, compulsion, emergency, pressure.

dusky (SYN.) sable, black, dark, darkish, swarthy, tawny, gloomy, overcast, misty, obscure, opaque, shadowy.

(ANT.) light, fair, white, pale, shining, clear, bright.

dutiful (SYN.) docile, faithful, obedient.

(ANT.) disobedient, willful, unruly, headstrong.

duty (SYN.) bond, responsibility, accountability, faithfulness, function, obligation, assignment, engagement.

(ANT.) freedom, choice.

dwarf (SYN.) midget, runt, reduce, stunt, minimize, tiny.

(ANT.) mammoth, colossus, monster, giant.

dwell (SYN.) inhabit, roost, settle, abide, live, reside.

dwindle (SYN.) wane, decrease, diminish, fade, subside, ebb, shrivel, lessen.

(ANT.) enlarge, increase, grow, gain.

dynamic (SYN.) active, forceful, kinetic, energetic, motive, mighty, vigorous.

(ANT.) sleepy, stable, inert, fixed, dead, still, uninspiring, ineffectual, listless.

eager *(SYN.)* avid, hot, anxious, fervent, enthusiastic, impatient, ardent, impassioned, yearning.
(ANT.) unconcerned, apathetic, impassioned, dull, uninterested, indifferent.

early *(SYN.)* betimes, opportune, first, beforehand, advanced, soon, shortly.
(ANT.) retarded, late, tardy, belated, overdue.

earmark *(SYN.)* peculiarity, characteristic, brand, sign, stamp, trademark.

earn *(SYN.)* attain, win, get, achieve, obtain, gain, deserve, realize, collect, net, acquire, merit.
(ANT.) lose, waste, consume, forfeit.

earnest *(SYN.)* sincere, decided, determined, intent, serious, eager, resolute.
(ANT.) indifferent, frivolous, insincere.

earnings *(SYN.)* wages, pay, salary, income.

earth *(SYN.)* globe, dirt, land, world, turf, soil, sod, ground.

earthly *(SYN.)* mundane, everyday, worldly.
(ANT.) heavenly.

earthy *(SYN.)* earthlike, coarse, earthen, crude, unrefined, vulgar.
(ANT.) tasteful, elegant, polished, refined.

ease *(SYN.)* lighten, alleviate, pacify, soothe, allay, comfort, contentedness.
(ANT.) worry, disturb, confound, ageffort, trouble, intensify, distress.

easily *(SYN.)* readily, effortlessly, smoothly, naturally, facilely.
(ANT.) hardly, ardously, painfully, laboriously.

easiness *(SYN.)* repose, comfort, satisfaction, contentment, liberty, leisure, facility, simplicity.
(ANT.) unrest, torment, arduousness, difficulty, discomfort.

easy *(SYN.)* light, simple, facile, gentle, effortless, unhurried, comfortable.
(ANT.) hard, demanding, awkward, strict, difficult, formal.

eat *(SYN.)* consume, swallow, dine, corrode, chew, lunch, devour, feast.

eavesdrop *(SYN.)* spy, listen, snoop, overhear.

ebb *(SYN.)* diminish, recede, decline, decrease, retreat, lessen.
(ANT.) wax, grow, thrive, increase, swell.

ebullient *(SYN.)* vivacious, buoyant, exuberant.
(ANT.) lethargic, sad, gloomy, depressed.

eccentric *(SYN.)* odd, irregular, unusual, abnormal, peculiar.
(ANT.) ordinary, conventional, normal.

eccentricity *(SYN.)* kink, idiosyncracy, whim, freak, caprice, foible, quirk, oddness, strangeness, aberration.
(ANT.) conventionality, ordinariness.

ecclesiastical *(SYN.)* religious, churchly, clerical.

echelon *(SYN.)* rank, level, grade, status.

echo *(SYN.)* response, imitation, suggestion, trace, reaction, imitate, repeat.

eclectic *(SYN.)* selective, diverse, broad, liberal, comprehensive.
(ANT.) limited, narrow, rigid, confined.

eclipse *(SYN.)* conceal, screen, hide, cover, obscure, overcast, veil.

economical *(SYN.)* saving, thrifty, careful, frugal, provident, sparing.
(ANT.) wasteful, extravagant, lavish, improvident, prodigal.

economy *(SYN.)* saving, thrift.

ecstasy *(SYN.)* frenzy, gladness, delight, madness, joy, glee, exaltation, pleasure, trance, rapture.
(ANT.) misery, melancholy, sadness.

ecstatic *(SYN.)* overjoyed, thrilled, delighted, happy, elated.

edge *(SYN.)* margin, brim, verge, brink, border, keenness, extremity, boundary, trim, periphery, hem, rim, sting.
(ANT.) dullness, center, bluntness.

edgy *(SYN.)* tense, touchy, nervous, irritable.

edict *(SYN.)* declaration, order, ruling, decree, pronouncement, command, law, proclamation.

edifice *(SYN.)* construction, building, establishment.

edit *(SYN.)* check, revise, correct, amend.

educate *(SYN.)* instruct, teach, school, train.

education *(SYN.)* training, development, knowledge, learning, cultivation, schooling, instruction, study.

eerie *(SYN.)* weird, fearful, ghastly, spooky, strange.

efface *(SYN.)* obliterate, erase.

effect *(SYN.)* produce, consequence, evoke, cause, make, complete, outcome, result, determine.

effective *(SYN.)* efficient, practical,

productive.

(ANT.) useless, wasteful, ineffective.

efficiency *(SYN.)* efficacy, capability, effectiveness, competency, ability.

(ANT.) wastefulness, inability.

efficient *(SYN.)* efficacious, skillful, capable, adept, competent, useful, effectual, effective, apt, proficient.

(ANT.) inefficient, unskilled, ineffectual, incompetent.

effort *(SYN.)* labor, endeavor, pains, essay, trial, exertion, struggle, strain.

egg *(SYN.)* stir, ovum, incite, urge, arouse, embryo, provoke.

egghead *(SYN.)* scholar, intellectual, pedant.

egoism *(SYN.)* self-interest, conceit, pride, selfishness, egotism.

(ANT.) modesty, generosity, selflessness.

eject *(SYN.)* expel, remove, oust, eliminate.

(ANT.) include.

elaborate *(SYN.)* detail, develop, decorated, decorative, ornate, complex.

(ANT.) simplify, simple, unadorned.

elapse *(SYN.)* expire.

elastic *(SYN.)* yielding, flexible, adaptable, pliable.

elated *(SYN.)* delighted, rejoicing, overjoyed, jubilant.

(ANT.) sad, unhappy.

elder *(SYN.)* senior.

(ANT.) younger.

elderly *(SYN.)* aged, old.

(ANT.) young, youthful.

elect *(SYN.)* pick, appoint, choose.

electrify *(SYN.)* shock, charge, stir, upset, generate, agitate.

elegant *(SYN.)* tasteful, refined, cultivated, choice, polished, superior, fine.

(ANT.) crude, coarse, unpolished, tasteless.

elementary *(SYN.)* simple, primary, basic, uncomplicated, initial, beginning, fundamental.

(ANT.) involved, complex, sophisticated, complicated.

elevate *(SYN.)* raise, lift.

(ANT.) lower, drop.

elf *(SYN.)* devil, fairy, imp.

elicit *(SYN.)* summon.

eligible *(SYN.)* fit, suitable, qualified.

eliminate *(SYN.)* expel, eject, remove, dislodge, extirpate, erase, oust.

(ANT.) admit, involve.

elite *(SYN.)* nobility, upper-class, aristocracy, gentry.

(ANT.) mob, proletariat.

elongate *(SYN.)* extend, prolong, lengthen.

elope *(SYN.)* escape, flee.

eloquent *(SYN.)* expressive, fluent, articulate, glib, meaningful.

(ANT.) inarticulate.

else *(SYN.)* different, another, other.

elude *(SYN.)* escape, miss, avoid, dodge.

(ANT.) add, include.

emaciated *(SYN.)* wasted, thin, starved, withered, shriveled, gaunt, shrunken, drawn, undernourished.

emancipate *(SYN.)* liberate, free, deliver, save.

(ANT.) restrain.

embankment *(SYN.)* shore, dam, bank, fortification, buttress.

embargo *(SYN.)* prohibition, restriction, restraint.

embark *(SYN.)* board, depart.

embarrass *(SYN.)* discomfit, rattle, distress, hamper, fluster, entangle, abash, mortify, hinder, perplex, confuse, shame, trouble.

(ANT.) relieve, encourage, help.

embassy *(SYN.)* ministry, legation, consulate.

embed *(SYN.)* root, inset, enclose, plant.

embellish *(SYN.)* adorn, decorate, ornament.

embezzle *(SYN.)* pilfer, misuse, rob, misappropriate, steal, take.

embitter *(SYN.)* provoke, arouse, alienate, anger, inflame.

emblem *(SYN.)* token, mark, symbol, badge.

embody *(SYN.)* comprise, cover, embrace, include.

embrace *(SYN.)* espouse, accept, receive, comprehend, contain, welcome, comprise, cover, clasp, include, adopt, hug.

(ANT.) spurn, reject, bar, exclude, repudiate.

embroider *(SYN.)* decorate, adorn, stitch, trim, overstate, embellish, ornament, exaggerate, magnify.

emerge *(SYN.)* surface, show, appear.

emergency *(SYN.)* strait, pass, crisis, urgency, predicament, pinch.

eminent *(SYN.)* renowned, glorious, dis-

glorious, important, conspicuous, prominent, famous.
(ANT.) ordinary, commonplace, unknown, undistinguished, common.
emissary *(SYN.)* envoy, minister, delegate, agent, spy.
emit *(SYN.)* expel, breathe, shoot, hurl, ooze, vent, belch, discharge.
emotion *(SYN.)* passion, turmoil, perturbation, affection, sentiment, feeling, trepidation, agitation.
(ANT.) dispassion, indifference, tranquillity, calm, restraint.
emotional *(SYN.)* ardent, passionate, stirring, zealous, impetuous, overwrought, enthusiastic.
(ANT.) tranquil, calm, placid.
emphasis *(SYN.)* accent, stress, insistence.
emphatic *(SYN.)* positive, definite, forceful, energetic, strong.
(ANT.) lax, quiet, unforceful.
employ *(SYN.)* avail, use, devote, apply, utilize, engage, sign, hire, retain, service, contract.
(ANT.) reject, discard.
employee *(SYN.)* laborer, worker, servant.
(ANT.) boss, employer.
employer *(SYN.)* owner, boss, management, proprietor, manager, superintendent, supervisor.
(ANT.) employee, worker.
employment *(SYN.)* occupation, work, business, position, job, service, engagement.
(ANT.) leisure, idleness, slothfulness.
empower *(SYN.)* enable, sanction, permit, warrant.
empty *(SYN.)* void, devoid, unfilled, barren, senseless, unoccupied, unfurnished, vacant, blank, evacuate, unload, hollow.
(ANT.) supplied, full, occupied.
emulate *(SYN.)* follow, imitate, copy.
enable *(SYN.)* authorize, empower, sanction, qualify.
enact *(SYN.)* legislate, portray, pass, stage, represent.
enchant *(SYN.)* charm, titillate, fascinate, bewitch, delight, thrill, captivate.
(ANT.) tire, bore.
encircle *(SYN.)* comprise, include, bound, encompass.
enclose *(SYN.)* envelop, confine, bound,

enclose *(SYN.)* envelop, confine, bound, surround, encompass, encircle, circumscribe.
(ANT.) open, exclude, distend, expose, develop.
encompass *(SYN.)* include, surround, encircle.
encore *(SYN.)* repetition, repeat, again.
encounter *(SYN.)* battle, meet, oppose, run into, face, collide.
encourage *(SYN.)* incite, favor, cheer, impel, countenance, inspirit, exhilarate, animate, hearten, embolden, support.
(ANT.) deter, dispirit, deject, dissuade.
encroach *(SYN.)* interfere, trespass, intrude, infringe.
encumber *(SYN.)* hamper, load, burden.
end *(SYN.)* completion, object, close, aim, result, conclusion, finish, extremity, intent, halt, stop, limit, purpose, cessation, expiration, termination.
(ANT.) opening, start, introduction, beginning, launch, inception.
endanger *(SYN.)* imperil, hazard, risk.
(ANT.) secure.
endear *(SYN.)* allure, charm.
endeavor *(SYN.)* strive, struggle, exertion, attempt, try, labor.
endless *(SYN.)* constant, nonstop, continuous, incessant, everlasting.
endorse *(SYN.)* approve, accept, sign, confirm, pass.
endow *(SYN.)* provide, furnish, bestow, give, contribute.
(ANT.) divest.
endure *(SYN.)* experience, undergo, sustain, last, bear, continue, remain, undergo, persist, brook, tolerate, suffer.
(ANT.) wane, die, perish, succumb, fail.
enemy *(SYN.)* foe, antagonist, rival, opponent, competitor, adversary, opposition.
(ANT.) colleague, ally, friend, accomplice.
energy *(SYN.)* strength, vim, force, power, stamina, vigor, might.
(ANT.) feebleness, lethargy.
enervate *(SYN.)* enfeeble, weaken, debilitate, exhaust, devitalize.
(ANT.) invigorate.
enfold *(SYN.)* clasp, surround, wrap, embrace, hug.
enforce *(SYN.)* make, drive, compel, execute, force.

engage *(SYN.)* absorb, occupy, employ, hold, involve, hire, agree, engross, retain, promise, commit, entangle.
(ANT.) fire, disengage, discharge, dismiss.

engaged *(SYN.)* affianced, betrothed, busy, occupied.

engaging *(SYN.)* fascinating, appealing, enticing, interesting, tempting, lovely, beguiling, charming, enchanting, engrossing, delightful, exquisite.
(ANT.) ordinary, boring.

engender *(SYN.)* develop, breed, cause, generate, produce.

engineer *(SYN.)* direct, conduct, guide, lead, manage.

engrave *(SYN.)* print, cut, impress, inscribe, carve, sketch.

engross *(SYN.)* engage, enthrall, occupy, fascinate, absorb.

engulf *(SYN.)* flood, swallow.

enhance *(SYN.)* better, uplift, improve.

enigma *(SYN.)* mystery, stumper, riddle.

enigmatic *(SYN.)* perplexing, confusing, puzzling, baffling, mystifying.

enjoy *(SYN.)* savor, like, relish.

enjoyment *(SYN.)* pleasure, delight, gratification.
(ANT.) abhorrence, displeasure.

enlarge *(SYN.)* widen, distend, amplify, broaden, extend, increase, augment, expand, dilate.
(ANT.) diminish, shrink, contract, decrease, wane, restrict.

enlighten *(SYN.)* inform, illuminate, clarify, teach, instruct.
(ANT.) confuse.

enlist *(SYN.)* enroll, prompt, join, induce, enter, register, persuade.
(ANT.) quit, leave, abandon.

enliven *(SYN.)* inspire, brighten, stimulate.

enmity *(SYN.)* antagonism, hatred, animosity, malignity, ill-will, antipathy, hostility, unfriendliness.
(ANT.) love, like, friendliness.

enormity *(SYN.)* heinousness, wickedness, barbarity, atrociousness.

enormous *(SYN.)* vast, huge, colossal, immense, gargantuan, elephantine, gigantic, stupendous, large.
(ANT.) small, slight, tiny, minute, infinitesimal, diminutive, little.

enough *(SYN.)* ample, adequate, sufficient, plenty.
(ANT.) inadequate, insufficient.

enrage *(SYN.)* anger, provoke, madden, inflame.
(ANT.) appease, soothe, calm.

enrich *(SYN.)* better, improve.

enroll *(SYN.)* record, list, recruit, register, enlist, write, induct.
(ANT.) quit, leave, abandon.

enshrine *(SYN.)* bury, entomb.

ensign *(SYN.)* banner, colors, flag, officer.

enslave *(SYN.)* keep, hold, capture.

ensue *(SYN.)* arise, succeed, follow, result.

ensure *(SYN.)* guarantee, assure, protect, defend, cover.

entangle *(SYN.)* confuse, snare, involve, ravel, snarl, tangle, trap.

enter *(SYN.)* join, go inside.

enterprise *(SYN.)* fete, deed, venture, project, adventure, undertaking, ambition, business, exploit.

enterprising *(SYN.)* energetic, resourceful.
(ANT.) lazy, indolent, sluggish, unresourceful.

entertain *(SYN.)* cheer, gladden, hold, consider, please, contemplate, divert, amuse, harbor, fascinate, interest.
(ANT.) repulse, tire, bore, disgust, annoy.

enthrall *(SYN.)* captivate, fascinate, enchant, charm, thrill.

enthusiasm *(SYN.)* fervor, fanaticism, zeal, ardor, intensity, devotion, excitement, eagerness, fervency, earnestness.
(ANT.) indifference, ennui, apathy, unconcern, detachment.

enthusiastic *(SYN.)* earnest, zealous, eager.
(ANT.) aloof, indifferent, unconcerned.

entice *(SYN.)* lure, attract, seduce.

entire *(SYN.)* complete, intact, whole, undivided.
(ANT.) divided, separated, incomplete, partial.

entirely *(SYN.)* altogether, thoroughly, wholly, solely.

entitle *(SYN.)* call, label, name, empower, allow, authorize, license, title.

entourage *(SYN.)* train, company, retinue, escort.

entrance *(SYN.)* inlet, portal, doorway, fascinate, entry, intrigue, door, thrill.

entreat *(SYN.)* implore, beg, plead.

entreaty *(SYN.)* plea, appeal.

entrust *(SYN.)* commit, charge, assign, delegate, consign, commission.

enumerate *(SYN.)* count, tally, list, number.

enunciate *(SYN.)* announce, express, speak, state.

envelop *(SYN.)* embrace, cover, conceal, surround, wrap.

environment *(SYN.)* neighborhood, habitat, surroundings, setting.

envision *(SYN.)* picture, imagine, visualize.

envoy *(SYN.)* delegate, emissary, representative, agent, messenger.

envy *(SYN.)* covetousness, jealousy, spitefulness, covet.

(ANT.) indifference, generosity.

epicure *(SYN.)* gourmand, gourmet, connoisseur, gastronome, epicurean, aesthete.

epidemic *(SYN.)* prevalent, scourge, plague, catching, widespread, pestilence, infectious.

episode *(SYN.)* happening, affair, occurrence, event, experience.

epoch *(SYN.)* age.

equal *(SYN.)* even, uniform, like, alike, equitable, same, identical, commensurate, equivalent, regular, parallel.

(ANT.) different, unequal, irregular, uneven.

equilibrium *(SYN.)* stability, steadiness, balance, firmness.

equip *(SYN.)* fit, rig, provide, outfit, prepare, furnish.

equipment *(SYN.)* utensils, material, apparatus.

equitable *(SYN.)* square, rightful, fair, due, just, fit.

(ANT.) partial, biased, unjust, uneven.

equity *(SYN.)* impartiality, fairness, justness, justice, fair-mindedness, evenhandedness.

equivalent *(SYN.)* match, rival, equal, like, replacement.

equivocal *(SYN.)* oblique, ambiguous, vague, indeterminate, uncertain, obscure.

(ANT.) clear, precise, explicit, certain, clear-cut, definite.

equivocate *(SYN.)* temporize, evade, hedge, quibble, fudge, waffle, straddle.

hedge, quibble, fudge, waffle, straddle.

era *(SYN.)* epoch, cycle, age, time, period.

eradicate *(SYN.)* remove, demolish, eliminate.

erase *(SYN.)* obliterate, remove, cancel.

(ANT.) add, include.

erect *(SYN.)* upright, build, straight, raise, construct, vertical.

(ANT.) flat, horizontal, raze, flatten, demolish.

erection *(SYN.)* building, construction, raising, fabrication.

erode *(SYN.)* rust, consume, disintegrate.

erotic *(SYN.)* carnal, fleshy, amatory, prurient, lewd, wanton, passionate, lecherous.

err *(SYN.)* slip, misjudge.

errand *(SYN.)* chore, duty, task, exercise.

errant *(SYN.)* roving, rambling, wandering, vagrant.

erratic *(SYN.)* irregular, abnormal, uneven, occasional, sporadic, changeable, unsteady, odd, eccentric, strange, extraordinary, unconventional, bizarre, peculiar, uncertain, unusual, unstable.

(ANT.) regular, steady, normal, ordinary.

erroneous *(SYN.)* wrong, mistaken, incorrect, inaccurate, false, untrue.

(ANT.) true, right, correct, accurate.

error *(SYN.)* inaccuracy, fault, slip, oversight, fallacy, mistake, blunder.

erudite *(SYN.)* sage, wise, learned, deep, profound.

erupt *(SYN.)* vomit.

escapade *(SYN.)* caper, antic, stunt, trick, prank.

escape *(SYN.)* shun, avoid, flee, decamp, elude, flight, avert, departure, abscond, fly, evade.

(ANT.) meet, confront, invite, catch.

escort *(SYN.)* conduct, lead, attend, accompany, protection, guard, guide, convoy, usher, squire.

especially *(SYN.)* unusually, principally, mainly, particularly, primarily.

essay *(SYN.)* test, thesis, undertake, paper, try.

essence *(SYN.)* substance, character, nature, principle, odor, meaning, basis, smell, perfume.

essential *(SYN.)* vital, intrinsic, basic, requisite, fundamental, indispensable, critical, requirement, necessity, necessary, important.

(ANT.) dispensable, unimportant, inessential.

establish *(SYN.)* prove, fix, found, settle, institute, raise, verify, conform, form, sanction, ordain, begin, organize.

(ANT.) upset, discontinue, scatter, disperse, refute, abolish, unsettle.

esteem *(SYN.)* revere, deem, appreciate, honor, value, think, admire, respect, hold, prize, reverence, regard.

(ANT.) scorn, disdain, depreciate, disregard, contempt, abhor.

estimate *(SYN.)* calculate, gauge, judge, rate, evaluate, compute, value, figure.

estimation *(SYN.)* judgment, viewpoint, opinion.

etch *(SYN.)* stamp, engrave, impress.

eternal *(SYN.)* undying, immortal, ceaseless, infinite, everlasting, deathless, perpetual, endless, timeless.

(ANT.) mortal, transient, finite, brief, temporary, passing.

etiquette *(SYN.)* decorum, formality.

evacuate *(SYN.)* withdraw, depart, leave, vacate.

evade *(SYN.)* miss, avoid, bypass.

(ANT.) confront, meet, face.

evaluate *(SYN.)* value, appraise, assay.

evaporate *(SYN.)* disappear, vanish.

(ANT.) condense, appear.

even *(SYN.)* smooth, level, still, square, same, flat, balanced, equal, parallel, identical.

(ANT.) irregular, bumpy, unbalanced, unequal, divergent.

evening *(SYN.)* twilight, dusk, sunset.

(ANT.) sunrise, dawn.

event *(SYN.)* issue, end, result, circumstance, occurrence, incident, consequence, happening, episode, outcome.

even-tempered *(SYN.)* composed, calm, cool.

(ANT.) hotheaded.

eventual *(SYN.)* consequent, ultimate.

(ANT.) present, current.

eventually *(SYN.)* ultimately.

ever *(SYN.)* continuously, always, constantly.

(ANT.) never.

everlasting *(SYN.)* permanent, ceaseless, endless, continual.

evermore *(SYN.)* always.

everyday *(SYN.)* commonplace, common,

usual, ordinary, customary.

(ANT.) rare.

evict *(SYN.)* oust, put out, expel.

evidence *(SYN.)* grounds, clue, facts, testimony, data, sign, proof.

evident *(SYN.)* apparent, clear, obvious, indubitable, plain, conspicuous, patent, manifest, open, unmistakable.

(ANT.) hidden, unclear, uncertain, obscure, concealed.

evil *(SYN.)* immoral, harmful, badness, sinful, injurious, woe, bad, wicked.

(ANT.) goodness, moral, useful, upright, virtuous, beneficial, virtue, advantageous.

evoke *(SYN.)* summon, prompt.

evolve *(SYN.)* grow, advance, develop, result, emerge, unfold.

exact *(SYN.)* correct, faultless, errorless, detailed, accurate.

(ANT.) inaccurate, inexact, faulty.

exaggerate *(SYN.)* stretch, expand, amplify, embroider, heighten, overstate, caricature, magnify, enlarge.

(ANT.) understate, minimize, diminish, depreciate.

exalt *(SYN.)* erect, consecrate, raise, elevate, extol, dignify.

(ANT.) humble, degrade, humiliate.

examination *(SYN.)* investigation, inspection, test, scrutiny.

examine *(SYN.)* assess, contemplate, question, review, audit, notice, inquire, analyze, check, investigate, dissect, inspect, survey.

(ANT.) omit, disregard, overlook.

example *(SYN.)* pattern, archetype, specimen, illustration, model, instance, prototype, sample.

(ANT.) rule, concept, principle.

exasperate *(SYN.)* aggravate, anger, madden, irritate.

excavate *(SYN.)* unearth, dig, burrow.

exceed *(SYN.)* excel, beat, surpass, top.

exceedingly *(SYN.)* extremely, very, especially, unusually, surprisingly.

excel *(SYN.)* better, beat, surpass.

excellence *(SYN.)* distinction, superiority.

(ANT.) poorness, inferiority, badness.

excellent *(SYN.)* wonderful, fine, marvelous, superior.

(ANT.) poor, terrible, bad, inferior.

except *(SYN.)* omitting, barring, but, reject, excluding, save, exclude.

exception *(SYN.)* affront, offense, exclusion, deviation, omission, anomaly.

exceptional *(SYN.)* different, irregular, strange, unusual, abnormal.

excerpt *(SYN.)* abstract, extract.

excess *(SYN.)* surplus, intemperance, extravagance, immoderation, profusion, abundant, profuse, superfluity.

(ANT.) want, sparse, lack, dearth.

exchange *(SYN.)* barter, interchange, substitute, trade, change, swap.

excite *(SYN.)* arouse, incite, agitate, stimulate, awaken, disquiet.

(ANT.) lull, quiet, bore, pacify.

exclaim *(SYN.)* vociferate, cry, call out, cry out, ejaculate, shout.

exclamation *(SYN.)* shout, outcry, clamor.

exclude *(SYN.)* omit, restrain, hinder, bar, except, prevent.

(ANT.) welcome, involve, embrace, admit, accept, include.

exclusion *(SYN.)* exception, bar, rejection.

(ANT.) inclusion.

exclusive *(SYN.)* restricted, limited, restrictive, choice, selective, fashionable.

(ANT.) common, general, ordinary, unrestricted, unfashionable.

excursion *(SYN.)* voyage, tour, trip.

excuse *(SYN.)* exculpate, forgive, remit, acquit, free, pardon, condone, explanation, overlook, exempt, reason, justify, absolve.

(ANT.) revenge, punish, convict.

execute *(SYN.)* complete, accomplish, do, achieve, kill, perform.

exemplify *(SYN.)* show, illustrate.

exempt *(SYN.)* excuse, free, except, release.

exercise *(SYN.)* drill, task, use, activity, lesson, training, exertion, application, gymnastics, operation, practice.

(ANT.) rest, indolence, repose.

exertion *(SYN.)* attempt, effort, strain, endeavor.

exhale *(SYN.)* blow, breathe out.

exhaust *(SYN.)* drain, tire, empty, wear out, use, finish, fatigue.

(ANT.) renew, refresh, replace.

exhaustive *(SYN.)* comprehensive, thorough, extensive, complete.

(ANT.) incomplete.

exhibit *(SYN.)* demonstrate, display, reveal, betray, present, show, flaunt.

(ANT.) hide conceal, disguise.

exhilarate *(SYN.)* gladden, refresh, cheer, excite, stimulate.

exhort *(SYN.)* advise, coax, press, urge, prompt.

exile *(SYN.)* expulsion, proscription, deportation, ostracism, expatriation, deport, extradition, expel, banishment.

(ANT.) retrieval, welcome, recall, admittance, reinstatement.

exist *(SYN.)* stand, live, occur, be.

exit *(SYN.)* leave, depart.

exodus *(SYN.)* leaving, exit, parting, departure.

exonerate *(SYN.)* acquit, clear.

exorbitant *(SYN.)* unreasonable, outrageous, overpriced, preposterous, excessive.

(ANT.) normal, reasonable.

exotic *(SYN.)* strange, vivid, foreign, gay.

(ANT.) dull, native.

expand *(SYN.)* unfold, enlarge, broaden, spread, inflate, swell, grow.

(ANT.) contract, shrivel, shrink.

expect *(SYN.)* await, think, hope, anticipate.

expedient *(SYN.)* helpful, desirable, rush, hasten, useful, fitting, sensible.

(ANT.) delay.

expedition *(SYN.)* trek, speed, trip, haste, voyage, journey, hurry.

expel *(SYN.)* exile, dislodge, discharge, excommunicate, oust, eject, dismiss, banish, disown.

(ANT.) favor, recall, invite, admit.

expend *(SYN.)* consume, waste, spend, exhaust.

(ANT.) ration, reserve, conserve.

expense *(SYN.)* charge, cost, payment, price.

expensive *(SYN.)* costly, dear.

(ANT.) modest, inexpensive, cheap.

experience *(SYN.)* occurrence, episode, sensation, happening, existence, background, feeling, living, encountering, knowledge.

experienced *(SYN.)* expert, qualified, accomplished, skilled, practiced.

(ANT.) untutored, inexperienced, naive.

experiment *(SYN.)* trial, test, prove, research, examine, try, verify.

expert *(SYN.)* adept, handy, skillful, clever, specialist, authority, skilled, knowledgeable, ingenious.

(ANT.) untrained, unskilled, inexperienced.

expire *(SYN.)* terminate, die, cease, perish, pass, end, disappear.

(ANT.) commence, continue.

explain *(SYN.)* illustrate, decipher, expound, clarify, resolve, define, unravel, elucidate, unfold, justify, interpret.

(ANT.) darken, baffle, obscure.

explanation *(SYN.)* definition, description, interpretation, account, reason, justification, excuse.

explicit *(SYN.)* lucid, definitive, specific, express, clear, manifest.

(ANT.) vague, implicit, ambiguous.

exploit *(SYN.)* feat, deed, accomplishment, adventure.

explore *(SYN.)* research, hunt, probe, search, investigate, look, examine.

explosion *(SYN.)* bang, boom, blowup, flare-up, blast, detonation, outbreak, convulsion, furor, tantrum, paroxysm.

explosive *(SYN.)* fiery, rabid, eruptive, volcanic, fulminatory, inflammatory.

(ANT.) stable, inert, peaceful, calm.

exponent *(SYN.)* explicator, spokesman, supporter, expounder, interpreter.

expose *(SYN.)* uncover, display, bare, open, unmask, reveal.

(ANT.) hide, conceal, mask, covered.

exposition *(SYN.)* fair, bazaar, show, expo, exhibition.

expound *(SYN.)* clarify, present, explain, lecture, demonstrate.

express *(SYN.)* voice, tell, send, say, ship, declare, state, precise, specific, swift, describe.

expression *(SYN.)* declaration, statement, look.

expressive *(SYN.)* suggestive, meaningful, telling, significant, thoughtful.

(ANT.) unthinking, meaningless, nondescript.

expressly *(SYN.)* precisely, exactly, definitely, clearly.

(ANT.) tentatively, vaguely, ambiguously.

expulsion *(SYN.)* ejection, discharge, removal, elimination.

expunge *(SYN.)* blot out, erase, cancel, obliterate, delete, efface, remove.

expurgate *(SYN.)* cleanse, purge, censor, edit, emasculate, abridge, blip.

exquisite *(SYN.)* delicate, delightful, attractive, dainty, beautiful, elegant, fine, superb, lovely, excellent, perfect.

(ANT.) vulgar, dull, ugly, unattractive.

extant *(SYN.)* subsisting, remaining, surviving, present, existing.

(ANT.) lost, defunct, extinct, vanished.

extemporize *(SYN.)* improvise, devise.

extend *(SYN.)* lengthen, stretch, increase, offer, give, grant, magnify, expand.

(ANT.) abbreviate, shorten, curtail.

extension *(SYN.)* expansion, increase, stretching, enlargement.

extensive *(SYN.)* vast, wide, spacious.

(ANT.) cramped, confined, restricted.

extent *(SYN.)* length, degree, range, amount, measure, size, compass, reach, magnitude, scope, expanse, area.

extenuating *(SYN.)* exculpating, excusable, qualifying, justifying, softening.

exterior *(SYN.)* surface, face, outside, covering, outer, external.

(ANT.) inside, interior, inner, internal.

exterminate *(SYN.)* slay, kill, destroy.

external *(SYN.)* outer, exterior, outside.

(ANT.) inner, internal, inside, interior.

externals *(SYN.)* images, effects, look, appearance, veneer, aspect.

extinct *(SYN.)* lost, dead, gone, vanished.

(ANT.) present, flourishing, alive, extant.

extinction *(SYN.)* eclipse, annihilation, obliteration, death, extirpation.

extol *(SYN.)* laud, eulogize, exalt, praise.

(ANT.) denounce, discredit, disparage.

extra *(SYN.)* surplus, spare, additional.

extract *(SYN.)* remove, essence.

(ANT.) penetrate, introduce.

extraordinary *(SYN.)* unusual, wonderful, marvelous, peculiar, noteworthy.

(ANT.) commonplace, ordinary, usual.

extravagant *(SYN.)* excessive, exaggerated, lavish, wasteful, extreme.

(ANT.) prudent, frugal, thrifty, economical, provident.

extreme *(SYN.)* excessive, overdone, outermost, limit, greatest, utmost, furthest.

(ANT.) reasonable, modest, moderate.

extricate *(SYN.)* rescue, free, clear, release, liberate.

exuberant *(SYN.)* buoyant, ebullient, vivacious.

(ANT.) sad, depressed.

exult *(SYN.)* rejoice, delight.

eye *(SYN.)* watch, view, stare, look, inspect, glance.

fable *(SYN.)* legend, parable, myth, fib, falsehood, fiction, tale, story.

fabled *(SYN.)* legendary, famous, famed, historic.

fabric *(SYN.)* goods, textile, material, cloth, yard goods.

fabricate *(SYN.)* assemble, make, construct, produce, create, manufacture, form.
(ANT.) raze, destroy, demolish.

fabrication *(SYN.)* deceit, lie, falsehood, untruth, forgery, prevarication, deception.
(ANT.) verity, reality, actuality, truth, fact.

fabulous *(SYN.)* amazing, marvelous, unbelievable, fantastic, astounding, astonishing, striking.
(ANT.) ordinary, commonplace, credible, proven, factual.

facade *(SYN.)* deception, mask, front, show, pose, veneer, guise, affectation.

face *(SYN.)* cover, mug, front, assurance, countenance, audacity, visage, expression, look, features, facade, encounter, meet, surface.
(ANT.) rear, shun, avoid, evade, back, timidity.

facet *(SYN.)* perspective, view, side, phase.

facetious *(SYN.)* jocular, pungent, humorous, funny, clever, droll, witty, playful, jesting.
(ANT.) sober, serious, grave, weighty.

face to face *(SYN.)* opposing, nose to nose, confronting.

facile *(SYN.)* simple, easy, quick, uncomplicated, clever, fluent, skillful.
(ANT.) complex, difficult, complicated, laborious, hard, ponderous, painstaking, arduous.

facilitate *(SYN.)* help, speed, ease, promote, accelerate, expedite.

facilities *(SYN.)* aid, means, resources, conveniences.

facility *(SYN.)* ability, skill, ease, skillfulness, material.
(ANT.) effort, difficulty, labor.

facsimile *(SYN.)* reproduction, likeness, replica.

fact *(SYN.)* reality, deed, certainty, act, incident, circumstance, occurrence, event, truth, actuality.
(ANT.) falsehood, fiction, delusion.

faction *(SYN.)* clique, party, sect.

factitious *(SYN.)* false, sham, artificial, spurious, unnatural, affected.
(ANT.) natural, real, genuine, artless.

factor *(SYN.)* part, certain, element, basis, cause.

factory *(SYN.)* installation, plant, mill, works.

factual *(SYN.)* true, correct, accurate, sure, genuine, authentic.
(ANT.) incorrect, erroneous, fabricated, invented.

faculty *(SYN.)* power, capacity, talent, staff, gift, ability, qualification, ability, skill.

fad *(SYN.)* fashion, vogue, mania, rage.

faddish *(SYN.)* ephemeral, modish, temporary, passing, fleeting.
(ANT.) lasting, permanent, enduring, classic.

fade *(SYN.)* pale, bleach, weaken, dim, decline, sink, discolor, fail, diminish, droop.

fagged *(SYN.)* exhausted, tired, weary, jaded, pooped, worn.

fail *(SYN.)* neglect, weaken, flunk, miss, decline, disappoint, fade.
(ANT.) succeed, achieve, accomplish.

failing *(SYN.)* fault, foible, imperfection, frailty, defect, peccadillo, shortcoming.
(ANT.) steadiness, strength, integrity, firmness.

failure *(SYN.)* miscarriage, omission, decline, deficiency, fiasco, lack, dereliction, failing, unsuccessfulness, loss, default, want, insufficiency, decay.
(ANT.) conquest, accomplishment, success, triumph, victory, hit, luck, achievement.

faint *(SYN.)* timid, faded, languid, halfhearted, dim, pale, wearied, feeble, indistinct, weak.
(ANT.) strong, sharp, forceful, glaring, clear, distinct, conspicuous, brave.

faint-hearted *(SYN.)* shy, cowardly, timid, bashful.
(ANT.) fearless, brave, stouthearted, courageous.

fair *(SYN.)* pale, average, light, sunny, mediocre, bright, just, clear, lovely, market, blond, honest, equitable, impartial, reasonable, comely, exposition.
(ANT.) ugly, fraudulent, foul, outstanding, dishonorable, unfair.

fairly *(SYN.)* equally, evenly, rather, impartially, passably, justly, squarely, somewhat.

fair-minded *(SYN.)* reasonable, fair, just, open-minded, honest, unprejudiced, impartial, evenhanded.

(ANT.) bigoted, narrow-minded, unjust, close-minded, partisan.

fairness *(SYN.)* equity, justice, evenhandedness, honesty.

(ANT.) favoritism, partiality, bias, onesidedness.

fairy *(SYN.)* leprechaun, gnome, elf, pixie, sprite.

faith *(SYN.)* dependence, trust, reliance, creed, loyalty, doctrine, confidence, dogma, tenet, persuasion, constancy, credence, fidelity, religion, belief.

(ANT.) mistrust, disbelief, doubt, infidelity.

faithful *(SYN.)* staunch, true, devoted, trusty, loyal, constant, credible, steadfast, strict, trust-worthy, accurate.

(ANT.) untrustworthy, faithless, inaccurate, wrong, false, disloyal, erroneous, treacherous.

faithless *(SYN.)* treacherous, unfaithful, disloyal, perfidious, untrue.

(ANT.) loyal, true, unwavering, constant, faithful.

fake *(SYN.)* falsify, distort, pretend, feign, fraud, counterfeit, cheat, false, artificial, phony, imitation, forgery, mock.

(ANT.) honest, pure, real, genuine, authentic.

falderal *(SYN.)* foolery, jargon, nonsense, gibberish, blather, balderdash.

fall *(SYN.)* drop, decline, diminish, droop, topple, decrease, sink, hang, descend, subside, plunge, collapse.

(ANT.) soar, climb, steady, rise, ascend.

fallacious *(SYN.)* untrue, false, wrong, erroneous, deceptive, illusory, delusive.

(ANT.) accurate, true, exact, real, factual.

fallacy *(SYN.)* mistake, error, illusion, sophism, misconception, deception.

fall back *(SYN.)* retreat, recede, retire, withdraw, concede.

(ANT.) progress, advance, gain, prosper, proceed.

fallow *(SYN.)* idle, unprepared, unproductive. inactive.

(ANT.) prepared, productive, cultivated.

false *(SYN.)* incorrect, wrong, deceitful, fake, imitation, counterfeit.

(ANT.) genuine, loyal, true, honest.

falsehood *(SYN.)* untruth, lie, fib, story.

(ANT.) truth.

falsify *(SYN.)* misquote, distort, misstate, mislead, adulterate.

falter *(SYN.)* stumble, tremble, waver, hesitate, flounder.

fame *(SYN.)* distinction, glory, mane, eminence, credit, reputation, renown, acclaim, notoriety.

(ANT.) infamy, obscurity, anonymity, disrepute.

famed *(SYN.)* known, renowned, famous.

(ANT.) obscure, unknown, anonymous.

familiar *(SYN.)* informal, intimate, close, acquainted, amicable, knowing, cognizant, well-acquainted, versed, unreserved, friendly, sociable, affable, aware, known, courteous, intimate.

(ANT.) unfamiliar, distant, affected, reserved.

familiarity *(SYN.)* sociability, acquaintance, awareness, frankness, intimacy, understanding, knowledge, fellowship.

(ANT.) distance, ignorance, reserve, presumption, constraint, haughtiness.

family *(SYN.)* kin, tribe, folks, group, relatives.

famine *(SYN.)* want, deficiency, starvation, need.

(ANT.) excess, plenty.

famous *(SYN.)* distinguished, noted, glorious, illustrious, famed, celebrated, well-known, eminent, renowned, prominent, esteemed.

(ANT.) obscure, hidden, unknown.

fan *(SYN.)* arouse, spread, admirer, enthusiast, devotee, stir, aficionado, whip, follower.

fanatic *(SYN.)* bigot, enthusiast, zealot.

fancy *(SYN.)* love, dream, ornate, imagine, suppose, imagination, taste, fantasy, ornamented, elaborate, think.

(ANT.) plain, undecorated, simple, unadorned.

fantastic *(SYN.)* strange, unusual, odd, wild, unimaginable, incredible, unbelievable, unreal, bizarre, capricious.

(ANT.) mundane, ordinary, staid, humdrum.

fantasy *(SYN.)* illusion, dream, whim, hallucination, delusion, caprice, mirage, daydream, fancy.

(ANT.) bore.

far *(SYN.)* removed, much, distant, remote, estranged, alienated.

(ANT.) close, near.

fare *(SYN.)* prosper, eat, passenger, thrive, toll, progress, succeed.

farewell *(SYN.)* good-by, valediction, departure, leaving.

(ANT.) welcome, greeting.

farm *(SYN.)* grow, harvest, cultivate, ranch, hire, charter, plantation.

fascinate *(SYN.)* charm, enchant, bewitch, attract, enthrall.

fashion *(SYN.)* create, shape, style, mode, make, custom, form, manner, method, way, vogue.

fashionable *(SYN.)* chic, smart, stylish, modish, elegant, voguish.

(ANT.) dowdy, unfashionable.

fast *(SYN.)* fleet, firm, quick, swift, inflexible, stable, secure, expeditious, rapid, steady, solid, constant, speedy.

(ANT.) insecure, sluggish, unstable, loose, slow, unsteady.

fasten *(SYN.)* secure, bind, tie, join, fix, connect, attach, unite.

(ANT.) open, loose, free, loosen, release, separate.

fastidious *(SYN.)* choosy, selective, discriminating, picky, meticulous.

fat *(SYN.)* stout, plump, chubby, pudgy, obese, oily, fleshy, greasy, fatty, portly, corpulent, paunchy, wide, thick, rotund.

(ANT.) slim, gaunt, emaciated, thin, slender.

fatal *(SYN.)* killing, lethal, doomed, disastrous, deadly, fateful, mortal.

(ANT.) nonfatal.

fate *(SYN.)* end, fortune, doom, issue, destiny, necessity, portion, result, lot, chance, luck, outcome, consequence, kismet.

father *(SYN.)* cause, sire, breed, originate, founder, inventor.

fatherly *(SYN.)* protective, paternal, kind, paternalistic.

fathom *(SYN.)* penetrate, understand, interpret, comprehend.

fatigue *(SYN.)* weariness, lassitude, exhaustion, enervation, languor, tiredness.

(ANT.) vivacity, rejuvenation, energy, vigor.

fault *(SYN.)* defect, flaw, mistake, imperfection, shortcoming, error, weakness, responsibility, omission, blemish, blame, failure.

(ANT.) perfection, completeness.

faultfinding *(SYN.)* carping, censorious, critical, caviling, nitpicking.

faulty *(SYN.)* imperfect, broken, defective, damaged, impaired.

(ANT.) flawless, perfect, whole.

favor *(SYN.)* rather, resemble, liking, service, prefer, approval, like, support, patronize, benefit.

(ANT.) deplore, disapprove.

favorite *(SYN.)* prized, pet, choice, darling, treasured, preferred.

favoritism *(SYN.)* prejudice, bias, partiality.

(ANT.) fairness, impartiality.

fear *(SYN.)* horror, terror, fright, trepidation, alarm, consternation, dismay, cowardice, panic, anxiety, dread, scare, apprehension.

(ANT.) fearlessness, boldness, courage, assurance.

fearless *(SYN.)* bold, brave, courageous, gallant, dauntless, confident.

(ANT.) timid, fearful, cowardly.

feast *(SYN.)* dinner, banquet, barbecue.

feat *(SYN.)* performance, act, operation, accomplishment, achievement, doing, transaction, deed.

(ANT.) intention, deliberation, cessation.

feature *(SYN.)* trait, quality, characteristic, highlight, attribute.

fee *(SYN.)* payment, pay, remuneration, charge, recompense.

feeble *(SYN.)* faint, puny, exhausted, impair, delicate, weak, enervated, frail, powerless, forceless, sickly, decrepit, ailing.

(ANT.) strong, forceful, powerful, vigorous, stout.

feed *(SYN.)* satisfy, nourish, food, fodder, forage.

feel *(SYN.)* sense, experience, perceive.

feeling *(SYN.)* opinion, sensibility, tenderness, affection, impression, belief, sensation, sympathy, thought, passion, sentiment, attitude, emotion.

(ANT.) fact, imperturbability, anesthesia, insensibility.

fellowship *(SYN.)* clan, society, brotherhood, fraternity, camaraderie, companionship, comradeship, association.

(ANT.) dislike, discord, distrust, enmity, strife, acrimony.

felonious *(SYN.)* murderous, criminal, larcenous.

feminine *(SYN.)* womanly, girlish, ladylike, female, maidenly, womanish.

(ANT.) masculine, male, virile.

ferocious *(SYN.)* savage, fierce, wild, blood-thirsty, brutal.

(ANT.) playful, gentle, harmless, calm.

fertile *(SYN.)* rich, fruitful, teeming, plenteous, bountiful, prolific, luxuriant, productive, fecund.

(ANT.) unproductive, barren, sterile.

festival *(SYN.)* feast, banquet, regalement, celebration.

festive *(SYN.)* joyful, gay, joyous, merry, gala, jovial, jubilant.

(ANT.) sad, gloomy, mournful, morose.

fetching *(SYN.)* charming, attractive, pleasing, captivating, winsome.

feud *(SYN.)* dispute, quarrel, strife, argument, conflict, controversy.

(ANT.) amity, understanding, harmony, peace.

fiber *(SYN.)* line, strand, thread, string.

fickle *(SYN.)* unstable, capricious, restless, changeable, inconstant, variable.

(ANT.) stable, constant, trustworthy, steady, reliable, dependable.

fiction *(SYN.)* fabrication, romance, falsehood, tale, allegory, narrative, fable, novel, story, invention.

(ANT.) verity, reality, fact, truth.

fictitious *(SYN.)* invented, make-believe, imaginary, fabricated, unreal, counterfeit, feigned.

(ANT.) real, true, genuine, actual, proven.

fidelity *(SYN.)* fealty, devotion, precision, allegiance, exactness, constancy, accuracy, faithfulness, loyalty.

(ANT.) treachery, disloyalty.

fidget *(SYN.)* squirm, twitch, wriggle.

fiendish *(SYN.)* devilish, demonic, diabolical, savage, satanic.

fierce *(SYN.)* furious, wild, savage, violent, ferocious, vehement.

(ANT.) calm, meek, mild, gentle, placid.

fight *(SYN.)* contend, scuffle, struggle, battle, wrangle, combat, brawl, quarrel, dispute, war, skirmish, conflict.

figure *(SYN.)* design, pattern, mold, shape, form, frame, reckon, calculate, compute, determine.

fill *(SYN.)* glut, furnish, store, stuff, occupy, gorge, pervade, content, stock, fill up, supply, sate, replenish, satisfy.

(ANT.) void, drain, exhaust, deplete, empty.

filter *(SYN.)* screen, strainer, sieve.

filth *(SYN.)* pollution, dirt, sewage, foulness.

(ANT.) cleanliness, innocence, purity.

filthy *(SYN.)* foul, polluted, dirty, stained, unwashed, squalid.

(ANT.) pure, clean, unspoiled.

final *(SYN.)* ultimate, decisive, concluding, ending, terminal, last, conclusive, eventual, latest.

(ANT.) inaugural, rudimentary, beginning, initial, incipient, first, original.

finally *(SYN.)* at last, eventually, ultimately.

find *(SYN.)* observe, detect, discover, locate.

fine *(SYN.)* thin, pure, choice, small, elegant, dainty, splendid, handsome, delicate, nice, powdered, beautiful, minute, exquisite, subtle,pretty, refined.

(ANT.) thick, coarse, rough, blunt, large.

finicky *(SYN.)* fussy, meticulous, finical, fastidious, prim.

finish *(SYN.)* consummate, close, get done, terminate, accomplish, conclude, execute, perform, complete, end, achieve, fulfill, do, perfect.

(ANT.) open, begin, start, beginning.

fire *(SYN.)* vigor, glow, combustion, passion, burning, conflagration, ardor, flame, blaze, intensity, fervor.

(ANT.) apathy, cold.

firm *(SYN.)* solid, rigid, inflexible, stiff, unchanging, steadfast, dense, hard, unshakable, compact, business, company, corporation, partnership.

(ANT.) weak, limp, soft, drooping.

first *(SYN.)* chief, primary, initial, pristine, beginning, foremost, primeval, earliest, prime, primitive, original.

(ANT.) subordinate, last, least, hindmost, latest.

fishy *(SYN.)* suspicious, questionable, doubtful.

(ANT.) believable, credible.

fit *(SYN.)* adjust, suit, suitable, accommodate, conform, robust, harmonize,

belong, seizure, spasm, attack, suited, appropriate, healthy, agree, adapt.
(ANT.) misfit, disturb, improper.

fitful (SYN.) variable, restless, fickle, capricious, unstable, changeable.
(ANT.) trustworthy, stable, constant, steady.

fitting (SYN.) apt, due, suitable, proper.
(ANT.) improper, unsuitable, inappropriate.

fix (SYN.) mend, regulate, affix, set, tie, repair, attach, settle, link, bind, determine, establish, define, place, rectify, stick, limit, adjust, fasten.
(ANT.) damage, change, mistreat, displace, alter, disturb, mutilate.

fixation (SYN.) fetish, obsession, infatuation, compulsion.

flair (SYN.) style, dash, flamboyance, drama, gift, knack, aptitude.

flamboyant (SYN.) showy, flashy, ostentatious, gaudy, ostentatious.

flame (SYN.) blaze, fire.

flash (SYN.) flare, flame, wink, twinkling, instant, gleam.

flashy (SYN.) tawdry, tasteless, pretentious, garish, flamboyant.

flat (SYN.) vapid, stale, even, smooth, tasteless, horizontal, dull, level, insipid, uninteresting, lifeless, boring.
(ANT.) tasty, racy, hilly, savory, stimulating, interesting, broken, sloping.

flattery (SYN.) compliment, praise, applause, blarney, acclaim.

flaunt (SYN.) exhibit, show off, display, parade.
(ANT.) conceal, hide, disguise.

flavor (SYN.) tang, taste, savor, essence, quality, character, season, spice.

flaw (SYN.) spot, imperfection, blemish, fault, deformity, blotch.

flee (SYN.) fly, abscond, hasten, escape, run away, decamp, evade.
(ANT.) remain, appear, stay, arrive.

fleece (SYN.) filch, rob, purloin, swindle, defraud, pilfer, cheat.

fleet (SYN.) rapid, swift, quick, fast.
(ANT.) unhurried, sluggish, slow.

fleeting (SYN.) brief, swift, passing, temporary.
(ANT.) stable, fixed, lasting, permanent.

fleshy (SYN.) overweight, chubby, stocky, plump, obese, stout.
(ANT.) spare, underweight, skinny.

flexible (SYN.) lithe, resilient, pliable, tractable, complaint, elastic, yielding, adaptable, agreeable, supple, pliant, easy, ductile.
(ANT.) hard, unbending, firm, brittle, inflexible, rigid, fixed.

flighty (SYN.) giddy, light-headed, frivolous, irresponsible.
(ANT.) solid, responsible, steady.

flimsy (SYN.) wobbly, weak, frail, fragile, unsteady, delicate, thin.
(ANT.) durable, stable, firm, strong.

fling (SYN.) pitch, throw, toss, fun, celebration, party.

flippant (SYN.) disrespectful, sassy, insolent, brazen, rude, impertinent.
(ANT.) courteous, polite, mannerly.

flit (SYN.) flutter, scurry, hasten, dart, skim.

flock (SYN.) gathering, group, flight, swarm, herd, school.

flog (SYN.) thrash, lash, switch, strike, paddle.

flood (SYN.) overflow, deluge, inundate, cascade.

florid (SYN.) gaudy, fancy, ornate, embellished.
(ANT.) spare, simple, plain, unadorned.

flourish (SYN.) succeed, grow, prosper, wave, thrive, bloom.
(ANT.) wither, wane, die, decline.

flout (SYN.) disdain, scorn, spurn, ignore, taunt, ridicule, mock.

flow (SYN.) proceed, abound, spout, come, stream, run, originate, emanate, result, pour, squirt, issue, gush, spurt.

fluctuate (SYN.) vary, oscillate, change, waver, hesitate, vacillate.
(ANT.) persist, stick, adhere, resolve.

fluent (SYN.) graceful, glib, flowing.

fluid (SYN.) liquid, running, liquefied.

flush (SYN.) abundant, flat, even, level.

fluster (SYN.) rattle, flurry, agitate, upset, perturb, quiver, vibrate.

fly (SYN.) flee, mount, shoot, decamp, hover, soar, flit, flutter, sail, escape, rush, spring, glide, abscond, dart, float.
(ANT.) sink, descend, plummet.

foam (SYN.) suds, froth, lather.

foe (SYN.) opponent, enemy, antagonist, adversary.
(ANT.) associate, ally, friend, comrade.

fog (SYN.) haze, mist, cloud, daze, confusion, stupor, vapor, smog.

foible *(SYN.)* frailty, weakness, failing, shortcoming, kink.

foist *(SYN.)* misrepresent, insinuate, falsify.

fold *(SYN.)* lap, double, overlap, clasp, pleat, tuck.

follow *(SYN.)* trail, observe, succeed, ensue, obey, chase, comply, accompany, copy, result, imitate, heed, adopt.
(ANT.) elude, cause, precede, avoid, flee.

follower *(SYN.)* supporter, devotee, henchman, adherent, partisan, votary, attendant, disciple, successor.
(ANT.) master, head, chief, dissenter.

following *(SYN.)* public, disciples, supporters, clientele, customers.

folly *(SYN.)* imprudence, silliness, foolishness, indiscretion, absurdity, imprudence, imbecility, stupidity, extravagance.
(ANT.) reasonableness, judgment, sense, prudence, wisdom.

fond *(SYN.)* affectionate, loving, attached, tender, devoted.
(ANT.) hostile, cool, distant, unfriendly.

fondness *(SYN.)* partiality, liking, affection.
(ANT.) hostility, unfriendliness.

food *(SYN.)* viands, edibles, feed, repast, nutriment, sustenance, diet, bread, provisions, meal, rations, victuals, fare.
(ANT.) want, hunger, drink, starvation.

fool *(SYN.)* oak, dunce, jester, idiot, simpleton, buffoon, harlequin, dolt, blockhead, numskull, clown, dope, trick, deceive, nincompoop.
(ANT.) scholar, genius, sage.

foolish *(SYN.)* senseless, irrational, crazy, silly, brainless, idiotic, simple, nonsensical, stupid, preposterous, asinine.
(ANT.) sane, sound, sensible, rational, judicious, wise, reasonable, prudent.

footing *(SYN.)* base, basis, foundation.

footloose *(SYN.)* uncommitted, free, detached, independent.
(ANT.) engaged, rooted, involved.

forbearance *(SYN.)* moderation, abstinence, abstention, continence.
(ANT.) greed, excess, intoxication.

forbid *(SYN.)* disallow, prevent, ban, prohibit, taboo, outlaw.
(ANT.) approve, let, allow, permit.

forbidding *(SYN.)* evil, hostile, unfriendly, sinister, scary, repulsive.

(ANT.) pleasant, beneficent, friendly.

force *(SYN.)* energy, might, violence, vigor, intensity, dint, power, constraint, coercion, vigor, compel, compulsion, oblige, make, coerce, strength.
(ANT.) weakness, frailty, persuasion, feebleness, impotence, ineffectiveness.

forceful *(SYN.)* dynamic, vigorous, energetic, potent, drastic, intense.
(ANT.) lackadaisical, insipid, weak.

foreboding *(SYN.)* misgiving, suspicion, apprehension, presage, intuition.

forecast *(SYN.)* prophesy, predict, predetermine.

foregoing *(SYN.)* above, former, preceding, previous, prior.
(ANT.) later, coming, below, follow.

foreign *(SYN.)* alien, strange, exotic, different, unfamiliar.
(ANT.) commonplace, ordinary, familiar.

foreigner *(SYN.)* outsider, alien, newcomer, stranger.
(ANT.) native.

foreman *(SYN.)* super, boss, overseer, supervisor.

forerunner *(SYN.)* harbinger, proclaimer, informant.

foresee *(SYN.)* forecast, expect, anticipate, surmise, envisage.

forest *(SYN.)* grove, woodland, wood, copse, woods.

forestall *(SYN.)* hinder, thwart, prevent, obstruct, repel.

foretell *(SYN.)* soothsay, divine, predict.

forever *(SYN.)* evermore, always, everlasting, hereafter, endlessly.
(ANT.) fleeting, temporarily.

forfeit *(SYN.)* yield, resign, lose, sacrifice.

forgive *(SYN.)* exonerate, clear, excuse, pardon.
(ANT.) impeach, accuse, blame, censure.

forgo *(SYN.)* relinquish, release, surrender, waive, abandon.
(ANT.) keep, retain, safeguard.

forlorn *(SYN.)* pitiable, desolate, dejected, woeful, wretched.
(ANT.) optimistic, cherished, cheerful.

form *(SYN.)* frame, compose, fashion, arrange, construct, make up, devise, create, invent, mold, shape, forge, organize, produce, constitute, make.
(ANT.) wreck, dismantle, destroy, misshape.

formal *(SYN.)* exact, stiff, correct, outward, conformist, conventional, affected, regular, proper, ceremonious, decorous, methodical, precise, solemn, external, perfunctory.

(ANT.) heartfelt, unconstrained, easy, unconventional.

former *(SYN.)* earlier, previous, erstwhile, prior.

formidable *(SYN.)* alarming, frightful, imposing, terrible, terrifying, dire, fearful, forbidding.

(ANT.) weak, unimpressive, ordinary.

forsake *(SYN.)* abandon, desert, forgo, quit, discard, neglect.

forte *(SYN.)* gift, capability, talent, specialty, aptitude, bulwark.

forth *(SYN.)* out, onward, forward.

forthright *(SYN.)* honest, direct, candid, outspoken, blunt sincere, plain, explicit.

forthwith *(SYN.)* instantly, promptly, immediately.

(ANT.) afterward, later, ultimately, slowly.

fortify *(SYN.)* bolster strengthen, buttress, barricade, defend.

fortuitous *(SYN.)* successful, benign, lucky, advantageous, propitious, happy, favored, chance.

(ANT.) unlucky, condemned, persecuted.

fortunate *(SYN.)* happy, auspicious, fortuitous, successful, favored, advantageous, benign, charmed, lucky, felicitous, blessed, propitious, blissful.

(ANT.) ill-fated, cheerless, unlucky, unfortunate, cursed, condemned.

fortune *(SYN.)* chance, fate, lot, luck, riches, wealth, kismet, destiny.

fortuneteller *(SYN.)* soothsayer, clairvoyant, forecaster, oracle, medium.

forward *(SYN.)* leading, front, promote, elevate, advance, first, ahead, onward, further, foremost, aggrandize.

(ANT.) withhold, retard, hinder, retreat, oppose.

foul *(SYN.)* base, soiled, dirty, mean, unclean, polluted, impure, vile, evil, muddy, wicked, rainy, stormy, despicable, filthy.

(ANT.) pure, neat, wholesome, clean.

found *(SYN.)* organize, establish.

foundation *(SYN.)* support, root, base, underpinning, ground-work, bottom, establishment, substructure, basis.

(ANT.) top, cover, building.

foxy *(SYN.)* cunning, sly, artful, crafty, wily, sharp, shrewd, slick.

fraction *(SYN.)* fragment, part, section, morsel, share, piece.

fracture *(SYN.)* crack, break, rupture.

fragile *(SYN.)* delicate, frail, weak, breakable, infirm, brittle, feeble.

(ANT.) tough, hardy, sturdy, strong, stout, durable.

fragment *(SYN.)* scrap, piece, bit, remnant, part, splinter, segment.

fragrance *(SYN.)* odor, smell, scent, perfume, aroma.

fragrant *(SYN.)* aromatic, scented, perfumed.

frail *(SYN.)* feeble, weak, delicate, breakable, fragile.

(ANT.) sturdy, strong, powerful.

frame *(SYN.)* support, framework, skeleton, molding, border, mount.

frank *(SYN.)* honest, candid, open, unreserved, direct, sincere, straight-forward.

(ANT.) tricky, dishonest.

frantic *(SYN.)* frenzied, crazed, raving, panicky.

(ANT.) composed, stoic.

fraud *(SYN.)* deception, guile, swindle, deceit, artifice, imposture, trick, cheat, imposition, duplicity, chicanery.

(ANT.) sincerity, fairness, integrity.

fraudulent *(SYN.)* tricky, fake, dishonest, deceitful

fray *(SYN.)* strife, fight, battle, struggle, tussle, combat, brawl, melee, skirmish.

(ANT.) truce, agreement, peace, concord.

freak *(SYN.)* curiosity, abnormality, monster, oddity.

free *(SYN.)* munificent, clear, autonomous, immune, open, freed, bountiful, liberated, unfastened, immune, emancipated, unconfined, unobstructed, easy, artless, loose, familiar, bounteous, unrestricted, liberal, independent, careless, frank, exempt.

(ANT.) stingy, clogged, illiberal, confined, parsimonious.

freedom *(SYN.)* independence, privilege, familiarity, unrestraint, liberty, exemption, liberation, immunity, license.

(ANT.) servitude, constraint, bondage, slavery, necessity.

freely *(SYN.)* liberally, generously, unstintingly.

freight *(SYN.)* chipping, cargo, load, shipment.

frenzy *(SYN.)* craze, agitation, excitement.

frequent *(SYN.)* usual, habitual, common, often, customary, general.
(ANT.) unique, rare, solitary, uncommon, exceptional, infrequent, scanty.

fresh *(SYN.)* recent, new, additional, modern, further, refreshing, natural, brisk, novel, inexperienced, late, current, sweet, pure, cool.
(ANT.) stagnant, decayed, musty, faded.

fret *(SYN.)* torment, worry, grieve, anguish.

fretful *(SYN.)* testy, irritable, touchy, peevish, short-tempered.
(ANT.) calm.

friend *(SYN.)* crony, supporter, ally, companion, intimate, associate, advocate, comrade, mate, patron, acquaintance, chum, defender.
(ANT.) stranger, adversary.

friendly *(SYN.)* sociable, kindly, affable, genial, companionable, social, neighborly, amicable.
(ANT.) hostile, antagonistic, reserved.

friendship *(SYN.)* knowledge, familiarity, fraternity, acquaintance, intimacy, fellowship, comradeship, cognizance.
(ANT.) unfamiliarity, ignorance.

fright *(SYN.)* alarm, fear, panic, terror.

frighten *(SYN.)* scare, horrify, daunt, affright, appall, terrify, alarm, terrorize, astound, dismay, startle, panic.
(ANT.) soothe, embolden, compose, reassure.

frigid *(SYN.)* cold, wintry, icy, glacial, arctic, freezing.

fringe *(SYN.)* hem, edge, border, trimming, edging.

frisky *(SYN.)* animated, lively, peppy, vivacious.

frolic *(SYN.)* play, cavort, romp, frisk.

front *(SYN.)* facade, face, start, beginning, border, head.
(ANT.) rear, back.

frontier *(SYN.)* border, boundary.

frugal *(SYN.)* parsimonious, saving, stingy, provident, temperate, economical, sparing.
(ANT.) extravagant, wasteful, self-indulgent, intemperate.

fruitful *(SYN.)* fertile, rich, bountiful,

teeming, fecund, productive, luxuriant.
(ANT.) lean, barren, sterile.

fruitless *(SYN.)* barren, futile, vain, sterile, unproductive.
(ANT.) fertile, productive.

frustrate *(SYN.)* hinder, defeat, thwart, circumvent, outwit, foil, baffle, disappoint, balk, discourage, prevent.
(ANT.) promote, accomplish, further.

fulfill *(SYN.)* do, effect, complete, accomplish, realize.

full *(SYN.)* baggy, crammed, entire, satiated, flowing, perfect, gorged, soaked, complete, filled, packed, extensive.
(ANT.) lacking, partial, empty, depleted.

full-grown *(SYN.)* ripe, adult, mature, developed, grown-up, complete.
(ANT.) green, young, unripe, adolescent.

fulsome *(SYN.)* disgusting, repulsive, nauseating, repellent, revolting.

fume *(SYN.)* gas, steam, smoke, rage, rave, vapor.

fun *(SYN.)* merriment, pleasure, enjoyment, gaiety, sport, amusement.

function *(SYN.)* operation, activity, affair, ceremony, gathering, party.

fundamental *(SYN.)* basic, essential, primary, elementary.

funny *(SYN.)* odd, droll, ridiculous, farcical, laughable, comic, curious, amusing.
(ANT.) solemn, sad, sober, melancholy.

furious *(SYN.)* angry, enraged.
(ANT.) serene, calm.

furnish *(SYN.)* yield, give, endow, fit, produce, equip, afford, decorate, supply.
(ANT.) divest, denude, strip.

furor *(SYN.)* commotion, tumult, turmoil.

furtive *(SYN.)* surreptitious, secret, hidden, clandestine.
(ANT.) honest, open.

fury *(SYN.)* wrath, anger, frenzy, rage, violence, fierceness.
(ANT.) calmness, serenity.

fuss *(SYN.)* commotion, bother, pester, annoy, irritate.

futile *(SYN.)* pointless, idle, vain, useless, worthless, minor.
(ANT.) weighty, important, worth-while, serious, valuable.

future *(SYN.)* approaching, imminent, coming, impending.
(ANT.) former, past.

fuzzy *(SYN.)* indistinct, blurred.
(ANT.) lucid, clear.

gab *(SYN.)* jabber, babble, chatter, prattle, gossip.

gabble *(SYN.)* chatter, babble, jabber, blab, prate, gaggle, prattle, gibberish.

gabby *(SYN.)* chatty, talkative, wordy, verbose.

gad *(SYN.)* wander, roam, rove, ramble, meander, cruise.

gadget *(SYN.)* contrivance, device, doodad, jigger, thing, contraption.

gaffe *(SYN.)* blunder, boner, mistake, gaucherie, error, howler.

gag *(SYN.)* witticism, crack jest, joke.

gaiety *(SYN.)* joyousness, cheerfulness, joyfulness, light-heartedness.
(ANT.) melancholy, sadness, depression.

gain *(SYN.)* acquire, avail, account, good, interest, attain, favor, achieve, get, secure, advantage, earn, profit, procure.
(ANT.) trouble, lose, calamity, forfeit, handicap, lose, distress.

gainful *(SYN.)* lucrative, rewarding, profitable, beneficial, payable, productive.
(ANT.) unprofitable, unrewarding.

gainsay *(SYN.)* refute, contradict, controvert, deny, refuse, inpugn, contravene, disavow, differ.
(ANT.) aver, affirm, asseverate.

gait *(SYN.)* stride, walk, tread, step.

gala *(SYN.)* ball, party, carnival, festival.

gale *(SYN.)* burst, surge, outburst.

gall *(SYN.)* nerve, audacity, impudence, annoy, vex, anger, provoke, irritate.

gallant *(SYN.)* bold, brave, courageous, valorous, valiant, noble, polite, fearless, heroic, chivalrous.

gallantry *(SYN.)* valor, daring, courage, prowess, heroism, manliness, dauntlessness, graciousness, attentiveness.
(ANT.) poltroonery, timidity, cowardice, cravenness, cloddishness.

gallery *(SYN.)* passageway, hall, aisle, hallway, passage, corridor.

galling *(SYN.)* vexing, irritating, annoying, distressful, irksome.

galore *(SYN.)* abounding, plentiful, profuse, rich, overflowing.

gamble *(SYN.)* game, wager, bet, hazard, risk, venture, chance.

gambol *(SYN.)* romp, dance, cavort, frolic.

game *(SYN.)* fun, contest, merriment, pastime, match, play, amusement, recreation, diversion, entertainment.

(ANT.) labor, hardship, work, business.

gamut *(SYN.)* extent, scope, sweep, horizon, range.

gang *(SYN.)* group, troop, band, company, horde, crew.

gangling *(SYN.)* rangy, lean, skinny, tall, lanky.

gangster *(SYN.)* crook, hoodlum, gunman, criminal.

gap *(SYN.)* cavity, chasm, pore, gulf, aperture, abyss, interval, space, hole, void, pore, break, opening.

gape *(SYN.)* ogle, stare, gawk.

garb *(SYN.)* clothing, dress, vesture, array, attire, clothes, drapery, apparel, garments, costume, raiment.
(ANT.) nudity, nakedness.

garbage *(SYN.)* refuse, waste, trash, rubbish.

gargantuan *(SYN.)* colossal, monumental, giant, huge, large, enormous.

garments *(SYN.)* drapery, dress, garb, apparel, array, attire, clothes, vesture.
(ANT.) nakedness, nudity.

garnish *(SYN.)* decorate, embellish, trim, adorn, enrich, beautify, deck, ornament.
(ANT.) expose, strip, debase, uncover, defame.

garrulous *(SYN.)* chatty, glib, verbose, talkative, communicative, voluble.
(ANT.) silent, uncommunicative, laconic, reticent, taciturn.

gash *(SYN.)* lacerate, slash, pierce, cut, hew, slice.

gasp *(SYN.)* pant, puff, wheeze.

gather *(ANT.)* assemble, collect, garner, harvest, reap, deduce, judge, amass, congregate, muster, cull, glean, accumulate, convene.
(ANT.) scatter, disperse, distribute, disband, separate.

gathering *(SYN.)* meeting, crowd, throng, company, assembly.

gaudy *(SYN.)* showy, flashy, loud, bold, ostentatious.

gaunt *(ANT.)* lank, diaphanous, flimsy, gauzy, narrow, rare, scanty, meager, gossamer, emaciated, scrawny, tenuous, thin, fine, lean, skinny, spare, slim, slight, slender, diluted.
(ANT.) wide, fat, thick, broad, bulky.

gay *(SYN.)* merry, lighthearted, joyful, cheerful, sprightly, jolly, happy, joyous, gleeful, jovial, colorful, bright, glad.

(ANT.) glum, mournful, sad, depressed, sorrowful, somber, sullen.

gaze *(SYN.)* look, stare, view, watch, examine, observe, glance, behold, discern, seem, see, survey, witness, inspect, goggle, appear.

(ANT.) hide, overlook, avert, miss.

geld *(SYN.)* neuter, alter, spay, castrate.

gem *(SYN.)* jewel, semiprecious stone.

general *(SYN.)* ordinary, universal, usual, common, customary, regular, vague, miscellaneous, indefinite, inexact.

(ANT.) definite, particular, exceptional, singular, rare, particular, precise, exact, specific.

generally *(SYN.)* ordinarily, usually, customarily, normally, mainly.

(ANT.) seldom, infrequently, rare.

generate *(SYN.)* produce, bestow, impart, concede, permit, acquiesce, cede, relent, succumb, surrender, pay, supply, grant, relent, bear, afford, submit, waive, allow, breed, accord, accede, abdicate, resign, relinquish, surrender, quit.

(ANT.) assert, refuse, struggle, resist, dissent, oppose, deny, strive.

generation *(SYN.)* age, date, era, period, seniority, senescence, senility, time, epoch, dotage.

(ANT.) infancy, youth, childhood.

generosity *(SYN.)* magnanimity, benevolence, humanity, kindness, philanthropy, tenderness, altruism, liberality, charity, beneficence.

(ANT.) selfishness, malevolence, cruelty, inhumanity, unkindness.

generous *(SYN.)* giving, liberal, unselfish, magnanimous, bountiful, munificent, charitable, big, noble, beneficent.

(ANT.) greedy, stingy, selfish, covetous, mean, miserly.

genesis *(SYN.)* birth, root, creation, source, origin, beginning.

genius *(SYN.)* intellect, adept, intellectual, sagacity, proficient, creativity, ability, inspiration, faculty, originality, aptitude, brain, gift, prodigy, talent.

(ANT.) dullard, stupidity, dolt, shallowness, moron, ineptitude, obtuseness.

genre *(SYN.)* chaste, order, set, elegance, class, excellence, kind, caste, denomination, grade.

genteel *(SYN.)* cultured, polished, polite, refined, elegant.

(ANT.) discourteous, churlish, common.

gentle *(SYN.)* peaceful, placid, tame, serene, relaxed, docile, benign, soothing, calm, soft, mild, amiable, friendly, kindly, cultivated.

(ANT.) nasty, harsh, rough, fierce, mean, violent, savage.

genuine *(SYN.)* real, true, unaffected, authentic, sincere, bona fide, unadulterated, legitimate, actual, veritable, definite, proven.

(ANT.) false, sham, artificial, fake, counterfeit, bogus, pretended, insincere, sham.

genus *(SYN.)* kind, race, species, type, variety, character, family, breed, sort.

germ *(SYN.)* pest, virus, contamination, disease, pollution, taint, infection, contagion, poison, ailment.

germinate *(SYN.)* vegetate, pullulate, sprout, develop, grow.

gesture *(SYN.)* omen, signal, symbol, emblem, indication, note, token, symptom, movement, sign, motion, indication.

get *(SYN.)* obtain, receive, attain, gain, achieve, acquire, procure, earn, fetch, carry, remove, prepare, take, ready, urge, induce, secure.

(ANT.) lose, surrender, forfeit, leave, renounce.

ghastly *(SYN.)* frightful, horrible, horrifying, frightening, grisly, hideous, dreadful.

ghost *(SYN.)* phantom, spook, apparition, specter, trace, hint, vestige, spirit.

ghoulish *(SYN.)* weird, eerie, horrifying, gruesome, sinister, scary.

giant *(SYN.)* monster, colossus, mammoth, superman, gigantic.

(ANT.) small, tiny, dwarf, runt, midget, infinitesimal.

gibe *(SYN.)* sneer, jeer, mock, scoff, boo, hoot, hiss.

(ANT.) approve.

giddy *(SYN.)* reeling, dizzy, flighty, silly, scatterbrained.

(ANT.) serious.

gift *(SYN.)* endowment, favor, gratuity, bequest, talent, charity, present, largess, donation, grant, aptitude, boon, offering, faculty, genius, benefaction.

(ANT.) purchase, loss, ineptitude, deprivation, earnings, incapacity.

gigantic *(SYN.)* huge, colossal, immense, large, vast, elephantine, gargantuan,

prodigious, mammoth, monumental, enormous.
(ANT.) small, tiny, minute, diminutive, little.

giggle *(SYN.)* chuckle, jeer, laugh, roar, snicker, titter, cackle, guffaw, mock.

gild *(SYN.)* cover, coat, paint, embellish, sweeten, retouch, camouflage.

gingerly *(SYN.)* gentle, cautiously, carefully, gently.
(ANT.) roughly.

gird *(SYN.)* wrap, tie, bind, belt, encircle, surround, get set, prepare.
(ANT.) untie.

girl *(SYN.)* female, lass, miss, maiden, damsel.

girth *(SYN.)* measure, size, width, dimensions, expanse, proportions.

gist *(SYN.)* connotation, explanation, purpose, significance, acceptation, implication, interpretation, meaning.
(ANT.) redundancy.

give *(SYN.)* bestow, contribute, grant, impart, provide, donate, confer, deliver, present, furnish, yield, develop, offer, produce, hand over, award, allot, deal out, mete out, bend, sacrifice, supply.
(ANT.) withdraw, take, retain, keep, seize.

given *(SYN.)* handed over, presented, supposed, stated, disposed, assumed, inclined, bent.

glacier *(SYN.)* frigid, icy, iceberg.

glad *(SYN.)* happy, cheerful, gratified, delighted, joyous, merry, pleased, exulting, charmed, thrilled, satisfied, tickled, gay, bright.
(ANT.) sad, depressed, dejected, melancholy, unhappy, morose, somber, despondent.

gladness *(SYN.)* bliss, contentment, happiness, pleasure, well-being, beatitude, delight, satisfaction, blessedness.
(ANT.) sadness, sorrow, despair, misery, grief.

glade *(SYN.)* clearing.

gladiator *(SYN.)* battler, fighter, competitor, combatant, contender, contestant.

glamorous *(SYN.)* spellbinding, fascinating, alluring, charming, bewitching, entrancing, captivating, enchanting, attractive, appealing, enticing, enthralling.

glamour *(SYN.)* charm, allure, attraction, magnetism, fascination.

glance *(SYN.)* eye, gaze, survey, view, examine, inspect, discern, look, see, witness, peek, regard, skim, reflect, glimpse, behold, observe.
(ANT.) hide, miss, avert, overlook.

glare *(SYN.)* flash, dazzle, stare, glower, glow, shine, glaze, burn, brilliance, flare, blind, scowl.

glaring *(SYN.)* flagrant, obvious, blatant, prominent, dazzling.

glass *(SYN.)* cup, tumbler, goblet, pane, crystal.

glassy *(SYN.)* blank, empty, emotionless, vacant, fixed, expressionless.

glaze *(SYN.)* buff, luster, cover, wax, gloss, coat, polish, shellac.

gleam *(SYN.)* flash, glimmer, glisten, shimmer, sparkle, twinkle, glare, beam, glow, radiate, glimmering, shine, burn, reflection, blaze.

glean *(SYN.)* reap, gather, select, harvest, pick, separate, cull.

glee *(SYN.)* mirth, joy, gladness, enchantment, delight, cheer, bliss, elation, merriment.
(ANT.) depression, misery, dejection.

glen *(SYN.)* ravine, valley.

glib *(SYN.)* smooth, suave, flat, plain, polished, sleek, urbane.
(ANT.) rough, rugged, blunt, harsh, bluff.

glide *(SYN.)* sweep, sail, fly, flow, slip, coast, cruise, move easily, skim, slide.

glimmer *(SYN.)* blink, shimmer, flicker, indication, hint, clue, suggestion.

glimpse *(SYN.)* notice, glance, peek, see, impression, look, flash.

glint *(SYN.)* flash, gleam, peek, glance, glimpse, sparkle, glitter.

glisten *(SYN.)* shimmer, shine, glimmer, twinkle, glitter, glister, sparkle.

glitch *(SYN.)* mishap, snag, hitch, malfunction.

glitter *(SYN.)* glisten, glimmer, sparkle, shine, twinkle.

gloat *(SYN.)* triumph, exult, glory, rejoice, revel.

global *(SYN.)* universal, international, worldwise.

globe *(SYN.)* orb, ball, world, earth, map, universe, sphere.

gloom *(SYN.)* bleakness, despondency, misery, sadness, woe, darkness, dejection, obscurity, blackness, shadow, shade, dimness, shadows, melancholy.

(ANT.) joy, mirth, exultation, cheerfulness, light, happiness, brightness, frivolity.

gloomy *(SYN.)* despondent, dismal, glum, somber, sorrowful, sad, dejected, disconsolate, dim, dark, morose, dispirited, moody, grave, pensive.
(ANT.) happy, merry, cheerful, high-spirited, bright, sunny, joyous.

glorify *(SYN.)* enthrone, exalt, honor, revere, adore, dignify, enshrine, consecrate, praise, worship, laud, venerate.
(ANT.) mock, dishonor, debase, abuse, degrade.

glorious *(SYN.)* exalted, high, noble, splendid, supreme, elevated, lofty, raised, majestic, famous, noted, stately, distinguished, celebrated, renowned, famed, magnificent, grand, proud, impressive, elegant, sublime.
(ANT.) ridiculous, low, base, ignoble, terrible, ordinary.

glory *(SYN.)* esteem, praise, respect, reverence, admiration, honor, dignity, worship, eminence, homage, deference.
(ANT.) dishonor, disgrace, contempt, reproach, derision.

gloss *(SYN.)* luster, shine, glow, sheen.

glossary *(SYN.)* dictionary, thesaurus, wordbook, lexicon.

glossy *(SYN.)* smooth, glistening, shiny, sleek, polished.
(ANT.) matte, dull.

glow *(SYN.)* beam, glisten, radiate, shimmer, sparkle, glare, blaze, scintillate, shine, light, gleam, burn, flare, flame, radiate, dazzle, blush, redden, heat, warmth, flicker.

glower *(SYN.)* scowl, stare, frown, glare.
(ANT.) beam, grin, smile.

glowing *(SYN.)* fiery, intense, passionate, zealous, enthusiastic, ardent, eager, fervent, favorable, impassioned, keen, complimentary, vehement.
(ANT.) cool, indifferent, apathetic, nonchalant.

glue *(SYN.)* bind, fasten, cement, paste.

glum *(SYN.)* morose, sulky, fretful, crabbed, sullen, dismal, dour, moody.
(ANT.) joyous, merry, amiable, gay, pleasant.

glut *(SYN.)* gorge, sate, content, furnish, fill, pervade, satiate, stuff, replenish, fill up, satisfy, stock.
(ANT.) empty, exhaust, deplete, void,

drain.

glutton *(SYN.)* pig, hog, greedy eater.

gluttony *(SYN.)* ravenousness, piggishness, devouring, hoggishness, insatiability, swinishness, voraciousness.
(ANT.) satisfaction, fullness.

gnarled *(SYN.)* twisted, knotted, rugged, knobby, nodular.

gnash *(SYN.)* gnaw, crunch, grind.

gnaw *(SYN.)* chew, eat, gnash, grind, erode.

go *(SYN.)* proceed, depart, flee, move, vanish, exit, walk, quit, fade, progress, travel, become, fit, agree, leave, suit, harmonize, pass, travel, function, operate, withdraw.
(ANT.) stay, arrive, enter, stand, come.

goad *(SYN.)* incite, prod, drive, urge, push, shove, jab, provoke, stimulate.

goal *(SYN.)* craving, destination, desire, longing, objective, finish, end, passion, aim, object, aspiration.

gobble *(SYN.)* devour, eat fast, gorge, gulp, stuff.

goblet *(SYN.)* cup, glass.

goblin *(SYN.)* troll, elf, dwarf, spirit.

godlike *(SYN.)* holy, supernatural, heavenly, celestial, divine, transcendent.
(ANT.) profane, wicked, blasphemous, diabolical, mundane.

godly *(SYN.)* pious, religious, holy, pure, divine, spiritual, righteous, saintly.

golden *(SYN.)* shining, metallic, bright, fine, superior, nice, excellent, valuable.
(ANT.) dull, inferior.

gong *(SYN.)* chimes, bells.

good *(SYN.)* honest, sound, valid, cheerful, honorable, worthy, conscientious, moral, genuine, humane, kind, fair, useful, skillful, adequate, friendly, genial, proficient, pleasant, exemplary, admirable, virtuous, reliable, precious, benevolent, excellent, pure, agreeable, gracious, safe, commendable.
(ANT.) bad, imperfect, vicious, undesirable, unfriendly, unkind, evil.

good-by *(SYN.)* so long, farewell.

good-bye *(SYN.)* farewell.

good-hearted *(SYN.)* good, kind, thoughtful, kindhearted, considerate.
(ANT.) evil-hearted.

good-humored *(SYN.)* pleasant, good-natured, cheerful, sunny, amiable.
(ANT.) petulant, cranky.

goodness *(SYN.)* good, honesty, integrity, virtue, righteousness.
(ANT.) sin, evil, dishonesty, corruption, badness.

goods *(SYN.)* property, belongings, holdings, possessions, merchandise, wares.

good will *(SYN.)* agreeability, harmony, willingness, readiness.

gore *(SYN.)* impale, penetrate, puncture, gouge.

gorge *(SYN.)* ravine, devour, stuff, gobble, valley, defile, pass, cram, fill.

gorgeous *(SYN.)* grand, ravishing, glorious, stunning, brilliant, divine, splendid, dazzling, beautiful, magnificent.
(ANT.) homely, ugly, squalid.

gory *(SYN.)* bloody.

gossamer *(SYN.)* dainty, fine, filmy, delicate, sheer, transparent.

gossip *(SYN.)* prate, rumor, prattle, hearsay, meddler, tattler, chatter, talk, chat, blabbermouth.

gouge *(SYN.)* scoop, dig, carve, burrow, excavate, chisel, notch.

gourmet *(SYN.)* gourmand, gastronome, connoisseur.

govern *(SYN.)* manage, oversee, reign, preside over, supervise, direct, command, sway, administer, control, regulate, determine, influence, guide, lead, head, rule.
(ANT.) assent, submit, acquiesce, obey, yield.

government *(SYN.)* control, direction, rule, command, authority.

governor *(SYN.)* controller, administrator, director, leader, manager.

gown *(SYN.)* garment, robe, frock, dress, costume, attire.

grab *(SYN.)* snatch, grip, clutch, seize, grasp, capture, pluck.

grace *(SYN.)* charm, beauty, handsomeness, loveliness, dignify, fairness, honor, distinguish, sympathy, attractiveness, elegance, clemency, excuse, pardon, thanks, blessing, prayer, pulchritude.
(ANT.) eyesore, homeliness, deformity, ugliness, disfigurement.

graceful *(SYN.)* elegant, fluid, natural, supple, beautiful, comely, flowing, lithe.
(ANT.) clumsy, awkward, gawky, ungainly, deformed.

gracious *(SYN.)* warm-hearted, pleasing, friendly, engaging, agreeable, kind, amiable, kindly, nice, good, courteous, polite, generous, good-natured.
(ANT.) surly, hateful, churlish, rude, disagreeable, impolite, thoughtless, discourteous, ill-natured.

grade *(SYN.)* kind, rank, elegance, denomination, sort, arrange, category, classify, rate, group, place, mark, incline, slope, excellence, caste, order.

gradual *(SYN.)* deliberate, sluggish, dawdling, laggard, slow, leisurely, moderate, easy, delaying.
(ANT.) quick, swift, fast, speedy, rapid.

graduate *(SYN.)* pass, finish, advance.

graft *(SYN.)* fraud, theft, cheating, bribery, dishonesty, transplant, corruption.

grain *(SYN.)* speck, particle, plant, bit, seed, temper, fiber, character, texture, markings, nature, tendency.

grand *(SYN.)* great, elaborate, splendid, royal, stately, noble, considerable, outstanding, distinguished, impressive, prominent, majestic, fine, dignified, large, main, principal.
(ANT.) unassuming, modest, insignificant, unimportant, humble.

grandeur *(SYN.)* resplendence, majesty, distinction, glory.

grandiose *(SYN.)* grand, lofty, magnificent, stately, noble, pompous, dignified, imposing, sublime, majestic.
(ANT.) lowly, ordinary, common, undignified, humble.

grandstand *(SYN.)* bleachers, gallery.

granite *(SYN.)* stone, rock.

grant *(SYN.)* confer, allocate, deal, divide, mete, appropriation, assign, benefaction, distribute, allowance, donate, award, mete out, deal out, consent, bestow, give, measure.
(ANT.) refuse, withhold, confiscate, keep, retain.

granular *(SYN.)* grainy, sandy, crumbly, rough, gritty.

graph *(SYN.)* design, plan, stratagem, draw up, chart, sketch, cabal, machination, outline, plot, scheme, diagram.

graphic *(SYN.)* vivid, lifelike, significant, meaningful, pictorial, descriptive, representative.

grapple *(SYN.)* grip, seize, clutch, clasp, grasp, fight, struggle.

grasp *(SYN.)* clutch, grip, seize, apprehend, capture, snare, hold, clasp, comprehend, reach, grab, understand, grapple, possession, control, domination, command, perceive, trap.

(ANT.) release, lose, throw, liberate.

grasping *(SYN.)* possessive, greedy, selfish, acquisitive, mercenary.

(ANT.) liberal, unselfish, generous.

grate *(SYN.)* file, pulverize, grind, scrape, scratch, scrape, annoy, irritate.

grateful *(SYN.)* beholden, obliged, appreciative, thankful, indebted.

(ANT.) ungrateful, unappreciative, grudging, thankless.

gratify *(SYN.)* charm, gladden, please, satisfy.

(ANT.) frustrate.

gratifying *(SYN.)* contentment, solace, relief, comfort, ease, succor, consolation, enjoyment.

(ANT.) suffering, torment, affliction, discomfort, torture, misery.

grating *(SYN.)* harsh, rugged, severe, stringent, coarse, gruff, jarring, rigorous, strict.

(ANT.) smooth, melodious, mild, gentle, soft.

gratis *(SYN.)* complimentary, free.

gratitude *(SYN.)* gratefulness, thankfulness, appreciation.

(ANT.) ungratefulness.

gratuity *(SYN.)* tip, bonus, gift, donation.

grave *(SYN.)* sober, grim, earnest, serious, important, momentous, sedate, solemn, somber, imposing, vital, essential, staid, consequential, thoughtful.

(ANT.) light, flighty, trivial, insignificant, unimportant, trifling, merry, gay, cheery, frivolous.

gravel *(SYN.)* stones, pebbles, grain.

gravitate *(SYN.)* incline, tend, lean, approach, toward.

gravity *(SYN.)* concern, importance, seriousness, pull, movement.

(ANT.) triviality.

graze *(SYN.)* scrape, feed, rub, brush, contact, skim.

grease *(SYN.)* fat, oil, lubrication.

greasy *(SYN.)* messy, buttery, waxy, fatty.

great *(SYN.)* large, numerous, eminent, illustrious, big, gigantic enormous, immense, vast, weighty, fine, important, countless, prominent, vital, huge, momentous, serious, famed, dignified, excellent, critical, renowned, majestic,

august, elevated, noble, grand.

(ANT.) minute, common, menial, ordinary, diminutive, small, paltry, unknown.

greed *(SYN.)* piggishness, lust, desire, greediness, avarice, covetousness.

(ANT.) unselfishness, selflessness, generosity.

greedy *(SYN.)* selfish, devouring, ravenous, avaricious, covetous, rapacious, gluttonous, insatiable, voracious.

(ANT.) full, generous, munificent, giving, satisfied.

green *(SYN.)* inexperienced, modern, novel, recent, further, naive, fresh, natural, raw, unsophisticated, undeveloped, immature, unripe, additional, brisk, artless.

(ANT.) hackneyed, musty, decayed, faded, stagnant.

greenhorn *(SYN.)* tenderfoot, beginner, apprentice, amateur, novice.

greenhouse *(SYN.)* hothouse.

greet *(SYN.)* hail, accost, meet, address, talk to, speak to, welcome, approach.

(ANT.) pass by, avoid.

gregarious *(SYN.)* outgoing, civil, affable, communicative, hospitable, sociable.

(ANT.) inhospitable, antisocial, disagreeable, hermitic.

grief *(SYN.)* misery, sadness, tribulation, affliction, heartache, woe, trial, anguish, mourning, distress, lamentation.

(ANT.) happiness, solace, consolation, comfort, joy.

grief-stricken *(SYN.)* heartsick, ravaged, devastated, wretched, forlorn, desolate, wretched.

(ANT.) joyous, blissful, content.

grievance *(SYN.)* injury, wrong, injustice, detriment, complaint, damage, prejudice, evil, objection, protest, accusation, harm.

(ANT.) improvement, benefit, repair.

grieve *(SYN.)* lament, brood over, mourn, weep, wail, sorrow, distress, bemoan, hurt, deplore.

(ANT.) revel, carouse, celebrate, rejoice, gladden, soothe.

grieved *(SYN.)* contrite, remorseful, beggarly, mean, pitiful, shabby, vile, sorrowful, pained, hurt, sorry, contemptible, worthless.

(ANT.) splendid, delighted, cheerful, impenitent, unrepentant.

grievous *(SYN.)* gross, awful, outrageous, shameful, lamentable, regrettable.
(ANT.) agreeable, comforting pleasurable.

grill *(SYN.)* cook, broil, question, interrogate, barbecue, grating, gridiron, cross-examine.

grim *(SYN.)* severe, harsh, strict, merciless, fierce, horrible, inflexible, adamant, ghastly, frightful, unyielding, rigid, stern.
(ANT.) pleasant, lenient, relaxed, amiable, congenial, smiling.

grimace *(SYN.)* expression, sneer, scowl, mope.

grimy *(SYN.)* unclean, grubby, soiled.

grin *(SYN.)* beam, smile, smirk.

grind *(SYN.)* mill, mash, powder, crush, crumble, pulverize, smooth, grate, sharpen, even.

grip *(SYN.)* catch, clutch, apprehend, trap, arrest, grasp, hold, bag, suitcase, lay hold of, clench, command, control, possession, domination, comprehension, understanding, seize.
(ANT.) release, liberate, lose, throw.

gripe *(SYN.)* protest, lament, complaint, grumbling.

grit *(SYN.)* rub, grind, grate, sand, gravel, pluck, courage, stamina.

groan *(SYN.)* sob, wail, howl, moan, whimper, wail, complain.

groggy *(SYN.)* dazed, dopy, stupefied, stunned, drugged, unsteady.
(ANT.) alert.

groom *(SYN.)* tend, tidy, preen, curry, spouse, consort.

groove *(SYN.)* furrow, channel, track, routine, slot, scratch.

groovy *(SYN.)* marvelous, delightful, wonderful.

grope *(SYN.)* fumble, feel around.

gross *(SYN.)* glaring, coarse, indelicate, obscene, bulky, great, total, whole, brutal, grievous, aggregate, earthy, rude, vulgar, entire, enormous, plain, crass, rough, large.
(ANT.) appealing, delicate, refined, proper, polite, cultivated, slight, comely, trivial, decent.

grotesque *(SYN.)* strange, weird, odd, incredible, fantastic, monstrous, absurd, freakish, bizarre, peculiar, deformed, disfigured, unnatural, queer.

grotto *(SYN.)* tunnel, cave, hole, cavern.

grouch *(SYN.)* protest, remonstrate, whine, complain, grumble, murmur, mope, mutter, repine.
(ANT.) praise, applaud, rejoice, approve.

grouchy *(SYN.)* cantankerous, grumpy, surly.
(ANT.) cheerful, contented, agreeable, pleasant.

ground *(SYN.)* foundation, presumption, surface, principle, underpinning, premise, base, bottom, fix, basis, soil, land, earth, set, root, support, establish, dirt, presupposition.
(ANT.) implication, superstructure, trimming, derivative.

groundless *(SYN.)* baseless, unfounded, unwarranted, needless.

grounds *(SYN.)* garden, lawns, dregs, foundation, leftovers, reason, sediment, cause, basis, premise, motive.

groundwork *(SYN.)* support, bottom, base, underpinning, premise, presupposition, principle, basis.
(ANT.) trimming, implication, derivative, superstructure.

group *(SYN.)* crowd, clock, party, troupe, swarm, bunch, brook, assembly, herd, band, mob, brood, class, throng, cluster, flock, lot, collection, pack, horde, gathering, aggregation.
(ANT.) disassemble.

grouse *(SYN.)* mutter, grumble, gripe, scold, growl, complain.

grovel *(SYN.)* creep, crawl, cower, cringe, slouch, stoop, scramble.

groveling *(SYN.)* dishonorable, lowly, sordid, vile, mean, abject, despicable, ignoble, menial, servile, vulgar, ignominious.
(ANT.) lofty, noble, esteemed, exalted, righteous.

grow *(SYN.)* extend, swell, advance, develop, enlarge, enlarge, germinate, mature, expand, flower, raise, become, cultivate, increase, distend.
(ANT.) wane, shrink, atrophy, decay, diminish, contract.

growl *(SYN.)* complain, snarl, grumble, gnarl, roar, clamor, bellow.

grown-up *(SYN.)* full-grown, adult, of age, mature, big, senior.
(ANT.) little, childish, budding, junior, juvenile.

growth *(SYN.)* expansion, development, unfolding, maturing, progress, elaboration, evolution.

(ANT.) degeneration, deterioration, curtailment, abbreviation, compression.

grub *(SYN.)* gouge, dig, scoop out, burrow, tunnel, excavate, plod, toil, drudge.

grubby *(SYN.)* unkempt, grimy, slovenly, dirty.

(ANT.) tidy, spruce, neat, clean, well-groomed.

grudge *(SYN.)* malevolence, malice, resentment, bitterness, spite, animosity, enmity, rancor, ill will.

(ANT.) kindness, love, benevolence, affection, good will, friendliness, toleration.

grudgingly *(SYN.)* reluctantly, unwillingly, under protest, involuntarily.

grueling *(SYN.)* taxing, exhausting, excruciating, trying, arduous, grinding, crushing.

(ANT.) effortless, easy, light, simple.

gruesome *(SYN.)* hideous, frightful, horrible, loathsome, ghastly, horrifying, grisly.

(ANT.) agreeable, soothing, delightful, charming.

gruff *(SYN.)* scratchy, crude, incomplete, unpolished, stormy, brusque, rude, rough, uncivil, churlish, violent, harsh, imperfect, craggy, irregular, deep, husky, approximate, tempestuous, blunt.

(ANT.) civil, courteous, polished, calm, even, sleek, smooth, finished, gentle, placid, pleasant, tranquil. **grumble** *(SYN.)* protest, mutter, complain.

grumpy *(SYN.)* ill-tempered, cranky, grouchy, surly, cross-grained, crabbed, fractious, pettish, disgruntled, moody.

(ANT.) winsome, amiable, pleasant, cheery.

guarantee *(SYN.)* bond, pledge, token, warrant, earnest, surety, bail, commitment, promise, secure, swear, assure, sponsor, certify, warranty, insure, endorse, security.

guarantor *(SYN.)* voucher, sponsor, warrantor, signatory, underwriter, surety, seconder.

guaranty *(SYN.)* warranty, token, deposit, earnest, pledge, gage, collateral, stake.

guard *(SYN.)* protect, shield, veil, cloak, conceal, disguise, envelop, preserve, hide, defend, cover, sentry, protector, shroud, curtain.

(ANT.) unveil, expose, ignore, neglect, bare, reveal, disregard, divulge.

guarded *(SYN.)* discreet, cautious, careful.

(ANT.) audacious, reckless, indiscreet, careless.

guardian *(SYN.)* curator, keeper, protector, custodian, patron, champion.

guess *(SYN.)* estimate, suppose, think, assume, reason, believe, reckon, speculate, notion, surmise, hypothesis, imagine, consider, opinion, conjecture.

(ANT.) know.

guest *(SYN.)* caller, client, customer, patient, visitor, company.

(ANT.) host.

guide *(SYN.)* manage, supervise, conduct, direct, lead, steer, escort, pilot, show, squire, usher, control, affect, influence, regulate.

(ANT.) follower, follow.

guild *(SYN.)* association, union, society.

guile *(SYN.)* deceitfulness, fraud, wiliness, trick, deceit, chicanery, cunning, deception, craftiness, sham, sneakiness, cheat.

(ANT.) sincerity, openness, honesty, truthfulness, candor, frankness.

guilt *(SYN.)* sin, blame, fault, offense.

guilty *(SYN.)* culpable, to blame, responsible, at fault, criminal, blameworthy.

(ANT.) blameless, innocent, guiltless.

guise *(SYN.)* aspect, pretense, mien, look, air, advent, apparition, appearance.

gulch *(SYN.)* gorge, valley, gully, ravine.

gullible *(SYN.)* trustful, naive, innocent, deceivable, unsuspicious, believing.

(ANT.) skeptical, sophisticated.

gully *(SYN.)* ditch, gorge, ravine, valley, gulch, gulf.

gulp *(SYN.)* devour, swallow, gasp, repress, choke.

gun *(SYN.)* fire, shoot, weapon, discharge, pistol, firearm, revolver.

gust *(SYN.)* blast, wind, outbreak, outburst, eruption.

gutter *(SYN.)* ditch, groove, drain, channel, trench, sewer, trough.

gymnasium *(SYN.)* playground, arena, court, athletic field.

gymnastics *(SYN.)* drill, exercise, acrobatics, calisthenics.

gyp *(SYN.)* swindle, cheat, defraud.

gypsy *(SYN.)* nomad.

habit *(SYN.)* usage, routine, compulsion, use, wont, custom, disposition, practice, addiction, fashion.

habitation *(SYN.)* abode, domicile, lodgings, dwelling, home.

habitual *(SYN.)* general, usual, common, frequent, persistent, customary, routine, regular, often.

(ANT.) solitary, unique, exceptional, occasional, unusual, scanty, rare.

habituated *(SYN.)* used, accustomed, adapted, acclimated, comfortable, familiarized, addicted, settled.

hack *(SYN.)* cleave, chop, slash, hew, slice, pick, sever, mangle.

hag *(SYN.)* beldam, crone, vixen, granny, ogress, harridan, virage.

haggard *(SYN.)* drawn, careworn, debilitated, spent, gaunt, worn.

(ANT.) bright, fresh, animated.

haggle *(SYN.)* dicker, bargain.

hail *(SYN.)* welcome, approach, accost, speak to, address, greet.

(ANT.) pass by, avoid.

hair-do *(SYN.)* hairstyle, coiffure, haircut.

hairdresser *(SYN.)* beautician, barber.

hairless *(SYN.)* shorn, glabrous, bald, baldpated, depilitated.

(ANT.) hirsute, hairy, unshaven.

hairy *(SYN.)* bearded, shaggy, hirsute, bewhiskered.

hale *(SYN.)* robust, well, wholesome, hearty, healthy, sound, strong, vigorous, salubrious.

(ANT.) noxious, frail, diseased, delicate, infirm, injurious.

half-baked *(SYN.)* crude, premature, makeshift, illogical, shallow.

half-hearted *(SYN.)* uncaring, indifferent, unenthusiastic, cool.

(ANT.) eager, enthusiastic, earnest.

half-wit *(SYN.)* dope, simpleton, nitwit, dunce, idiot, fool.

hall *(SYN.)* corridor, lobby, passage, hallway, vestibule, foyer.

hallow *(SYN.)* glorify, exalt, dignify, aggrandize, consecrate, elevate, ennoble, raise, erect.

(ANT.) dishonor, humiliate, debase, degrade.

hallowed *(SYN.)* holy, sacred, sacrosanct, blessed, divine.

hallucination *(SYN.)* fantasy, mirage, dream, vision, phantasm, appearance, aberration, illusion.

halt *(SYN.)* impede, obstruct, terminate, stop, hinder, desist, check, arrest, abstain, discontinue, hold, end, cork, interrupt, bar, cease.

(ANT.) start, begin, proceed, speed, beginning, promote.

halting *(SYN.)* imperfect, awkward, stuttering, faltering, hobbling, doubtful, limping, wavering.

(ANT.) decisive, confident, smooth, graceful, facile.

hammer *(SYN.)* beat, bang, whack, pound, batter, drive, tap, cudgel.

hamper *(SYN.)* prevent, impede, thwart, restrain, hinder, obstruct.

(ANT.) help, assist, expedite, encourage, facilitate.

hamstrung *(SYN.)* disabled, helpless, paralyzed.

hand *(SYN.)* assistant, helper, support, aid, farmhand, laborer.

handicap *(SYN.)* retribution, penalty, disadvantage, forfeiture, hindrance, chastisement.

(ANT.) reward, pardon, compensation, remuneration.

handily *(SYN.)* readily, skillfully, easily, dexterously, smoothly, adroitly, deftly.

handkerchief *(SYN.)* bandanna, kerchief, scarf.

handle *(SYN.)* hold, touch, finger, clutch, grip, manipulate, feel, grasp, control, oversee, direct, treat, steer, supervise, run, regulate.

hand out *(SYN.)* disburse, distribute, deal, mete, circulate.

hand over *(SYN.)* release, surrender, deliver, yield, present, fork over.

handsome *(SYN.)* lovely, pretty, fair, comely, beautiful, charming, elegant, good-looking, large, generous, liberal, beauteous, fine.

(ANT.) repulsive, ugly, unattractive, stingy, small, mean, petty, unsightly, meager, homely, foul, hideous.

handy *(SYN.)* suitable, adapted, appropriate, favorable, fitting, near, ready, close, nearby, clever, helpful, useful, timely, accessible.

(ANT.) inopportune, troublesome,

awkward, inconvenient.

hang *(SYN.)* drape, hover, dangle, suspend, kill, sag, execute, lynch.

hang in *(SYN.)* continue, endure, remain, perservere, resist, persist.

hang-up *(SYN.)* inhibition, difficulty, snag, hindrance, block.

hanker *(SYN.)* wish, yearn, long, desire, pine, thirst, covet.

haphazard *(SYN.)* aimless, random, purposeless, casual, indiscriminate, accidental.

(ANT.) determined, planned, designed, deliberate.

hapless *(SYN.)* ill-fated, unfortunate, jinxed, luckless, wretched.

happen *(SYN.)* occur, take place, bechance, betide, transpire, come to pass, chance, befall.

happening *(SYN.)* episode, event, scene, incident, affair, experience, phenomenon, transaction.

happiness *(SYN.)* pleasure, gladness, delight, beatitude, bliss, contentment, satisfaction, joy, joyousness, blessedness, joyfulness, felicity, elation, well-being.

(ANT.) sadness, sorrow, despair, misery, grief.

happy *(SYN.)* gay, joyous, cheerful, fortunate, glad, merry, contented, satisfied, lucky, blessed, pleased, opportune, delighted.

(ANT.) gloomy, morose, sad, sorrowful, miserable, inconvenient, unlucky, depressed, blue.

happy-go-lucky *(SYN.)* easygoing, carefree, unconcerned.

(ANT.) prudent, responsible, concerned.

harangue *(SYN.)* oration, diatribe, lecture, tirade, exhortation.

harass *(SYN.)* badger, irritate, molest, pester, taunt, torment, provoke, tantalize, worry, aggravate, annoy, nag, plague, vex.

(ANT.) please, soothe, comfort, delight, gratify.

harbinger *(SYN.)* sign, messenger, proclaim, forerunner, herald.

harbor *(SYN.)* haven, port, anchorage, cherish, entertain, protect, shelter.

hard *(SYN.)* difficult, burdensome,

arduous, rigid, puzzling, cruel, strict, unfeeling, severe, stern, impenetrable, compact, tough, solid, onerous, rigorous, firm, intricate, harsh, perplexing.

(ANT.) fluid, brittle, effortless, gentle, tender, easy, simple, plastic, soft, lenient, flabby, elastic.

hard-boiled *(SYN.)* unsympathetic, tough, harsh, unsentimental.

harden *(SYN.)* petrify, solidify.

(ANT.) loose, soften.

hardheaded *(SYN.)* stubborn, obstinate, unyielding, headstrong.

hardhearted *(SYN.)* merciless, hard, unmerciful, callous, pitiless, ruthless.

hardly *(SYN.)* barely, scarcely.

hard-nosed *(SYN.)* shrewd, tough, practical.

hardship *(SYN.)* ordeal, test, effort, affliction, misfortune, trouble, experiment, proof, essay, misery, examination, difficulty, tribulation.

(ANT.) consolation, alleviation.

hardy *(SYN.)* sturdy, strong, tough, vigorous.

(ANT.) frail, decrepit, feeble, weak, fragile.

harm *(SYN.)* hurt, mischief, misfortune, mishap, damage, wickedness, cripple, injury, evil, detriment, ill, infliction, wrong.

(ANT.) favor, kindness, benefit, boon.

harmful *(SYN.)* damaging, injurious, mischievous, detrimental, hurtful, deleterious.

(ANT.) helpful, salutary, profitable,, advantageous, beneficial.

harmless *(SYN.)* protected, secure, snag, dependable, certain, painless, innocent, trustworthy.

(ANT.) perilous, hazardous, insecure, dangerous, unsafe.

harmonious *(SYN.)* tuneful, melodious, congenial, amicable.

(ANT.) dissonant, discordant, disagreeable.

harmony *(SYN.)* unison, bargain, contract, stipulation, pact, agreement, accordance, concord, accord, understanding, unity, coincidence.

(ANT.) discord, dissension, dif-

ference, variance, disagreement.

harness *(SYN.)* control, yoke.

harry *(SYN.)* vex, pester, harass, bother, plague.

harsh *(SYN.)* jarring, gruff, rugged, severe, stringent, blunt, grating, unpleasant, tough, stern, strict, unkind, rigorous, cruel, coarse.

(ANT.) smooth, soft, gentle, melodious, soothing, easy, mild.

harvest *(SYN.)* reap, gather, produce, yield, crop, gain, acquire, fruit, result, reaping, product, proceeds, glean, garner.

(ANT.) plant, squander, lose, sow.

haste *(SYN.)* speed, hurry, rush, rapidity, flurry, scramble.

(ANT.) sloth, sluggishness.

hasten *(SYN.)* hurry, sprint, quicken, rush, precipitate, accelerate, scurry, run, scamper, dispatch, press, urge, dash, expedite, speed.

(ANT.) retard, tarry, detain, linger, dawdle, delay, hinder.

hasty *(SYN.)* quick, swift, irascible, lively, nimble, brisk, active, speedy, impatient, testy, sharp, fast, rapid.

(ANT.) slow, dull, sluggish.

hat *(SYN.)* helmet, bonnet.

hatch *(SYN.)* breed, incubate, brood.

hate *(SYN.)* loathe, detest, despise, disfavor, hatred, abhorrence, abominate, abhor, dislike.

(ANT.) love, cherish, approve, admire, like.

hateful *(SYN.)* loathsome, detestable, offensive.

(ANT.) likable, loving, admirable.

hatred *(SYN.)* detestation, dislike, malevolence, enmity, rancor, ill will, loathing, hate, hostility, abhorrence, aversion, animosity.

(ANT.) friendship, love, affection, attraction.

haughty *(SYN.)* proud, stately, vainglorious, arrogant, disdainful, overbearing, supercilious, vain.

(ANT.) meek, ashamed, lowly, humble.

haul *(SYN.)* draw, pull, drag, tow.

have *(SYN.)* own, possess, seize, hold, control, occupy, acquire, undergo, maintain, experience, receive, gain, affect, include, con-

tain, get, take, obtain.

(ANT.) surrender, abandon, renounce, lose.

havoc *(SYN.)* devastation, ruin, destruction.

hazard *(SYN.)* peril, chance, dare, risk, offer, conjecture, jeopardy, danger.

(ANT.) safety, defense, protection, immunity.

hazardous *(SYN.)* perilous, precarious, threatening, unsafe, dangerous, critical, menacing, risky.

(ANT.) protected, secure, safe.

hazy *(SYN.)* uncertain, unclear, ambiguous, dim, obscure, undetermined, vague, unsettled, indefinite.

(ANT.) specific, clear, lucid, precise, explicit.

head *(SYN.)* leader, summit, top, culmination, director, chief, master, commander, supervisor, start, source, crest, beginning, crisis.

(ANT.) foot, base, bottom, follower, subordinate, underling.

headstrong *(SYN.)* obstinate, stubborn, willful.

(ANT.) easygoing, amenable.

headway *(SYN.)* movement, progress.

heady *(SYN.)* thrilling, intoxicating, exciting, electrifying.

heal *(SYN.)* restore, cure.

healthy *(SYN.)* wholesome, hale, robust, sound, well, vigorous, strong, hearty, healthful, hygienic, salubrious, salutary.

(ANT.) noxious, diseased, unhealthy, delicate, frail, infirm, injurious.

heap *(SYN.)* collection, mound, increase, store, stack, pile, gather, accumulate, amass, accrue, accumulation, collect.

(ANT.) dissipate, scatter, waste, diminish, disperse.

hear *(SYN.)* heed, listen, detect, harken, perceive, regard.

heart *(SYN.)* middle, center, sympathy, nucleus, midpoint, sentiment, core, feeling, midst.

(ANT.) outskirts, periphery, border, rim, boundary.

heartache *(SYN.)* anguish, mourning, sadness, sorrow, affliction, distress,

grief, lamentation, tribulation.
(ANT.) happiness, joy, solace, comfort, consolation.

heartbroken *(SYN.)* distressed, forlorn, mean, paltry, worthless, contemptible, wretched, crestfallen, disconsolate, downhearted, comfortless, brokenhearted, low.
(ANT.) noble, fortunate, contented, significant.

hearten *(SYN.)* encourage, favor, impel, urge, promote, sanction, animate, cheer, exhilarate, cheer.
(ANT.) deter, dissuade, deject, discourage, dispirit.

heartless *(SYN.)* mean, cruel, ruthless, hardhearted, pitiless.
(ANT.) sympathetic, kind.

heart-rending *(SYN.)* heartbreaking, depressing, agonizing.

hearty *(SYN.)* warm, earnest, ardent, cordial, sincere, gracious, sociable.
(ANT.) taciturn, aloof, cool, reserved.

heat *(SYN.)* hotness, warmth, temperature, passion, ardor, zeal, inflame, cook, excitement, warm.
(ANT.) cool, chill, coolness, freeze, coldness, chilliness, iciness, cold.

heated *(SYN.)* vehement, fiery, intense, passionate.

heave *(SYN.)* boost, hoist, raise.

heaven *(SYN.)* empyrean, paradise.

heavenly *(SYN.)* superhuman, godlike, blissful, saintly, holy, divine, celestial, angelic, blessed.
(ANT.) wicked, mundane, profane, blasphemous, diabolical.

heavy *(SYN.)* weighty, massive, gloomy, serious, ponderous, cumbersome, trying, burdensome, harsh, grave, intense, dull, grievous, concentrated, severe, oppressive, sluggish.
(ANT.) brisk, light, animated.

heckle *(SYN.)* torment, harass, tease, hector, harry.

heed *(SYN.)* care, alertness, circumspection, mindfulness, consider, watchfulness, reflection, study, attention, notice, regard, obey, ponder, respect, meditate, mind, observe, deliberate, examine, contemplate, weigh, esteem, applica-

tion.
(ANT.) negligence, oversight, over look, neglect, ignore, disregard, indifference, omission.

heedless *(SYN.)* sightless, headlong, rash, unmindful, deaf, unseeing, oblivious, ignorant, inattentive, disregardful, blind.
(ANT.) perceiving, sensible, aware, calculated, discerning.

height *(SYN.)* zenith, peak, summit, tallness, mountain, acme, apex, elevation, altitude, prominence, maximum, pinnacle, culmination.
(ANT.) base, depth, anticlimax.

heighten *(SYN.)* increase, magnify, annoy, chafe, intensify, amplify, aggravate, provoke, irritate, concentrate, nettle.
(ANT.) soothe, mitigate, palliate, soften, appease.

heinous *(SYN.)* abominable, grievous, atrocious.

hello *(SYN.)* greeting, good evening, good afternoon, good morning.
(ANT.) farewell, good-bye, so long.

help *(SYN.)* assist, support, promote, relieve, abet, succor, back, uphold, further, remedy, encourage, aid, facilitate, mitigate.
(ANT.) afflict, thwart, resist, hinder, impede.

helper *(SYN.)* aide, assistant, supporter.

helpful *(SYN.)* beneficial, serviceable, wholesome, useful, profitable, advantageous, good, salutary.
(ANT.) harmful, injurious, useless, worthless, destructive, deleterious, detrimental.

helpfulness *(SYN.)* assistance, cooperation, usefulness, serviceability, kindness, neighborliness, willingness, collaboration, supportiveness, readiness.
(ANT.) antagonism, hostility, opposition.

helpless *(SYN.)* weak, feeble, dependent, disabled, inept, unresourceful, incapable, incompetent.
(ANT.) resourceful, competent, enterprising.

helplessness *(SYN.)* impotence,

feebleness, weakness, incapacity, ineptitude, invalidism, shiftless, awkwardness.

(ANT.) power, strength, might, potency.

helter-skelter *(SYN.)* haphazardly, chaotically, irregularly.

hem *(SYN.)* bottom, border, edge, rim, margin, pale, verge, flounce, boundary, fringe, brim, fence, hedge, frame.

hem in *(SYN.)* enclose, shut in, confine, restrict, limit.

hence *(SYN.)* consequently, thence, therefore, so, accordingly.

herald *(SYN.)* harbinger, crier, envoy, forerunner, precursor, augury, forecast.

herculean *(SYN.)* demanding, heroic, titanic, mighty, prodigious, laborious, arduous, overwhelming, backbreaking.

herd *(SYN.)* group, pack, drove, crowd, flock, gather.

heretic *(SYN.)* nonconformist, sectarian, unbeliever, sectary, schismatic, apostate, dissenter.

heritage *(SYN.)* birthright, legacy, patrimony, inheritance.

hermit *(SYN.)* recluse, anchorite, eremite.

hero *(SYN.)* paladin, champion, idol.

heroic *(SYN.)* bold, courageous, fearless, gallant, valiant, valorous, brave, chivalrous, adventurous, dauntless, intrepid, magnanimous.

(ANT.) fearful, weak, cringing, timid, cowardly.

heroism *(SYN.)* valor, bravery, gallant, dauntless, bold, courageous, fearless.

hesitant *(SYN.)* reluctant, unwilling, disinclined, loath, slow, averse.

(ANT.) willing, inclined, eager, ready, disposed.

hesitate *(SYN.)* falter, waver, pause, doubt, demur, delay, vacillate, wait, stammer, stutter, scruple.

(ANT.) proceed, resolve, continue, decide, persevere.

hesitation *(SYN.)* distrust, scruple, suspense, uncertainty, unbelief, ambiguity, doubt, incredulity, skepticism.

(ANT.) determination, belief, certainty, faith, conviction.

hidden *(SYN.)* undeveloped, unseen dormant, concealed, quiescent, latent, potential, inactive.

(ANT.) visible, explicit, conspicuous, evident.

hide *(SYN.)* disguise, mask, suppress, withhold, veil, cloak, conceal, screen, camouflage, shroud, pelt, skin, leather, cover.

(ANT.) reveal, show, expose, disclose, uncover, divulge.

hideous *(SYN.)* frightful, ugly, shocking, frightening, horrible, terrible, horrifying, terrifying, grisly, gross.

(ANT.) lovely, beautiful, beauteous.

high *(SYN.)* tall, eminent, exalted, elevated, high-pitched, sharp, lofty, proud, shrill, raised, strident, prominent, important, powerful, expensive, dear, high-priced, costly, grave, serious, extreme, towering.

(ANT.) low, mean, tiny, stunted, short, base, lowly, deep, insignificant, unimportant, inexpensive, reasonable, trivial, petty, small.

highly *(SYN.)* extremely, very, extraordinarily, exceedingly.

high-minded *(SYN.)* lofty, noble, honorable.

(ANT.) dishonorable, base.

high-priced *(SYN.)* dear, expensive, costly.

(ANT.) economical, cheap.

high-strung *(SYN.)* nervous, tense, wrought-up, intense.

(ANT.) calm.

highway *(SYN.)* parkway, speedway, turnpike, superhighway, freeway.

hilarious *(SYN.)* funny, side-splitting, hysterical.

(ANT.) depressing, sad.

hinder *(SYN.)* hamper, impede, block, retard, stop, resist, thwart, obstruct, check, prevent, interrupt, delay, slow, restrain.

(ANT.) promote, further, assist, expedite, advance, facilitate.

hindrance *(SYN.)* interruption, delay, interference, obstruction, obstacle, barrier.

hinge *(SYN.)* rely, depend, pivot.

hint *(SYN.)* reminder, allusion, suggestion, clue, tip, taste, whisper, implication, intimate, suspicion, mention, insinuation.

(ANT.) declaration, affirmation, statement.

hire *(SYN.)* employ, occupy, devote, apply, enlist, lease, rent, charter, rental, busy, engage, utilize, retain, let, avail.

(ANT.) reject, banish, discard, fire, dismiss, discharge.

history *(SYN.)* narration, relation, computation, record, account, chronicle, detail, description, narrative, annal, tale, recital.

(ANT.) confusion, misrepresentation, distortion, caricature.

hit *(SYN.)* knock, pound, strike, hurt, pummel, beat, come upon, find, discover, blow, smite.

hitch *(SYN.)* tether, fasten, harness, interruption, hindrance, interference.

hoard *(SYN.)* amass, increase, accumulate, gather, save, secret, store, cache, store, accrue, heap.

(ANT.) dissipate, scatter, waste, diminish, squander, spend, disperse.

hoarse *(SYN.)* deep, rough, husky, raucous, grating, harsh.

(ANT.) clear.

hoax *(SYN.)* ploy, ruse, wile, device, cheat, deception, antic, imposture, stratagem, stunt, guile, fraud.

(ANT.) openness, sincerity, candor, exposure, honesty.

hobbling *(SYN.)* deformed, crippled, halt, lame, unconvincing, unsatisfactory, defective, feeble, disabled maimed, weak.

(ANT.) robust, vigorous, agile, sound, athletic.

hobby *(SYN.)* diversion, pastime, avocation.

(ANT.) vocation, profession.

hobo *(SYN.)* derelict, vagrant, vagabond, tramp.

hoist *(SYN.)* heave, lift, elevate, raise, crane, elevator, derrick.

hold *(SYN.)* grasp, occupy, possess, curb, contain, stow, carry, adhere, have, clutch, keep, maintain, clasp, grip, retain, detain, accommodate, restrain, observe, conduct, check, support.

(ANT.) vacate, relinquish, surrender, abandon.

holdup *(SYN.)* heist, robbery, stickup, delay, interruption, slowdown.

hole *(SYN.)* cavity, void, pore, opening, abyss, chasm, gulf, aperture, tear, pit, burrow, lair, den, gap.

hollow *(SYN.)* unfilled, vacant, vain, meaningless, flimsy, false, hole, cavity, depression, hypocritical, depressed, empty, pit, insincere.

(ANT.) sound, solid, genuine, sincere, full.

holocaust *(SYN.)* fire, burning, extermination, butchery, disaster, massacre.

holy *(SYN.)* devout, divine, blessed, consecrated, sacred, spiritual, pious, sainted, religious, saintly, hallowed.

(ANT.) worldly, sacrilegious, unconsecrated, evil, profane, secular.

homage *(SYN.)* reverence, honor, respect.

home *(SYN.)* dwelling, abode, residence, seat, quarters, hearth, domicile, family, house, habitat.

homely *(SYN.)* uncommonly, disagreeable, ill-natured, ugly, vicious, plain, hideous, unattractive, deformed, surly, repellent, spiteful.

(ANT.) fair, handsome, pretty, attractive, comely, beautiful.

homesick *(SYN.)* lonely, nostalgic.

honest *(SYN.)* sincere, trustworthy, truthful, fair, ingenuous, candid, conscientious, moral, upright, open, frank, forthright, honorable, just, straightfoward.

(ANT.) fraudulent, tricky, deceitful, dishonest, lying.

honesty *(SYN.)* frankness, openness, fairness, sincerity, trustworthiness, justice, candor, honor, integrity, responsibility, uprightness.

(ANT.) deceit, dishonesty, trickery, fraud, cheating.

honor *(SYN.)* esteem, praise, worship, admiration, homage, glory, respect, admire, heed, dignity, revere, value, deference, venerate, reverence, consider, distinction, character, principle, uprightness, honesty, adoration.

(ANT.) scorn, dishonor, despise, neglect, abuse, shame, reproach, disdain, contempt, derision, disgrace.

honorable (SYN.) fair, noble, creditable, proper, reputable, honest, admirable, true, trusty, eminent, respectable, esteemed, just, famed, illustrious, noble, virtuous, upright.

(ANT.) infamous, disgraceful, shameful, dishonorable, ignominious.

honorary (SYN.) gratuitous, complimentary.

hoodlum (SYN.) crook, gangster, criminal, hooligan, mobster.

hop (SYN.) jump, leap.

hope (SYN.) expectation, faith, optimism, anticipation, expectancy, confidence, desire, trust.

(ANT.) pessimism, despair, despondency.

hopeful (SYN.) optimistic, confident.

(ANT.) despairing, hopeless.

hopeless (SYN.) desperate, despairing, forlorn, fatal, incurable, disastrous.

(ANT.) promising, hopeful.

hopelessness (SYN,) gloom, discouragement, depression, pessimism, despondency.

(ANT.) hope, optimism, confidence, elation.

horde (SYN.) host, masses, press, rabble, swarm, throng, bevy, crush, mob, multitude, crowd, populace.

horizontal (SYN.) even, level, plane, flat, straight, sideways.

(ANT.) upright, vertical.

horrendous (SYN.) awful, horrifying, terrible, dreadful, horrid, ghastly.

(ANT.) splendid, wonderful.

horrible (SYN.) awful, dire, ghastly, horrid, terrible, repulsive, frightful, appalling, horrifying, dreadful, ghastly, fearful.

(ANT.) enjoyable, enchanting, beautiful, lovely, fascinating.

horrid (SYN.) repulsive, terrible, appalling, dire, awful, frightful, fearful, shocking, horrible, horrifying, horrid, ghastly, dreadful, revolting, hideous.

(ANT.) fascinating, enchanting, enjoyable, lovely, beautiful.

horror (SYN.) dread, awe, hatred, loathing, foreboding, alarm, apprehension, aversion, terror.

(ANT.) courage, boldness, assurance, confidence.

horseplay (SYN.) tomfoolery, clowning, shenanigans.

hospital (SYN.) infirmary, clinic, sanatorium, rest home, sanitarium.

hospitality (SYN.) warmth, liberality, generosity, graciousness, welcome.

hostile (SYN.) unfriendly, opposed, antagonistic, inimical, adverse, warlike.

(ANT.) friendly, favorable, amicable, cordial.

hostility (SYN.) grudge, hatred, rancor, spite, bitterness, enmity, malevolence.

(ANT.) love, friendliness, good will.

hot (SYN.) scorching, fervent, hotblooded, passionate, peppery, ardent, burning, fiery, impetuous, scalding, heated, sizzling, blazing, frying, roasting, warm, intense, torrid, pungent.

(ANT.) indifferent, apathetic, impassive, passionless, bland, frigid, cold, freezing, cool, phlegmatic.

hot air (SYN.) bombast, blather, jabber, gabble.

hotbed (SYN.) sink, nest, well, den, nursery, cradle, source, incubator, seedbed.

hot-blooded (SYN.) passionate, ardent, excitable, wild, fervent, fiery, impetuous, rash, brash, intense, impulsive.

(ANT.) stolid, impassive, cold, staid.

hotel (SYN.) hostel, motel, inn, hostelry.

hotheaded (SYN.) rash, touchy, short-tempered, reckless, unruly.

(ANT.) levelheaded, cool-headed, calm.

hound (SYN.) harry, pursue, pester, harass.

hourly (SYN.) frequently, steadily, constantly, unfailingly, periodically, perpetually, ceaselessly, continually, incessantly.

(ANT.) occasionally, seldom.

house *(SYN.)* building, residence, abode, dwelling.

housebreaker *(SYN.)* robber, thief, prowler, cracksman, burglar.

household *(SYN.)* manage, family, home.

householder *(SYN.)* homeowner, occupant.

housing *(SYN.)* lodgings, shelter, dwelling, lodgment, case, casing, quarters, domicile, enclosure, console, bracket.

hovel *(SYN.)* cabin, hut, sty, shack, hole, shed.

hover *(SYN.)* hang, drift, poise, stand by, linger, impend, waver, hand around.

however *(SYN.)* notwithstanding, still, nevertheless, but, yet.

howl *(SYN.)* bellow, yowl, wail, yell, cry.

hub *(SYN.)* pivot, center, core, heart, axis, basis, focus, nucleus.

hubbub *(SYN.)* uproar, tumult, commotion, clamor, bustle, turmoil, racket, confusion.

(ANT.) peacefulness, stillness, silence, quiet, quiescence.

huckster *(SYN)* peddler, adman, hawker, salesman, pitchman.

huddle *(SYN.)* mass, herd, bunch, crowd, cram, gather, shove, pack, flock, ball, conglomeration, knot, clump, medley, scrum.

hue *(SYN.)* pigment, tint, shade, dye, complexion, paint, stain, color, tone, tincture.

(ANT.) transparency, achromatism, paleness.

huffy *(SYN.)* sensitive, vulnerable, testy, offended, thin-skinned, touchy, irascible, cross, offended.

(ANT.) tough, placid, stolid, impassive.

hug *(SYN.)* embrace, coddle, caress, kiss, pet, press, clasp, fondle, cuddle.

(ANT.) tease, vex, spurn, buffet, annoy.

huge *(SYN.)* great, immense, vast, ample, big, capacious, extensive, gigantic, enormous, vast, tremendous, large, wide, colossal.

(ANT.) short, small, mean, little, tiny.

hulking *(SYN.)* massive, awkward, bulky, ponderous, unwieldy, overgrown, lumpish, oafish.

hullabaloo *(SYN.)* clamor, uproar, din, racket, tumult, hubbub, commotion, noise, blare.

(ANT.) calm, peace, silence.

hum *(SYN.)* whir, buzz, whizz, purr, croon, murmur, intone, vibrate.

human *(SYN.)* manlike, hominid, mortal, fleshly, individual, person, tellurian.

humane *(SYN.)* lenient, tender, tolerant, compassionate, clement, forgiving, kind, forbearing, thoughtful, kindhearted, kindly, gentle, merciful.

(ANT.) remorseless, cruel, heartless, pitiless, unfeeling, brutal.

humanist *(SYN.)* scholar, sage, classicist, savant.

humanitarian *(SYN.)* benefactor, philanthropist.

humanitarianism *(SYN.)* good will, beneficence, philanthropy, welfarism, humanism.

humanity *(SYN.)* generosity, magnanimity, tenderness, altruism, beneficence, kindness, charity, philanthropy.

(ANT.) selfishness, unkindness, cruelty, inhumanity.

humble *(SYN.)* modest, crush, mortify, simple, shame, subdue, meek, abase, break, plain, submissive, compliant, unpretentious, unassuming, abash, unostentatious, lowly, polite, courteous, unpretending, degrade.

(ANT.) praise, arrogant, exalt, illustrious, boastful, honor, elevate.

humbly *(SYN.)* deferentially, meekly, respectfully, unassumingly, diffidently, modestly, subserviently, submissively.

(ANT.) insolently, proudly, grandly, arrogantly.

humbug *(SYN.)* drivel, gammon, bosh, nonsense, rubbish, inanity.

humdrum *(SYN.)* commonplace, prosy, mundane, insipid, tedious, routine, dull, boring.

(ANT.) interesting, stimulating, ar-

resting, striking, exciting.

humid *(SYN.)* moist, damp, misty, muggy, wet, watery, vaporous.

(ANT.) parched, dry, desiccated.

humiliate *(SYN.)* corrupt, defile, depress, pervert, abase, degrade, disgrace, adulterate, humble, shame, lower, impair, deprave, depress.

(ANT.) restore, raise, enhance, improve, vitalize.

humiliation *(SYN.)* chagrin, dishonor, ignominy, scandal, abasement, mortification, disrepute, odium, disgrace, shame.

(ANT.) honor, praise, glory, dignity, renown.

humor *(SYN.)* jocularity, wit, temperament, sarcasm, irony, joking, amusement, facetiousness, joke, disposition, waggery, fun, clowning, satire, mood.

(ANT.) sorrow, gravity, seriousness.

humorous *(SYN.)* funny, ludicrous, witty, curious, queer, amusing, comical, farcical, laughable, droll.

(ANT.) sober, unfunny, melancholy, serious, sad, solemn.

hunger *(SYN.)* desire, longing, inclination, relish, stomach, zest, craving, liking, passion.

(ANT.) satiety, repugnance, disgust, distaste, renunciation.

hungry *(SYN.)* famished, thirsting, craving, avid, longing, starved, ravenous.

(ANT.) gorged, satisfied, full, sated.

hunt *(SYN.)* pursuit, investigation, examination, inquiry, pursue, track.

(ANT.) cession, abandonment.

hurl *(SYN.)* throw, cast, propel, fling, toss, pitch, thrust.

(ANT.) retain, pull, draw, haul, hold.

hurried *(SYN.)* rushed, hasty, swift, headlong, slipshod, careless, impulsive, superficial.

(ANT.) deliberate, slow, dilatory, thorough, prolonged.

hurry *(SYN.)* quicken, speed, ado, rush, accelerate, run, hasten, race, urge, bustle, expedite, precipitate.

(ANT.) retard, tarry, hinder, linger, dawdle, delay, hinder.

hurt *(SYN.)* damage, harm, grievance, detriment, pain, injustice, injure, abuse, distress, disfigured, mar, afflict, spoil, affront, insult.

(ANT.) improvement, repair, compliment, help, praise, benefit.

hurtle *(SYN.)* charge, collide, rush, crash, lunge, bump, fling.

husband *(SYN.)* spouse, mate.

hush *(SYN.)* quiet, silence, still.

husk *(SYN.)* shell, hull, pod, skin, covering, crust, bark.

husky *(SYN.)* strong, brawny, strapping, muscular.

(ANT.) feeble, weak.

hustle *(SYN.)* hasten, run, race, hurry, speed.

hut *(SYN.)* cottage, shanty, cabin, shed.

hutch *(SYN.)* box, chest, locker, trunk, coffer, bin.

hybrid *(SYN.)* mule, mixture, crossbreed, cross, mongrel, mutt.

hygiene *(SYN.)* cleanliness, sanitation, health, prophylaxis.

hygienic *(SYN.)* robust, strong, well, wholesome, hale, healthy, sound.

(ANT.) frail, noxious, infirm, delicate, diseased, injurious.

hyperbole *(SYN.)* puffery, exaggeration, embellishment, overstatement.

hypercritical *(SYN.)* faultfinding, captious, censorious, finicky, exacting, carping, querulous, nagging, finical, hairsplitting.

(ANT.) lax, easygoing, indulgent, lenient, tolerant.

hypnotic *(SYN.)* soothing, opiate, sedative, soporific, entrancing, spellbinding, arresting, charming.

hypnotize *(SYN.)* entrance, dazzle, mesmerize, fascinate, spellbind.

hypocrisy *(SYN.)* pretense, deceit, dissembling, fakery, feigning, pharisaism, sanctimony, cant.

(ANT.) openness, candor, truth, directness, honesty, frankness.

hypocrite *(SYN.)* cheat, deceiver, pretender, dissembler, fake, fraud.

hypothesis *(SYN.)* law, theory, supposition, conjecture.

(ANT.) proof, fact, certainty.

hypothetical *(SYN.)* conjectural, speculative, theoretical.

(ANT.) actual.

idea (SYN.) conception, image, opinion, sentiment, concept, fancy, notion, thought, impression.
(ANT.) thing, matter, entity, object, substance.

ideal (SYN.) imaginary, supreme, unreal, visionary, perfect, faultless, fancied, exemplary, utopian.
(ANT.) imperfect, actual, material, real, faulty.

idealistic (SYN.) extravagant, dreamy, fantastic, fanciful, ideal, maudlin, imaginative, mawkish, sentimental, poetic, picturesque.
(ANT.) practical, literal, factual, prosaic.

identify (ANT.) recollect, apprehend, perceive, remember, confess, acknowledge, name, describe, classify.
(ANT.) ignore, forget, overlook, renounce, disown, repudiate.

identity (SYN.) uniqueness, personality, character, individuality.

ideology (SYN.) credo, principles, belief.

idiom (SYN.) language, speech, vernacular, lingo, dialect, jargon, slang, tongue.
(ANT.) babble, gibberish, drivel, nonsense.

idiot (SYN.) buffoon, harlequin, dolt, jester, dunce, blockhead, imbecile, numb-skull, simpleton, oaf, nincompoop, fool, moron.
(ANT.) philosopher, genius, scholar, sage.

idiotic (SYN.) asinine, absurd, brainless, irrational, crazy, nonsensical, senseless, preposterous, silly, ridiculous, simple, stupid, foolish, inane, moronic, half-witted, simpleminded, dimwitted.
(ANT.) prudent, wise, sagacious, judicious, sane, intelligent, bright, brilliant, smart.

idle (SYN.) unemployed, dormant, lazy, inactive, unoccupied, indolent, slothful, inert, unused.
(ANT.) occupied, working, employed, active, industrious, busy, engaged.

idol (SYN.) unoccupied, unused, inactive, unemployed.

idolize (SYN.) revere, worship, adore.
(ANT.) despise.

ignoble (SYN.) dishonorable, ignominious, lowly, menial vile, sordid, vulgar, abject, base, despicable, groveling, mean, vile.

(ANT.) righteous, lofty, honored, esteemed, noble, exalted.

ignominious (SYN.) contemptible, abject, despicable, groveling, dishonorable, ignoble, lowly, low, menial, mean, sordid, servile, vulgar, vile.
(ANT.) lofty, noble, esteemed, righteous, exalted.

ignorant (SYN.) uneducated, untaught, uncultured, illiterate, uninformed, unlearned, unlettered, untrained, unaware, unmindful.
(ANT.) cultured, literate, educated, erudite, informed, cultivated, schooled, learned, lettered.

ignore (SYN.) omit, slight, disregard, overlook, neglect, skip.
(ANT.) notice, regard, include.

ill (SYN.) diseased, ailing, indisposed, morbid, infirm, unwell, unhealthy, sick, unhealthy.
(ANT.) robust, strong, healthy, well, sound, fit.

ill-use (SYN.) defame, revile, vilify, misemploy, disparage, abuse, traduce, asperse, misapply, misuse.
(ANT.) protect, cherish, respect, honor, praise.

ill-advised (SYN.) injudicious, ill-considered, imprudent.

ill-at-ease (SYN.) nervous, uncomfortable, uneasy.
(ANT.) comfortable.

illegal (SYN.) prohibited, unlawful, criminal, illicit, outlawed, illegitimate.
(ANT.) permitted, lawful, honest, legal, legitimate.

illiberal (SYN.) fanatical, bigoted, intolerant, narrow-minded, dogmatic, prejudiced.
(ANT.) progressive, liberal radical.

illicit (SYN.) illegitimate, criminal, outlawed, unlawful, prohibited, illegal, unauthorized.
(ANT.) legal, honest, permitted, lawful, licit.

ill-natured (SYN.) crabby, cranky, grouchy, cross, irascible.

illness (SYN.) complaint, infirmity, ailment, disorder, malady, sickness.
(ANT.) healthiness, health, soundness, vigor.

illogical (SYN.) absurd, irrational, preposterous.

ill-tempered *(SYN.)* crabby, cranky, cross, grouchy.

ill-treated *(SYN.)* harmed, mistreated, abused, maltreated.

illuminate *(SYN.)* enlighten, clarify, irradiate, illustrate, light, lighten, explain, interpret, clarify, elucidate, brighten, illumine.
(ANT.) obscure, confuse, darken, obfuscate, shadow, complicate.

illusion *(SYN.)* hallucination, vision, phantom, delusion, fantasy, dream, mirage.
(ANT.) substance, actuality, reality.

illusive *(SYN.)* fallacious, delusive, false, specious, misleading, deceptive, deceitful, delusory.
(ANT.) real, truthful, authentic, genuine, honest.

illustrate *(SYN.)* decorate, illuminate, adorn, show, picture, embellish, demonstrate.

illustration *(SYN.)* likeness, painting, picture, print, scene, sketch, view, engraving, drawing, panorama, photograph, cinema, etching, effigy, film, appearance, portrayal, resemblance, image, portrait.

illustrator *(SYN.)* painter, artist.

illustrious *(SYN.)* prominent, eminent, renowned, famed, great, vital, elevated, majestic, noble, excellent, dignified, big, gigantic, enormous, immense, huge, vast, large, countless, numerous, celebrated, critical, momentous, august, weighty, grand, fine, magnificent, serious, important.
(ANT.) menial, common, minute, diminutive, small, obscure, ordinary, little.

image *(SYN.)* reflection, likeness, idea, representation, notion, picture, conception.

imaginary *(SYN.)* fanciful, fantastic, unreal, whimsical.
(ANT.) actual, real.

imagination *(SYN.)* creation, invention, fancy, notion, conception, fantasy, idea.

imaginative *(SYN.)* inventive, poetical, fanciful, clever, creative, mystical, visionary.
(ANT.) prosaic, dull, unromantic, literal.

imagine *(SYN.)* assume, surmise, suppose, conceive, dream, pretend, conjec-ture, fancy, opine, envisage, think, envision, guess, picture.

imbecile *(SYN.)* idiot, numbskull, simpleton, blockhead, dolt, dunce, jester, buffoon, harlequin, nincompoop, clown, fool, oaf.
(ANT.) scholar, genius, philosopher, sage.

imbibe *(SYN.)* absorb, consume, assimilate, engulf, engage, occupy, engross.
(ANT.) dispense, exude, discharge, emit.

imitate *(SYN.)* duplicate, mimic, follow, reproduce, mock, ape, counterfeit, copy, simulate, impersonate.
(ANT.) invent, distort, alter, diverge.

imitation *(SYN.)* replica, reproduction copy, duplicate, facsimile, transcript, exemplar.
(ANT.) prototype, original.

immaculate *(SYN.)* clean, spotless, unblemished.
(ANT.) dirty.

immature *(SYN.)* young, boyish, childish, youthful, childlike, puerile, girlish, juvenile, callow.
(ANT.) old, senile, aged, elderly, mature.

immeasurable *(SYN.)* unlimited, endless, eternal, immense, interminable, unbounded, immeasurable, boundless, illimitable, infinite.
(ANT.) limited, confined, bounded, finite, circumscribed.

immediate *(SYN.)* present, instant, instantaneous, near, close, next, prompt, direct.
(ANT.) distant, future.

immediately *(SYN.)* now, presently, instantly, promptly, straightway, directly, instantaneously, forthwith.
(ANT.) sometime, hereafter, later, shortly, distantly.

immense *(SYN.)* enormous, large, gigantic, huge, colossal, elephantine, great, gargantuan, vast.
(ANT.) small, diminutive, little, minuscule, minute, petit, tiny.

immensity *(SYN.)* hugeness, enormousness, vastness.

immerse *(SYN.)* plunge, dip, dunk, sink, submerge, engage, absorb, engross, douse.
(ANT.) uplift, elevate, recover.

immigration *(SYN.)* settlement, colonization.
(ANT.) exodus, emigration.

imminent *(SYN.)* nigh, impending, overhanging, approaching, menacing, threatening.

(ANT.) retreating, afar, distant, improbable, remote.

immoderation *(SYN.)* profusion, surplus, extravagance, excess, intemperance, superabundance.

(ANT.) lack, want, deficiency, dearth, paucity.

immoral *(SYN.)* sinful, wicked, corrupt, bad, indecent, profligate, unprincipled, antisocial, dissolute.

(ANT.) pure, high-minded, chaste, virtuous, noble.

immortal *(SYN.)* infinite, eternal, timeless, undying, perpetual, ceaseless, endless, deathless, everlasting.

(ANT.) mortal, transient, finite, ephemeral, temporal.

immune *(SYN.)* easy, open, autonomous, unobstructed, free, emancipated, clear, independent, unrestricted, exempt, liberated, familiar, loose, unconfined, frank, unfastened, careless, freed.

(ANT.) confined, impeded, restricted, subject.

immutable *(SYN.)* constant, faithful, invariant, persistent, unchanging, unalterable, continual, ceaseless, enduring, fixed, permanent, abiding, perpetual, unwavering.

(ANT.) mutable, vacillating, wavering, fickle.

impact *(SYN.)* striking, contact, collision.

impair *(SYN.)* harm, injure, spoil, deface, destroy, hurt, damage, mar.

(ANT.) repair, mend, ameliorate, enhance, benefit.

impart *(SYN.)* convey, disclose, inform, tell, reveal, transmit, notify, confer, divulge, communicate, relate.

(ANT.) hide, withhold, conceal.

impartial *(SYN.)* unbiased, just, honest, fair, reasonable, equitable.

(ANT.) fraudulent, dishonorable, partial.

impartiality *(SYN.)* indifference, unconcern, impartiality, neutrality, disinterestedness, apathy, insensibility.

(ANT.) passion, ardor, fervor, affection.

impasse *(SYN.)* standstill, deadlock, stalemate.

impede *(SYN.)* hamper, hinder, retard, thwart, check, encumber, interrupt, bar,

clog, delay, obstruct, block, frustrate, restrain, stop.

(ANT.) assist, promote, help, advance, further.

impediment *(SYN.)* barrier, bar, block, difficulty, check, hindrance, snag, obstruction.

(ANT.) assistance, help, aid, encouragement.

impel *(SYN.)* oblige, enforce, drive, coerce, force, constrain.

(ANT.) induce, prevent, convince, persuade.

impending *(SYN.)* imminent, nigh, threatening, overhanging, approaching, menacing.

(ANT.) remote, improbable, afar, distant, retreating.

impenetrable *(SYN)* rigid, tough, harsh, strict, unfeeling, rigorous, intricate, arduous, penetrable, cruel, difficult, severe, stern, firm, hard, compact.

(ANT.) soft, simple, gentle, tender, brittle, fluid, flabby, elastic, lenient, easy, effortless.

imperative *(SYN.)* critical, instant, important, necessary, serious, urgent, cogent, compelling, crucial, pressing, impelling, importunate, exigent, insistent.

(ANT.) trivial, insignificant, unimportant, petty.

imperceptible *(SYN.)* invisible, indiscernible, unseen, indistinguishable.

(ANT.) seen, evident, visible, perceptible.

imperfection *(SYN.)* flaw, shortcoming, vice, defect, blemish, failure, mistake, omission, fault, error.

(ANT.) correctness, perfection, completeness.

imperil *(SYN.)* jeopardize, risk, endanger, hazard, risk.

(ANT.) guard, insure.

impersonal *(SYN.)* objective, detached, disinterested.

(ANT.) personal.

impersonate *(SYN.)* mock, simulate, imitate, ape, counterfeit, mimic, copy, duplicate.

(ANT.) alter, invent, diverge, distort.

impertinence *(SYN)* impudence, presumption, sauciness, effrontery, audacity, rudeness, assurance, boldness, insolence.

(ANT.) truckling, politeness, diffidence,

subserviency.

impertinent *(SYN.)* rude, offensive, insolent, disrespectful, arrogant, brazen, impudent, insulting, contemptuous, abusive.

(ANT.) polite, respectful, considerate, courteous.

impetuous *(SYN.)* rash, heedless, quick, hasty, careless, passionate, impulsive.

(ANT.) cautious, reasoning, careful, prudent, thoughtful, calculating.

implicate *(SYN.)* reproach, accuse, blame, involve, upbraid, condemn, incriminate, rebuke, censure.

(ANT.) exonerate, absolve, acquit.

implore *(SYN.)* beg, pray, request, solicit, crave, entreat, beseech, ask, importune, supplicate, adjure, appeal, petition.

(ANT.) give, cede, bestow, favor, grant.

imply *(SYN.)* mean, involve, suggest, connote, hint, mention, indicate, insinuate, signify.

(ANT.) state, assert, declare, express.

impolite *(SYN.)* rude, unpolished, impudent, boorish, blunt, discourteous, rough, saucy, surly, savage, insolent, gruff, uncivil, coarse, ignorant, crude, illiterate, raw, primitive, vulgar, untaught.

(ANT.) genteel, courteous, courtly, dignified, polite, stately, noble, civil.

import *(SYN.)* influence, significance, stress, emphasis, importance, value, weight.

(ANT.) triviality, insignificance.

important *(SYN.)* critical, grave, influential, momentous, well-known, pressing, relevant, prominent, primary, essential, weighty, material, considerable, famous, principle, famed, sequential, notable, significant, illustrious, decisive.

(ANT.) unimportant, trifling, petty, trivial, insignificant, secondary, anonymous, irrelevant.

impose *(SYN.)* levy, require, demand.

imposing *(SYN.)* lofty, noble, majestic, magnificent, august, dignified, grandiose, high, grand, impressive, pompous, stately.

(ANT.) ordinary, undignified, humble, common, lowly.

imposition *(SYN.)* load, onus, burden.

impossible *(SYN.)* preposterous.

impregnable *(SYN.)* safe, invulnerable,

secure, unassailable.

(ANT.) vulnerable.

impress *(SYN.)* awe, emboss, affect, mark, imprint, indent, influence.

impression *(SYN.)* influence, indentation, feeling, opinion, mark, effect, depression, guess, thought, belief, dent, sensibility.

(ANT.) fact, insensibility.

impressive *(SYN.)* arresting, moving, remarkable, splendid, thrilling, striking, majestic, grandiose, imposing, commanding, affecting, exciting, touching, stirring.

(ANT.) regular, unimpressive, commonplace.

impromptu *(SYN.)* casual, unprepared, offhand, extemporaneous.

improper *(SYN.)* unfit, unsuitable, inappropriate, naughty, indecent, unbecoming.

(ANT.) fitting, proper, appropriate.

improve *(SYN.)* better, reform, refine, ameliorate, amend, help, upgrade, rectify.

(ANT.) debase, vitiate, impair, corrupt, damage.

improvement *(SYN)* growth, advance, progress, betterment, development, advancement, progression.

(ANT.) relapse, regression, decline, retrogression, delay.

imprudent *(SYN.)* indiscreet, thoughtless, desultory, lax, neglectful, remiss, careless, inattentive, heedless, inconsiderate, reckless, ill-advised, irresponsible, unconcerned.

(ANT.) careful, meticulous, accurate.

impudence *(SYN.)* boldness, insolence, rudeness, sauciness, assurance, effrontery, impertinence, presumption, audacity.

(ANT.) politeness, truckling, subserviency, diffidence.

impudent *(SYN.)* forward, rude, abrupt, prominent, striking, bold, fresh, impertinent, insolent, pushy, insulting, brazen.

(ANT.) bashful, flinching, polite, courteous, cowardly, retiring, timid.

impulse *(SYN.)* hunch, whim, fancy, urge, caprice, surge, pulse.

impulsive *(SYN.)* passionate, rash, spontaneous, heedless, careless, hasty, quick, impetuous.

(ANT.) reasoning, calculating, careful, prudent, cautious.

impure *(SYN.)* dishonest, spoiled, tainted, contaminated, debased, corrupt, profligate, unsound, putrid, corrupted, crooked, depraved, vitiated, venal.

imputation *(SYN.)* diary, incrimination, arraignment, indictment.

(ANT.) exoneration, pardon, exculpation.

inability *(SYN.)* incompetence, incapacity, handicap, disability, impotence, weakness.

(ANT.) power, strength, ability, capability.

inaccurate *(SYN.)* false, incorrect, mistaken, untrue, askew, wrong, awry, erroneous, fallacious, imprecise, faulty, amiss.

(ANT.) right, accurate, true, correct.

inactive *(SYN.)* lazy, unemployed, indolent, motionless, still, inert, dormant, idle, unoccupied.

(ANT.) employed, working, active, industrious, occupied.

inadequate *(SYN.)* insufficient, lacking, short, incomplete, defective, scanty.

(ANT.) satisfactory, enough, adequate, ample, sufficient.

inadvertent *(SYN.)* careless, negligent, unthinking, thoughtless.

inane *(SYN.)* trite, insipid, banal, absurd, silly, commonplace, vapid, foolish, stupid, hackneyed.

(ANT.) stimulating, novel, fresh, original, striking.

inanimate *(SYN.)* deceased, spiritless, lifeless, gone, dull, mineral, departed, dead, insensible, vegetable, unconscious.

(ANT.) living, stirring, alive, animate.

inattentive *(SYN.)* absent-minded, distracted, abstracted, preoccupied.

(ANT.) watchful, attending, attentive.

inaugurate *(SYN.)* commence, begin, open, originate, start, arise, launch, enter, initiate.

(ANT.) end, terminate, close, complete, finish.

incense *(SYN.)* anger, enrage, infuriate.

incentive *(SYN.)* impulse, stimulus, inducement, encouragement.

(ANT.) discouragement.

inception *(SYN.)* origin, start, source, opening, beginning, outset, commencement.

(ANT.) end, termination, close, completion, consummation.

incessant *(SYN.)* perennial, uninterrupted, continual, ceaseless, continuous, unremitting, eternal, constant, unceasing, unending, perpetual, everlasting.

(ANT.) rare, occasional, periodic, interrupted.

incident *(SYN.)* happening, situation, occurrence, circumstance, condition, event, fact.

incidental *(SYN.)* casual, contingent, trivial, undesigned, chance, fortuitous, accidental, secondary, unimportant, unintended.

(ANT.) intended, fundamental, planned, calculated, willed, decreed.

incidentally *(SYN.)* by the way.

incinerate *(SYN.)* sear, char, blaze, scald, singe, consume, scorch, burn.

(ANT.) quench, put out, extinguish.

incisive *(SYN.)* neat, succinct, terse, brief, compact, condensed, neat, summary, concise.

(ANT.) wordy, prolix, verbose, lengthy.

incite *(SYN.)* goad, provoke, urge, arouse, encourage, cause, stimulate, induce, instigate, foment.

(ANT.) quiet, bore, pacify, soothe.

inclination *(SYN.)* bent, preference, desire, slope, affection, bent, bias, disposition, bending, penchant, incline, attachment, predisposition, predication, tendency, prejudice, slant, lean, leaning.

(ANT.) nonchalance, apathy, distaste, aversion, reluctance, disinclination, uprightness, repugnance.

incline *(SYN.)* slope, nod, lean.

(ANT.) straighten.

include *(SYN.)* contain, hold, accommodate, embody, encompass, involve, comprise, embrace.

(ANT.) omit, exclude, discharge.

income *(SYN.)* earnings, salary, wages, revenue, pay, return, receipts.

incomparable *(SYN.)* peerless, matchless, unequaled.

incompetency *(SYN.)* inability, weakness, handicap, impotence, disability, incapacity.

(ANT.) strength, ability, power, capability.

incomprehensible *(SYN.)* unintelligible, indecipherable.

inconceivable *(SYN.)* unbelievable, unimaginable, impossible.
(ANT.) possible, believable.

incongruous *(SYN.)* inconsistent, contrary, incompatible, irreconcilable, contradictory, unsteady, incongruous, wavering, paradoxical, vacillating, discrepant, illogical.
(ANT.) consistent, compatible, correspondent.

inconsiderate *(SYN.)* unthinking, careless, unthoughtful, unmindful.
(ANT.) logical, consistent.

inconsistency *(SYN)* discord, variance, contention, conflict, controversy, interference.
(ANT.) harmony, concord, amity, consonance.

inconsistent *(SYN.)* fickle, wavering, variable, changeable, contrary, unstable, illogical, contradictory, irreconcilable, discrepant, paradoxical, incompatible, self-contradictory, incongruous, unsteady, fitful, shifting.
(ANT.) unchanging, steady, logical, stable, uniform, constant.

inconspicuous *(SYN.)* retiring, unnoticed, unostentatious.
(ANT.) obvious, conspicuous.

inconstant *(SYN.)* fickle, shifting, changeable, fitful, vacillating, unstable, wavering.
(ANT.) stable, constant, steady, uniform, unchanging.

inconvenient *(SYN.)* awkward, inappropriate, untimely, troublesome.
(ANT.) handy, convenient.

incorrect *(SYN.)* mistaken, wrong, erroneous, inaccurate.
(ANT.) proper, accurate, suitable.

increase *(SYN.)* amplify, enlarge, grow, magnify, multiply, augment, enhance, expand, intensify, swell, raise, greaten, prolong, broaden, lengthen, expansion, accrue, extend, heighten.
(ANT.) diminish, reduce, atrophy, shrink, shrinkage, decrease, lessening, lessen, contract.

incredible *(SYN.)* improbable, unbelievable.
(ANT.) plausible, credible, believable.

incriminate *(SYN.)* charge, accuse, indict, arraign, censure.
(ANT.) release, exonerate, acquit, absolve, vindicate.

incrimination *(SYN.)* imputation, indictment, accusation, charge, arraignment.
(ANT.) exoneration, pardon, exculpation.

indebted *(SYN.)* obliged, grateful, beholden, thankful, appreciative.
(ANT.) unappreciative, thankless.

indecent *(SYN.)* impure, obscene, pornographic, coarse, dirty, filthy, smutty, gross, disgusting.
(ANT.) modest, refined, decent, pure.

indeed *(SYN.)* truthfully, really, honestly, surely.

indefinite *(SYN.)* unsure, uncertain, vague, confused, unsettled, confusing.
(ANT.) decided, definite, equivocal.

independence *(SYN.)* liberation, privilege, freedom, immunity, familiarity, liberty, exemption, license.
(ANT.) necessity, constraint, compulsion, reliance, dependence, bondage, servitude.

independent *(SYN.)* free, unrestrained, voluntary, autonomous, self-reliant, uncontrolled, unrestricted.
(ANT.) enslaved, contingent, dependent, restricted.

indestructible *(SYN.)* enduring, lasting, permanent, unchangeable, abiding, constant, fixed, stable, changeless.
(ANT.) unstable, temporary, transitory, ephemeral.

indicate *(SYN.)* imply, denote, signify, specify, intimate, designate, symbolize, show, manifest, disclose, mean, reveal.
(ANT.) mislead, falsify, distract, conceal, falsify.

indication *(SYN.)* proof, emblem, omen, sign, symbol, token, mark, portent, gesture, signal.

indict *(SYN.)* charge, accuse, incriminate, censure, arraign.
(ANT.) acquit, vindicate, absolve, exonerate.

indictment *(SYN.)* incrimination, arraignment, imputation, charge.
(ANT.) pardon, exoneration, exculpation.

indifference *(SYN.)* unconcern, apathy, impartiality, disinterestedness, insensibility, neutrality.
(ANT.) ardor, passion, affection, fervor.

indifferent *(SYN.)* uncaring, insensitive, cool, unconcerned.

(ANT.) caring, concerned, earnest.

indigence *(SYN.)* necessity, destitution, poverty, want, need, privation, penury.

(ANT.) wealth, abundance, plenty, riches, affluence.

indigenous *(SYN.)* inborn, native, inherent, domestic, aboriginal, plenty, endemic, innate, natural.

indigent *(SYN.)* wishing, covetous, demanding, lacking, requiring, wanting, claiming, craving.

indignant *(SYN.)* irritated, irate, angry, aroused, exasperated.

(ANT.) calm, serene, content.

indignation *(SYN.)* ire, petulance, passion, choler, anger, wrath, temper, irritation, exasperation, animosity, resentment, rage.

(ANT.) self-control, peace, forbearance, patience.

indignity *(SYN.)* insolence, insult, abuse, affront, offense.

(ANT.) homage, apology, salutation.

indirect *(SYN.)* winding, crooked, devious, roundabout, cunning, tricky, tortuous, circuitous, distorted, erratic, swerving.

(ANT.) straightforward, direct, straight, honest.

indiscretion *(SYN.)* imprudence, folly, absurdity, extravagance.

(ANT.) prudence, sense, wisdom, reasonableness, judgment.

indispensable *(SYN.)* necessary, fundamental, basic, essential, important, intrinsic, vital.

(ANT.) optional, expendable, peripheral, extrinsic.

indistinct *(SYN.)* cloudy, dark, mysterious, vague, blurry, ambiguous, cryptic, dim, obscure, enigmatic, abstruse, hazy, blurred, unintelligible.

(ANT.) clear, lucid, bright, distinct.

indistinguishable *(SYN.)* identical, like, coincident, equal, same, equivalent.

(ANT.) dissimilar, opposed, contrary, disparate, distinct.

individual *(SYN.)* singular, specific, unique, distinctive, single, particular, undivided, human, apart, marked, person, different, special, separate.

(ANT.) universal, common, general, ordinary.

individuality *(SYN.)* symbol, description,

mark, kind, character, repute, class, standing, sort, nature, disposition, reputation, sign.

indolent *(SYN.)* slothful, lazy, idle, inactive, slow, sluggish, torpid, supine, inert.

(ANT.) diligent, active, assiduous, vigorous, zestful, alert.

indomitable *(SYN.)* insurmountable, unconquerable, invulnerable, impregnable, unassailable.

(ANT.) weak, puny, powerless, vulnerable.

induce *(SYN.)* evoke, cause, influence, persuade, effect, make, originate, prompt, incite, create.

inducement *(SYN.)* incentive, motive, purpose, stimulus, reason, impulse, cause, principle, spur, incitement.

(ANT.) result, attempt, action, effort, deed.

induct *(SYN.)* instate, establish, install.

(ANT.) eject, oust.

indulge *(SYN.)* humor, satisfy, gratify.

indulgent *(SYN.)* obliging, pampering, tolerant, easy.

indurate *(SYN.)* impenitent, hard, insensible, tough, obdurate, callous, unfeeling.

(ANT.) soft, compassionate, tender, sensitive.

industrious *(SYN.)* hard-working, perseverant, busy, active, diligent, assiduous, careful, patient.

(ANT.) unconcerned, indifferent, lethargic, careless, apathetic, lazy, indolent, shiftless.

inebriated *(SYN.)* drunk, tight, drunken, intoxicated, tipsy.

(ANT.) sober, clearheaded, temperate.

ineffective *(SYN.)* pliant, tender, vague, wavering, defenseless, weak, inadequate, poor, irresolute, frail, decrepit, delicate, vacillating, assailable, exposed, vulnerable.

(ANT.) sturdy, robust, strong, potent, powerful.

inept *(SYN.)* clumsy, awkward, improper, inappropriate.

(ANT.) adroit, dexterous, adept, appropriate, proper, apt, fitting.

inequity *(SYN.)* wrong, injustice, unfairness, grievance, injury.

(ANT.) righteousness, lawfulness, equity, justice.

inert *(SYN.)* lazy, dormant, slothful, inactive, idle, indolent, motionless, unmoving, fixed, static.
(ANT.) working, active, industrious, occupied.

inertia *(SYN.)* indolence, torpidity, idleness, slothfulness, indolence, sluggishness, supineness.
(ANT.) assiduousness, activity, alertness, diligence.

inevitable *(SYN.)* definite, fixed, positive, sure, undeniable, indubitable, certain, assured, unquestionable, secure.
(ANT.) uncertain, probable, doubtful, questionable.

inexpensive *(SYN.)* low-priced, cheap, inferior, mean, beggarly, common, poor, shabby, modest, economical.
(ANT.) expensive, costly, dear.

inexperienced *(SYN.)* naive, untrained, uninformed, green.
(ANT.) experienced, skilled, sophisticated, trained, seasoned.

inexplicable *(SYN.)* hidden, mysterious, obscure, secret, dark, cryptic, enigmatical, incomprehensible, occult, recondite, inscrutable, dim.
(ANT.) plain, simple, clear, obvious, explained.

infamous *(SYN.)* shocking, shameful, scandalous.

infantile *(SYN.)* babyish, naive, immature, childish.
(ANT.) mature, grownup, adult.

infect *(SYN.)* pollute, poison, contaminate, defile, sully, taint.
(ANT.) purify, disinfect.

infection *(SYN.)* virus, poison, ailment, disease, pollution, pest, germ, taint, contamination, contagion.

infectious *(SYN.)* contagious, virulent, catching, communicable, pestilential, transferable.
(ANT.) noncommunicable, hygienic, healthful.

infer *(SYN.)* understand, deduce, extract.

inference *(SYN.)* consequence, result, conclusion, corollary, judgment, deduction.
(ANT.) preconception, foreknowledge, assumption, presupposition.

inferior *(SYN.)* secondary, lower, poorer, minor, subordinate, mediocre.
(ANT.) greater, superior, better, higher.

infinite *(SYN.)* immeasurable, interminable, unlimited, unbounded, eternal, boundless, illimitable, immense, endless, vast, innumerable, numberless, limitless.
(ANT.) confined, limited, bounded, circumscribed, finite.

infinitesimal *(SYN.)* minute, microscopic, tiny, submicroscopic.
(ANT.) gigantic, huge, enormous.

infirm *(SYN.)* feeble, impaired, decrepit, forceless, languid, puny, powerless, enervated, weak, exhausted.
(ANT.) stout, vigorous, forceful, lusty, strong.

infirmity *(SYN.)* disease, illness, malady, ailment, sickness, disorder, complaint.
(ANT.) soundness, health, vigor, healthiness.

inflame *(SYN.)* fire, incite, excite, arouse.
(ANT.) soothe, calm.

inflammation *(SYN.)* infection, soreness, irritation.

inflammatory *(SYN.)* instigating, inciting, provocative.

inflate *(SYN.)* expand, swell, distend.
(ANT.) collapse, deflate.

inflexible *(SYN.)* firm, stubborn, headstrong, immovable, unyielding, uncompromising, dogged, contumacious, determined, obstinate, rigid, unbending, unyielding, steadfast.
(ANT.) submissive, compliant, docile, amenable, yielding, flexible, giving, elastic.

inflict *(SYN.)* deliver, deal, give, impose, apply.

influence *(SYN.)* weight, control, effect, sway.

influenced *(SYN.)* sway, affect, bias, control, actuate, impel, stir, incite.

influential *(SYN.)* important, weighty, prominent, significant, critical, decisive, momentous, relevant, material, pressing, consequential, grave.
(ANT.) petty, irrelevant, mean, trivial, insignificant.

inform *(SYN.)* apprise, instruct, tell, notify, advise, acquaint, enlighten, impart, warn, teach, advise, relate.
(ANT.) delude, mislead, distract, conceal.

informal *(SYN.)* simple, easy, natural, unofficial, familiar.

(ANT.) formal, distant, reserved, proper.

informality *(SYN.)* friendship, frankness, liberty, acquaintance, sociability, intimacy, unreserved.

(ANT.) presumption, constraint, reserve, distance, haughtiness.

information *(SYN.)* knowledge, data, intelligence, facts.

informative *(SYN.)* educational, enlightening, instructive.

informer *(SYN.)* tattler, traitor, betrayer.

infrequent *(SYN.)* unusual, rare, occasional, strange.

(ANT.) commonplace, abundant, usual, ordinary, customary, frequent, numerous.

ingenious *(SYN.)* clever, skillful, talented, adroit, dexterous, quick-witted, bright, smart, witty, sharp, apt, resourceful, imaginative, inventive, creative.

(ANT.) dull, slow, awkward, bungling, unskilled, stupid.

ingenuity *(SYN.)* cunning, inventiveness, resourcefulness, aptitude, faculty, cleverness, ingenuousness.

(ANT.) ineptitude, clumsiness, dullness, stupidity.

ingenuous *(SYN.)* open, sincere, honest, candid, straightforward, plain, frank, truthful, free, naive, simple, innocent, unsophisticated.

(ANT.) scheming, sly, contrived, wily.

ingredient *(SYN.)* component, element, constituent.

inhabit *(SYN.)* fill, possess, absorb, dwell, occupy, live.

(ANT.) relinquish, abandon, release.

inherent *(SYN.)* innate, native, congenital, inherent, intrinsic, inborn, inbred, natural, real.

(ANT.) extraneous, acquired, external, extrinsic.

inhibit *(SYN.)* curb, constrain, hold back, restrain, bridle, hinder, repress, suppress, stop, limit.

(ANT.) loosen, aid, incite, encourage.

inhuman *(SYN.)* merciless, cruel, brutal, ferocious, savage, ruthless, malignant, barbarous, barbaric, bestial.

(ANT.) kind, benevolent, forbearing, gentle, compassionate, merciful, humane, humane.

inimical *(SYN.)* hostile, warlike, adverse, antagonistic, opposed, unfriendly.

(ANT.) favorable, amicable, cordial.

iniquitous *(SYN.)* baleful, immoral, pernicious, sinful, wicked, base, bad, evil, noxious, unsound, villainous, unwholesome.

(ANT.) moral, good, excellent, honorable, reputable.

iniquity *(SYN.)* injustice, wrong, grievance, unfairness, injury.

(ANT.) lawful, equity, righteousness, justice.

initial *(SYN.)* original, first, prime, beginning, earliest, pristine, chief, primeval, primary, foremost, basic, elementary.

(ANT.) latest, subordinate, last, least, hindmost, final, terminal.

initiate *(SYN.)* institute, enter, arise, inaugurate, commence, originate, start, open, begin.

(ANT.) terminate, complete, end, finish, close, stop.

initiative *(SYN.)* enthusiasm, energy, vigor, enterprise.

injure *(SYN.)* harm, wound, abuse, dishonor, damage, hurt, impair, spoil, disfigure, affront, insult, mar.

(ANT.) praise, ameliorate, help, preserve, compliment, benefit.

injurious *(SYN.)* detrimental, harmful, mischievous, damaging, hurtful, deleterious, harmful, destructive.

(ANT.) profitable, helpful, advantageous, salutary, beneficial, useful.

injury *(SYN.)* harm, detriment, damage, injustice, wrong, prejudice, grievance, mischief.

(ANT.) repair, benefit, improvement.

injustice *(SYN.)* unfairness, grievance, iniquity, wrong, injury.

(ANT.) righteousness, justice, equity, lawfulness.

inmate *(SYN.)* patient, prisoner.

inn *(SYN.)* motel, lodge, hotel.

innate *(SYN.)* native, inherent, congenital, innate, real, inborn, natural, intrinsic, inbred.

(ANT.) extraneous, acquired, external, extrinsic.

innocent *(SYN.)* pure, sinless, blameless, innocuous, lawful, naive, faultless, virtuous, not guilty.

(ANT.) guilty, corrupt, sinful, culpable, sophisticated, wise, worldly.

innocuous *(SYN.)* naive, pure, innocent,

blameless, virtuous, lawful, faultless, innocuous, sinless.
(ANT.) sinful, corrupt, unrighteous, culpable, guilty.

inquire *(SYN.)* ask, solicit, invite, demand, claim, entreat, interrogate, query, beg, request, question, investigate, examine.
(ANT.) dictate, insist, reply, command, order.

inquiring *(SYN.)* prying, searching, curious, inquisitive, peering, snoopy, peeping, meddling, interrogative.
(ANT.) unconcerned, indifferent, uninterested, incurious.

inquiry *(SYN.)* investigation, quest, research, examination, interrogation, exploration, query, question, scrutiny, study.
(ANT.) inattention, inactivity, disregard, negligence.

inquisitive *(SYN.)* meddling, peeping, nosy, interrogative, peering, searching, prying, snoopy, inquiring, curious.
(ANT.) unconcerned, indifferent, incurious, uninterested.

insane *(SYN.)* deranged, mad, foolish, idiotic, demented, crazy, delirious, maniacal, lunatic.
(ANT.) sane, rational, reasonable, sound, sensible, coherent.

insanity *(SYN.)* delirium, aberration, dementia, psychosis, lunacy, madness, frenzy, mania, craziness, derangement.
(ANT.) stability, rationality, sanity.

insecure *(SYN.)* uneasy, nervous, uncertain, shaky.
(ANT.) secure.

insensitive *(SYN.)* unfeeling, impenitent, callous, hard, indurate, obdurate, tough.
(ANT.) soft, compassionate, tender, sensitive.

insight *(SYN.)* intuition, acumen, penetration, discernment, perspicuity.
(ANT.) obtuseness.

insignificant *(SYN.)* trivial, paltry, petty, small, frivolous, unimportant, insignificant, trifling.
(ANT.) momentous, serious, important, weighty.

insincere *(SYN.)* false, dishonest, deceitful.
(ANT.) honest, sincere.

insinuate *(SYN.)* imply, mean, suggest,

connote, signify, involve.
(ANT.) express, state, assert.

insipid *(SYN.)* tasteless, dull, stale, flat, vapid.
(ANT.) racy, tasty, savory, exciting.

insist *(SYN.)* command, demand, require.

insolence *(SYN.)* boldness, presumption, sauciness, effrontery, audacity, assurance, impertinence, rudeness.
(ANT.) politeness, truckling, diffidence, subserviency.

insolent *(SYN.)* arrogant, impertinent, insulting, rude, brazen, contemptuous, abusive, offensive, disrespectful.
(ANT.) respectful, courteous, polite, considerate.

inspect *(SYN.)* observe, discern, eye, behold, glance, scan, stare, survey, view, regard, see, watch, witness, examine, investigate.
(ANT.) overlook, miss, avert, hide.

inspection *(SYN.)* examination, retrospect, survey, revision, reconsideration, critique, criticism, review.

inspiration *(SYN.)* creativity, aptitude, genius, originality, ability, faculty, sagacity, talent, proficient, master, gift, adept, intellectual, thought, impulse, idea, notion, hunch.
(ANT.) dullard, moron, shallowness, ineptitude, stupidity, obtuseness, dolt.

install *(SYN.)* establish.

instance *(SYN.)* occasion, illustration, occurrence, example, case.

instant *(SYN.)* flash, moment.

instantaneous *(SYN.)* hasty, sudden unexpected, rapid, abrupt, immediate.
(ANT.) slowly, anticipated, gradual.

instantly *(SYN.)* now, presently, directly, forthwith, immediately, rapidly straight-away, at once, instantaneously.
(ANT.) sometime, distantly, hereafter, later, shortly.

instinct *(SYN.)* intuition, feeling.

instinctive *(SYN.)* offhand, voluntary, willing, spontaneous, automatic, impulsive, extemporaneous.
(ANT.) rehearsed, planned, compulsory, prepared, forced.

institute *(SYN.)* ordain, establish, raise, form, organize, sanction, fix, found, launch, begin, initiate.
(ANT.) overthrow, upset, demolish,

abolish, unsettle.

instruct (*SYN.*) teach, tutor, educate, inform, school, instill, train, inculcate, drill.

(*ANT.*) misinform, misguide.

instruction (*SYN.*) advise, warning, information, exhortation, notification, admonition, caution, recommendation, counsel, suggestion, teaching, training, education, command, order.

instrument (*SYN.*) channel, device, utensil, tool, agent, apparatus, means, vehicle, medium, agent, implement.

(*ANT.*) obstruction, hindrance, preventive, impediment.

insubordinate (*SYN.*) rebellious, unruly, defiant, disorderly, disobedient, undutiful, refractory, intractable, mutinous.

(*ANT.*) obedient, compliant, submissive, dutiful.

insufficient (*SYN.*) limited, lacking, deficient, short, inadequate.

(*ANT.*) ample, protracted, abundant, big, extended.

insulation (*SYN.*) quarantine, segregation, seclusion, withdrawal, isolation, loneliness, alienation, solitude.

(*ANT.*) union, communion, association, fellowship, connection.

insult (*SYN.*) insolence, offense, abuse, dishonor, affront, insult, indignity, offend, humiliate, outrage.

(*ANT.*) compliment, homage, apology, salutation, flatter, praise.

integrated (*SYN.*) mingled, mixed, combined, interspersed, desegregated, nonsectarian, interracial.

(*ANT.*) separated, divided, segregated.

integrity (*SYN.*) honesty, openness, trustworthiness, fairness, candor, justice, rectitude, sincerity, uprightness, soundness, wholeness, honor, principle, virtue.

(*ANT.*) fraud, deceit, cheating, trickery, dishonesty.

intellect (*SYN.*) understanding, judgment.

intellectual (*SYN.*) intelligent.

intelligence (*SYN.*) reason, sense, intellect, understanding, mind, ability, skill, aptitude.

(*ANT.*) feeling, passion, emotion.

intelligent (*SYN.*) clever, smart, knowledgeable, well-informed, alert,

discerning, astute, quick, enlightened, smart, bright, wise.

(*ANT.*) insipid, obtuse, dull, stupid, slow, foolish, unintelligent, dumb.

intend (*SYN.*) plan, prepare, scheme, contrive, outline, design, sketch, plot, project, delineate.

intense (*SYN.*) brilliant, animated, graphic, lucid, bright, expressive, vivid, deep, profound, concentrated, serious, earnest.

(*ANT.*) dull, vague, dusky, dim, dreary.

intensify (*SYN.*) accrue, augment, amplify, enlarge, enhance, extend, expand, heighten, grow, magnify, raise, multiply.

(*ANT.*) reduce, decrease, contract, diminish.

intent (*SYN.*) purpose, design, objective, intention, aim.

(*ANT.*) accidental, result, chance.

intensity (*SYN.*) force, potency, power, toughness, activity, durability, fortitude, vigor, stamina.

(*ANT.*) weakness, feebleness, infirmity, frailty.

intention (*SYN.*) intent, purpose, objective, plan, expectation, aim, object.

(*ANT.*) chance, accident.

intentional (*SYN.*) deliberate, intended, studied, willful, contemplated, premeditated, designed, voluntary, purposeful, planned.

(*ANT.*) fortuitous, accidental, chance.

intentionally (*SYN.*) purposefully, deliberately, maliciously.

(*ANT.*) accidentally.

interest (*SYN.*) attention, concern, care, advantage, benefit, profit, ownership, credit, attract, engage, amuse, entertain.

(*ANT.*) apathy, weary, disinterest.

interested (*SYN.*) affected, concerned.

(*ANT.*) unconcerned, indifferent, uninterested.

interesting (*SYN.*) engaging, inviting, fascinating, attractive.

(*ANT.*) boring, tedious, uninteresting, wearisome.

interfere (*SYN.*) meddle, monkey, interpose, interrupt, tamper, butt in, intervene.

interference (*SYN.*) prying, intrusion, meddling, obstacle, obstruction.

interior (*SYN.*) internal, inmost, inner, inward, inside, center.

(ANT.) *outer, adjacent, exterior, external, outside.*

interject (SYN.) intrude, introduce, insert, inject, interpose.

(ANT.) *overlook, avoid, disregard.*

interminable (SYN) immense, endless, immeasurable, unlimited, vast, unbounded, boundless, eternal, infinite.

(ANT.) *limited, bounded, circumscribed, confined.*

internal (SYN.) inner, interior, inside, intimate, private.

(ANT.) *outer, external, surface.*

interpose (SYN.) arbitrate, inject, intervene, meddle, insert, interject, introduce, intercede, intrude, interfere.

(ANT.) *overlook, avoid, disregard.*

interpret (SYN.) explain, solve, translate, construe, elucidate, decode, explicate, render, unravel, define, understand.

(ANT.) *misinterpret, falsify, confuse, distort, misconstrue.*

interrogate (SYN.) quiz, analyze, inquire, audit, question, contemplate, assess, dissect, notice, scan, review, view, check, survey, scrutinize, examine.

(ANT.) *overlook, omit, neglect, disregard.*

interrupt (SYN.) suspend, delay, postpone, defer, adjourn, stay, discontinue, intrude, interfere.

(ANT.) *prolong, persist, continue, maintain, proceed.*

interval (SYN.) pause, gap.

intervene (SYN.) insert, intercede, meddle, inject, introduce, interpose, mediate, interfere, interrupt, intrude.

(ANT.) *overlook, avoid, disregard.*

intimacy (SYN.) fellowship, friendship, acquaintance, frankness, familiarity, unreserved, liberty.

(ANT.) *presumption, distance, haughtiness, constraint, reserve.*

intimate (SYN.) chummy, confidential, friendly, loving, affectionate, close, familiar, near, personal, private, secret.

(ANT.) *conventional, formal, ceremonious, distant.*

intimation (SYN.) reminder, implication, allusion, hint, insinuation.

(ANT.) *declaration, statement, affirmation.*

intolerant (SYN.) fanatical, narrowminded, prejudiced, bigoted, illiberal, dogmatic, biased.

(ANT.) *tolerant, radical, liberal, progressive, broad-minded, fair.*

intoxicated (SYN.) inebriated, tipsy, drunk, tight, drunken, high.

(ANT.) *sober, temperate, clearheaded.*

intrepid (SYN.) brave, fearless, insolent, abrupt, rude, pushy, adventurous, daring, courageous, prominent, striking, forward, imprudent.

(ANT.) *timid, bashful, flinching, cowardly, retiring.*

intricate (SYN.) compound, perplexing, complex, involved, complicated.

(ANT.) *simple, plain, uncompounded.*

intrigue (SYN.) design, plot, cabal, machination, stratagem, scheme, attract, charm, interest, captivate.

intrinsic (SYN.) natural, inherent, inbred, congenital, inborn, native.

(ANT.) *extraneous, acquired, external, extrinsic.*

introduce (SYN.) acquaint, present, submit, present, offer, propose.

introduction (SYN.) preamble, prelude, beginning, prologue, start, preface.

(ANT.) *finale, conclusion, end, epilogue, completion.*

intrude (SYN.) invade, attack, encroach, trespass, penetrate, infringe, interrupt.

(ANT.) *vacate, evacuate, abandon, relinquish.*

intruder (SYN.) trespasser, thief, prowler, robber.

intuition (SYN.) insight, acumen, perspicuity, penetration, discernment, instinct, clairvoyance.

invade (SYN.) intrude, violate, infringe, attack, penetrate, encroach, trespass.

(ANT.) *vacate, abandon, evacuate, relinquish.*

invalidate (SYN.) annul, cancel, abolish, revoke, abrogate.

(ANT.) *promote, restore, sustain, establish, continue.*

invaluable (SYN.) priceless, precious, valuable.

(ANT.) *worthless.*

invasion (SYN.) assault, onslaught, aggression, attack, intrusion.

(ANT.) *surrender, opposition, resistance, defense.*

invective (SYN.) insult, abuse, disparagement, upbraiding, reproach, defamation, aspersion.

(ANT.) laudation, plaudit, commendation.

invent *(SYN.)* devise, fabricate, design, concoct, frame, conceive, contrive, create, originate, devise.

(SYN.) reproduce, copy, imitate.

inventive *(SYN.)* fanciful, imaginative, visionary, poetical, clever, creative.

(ANT.) unromantic, literal, dull, prosaic.

inventiveness *(SYN)* cunning, cleverness, ingeniousness, aptitude.

(ANT.) ineptitude, clumsiness, dullness, stupidity.

invert *(SYN.)* upset, turn about, transpose, countermand, revoke, reverse.

(ANT.) maintain, stabilize, endorse.

investigate *(SYN.)* look, probe, ransack, scrutinize, ferret, examine, seek, explore, search, scour, inspect, study.

investigation *(SYN.)* exploration, interrogation, quest, question, scrutiny, inquiry, query, examination, study, research.

(ANT.) inattention, disregard, inactivity, negligence.

invigorating *(SYN.)* bracing, fortifying, vitalizing, stimulating.

invincible *(SYN.)* insurmountable, unconquerable, impregnable, indomitable, invulnerable, unassailable.

(ANT.) powerless, weak, vulnerable.

invisible *(SYN.)* indistinguishable, unseen, imperceptible, indiscernible.

(ANT.) evident, visible, seen, perceptible.

invite *(SYN.)* bid, ask, encourage, request, urge.

inviting *(SYN.)* appealing, attractive, tempting, luring, alluring.

(ANT.) unattractive, uninviting.

involuntary *(SYN.)* reflex, uncontrolled, automatic, unintentional.

(SYN.) voluntary, willful.

involve *(SYN.)* include, embrace, entangle, envelop, incriminate, embroil, implicate, contain, complicate, confuse.

(ANT.) separate, extricate, disengage.

involved *(SYN.)* compound, intricate, complicated, complex, perplexing.

(ANT.) plain, uncompounded, simple.

invulnerable *(SYN.)* indomitable, unassailable, invincible, unconquerable, insurmountable, impregnable.

(ANT.) weak, puny, powerless, vulnerable.

irate *(SYN.)* incensed, enraged, angry.

ire *(SYN.)* indignation, irritation, wrath, anger, animosity, fury, passion, temper, exasperation, petulance, rage.

(ANT.) peace, patience, conciliation, self-control, forbearance.

irk *(SYN.)* irritate, bother, disturb, pester, trouble, vex, tease, chafe, annoy.

(ANT.) console, accommodate, gratify.

irrational *(SYN.)* inconsistent, preposterous, unreasonable, absurd, foolish, nonsensical, ridiculous.

(ANT.) sensible, sound, rational consistent, reasonable.

irregular *(SYN.)* eccentric, unusual, aberrant, devious, abnormal, unnatural.

(ANT.) regular, methodical, fixed, usual, ordinary, even.

irrelevant *(SYN.)* foreign, unconnected, remote, alien, strange.

(ANT.) germane, relevant, akin, kindred.

irresolute *(SYN.)* frail, pliant, vacillating, ineffective, wavering, weak, yielding, fragile, pliable.

(ANT.) robust, potent, sturdy, strong, powerful.

irresponsible *(SYN.)* unreliable.

irritable *(SYN.)* hasty, hot, peevish, testy, irascible, fiery, snappish, petulant.

(ANT.) composed, tranquil, calm.

irritate *(SYN.)* irk, molest, bother, annoy, tease, disturb, inconvenience, vex, trouble, pester, inflame, chafe.

(ANT.) console, gratify, accommodate, soothe, pacify, calm.

irritation *(SYN.)* chagrin, mortification, vexation, annoyance, exasperation, pique.

(ANT.) pleasure, comfort, gratification, appeasement.

isolate *(SYN.)* detach, segregate, separate, disconnect.

(ANT.) happy, cheerful.

isolated *(SYN.)* lone, single, alone, desolate, secluded, solitary, deserted, sole.

(ANT.) surrounded, accompanied.

isolation *(SYN.)* quarantine, seclusion, separation, solitude, alienation, retirement, segregation, detachment.

(ANT.) fellowship, union, association, communion, connection.

issue *(SYN.)* flow, proceed, result, come, emanate, originate, abound, copy, number, edition, problem, question.

itemize *(SYN.)* register, detail, record.

jab *(SYN.)* thrust, poke, nudge, prod, shove, jolt, boost, tap, slap, rap, thwack, push.

jabber *(SYN.)* mumble, gossip, prattle, chatter, gab, palaver.

jacent *(SYN.)* level, flatness, plane, proneness, recline.

jacinth *(SYN.)* decoration, ornament, embellishment.

jack *(SYN.)* fellow, guy, boy, toiler, guy, man, worker.

jackal *(SYN.)* puppet, drone, slave, legman, flunky, slavery, tool, servility, vassal.

jackass *(SYN.)* fool, idiot, dope, dunce, ignoramus, imbecile, ninny, simpleton, blockhead.

jacket *(SYN.)* wrapper, envelope, coat, sheath, cover, casing, folder, enclosure, skin.

jack-of-all-trades *(SYN.)* man friday, expert, proficient, amateur, adept, handyman, dab, master, specialist, mastermind, generalist.

jade *(SYN.)* hussy, wanton, trollop, harlot, common, whore, ignoble, wench, hag, shrew.

jaded *(SYN.)* exhausted, bored, tired, fatigued, satiated, weary, hardened.

jag *(SYN.)* notch, snag, protuberance, barb, dent, cut, nick, serration, indentation, point.

jagged *(SYN.)* crooked, bent, ragged, pointy, notched, aquiline, furcated, aduncous, serrated.

(ANT.) smooth.

jail *(SYN.)* stockade, prison, reformatory, penitentiary, keep, dungeon, brig, confine, lock up, detain, imprison, hold captive, coop, cage, house of detention, incarcerate.

jailbird *(SYN.)* convict, parolee, con, inmate, prisoner.

jailer *(SYN.)* guard, keeper, turnkey, warden.

jam *(SYN.)* force, pack, ram, crowd, push, wedge, squeeze, stuff, load, cram, press, crush, marmalade, jelly, conserve, preserve.

jamboree *(SYN.)* celebration, fete, spree, festival, festivity, carousal.

jangle *(SYN.)* rattle, vibrate, clank, clatter, dissonance, discord, quarrel, din, discord, dispute.

janitor *(SYN.)* custodian, door-keeper, caretaker, superintendent, gatekeeper.

jape *(SYN.)* lampoon, banter, joke, jest, tease, ridicule.

jar *(SYN.)* rattle, shake, bounce, jolt.

jargon *(SYN.)* speech, idiom, dialect, vernacular, diction, argot, phraseology, language, patois, parlance, slang.

(ANT.) gibberish, babble, nonsense, drivel.

jaundiced *(SYN.)* biased, prejudiced.

(ANT.) fair.

jaunt *(SYN.)* journey, trip, tour, excursion, outing, voyage, expedition.

jaunty *(SYN.)* lively, vivacious, bouyant, winsome, frisky, showy, dapper, breezy, airy.

jazzy *(SYN.)* garish, vivacious, loud, splashy, exaggerated, flashy.

jealous *(SYN.)* covetqus, desirous of, envious.

jealousy *(SYN.)* suspicion, envy, resentfulness, greed, covetousness.

(ANT.) tolerance, indifference, geniality, liberality.

jeer *(SYN.)* taunt, mock, scoff, deride, make fun of, gibe, sneer.

(ANT.) flatter, praise, compliment, laud.

jeering *(SYN.)* mockery, sneering, derision, sarcasm, irony, ridicule.

jell *(SYN.)* finalize, congeal, set, solidify, shape up, take form.

jeopardize *(SYN.)* risk, dare, expose, imperil, chance, venture, conjecture, hazard, endanger.

(ANT.) know, guard, determine.

jerk *(SYN.)* quiver, twitch, shake, spasm, jolt, yank, fool.

jerkwater *(SYN.)* remote, hick, backwoods, unimportant, one-horse.

jest *(SYN.)* mock, joke, tease, fun, witticism, quip.

jester *(SYN.)* fool, buffoon, harlequin, clown.

(ANT.) sage, genius, scholar, philosopher.

jet *(SYN.)* squirt, spurt, gush, inky, coal-black, nozzle.

jettison *(SYN.)* heave, discharge, throw, eject, cast off, dismiss.

jetty *(SYN.)* pier, breakwater, bulwark, buttress.

jewel *(SYN.)* ornament, gemstone, gem, bauble, stone.

jib *(SYN.)* shrink, shy, dodge, retreat, balk.

jig *(SYN.)* caper, prance, jiggle, leap, skip.

jiggle *(SYN.)* shimmy, agitate, jerk, twitch, wiggle.

jilt *(SYN.)* abandon, get rid of, reject, desert, forsake, leave.

jingle *(SYN.)* chime, ring, tinkle.

jinx *(SYN.)* hex, whammy, nemesis, curse, evil eye.

jittery *(SYN.)* jumpy, nervous, quivering, shaky, skittery.

job *(SYN.)* toil, business, occupation, post, chore, stint, career, duty, employment, profession, trade, work, situation, labor, assignment, position, undertaking, calling, task.

jobless *(SYN.)* idle, unoccupied, inactive, unemployed.

jocularity *(SYN.)* humor, wit, joke, facetiousness, waggery.
(ANT.) sorrow, gravity.

jocund *(SYN.)* mirthful, elated, pleasant, cheerful, merry, gay, jovial, frolicsome.

jog *(SYN.)* gait, trot, sprint, run, lope.

join *(SYN.)* conjoin, unite, attach, accompany, associate, assemble, fit, couple, combine, fasten, unite, clasp, put together, go with, adjoin, link, connect.
(ANT.) separate, disconnect, split, sunder, part, divide, detach.

joint *(SYN.)* link, union, connection, junction, coupling, common, combined, mutual, connected.
(ANT.) divided, separate.

joke *(SYN.)* game, jest, caper, prank, anecdote, quip, tease, antic, banter, laugh.

joker *(SYN.)* wisecracker, humorist, comedian, trickster, comic, jester, wit, punster.

jolly *(SYN.)* merry, joyful, gay, happy, sprightly, pleasant, jovial, gleeful, spirited, cheerful, glad.
(ANT.) mournful, depressed, sullen, glum.

jolt *(SYN.)* sway, waver, startle, rock, jar, totter, jerk, bounce, quake, bump, shake.

josh *(SYN.)* poke fun at, kid, tease, ridicule.

jostle *(SYN.)* shove, push, bump, thrust.

jot *(SYN.)* note, write, record.

jounce *(SYN.)* bounce, jolt, bump, jostle, jar, shake.

journal *(SYN.)* account, diary, log, chronicle, magazine, newspaper, record.

journey *(SYN.)* tour, passage, cruise, voyage, pilgrimage, jaunt, trip, outing, expedition, junket, excursion, travel.

joust *(SYN.)* tournament, contest, skirmish, competition, fight.

jovial *(SYN.)* good-natured, kindly, merry, good-humored, good-hearted, joyful, jolly, gleeful.
(ANT.) solemn, sad, serious, grim.

joy *(SYN.)* pleasure, glee, bliss, elation, mirth, felicity, rapture, delight, transport, exultation, gladness, happiness, festivity, satisfaction, merriment, ecstasy.
(ANT.) grief, depression, unhappiness, sorrow, misery, gloom, sadness, affliction.

joyful *(SYN.)* gay, lucky, opportune, cheerful, happy, blissful, jovial, merry, gleeful, delighted, glad, contented, fortunate.
(ANT.) gloomy, sad, blue, solemn, serious, grim, morose, glum, depressed.

joyous *(SYN.)* jolly, gay, blithe, merry, gleeful, cheerful, jovial.
(ANT.) sad, gloomy, sorrowful, melancholy.

jubilant *(SYN.)* exulting, rejoicing, overjoyed, triumphant, gay, elated, delighted.
(ANT.) dejected.

jubilee *(SYN.)* gala, holiday, celebration, festival, fete.

judge *(SYN.)* umpire, think, estimate, decide, arbitrator, condemn, decree, critic, appreciate, adjudicator, determine, arbiter, magistrate, arbitrate, justice, consider, mediate, referee, evaluate.

judgment *(SYN.)* wisdom, perspicacity, discernment, decision, common sense, estimation, verdict, understanding, intelligence, discretion, opinion, sense, discrimination.
(ANT.) thoughtlessness, senselessness, arbitrariness.

judicial *(SYN.)* legal, judicatory, forensic.

judicious *(SYN.)* sensible, wise, well-advised, thoughtful.
(ANT.) ignorant.

jug *(SYN.)* bottle, jar, flask, flagon, pitcher.

juice *(SYN.)* broth, liquid, sap, distillation, serum, fluid.

jumble *(SYN.)* disarrangement, tumult, agitation, ferment, turmoil, commotion, confuse, mix, muddle, scramble, disorder.

(ANT.) peace, arrange, compose, certainty, tranquillity.

jumbo *(SYN.)* huge, big, immense, enormous, giant, colossal, monstrous, mammoth, gigantic, tremendous.

(ANT.) mini, midget, dwarf, small, little, tiny.

jump *(SYN.)* leap, caper, skip, bound, jerk, vault, hop, spring.

jumpy *(SYN.)* touchy, excitable, nervous, sensitive.

(ANT.) tranquil, calm, unruffled.

junction *(SYN.)* coupling, joining, union, crossroads, intersection, weld, connection, linking, meeting, tie-up, seam, joint.

(ANT.) separation.

jungle *(SYN.)* woods, thicket, undergrowth, forest, bush.

junior *(SYN.)* secondary, inferior, minor, lower, younger.

junk *(SYN.)* rubbish, scraps, trash, waste, dump, discard, castoffs, debris.

junky *(SYN.)* tawdry, ramshackle, tattered, tacky, shoddy.

jurisdiction *(SYN.)* power, commission, warrant, authority, authorization, magistacy, sovereignty.

just *(SYN.)* fair, trustworthy, precise, exact, candid, upright, honest, impartial, lawful, rightful, proper, legal, truthful, merely, only, conscientious.

(ANT.) tricky, dishonest, unjust, corrupt, lying, deceitful.

justice *(SYN.)* justness, rectitude, equity, law, fairness, impartiality, right.

(ANT.) inequity, wrong, partiality.

justifiable *(SYN.)* allowable, tolerable, admissible, warranted.

(ANT.) unsuitable, inadmissible.

justify *(SYN.)* uphold, excuse, defend, acquit, exonerate, absolve, clear, vindicate.

(ANT.) convict.

jut *(SYN.)* project, protrude, stick out.

(ANT.) indent, recess.

juvenile *(SYN.)* puerile, youthful, childish, youngster, youth, young, child.

(ANT.) old, aged, adult, mature.

kaiser *(SYN.)* czar, caesar, caliph, mogul, padishah, tycoon, khan, landamman, cazique.

kavass *(SYN.)* badel, macebearer, constable.

keck *(SYN.)* vomit, belch, retch.

keen *(SYN.)* clever, cunning, acute, penetrating, exact, severe, shrewd, wily, astute, sharp, bright, intelligent, smart, sharp-witted, witty, cutting, fine, quick.

(ANT.) stupid, shallow, dull, blunted, slow, bland, gentle, obtuse, blunt.

keep *(SYN.)* maintain, retain, observe, protect, confine, sustain, continue, preserve, save, guard, restrain, reserve, obey, support, honor, execute, celebrate, conserve, have, tend, detain, commemorate, hold.

(ANT.) abandon, disobey, dismiss, discard, ignore, neglect, lose, reject, relinquish.

keeper *(SYN.)* warden, jailer, ranger, gaoler, guard, turnkey, watchman, escort, custodian.

keeping *(SYN.)* congeniality, uniformity, consentaneousness, conformance, congruity, union.

keepsake *(SYN.)* reminder, memorial, relic, souvenir, memento, hint, remembrance.

keg *(SYN.)* container, drum, tub, barrel, receptacle, reservatory, capsule, cask, tank.

kelpie *(SYN.)* sprite, nixie, naiad, pixy.

kelson *(SYN.)* bottom, sole, toe, foot, root, keel.

kempt *(SYN.)* neat, trim, tidy, spruce, cleaned.

ken *(SYN.)* field, view, vision, range, scope.

kennel *(SYN.)* swarm, flock, covy, drove, herd, pound, doghouse.

kerchief *(SYN.)* neckcloth, hankerchief, scarf, headpiece, babushka.

kern *(SYN.)* peasant, carle, serf, tike, tyke, countryman.

kernel *(SYN.)* marrow, pith, backbone, soul, heart, core, nucleus.

ketch *(SYN.)* lugger, cutter, clipper, ship, barge, sloop.

kettle *(SYN.)* pan, caldron, vat, pot, teapot, vessel, receptacle, receiver, tureen.

key *(SYN.)* opener, explanation, tone,

lead, cause, source, note, pitch, answer, clue.

keynote *(SYN.)* core, model, theme, pattern, standard, gist.

keystone *(SYN.)* backbone, support.

khan *(SYN.)* master, czar, kaiser, padishah, caesar.

kick *(SYN.)* punt, remonstrate, boot.

kickback *(SYN.)* repercussion, backfire, rebound.

kickoff *(SYN.)* beginning, opening, commencement, outset, start.

kid *(SYN.)* joke, tease, fool, jest, tot, child.

kidnap *(SYN.)* abduct, snatch, shanghai.

kill *(SYN.)* execute, put to death, slay, butcher, assassinate, murder, cancel, destroy, slaughter, finish, end, annihilate, massacre.
(ANT.) save, protect, animate, resuscitate, vivify.

killing *(SYN.)* massacre, genocide, slaughter, carnage, butchery, bloodshed.

killjoy *(SYN.)* wet blanket, sourpuss, party-pooper.

kin *(SYN.)* relatives, family, folks, relations.

kind *(SYN.)* humane, affable, compassionate, benevolent, merciful, tender, sympathetic, breed, indulgent, forbearing, kindly, race, good, thoughtful, character, benign, family, sort, species, variety, class, type, gentle.
(ANT.) unkind, cruel, merciless, severe, mean, inhuman.

kindle *(SYN.)* fire, ignite, light, arouse, excite, set afire, stir up, trigger, move, provoke, inflame.
(ANT.) pacify, extinguish, calm.

kindly *(SYN.)* warm, kind-hearted, kind, warm-hearted.
(ANT.) mean, cruel.

kindred *(SYN.)* family, relations, relatives, consanguinity, kinsfolk, affinity.
(ANT.) strangers, disconnection.

kinetic *(SYN.)* vigorous, active, dynamic, energetic, mobile, forceful.

king *(SYN.)* sovereign, ruler, chief, monarch, potentate.

kingdom *(SYN.)* realm, empire, monarchy, domain.

kingly *(SYN.)* kinglike, imperial, regal, royal, majestic.

kink *(SYN.)* twist, curl, quirk, complication.

kinship *(SYN.)* lineage, blood, family, stock, relationship.

kismet *(SYN.)* fate, end, fortune, destiny.

kiss *(SYN.)* pet, caress, fondle, cuddle, osculate, embrace.
(ANT.) vex, spurn, annoy, tease, buffet.

kit *(SYN.)* outfit, collection, furnishings, equipment, rig, gear, set.

knack *(SYN.)* cleverness, readiness, deftness, ability, ingenuity, skill, talent; aptitude, talent, know-how, art, adroitness, skillfulness.
(ANT.) inability, clumsiness, awkwardness, ineptitude.

knave *(SYN.)* rogue, rascal, villain, scoundrel.

knead *(SYN.)* combine, massage, blend.

knickknack *(SYN.)* trinket, bric-a-brac, trifle.

knife *(SYN.)* sword, blade.

knightly *(SYN.)* valiant, courageous, gallant, chivalrous, noble.

knit *(SYN.)* unite, join, mend, fasten, connect, combine, heal.

knob *(SYN.)* doorknob, handle, protuberance, bump.

knock *(SYN.)* thump, tap, rap, strike, hit, jab, punch, beat, pound, bang, hammer.

knoll *(SYN.)* hill, elevation, hump, mound, butte.

knot *(SYN.)* cluster, gathering, collection, group, crowd, twist, snarl, tangle.

know *(SYN.)* perceive, comprehend, apprehend, recognize, understand, discern, discriminate, ascertain, identify, be aware, distinguish.
(ANT.) doubt, suspect, dispute, ignore.

knowing *(SYN.)* sage, smart, wise, clever, sagacious, shrewd.

knowledge *(SYN.)* information, wisdom, erudition, learning, apprehension, scholarship, lore, cognizance.
(ANT.) misunderstanding, ignorance, stupidity, illiteracy.

knurl *(SYN.)* gnarl, knot, projection, burl, node, lump.

kosher *(SYN.)* permitted, okay, fit, proper, acceptable.

kowtow *(SYN.)* stoop, bend, kneel, genuflect, bow.

kudos *(SYN.)* acclaim, praise, approbation, approval.

label *(SYN.)* mark, tag, title, name, marker, stamp, sticker, ticket, docket, identity.

labor *(SYN.)* toil, travail, effort, task, childbirth, work, parturition, striving, workers, effort, industry, workingmen, strive, exertion, employment, drudgery, endeavor.

(ANT.) recreation, indolence, idleness, leisure.

laboratory *(SYN.)* lab, workroom, workshop.

laborer *(SYN.)* wage earner, helper, worker, toiler, coolie, blue-collar worker.

laborious *(SYN.)* tiring, difficult, hard, burdensome, industrious, painstaking.

(ANT.) simple, easy, relaxing, restful.

labyrinth *(SYN.)* complex, maze, tangle.

lace *(SYN.)* openwork, fancywork, embroidery, edging.

lacerate *(SYN.)* mangle, tear roughly.

laceration *(SYN.)* cut, wound, puncture, gash, lesion, injury.

lack *(SYN.)* want, need, shortage, dearth, scarcity, require.

(ANT.) profusion, quantity, plentifulness.

lackey *(SYN.)* yesman, stooge, flatterer, flunky.

lacking *(SYN.)* insufficient, short, deficient, incomplete, defective, scanty.

(ANT.) satisfactory, enough, ample, sufficient, adequate.

lackluster *(SYN.)* dull, pallid, flat, lifeless, drab, dim.

laconic *(SYN.)* short, terse, compact, brief, curt, succinct, concise.

lacquer *(SYN.)* polish, varnish, gild.

lad *(SYN.)* youth, boy, fellow, stripling.

laden *(SYN.)* burdened, loaded, weighted.

ladle *(SYN.)* scoop, dipper.

lady *(SYN.)* matron, woman, dame, gentlewoman.

ladylike *(SYN.)* feminine, womanly, maidenly, womanish, female.

(ANT.) masculine, male, virile, mannish, manly.

lag *(SYN.)* dawdle, loiter, linger, poke, dilly-dally, straggle, delay, tarry, slowdown.

laggard *(SYN.)* dallier, idler, lingerer, slowpoke, dawdler.

lair *(SYN.)* retreat, burrow, den, nest, mew, hole.

lambaste *(SYN.)* berate, castigate, scold, censure.

lame *(SYN.)* feeble, maimed, disabled, crippled, deformed, hobbling, unconvincing, weak, poor, inadequate, halt, defective, limping.

(ANT.) vigorous, convincing, plausible, athletic, robust, agile, sound.

lament *(SYN.)* deplore, wail, bemoan, bewail, regret, grieve, mourning, lamentation, moaning, wailing, weep, mourn, sorrow.

(ANT.) celebrate, rejoice.

lamentable *(SYN.)* unfortunate, deplorable.

lamp *(SYN.)* light, beam, illumination, shine, insight, knowledge, understanding, radiance, luminosity, incandescence.

(ANT.) shadow, darkness, obscurity, gloom.

lampoon *(SYN.)* skit, tirade, burlesque, parody, satire.

lance *(SYN.)* cut, pierce, perforate, stab, puncture, impale, knife.

land *(SYN.)* earth, continent, ground, soil, domain, estate, field, realm, plain, surface, arrive, descend, country, island, region, alight, shore, sod, tract, farm.

landlord *(SYN.)* owner, landholder, landowner, proprietor.

landmark *(SYN.)* keystone, monument, milestone, point, cornerstone.

landscape *(SYN.)* panorama, environs, countryside, scenery, scene.

landslide *(SYN.)* rockfall, glissade, avalanche.

lane *(SYN.)* alley, way, road, path, aisle, pass, channel, avenue, artery, passage.

language *(SYN.)* dialect, tongue, speech, lingo, jargon, cant, diction, idiom, patter, phraseology, vernacular, words, lingo, talk, slang.

(ANT.) gibberish, nonsense, babble, drivel.

languid *(SYN.)* feeble, drooping, irresolute, debilitated, dull, lethargic, weak, faint, listless, wearied.

(ANT.) forceful, strong, vigorous.

languish *(SYN.)* decline, sink, droop, wither, waste, fail, wilt, weaken.

(ANT.) revive, rejuvenate, refresh, renew.

languor *(SYN.)* weariness, depression, torpor, inertia, apathy.

lanky *(SYN.)* skinny, gaunt, lean, scrawny, slender, thin.
(ANT.) chunky, stocky, obese, fat.

lantern *(SYN.)* torch, light, lamp, flashlight.

lap *(SYN.)* drink, lick, fold over.

lapse *(SYN.)* decline, sink, go down, slump.

larceny *(SYN.)* pillage, robbery, stealing, theft, burglary, plunder.

lard *(SYN.)* grease, fat.

large *(SYN.)* great, vast, colossal, ample, extensive, capacious, sizable, broad, massive, grand, immense, big, enormous, huge, giant, mammoth, wide.
(ANT.) tiny, little, short, small.

largely *(SYN.)* chiefly, mainly, principally, mostly.

lariat *(SYN.)* lasso, rope.

lark *(SYN.)* fling, frolic, play, fun, spree, joke, revel, celebration.

lascivious *(SYN.)* lecherous, raunchy, lustful, wanton, lewd.

lash *(SYN.)* thong, whip, rod, cane, blow, strike, hit, beat, knout.

lass *(SYN.)* maiden, girl, damsel.
(ANT.) woman.

lasso *(SYN.)* lariat, rope, noose, snare.

last *(SYN.)* terminal, final, ultimate, remain, endure, concluding, latest, utmost, end, conclusive, hindmost, continue, extreme.
(ANT.) first, initial, beginning, opening, starting, foremost.

latch *(SYN.)* clasp, hook, fastener, lock, closing, seal, catch.

late *(SYN.)* overdue, tardy, behind, advanced, delayed, new, slow, recent.
(ANT.) timely, early.

lately *(SYN.)* recently, yesterday.

latent *(SYN.)* potential, undeveloped, unseen, dormant, secret, concealed, inactive, hidden, obscured, covered, quiescent.
(ANT.) visible, evident, conspicuous, explicit, manifest.

lather *(SYN.)* suds, foam, froth.

lateral *(SYN.)* sideways, glancing, tangential, marginal, skirting, side.

latitude *(SYN.)* range, scope, freedom, extent.

latter *(SYN.)* more recent, later.
(ANT.) former.

lattice *(SYN.)* grating, screen, frame, trel-
lis, openwork, framework, grid.

laud *(SYN.)* commend, praise, extol, glorify, compliment.
(ANT.) criticize, belittle.

laudable *(SYN.)* creditable, praiseworthy, commendable, admirable.

laudation *(SYN.)* applause, compliment, flattery, praise, commendation, acclaim, extolling, glorification.
(ANT.) criticizing, condemnation, reproach, disparagement, censure.

laugh *(SYN.)* chuckle, giggle, snicker, cackle, titter, grin, smile, roar, guffaw, jeer, mock.

laughable *(SYN.)* funny, amusing, comical, humorous, ridiculous.

launch *(SYN.)* drive, fire, propel, start, begin, originate, set afloat, initiate.
(ANT.) finish, stop, terminate.

launder *(SYN.)* bathe, wash, scrub, scour.

laurels *(SYN.)* glory, distinction, recognition, award, commendation, reward, honor.

lavatory *(SYN.)* toilet, washroom, bathroom, latrine.

lavish *(SYN.)* squander, waste, dissipate, scatter, abundant, free, plentiful, liberal, extravagant, ample, wear out, prodigal, generous, spend.
(ANT.) economize, save, conserve, accumulate, sparing, stingy, preserve.

law *(SYN.)* decree, formula, statute, act, rule, ruling, standard, principle, ordinance, proclamation, regulation, order, edict.

lawful *(SYN.)* legal, permissible, allowable, legitimate, authorized, constitutional, rightful.
(ANT.) prohibited, criminal, illicit, illegal, illegitimate.

lawless *(SYN.)* uncivilized, uncontrolled, wild, savage, untamed, violent.
(ANT.) obedient, law-abiding, tame.

lawlessness *(SYN.)* chaos, anarchy.

lawn *(SYN.)* grass, meadow, turf.

lawyer *(SYN.)* counsel, attorney, counselor.

lax *(SYN.)* slack, loose, careless, vague, lenient, lazy.
(ANT.) firm, rigid.

lay *(SYN.)* mundane, worldly, temporal, place, dispose, bet, wager, hazard, risk, stake, site, earthly, profane, laic, arrange, location, put, set, ballad, deposit, position, song, secular.

(ANT.) spiritual, unworldly, remove, misplace, disturb, mislay, disarrange, ecclesiastical, religious.

lay off *(SYN.)* discharge, bounce, fire, dismiss.

layout *(SYN.)* plan, arrangement, design.

lazy *(SYN.)* slothful, supine, idle, inactive, sluggish, inert, indolent, torpid.

(ANT.) alert, ambitious, forceful, diligent, active, assiduous.

lea *(SYN.)* pasture, meadow.

leach *(SYN.)* remove, extract, seep, dilute, wash out.

lead *(SYN.)* regulate, conduct, guide, escort, direct, supervise, command, come first, steer, control.

(ANT.) follow.

leader *(SYN.)* master, ruler, captain, chief, commander, principal, director, head, chieftain.

(ANT.) follower, servant, disciple, subordinate, attendant.

leading *(SYN.)* dominant, foremost, principal, first, main, primary.

league *(SYN.)* entente, partnership, association, confederacy, coalition, society, alliance, federation, union.

(ANT.) separation, schism.

leak *(SYN.)* dribble, flow, drip, opening, perforation.

lean *(SYN.)* rely, tilt, slim, slender, slope, incline, tend, trust, bend, tendency, slant, depend, spare, scant, lanky, thin, meager, inclination, narrow, sag.

(ANT.) rise, heavy, fat, erect, straighten, portly, raise.

leaning *(SYN.)* trend, proclivity, bias, tendency, bent, predisposition, proneness.

(ANT.) disinclination, aversion.

leap *(SYN.)* vault, skip, caper, dive, hurdle, jump, bound, start, hop, plunge, spring.

learn *(SYN.)* gain, find out, memorize, acquire, determine.

learned *(SYN.)* erudite, knowing, enlightened, deep, wise, discerning, scholarly, intelligent, educated, sagacious.

(ANT.) simple, uneducated, ignorant, illiterate, unlettered, foolish.

learning *(SYN.)* science, education, lore, apprehension, wisdom, knowledge, scholarship, erudition.

(ANT.) misunderstanding, ignorance, stupidity.

lease *(SYN.)* charter, let, rent, engage.

leash *(SYN.)* chain, strap, shackle, collar.

least *(SYN.)* minutest, smallest, tiniest, trivial, minimum, fewest, slightest.

(ANT.) most.

leave *(SYN.)* give up, retire, desert, abandon, withdraw, relinquish, will, depart, quit, liberty, renounce, go, bequeath, consent, allowance, permission, freedom, forsake.

(ANT.) come, stay, arrive, tarry, remain, abide.

lecherous *(SYN.)* lustful, sensual, carnal, lascivious.

lecture *(SYN.)* talk, discussion, lesson, instruct, speech, conference, sermon, report, recitation, address, oration, discourse.

(ANT.) writing, meditation, correspondence.

ledge *(SYN.)* eaves, ridge, shelf, rim, edge.

lee *(SYN.)* shelter, asylum, sanctuary, haven.

leech *(SYN.)* barnacle, bloodsucker, parasite.

leer *(SYN.)* eye, grimace, ogle, wink, squint.

leeway *(SYN.)* reserve, allowance, elbowroom, slack, clearance.

leftovers *(SYN.)* scraps, remains, residue, remainder.

legacy *(SYN.)* bequest, inheritance, heirloom.

legal *(SYN.)* legitimate, rightful, honest, allowable, allowed, permissible, lawful, permitted, authorized.

(ANT.) illicit, illegal, prohibited, illegitimate.

legalize *(SYN.)* authorize, ordain, approve, sanction.

legate *(SYN.)* envoy, agent, representative, emissary.

legend *(SYN.)* saga, fable, allegory, myth, parable, tale, story, folklore, fiction, chronicle.

(ANT.) history, facts.

legendary *(SYN.)* fictitious, traditional, mythical, imaginary, fanciful.

legible *(SYN.)* plain, readable, clear, distinct.

(ANT.) illegible.

legion *(SYN.)* outfit, unit, troop, regiment, company, battalion, force, army, team, division.

legislation *(SYN.)* resolution, ruling, lawmaking, regulation, enactment, statute, decree.

legislator *(SYN.)* statesman, congressman, senator, politician, lawmaker.

legitimate *(SYN.)* true, real, bona fide, lawful, proper, right, valid, correct, unadulterated, authentic, rightful, legal, sincere.

(ANT.) sham, counterfeit, artificial, false.

leisure *(SYN.)* respite, intermission, ease, relaxation, rest, calm, tranquillity, recreation, peace, pause.

(ANT.) motion, commotion, tumult, agitation, disturbance.

leisurely *(SYN.)* sluggish, laggard, unhurried, relaxed, casual, dawdling, slow, deliberate.

(ANT.) hurried, swift, pressed, rushed, forced, fast, speedy, quick.

lend *(SYN.)* entrust, advance, confer.

length *(SYN.)* reach, measure, extent, distance, span, longness, stretch.

lengthen *(SYN.)* stretch, prolong, draw, reach, increase, grow, protract, extend.

(ANT.) shrink, contract, shorten.

leniency *(SYN.)* grace, pity, compassion, mildness, charity, mercy, clemency.

(ANT.) vengeance, punishment, cruelty.

lenient *(SYN.)* tender, humane, clement, tolerant, compassionate, merciful, relaxed, forgiving, gentle, mild, lax, kind.

(ANT.) unfeeling, pitiless, brutal, remorseless.

leprechaun *(SYN.)* gnome, imp, goblin, fairy, elf, sprite, banshee.

lesion *(SYN.)* wound, blemish, sore, trauma, injury.

less *(SYN.)* fewer, smaller, reduced, negative, stinted.

(ANT.) more.

lessen *(SYN.)* shorten, reduce, deduct, subtract, curtail, diminish, shrink, dwindle, decline, instruction, teaching, remove, decrease.

(ANT.) swell, grow, enlarge, increase, expand, multiply, amplify.

lesson *(SYN.)* exercise, session, class, assignment, section, recitation.

let *(SYN.)* admit, hire out, contract, allow, permit, consent, leave, grant, rent.

(ANT.) deny.

letdown *(SYN.)* disillusionment, disappointment.

lethal *(SYN.)* mortal, dangerous, deadly, fatal, devastating.

lethargic *(SYN.)* sluggish, logy, slow, listless, phlegmatic, lazy.

(ANT.) vivacious, energetic.

lethargy *(SYN.)* numbness, stupor, daze, insensibility, torpor.

(ANT.) wakefulness, liveliness, activity, readiness.

letter *(SYN.)* note, letter, mark, message, character, symbol, sign, memorandum.

letup *(SYN.)* slowdown, slackening, lessening, abatement, reduction.

levee *(SYN.)* dike, breakwater, dam, embankment.

level *(SYN.)* smooth, even, plane, equivalent, uniform, horizontal, equal, flatten, equalize, raze, demolish, flat.

(ANT.) uneven, sloping, hilly, broken.

level-headed *(SYN.)* reasonable, sensible, calm, collected, cool.

leverage *(SYN.)* clout, power, influence, weight, rank.

levity *(SYN.)* humor, triviality, giddiness. hilarity, fun, frivolity.

levy *(SYN.)* tax, duty, tribute, rate, assessment, exaction, charge, custom.

(ANT.) wages, remuneration, gift.

lewd *(SYN.)* indecent, smutty, course, gross, disgusting, impure.

(ANT.) pure, decent, refined.

liability *(SYN.)* indebtedness, answerability, obligation, vulnerability.

liable *(SYN.)* answerable, responsible, likely, exposed to, subject, amenable, probable, accountable.

(ANT.) immune, exempt, independent.

liaison *(SYN.)* union, coupling, link, connection, alliance.

liar *(SYN.)* fibber, falsifier, storyteller, fabricator, prevaricator.

libel *(SYN.)* slander, calumny, vilification, aspersion, defamation.

(ANT.) defense, praise, applause, flattery.

liberal *(SYN.)* large, generous, unselfish, openhanded, broad, tolerant, kind, unprejudiced, open-minded, lavish, plentiful, ample, abundant, extravagant, extensive.

(ANT.) restricted, conservative, stingy,

confined.

liberality *(SYN.)* kindness, philanthropy, beneficence, humanity, altruism, benevolence, generosity, charity.
(ANT.) selfishness, cruelty, malevolence.

liberate *(SYN.)* emancipate, loose, release, let go, deliver, free, discharge.
(ANT.) subjugate, oppress, jail, confine, restrict, imprison.

liberated *(SYN.)* loose, frank, emancipated, careless, liberal, freed, autonomous, exempt, familiar.
(ANT.) subject, clogged, restricted, impeded.

liberty *(SYN.)* permission, independence, autonomy, license, privilege, emancipation, self-government, freedom.
(ANT.) constraint, imprisonment, bondage, captivity.

license *(SYN.)* liberty, freedom, liberation, permission, exemption, authorization, warrant, allow, consent, permit, sanction, approval, unrestraint.
(ANT.) servitude, constraint, bondage, necessity.

lick *(SYN.)* taste, lap, lave.

lid *(SYN.)* top, cover, cap, plug, cork, stopper.

lie *(SYN.)* untruth, fib, illusion, delusion, falsehood, fiction, equivocation, prevarication, repose, location, perjury, misinform, site, recline, similitude.
(ANT.) variance, truth, difference.

life *(SYN.)* sparkle, being, spirit, vivacity, animation, buoyancy, vitality, existence, biography, energy, liveliness, vigor.
(ANT.) demise, lethargy, death, languor.

lift *(SYN.)* hoist, pick up, elevate, raise, heft.

light *(SYN.)* brightness, illumination, beam, gleam, lamp, knowledge, brilliance, fixture, bulb, candle, fire, ignite, burn, dawn, incandescence, flame, airy, unsubstantial, dainty, luminosity, shine, radiance, giddy, enlightenment, weightless, understanding.
(ANT.) darken, gloom, shadow, extinguish, darkness.

lighten *(SYN.)* diminish, unburden, reduce, brighten.

light-headed *(SYN.)* giddy, silly, dizzy, frivolous.
(ANT.) sober, clear-headed, rational.

lighthearted *(SYN.)* carefree, merry, gay, cheerful, happy, glad.
(ANT.) somber, sad, serious, melancholy.

like *(SYN.)* fancy, esteem, adore, love, admire, care for, prefer, cherish.
(ANT.) disapprove, loathe, hate, dislike.

likely *(SYN.)* liable, reasonable, probable, possible.

likeness *(SYN.)* similarity, resemblance, representation, image, portrait.
(ANT.) difference.

likewise *(SYN.)* besides, as well, also, too, similarly.

liking *(SYN.)* fondness, affection, partiality.
(ANT.) antipathy, dislike.

limb *(SYN.)* arm, leg, member, appendage, part, bough.

limber *(SYN.)* bending, flexible, elastic, pliable.
(ANT.) inflexible, stiff.

limbo *(SYN.)* exile, banishment, purgatory.

limelight *(SYN.)* spotlight, notice, notoriety, fame, prominence.

limerick *(SYN.)* jingle, rhyme.

limit *(SYN.)* terminus, bound, extent, confine, border, restriction, boundary, restraint, edge, frontier, check, end, limitation.
(ANT.) endlessness, vastness, boundlessness.

limn *(SYN.)* depict, portray, sketch, paint, illustrate.

limp *(SYN.)* soft, flabby, drooping, walk, limber, supple, flexible, hobble, stagger.
(ANT.) stiff.

limpid *(SYN.)* clear, open, transparent, unobstructed.
(ANT.) cloudy.

line *(SYN.)* row, file, series, array, sequence, wire, seam, wrinkle, crease, boundary, arrangement, kind, type, division.

lineage *(SYN.)* race, family, tribe, nation, strain, folk, people, ancestry, clan.

linger *(SYN.)* wait, rest, bide, delay, dwadle, stay, loiter, remain, dilly-dally, tarry.
(ANT.) leave, expedite.

lingo *(SYN.)* vernacular, dialect, language, jargon, speech.

link *(SYN.)* unite, connector, loop, couple, attach, connective, connection, coupling, juncture, bond.

(ANT.) separate, disconnect, split.
lip *(SYN.)* edge, brim, rim.
liquid *(SYN.)* watery, fluent, fluid, flowing.
(ANT.) solid, congealed.
liquidate *(SYN.)* pay off, settle, defray.
liquor *(SYN.)* spirits, alcohol, drink, booze.
lissom *(SYN.)* nimble, quick, lively, flexible, agile.
list *(SYN.)* roll, register, slate, enumeration, series.
listen *(SYN.)* overhear, attend to, heed, hear, list, hearken.
(ANT.) ignore, scorn, disregard, reject.
listless *(SYN.)* uninterested, tired, lethargic, unconcerned, apathetic.
(ANT.) active.
literal *(SYN.)* exact, verbatim, precise, strict, faithful.
literally *(SYN.)* actually, exactly, really.
literate *(SYN.)* informed, educated, learned, intelligent, versed, knowledgeable.
(ANT.) unread, illiterate, ignorant, unlettered.
literature *(SYN.)* books, writings, publications.
lithe *(SYN.)* supple, flexible, bending, limber, pliable.
(ANT.) stiff.
litigious *(SYN.)* quarrelsome, disputatious, argumentative.
litter *(SYN.)* rubbish, trash, scatter, clutter, strew, debris, rubble, disorder.
little *(SYN.)* tiny, petty, miniature, diminutive, puny, wee, significant, small, short, brief, bit, trivial.
(ANT.) huge, large, big, long, immense.
liturgy *(SYN.)* ritual, sacrament, worship, service.
live *(SYN.)* dwell, reside, abide, survive, exist, alive, occupy, stay, active, surviving.
(ANT.) die.
livelihood *(SYN.)* keep, sustenance, support, subsistence, job, trade, profession, vocation.
lively *(SYN.)* blithe, vivaciousness, clear, vivid, active, frolicsome, brisk, fresh, animated, energetic, live, spry, vigorous, quick, nimble, bright, exciting, supple.
(ANT.) stale, dull, listless, slow, vapid.
livestock *(SYN.)* animals, cattle.

livid *(SYN.)* grayish, furious, pale, enraged.
living *(SYN.)* support, livelihood, existent, alive.
load *(SYN.)* oppress, trouble, burden, weight, freight, afflict, encumber, pack, shipment, cargo, lade, tax.
(ANT.) lighten, console, unload, mitigate, empty, ease.
loafer *(SYN.)* loiterer, bum, idler, sponger, deadbeat.
loan *(SYN.)* credit, advance, lend.
loath *(SYN.)* reluctant, unwilling, opposed.
loathe *(SYN.)* dislike, despise, hate, abhor, detest, abominate.
(ANT.) love, approve, like, admire.
loathsome *(SYN.)* foul, vile, detestable, revolting, abominable, atrocious, offensive, odious.
(ANT.) pleasant, commendable, alluring, agreeable, delightful.
lob *(SYN.)* toss, hurl, pitch, throw, heave.
lobby *(SYN.)* foyer, entry, entrance, vestibule, passageway, entryway.
local *(SYN.)* limited, regional, restricted, particular.
locality *(SYN.)* nearness, neighborhood, district, vicinity.
(ANT.) remoteness.
locate *(SYN.)* discover, find, unearth, site, situate, place.
located *(SYN.)* found, residing, positioned, situated, placed.
location *(SYN.)* spot, locale, station, locality, situation, place, area, site, vicinity, position, zone, region.
lock *(SYN.)* curl, hook, bolt, braid, ringlet, plait, close, latch, tuft, fastening, bar, hasp, fasten, tress.
(ANT.) open.
locker *(SYN.)* wardrobe, closet, cabinet, chest.
locket *(SYN.)* case, lavaliere, pendant.
locomotion *(SYN.)* movement, travel, transit, motion.
locution *(SYN.)* discourse, cadence, manner, accent.
lodge *(SYN.)* cabin, cottage, hut, club, chalet, society, room, reside, dwell, live, occupy, inhabit, abide, board, fix, settle.
lodger *(SYN.)* guest, tenant, boarder, occupant.
lofty *(SYN.)* high, stately, grandiose,

towering, elevated, exalted, sublime, majestic, scornful, proud, grand, tall, pompous.
(ANT.) undignified, lowly, common, ordinary.

log *(SYN.)* lumber, wood, board, register, record, album, account, journal, timber.

logical *(SYN.)* strong, effective, telling, convincing, reasonable, sensible, rational, sane, sound, cogent.
(ANT.) crazy, illogical, irrational, unreasonable, weak.

logy *(SYN.)* tired, inactive, lethargic, sleepy, weary.

loiter *(SYN.)* idle, linger, wait, stay, tarry, dilly-dally, dawdle.

loll *(SYN.)* hang, droop, recline, repose, relax.

lone *(SYN.)* lonely, sole, unaided, single, deserted, isolated, secluded, apart, alone, solitary.
(ANT.) surrounded, accompanied.

loner *(SYN.)* recluse, maverick, outsider, hermit.

loneliness *(SYN.)* solitude, isolation, seclusion, alienation.

lonely *(SYN.)* unaided, isolated, single, solitary, lonesome, unaccompanied, deserted, alone, desolate.
(ANT.) surrounded, attended.

lonesome *(SYN.)* secluded, remote, unpopulated, barren, empty, desolate.

long *(SYN.)* lengthy, prolonged, wordy, elongated, extended, lingering, drawn out, lasting, protracted, extensive, length, prolix, far-reaching, extended.
(ANT.) terse, concise, abridged, short.

long-standing *(SYN.)* persistent, established.

long-winded *(SYN.)* boring, dull, wordy.
(ANT.) curt, terse.

look *(SYN.)* gaze, witness, seem, eye, behold, see, watch, scan, view, appear, stare, discern, glance, examine, examination, peep, expression, appearance, regard, study, contemplation, survey.
(ANT.) overlook, hide, avert, miss.

loom *(SYN.)* emerge, appear, show up.

loop *(SYN.)* ringlet, noose, spiral, fastener.

loose *(SYN.)* untied, unbound, lax, vague, unrestrained, dissolute, limp, undone, baggy, disengaged, indefinite, slack,

careless, heedless, unfastened, free, wanton.
(ANT.) restrained, steady, fastened, secure, tied, firm, fast, definite, inhibited.

loosen *(SYN.)* untie, undo, loose, unchain.
(ANT.) tie, tighten, secure.

loot *(SYN.)* booty, plunder, take, steal, rob, sack, rifle, pillage, ravage, devastate.

lope *(SYN.)* run, race, bound, gallop.

lopsided *(SYN.)* unequal, twisted, uneven, askew, distorted.

loquacious *(SYN.)* garrulous, wordy, profuse, chatty, verbose.

lord *(SYN.)* peer, ruler, proprietor, nobleman, master, owner, boss, governor.

lore *(SYN.)* learning, knowledge, wisdom, stories, legends beliefs, teachings.

lose *(SYN.)* misplace, flop, fail, sacrifice, forfeit, mislay, vanish, surrender.
(ANT.) succeed, locate, place, win, discover, find.

loss *(SYN.)* injury, damage, want, hurt, need, bereavement, trouble, death, failure, deficiency.

lost *(SYN.)* dazed, wasted, astray, forfeited, preoccupied, used, adrift, bewildered, missing, distracted, consumed, misspent, absorbed, confused, mislaid, gone, destroyed.
(ANT.) found, anchored.

lot *(SYN.)* result, destiny, bunch, many, amount, fate, cluster, group, sum, portion, outcome, number, doom, issue.

lotion *(SYN.)* cosmetic, salve, balm, cream.

lottery *(SYN.)* wager, chance, drawing, raffle.

loud *(SYN.)* vociferous, noisy, resounding, stentorian, clamorous, sonorous, thunderous, shrill, blaring, roaring, deafening.
(ANT.) soft, inaudible, murmuring, subdued, quiet, dulcet.

lounge *(SYN.)* idle, loaf, laze, sofa, couch, davenport, relax, rest, lobby, salon, divan.

louse *(SYN.)* scoundrel, knave, cad, rat.

lousy *(SYN.)* revolting, grimy, rotten, dirty, disgusting.

lovable *(SYN.)* charming, attractive,

delightful, amiable, sweet, cuddly, likeable.

love *(SYN.)* attachment, endearment, affection, adoration, liking, devotion, warmth, tenderness, friendliness, adore, worship, like, cherish, fondness.
(ANT.) *loathing, detest, indifference, dislike, hate, hatred.*

loveliness *(SYN.)* grace, pulchritude, elegance, charm, attractiveness, comeliness, fairness, beauty.
(ANT.) *ugliness, eyesore, disfigurement, deformity.*

lovely *(SYN.)* handsome, fair, charming, pretty, attractive, delightful, beautiful, beauteous, exquisite, comely.
(ANT.) *ugly, unsightly, homely, foul, hideous, repulsive.*

lover *(SYN.)* fiance, suitor, courter, sweetheart, beau.

loving *(SYN.)* close, intimate, confidential, affectionate, friendly.
(ANT.) *formal, conventional, ceremonious, distant.*

low *(SYN.)* mean, vile, despicable, vulgar, abject, groveling, contemptible, lesser, menial.
(ANT.) *righteous, lofty, esteemed, noble.*

lower *(SYN.)* subordinate, minor, secondary, quiet, soften, disgrace, degrade, decrease, reduce, diminish, inferior.
(ANT.) *greater, superior, increase, better.*

loyal *(SYN.)* earnest, ardent, addicted, inclined, faithful, devoted, affectionate, prone, fond, patriotic, dependable, true.
(ANT.) *indisposed, detached, disloyal, traitorous, untrammeled.*

loyalty *(SYN.)* devotion, steadfastness, constancy, faithfulness, fidelity, patriotism, allegiance.
(ANT.) *treachery, falseness, disloyalty.*

lubricate *(SYN.)* oil, grease, anoint.

lucent *(SYN.)* radiant, beaming, vivid, illuminated, lustrous.

lucid *(SYN.)* plain, visible, clear, intelligible, unmistakable, transparent, limpid, translucent, open, shining, light.
(ANT.) *unclear, vague, obscure.*

luck *(SYN.)* chance, fortunate, fortune, lot, fate, fluke, destiny, karma.
(ANT.) *misfortune.*

lucrative *(SYN.)* well-paying, profitable, high-paying, productive, beneficial.

ludicrous *(SYN.)* absurd, ridiculous, preposterous.

lug *(SYN.)* pull, haul, drag, tug.

luggage *(SYN.)* bags, valises, baggage, suitcases, trunks.

lugubrious *(SYN.)* mournful, sad, gloomy, somber, melancholy.

lukewarm *(SYN.)* unenthusiastic, tepid, spiritless, detached, apathetic, mild.

lull *(SYN.)* quiet, calm, soothe, rest, hush, stillness, pause, break, intermission.

lumber *(SYN.)* logs, timber, wood.

luminous *(SYN.)* beaming, lustrous, shining, glowing, gleaming, bright, light.
(ANT.) *murky, dull, dark.*

lummox *(SYN.)* yokel, oaf, bumpkin, clown, klutz.

lump *(SYN.)* swelling, protuberance, mass, chunk, hunk, bump.

lunacy *(SYN.)* derangement, madness, aberration, psychosis, craziness.
(ANT.) *stability, rationality.*

lunge *(SYN.)* charge, stab, attack, thrust, push.

lurch *(SYN.)* topple, sway, toss, roll, rock, tip, pitch.

lure *(SYN.)* draw, tug, drag, entice, attraction, haul, attract, temptation, persuade, pull, draw on, allure.
(ANT.) *drive, alienate, propel.*

lurid *(SYN.)* sensational, terrible, melodramatic, startling.

lurk *(SYN.)* sneak, hide, prowl, slink, creep.

luscious *(SYN.)* savory, delightful, juicy, sweet, pleasing, delectable, palatable, delicious, tasty.
(ANT.) *unsavory, nauseous, acrid.*

lush *(SYN.)* tender, succulent, ripe, juicy.

lust *(SYN.)* longing, desire, passion, appetite, craving, aspiration, urge.
(ANT.) *hate, aversion, loathing, distaste.*

lusty *(SYN.)* healthy, strong, mighty, powerful, sturdy, strapping, hale, hardy.
(ANT.) *weak.*

luxuriant *(SYN.)* abundant, flourishing, dense, lush, rich.

luxurious *(SYN.)* rich, lavish, deluxe, splendid.
(ANT.) *simple, crude, sparse.*

luxury *(SYN.)* frills, comfort, extravagance, elegance, splendor.
(ANT.) *poverty.*

lyric *(SYN.)* musical, text, words, libretto.

lyrical *(SYN.)* poetic, musical.

macabre *(SYN.)* ghastly, grim, horrible, gruesome.

maceration *(SYN.)* dilution, washing.

machination *(SYN.)* hoax, swindle, cardsharping, cunning, plot, cabal, conspriracy.

machinator *(SYN.)* stragetist, schemer, schemist.

machine *(SYN.)* motor, mechanism, device, contrivance.

machinist *(SYN.)* engineer.

macilent *(SYN.)* gaunt, lean, lank, meager, emaciated.

mactation *(SYN.)* immolation, self-immolation, infanticide.

macula *(SYN.)* mole, patch, freckle, spot.

maculate *(SYN.)* bespot, stipple.

maculation *(SYN.)* irisation, striae, iridescence, spottiness.

mad *(SYN.)* incensed, crazy, insane, angry, furious, delirious, provoked, enraged, demented, maniacal, exasperated, wrathful, crazy, deranged.

(ANT.) sane, calm, healthy, rational, lucid, cheerful, happy.

madam *(SYN.)* dame, woman, lady, matron, mistress.

madden *(SYN.)* anger, annoy, infuriate, enrage, provoke, asperate, outrage.

(ANT.) please, mollify, calm.

madder *(SYN.)* ruddle.

madness *(SYN.)* derangement, delirium, aberration, mania, insanity, craziness, frenzy, psychosis.

(ANT.) stability, rationality.

maelstrom *(SYN.)* surge, rapids, eddy, white water, riptide.

magazine *(SYN.)* journal, periodical, arsenal, armory.

magic *(SYN.)* sorcery, wizardry, charm, legerdemain, enchantment, black art, necromancy, conjuring.

magical *(SYN.)* mystical, marvelous, magic, miraculous, bewitching, spellbinding.

magician *(SYN.)* conjuror, sorcerer, wizard, witch, artist, trickster.

magistrate *(SYN.)* judge, adjudicator.

magnanimous *(SYN.)* giving, bountiful, beneficent, unselfish.

(ANT.) stingy, greedy, selfish.

magnate *(SYN.)* leader, bigwig, tycoon, chief, giant.

magnet *(SYN.)* enticer, enticement, lure, temptation.

magnetic *(SYN.)* pulling, attractive, alluring, drawing, enthralling, seductive.

magnetism *(SYN.)* allure, irresistibility, attraction, appeal.

magnificence *(SYN.)* luxury, grandeur, splendor, majesty, dynamic, mesmerizing.

magnificent *(SYN.)* rich, lavish, luxurious, splendid, wonderful, extraordinary, impressive.

(ANT.) simple, plain.

magnify *(SYN.)* heighten, exaggerate, amplify, expand, stretch, caricature, increase, enhance.

(ANT.) compress understate, depreciate, belittle.

magnitude *(SYN.)* mass, bigness, size, area, volume, dimensions, greatness, extent, measure, importance, consequence, significance.

maid *(SYN.)* chambermaid, servant, maidservant.

maiden *(SYN.)* original, foremost, first, damsel, lass, miss.

(ANT.) accessory, secondary.

mail *(SYN.)* dispatch, send, letters, post, correspondence.

maim *(SYN.)* disable, cripple, hurt, wound, injure, mangle, mutilate, incapacitate.

main *(SYN.)* essential, chief, highest, principal, first, leading, cardinal, supreme, foremost.

(ANT.) supplemental, subordinate, auxiliary.

mainstay *(SYN.)* buttress, pillar, refuge, reinforcement, support, backbone.

maintain *(SYN.)* claim, support, uphold, defend, vindicate, sustain, continue, allege, contend, preserve, affirm, keep, justify, keep up.

(ANT.) neglect, oppose, discontinue, resist, deny.

maintenance *(SYN.)* subsistence, livelihood, living, support, preservation, upkeep.

majestic *(SYN.)* magnificent, stately, noble, august, grand, imposing, sublime, lofty, high, grandiose, dignified, royal, kingly, princely, regal.

(ANT.) humble, lowly, undignified, common, ordinary.

majesty *(SYN.)* grandeur, dignity, nobility, splendor, distinction, eminence.

major *(SYN.)* important, superior, larger, chief, greater, uppermost.
(ANT.) inconsequential, minor.

make *(SYN.)* execute, cause, produce, establish, assemble, create, shape, compel, fashion, construct, build, fabricate, manufacture, form, become.
(ANT.) unmake, break, undo, demolish.

make-believe *(SYN.)* pretend, imagined, simulated, false, fake, unreal.

maker *(SYN.)* inventor, creator, producer, builder, manufacturer, originator.

makeshift *(SYN.)* proxy, deputy, understudy, expedient, agent, lieutenant, alternate, substitute, equivalent.
(ANT.) sovereign, head, principal.

make-up *(SYN.)* composition, formation, structure, cosmetics.

malady *(SYN.)* disease, illness, sickness, ailment, infirmity, disorder, affliction.
(ANT.) vigor, healthiness, health.

malaise *(SYN.)* anxiety, apprehension, dissatisfaction, uneasiness, nervousness, disquiet, discontent.

male *(SYN.)* masculine, virile.
(ANT.) female, womanly, feminine.

malcontent *(SYN.)* displeased, ill-humored, querulous, discontented, quarrelsome.

malefactor *(SYN.)* perpetrator, gangster, hoodlum, wrongdoer, troublemaker, criminal, scoundrel, evildoer, lawbreaker.

malevolence *(SYN.)* spite, malice, enmity, rancor, animosity.
(ANT.) love, affection, toleration, kindness.

malfunction *(SYN.)* flaw, breakdown, snag, glitch, failure.

malice *(SYN.)* spite, grudge, enmity, ill will, malignity, animosity, rancor, resentment, viciousness, grudge, bitterness.
(ANT.) love, affection, toleration, benevolence, charity.

malicious *(SYN.)* hostile, malignant, virulent, bitter, rancorous, evil-minded, malevolent, spiteful, wicked.
(ANT.) kind, benevolent, affectionate.

malign *(SYN.)* misuse, defame, revile, abuse, traduce, asperse, misapply, disparage.

(ANT.) praise, cherish, protect, honor.

malignant *(SYN.)* harmful, deadly, killing, lethal, mortal, destructive, hurtful, malicious.
(ANT.) benign, harmless.

malingerer *(SYN.)* quitter, idler, goldbrick.

malleable *(SYN.)* meek, tender, soft, lenient, flexible, mild, compassionate, supple.
(ANT.) tough, rigid, unyielding, hard.

malodorous *(SYN.)* reeking, fetid, smelly, noxious, vile, rancid, offensive,

malpractice *(SYN.)* wrongdoing, misdeed, abuse, malfeasance, error, mismanagement, dereliction, fault, sin, misconduct.

maltreat *(SYN.)* mistreat, ill-treatment, abuse.

maltreatment *(SYN.)* disparagement, perversion, aspersion, invective, defamation, profanation.
(ANT.) respect, approval, laudation, commendation.

mammoth *(SYN.)* enormous, immense, huge, colossal, gigantic, gargantuan, ponderous.
(ANT.) minuscule, tiny, small.

man *(SYN.)* person, human-being, society, folk, soul, individual, mortal, fellow, male, gentleman.
(ANT.) woman.

manacle *(SYN.)* chain, shackle, cuff, handcuff, bond.

manage *(SYN.)* curb, govern, direct, bridle, command, regulate, repress, check, restrain, dominate, guide, lead, supervise, superintend, control, rule.
(ANT.) forsake, submit, abandon, mismanage, bungle.

manageable *(SYN.)* willing, obedient, docile, controllable, tractable, submissive, governable, wieldy, untroublesome.
(ANT.) recalcitrant, unmanageable, wild.

management *(SYN.)* regulation, administration, supervision, direction, control.

manager *(SYN.)* overseer, superintendent, supervisor, director, boss, executive.

mandate *(SYN.)* order, injunction, command, referendum, dictate, writ, directive, commission.

mandatory *(SYN.)* compulsory, required, obligatory, imperative, necessary. *(ANT.) optional.*

maneuver *(SYN.)* execution, effort, proceeding, enterprise, working, action, operation, agency, instrumentality. *(ANT.) rest, inaction, cessation.*

mangle *(SYN.)* tear apart, cut, maim, wound, mutilate, injure, break, demolish.

mangy *(SYN.)* shoddy, frazzled, seedy, threadbare, shabby, ragged, sordid.

manhandle *(SYN.)* maltreat, maul, abuse, ill-treat.

manhood *(SYN.)* maturity, manliness. *(ANT.) youth.*

mania *(SYN.)* insanity, enthusiasm, craze, desire, madness.

manic *(SYN.)* excited, hyped up, agitated.

manifest *(SYN.)* open, evident, lucid, clear, distinct, unobstructed, cloudless, apparent, intelligible, apparent. *(ANT.) vague, overcast, unclear, cloudy, hidden, concealed.*

manifesto *(SYN.)* pronouncement, edict, proclamation, statement, declaration.

manifold *(SYN.)* various, many, multiple, numerous, abundant, copious, profuse. *(ANT.) few.*

manipulate *(SYN.)* manage, feel, work, operate, handle, touch, maneuver.

manly *(SYN.)* strong, brave, masculine, manful, courageous, stalwart.

man-made *(SYN.)* artificial. *(ANT.) natural.*

manner *(SYN.)* air, demeanor, custom, style, method, deportment, mode, habit, practice, way, behavior, fashion.

mannerism *(SYN.)* eccentricity, quirk, habit, peculiarity, idiosyncrasy, trait.

mannerly *(SYN.)* well-bred, gentlemanly, courteous, suave, polite, genteel.

manor *(SYN.)* land, mansion, estate, domain, villa, castle, property, palace.

manslaughter *(SYN.)* murder, killing, assassination, homicide, elimination.

mantle *(SYN.)* serape, garment, overgarment, cover, cloak, wrap.

manual *(SYN.)* directory, guidebook, handbook, physical, laborious, menial.

manufacture *(SYN.)* construct, make, assemble, fabricate, produce, fashion, build.

manure *(SYN.)* fertilizer, droppings, waste, compost.

manuscript *(SYN.)* copy, writing, work, paper, composition, document.

many *(SYN.)* numerous, various, divers, multitudinous, sundry, multifarious, several, manifold, abundant, plentiful. *(ANT.) infrequent, meager, few, scanty.*

map *(SYN.)* sketch, plan, chart, graph, itinerary.

mar *(SYN.)* spoil, hurt, damage, impair, harm, deface, injure. *(ANT.) repair, benefit, mend.*

marathon *(SYN.)* relay, race, contest.

maraud *(SYN.)* invade, plunder, loot, ransack, ravage, raid.

march *(SYN.)* promenade, parade, pace, hike, walk, tramp.

margin *(SYN.)* boundary, border, rim, edge.

marginal *(SYN.)* unnecessary, nonessential, borderline, noncritical. *(ANT.) essential.*

marine *(SYN.)* naval, oceanic, nautical, ocean, maritime.

mariner *(SYN.)* seafarer, gob, seaman, sailor.

marionette *(SYN.)* doll, puppet.

maritime *(SYN.)* shore, coastal, nautical.

mark *(SYN.)* stain, badge, stigma, vestige, sign, feature, label, characteristic, trace, brand, trait, scar, indication, impression, effect, imprint, stamp, brand.

marked *(SYN.)* plain, apparent, noticeable, evident, decided, noted, special, noteworthy.

market *(SYN.)* supermarket, store, bazaar, mart, stall, marketplace, plaza, emporium.

maroon *(SYN.)* desert, leave behind, forsake, abandon, jettison.

marriage *(SYN.)* wedding, matrimony, nuptials, espousal, union, alliance, association. *(ANT.) divorce, celibacy, separation.*

marrow *(SYN.)* center, core, gist, essential, soul.

marry *(SYN.)* wed, espouse, betroth.

marsh *(SYN.)* bog, swamp, mire, everglade, estuary.

marshal *(SYN.)* adjutant, officer, order, arrange, rank.

mart *(SYN.)* shop, market, store.

martial *(SYN.)* warlike, combative, militant, belligerent.

(ANT.) peaceful.

martyr *(SYN.)* victim, sufferer, tortured, torment, plague, harass, persecute.

marvel *(SYN.)* phenomenon, wonder, miracle, astonishment, sensation.

marvelous *(SYN.)* rare, wonderful, extraordinary, unusual, exceptional, miraculous, wondrous, amazing, astonishing, astounding.

(ANT.) usual, common, ordinary. commonplace.

mascot *(SYN.)* pet, amulet, charm.

masculine *(SYN.)* robust, manly, virile, strong, bold, male, lusty, vigorous, hardy, mannish.

(ANT.) weak, emasculated, feminine, effeminate, womanish, female, unmasculine.

mash *(SYN.)* mix, pulverize, crush, grind, crumble, granulate.

mask *(SYN.)* veil, disguise, cloak, secrete, withhold, hide, cover, protection, protector, camouflage, conceal, screen.

(ANT.) uncover, reveal, disclose, show, expose.

masquerade *(SYN.)* pretend, disguise, pose, impersonate, costume party.

mass *(SYN.)* society, torso, body, remains, association, carcass, bulk, company, pile, heap, quantity, aggregation.

(ANT.) spirit, mind, intellect.

massacre *(SYN.)* butcher, murder, carnage, slaughter, execute, slay, genocide, killing, butchery, extermination.

(ANT.) save, protect, vivify, animate.

massage *(SYN.)* knead, rub, stroke.

masses *(SYN)* populace, crowd, multitude, people.

massive *(SYN.)* grave, cumbersome, heavy, sluggish, ponderous, serious, burdensome, huge, immense, tremendous, gigantic.

(ANT.) light, animated, small, tiny, little.

mast *(SYN.)* pole, post.

master *(SYN.)* owner, employer, leader, ruler, chief, head, lord, teacher, manager, holder, commander, overseer, expert, maestro, genius, captain, director, boss.

(ANT.) slave, servant.

masterful *(SYN.)* commanding, bossy, domineering, dictatorial, cunning, wise, accomplished, skillful, sharp.

masterly *(SYN.)* adroit, superb, skillful,

expert.

(ANT.) awkward, clumsy.

mastermind *(SYN.)* prodigy, sage, guru, mentor.

masterpiece *(SYN.)* prizewinner, classic, perfection, model.

mastery *(SYN.)* sway, sovereignty, domination, transcendence, ascendancy, influence, jurisdiction, prestige.

masticate *(SYN.)* chew.

mat *(SYN.)* cover, rug, pallet, bedding, pad.

match *(SYN.)* equivalent, equal, contest, balance, resemble, peer, mate.

matchless *(SYN.)* peerless, incomparable, unequaled, unrivaled, excellent.

(ANT.) ordinary, unimpressive.

mate *(SYN.)* friend, colleague, associate, partner, companion, comrade.

(ANT.) stranger, adversary.

material *(SYN.)* sensible, momentous, germane, bodily, palpable, important, physical, essential, corporeal, tangible, substance, matter, fabric.

(ANT.) metaphysical, spiritual, insignificant, mental, immaterial, irrelevant, intangible.

materialize *(SYN.)* take shape, finalize, embody, incarnate, emerge, appear.

maternal *(SYN.)* motherly.

(ANT.) fatherly.

mathematics *(SYN.)* measurements, computations, numbers, calculation, figures.

matrimony *(SYN.)* marriage, wedding, espousal, union.

(ANT.) virginity, divorce.

matrix *(SYN.)* template, stamp, negative, stencil, mold, form, die, cutout.

matron *(SYN.)* lady.

matted *(SYN.)* tangled, clustered, rumpled, shaggy, knotted, gnarled, tousled.

matter *(SYN.)* cause, thing, substance, occasion, material, moment, topic, stuff, concern, theme, subject, consequence, affair, business, interest.

(ANT.) spirit, immateriality.

mature *(SYN.)* ready, matured, complete, ripe, consummate, mellow, aged, seasoned, full-grown.

(ANT.) raw, crude, undeveloped, young, immature, innocent.

maudlin *(SYN.)* emotional, mushy, sentimental, mawkish.

maul *(SYN.)* pummel, mistreat,

manhandle, beat, batter, bruise, abuse.

mausoleum *(SYN.)* shrine, tomb, vault.

maverick *(SYN.)* nonconformist, oddball, outsider, dissenter, loner.

mawkish *(SYN.)* sentimental, emotional, nostalgic.

maxim *(SYN.)* rule, code, law, proverb, principle, saying, adage, motto.

maximum *(SYN.)* highest, largest, head, greatest, supremacy, climax.
(ANT.) minimum.

may *(SYN.)* can, be able.

maybe *(SYN.)* feasibly, perchance, perhaps, possibly.
(ANT.) definitely.

mayhem *(SYN.)* brutality, viciousness, ruthlessness.

maze *(SYN.)* complex, labyrinth, network, muddle, confusion, snarl, tangle.

meadow *(SYN.)* field, pasture, lea, range, grassland.

meager *(SYN.)* sparse, scanty, mean, frugal, deficient, slight, paltry, inadequate.
(ANT.) ample, plentiful, abundant, bountiful.

meal *(SYN.)* refreshment, dinner, lunch, repast, breakfast.

mean *(SYN.)* sordid, base, intend, plan, propose, expect, indicate, denote, say, signify, suggest, express, average, nasty, middle, contemptible, offensive, vulgar, unkind, cruel, despicable, vile, low, medium.
(ANT.) dignified, noble, exalted, thoughtful, gentle, openhanded, kind, generous, admirable.

meander *(SYN.)* wind, stray, wander, twist

meaning *(SYN.)* gist, connotation, intent, purport, drift, acceptation, implication, sense, import, interpretation, denotation, signification, explanation, purpose, significance.

meaningful *(SYN.)* profound, deep, expressive, important, crucial.

meaningless *(SYN.)* nonsensical, senseless, unreasonable, preposterous.

means *(SYN.)* utensil, channel, agent, money, riches, vehicle, apparatus, device, wealth, support, medium, instrument.
(ANT.) preventive, impediment, hindrance.

measly *(SYN.)* scanty, puny, skimpy, meager, petty.

measure *(SYN.)* law, bulk, rule, criterion, size, volume, weight, standard, dimension, breadth, depth, test, touchstone, trial, length, extent, gauge.
(ANT.) guess, chance, supposition.

measureless *(SYN.)* immeasurable, immense, boundless, limitless, infinite, vast.
(ANT.) figurable, ascertainable, measurable.

meat *(SYN.)* lean, flesh, food.

mecca *(SYN.)* target, shrine, goal, sanctuary, destination.

mechanic *(SYN.)* repairman, machinist.

mechanism *(SYN.)* device, contrivance, tool, machine, machinery.

medal *(SYN.)* decoration, award, badge, medallion, reward, ribbon, prize, honor.

meddle *(SYN.)* tamper, interpose, pry, snoop, intrude, interrupt, interfere, monkey.

meddlesome *(SYN.)* forward, bothersome, intrusive, obtrusive.

media *(SYN.)* tools, instruments, implements.

mediate *(SYN.)* settle, intercede, umpire, intervene, negotiate, arbitrate, referee.

medicinal *(SYN.)* helping, healing, remedial, therapeutic, corrective.

medicine *(SYN.)* drug, medication, remedy, cure, prescription, potion.

mediocre *(SYN.)* medium, mean, average, moderate, fair, ordinary.
(ANT.) outstanding, exceptional.

meditate *(SYN.)* remember, muse, think, judge, mean, conceive, contemplate, deem, suppose, purpose, consider, picture, reflect, believe, plan, reckon.

medium *(SYN.)* modicum, average, middling, median.
(ANT.) extreme.

medley *(SYN.)* hodgepodge, mixture, assortment, conglomeration, mishmash, miscellany.

meek *(SYN.)* subdued, dull, tedious, flat, docile, domesticated, tame, insipid, domestic.
(ANT.) spirited, exciting, savage, wild.

meet *(SYN.)* fulfill, suffer, find, collide, gratify, engage, connect, converge, encounter, unite, join, satisfy, settle, greet, answer, undergo, answer, meeting, contest, match, assemble, discharge, gather, convene, congregate, confront, intersect.

(ANT.) scatter, disperse, separate, cleave.

melancholy *(SYN.)* disconsolate, dejected, despondent, glum, somber, pensive, moody, dispirited, depressed, gloomy, dismal, doleful, depression, downcast, gloom, sadness, sad, grave, downhearted, sorrowful.

(ANT.) happy, cheerful, merry.

meld *(SYN.)* unite, mix, combine, fuse, merge, blend, commingle, amalgamate.

melee *(SYN.)* battle royal, fight, brawl, free-for-all, fracas.

mellow *(SYN.)* mature, ripe, aged, cured, full-flavored, sweet, smooth, melodious, develop, soften.

(ANT.) unripened, immature.

melodious *(SYN.)* lilting, musical, lyric, dulcet, mellifluous, tuneful, melodic.

melodramatic *(SYN.)* dramatic, ceremonious, affected, stagy, histrionic, overwrought, sensational, stagy.

(ANT.) unemotional, subdued, modest.

melody *(SYN.)* strain, concord, music, air, song, tune, harmony.

melt *(SYN.)* dissolve, liquefy, blend, fade out, vanish, dwindle, disappear, thaw.

(ANT.) freeze, harden, solidify.

member *(SYN.)* share, part, allotment, moiety, element, concern, interest, lines, faction, role, apportionment.

(ANT.) whole.

membrane *(SYN.)* layer, sheath, tissue, covering.

memento *(SYN.)* keepsake, token, reminder, trophy, sign, souvenir, remembrance.

memoirs *(SYN.)* diary, reflections, experiences, autobiography, journal, confessions.

memorable *(SYN.)* important, historic, significant, unforgettable, noteworthy, momentous, crucial, impressive.

(ANT.) passing, forgettable, transitory, commonplace.

memorandum *(SYN.)* letter, mark, token, note, indication, remark, message.

memorial *(SYN.)* monument, souvenir, memento, remembrance, commemoration, reminiscent, ritual, testimonial.

memorize *(SYN.)* study, remember.

memory *(SYN.)* renown, remembrance, reminiscence, fame, retrospection, recollection, reputation.

(ANT.) oblivion.

menace *(SYN.)* warning, threat, intimidation, warn, threaten, imperil, forebode.

menagerie *(SYN.)* collection, zoo, kennel.

mend *(SYN.)* restore, better, refit, sew, remedy, patch, correct, repair, rectify, ameliorate, improve, reform, recover, fix.

(ANT.) hurt, deface, rend, destroy.

mendacious *(SYN.)* dishonest, false, lying, deceitful, deceptive, tricky.

(ANT.) honest, truthful, sincere, creditable.

mendicant *(SYN.)* ragamuffin, vagabond, beggar.

menial *(SYN.)* unskilled, lowly, degrading, tedious, humble, routine.

mental *(SYN.)* reasoning, intellectual, rational, thinking, conscious, reflective, thoughtful.

(ANT.) physical.

mentality *(SYN.)* intellect, reason, understanding, liking, disposition, judgment, brain, inclination, faculties, outlook.

(ANT.) materiality, corporeality.

mention *(SYN.)* introduce, refer to, reference, allude, enumerate, speak of.

mentor *(SYN.)* advisor, tutor, sponsor, guru, teacher, counselor, master, coach.

mercenary *(SYN.)* sordid, corrupt, venal, covetous, grasping, avaricious, greedy.

(ANT.) liberal, generous.

merchandise *(SYN.)* stock, wares, goods, sell, commodities, promote, staples, products.

merchant *(SYN.)* retailer, dealer, trader, storekeeper, salesman, businessman.

merciful *(SYN.)* humane, kindhearted, tender, clement, sympathetic, forgiving, tolerant, forbearing, lenient, compassionate, tenderhearted, kind.

(ANT.) remorseless, cruel, unjust, mean, harsh, unforgiving, vengeful, brutal, unfeeling, pitiless.

merciless *(SYN.)* carnal, ferocious, brute, barbarous, gross, ruthless, cruel, remorseless, bestial, savage, rough, pitiless, inhuman.

(ANT.) humane, courteous, merciful, openhearted, kind, civilized.

mercurial *(SYN.)* fickle, unstable, volatile, changeable, inconstant, capricious, flighty.

mercy *(SYN.)* grace, consideration, kindness, clemency, mildness, forgiveness, pity, charity, sympathy, leniency, compassion.

(ANT.) punishment, retribution, ruthlessness, cruelty, vengeance.

mere *(SYN.)* only, simple, scant, bare.

(ANT.) substantial, considerable.

merely *(SYN.)* only, barely, simply, hardly.

meretricious *(SYN.)* gaudy, sham, bogus, tawdry, flashy, garish.

merge *(SYN.)* unify, fuse, combine, amalgamate, unite, blend, commingle.

(ANT.) separate, decompose, analyze.

merger *(SYN.)* cartel, union, conglomerate, trust, incorporation, combine, pool.

meridian *(SYN.)* climax, summit, pinnacle, zenith, peak, acme, apex, culmination.

merit *(SYN.)* worthiness, earn, goodness, effectiveness, power, value, virtue, goodness, quality, deserve, excellence, worth.

(ANT.) sin, fault, lose, consume.

merited *(SYN.)* proper, deserved, suitable, adequate, earned.

(ANT.) unmerited, improper.

meritorious *(SYN.)* laudable, excellent, commendable, good, praise-worthy, deserving.

merry *(SYN.)* hilarious, lively, festive, joyous, sprightly, mirthful, blithe, gay, cheery, joyful, jolly, happy, gleeful, jovial, cheerful.

(ANT.) sorrowful, doleful, morose, gloomy, sad, melancholy.

mesh *(SYN.)* grid, screen, net, complex.

mesmerize *(SYN.)* enthrall, transfix, spellbind, bewitch, charm, fascinate, hypnotize.

mess *(SYN.)* dirtiness, untidiness, disorder, confusion, muddle, trouble, jumble, difficulty, predicament, confuse, dirty.

message *(SYN.)* letter, annotation, memo, symbol, indication, sign, note, communication, memorandum, observation, token.

messenger *(SYN.)* bearer, agent, runner, courier, liaison, delegate, page.

messy *(SYN.)* disorderly, dirty, confusing, confused, disordered, sloppy, untidy, slovenly.

(ANT.) orderly, neat, tidy.

metallic *(SYN.)* grating, harsh, clanging, brassy, brazen.

metamorphosis *(SYN.)* transfiguration, change, alteration, rebirth, mutation.

mete *(SYN.)* deal, assign, apportion, divide, give, allocate, allot, measure.

(ANT.) withhold, keep, retain.

meteoric *(SYN.)* flashing, blazing, swift, brilliant, spectacular, remarkable.

meter *(SYN.)* record, measure, gauge.

method *(SYN.)* order, manner, plan, way, mode, technique, fashion, approach, design, procedure.

(ANT.) disorder.

methodical *(SYN.)* exact, definite, ceremonious, stiff, accurate, distinct, unequivocal.

(ANT.) easy, loose, informal, rough.

meticulous *(SYN.)* precise, careful, exacting, fastidious, fussy, perfectionist.

metropolitan *(SYN.)* civic, city, municipal.

mettle *(SYN.)* intrepidity, resolution, boldness, prowess, bravery, fearlessness.

(ANT.) fear, timidity, cowardice.

microscopic *(SYN.)* tiny, precise, fine, detailed, minute, infinitesimal, minimal.

(ANT.) general, huge, enormous.

middle *(SYN.)* midpoint, nucleus, center, midst, median, central, intermediate, core.

(ANT.) end, rim, outskirts, beginning, border, periphery.

middleman *(SYN.)* dealer, agent, distributor, broker, representative, intermediary.

midget *(SYN.)* gnome, shrimp, pygmy, runt, dwarf.

(ANT.) giant.

midst *(SYN.)* center, heart, middle, thick.

midway *(SYN.)* halfway, midmost, inside, central, middle.

mien *(SYN.)* way, semblance, manner, behavior, demeanor, expression, deportment.

miff *(SYN.)* provoke, rile, chagrin, irk, irritate, affront, offend, annoy, exasperate.

might *(SYN.)* force, power, vigor, potency, ability, strength.

(ANT.) frailty, vulnerability, weakness.

mighty *(SYN.)* firm, fortified, powerful, athletic, potent, muscular, robust, strong, cogent.

(ANT.) *feeble, weak, brittle, insipid, frail, delicate.*

migrant *(SYN.)* traveling, roaming, straying, roving, rambling, transient, meandering.

(ANT.) *stationary.*

migrate *(SYN.)* resettle, move, emigrate, immigrate, relocate, journey.

(ANT.) *stay, remain, settle.*

migratory *(SYN.)* itinerant, roving, mobile, vagabond, unsettled, nomadic, wandering.

mild *(SYN.)* soothing, moderate, gentle, tender, bland, pleasant, kind, meek, calm, amiable, compassionate, temperate, peaceful, soft.

(ANT.) *severe, turbulent, stormy, excitable, violent, harsh, bitter.*

milieu *(SYN.)* environment, background, locale, setting, scene, circumstances.

militant *(SYN.)* warlike, belligerent, hostile, fighting, pugnacious, aggressive, combative.

(ANT.) *peaceful.*

military *(SYN.)* troops, army, service, soldiers.

milksop *(SYN.)* namby-pamby, weakling, sissy, coward.

mill *(SYN.)* foundry, shop, plant, factory, manufactory.

millstone *(SYN.)* load, impediment, burden, encumbrance, hindrance.

mimic *(SYN.)* simulate, duplicate, copy, imitate, mock, counterfeit, simulate.

(ANT.) *invent, distort, alter.*

mince *(SYN.)* shatter, fragment, chop, smash.

mind *(SYN.)* intelligence, psyche, disposition, intention, understanding, intellect, spirit, brain, inclination, mentality, soul, wit, liking, brain, sense, watch, faculties, judgment, reason.

(ANT.) *matter, corporeality.*

mindful *(SYN.)* alert, aware, watchful, cognizant, watchful, sensible, heedful.

mine *(SYN.)* shaft, lode, pit, excavation, drill, dig, quarry, source.

mingle *(SYN.)* unite, coalesce, fuse, merge, combine, amalgamate, unify, conjoin, mix, blend, commingle.

(ANT.) *separate, analyze, sort, disintegrate.*

miniature *(SYN.)* small, little, tiny, midget, minute, minuscule, wee, petite, diminutive.

(ANT.) *outsize.*

minimize *(SYN.)* shorten, deduct, belittle, decrease, reduce, curtail, lessen, diminish, subtract.

(ANT.) *enlarge, increase, amplify.*

minimum *(SYN.)* lowest, least, smallest, slightest.

(ANT.) *maximum.*

minister *(SYN.)* pastor, clergyman, vicar, parson, curate, preacher, prelate, chaplain, cleric, deacon, reverend.

minor *(SYN.)* poorer, lesser, petty, youth, inferior, secondary, smaller, unimportant, lower.

(ANT.) *higher, superior, major, greater.*

minority *(SYN.)* youth, childhood, immaturity.

minstrel *(SYN.)* bard, musician.

mint *(SYN.)* stamp, coin, strike, punch.

minus *(SYN.)* lacking, missing, less, absent, without.

minute *(SYN.)* tiny, particular, fine, precise, jiffy, instant, moment, wee, exact, detailed, microscopic.

(ANT.) *large, general, huge, enormous.*

miraculous *(SYN.)* spiritual, supernatural, wonderful, marvelous, incredible, preternatural.

(ANT.) *commonplace, natural, common, plain, everyday, human.*

mirage *(SYN.)* vision, illusion, fantasy, dream, phantom.

(ANT.) *reality, actuality.*

mire *(SYN.)* marsh, slush, slime, mud.

mirror *(SYN.)* glass, reflector, reflect.

mirth *(SYN.)* joy, glee, jollity, joyousness, gaiety, joyfulness, laughter, merriment.

(ANT.) *sadness, gloom, seriousness.*

misadventure *(SYN.)* accident, adversity, reverse, calamity, catastrophe, hardship, mischance, setback.

misappropriate *(SYN.)* embezzle, steal, purloin, plunder, cheat, filch, defraud.

misbehave *(SYN.)* trespass, act badly.

(ANT.) *behave.*

miscalculate *(SYN.)* miscount, blunder, confuse, err, mistake, misconstrue.

miscarriage *(SYN.)* omission, want, decay, fiasco, default, deficiency, loss, abortion, prematurity.

(ANT.) *success, sufficiency, achievement.*

miscarry *(SYN.)* flounder, fall short, falter, go wrong, fail.

(ANT.) succeed.

miscellaneous *(SYN.)* diverse, motley, indiscriminate, assorted, sundry, heterogeneous, mixed, varied.
(ANT.) classified, selected, homogeneous, alike, ordered.

miscellany *(SYN.)* medley, gallimaufry, jumble, potpourri, mixture, collection.

mischief *(SYN.)* injury, harm, damage, evil, ill, prankishness, rascality, roguishness, playfulness, wrong, detriment, hurt.
(ANT.) kindness, boon, benefit.

mischievous *(SYN.)* roguish, prankish, naughty, playful.
(ANT.) well-behaved, good.

misconduct *(SYN.)* transgression, delinquency, wrongdoing, negligence.

miscreant *(SYN.)* rascal, wretch, rogue, sinner, criminal, villain, scoundrel.

miscue *(SYN.)* blunder, fluff, mistake, error, lapse.

misdemeanor *(SYN.)* infringement, transgression, violation, offense, wrong.

miser *(SYN.)* cheapskate, tightwad, skinflint. *(ANT.) philanthropist.*

miserable *(SYN.)* abject, forlorn, comfortless, low, worthless, pitiable, distressed, heartbroken, disconsolate, despicable, wretched, uncomfortable, unhappy, poor, unlucky, paltry, contemptible, mean.
(ANT.) fortunate, happy, contented, joyful, content, wealthy, honorable, lucky, noble, significant.

miserly *(SYN.)* stingy, greedy, acquisitive, tight, tightfisted, cheap, mean, parsimonious, avaricious.
(ANT.) bountiful, generous, spendthrift, munificent, extravagant, openhanded, altruistic.

misery *(SYN.)* suffering, woe, evil, agony, torment, trouble, distress, anguish, grief, unhappiness, anguish, tribulation, calamity, sorrow.
(ANT.) fun, pleasure, delight, joy.

misfit *(SYN.)* crank, loner, deviate, fifth wheel, individualist.

misfortune *(SYN.)* adversity, distress, mishap, calamity, accident, catastrophe, hardship, ruin, disaster, affliction.
(ANT.) success, blessing, prosperity.

misgiving *(SYN.)* suspicion, doubt, mistrust, hesitation, uncertainty.

misguided *(SYN.)* misdirected, misled, misinformed, wrong, unwise, foolish, erroneous, unwarranted, ill-advised.

mishap *(SYN.)* misfortune, casualty, accident, disaster, adversity, reverse.
(ANT.) intention, calculation, purpose.

mishmash *(SYN.)* medley, muddle, gallimaufry, hodge-podge, hash.

misjudge *(SYN.)* err, mistake, miscalculate.

mislay *(SYN.)* misplace, lose.
(ANT.) discover, find.

mislead *(SYN.)* misdirect, deceive, misinform, deceive, delude.

misleading *(SYN.)* fallacious, delusive, deceitful, false, deceptive, illusive.
(ANT.) real, genuine, truthful, honest.

mismatched *(SYN.)* unfit, unsuitable, incompatible, unsuited.

misplace *(SYN.)* lose, mislay, miss.
(ANT.) find.

misrepresent *(SYN.)* misstate, distort, falsify, twist, belie, garble, disguise.

miss *(SYN.)* lose, want, crave, yearn for, fumble, drop, error, slip, default, omit, lack, need, desire, fail.
(ANT.) suffice, have, achieve, succeed.

misshapen *(SYN.)* disfigured, deformed, grotesque, malformed, ungainly, gnarled, contorted.

missile *(SYN.)* grenade, shot, projectile.

missing *(SYN.)* wanting, lacking, absent, lost, gone, vanished.

mission *(SYN.)* business, task, job, stint, work, errand, assignment, delegation.

missionary *(SYN.)* publicist, evangelist, propagandist.

mist *(SYN.)* cloud, fog, haze, steam, haze.

mistake *(SYN.)* slip, misjudge, fault, blunder, misunderstand, confuse, inaccuracy, misinterpret, error.
(ANT.) truth, accuracy.

mistaken *(SYN.)* false, amiss, incorrect, awry, wrong, misinformed, confused, inaccurate, askew.
(ANT.) true, correct, suitable, right.

mister *(SYN.)* young man, gentleman, esquire, fellow, buddy.

mistreat *(SYN.)* wrong, pervert, oppress, harm, maltreat, abuse.

mistrust *(SYN.)* suspect, doubt, distrust, dispute, question, skepticism, apprehension.

(ANT.) trust.

misunderstand (SYN.) misjudge, misinterpret, jumble, confuse, mistake.

(ANT.) perceive, comprehend.

misunderstanding (SYN) clash, disagreement, dispute, conflict, misinterpretation.

misuse (SYN.) defame, malign, abuse, misapply, traduce, asperse, revile, vilify.

(ANT.) protect, honor, respect, cherish.

mite (SYN.) particle, mote, smidgen, trifle, iota, corpuscle.

mitigate (SYN.) soften, soothe, abate, assuage, relieve, allay, diminish.

(ANT.) irritate, agitate, increase.

mix (SYN.) mingle, blend, consort, fuse, alloy, combine, jumble, fraternize, associate, concoct, commingle, amalgamate, confound, compound, join.

(ANT.) divide, sort, segregate, dissociate, separate.

mixture (SYN.) diversity, variety, strain, scrt, change, kind, confusion, heterogeneity, jumble, mess, assortment, breed, mix, hodge-podge, subspecies.

(ANT.) likeness, sameness, homogeneity, monotony.

moan (SYN.) wail, groan, cry, lament.

moat (SYN.) fortification, ditch, trench, entrenchment.

mob (SYN.) crowd, host, populace, swarm, riot, bevy, horde, rabble, throng, multitude.

mobile (SYN.) free, movable, portable.

(ANT.) stationary, immobile, fixed.

mock (SYN.) taunt, jeer, deride, scoff, scorn, fleer, ridicule, tease, fake, imitation, sham, gibe, sneer, fraudulent, flout.

(ANT.) praise, applaud, real, genuine, honor, authentic, compliment.

mockery (SYN.) gibe, ridicule, satire, derision, sham, banter, irony, sneering, scorn, travesty, jeering.

(ANT.) admiration, praise.

mode (SYN.) method, fashion, procedure, design, manner, technique, way, style, practice, plan.

(ANT.) disorder, confusion.

model (SYN.) copy, prototype, type, example, ideal, imitation, version, facsimile, design, style, archetype, pattern, standard, mold.

(ANT.) reproduction, imitation.

moderate (SYN.) lower, decrease, average, fair, reasonable, abate, medium, conservative, referee, umpire, suppress, judge, lessen, assuage.

(ANT.) intensify, enlarge, amplify.

moderation (SYN.) sobriety, forbearance, self-control, restraint, continence, temperance.

(ANT.) greed, excess, intoxication.

moderator (SYN.) referee, leader, arbitrator, chairman, chairperson, master of cermonies, emcee.

modern (SYN.) modish, current, recent, novel, fresh, contemporary, new.

(ANT.) old, antiquated, past, bygone, ancient.

modernize (SYN.) refurnish, refurbish, improve, rebuild, renew, renovate.

modest (SYN.) unassuming, virtuous, bashful, meek, shy, humble, decent, demure, unpretentious, prudish, moderate, reserved.

(ANT.) forward, bold, ostentatious, conceited, immodest, arrogant.

modesty (SYN.) decency, humility, propriety, simplicity, shyness.

(ANT.) conceit, vanity, pride.

modicum (SYN.) particle, fragment, grain, trifle, smidgen, bit.

modification (SYN.) alternation, substitution, variety, change, alteration.

(ANT.) uniformity, monotony.

modify (SYN.) shift, vary, alter, change, convert, adjust, temper, moderate, curb, exchange, transform, veer.

(ANT.) settle, establish, retain, stabilize.

modish (SYN.) current, fashionable, chick, stylish, voguish.

modulate (SYN.) temper, align, balance, correct, regulate, adjust, modify.

module (SYN.) unit, measure, norm, dimension, component, gauge.

modus operandi (SYN.) method, technique, system, means, process, workings, procedure.

mogul (SYN.) bigwig, personage, figure, tycoon, magnate, potentate.

moiety (SYN.) part, scrap, share, allotment, piece, division, portion.

moist (SYN.) damp, humid, dank, muggy, clammy.

moisten (SYN.) wet, dampen, sponge.

(ANT.) dry.

moisture *(SYN.)* wetness, mist, dampness, condensation, evaporation, vapor, humidity.
(ANT.) aridity, dryness.

mold *(SYN.)* make, fashion, organize, produce, forge, constitute, create, combine, construct, form, pattern, format.
(ANT.) wreck, dismantle, destroy, misshape.

moldy *(SYN.)* dusty, crumbling, dank, old, deteriorating.

molest *(SYN.)* irk, disturb, trouble, annoy, pester, bother, vex, inconvenience.
(ANT.) console, accommodate.

mollify *(SYN.)* soothe, compose, quiet, humor, appease, tranquilize, pacify.

molt *(SYN.)* slough off, shed, cast off.

molten *(SYN.)* fusible, melted, smelted, redhot.

moment *(SYN.)* flash, jiffy, instant, twinkling, gravity, importance, consequence, seriousness.

momentary *(SYN.)* concise, pithy, brief, curt, terse, laconic, compendious.
(ANT.) long, extended, prolonged.

momentous *(SYN.)* critical, serious, essential, grave, material, weighty, consequential, decisive, important.
(ANT.) unimportant, trifling, mean, trivial, tribial, insignificant.

momentum *(SYN.)* impetus, push, thrust, force, impulse, drive, vigor, propulsion, energy.

monarch *(SYN.)* ruler, king, queen, empress, emperor, sovereign.

monastic *(SYN.)* withdrawn, dedicated, austere, unworldly, celibate, abstinent, ascetic.

monastery *(SYN.)* convent, priory, abbey, hermitage, cloister.

money *(SYN.)* cash, bills, coin, notes, currency, funds, specie, capital.

monger *(SYN.)* seller, hawker, huckster, trader, merchant, shopkeeper, retailer, vendor.

mongrel *(SYN.)* mixed-breed, hybrid, mutt.

monitor *(SYN.)* director, supervisor, advisor, observe, watch, control.

monkey *(SYN.)* tamper, interfere, interrupt, interpose.

monogram *(SYN.)* mark, stamp, signature

monograph *(SYN.)* publication, report, thesis, biography, treatise, paper, dissertation.

monologue *(SYN.)* discourse, lecture, sermon, talk, speech, address, soliloquy, oration.

monomania *(SYN.)* obsessiveness, passion, single-mindedness, extremism.

monopoly *(SYN.)* corner, control, possession.

monotonous *(SYN.)* dull, slow, tiresome, boring, humdrum, dilatory, tiring, irksome, tedious, burdensome, wearisome.
(ANT.) interesting, riveting, quick, fascinating, exciting, amusing.

monsoon *(SYN.)* storm, rains.

monster *(SYN.)* brute, beast, villain, demon, fiend, wretch.

monstrous *(SYN.)* tremendous, huge, gigantic, immense, enormous, revolting, repulsive, shocking, horrible, hideous, terrible.
(ANT.) diminutive, tiny, miniature, small.

monument *(SYN.)* remembrance, memento, commemoration, souvenir, statue, shrine.

monumental *(SYN.)* enormous, huge, colossal, immense, gigantic, important, significant.
(ANT.) trivial, insignificant, tiny, miniature.

mood *(SYN.)* joke, irony, waggery, temper, disposition, temperament, sarcasm.
(ANT.) sorrow, gravity.

moody *(SYN.)* morose, fretful, crabbed, changeable, sulky, dour, short-tempered, testy, temperamental, irritable, peevish, glum.
(ANT.) good-natured, even-tempered, merry, gay, pleasant, joyous.

moor *(SYN.)* tether, fasten, tie, dock, anchor, bind.

moorings *(SYN.)* marina, slip, harbor, basin, landing, dock, wharf, pier, anchorage.

moot *(SYN.)* unsettled, questionable, problematical, controversial, contestable.

mop *(SYN.)* wash, wipe, swab, scrub.

mope *(SYN.)* gloom, pout, whine, grumble, grieve, sulk, fret.
(ANT.) rejoice.

moral *(SYN.)* just, right, chaste, good, virtuous, pure, decent, honest, upright, ethical, righteous, honorable, scrupulous.

(ANT.) libertine, immoral, unethical, licentious, amoral, sinful.

morale (SYN.) confidence, spirit, assurance.

morality (SYN.) virtue, strength, worth, chastity, probity, force, merit.

(ANT.) fault, sin, corruption, vice.

morals (SYN.) conduct, scruples, guidelines, behavior, life style, standards.

morass (SYN.) fen, march, swamp, mire.

morbid (SYN.) sickly, unwholesome, unhealthy, ghastly, awful, horrible, shocking.

(ANT.) pleasant, healthy.

more (SYN.) further, greater, farther, extra, another.

(ANT.) less.

moreover (SYN.) further, in addition, also, furthermore, besides.

mores (SYN.) standards, rituals, rules, customs, conventions, traditions.

moron (SYN.) subnormal, dunce, blockhead, imbecile, retardate, simpleton.

morose (SYN.) gloomy, moody, fretful, crabbed, sulky, glum, dour, surly, down-cast, sad, unhappy.

(ANT.) merry, gay, amiable, joyous, pleasant.

morsel (SYN.) portion, fragment, bite, bit, scrap. amount, piece, taste, tidbit.

(ANT.) whole, all, sum.

mortal (SYN.) fatal, destructive, human, perishable, deadly, temporary, momentary, final.

(ANT.) superficial, divine, immortal.

mortgage (SYN.) stake, post, promise, pledge.

mortician (SYN.) funeral director, embalmer.

mortified (SYN.) embarrassed, humiliated, abashed, ashamed.

mortify (SYN.) humiliate, crush, subdue, abase, degrade, shame.

(ANT.) praise, exalt, elevate.

mortuary (SYN.) morgue, crematory, funeral parlor.

most (SYN.) extreme, highest, supreme, greatest, majority.

(ANT.) least.

mostly (SYN.) chiefly, generally, largely, mainly, principally, especially, primarily.

mother (SYN.) bring about, produce,

breed, mom, mama, watch, foster, mind, nurse, originate, nurture.

(ANT.) father.

motif (SYN.) keynote, topic, subject, theme.

motion (SYN.) change, activity, movement, proposition, action, signal, gesture, move, proposal.

(ANT.) stability, immobility, equilibrium, stillness.

motionless (SYN.) still, undisturbed, rigid, fixed, stationary, unresponsive, immobilized.

motivate (SYN.) move, prompt, stimulate, induce, activate, propel, arouse.

motive (SYN.) inducement, purpose, cause, incentive, reason, incitement, idea, ground, principle, stimulus, impulse, spur.

(ANT.) deed, result, attempt, effort.

motley (SYN.) heterogeneous, mixed, assorted, sundry, diverse, miscellaneous.

(ANT.) ordered, classified.

motor (SYN.) engine, generator, machine.

mottled (SYN.) streaked, flecked, dappled, spotted, speckled.

motto (SYN.) proverb, saying, adage, byword, saw, slogan, catchword, aphorism.

mound (SYN.) hillock, hill, heap, pile, stack, knoll, accumulation, dune.

mount (SYN.) scale, climb, increase, rise, prepare, ready, steed, horse, tower.

(ANT.) sink, descend.

mountain (SYN.) alp, mount, pike, peak, ridge, height, range.

mountebank (SYN.) faker, rascal, swindler, cheat, fraud.

mounting (SYN.) backing, pedestal, easel, support, framework, background.

mourn (SYN.) suffer, grieve, bemoan, sorrow, lament, weep, bewail.

(ANT.) revel, celebrate, carouse.

mournful (SYN.) gloomy, sorrowful, sad, melancholy, woeful, disconsolate.

(ANT.) joyful, cheerful, happy.

mourning (SYN.) misery, trial, distress, affliction, tribulation, sorrow, woe.

(ANT.) happiness, solace, comfort, joy.

mousy (SYN.) quiet, reserved, dull, colorless, withdrawn, shy, bashful.

move (SYN.) impel, agitate, persuade, induce, push, instigate, advance, stir, progress, propel, shift, drive, retreat, proceed, stir, transfer, budge, actuate.

(ANT.) halt, stop, deter, rest.

moving *(SYN.)* stirring, touching.

mow *(SYN.)* prune, cut, shave, crop, clip.

much *(SYN.)* abundance, quantity, mass, ample, plenty, sufficient, substantial.

mucilage *(SYN.)* adhesive, glue, paste.

muck *(SYN.)* filth, mire, dirt, rot, sludge.

muddle *(SYN.)* disorder, chaos, mess.

muddled *(SYN.)* disconcerted, confused, mixed, bewildered, perplexed.

(ANT.) plain, lucid, organized.

muff *(SYN.)* blunder, spoil, mess, fumble.

muffle *(SYN.)* soften, deaden, mute, quiet, drape, shroud, veil, cover.

(ANT.) louden, amplify.

mug *(SYN.)* cup, stein, goblet, tankard.

muggy *(SYN.)* damp, warm, humid, stuffy, sticky, dank.

mulct *(SYN.)* amerce, punish, penalize.

mulish *(SYN.)* obstinate, stubborn, head-strong, rigid, tenacious, willful.

multifarious *(SYN.)* various, many, numerous, diversified, several, manifold.

(ANT.) scanty, infrequent, scarce, few.

multiply *(SYN.)* double, treble, increase, triple, propagate, spread, expand.

(ANT.) lessen, decrease.

multitude *(SYN.)* crowd, throng, mass, swarm, host, mob, army, legion.

(ANT.) scarcity, handful.

mumble *(SYN.)* stammer, whisper, hesitate, mutter.

(ANT.) shout, yell.

mundane *(SYN.)* temporal, earthly, profane, worldly, lay, secular, common.

(ANT.) unworldly, religious.

municipal *(SYN.)* urban, metropolitan.

munificent *(SYN.)* bountiful, full, generous, forthcoming, satisfied.

(ANT.) voracious, insatiable, grasping, ravenous, devouring.

murder *(SYN.)* homicide, kill, slay, slaughter, butcher, killing, massacre, assassinate, execute.

(ANT.) save, protect, vivify, animate.

murky *(SYN.)* gloomy, dark, obscure, unclear, impenetrable.

(ANT.) cheerful, light.

murmur *(SYN.)* mumble, whine, grumble, whimper, lament, mutter.

(ANT.) praise, applaud, rejoice.

muscle *(SYN.)* brawn, strength, power, fitness, vigor, vim, stamina, robustness.

muse *(SYN.)* ponder, brood, think,

meditate, ruminate, reflect.

museum *(SYN.)* exhibit hall, treasure house, gallery, repository.

mushroom *(SYN.)* multiply, proliferate, flourish, spread, grow, pullulate.

musical *(SYN.)* tuneful, melodious, dulcet, lyrical, harmonious.

muss *(SYN.)* mess, disarray, rumple, litter, clutter, disarrange.

(ANT.) fix, arrange.

must *(SYN.)* ought to, should, duty, obligation, ultimatum.

muster *(SYN.)* cull, pick, collect, harvest, accumulate, garner, reap, deduce.

(ANT.) separate, disband, scatter.

musty *(SYN.)* mildewed, rancid, airless, dank, stale, decayed, rotten, funky.

mute *(SYN.)* quiet, noiseless, dumb, taciturn, hushed, peaceful, speechless, uncommunicative, silent.

(ANT.) raucous, clamorous, noisy.

mutilate *(SYN.)* tear, cut, clip, amputate, lacerate, dismember, deform, castrate.

mutinous *(SYN.)* revolutionary, rebellious, unruly, turbulent, riotous.

(ANT.) dutiful, obedient, complaint.

mutiny *(SYN.)* revolt, overthrow, rebellion, rebel, coup, uprising, insurrection.

mutter *(SYN.)* complain, mumble, whisper, grumble, murmur.

mutual *(SYN.)* correlative, interchangeable, shared, alternate, joint, common.

(ANT.) unshared, unrequited, separate, dissociated.

muzzle *(SYN.)* restrain, silence, bridle, bind, curb, suppress, gag, stifle, censor.

myopia *(SYN.)* incomprehension, folly, shortsightedness, obtuseness.

myriad *(SYN.)* considerable, many.

mysterious *(SYN.)* hidden, mystical, secret, cryptic, incomprehensible, occult, dim, dark, inexplicable, enigmatical.

(ANT.) simple, obvious, clear, plain.

mystery *(SYN.)* riddle, difficulty, enigma, puzzle, strangeness, conundrum.

(ANT.) solution, key, answer, resolution.

mystical *(SYN.)* secret, cryptic, hidden, dim, obscure, dark, cabalistic.

(ANT.) simple, explained, plain, clear.

mystify *(SYN.)* puzzle, confound, bewilder, stick, get, floor, bamboozle.

myth *(SYN.)* fable, parable, allegory, fiction, tradition, lie, saga, legend.

(ANT.) history.

nag *(SYN.)* badger, harry, provoke, tease, bother, annoy, molest, taunt, vex, torment, worry, annoy, pester, irritate, pick on, horse, torment.
(ANT.) please, comfort, soothe.

nail *(SYN.)* hold, fasten, secure, fix, seize, catch, snare, hook, capture.
(ANT.) release.

naive *(SYN.)* frank, unsophisticated, natural, artless, ingenuous, simple, candid, open, innocent.
(ANT.) worldly, cunning, crafty.

naked *(SYN.)* uncovered, unfurnished, nude, bare, open, unclad, stripped, exposed, plain, mere, simple, barren, unprotected, bald, defenseless, unclothed.
(ANT.) covered, protected, dressed, clothed, concealed, suppressed.

name *(SYN.)* title, reputation, appellation, style, fame, repute, renown, denomination, appoint, character, designation, surname, distinction, christen, denominate, mention, specify, epithet, entitle, call, label.
(ANT.) anonymity, hint, misname.

nap *(SYN.)* nod, doze, sleep, snooze, catnap, slumber, drowse.

narcissistic *(SYN.)* egotistical, egocentric, self-centered, egotistic.

narcotics *(SYN.)* opiates, drugs, sedatives, tranquilizers, barbiturates.

narrate *(SYN.)* recite, relate, declaim, detail, rehearse, deliver, review, tell, describe, recount.

narrative *(SYN.)* history, relation, account, record, chronicle, detail, recital, description, story, tale.
(ANT.) distortion, caricature, misrepresentation.

narrow *(SYN.)* narrow-minded, illiberal, bigoted, fanatical, prejudiced, close, restricted, slender, cramped, confined, meager, thin, tapering, tight.
(ANT.) progressive, liberal, wide,

narrow-minded *(SYN.)* close-minded, intolerant, partisan, arbitrary, bigoted.
(ANT.) tolerant, liberal, broad-minded.

nascent *(SYN.)* prime, introductory, emerging, elementary.

nasty *(SYN.)* offensive, malicious, selfish, mean, disagreeable, unpleasant, foul, dirty, filthy, loathsome, disgusting, polluted, obscene, indecent, sickening, nauseating, obnoxious, revolting.

(ANT.) generous, dignified, noble, admirable, pleasant.

nation *(SYN.)* state, community, realm, nationality, commonwealth, kingdom, country, republic, land, society, tribe.

native *(SYN.)* domestic, inborn, inherent, natural, aboriginal, endemic, innate, inbred, indigenous, hereditary, original, local.
(ANT.) alien, stranger, foreigner, outsider, foreign.

natty *(SYN.)* chic, well-dressed, sharp, dapper.

natural *(SYN.)* innate, genuine, real, unaffected, characteristic, native, normal, regular, inherent, original, simple, inbred, inborn, hereditary, typical, authentic, honest, legitimate, pure, customary.
(ANT.) irregular, false, unnatural, formal, abnormal.

naturally *(SYN.)* typically, ordinarily, usually, indeed, normally, plainly, of course, surely, certainly.
(ANT.) artificially.

nature *(SYN.)* kind, disposition, reputation, character, repute, world, quality, universe, essence, variety, features, traits.

naught *(SYN.)* nought, zero, nothing.

naughty *(SYN.)* unmanageable, insubordinate, disobedient, mischievous, unruly, bad, misbehaving, disorderly, wrong, evil, rude, improper, indecent.
(ANT.) obedient, good, well-behaved.

nausea *(SYN.)* sickness, vomiting, upset, queasiness, seasickness.

nauseated *(SYN.)* unwell, sick, queasy, squeamish.

nautical *(SYN.)* naval, oceanic, marine, ocean.

naval *(SYN.)* oceanic, marine, nautical, maritime.

navigate *(SYN.)* sail, cruise, pilot, guide, steer.

near *(SYN.)* close, nigh, dear, adjacent, familiar, at hand, neighboring, approaching, impending, proximate, imminent, bordering.
(ANT.) removed, distant, far, remote.

nearly *(SYN.)* practically, close to, approximately, almost.

neat *(SYN.)* trim, orderly, precise, clear, spruce, nice, tidy, clean, well-kept,

clever, skillful, adept, apt, tidy, dapper, smart, proficient, expert, handy, well-done, shipshape, elegant, well-organized.
(ANT.) unkempt, sloppy, dirty, slovenly, messy, sloppy, disorganized.

nebulous *(SYN.)* fuzzy, indistinct, indefinite, clouded, hazy.
(ANT.) definite, distinct, clear.

necessary *(SYN.)* needed, expedient, unavoidable, required, essential, indispensable, urgent, imperative, inevitable, compelling, compulsory, obligatory, needed, exigent.
(ANT.) optional, nonessential, contingent, casual, accidental, unnecessary, dispensable, unneeded.

necessity *(SYN.)* requirement, fate, destiny, constraint, requisite, poverty, exigency, compulsion, want, essential, prerequisite.
(ANT.) option, luxury, freedom, choice, uncertainty.

necromancy *(SYN.)* witchcraft, charm, sorcery, conjuring, wizardry.

need *(SYN.)* crave, want, demand, claim, desire, covet, wish, lack, necessity, requirement, poverty, require, pennilessness.

needed *(SYN.)* necessary, indispensable, essential, requisite.
(ANT.) optional, contingent.

needle *(SYN.)* goad, badger, tease, nag, prod, provoke.

needless *(SYN.)* nonessential, unnecessary, superfluous, useless, purposeless.

needy *(SYN.)* poor, indigent, impoverished penniless, destitute.
(ANT.) affluent, well-off, wealthy, well-to-do.

nefarious *(SYN.)* detestable, vicious, wicked, atrocious, horrible, vile.

negate *(SYN.)* revoke, void, cancel, nullify.

neglect *(SYN.)* omission, default, heedlessness, carelessness, thoughtlessness, disregard, negligence, oversight, omission, ignore, slight, failure, overlook, omit, skip, pass over, be inattentive, miss.
(ANT.) diligence, do, protect, watchfulness, care, attention, careful, attend, regard, concern.

negligent *(SYN.)* imprudent, thoughtless,

lax, careless, inattentive, indifferent, remiss, neglectful.
(ANT.) careful, nice, accurate, meticulous.

negligible *(SYN.)* trifling, insignificant, trivial, inconsiderable.
(ANT.) major, vital, important.

negotiate *(SYN.)* intervene, talk over, mediate, transact, umpire, referee, arbitrate, arrange, settle, bargain.

neighborhood *(SYN.)* environs, nearness, locality, district, vicinity, area, section, locality.
(ANT.) remoteness.

neighboring *(SYN.)* bordering, near, adjacent, next to, surrounding, adjoining.

neighborly *(SYN.)* friendly, sociable, amiable, affable, companionable, congenial, kind, cordial, amicable.
(ANT.) distant, reserved, cool, unfriendly, hostile.

neophyte *(SYN.)* greenhorn, rookie, amateur, beginner, apprentice, tyro, student.

nepotism *(SYN.)* bias, prejudice, patronage, favoritism.

nerve *(SYN.)* bravery, spirit, courage, boldness, rudeness, strength, stamina, bravado, daring, impudence, mettle, impertinence.
(ANT.) frailty, cowardice, weakness.

nervous *(SYN.)* agitated, restless, excited, shy, timid, upset, disturbed, shaken, rattle, high-strung, flustered, tense, jittery, strained, edgy, perturbed, fearful.
(ANT.) placid, courageous, confident, calm, tranquil, composed, bold.

nest *(SYN.)* den, refuge, hideaway.

nestle *(SYN.)* cuddle, snuggle.

net *(SYN.)* snare, trap, mesh, earn, gain, web, get, acquire, secure, obtain.

nettle *(SYN.)* irritate, vex, provoke, annoy, disturb, irk, needle, pester.

neurotic *(SYN.)* disturbed, psychoneurotic.

neutral *(SYN.)* nonpartisan, uninvolved, detached, impartial, cool, unprejudiced, indifferent, inactive.
(ANT.) involved, biased, partisan.

neutralize *(SYN.)* offset, counteract, nullify, negate.

nevertheless *(SYN.)* notwithstanding, however, although, anyway, but, regardless.

new *(SYN.)* modern, original, newfangled, late, recent, novel, young, firsthand, fresh, unique, unusual.
(ANT.) antiquated, old, ancient, obsolete, outmoded.

newborn *(SYN.)* baby, infant, cub, suckling.

news *(SYN.)* report, intelligence, information, copy, message, advice, tidings, knowledge, word, story, data.

next *(SYN.)* nearest, following, closest, successive, succeeding, subsequent.

nibble *(SYN.)* munch, chew, bit.

nice *(SYN.)* pleasing, pleasant, agreeable, thoughtful, satisfactory, friendly, enjoyable, gratifying, desirable, fine, good, cordial.
(ANT.) nasty, unpleasant, disagreeable, unkind, inexact, careless, thoughtless.

niche *(SYN.)* corner, nook, alcove, cranny, recess.

nick *(SYN.)* cut, notch, indentation, dash, score, mark.

nickname *(SYN.)* byname, sobriquet.

nigh *(SYN.)* close, imminent, near, adjacent, approaching, bordering, neighboring, impending.
(ANT.) removed, distant.

nightmare *(SYN.)* calamity, horror, torment, bad dream.

nil *(SYN.)* zero, none, nought, nothing.

nimble *(SYN.)* brisk, quick, active, supple, alert, lively, spry, light, fast, speedy, swift, agile.
(ANT.) slow, heavy, sluggish, clumsy.

nincompoop *(SYN.)* nitwit, idiot, fool, moron, blockhead, ninny, idiot, simpleton.

nip *(SYN.)* bite, pinch, chill, cold, squeeze, crispness, sip, small.

nippy *(SYN.)* chilly, sharp, bitter, cold, penetrating.

nit-picker *(SYN.)* fussbudget, precise, purist, perfectionist.

nitty-gritty *(SYN.)* essentials, substance, essence.

noble *(SYN.)* illustrious, exalted, dignified, stately, eminent, lofty, grand, elevated, honorable, honest, virtuous, great, distinguished, majestic, important, prominent, magnificent, grandiose, aristocratic, upright, well-born.
(ANT.) vile, low, base, mean, dishonest, common, ignoble.

nod *(SYN.)* bob, bow, bend, tip, signal.

node *(SYN.)* protuberance, growth, nodule, cyst, lump, wen.

noise *(SYN.)* cry, sound, din, babel, racket, uproar, clamor, outcry, tumult, outcry, sounds, hubbub, bedlam, commotion, rumpus, clacter.
(ANT.) quiet, stillness, hush, silence, peace.

noisome *(SYN.)* repulsive, disgusting, revolting, obnoxious, malodorous, rotten, rancid.

noisy *(SYN.)* resounding, loud, clamorous, vociferous, stentorian, tumultuous.
(ANT.) soft, dulcet, subdued, quiet, silent, peaceful.

nomad *(SYN.)* gypsy, rover, traveler, roamer, migrant, vagrant, wanderer.

nominate *(SYN.)* propose, choose, select.

nomination *(SYN.)* appointment, naming, choice, selection, designation.

nominee *(SYN.)* aspirant, contestant, candidate, competitor.

nonbeliever *(SYN.)* skeptic, infidel, atheist, heathen.

nonchalant *(SYN.)* unconcerned, indifferent, cool, casual, easygoing.

noncommittal *(SYN.)* neutral, tepid, undecided, cautious, guarded, uncommunicative.

nonconformist *(SYN.)* protester, rebel, radical, dissenter, renegade, dissident, eccentric.

nondescript *(SYN.)* unclassifiable, indescribable, indefinite.

nonentity *(SYN.)* nothing, menial, nullity.

nonessential *(SYN.)* needless, unnecessary.

nonpareil *(SYN.)* unsurpassed, exceptional, paramount, unrivaled.

nonplus *(SYN.)* confuse, perplex, dumfound, mystify, confound, puzzle, baffle, bewilder.
(ANT.) illumine, clarify, solve, explain.

nonsense *(SYN.)* balderdash, rubbish, foolishness, folly, ridiculousness, stupidity, absurdity, poppycock, trash.

nonsensical *(SYN.)* silly, preposterous, absurd, unreasonable, foolish, irrational, ridiculous, stupid, senseless.
(ANT.) sound, consistent, reasonable.

nonstop *(SYN.)* constant, continuous, unceasing, endless.

nook *(SYN.)* niche, corner, recess, cranny,

nook *(SYN.)* niche, corner, recess, cranny, alcove.

noose *(SYN.)* snare, rope, lasso, loop.

normal *(SYN.)* ordinary, uniform, natural, unvaried, customary, regular, healthy, sound, whole, usual, typical, characteristic, routine, standard.
(ANT.) rare, erratic, unusual, abnormal.

normally *(SYN.)* regularly, frequently, usually, customarily.

nosy *(SYN.)* inquisitive, meddling, peering, searching, prying, snooping.
(ANT.) unconcerned, incurious, uninterested.

notable *(SYN.)* noted, unusual, uncommon, noteworthy, remarkable, conspicuous, distinguished, distinctive, celebrity, starts, important, striking, special, memorable, extraordinary, rare, exceptional, personality.
(ANT.) commonplace, ordinary, usual.

notch *(SYN.)* cut, nick, indentation, gash.

note *(SYN.)* sign, annotation, letter, indication, observation, mark, symbol, comment, remark, token, message, memorandum, record, memo, write, list, inscribe, notice.

noted *(SYN.)* renowned, glorious, celebrated, famous, illustrious, well-known, distinguished, famed, notable.
(ANT.) unknown, hidden, infamous, ignominious.

noteworthy *(SYN.)* consequential, celebrated, exceptional, prominent.

notice *(SYN.)* heed, perceive, hold, mark, behold, descry, recognize, observe, attend to, remark, note, regard, see, sign, announcement, poster, note, advertisement, observation, warning.
(ANT.) overlook, disregard, skip.

notify *(SYN.)* apprise, acquaint, instruct, tell, advise, warn, teach, inform, report, remind, announce, mention, reveal.
(ANT.) mislead, delude, conceal.

notion *(SYN.)* image, conception, sentiment, abstraction, thought, idea, impression, fancy, understanding, view, opinion, concept.
(ANT.) thing, matter, substance, entity.

notorious *(SYN.)* celebrated, renowned, famous, well-known, popular, infamous.

nourish *(SYN.)* strengthen, nurse, feed, supply, nurture, sustain, support.

nourishment *(SYN.)* nutriment, food, sustenance, support.
(ANT.) starvation, deprivation.

novel *(SYN.)* fiction, narrative, allegory, tale, fable, story, romance, invention, different, unusual, strange, original.
(ANT.) verity, history, truth, fact.

novice *(SYN.)* beginner, amateur, newcomer, greenhorn, learner, apprentice, freshman, dilettante.
(ANT.) expert, professional, adept, master.

now *(SYN.)* today, at once, right away, immediately, at this time, present.
(ANT.) later.

noxious *(SYN.)* poisonous, harmful, damaging, toxic, detrimental.
(ANT.) harmless.

nucleus *(SYN.)* core, middle, heart, focus, hub, kernel.

nude *(SYN.)* naked, unclad, plain, open, defenseless, mere, bare, exposed, unprotected, simple, stripped, uncovered.
(ANT.) dressed, concealed, protected, clothed, covered.

nudge *(SYN.)* prod, push, jab, shove, poke, prompt.

nugget *(SYN.)* clump, mass, lump, wad, chunk, hunk.

nuisance *(SYN.)* annoyance, bother, irritation, pest.

nullify *(SYN.)* abolish, cross out, delete, invalidate, obliterate, cancel, expunge, repeal, annul, revoke, quash, rescind.
(ANT.) perpetuate, confirm, enforce.

numb *(SYN.)* unfeeling, dull, insensitive, deadened, anesthetized, stupefied.

numeral *(SYN.)* figure, symbol, digit.

numerous *(SYN.)* many, several, manifold, multifarious, various, multitudinous, diverse, abundant, sundry.
(ANT.) infrequent, meager, few, scarce.

nuptials *(SYN.)* marriage, wedding, espousal, wedlock, matrimony.
(ANT.) virginity, divorce, celibacy.

nurse *(SYN.)* tend, care for, nourish, nurture, feed, train, mind, attend.

nurture *(SYN.)* hold dear, foster, sustain, appreciate, prize, rear, value, treasure.
(ANT.) dislike, disregard, abandon.

nutriment *(SYN.)* food, diet, sustenance, repast, meal, fare, edibles.
(ANT.) hunger, want, starvation.

nutrition *(SYN.)* nourishment, sustenance, food, nutriment.

oaf *(SYN.)* boor, clod, clown, lummox, fool, lout, dunce, bogtrotter.

oasis *(SYN.)* shelter, haven, retreat, refuge.

oath *(SYN.)* promise, pledge, vow, profanity, curse, agreement, commitment.

obdurate *(SYN.)* insensible, callous, hard, tough, unfeeling, insensitive.

(ANT.) soft, compassionate, tender.

obedience *(SYN.)* docility, submission, subservience, compliance.

(ANT.) rebelliousness, disobedience.

obedient *(SYN.)* dutiful, yielding, tractable, compliant, submissive.

(ANT.) rebellious, intractable, insubordinate, obstinate.

obese *(SYN.)* portly, fat, pudgy, chubby, plump, rotund, stout, thickset, corpulent, stocky.

(ANT.) slim, gaunt, lean, thin, slender.

obey *(SYN.)* submit, yield, mind, comply, listen to, serve, conform.

(ANT.) resist, disobey.

obfuscate *(SYN.)* bewilder, complicate, fluster, confuse.

object *(SYN.)* thing, aim, intention, design, end, objective, particular, mark, purpose, goal, target, article.

(ANT.) assent, agree, concur, approve, acquiesce.

objection *(SYN.)* disagreement, protest, rejection, dissent, challenge, noncompliance, difference, nonconformity, recusancy, disapproval, criticism, variance.

(ANT.) acceptance, compliance, agreement, assent.

objectionable *(SYN.)* improper, offensive, unbecoming, deplorable.

objective *(SYN.)* aspiration, goal, passion, desire, aim, hope, purpose, drift, design, ambition, end, object, intention, intent, longing, craving.

(ANT.) biased, subjective.

objectivity *(SYN.)* disinterest, neutrality, impartiality.

obligate *(SYN.)* oblige, require, pledge, bind, force, compel.

obligation *(SYN.)* duty, bond, engagement, compulsion, account, contract, ability, debt.

(ANT.) freedom, choice, exemption.

oblige *(SYN.)* constrain, force, impel, enforce, coerce, drive, gratify.

(ANT.) persuade, convince, allure, free,

induce, disoblige, prevent.

obliging *(SYN.)* considerate, helpful, thoughtful, well-meaning, accommodating.

(ANT.) discourteous.

obliterate *(SYN.)* terminate, destroy, eradicate, raze, extinguish, exterminate, annihilate, devastate, wipe out, ravage.

(ANT.) make, save, construct, establish, preserve.

oblivious *(SYN.)* sightless, unmindful, headlong, rash, blind, senseless, ignorant, forgetful, undiscerning, preoccupied, unconscious, heedless.

(ANT.) sensible, aware, calculated, perceiving, discerning.

obloquy *(SYN.)* defamation, rebuke, censure.

obnoxious *(SYN.)* hateful, offensive, nasty, disagreeable, repulsive, loathsome, vile, disgusting, detestable, wretched, terrible, despicable, dreadful.

obscene *(SYN.)* indecent, filthy, impure, dirty, gross, lewd, pornographic, coarse, disgusting, bawdy, offensive, smutty.

(ANT.) modest, pure, decent, refined.

obscure *(SYN.)* cloudy, enigmatic, mysterious, abstruse, cryptic, dim, indistinct, dusky, ambiguous, dark, indistinct, unintelligible, unclear, shadowy, fuzzy, blurred, vague.

(ANT.) clear, famous, distinguished, noted, illumined, lucid, bright, distinct.

obsequious *(SYN.)* fawning, flattering.

observance *(SYN.)* protocol, ritual, ceremony, rite, parade, pomp, solemnity.

(ANT.) omission.

observant *(SYN.)* aware, alert, careful, mindful, watchful, heedful, considerate, attentive, anxious, circumspect, cautious, wary.

(ANT.) unaware, indifferent, oblivious.

observation *(SYN.)* attention, watching, comment, opinion, remark, notice.

observe *(SYN.)* note, behold, discover, notice, perceive, eye, detect, inspect, keep, commemorate, mention, utter, watch, examine, mark, view, express, see, celebrate.

(ANT.) neglect, overlook, disregard, ignore.

observer *(SYN.)* examiner, overseer, lookout, spectator, bystander, witness, watcher.

obsession *(SYN.)* preoccupation, mania, compulsion, passion, fetish, infatuation.

obsolete *(SYN.)* old, out-of-date, ancient, archaic, extinct, old-fashioned, discontinued, obsolescent, venerable, dated, antiquated.
(ANT.) modern, stylish, current, recent, fashionable, extant.

obstacle *(SYN.)* block, hindrance, barrier, impediment, snag, check, deterrent, stoppage, hitch, bar, difficulty, obstruction.
(ANT.) help, aid, assistance, encouragement.

obstinate *(SYN.)* firm, headstrong, immovable, stubborn, determined, dogged, intractable, uncompromising, inflexible, willful, bullheaded, contumacious, obdurate, unbending, unyielding, pertinacious.
(ANT.) yielding, docile, amenable, submissive, pliable, flexible, compliant.

obstruct *(SYN.)* clog, barricade, impede, block, delay, hinder, stop, close, bar.
(ANT.) promote, clear, aid, help, open, further.

obstruction *(SYN.)* block, obstacle, barrier, blockage, interference.

obtain *(SYN.)* get, acquire, secure, win, procure, attain, earn, gain, receive, assimilate.
(ANT.) surrender, forfeit, lose, forego, miss.

obtrusive *(SYN.)* blatant, garish, conspicuous.

obtuse *(SYN.)* blunt, dull, slow-witted, unsharpened, stupid, dense, slow.
(ANT.) clear, interesting, lively, bright, animated, sharp.

obviate *(SYN.)* prevent, obstruct, forestall, preclude, intercept, avert, evade.

obvious *(SYN.)* plain, clear, evident, palpable, patent, self-evident, apparent, distinct, understandable, manifest, unmistakable.
(ANT.) concealed, hidden, abstruse, obscure.

obviously *(SYN.)* plainly, clearly, surely, evidently, certainly.

occasion *(SYN.)* occurrence, time, happening, excuse, opportunity, chance.

occasional *(SYN.)* random, irregular, sporadic, infrequent, periodically, spasmodic.

(ANT.) chronic, regular, constant.

occasionally *(SYN.)* seldom, now and then, infrequently, sometimes, irregularly.
(ANT.) regularly, often.

occlude *(SYN.)* clog, obstruct, choke, throttle.

occupant *(SYN.)* tenant, lodger, boarder, dweller, resident, inhabitant.

occupation *(SYN.)* employment, business, enterprise, job, trade, vocation, work, profession, matter, interest, concern, affair, activity, commerce, trading, engagement.
(ANT.) hobby, pastime, avocation.

occupy *(SYN.)* dwell, have, inhabit, absorb, hold, possess, fill, busy, keep.
(ANT.) relinquish, abandon, release.

occur *(SYN.)* take place, bechance, come about, befall, chance, transpire, betide, happen.

occurrence *(SYN.)* episode, event, issue, end, result, consequence, happening, circumstance, outcome.

ocean *(SYN.)* deep, sea, main, briny.

odd *(SYN.)* strange, bizarre, eccentric, unusual, single, uneven, unique, queer, quaint, peculiar, curious, unmatched, remaining, singular.
(ANT.) matched, common, typical, normal, familiar, even, usual, regular.

odious *(SYN.)* obscene, depraved, vulgar, despicable, mean, wicked, sordid, foul, base, loathsome, depraved, vicious, displeasing, hateful, revolting, offensive, repulsive, horrible, obnoxious, vile.
(ANT.) decent, upright, laudable, attractive, honorable.

odor *(SYN.)* fume, aroma, fragrance, redolence, smell, stink, scent, essence, stench.

odorous *(SYN.)* scented, aromatic, fragrant.

odyssey *(SYN.)* crusade, quest, journey, voyage.

offbeat *(SYN.)* uncommon, eccentric, strange, unconventional, peculiar.

off-color *(SYN.)* rude, improper, earthy, suggestive, salty.

offend *(SYN.)* annoy, anger, vex, irritate, displease, provoke, hurt, grieve, pain, disgust, wound, horrify, stricken, insult, outrage.
(ANT.) flatter, please, delight.

offender *(SYN.)* criminal, culprit, lawbreaker, miscreant.

offense *(SYN.)* indignity, injustice, transgression, affront, outrage, misdeed, sin, insult, atrocity, aggression, crime.

(ANT.) morality, gentleness, innocence, right.

offensive *(SYN.)* attacking, aggressive, unpleasant, revolting, disagreeable, nauseous, disgusting.

(ANT.) pleasing, defending, defensive, pleasant, attractive, agreeable.

offer *(SYN.)* suggestion, overture, proposal, present, suggest, propose, try, submit, attempt, tender.

(ANT.) withdrawal, denial, rejection.

offhand *(SYN.)* informal, unprepared, casual, impromptu, spontaneous.

(ANT.) considered, planned, calculated.

office *(SYN.)* position, job, situation, studio, berth, incumbency, capacity, headquarters, duty, task, function, work, post.

officiate *(SYN.)* regulate, administer, superintend, oversee, emcee.

offset *(SYN.)* compensate, counterbalance, cushion, counteract, neutralize, soften, balance.

offshoot *(SYN.)* outgrowth, addition, byproduct, supplement, appendage, accessory, branch.

offspring *(SYN.)* issue, children, progeny, descendants.

often *(SYN.)* frequently, repeatedly, commonly, generally, many times, recurrently.

(ANT.) seldom, infrequently, rarely, occasionally, sporadically.

ogle *(SYN.)* gaze, stare, eye, leer.

ogre *(SYN.)* fiend, monster, devil, demon.

ointment *(SYN.)* lotion, pomade, balm, emollient.

old *(SYN.)* antique, senile, ancient, archaic, old-fashioned, superannuated, obsolete, venerable, antiquated, elderly, discontinued, abandoned, aged.

(ANT.) new, youthful, recent, modern, young.

old-fashioned *(SYN.)* outmoded, old, dated, ancient.

(ANT.) modern, fashionable, current, new.

olio *(SYN.)* potpourri, variety, mixture, jumble.

omen *(SYN.)* sign, gesture, indication, proof, portent, symbol, token, emblem, signal.

ominous *(SYN.)* unfavorable, threatening, sinister, menacing.

omission *(SYN.)* failure, neglect, oversight, default.

(ANT.) inclusion, notice, attention, insertion.

omit *(SYN.)* exclude, delete, cancel, eliminate, ignore, neglect, skip, leave out, drop, miss, bar, overlook, disregard.

(ANT.) insert, notice, enter, include, introduce.

omnipotent *(SYN.)* all-powerful, almighty, divine.

oncoming *(SYN.)* imminent, approaching, arriving, nearing.

onerous *(SYN.)* intricate, arduous, hard, perplexing, difficult, burdensome, puzzling.

(ANT.) simple, easy, facile, effortless.

one-sided *(SYN.)* unfair, partial, biased, prejudiced.

(ANT.) impartial, neutral.

ongoing *(SYN.)* advancing, developing, continuing, progressive.

onlooker *(SYN.)* witness, spectator, observer, bystander.

only *(SYN.)* lone, sole, solitary, single, merely, but, just.

onset *(SYN.)* commencement, beginning, opening, start, assault, attack, charge, offense, onslaught.

(ANT.) end.

onslaught *(SYN.)* invasion, aggression, attack, assault, offense, drive, criticism, onset, charge, denunciation.

(ANT.) vindication, defense, surrender, opposition, resistance.

onus *(SYN.)* load, weight, burden, duty.

onward *(SYN.)* ahead, forward, frontward.

(ANT.) backward.

ooze *(SYN.)* seep, leak, drip, flow, filter.

opacity *(SYN.)* obscurity, thickness, imperviousness.

opaque *(SYN.)* murky, dull, cloudy, filmy, unilluminated, dim, obtuse, indistinct, shadowy, dark, obscure.

(ANT.) light, clear, bright.

open *(SYN.)* uncovered, overt, agape, unlocked, passable, accessible, unrestricted, candid, plain, clear, exposed, unclosed, unobstructed, free, disengaged, frank, unoccupied, public, honest, ajar, available.

open *(SYN.)* unbar, unfold, exhibit, spread, unseal, expand, unfasten.
(ANT.) close, shut, conceal, hide.

open-handed *(SYN.)* kind, generous, charitable, lavish, extravagant, bountiful.
(ANT.) mean, stingy.

openhearted *(SYN.)* frank, honest, candid, sincere, ingenuous, straightforward.
(ANT.) insincere, devious.

opening *(SYN.)* cavity, hole, void, abyss, aperture, chasm, pore, gap, loophole.

openly *(SYN.)* sincerely, frankly, freely.
(ANT.) secretly.

open-minded *(SYN.)* tolerant, fair, just, liberal, impartial, reasonable, unprejudiced.
(ANT.) prejudiced, bigoted.

operate *(SYN.)* comport, avail, behave, interact, apply, manage, utilize, demean, run, manipulate, employ, act, exploit, exert, exercise, practice, conduct.
(ANT.) neglect, waste.

operation *(SYN.)* effort, enterprise, mentality, maneuver, action, instrumentality, performance, working, proceeding, agency.
(ANT.) inaction, cessation, rest, inactivity.

operative *(SYN.)* busy, active, industrious, working, effective, functional.
(ANT.) inactive, dormant.

opiate *(SYN.)* hypnotic, tranquilizer, narcotic.

opinion *(SYN.)* decision, feeling, notion, view, idea, conviction, belief, judgment, sentiment, persuasion, impression.
(ANT.) knowledge, fact, misgiving, skepticism.

opinionated *(SYN.)* domineering, overbearing, arrogant, dogmatic, positive, magisterial, obstinate, pertinacious.
(ANT.) questioning, fluctuating, indecisive, skeptical, open-minded, indecisive.

opponent *(SYN.)* competitor, foe, adversary, contestant, enemy, rival, contender, combatant, antagonist.
(ANT.) comrade, team, ally, confederate.

opportune *(SYN.)* fitting, suitable, ap-

propriate, proper, favorable, felicitous.

opportunity *(SYN.)* possibility, chance, occasion, time, contingency, opening.
(ANT.) obstacle, disadvantage, hindrance.

oppose *(SYN.)* defy, resist, withstand, combat, bar, counteract, confront, thwart, struggle, fight, contradict, hinder, obstruct.
(ANT.) submit, support, agree, cooperate, succumb.

opposed *(SYN.)* opposite, contrary, hostile, adverse, counteractive, unlucky, antagonistic, unfavorable, disastrous.
(ANT.) lucky, benign, propitious, fortunate, favorable.

opposite *(SYN.)* reverse, contrary, different, unlike, opposed.
(ANT.) like, same, similar.

opposition *(SYN.)* combat, struggle, discord, collision, conflict, battle, fight, encounter, discord, controversy, inconsistency, variance.
(ANT.) harmony, amity, concord, consonance.

oppress *(SYN.)* harass, torment, vex, afflict, annoy, harry, pester, hound, worry, persecute.
(ANT.) encourage, support, comfort, assist, aid.

oppression *(SYN.)* cruelty, tyranny, persecution, injustice, despotism, brutality, abuse.
(ANT.) liberty, freedom.

oppressive *(SYN.)* difficult, stifling, burdensome, severe, domineering, harsh, unjust, overbearing, overwhelming.

oppressor *(SYN.)* bully, scourge, slave-driver.

opprobrium *(SYN.)* disgrace, contempt, reproach, shame, discredit.

opt *(SYN.)* choose, prefer, pick, select.

optical *(SYN.)* seeing, visual.

optimism *(SYN.)* faith, expectation, optimism, anticipation, trust, expectancy, confidence, hope.
(ANT.) despair, pessimism, despondency.

optimistic *(SYN.)* happy, cheerful, bright, glad, pleasant, radiant, lighthearted.
(ANT.) pessimistic.

option *(SYN.)* preference, choice, selection, alternative, election, self-determination.

optional *(SYN.)* selective, elective, voluntary.

(ANT.) required.

opulence *(SYN.)* luxury, abundance, fortune, riches, wealth, plenty, affluence.

(ANT.) need, indigence, want, poverty.

opulent *(SYN.)* wealthy, rich, prosperous, well-off, affluent, well-heeled.

oracle *(SYN.)* authority, forecaster, wizard, seer, mastermind, clairvoyant.

oral *(SYN.)* voiced, sounded, vocalized, said, uttered, verbal, vocal, spoken.

(ANT.) recorded, written, documentary.

orate *(SYN.)* preach, lecture, sermonize.

oration *(SYN.)* address, lecture, speech, sermon, discourse, recital, declamation.

orb *(SYN.)* globe, sphere, ball, moon.

orbit *(SYN.)* path, lap, course, circuit, revolution, revolve, circle.

orchestra *(SYN.)* ensemble, band.

orchestrate *(SYN.)* coordinate, direct, synchronize, organize.

ordain *(SYN.)* constitute, create, order, decree, decide, dictate, command, rule, bid, sanction, appoint.

(ANT.) terminate, disband.

ordeal *(SYN.)* hardship, suffering, test, affliction, trouble, fortune, proof, examination, trial, experiment, tribulation, misery.

(ANT.) consolation, alleviation.

order *(SYN.)* plan, series, decree, instruction, command, system, method, aim, arrangement, class, injuction, mandate, instruct, requirement, dictate, bidding.

(ANT.) consent, license, confusion, disarray, irregularity, permission.

order *(SYN.)* guide, command, rule, direct, govern, manage, regulate, bid, conduct.

(ANT.) misguide, deceive, misdirect, distract.

orderly *(SYN.)* regulated, neat, well-organized, disciplined, methodical, shipshape.

(ANT.) sloppy, messy, haphazard, disorganized.

ordinarily *(SYN.)* commonly, usually, generally, mostly, customarily, normally.

ordinary *(SYN.)* common, habitual, normal, typical, usual, conventional, familiar, accustomed, customary, average, standard, everyday, inferior, mediocre, regular, vulgar, plain.

(ANT.) uncommon, marvelous, extraor-

dinary, remarkable, strange.

ordance *(SYN.)* munitions, artillery.

organ *(SYN.)* instrument, journal, voice.

organic *(SYN.)* living, biological, animate.

organism *(SYN.)* creature, plant, micro-organism.

organization *(SYN.)* order, rule, system, arrangement, method, plan, regularity, scheme, mode, process.

(ANT.) irregularity, chaos, disarrangement, chance, disorder, confusion.

organize *(SYN.)* assort, arrange, plan, regulate, systematize, devise, categorize, classify, prepare.

(ANT.) jumble, disorder, disturb, confuse, scatter.

organized *(SYN.)* planned, neat, orderly, arranged.

orient *(SYN.)* align, fit, accustom, adjust.

orifice *SYN.)* vent, slot, opening, hole.

origin *(SYN.)* birth, foundation, source, start, commencement, inception, beginning, derivation, infancy, parentage, spring, cradle.

(ANT.) product, issue, outcome, end.

original *(SYN.)* primary, fresh, new, initial, pristine, creative, first, primordial, inventive, primeval, novel, introductory.

(ANT.) banal, trite, subsequent, derivative, later, modern, terminal.

originality *(SYN.)* unconventionality, genius, novelty, creativity, imagination.

originate *(SYN.)* fashion, invent, cause, create, make, initiate, inaugurate, organize, institute, produce, engender, commence, found, establish, form, begin, arise, generate, formulate.

(ANT.) demolish, terminate, annihilate, disband, destroy.

originator *(SYN.)* creator, inventor, discoverer.

(ANT.) follower, imitator.

ornament *(SYN.)* decoration, ornamentation, adornment, embellishment, trimming, garnish.

ornamental *(SYN.)* ornate, decorative.

ornate *SYN.)* florid, overdone, elaborate, showy, flowery, pretentious.

ornery *(SYN.)* disobedient, firm, unruly, stiff, rebellious, stubborn, headstrong, willful, contrary, rigid, mean, difficult, malicious, cross, disagreeable.

(ANT.) pleasant.

orthodox *(SYN.)* customary, usual, conventional, correct, proper, accepted.
(ANT.) different, unorthodox.

oscillate *(SYN.)* vary, change, hesitate, waver, undulate, fluctuate, vacillate.
(ANT.) persist, resolve, adhere, stick, decide.

ostentation *(SYN.)* parade, show, boasting, pageantry, vaunting, pomp, display, flourish.
(ANT.) reserve, humility, unobtrusiveness, modesty.

ostentatious *(SYN.)* flashy, showy, overdone, fancy, pretentious, garish.

ostracize *(SYN.)* hinder, omit, bar, exclude, blackball, expel, prohibit, shout out, prevent, except.
(ANT.) welcome, accept, include, admit.

other *(SYN.)* distinct, different, extra, further, new, additional, supplementary.

ought *(SYN.)* must, should, be obliged.

oust *(SYN.)* eject, banish, exclude, expatriate, ostracize, dismiss, exile, expel.
(ANT.) shelter, accept, receive, admit, harbor.

ouster *(SYN.)* expulsion, banishment, ejection, overthrow.

outbreak *(SYN.)* riot, revolt, uprising, disturbance, torrent, eruption, outburst.

outburst *(SYN.)* outbreak, eruption, torrent, ejection, discharge.

outcast *(SYN.)* friendless, homeless, deserted, abandoned, forsaken, disowned, derelict, forlorn, rejected.

outclass *(SYN.)* outshine, surpass.

outcome *(SYN.)* fate, destiny, necessity, doom, portion, consequence, result, end, fortune, effect, issue, aftermath.

outcry *(SYN.)* scream, protest, clamor, noise, uproar.

outdated *(SYN.)* old-fashioned, unfashionable, old, outmoded.
(ANT.) stylish.

outdo *(SYN.)* outshine, defeat, excel, beat, surpass.

outer *(SYN.)* remote, exterior, external.

outfit *(SYN.)* garb, kit, gear, furnish, equip, rig, clothing, provisions.

outgoing *(SYN.)* leaving, departing, friendly, congenial, amicable.
(ANT.) unfriendly, incoming.

outgrowth *(SYN.)* effect, outcome, upshot, fruit, result, consequence, product.

outing *(SYN.)* journey, trip, excursion, jaunt, expedition, junket.

outlandish *(SYN.)* peculiar, odd, weird, curious, strange, queer, exotic, bazaar.
(ANT.) ordinary, common.

outlast *(SYN.)* survive, endure, outlive.

outlaw *(SYN.)* exile, bandit, outcast, badman, convict, criminal, fugitive, desperado.

outlay *(SYN.)* expense, costs, spending, disbursement, expenditure, charge.

outlet *(SYN.)* spout, opening, passage.

outline *(SYN.)* form, sketch, brief, draft, figure, profile, contour, chart, diagram, skeleton, delineation, plan, silhouette.

outlook *(SYN.)* viewpoint, view, prospect, opportunity, position, attitude, future.

outlying *(SYN.)* external, remote, outer, out-of-the-way, surburban, rural.

outmoded *(SYN.)* unfashionable, old-fashioned.
(ANT.) up-to-date, modern.

outnumber *(SYN.)* exceed.

output *(SYN.)* yield, crop, harvest, proceeds, productivity, production.

outrage *(SYN.)* aggression, transgression, vice, affront, offense, insult, indignity, atrocity, misdeed, trespass, wrong.
(ANT.) morality, right, gentleness, innocence.

outrageous *(SYN.)* shameful, shocking, disgraceful, insulting, nonsensical, absurd, foolish, crazy, excessive, ridiculous, bizarre, preposterous, offensive.
(ANT.) prudent, reasonable, sensible.

outright *(SYN.)* entirely, altogether, completely, quite, fully, thoroughly.

outset *(SYN.)* inception, origin, start, commencement, opening, source.
(ANT.) end, completion, termination, consummation, close.

outside *(SYN.)* covering, exterior, surface, facade, externals, appearance.
(ANT.) intimate, insider.

outsider *(SYN.)* immigrant, stranger, foreigner, alien, newcomer, bystander.
(ANT.) countryman, friend, acquaintance, neighbor, associate.

outsmart *(SYN.)* outmaneuver, outwit.

outspoken *(SYN.)* rude, impolite, unceremonious, brusque, unrestrained, vocal, open, straight-foward, blunt, unreserved, frank, forthright, rough.
(ANT.) suave, tactful, shy, polished, polite, subtle.

outstanding *(SYN.)* well-known, important, prominent, leading, eminent, distinguished, significant, conspicuous.
(ANT.) insignificant, unimportant.

outward *(SYN.)* apparent, outside, exterior, visible.

outweigh *(SYN.)* predominate, supersede, counteract, dwarf.

outwit *(SYN.)* baffle, trick, outsmart, bewilder, outdo, outmaneuver, confuse.

oval *(SYN.)* egg-shaped, elliptical, ovular.

ovation *(SYN.)* fanfare, homage, applause, tribute, cheers, acclamation.

overall *(SYN.)* comprehensive, complete, general, extensive, wide-spread, entire.

overbearing *(SYN.)* domineering, masterful, autocratic, dictatorial, arrogant, bossy, imperious, haughty.
(ANT.) humble.

overcast *(SYN.)* dim, shadowy, cloudy, murky, dark, mysterious, gloomy, somber, dismal, hazy, indistinct.
(ANT.) sunny, bright, limpid, clear.

overcome *(SYN.)* quell, beat, crush, surmount, rout, humble, conquer, subjugate, defeat, subdue, upset, vanquish.
(ANT.) retreat, surrender, capitulate, cede, lose.

overconfident *(SYN.)* egotistical, presumptuous, arrogant, conceited.

overdo *(SYN.)* stretch, exaggerate, enlarge, magnify, exhaust, overexert.

overdue *(SYN.)* tardy, advanced, slow, delayed, new.
(ANT.) timely, early, beforehand.

overflow *(SYN.)* run over, flood, spill, cascade, inundate.

overflowing *(SYN.)* ample, plentiful, teeming, abundant, copious, profuse.
(ANT.) insufficient, deficient, scarce.

overhang *(SYN.)* protrude, extend.

overhaul *(SYN.)* recondition, rebuild, service, repair, condition, revamp.

overhead *(SYN.)* high, above, aloft, expenses, costs.

overjoyed *(SYN.)* enchanted, delighted, ecstatic, enraptured, elated, blissful.
(ANT.) depressed.

overlap *(SYN.)* overhang, extend, superimpose.

overload *(SYN.)* burden, weight, oppress, afflict, weigh, trouble, encumber, tax.
(ANT.) ease, lighten, console, alleviate, mitigate.

overlook *(SYN.)* miss, disregard, exclude, cancel, omit, skip, ignore, drop, delete, neglect, exclude, watch, eliminate.
(ANT.) notice, include, introduce, insert.

overly *(SYN.)* exceedingly, unreasonably.

overpass *(SYN.)* span, bridge, viaduct.

overpower *(SYN.)* overcome, conquer, defeat, surmount, vanquish, overwhelm.
(ANT.) surrender.

overrule *(SYN.)* disallow, nullify, cancel, override, repeal, revoke.

overrun *(SYN.)* spread, exceed, beset, infest, flood, abound.

oversee *(SYN.)* direct, run, operate, administer, boss, manage, supervise.

overseer *(SYN.)* leader, ruler, master, teacher, chief, commander, lord, employer, manager, head.
(ANT.) slave, servant.

overshadow *(SYN.)* dominate, control, outclass, surpass, domineer.

oversight *(SYN.)* omission, charge, superintendence, surveillance, inattention, error, inadvertence, neglect, mistake, inspection, control, slip, management.
(ANT.) scrutiny, attention, observation.

overstep *(SYN.)* surpass, exceed, trespass, transcend, impinge, violate, intrude.

overt *(SYN.)* honest, candid, frank, plain, open, apparent, straightforward.

overtake *(SYN.)* outdistance, reach, catch, pass.

overthrow *(SYN.)* defeat, demolish, overcome, destroy, ruin, rout, vanquish, subvert, reverse, supplant, overturn, overpower, upset.
(ANT.) revive, restore, construct, regenerate, reinstate.

overturn *(SYN.)* demolish, overcome, vanquish, upset, supplant, destroy.
(ANT.) uphold, construct, build, preserve, conserve.

overweight *(SYN.)* pudgy, stout, heavy, obese, fat.

overwhelm *(SYN.)* crush, surmount, vanquish, conquer, astonish, surprise, bewilder, astound, startle, overcome.

overwrought *(SYN.)* distraught, hysterical.

owe *(SYN.)* be liable, be indebted.

own *(SYN.)* monopolize, hold, possess, maintain, have.

owner *(SYN.)* landholder, partner, proprietor, possessor.

pace *(SYN.)* rate, gait, step.

pacify *(SYN.)* appease, lull, relieve, quell, soothe, allay, assuage, calm, satisfy, compose, placate, alleviate.

(ANT.) incense, inflame, arouse, excite.

pack *(SYN.)* prepare, stow, crowd, stuff, bundle, parcel, load, crowd, gang, mob.

package *(SYN.)* parcel, packet, load, bundle, box, bottle, crate.

packed *(SYN.)* filled, complete, plentiful, crammed, fall, replete, gorged, satiated.

(ANT.) lacking, depleted, devoid, vacant, insufficient, partial, empty.

pageant *(SYN.)* show, display, spectacle.

pain *(SYN.)* twinge, ache, pang, agony, distress, grief, anguish, throe, paroxysm.

(ANT.) happiness, pleasure, comfort, relief, solace, ease, delight, joy.

painful *(SYN.)* hurting, galling, poignant, bitter, grievous, agonizing, aching.

(ANT.) sweet, pleasant, soothing.

painting *(SYN.)* image, picture, portrayal, scene, view, sketch, illustration, panorama, likeness, representation.

pair *(SYN.)* team, couple, mate, match.

palatial *(SYN.)* majestic, magnificent, sumptuous, luxurious.

pale *(SYN.)* colorless, white, pallid, dim, faint, whiten, blanch.

(ANT.) flushed, ruddy, bright, dark.

pamphlet *(SYN.)* leaflet, brochure.

pang *(SYN.)* throb, pain, hurt.

panic *(SYN.)* fear, terror, fright, alarm, apprehension, trembling, horror, dread.

(ANT.) tranquillity, composure, calmness, serenity, calm, soothe.

pant *(SYN.)* wheeze, puff, gasp.

pantry *(SYN.)* cupboard, storeroom.

paper *(SYN.)* journal, newspaper, document, article, essay.

parable *(SYN.)* fable, saga, legend, myth, allegory, chronicle, fiction.

(ANT.) history, fact.

parade *(SYN.)* procession, cavalcade, succession, train, file, cortege, retinue, sequence, march, review, pageant, strut.

paradise *(SYN.)* utopia, heaven.

paradoxical *(SYN.)* unsteady, contradictory, discrepant, incompatible, inconsistent, vacillating, wavering, illogical.

(ANT.) correspondent, compatible, congruous, consistent.

parallel *(SYN.)* allied, analogous, comparable, corresponding, akin, similar, correlative, alike, like, resembling, equal, counterpart, likeness, correspondence, resemble, equal, match.

(ANT.) opposed, different, incongruous.

paralyze *(SYN.)* numb, deaden.

paraphernalia *(SYN.)* effect, gear, belonging, equipment.

parcel *(SYN.)* packet, package, bundle.

parched *(SYN.)* dry, arid, thirsty, drained, dehydrated, desiccated.

(ANT.) moist, damp.

pardon *(SYN.)* absolution, forgiveness, remission, acquittal, amnesty, excuse, exoneration, forgive, acquit.

(ANT.) sentence, penalty, conviction, punishment, condemn.

pardon *(SYN.)* condone, overlook, remit, absolve, acquit, forgive, excuse, remit.

(ANT.) punish, chastise, accuse, condemn, convict.

pare *(SYN.)* skin, peel, reduce, trim, shave, crop.

parley *(SYN.)* interview, talk, conference, chat, dialogue, colloquy.

paroxysm *(SYN.)* twinge, pang, ache, pain.

(ANT.) ease, relief, comfort.

parsimonious *(SYN.)* avaricious, miserly, penurious, stingy, acquisitive, greedy.

(ANT.) munificent, extravagant, bountiful, altruistic, generous.

part *(SYN.)* piece, section, allotment, portion, segment, element, member, concern, side, interest, lines, role, apportionment, division, share, fragment, ingredient, organ, party, moiety, section, fraction, participation, divide.

(ANT.) whole, entirety.

part *(SYN.)* separate, sever, divide, sunder.

(ANT.) join, combine, unite, convene.

partake *(SYN.)* dispense, parcel, allot, assign, distribute, partition, appropriate, divide, portion, share.

(ANT.) condense, aggregate, combine.

partial *(SYN.)* unfinished, undone, incomplete, prejudiced, unfair.

(SYN.) comprehensive, complete.

partiality *(SYN.)* preconception, bias, predisposition, bigotry.

(ANT.) reason, fairness, impartiality.

participant *(SYN.)* associate, colleague, partner, shareholder.

participate *(SYN.)* join, share, partake.

participation *(SYN.)* communion, sacrament, union, intercourse, association, fellowship.
(ANT.) nonparticipation, alienation.

particle *(SYN.)* mite, crumb, scrap, atom, corpuscle, grain, iota, shred, smidgen, grain, speck, bit, spot.
(ANT.) quantity, bulk, mass.

particular *(SYN.)* peculiar, unusual, detailed, specific, fastidious, individual, distinctive, singular, circumstantial, exact, careful, squeamish, special.
(ANT.) general, rough, universal, comprehensive, undiscriminating.

partisan *(SYN.)* follower, successor, adherent, attendant, henchman, devotee, disciple, votary.
(ANT.) leader, chief, master, head.

partition *(SYN.)* distribution, division, separation, screen, barrier, separator, divider, wall.
(ANT.) unification, joining.

partly *(SYN.)* comparatively, partially, somewhat.

partner *(SYN.)* colleague, comrade, friend, crony, consort, associate, companion, mate, participant.
(ANT.) stranger, enemy, adversary.

party *(SYN.)* company, gathering, crowd, group.

pass *(SYN.)* proceed, continue, move, go, disregard, ignore, exceed, gap, permit, permission, admission, throw, toss.
(ANT.) note, consider, notice.

pass by *(SYN.)* dodge, avert, elude, free, ward, shun, eschew avoid, forbear.
(ANT.) meet, confront, oppose, encounter.

passable *(SYN.)* fair, average, mediocre, acceptable, adequate, satisfactory.
(ANT.) worst, excellent, first-rate, exceptional, extraordinary, superior.

passage *(SYN.)* section, passageway, corridor, section, voyage, tour; crossing.

passenger *(SYN.)* traveler, tourist, rider, voyager, commuter.

passion *(SYN.)* feeling, affection, turmoil, sentiment, perturbation, agitation, emotion, trepidation, zeal, rapture, excitement, desire, love, liking, fondness, enthusiasm.
(ANT.) tranquillity, indifference, calm, restraint, dispassion, apathy, coolness.

passionate *(SYN.)* fiery, ardent, burning, glowing, irascible, fervid, excitable hot, impetuous, emotional, impulsive, excited, zealous, enthusiastic, earnest, sincere.
(ANT.) quiet, calm, cool, apathetic, deliberate.

passive *(SYN.)* relaxed, idle, stoical, enduring, inert, inactive, patient, submissive.
(ANT.) dynamic, active, aggressive.

password *(SYN.)* watchword.

past *(SYN.)* done, finished, gone, over, former.
(ANT.) future, present, ahead.

pastime *(SYN.)* match, amusement, diversion, fun, play, sport, contest, merriment, recreation, entertainment, hobby.
(ANT.) quiescence, labor, apathy, business.

patch *(SYN.)* restore, fix, repair, ameliorate, correct, rectify, remedy, sew, mend, better.
(ANT.) rend, deface, destroy, hurt, injure.

patent *(SYN.)* conspicuous, apparent, obvious, clear, evident, unmistakable, open, overt, manifest, indubitable, protection, control, copyright, permit.
(ANT.) hidden, concealed, obscure, covert.

path *(SYN.)* avenue, street, trail, walk, course, road, route, thoroughfare, channel, way, track, lane, footpath, pathway, walkway.

pathetic *(SYN.)* piteous, sad, affecting, moving, poignant, pitiable, touching, pitiful, touching.
(ANT.) funny, comical, ludicrous.

patience *(SYN.)* perseverance, composure, endurance, fortitude, long-suffering, forbearance, calmness, passiveness, serenity, courage, persistence.
(ANT.) restlessness, nervousness, impatience, unquite, impetuosity.

patient *(SYN.)* indulgent, stoical, forbearing, composed, assiduous, passive, uncomplaining, resigned, persistent, untiring, persevering, submissive, resigned, serene, calm, quiet, unexcited, unruffled.
(ANT.) turbulent, high-strung, chafing, clamorous, hysterical.

patrol *(SYN.)* inspect, watch, guard.

patron *(SYN.)* purchaser, buyer, client, customer.

patronize *(SYN.)* support.

pattern *(SYN.)* guide, example, original, model, design, figure, decoration.

paunchy *(SYN.)* fat, pudgy, stout, plump, portly, rotund, corpulent, obese, stocky.
(ANT.) slim, slender, gaunt, lean, thin.

pause *(SYN.)* falter, hesitate, waver, demur, doubt, scruple, delay, vacillate, hesitation, rest, interruption, break, delay, intermission, recess.
(ANT.) proceed, continue, decide, resolve, persevere, continuity, perpetuate.

pawn *(SYN.)* tool, puppet, stooge.

pay *(SYN.)* earnings, salary, allowance, stipend, wages, payment, compensation, recompense.
(ANT.) gratuity, present, gift.

payable *(SYN.)* unpaid, due, owed, owing.

peace *(SYN.)* hush, repose, serenity, tranquillity, silence, stillness, calmness, quiescence, calm, quietude, rest, quiet, peacefulness, pact.
(ANT.) noise, tumult, agitation, disturbance, excitement.

peaceable *(SYN.)* mild, calm, friendly, peaceful, amiable, gentle, pacific.
(ANT.) aggressive, hostile, warlike.

peaceful *(SYN.)* pacific, calm, undisturbed, quiet, serene, mild, placid, gentle, tranquil, peaceable.
(ANT.) noisy, violent, agitated, turbulent, disturbed, disrupted, riotous.

peak *(SYN.)* climax, culmination, summit, zenith, height, acme, consummation, apex, top, point, crest.
(ANT.) depth, floor, base, anticlimax, base, bottom.

peculiar *(SYN.)* odd, eccentric, extraordinary, unusual, individual, particular, striking, rare, exceptional, distinctive, strange, unfamiliar, uncommon, queer, curious, outlandish.
(ANT.) ordinary, common, normal, general, regular, unspecial.

peculiarity *(SYN.)* characteristic, feature, mark, trait, quality, attribute, property, distinctiveness.

pedantic *(SYN.)* formal, scholastic, erudite, academic, learned, bookish, theoretical, scholarly.
(ANT.) simple, commonsense, ignorant, practical, unlearned.

peddle *(SYN.)* sell, vend, hawk.

pedestrian *(SYN.)* stroller, walker.

pedigree *(SYN.)* descent, line, parentage, lineage, ancestry, family.

peek *(SYN.)* glimpse, look, peer, peep.

peel *(SYN.)* rind, skin, peeling.

peep *(SYN.)* squeak, cheep, chirp.

peer *(SYN.)* match, rival, equal, parallel, peep, glimpse, examine, peek, scrutinize.

peeve *(SYN.)* nettle, irk, irritate, annoy, vex.

peevish *(SYN.)* ill-natured, irritable, waspish, touchy, petulant, snappish, fractious, ill-tempered, fretful.
(ANT.) pleasant, affable, good-tempered, , genial, good-natured.

pen *(SYN.)* coop, enclosure, cage.

penalize *(SYN.)* dock, punish.

penalty *(SYN.)* fine, retribution, handicap, punishment, chastisement, disadvantage, forfeiture, forfeit.
(ANT.) remuneration, compensation, reward, pardon.

penchant *(SYN.)* disposition, propensity, tendency, partiality, inclination, bent, tendency, slant, bias.
(ANT.) justice, fairness, equity, impartiality.

penetrate *(SYN.)* bore, hole, pierce, enter.

penetrating *(SYN.)* profound, recondite, abstruse, deep, solemn, piercing, puncturing, boring, sharp, acute.
(ANT.) superficial, trivial, shallow, slight.

peninsula *(SYN.)* spit, headland, neck, point.

penitent *(SYN.)* remorseful, sorrowful, regretful, contrite, sorry, repentant.
(ANT.) remorseless, objurgate.

penniless *(SYN.)* poor, destitute, impecunious, needy, poverty-stricken, needy.
(ANT.) rich, wealthy, affluent, opulent, prosperous, well-off.

pensive *(SYN.)* dreamy, meditative, thoughtful, introspective, reflective, contemplative.
(ANT.) thoughtless, heedless, inconsiderate, precipitous, rash.

penurious *(SYN.)* avaricious, greedy, parsimonious, miserly, stingy, acquisitive, tight.
(ANT.) munificent, extravagant, bountiful, generous, altruistic.

penury *(SYN.)* poverty, want, destitution, necessity, indigence, need, privation.

(ANT.) riches, affluence, abundance, plenty, wealth.

people *(SYN.)* humans, person.

perceive *(SYN.)* note, conceive, see, comprehend, understand, discern, recognize, apprehend, notice, observe, distinguish, understand, grasp.
(ANT.) overlook, ignore, miss.

perceptible *(SYN.)* sensible, appreciable, apprehensible.
(ANT.) imperceptible, absurd, impalpable.

perception *(SYN.)* understanding, apprehension, conception, insight, comprehension, discernment.
(ANT.) misconception, ignorance, misapprehension, insensibility.

perceptive *(SYN.)* informed, observant, apprised, cognizant, aware, conscious, sensible, mindful, discerning, sharp, acute, observant.
(ANT.) unaware, ignorant, oblivious, insensible.

perfect *(SYN.)* ideal, whole, faultless, immaculate, complete, superlative, absolute, unqualified, utter, sinless, holy, finished, blameless, entire, excellent, pure, flawless, ideal.
(ANT.) incomplete, defective, imperfect, deficient, blemished, lacking, faulty, flawed.

perfectionist *(SYN.)* purist, pedant.

perform *(SYN.)* impersonate, pretend, act, play, do, accomplish, achieve, complete.

performance *(SYN.)* parade, entertainment, demonstration, movie, show, production, ostentation, spectacle, presentation, offering.

performer *(SYN.)* entertainer, actress, actor.

perfume *(SYN.)* cologne, scent, essence.

perfunctory *(SYN.)* decorous, exact, formal, external, correct, affected, methodical, precise, stiff, outward, proper, solemn.
(ANT.) unconventional, easy, unconstrained, natural, heartfelt.

perhaps *(SYN.)* conceivable, possible, maybe.
(ANT.) absolutely, definitely.

peril *(SYN.)* jeopardy, risk, danger, hazard.
(ANT.) safety, immunity, protection, defense, security.

perilous *(SYN.)* menacing, risky, hazardous, critical, dangerous, precarious, unsafe, insecure, threatening.
(ANT.) safe, firm, protected, secure.

period *(SYN.)* era, age, interval, span, tempo, time, epoch, duration, spell, date.

periodical *(SYN.)* uniform, customary, orderly, systematic, regular, steady.
(ANT.) exceptional, unusual, abnormal, rare, erratic.

perish *(SYN.)* die, sink cease, decline, decay, depart, wane, wither, languish, expire, cease, pass away.
(ANT.) grow, survive, flourish, begin, live.

perishable *(SYN.)* decomposable, decayable.

permanent *(SYN.)* constant, durable, enduring, abiding, fixed, changeless, unchangeable, lasting, indestructible, stable, continuing, long-lived, persistent, persisting, everlasting, unchanging, unaltered.
(ANT.) unstable, transient, ephemeral, temporary, transitory, passing, inconstant, fluctuating.

permeate *(SYN.)* penetrate, pervade, run through, diffuse, fill, saturate, infiltrate.

permissible *(SYN.)* allowable, fair, tolerable, admissible, justifiable, probable, warranted.
(ANT.) unsuitable, inadmissible, irrelevant.

permission *(SYN.)* authorization, liberty, permit, authority, consent, leave, license, freedom.
(ANT.) refusal, prohibition, denial, opposition.

permissive *(SYN.)* easy, tolerant, open-minded, unrestrictive.
(ANT.) restrictive.

permit *(SYN.)* let, tolerate, authorize, sanction, allow, grant, give.
(ANT.) refuse, resist, forbid, protest, object, prohibit, disallow.

perpendicular *(SYN.)* standing, upright, vertical.
(ANT.) horizontal.

perpetrate *(SYN.)* commit, perform, do.
(ANT.) neglect, fail, miscarry.

perpetual *(SYN.)* everlasting, immortal, ceaseless, endless, timeless, undying, infinite, eternal, unceasing, continuing, continual, continuous, permanent, constant, eternal.

(ANT.) *transient, mortal, finite, temporal ephemeral, inconstant, intermittent, fluctuating.*

perpetually (SYN.) continually, ever, incessantly, eternally, forever, always, constantly.

(ANT.) *rarely, sometimes, never, occasionally, fitfully.*

perplex (SYN.) confuse, dumbfound, mystify, puzzle, bewilder, confound, nonplus.

(ANT.) *solve, explain, illumine, instruct, clarify.*

perplexed (SYN.) confused, disorganized, mixed, bewildered, deranged, disordered, muddled, disconcerted.

(ANT.) *plain, obvious, clear, lucid, organized.*

perplexing (SYN.) intricate, complex, involved, compound, complicated.

(ANT.) *uncompounded, plain, simple.*

persecute (SYN.) harass, hound, torment, worry, vex, torture, harry, afflict, annoy, oppress, pester, ill-treat, victimize, maltreat.

(ANT.) *support, comfort, assist, encourage, aid.*

persevere (SYN.) remain, abide, endure, last, persist, continue.

(ANT.) *vacillate, desist, discontinue, cease, waver, lapse.*

perseverance (SYN.) persistency, constancy, pertinacity, steadfastness, tenacity, industry.

(ANT.) *sloth, cessation, laziness, idleness, rest.*

persist (SYN.) endure, remain, abide, persevere, continue, last.

(ANT.) *vacillate, waver, desist, cease, discontinue, stop.*

persistence (SYN.) persistency, constancy, perseverance, steadfastness, tenacity.

(ANT.) *cessation, rest, sloth, idleness.*

persistent (SYN.) lasting, steady, obstinate, stubborn, fixed, enduring, immovable, constant, indefatigable, dogged.

(ANT.) *wavering, unsure, hesitant, vacillating.*

person (SYN.) human, individual, somebody, someone.

personal (SYN.) secret, private.

(ANT.) *general, public.*

personality (SYN.) make-up, nature, disposition, character.

perspicacity (SYN.) intelligence, understanding, discernment, judgment, wisdom, sagacity.

(ANT.) *thoughtlessness, stupidity, arbitrariness, senselessness.*

persuade (SYN.) entice, coax, exhort, prevail upon, urge, allure, induce, influence, win over, convince.

(ANT.) *restrain, deter, compel, dissuade, coerce, discourage.*

persuasion (SYN.) decision, feeling, notion, view, sentiment, conviction, belief, opinion.

(ANT.) *knowledge, skepticism, fact, misgiving.*

persuasive (SYN.) winning, alluring, compelling, convincing, stimulating, influential.

(ANT.) *dubious, unconvincing.*

pertain (SYN.) refer, relate, apply.

pertinacious (SYN.) firm, obstinate, contumacious, head-strong, dogged, inflexible, obdurate, uncompromising, determined, immovable, unyielding.

(ANT.) *yielding, docile, amenable, submissive, compliant.*

pertinent (SYN.) apt, material, relevant, relating, applicable, to the point, germane, apropos, apposite, appropriate.

(ANT.) *unrelated, foreign, alien, extraneous.*

perturbed (SYN.) agitated, disturbed, upset, flustered.

pervade (SYN.) penetrate, saturate, fill, diffuse, infiltrate, run through, permeate.

perverse (SYN.) obstinate, ungovernable, sinful, contrary, fractious, peevish, forward, disobedient, wicked, intractable, petulant.

(ANT.) *docile, agreeable, tractable, obliging.*

perversion (SYN.) maltreatment, outrage, desecration, abuse, profanation, misuse, reviling.

(ANT.) *respect.*

pervert (SYN.) deprave, humiliate, impair, debase, corrupt, degrade, abase, defile.

(ANT.) *improve, raise, enhance.*

perverted *(SYN.)* wicked, perverse, sinful.

pest *(SYN.)* annoyance, bother, nuisance, bother, irritant, irritation.

pester *(SYN.)* disturb, annoy, irritate, tease, bother, chafe, inconvenience, molest, trouble, vex, harass, torment, worry.
(ANT.) console, soothe, accommodate, gratify.

pet *(SYN.)* darling, favorite, caress.

petition *(SYN.)* invocation, prayer, request, appeal, entreaty, supplication, suit, plea, application, solicitation, entreaty.

petty *(SYN.)* paltry, trivial, frivolous, small, unimportant, trifling, insignificant.
(ANT.) important, serious, weighty, momentous, grand, vital, significant, generous.

petulant *(SYN.)* irritable, ill-natured, fretful, snappish, peevish, ill-tempered, waspish, touchy.
(ANT.) pleasant, affable, good-tempered, genial, good-natured.

phantom *(SYN.)* apparition, ghost, specter.

phase *(SYN.)* period, stage, view, condition.

phenomenon *(SYN.)* occurrence, fact, happening, incident.

philanthropy *(SYN.)* kindness, benevolence, charity, generosity, tenderness, liberality, humanity, magnanimity, altruism.
(ANT.) unkindness, inhumanity, cruelty, malevolence, selfishness.

phlegmatic *(SYN.)* unfeeling, passionless, listless, cold, lethargic, sluggish, slow, lazy.
(ANT.) passionate, ardent, energetic.

phony *(SYN.)* counterfeit, artificial, ersatz, fake, synthetic, unreal, spurious, feigned, assumed, bogus, sham, false, forged.
(ANT.) real, genuine, natural, true.

phrase *(SYN.)* expression, term, word, name.

physical *(SYN.)* material, bodily, carnal, corporeal, natural, somatic, corporal.
(ANT.) spiritual, mental.

pick *(SYN.)* cull, opt, select, elect, choose.
(ANT.) reject, refuse.

picture *(SYN.)* etching, image, painting, portrait, print, representation, sketch, appearance, cinema, effigy, engraving, scene, view, illustration, panorama, resemblance, likeness, drawing, photograph.

piece *(SYN.)* portion, bit, fraction, morsel, scrap, fragment, amount, part, quantity, unit, section, portion.
(ANT.) sum, whole, entirety, all, total.

piecemeal *(SYN.)* gradually, partially.
(ANT.) whole, complete, entire.

pierce *(SYN.)* puncture, perforate.

pigheaded *(SYN.)* inflexible, stubborn, obstinate.

pigment *(SYN.)* shade, tint, color, dye, hue, complexion, tincture, stain, tinge.
(ANT.) transparency, paleness.

pile *(SYN.)* accumulation, heap, collection, amass.

pilgrim *(SYN.)* wanderer, traveler.

pilgrimage *(SYN.)* trip, journey, tour, expedition.

pillar *(SYN.)* support, prop, column, shaft.

pillow *(SYN.)* bolster, cushion, pad.

pilot *(SYN.)* helmsman, aviator, steersman.

pin *(SYN.)* clip, fastening, peg, fastener.

pinch *(SYN.)* squeeze, nip.

pinnacle *(SYN.)* crown, zenith, head, summit, chief, apex, crest, top.
(ANT.) bottom, foundation, base, foot.

pioneer *(SYN.)* guide, pilgrim, pathfinder, explorer.

pious *(SYN.)* devout, religious, spiritual, consecrated, divine, hallowed, holy, saintly, sacred, reverent.
(ANT.) worldly, sacrilegious, evil, secular, profane, irreligious, impious.

pirate *(SYN.)* plunderer, buccaneer, privateer.

pistol *(SYN.)* gun, revolver, weapon, handgun.

pit *(SYN.)* well, cavity, hole, excavation.

pitch *(SYN.)* throw, cast, toss, propel, hurl, fling, thrust, establish.
(ANT.) retain, draw, hold, pull, haul.

pitcher *(SYN.)* jug.

piteous *(SYN.)* poignant, touching, affecting, moving, pitiable, sad, pathetic.
(ANT.) funny, ludicrous, comical.

pitfall *(SYN.)* lure, snare, wile, ambush, bait, intrigue, trick, trap, artifice, net, snare.

pitiable *(SYN.)* poignant, touching, moving, affecting, sad.
(ANT.) ludicrous, funny, comical.

pitiful *(SYN.)* distressing, pathetic, pitiable.

pitiless *(SYN.)* unmerciful, mean, unpitying, merciless, cruel.
(ANT.) gentle, kind.

pity *(SYN.)* sympathy, commiseration, condolence, mercy, compassion, charity, mercy.
(ANT.) ruthlessness, hardness, cruelty, inhumanity, brutality, vindictiveness.

pivotal *(SYN.)* crucial, critical, essential, central.
(ANT.) peripheral, unimportant.

place *(SYN.)* lay, arrange, dispose, put, deposit, space, region, location, plot, area, spot.
(ANT.) mislay, remove, disarrange, disturb, misplace.

placid *(SYN.)* pacific, serene, tranquil, calm, imperturbable, composed, peaceful, quiet, still, undisturbed, unruffled.
(ANT.) wild, frantic, turbulent, stormy, excited.

plagiarize *(SYN.)* recite, adduce, cite, quote, paraphrase, repeat, extract.
(ANT.) retort, contradict, misquote, refute.

plague *(SYN.)* hound, pester, worry, harass, annoy, persecute, torment, vex, afflict, badger, torture, epidemic, trouble.
(ANT.) encourage, aid, comfort, assist, support.

plain *(SYN.)* candid, simple, flat, smooth, clear, evident, sincere, unpretentious, level, distinct, absolute, visible, open, frank, palpable, undecorated, ordinary, unembellished, unadorned.
(ANT.) embellished, abstruse, abrupt, rough, broken, insincere, adorned, fancy, elaborate, beautiful, ornamented.

plan *(SYN.)* design, purpose, sketch, devise, invent, contrive, intend, draw, create, scheme, plot, method, procedure.

plane *(SYN.)* level, airplane.

plastic *(SYN.)* pliable, moldable, supple, flexible, synthetic.

platform *(SYN.)* stage, pulpit.

plausible *(SYN.)* likely, practical, credible, feasible, possible, probable.

(ANT.) impracticable, impossible, visionary.

play *(SYN.)* entertainment, amusement, pastime, sport, game, fun, diversion, recreation, show, performance, drama, theatrical.
(ANT.) work, labor, boredom, toil.

playful *(SYN.)* sportive, frolicsome, frisky.

plaything *(SYN.)* game, trinket, toy, gadget.

playwright *(SYN.)* scriptwriter, dramatist.

plea *(SYN.)* invocation, request, appeal, entreaty, supplication, petition, suit.

plead *(SYN.)* beseech, defend, rejoin, supplicate, discuss, beg, appeal, ask, implore, argue, entreat.
(ANT.) deprecate, deny, refuse.

pleasant *(SYN.)* agreeable, welcome, suitable, charming, pleasing, amiable, gratifying, acceptable, pleasurable, enjoyable, nice, satisfying, satisfactory, acceptable, affable, mild, friendly.
(ANT.) offensive, disagreeable, obnoxious, unpleasant, horrid, sour, difficult, nasty.

please *(SYN.)* satisfy, suffice, fulfill, content, appease, gratify, satiate, compensate, remunerate.
(ANT.) dissatisfy, annoy, tantalize, frustrate, displease, vex.

pleasing *(SYN.)* luscious, melodious, sugary, delightful, agreeable, honeyed, mellifluous, engaging, pleasant, charming, engaging.
(ANT.) repulsive, sour, acrid, bitter, offensive, irritating, annoying.

pleasure *(SYN.)* felicity, delight, amusement, enjoyment gratification, happiness, joy, satisfaction, gladness, well-being.
(ANT.) suffering, pain, vexation, trouble, affliction, discomfort, torment.

pledge *(SYN.)* promise, statement, assertion, declaration, assurance, agreement, oath, commitment, agree, vow, swear.

pledge *(SYN.)* bind, obligate, commit.
(ANT.) renounce, release, neglect, mistrust.

plentiful *(SYN.)* ample, profuse, replete, bountiful, abundant, plenteous, luxurious, fullness, fruitful, copious.
(ANT.) rare, scanty, deficient, scarce, in-

sufficient.

plenty *(SYN.)* fruitfulness, bounty, fullness, abundance.

(ANT.) want, scarcity, need.

pliable *(SYN.)* elastic, supple, flexible, compliant, pliant, resilient, ductile.

(ANT.) rigid, unbending, hard, brittle, stiff.

plight *(SYN.)* dilemma, situation, difficulty, condition, predicament, fix, scrape, state.

(ANT.) satisfaction, ease, comfort, calmness.

plot *(SYN.)* design, plan, scheme, cabal, conspiracy, diagram, sketch, graph, chart, machination, intrigue.

plotting *(SYN.)* cunning, scheming, objective, artfulness, contrivance, purpose, intent, design.

(ANT.) accident, chance, result, candor, sincerity.

ploy *(SYN.)* ruse, guile, antic, deception, hoax, subterfuge, wile, cheat, artifice, fraud, trick.

(ANT.) honesty, sincerity, openness, exposure, candor.

pluck *(SYN.)* yank, snatch, jerk, pull.

plug *(SYN.)* cork, stopper.

plump *(SYN.)* obese, portly, stout, thick-set, rotund, chubby, fat, paunchy, stocky, corpulent, pudgy, stout, fleshy.

(ANT.) slim, thin, gaunt, lean, slender, skinny.

plunder *(SYN.)* ravage, strip, sack, rob, pillage, raid, loot.

plunge *(SYN.)* immerse, dip, submerge.

pocketbook *(SYN.)* purse, handbag.

poem *(SYN.)* lyric, verse, poetry.

poetry *(SYN.)* rhyme, verse.

pogrom *(SYN.)* massacre, carnage, slaughter, butchery.

poignant *(SYN.)* pitiable, touching, affecting, impressive, sad, tender, moving, heart-rending.

point *(SYN.)* direct, level, train, aim, locality, position, spot, location.

(ANT.) distract, misguide, deceive, misdirect.

pointed *(SYN.)* keen, sharp, penetrating, shrewd, witty, quick, acute, penetrating, cutting, piercing, astute, severe.

(ANT.) shallow, stupid, bland, blunt, gentle.

pointless *(SYN.)* vain, purposeless.

poise *(SYN.)* composure, self-possession, equanimity, equilibrium, carriage, calmness, balance, self-control, assurance, control, dignity.

(ANT.) rage, turbulence, agitation, anger, excitement.

poison *(SYN.)* corrupt, sully, taint, infect, befoul, defile, contaminate, venom, toxin, virus.

(ANT.) purify, disinfect.

poke *(SYN.)* punch, stab, thrust, jab.

policy *(SYN.)* procedure, system, rule, approach, tactic.

polish *(SYN.)* brighten, shine, finish, brightness, gloss.

(ANT.) tarnish, dull.

polished *(SYN.)* glib, diplomatic, urbane, refined, sleek, suave, slick.

(ANT.) rough, blunt, bluff, harsh, rugged.

polite *(SYN.)* civil, refined, well-mannered, accomplished, courteous, genteel, urbane, well-bred, cultivated, considerate, thoughtful, mannerly, respectful.

(ANT.) uncouth, impertinent, rude, boorish, uncivil, discourteous.

pollute *(SYN.)* contaminate, poison, taint, sully, infect, befoul, defile, dirty.

(ANT.) purify, disinfect, clean, clarify.

pomp *(SYN.)* flourish, pageantry, vaunting, show, boasting, ostentation, parade, display.

(ANT.) reserve, humility, modesty.

pompous *(SYN.)* high, magnificent, stately, august, dignified, grandiose, noble, majestic, lofty, imposing, arrogant, vain, pretentious.

(ANT.) lowly, undignified, humble, common, ordinary.

ponder *(SYN.)* examined, study, contemplate, investigate, meditate, muse, scrutinize, cogitate, reflect, weigh, deliberate, consider.

ponderous *(SYN.)* burdensome, trying, gloomy, serious, sluggish, massive, heavy, cumbersome, grievous, grave, dull, weighty.

(ANT.) light, animated, brisk.

poor *(SYN.)* penniless, bad, deficient, destitute, inferior, shabby, wrong, scanty, pecunious, indigent, needy, poverty-stricken, unfavorable, impoverished, penniless.

(ANT.) wealthy, prosperous, rich, for-

tunate, good, excellent.

poppycock *(SYN.)* rubbish, babble, twaddle, nonsense.

popular *(SYN.)* favorite, general, common, familiar, prevalent, liked, prevailing, well-liked, approved, accepted, celebrated, admired, ordinary.

(ANT.) unpopular, esoteric, restricted, exclusive.

populous *(SYN.)* dense, thronged, crowded.

porch *(SYN.)* patio, veranda.

pornographic *(SYN.)* impure, indecent, obscene, coarse, dirty, filthy, lewd, smutty, offensive, disgusting.

(ANT.) refined, modest, pure, decent.

port *(SYN.)* harbor, refuge, anchorage.

portable *(SYN.)* transportable, movable.

portal *(SYN.)* entry, doorway, opening, inlet, entrance.

(ANT.) exit, departure.

portend *(SYN.)* foreshadow, presage, foretoken.

portentous *(SYN.)* significant, critical, momentous.

(ANT.) trivial.

portion *(SYN.)* share, bit, parcel, part, piece, section, fragment, division, quota, segment, allotment.

(ANT.) whole, bulk.

portly *(SYN.)* majestic, grand, impressive, dignified, stout, fat, heavy, obese.

(ANT.) slender, thin, slim.

portrait *(SYN.)* painting, representation, picture, likeness.

portray *(SYN.)* depict, picture, represent, sketch, describe, delineate, paint.

(ANT.) misrepresent, caricature, suggest.

pose *(SYN.)* model.

position *(SYN.)* caste, site, locality, situation, condition, standing, incumbency, office, bearing, posture, berth, place, job, pose, rank, attitude, location, place, spot, station, job, situation, occupation.

positive *(SYN.)* sure, definite, fixed, inevitable, undeniable, indubitable, assured, certain, unquestionable, unmistakable.

(ANT.) uncertain, doubtful, questionable, probably, unsure, dubious, confused, negative, adverse.

positively *(SYN.)* unquestionably, surely, certainly, absolutely.

possess *(SYN.)* own, obtain, control,

have, seize, hold, occupy, affect, hold, control.

(ANT.) surrender, abandon, lose, renounce.

possessed *(SYN.)* entranced, obsessed, consumer, haunted, enchanted.

possession *(SYN.)* custody, ownership, occupancy.

possessions *(SYN.)* commodities, effects, goods, property, merchandise, wares, wealth, belongings, stock.

possible *(SYN.)* likely, practical, probable, feasible, plausible, credible, practicable.

(ANT.) visionary, impossible, improbable.

possibility *(SYN.)* opportunity, chance, contingency, occasion.

(ANT.) obstacle, disadvantage, hindrance.

possible *(SYN.)* feasible, practical, practicable, doable.

possibly *(SYN.)* perchance, perhaps, maybe.

post *(SYN.)* position, job, berth, incumbency, situation, shaft, pole, fort, base, station.

postpone *(SYN.)* delay, stay, suspend, discontinue, defer, adjourn, interrupt, put off.

(ANT.) persist, prolong, maintain, continue, proceed.

postulate *(SYN.)* principle, adage, saying, proverb, truism, byword, aphorism, axiom, fundamental, maxim.

potency *(SYN.)* effectiveness, capability, skillfulness, efficiency, competency, ability.

(ANT.) wastefulness, inability, ineptitude.

potent *(SYN.)* mighty, influential, convincing, effective.

(ANT.) feeble, weak, powerless, impotent.

potential *(SYN.)* likely, possible, dormant, hidden, latent.

pouch *(SYN.)* container, bag, sack.

pound *(SYN.)* buffet, beat, punch, strike, thrash, defeat, subdue, pulse, smite, belabor, knock, thump, overpower, palpitate, rout, vanquish.

(ANT.) fail, surrender, stroke, defend, shield.

pour *(SYN.)* flow.

pout *(SYN.)* brood, sulk, mope.

poverty *(SYN.)* necessity, need, want, des-

titution, privation, indigence, distress.
(ANT.) plenty, abundance, wealth, riches, affluence, richness, comfort.

power *(SYN.)* potency, might, authority, control, predominance, capability, faculty, validity, force, vigor, command, influence, talent, ability, dominion, competency.
(ANT.) incapacity, fatigue, weakness, disablement, impotence, ineptitude.

powerful *(SYN.)* firm, strong, concentrated, enduring, forcible, robust, sturdy, tough, athletic, forceful, hale, impregnable, hardy, mighty, potent.
(ANT.) feeble, insipid, brittle, delicate, fragile, weak, ineffectual, powerless.

practical *(SYN.)* sensible, wise, prudent, reasonable, sagacious, sober, sound, workable, attainable.
(ANT.) stupid, unaware, impalpable, imperceptible, absurd, impractical.

practically *(SYN.)* almost, nearly.

practice *(SYN.)* exercise, habit, custom, manner, wont, usage, drill, tradition, performance, action, repetition.
(ANT.) inexperience, theory, disuse, idleness, speculation.

practiced *(SYN.)* able, expert, skilled, adept.
(ANT.) inept.

prairie *(SYN.)* plain, grassland.

praise *(SYN.)* applaud, compliment, extol, laud, glorify, commend, acclaim, eulogize, flatter, admire, celebrate, commendation, approval.
(ANT.) criticize, censure, reprove, condemn, disparage, disapprove, criticism, negation.

pray *(SYN.)* supplicate, importune, beseech, beg.

prayer *(SYN.)* plea, suit, appeal, invocation, supplication, petition, entreaty, request.

preach *(SYN.)* teach, urge, moralize, lecture.

preamble *(SYN.)* overture, prologue, beginning, introduction, prelude, start, foreword, preface.
(ANT.) end, finale, completion, conclusion, epilogue.

precarious *(SYN.)* dangerous, perilous, threatening, menacing, critical, risky, unsafe, hazardous.
(ANT.) secure, firm, protected, safe.

precaution *(SYN.)* foresight, forethought, care.

precedence *(SYN.)* preference, priority.

precedent *(SYN.)* model, example.

precept *(SYN.)* doctrine, tenet, belief, creed, teaching, dogma.
(ANT.) practice, conduct, performance, deed.

precious *(SYN.)* dear, useful, valuable, costly, esteemed, profitable, expensive, priceless, dear.
(ANT.) poor, worthless, cheap, mean, trashy.

precipice *(SYN.)* bluff, cliff.

precipitate *(SYN.)* speedy, swift, hasty, sudden.

precipitous *(SYN.)* unannounced, sudden, harsh, rough, unexpected, sharp, abrupt, hasty, craggy, steep, precipitate.
(ANT.) expected, smooth, anticipated, gradual.

precise *(SYN.)* strict, exact, formal, rigid, definite, unequivocal, prim, ceremonious, distinct, accurate, correct.
ANT.) loose, easy, vague, informal, careless, erroneous.

precisely *(SYN.)* specifically, exactly.

precision *(SYN.)* correction, accuracy, exactness.

preclude *(SYN.)* hinder, prevent, obstruct, forestall, obviate, thwart, impede.
(ANT.) permit, aid, expedite, encourage, promote.

preclusion *(SYN.)* omission, exception, exclusion.
(ANT.) standard, rule, inclusion.

predicament *(SYN.)* dilemma, plight, situation, condition, fix, difficulty, strait, scrape.
(ANT.) satisfaction, comfort, east, calmness.

predict *(SYN.)* forecast, foretell.

prediction *(SYN.)* forecast, prophecy.

predilection *(SYN.)* attachment, inclination, affection, bent, desire, penchant, disposition, preference.
ANT.) repugnance, aversion, apathy, distaste, nonchalance.

predominant *(SYN.)* highest, paramount, cardinal, foremost, main, first, leading, supreme, principal, essential, prevalent, dominant, prevailing.
(ANT.) subsidiary, auxiliary, supplemen-

tal, minor, subordinate.

predominate *(SYN.)* prevail, outweigh, rule.

preface *(SYN.)* foreword, introduction, preliminary, prelude, prologue, preamble.

prefer *(SYN.)* select, favor, elect, fancy.

preference *(SYN.)* election, choice, selection, alternative, option.

prejudice *(SYN.)* bias, favoritism, unfairness, partiality.

prejudiced *(SYN.)* fanatical, narrow-minded, dogmatic, bigoted, illiberal, intolerant.

(ANT.) radical, liberal, tolerant, progressive.

preliminary *(SYN.)* introductory, preparatory, prelude, preface.

premature *(SYN.)* early, untimely, unexpected.

(ANT.) timely.

premeditated *(SYN.)* intended, voluntary, contemplated, designed, intentional, willful, deliberate, studied.

(ANT.) fortuitous, accidental.

premeditation *(SYN.)* intention, deliberation, forethought, forecast.

(ANT.) hazard, accident, impromptu, extemporization.

premise *(SYN.)* basis, presupposition, assumption, postulate, principle, presumption.

(ANT.) superstructure, derivative, trimming, implication.

preoccupied *(SYN.)* abstracted, distracted, absorbed, meditative, inattentive, absent, absent-minded.

(ANT.) attentive, alert, conscious, present, attending, watchful.

prepare *(SYN.)* contrive, furnish, ready, predispose, condition, fit, arrange, plan, qualify, make ready, get ready.

preposterous *(SYN.)* foolish, nonsensical, silly, contradictory, unreasonable, absurd, inconsistent, irrational, self-contradictory.

(ANT.) sensible, rational, consistent, sound, reasonable.

prerequisite *(SYN.)* essential, requirement, necessity, condition, demand.

prerogative *(SYN.)* grant, right, license, authority, privilege.

(ANT.) violation, encroachment, wrong,

injustice.

prescribe *(SYN.)* order, direct, designate.

presence *(SYN.)* nearness, attendance, closeness, vicinity, appearance, bearing, personality.

present *(SYN.)* donation, gift, today, now, existing, current, largess, donate, acquaint, introduce, being, give, gratuity, boon, grant.

(ANT.) reject, spurn, accept, retain, receive.

presentable *(SYN.)* polite, well-bred, respectable, well-mannered.

presently *(SYN.)* shortly, soon, directly, immediately.

preserve *(SYN.)* protect, save, conserve, maintain, secure, rescue, uphold, spare, keep, can, safeguard, defend, rescue.

(ANT.) impair, abolish, destroy, abandon, squander, injure.

preside *(SYN.)* officiate, direct, administrate.

press SYN.) impel, shove, urge, hasten, push, compress, squeeze, hug, crowd, propel, force, drive, embrace, smooth, iron, insist on, pressure, promote, urgency, jostle.

(ANT.) oppose, pull, falter, drag, retreat, ignore.

pressing *(SYN.)* impelling, insistent, necessary, urgent, compelling imperative, instant, serious, important, cogent, exigent, importunate.

(ANT.) unimportant, trifling, insignificant, petty, trivial.

pressure *(SYN.)* force, influence, stress, press, compulsion, urgency, constraint, compression.

(ANT.) relaxation, leniency, ease, recreation.

prestige *(SYN.)* importance, reputation, weight, influence, renown, fame, distinction.

presume *(SYN.)* guess, speculate, surmise, imagine, conjecture, apprehend, believe, think, assume, suppose, deduce.

(ANT.) prove, ascertain, demonstrate, know, conclude.

presumption *(SYN.)* boldness, impertinence, insolence, rudeness, assurance, effrontery, impudence, assumption, audacity, supposition, sauciness.

(ANT.) politeness, truckling, diffidence.

presumptuous *(SYN.)* bold, impertinent,

fresh, imprudent, rude, forward, arrogant.

presupposition *(SYN.)* basis, principle, premise, assumption, postulate.
(ANT.) superstructure, derivative, implication.

pretend *(SYN.)* feign, stimulate, act, profess, make believe, imagine, fake, sham, affect.
(ANT.) expose, reveal, display, exhibit.

pretense *(SYN.)* mask, pretext, show, affection, disguise, garb, semblance, simulation, fabrication, lie, excuse, falsification, deceit, subterfuge.
(ANT.) sincerity, actuality, truth, fact, reality.

pretentious *(SYN.)* gaudy, ostentatious.
(ANT.) simple, humble.

pretty *(SYN.)* charming, handsome, lovely, beauteous, fair, comely, attractive, beautiful, elegant.
(ANT.) repulsive, foul, unsightly, homely, plain, hideous.

prevail *(SYN.)* win, succeed, predominate, triumph.
(ANT.) yield, lose.

prevailing *(SYN.)* common, current, general, habitual, steady, regular, universal.

prevalent *(SYN.)* ordinary, usual, common, general, familiar, popular, prevailing, widespread, universal, frequent.
(ANT.) odd, scarce, exceptional, extraordinary.

prevent *(SYN.)* impede, preclude, forestall, stop, block, check, halt, interrupt, deter, slow, obviate, hinder, obstruct, thwart.
(ANT.) expedite, help, allow, abet, aid, permit, encourage, promote.

previous *(SYN.)* former, anterior, preceding, prior, antecedent, earlier, aforesaid, foregoing.
(ANT.) subsequent, following, consequent, succeeding, later.

prey *(SYN.)* raid, seize, victimize.

price *(SYN.)* worth, cost, expense, charge, value.

pride *(SYN.)* self-respect, vanity, glory, superciliousness, haughtiness, conceit, arrogance, self-importance, pretension, egotism, satisfaction, fulfillment, enjoyment, self-esteem.
(ANT.) modesty, shame, humbleness,

lowliness, meekness, humility.

prim *(SYN.)* formal, puritanical, priggish, prudish.

primarily *(SYN.)* mainly, chiefly, firstly, essentially, originally.
(ANT.) secondarily.

primary *(SYN.)* first, principal, primeval, pristine, beginning, original, initial, fundamental, elementary, chief, foremost, earliest, main, prime.
(ANT.) subordinate, last, secondary, least, hindmost, latest.

prime *(SYN.)* first, primary, chief, excellent, best, superior, ready.

primeval *(SYN.)* fresh, primary, novel, inventive, creative, primordial, original, first, new, initial.
(ANT.) trite, modern, subsequent, banal, later, terminal, derivative.

primitive *(SYN.)* antiquated, early, primeval, prehistoric, uncivilized, uncultured, simple, pristine, old, aboriginal, unsophisticated, rude, rough, primary.
(ANT.) sophisticated, modish, civilized, cultured, cultivated, late.

primordial *(SYN.)* pristine, inventive, novel, creative, original, first, initial, new, primary.
(ANT.) trite, terminal, banal, modern, derivative, subsequent, later.

principal *(SYN.)* first, leading, main, supreme, predominant, chief, foremost, highest, prime, primary, leader, headmaster, paramount, essential, cardinal.
(ANT.) supplemental, secondary, auxiliary, subsidiary, accessory, minor, subordinate.

principle *(SYN.)* law, method, axiom, rule, propriety, regulation, maxim, formula, order, statute.
(ANT.) exception, hazard, chance, deviation.

print *(SYN.)* issue, reprint, publish, letter, sign, fingerprint, mark, picture, lithograph, engraving, etching.

prior *(SYN.)* previous, aforesaid, antecedent, sooner, earlier, preceding, former, foregoing.
(ANT.) succeeding, following, later, consequent, subsequent.

prison *(SYN.)* brig, jail, stockade, penitentiary.

pristine *(SYN.)* primordial, creative, first, original, fresh, inventive, novel, primary, initial.

(ANT.) trite, terminal, derivative, modern, banal, subsequent, plagiarized, later.

private *(SYN.)* concealed, hidden, secret, clandestine, unknown, personal, surreptitious, covert, individual, particular, special, latent.

(ANT.) exposed, known, closed, general, public, conspicuous, disclosed, obvious.

privation *(SYN.)* necessity, penury, destitution, need, poverty, want.

(ANT.) wealth, affluence, abundance, plenty, riches.

privilege *(SYN.)* liberty, right, advantage, immunity, freedom, license, favor, sanction.

(ANT.) restriction, inhibition, prohibition, disallowance.

prize *(SYN.)* compensation, bonus, award, premium, remuneration, reward, bounty, esteem, value, rate, recompense, requital.

(ANT.) charge, punishment, wages, earnings, assessment.

probable *(SYN.)* presumable, likely.

probe *(SYN.)* stretch, reach, investigate, examine, examination, scrutiny, scrutinize, inquire, explore, inquiry, investigation, extend.

(ANT.) miss, short.

problem *(SYN.)* dilemma, question, predicament, riddle, difficulty, puzzle.

procedure *(SYN.)* process, way, fashion, form, mode, conduct, practice, manner, habit, system, operation, management, plan.

proceed *(SYN.)* progress, continue, issue, result, spring, thrive, improve, advance, emanate, rise.

(ANT.) retard, withhold, withdraw, hinder, retreat, oppose.

proceeding *(SYN.)* occurrence, business, affair, deal, negotiation, transaction, deed.

proceedings *(SYN.)* account, record, document.

proceeds *(SYN.)* result, produce, income, reward, intake, fruit, profit, store, yield, product, return, harvest, crop.

process *(SYN.)* method, course, system, procedure, operation, prepare, treat.

procession *(SYN.)* cortege, parade, sequence, train, cavalcade, file, retinue,

succession.

proclaim *(SYN.)* declare, assert, make known, promulgate, state, assert, broadcast, express, announce, aver, advertise, tell, publish, profess.

proclamation *(SYN.)* declaration, announcement, promulgation.

procrastinate *(SYN.)* waver, vacillate, defer, hesitate, delay, postpone.

procreate *(SYN.)* generate, produce, beget, engender, originate, propagate, sire, create, father.

(ANT.) murder, destroy, abort, kill, extinguish.

procure *(SYN.)* secure, gain, win, attain, obtain, get, acquire, earn.

(ANT.) lose.

prod *(SYN.)* goad, nudge, jab, push.

prodigious *(SYN.)* astonishing, enormous, immense, monstrous, remarkable, marvelous, huge, amazing, astounding, stupendous, monumental.

(ANT.) insignificant, commonplace, small.

produce *(SYN.)* harvest, reaping, bear, result, originate, bring about, store, supply, make, create, crop, proceeds, bring forth, occasion, breed, generate, cause, exhibit, show, demonstrate, fabricate, hatch, display, manufacture, exhibit, give, yield.

(ANT.) conceal, reduce, destroy, consume, waste, hide.

product *(SYN.)* outcome, result, output, produce, goods, commodity, stock, merchandise.

productive *(SYN.)* fertile, luxuriant, rich, bountiful, fruitful, creative, fecund, teeming, plenteous, prolific.

(ANT.) wasteful, unproductive, barren, impotent, useless, sterile.

profanation *(SYN.)* dishonor, insult, outrage, aspersion, defamation, invective, misuse, abuse, reviling, maltreatment, desecration, perversion.

(ANT.) plaudit, commendation, laudation, respect, approval.

profane *(SYN.)* deflower, violate, desecrate, pollute, dishonor, ravish, debauch.

profess *(SYN.)* declare, assert, make known, state, protest, announce, aver, express, broadcast, avow, tell.

(ANT.) suppress, conceal, repress,

withhold.

profession *(SYN.)* calling, occupation, vocation, employment.

(ANT.) hobby, avocation, pastime.

proffer *(SYN.)* extend, tender, volunteer, propose, advance.

(ANT.) reject, spurn, accept, receive, retain.

proficient *(SYN.)* competent, adept, clever, able, cunning, practiced, skilled, versed, ingenious, accomplished, skillful, expert.

(ANT.) untrained, inexpert, bungling, awkward, clumsy.

profit *(SYN.)* gain, service, advantage, return, earnings, emolument, improvement, benefit, better, improve, use, avail.

(ANT.) waste, loss, detriment, debit, lose, damage, ruin.

profitable *(SYN.)* beneficial, advantageous, helpful, wholesome, useful, gainful, favorable, beneficial, serviceable, salutary, productive, good.

(ANT.) harmful, destructive, injurious, deleterious, detrimental.

profligate *(SYN.)* corrupt, debased, tainted, unsound, vitiated, contaminated, crooked, depraved, impure, venal.

profound *(SYN.)* deep, serious, knowing, wise, intelligent, knowledgeable, recondite, solemn, abstruse, penetrating.

(ANT.) trivial, slight, shallow, superficial.

profuse *(SYN.)* lavish, excessive, extravagant, improvident, luxuriant, prodigal, wasteful, exuberant, immoderate, plentiful.

(ANT.) meager, poor, economical, sparse, skimpy.

profusion *(SYN.)* immoderation, superabundance, surplus, extravagance, intemperance, superfluity.

(ANT.) lack, paucity, death, want, deficiency.

program *(SYN.)* record, schedule, plan, agenda, calendar.

progress *(SYN.)* advancement, improvement, development, betterment, advance, movement, improve, progression.

(ANT.) delay, regression, relapse, retrogression, decline.

progression *(SYN.)* gradation, string, train, chain, arrangement, following, arrangement, order.

prohibit *(SYN.)* hinder, forbid, disallow, obstruct, prevent, stop, ban, interdict, debar.

(ANT.) help, tolerate, allow, sanction, encourage, permit.

prohibition *(SYN.)* prevention, ban, embargo, restriction.

(ANT.) allowance, permission.

prohibitive *(SYN.)* forbidding, restrictive.

project *(SYN.)* design, proposal, scheme, contrivance, outline, homework, activity, purpose, bulge, protrude, throw, cast, device, plan.

(ANT.) production, accomplishment, performance.

prolific *(SYN.)* fertile, rich, fruitful, teeming, fecund, bountiful, luxuriant, productive, plenteous.

(ANT.) unproductive, barren, sterile, impotent.

prolong *(SYN.)* extend, increase, protract, draw, stretch, lengthen.

(ANT.) shorten.

prominent *(SYN.)* distinguished, illustrious, outstanding, renowned, influential, famous, well-known, noted, notable, important, conspicuous, eminent, leading, celebrated.

(ANT.) low, vulgar, ordinary, common.

promise *(SYN.)* assurance, guarantee, pledge, undertaking, agreement, bestowal, word, contract, oath, vow.

promote *(SYN.)* advance, foster, encourage, assist, support, further, aid, help, elevate, raise, facilitate, forward.

(ANT.) obstruct, demote, hinder, impede.

prompt *(SYN.)* punctual, timely, exact, arouse, evoke, occasion, induce, urge, ineffect, cite, suggest, hint, cause, mention, propose, make, precise, originate.

(ANT.) laggardly, slow, tardy, dilatory.

promptly *(SYN.)* immediately, instantly, straightway, forthwith, directly, instantaneously, presently.

(ANT.) later, sometime, hereafter, distantly, shortly.

promulgate *(SYN.)* declare, known, protest, affirm, broadcast, profess, assert, proclaim, state, aver, tell.

(ANT.) repress, conceal, withhold.

prone *(SYN.)* apt, inclined, disposed, likely, predisposed.

pronounce *(SYN.)* proclaim, utter, announce, articulate, enunciate.

pronounced *(SYN.)* clear, definite.

(ANT.) minor, unnoticeable.

proof *(SYN.)* evidence, verification, confirmation, experiment, demonstration, testimony, trial, protected, impenetrable, corroboration, test.

(ANT.) fallacy, invalidity, failure.

propagate *(SYN.)* create, procreate, sire, beget, breed, father, originate, produce.

(ANT.) extinguish, kill, abort, destroy.

propel *(SYN.)* drive, push, transfer, actuate, induce, shift, persuade, move.

(ANT.) stay, deter, halt, rest, stop.

propensity *(SYN.)* leaning, proneness, trend, drift, aim, inclination, bias, proclivity, tendency, predisposition.

(ANT.) disinclination, aversion.

proper *(SYN.)* correct, suitable, decent, peculiar, legitimate, right, conventional.

property *(SYN.)* real estate, effects, possessions, quality, characteristic, merchandise, stock, possession, land.

(ANT.) poverty, destitution, want, deprivation.

prophecy *(SYN.)* augury, prediction.

prophesy *(SYN.)* foretell, predict, augur.

prophet *(SYN.)* fortuneteller, oracle, seer, soothsayer, clairvoyant.

propitious *(SYN.)* lucky, opportune, advantageous, favorable, fortunate, promising, happy.

proportion *(SYN.)* steadiness, poise, composure, relation, balance, equilibrium.

(ANT.) unsteadiness, imbalance, fall.

proposal *(SYN.)* plan, proposition, tender, scheme, program, offer, suggestion, overture.

(ANT.) rejection, acceptance, denial.

propose *(SYN.)* offer, proffer, recommend, plan, mean, expect, move, design, propound, present, tender.

(ANT.) fulfill, perform, effect.

proposition *(SYN.)* proposal, motion.

propound *(SYN.)* bring forward, offer, advance, allege, propose, assign.

(ANT.) retreat, hinder, withhold, retard.

proprietor *(SYN.)* master, owner.

(ANT.) slave, servant.

prosaic *(SYN.)* commonplace, common, everyday, ordinary, routine.

(ANT.) exciting, different, extraordinary.

proscribe *(SYN.)* forbid, ban, prohibit.

(ANT.) permit, allow.

prospect *(SYN.)* anticipation, expectation, candidate, buyer, explore, search.

prospective *(SYN.)* planned, proposed.

prosper *(SYN.)* succeed, win, achieve, gain, rise, prevail, flourish, thrive.

(ANT.) miscarry, wane, miss, fail.

prosperous *(SYN.)* rich, wealthy, affluent, well-to-do, sumptuous, well-off, flourishing, thriving, opulent, luxurious.

(ANT.) impoverished, indigent, beggarly, needy, destitute, poor.

prostrate *(SYN.)* prone, supine, overcome, recumbent, crushed.

protect *(SYN.)* defend, preserve, save, keep, conserve, safeguard, maintain, guard, shield, secure.

(ANT.) impair, abandon, destroy, abolish, injure.

protest *(SYN.)* dissent, noncompliance, disagree, objection, disagreement, challenge, difference, complaint, nonconformity, variance, opposition.

(ANT.) acquiesce, assent, compliance, concur, comply, acceptance, approval.

prototype *(SYN.)* model, archetype, specimen, instance, illustration, example, pattern, sample.

(ANT.) rule, concept, precept, principle.

protract *(SYN.)* extend, strain, distend, expand, spread, stretch, elongate, distort, lengthen.

(ANT.) tighten, contract, loosen, shrink.

protuberance *(SYN.)* prominence, projection, bulge, protrusion, swelling.

proud *(SYN.)* overbearing, vain, arrogant, haughty, stately, vain, glorious, disdainful, prideful, conceited, egotistical, self-important, supercilious.

(ANT.) humble, meek, ashamed, lowly.

prove *(SYN.)* manifest, verify, confirm, demonstrate, establish, show, affirm, examine, corroborate, try, test.

(ANT.) contradict, refute, disprove.

proverb *(SYN.)* maxim, byword, saying, adage, byword, saw, motto, apothegm.

proverbial *(SYN.)* common, well-known.

provide *(SYN.)* supply, endow, afford, produce, yield, give, fit, equip, furnish.

(ANT.) strip, denude, divest, despoil.

provident *(SYN.)* saving, thrifty, economical, frugal, sparing.

(ANT.) wasteful, lavish, extravagant.

provision *(SYN.)* supply, fund, condition,

arrangement, accumulation, reserve, store, hoard.

provisions *(SYN.)* stock, supplies, store.

provoke *(SYN.)* excite, stimulate, agitate, arouse, incite, stir up, vex, bother, disquiet, excite, irritate, annoy, anger.

(ANT.) quell, allay, pacify, calm, quiet.

prowess *(SYN.)* fortitude, mettle, boldness, fearlessness, courage, chivalry, bravery, resolution.

(ANT.) fear, cowardice, timidity.

prowl *(SYN.)* sneak, slink, lurk.

proximate *(SYN.)* nigh, imminent, adjacent, neighboring, bordering, close.

(ANT.) removed, distant, far.

proximity *(SYN.)* vicinity, nearness.

proxy *(SYN.)* representative, equivalent, makeshift, alternate, deputy, substitute.

(ANT.) sovereign, head, principal, master.

prudence *(SYN.)* watchfulness, care, heed, vigilance, wariness, carefulness, tact, judgment, wisdom, common, foresight, caution.

(ANT.) rashness, recklessness, abandon, foolishness, carelessness.

prudent *(SYN.)* reasonable, sensible, sound, discreet, practical, judicious.

(ANT.) stupid, unaware, absurd.

pry *(SYN.)* peer, peep, meddle, peek.

prying *(SYN.)* inquisitive, meddling, curious, inquiring, nosy, peering, searching, interrogative, snoopy.

(ANT.) unconcerned, incurious, indifferent, uninterested.

psyche *(SYN.)* judgment, reason, understanding, brain, intellect, mentality, soul, mind, faculties, spirit.

(ANT.) materiality, body, matter, corporality.

psychosis *(SYN.)* derangement, insanity, madness, delirium, dementia, frenzy, lunacy, mania, aberration.

(ANT.) stability, rationality, sanity.

public *(SYN.)* common, civil, governmental, federal, unrestricted, people, society, open.

publish *(SYN.)* distribute, issue, declare, announce, reveal, proclaim, publicize.

pull *(SYN.)* attract, induce, prolong, draw, tow, drag, remove, take out, persuade, allure, entice, extract.

(ANT.) shorten, alienate, drive, propel.

pulsate *(SYN.)* beat, throb, palpitate.

pummel *(SYN.)* punish, correct, castigate,

discipline, chastise, strike.

(ANT.) release, acquit, free, exonerate.

pump *(SYN.)* interrogate, question, ask, inquire, quiz, examine, query.

(ANT.) state, answer, respond, reply.

punctual *(SYN.)* timely, prompt, exact, ready, nice, precise.

(ANT.) laggardly, tardy, dilatory, late.

punish *(SYN.)* correct, pummel, chasten, reprove, strike, castigate, chastise.

(ANT.) release, exonerate, reward, pardon, acquit, free.

puny *(SYN.)* feeble, impaired, exhausted, infirm, unimportant, weak, decrepit.

(ANT.) strong, forceful, lusty, vigorous.

purchase *(SYN.)* get, procure, buy, shopping, acquire, obtain.

(ANT.) sell, dispose of, vend.

pure *(SYN.)* chaste, absolute, clean, immaculate, untainted, spotless, guiltless, modest, virgin, bare, unmixed, simple.

(ANT.) corrupt, mixed, defiled, foul, tainted, adulterated, polluted, tarnished.

puritanical *(SYN.)* prim, stiff.

(ANT.) permissive.

purport *(SYN.)* import, meaning, explanation, acceptation, drift, sense, significance, purpose, intent, gist.

purpose *(SYN.)* intention, end, goal, aim, objective, application, use, drift, object.

(ANT.) hazard, accident, fate.

pursue *(SYN.)* persist, track follow, hunt, hound, chase, trail.

(ANT.) evade, abandon, flee, elude.

pursuit *(SYN.)* hunt, chase.

push *(SYN.)* jostle, shove, urge, press, thrust, force, drive, crowd, hasten, shove, propel, promote.

(ANT.) ignore, falter, halt, drag, oppose.

pushy *(SYN.)* impudent, abrupt, prominent, insolent, forward, brazen, conspicuous, bold, striking.

(ANT.) retiring, timid, cowardly, bashful.

put *(SYN.)* set, place, state, express, say, assign, attach, establish.

putrefy *(SYN.)* disintegrate, decay, rot, waste, spoil, decompose.

(ANT.) grow, increase, luxuriate.

putrid *(SYN.)* decayed, rotten, moldy, decomposed.

puzzle *(SYN.)* mystery, mystify, confound, perplex, riddle, conundrum, confusion.

(ANT.) key, solution, solve, explain, answer, resolution, illumine, clue.

quack *(SYN.)* faker, fake, fraud, gaggle, clack, gabble, bluffer, cackle, dissembler, charlatan, impostor.

quackery *(SYN.)* charlatanism, deceit, make-believe, fakery, duplicity, dissimulation, pretense, fraudulence, sham, counterfeiting, show.

(ANT.) integrity, probity, veracity, sincerity, honesty.

quaff *(SYN.)* swig, swill, swallow, lap up, sip, drink, ingurgitate, guzzle, imbibe.

quagmire *(SYN.)* swamp, bog, fen, ooze, morass, slough, marsh, plight, predicament, dilemma, impasse, fix, entanglement, quicksand, hole, quandary.

quail *(SYN.)* recoil, cower, flinch, blench, wince, falter, shrink, shake, hesitate, faint, droop.

(ANT.) brave, resist, defy, withstand.

quaint *(SYN.)* odd, uncommon, old-fashioned, antique, antiquated, queer, unusual, curious, eccentric, peculiar, picturesque, singular, whimsical, droll, charming, fanciful, droll, strange.

(ANT.) usual, normal, common, novel, ordinary, modern, current, commonplace, familiar.

quake *(SYN.)* shake, tremble, shudder, quiver, pulsate, stagger, shiver, temblor, vibrate, quaver, throb, earthquake.

qualification *(SYN.)* efficiency, adaptation, restriction, aptness, skill, ability, faculty, talent, power, aptitude, competence, suitability, capability, fitness, condition, dexterity.

(ANT.) unreadiness, incapacity, disability.

qualified *(SYN.)* clever, skillful, efficient, suitable, able, capable, fit, fitted, suited, bounded, limited, contingent, eligible, delimited, adept, circumscribed, equipped, modified, competent.

(ANT.) deficient, inept, impotent, categorical, unlimited, unfitted, unfit, incapable, unsuitable, inadequate.

qualify *(SYN.)* fit, suit, befit, ready, prepare, empower, lessen, moderate, soften, capacitate, condition, adapt, label, designate, name, call, equip, train, restrict, restrict, limit, change.

(ANT.) unfit, incapacitate, disable, disqualify, enlarge, reinforce, aggravate.

quality *(SYN.)* trait, feature, attribute, value, peculiarity, grade, caliber, charac-

ter, distinction, rank, condition, status, characteristic, kind, nature, constitution, mark, type, property.

(ANT.) nature, inferiority, mediocrity, triviality, indifference, inferior, shoddy, second-rate, being, substance, essence.

qualm *(SYN.)* doubt, uneasiness, anxiety, suspicion, skepticism, question, pang, compunction, twinge, regret, uncertainty, demur, fear, remorse, misgiving.

(ANT.) security, comfort, confidence, easiness, invulnerability, firmness.

quandary *(SYN.)* predicament, perplexity, confusion, uncertainty, puzzle, plight, bewilderment, fix, difficulty, entanglement, impasse, doubt, dilemma.

(ANT.) ease, relief, certainty, assurance.

quantity *(SYN.)* sum, measure, volume, content, aggregate, bulk, mass, portion, amount, number, multitude, extent.

(ANT.) zero, nothing.

quarantine *(SYN.)* segregate, separate, confine, isolate, seclude.

quarrel *(SYN.)* contention, argument, affray, dispute, altercation, squabble, feud, difference, disagree, bicker, differ, spar, fight, bickering, tiff, argue, disagreement, spat.

(ANT.) peace, friendliness, reconciliation, amity, agreement, sympathy, accord, concur, support, agree, unity, harmony.

quarrelsome *(SYN.)* testy, contentious, edgy, peevish, irritable, snappish, argumentative, disputatious, cranky, belligerent, combative, disagreeable.

(ANT.) genial, friendly, peaceful, easygoing, peaceable, tempered.

quarry *(SYN.)* prey, quest, game, victim, goal, aim, prize, objective.

quarter *(SYN.)* place, source, fount, well, origin, mainspring, ruth, mercy, pity, compassion, clemency, spring, benevolence, forbearance.

(ANT.) ruthlessness, brutality, cruelty, barbarity, harshness, ferocity.

quarters *(SYN.)* residence, rooms, lodgings, dwelling, flat, billets, chambers, accommodations.

quash *(SYN.)* void, annul, overthrow, nullify, suppress, cancel, quench, quell, repress, invalidate.

(ANT.) reinforce, sustain, authorize, sanction, validate, incite.

quasi *(SYN.)* would-be, partial, synthetic,

nominal, imitation, bogus, sham, counterfeit, mock.

(ANT.) certified, real, legitimate.

quaver *(SYN.)* tremble, shake, hesitate, trill, oscillate, waver, vibrate, shiver, quiver, falter, quake.

quay *(SYN.)* dock, wharf, pier, jetty, bank.

queasy *(SYN.)* sick, squeamish, nauseated, uneasy, queer, restless, nauseous, uncomfortable.

(ANT.) untroubled, comfortable, easy, relaxed.

queen *(SYN.)* empress, diva, doyenne, goddess, star.

queer *(SYN.)* odd, quaint, curious, unusual, droll, strange, peculiar, extraordinary, singular, uncommon, eccentric, weird, funny, nutty, screwy, wacky, deviant, whimsical.

(ANT.) familiar, usual, normal, common, commonplace, plain, patent, conventional, ordinary.

queerness *(SYN.)* oddity, oddness, freakishness, strangeness, singularity, outlandishness, anomaly, weirdness.

(ANT.) normality, familiarity, commonness, standardization.

quell *(SYN.)* subdue, calm, pacify, quiet, cool, hush, appease, lull, mollify, reduce, crush, smother, suppress, stifle, extinguish.

(ANT.) encourage, foment, arouse, foster, incite.

quench *(SYN.)* extinguish, stop, suppress, sate, allay, abate, stifle, slacken, put out, slake, satisfy.

(ANT.) set, light, begin, start, kindle.

querulous *(SYN.)* faultfinding, fretful, carping, critical, complaining, censorious, captious, petulant.

(ANT.) pleased, easygoing, contented, carefree.

query *(SYN.)* inquire, interrogate, demand, investigate, probe, examine, question, inquiry, ask.

(ANT.) answer.

quest *(SYN.)* investigation, interrogation, research, examination, search, question, exploration, seek, pursue, journey, hunt, pursuit, explore, query.

(ANT.) negligence, inactivity, disregard.

question *(SYN.)* interrogate, quiz, doubt, ask, pump, challenge, inquiry, uncertainty, interview, suspect, inquire, dispute, demand, examine, query.

(ANT.) accept, solution, reply, assurance, rejoinder, state, answer, result, response, attest, avow, confidence, respond.

questionable *(SYN.)* uncertain, doubtful, dubious, implausible, debatable, hypothetical, unlikely.

(ANT.) obvious, assured, indubitable, proper, unimpeachable, seemly, conventional, sure, certain.

queue *(SYN.)* file, row, line, series, chain, tier, sequence, string.

quibble *(SYN.)* cavil, shift, evasion, equivocation, dodge, sophism, prevaricate, quiddity, palter.

quick *(SYN.)* rapid, touchy, shrewd, active, hasty, testy, nimble, irascible, discerning, fast, swift, precipitate, excitable, speedy, sharp, impatient, acute, abrupt, curt, brisk, clever, keen, sensitive, lively.

(ANT.) inattentive, dull, gradual, patient, slow, unaware, unhurried, backward, deliberate, sluggish.

quicken *(SYN.)* expedite, forward, rush, hurry, accelerate, push, hasten, dispatch, facilitate, speed.

(ANT.) slow, impede, hinder, hamper, delay, kill, deaden, retard, block.

quickly *(SYN.)* soon, rapidly, fast, at once, promptly, presently, swiftly, hastily, fleety, headlong.

(ANT.) deliberately, later, gradually.

quickness *(SYN.)* energy, vigor, intensity, action, movement, briskness, exercise, motion, rapidity, agility, enterprise.

(ANT.) sloth, idleness, inertia, dullness.

quick-witted *(SYN.)* astute, shrewd, alert, keen, penetrating, quick, intelligent.

(ANT.) slow, dull, unintelligent, plodding.

quiescent *(SYN.)* latent, resting, silent, tranquil, undeveloped, still, quiet, dormant, secret, unseen, inactive.

(ANT.) visible, aroused, evident, active, patent, astir, manifest.

quiet *(SYN.)* meek, passive, hushed, peaceful, calm, patient, quiescent, motionless, tranquil, gentle, undisturbed, mild, peace, silent, quiescence, hush, modest, quietude, rest, tranquillity.

(ANT.) disturbed, agitation, excitement, loud, disturbance, restless, noisy, bois-

terous, perturbed, noise, agitated.

quietness *(SYN.)* tranquillity, repose, calm, silence, quietude, stillness.

(ANT.) flurry, disturbance, fuss, turbulence, agitation, uproar, tumult.

quintessence *(SYN.)* heart, soul, extract, essence, distillation, core.

(ANT.) contingency, adjunct, excrescence, nonessential.

quip *(SYN.)* jest, sally, wisecrack, witticism, joke, jibe, pleasantry.

quirk *(SYN.)* mannerism, idiosyncrasy, foible, peculiarity, oddity, quiddity, vagary, habit, trait, eccentricity.

quirky *(SYN.)* odd, weird, whimsical, peculiar, pixilated, erratic, kinky.

(ANT.) normal, conventional, steady.

quisling *(SYN.)* collaborationist, traitor, subversive, betrayer.

(ANT.) partisan, loyalist.

quit *(SYN.)* leave, stop, desist, depart, abandon, resign, withdraw, refrain, retreat, cease, vacate, end, relinquish, discontinue, halt, lay off, surrender.

(ANT.) persevere, remain, stay, endure, persist, abide, continue.

quite *(SYN.)* somewhat, rather, completely, truly, absolutely, really, entirely.

(ANT.) hardly, merely, barely, somewhat.

quitter *(SYN.)* shirker, dropout, defeatist, piker, loser, malingerer.

quiver *(SYN.)* quake, shake, shudder, tremble, vibrate, shiver.

quixotic *(SYN.)* unrealistic, romantic, visionary, impractical, idealistic, chimerical, lofty, fantastic, frail.

(ANT.) pragmatic, realistic, practical.

quiz *(SYN.)* challenge, interrogate, inquire, pump, doubt, question, ask, dispute, test, query, examine.

(ANT.) reply, say, inform, respond, accept, answer, state.

quizzical *(SYN.)* teasing, coy, mocking, derisive, insolent, arch, bantering, puzzled, questioning, baffled.

(ANT.) respectful, obsequious, uninterested, normal, usual, serious, attentive.

quota *(SYN.)* share, portion, apportionment, ratio, proportion, allotment.

quotation *(SYN.)* quote, selection, excerpt, repetition, cutting, reference.

quote *(SYN.)* refer to, recite, paraphrase, adduce, repeat, illustrate, cite, echo.

(ANT.) retort, contradict, refute.

rabble *(SYN.)* throng, mob, horde, crowd.

rabid *(SYN.)* frantic, frenzied, violent, raging, raving, zealous, fanatical.

(ANT.) normal, sound, sober, moderate.

race *(SYN.)* meet, run, clan, stock, lineage, strain, match, course, stream, hasten, compete, folk, competition.

(ANT.) linger, dawdle, dwell.

rack *(SYN.)* frame, framework, bracket, scaffold, skeleton.

racket *(SYN.)* sound, cry, babel, noise, uproar, hubbub, clamor, fuss, disturbance, din, tumult, fracas, clatter.

(ANT.) stillness, hush, silence, quiet, tranquillity, peace.

racy *(SYN.)* interesting, vigorous, lively, spirited, animated, entertaining.

radiance *(SYN.)* luster, brilliancy, brightness, splendor, effulgence, glowing.

(ANT.) gloom, darkness, obscurity.

radiant *(SYN.)* showy, superb, brilliant, illustrious, dazzling, grand, shining, bright, effulgent, beaming, sumptuous.

(ANT.) dark, unimpressive, dull, dim, lusterless, ordinary.

radiate *(SYN.)* spread, emit, diffuse, shed, irradiate, shine, gleam, illuminate.

radical *(SYN.)* ultra, innate, essential, organic, complete, revolutionary, insurgent, natural, total, fundamental, extreme, basic, original, thorough.

(ANT.) extraneous, moderate, conservative, superficial, shallow, established.

radius *(SYN.)* orbit, reach, extent, scope, sphere, range, sweep.

raft *(SYN.)* pontoon, platform, float.

rag *(SYN.)* dishcloth, dishrag, cloth.

rage *(SYN.)* passion, ire, exasperation, fashion, fad, vogue, craze, anger, temper, fury, irritation, mania, rave, rant, storm, fume, overflow, wrath.

(ANT.) peace, forbearance, patience.

raging *(SYN.)* raving, severe, passionate, boisterous, violent, fierce, wild, passionate, acute, intense, powerful.

(ANT.) feeble, soft, calm, quiet.

ragged *(SYN.)* tattered, torn, worn, shredded, seedy, threadbare, shabby.

raid *(SYN.)* assault, attack, invasion, arrest, invade, seizure, maraud, foray.

rail *(SYN.)* railing, fence, bar.

railing *(SYN.)* balustrade, banister, barrier, fence.

rain *(SYN.)* shower, drizzle, rainstorm,

sprinkle, deluge, down-pour.

raise *(SYN.)* grow, muster, elevate, heave, cultivate, awake, rouse, excite, enlarge, increase, rise, breed, hoist, bring up.
(ANT.) destroy, decrease, lessen, cut, depreciate, lower, abase, debase, drop, demolish, level.

rakish *(SYN.)* dapper, dashing, smart, debonair, natty, swanky, showy.

rally *(SYN.)* muster, convoke, summon, convene, convention, assemblage.

ramble *(SYN.)* err, amble, saunter, wander, roam, saunter, walk, deviate.
(ANT.) stop, linger, stay, halt, settle.

rambling *(SYN.)* incoherent, erratic.
(ANT.) straightfoward, coherent.

rambunctious *(SYN.)* stubborn, defiant, unruly, aggressive, contrary.

ramification *(SYN.)* aftermath, extension, branch, offshoot, result, consequence.

rampage *(SYN.)* tumult, outbreak, uproar, rage, frenzy, ebullition, storm.

rampant *(SYN.)* excessive, flagrant, boisterous, menacing.
(ANT.) bland, calm, mild.

ramshackle *(SYN.)* rickety, decrepit, flimsy, dilapidated, shaky.

rancid *(SYN.)* spoiled, rank, tainted, sour, musty, putrid, rotten, purtrescent.
(ANT.) pure, fresh, wholesome, fragrant.

rancor *(SYN.)* spite, grudge, malice, animosity, malevolence, hostility.
(ANT.) kindness, toleration, affection.

random *(SYN.)* haphazard, chance, unscheduled, unplanned, casual.
(ANT.) intentional, specific, particular.

range *(SYN.)* expanse, extent, limit, area, grassland, pasture, plain, change, wander, roam, travel, rove.

ransack *(SYN.)* pillage, loot, rummage, plunder, despoil, ravish, search.

ransom *(SYN.)* release, deliverance, compensation, redeem.

rant *(SYN.)* declaim, rave, harangue.

rap *(SYN.)* thump, knock, blow, whack.

rapacious *(SYN.)* greedy, wolfish, avaricious, ravenous, grasping, predatory.

rapid *(SYN.)* speedy, quick, swift, fast.
(ANT.) deliberate, halting, sluggish, slow.

rapine *(SYN.)* destruction, pillage, robbery, marauding, spoiling.

rapport *(SYN.)* harmony, fellowship, agreement, mutuality, accord, empathy.

rapture *(SYN.)* joy, gladness, ecstasy,

bliss, transport, exultation, delight, happiness, enchantment, ravishment.
(ANT.) woe, misery, wretch, depression.

rare *(SYN.)* unique, strange, precious, uncommon, infrequent, choice, singular, occasional, unusual, fine, matchless.
(ANT.) worthless, common, commonplace, usual, everyday, customary.

rarely *(SYN.)* scarcely, hardly infrequently, occasionally, sparingly, barely.
(ANT.) usually, continually, often.

rascal *(SYN.)* scoundrel, villain, trickster, rogue, scamp, swindler, imp, prankster.

rash *(SYN.)* quick, careless, passionate, thoughtless, hotheaded, reckless, foolhardy, eruption, dermatitis, heedless.
(ANT.) thoughtful, considered, prudent, reasoning, calculating, careful.

raspy *(SYN.)* gruff, harsh, dissonant, grinding, hoarse, grating, strident.

rate *(SYN.)* try, adjudicate, consider, decide, condemn, decree, estimate, speed, pace, measure, judge, arbitrate.

ratify *(SYN.)* validate, certify, confirm, establish, support, endorse, uphold.

rating *SYN.)* assessment, position, assignment, status, classification.

ration *(SYN.)* portion, allowance, distribute, measure, allotment, share, percentage.

rational *(SYN.)* sound, wise, sane, intelligent, sober, sensible, judicious, sober.
(ANT.) irrational, absurd, insane.

rationality *(SYN.)* cause, aim, intelligence, reason, basis, understanding, ground, argument, mind, sense.

raucous *(SYN.)* raspy, harsh, grating, hoarse, discordant, rowdy.
(ANT.) dulcet, pleasant, sweet.

ravage *(SYN.)* ruin, despoil, strip, waste, destroy, pillage, plunder, sack, havoc.
(ANT.) conserve, save, accumulate.

rave *(SYN.)* rage, storm, laud, praise.

ravenous *(SYN.)* hungry, voracious, craving, starved, gluttonous, famished.
(ANT.) replete, gorged, satiated, full.

ravine *(SYN.)* chasm, gorge, crevasse, canyon, abyss.

ravish *(SYN.)* violate, debauch.

ravishing *(SYN.)* enchanting, captivating, bewitching, fascinating, alluring.
(ANT.) loathsome, disgusting, repulsive.

raw *(SYN.)* harsh, rough, coarse, unrefined, undone, uncooked, unprocessed, crude, unpolished, natural. *(ANT.) finished, refined, processed.*

ray *(SYN.)* beam.

raze *(SYN.)* ravage, wreck, destroy, flatten, annihilate, obliterate, demolish. *(ANT.) make, erect, construct, preserve, establish, save.*

reach *(SYN.)* overtake, arrive at, extent, distance, scope, range, extend, attain, stretch. *(ANT.) fail, miss.*

react *(SYN.)* result, reply, respond. *(ANT.) overlook, disregard.*

reaction *(SYN.)* result, response, reception, repercussion.

readable *(SYN.)* understandable, distinct, legible, plain, clear, comprehensible. *(ANT.) obliterated, illegible, defaced.*

readily *(SYN.)* quickly, promptly, easily.

ready *(SYN.)* mature, ripe, complete, seasonable, done, arrange, prompt, prepared, completed, quick, mellow. *(ANT.) undeveloped, immature, green.*

real *(SYN.)* true, actual, positive, authentic, genuine, veritable. *(ANT.) counterfeit, unreal, fictitious, false, sham, supposed.*

realization *(SYN.)* completion, achievement, performance, accomplishment, comprehension, insight. *(ANT.) failure.*

realize *(SYN.)* discern, learn, comprehend, appreciate, perfect, actualize, understand, apprehend, know, see. *(ANT.) misunderstand, misapprehend.*

really *(SYN.)* truly, actually, honestly, undoubtedly, positively, genuinely. *ANT.) questionably, possibly, doubtfully.*

realm *(SYN.)* land, domain, farm, kingdom, sphere, department, estate, world.

reap *(SYN.)* gather, harvest, gain, glean, produce, cut, pick, acquire, garner. *(ANT.) plant, seed, sow, lose, squander.*

reaping *(SYN.)* proceeds, result, crop, yield, fruit, produce.

rear *(SYN.)* posterior, raise, lift, train, nurture, rump, back, elevate, construct, build, foster.

reason *(SYN.)* intelligence, objective, understanding, mind, aim, argument, cause, aim, judgment, common sense, sanity, gather, assume, sake, motive.

reasonable *(SYN.)* prudent, rational, logical, sage, sound, moderate, intelligent, sensible, discreet. *(ANT.) unaware, imperceptible, insane, absurd, stupid, illogical, irrational.*

rebel *(SYN.)* revolutionary, traitor, mutineer, mutiny, revolt, disobey.

rebellion *(SYN.)* revolt, uprising, coup, overthrow, insurrection, revolution. *(ANT.) submission, obedience, repression, peace.*

rebellious *(SYN.)* unruly, forward, defiant, undutiful, disobedient. *(ANT.) obedient, compliant, submissive.*

rebirth *(SYN.)* renascence, renaissance, revival.

rebuff *(SYN.)* snub, oppose, resist, reject, refuse, slight, opposition. *(ANT.) welcome, encourage, support.*

rebuild *(SYN.)* restore, renew, refresh, reconstruct, renovate.

rebuke *(SYN.)* chide, scold, reproach, censure, upbraid, scolding, condemn. *(ANT.) praise, exonerate, absolve.*

rebuttal *(SYN.)* contradiction, defense, answer. *(ANT.) argument, validation, corroboration.*

recall *(SYN.)* recollect, remembrance, withdraw, retract, remember, recollection, reminisce, mind, memory, remind. *(ANT.) forget, overlook, ignore.*

recede *(SYN.)* withdraw, ebb, retire, retreat.

receive *(SYN.)* entertain, acquire, admit, accept, shelter, greet, obtain, welcome. *(ANT.) reject, offer, give, bestow, discharge, impart.*

recent *(SYN.)* novel, original, late, new, newfangled, fresh, modern, current. *(ANT.) old, antiquated, ancient.*

reception *(SYN.)* gathering, party.

recess *(SYN.)* hollow, opening, nook, cranny, dent, respite, rest, break, pause. *(ANT.) gather, convene.*

recession *(SYN.)* slump, depression.

recipe *(SYN.)* instructions, formula, prescriptions, procedure, method.

recital *(SYN.)* history, account, relation, chronicle, narrative, detail, narration. *(ANT.) distortion, confusion, misrepresentation.*

recite *(SYN.)* describe, narrate, declaim, rehearse, tell, mention, repeat, detail, recapitulate, report, list, relate, deliver.

reckless *(SYN.)* thoughtless, inconsiderate, careless, imprudent, rash, indiscreet, unconcerned.
(ANT.) careful, nice, accurate.

reclaim *(SYN.)* reform, rescue, reinstate, regenerate, recycle.

recline *(SYN.)* stretch, sprawl, repose, rest, lounge, loll, incline.

recluse *(SYN.)* hermit, eremite, loner, anchorite.

recognize *(SYN.)* remember, avow, own, know, admit, apprehend, recollect, recall, concede, acknowledge, confess.
(ANT.) disown, ignore, renounce.

recollect *(SYN.)* recall, remember, memory, reflect, call to mind, reminisce.
(ANT.) forget.

recollection *(SYN.)* remembrance, retrospection, impression, recall.
(ANT.) forgetfulness, oblivion.

recommend *(SYN.)* hind, refer, advise, commend, suggest, counsel, allude, praise, approve, intimate, advocate.
(ANT.) disapprove, declare, insist.

recommendation *(SYN.)* instruction, justice, trustworthiness, counsel, admonition, caution, integrity, uprightness.
(ANT.) fraud, deceit, trickery, cheating.

reconcile *(SYN.)* meditate, unite, adapt, adjust, settle, reunite, appease.

recondition *(SYN.)* rebuild, overhaul, restore, service.

reconsider *(SYN.)* ponder, reevaluate, mull over, reflect, reassess.

record *(SYN.)* enter, write, register, chronicle, history, account, doeument.

recount *(SYN.)* report, convey, narrate, tell, detail, recite, describe, repeat.

recoup *(SYN.)* regain, recover, repay, retrieve.

recover *(SYN.)* regain, redeem, recapture, retrieve, salvage, better, improve, mend, heal.
(ANT.) debilitate, succumb, worsen.

recreation *(SYN.)* entertainment, amusement, enjoyment, diversion, fun.

recrimination *(SYN.)* vindication, reproach, dissension, accusation, countercharge.

recruit *(SYN.)* trainee, beginner, volunteer, draftee, select, enlist, novice.

recuperate *(SYN.)* regain, retrieve, cure, recapture, redeem, rally, convalesce,

revive, recover, repossess, restore.
(ANT.) sicken, weaken, lose, regress, forfeit.

redeem *(SYN.)* claim, recover, repossess, regain, reclaim, cash in, retrieve.

reduce *(SYN.)* lessen, decrease, lower, downgrade, degrade, suppress, lower, abate, diminish.
(ANT.) enlarge, swell, raise, elevate, revive, increase, amplify.

reduction *(SYN.)* shortening, abridgment, abbreviation.
(ANT.) amplification, extension, enlargement.

reek *(SYN.)* odor, stench, stink, smell.

refer *(SYN.)* recommend, direct, commend, regard, concern, relate, suggest, mention.

referee *(SYN.)* judge, arbitrator, umpire, arbiter, moderator, mediator, intermediary.

reference *(SYN.)* allusion, direction, mention, concern, respect, referral.

refine *(SYN.)* purify, clarify, improve, clean.
(ANT.) pollute, debase, muddy, downgrade.

refined *(SYN.)* purified, cultured, cultivated, courteous, courtly.
(ANT.) rude, coarse, crude, vulgar.

refinement *(SYN.)* culture, enlightenment, education, civilization.
(ANT.) vulgarity, ignorance, boorishness.

reflect *(SYN.)* muse, mirror, deliberate, cogitate, think, reproduce, ponder, consider, reason, meditate, contemplate.

reflection *(SYN.)* warning, conception, intelligence, appearance, likeness, image, cogitation, notification.

reform *(SYN.)* right, improve, correction, change, amend, improvement, better, betterment, correct, rectify.
(ANT.) spoil, damage, aggravate, vitiate.

refresh *(SYN.)* exhilarate, renew, invigorate.
(ANT.) exhaust, tire.

refreshing *(SYN.)* bracing, cool, brisk, fresh.

refreshment *(SYN.)* food, snack, drink, nourishment, exhilaraton, stimulation.

refuge *(SYN.)* safety, retreat, shelter, asylum, sanctuary, harbor.
(ANT.) peril, exposure, jeopardy, danger.

refuse *(SYN.)* spurn, rebuff, decline,

reject, trash, rubbish, withhold, disallow, waste, garbage, deny, demur.
(ANT.) allow, accept, welcome, grant.
refute *(SYN.)* rebut, disprove, confute, falsify, controvert, contradict.
(ANT.) prove, confirm, accept, establish.
regain *(SYN.)* redeem, retrieve, recover, repossess, recapture.
(ANT.) lose.
regalement *(SYN.)* feast, dinner, celebration, entertainment.
regard *(SYN.)* estimate, value, honor, affection, notice, care, consideration, consider, relation, respect, attend, thought, reference, care, attention, esteem, concern, liking.
(ANT.) neglect, disgust, antipathy.
regards *(SYN.)* salutations, greetings, good wishes, respects, remembrances.
regenerate *(SYN.)* improve, reconstruct, remedy, reestablish, rebuild.
regime *(SYN.)* direction, government, administration, management, dynasty, command, leadership.
regimented *(SYN.)* ordered, directed controlled, orderly, rigid, disciplined.
(ANT.) loose, free, unstructured.
region *(SYN.)* belt, place, spot, territory, climate, area, zone, locality, station, locale.
register *(SYN.)* catalog, record, book, list, roll, enter, roster, chronicle.
regressive *(SYN.)* revisionary, retrograde.
(ANT.) progressive, civilized, advanced.
regret *(SYN.)* sorrow, qualm, lament, grief, compunction, bemoan, concern, scruple, misgiving, remorse, contrition.
(ANT.) obduracy, complacency.
regular *(SYN.)* steady, orderly, natural, normal, customary, usual, habitual, even, uniform, systematic, unvaried, methodical, symmetrical.
(ANT.) odd, exceptional, unusual, irregular, abnormal, rare.
regulate *(SYN.)* control, manage, govern, direct, legislate, set, adjust, systematize.
regulation *(SYN.)* method, rule, axiom, guide, control, standard, canon, precept, restraint, requirement.
(ANT.) chaos, deviation, hazard, turbulence, confusion.
rehabilitate *(SYN.)* renew, restore, rebuild, reestablish, repair, reconstruct.

rehearse *(SYN.)* repeat, practice, train, learn, coach, prepare, perfect, direct.
reign *(SYN.)* dominion, power, rule, sovereignty, govern, domination.
reimburse *(SYN.)* recompense, remunerate, compensate, remit.
rein *(SYN.)* restriction, bridle, check, deterrent, curb, restraint, barrier, control.
reinforce *(SYN.)* brace, strengthen, fortify, intensify, support.
reiterate *(SYN.)* reproduce, recapitulate, duplicate, repeat, rephrase.
reject *(SYN.)* spurn, rebuff, decline, renounce, expel, discard, withhold, deny, refuse.
(ANT.) endorse, grant, welcome, accept.
rejection *(SYN.)* dissent, nonconformity, variance, challenge, remonstrance, difference, noncompliance.
(ANT.) assent, acceptance, compliance.
rejoice *(SYN.)* celebrate, delight, enjoy, revel, exhilarate, elate.
rejuvenate *(SYN.)* refresh, rekindle, overhaul, revitalize, animate, invigorate.
(ANT.) deplete, weaken, exhaust, eneverate.
relapse *(SYN.)* worsen, deteriorate, regress, weaken, fade, worsen, sink fail.
(ANT.) strengthen, progress, advance, get well, rehabilitate.
relate *(SYN.)* refer, beat, report, describe, tell, correlate, narrate, recount, compare, connect.
relation *(SYN.)* entente, compact, coalition, alliance, connection, relationship, association, partnership, similarity, kinsman, treaty, marriage.
(ANT.) separation, divorce.
relationship *(SYN.)* link, tie, alliance, connection, union, bond, affinity, conjunction.
(ANT.) separation, disunion.
relative *(SYN.)* dependent, proportional, about, pertinent, regarding.
relax *(SYN.)* slacken, loosen, repose, rest, recline, unwind.
(ANT.) increase, tighten, intensify.
relaxation *(SYN.)* comfort, ease, rest, enjoyment, lull, recess, breather, loafing.
relaxed *(SYN.)* welcome, pleasing, casual, acceptable, informal, restful, agreeable.
(ANT.) formal, planned, wretched, distressing, troubling.

release (SYN.) liberate, emancipate, relinquish, proclaim, publish, liberation, announce, deliver, free, discharge.
(ANT.) restrict, imprison, subjugate.

relegate (SYN.) entrust, authorize, remand, refer, assign.

relent (SYN.) cede, yield, surrender, give, relax, abdicate, relinquish, waive.
(ANT.) strive, assert, struggle.

relentless (SYN.) eternal, stubborn, tenacious, dogged, ceaseless, incessant, ceaseless, persistent, determined.

relevant (SYN.) related, material, apt, applicable, fit, relating, germane.
(ANT.) foreign, alien, unrelated.

reliable (SYN.) trusty, tried, certain, secure, trustworthy, dependable.
(ANT.) unreliable, eccentric, questionable, erratic, dubious.

reliance (SYN.) faith, confidence, trust.
(ANT.) mistrust, doubt, skepticism.

relic (SYN.) remains, fossil, throwback, heirloom, souvenir, keepsake, heirloom.

relief (SYN.) help, aid, comfort, ease, backing, patronage, alms, support.
(ANT.) hostility, defiance, antagonism, resistance.

relieve (SYN.) diminish, soothe, calm, abate, pacify, ease, lessen, replace, spell, lighten, comfort, alleviate.
(ANT.) disturb, irritate, agitate, trouble, aggravate, worry.

religion (SYN.) tenet, belief, dogma, faith, creed, persuasion.

religious (SYN.) godly, reverent, faithful, devout, zeal, pious, divine, holy, devoted, sacred, theological.
(ANT.) profane, irreligious, skeptical, impious, lax, atheistic.

religiousness (SYN.) love, zeal, affection, devoutness, fidelity, ardor.
(ANT.) indifference, apathy, unfaithfulness.

relinquish (SYN.) capitulate, submit, yield, abandon, cede, sacrifice, disclaim.
(ANT.) overcome, conquer, rout, resist.

relish (SYN.) enjoyment, satisfaction, delight, gusto, appreciation, condiment, like, enjoy, enthusiasm.
(ANT.) distaste, antipathy, disfavor, dislike.

reluctance (SYN.) disgust, hatred, repulsion, abhorrence, distaste, repugnance, aversion.

(ANT.) enthusiasm, affection, devotion.

reluctant (SYN.) slow, averse, hesitant, unwilling, loath, disinclined, balky.
(ANT.) ready, eager, willing, disposed.

rely (SYN.) confide, trust, lean, depend.
(ANT.) mistrust, disbelieve, question, distrust.

remain (SYN.) survive, rest, stay, abide, halt, endure, dwell, tarry, continue, linger.
(ANT.) finish, leave, terminate, dissipate.

remainder (SYN.) leftover, residue, rest, surplus, balance, excess.

remains (SYN.) residue, balance, rest, remnants, relics, discards, waste, junk.

remark (SYN.) comment, state, utterance, mention, note, observe, observation, annotation, declaration, statement.

remarkable (SYN.) exciting, impressive, overpowering, unusual, affecting, thrilling, splendid, special, noteworthy, extraordinary, touching, august.
(ANT.) ordinary, unimpressive, commonplace, average, regular.

remedy (SYN.) redress, help, cure, relief, medicine, restorative, rectify, alleviate, medication, correct, reparation.

remember (SYN.) recollect, reminisce, recall, memorize, mind, retain, remind.
(ANT.) forget, overlook, disregard.

remembrance (SYN.) monument, memory, recollection, memento, recall, keepsake, souvenir, retrospection.

remiss (SYN.) delinquent, lax, careless, negligent, oblivious, forgetful, absentminded, sloppy, irresponsible.

remit (SYN.) send, pay, forward, forgive, pardon, overlook, excuse, reimburse.

remittance (SYN.) payment.

remnant (SYN.) remains, remainder, rest, residue, trace, relic.

remodel (SYN.) remake, reshape, rebuild, redecorate, renovate, modify, change, alter, convert, refurbish, update.

remonstrate (SYN.) grouch, protest, complain, grumble, murmur, repine, dispute.
(ANT.) rejoice, applaud, praise.

remorse (SYN.) sorrow, qualm, contrition, regret, compunction, repentance.
(ANT.) obduracy, complacency.

remorseless (SYN.) savage, unrelenting, crude, barbaric, merciless, cruel, fiendish, brutal, callous.

(ANT.) kind, refined, polite, civilized.

remote (SYN.) inconsiderable, removed, slight, far, unlikely, distant, inaccessible, unreachable, isolated, sequestered.

(ANT.) visible, nearby, current, near, close.

remove (SYN.) transport, eject, move, vacate, withdraw, dislodge, transfer, doff, displace, eliminate, murder, kill, oust, extract.

(ANT.) insert, retain, leave, stay, keep.

removed (SYN.) aloof, distant, cool, remote.

remuneration (SYN.) wages, payment, pay, salary, compensation, reimbursement, reward.

render (SYN.) become, make, perform, do, offer, present, give, submit.

rendition (SYN.) interpretation, version, depiction, expression, characterization.

renegade (SYN.) defector, insurgent, dissenter, rebel, maverick, mutineer, betrayer.

renege (SYN.) let down, doublecross, deceive.

renew (SYN.) restore, renovate, overhaul, revise, modernize, reshape, redo.

renounce (SYN.) resign, disown, revoke, abandon, quit, retract, forgo, leave, forsake, abdicate, reject, relinquish, deny.

(ANT.) assert, uphold, recognize, maintain.

renovate (SYN.) restore, rehabilitate, rebuild, refresh, renew, overhaul, redesign.

renown (SYN.) honor, reputation, eminence, acclaim, glory, repute, luster, fame, notability.

(ANT.) obscurity, anonymity, disgrace.

renowned (SYN.) noted, famous, distinguished, well-known, glorious, celebrated.

(ANT.) unknown, infamous, hidden, obscure.

rent (SYN.) payment, rental, let, lease, hire.

repair (SYN.) rebuilding, mend, renew, tinker, correct, patch, restore, adjust, reconstruction, remedy, amend, rehabilitation, retrieve.

(ANT.) harm, break.

repartee (SYN.) badinage, banter.

repast (SYN.) feast, banquet, meal, refreshment, snack.

repeal (SYN.) end, cancel, nullify, annul, quash, abolish, cancellation, rescind, abolition, abrogate.

repeat (SYN.) reiterate, restate, redo, rehearse, quote, remake, relate, iterate, reproduce.

repeated (SYN.) continuous, frequent, recurrent, continual.

repel (SYN.) check, repulse, rebuff, reject, decline, discourage.

(ANT.) lure, attract.

repellent (SYN.) sickening, offensive, disgusting, nauseating, repugnant, obnoxious.

repent (SYN.) deplore, regret, rue, lament.

repentance (SYN.) penitence, remorse, sorrow, compunction, qualm, grief.

(ANT.) obduracy, complacency.

repentant (SYN.) regretful, sorrowful, contrite, sorry, penitent.

(ANT.) remorseless, obdurate.

repetitious (SYN.) repeated, monotonous, boring, tiresome, humdrum.

repine (SYN.) protest, lament, complain, whine, regret, grouch, murmur, grumble.

(ANT.) rejoice, applaud, praise.

replace (SYN.) alternate, return, reinstate.

replacement (SYN.) understudy, proxy, second, alternate, substitute, replica, surrogate.

replenish (SYN.) store, pervade, fill, stock, occupy, supply.

(ANT.) empty, void, deplete, exhaust, drain.

replica (SYN.) reproduction, copy, exemplar, imitation, duplicate, facsimile.

(ANT.) prototype.

reply (SYN.) retort, rejoinder, answer, retaliate, respond, confirmation.

(ANT.) summoning, inquiry.

report (SYN.) declare, herald, publish, announce, summary, publish, advertise.

(ANT.) suppress, conceal, withhold, bury.

reporter (SYN.) journalist.

repose (SYN.) hush, quiet, tranquillity, rest, peace, slumber, calm, stillness, sleep, calmness, dormancy.

(ANT.) tumult, excitement, agitation.

reprehensible (SYN.) criminal, immoral,

damnable, culpable, wrong, wicked.

represent *(SYN.)* picture, draw, delineate, portray, depict, denote, symbolize.

(ANT.) misrepresent, caricature.

representation *(SYN.)* effigy, film, likeness, portrait, print, scene, appearance, drawing, scene, view, cinema.

representative *(SYN.)* delegate, agent, substitute, surrogate.

repress *(SYN.)* limit, stop, check, bridle, curb, restrain, constrain, suppress.

(ANT.) loosen, aid, incite, liberate, encourage.

reprimand *(SYN.)* rate, scold, vituperate, berate, lecture, blame, admonish, upbraid.

(ANT.) praise, approve.

reproach *(SYN.)* defamation, dishonor, insult, profanation, abuse, disparagement, misuse, reviling.

(ANT.) respect, laudation, approval, plaudit.

reproduction *(SYN.)* replica, copy, exemplar, transcript, duplicate, photocopy.

reproof *(SYN.)* rebuke, punishment, blame, censure, disapproval, scorn, disdain, admonition.

repugnance *(SYN.)* disgust, hatred, reluctance, abhorrence, aversion, loathing, antipathy, distaste, repulsion.

(ANT.) devotion, affection, enthusiasm, attachment.

repulsive *(SYN.)* repellent, ugly, homely, deformed, horrid, offensive, plain, uncomely.

(ANT.) fair, pretty, attractive, handsome.

reputable *(SYN.)* honest, upstanding, trustworthy, straightforward, upright, reliable.

(ANT.) notorious, corrupt, disreputable.

reputation *(SYN.)* class, nature, standing, name, fame, kind, renown, prominence, character, distinction, disposition, repute.

repute *(SYN.)* class, nature, standing, kind, character, reputation, disposition, sort.

request *(SYN.)* sue, implore, petition, desire, appeal, question, entreaty, beseech, ask, pray, supplicate.

(ANT.) require.

require *(SYN.)* exact, need, order, command, order, lack, claim, demand, want.

requirement *(SYN.)* demand, need, necessity, condition, provision, prerequisite.

requisite *(SYN.)* vital, necessary, basic, fundamental, indispensable, essential, needed.

(ANT.) casual, nonessential, peripheral, accidental.

rescind *(SYN.)* annul, quash, revoke, abolish, invalidate, abrogate, withdraw.

rescue *(SYN.)* liberate, ransom, release, deliver, deliverance, liberation.

research *(SYN.)* exploration, quest, scrutiny, exploration, interrogation, query, examination, study, investigation.

(ANT.) inattention, disregard, negligence.

resemblance *(SYN.)* parity, similitude, analogy, likeness, correspondence.

(ANT.) distinction, difference.

resemble *(SYN.)* duplicate, mirror, look like.

resentfulness *(SYN.)* envy, jealousy, covetousness, suspicion.

(ANT.) liberality, geniality, tolerance, difference.

resentment *(SYN.)* displeasure, bitterness, indignation, rancor, outrage, hostility.

(ANT.) complacency, understanding, good will.

reservation *(SYN.)* skepticism, restriction, objection, limitation, doubt.

reserve *(SYN.)* fund, hold, keep, store, accumulation, save, stock, maintain, supply.

(ANT.) waste, squander.

reserved *(SYN.)* cautious, fearful, timorous, wary, aloof, chary, sheepish, restrained, proper, unfriendly, bashful, diffident.

(ANT.) forward, bold, wild, immodest, brazen, abandoned, friendly.

reside *(SYN.)* inhabit, dwell, abide, live, lie.

residence *(SYN.)* home, dwelling, stay, seat, abode, quarters, domicile, living quarters.

residue *(SYN.)* balance, remainder, rest, ashes, remnants, dregs, leftovers, ends.

resign *(SYN.)* vacate, withdraw, leave, surrender, quit.

resignation *(SYN.)* perseverance, endurance, fortitude, composure, forbearance.

(ANT.) unquiet, nervousness, impatience.

resigned (SYN.) forbearing, stoical, assiduous, passive, accepting, composed, uncomplaining.

(ANT.) turbulent, chafing.

resilience (SYN.) rubbery, springy, buoyant, elasticity.

(ANT.) unresponsive, fixed, rigid, stolid.

resist (SYN.) defy, attack, withstand, hinder, confront, oppose.

(ANT.) relent, allow, yield, accede.

resolute (SYN.) firm, resolved, set, determined, decided.

(ANT.) irresolute, wavering, vacillating.

resolution (SYN.) resolve, courage, determination, persistence, statement, verdict, recommendation, decision, steadfastness, dedication, perseverance.

(ANT.) indecision, inconstancy.

resolve (SYN.) determination, resolution, courage, settle, decide, persistence, determine, confirm, decision, steadfastness.

(ANT.) integrate, indecision, inconstancy.

resort (SYN.) motel, lodge, hotel, solve.

resound (SYN.) echoe, ring, reverberate.

resource (SYN.) store, source, supply, reserve.

resourceful (SYN.) inventive, ingenious, creative, clever, imaginative, skillful.

respect (SYN.) honor, approval, revere, heed, value, admire, esteem, point, detail, admiration, reverence, regard, feature, particular, venerate, consider.

(ANT.) disrespect, neglect, abuse, scorn, disregard, despise.

respectable (SYN.) becoming, respected, proper, seemly, tolerable, decent, acceptable, fair, adequate, passable, suitable, honorable, valuable.

(ANT.) unsavory, vulgar, gross, disreputable, reprehensible.

respectful (SYN.) courteous, polite, well-behaved, well-bred, compliant, submssive.

(ANT.) disobedient, impertinent, rude, flippant.

respite (SYN.) deferment, adjournment, suspension.

respond (SYN.) rejoin, answer, reply, acknowledge, retort.

(ANT.) overlook, disregard.

response (SYN.) reply, acknowledgment,

answer, retort, rejoinder.

(ANT.) summoning, inquiry.

responsibility (SYN.) duty, obligation, accountability, trust-worthiness, trust, liability, commitment.

responsible (SYN.) answerable, chargeable, trustworthy, liable, accountable, able, capable, upstanding, reliable, solid, indebted, creditable.

(ANT.) careless, free, negligent.

rest (SYN.) ease, intermission, calm, quiet, balance, surplus, repose, lounge, inactivity, motionlessness, immobility, standstill, relax, remainder, excess, surplus, relaxation, slumber, peace, tranquillity, leisure.

(ANT.) tumult, commotion, motion, agitation.

restful (SYN.) peaceful, quiet, tranquil, calm.

(ANT.) tumultuous, upsetting, agitated, disturbed.

restitution (SYN.) recompense, satisfaction, refund, amends, retrieval.

restive (SYN.) balky, disobedient, fractious, impatient, unruly, fidgety, uneasy.

restless (SYN.) sleepless, unquiet, transient, active, agitated, disturbed, jumpy, nervous, uneasy, disquieted, irresolute.

(ANT.) quiet, tranquil, calm, peaceable.

restore (SYN.) repair, recover, rebuild, reestablish, renovate, return, renew, mend, reinstall, revive, rehabilitate, replace.

restrain (SYN.) limit, curb, constraint, stop, bridle, control, reserve, constrain, repress, check, suppress, hinder.

(ANT.) incite, aid, loosen.

restraint (SYN.) order, self-control, reserve, control, regulation, limitation, confinement.

(ANT.) freedom, liberty, confusion.

restrict (SYN.) fetter, restrain, confine, limit, engage, attach, connect, link, tie, bind.

(ANT.) broaden, enlarge, untie, loose, free.

restriction (SYN.) curb, handicap, check, boundary, ban, limitation, control, deterrent.

result (SYN.) effect, issue, outcome, resolve, end, consequence, happen, determination, conclusion, reward, aftermath.

(ANT.) cause, beginning, origin.
resume *(SYN.)* restart, continue, recommence, reassume.
resurgence *(SYN.)* rebirth, comeback, recovery, revival, resuscitation, rejuvenation, renewal.
resuscitate *(SYN.)* restore, revive, resurrect.
retain *(SYN.)* keep, hold, recall, remember, employ, hire, engage.
retainer *(SYN.)* aide, assistant, lackey, attendant, servant.
retaliate *(SYN.)* repay, revenge, return, avenge.
(ANT.) condone, forgive, overlook, excuse, forget.
retard *(SYN.)* detain, slacken, defer, impede, hold back, delay, postpone.
(ANT.) accelerate, speed, hasten, rush.
retention *(SYN.)* reservation, acquisition, holding, tenacity, possession.
reticent *(SYN.)* reserved, subdued, quiet, shy, withdrawn, restrained, bashful, silent.
(ANT.) outspoken, forward, opinionated.
retire *(SYN.)* resign, quit, abdicate, depart, vacate.
retiring *(SYN.)* timid, bashful, withdrawn, modest, reticent, quiet, reserved.
(ANT.) gregarious, assertive, bold.
retort *(SYN.)* reply, answer, response, respond, rejoin, rejoinder, retaliate.
(ANT.) summoning, inquiry.
retreat *(SYN.)* leave, depart, retire, withdraw, retirement, withdrawal, departure, shelter, refuge.
(ANT.) advanced.
retrench *(SYN.)* reduce, scrape, curtail.
retribution *(SYN.)* justice, vengeance, reprisal, punishment, comeuppance, vindictiveness, revenge, retaliation.
retrieve *(SYN.)* regain, recover, recapture, repossess, reclaim, salvage, recoup.
retrograde *(SYN.)* regressive, backward, declining, deteriorating, worsening.
(ANT.) onward, progression, advanced.
return *(SYN.)* restoration, replace, revert, recur, restore, retreat.
(ANT.) keep, take, retain.
reveal *(SYN.)* discover, publish, communicate, impart, uncover, tell, betray, divulge, disclose.
(ANT.) conceal, cover, obscure, cloak, hide.

revel *(SYN.)* rejoice, wallow, bask, enjoy, delight, savor, gloat, luxuriate, relish.
revelation *(SYN.)* hallucination, dream, phantoms, apparition, ghost, mirage, specter, daydream, suprise, shocker.
(ANT.) verity, reality.
revelry *(SYN.)* merriment, merry-making, carousal, feasting, gala, festival.
revenge *(SYN.)* vindictiveness, reprisal, requital, vengeance, repayment, repay, retribution, reparation.
(ANT.) reconcile, forgive, pity.
revenue *(SYN.)* take, proceeds, income, profit, return.
revere *(SYN.)* admire, honor, worship, respect, venerate, adore.
(ANT.) ignore, despise.
reverence *(SYN.)* glory, worship, homage, admiration, dignity, renown, respect, esteem, veneration, adoration, honor.
(ANT.) dishonor, derision, reproach.
reverent *(SYN.)* honoring, respectful, adoring, pious, devout, humble.
(ANT.) impious, disrespectful.
reverse *(SYN.)* overthrow, unmake rescind, opposite, invert, contrary, rear, back, misfortune, defeat, catastrophe, upset, countermand, revoke.
(ANT.) vouch, stabilize, endorse, affirm.
revert *(SYN.)* revive, relapse, backslide, rebound, retreat, recur, go back.
(ANT.) keep, take, appropriate.
review *(SYN.)* reconsideration, examination, commentary, retrospection, restudy, journal, synopsis, study, reexamine, critique, inspection.
revile *(SYN.)* defame, malign, vilify, abuse, traduce, asperse, scandalize, smear.
(ANT.) honor, respect, cherish, protect.
revise *(SYN.)* change, alter, improve, correct, amend, update, rewrite, polish.
revision *(SYN.)* inspection, survey, retrospection, commentary, critique.
revival *(SYN.)* renaissance, exhumation, resurgence, renewal, revitalization.
revive *(SYN.)* refresh, lessen, decrease, renew, reduce, lower, abate, reanimate, diminish, reawaken, rejuvenate, suppress.
(ANT.) increase, amplify, intensify.
revoke *(SYN.)* nullify, cancel, abolish, quash, rescind, abrogate.
revolt *(SYN.)* mutiny, rebel, disgust,

revolution, uprising, rebellion, upheaval, takeover, insurgence, abolish.

revolting *(SYN.)* hateful, odious, abominable, foul, vile, detestable, loathsome, repugnant, obnoxious, sickening.
(ANT.) delightful, agreeable, pleasant.

revolution *(SYN.)* rebellion, mutiny, turn, coup, revolt, overthrow, cycle, spin, uprising.

revolutionary *(SYN.)* insurgent, extremist, radical, subversive, mutinous.

revolve *(SYN.)* spin, wheel, rotate, circle, circle, turn, whirl, gyrate.
(ANT.) travel, proceed, wander.

revolver *(SYN.)* gun, pistol.

revulsion *(SYN.)* reversal, rebound, backlash, withdrawal, recoil.

reward *(SYN.)* bounty, premium, meed, award, compensation, prize, recompense, bonus, remuneration, accolade, wages.
(ANT.) charge, wages, punishment.

rewarding *(SYN.)* pleasing, productive, fruitful, profitable, favorable, satisfying, gratifying, fulfilling.

rhetoric *(SYN.)* style, verbosity, expressiveness, eloquence, fluency, flamboyance.

rhyme *(SYN.)* poem, verse, poetry, ballad, ditty, rhapsody, sonnet.

ribald *(SYN.)* suggestive, off-color, indecent, spicy, rude, vulgar.

rich *(SYN.)* ample, costly, wealthy, fruitful, prolific, abundant, well-off, affluent, plentiful, fertile, bountiful, luxuriant.
(ANT.) poor, unfruitful, beggarly, barren, impoverished, scarce, scanty, unproductive, destitute.

rickety *(SYN.)* unsound, unsteady, flimsy, unstable, shaky, decrepit, wobbly.
(ANT.) steady, solid, sturdy.

ricochet *(SYN.)* recoil, backfire, rebound, bounce, deviate, boomerang.

rid *(SYN.)* free, clear, shed, delivered, eliminate, disperse, unload, purge.

riddle *(SYN.)* puzzle, mystery, conundrum, problem, question, enigma.
(ANT.) key, solution, answer, resolution.

ride *(SYN.)* tour, journey, motor, manage, drive, control, guide.

ridge *(SYN.)* hillock, backbone, spine, crest, mound, hump.

ridicule *(SYN.)* gibe, banter, mock, jeering, deride, tease, taunt, satire, mockery, derision.
(ANT.) praise, respect.

ridiculous *(SYN.)* silly, nonsensical, absurd, accurate, inconsistent, farcical, proper, laughable, apt, preposterous, foolish.
(ANT.) sound, reasonable, consistent.

rife *(SYN.)* widespread, abundant, innumerable, rampant, teeming.

rifle *(SYN.)* plunder, pillage, rummage, ransack, rob, steal.

rift *(SYN.)* crevice, fault, opening, crack, flaw, fissure, split, breach, opening.

right *(SYN.)* correct, appropriate, suitable, ethical, fit, real, legitimate, justice, factual, just, directly, virtue, true, definite, straight, honorably, seemly.
(ANT.) immoral, unfair, wrong, bad, improper.

righteous *(SYN.)* ethical, chaste, honorable, good, virtuous, good, noble.
(ANT.) sinful, libertine, amoral, licentious.

rigid *(SYN.)* strict, unyielding, stiff, stern, austere, rigorous, inflexible, stringent, unbendable, severe, harsh, unbending.
(ANT.) supple, flexible, mild, compassionate, pliable, limp, relaxed.

rigorous *(SYN.)* unfeeling, rough, strict, blunt, cruel, hard, severe, grating, coarse, jarring, stern, stringent.
(ANT.) soft, mild, tender, gentle, smooth.

rile *(SYN.)* irritate, nettle, hector, exasperate, provoke, gripe.

rim *(SYN.)* verge, frontier, border, outskirts, edge, brink, lip, limit, termination, boundary, fringe, brim, margin.
(ANT.) core, mainland, center.

rind *(SYN.)* layer, cover, skin, hide, peel, crust, bark.

ring *(SYN.)* fillet, band, loop, circlet, circle, surround, encircle, peal, sound, resound, jingle, tinkle.

ringleader *(SYN.)* provoker, troublemaker, leader, instigator, chief, inciter, agitator.

rinse *(SYN.)* launder, cleanse, wash, soak, immerse, laundering, rinsing, immerse, bathe, clean.

riot *(SYN.)* disturbance, disorder, outburst, commotion, insurgence, uproar, panic, boisterousness, lark, hoot, wow, sensation, caper, roister, frolic, eruption, confusion, tumult, revolt.

riotous *(SYN.)* boisterous, wild, rambunctious, roisterous, tumultuous, turbulent, noisy, loud, rowdy, rollicking.

rip *(SYN.)* tear, rend, wound, rive, cleave, cut, slit, slash, lacerate, shred, scramble, dart, dash, split, disunite.

(ANT.) unite, join, repair.

ripe *(SYN.)* ready, finished, mature, complete, full-grown, develop, mellow, seasonable, full-fledged, primed, disposed, keen, avid, consummate.

(ANT.) raw, crude, undeveloped, premature, unprepared, unripe, immature.

ripen *(SYN.)* grow, season, age, mature, mellow, develop, progress, maturate.

rip into *(SYN.)* assail, lash out at, attack, charge.

rip-off *(SYN.)* fraud, dishonesty, gyp, racket, swindle, exploitation, heist, theft, extortion, thievery, larceny, shakedown.

riposte *(SYN.)* rejoinder, comeback, quip, retort, response, reply, wisecrack.

ripple *(SYN.)* wave, ruffle, wavelet, gurgle, undulate, gurgle, corrugation, rumple, crumple, spurtle, dribble, bubble.

rise *(SYN.)* thrive, awaken, ascend, climb, mount, tower, arise, wake, scale, flourish, prosper, advance, proceed, soar.

(ANT.) fall, drop, plunge, fade, slump, decline, sinking, depression, waning, comedown, setback, retrogression, descend.

risk *(SYN.)* hazard, peril, danger, endanger, chance, jeopardy, threat, vulnerability, contingency, precariousness, shakiness.

(ANT.) protection, safety, immunity, defense.

risky *(SYN.)* menacing, chancy, threatening, critical, perilous, insecure, unsafe, dicey, unsound, dangerous.

(ANT.) guarded, safe, certain, firm, secure.

rite *(SYN.)* pomp, solemnity, ceremony, observance, ceremonial, formality.

ritual *(SYN.)* pomp, solemnity, ceremony, parade, rite, ritualism, prescription, routine, custom, tradition.

rival *(SYN.)* enemy, opponent, contestant, compete, foe, adversary, oppose, competitor, contest, antagonist.

(ANT.) colleague, confederate, allay, col-laborator, helpmate, teammate.

rivalry *(SYN.)* contest, struggle, duel, race, vying, opposition, contention, competition.

(ANT.) alliance, collaboration, partnership, cooperation, teamwork, coalition.

river *(SYN.)* brook, stream, headstream, watercourse, tributary, creek.

rivet *(SYN.)* weld, bolt, fasten, attach, secure, bind, join, staple, nail, couple.

road *(SYN.)* street, way, highway, pike, drive, highway, expressway, boulevard.

roam *(SYN.)* err, saunter, deviate, rove, range, wander, digress, ramble, stroll.

(ANT.) stop, linger, stay, halt, settle.

roar *(SYN.)* cry, bellow, yell, shout, yowl, howl, bawl, hoot, bang, boom, blast, blare, scream, whoop, holler, yelp.

roast *(SYN.)* deride, ridicule, kid, ride, mock, tease, twit, parody, burlesque.

rob *(SYN.)* fleece, steal, despoil, pilfer, pillage, sack, loot, plunder, burglarize, ransack, hold up, rip off, thieve.

robbery *(SYN.)* larceny, plundering, thievery, stealing, theft, pillage, swiping, caper, snatching, burglary, plunder.

robe *(SYN.)* housecoat, bathrobe, dressing gown, caftan, muumuu, smock, cape.

robot *(SYN.)* computer, android, automaton, pawn, workhorse, drudge, laborer.

robust *(SYN.)* well, hearty, hale, sound, healthy, strong, able-bodied, stalwart.

(ANT.) fragile, feeble, debilitated, reserved, refined, puny, frail, delicate, infirm.

rock *(SYN.)* pebble, boulder, stone, gravel, granite, roll, sway, swagger, limestone.

rocky *(SYN.)* unstable, faint, rocklike, stony, pebbly, gravelly, trembly, rough, bumpy, formidable, quavering, challenging, unsteady, dizzy.

(ANT.) effortless, easy, slight, simple, sound, rugged, stout, hardy, strong, robust.

rod *(SYN.)* bar, pole, wand, stick, pike, staff, billy, baton.

rogue *(SYN.)* criminal, rascal, outlaw, scoundrel, scamp, good-for-nothing, villain.

roguish *(SYN.)* prankish, playful, mischievous, elfish, waggish, devilish, tricky.

(ANT.) grave, humorless, solemn, staid,

lawabiding.

roil *(SYN.)* churn, muddy, rile, mire, disturb.

roister *(SYN.)* bluster, swagger, swashbuckle, vaunt, bluff, flourish, rollick.

role *(SYN.)* task, part, function, characterization, portrayal, face, character.

roll *(SYN.)* revolve, rotate, whirl, swing, rock, waver, reel, lumber, swagger, stagger, progress, proceed, turn, spin.

rollicking *(SYN.)* spirited, animated, frolicsome, exuberant, lighthearted, carefree.

roll up *(SYN.)* amass, collect, accumulate, gather.

romance *(SYN.)* affair, enchantment, novel, tale, adventure, enterprise, daring, story.

romantic *(SYN.)* poetic, mental, dreamy, fanciful, imaginative, extravagant, impractical, exaggerated, wild, idealistic, mawkish, ideal, maudlin.

(ANT.) homely, faint-hearted, familiar, unromantic, pessimistic, unemotional, cynical, literal, prosaic, factual.

romp *(SYN.)* caper, gambol, frolic, play, conquer, triumph, horseplay, frisk.

(ANT.) defeat, rout.

room *(SYN.)* enclosure, cell, chamber, space, stay, lodge, cubicle, reside.

roomy *(SYN.)* broad, large, wide, sizable, generous, capacious, ample, spacious, extensive, commodious, vast.

(ANT.) tight, limited, crowded, confined, narrow.

roost *(SYN.)* coop, henhouse, perch, hutch, residence, abode, hearth, lodgings.

root *(SYN.)* reason, bottom, groundwork, cause, support, base, underpinning, beginning, mainspring, source, basis.

(ANT.) cover, top, building.

rooted *(SYN.)* fixed, fast, firm, steadfast, immovable, stationary.

root for *(SYN.)* back, support, boost, sponsor, promote, bolster, encourage, hail, cheer.

root out *(SYN.)* dispose of, uproot, cut out, pluck out.

rope *(SYN.)* string, wire, cord, cable, line, strand, rigging, ropework, cordage.

ropy *(SYN.)* wiry, stringy, viscous, threadlike, viscoid.

roster *(SYN.)* list, census, muster, enrollment, listing, register.

rosy *(SYN.)* reddish, pink, healthy, fresh, cheerful, bright, happy, glowing, flushed, promising, favorable.

(ANT.) pale, pallid, gray, wan, disheartening, ashen, unfavorable, gloomy.

rot *(SYN.)* putrefy, waste, decay, mold, decompose, dwindle, spoil, decline, decomposition, wane, rotting, ebb.

(ANT.) increase, rise, grow, luxuriate.

rotary *(SYN.)* axial, rotating, turning, gyral, revolving, rolling, whirling, rotational.

rotate *(SYN.)* spin, twirl, wheel, circle, twist, orbit, invert, swivel, gyrate, wind, alternate, recur, intermit, pivot.

(ANT.) stop, arrest, stand.

rote *(SYN.)* repetition, system, convention, routine, mechanization, habitude, habit, custom, perfunctoriness.

rough *(SYN.)* jagged, scratchy, crude, incomplete, severe, craggy, stormy, rugged, unpolished, approximate, uneven, irregular, bumpy, coarse.

(ANT.) calm, polished, civil, mild, refined, placid, gentle, smooth, sleek, sophisticated, suave.

round *(SYN.)* round, chubby, curved, bulbous, entire, complete, spherical, circular, bowed.

(ANT.) slender, trim, slim, thin, lean.

rouse *(SYN.)* waken, awaken, stimulate, excite, summon, arise, stir.

(ANT.) rest, calm, sleep, restrain, sedate.

rousing *(SYN.)* exciting, galvanic, stimulating, electric, moving, exhilarating, stirring, breathtaking, inciting.

(ANT.) flat, uninteresting, drab, monotonous, boring, tiresome, slow, dull.

rout *(SYN.)* defeat, beat, quell, vanquish, conquer, humble, subdue, scatter.

(ANT.) cede, retreat, surrender.

route *(SYN.)* street, course, trail, way, avenue, passage, thoroughfare, track.

routine *(SYN.)* way, habit, use, custom, practice, fashion, method, system.

(ANT.) unusual, rate, uncommon.

rover *(SYN.)* traveler, adventurer, wanderer, voyager.

row *(SYN.)* file, order, series, rank, progression, sequence, arrangement.

rowdy *(SYN.)* disorderly, unruly, brawling, roughneck, scrapper.

royal *(SYN.)* lordly, regal, noble, courtly,

ruling, stately, dignified, supreme, majestic, sovereign, imperial, kingly. (ANT.) *servile, common, low, humble, vulgar.*

rub (SYN.) shine, polish, scour, scrape.

rubbish (SYN.) debris, garbage, trash, waste, junk, clutter.

ruddy (SYN.) rosy, reddish, healthy, robust, blushing, sanguine.

rude (SYN.) gruff, impudent, blunt, impolite, boorish, insolent, saucy, rough, crude, unmannerly, coarse, impertinent. (ANT.) *courtly, civil, stately, genteel, calm, dignified, polished, courteous, cultivated, polite.*

rudimentary (SYN. essential, primary, fundamental, original, imperfect.

rue (SYN.) lament, repine, sorrow, deplore, regret, bemoan.

ruffian (SYN.) crook, hoodlum, thug.

ruffle (SYN.) rumple, disarrange, disorder, disturb, trimming, frill.

rug (SYN.) floor-covering, carpet.

rugged (SYN.) jagged, craggy, scratchy, irregular, uneven, harsh, severe, tough. (ANT.) *smooth, level, even.*

ruin (SYN.) wreck, exterminate, devastate, annihilate, raze, demolish, spoil. (ANT.) *save, establish, preserve.*

rule (SYN.) law, guide, order, regulation, dominion, sovereignty, control.

ruler (SYN.) commander, chief, leader, governor, yardstick.

ruling (SYN.) judgment, decision, decree.

ruminate (SYN.) brood, reflect, meditate, ponder, consider, speculate, mull.

rummage (SYN.) root, scour, ransack.

rumor (SYN.) innuendo, hearsay, gossip.

rumple (SYN.) tousle, furrow, crease, wrinkle, dishevel.

run (SYN.) race, hurry, speed, hasten, sprint, dart, scamper, dash.

runaway (SYN.) refugee, deserter, fugitive.

run-down (SYN.) ramshackle, dilapidated, tumble-down, weakened.

rupture (SYN.) fracture, fissure, cleft, severance.

rural (SYN.) country, farm, rustic, backwoods. (ANT.) *citified, urban.*

rush (SYN.) dash, speed, hurry, hasten, run, scoot, hustle, scurry. (ANT.) *tarry, linger.*

sabotage (SYN.) subversion, treason, treachery, damage, disable, subvert.

sack (SYN.) pouch, bag.

sacrament (SYN.) communion, fellowship, association, participation, union. (ANT.) *nonparticipation, alienation.*

sacred (SYN.) consecrated, blessed, devout, divine, holy, hallowed, pious, religious, spiritual, saintly. (ANT.) *profane, evil, sacrilegious, worldly, secular, blasphemous.*

sad (SYN.) dejected, cheerless, despondent, depressed, disconsolate, doleful, downhearted, glum, saddening. (ANT.) *happy, cheerful, glad, merry.*

safe (SYN.) dependable, certain, harmless, secure, snug, trustworthy. (ANT.) *hazardous, dangerous, unsafe, insecure, perilous.*

sag (SYN.) incline, bend, lean, slant, tend, depend, rely, trust, fail. (ANT.) *rise, raise, erect, straighten.*

sagacity (SYN.) erudition, discretion, foresight, insight, information, judgment, intelligence, knowledge, learning. (ANT.) *foolishness, imprudence, stupidity, nonsense.*

sage (SYN.) intellectual, disciple, learner, savant, scholar, pupil, student, wise, judicious, sagacious, rational, logical. (ANT.) *dunce, fool, dolt, idiot.*

saintly (SYN.) virtuous, moral, holy, devout, righteous, good.

sake (SYN.) motive, reason, purpose; benefit, advantage, welfare.

salary (SYN.) compensation, allowance, earnings, pay, fee, payment, recompense, wages. (ANT.) *gratuity, present, gift.*

salubrious (SYN.) healthy, hale, sound, robust, strong, well, hygienic, wholesome, salutary. (ANT.) *diseased, delicate, frail, injurious, infirm, noxious.*

saloon (SYN.) pub, bar.

salutary (SYN.) beneficial, advantageous, profitable, useful, wholesome. (ANT.) *destructive, deleterious, detrimental, injurious, harmful.*

salute (SYN.) receive, greet.

salvage (SYN.) retrieve, rescue, recover.

salvation (SYN.) release, rescue, deliverance.

same (SYN.) equal, coincident, equivalent, like, indistinguishable.

(ANT.) disparate, contrary, dissimilar, opposed, distinct.

sample (SYN.) example, case, illustration, model, instance, pattern, prototype, specimen, token.

sanction (SYN.) approval, approbation, authorization, authority, let, permit.

(ANT.) reproach, reprimand, stricture, censure, object, forbid, refuse, resist.

sanctuary (SYN.) harbor, haven, asylum, refuge, retreat, shelter.

(ANT.) danger, hazard, exposure, jeopardy, peril.

sane (SYN.) balanced, rational, normal, sound, reasonable.

(ANT.) crazy, insane, irrational.

sanitary (SYN.) purified, clean, hygienic, disinfected.

(ANT.) soiled, fouled, unclean, dirty.

sap (SYN.) exhausted, drain, weaken.

sarcastic (SYN.) biting, acrimonious, cutting, caustic, derisive, sardonic, satirical, ironic, sneering.

(ANT.) agreeable, affable, pleasant.

sardonic (SYN.) bitter, caustic, acrimonious, severe, harsh.

(ANT.) mellow, pleasant, sweet.

satanic (SYN.) demonic, fiendish, diabolic, diabolical.

sate (SYN.) fill up, fill, occupy, furnish, pervade, stock, replenish, store, supply, content, gorge, satiate, stuff, satisfy.

(ANT.) empty, drain, deplete, void.

satire (SYN.) cleverness, fun, banter, humor, irony, raillery, pleasantry.

(ANT.) platitude, sobriety, commonplace, solemnity, stupidity.

satirical (SYN.) biting, caustic, acrimonious, cutting, ironic, derisive, sarcastic, sneering, sardonic, taunting.

(ANT.) agreeable, affable, pleasant.

satisfactory (SYN.) ample, capable, adequate, commensurate, enough, sufficient, fitting, suitable, okay.

(ANT.) scant, lacking, deficient, unsatisfactory, poor.

satisfy (SYN.) compensate, appease, content, gratify, fulfill, suitable.

(ANT.) displease, dissatisfy, annoy, frustrate, tantalize.

saturate (SYN.) fill, diffuse, infiltrate, penetrate, permeate, run through.

saucy (SYN.) insolent, bold, impudent,

impertinent.

(ANT.) shy, demure.

savage (SYN.) brutal, cruel, barbarous, ferocious, inhuman, merciless.

(ANT.) compassionate, gentle, humane, kind, merciful, tame, cultivated.

save (SYN.) defend, conserve, keep, maintain, guard, preserve, protect, safeguard, rescue, secure, uphold, spare.

(ANT.) abolish, destroy, abandon, impair, injure.

savory (SYN.) delectable, delightful, delicious, palatable, luscious, tasty.

(ANT.) distasteful, nauseous, acrid, unpalatable, unsavory.

say (SYN.) converse, articulate, declare, express, discourse, harangue, talk, speak, tell, utter, remark, state.

(ANT.) hush, refrain, be silent.

saying (SYN.) aphorism, adage, byword, maxim, proverb, motto.

scalding (SYN.) hot, scorching, burning, torrid, warm, fervent, ardent, fiery.

(ANT.) cool, cold, freezing, passionless, frigid, bland.

scale (SYN.) balance, proportion, ration, range, climb, mount.

scamp (SYN.) troublemaker, rascal.

scan (SYN.) examine, study.

scandal (SYN.) chagrin, humiliation, abashment, mortification, dishonor, disgrace, disrepute, odium.

(ANT.) glory, honor, dignity, praise.

scandalize (SYN.) asperse, defame, abuse, disparage, revile, vilify, traduce.

(ANT.) honor, respect, cherish.

scandalous (SYN.) disgraceful, discreditable, dishonorable, ignominious, disreputable, shameful.

(ANT.) honorable, renowned, esteemed.

scant (SYN.) succinct, summary, concise, terse, inadequate, deficient, insufficient.

(ANT.) ample, big, extended, abundant, protracted.

scarce (SYN.) occasional, choice, infrequent, exceptional, incomparable, precious, singular, rare, uncommon.

(ANT.) frequent, ordinary, usual, customary, abundant, numerous, worthless.

scarcely (SYN.) barely, hardly.

scarcity (SYN.) want, insufficiency, lack, need, dearth.

(ANT.) abundance.

scare (SYN.) alarm, papal, affright, as-

tound, dismay, daunt, frighten, intimidate, horrify, terrorize, shock.
(ANT.) compose, reassure, soothe.

scared *(SYN.)* apprehensive, afraid, faint-hearted, frightened, fearful, timid.
(ANT.) bold, assured, courageous, composed, sanguine.

scarf *(SYN.)* kerchief.

scatter *(SYN.)* dispel, disperse, diffuse, disseminate, separate, dissipate, spread.
(ANT.) assemble, accumulate, amass, gather, collect.

scene *(SYN.)* exhibition, view, display.

scent *(SYN.)* fragrance, fume, aroma, incense, perfume, odor, redolence, stench, stink, smell.

schedule *(SYN.)* program, timetable.

scheme *(SYN.)* conspiracy, cabal, design, machination, intrigue, plot, plan, chart.

scholar *(SYN.)* intellectual, pupil, learner, disciple, sage, student, savant, teacher.
(ANT.) dunce, idiot, fool, ignoramus.

scholarly *(SYN.)* bookish, erudite, formal, academic, learned, pedantic, theoretical, scholastic.
(ANT.) practical, simple, ignorant.

scholarship *(SYN.)* cognizance, erudition, apprehension, information, learning, knowledge, science, wisdom.
(ANT.) illiteracy, stupidity, ignorance, misunderstanding.

science *(SYN.)* enlightenment, discipline, knowledge, scholarship.
(ANT.) superstition, ignorance.

scoff *(SYN.)* ridicule, belittle, mock.

scold *(SYN.)* berate, blame, lecture, rate, rebuke, censure, admonish, reprehend, upbraid, reprimand, criticize.
(ANT.) commend, praise, approve.

scope *(SYN.)* area, compass, expanse, amount, extent, magnitude, degree, measure, reach, size, range.

scorch *(SYN.)* burn, char, consume, blaze, incinerate, sear, singe, scald.
(ANT.) put out, quench, extinguish.

score *(SYN.)* reckoning, tally, record, mark, rating.

scorn *(SYN.)* contumely, derision, contempt, detestation, hatred, disdain, despise, hate, spurn, refuse, reject.
(ANT.) esteem, respect, awe.

scornful *(SYN.)* disdainful, contemptuous.

scoundrel *(SYN.)* rogue, villain, cad.

scour *(SYN.)* wash, clean, scrub.

scourge *(SYN.)* affliction, lash, whip.

scowl *(SYN.)* glower, frown, glare.

scramble *(SYN.)* combine, mix, blend, hasten, clamber, climb.

scrap *(SYN.)* fragment, rag, apportionment, part, portion, piece, section, share, segment, crumb, junk.
(ANT.) whole, entirety.

scrape *(SYN.)* difficulty, dilemma, condition, fix, predicament, plight, situation, strait, scour, rub, scratch.
(ANT.) comfort, ease, calmness.

scratch *(SYN.)* scrape, scar.

scrawny *(SYN.)* gaunt, skinny, spindly.
(ANT.) husky, burly.

scream *(SYN.)* screech, shriek, yell.

screech *(SYN.)* yell, cry, scream, shriek.

screen *(SYN.)* partition, cover, separation, protection.

scrimp *(SYN.)* skimp, save, economize, conserve.

script *(SYN.)* penmanship, hand, handwriting, text, lines.

scrounge *(SYN.)* sponge, borrow.

scrub *(SYN.)* cleanse, mop, purify, clean, sweep, wash, scour.
(ANT.) pollute, dirty, stain, sully.

scrupulous *(SYN.)* conscientious, candid, honest, honorable, fair, just sincere, truthful, upright, painstaking, critical.
(ANT.) dishonest, fraudulent, lying deceitful, tricky, careless.

scrutinize *(SYN.)* criticize, appraise, evaluate, examine, inspect, analyze.
(ANT.) neglect, overlook, approve.

scurrilous *(SYN.)* insulting, outrageous.

scurry *(SYN.)* scamper, scramble, hasten, hustle, hurry.

scuttle *(SYN.)* swamp, ditch, sink.

seal *(SYN.)* emblem, stamp, symbol, crest, signet.

search *(SYN.)* exploration, examination, investigation, inquiry, pursuit, quest, explore, scrutinize, investigate, hunt, probe, rummage, ransack, seek, scour.
(ANT.) resignation, abandonment.

searching *(SYN.)* inquiring, inquisitive, interrogative, nosy, curious, peeping, peering, snoopy, prying.
(ANT.) indifferent, unconcerned, incurious, uninterested.

season *(SYN.)* mature, perfect, ripen, develop, age.

seasoned *(SYN.)* veteran, skilled.

secede *(SYN.)* quit, withdraw, resign.

secluded *(SYN.)* deserted, desolate, isolated, alone, lonely, lone, unaided, only, sole, solitary, single, separate, isolated, sheltered, hidden, secret.
(ANT.) attended, surrounded, accompanied.

seclusion *(SYN.)* insulation, isolation, loneliness, alienation, quarantine, segregation, separation, retirement.
(ANT.) fellowship, union, connection, association, communion.

secondary *(SYN.)* minor, poorer, inferior, lower, subordinate.
(ANT.) greater, higher, superior.

secret *(SYN.)* concealed, hidden, latent, covert, private, surreptitious, unknown.
(ANT.) disclosed, exposed, known, obvious, conspicuous, open, public.

secrete *(SYN.)* clothe, conceal, cover, cloak, curtain, envelop, disguise, hide, mask, guard, protect, shroud, veil.
(ANT.) divulge, reveal, expose, unveil.

sect *(SYN.)* segment, denomination, faction, group.

section *(SYN.)* district, country, domain, dominion, division, land, place, province, territory, subdivision.

secular *(SYN.)* lay earthly, laic, mundane, temporal, profane, worldly, temporal.
(ANT.) religious, spiritual, unworldly, ecclesiastical.

secure *(SYN.)* certain, definite, fixed, assured, indubitable, positive, inevitable, undeniable, sure, unquestionable, firm,
(ANT.) probable, questionable, uncertain, doubtful, loose, endangered, free.

security *(SYN.)* bond, earnest, pawn, bail, guaranty, pledge, token, surety.

sedate *(SYN.)* controlled, serene, calm, composed, unruffled.

sediment *(SYN.)* residue, lees, dregs, grounds.

see *(SYN.)* contemplate, descry, behold, discern, espy, distinguish, glimpse, inspect, look at, observe, perceive, scan, watch, view, witness, regard, examine, study, notice, eye.

seek *(SYN.)* explore, hunt, examine, look, investigate, probe, ransack, search, scour, rummage, scrutinize.

seem *(SYN.)* look, appeal.
(ANT.) exist, be, disappear, withdraw,

vanish.

segment *(SYN.)* apportionment, division, fragment, moiety, allotment, part, portion, piece, scrap, share, section, element, faction, ingredient, interest, side.
(ANT.) whole, entirety.

segregate *(SYN.)* exclude, separate.
(ANT.) include, combine.

seize *(SYN.)* check, detain, hinder, apprehend, arrest, obstruct, stop, restrain, withhold, grab, grasp, clutch.
(ANT.) free, liberate, release, activate, discharge, loosen.

seldom *(SYN.)* infrequently, scarcely, rarely.

select *(SYN.)* cull, opt, pick, choose, elect, prefer.
(ANT.) reject, refuse.

selection *(SYN.)* election, choice, alternative, option, preference.

self-denial *(SYN.)* abstinence, continence, abstention, forbearance, fasting, sobriety, moderation, temperance.
(ANT.) gluttony, excess, greed, intoxication, self-indulgence.

self-important *(SYN.)* egotistical, proud, conceited, egocentric.

self-indulgence *(SYN.)* egotism, narrowness, self-centeredness, self-seeking, stinginess, ungenerousness.
(ANT.) charity, magnanimity, altruism, liberality.

selfish *(SYN.)* illiberal, narrow, self-centered, self-seeking, mercenary, stingy, ungenerous, greedy, mean, miserly.
(ANT.) charitable.

self-satisfied *(SYN.)* smug, complacent.

sell *(SYN.)* market, retail, merchandise, vend, trade, barter.

send *(SYN.)* discharge, emit, dispatch, cast, propel, impel, throw, transmit, forward, ship, convey, mail.
(ANT.) get, hold, retain, receive, bring.

senescence *(SYN.)* dotage, senility, age, seniority.
(ANT.) infancy, youth, childhood.

senile *(SYN.)* antiquated, antique, aged, ancient, archaic, obsolete, old, elderly, old-fashioned, venerable.
(ANT.) new, youthful, young, modern.

senior *(SYN.)* superior, older, elder.
(ANT.) minor, junior.

sensation *(SYN.)* feeling, image, impression, apprehension, sense, sensibility, perception, sensitiveness.

(ANT.) *insensibility, torpor, stupor, apathy.*

sensational *(SYN.)* exciting, marvelous, superb, thrilling, startling, spectacular.

sense *(SYN.)* drift, connotation, acceptation, explanation, gist, implication, intent, import, interpretation, purport, meaning, purpose, signification, significance, sensation, perception.

sense *(SYN.)* perception, sensation, feeling, awareness, insight, consciousness, appreciate, discern, perceive.

senseless *(SYN.)* dense, dull, crass, brainless, dumb, obtuse, foolish, stupid.

(ANT.) *discerning, intelligent, alert, clever, bright.*

sensibility *(SYN.)* sensation, emotion, feeling, passion, tenderness, sentiment.

(ANT.) *coldness, imperturbability, anesthesia, insensibility, fact.*

sensible *(SYN.)* apprehensible, perceptible, appreciable, alive, aware, awake, cognizant, comprehending, perceiving, conscious, sentient, intelligent, discreet, practical, judicious, prudent, sagacious, reasonable, sage, sober, wise, sound.

(ANT.) *impalpable, imperceptible, absurd, stupid, unaware, foolish.*

sensitive *(SYN.)* perceptive, prone, impressionable, responsive, susceptible, sentient, tender, sore, delicate, tender, tense, touchy, nervous, keen.

(ANT.) *dull, hard, callous, insensitive.*

sensual *(SYN.)* lascivious, earthy, lecherous, carnal, sensory, voluptuous, wanton, erotic, lustful, sexual, indecent.

(ANT.) *chaste, ascetic, abstemious, virtuous, continent.*

sentence *(SYN.)* convict, condemn.

(ANT.) *acquit, pardon, absolve acquit.*

sentiment *(SYN.)* affection, emotion, sensation, feeling, sensibility, passion, tenderness, impression, opinion, attitude.

(ANT.) *coldness, imperturbability, anesthesia, insensibility, fact.*

sentimental *(SYN.)* extravagant, fanciful, fantastic, dreamy, fictitious, idealistic, ideal, maudlin, imaginative, mawkish, poetic, romantic, picturesque.

(ANT.) *literal, practical, prosaic.*

separate *(SYN.)* part sever, sunder, divide, allot, dispense, share, distribute,

disconnect, split, isolate, segregate, different, distinct, independent.

(ANT.) *convene, join, gather, combine.*

separation *(SYN.)* insulation, isolation, loneliness, alienation, quarantine, seclusion, retirement, solitude, segregation, withdrawal.

(ANT.) *communion, fellowship, union, association, connection.*

sequence *(SYN.)* chain, graduation, order, progression, arrangement, following, series, succession, train, string.

serene *(SYN.)* composed, imperturbable, calm, dispassionate, pacific, placid, peaceful, quiet. tranquil, still, undisturbed, unruffled.

(ANT.) *frantic, turbulent, wild, excited, stormy, agitated, turbulent.*

serenity *(SYN.)* calmness, hush, calm, quiet, peace, quiescence, quietude, rest, repose, stillness, silence, tranquillity.

(ANT.) *tumult, excitement, noise, agitation, disturbance.*

series *(ANT.)* following, chain, arrangement, graduation, progression, order, sequence, train, string.

serious *(SYN.)* important, momentous, great, earnest, grave, sedate, sober, staid, alarming, solemn, critical, dangerous, risky, solemn.

(ANT.) *trivial, informal, relaxed, small.*

servant *(SYN.)* attendant, butler, domestic, valet, manservant, maid.

serve *(SYN.)* assist, attend, help, succor, advance, benefit, forward, answer, promote, content, satisfy, suffice, supply, distribute, wait on, aid.

(ANT.) *command, direct, dictate, rule.*

service *(SYN.)* advantage, account, avail, benefit, behalf, favor, good, gain, profit, interest.

(ANT.) *distress, calamity, trouble, handicap.*

serviceable *(SYN.)* beneficial, good, helpful, advantageous, profitable, salutary, wholesome, useful.

(ANT.) *destructive, deleterious, detrimental, injurious, harmful.*

servile *(SYN.)* base, contemptible, despicable, abject, groveling, dishonorable, ignominious, ignoble, lowly, low, menial, mean, sordid, vulgar, vile.

(ANT.) *honored, exalted, lofty, esteemed,*

righteous, noble.

servitude *(SYN.)* confinement, captivity, bondage, imprisonment, slavery.

(ANT.) liberation, freedom.

set *(SYN.)* deposit, dispose, lay, arrange, place, put, position, pose, station, appoint, fix, assign, settle, establish.

(ANT.) mislay, misplace, disturb, remove, disarrange.

settle *(SYN.)* close, conclude, adjudicate, decide, end, resolve, agree upon, establish, satisfy, pay, lodge, locate, reside, determine, abide, terminate.

(ANT.) suspend, hesitate, doubt, vacillate, waver.

settlement *(SYN.)* completion, close, end, finale, issue, conclusion, termination, deduction, decision, inference.

(ANT.) commencement, prelude, start, inception, beginning.

sever *(SYN.)* part, divide, sunder, split, cut, separate.

(ANT.) convene, connect, gather, join, unite, combine.

several *(SYN.)* some, few, a handful.

severe *(SYN.)* arduous, distressing, acute, exacting, hard, harsh, intense, relentless, rigorous, sharp, stern, rigid, stringent, strict, cruel, firm, unyielding, unmitigated, difficult, unpleasant, dangerous, violent.

(ANT.) genial, indulgent, lenient, yielding, merciful, considerate.

sew *(SYN.)* mend, patch, fix, stitch, refit, restore, repair.

(ANT.) destroy, hurt, deface, injure.

shabby *(SYN.)* indigent, impecunious, needy, penniless, worn, ragged, destitute, poor, threadbare, deficient, inferior, scanty.

(ANT.) rich, wealthy, ample, affluent, opulent, right, sufficient, good.

shack *(SYN.)* hovel, hut, shanty, shed.

shackle *(SYN.)* chain, fetter, handcuff.

shade *(SYN.)* complexion, dye, hue, paint, color, stain, pigment, darkness, shadow, tincture, dusk, gloom, blacken, darken, conceal, screen, tint, tinge.

(ANT.) transparency, paleness.

shadowy *(SYN.)* dark, dim, gloomy, murky, black, obscure, dusky, unilluminated, dismal, evil, gloomy, sinister, indistinct, hidden, vague, undefined, wicked, indefinite, mystic, secret, occult.

(ANT.) bright, clear, light, pleasant, lucid.

shady *(SYN.)* shifty, shaded, questionable, doubtful, devious.

shaggy *(SYN.)* hairy, unkempt, uncombed, woolly.

shake *(SYN.)* flutter, jar, jolt, quake, agitate, quiver, shiver, shudder, rock, totter, sway, tremble, vibrate, waver.

shaky *(SYN.)* questionable, uncertain, iffy, faltering, unsteady.

(ANT.) sure, definite, positive, certain.

shallow *(SYN.)* exterior, cursory, flimsy, frivolous, slight, imperfect, superficial.

(ANT.) complete, deep, abstruse, profound, thorough.

sham *(SYN.)* affect, act, feign, assume, pretend, simulate, profess.

(ANT.) exhibit, display, reveal, expose.

shame *(SYN.)* chagrin, humiliation, abashment, disgrace, mortification, dishonor, ignominy, embarrassment, disrepute, odium mortify, humiliate, abash, humble, opprobrium, scandal.

(ANT.) pride, glory, praise, honor.

shameful *(SYN.)* disgraceful, dishonorable, disreputable, discreditable, humiliating, ignominious, scandalous.

(ANT.) honorable, renowned, respectable, esteemed.

shameless *(SYN.)* unembarrassed, unashamed, brazen, bold, impudent.

(ANT.) demure, modest.

shape *(SYN.)* create, construct, forge, fashion, form, make, produce, mold, constitute, compose, arrange, combine, organize, frame, outline, figure, invent, appearance, pattern, cast, model, devise.

(ANT.) disfigure, misshape, dismantle, wreck.

shapeless *(SYN.)* rough, amorphous, vague.

shapely *(SYN.)* attractive, well-formed, curvy, alluring.

(ANT.) shapeless.

share *(SYN.)* parcel, bit, part, division, portion, ration, piece, fragment, allotment, partake, apportion, participate, divide, section.

(ANT.) whole.

shared *(SYN.)* joint, common, reciprocal, correlative, mutual.

(ANT.) unrequited, dissociated.

sharp *(SYN.)* biting, pointed, cunning, acute, keen, rough, fine, cutting, shrill, cutting, pungent, witty, acrid, blunt, steep, shrewd.
(ANT.) gentle, bland, shallow, smooth, blunt.

sharpen *(SYN.)* whet, hone, strop.

shatter *(SYN.)* crack, rend, break, pound, smash, burst, demolish, shiver, infringe.
(ANT.) renovate, join, repair, mend.

shattered *(SYN.)* fractured, destroyed, reduced, separated, broken, smashed, flattened, rent, wrecked.
(ANT.) united, integral, whole.

shawl *(SYN.)* stole, scarf.

sheepish *(SYN.)* coy, embarrassed, shy, humble, abashed, diffident, timid, modest, timorous.
(ANT.) daring, outgoing, adventurous, gregarious.

sheer *(SYN.)* thin, transparent, clear, simple, utter, absolute, abrupt, steep, see-through.

sheet *(SYN.)* leaf, layer, coating, film.

shelter *(SYN.)* retreat, safety, cover, asylum, protection, sanctuary, harbor, guard, haven, security.
(ANT.) unveil, expose, bare, reveal.

shield *(SYN.)* envelop, cover, clothe, curtain, protest, protection, cloak, guard, conceal, defense, shelter, hide, screen, veil, shroud.
(ANT.) unveil, divulge, reveal, bare.

shift *(SYN.)* move, modify, transfer, substitute, vary, change, alter, spell, turn, transfigure.
(ANT.) settle, establish, stabilize.

shifting *(SYN.)* wavering, inconstant, changeable, fitful, variable, fickle.
(ANT.) uniform, stable, unchanging.

shiftless *(SYN.)* idle, lazy, slothful.
(ANT.) energetic.

shifty *(SYN.)* shrewd, crafty, tricky.

shilly-shally *(SYN.)* fluctuate, waver, hesitate, vacillate.

shimmer *(SYN.)* glimmer, shine, gleam.
(ANT.) dull.

shine *(SYN.)* flicker, glisten, glow, blaze, glare, flash, beam, shimmer, glimmer, radiate, brush, polish, twinkle, buff, luster, gloss, scintillate, radiance, gleam.

shining *(SYN.)* dazzling, illustrious, showy, superb, brilliant, effulgent, magnificent, splendid, bright.

(ANT.) ordinary, dull, unimpressive.

shiny *(SYN.)* bright, glossy, polished, glistening.
(ANT.) lusterless, dull.

shipshape *(SYN.)* clean, neat.
(ANT.) sloppy, messy.

shiver *(SYN.)* quiver, quake, quaver, tremble, shudder, shake, break, shatter.

shock *(SYN.)* disconcert, astonish, surprise, astound, amaze, clash, disturbance, bewilder, outrage, horrify, revolt, agitation, stagger, blow, impact, collision, surprise, startle, upset, stun.
(ANT.) prepare, caution, admonish.

shocking *(SYN.)* hideous, frightful, severe, appalling, horrible, awful, terrible, dire, fearful.
(ANT.) safe, happy, secure, joyous.

shore *(SYN.)* seaside, beach, coast.
(ANT.) inland.

short *(SYN.)* abrupt, squat, concise, brief, low, curtailed, dumpy, terse, inadequate, succinct, dwarfed, small, abbreviated, lacking, abridge, condensed, undersized, slight, little.
(ANT.) extended, ample, protracted.

shortage *(SYN.)* deficiency, deficit, shortfall.
(ANT.) surplus, enough.

shortcoming *(SYN.)* error, vice, blemish, failure, flaw, omission, failing.
(ANT.) perfection, completeness.

shorten *(SYN.)* curtail, limit, cut, abbreviate, reduce, abridge, lessen, restrict.
(ANT.) lengthen, elongate.

shortening *(SYN.)* reduction, abridgment, abbreviation.
(ANT.) enlargement, amplification.

short-handed *(SYN.)* understaffed.

shortly *(SYN.)* soon, directly, presently.

shortsighted *(SYN.)* myopic, nearsighted, unimaginative, unthinking, thoughtless.

shout *(SYN.)* ejaculate, cry, yell, roar, vociferate, bellow, exclaim.
(ANT.) whisper, intimate.

shove *(SYN.)* propel, drive, urge, crowd, jostle, force, push, promote.
(ANT.) retreat, falter, oppose, drag, halt.

shovel *(SYN.)* spade.

show *(SYN.)* flourish, parade, point, reveal, explain, array, movie, production, display, exhibit, note, spectacle, demonstrate, entertainment, tell, usher, guide, prove, indicate, present, lead, demonstration.

showy *(SYN.)* ceremonious, stagy, affected, theatrical, artificial.
(ANT.) *unaffected, modest, unemotional, subdued.*

shred *(SYN.)* particle, speck, iota, mite, bit, smidgen, tear, slit, cleave, rip, disunite, wound, rend, mince, tatter, lacerate.
(ANT.) *bulk, unite, quantity, mend, aggregate, repair.*

shrewd *(SYN.)* cunning, covert, artful, stealthy, foxy, astute, ingenious, guileful, crafty, sly, surreptitious, wily, tricky, clever, intelligent, clandestine.
(ANT.) *frank, sincere, candid, open.*

shriek *(SYN.)* screech, scream, howl, yell.

shrill *(SYN.)* keen, penetrating, sharp, acute, piercing, severe.
(ANT.) *gentle, bland, shallow.*

shrink *(SYN.)* diminish, shrivel, dwindle.

shrivel *(SYN.)* wizen, waste, droop, decline, sink, dry, languish, wither.
(ANT.) *renew, refresh, revive, rejuvenate.*

shun *(SYN.)* escape, avert, forestall, avoid, forbear, evade, ward, elude, dodge, free.
(ANT.) *encounter, confront, meet.*

shut *(SYN.)* seal, finish, stop, close, terminate, conclude, clog, end, obstruct.
(ANT.) *begin, open, start, unbar, inaugurate, unlock, commence.*

shy *(SYN.)* reserved, fearful, bashful, retiring, cautious, demure, timid, shrinking, wary, chary.
(ANT.) *brazen, bold, immodest, self-confident, audacious.*

sick *(SYN.)* ill, morbid, ailing, unhealthy, diseased, unwell, infirm.
(ANT.) *sound, well, robust, strong.*

sickness *(SYN.)* illness, ailment, disease, complaint, disorder.
(ANT.) *soundness, healthiness, vigor.*

side *(SYN.)* surface, face, foe, opponent, rival, indirect, secondary, unimportant.

siege *(SYN.)* blockade.

sieve *(SYN.)* screen, strainer, riddle, colander.

sight *(SYN.)* eyesight, vision, scene, view, display, spectacle, eyesore.

sightless *(SYN.)* unmindful, oblivious, blind, unseeing, heedless, ignorant.
(ANT.) *sensible, discerning, aware, perceiving.*

sign *(SYN.)* omen, mark, emblem, token, suggestion, indication, clue, hint, approve, authorize, signal, gesture, symbol, portent.

signal *(SYN.)* beacon, sign, alarm.

significance *(SYN.)* connotation, drift, acceptation, explanation, implication, gist, importance, interpretation, intent, weight, meaning, purpose, purport, sense, signification.

significant *(SYN.)* grave, important, critical, material, indicative, meaningful, crucial, momentous, telling, vital, weighty.
(ANT.) *irrelevant, insignificant, meaningless, unimportant, negligible.*

signify *(SYN.)* designate, imply, denote, intimate, reveal, indicate, manifest, mean, communicate, show, specify.
(ANT.) *distract, divert, mislead, conceal, conceal.*

silence *(SYN.)* motionless, peaceful, placid, hushed, stillness, quiescent, still, soundlessness, quiet, tranquil, noiselessness, hush, muteness, undisturbed.
(ANT.) *strident, loud, racket, disturbed, clamor, agitated, perturbed.*

silent *(SYN.)* dumb, hushed, mute, calm, noiseless, quiet, peaceful, still, soundless, speechless, tranquil, uncommunicative, taciturn.
(ANT.) *communicative, loud, noisy, raucous, talkative, clamorous.*

silhouette *(SYN.)* contour, delineation, brief, draft, form, figure, outline, profile, plan, sketch.

silly *(SYN.)* asinine, brainless, crazy, absurd, foolish, irrational, witless, nonsensical, simple, ridiculous, stupid.
(ANT.) *sane, wise, judicious, prudent.*

similar *(SYN.)* alike, akin, allied, comparable, analogous, correlative, corresponding, correspondent, parallel, resembling, like.
(ANT.) *dissimilar, divergent, opposed, different, incongruous.*

similarity *(SYN.)* likeness, parity, analogy, correspondence, resemblance, similitude.
(ANT.) *distinction, variance, difference.*

simple *(SYN.)* effortless, elementary, pure, easy, facile, mere, single, uncompounded, homely, humble, unmixed, plain, artless, naive, frank, natural, unsophisticated, open, asinine, foolish, credulous, silly.

(ANT.) artful, complex, intricate, adorned, wise.

simpleton *(SYN.)* idiot, fool, ignoramus.

simulate *(SYN.)* copy, counterfeit, duplicate, ape, imitate, impersonate, mock, mimic.

(ANT.) distort, diverge, alter, invent.

sin *(SYN.)* evil, crime, iniquity, transgress, guilt, offense, ungodliness, trespass, vice, transgression, wickedness, wrong.

(ANT.) purity, goodness, purity, virtue, righteousness.

sincere *(SYN.)* earnest, frank, heartfelt, genuine, candid, honest, open, true, straightforward, faithful, truthful, upright, trustworthy, unfeigned.

(ANT.) hypocritical, insincere, affected, dishonest, untruthful.

sincerity *(SYN.)* fairness, frankness, honesty, justice, candor, integrity, openness, responsibility, rectitude, uprightness.

(ANT.) deceit, dishonesty, cheating.

sinful *(SYN.)* bad, corrupt, dissolute, antisocial, immoral, licentious, profligate, evil, indecent, unprincipled, vicious.

(ANT.) pure, noble, virtuous.

sing *(SYN.)* chant, croon, hum, carol, intone, lilt, warble.

singe *(SYN.)* burn, char, consume, blaze, incinerate, scorch, sear, scald.

(ANT.) put out, quench, extinguish.

single *(SYN.)* individual, marked, particular, distinctive, separate, special, specific, lone, one, solitary, sole, unwed, unmarried, singular, unique.

(ANT.) ordinary, universal, general.

singular *(SYN.)* exceptional, eccentric, odd, peculiar, rare, extraordinary, strange, unusual, striking, characteristic, remarkable, rare, individual, distinctive, uncommon, special.

(ANT.) general, normal, ordinary.

sink *(SYN.)* diminish, droop, subside, hang, decline, fall, extend, downward, drop, descend.

(ANT.) mount, climb, soar, steady, arise.

sinless *(SYN.)* faultless, holy, immaculate, perfect, blameless, holy, consummate, ideal, excellent, superlative, supreme.

(ANT.) defective, faulty, blemished, imperfect.

sip *(SYN.)* drink, taste, swallow.

sire *(SYN.)* breed, create, father, engender, beget, generate, procreate, originate, produce, propagate.

(ANT.) destroy, ill, extinguish, murder, abort.

site *(SYN.)* place, position, location, situation, station, locality.

situation *(SYN.)* circumstance, plight, state, site, location, placement, locale, predicament, position, state, condition.

size *(SYN.)* bigness, bulk, dimensions, expanse, amplitude, measurement, area, extent, largeness, magnitude, mass, greatness, volume.

skeptic *(SYN.)* doubter, infidel, agnostic, deist, questioner, unbeliever.

(ANT.) believer, worshiper, adorer.

skepticism *(SYN.)* hesitation, questioning, wavering, doubting, distrust, mistrust, suspicion.

(ANT.) confidence, reliance, trust.

sketch *(SYN.)* draft, figure, form, outline, contour, delineation, drawing, picture, represent, silhouette, draw, profile.

sketchy *(SYN.)* indefinite, vague, incomplete, indistinct.

(ANT.) definite, detailed, complete.

skill *(SYN.)* cunning, deftness, dexterity, ability, adroitness, cleverness, talent, readiness, skillfulness.

(ANT.) ineptitude, inability.

skillful *(SYN.)* adept, clever, able, accomplished, competent, expert, ingenious, cunning, proficient, practiced, versed, skilled.

(ANT.) untrained, inept, clumsy, inexpert, bungling, awkward.

skimpy *(SYN.)* cheap, scanty, meager.

(ANT.) abundant, generous.

skin *(SYN.)* outside, covering, peel, rind, shell, pare.

skinny *(SYN.)* gaunt, thin, raw-boned.

(ANT.) fat, hefty, heavy.

skip *(SYN.)* drop, eliminate, ignore, exclude, cancel, delete, disregard, omit, overlook neglect, miss.

(ANT.) notice, introduce, include, insert.

skirmish *(SYN.)* brawl, battle, conflict, combat, dispute, encounter, contend, quarrel, squabble, scuffle, wrangle, struggle.

slack *(SYN.)* lax, limp, indefinite, free, disengaged, unbound, untied, unfastened, vague, dissolute, heedless, careless, unrestrained, limp, lazy, loose, inactive, sluggish, wanton.

(ANT.) restrained, tied, right, stiff, taunt, rigid, fast, inhibited.

slander *(SYN.)* libel, calumny, backbiting, aspersion, scandal, vilification.

(ANT.) praise, flattery, commendation, defense.

slang *(SYN.)* jargon, dialect.

slant *(SYN.)* disposition, inclination, bias, bent, partiality, slope, tilt, pitch, penchant, prejudice, proneness, proclivity, turn, incline, lean, tendency.

(ANT.) justice, fairness, impartiality, equity.

slash *(SYN.)* gash, cut, slit, lower, reduce.

slaughter *(SYN.)* butcher, kill, massacre, slay, butchering, killing.

slave *(SYN.)* bondservant, serf.

slavery *(SYN.)* captivity, imprisonment, serfdom, confinement, bondage, thralldom, servitude, enslavement.

(ANT.) freedom, liberation.

slay *(SYN.)* assassinate, kill, murder.

sleek *(SYN.)* smooth, polished, slick.

(ANT.) blunt, harsh, rough, rugged.

sleep *(SYN.)* drowse, nap, nod, catnap, repose, doze, rest, slumber, snooze.

sleepy *(SYN.)* tired, drowsy, nodding.

slender *(SYN.)* lank, lean, meager, emaciated, gaunt, scanty, rare, skinny, scrawny, slight, spare, trim, slim, tenuous, thin.

(ANT.) fat, broad, overweight, thick, wide, bulky.

slide *(SYN.)* glide, slip, skim, skid.

slight *(SYN.)* lank, lean, meager, emaciated, gaunt, fine, narrow, scanty, scrawny, skinny, sparse, small, rare, slender, spare, insignificant, tenuous, unimportant, slim, thin.

(ANT.) regard, notice, enormous, large, major, huge, include.

slim *(SYN.)* thin, slender, lank, slight, weak, insignificant, unimportant.

slip *(SYN.)* error, fault, inaccuracy, shift, err, slide, mistake, glide, blunder.

(ANT.) precision, truth, accuracy.

slipshod *(SYN.)* sloppy, careless.

(ANT.) careful.

slit *(SYN.)* slash, cut, tear, slot.

slogan *(SYN.)* catchword, motto.

slope *(SYN.)* incline, leaning, inclination, bending, slant.

sloth *(SYN.)* indolence, idleness, inactivity, inertia, supineness, sluggishness, torpidity.

(ANT.) alertness, assiduousness, diligence, activity.

slothful *(SYN.)* indolent, idle, inactive, lazy, inert, supine, sluggish, torpid.

(ANT.) alert, diligent, active, assiduous.

slovenly *(SYN.)* sloppy, bedraggled, unkempt, messy.

(ANT.) meticulous, neat.

slow *(SYN.)* deliberate, dull, delaying, dawdling, gradual, leisurely, tired, sluggish, unhurried, late, behindhand, delayed.

(ANT.) rapid, quick, swift, speedy, fast.

sluggish *(SYN.)* dull, deliberate, dawdling, delaying, laggard, gradual, leisurely, tired, slow, lethargic.

(ANT.) quick, rapid, fast, speedy, swift, energetic, vivacious.

slumber *(SYN.)* drowse, catnap, nod, doze, repose, sleep, rest, snooze.

slump *(SYN.)* drop, decline, descent.

sly *(SYN.)* covert, artful, astute, crafty, clandestine, foxy, furtive, cunning, insidious, guileful, stealthy, subtle, shrewd, tricky, surreptitious, underhand, wily, secretive.

(ANT.) sincere, ingenuous, open, candid.

small *(SYN.)* little, minute, petty, diminutive, puny, wee, tiny, trivial, slight, miniature.

(ANT.) immense, enormous, large, huge.

smart *(SYN.)* dexterous, quick, skillful, adroit, apt, clever, bright, witty, ingenious, sharp, intelligent.

(ANT.) foolish, stupid, unskilled, awkward, clumsy, bungling, slow, dumb.

smash *(SYN.)* burst, crush, demolish, destroy, break, crack, fracture, pound, fringe, rack, rupture, shatter, rend.

(ANT.) mend, renovate, restore, repair.

smear *(SYN.)* wipe, rub, spread.

smell *(SYN.)* fragrance, fume, odor, perfume, incense, aroma, fetidness, stench, stink, scent, sniff, detect, bouquet.

smidgen *(SYN.)* crumb, mite, small, bit, particle, shred, speck, scrap.

(ANT.) bulk, mass, quantity, aggregate.

smile grin.
(ANT.) frown.

smite *(SYN.)* knock, hit, dash, beat, belabor, buffet, pound, punch, pummel, thrash, thump, defeat, overthrow, overpower, subdue, vanquish, rout.
(ANT.) surrender, fail, defend, shield, stroke.

smooth *(SYN.)* polished, sleek, slick, glib, diplomatic, flat, level, plain, suave, urbane, even, unwrinkled.
(ANT.) rugged, harsh, rough, blunt, bluff, uneven.

smother *(SYN.)* suffocate, asphyxiate, stifle.

smutty *(SYN.)* disgusting, filthy, impure, coarse, dirty, lewd, offensive, obscene, pornographic.
(ANT.) modest, refined, decent, pure.

snag *(SYN.)* difficulty, bar, barrier, check, hindrance, obstruction.
(ANT.) assistance, help, encouragement.

snappish *(SYN.)* ill-natured, ill-tempered, fractious, irritable, fretful, peevish, testy, touchy, petulant.
(ANT.) good-tempered, pleasant, good-natured, affable, genial.

snappy *(SYN.)* quick, stylish, chic.

snare *(SYN.)* capture, catch, arrest, clutch, grasp, grip, lay, apprehend, seize, trap, net.
(ANT.) throw, release, lose, liberate.

snarl *(SYN.)* growl.

snatch *(SYN.)* grasp, seize, grab.

sneak *(SYN.)* steal, skulk, slink.

sneer *(SYN.)* fleer, flout, jeer, mock, gibe, deride, taunt, scoff, scorn,
(ANT.) laud, flatter, praise, compliment.

sneering *(SYN.)* derision, gibe, banter, jeering, mockery, raillery, sarcasm, ridicule, satire.

sniveling *(SYN.)* whimpering, sniffling, weepy, whining, blubbering.

snobbish *(SYN.)* uppity, conceited, snooty, snobby, snotty.

snoopy *(SYN.)* inquisitive, interrogative, curious, inquiring, meddling, peeping, prying, peering.
(ANT.) uninterested, incurious, unconcerned, indifferent.

snub *(SYN.)* rebuke, insult, slight.

snug *(SYN.)* constricted, close, contracted, compact, firm, narrow, taut, tense, stretched, tight, cozy, comfort-

able, sheltered.
(ANT.) loose, lax, slack, relaxed, open.

soak *(SYN.)* saturate, drench, steep, wet.

soar *(SYN.)* flutter, fly, flit, float, glide, sail, hover, mount.
(ANT.) plummet, sink, fall, descend.

sob *(SYN.)* weep, cry, lament.

sober *(SYN.)* sedate, serious, staid, earnest, grave, solemn, moderate.
(ANT.) ordinary, joyful, informal, boisterous, drunk, fuddled, inebriated.

sobriety *(SYN.)* forbearance, abstinence, abstention, self-denial, moderation, temperance.
(ANT.) self-indulgence, excess, intoxication.

social *(SYN.)* friendly, civil, gregarious, affable, communicative, hospitable, sociable, group, common, genial, polite.
(ANT.) inhospitable, hermitic, antisocial, disagreeable.

society *(SYN.)* nation, community, civilization, organization, club, association, fraternity, circle, association, company, companionship.

soft *(SYN.)* gentle, lenient, flexible, compassionate, malleable, meek, mellow, subdued, mild, tender, supple, yielding, pliable, elastic, pliant.
(ANT.) unyielding, rough, hard, tough, rigid.

soften *(SYN.)* assuage, diminish, abate, allay, alleviate, mitigate, relieve, soothe, solace.
(ANT.) irritate, increase, aggravate, agitate.

soil *(SYN.)* defile, discolor, spot, befoul, blemish, blight, stain, sully, earth, dirt, loam, dirty.
(ANT.) purify, honor, cleanse, bleach, decorate.

solace *(SYN.)* contentment, ease, enjoyment, comfort, consolation, relief, succor.
(ANT.) torture, torment, misery, affliction, discomfort.

sole *(SYN.)* isolated, desolate, deserted, secluded, unaided, lone, alone, only, single, solitary.
(ANT.) surrounded, accompanied, attended.

solemn*(SYN.)* ceremonious, imposing, formal, impressive, reverential, ritualistic, grave, sedate, earnest, sober, staid, serious, dignified.

(ANT.) ordinary, joyful, informal, boisterous, cheerful, gay, happy.

solicit (SYN.) beg, beseech, request, seek, pray.

solicitous (SYN.) anxious, concerned.

solicitude (SYN.) concern, worry, anxiety, care, attention, regard, vigilance, caution, wariness.

(ANT.) indifference, disregard, neglect, negligence.

solid (SYN.) hard, dense, compact, firm.

(ANT.) loose.

solitary (SYN.) isolated, alone, lonely, deserted, unaided, secluded, only, single, lone, sole.

(ANT.) surrounded, attended, accompanied.

solitude (SYN.) loneliness, privacy, refuge, retirement, seclusion, retreat, alienation, asylum, concealment.

(ANT.) publicity, exposure, notoriety.

solution (SYN.) explanation, answer.

solve (SYN.) explain, answer, unravel.

somatic (SYN.) corporeal, corporal, natural, material, bodily, physical.

(ANT.) spiritual, mental.

somber (SYN.) dismal, dark, bleak, doleful, cheerless, natural, physical, serious, sober, gloomy, grave.

(ANT.) lively, joyous, cheerful, happy.

sometimes (SYN.) occasionally.

(ANT.) invariably, always.

soon (SYN.) shortly, early, betimes, beforehand.

(ANT.) tardy, late, overdue, belated.

soothe (SYN.) encourage, console, solace, comfort, cheer, gladden, sympathize, calm, pacify.

(ANT.) dishearten, depress, antagonize, aggravate, disquiet, upset, unnerve.

soothing (SYN.) gentle, benign, docile, calm, mild, placid, peaceful, serene, soft, relaxed, tractable, tame.

(ANT.) violent, savage, fierce, harsh.

sophisticated (SYN.) cultured, worldly, blase, cultivated, urbane, cosmopolitan, suave, intricate, complex, advanced.

(ANT.) uncouth, ingenuous, simple, naive, crude.

sorcery (SYN.) enchantment, conjuring, art, charm, black, magic, voodoo, witchcraft, wizardry.

sordid (SYN.) vicious, odious, revolting, obscene, foul, loathsome, base, depraved, debased, vile, vulgar, abject, wicked, ignoble, despicable, mean, low, worthless, wretched, dirty, unclean.

(ANT.) upright, decent, honorable.

sore (SYN.) tender, sensitive, aching, hurting, painful.

sorrow (SYN.) grief, distress, heartache, anguish, misery, sadness, mourning, trial, tribulation, gloom, depression.

(ANT.) consolation, solace, joy, happiness, comfort.

sorrowful (SYN.) dismal, doleful, dejected, despondent, depressed, disconsolate, gloomy, melancholy, glum, moody, somber, sad, grave, aggrieved.

(ANT.) merry, happy, cheerful, joyous.

sorry (SYN.) hurt, pained, sorrowful, afflicted, grieved, contrite, repentant, paltry, poor, wretched, remorseful, mean, shabby, contemptible, worthless, vile, regretful, apologetic.

(ANT.) delighted, impenitent, cheerful, unrepentant, splendid.

sort (SYN.) class, stamp, category, description, nature, character, kind, type, variety.

(ANT.) peculiarity, deviation.

sound (SYN.) effective, logical, telling, binding, powerful, weighty, legal, strong, conclusive, valid.

(ANT.) weak, null, counterfeit.

sour (SYN.) glum, sullen, bitter, peevish, acid, rancid, tart, acrimonious, sharp, bad-tempered, unpleasant, cranky.

(ANT.) wholesome, kindly, genial, benevolent, sweet.

source (SYN.) birth, foundation, agent, determinant, reason, origin, cause, start, incentive, motive, spring, inducement, principle, beginning.

(ANT.) product, harvest, outcome, issue, consequence, end.

souvenir (SYN.) memento, monument, commemoration, remembrance.

sovereign (SYN.) monarch, king, emperor, queen, empress.

sovereignty (SYN.) command, influence, authority, predominance, control, sway.

(ANT.) debility, incapacity, disablement, ineptitude, impotence.

space (SYN.) room, area, location.

spacious (SYN.) capacious, large, vast, ample, extensive, wide, roomy, large.

(ANT.) limited, confined, narrow, small, cramped.

span *(SYN.)* spread, extent.

spare *(SYN.)* preserve, safeguard, uphold, conserve, protect, defend, rescue, reserve, additional, unoccupied.

(ANT.) impair, abolish, injure, abandon.

sparing *(SYN.)* economical, thrifty, frugal.

(ANT.) lavish.

sparkle *(SYN.)* gleam, glitter, twinkle, beam, glisten, radiate, shine, blaze.

spat *(SYN.)* quarrel, dispute, affray, wrangle, altercation.

(ANT.) peace, friendliness, agreement, reconciliation.

spawn *(SYN.)* yield, bear.

speak *(SYN.)* declare, express, say, articulate, harangue, converse, talk, utter.

(ANT.) refrain, hush, quiet.

special *(SYN.)* individual, uncommon, distinctive, peculiar, exceptional, unusual, extraordinary, different, particular.

(ANT.) general, widespread, broad, prevailing, average, ordinary.

specialist *(SYN.)* authority, expert.

species *(SYN.)* variety, type, kind, class, sort.

specific *(SYN.)* limited, characteristic, definite, peculiar, explicit, categorical, particular, distinct, precise.

(ANT.) generic, general, nonspecific.

specify *(SYN.)* name, call, mention, appoint, denominate, designate, define.

(ANT.) miscall, hint.

specimen *(SYN.)* prototype, example, sample, model, pattern, type.

speck *(SYN.)* scrap, jot, bit, mite, smidgen, crumb, iota, particle, spot.

(ANT.) quantity, bulk, aggregate.

spectacle *(SYN.)* demonstration, ostentation, movie, array, exhibition, show, display, performance, parade, splurge.

spectator *(SYN.)* viewer, observer.

speculate *(SYN.)* assume, deduce, surmise, apprehend, imagine, consider, view, think, guess, suppose, conjecture.

(ANT.) prove, demonstrate, conclude.

speech *(SYN.)* gossip, discourse, talk, chatter, lecture, conference, discussion, address, dialogue, articulation, accent.

(ANT.) silence, correspondence, writing, meditation.

speed *(SYN.)* forward, push, accelerate, hasten, rapidity, dispatch, swiftness.

(ANT.) impede, slow, block, retard.

spellbound *(SYN.)* fascinated, entranced, hypnotized, mesmerized, rapt.

spend *(SYN.)* pay, disburse, consume.

(ANT.) hoard, save.

spendthrift *(SYN.)* squanderer, profligate.

sphere *(SYN.)* globe, orb, ball, environment, area, domain.

spherical *(SYN.)* round, curved, globular.

spicy *(SYN.)* indecent, off-color, suggestive, indelicate.

spin *(SYN.)* revolve, turn, rotate, whirl, twirl, tell, narrate, relate.

spine *(SYN.)* vertebrae, backbone.

spineless *(SYN.)* weak, limp, cowardly.

(ANT.) brave, strong, courageous.

spirit *(SYN.)* courage, phantom, verve, fortitude, apparition, mood, soul, ghost.

(ANT.) listlessness, substance, languor.

spirited *(SYN.)* excited, animated, lively, active, vigorous, energetic.

(ANT.) indolent, lazy, sleepy.

spiritless *(SYN.)* gone, lifeless, departed, dead, insensible, deceased, unconscious.

(ANT.) stirring, alive, living.

spiritual *(SYN.)* sacred, unearthly, holy, divine, immaterial, supernatural.

(ANT.) material, physical, corporeal.

spite *(SYN.)* grudge, rancor, malice, animosity, malevolence, malignity.

(ANT.) kindness, toleration, affection.

spiteful *(SYN.)* vicious, disagreeable, surly, ill-natured.

(ANT.) pretty, beautiful, attractive, fair.

splendid *(SYN.)* glorious, illustrious, radiant, brilliant, showy, superb, bright.

(ANT.) ordinary, mediocre, dull.

splendor *(SYN.)* effulgence, radiance, brightness, luster, magnificence, display.

(ANT.) darkness, obscurity, dullness.

splinter *(SYN.)* fragment, piece, sliver, chip, shiver.

split *(SYN.)* rend, shred, cleave, disunite, sever, break, divide, opening, lacerate.

(ANT.) repair, unite, join, sew.

spoil *(SYN.)* rot, disintegrate, waste, decay, ruin, damage, mold, destroy.

(ANT.) luxuriate, grow, flourish.

spoken *(SYN.)* verbal, pronounced, articulated, vocal, uttered, oral.

(ANT.) written, documentary.

spokesman *(SYN.)* agent, representative.

spontaneous *(SYN.)* impulsive, voluntary, automatic, instinctive, willing, extemporaneous, natural, unconscious.
(ANT.) *planned, rehearsed, forced, studied, prepared.*

sport *(SYN.)* match, play, amusement, fun, pastime, entertainment, athletics.

sporting *(SYN.)* considerate, fair, sportsmanlike.

spot *(SYN.)* blemish, mark, stain, flaw, blot, location, place, site, splatter.

spotty *(SYN.)* erratic, uneven, irregular, inconsistent.
(ANT.) *regular, even.*

spout *(SYN.)* spurt, squirt, tube, nozzle.

spray *(SYN.)* splash, spatter, sprinkle.

spread *(SYN.)* unfold, distribute, open, disperse, unroll, unfurl, scatter, jelly.
(ANT.) *shut, close, hide, conceal.*

sprightly *(SYN.)* blithe, hopeful, vivacious, buoyant, lively, light, nimble.
(ANT.) *hopeless, depressed, sullen, dejected, despondent.*

spring *(SYN.)* commencement, foundation, start, beginning, inception, jump, cradle, begin, birth, bound, originate.
(ANT.) *issue, product, end.*

sprinkle *(SYN.)* strew, spread, scatter, rain.

spruce *(SYN.)* orderly, neat, trim, clear, nice.
(ANT.) *unkempt, sloppy, dirty.*

spry *(SYN.)* brisk, quick, agile, nimble, energetic, supple, alert, active, lively.
(ANT.) *heavy, sluggish, inert, clumsy.*

spur *(SYN.)* inducement, purpose, cause, motive, impulse, reason, incitement.
(ANT.) *effort, action, result, attempt.*

squabble *(SYN.)* bicker, debate, altercate, contend, discuss, argue, quarrel.
(ANT.) *concede, agree, assent.*

squalid *(SYN.)* base, indecent, grimy, dirty, pitiful, filthy, muddy, nasty.
(ANT.) *wholesome, clean, pure.*

squander *(SYN.)* scatter, lavish, consume, dissipate, misuse.
(ANT.) *preserve, conserve, save, accumulate.*

squeamish *(SYN.)* particular, careful.

stab *(SYN.)* stick, gore, pierce, knife, spear, bayonet.

stability *(SYN.)* steadiness, balance, proportion, composure, symmetry.
(ANT.) *imbalance, fall, unsteadiness.*

stable *(SYN.)* firm, enduring, constant, fixed, unwavering, steadfast, steady.
(ANT.) *irresolute, variable, changeable.*

stack *(SYN.)* mass, pile, mound, heap, accumulate.

staff *(SYN.)* pole, stick, club, personnel, crew, employees.

stage *(SYN.)* frame, platform, boards, theater, scaffold, period, phase, step, direct, produce, present.

stagger *(SYN.)* totter, sway, reel, vary, falter, alternate.

staid *(SYN.)* solemn, sedate, earnest, sober, grave.
(ANT.) *joyful, informal, ordinary.*

stain *(SYN.)* blight, dye, tint, befoul, spot, defile, mark, dishonor, disgrace, smirch, blot, tint, blemish, discolor, color, tinge.
(ANT.) *honor, bleach, decorate, purify.*

stair *(SYN.)* staircase, stairway, steps.

stake *(SYN.)* rod, pole, picket, post, pale, bet, wager, concern, interest.

stale *(SYN.)* tasteless, spoiled, old, inedible, dry, uninteresting, trite, flat, dull, vapid, insipid.
(ANT.) *new, fresh, tasty.*

stalk *(SYN.)* dog, follow, track, shadow, hunt.

stall *(SYN.)* hesitate, stop, delay, postpone.

stammer *(SYN.)* falter, stutter.

stamp *(SYN.)* crush, trample, imprint, mark, brand, block, seal, die.

stand *(SYN.)* tolerate, suffer, stay, stand up, endure, bear, abide, halt, arise, rise, remain, sustain, rest.
(ANT.) *run, yield, advance.*

standard *(SYN.)* law, proof, pennant, emblem, touchstone, measure, example, gauge, model, banner, symbol, test.
(ANT.) *guess, chance, irregular, unusual, supposition.*

standing *(SYN.)* rank, position, station, status.

standpoint *(SYN.)* position, viewpoint, attitude.

staple *(SYN.)* main, principal, chief, essential, necessary.

stare *(SYN.)* gaze.

stark *(SYN.)* utter, absolute, sheer, complete, rough, severe, harsh, grim.

start *(SYN.)* opening, source, commence, onset, surprise, shock, beginning, origin, begin, initiate, jerk, jump, advantage,

lead, commencement, outset.
(ANT.) end, completion, termination, close.

startle (SYN.) astonish, disconcert, aback, alarm, shock, agitate, surprise, astound, amaze, stun.
(ANT.) caution, prepare, admonish, forewarn.

starved (SYN.) longing, voracious, hungry, craving, avid, famished.
(ANT.) satisfied, sated, gorged, full.

state (SYN.) circumstance, predicament, case, situation, condition, affirm, declare, express, nation, country, status, assert, recite, tell, recount.
(ANT.) imply, conceal, retract.

stately (SYN.) lordly, elegant, regal, sovereign, impressive, magnificent, courtly, grand, imposing, majestic, noble, supreme, dignified.
(ANT.) low, common, mean, servile, humble, vulgar.

statement (SYN.) announcement, mention, allegation, declaration, thesis, assertion, report.

station (SYN.) post, depot, terminal, position, place.

statuesque (SYN.) imposing, stately, regal, majestic, dignified.

status (SYN.) place, caste, standing, condition, state, rank, position.

statute (SYN.) law, ruling, decree, rule.
(ANT.) intention, deliberation.

staunch (SYN.) faithful, true, constant, reliable, loyal, devoted.
(ANT.) treacherous, untrustworthy.

stay (SYN.) delay, continue, hinder, check, hold, hindrance, support, brace, line, rope, linger, sojourn, abide, halt, stand, rest, remain, tarry, arrest, wait.
(ANT.) hasten, progress, go, depart, advance, leave.

stead (SYN.) place.

steadfast (SYN.) solid, inflexible, constant, stable, unyielding, secure.
(ANT.) unstable, insecure, unsteady.

steadfastness (SYN.) persistence, industry, tenacity, constancy, persistency.
(ANT.) laziness, sloth, cessation.

steady (SYN.) regular, even, unremitting, stable, steadfast, firm, reliable, solid.

steal (SYN.) loot, rob, swipe, burglarize, pilfer, shoplift, embezzle, snitch.
(ANT.) restore, buy, return, refund.

stealthy (SYN.) sly, secret, furtive.
(ANT.) direct, open, obvious.

steep (SYN.) sharp, hilly, sheer, abrupt, perpendicular, precipitous.
(ANT.) gradual, level, flat.

steer (SYN.) manage, guide, conduct, lead, supervise, escort, navigate, drive, control, direct.

stem (SYN.) stalk, trunk, arise, check, stop, originate, hinder.

stench (SYN.) odor, fetor, fetidness, stink, aroma, smell, fume, scent.

step (SYN.) stride, pace, stage, move, action, measure, come, go, walk.

stern (SYN.) harsh, rigid, exacting, rigorous, sharp, severe, strict, hard, unyielding, unmitigated, stringent.
(ANT.) indulgent, forgiving, yielding, lenient, considerate.

stew (SYN.) ragout, goulash, boil, simmer.

stick (SYN.) stalk, twig, rod, staff, pole, pierce, spear, stab, puncture, gore, cling, adhere, hold, catch, abide, remain, persist.

stickler (SYN.) nitpicker, perfectionist, disciplinarian.

sticky (SYN.) tricky, delicate, awkward.

stiff (SYN.) severe, unbendable, unyielding, harsh, inflexible, unbending, rigid, firm, hard, solid, rigorous.
(ANT.) supple, yielding, compassionate, mild, lenient, resilient.

stifle (SYN.) choke, strangle, suffocate.

stigma (SYN.) trace, scar, blot, stain, mark, vestige.

still (SYN.) peaceful, undisturbed, but, mild, hushed, calm, patient, modest, nevertheless, motionless, meek, quiescent, stationary, besides, however, quiet, hush, tranquil, serene, placid.
(ANT.) agitated, perturbed, loud.

stimulate (SYN.) irritate, excite, arouse, disquiet, rouse, activate, urge, invigorate, animate, provoke.
(ANT.) quell, calm, quiet, allay.

stimulus (SYN.) motive, goad, arousal, provocation, encouragement.
(ANT.) discouragement, depressant.

stingy (SYN.) greedy, penurious, avaricious, mean, penny-pinching, cheap, selfish, miserly, tight, tightfisted.
(ANT.) munificent, generous, giving, extravagant, openhanded, bountiful.

stipend *(SYN.)* payment, earnings, salary, allowance, pay, compensation, wages.
(ANT.) gratuity, gift.

stipulate *(SYN.)* require, demand.

stir *(SYN.)* instigate, impel, push, agitate, induce, mix, rouse, move, propel.
(ANT.) halt, stop, deter.

stock *(SYN.)* hoard, store, strain, accumulation, supply, carry, keep, provision, fund, breed, sort.
(ANT.) sameness, likeness, homogeneity, uniformity.

stoical *(SYN.)* passive, forbearing, uncomplaining, composed, patient.
(ANT.) turbulent, chafing, hysterical.

stolid *(SYN.)* obtuse, unsharpened, dull, blunt, edgeless.
(ANT.) suave, tactful, polished, subtle.

stone *(SYN.)* pebble, gravel, rock.

stony *(SYN.)* insensitive, unsentimental, cold.

stoop *(SYN.)* bow, bend, lean, crouch.

stop *(SYN.)* terminate, check, abstain, hinder, arrest, close, bar, cork, halt, end, conclude, obstruct, finish, quit, pause, discontinue, stay, impede, cease.
(ANT.) start, proceed, speed, begin.

store *(SYN.)* amass, hoard, collect, market, shop, reserve, supply, deposit, bank, save, accrue, increase, stock.
(ANT.) dissipate, waste, disperse.

storm *(SYN.)* gale, tempest, tornado, thunderstorm, hurricane, rage, rant, assault, besiege.

stormy *(SYN.)* rough, inclement, windy, blustery, roaring, tempestuous.
(ANT.) quiet, calm, tranquil, peaceful.

story *(SYN.)* yarn, novel, history, tale, falsehood, account, fable, anecdote, narrative, fabrication, lie, level, floor, fiction, report.

stout *(SYN.)* plump, obese, chubby, fat, paunchy, overweight, portly, heavy, sturdy, strong, pudgy, thickset.
(ANT.) thin, slender, flimsy, gaunt, slim.

straight *(SYN.)* erect, honorable, square, just, direct, undeviating, unbent, right, upright, honest, uncurving, directly, moral, correct, orderly, vertical.
(ANT.) dishonest, bent, circuitous, twisted, crooked.

straightforward *(SYN.)* forthright, direct, open, candid, aboveboard.
(ANT.) devious.

strain *(SYN.)* stock, kind, variety, stretch, breed, tighten, harm, injure, screen, filter, sprain, sort.

strainer *(SYN.)* colander, sieve, filter.

strait *(SYN.)* fix, situation, passage, condition, dilemma, channel, trouble, predicament, difficulty, distress, crisis.
(ANT.) ease, calmness, satisfaction, comfort.

strange *(SYN.)* bizarre, peculiar, odd, abnormal, irregular, unusual, curious, uncommon, singular, extraordinary, foreign, eccentric, unfamiliar, queer.
(ANT.) regular, common, familiar, conventional.

stranger *(SYN.)* foreigner, outsider, newcomer, alien, outlander, immigrant.
(ANT.) friend, associate, acquaintance.

strap *(SYN.)* strip, belt, thong, band.

stratagem *(SYN.)* design, ruse, cabal, plot, machination, subterfuge, trick, wile, conspiracy.

strategy *(SYN.)* technique, management, tactics, approach.

stray *(SYN.)* ramble, rove, deviate, lost, strayed, wander, digress, roam, stroll.
(ANT.) linger, stop, halt, settle.

stream *(SYN.)* issue, proceed, flow, come, abound, spout, run, brook.

street *(SYN.)* way, road, boulevard, avenue.

strength *(SYN.)* power, might, toughness, durability, lustiness, soundness, vigor, potency.
(ANT.) weakness, frailty, feebleness.

strengthen *(SYN.)* verify, assure, confirm, fix, sanction, ratify, substantiate.

strenuous *(SYN.)* forceful, energetic, active, vigorous, determined.

stress *(SYN.)* urgency, press, emphasize, accentuate, accent, weight, strain, importance, compulsion, pressure.
(ANT.) relaxation, lenience, ease.

stretch *(SYN.)* strain, expand, elongate, extend, lengthen, spread, distend, protract, distort.
(ANT.) tighten, loosen, slacken, contract.

strict *(SYN.)* rough, stiff, stringent, harsh, unbending, severe, rigorous.
(ANT.) easygoing, lenient, mild.

strife *(SYN.)* disagreement, conflict, discord, quarrel, difference, unrest.
(ANT.) tranquillity, peace, concord.

strike *(SYN.)* pound, hit, smite, beat, assault, attack, affect, impress, overwhelm, sitdown, walkout, slowdown.

striking *(SYN.)* arresting, imposing, splendid, august, impressive, thrilling, stirring, awesome, aweinspiring.
(ANT.) ordinary, unimpressive, commonplace, regular.

stringent *(SYN.)* harsh, rugged, grating, severe, gruff.

strip *(SYN.)* disrobe, undress, remove, uncover, peel, ribbon, band, piece.

stripped *(SYN.)* open, simple, bare, nude, uncovered, exposed, bald, plain, naked, barren, defenseless.
(ANT.) protected, dressed, concealed.

strive *(SYN.)* aim, struggle, attempt, undertake, design, endeavor, try.
(ANT.) omit, abandon, neglect, decline.

stroke *(SYN.)* rap, blow, tap, knock, feat, achievement, accomplishment, caress.

stroll *(SYN.)* amble, walk, ramble.

strong *(SYN.)* potent, hale, athletic, mighty, sturdy, impregnable, resistant.
(ANT.) feeble, insipid, brittle, weak, bland, fragile.

structure *(SYN.)* construction, framework, arrangement.

struggle *(SYN.)* fray, strive, fight, contest, battle, skirmish, oppose, clash.
(ANT.) peace, agreement, truce.

stubborn *(SYN.)* obstinate, firm, determined, inflexible, obdurate, uncompromising, pigheaded, contumacious, rigid, unbending, intractable.
(ANT.) docile, yielding, amenable, submissive.

student *(SYN.)* pupil, observer, disciple, scholar, learner.

studio *(SYN.)* workroom, workshop.

study *(SYN.)* weigh, muse, master, contemplate, reflect; examination, examine.

stuff *(SYN.)* thing, subject, material, theme, matter, substance, fill, ram, cram, pack, textile, cloth, topic.
(ANT.) spirit, immateriality.

stumble *(SYN.)* sink, collapse, tumble, drop, topple, lurch, trip, fall.
(ANT.) steady, climb, soar, arise.

stun *(SYN.)* shock, knock out, dumbfound, take, amaze, alarm.
(ANT.) forewarn, caution, prepare.

stunning *(SYN.)* brilliant, dazzling, exquisite, ravishing.
(ANT.) drab, ugly.

stunt *(SYN.)* check, restrict, hinder.

stupid *(SYN.)* dull, obtuse, half-witted, brainless, foolish, dumb, witless, idiotic.
(ANT.) smart, intelligent, clever, quick, bright, alert, discerning.

stupor *(SYN.)* lethargy, torpor, daze, languor, drowsiness, numbness.
(ANT.) wakefulness, liveliness, activity.

sturdy *(SYN.)* hale, strong, rugged, stout, mighty, enduring, hardy, well-built.
(ANT.) fragile, brittle, insipid, delicate.

style *(SYN.)* sort, type, kind, chic, smartness, elegance.

subdue *(SYN.)* crush, overcome, rout, beat, reduce, lower, defeat, vanquish.
(ANT.) retreat, cede, surrender.

subject *(SYN.)* subordinate, theme, case, topic, dependent, citizen, matter.

sublime *(SYN.)* lofty, raised, elevated, supreme, exalted, splendid, grand.
(ANT.) ordinary, vase, low, ridiculous.

submerge *(SYN.)* submerse, dunk, sink, dip, immerse, engage, douse, engross.
(ANT.) surface, rise, uplift, elevate.

submissive *(SYN.)* deferential, yielding, dutiful, compliant.
(ANT.) rebellious, intractable, insubordinate.

submit *(SYN.)* quit, resign, waive, yield, tender, offer, abdicate, cede, surrender.
(ANT.) fight, oppose, resist, struggle, deny, refuse.

subordinate *(SYN.)* demean, reduce, inferior, assistant, citizen, liegeman.
(ANT.) superior.

subsequent *(SYN.)* later, following.
(ANT.) preceding, previous.

subside *(SYN.)* decrease, lower, sink, droop, hang, collapse, downward.
(ANT.) mount, steady, arise, climb.

subsidy *(SYN.)* support, aid, grant.

substance *(SYN.)* stuff, essence, importance, material, moment, matter.
(ANT.) spirit, immaterial.

substantial *(SYN.)* large, considerable, sizable, actual, real, tangible, influential.
(ANT.) unimportant, trivial.

substantiate *(SYN.)* strengthen, corroborate, confirm.

substitute *(SYN.)* proxy, expedient, deputy, makeshift, replacement, alternate, lieutenant, representative, surrogate, displace, exchange, equivalent.
(ANT.) sovereign, master, head.

substitution *(SYN.)* change, mutation, vicissitude, alteration, modification.
(ANT.) uniformity, monotony.

subterfuge *(SYN.)* pretext, excuse, cloak, simulation, disguise, garb, pretension.
(ANT.) reality, truth, actuality, sincerity.

subtle *(SYN.)* suggestive, indirect.
(ANT.) overt, obvious.

subtract *(SYN.)* decrease, reduce, curtail, deduct, diminish, remove, lessen.
(ANT.) expand, increase, add, enlarge, grow.

succeed *(SYN.)* thrive, follow, replace, achieve, win, flourish, prevail, inherit.
(ANT.) flop, miscarry, anticipate, fail, precede.

success *(SYN.)* advance, prosperity, luck.
(ANT.) failure.

successful *(SYN.)* fortunate, favorable, lucky, triumphant.

succession *(SYN.)* chain, course, series, order, string, arrangement, progression, train, following.

successive *(SYN.)* serial, sequential.

succinct *(SYN.)* pithy, curt, brief, short, compendious, terse.
(ANT.) prolonged, extended, long, protracted.

succor *(SYN.)* ease, solace, comfort, enjoyment, consolation.
(ANT.) suffering, discomfort, torture, affliction, torment.

sudden *(SYN.)* rapid, swift, immediate, abrupt, unexpected, unforeseen, hasty.
(ANT.) slowly, anticipated.

suffer *(SYN.)* stand, experience, endure, bear, feel, allow, let, permit, sustain.
(ANT.) exclude, banish, overcome.

suffering *(SYN.)* distress, ache, anguish, pain, woe, misery, torment.
(ANT.) ease, relief, comfort.

sufficient *(SYN.)* fitting, enough, adequate, commensurate, satisfactory.
(ANT.) scant, deficient.

suffix *(SYN.)* ending.
(ANT.) prefix.

suggest *(SYN.)* propose, offer, refer, advise, hint, insinuate, recommend, allude.
(ANT.) dictate, declare, insist.

suggestion *(SYN.)* exhortation, recommendation, intelligence, caution, admonition, warning, advice.

suit *(SYN.)* conform, accommodate, fit.
(ANT.) misapply, disturb.

suitable *(SYN.)* welcome, agreeable, acceptable, gratifying.
(ANT.) offensive, disagreeable.

sullen *(SYN.)* moody, fretful, surly, crabbed, morose, dour.
(ANT.) merry, gay, pleasant, amiable.

sullen *(SYN.)* fretful, morose, crabbed, dismal, silent, sulky, bitter, sad, somber, glum, gloomy, dour, moody.
(ANT.) pleasant, joyous, amiable, merry.

sultry *(SYN.)* close, hot, stifling.

sum *(SYN.)* amount, total, aggregate, whole, increase, append, add.
(ANT.) sample, fraction, reduce, deduct.

summarize *(SYN.)* abstract, abridge.
(ANT.) restore, add, unite, return.

summary *(SYN.)* digest, outline, abstract, synopsis, concise, brief, short, compact.

summit *(SYN.)* peak, top, head, crest, zenith, apex, crown, pinnacle.
(ANT.) bottom, foundation, base, foot.

summon *(SYN.)* invoke, call, invite.
(ANT.) dismiss.

sundry *(SYN.)* miscellaneous, several, different, various, divers.
(ANT.) similar, identical, alike, same, congruous.

sunny *(SYN.)* cheery, cheerful, fair, joyful, happy, cloudless.
(ANT.) overcast, cloudy.

superannuated *(SYN.)* old, archaic, aged, senile, ancient, venerable, elderly.
(ANT.) youthful, modern, young.

superb *(SYN.)* splendid, wonderful, extraordinary, marvelous.

supercilious *(SYN.)* contemptuous, snobbish, overbearing, vainglorious, arrogant, haughty, stately.
(ANT.) meek, ashamed, lowly.

superficial *(SYN.)* flimsy, shallow, cursory, slight, exterior.
(ANT.) thorough, deep, abstruse, profound.

superintend *(SYN.)* control, govern, rule, command, manage, direct, regulate.
(ANT.) ignore, follow, submit, abandon.

superintendence *(SYN.)* control, oversight, surveillance, management.

superintendent *(SYN.)* manager, supervisor, overseer, director, administrator.

superiority *(SYN.)* profit, mastery, advantage, good, service, edge, utility.
(ANT.) harm, detriment, impediment.

superlative *(SYN.)* pure, consummate,

sinless, blameless, holy, perfect, fault-less, ideal, unqualified, immaculate.
(ANT.) *lacking, defective, imperfect, deficient, blemished.*
supernatural *(SYN.)* unearthly, preter-natural, marvelous, miraculous.
(ANT.) *plain, human, physical, common.*
supervise *(SYN.)* rule, oversee, govern, command, direct, superintend, manage.
(ANT.) *submit, forsake, abandon.*
supervision *(SYN.)* oversight, inspection, surveillance, charge, management.
supervisor *(SYN.)* manager, boss, foreman, director.
supplant *(SYN.)* overturn, overcome.
(ANT.) *uphold, conserve.*
supple *(SYN.)* lithe, pliant, flexible, lim-ber, elastic, pliable.
(ANT.) *stiff, brittle, rigid, unbending.*
supplement *(SYN.)* extension, comple-ment, addition, extend, add.
supplicate *(SYN.)* beg, petition, solicit, adjure, beseech, entreat, ask, pray, crave.
(ANT.) *cede, give, bestow, grant.*
supplication *(SYN.)* invocation, plea, ap-peal, request, entreaty.
supply *(SYN.)* provide, inventory, hoard, reserve, store, accumulation, stock, fur-nish, endow, give.
support *(SYN.)* groundwork, aid, favor, base, prop, assistance, comfort, basis, succor, living, subsistence, encourage-ment, backing, livelihood, help.
(ANT.) *discourage, abandon, oppose, opposition, attack.*
supporter *(SYN.)* follower, devotee, adherent, henchman, attendant, dis-ciple, votary.
(ANT.) *master, head, chief.*
suppose *(SYN.)* believe, presume, deduce, apprehend, think, assume, imagine, speculate, guess, conjecture.
(ANT.) *prove, demonstrate, ascertain.*
supposition *(SYN.)* theory, conjecture.
(ANT.) *proof, fact.*
suppress *(SYN.)* diminish, reduce, over-power, abate, lessen, decrease, subdue.
(ANT.) *revive, amplify, intensify, enlarge.*
supremacy *(SYN.)* domination, pre-dominance, ascendancy, sovereignty.
supreme *(SYN.)* greatest, best, highest, main, principal, cardinal, first, chief, foremost, paramount.

(ANT.) *supplemental, minor, subsidiary, auxiliary.*
sure *(SYN.)* confident, fixed, inevitable, certain, positive, trustworthy, reliable, unquestionable, convinced, steady.
(ANT.) *probable, uncertain, doubtful.*
surface *(SYN.)* outside, exterior, cover, covering.
surge *(SYN.)* heave, swell, grow.
(ANT.) *wane, ebb, diminish.*
surly *(SYN.)* disagreeable, hostile, un-friendly, ugly, antagonistic.
surmise *(SYN.)* judge, think, believe, as-sume, suppose, presume, guess.
surpass *(SYN.)* pass, exceed, excel, out-strip, outdo.
surplus *(SYN.)* extravagance, intem-perance, superabundance, excess, im-moderation, remainder, extra, profu-sion, superfluity.
(ANT.) *want, lack, dearth, paucity.*
surprise *(SYN.)* miracle, prodigy, wonder, awe, phenomenon, marvel, bewilder-ment, wonderment, rarity.
(ANT.) *expectation, triviality, indif-ference, familiarity.*
surrender *(SYN.)* relinquish, resign, yield, abandon, sacrifice, submit, cede.
(ANT.) *overcome, rout, conquer.*
surreptitious *(SYN.)* sneaky, sneaking, underhead, sly, furtive.
(ANT.) *openhanded, open, straight-forward.*
surround *(SYN.)* confine, encompass, circle, encircle, girdle, fence, cir-cumscribe, limit, envelop.
(ANT.) *open, distend, expose, enlarge.*
surveillance *(SYN.)* inspection, oversight, supervision, management, control.
survey *(SYN.)* scan, inspect, view, ex-amine, inspection, examination.
survive *(SYN.)* live, remain, continue, persist.
(ANT.) *die, fail, succumb.*
suspect *(SYN.)* waver, disbelieve, presume, suppose, mistrust, distrust.
suspend *(SYN.)* delay, hang, withhold, in-terrupt, postpone, dangle, adjourn, poise.
(ANT.) *persist, proceed, maintain.*
suspicion *(SYN.)* unbelief, distrust, suspense, uncertainty, doubt.
(ANT.) *determination, conviction, faith, belief.*
sustain *(SYN.)* bear, carry, undergo,

foster, keep, prop, help, advocate, back.
(ANT.) discourage, oppose, destroy.
sustenance *(SYN.)* fare, food, diet, rations, nutriment, edibles, victuals.
(ANT.) hunger, want, drink.
swallow *(SYN.)* gorge, eat, mouthful.
swallow up *(SYN.)* consume, absorb, engulf, assimilate.
(ANT.) exude, dispense, expel, discharge.
swarm *(SYN.)* throng, horde, crowd.
swarthy *(SYN.)* sable, dark.
(ANT.) bright, light.
swear *(SYN.)* declare, state, affirm, vouchsafe, curse, maintain.
(ANT.) demur, oppose, deny, contradict.
sweat *(SYN.)* perspiration, perspire.
sweeping *(SYN.)* extensive, wide, general, broad, tolerant, comprehensive, vast.
(ANT.) restricted, confined.
sweet *(SYN.)* engaging, luscious, pure, clean, fresh, melodious, pleasant.
(ANT.) bitter, harsh, nasty, irascible, discordant, irritable, acrid.
swell *(SYN.)* increase, grow, expand, enlarge.
(ANT.) diminish, shrink.
swift *(SYN.)* quick, fast, fleet, speedy, rapid, expeditious.
swindle *(SYN.)* bilk, defraud, con, deceive, cheat, guile, deception, deceit.
(ANT.) sincerity, honesty, fairness.
swing *(SYN.)* rock, sway, wave.
switch *(SYN.)* shift, change, turn.
swoon *(SYN.)* faint.
symbol *(SYN.)* sign, character.
sympathetic *(SYN.)* considerate, compassionate, gentle, benevolent, good, tender, affable, merciful, thoughtful.
(ANT.) unkind, merciless, unsympathetic, indifferent, intolerant, cruel.
sympathy *(SYN.)* compassion, agreement, tenderness, commiseration, pity.
(ANT.) indifference, unconcern, antipathy, malevolence.
symptom *(SYN.)* indication, sign.
synopsis *(SYN.)* outline, digest.
synthetic *(SYN.)* counterfeit, artificial, phony, unreal, bogus, sham.
(ANT.) natural, true, genuine.
system *(SYN.)* organization, procedure, regularity, arrangement, mode, order.
(ANT.) confusion, chance, disorder.
systematic *(SYN.)* orderly, organized.
(ANT.) irregular, random.

table *(SYN.)* catalog, list, schedule, postpone, chart, index, shelve, delay, put off.
tablet *(SYN.)* pad, notebook, capsule, sketchpad, pill, lozenge.
taboo *(SYN.)* banned, prohibited, forbidden, restriction.
(ANT.) accepted, allowed, sanctioned.
tacit *(SYN.)* understood, assumed, implied.
taciturn *(SYN.)* quiet, withdrawn, reserved.
tack *(SYN.)* add, join, attach, clasp, fasten.
tackle *(SYN.)* rigging, gear, apparatus, equipment, grab, seize, catch, down, throw, try, undertake.
tacky *(SYN.)* gummy, sticky, gooey.
tact *(SYN.)* dexterity, poise, diplomacy, judgment, savoirfaire, skill, finesse, sense, prudence, adroitness, address.
(ANT.) incompetence, vulgarity, blunder, rudeness, insensitivity, grossness.
tactical *(SYN.)* foxy, cunning, proficient, deft, adroit, clever, expert.
(ANT.) blundering, gauche, clumsy, inept.
tactics *(SYN.)* plan, strategy, approach, maneuver, course, scheme.
tag *(SYN.)* sticker, label, mark, identification, marker, name.
tail *(SYN.)* rear, back, follow, end, shadow, pursue, trail, heel.
tailor *(SYN.)* modiste, couturier, modify, redo, shape, fashion.
taint *(SYN.)* spot, stain, tarnish, soil, mark, discolor.
(ANT.) cleanse, disinfect, clean.
tainted *(SYN.)* crooked, impure, vitiated, profligate, debased, spoiled, corrupted, depraved, dishonest, contaminated, putrid, unsound.
take *(SYN.)* accept, grasp, catch, confiscate, clutch, adopt, assume, receive, bring, attract, claim, necessitate, steal, ensnare, capture, demand, select, appropriate, obtain, captivate, hold, seize, win, escort, note, record, rob, shoplift, get, remove, gain, choose.
taking *(SYN.)* charming, captivating, winning, attractive.
takeover *(SYN.)* revolution, merger, usurpation, confiscation.
tale *(SYN.)* falsehood, history, yarn,

chronicle, account, fable, fiction, narration, story, narrative, anecdote.

talent *(SYN.)* capability, knack, skill, endowment, gift, cleverness, aptitude, ability, cleverness, genius.
(ANT.) *ineptitude, incompetence, stupidity.*

talented *(SYN.)* skillful, smart, adroit, dexterous, clever, apt, quick-witted, witty, ingenious.
(ANT.) *dull, clumsy, awkward, unskilled, stupid, slow.*

talk *(SYN.)* conversation, gossip, report, speech, communicate, discuss, confer, chatter, conference, preach, dialogue, reason, jabber, discourse, lecture, communication, consul, plead, argue, converse, rant, chat, mutter, speak, rangue, rumor, deliberate, discussion.
(ANT.) *silence, correspondence, meditation, writing.*

talkative *(SYN.)* glib, communicative, chattering, loquacious, voluble, garrulous, chatty.
(ANT.) *uncommunicative, laconic, reticent, silent.*

tall *(SYN.)* elevated, high, towering, big, lofty, imposing, gigantic.
(ANT.) *tiny, low, short, small, stunted.*

tally *(SYN.)* score, count, compute, reckon, calculate, estimate, list, figure, correspond, agree, match, check.

tame *(SYN.)* domesticated, dull, insipid, docile, broken, uninteresting, gentle, subdued, insipid, flat, unexciting, boring, empty, break, domesticate, mild, tedious, domestic, submissive.
(ANT.) *spirited, savage, wild, exciting, animated, undomesticated.*

tamper *(SYN.)* mix in, interrupt, interfere, meddle, interpose.

tang *(SYN.)* zest, sharpness, tartness, taste.

tangible *(SYN.)* material, sensible, palpable, corporeal, bodily.
(ANT.) *metaphysical, mental, spiritual.*

tangle *(SYN.)* confuse, knot, snarl, twist, ensnare, embroil, implicate.

tangy *(SYN.)* pungent, peppery, seasoned, sharp, tart.

tantalize *(SYN.)* tease, tempt, entice, titillate, stimulate, frustrate.

tantrum *(SYN.)* outburst, fit, fury, flareup, conniption, rampage.

tap *(SYN.)* pat, rap, hit, strike, blow, faucet, spout, spigot, bunghole.

tape *(SYN.)* ribbon, strip, fasten, bandage, bind, record, tie.

taper *(SYN.)* narrow, candle, decrease, lessen.

tardy *(SYN.)* slow, delayed, overdue, late, belated.
(ANT.) *prompt, timely, punctual, early.*

target *(SYN.)* aim, goal, object, objective.

tariff *(SYN.)* duty, tax, levy, rate.

tarnish *(SYN.)* discolor, blight, defile, sully, spot, befoul, disgrace, stain.
(ANT.) *honor, purify, cleanse, bleach, decorate, shine, gleam, sparkle.*

tarry *(SYN.)* dawdle, loiter, linger, dally, remain, delay, procrastinate.

tart *(SYN.)* sour, acrid, pungent, acid, sharp, distasteful, bitter.
(ANT.) *mellow, sweet, delicious, pleasant.*

task *(SYN.)* work, job, undertaking, labor, chore, duty, stint.

taste *(SYN.)* tang, inclination, liking, sensibility, flavor, savor, try, sip, sample, zest, experience, undergo, appreciation, relish, discrimination, discernment, judgment.
(ANT.) *indelicacy, disinclination, antipathy, insipidity.*

tasteful *(SYN.)* elegant, choice, refined, suitable, artistic.
(ANT.) *offensive, unbecoming.*

tasteless *(SYN.)* flavorless, insipid, unpalatable, rude, unrefined, uncultivated, boorish, uninteresting.

tasty *(SYN.)* delectable, delicious, luscious, palatable, tempting.

tattered *(SYN.)* ragged, torn, shoddy, shabby, frazzled, frayed, tacky, seedy.

tattle *(SYN.)* inform, divulge, disclose, blab, reveal.

taunt *(SYN.)* tease, deride, flout, scoff, sneer, mock, annoy, pester, bother, ridicule, jeer.
(ANT.) *praise, compliment, laud, flatter.*

taunting *(SYN.)* ironic, caustic, cutting, sardonic, derisive, biting, acrimonious, sarcastic, satirical, sneering.
(ANT.) *pleasant, agreeable, affable, amiable.*

taut *(SYN.)* tight, constricted, firm, stretched, snug, tense, extended.
(ANT.) *slack, loose, relaxed, open, lax.*

tavern *(SYN.)* pub, bar, cocktail lounge.

tawdry *(SYN.)* pretentious, showy, vulgar, tasteless, sordid, garish.

tax *(SYN.)* duty, assessment, excise, levy, toll, burden, strain, tribute, tariff, assess, encumber, overload, impost, custom, exaction, rate.
(ANT.) reward, gift, remuneration, wages.

taxi *(SYN.)* cab, taxicab.

teach *(SYN.)* inform, school, educate, train, inculcate, instruct, instill, tutor.
(ANT.) misinform, misguide.

teacher *(SYN.)* tutor, instructor, professor, lecturer.

team *(SYN.)* company, band, party, crew, gang, group.

teamwork *(SYN.)* collaboration, cooperation.

tear *(SYN.)* rend, shred, sunder, cleave, rip, lacerate, teardrop, disunite, rend, divide, drop, wound, split, slit, sever.
(ANT.) mend, repair, join, unite, sew.

tearful *(SYN.)* sad, weeping, crying, sobbing, weepy, lachrymose.

tease *(SYN.)* badger, harry, bother, irritate, nag, pester, taunt, vex, annoy, disturb, harass, worry, tantalize, plague, aggravate, provoke, torment.
(ANT.) please, delight, soothe, comfort, gratify.

technical *(SYN.)* industrial, technological, specialized, mechanical.

technique *(SYN.)* system, method, routine, approach, procedure.

tedious *(SYN.)* boring, dilatory, humdrum, sluggish, monotonous, irksome, dreary, dull, tiring, burdensome, tiresome, wearisome, tardy.
(ANT.) interesting, entertaining, engaging, exciting, amusing, quick.

teem *(SYN.)* abound, swarm.

teeming *(SYN.)* overflowing, bountiful, abundant, ample, profuse, plenteous, rich, copious.
(ANT.) scant, scarce, deficient, insufficient.

teeter *(SYN.)* sway, hesitate, hem and haw, waver.

telecast *(SYN.)* broadcast.

televise *(SYN.)* telecast.

tell *(SYN.)* report, mention, state, betray, announce, recount, relate, narrate, rehearse, mention, utter, confess, disclose, direct, request, acquaint, instruct, notify, inform, discover, determine, reveal, divulge.

telling *(SYN.)* persuasive, convincing, forceful, effective.

telltale *(SYN.* revealing, informative, suggestive, meaningful.

temerity *(SYN.)* rashness, foolhardiness, audacity, boldness, recklessness, precipitancy.
(ANT.) prudence, wariness, caution, hesitation, timidity.

temper *(SYN.)* fury, choler, exasperation, anger, passion, petulance, disposition, nature, rage, soothe, soften, wrath, indignation, irritation, pacify, animosity, mood, resentment.
(ANT.) peace, self-control, forbearance, conciliation.

temperament *(SYN.)* humor, mood, temper, nature, disposition.

temperamental *(SYN.)* testy, moody, touchy, sensitive, irritable.
(ANT.) calm, unruffled, serene.

temperance *(SYN.)* abstinence, sobriety, self-denial, forbearance, abstention.
(ANT.) intoxication, excess, self-indulgence, gluttony, wantonness.

temperate *(SYN.)* controlled, moderate, cool, calm, restrained.
(ANT.) excessive, extreme, prodigal.

tempest *(SYN.)* draft, squall, wind, blast, gust, storm, hurricane, commotion, tumult, zephyr.
(ANT.) calm, tranquillity, peace.

tempo *(SYN.)* measure, beat, cadence, rhythm.

temporal *(SYN.)* mundane, earthly, lay, profane, worldly, terrestrial, laic.
(ANT.) spiritual, ecclesiastical, unworldly, religious, heavenly.

temporary *(SYN.)* brief, momentary, shortlived, fleeting, ephemeral, passing, short, transient.
(ANT.) lasting, permanent, immortal, everlasting, timeless, abiding.

tempt *(SYN.)* entice, allure, lure, attract, seduce, invite, magnetize.

tenacious *(SYN.)* persistent, determined, unchanging, unyielding.

tenable *(SYN.)* correct, practical, rational, reasonable, sensible, defensible.

tenacity *(SYN.)* perseverance, steadfastness, industry, constancy, persistence, pertinacity.

(ANT.) laziness, rest, cessation, idleness, sloth.

tenant *(SYN.)* renter, lessee, lodger, lease-holder, dweller, resident.

tend *(SYN.)* escort, follow, care for, lackey, watch, protect, take care of, attend, guard, serve.

tendency *(SYN.)* drift, inclination, proneness, leaning, bias, aim, leaning, disposition, predisposition, propensity, trend, impulse.

(ANT.) disinclination, aversion, deviation.

tender *(SYN.)* sympathetic, sore, sensitive, painful, gentle, meek, delicate, fragile, proffer, bland, mild, loving, offer, affectionate, soothing, propose, moderate, soft.

(ANT.) rough, severe, fierce, chewy, tough, cruel, unfeeling, harsh.

tenderfoot *(SYN.)* novice, apprentice, beginner, amateur.

tenderhearted *(SYN.)* kind, sympathetic, merciful, softhearted, understanding, sentimental, affectionate, gentle, sensitive.

tenderness *(SYN.)* attachment, kindness, love, affection, endearment.

(ANT.) repugnance, indifference, aversion, hatred, repulsive.

tenet *(SYN.)* dogma, belief, precept, doctrine, creed, opinion.

(ANT.) deed, conduct, practice, performance.

tense *(SYN.)* strained, stretched, excited, tight, nervous.

(ANT.) loose, placid, lax, relaxed.

tension *(SYN.)* stress, strain, pressure, anxiety, apprehension, distress.

tentative *(SYN.)* hypothetical, indefinite, probationary, conditional.

tenure *(SYN.)* administration, time, regime, term.

tepid *(SYN.)* temperate, mild, lukewarm.

(ANT.) boiling, scalding, passionate, hot.

term *(SYN.)* period, limit, time, boundary, duration, name, phrase, interval, session, semester, expression, word.

terminal *(SYN.)* eventual, final, concluding, decisive, ending, fatal, latest, last, ultimate, conclusive.

(ANT.) original, first, rudimentary, incipient, inaugural.

terminate *(SYN.)* close, end, finish,

abolish, complete, cease, stop, conclude, expire, culminate.

(ANT.) establish, begin, initiate, start, commence.

terminology *(SYN.)* vocabulary, nomenclature, terms, phraseology.

terms *(SYN.)* stipulations, agreement, conditions, provisions.

terrible *(SYN.)* frightful, dire, awful, gruesome, horrible shocking, horrifying, terrifying, horrid, hideous, appalling, shocking.

(ANT.) secure, happy, joyous, pleasing, safe.

terrific *(SYN.)* superb, wonderful, glorious, great, magnificent, divine, colossal, sensational, marvelous.

terrify *(SYN.)* dismay, intimidate, startle, terrorize, appall, frighten, petrify, astound, alarm, affright, horrify, scare.

(ANT.) soothe, allay, reassure, compose, embolden.

territory *(SYN.)* dominion, province, quarter, section, country, division, region, domain, area, place, district.

terror *(SYN.)* fear, alarm, dismay, horror, dread, consternation, fright, panic.

(ANT.) calm, security, assurance, peace.

terse *(SYN.)* concise, incisive, succinct, summary, condensed, compact, neat, pithy, summary.

(ANT.) verbose, wordy, lengthy, prolix.

test *(SYN.)* exam, examination, trial, quiz, analyze, verify, validate.

testify *(SYN.)* depose, warrant, witness, state, attest, swear.

testimony *(SYN.)* evidence, attestation, declaration, proof, witness, confirmation.

(ANT.) refutation, argument, disproof, contradiction.

testy *(SYN.)* ill-natured, irritable, snappish, waspish, fractious, fretful, touchy, ill-tempered, peevish, petulant.

(ANT.) pleasant, affable, good-tempered, genial, good-natured.

tether *(SYN.)* tie, hamper, restraint, bridle.

text *(SYN.)* textbook, book, manual.

textile *(SYN.)* material, cloth, goods, fabric.

texture *(SYN.)* construction, structure, make-up, composition, grain, finish.

thankful *(SYN.)* obliged, grateful, appreciative.

(ANT.) thankless, ungrateful, resenting.

thaw *(SYN.)* liquefy, melt, dissolve.

(ANT.) solidify, freeze.

theater *(SYN.)* arena, playhouse, battlefield, stadium, hall.

theatrical *(SYN.)* ceremonious, melodramatic, stagy, artificial, affected, dramatic, showy, dramatic, compelling.

(ANT.) unemotional, subdued, modest, unaffected.

theft *(SYN.)* larceny, robbery, stealing, plunder, burglary, pillage, thievery, depredation.

theme *(SYN.)* motive, topic, argument, subject, thesis, text, point, paper, essay, composition.

theoretical *(SYN.)* bookish, learned, scholarly, pedantic, academic, formal, erudite, scholastic.

(ANT.) practical, ignorant, commonsense, simple.

theory *(SYN.)* doctrine, guess, presupposition, postulate, assumption, hypothesis, speculation.

(ANT.) practice, verity, fact, proof.

therefore *(SYN.)* consequently, thence so, accordingly, hence, then.

thick *(SYN.)* compressed, heavy, compact, viscous, close, concentrated, crowded, syrupy, dense.

(ANT.) watery, slim, thin, sparse, dispersed, dissipated.

thief *(SYN.)* burglar, robber, criminal.

thin *(SYN.)* diluted, flimsy, lean, narrow, slender, spare, emaciated, diaphanous, gauzy, meager, slender, tenuous, slim, rare, sparse, scanty, lank, gossamer, scanty, slight.

(ANT.) fat, wide, broad, thick, bulky.

think *(SYN.)* picture, contemplate, ponder, esteem, intend, mean, imagine, deliberate, contemplate, recall, speculate, recollect, deem, apprehend, consider, devise, plan, judge, purpose, reflect, suppose, assume, meditate, muse.

(ANT.) forget, conjecture, guess.

thirst *(SYN.)* appetite, desire, craving, longing.

thirsty *(SYN.)* arid, dry, dehydrated, parched, craving, desirous.

(ANT.) satisfied.

thorn *(SYN.)* spine, barb, prickle, nettle, bramble.

thorough *(SYN.)* entire, complete, perfect, total, finished, unbroken, perfect, careful, thoroughgoing, consummate, undivided.

(ANT.) unfinished, careless, slapdash, imperfect, haphazard, lacking.

thoroughfare *(SYN.)* avenue, street, parkway, highway, boulevard.

(ANT.) byway.

though *(SYN.)* in any case, notwithstanding, however, nevertheless.

thought *(SYN.)* consideration, pensive, attentive, heedful, prudent, dreamy, reflective, introspective, meditation, notion, view, deliberation, sentiment, fancy, idea, impression, reasoning, contemplation, judgment, regard.

(ANT.) thoughtlessness.

thoughtful *(SYN.)* considerate, attentive, dreamy, pensive, provident, introspective, meditative, cautious, heedful, kind, courteous, friendly, pensive.

(ANT.) thoughtless, heedless, inconsiderate, rash, precipitous, selfish.

thoughtless *(SYN.)* inattentive, unconcerned, negligent, lax, desultory, inconsiderate, careless, imprudent, inaccurate, neglectful, indiscreet, remiss.

(ANT.) meticulous, accurate, nice, careful.

thrash *(SYN.)* whip, beat, defeat, flog, punish, flog, strap, thresh.

thread *(SYN.)* yarn, strand, filament, fiber, string, cord.

threadbare *(SYN.)* shabby, tacky, worn, ragged, frayed.

threat *(SYN.)* menace, warning, danger, hazard, jeopardy, omen.

threaten *(SYN.)* caution, warning, forewarn, menace, intimidate, loom.

threatening *(SYN.)* imminent, nigh, approaching, impending, overhanging, sinister, foreboding.

(ANT.) improbable, retreating, afar, distant, remote.

threshold *(SYN.)* edge, verge, start, beginning, doorsill, commencement.

thrift *(SYN.)* prudence, conservation, saving, economy.

thrifty *(SYN.)* saving, economical, sparing, frugal, provident, stingy, saving, parsimonious.

(ANT.) wasteful, spendthrift, intemperate

self-indulgent, extravagant.

thrill *(SYN.)* arouse, rouse, excite, stimulation, excitement, tingle.
(ANT.) bore.

thrive *(SYN.)* succeed, flourish, grow, prosper.
(ANT.) expire, fade, shrivel, die, fail, languish.

throb *(SYN.)* pound, pulsate, palpitate, beat, pulse.

throe *(SYN.)* pang, twinge, distress, suffering, pain, ache, grief, agony.
(ANT.) pleasure, relief, ease, solace, comfort.

throng *(SYN.)* masses, press, crowd, bevy, populace, swarm, rabble, horde, host, mass, teem, mob, multitude.

throttle *(SYN.)* smother, choke, strangle.

through *(SYN.)* completed, done, finished, over.

throughout *(SYN.)* all over, everywhere, during.

throw *(SYN.)* propel, cast, pitch, toss, hurl, send, thrust, fling.
(ANT.) retain, pull, draw, haul, hold

thrust *(SYN.)* jostle, push, promote, crowd, force, drive, hasten, push, press, shove, urge.
(ANT.) ignore, falter, retreat, drag, oppose, halt.

thug *(SYN.)* mobster, hoodlum, mugger, gangster, assassin, gunman.

thump *(SYN.)* blow, strike, knock, jab, poke, pound, beat, clout, bat, rap, bang.

thunderstruck *(SYN.)* amazed, astounded, astonished, awed, flabbergasted, surprised, dumbfounded, bewildered, spellbound.

thus *(SYN.)* hence, therefore, accordingly, so, consequently.

thwart *(SYN.)* defeat, frustrate, prevent, foil, stop, baffle, circumvent hinder, obstruct, disappoint, balk, outwit.
(ANT.) promote, accomplish, fulfill, help, further.

ticket *(SYN.)* stamp, label, tag, seal, token, pass, summons, certificate, ballot, sticker, slate, citation.

tickle *(SYN.)* delight, entertain, thrill, amuse, titillate, excite.

ticklish *(SYN.)* fragile, delicate, tough, difficult.

tidings *(SYN.)* message, report, information, word, intelligence, news.

tidy *(SYN.)* trim, clear, neat, precise, spruce, orderly, shipshape.
(ANT.) disheveled, unkempt, sloppy, dirty, slovenly.

tie *(SYN.)* bond, join, relationship, bind, restrict, fetter, connect, conjunction, association, alliance, union, fasten, engage, attach, restrain, oblige, link, affinity.
(ANT.) separation, disunion, unfasten, open, loose, untie, free, isolation.

tier *(SYN.)* line, row, level, deck, layer.

tiff *(SYN.)* bicker, squabble, argue, row, clash, dispute, altercation.

tight *(SYN.)* firm, taut, penny-pinching, constricted, snug, taut, parsimonious, secure, fast, strong, sealed, fastened, watertight, locked, close, compact, stingy.
(ANT.) slack, lax, open, relaxed, loose.

till *(SYN.)* plow, work, moneybox, depository, cultivate, vault.

tilt *(SYN.)* slant, slope, incline, tip, lean.

timber *(SYN.)* lumber, wood, logs.

time *(SYN.)* epoch, span, term, age, duration, interim, period, tempo, interval, space, spell, season.

timeless *(SYN.)* unending, lasting, perpetual, endless, immemorial.
(ANT.) temporary, mortal, temporal.

timely *(SYN.)* prompt, exact, punctual, ready, precise.
(ANT.) slow, dilatory, tardy, late.

timepiece *(SYN.)* clock, watch.

timetable *(SYN.)* list, schedule.

timid *(SYN.)* coy, humble, sheepish, abashed, embarrassed, modest, bashful, diffident, shamefaced, retiring, fearful, faint-hearted, shy, timorous.
(ANT.) gregarious, bold, daring, adventurous, fearless, outgoing.

tinge *(SYN.)* color, tint, dye, stain, flavor, imbue, season, impregnate.

tingle *(SYN.)* shiver, chime, prickle.

tinker *(SYN.)* potter, putter, fiddle with, dawdle, dally, dabble.

tinkle *(SYN.)* sound, peal, ring, jingle, chime, toll.

tint *(SYN.)* color, tinge, dye, stain, hue, tone, shade.

tiny *(SYN.)* minute, little, petty, wee, slight, diminutive, miniature, small, insignificant, trivial, puny.
(ANT.) huge, large, immense, big, enor-

mous.

tip *(SYN.)* point, end, top, peak, upset, tilt, reward, gift, gratuity, clue, hint, suggestion, inkling.

tirade *(SYN.)* outburst, harangue, scolding.

tire *(SYN.)* jade, tucker, bore, weary, exhaust, weaken, wear out, fatigue.

(ANT.) restore, revive, exhilarate, amuse, invigorate, refresh.

tired *(SYN.)* weary, exhausted, fatigued, run-down, sleepy, faint, spent, wearied, worn, jaded.

(ANT.) rested, fresh, hearty, invigorated, energetic, tireless, eager.

tireless *(SYN.)* active, enthusiastic, energetic, strenuous.

(ANT.) exhausted, wearied, fatigued.

tiresome *(SYN.)* dull, boring, monotonous, tedious.

(ANT.) interesting.

titan *SYN.)* colossus, powerhouse, mammoth.

title *(SYN.)* epithet, privilege, name, appellation, claim, denomination, due, heading, ownership, right, deed, designation.

toast *(SYN.)* salutation, pledge, celebration.

toddle *(SYN.)* stumble, wobble, shuffle.

toil *(SYN.)* labor, drudgery, work, travail, performance, business, achievement, employment, occupation, slave, sweat, effort.

(ANT.) recreation, ease, vacation, relax, loll, play, leisure, repose.

token *(SYN.)* mark, sign, sample, indication, evidence, symbol.

tolerant *(SYN.)* extensive, vast, considerate, broad, patient, large, sweeping, liberal, wide.

(ANT.) intolerant, bigoted, biased, restricted, narrow, confined.

tolerate *(SYN.)* endure, allow, bear, authorize, permit, brook, stand, abide.

(ANT.) forbid, protest, prohibit, discriminating, unreasonable.

toll *(SYN.)* impost, burden, rate, assessment, duty, custom, excise, tribute, levy, burden, strain.

(ANT.) reward, wages, gift, remuneration.

tomb *(SYN.)* vault, monument, catacomb, grave, mausoleum.

tone *(SYN.)* noise, sound, mood, manner,

expression, cadence.

tongs *(SYN.)* tweezers, hook, grapnel, forceps.

tongue *(SYN.)* diction, lingo, cant, jargon, vernacular, dialect, idiom, speech, phraseology.

(ANT.) nonsense, drivel, babble, gibberish.

too *(SYN.)* furthermore, moreover, similarly, also, in addition, besides, likewise.

tool *(SYN.)* devise, medium, apparatus, agent, implement, utensil, agent, vehicle, instrument.

(ANT.) preventive, hindrance, impediment, obstruction.

top *(SYN.)* crown, pinnacle, peak, tip, cover, cap, zenith, apex, crest, chief, head, summit.

(ANT.) bottom, foundation, base, foot.

topic *(SYN.)* subject, thesis, issue, argument, matter, theme, point.

topple *(SYN.)* collapse, sink, fall, tumble.

torment *(SYN.)* pain, woe, pester, ache, distress, misery, harass, throe, annoy, vex, torture, anguish, suffering, misery.

(ANT.) relief, comfort, ease, gratify, delight.

torpid *(SYN.)* sluggish, idle, lazy, inert, inactive, supine, slothful, indolent, motionless, lethargic.

(ANT.) alert, assiduous, diligent, active.

torpor *(SYN.)* lethargy, daze, numbness, stupor, drowsiness, insensibility, languor.

(ANT.) wakefulness, liveliness, activity, alertness, readiness.

torrent *(SYN.)* flood, downpour, deluge.

torrid *(SYN.)* scorching, ardent, impetuous, passionate, scalding, warm, fiery, hot-blooded, sultry, tropical, intense, sweltering, burning, hot.

(ANT.) passionless, impassive, cold, frigid, apathetic, freezing, phlegmatic, indifferent, temperate.

torso *(SYN.)* form, frame, body.

(ANT.) soul, mind, spirit, intellect.

torture *(SYN.)* anguish, badger, plague, distress, ache, torment, pester, pain, hound, agony, woe, worry, vex, persecute, suffering, throe, afflict, misery.

(ANT.) aid, relief, comfort, ease, support, encourage, mitigation.

toss *(SYN.)* throw, cast, hurl, pitch,

tumble, thrust, pitch, fling, propel.
(ANT.) retain, pull, draw, haul, hold.

total *(SYN.)* entire, complete, concluded, finished, thorough, whole, entirely, collection, aggregate, conglomeration, unbroken, perfect, undivided, consummate, full.
(ANT.) part, element, imperfect, unfinished, ingredient, particular, lacking.

tote *(SYN.)* move, transfer, convey, drag, carry.

totter *(SYN.)* falter, stagger, reel, sway, waver, stumble, wobble.

touch *(SYN.)* finger, feel, handle, move, affect, concern, mention, hint, trace, suggestion, knack, skill, ability, talent.

touch-and-go *(SYN.)* dangerous, risky, perilous, hazardous.

touching *(SYN.)* pitiable, affecting, moving, sad, adjunct, bordering, tangent, poignant, tender, effective, impressive, adjacent.
(ANT.) removed, enlivening, animated, exhilarating.

touchy *(SYN.)* snappish, irritable, fiery, choleric, testy, hot, irascible, nervous, excitable, petulant, sensitive, short-tempered, jumpy, peevish.
(ANT.) composed, agreeable, tranquil, calm, serene, stolid, cool.

tough *(SYN.)* sturdy, difficult, trying, vicious, incorrigible, troublesome, hard, stout, leathery, strong, laborious, inedible, sinewy, cohesive, firm, callous, obdurate, vicious.
(ANT.) vulnerable, submissive, easy, brittle, facile, weak, fragile, compliant, tender, frail.

toughness *(SYN.)* stamina, sturdiness, fortitude, durability, intensity, force, might, stoutness, power, sturdiness, vigor.
(ANT.) weakness, feebleness, infirmity, frailty.

tour *(SYN.)* rove, travel, go, visit, excursion, ramble, journey, roam.
(ANT.) stop, stay.

tourist *(SYN.)* traveler, sightseer, vagabond, voyager.

tournament *(SYN.)* tourney, match, contest, competition.

tout *(SYN.)* vend, importune, peddle, solicit, sell, hawk.

tow *(SYN.)* tug, take out, unsheathe, haul,

draw, remove, extract, pull, drag.
(ANT.) propel, drive.

towering *(SYN.)* elevated, exalted, high, lofty, tall, proud, eminent.
(ANT.) base, mean, stunted, small, tiny, low.

town *(SYN.)* hamlet, village, community, municipality.

toxic *(SYN.)* deadly, poisonous, fatal, lethal, harmful.
(ANT.) beneficial.

toy *(SYN.)* play, romp, frolic, gamble, stake, caper, plaything, wager, revel.

trace *(SYN.)* stigma, feature, indication, trait, mark, stain, scar, sign, trial, trace, suggestion, characteristic, vestige, symptoms.

track *(SYN.)* persist, pursue, follow, sign, mark, spoor, trace, path, route, road, carry, hunt, chase.
(ANT.) escape, evade, abandon, flee, elude.

tract *(SYN.)* area, region, territory, district, expanse, domain.

tractable *(SYN.)* yielding, deferential, submissive, dutiful, compliant, obedient.
(ANT.) rebellious, intractable, insubordinate, obstinate.

trade *(SYN.)* business, traffic, commerce, dealing, craft, occupation, profession, livelihood, swap, barter, exchange.

trademark *(SYN.)* logo, brand name, identification, emblem, insignia, monogram.

tradition *(SYN.)* custom, legend, folklore, belief, rite, practice.

traduce *(SYN.)* defame, malign, vilify, revile, abuse, asperse, scandalize, disparage.
(ANT.) protect, honor, cherish, praise, respect, support, extol.

tragedy *(SYN.)* unhappiness, misfortune, misery, adversity, catastrophe.

tragic *(SYN.)* miserable, unfortunate, depressing, melancholy, mournful.
(ANT.) happy, cheerful, comic.

trail *(SYN.)* persist, pursue, chase, follow, drag, draw, hunt, track.
(ANT.) evade, flee, abandon, elude, escape.

train *(SYN.)* direct, prepare, aim, point, level, teach, drill, tutor, bid, instruct, order, command.
(ANT.) distract, deceive, misguide, mis-

direct.

traipse *(SYN.)* roam, wander, saunter, meander.

trait *(SYN.)* characteristic, feature, attribute, peculiarity, mark, quality, property.

traitor *(SYN.)* turncoat, betrayer, spy, double-dealer, conspirator.

traitorous *(SYN.)* disloyal, faithless, apostate, false, recreant, perfidious, treasonable, treacherous.

(ANT.) devoted, true, loyal, constant.

tramp *(SYN.)* bum, beggar, rover, hobo, march, stamp, stomp, vagabond, wanderer, vagrant.

(ANT.) laborer, worker, gentleman.

trample *(SYN.)* crush, stomp, squash.

tranquil *(SYN.)* composed, calm, dispassionate, imperturbable, peaceful, pacific, placid, quiet, still, serene, undisturbed, unruffled.

(ANT.) frantic, stormy, excited, disturbed, upset, turbulent, wild.

tranquillity *(SYN.)* calmness, calm, hush, peace, quiet, quiescence, quietude, repose, serenity, rest, stillness, silence, placid.

(ANT.) disturbance, agitation, excitement, tumult, noise.

transact *(SYN.)* conduct, manage, execute, treat, perform.

transaction *(SYN.)* business, deal, affair, deed, settlement, occurrence, negotiation, proceeding.

transcend *(SYN.)* overstep, overshadow, exceed.

transcribe *(SYN.)* write, copy, rewrite, record.

transfer *(SYN.)* dispatch, send, transmit, remove, transport, transplant, consign, move, shift, reasign, assign, relegate.

transform *(SYN.)* change, convert, alter, modify, transfigure, shift, vary, veer.

(ANT.) establish, continue, settle, preserve, stabilize.

transgression *(SYN.)* atrocity, indignity, offense, insult, outrage, aggression, injustice, crime, misdeed, trespass, sin, wrong, vice.

(ANT.) innocence, morality, gentleness, right.

transient *(SYN.)* ephemeral, evanescent, brief, fleeting, momentary, temporary, short-lived.

(ANT.) immortal, abiding, permanent, lasting, timeless, established.

transition *(SYN.)* change, variation, modification.

translate *(SYN.)* decipher, construe, decode, elucidate, explicate, explain, interpret, solve, render, unravel.

(ANT.) distort, falsify, misinterpret, confuse, misconstrue.

transmit *(SYN.)* confer, convey, communicate, divulge, disclose, impart, send, inform, relate, notify, reveal, dispatch, tell.

(ANT.) withhold, hide, conceal.

transparent *(SYN.)* crystalline, clear, limpid, lucid, translucent, thin, evident, manifest, plain, evident, explicit, obvious, open.

(ANT.) opaque, muddy, turbid, thick, questionable, ambiguous.

transpire *(SYN.)* befall, bechance, betide, happen, chance, occur.

transport *(SYN.)* carry, bear, convey, remove, move, shift, enrapture, transfer, lift, entrance, ravish, stimulate.

transpose *(SYN.)* change, switch, reverse.

trap *(SYN.)* artifice, bait, ambush, intrigue, net, lure, pitfall, ensnare, deadfall, snare, ruse, entrap, bag, trick, stratagem, wile.

trash *(SYN.)* refuse, garbage, rubbish, waste.

trashy *(SYN.)* insignificant, worthless, slight.

trauma *(SYN.)* ordeal, upheaval, jolt, shock, disturbance.

travail *(SYN.)* suffering, torment, anxiety, distress, anguish, misery, ordeal.

travel *(SYN.)* journey, go, touring, ramble, rove, voyage, cruise, tour, roam.

(ANT.) stop, stay, remain, hibernate.

travesty *(SYN.)* farce, joke, misrepresentation, counterfeit, mimicry.

treachery *(SYN.)* collusion, cabal, combination, intrigue, conspiracy, machination, disloyalty, betrayal, treason, plot.

(ANT.) allegiance, steadfastness, loyalty.

treason *(SYN.)* cabal, combination, betrayal, sedition, collusion, intrigue, conspiracy, machination, disloyalty, treachery, plot.

treasure *(SYN.)* cherish, hold dear, abundance, guard, prize, appreciate, value, riches, wealth, foster, sustain, nurture.

(ANT.) disregard, neglect, dislike, abandon, reject.

treat *(SYN.)* employ, avail, manipulate, exploit, operate, utilize, exert, act, exercise, practice, handle, manage, deal, entertain, indulge, host, negotiate, tend, attend, heal, use.
(ANT.) neglect, overlook, ignore, waste.

treaty *(SYN.)* compact, agreement, pact, bargain, covenant, alliance, marriage.
(ANT.) schism, separation, divorce.

trek *(SYN.)* tramp, hike, plod, trudge.

tremble *(SYN.)* flutter, jolt, jar, agitate, quake, quiver, quaver, rock, shake shudder, shiver, totter, sway, vibrate, waver.

trembling *(SYN.)* apprehension, alarm, dread, fright, fear, horror, terror, panic.
(ANT.) composure, calmness, tranquillity, serenity.

tremendous *(SYN.)* enormous, huge, colossal, gigantic, great, large.

tremor *(SYN.)* flutter, vibration, palpitation.

trench *(SYN.)* gully, gorge, ditch, gulch, moat, dugout, trough.

trenchant *(SYN.)* clear, emphatic, forceful, impressive, meaningful.

trend *(SYN.)* inclination, tendency, drift, course, tendency, direction.

trendy *(SYN.)* modish, faddish, stylish, voguish, popular, current.

trepidation *(SYN.)* apprehension, alarm, dread, fright, fear, horror, panic, terror.
(ANT.) boldness, bravery, fearlessness, courage, assurance.

trespass *(SYN.)* atrocity, indignity, affront, insult, outrage, offense, aggression, crime, misdeed, injustice, vice, wrong, sin.
(ANT.) evacuate, vacate, relinquish, abandon.

trespasser *(SYN.)* invader, intruder, encroacher.

trial *(SYN.)* experiment, ordeal, proof, test, examination, attempt, effort, endeavor, essay, affliction, misery, hardship, suffering, difficulty, misfortune, tribulation, trouble.
(ANT.) consolation, alleviation.

tribe *(SYN.)* group, race, clan, bunch.

tribulation *(SYN.)* anguish, distress, agony, grief, misery, sorrow, torment, suffering, woe, disaster, calamity, evil, trouble, misfortune.

(ANT.) elation, delight, joy, fun, pleasure.

tribunal *(SYN.)* arbitrators, judges, decision-makers, judiciary.

trick *(SYN.)* artifice, antic, deception, device, cheat, fraud, hoax, guile, imposture, ruse, ploy, stratagem, trickery, deceit, jest, joke, prank, defraud, subterfuge, wile, stunt.
(ANT.) exposure, candor, openness, honesty, sincerity.

trickle *(SYN.)* drip, drop, dribble, leak, seep.

tricky *(SYN.)* artifice, antic, covert, cunning, foxy, crafty, furtive, guileful, insidious, sly, shrews, stealthy, surreptitious, subtle, underhand, wily.
(ANT.) frank, candid, ingenuous, sincere, open.

trifling *(SYN.)* insignificant, frivolous, paltry, petty, trivial, small, unimportant.
(ANT.) momentous, serious, important, weighty.

trigger *(SYN.)* generate, provoke, prompt, motivate, activate.

trim *(SYN.)* nice, clear, orderly, precise, tidy, spruce, adorn, bedeck, clip, shave, prune, cut, shear, compact, neat, decorate, embellish, garnish.
(ANT.) deface, deform, spoil, mar, important, serious, momentous, weighty.

trimmings *(SYN.)* accessories, adornments, decorations, garnish, ornaments.

trinket *(SYN.)* bead, token, memento, bauble, charm, knickknack.

trio *(SYN.)* threesome, triad, triple.

trip *(SYN.)* expedition, cruise, stumble, err, journey, jaunt, passage, blunder, bungle, slip, excursion, tour, pilgrimage, voyage, travel.

trite *(SYN.)* common, banal, hackneyed, ordinary, stereotyped, stale.
(ANT.) modern, fresh, momentous, stimulating, novel, new.

triumph *(SYN.)* conquest, achievement, success, prevail, win, jubilation, victory, ovation.
(ANT.) succumb, failure, defeat.

triumphant *(SYN.)* celebrating, exultant, joyful, exhilarated, smug.

trivial *(SYN.)* insignificant, frivolous, paltry, petty, trifling, small, unimportant.
(ANT.) momentous, important weighty, serious.

troops *(SYN.)* militia, troopers, recruits, soldiers, enlisted men.

trophy *(SYN.)* award, memento, honor, testimonial, prize.

tropical *(SYN.)* sultry, sweltering, humid, torrid.

trouble *(SYN.)* anxiety, affliction, calamity, distress, hardship, grief, pain, misery, sorrow, woe, bother, annoyance, care, embarrassment, irritation, torment, pains, worry, disorder, problem, disturbance, care, effort, exertion, toil, inconvenience, misfortune, labor.

(ANT.) console, accommodate, gratify, soothe, joy, peace.

troublemaker *(SYN.)* rebel, scamp, agitator, demon, devil, ruffian.

troublesome *(SYN.)* bothersome, annoying, distressing, irksome, disturbing, trying, arduous, vexatious, arduous, difficult, burdensome, laborious, tedious.

(ANT.) amusing, accommodating, gratifying, easy, pleasant.

trounce *(SYN.)* lash, flog, switch, whack, punish, whip, stomp.

truant *(SYN.)* delinquent, absentee, vagrant, malingerer.

truce *(SYN.)* armistice, cease-fire, interval, break, intermission, respite.

trudge *(SYN.)* march, trek, lumber, hike.

true *(SYN.)* actual, authentic, accurate, correct, exact, genuine, real, veracious, veritable, constant, honest, faithful, loyal, reliable, valid, legitimate, steadfast, sincere, trustworthy.

(ANT.) erroneous, counterfeit, false, spurious, fictitious, faithless, inconstant, fickle.

truly *(SYN.)* indeed, actually, precisely, literally, really, factually.

truncate *(SYN.)* prune, clip, pare, shorten.

truss *(SYN.)* girder, brace, framework, shoring.

trust *(SYN.)* credence, confidence, dependence, reliance, faith, trust, depend on, rely on, reckon on, believe, hope, credit, commit, entrust, confide.

(ANT.) incredulity, doubt, skepticism, mistrust.

trusted *(SYN.)* trustworthy, reliable, true, loyal, staunch, devoted.

trustworthy *(SYN.)* dependable, certain, reliable, secure, safe, sure, tried, trust.

(ANT.) fallible, dubious, questionable, unreliable, uncertain.

truth *(SYN.)* actuality, authenticity, accuracy, correctness, exactness, honesty, fact, rightness, truthfulness, veracity, verisimilitude, verity.

(ANT.) falsity, fiction, lie, untruth.

truthful *(SYN.)* frank, candid, honest, sincere, open, veracious, accurate, correct.

(ANT.) misleading, sly, deceitful.

try *(SYN.)* endeavor, attempt, strive, struggle, undertake, afflict, test, prove, torment, trouble, essay, examine, analyze, investigate, effort, aim, design, aspire, intend, mean.

(ANT.) decline, ignore, abandon, omit, neglect, comfort, console.

trying *(SYN.)* bothersome, annoying, distressing, disturbing, troublesome, arduous, vexatious, difficult, tedious.

(ANT.) amusing, easy, accommodating, pleasant, gratifying.

tryout *(SYN.)* audition, trial, chance, test.

tryst *(SYN.)* rendezvous, meeting, appointment.

tub *(SYN.)* basin, vessel, sink, bowl.

tube *(SYN.)* hose, pipe, reed.

tubular *(SYN.)* hollow, cylindrical.

tuck *(SYN.)* crease, fold, gather, bend.

tuft *(SYN.)* bunch, group, cluster.

tug *(SYN.)* pull, wrench, tow, haul, jerk.

tuition *(SYN.)* instruction, schooling, teaching, education.

tumble *(SYN.)* toss, trip, fall, sprawl, wallow, lurch, flounder, plunge, topple.

tumult *(SYN.)* chaos, agitation, commotion, confusion, disarray, disarrangement, disorder, noise, hubbub, ferment.

(ANT.) peacefulness, order, peace, certainty, tranquillity.

tune *(SYN.)* song, concord, harmony, air, melody, strain.

(ANT.) aversion, discord, antipathy.

tunnel *(SYN.)* passage, grotto, cave.

turbid *(SYN.)* dark, cloudy, thick, muddy, murky.

turf *(SYN.)* lawn, grassland, sod, grass.

turmoil *(SYN.)* chaos, agitation, commotion, confusion, disarray, disorder.

(ANT.) order, peace, certainty, quiet, tranquillity.

turn *(SYN.)* circulate, circle, invert, rotate, revolve, spin, twist, twirl, whirl,

wheel, avert, reverse, become, sour.
(ANT.) fix, stand, arrest, stop, continue, endure, proceed, perpetuate.
turncoat *(SYN.)* renegade, defector, deserter, rat, betrayer, traitor.
(ANT.) loyalist.
turret *(SYN.)* watchtower, belfry, steeple, tower, cupola, lookout.
tussle *(SYN.)* wrestle, struggle, contend, battle, fight, scuffle.
tutor *(SYN.)* instruct, prime, school, teach, train, prepare, drill.
tweak *(SYN.)* squeeze, pinch, nip.
twig *(SYN.)* sprig, branch, shoot, stem.
twilight *(SYN.)* sunset, sundown, nightfall, eventide, dusk.
twin *(SYN.)* lookalike, imitation, copy, double, replica.
twine *(SYN.)* string, cordage, rope, cord.
twinge *(SYN.)* smart, pang, pain.
twinkle *(SYN.)* shine, gleam, glisten, sparkle, glitter, shimmer, scintillate.
twirl *(SYN.)* rotate, spin, wind, turn, pivot, wheel, swivel, whirl.
twist *(SYN.)* bow, bend, crook, intertwine, curve, incline, deflect, lean, braid, distort, contort, warp, interweave, stoop, turn.
(ANT.) resist, break, straighten, stiffen.
twitch *(SYN.)* fidget, shudder, jerk.
two-faced *(SYN.)* deceitful, insincere, hypocritical, false, untrustworthy.
(ANT.) straightforward, honest.
tycoon *(SYN.)* millionaire, industrialist, businessman.
tyke *(SYN.)* rascal, urchin, brat, ragamuffin, imp.
typhoon *(SYN.)* hurricane, cyclone, storm, tornado, whirlwind, twister.
typical *(SYN.)* common, accustomed, conventional, familiar, customary.
(ANT.) marvelous, extraordinary, odd, atypical, uncommon, strange.
typify *(SYN.)* symbolize, illustrate, signify, represent, incarnate, indicate.
tyrannize *(SYN.)* oppress, victimize, threaten, brutalize, coerce.
tyrannous *(SYN.)* arbitrary, absolute, authoritative, despotic.
(ANT.) conditional, accountable, contingent, qualified, dependent.
tyrant *(SYN.)* dictator, autocrat, despot, oppressor, slave driver, martinet, disciplinarian, persecutor.

ugly *(SYN.)* hideous, homely, plain, deformed, repellent, uncomely, repulsive, ill-natured, unsightly, nasty, unpleasant, wicked, disagreeable, spiteful, surly, vicious.
(ANT.) beautiful, fair, pretty, attractive, handsome, comely, good.
ultimate *(SYN.)* extreme, latest, final, concluding, decisive, hindmost, last, terminal, utmost, greatest, maximum.
(ANT.) foremost, opening, first, beginning, initial.
umbrage *(SYN.)* anger, displeasure.
umpire *(SYN.)* judge, referee, arbitrator.
unadulterated *(SYN.)* genuine, clear, clean, immaculate, spotless, pure, absolute, untainted, sheer, bare.
(ANT.) foul, sullied, corrupt, tainted, polluted, tarnished, defiled.
unalterable *(SYN.)* fixed, unchangeable, steadfast, inflexible.
unanimity *(SYN.)* accord, unity, agreement.
unannounced *(SYN.)* hasty, precipitate, abrupt, unexpected.
(ANT.) courteous, expected, anticipated.
unassuming *(SYN.)* humble, lowly, compliant, modest, plain, meek, simple, unostentatious, retiring, submissive, unpretentious.
(ANT.) haughty, showy, pompous, proud, vain, arrogant, boastful.
unattached *(SYN.)* apart, separate, unmarried, single, free, independent.
(ANT.) committed, involved, entangled.
unavoidable *(SYN.)* inescapable, certain, inevitable, unpreventable.
unawares *(SYN.)* abruptly, suddenly, unexpectedly, off guard.
unbalanced *(SYN.)* crazy, mad, insane, deranged.
unbearable *(SYN.)* insufferable, intolerable.
(ANT.) tolerable, acceptable.
unbeliever *(SYN.)* dissenter, apostate, heretic, schismatic, nonconformist, sectary, sectarian.
unbending *(SYN.)* firm, inflexible, decided, determined, obstinate.
(ANT.) flexible.
unbiased *(SYN.)* honest, equitable, fair, impartial, reasonable, unprejudiced, just.
(ANT.) partial, fraudulent, dishonorable.

unbroken *(SYN.)* complete, uninterrupted, continuous, whole.

unburden *(SYN.)* clear, disentangle, divest, free.

uncanny *(SYN.)* amazing, remarkable, extraordinary, strange.

uncertain *(SYN.)* dim, hazy, indefinite, obscure, indistinct, unclear, undetermined, unsettled, ambiguous, unsure, doubtful, questionable, dubious, vague.
(ANT.) explicit, lucid, specific, certain, unmistakable, precise, clear.

uncertainty *(SYN.)* distrust, doubt, hesitation, incredulity, scruple, ambiguity, skepticism, uncertainty, suspense, suspicion, unbelief.
(ANT.) faith, belief, certainty, conviction, determination.

uncivil *(SYN.)* impolite, rude, discourteous.
(ANT.) polite.

uncivilized *(SYN.)* barbaric, barbarous, barbarian, brutal, crude, inhuman, cruel, merciless, rude, remorseless, uncultured, savage, unrelenting.
(ANT.) humane, kind, polite, civilized, refined.

unclad *(SYN.)* exposed, nude, naked, bare, stripped, defenseless, uncovered, open, unprotected.
(ANT.) concealed, protected, clothed, covered, dressed.

uncommon *(SYN.)* unusual, rare, odd, scarce, strange, peculiar, queer, exceptional, remarkable.
(ANT.) ordinary, usual.

uncompromising *(SYN.)* determined, dogged, firm, immovable, contumacious, headstrong, inflexible, obdurate, intractable, obstinate, pertinacious, stubborn, unyielding.
(ANT.) docile, compliant, amenable, yielding, submissive, pliable.

unconcern *(SYN.)* disinterestedness, impartiality, indifference, apathy, insensibility, neutrality.
(ANT.) affection, fervor, passion, ardor.

unconditional *(SYN.)* unqualified, unrestricted, arbitrary, absolute, pure, complete, actual, authoritative, perfect, entire, ultimate, tyrannous.
(ANT.) conditional, contingent, accountable, dependent, qualified.

unconscious *(SYN.)* lethargic, numb, comatose.

uncouth *(SYN.)* green, harsh, crude, coarse, ill-prepared, rough, raw, unfinished, unrefined, vulgar, rude, impolite, discourteous, unpolished, ill-mannered, crass.
(ANT.) well-prepared, cultivated, refined, civilized, finished.

uncover *(SYN.)* disclose, discover, betray, divulge, expose, reveal, impart, show.
(ANT.) conceal, hide, cover, obscure, cloak.

undependable *(SYN.)* changeable, unstable, uncertain, shifty, irresponsible.
(ANT.) stable, dependable, trustworthy.

under *(SYN.)* beneath, underneath, following, below, lower, downward.
(ANT.) over, above, up, higher.

undercover *(SYN.)* hidden, secret.

undergo *(SYN.)* endure, feel, stand, bear, indulge, suffer, sustain, experience, let, allow, permit, feel, tolerate.
(ANT.) overcome, discard, exclude, banish.

underhand *(SYN.)* sly, secret, sneaky, secretive, stealthy, crafty.
(ANT.) honest, open, direct, frank.

undermine *(SYN.)* demoralize, thwart, erode, weaken, subvert, sabotage.

underscore *(SYN.)* emphasize, stress.

understand *(SYN.)* apprehend, comprehend, appreciate, conceive, discern, know, grasp, hear, learn, realize, see, perceive.
(ANT.) misunderstand, mistake, misapprehend, ignore.

understanding *(SYN.)* agreement, coincidence, concord, accordance, concurrence, harmony, unison, compact, contract, arrangement, bargain, covenant, stipulation.
(ANT.) variance, difference, discord, dissension, disagreement.

understudy *(SYN.)* deputy, agent, proxy, representative, agent, alternate, lieutenant, substitute.
(ANT.) head, principal, sovereign, master.

undertake *(SYN.)* venture, attempt.

undertaking *(SYN.)* effort, endeavor, attempt, experiment, trial, essay.
(ANT.) laziness, neglect, inaction.

undersigned *(SYN.)* casual, chance, contingent, accidental, fortuitous, incidental, unintended.

(ANT.) decreed, planned, willed, calculated.

undesirable *(SYN.)* obnoxious, distasteful, objectionable, repugnant.

(ANT.) appealing, inviting, attractive.

undivided *(SYN.)* complete, intact, entire, integral, total, perfect, unimpaired, whole.

(ANT.) partial, incomplete.

undoing *(SYN.)* ruin, downfall, destruction, failure, disgrace.

undying *(SYN.)* endless, deathless, eternal, everlasting, ceaseless, immortal, infinite, perpetual, timeless.

(ANT.) transient, mortal, temporal, ephemeral, finite, impermanent.

unearthly *(SYN.)* metaphysical, ghostly, miraculous, marvelous, preternatural, superhuman, spiritual, foreign, strange, weird, supernatural.

(ANT.) physical, plain, human, natural, common, mundane.

uneducated *(SYN.)* uncultured, ignorant, illiterate, uninformed, unlearned, untaught, unlettered.

(ANT.) erudite, cultured, educated, literate, formed.

unemployed *(SYN.)* inert, inactive, idle, jobless, unoccupied.

(ANT.) working, occupied, active, industrious, employed.

uneven *(SYN.)* remaining, single, odd, unmatched, rugged, gnarled, irregular.

(ANT.) matched, even, flat, smooth.

unexceptional *(SYN.)* commonplace, trivial, customary.

unexpected *(SYN.)* immediate, hasty, surprising, instantaneous, unforeseen, abrupt, rapid, startling, sudden.

(ANT.) slowly, expected, gradual, predicted, anticipated, planned.

unfaithful *(SYN.)* treacherous, disloyal, deceitful,capricious.

(ANT.) true, loyal, steadfast, faithful.

unfasten *(SYN.)* open, expand, spread, exhibit, unbar, unlock, unfold, unseal.

(ANT.) shut, hide, conceal, close.

unfavorable *(SYN.)* antagonistic, contrary, adverse, opposed, opposite, disastrous, counteractive, unlucky.

(ANT.) benign, fortunate, lucky, propitious.

unfeeling *(SYN.)* hard, rigorous, cruel,

stern, callous, numb, hard, strict, unsympathetic, severe.

(ANT.) tender, gentle, lenient. humane.

unfold *(SYN.)* develop, create, elaborate, amplify, evolve, mature, expand.

(ANT.) wither, restrict, contract, stunt, compress.

unfurnished *(SYN.)* naked, mere, bare, exposed, stripped, plain, open, simple.

(ANT.) concealed, protected, covered.

ungainly *(SYN.)* clumsy, awkward, bungling, clownish, gawky.

(ANT.) dexterous, graceful, elegant.

unhappy *(SYN.)* sad, miserable, wretched, melancholy, distressed, depressed, wretched.

(ANT.) joyful, happy, joyous, cheerful.

unhealthy *(SYN.)* infirm, sick, diseased, sickly.

(ANT.) vigorous, well, healthy, hale.

uniform *(SYN.)* methodical, natural, customary, orderly, normal, consistent, ordinary, regular, unvarying, unchanging, systematic, steady, unvaried.

(ANT.) rare, unusual, erratic, abnormal, exceptional, changeable.

unimportant *(SYN.)* petty, trivial, paltry, trifling, insignificant, indifferent, minor, petty.

uninformed *(SYN.)* illiterate, uncultured, uneducated, ignorant, unlearned, untaught, unlettered.

(ANT.) informed, literate, erudite, cultured, educated.

uninhibited *(SYN.)* loose, open, liberated, free.

(ANT.) constrained, tense, suppressed.

unintelligible *(SYN.)* ambiguous, cryptic, dark, cloudy, abstruse, dusky, mysterious, indistinct, obscure, vague.

(ANT.) lucid, distinct, bright, clear.

uninteresting *(SYN.)* burdensome, dilatory, dreary, dull, boring, slow humdrum, monotonous, sluggish, tedious, tardy, wearisome, tiresome.

(ANT.) entertaining, exciting, quick, amusing.

union *(SYN.)* fusion, incorporation, combination, joining, concurrence, solidarity, agreement, unification, concord, harmony, alliance, unanimity, coalition, confederacy, amalgamation, league, concert, marriage.

(ANT.) schism, disagreement, separation,

discord.

unique *(SYN.)* exceptional, matchless, distinctive, choice, peculiar, singular, rare, sole, single, incomparable, uncommon, solitary, unequaled.

(ANT.) typical, ordinary, commonplace, frequent, common.

unison *(SYN.)* harmony, concurrence, understanding, accordance, concord, agreeable, coincidence.

(ANT.) disagreement, difference, discord, variance.

unite *(SYN.)* attach, blend, amalgamate, combine, conjoin, associate, connect, embody, consolidate, join, link, fuse, unify, merge.

(ANT.) sever, divide, separate, sever, disrupt, disconnect.

universal *(SYN.)* frequent, general, popular, common, familiar, prevailing, prevalent, usual.

(ANT.) scarce, odd, regional, local, extraordinary, exceptional.

unkempt *(SYN.)* sloppy, rumpled, untidy, messy, bedraggled.

(ANT.) presentable, well-groomed, tidy, neat.

unkind *(SYN.)* unfeeling, unsympathetic, unpleasant, cruel, harsh.

(ANT.) considerate, sympathetic, amiable, kind.

unlawful *(SYN.)* illegitimate, illicit, illegal, outlawed, criminal, prohibited.

(ANT.) permitted, law, honest, legal, legitimate, authorized.

unlike *(SYN.)* dissimilar, different, distinct, contrary, diverse, divergent, opposite, incongruous, variant, miscellaneous, divers.

(ANT.) conditional, accountable, contingent, qualified, dependent.

unlucky *(SYN.)* cursed, inauspicious, unfortunate.

(ANT.) prosperous, fortunate, blessed.

unmerciful *(SYN.)* cruel, merciless, heartless, brutal.

unmistakable *(SYN.)* clear, patent, plain, visible, obvious.

unnecessary *(SYN.)* pointless, needless, superfluous, purposeless.

unoccupied *(SYN.)* empty, vacant, uninhabited.

unparalleled *(SYN.)* peerless, unequaled, rare, unique, unmatched.

unpleasant *(SYN.)* offensive, disagreeable, repulsive, obnoxious, unpleasing.

unqualified *(SYN.)* inept, unfit, incapable, incompetent, unquestioned, absolute, utter.

unreasonable *(SYN.)* foolish, absurd, irrational, inconsistent, nonsensical, ridiculous, silly.

(ANT.) reasonable, sensible, sound, consistent, rational.

unruffled *(SYN.)* calm, smooth, serene, unperturbed.

unruly *(SYN.)* unmanageable, disorganized, disorderly, disobedient.

(ANT.) orderly.

unsafe *(SYN.)* hazardous, insecure, critical, dangerous, perilous, menacing, risky, precarious, threatening.

(ANT.) protected, secure, firm, safe.

unselfish *(SYN.)* bountiful, generous, liberal, giving, beneficent, magnanimous, openhanded, munificent.

(ANT.) miserly, stingy, greedy, selfish, covetous.

unsightly *(SYN.)* ugly, unattractive, hideous.

unsophisticated *(SYN.)* frank, candid, artless, ingenuous, naive, open, simple, natural.

(ANT.) sophisticated, worldly, cunning, crafty.

unsound *(SYN.)* feeble, flimsy, weak, fragile, sick, unhealthy, diseased, invalid, faulty, false.

unstable *(SYN.)* fickle, fitful, inconstant, capricious, changeable, restless, variable.

(ANT.) steady, stable, trustworthy, constant.

unswerving *(SYN.)* fast, firm, inflexible, constant, secure, stable, solid, steady, steadfast, unyielding.

(ANT.) sluggish, insecure, unsteady, unstable, loose, slow.

untainted *(SYN.)* genuine, pure, spotless, clean, clear, unadulterated, guiltless, innocent, chaste, modest, undefiled, sincere, virgin.

(ANT.) polluted, tainted, sullied, tarnished, defiled, corrupt, foul.

untamed *(SYN.)* fierce, savage, uncivilized, barbarous, outlandish, rude, undomesticated, desert, wild, frenzied, mad, turbulent, impetuous, wanton, boisterous, wayward, stormy, extravagant, tempestuous, foolish, rash, giddy, reckless.

(ANT.) quiet, gentle, calm, civilized, placid.

untidy *(SYN.)* messy, sloppy, disorderly, slovenly.

untoward *(SYN.)* disobedient, contrary, peevish, fractious, forward, petulant, obstinate, intractable, stubborn, perverse, ungovernable.

(ANT.) docile, tractable, obliging, agreeable.

unusual *(SYN.)* capricious, abnormal, devious, eccentric, aberrant, irregular, variable, remarkable, extraordinary, odd, peculiar, uncommon, strange, exceptional, unnatural.

(ANT.) methodical, regular, usual, fixed, ordinary.

unyielding *(SYN.)* fast, firm, inflexible, constant, solid, secure, stable, steadfast, unswerving, steady.

(ANT.) sluggish, slow, insecure, loose, unsteady, unstable.

upbraid *(SYN.)* blame, censure, berate, admonish, rate, lecture, rebuke, reprimand, reprehend, scold, vituperate.

(ANT.) praise, commend, approve.

uphold *(SYN.)* justify, espouse, assert, defend, maintain, vindicate.

(ANT.) oppose, submit, assault, deny, attack.

upright *(SYN.)* undeviating, right, unswerving, direct, erect, unbent, straight, fair, vertical.

(ANT.) bent, dishonest, crooked, circuitous, winding.

uprising *(SYN.)* revolution, mutiny, revolt, rebellion.

uproar *(SYN.)* noise, disorder, commotion, tumult, disturbance.

upset *(SYN.)* disturb, harass, bother, annoy, haunt, molest, inconvenience, perplex, pester, tease, plague, trouble, worry, overturned, toppled, upend, capsize, fluster, agitate.

(ANT.) soothe, relieve, please, gratify.

urbane *(SYN.)* civil, considerate, cultivated, courteous, genteel, polite, accomplished, refined, well-mannered.

(ANT.) rude, uncouth, boorish, uncivil.

urge *(SYN.)* craving, desire, longing, lust, appetite, aspiration, yearning, incite,

coax, entice, force, drive, prod, press, plead, persuade, implore, beg, recommend, advise.

(ANT.) loathing, hate, distaste, aversion, coerce, deter, dissuade, discourage.

urgency *(SYN.)* emergency, exigency, pass, pinch, strait, crisis.

urgent *(SYN.)* critical, crucial, exigent, imperative, impelling, insistent, necessary, instant, serious, pressing, cogent, important, importunate, immediate.

(ANT.) trivial, unimportant, insignificant.

usage *(SYN.)* use, treatment, custom, practice, tradition.

use *(SYN.)* custom, practice, habit, training, usage, manner, apply, avail employ, operate, utilize, exert, exhaust, handle, manage, accustom, inure, train, exploit, manipulate, spend, expend, consume.

(ANT.) disuse, neglect, waste, ignore, overlook, idleness.

useful *(SYN.)* beneficial, helpful, good, serviceable, wholesome, advantageous.

(ANT.) harmful, injurious, deleterious, destructive, detrimental.

usefulness *(SYN.)* price, merit, utility, excellence, virtue, worth, worthiness.

(ANT.) useless, cheapness, valuelessness, uselessness.

useless *(SYN.)* bootless, empty, idle, pointless, vain, valueless, worthless, abortive, fruitless, unavailing, ineffectual, vapid.

(ANT.) profitable, potent, effective.

usher *(SYN.)* guide, lead.

usual *(SYN.)* customary, common, familiar, general, normal, habitual, accustomed, everyday, ordinary, regular.

(ANT.) irregular, exceptional, rare, extraordinary, abnormal.

utensil *(SYN.)* instrument, tool, vehicle, apparatus, device, implement.

(ANT.) preventive, obstruction.

utilize *(SYN.)* use, apply, devote, busy, employ, occupy, avail.

(ANT.) reject, banish, discharge, discard.

utopian *(SYN.)* perfect, ideal, faultless, exemplary, supreme, visionary, unreal.

(ANT.) real, imperfect, actual, faulty.

utter *(SYN.)* full, perfect, whole, finished, entire, speak, say, complete, superlative.

(ANT.) imperfect, deficient, lacking, faulty, incomplete.

vacancy *(SYN.)* void, emptiness, vacuum, hollowness, blankness, vacuity, depletion, nothingness.

(ANT.) plenitude, fullness, profusion, completeness.

vacant *(SYN.)* barren, empty, blank, bare, unoccupied, void, vacuous.

(ANT.) filled, packed, employed, full, replete, busy, engaged.

vacate *(SYN.)* abjure, relinquish, abdicate, renounce, abandon, resign, surrender, desert, waive, quit, leave.

(ANT.) stay, support, uphold, maintain.

vacation rest, holiday, recess, break.

(ANT.) labor, work, routine.

vacillate *(SYN.)* hesitate, oscillate, undulate, change, fluctuate, vary, waver.

(ANT.) adhere, persist, stick, decide.

vacillating *(SYN.)* contrary, illogical, contradictory, contrary, inconsistent, incongruous, incompatible, paradoxical, irreconcilable, unsteady, wavering.

(ANT.) correspondent, congruous, consistent, compatible.

vacuity *(SYN.)* space, emptiness, vacuum, void, blank, nothingness, ignorance, unawareness, senselessness, mindlessness, chatter, nonsense, froth, absurdity.

(ANT.) matter, fullness, content, substance, knowledge, intelligence.

vacuous *(SYN.)* dull, blank, uncomprehending, imbecillic, foolish, thoughtless, distracted, absent-minded.

(ANT.) responsive, alert, attentive, bright, intelligent, aware.

vacuum *(SYN.)* void, gap, emptiness, hole, chasm, nothingness, abyss.

vagabond *(SYN.)* pauper, ragamuffin, scrub, beggar, mendicant, starveling, wretch, tatterdemalion, hobo, tramp.

(ANT.) responsible, established, rooted, installed, reliable.

vagary *(SYN.)* notion, whim, fantasy, fancy, daydream, caprice, conceit, quirk, whimsy, impulse.

vagrant *(SYN.)* hobo, rover, tramp, beggar, bum, wanderer, vagabond.

(ANT.) settled, worker, laborer, rooted, ambitious, gentleman.

vague *(SYN.)* indefinite, hazy, dim, indistinct, ambiguous, obscure, undetermined, unclear, unsure, unsettled.

(ANT.) certain, spelled out, specific, lucid, clear, definite, distinct, explicit, precise, unequivocal.

vain *(SYN.)* fruitless, empty, bootless, futile, idle, abortive, ineffectual, unavailing, vapid, pointless, valueless, useless, trivial, unfruitful, worthless, unsuccessful, proud, conceited.

(ANT.) meek, modest, potent, rewarding, self-effacing, diffident, profitable, effective, humble.

vainglory *(SYN.)* conceit, pride, self-esteem, arrogance, self-respect, superciliousness, haughtiness, vanity.

(ANT.) shame, modesty, meekness, humility, lowliness.

valet *(SYN.)* groom, dresser, attendant, manservant.

valiant *(SYN.)* bold, brave, courageous, adventurous, audacious, chivalrous, daring, fearless, dauntless, heroic, brave, gallant, magnanimous, intrepid, unafraid, valorous, dauntless.

(ANT.) weak, fearful, cowardly, timid.

valid *(SYN.)* cogent, conclusive, effective, convincing, binding, efficacious, logical, powerful, legal, sound, weighty, well-founded, real, genuine, actual, true, trustworthy, authentic, strong, telling, logical, authentic.

(ANT.) weak, unconvincing, void, unproved, null, spurious, counterfeit.

validate *(SYN.)* corroborate, substantiate, support, confirm, prove, uphold, sustain, authenticate.

(ANT.) disprove, contradict, cancel.

valise *(SYN.)* satchel, bag, baggage.

valley *(SYN.)* dale, dell, lowland, basin, gully, vale, ravine.

(ANT.) highland, hill, upland, headland.

valor *(SYN.)* courage, heroism, bravery, boldness, intrepidity, fearlessness.

valuable *(SYN.)* profitable, useful, costly, precious, dear, expensive, worthy, important, high-priced, esteemed.

(ANT.) trashy, poor, cheap, worthless.

value *(SYN.)* price, merit, usefulness, value, virtue, utility, appreciate, prize, hold dear, treasure, excellence, benefit, cost, rate, evaluate, appraise, esteem, importance, worth, worthiness.

(ANT.) valuelessness, uselessness, cheapness.

vanish *(SYN.)* evaporate, disappear.

(ANT.) appear.

vanity *(SYN.)* complacency, egotism,

pride, self-esteem, conceit, caprice, fancy, idea, conception, notion, haughtiness, self-respect, whim, smugness, vainglory, arrogance, imagination.
(ANT.) meekness, humility, diffidence.

vanquish (SYN.) defeat, crush, humble, surmount, master, beat, conquer, overcome, rout, quell, subjugate, subdue.
(ANT.) surrender, cede, lose, retreat, capitulate.

vapid (SYN.) hackneyed, inane, insipid, trite, banal, commonplace.
(ANT.) striking, novel, fresh, original, stimulating.

vapor (SYN.) steam, fog, mist, smog, haze, steam.

variable (SYN.) fickle, fitful, inconstant, unstable, shifting, changeable, unsteady, wavering, vacillating.
(ANT.) unchanging, uniform, stable, unwavering, steady, constant.

variant (SYN.) dissimilar, different, distinct, contrary, diverse, divergent, opposite, unlike, incongruous, divers, sundry, various, miscellaneous.
(ANT.) similar, same, congruous, identical, alike.

variation (SYN.) change, alternation, alteration, substitution, variety, substitute, mutation, exchange, vicissitude.
(ANT.) uniformity, stability, monotony.

variety (SYN.) dissimilarity, diversity, heterogeneity, assortment, change, difference, medley, mixture, miscellany, variousness, form, type, class, breed, sort, kind, strain, stock.
(ANT.) likeness, monotony, uniformity, sameness, homogeneity.

various (SYN.) miscellaneous, sundry, divers, several, contrary, distinct, dissimilar, divergent, unlike, incongruous, opposite, different.
(ANT.) identical, similar, same, alike, congruous.

vary (SYN.) exchange, substitute, alter, change, modify, shift, convert, transform, transfigure, diversify, veer.
(ANT.) settle, stabilize, continue, establish, preserve.

vassalage (SYN.) confinement, captivity, imprisonment, slavery, thralldom.
(ANT.) liberation, freedom.

vast (SYN.) big, capacious, extensive, huge, great, ample, immense, wide, un-limited, enormous, measureless, large.
(ANT.) tiny, small, short, little.

vault (SYN.) caper, jerk, jump, leap, bound, crypt, sepulcher, hop, spring, safe, start, tomb, grave, catacomb, skip.

vaunt (SYN.) crow, flaunt, glory, boast.
(ANT.) minimize, humble, deprecate, apologize.

vaunting (SYN.) flourish, display, ostentation, parade, show, pomp.
(ANT.) modesty, reserve, humility.

vehement (SYN.) excitable, fervent, ardent, burning, fiery, glowing, impetuous, hot, irascible, passionate.
(ANT.) calm, quiet, cool, apathetic, deliberate.

veil (SYN.) clothe, conceal, cover, cloak, web, hide, curtain, disguise, gauze, film, envelop, screen, mask, shield, film.
(ANT.) reveal, unveil, bare, divulge.

velocity (SYN.) quickness, rapidity, speed, swiftness.

venal (SYN.) greedy, mercenary, sordid, corrupt.
(ANT.) liberal, honorable, generous.

venerable (SYN.) antiquated, aged, antique, ancient, elderly, old, superannuated, old-fashion.
(ANT.) young, new, youthful, modern.

venerate (SYN.) approve, esteem, admire, appreciate, wonder, respect.
(ANT.) dislike, despise.

vengeance (SYN.) requital, reprisal, reparation, retribution, revenge.
(ANT.) forgiveness, remission, pardon, mercy.

venom (SYN.) toxin, poison, bitterness, spite, hate.

vent (SYN.) eject, emit, expel, shoot, spurt, emanate, hurl, shed, belch, discharge, breathe.

venture (ANT.) speculate, attempt, test, dare, hazard, gamble, chance, risk.
(ANT.) insure, secure, protect.

verbal (SYN.) oral, spoken, literal, unwritten, vocal.
(ANT.) printed, written, recorded.

verbose (SYN.) communicative, glib, chattering, chatty, garrulous, loquacious, talkative.
(ANT.) uncommunicative, silent.

verbosity (SYN.) long-windedness, verboseness, redundancy, wordiness.
(ANT.) terseness, laconic, conciseness.

verdict *(SYN.)* judgment, finding, opinion, decision.

verge *(SYN.)* lip, rim, edge, margin, brink, brim.

verification *(SYN.)* confirmation, demonstration, evidence, proof, test, experiment, testimony, trial.
(ANT.) terseness, laconic, conciseness.

verify *(SYN.)* confirm, substantiate, acknowledge, determine, assure, establish, approve, fix, settle, ratify, strengthen, corroborate, affirm, sanction.

veritable *(SYN.)* authentic, correct, genuine, real, true, accurate, actual.
(ANT.) false, fictitious, spurious, erroneous, counterfeit.

versed *(SYN.)* conversant, familiar, intimate, knowing, acquainted, aware.
(ANT.) inclined, level, prone, oblique.

version *(SYN.)* interpretation, rendition.

vertical *(SYN.)* erect, perpendicular, upright.
(ANT.) horizontal.

very *(SYN.)* exceedingly, extremely, greatly, considerably.

vessel *(SYN.)* craft, boat, ship.

vestige *(SYN.)* stain, scar, mark, brand, stigma, characteristic, trace, feature, trait, symptoms, hint, token, suggestion, indication.

veto *(SYN.)* refusal, denial, refuse, deny, negate, forbid, prohibit.
(ANT.) approve, approval.

vex *(SYN.)* embitter, exasperate, aggravate, annoy, chafe, bother, provoke, pester, plague, anger, nettle, anger.
(ANT.) soften soothe, palliate, mitigate.

vexation *(SYN.)* chagrin, irritation, annoyance, mortification, irritation, pique.
(ANT.) comfort, pleasure, appeasement, gratification.

vibrate *(SYN.)* flutter, jar, quake, jolt, quaver, agitate, transgression, wickedness, ungodliness, tremble, wrong.

vice *(SYN.)* iniquity, crime, offense, evil, guilt, sin, ungodliness, wickedness, depravity, corruption, wrong.
(ANT.) righteousness, virtue, goodness, innocence, purity.

vicinity *(SYN.)* district, area, locality, neighborhood, environs, proximity, nearness, adjacency.
(ANT.) remoteness, distance.

vicious *(SYN.)* bad, evil, wicked, sinful, corrupt, cruel, savage, dangerous.

victimize *(SYN.)* cheat, dupe, swindle, deceive, take advantage of.

victor *(SYN.)* champion, winner.
(ANT.) loser.

victory *(SYN.)* conquest, jubilation, triumph, success, achievement, ovation.
(ANT.) defeat, failure.

view *(SYN.)* discern, gaze, glance, behold, eye, discern, stare, watch, examine, witness, prospect, vision, vista, sight, look, panorama, opinion, judgment, belief, impression, perspective, range, regard, thought, observation, survey, scene, conception, outlook, inspect, observe.
(ANT.) miss, overlook, avert, hide.

viewpoint *(SYN.)* attitude, standpoint, aspect, pose, disposition, position, stand, posture.

vigilant *(SYN.)* anxious, attentive, careful, alert, circumspect, cautious, observant, wary, watchful, wakeful.
(ANT.) inattentive, neglectful, careless.

vigor *(SYN.)* spirit, verve, energy, zeal, fortitude, vitality, strength, liveliness.
(ANT.) listlessness.

vigorous *(SYN.)* brisk, energetic, active, blithe, animated, frolicsome, strong, spirited, lively, forceful, sprightly, vivacious, powerful, supple.
(ANT.) vapid, dull, listless, insipid.

vile *(SYN.)* foul, loathsome, base, depraved, debased, sordid, vulgar, wicked, abject, ignoble, mean, worthless, sinful, bad, low, wretched, evil, offensive, objectionable, disgusting.
(ANT.) honorable, upright, decent, laudable, attractive.

vilify *(SYN.)* asperse, defame, disparage, abuse, malign, revile, scandalize.
(ANT.) protect, honor, praise, cherish.

village *(SYN.)* hamlet, town.
(ANT.) metropolis, city.

villain *(SYN.)* rascal, rogue, cad, brute, scoundrel, devil, scamp.

villainous *(SYN.)* deleterious, evil, bad, base, iniquitous, unsound, sinful, unwholesome, wicked.
(ANT.) honorable, reputable, moral, good, excellent.

violate *(SYN.)* infringe, break.

violent *(SYN.)* strong, forcible, forceful.
(ANT.) gentle.

vindicate clear, assert, defend, absolve,

excuse, acquit, uphold, support.
(ANT.) accuse, convict, abandon.

violate (SYN.) disobey, invade, defile, break, desecrate, pollute, dishonor, debauch, profane, deflower, ravish.

violence (SYN.) constraint, force, compulsion, coercion.
(ANT.) weakness, persuasion, feebleness, impotence, frailty.

violent (SYN.) strong, forceful, powerful, forcible, angry, fierce, savage, passionate, furious.
(ANT.) gentle.

virgin (SYN.) immaculate, genuine, spotless, clean, clear, unadulterated, chaste, untainted, innocent, guiltless, pure, untouched, modest, maid, maiden, sincere, unused, undefiled, pure.
(ANT.) foul, tainted, defiled, sullied, polluted, corrupt.

virile (SYN.) hardy, male, mannish, lusty, bold, masculine, strong, vigorous.
(ANT.) feminine, unmanly, weak, effeminate, womanish, emasculated.

virtue (SYN.) integrity, probity, purity, chastity, goodness, rectitude, effectiveness, force, honor, power, efficacy, quality, strength, merit, righteousness.
(ANT.) fault, vice, lewdness, corruption.

virtuous (SYN.) good, ethical, chaste, honorable, moral, just, pure, righteous, upstanding, upright, scrupulous.
(ANT.) licentious, unethical, amoral, sinful, libertine, immoral.

virulent (SYN.) hostile, malevolent, malignant, bitter, spiteful, wicked.
(ANT.) kind, affectionate, benevolent.

vision (SYN.) dream, hallucination, mirage, eyesight, sight, fantasy, illusion, specter, revelation, phantom, spook.
(ANT.) verity, reality.

visionary (SYN.) faultless, ideal, perfect, unreal, supreme.
(ANT.) real, actual, imperfect, faulty.

visit (SYN.) attend, see, appointment.

visitor (SYN.) caller, guest.

vista (SYN.) view, scene, aspect.

vital (SYN.) cardinal, living, paramount, alive, essential, critical, basic, indispensable, urgent, life-and-death.
(ANT.) lifeless, unimportant, inanimate, nonessential.

vitality (SYN.) buoyancy, being, life, liveliness, existence, spirit, vigor.

(ANT.) death, lethargy, dullness, demise.

vitiate (SYN.) allay, abase, corrupt, adulterate, debase, defile, depress, deprave, degrade, impair, humiliate, pervert.

vivacious (SYN.) lively, spirited.

vivid (SYN.) brilliant, striking, clear, bright, intense, lively, strong, graphic.
(ANT.) dim, dusky, vague, dull, dreary.

vocal (SYN.) said, uttered, oral, spoken, definite, outspoken, specific.

vocation (SYN.) commerce, employment, business, art, job, profession, trade, occupation, career, calling, work, trading.
(ANT.) pastime, hobby, avocation.

void (SYN.) barren, emptiness, space, annul, cancel, empty, bare, unoccupied, meaningless, invalid, useless, invalidate, worthless, vacant, barren.
(ANT.) employed, full, replete, engaged.

volatile (SYN.) effervescent, resilient, buoyant, animated, cheerful, hopeful, lively, sprightly, spirited, vivacious.
(ANT.) depressed, sullen, hopeless, dejected, despondent.

volition (SYN.) desire, intention, pleasure, preference, choice, decision, resolution, testament, wish, will.
(ANT.) disinterest, compulsion, indifference.

voluble (SYN.) glib, communicative, verbose, loquacious, chatty, chattering.
(ANT.) uncommunicative, laconic, taciturn, silent.

volume (SYN.) capacity, skill, power, talent, faculty, magnitude, mass, book, dimensions, quantity, amount, size.
(ANT.) stupidity, inability, impotence, incapacity.

voluntary (SYN.) extemporaneous, free, automatic, spontaneous, offhand.
(ANT.) forced, planned, required, rehearsed, compulsory, prepared.

volunteer (SYN.) extend, offer, present, advance, propose, tender, sacrifice.
(ANT.) receive, spurn, reject, accept, retain.

voracious (SYN.) insatiable, ravenous.

vow (SYN.) oath, pledge, swear, promise.

voyage (SYN.) tour, journey, excursion.

vulgar (SYN.) ordinary, popular, common, general, crude, coarse, low, rude.
(ANT.) polite, refined, select, aristocratic.

vulnerable (SYN.) unguarded, defenseless, unprotected.

wacky *(SYN.)* strange, crazy, peculiar.

wad *(SYN.)* hunk, clump, chunk.

wafer *(SYN.)* cracker, lozenge.

waft *(SYN.)* convey, glide, sail, float.

wage *(SYN.)* conduct, pursue, make.

wager *(SYN.)* stake, bet, play, gamble, speculate, risk, chance.

wages *(SYN.)* payment, compensation, fee, allowance, pay, salary, earnings, rate, recompense.

wagon *(SYN.)* carriage, buggy, cart, surrey, stagecoach.

waif *(SYN.)* guttersnipe, ragamuffin, tramp, vagrant, urchin.

wail *(SYN.)* mourn, moan, cry, bewail, lament, bemoan, sorrow.

wait *(SYN.)* linger, tarry, attend, bide, watch, delay, await, abide, stay, serve, pause, remain, rest, minister, expect.
(ANT.) hasten, act leave, expedite.

waive *(SYN.)* renounce, abandon, surrender, relinquish, forgo.
(ANT.) uphold, maintain.

wake *(SYN.)* awaken, rouse, waken, arouse, stimulate, activate.
(ANT.) doze, sleep.

waken *(SYN.)* wake, arouse, rouse, awaken, stimulate, activate.
(ANT.) doze, sleep.

walk *(SYN.)* step, stroll, march, amble, saunter, hike, lane, path, passage.

wall *(SYN.)* barricade, divider, partition, panel, stockade.

wallow *(SYN.)* plunge, roll, flounder, grovel.

wan *(SYN.)* colorless, haggard, gaunt, pale, pallid, pasty, pale.

wander *(SYN.)* rove, stroll, deviate, ramble, digress, roam, traipse, range, err, meander, saunter.
(ANT.) linger, stop, settle.

wane *(SYN.)* abate, weaken, fade, ebb, decrease, wither, subside.

want *(SYN.)* penury, destitution, crave, desire, requirement, poverty, wish, require, need, privation.
(ANT.) wealth, plenty, abundance.

wanton *(SYN.)* lecherous, immoral, loose, lewd, salacious, lustful.

war *(SYN.)* battle, hostilities, combat, fight, strife, contention.

warble *(SYN.)* sing, trill, chirp.

ward *(SYN.)* annex, wing, section.

warden *(SYN.)* custodian, guard, guardian, keeper, turnkey, jailer, curator.

wares *(SYN.)* merchandise, staples, inventory, commodities, goods.

wariness *(SYN.)* heed, care, watchfulness, caution, vigilance.
(ANT.) carelessness, abandon.

warlike *(SYN.)* hostile, unfriendly, combative, belligerent, antagonistic, pugnacious, bellicose, opposed, aggressive.
(ANT.) cordial, peaceful, amicable.

warm *(SYN.)* sincere, cordial, hearty, earnest, sympathetic, ardent, heated, gracious, temperate, enthusiastic, lukewarm, tepid, eager, sociable.
(ANT.) cool, aloof, taciturn, brisk, indifferent.

warmhearted *(SYN.)* loving, kind, kindhearted, friendly, generous.

warmth *(SYN.)* friendliness, cordiality, geniality, understanding, compassion.

warn *(SYN.)* apprise, notify, admonish, caution, advise, inform.

warning *(SYN.)* advice, information, caution, portent, admonition, indication, notice, sign.

warp *(SYN.)* turn, bend, twist, distort, deprave.

warrant *(SYN.)* pledge, assurance, warranty, guarantee, authorize, approve, mandate, sanction.

warrior *(SYN.)* combatant, fighter, soldier, mercenary, guerrilla.

wary *(SYN.)* careful, awake, watchful, heedful, attentive, alive, mindful, cautious, thoughtful.
(ANT.) unaware, indifferent, careless, apathetic.

wash *(SYN.)* launder, cleanse, rub, touch, reach, border, wet, clean, scrub, bathe.
(ANT.) soil, dirty, stain.

washed-out *(SYN.)* bleached, dull, faded, pale, discolored, pallid.

waspish *(SYN.)* irritable, petulant, fractious, ill-tempered, testy, snappish, touchy.
(ANT.) pleasant, genial.

waste *(SYN.)* forlorn, bleak, wild, solitary, dissipate, abandoned, spend, deserted, bare, consume, dwindle, decay, misspend, decrease, wither, wear, effluent, useless, unused, garbage, rubbish, refuse, trash, squander, uninhabited.
(ANT.) cultivated, attended.

wasteful *(SYN.)* wanton, costly, lavish, extravagant.

watch *(SYN.)* inspect, descry, behold, distinguish, guard, attend, observe, contemplate, espy, perceive, look at, protect, chronometer, timepiece, patrol, vigil, duty, shift, regard, note, view, scan, sentinel, watchman, sentry, discern.

watchdog *(SYN.)* lookout, guard, sentinel, sentry.

watchful *(SYN.)* alert, careful, attentive, vigilant, wary, cautious.

waterfall *(SYN.)* cascade, cataract.

watertight *(SYN.)* impregnable, firm, solid.

wave *(SYN.)* ripple, whitecap, undulation, breaker, surf, swell, sea, surge, tide, flow, stream.

waver *(SYN.)* question, suspect, flicker, deliberate, doubt, distrust, hesitate, falter, stagger.
(ANT.) confide, trust, believe, decide.

wavering *(SYN.)* fickle, shifting, variable, changeable, vacillating, fitful.
(ANT.) unchanging, constant, uniform.

wavy *(SYN.)* rippling, serpentine, curly.

wax *(SYN.)* raise, heighten, expand, accrue, enhance, extend, multiply, enlarge, augment, amplify.
(ANT.) contract, reduce, atrophy, diminish.

way *(SYN.)* habit, road, course, avenue, route, mode, system, channel, track, fashion, method, walk, approach, manner, technique, means, procedure, trail, proceed, progress, path, style.

waylay *(SYN.)* surprise, accost, ambush, attack, pounce, intercept.

wayward *(SYN.)* stubborn, headstrong, contrary, obstinate, naughty, disobedient, rebellious, refractory.

weak *(SYN.)* frail, debilitated, delicate, poor, wavering, infirm, bending, lame, defenseless, vulnerable, fragile, pliant, feeble, watery, diluted, undecided, assailable, irresolute, unsteady, yielding, tender.
(ANT.) strong, potent, sturdy, powerful.

weaken *(SYN.)* exhaust, sap, disable, devitalize.

weakling *(SYN.)* sissy, namby-pamby, milksop, milquetoast.

weakness *(SYN.)* incompetence, inability, impotence, handicap, fondness, liking affection, disability, incapacity, feebleness.
(ANT.) strength, ability, dislike, power.

wealth *(SYN.)* fortune, money, riches, possessions, means, abundance, opulence, affluence, property, quantity, profession, luxury.
(ANT.) want, need.

wealthy *(SYN.)* rich, exorbitant, prosperous, affluent, successful.
(ANT.) poverty-stricken, poor, indigent, impoverished, beggarly, destitute, needy.

wear *(SYN.)* erode, fray, grind, apparel, clothes, garb, attire.

wearied *(SYN.)* weak, languid, faint, irresolute, feeble, timid.
(ANT.) brave, vigorous.

weary *(SYN.)* faint, spent, worn, tired, fatigued, exhausted, tiresome, bored, wearied, tedious, jaded.
(ANT.) rested, hearty, fresh.

weasel *(SYN.)* cheat, traitor, betrayer.

weave *(SYN.)* lace, interlace, plait, intertwine, braid, knit.

web *(SYN.)* netting, network, net, cobweb, trap, entanglement.

wed *(SYN.)* espouse, marry.

wedlock *(SYN.)* marriage, union, espousal, wedding, matrimony.

wedge *(SYN.)* chock, jam, lodge.

wee *(SYN.)* small, tiny, miniature, petite, microscopic, minute.

weep *(SYN.)* mourn, sob, bemoan, cry, lament, whimper, wail.

weigh *(SYN.)* heed, deliberate, consider, study, ponder, contemplate, reflect, evaluate.
(ANT.) neglect, ignore.

weight *(SYN.)* importance, emphasis, load, burden, import, stress, influence, heaviness, pressure, value, gravity, significance.
(ANT.) triviality, levity, insignificance, lightness, buoyancy.

weird *(SYN.)* odd, eerie, strange, unnatural, peculiar, spooky.

welcome *(SYN.)* take, entertain, greet, accept, receive, reception, gain, greeting, shelter.
(ANT.) reject, bestow, impart, discharge.

weld *(SYN.)* solder, connect, fuse, bond.

welfare *(SYN.)* good, well-being, prosperity.

well *(SYN.)* hearty, happy, sound, hale,

beneficial, good, convenient, expedient, healthy, favorably, fully, thoroughly, surely, adequately, satisfactorily, competently, certainly, completely, trim, undoubtedly, fit, profitable.

(ANT.) infirm, depressed, weak.

well-being *(SYN.)* delight, happiness, satisfaction, contentment, gladness.

(ANT.) sorrow, grief, sadness, despair.

well-bred *(SYN.)* cultured, polite, genteel, courtly, refined, cultivated.

(ANT.) crude, vulgar, boorish, rude.

well-known *(SYN.)* famous, illustrious, celebrated, noted, eminent, renowned.

(ANT.) unknown, ignominious, obscure, hidden.

wet *(SYN.)* moist, dank, soaked, damp, drenched, dampen, moisten.

(ANT.) arid, dry, parched.

wharf *(SYN.)* pier, dock.

wheedle *(SYN.)* coax, cajole, persuade.

whim *(SYN.)* fancy, notion, humor, quirk, caprice, whimsy, inclination, vagary.

whimsical *(SYN.)* quaint, strange, curious, odd, unusual, droll, queer, eccentric, peculiar.

(ANT.) normal, common, usual, familiar.

whine *(SYN.)* whimper, cry, moan, complain.

whip *(SYN.)* scourge, thrash, beat, lash.

whirl *(SYN.)* rotate, twirl, spin, revolve, reel.

whole *(SYN.)* total, sound, all, intact, complete, well, hale, integral, unimpaired, healed, entire, uncut, undivided, unbroken, undamaged, intact, perfect.

(ANT.) partial, defective, imperfect, deficient.

wholesome *(SYN.)* robust, well, hale, healthy, sound, salubrious, good, hygienic, salutary, nourishing, healthful, strong, nutritious, hearty.

(ANT.) frail, noxious, infirm, delicate, injurious, diseased.

wicked *(SYN.)* deleterious, iniquitous, immoral, bad, evil, base, ungodly, unsound, sinful, bitter, blasphemous, malicious, evil-minded, profane, baleful, hostile, rancorous, unwholesome.

(ANT.) moral, good, reputable, honorable.

wide *(SYN.)* large, broad, sweeping, extensive, vast, expanded.

(ANT.) restricted, narrow.

width *(SYN.)* wideness, extensiveness, breadth.

wield *(SYN.)* handle, brandish.

wild *(SYN.)* outlandish, uncivilized, untamed, irregular, wanton, foolish, mad, barbarous, rough, waste, desert, uncultivated, boisterous, unruly, savage, primitive, giddy, unrestrained, silly, wayward, uncontrolled, impetuous, crazy, ferocious, undomesticated, desolate.

(ANT.) quiet, gentle, placid, tame, restrained, civilized.

willful *(SYN.)* intentional, designed, contemplated, studied, premeditated.

(ANT.) fortuitous.

will *(SYN.)* intention, desire, volition, decision, resolution, wish, resoluteness, choice, determination, pleasure.

(ANT.) disinterest, coercion, indifference.

willing *(SYN.)* agreeing, energetic, enthusiastic, consenting, agreeable, eager.

wilt *(SYN.)* sag, droop, weaken.

wily *(SYN.)* cunning, foxy, sly, crafty.

win *(SYN.)* gain, succeed, prevail, achieve, thrive, obtain, get, acquire, earn, flourish.

(ANT.) lose, miss, forfeit, fail.

wind *(SYN.)* gale, breeze, storm, gust, blast, air, breath, flurry, puff, blow, hurricane, typhoon, cyclone, tornado, suggestion, hint, clue, zephyr, squall, coil, crank, screw, meander, wander, twist, weave, draft.

winsome *(SYN.)* winning, charming, agreeable.

wisdom *(SYN.)* insight, judgment, learning, sense, discretion, reason, prudence, erudition, foresight, intelligence, sageness, knowledge, information, sagacity.

(ANT.) nonsense, foolishness, stupidity, ignorance.

wise *(SYN.)* informed, sagacious, learned, penetrating, enlightened, advisable, prudent, profound, deep, erudite, scholarly, knowing, sound, intelligent, expedient, discerning.

(ANT.) simple, shallow, foolish.

wish *(SYN.)* crave, hanker, long, hunger, yearning, lust, craving, yearn, want, appetite, covet, longing, desire, urge.

(ANT.) hate, aversion, loathing, distaste.

wit *(SYN.)* sense, humor, pleasantry,

satire, intelligence, comprehension, understanding, banter, mind, wisdom, intellect, wittiness, fun, drollery, humorist, wag, comedian, raillery, irony, witticism. *(ANT.) solemnity, commonplace, sobriety.*

witch *(SYN.)* magician, sorcerer, enchanter, sorceress, enchantress, warlock.

witchcraft *(SYN.)* enchantment, magic, wizardry, conjuring, voodoo.

withdraw *(SYN.)* renounce, leave, abandon, recall, retreat, go, secede, desert, quit, retire, depart, retract, remove, forsake. *(ANT.) enter, tarry, abide, place, stay.*

wither *(SYN.)* wilt, languish, dry, shrivel, decline, fade, decay, sear, waste, wizen, weaken, droop, sink, fail, shrink. *(ANT.) renew, refresh, revive.*

withhold *(SYN.)* forbear, abstain, repress, check, refrain. *(ANT.) persist, continue.*

witness *(SYN.)* perceive, proof, spectator, confirmation, see, attestation, watch, observe, eyewitness, notice, testimony. *(ANT.) refutation, contradiction, argument.*

witty *(SYN.)* funny, talented, apt, bright, adroit, sharp, clever. *(ANT.) foolish, slow, dull, clumsy, awkward.*

wizard *(SYN.)* magician, conjuror, sorcerer.

wizardry *(SYN.)* voodoo, legerdemain, conjuring, witchcraft, charm.

woe *(SYN.)* sorrow, disaster, trouble, evil, agony, suffering, anguish, sadness, grief, distress, misery, torment, misfortune. *(ANT.) pleasure, delight, fun.*

womanly *(SYN.)* girlish, womanish, female, ladylike. *(ANT.) mannish, virile, male, masculine.*

wonder *(SYN.)* awe, curiosity, miracle, admiration, surprise, wonderment. *(ANT.) expectation, familiarity, indifference, apathy, triviality.*

wonderful *(SYN.)* extraordinary, marvelous, astonishing, amazing, remarkable, astounding.

wont *(SYN.)* practice, use, custom, training, habit, usage, manner. *(ANT.) inexperience, disuse.*

word *(SYN.)* phrase, term, utterance, expression, articulate.

wordy *(SYN.)* talkative, verbose, garrulous.

work *(SYN.)* opus, employment, achievement, performance, toil, business, exertion, occupation, labor, job, product. *(ANT.) recreation, leisure, vacation, ease.*

working *(SYN.)* busy, active, industrious. *(ANT.) lazy, dormant, passive, inactive.*

world *(SYN.)* globe, earth, universe.

worn *(SYN.)* tired, jaded, exhausted, wearied, faint, weary. *(ANT.) invigorated, fresh, rested.*

worry *(SYN.)* concern, trouble, disquiet, anxiety, fear, pain, harry, gall, grieve. *(ANT.) console, comfort, contentment, satisfaction, peace.*

worship *(SYN.)* honor, revere, adore, idolize, reverence, glorify, respect. *(ANT.) curse, scorn, blaspheme, despise.*

worth *(SYN.)* value, price, deserving, excellence, usefulness, utility, worthiness. *(ANT.) uselessness, valuelessness, cheapness.*

worthless *(SYN.)* empty, idle, abortive, ineffectual, bootless, vain, unavailing. *(ANT.) meek, effective, modest, potent.*

wound *(SYN.)* mar, harm, damage, hurt, dishonor, injure, injury, spoil, wrong. *(ANT.) compliment, preserve, help.*

wrap *(SYN.)* cover, protect, shield, cloak, mask, clothe, curtain, guard, conceal. *(ANT.) reveal, bare, unveil, expose.*

wrath *(SYN.)* fury, anger, irritation, rage, animosity, passion, temper, petulance. *(ANT.) patience, conciliation, peace.*

wreck *(SYN.)* ravage, devastation, extinguish, destroy, annihilate, damage, raze. *(ANT.) construct, preserve, establish.*

wrench *(SYN.)* tug, jerk, twist.

wrestle *(SYN.)* fight, tussle, grapple.

wretch *(SYN.)* cad, scoundrel, rogue.

wretched *(SYN.)* forlorn, miserable, comfortless, despicable, paltry, low. *(ANT.) contented, happy, significant.*

wring *(SYN.)* twist, extract.

writer *(SYN.)* creator, maker, author, father, composer.

writhe *(SYN.)* twist, squirm.

wrong *(SYN.)* awry, incorrect, improper, amiss, naughty, inappropriate, criminal, faulty, erroneous, bad, evil, imprecise. *(ANT.) proper, true, correct, suitable.*

wry *(SYN.)* amusing, witty, dry, droll.

yacht *(SYN.)* sailboat, boat, cruiser.

yank *(SYN.)* pull, wrest, draw, haul, tug, jerk, wrench, heave, extract.

yap *(SYN.)* howl, bark.

yard *(SYN.)* pen, confine, court, enclosure, compound, garden.

yardstick *(SYN.)* measure, criterion, gauge.

yarn *(SYN.)* wool, tale, narrative, thread, story, fiber, anecdote, spiel.

yaw *(SYN.)* tack, change course, pitch, toss. roll.

yawn *(SYN.)* open, gape.

yearly *(SYN.)* annually.

yearn *(SYN.)* pine, long for, want, desire, crave, wish.

yearning *(SYN.)* hungering, craving, desire, longing, appetite, lust, urge, aspiration, wish.

(ANT.) distaste, loathing, abomination, hate.

yell *(SYN.)* call, scream, shout, whoop, howl, roar, holler, wail, bawl.

yellow *(SYN.)* fearful, cowardly, chicken.

(ANT.) bold, brave.

yelp *(SYN.)* screech, squeal, howl, bark.

yen *(SYN.)* longing, craving, fancy, appetite, desire, lust, hunger.

yet *(SYN.)* moreover, also, additionally, besides.

yield *(SYN.)* produce, afford, breed, grant, accord, cede, relent, succumb, bestow, allow, permit, give way, submit, bear, surrender, supply, fruits, give up, abdicate, return, impart, harvest, permit, accede, acquiesce, crop, capitulate, pay, concede, generate, relinquish.

(ANT.) assert, deny, refuse, resist, struggle, oppose, strive.

yielding *(SYN.)* dutiful, submissive, compliant, obedient, tractable.

(ANT.) rebellious, intractable, insubordinate.

yoke *(SYN.)* tether, leash, bridle, harness.

yokel *(SYN.)* hick, peasant, hayseed, innocent.

young *(SYN.)* immature, undeveloped, youthful, underdeveloped, juvenile, junior, underage.

(ANT.) old, mature, elderly.

youngster *(SYN.)* kid, lad, stripling, minor, youth, child, fledgling.

(ANT.) adult, elder.

youthful *(SYN.)* childish, immature, young, boyish, childlike, callow, girlish, puerile.

(ANT.) old, elderly, senile, aged, mature.

yowl *(SYN.)* yell, shriek, cry, wail, whoop, howl, scream.

zany *(SYN.)* clownish, comical, foolish, silly, scatterbrained.

zap *(SYN.)* drive, vim, pep, determination.

zeal *(SYN.)* fervor, eagerness, passion, feverency, vehemence, devotion, intensity, excitement, earnestness, inspiration, warmth, ardor, fanaticism, enthusiasm.

(ANT.) unconcern, ennui, apathy, indifference.

zealot *(SYN.)* champion, crank, fanatic, bigot.

zealous *(SYN.)* enthusiastic, fiery, keen, eager, fervid, ardent, intense, vehement, fervent, glowing, hot, impassioned, passionate.

(ANT.) cool, nonchalant, apathetic.

zenith *(SYN.)* culmination, apex, height, acme, consummation, top, summit, pinnacle, climax, peak.

(ANT.) floor, nadir, depth, base, anticlimax.

zero *(SYN.)* nonexistent, nil, nothing, none.

zest *(SYN.)* enjoyment, savor, eagerness, relish, satisfaction, gusto, spice, tang, pleasure. exhilaration.

zestful *(SYN.)* delightful, thrilling, exciting, stimulating, enjoyable.

zip *(SYN.)* vigor, vim, energy, vitality, spirited, animation, provocative.

zone *(SYN.)* region, climate, tract, belt, sector, section, district, locality, precinct, territory.

zoo *(SYN.)* menagerie.

zoom *(SYN.)* zip, fly, speed, whiz, roar, race.